Dictionary of Business Biography

Dictionary of Business Biography

*A Biographical Dictionary of Business Leaders
Active in Britain in the Period 1860-1980*

edited by

David J Jeremy

Research Fellow, Business History Unit
London School of Economics and Political Science

deputy editor

Christine Shaw

Research Officer, Business History Unit
London School of Economics and Political Science

**Volume 4
Mc-R**

London
Butterworths
1985

England   Butterworth & Co (Publishers) Ltd, 88 Kingsway, LONDON WC2B 6AB
Australia   Butterworth Pty Ltd, SYDNEY, MELBOURNE, BRISBANE, ADELAIDE, and PERTH
Canada   Butterworth & Co (Canada) Ltd, TORONTO
                  Butterworth & Co (Western Canada) Ltd, VANCOUVER
New Zealand   Butterworths of New Zealand Ltd, WELLINGTON
Singapore   Butterworth & Co (Asia) Pte Ltd, SINGAPORE
South Africa   Butterworth Publishers (Pty) Ltd, DURBAN
USA   Mason Publishing Co, ST PAUL, Minnesota
                  Butterworth Legal Publishers, SEATTLE, Washington; BOSTON, Massachusetts;
                  and AUSTIN, Texas
                  D & S Publishers, CLEARWATER, Florida

© London School of Economics and Political Science 1985

ISBN for the complete set of volumes: 0 406 27340 5
       for this volume: 0 406 27344 8

Typeset by Whitefriars Composertype Ltd, Chichester
Printed by The Whitefriars Press Ltd, Tonbridge

Introduction and Acknowledgements

With Volume IV of the *Dictionary of Business Biography* another 245 business biographies are added to the 693 already published in volumes I, II and III. The *Dictionary*, as explained in Volume I, covers individuals in the whole gamut of business from mining and manufacturing to public utilities, construction, distribution and financial and miscellaneous services (as defined by the Central Statistical Office's *Standard Industrial Classification* (HMSO, 1968) Orders II–XXVI). Academics, civil servants (though not heads of nationalised industries) and agriculturalists have been excluded when their involvement in the business world was incidental to their central career. Those still active in business have also been omitted. Leaders of business based in Scotland are covered by a parallel project at the University of Glasgow.

Many of the acknowledgements in earlier volumes still apply because the *DBB* has continued to rely on the same individuals and institutions. The project owes its existence (and its final lease of life) as explained in Volume I, to the support of the Economic and Social Research Council. Some extra funding needed at the end of the project has come from the Business History Unit through the good offices of its acting director, Dr Geoffrey G Jones. Without the contributors (listed below) and the generous co-operation of referees (mostly academic economic historians) and advisors (listed in earlier volumes) the quality of entry that has been attained could not have been reached within the five-year life of the project.

Among the many learned institutions whose services we have not acknowledged previously are the Business Archives Council (Alison Turton), Brecon Public Library, Glasgow University Archives (Michael Moss and Iain Russell), the National Library of Wales, the National Motor Museum Library, the Official Publications Library and the Science Reference Library (branches of the British Library), the *Times* Archives (Ann Piggott and Sabina Sutherland), Trinity College Library Cambridge, Trinity College Library, Oxford, University of London Library. For all this outside help (and any more we have inadvertently omitted to mention) we in the editorial team are very grateful.

Within the editorial team high levels of commitment, co-operation and efficiency have been maintained as the project enters its last months. Miss Kiely and Mrs Peake have completed the enormous task of keying in the text of what is the largest volume in the series — a crucial task because, for each volume, the printer has used new technology so that their text is fed directly into his typesetter; and an onerous task, because editors and authors not infrequently require tiresome changes at the word processor proofing stage. In addition Mrs Peake has continued to maintain the *DBB* office's secretarial functions and Miss Kiely has searched for and collected birth and marriage certificates and probate data. The editors and Dr Tweedale have re-written sections of some entries to bring them in line with the generality of biographies. Dr Tweedale and Mr Francis Goodall have done most of the bibliographical research for the volume.

The editor has read and commented on every entry, normally imposing the usual *DBB* format; Dr Shaw has been responsible for the final editing of many of the M and R entries. Proofing has been shared between the editor, deputy editor, Dr Tweedale (who is preparing the computerised data bank of quantitative information derived from the biographies) and (at galley stage) Mr Michael Robbins, whose eagle eye and encyclopaedic knowledge have preserved us from a number of gross errors.

We are grateful to all those who have supplied us with the illustrations, assembled by Miss Kiely, and again, for any unwilling invasions of copyright (which we have tried to avoid or rectify) we apologise. Finally we are very appreciative of the speed with which our publishers, Butterworths have made up pages and seen our text through the press.

Again I would like to emphasise my gratitude to everyone who has in any way supported the *DBB* project, stressing that none besides the editors is responsible for the editorial faults that remain.

David J Jeremy

Contents

List of Contributors to Volume 4

(affiliations at the time of writing)

Geoffrey Alderman	Lecturer, Department of History, Royal Holloway College, University of London.
J K Almond	Senior Lecturer in Metallurgy, Teesside Polytechnic.
P J Atkins	Lecturer, Department of Geography, University of Durham.
J H Bamberg	Maidenhead, Berkshire.
T C Barker	Emeritus Professor of Economic History, London School of Economics and Political Science.
Hugh Barty-King	Wadhurst, East Sussex.
Victor Belcher	Assistant Editor, *Survey of London,* Greater London Council.
G T Bloomfield	Professor and Chairman of the Department of Geography, University of Guelph, Ontario.
Michael Bonavia	formerly Academic Visitor, Economic History Department, London School of Economics and Political Science.
John Booker	Archivist, Lloyds Bank plc, London.
Brian Bowers	Deputy Keeper, Department of Electrical Engineering and Communications, Science Museum, London.
Emily Boyle	Lecturer, School of Marketing and Business Organisation, University of Ulster.
Asa Briggs, Lord Briggs of Lewes	Provost, Worcester College, Oxford.
Keith Brooker	Lecturer, Department of Business Studies, East Yorkshire College of Further Education.
Peter W Brooks	Regional Executive, Aircraft Group, British Aerospace plc.
Jonathan Brown	Institute of Agricultural History and Museum of English Rural Life, University of Reading.
David Burgess-Wise	Co-ordinator of Car Product Information, Public Affairs, Ford of Europe.
Gill Burke	Senior Lecturer in Social Administration, School of Social Science and Business Studies, Polytechnic of Central London.

Gordon Bussey	Historical Adviser, Philips Electronics.
Michael Bywater	Librarian, Institute of Chartered Accountants in England and Wales.
Anne Channon	formerly Postgraduate Student, Department of Cultural History, Royal College of Art, London.
Geoffrey Channon	Principal Lecturer, Department of Humanities, Bristol Polytechnic.
S D Chapman	Pasold Reader in Business History, Department of History, University of Nottingham.
Martin Chick	formerly Research Student, Business History Unit, London School of Economics and Political Science.
J F Clarke	Principal Lecturer, Department of Geography and Humanities, Newcastle upon Tyne Polytechnic.
Hugh Cockerell	Visiting Professor in Business Studies, City University Business School.
Arthur G Codd	Manager, Press and Public Relations Department, Sir Robert McAlpine & Sons Ltd.
Howard Coles	Principal, Openshaw Technical College, Manchester.
D A Collier	Course Tutor, Department of Economic History, Mid-Warwickshire College of Further Education.
T A B Corley	Senior Lecturer, Department of Economics, University of Reading.
P L Cottrell	Lecturer, Department of Economic and Social History, University of Leicester.
Robin Craig	Senior Lecturer in Economic History, Department of History, University College, London.
M J Daunton	Lecturer, Department of History, University College, London.
R P T Davenport-Hines	Research Officer, Business History Unit, London School of Economics and Political Science.
Alun C Davies	Senior Lecturer, Department of Economic History, The Queen's University, Belfast.
P N Davies	Senior Lecturer and Head of Department of Economic History, University of Liverpool.
Martin Davis	Senior Lecturer, Department of Politics and History, Coventry (Lanchester) Polytechnic.
Francis Dick	Northwich, Cheshire.

Tom Donnelly	Senior Lecturer, Department of Politics and History, Coventry (Lanchester) Polytechnic.
Patricia A Dutton	Institute for Employment Research, University of Warwick.
J B F Earle	Kyle, Ross-shire.
D E H Edgerton	Temporary Lecturer, Department of Science and Technology Policy, University of Manchester.
J R Edwards	Senior Lecturer in Accountancy, Department of Accountancy, University College, Cardiff.
David M Fahey	Professor of History, Department of History, Miami University, Oxford, Ohio, USA.
Malcolm Falkus	Senior Lecturer, Department of Economic History, London School of Economics and Political Science.
D A Farnie	Reader in Economic History, Department of History, University of Manchester.
Peter Fearon	Senior Lecturer, Department of Economic and Social History, University of Leicester.
Alan Fowler	Senior Lecturer, Department of Economics and Economic History, Manchester Polytechnic.
G R M Garratt	Esher, Surrey.
S Martin Gaskell	Deputy Rector, Liverpool Polytechnic.
Francis Goodall	Bibliographer and Researcher, *Dictionary of Business Biography*, Business History Unit, London School of Economics and Political Science.
Edwin Green	Archivist, Midland Bank plc.
Robert Greenhill	Senior Lecturer, School of Business Studies, City of London Polytechnic.
A A Hall	NCB History Project.
Leslie Hannah	Professor of Business History and Director, Business History Unit, London School of Economics and Political Science.
Charles E Harvey	Senior Lecturer, Department of Humanities, Bristol Polytechnic.
*Martin Higham	formerly Group Recruitment Manager, Rowntree Mackintosh plc.
Robin Higham	Professor, Department of History, Kansas State University.

Len Holden	Research Student, School of Economic and Social Studies, University of East Anglia.
Graeme M Holmes	Senior Lecturer, Department of Economics and Banking, University of Wales Institute of Science and Technology.
Deian Hopkin	Lecturer, Department of History, University College of Wales, Aberystwyth.
A C Howe	Lecturer, Department of International History, London School of Economics and Political Science.
L B Hunt	formerly with Johnson, Matthey & Co Ltd.
Sandra Hunt	London.
John A Iredale	Lecturer, Project Planning Centre for Developing Countries, University of Bradford.
R J Irving	Personnel Director, Imperial Inns and Taverns Ltd.
D T Jenkins	Senior Lecturer, Department of Economic and Related Studies, University of York.
David J Jeremy	Research Fellow, Business History Unit, London School of Economics.
David S Johnson	Lecturer, Department of Economic and Social History, Queen's University, Belfast.
Charles A Jones	Lecturer, Department of International Studies, University of Warwick.
Edgar Jones	Group Historian, GKN plc.
Geoffrey Jones	Lecturer, Economic History Department, London School of Economic and Political Science.
*George A Jones	formerly Adviser in Photographic Technology, London.
Shirley Keeble	formerly Research Student, Business History Unit, London School of Economics and Political Science.
Dermot Keogh	Department of Modern History, University College, Cork.
Alexandra Kidner	formerly Researcher *Dictionary of Business Biography,* Business History Unit, London School of Economics and Political Science.
John R Killick	Lecturer, Department of Economics, University of Leeds.
N W Kirby	Lecturer in Economic History, Department of History, University of Stirling.

Derek Knee	Barr, South Glamorgan.
David Kynaston	formerly Research Student, Department of Economic History, London School of Economics and Political History.
Stephen Lawrence	Conference Officer, University College of Wales, Aberystwyth.
*Charles E Lee	London
Jonathan M Liebenau	Research Officer, Business History Unit, London School of Economics and Political Science.
William Lister	Curator of the Museum, Muirhead plc.
Joan Long	Sheringham, Norfolk.
Jane Lowe	Research Assistant, Department of Politics and History, Coventry (Lanchester) Polytechnic.
Arthur J McIvor	formerly Research Assistant, History Unit, Polytechnic of Central London.
Alan C McKinnon	Lecturer, Department of Geography, University of Leicester.
Roger Manville	University Professor and Professor of Film, School of Broadcasting and Film, College of Communication, Boston University, USA.
J D Marshall	Reader Emeritus, University of Lancaster.
Sir Peter Masefield	formerly Chairman of British European Airways and of the London Transport Executive.
T M Megaw	Consulting Engineer, Betchworth, Surrey.
Rosemary C E Milligan	Archivist, The Wellcome Foundation Ltd, London.
Robert M Morgan	Group Publicity and Public Relations Manager, BICC plc, Merseyside.
Peter Morris	Assistant Director (Synthetic Rubber), Centre for the History of Chemistry, Philadelphia, USA.
Jocelyn W F Morton	London.
Michael Moss	Archivist, University of Glasgow.
Robert Murphy	formerly Research Student, Department of Economic History, London School of Economics and Political Science.
Ian Nicholson	Archivist, Mullard Ltd.

G Oldfield	Retired Local Government Officer, Nottingham.
M J Orbell	Archivist, Baring Brothers Ltd, London.
R J Overy	Lecturer, Department of History, Kings College, London.
R H Parker	Professor of Accountancy, Department of Economics, University of Exeter.
Henry Parris	Research Consultant, Wokingham, Berkshire.
Linda Parry	Research Assistant, Department of Textile and Dress, Victoria and Albert Museum.
D C Phillips	Archivist, Institute of Agricultural History and Museum of English Rural Life, University of Reading.
D W Pittard	President, Pittard Group Limited, Yeovil, Somerset.
D C M Platt	Professor, Department of History, Oxford.
*K G Ponting	formerly Research Director, Pasold Research Fund.
Dilwyn Porter	Senior Lecturer, Department of History, Worcester College of Higher Education.
Joseph Rank	President, Ranks Hovis McDougall Ltd.
J Gordon Read	Keeper of Archives, Merseyside County Museums, Liverpool.
W J Reader	Texaco Visiting Fellow, Business History Unit, London School of Economics and Political Science.
Basil N Reckitt	Director, Reckitt & Coleman Ltd.
M C Reed	Honorary Lecturer, Department of History, University of Glasgow.
P N Reed	Assistant Director, Merseyside County Museums, Liverpool.
R W Rennison	New Works Engineer, Newcastle and Gateshead Water Co.
W G Rimmer	Professor and Head of the Department of Economic History, University of New South Wales, Australia.
Michael Robbins	formerly Managing Director (Railways), London Transport Executive.
Michael Robson	Research Student, Business History Unit, London School of Economics and Political History.
E A Rose	Hyde, Cheshire.

D J Rowe	Lecturer, Department of Economics, University of Newcastle upon Tyne.
C A Russell	Professor, Department of the History of Science and Technology, The Open University.
S P Russell	Bedford.
John P Scott	Lecturer, Department of Sociology, University of Leicester.
Christine Shaw	Research Officer, Business History Unit, London School of Economics and Political Science.
Sarah Silcox	Research Assistant, Business History Unit, London School of Economics and Political Science.
Judy Slinn	London.
P Eynon Smart	formerly with The Institute of Bankers, London.
Richard Storey	Archivist, Modern Records Centre, University of Warwick Library.
Geoffrey Stow	Cataloguer, Department of Manuscripts, National Maritime Museum.
Eric E G Street	Retired Agency Manager, The National Mutual Life Assurance Society.
Peter Sutcliffe	Senior Editor, Oxford University Press.
Philip Sykes	London.
Julian C Temple	Company Historian, Adwest Group plc, Reading.
W A Thomas	Senior Lecturer, Department of Economics, University of Liverpool.
J C Thompson	Peterborough.
David W Thoms	Principal Lecturer, Department of Politics and History, Coventry (Lanchester) Polytechnic.
L J Tolley	formerly with Renold plc.
G Tonge	Marketing Director, Austin Reed Ltd, London.
D Gordon Tucker	Honorary Professor and Senior Fellow in the History of Technology, University of Birmingham.
Geoffrey Tweedale	Researcher, Business History Unit, London School of Economics and Political Science.

R E Tyson   Senior Lecturer, Department of Economic History, University of Aberdeen.

David H E Wainwright   Economic and Social Research Council, London.

John Walton   Senior Lecturer, School of Library and Information Science, Loughborough Technical College.

Fred Wellings   Beckenham, Kent.

Brian West   Group Public Relations Adviser, The Littlewoods Organisation Ltd, Liverpool.

Oliver M Westall   Lecturer, Department of Economics, University of Lancaster.

Raymond R Wile   Associate Professor, Paul Klapper Library, Queen's College, Flushing, New York, USA.

L J Williams   Senior Lecturer, Department of Economic and Social History and Sociology, University College of Wales, Aberystwyth.

Ronald Wilson   Principal, Historical Aviation Service.

J R Winton   London.

Chris Wrigley   Reader of Economic History, Department of Economics, University of Loughborough.

* Now (July 1985) deceased

Notes to Readers

1 Biographies are in the alphabetical sequence of subjects' family names. In the case of *hyphenated* surnames the first name in the compound family name determines the sequence.

2 In entry headings the title 'Lord' has been confined to barons, holders of the lowest degree in the British peerage; holders of degrees above baron have been given their exact peerage title, 'Viscount', 'Duke' etc. Peers are all listed in the alphabetical sequence of *family* names, not titles.

3 Place names are normally used according to the contemporary usage pertaining to the particular entry.

4 County boundaries are usually those prevailing before the reorganisation of local government in 1975.

5 For a note on British currency usage, see abbreviations (below), under £.

6 Foreign words have not been italicised.

7 The place of publication in bibliographical references is London, unless otherwise stated.

8 In the case of books running to several editions, bibliographical information is provided for the first or major edition.

9 Cross references to entries in the *Dictionary of National Biography, Who's Who of British Members of Parliament* and *Who Was Who* are regularly provided in the lists of sources but in many cases contributors have relied on ampler or more recently discovered sources.

10 On probate: the biography of any *DBB* subject dying in England or Wales includes the gross valuation of his/her estate where this has been recorded in the probate calendars at Somerset House, London, under a civil system commenced in January 1858. These figures should however be used with great caution, bearing in mind the following caveats:

(a) Before 1898 probate was required in respect of personalty only ie only 'moveables' like personal effects, stocks and shares and bank credits but also leaseholds.

(b) From 1898 onwards (following the Land Transfer Act of 1897) the probate valuation included realty, or immovable property like land and houses.

(c) Valuations of both personalty and realty always included unsettled property ie property in the absolute possession of the testator and not preserved in any way for future generations by some legal act of settlement.

(d) Settled land (ie that tied up by acts of settlement) was included in the probate calendar figures from 1 January 1926 under the Settled Land Act of 1925.

(e) Inter vivos gifts were not included in probate.

(f) Gross probate valuations of estates are those made before the deduction of funeral expenses and debts due on the estate.

(g) Prior to 1881 the value of an estate was given in round figures eg not exceeding £450,000 or £500,000 etc.

(h) The figures given in these entries are taken from the calendars at Somerset House and therefore miss any Scottish, Irish or foreign probates, unless these are specifically identified.

For further historical notes on this complex subject see Josiah Wedgwood, *The Economics of Inheritance* (Harmondsworth, Middlesex: Penguin Books Ltd, 1939 ed); Colin D Harbury and D M W N Hitchens, *Inheritance and Wealth Inequality in Britain* (George Allen & Unwin, 1979); William D Rubinstein, *Men of Property. The Very Wealthy in Britain Since the Industrial Revolution* (Croom Helm, 1981).

11   Subjects' writings. These do not include unpublished works. Where these are known they are cited as an unpublished source. Subjects' writings have been checked against holdings recorded in the British Library and National Union catalogues as well as those of the BLPES.

12   Company reports have been regarded as an unpublished source.

13   Patents have been classed as writings.

Abbreviations

AA	Automobile Association *or* anti-aircraft
AC	Alternating current
& Co	and Company
ADC	aide-de-camp
AEG	Allgemeine Elektrizitäts Gesellschaft
AEI	Associated Electrical Industries
AFC	Air Force Cross
AG	Aktiengesellschaft (joint-stock company)
AGM	Annual General Meeting
AIOC	Anglo-Iranian Oil Co
am	ante meridiem (before noon)
APCM	Associated Portland Cement Manufacturers
APOC	Anglo Persian Oil Co
ARP	air-raid precautions
ASE	Amalgamated Society of Engineers
Aslef	Associated Society of Locomotive Engineers and Firemen
ATA	Air Transport Auxiliary
ATV	Associated Television
b	born
BA	Bachelor of Arts *or* British Airways
BASF	Badische Anilin-und-Soda Fabrik
BAT	British American Tobacco Co *or* British Automobile Traction Co Ltd
Bateman	John Bateman, *Great Landowners of Great Britain* (Harrison, 1879).
BBC	British Broadcasting Association

BBFT	British Bank for Foreign Trade
BC & CC	British Cocoa & Chocolate Co
BCe	Birth certificate from General Register Office, St Catherines House, London WC1B 6JP
BCe (Scots)	Scottish birth certificate from The Registrar General, New Register House, Edinburgh EH1 3YT
BDA	Bradford Dyers' Association
BDC	British Dyestuffs Corporation
BEA	British European Airways *or* British Electricity Authority
BEF	British Expeditionary Force
BET	British Electric Traction Co
bhp	brake horsepower
BICC	British Insulated Callender's Cables
BIDC	Bankers' Industrial Development Corporation
BISF	British Iron and Steel Federation
BL	British Library, Great Russell Street, London WC1B 3DG
BLPES	British Library of Political and Economic Science, London School of Economics, Portugal Street, London WC2A 2HD
BMC	British Motor Corporation *or* British Metal Corporation
BMH	British Motor Holdings
BMMO	Birmingham & Midland Motor Omnibus Co Ltd
BMPM	Bowater's Mersey Paper Mills Ltd
BOAC	British Overseas Airways Corporation
Boase	Frederic Boase, *Modern English Biography, Containing Memoirs of Persons Who Have Died since 1850* (6 vols, Truro: Netherton & Worth, 1892-1921).
BP	British Petroleum
BPC	British Printing Corporation

BPCM	British Portland Cement Manufacturers
Bros	Brothers (used in company titles)
BS	Bachelor of Surgery (Britain) *or* Bachelor of Science (USA) *or* Bristol-Siddeley
BSA	Birmingham Small Arms
BSc	Bachelor of Science (Britain)
BSC	British Steel Corporation
BST	British Stockbrokers' Trust Ltd
Bt	Baronet
BT	Board of Trade
BTC	British Transport Commission *or* British Trade Corporation
Burke's Landed Gentry	(Burke's Peerage Ltd. Various editions since 1836; edition identified by date).
Burke's Peerage and Baronetage	(Burke's Peerage [Genealogical Books] Ltd. Various editions since 1826; edition identified by date).
BVC	British Vacuum Cleaner
ca	circa
CB	Companion of the Bath
CBE	Commander of the Order of the British Empire
CBI	Confederation of British Industry
CEGB	Central Electricity Generating Board
ch	chapter
CIE	Companion of the Order of the Indian Empire
Cif	cost, insurance, freight
C-in-C	Commander-in-Chief
CIWL	Compagnie Internationale des Wagons-Lits
CME	Chief Mechanical Engineer

CMG	Companion of the Order of St Michael and St George
CND	Campaign for Nuclear Disarmament
Co	Company
Col	Colonel
comp	compiled, compiler
Complete Peerage	George Edward Cokayne, *The Complete Peerage of England, Scotland, Ireland, Great Britain and the United Kingdom, Extant Extinct or Dormant* (13 vols, St Catherine Press, 1910-59).
CPA	Calico Printers' Association
C Reg	Companies Registration Office file(s); microfiche versions of the files have been obtained from Companies Registration Office, 55 City Road, London EC1Y 1BB.
C Reg(w)	Notes made from company files subsequently despatched to the PRO and there subjected to a random destruction rate of 80–90 per cent.
CRO	County Record Office
Crockfords	*Crockfords Clerical Directory* (various editions, 1858 to present).
cwt	hundredweight (112 pounds, avoirdupois)
d	died
d (following a monetary figure)	pence [See note under £ at the end of this list]
DAB	*Dictionary of American Biography* edited by Allen Johnson and Dumas Malone (22 vols, New York: Charles Scribner's Sons, 1928-1944). The abbreviation also covers supplements to the *DAB*.
DBB	*Dictionary of Business Biography*
DCe	Death certificate from General Register Office, St Catherines House, London WC2B 6JP
DCL	Doctor of Civil Law *or* Distillers Co Ltd
DCM	Distinguished Conduct Medal
DCO	Dominion, Colonial and Overseas (Barclays Bank DCO)
DD	*Directory of Directors* (annual, East Grinstead: Thomas Skinner Directories, 1880-1983).

Debrett	*Debrett's Peerage, Baronetage, Knightage and Companionage with Her Majesty's Royal Warrant Holders* (Kingston upon Thames, Kelly's Directories. Numerous editions since 1803).
DH	de Havilland
DL	Deputy-Lieutenant
DLB	*Dictionary of Labour Biography* edited by Joyce M Bellamy and John Saville (6 vols, Macmillan, 1972-82, in progress).
DLitt	Doctor of Letters
DNB	*Dictionary of National Biography* edited by Leslie Stephen and Sidney Lee (63 vols, Oxford University Press, 1885-1933). The abbreviation also covers supplements to the *DNB*.
DOT	Department of Overseas Trade
DoT	Department of Trade
DSc	Doctor of Science
DSC	Distinguished Service Cross
DSIR	Department of Scientific and Industrial Research
DWB	*Dictionary of Welsh Biography down to 1940* edited by Sir John Edward Lloyd and R T Jenkins (London: The Honourable Society of Cymmrodorion, 1959).
EAC	Employers' Advisory Council
ECC	English China Clays
ECSC	European Coal and Steel Community
Edwards seminar paper.	Almost 450 papers, chiefly by businessmen and women presented in Professor Ronald S Edwards' Seminar at the LSE, 1946-1973, on 'Problems in Industrial Administration' (in BLPES Manuscripts). A number of these papers were published in *Business Enterprise* (Macmillan, 1959), *Studies in Business Organisation* (Macmillan, 1961) and *Business Growth* (Macmillan, 1966) edited by R S Edwards and H Townsend.
EE	English Electric
EEC	European Economic Community
EEF	Engineering Employers' Federation

EFTA	European Free Trade Association
Elliott research notes.	The biographical research notes on British MPs (mostly of the twentieth century) compiled by the late Anthony Elliott and kindly loaned to the *DBB* project by his widow Mrs Thea Elliott.
EMGAS	East Midlands Gas Board
EMI	Electric & Musical Industries
Erickson workcards.	Biographical workcards prepared by Professor Charlotte Erickson on steel and hosiery leaders, for her book *British Industrialists. Steel and Hosiery, 1850-1950* (Cambridge: Cambridge University Press for the National Institute of Economic and Social Research, 1959) and kindly loaned by her to the *DBB* project.
ESC	English Steel Corporation
ETU	Electrical Trades Union
F	Fahrenheit (temperature)
FBI	Federation of British Industries
FCS	Fellow of the Chemical Society (now FRCS)
FCSDA	Fine Cotton Spinners' & Doublers' Association
fl	floreat (flourished)
FO	Foreign Office
fob	free on board
Foster, *Alumni Oxonienses*.	Joseph Foster, *Alumni Oxonienses, The Members of the University of Oxford 1715-1886* (4 vols, Oxford: James Parker & Co, 1891).
FRS	Fellow of the Royal Society
GB	Great Britain (England, Wales and Scotland)
GBE	Knight *or* Dame Grand Cross of the Order of the British Empire
GCVO	Knight *or* Dame Grand Cross of the Royal Victorian Order
GDP	Gross Domestic Product
GEC	General Electric Co
GER	Great Eastern Railway

GHQ	General Headquarters
GKN	Guest, Keen & Nettlefolds
GL	Glaxo Laboratories
GLC	Greater London Council
GmbH	Gesellschaft mit beschränkter Haftung (private limited liability company)
GNP	Gross National Product
GRA	Greyhound Racing Association Ltd
GWR	Great Western Railway
HC	House of Commons
HLRO	House of Lords Record Office
HM	His/Her Majesty/Majesty's
HMS	His/Her Majesty's Ship
HMV	His Master's Voice
Hon	Honourable
HP	Handley Page
hp	horsepower
HT	High Tension
HTS	Hilton Transport Services
IAL	Imperial Airways Ltd
IBA	Independent Broadcasting Authority
ibid	ibidem (the same source as the one previously quoted)
ICAEW	Institute of Chartered Accountants in England and Wales
ICE	Institution of Civil Engineers
ICI	Imperial Chemical Industries
IEE	Institution of Electrical Engineers

IG	Interessengemeinschaft (combine)
IME	Institution of Mechanical Engineers
Inc	Incorporated
JISI	*Journal of the Iron and Steel Institute*
JP	Justice of the Peace
Jr	Junior
KBE	Knight Commander of the Order of the British Empire
KCB	Knight Commander of the Order of the Bath
KCIE	Knight Commander of the Order of the Indian Empire
KCMG	Knight Commander of the Order of St Michael and St George
KCVO	Knight Commander of the Royal Victorian Order
KG	Knight of the Order of the Garter
KLM	Koninklijke Luchtvaart Maatschappij NV (Royal Dutch Air Lines)
KT	Knight of the Order of the Thistle
kV	kilovolt
kW	kilowatt
£	£: see end of list
lb	pound(s), weight
LBC	Left Book Club *or* London Bicycle Co
LCC	London County Council
LCD	London, Chatham & Dover Railway
Lieut Col	Lieutenant Colonel
LLB	Bachelor of Laws
LLD	Doctor of Laws
LMS	London, Midland & Scottish Railway *or* London Missionary Society
LNER	London & North Eastern Railway

LNWR	London & North Western Railway
LSE	London School of Economics and Political Science
Ltd	Limited
MA	Master of Arts
MAP	Ministry of Aircraft Production
MBE	Member of the Order of the British Empire
MC	Military Cross
MCe	Marriage certificate from General Register Office, St Catherine's House, London WC2B 6JP
MCe (Scots)	Scottish marriage certificate from The Registrar General, New Register House, Edinburgh EH1 3YT
MCe (Irish)	Irish marriage certificate from The Registrar General, Oxford House, 49/55 Chichester Street, Belfast BT1 4HL (Northern Ireland), or The Registrar General, Custom House, Dublin 1 (Southern Ireland)
MCWF Co	Metropolitan Carriage, Wagon & Finance Co
MD	Doctor of Medicine
mk or MK	Mark
MM	Military Medal
MMS	Methodist Missionary Society
MP	Member of Parliament
MSc	Master of Science
MSS	Manuscripts
MVO	Member of the Royal Victorian Order
MW	megawatt(s)
NAAFI	Navy, Army, and Air Force Institutes
NATO	North Atlantic Treaty Organisation
NCB	National Coal Board
NCO	non-commissioned officer

nd	no date
NEDC	National Economic Development Council
NER	North-Eastern Railway
NHS	National Health Service
NLR	North London Railway
np	no place
NPA	Newspaper Proprietors' Association
NRA	National Register of Archives, Quality House, Quality Court, London WC2A 1HP
NSPCC	National Society for the Prevention of Cruelty to Children
NV	naamloze vennootschap (limited company)
OBE	Officer of the Order of the British Empire
OB St John	British Order of the Hospital of St John of Jerusalem
ODI	Overseas Development Institute
OPEC	Organisation of Petroleum Exporting Countries
OTC	Officers' Training Corps
P&O	Peninsular & Oriental Steamship Co
PA	Press Association
passim	here and there
PATA	Proprietary Articles Trade Association
PC	Privy Councillor
PD	*Parliamentary Debates* (Hansard)
PEP	Political and Economic Planning, now the Policy Studies Institute, London
PFR	Prototype Fast Reactor
pH	measure of hydrogen in concentration (indicating level of acidity)
PhD	Doctor of Philosophy

PLA	Port of London Authority
PLC (*or* plc)	public limited company
pm	post meridiem (afternoon)
PP	*Parliamentary Papers*
pp	privately printed or published
PrC	Probate Calendar in Principal Registry of the Family Division, Somerset House, Strand, London WC2R 1LP
PRO	Public Record Office, Chancery Lane, London WC2A 1LR, or Ruskin Avenue, Kew, Richmond, Surrey TW9 4DU
psi	pounds per square inch
Pty	Proprietary (private limited company in Australia and South Africa)
PVC	polyvinyl chloride
qqv	quae vide (which see; cross reference to several other entries)
qv	quod vide (which see; cross reference to another entry)
RA	Royal Artillery *or* Royal Academician
RAC	Royal Automobile Club
R&D	research and development
RAeS	Royal Aeronautical Society
RAF	Royal Air Force
RAFVR	Royal Air Force Volunteer Reserve
RAOC	Royal Army Ordnance Corps
RASC	Royal Army Service Corps
RC	Royal Commission
RCA	Radio Corporation of America
RE	Royal Engineers
REA	Royal Exchange Assurance
REME	Royal Electrical and Mechanical Engineers

rep	reprinted
RFC	Royal Flying Corps
RIBA	Royal Institute of British Architects
Rly	Railway
RM	Royal Marines
RN	Royal Navy
RNAS	Royal Naval Air Service
RNR	Royal Naval Reserve
RNVR	Royal Naval Volunteer Reserve
RO	Record Office
RPM	resale price maintenance
RR	Railroad (USA)
RSA	Royal Society of Arts
Rt Hon	Right Honourable
RTZ	Rio Tinto-Zinc Corporation
RUSI	Royal United Services Institute
s (following a monetary figure)	shillings [see note under £ at the end of this list]
SA	Société Anonyme (limited liability company)
SC	Select Committee
Scots DBB	*Scottish Dictionary of Business Biography,* Department of Economic History, Glasgow University
SE&CR	South Eastern & Chatham Railway
SHAEF	Supreme Headquarters, Allied Expeditionary Forces
Singer, *History of Technology.*	Charles Singer, E J Holmyard, A R Hall and Trevor Williams (eds), *A History of Technology* (7 vols, Oxford: Clarendon Press, 1954-78).
SMT	Securities Management Trust
SOAS	School of Oriental and African Studies, London University

SR	Southern Railway
Sr	Senior
SSRC Elites data.	Biographical workcards from SSRC project on 'The Economic Worth of Elites in British Society since 1880' conducted by Professor H J Perkin of Lancaster University, and kindly loaned by him to the *DBB* project.
STOL	Short take-off and landing
sv	sub verbo (under the heading cited)
TA	Territorial Army
TD	Territorial Decoration
TDG	Transport Development Group
Times *Prospectuses.*	*Prospectuses of Public Companies Including the Number of Bonds Drawn and Cancelled. Reprinted from the Advertisement Columns of the Times* (biannual, Times Publishing Co Ltd, 1891-1964).
TNPG	The Nuclear Power Group
TT	Tourist Trophy
TUC	Trades Union Congress
TV	television
TWA	Trans World Airlines
UAC	United Africa Company
UCL	University College, London
UDC	Urban District Council
UERL	Underground Electric Railway Co of London
UK	United Kingdom (England, Wales, Scotland and Northern Ireland)
USA	United States of America
USAF	United States Air Force
V	volt(s)
VCH	*Victoria History of the Counties of England*

Venn, *Alumni Cantabrigienses*	John Venn and J A Venn, *Alumni Cantabrigienses. A Biographical List of All Known Students, Graduates and Holders of Office at the University of Cambridge, from the Earliest Times to 1900* Part II *1752 to 1900* (6 vols, Cambridge: Cambridge University Press, 1946-54)
V/STOL	vertical or short take-off and landing
VTOL	vertical take-off and landing
Will	Will of subject (unless otherwise stated) in Principal Registry of the Family Division, Somerset House, London WC2R 1LP
WPM	Wallpaper Manufacturers
WW	*Who's Who* (annual, Adam & Charles Black, 1849-1983).
WWMP	Michael Stenton and Stephen Lees, *Who's Who of British Members of Parliament. A Biographical Dictionary of the House of Commons* (4 vols, Hassocks, Sussex: Harvester Press, 1976-81).
WWW	*Who Was Who, 1897-1980* (8 vols, Adam & Charles Black, 1920-81).
WWW Theatre	*Who Was Who in the Theatre, 1912-1976* (Detroit: Gale Research Co, 1978)
YMCA	Young Men's Christian Association
£	Pound (monetary). In all entries, for dates before 15 February 1971 (when Britain switched to a decimal currency) the pound quoted is the old one, ie divided into 20 shillings each of 12 pence. Monetary sums under this old system are expressed as follows: £2 12s 6d. The decimal system abandoned shillings and divided the pound into 100 pence. The conversion rate for shillings is therefore one (old) shilling of 12 pence to five decimal pence.

M

Sir Alfred McAlpine (courtesy of Sir Alfred McAlpine & Son).

McALPINE, Sir Alfred David

(1881-1944)

Builder and contractor

Alfred David McAlpine was born in Hamilton, Lanarkshire, on 6 November 1881, the fourth son of Robert (later Sir Robert) McAlpine of Newarthill (1847-1935) and his first wife Agnes née Hepburn. He was educated at Larchfield, Helensburgh and Kelvinside Academy, Glasgow.

In 1897, at the age of sixteen, Alfred followed his older brothers into his father's building and contracting firm. Robert McAlpine had started his own small business as a jobbing builder in 1869 and by 1878 was employing over 1,000 men on large building and civil engineering projects. The failure of the City of Glasgow Bank in that year, however, aggravated a depression in the property market and the firm underwent a massive contraction.

When Alfred joined, the firm had taken on a £393,000 contract for the extension of the West Highland Railway from Fort William to Mallaig, with a harbour on the coast, work supervised by his brothers Robert Jr and Tom (qv). Alfred was then involved in the Hebburn, Peterhead and Methil Dock contracts and was probably left in sole charge of a contract for the first time when the firm built College Station in Glasgow (1904-7). Alfred joined the family partnership in 1902. In 1911 he moved to North Wales for the construction of the Alwen Reservoir near Cerrig-y-Drudion. During the First World War he was in charge of a number of projects, including a £2.2 million expansion at the Huddersfield (Dalton) works of the British Dyes Ltd (later the British Dyestuffs Corporation), between November 1915 and October 1921.

Alfred took up residence at Marchwiel Hall, near Wrexham, in 1918 and thereafter North Wales and the North West was his home base and his major business territory. He had married in 1907 Ethel May Williams of Aboyne, Aberdeenshire; they had three children, James (b 1908), Gladys (b 1911) and Mary (b 1915).

In the period immediately after the war the firm was engaged in house-building, and Alfred controlled contracts which in three years turned out

3,000 houses, many for Manchester Corporation. In the 1920s Sir Robert McAlpine & Sons (London) Ltd (registered as a limited company in 1926) moved to London and became responsible, among other projects, for the construction of the Empire Exhibition at Wembley, Tilbury Docks and the construction of the Dorchester Hotel (on the site of Dorchester House). Alfred supervised various building works connected with electrical schemes in North Wales and wharves, docks, tunnels and railways for the Manchester Ship Canal, including considerable development at Ellesmere Port. He also supervised the McAlpine section of the Mersey Tunnel, begun in the late 1920s.

In 1930 the parent company established a subsidiary company for the business in North Wales and the North West, Sir Robert McAlpine & Sons (Midlands) Ltd, of which Alfred became chairman. Sir Robert died in 1934 at the age of eighty-seven and his eldest son, Robert, a few days later. In 1935 it was agreed by an amicable arrangement that Sir Alfred (he was knighted in 1932) should take complete control of the Midlands company and give up his interest in the parent company. The main reason appears to have been that business was relatively short in the Midlands and the directors of Sir Robert McAlpine & Sons (London) Ltd wanted to withdraw from the region and concentrate on Southern England. Despite the economic depression, Sir Alfred and his son, Jimmie, who by then had joined the firm, perceived long-term prospects in the Midlands.

From 1936 the company was deemed to be under Sir Alfred's control although it was not until 1940 that the share exchange was completed, the separation finalised and the name of the company changed to Sir Alfred McAlpine & Son Ltd. As part of the arrangement it was agreed that each firm would tender for orders only in its own geographical area, an arrangement which lasted in various forms for over forty years.

In its first year progress was slow for Sir Alfred McAlpine & Son Ltd, with turnover at only £500,000. As the country prepared for war, however there were contracts for factories, RAF stations and airfields and soon the small workforce and plant taken over from the parent company had to be expanded. A number of quarries were converted into underground factories or stores, a particularly large one at Corsham in Wiltshire being constructed for the Bristol Aeroplane Co. In 1943, in addition to the continuing building and repair work, the company, at the request of the Government, started open-cast coal-mining in order to provide more coal to meet the demand for power and fuel supplies.

Sir Alfred was known in the firm as a stickler for punctuality but he also inspired in his men great loyalty and affection. He ran the company in a paternal fashion. He was succeeded as chairman by his son, known in the company as 'Mr Jimmie', who presided over the subsequent growth of the company, now the Sir Alfred McAlpine Group, with diversified interests in the UK and overseas in all aspects of building and civil engineering, the raw materials and plant, pipelines, timber and motor distribution.

Outside business Sir Alfred was active in public life and local politics for thirty years. He was chairman of the Wrexham Division of the Conservative Party from 1921 until 1928 and in 1927 was appointed honorary treasurer of the North Wales Division of the National Union of Conservative and Unionist Associations. He was High Sheriff of Denbighshire in 1923 and a magistrate of Denbighshire from 1926 until his death. He was a life governor of Wrexham War Memorial Infirmary. His other interests were sporting — cricket (he was president of the North Wales Cricket Association) and football (he was a director of Wrexham Football Club). He also had a keen interest in horse-racing and owned a number of race-horses himself, some of which were moderately successful.

Sir Alfred McAlpine died on 25 May 1944, leaving £345,460 gross.

JUDY SLINN

Sources:

Unpublished

Sir Alfred McAlpine Group, London, company records.

PrC.

Published

WWW.

McALPINE, Sir Thomas Malcolm

(1877-1967)

Civil engineering and building contractor

Thomas Malcolm McAlpine (known in earlier years as Tom and later as Malcolm) was born in Hamilton, Lanarkshire, on 19 June 1877, the third son of Robert McAlpine, later the first baronet, and his wife Agnes, daughter of William Hepburn.

Thomas McAlpine was educated at Kelvinside Academy. He left school at the age of sixteen and, like his brothers Robert, William, Alfred (qv) and Granville, began working for his father's firm of building contractors, Robert McAlpine, Contractors. All the brothers joined the firm before they were seventeen, and none had any technical or professional skills or qualifications. The father proved a hard taskmaster to his sons, perhaps because the firm, though it had been operating for about twenty-five years, had not yet become firmly established. In later years Thomas McAlpine remarked that 'Father, even now, has no idea how hard was the grindstone to which he put our noses' {Childers (1925) 49}.

At the age of twenty-one Thomas was put in charge of the contract to build the Fort William to Mallaig extension of the West Highland

Railway, considered among the most arduous and hazardous civil engineering contracts ever undertaken in the United Kingdom. On this project, already distinguished by his own ingenious application of the principle of a water-driven dentist's drill to speed excavation through rock, he suffered grievous and near-fatal injuries as the result of a dynamiting operation. He survived by dint of his father's and workmen's efforts in carrying him the many miles to Fort William through countryside generously described as inhospitable, the consummate skills of the eminent Scottish surgeon, Professor (later Sir William) McEwan, and his own fierce determination to live. The spiritual impact of this experience on young Mr Tom, as he was known in the firm at that time, inspired an attitude to life and to living that remained steadfast throughout the long, active years that remained to him.

In 1907, eager to expand the firm's sphere of influence, and with stern parental admonitions to succeed quickly or return north, he came to London and opened an office from which he personally obtained and supervised the early Southern England contracts undertaken by the company. Indicative of his tenacity is the fact that, faced with being unknown amongst the all-important engineering fraternity, he set about acquiring sufficient skill at the billiard table to enter and win a tournament in a London club frequented by civil engineers, achieving a 'fame' sufficient to impress his contemporaries with his personal qualities and to open doors hitherto firmly closed. Soon after, he was elected an associate of the Institution of Civil Engineers, a distinction reserved for men who, though not qualified civil engineers, yet make notable contributions to the profession.

In the First World War, McAlpine was appointed chairman of the vitally important Home Ores Committee, charged with the procurement and control of this essential raw material. In 1921 he received a knighthood.

The post-war growth of the large London and Southern Counties area of company operations became a joint responsibility of the family, with Sir Malcolm (as Thomas was known) and his elder brother William playing a major part. This was and remains (1984) the pattern of the McAlpine family in commercial and industrial matters, each member assuming control of the work in defined areas of the country and a specific responsibility in the many related activities of the company. Although a private limited company, Sir Robert McAlpine & Sons Ltd, was incorporated in 1926, the firm continued to function as a partnership whose shares could only be held by working partners, who were all McAlpines.

In London Sir Malcolm and William brought a combination of talents to bear on such capital- and labour-intensive projects as the British Empire Exhibition and Stadium at Wembley in 1922-24, where 12,000 men were employed at the peak construction period and the completion, at the Government's urgent request, of the important Motor Transport Depot at Slough in 1919-20, a short-term contract worth £2 million.

Undertaking the construction of the prestigious Dorchester Hotel in London's Park Lane led to an extension of the family's interests. Within three years of its opening the hotel was in financial difficulties. The McAlpine family, who were joint owners with Gordon Hotels Ltd,

The McAlpine family with Thomas (later Sir Malcolm) McAlpine standing extreme left (courtesy of Sir Robert McAlpine & Sons plc).

proposed disposing of their interest to their partners. Whilst agreeing the wisdom of a change in ownership, Gordon Hotels Ltd proposed that McAlpines should be the ones to take control. Sir Malcolm, with the support of his brother William who deemed the proposal financially viable, persuaded the family that they could successfully undertake hotel management. They did so for more than forty years and to such effect that the Dorchester enjoyed an international reputation for excellence.

Sir Malcolm's strength lay in project organisation, an instinctive appreciation of construction techniques and the ability to make enduring friendships with people in all walks of life, a gregariousness that stood the company in good stead in many of their dealings. He would never talk of 'labour' but always of his men, believing each man should be recognised as an individual. William added the crucial element of financial acumen. Both showed a capacity to lead men, often by physical example, and in this way they were following the dictates of their father, as were all the other members of the family engaged in the firm. Sir Malcolm himself considered that the best training for construction bosses was to 'put 'em under a digger that needs repairing' {Turner (1969) 274}.

In May 1938 Sir Malcolm was appointed a member of the advisory and consultative body of businessmen appointed by Sir Kingsley Wood, Secretary of State for Air. During the Munich crisis, when it was realised that preparations made for camouflage of airfields were inadequate, he undertook to deal with the problem, and within forty-eight hours, McAlpines had surrounded the main airfields in the countryside with dummy fields, hedges and hangars. A number of major responsibilities occupied him heavily during the Second World War. As chairman of the Committee of Engineers and Contractors he advised on the efficient wartime use of manpower and plant and in his capacity as chairman of the Opencast Coal Technical Advisory Organisation he contributed to the production of coal with the minimum of manpower and the maximum utilisation of scarce equipment. In this role he personally organised the selection and transhipment of giant excavating equipment from America under the Lend-Lease arrangements, revelling in the honorary rank of admiral bestowed for his ocean journeys on the *Queen Mary*. By far the most dramatic deployment of his skills was reserved for his chairmanship of a committee formed to design and make the concrete breakwaters of Mulberry Harbours, so essential to the success of the build-up after the D-Day landings on the Normandy coast in 1944. Sir Robert McAlpine & Sons built more Phoenix caissons for the Mulberry Harbour than any other contractor.

In 1956 Sir Robert McAlpine & Sons Ltd was reconstructed, the new company, with a capital of 10,000 £1 ordinary shares, taking over the old, which had a share capital of £2,150,100. All seven directors were members of the McAlpine family. Soon 1,990,000 £1 ordinary shares were allotted to the directors as fully paid, as capitalisation of reserves. None of the shares were allotted to Sir Malcolm. By 1965 the total issued capital of the company was £10 million. (The company does not publish its results.) Though he did not undertake detailed supervision of projects, Sir Malcolm remained an active, potent force in the firm almost until his death.

Sir Malcolm assisted in the formation of the Federation of Civil Engineering Contractors, becoming its chairman in 1936 and then a vice-president. He was an enthusiastic and successful racehorse owner, his successes including the winning of the 1921 Grand National with *Shaun Spadah* and the 1952 1,000 Guineas at Newmarket with *Zabara*. He was a more than competent tennis player. To the end of his life he insisted on taking exercise, walking at least two miles a day.

In 1903 Malcolm McAlpine married Maud, second daughter of James Gibson Dees of Whitehaven. They had three sons, Robin (b 1906), Malcolm (b 1917) and Kenneth (b 1920). All entered the family firm at an early age: Robin (later Sir Robin) succeeded his father as chairman of the company on Sir Malcolm's death.

Sir Malcolm McAlpine died on 12 April 1967, at the age of ninety, leaving an estate proved at £151,799 gross.

ARTHUR G CODD

Sources:

Unpublished

Sir Robert McAlpine & Sons Ltd, London, archives.

C Reg: Sir Robert McAlpine & Sons Ltd (566,823).

PrC.

Published

J Saxon Childers, *Robert McAlpine — A Biography* (pp, 1925).

The First Hundred Years (Sir Robert McAlpine & Sons Ltd, 1972).

John Thomas, *The West Highland Railway* (Dawlish: David & Charles, 1965).

Times 13, 15 Apr, 4 May 1967.

Graham Turner, *Business in Britain* (Eyre & Spottiswoode, 1969).

WWW.

MACARA, Sir Charles Wright

(1845-1929)

Cotton manufacturer

Charles Wright Macara (from Sir Charles W Macara Recollections*).*

Charles Wright Macara was born in Strathmiglo, Fife, on 11 January 1845, the only son of William Macara, a Scottish Free Church minister and his wife, Charlotte née Cowpar, the daughter of a farmer and army colonel. Charles Macara later recorded that his parents inculcated in him a lifelong religious conviction (his affiliation was to the Presbyterian church) and a hatred of injustice. After education at Strathmiglo parish school and public school in Edinburgh, Macara was sent, aged seventeen, to work in a textile warehouse in Mosley Street, Manchester. After a brief migration to Glasgow, again employed by a firm of merchants, he returned to Manchester in 1868 as a representative for Cox Brothers (one of the brothers was related to Macara's mother), a large, well-known Dundee-based jute firm. He worked his way up to the position of head of Cox Brothers' business in Manchester, a job he held until 1880.

In 1875 Macara married Marion Young, grand-daughter of the founder of Henry Bannerman & Sons, cotton merchants, spinners and manufacturers, of Manchester; they had two sons (one of whom died young) and four daughters. Five years later Macara joined Henry Bannerman & Sons as the managing partner. Although he wrote little about the role he played at Bannermans, he was, nonetheless, a fairly dynamic, innovative and hard-working manager. In the 1880s he initiated an extensive reorganisation of the merchanting side of the business, switching the interests of the company almost exclusively to 'heavy' goods — including curtains, quilts, sheets, blankets, flannels and calicoes. The York Street warehouse was re-equipped, branches for distribution were extended to a number of towns, advertising improved considerably and the firm converted into a limited liability company — with Macara as managing director — in 1890. The production side of the business was also expanded under Macara's direction. The two Stalybridge spinning mills were re-equipped with ring frames and production shifted towards the more profitable finer grades of yarn. Weaving continued at the Old Hall Mill, Dukinfield, whilst the Brunswick Mill in Ancoats in an unusual way combined spinning with the making-up of finished garments, including the famous 'Banner' shirts. Macara also pioneered in Manchester the use of electric motors, introducing them into his Brunswick Mill in 1908.

Initially, Macara's managerial style was typical of the times: fairly firm, verging on the autocratic. The Brunswick Mill had a tradition of labour militancy and when 135 spinning operatives went on strike in 1884, Macara brought in replacement labour, organised protection, prosecuted pickets and any acts of violence and refused to take the men back, despite their eventual agreement to accept his terms. Macara was, on his own admission, a 'novice' in industrial relations at this stage {Macara *Recollections* 12}. By the early 1890s, his attitude towards the operatives had considerably mellowed. He developed a firm commitment to conciliation and fair play, and an aversion to industrial conflict for the rest of his life. Such conflict, he later argued, was futile. He also gained something of a reputation for being a 'welfarist' employer; the Brunswick Mill was reported in the 1920s to be a 'model mill' and Bannermans' business to be characterised by 'the harmonious relationship that exists between the workers and employers' {*Empire Mail* June 1925}.

Bannermans prospered up to the First World War. In the 1920s, however, the worldwide slump in demand for cotton goods seriously affected the firm's fortunes and Macara presided over a further process of rationalisation and reorganisation. The Stalybridge mills were sold off in the early 1920s and efforts were concentrated increasingly on made-up clothing, based at the newly-purchased mill in Hale, Cheshire, and the merchanting and distribution business. The Brunswick and Old Hall Mills only just survived Macara's death, being sold off to the Lancashire Cotton Corporation in March 1930.

Macara's reputation is primarily based on his involvement in the network of employers' organisations in textiles and his work to extend conciliation and regulate trading conditions in the cotton industry. However, it must be borne in mind that Macara was very effective in publicising himself, was pompous and extremely petulant (even by late nineteenth century standards) and throughout his life substantially overstated his contribution to the events of his time. He played a part in the formation of the Manchester Master Cotton Spinners' Association and was its chairman from 1892 to 1926. He did not, however, play a central role in 1890-91 in the formation of the Federation of Master Cotton Spinners' Associations, which was created on the initiative of the Oldham masters' association. Macara only came to prominence within the federation during the twenty-week 'Brooklands' lock-out in 1892-93 due to an accident, the illness of the president Arthur Reyner. During the dispute Macara worked for a constructive compromise and for acceptance of the conciliation proposals — incorporating a formal, industry-wide, three-stage disputes procedure — which were first drawn up by Robert Ascroft

Brunswick Mill, Ancoats, Manchester (from Henry Bannerman & Sons Diary and Buyers' Guide*).*

(1847-99), MP for Oldham and union solicitor. Macara was rewarded for his energy with the presidency of the Federation in 1894, a post he held for twenty-one years. This choice, however, was a politic one. As the Federation was initially dominated by the Oldham association, it was necessary to have a president from outside that area. Moreover, after Bolton joined in 1904-5, it suited most employers to have someone else to stand between the two largest local associations.

A new phase in the labour relations strategy of the Federation was inaugurated after Brooklands; a phase of procedural rather than coercive control, epitomised by the firm commitment of the employers' federation to the formalised 'constitutional' methods of the Brooklands conciliation agreement. Macara was voted chairman at every session of the final court of appeal under the disputes procedure during 1894-1913. Whilst the Brooklands Agreement restricted the ability of the operative spinners to use their bargaining power to secure wage rate increases, the procedure was relatively effective in reducing production time lost through industrial conflict, which was a positive gain for both management and men. The myth of the perfection of the Brooklands Agreement — vociferously propagated by the Webbs in the 1902 and 1926 editions of *Industrial Democracy* and contributed to by Macara himself — has, however, never been completely dispelled. Macara came to perceive its shortcomings and advocated modifications and a scheme for the automatic regulation of wages in cotton spinning according to the state of trade. The latter, however, was never accepted. He was also the originator of the Industrial Council, set up by the Liberal Government in 1911 as a final court of appeal when disputes procedures within any industry failed to produce a settlement. The Industrial Council was little utilised, though, and much to Macara's disgust was allowed to lapse during the First World War. Partly because of the Government's handling of the Industrial Council and its general lack of consultation with industry, Macara became increasingly critical of what he called the 'singularly stupid' state policy in industrial relations {Macara *New Industrial Situation* 23, 26}.

Macara did much to extend the concept and the popularity of collective organisation amongst employers. The Federation of Master Cotton Spinners' Associations grew considerably under his leadership, from representing around 35 per cent of the machine capacity in the cotton spinning trade in 1894, to representing around 65 per cent by 1914. He failed, however, in his objective of merging the spinning and weaving employers' organisations. Macara was also the founder and first president of the Cotton Employers' Parliamentary Association (1899-1911), formed to provide cotton employers with a parliamentary pressure group, representing all sections of the trade. In 1912, Macara extended this initiative by founding the Employers' Parliamentary Association, a broader confederation of employers providing a voice for capital on legislation affecting industry and commerce. This organisation grew to represent 40 employers' organisations and over 2,000 firms, in a number of industries, though the basis of its support lay in the Lancashire region. Macara was president of the latter association from its foundation until early 1917, when he resigned in protest against its merger with the Federation of British Industries.

Macara also worked to improve the trading conditions and organisation of the cotton trade. He helped reduce the cost of raw material and transportation for the industry by exerting pressure on shipping rings and railway companies to reduce freight rates, and by his promotion of a rival raw cotton market in Manchester through his position as first president of the Manchester Cotton Association, 1895-1900. He also played an important role in a number of initiatives to alleviate the problem of raw material shortage caused by poor crop yield, increasing world consumption and the operations of speculators. To combat the serious 'cotton corner' of 1903-4, Macara successfully organised, through the Federation, short-time working throughout Lancashire. He provided support for the Institute of Agriculture and became vice-president of the British Cotton Growing Association, formed in 1904 with the object of developing new sources of supply of raw cotton in areas of the Commonwealth. He also played a leading part in the formation of the International Cotton Federation in 1904 and was its chairman until 1915. This organisation combined almost all of the cotton growing and manufacturing countries of the world and did much to improve the quality and quantity of the world's cotton crop. (Bales produced in India, for example, doubled over 1904-13 from 3 million to 6 million.)

Macara was never drawn into any active involvement in politics and, despite a number of requests, he never sought municipal or parliamentary

Warehouse, 33 York Street, Manchester (from Henry Bannerman & Sons Diary and Buyers' Guide*).*

position. A lifelong champion of free trade, he was one of the most vociferous opponents, on business grounds, of the Conservative policy of Tariff Reform. As a vice-president of the Free Trade League, he played a significant and highly vocal role in the Free Trade movements in 1903, 1906, 1910 and 1917, organising joint action during the campaigns with the cotton trade unions. His involvement earned him the criticism of a number of Tory cotton manufacturers, who claimed that he abused his position within textile employers' organisations for political ends.

A number of philanthropic movements attracted Macara's attention and indeed, he tended to seek relaxation primarily in other forms of service to the community. From 1886 he became involved with the Royal National Lifeboat Institution, becoming chairman of the St Anne's committee of the Institution and occasionally going out to sea. In 1891, he originated the Lifeboat Saturday Movement, which considerably increased the finances of the RNLI, generating around £40,000 per annum. In 1897 and 1900 Macara also took a leading part in the organisation of the Lancashire Indian Famine Funds, which raised over £300,000. He travelled widely, addressed most European monarchs and heads of state in his capacity as chairman of the International Cotton Federation and received various foreign honours. For his services to industry he was created a baronet in 1911.

The First World War provoked a crisis in the cotton industry. Macara advocated a scheme for a wartime raw cotton reserve to prevent severe price fluctuations and the ruin of many cotton growers. When the Federation of Master Cotton Spinners' Associations rejected his proposals he resigned, accusing the organisation of pursuing sectional interests, and subsequently devoted himself to an outspokenly independent view on industrial questions. A sincere patriot, he provided advice and a number of services to wartime government departments. He played a leading role in the agitation for cotton to be made contraband of war due to its importance in the armaments industry; superintended the supply of aircraft cloth for the Admiralty; and considerably improved wartime labour mobilisation by his scheme for a national register of workpeople, which was incorporated in the National Registration Act (1915). His propaganda work for the revival of the Industrial Council and the abolition of Excess Profits Tax came, however, to nothing.

Despite advancing age, Macara remained active at Bannermans in the early 1920s and a prolific commentator on industrial affairs, publishing his memoirs (1921) and nine other books between 1918 and 1928. He was regarded as the doyen of the cotton trade and was a 'dove' in the employers' camp. He became a strong advocate of profit-sharing, continued to promote conciliation and firmly supported the sentiments behind the Mond-Turner conversations of 1928-29. He also openly criticised the severity of the employers' demands, the repressive anti-trade union legislation introduced after the General Strike and the tendency of employers to provoke confrontation and exploit slump conditions to administer a disciplinary lesson to labour.

Macara also became bitterly critical of the 'invertebrate policy' and 'gross mismanagement' {Rylands Library, Manchester and District Cotton Employers' Association, minutes 9 Oct 1925} of the leadership of the Federation of Master Cotton Spinners' Associations in the 1920s. The cotton industry engaged in an undercutting war, with disloyalty increasing and the proportion of the spinning trade organised by the Federation dropping from over 80 per cent in 1921-22 to 66 per cent by 1931. The Federation found it difficult, with the disintegration of consensus, to provide much decisive leadership. In September 1922, Macara was elected president of the Provisional Emergency Cotton Committee, which was an alternative focus of organisation by a group of master cotton spinners. With Macara as a figurehead, this organisation charged the Federation with a misguided, obsessional belief that the solution to the crisis in the industry lay in attacking wages and working conditions. It advocated instead a comprehensive reorganisation of the industry, integrating trade regulation policies (including compulsory price-fixing, action against speculators and the elimination of excess capacity) with an openly co-operative labour relations strategy, the formation of a Joint Cotton Control Board, and arming the Federation with effective disciplinary power, that is, legal compulsion. Macara, however, refused to weaken further the employers' solidarity and strenuously and successfully resisted attempts by the Provisional Committee for formal secession from the Federation.

Macara was a man who was convinced that his ideas were right, indeed infallible and, with age, he became more impatient of opposition and criticism from younger men whom he regarded, with some justification, as swayed purely by sectional interests. He wrote, as Bonar Law once remarked, 'as if he was the incarnation of the cotton trade' {Clarke (1971) 98-99}.

The records of the Manchester Master Cotton Spinners' Association in the 1920s indicate clearly that Macara's views and the direction of his leadership diverged from the opinions of the majority of master cotton spinners and consequently he resigned from the Association in February 1926, lamenting that he ceased to command the support of the organisation. Macara alienated fellow members by complaining of the apathy of the Association, by distancing himself publicly from the views of the vice-chairman, F Arrowsmith, and by devoting more and more of his time and energy to his work with the Provisional Committee. Sadly, he also remained passionately attached to the strategy of free trade at a time when most of the industry was seeking barriers against India, China and Japan as the only solution to protect domestic industry and employment. It is perhaps significant that no plea was made for Macara to reconsider his decision to resign and no official reference made by the Manchester Association three years later to the death of their long-serving chairman.

Nevertheless, Macara's vision was to some extent borne out by the fact that many of the reforms proposed by the Provisional Committee in the 1920s were adopted by the industry after 1931-32. Macara also developed a strong affinity towards moderate trade union leaders (including James Mawdsley (1848-1902)) and his enlightened liberal views and advocacy of complete collective organisation for both workers and employers as the prerequisite for industrial peace earned him the respect of the cotton operatives. A most fitting epitaph came from the operatives' paper:

> He stood out in a peculiar way from his fellows ... He was anything but the capitalist making haste to be rich at the expense of the toilers ... The idea of conciliation in disputes between capital and labour was ever before him ... He was a leader and a pioneer, and he will be remembered not only for what he did, but for what he tried to do {*Cotton Factory Times* 4 Jan 1929}.

Sir Charles Macara died on 2 January 1929 at his home in Hale, Cheshire, at the age of eighty-three and was buried at St Anne's on Sea. He left unsettled property of the gross value of £15,681, with a net personalty of £14,975.

ARTHUR J McIVOR

Writings:

Why Tariff Reform Must Be Rejected (Manchester: Sherratt & Hughes, 1910).

The International Federation of Master Cotton Spinners (Manchester: Sherratt & Hughes, 1911).

'The Industrial Council' *Financial Review of Reviews* Oct 1911.

'Leading the World' *Times* Textile Number 27 June 1913.

Social and Industrial Reform (Manchester: Sherratt & Hughes, 1918).

In Search of a Peaceful World: The Practical Views of a Leader of Industry (Manchester: Sherratt & Hughes, 1921).

Recollections (Cassell, 1921).

Getting the World to Work (Manchester: Sherratt & Hughes, 1922).

The New Industrial Situation; Bolshevism; Conscription of Wealth (Manchester: Sherratt & Hughes, 1922).

The New Industrial Era (Manchester: Sherratt & Hughes, 1923).

Trade Stability and How to Obtain It (Manchester: Sherratt & Hughes, 1925).

Modern Industrial Tendencies (Manchester: Sherratt & Hughes, 1926).

How the Cotton Industry Was Internationalised (Manchester: Sherratt & Hughes, 1927).

Pulling Together in the Industrial World (Manchester: Sherratt & Hughes, 1928).

MACARA Sir Charles Wright

Sources:

Unpublished

Courtaulds, Manchester, Lancashire Cotton Corporation files; sale no 40, Mar 1930.

Greater Manchester CRO, Ancoats, Manchester, Cotton Employers' Parliamentary Association, minutes, 1899-1911; Federation of Master Cotton Spinners' Association, Annual Reports 1891-1929.

Oldham Master Cotton Spinners' Association Archive, Oldham, Federation of Master Cotton Spinners' Associations, minutes, 1891-92.

John Rylands Library, Deansgate, Manchester, Manchester and District Cotton Employers' Association, minutes, 1892-1926.

C Reg: H Bannerman Co Ltd (514,606).

R F Dyson, 'The Development of Collective Bargaining in the Cotton Spinning Industry, 1893-1914' (Leeds PhD, 1971).

Published

George Askwith, *Industrial Problems and Disputes* (John Murray, 1920).

'Bannermans' *Manchester City News* 20 Mar 1926 (Business Centenary Supplement).

Henry Bannerman & Sons Ltd, *Diary and Buyers Guide* 1887-97.

Peter F Clarke, *Lancashire and the New Liberalism* (Cambridge University Press, 1971).

Cotton Factory Times 4 Jan 1929.

The Cotton Spinners and Manufacturers Directory 1894, 1914, 1921, 1931 (Manchester: J Worrall and Co Ltd).

DNB.

Manchester Guardian 3 Jan 1929.

W H Mills, *Sir Charles W Macara, Bart* (Manchester: Sherratt & Hughes, 1917).

John Mortimer, *Industrial Lancashire* (Manchester: Palmer & Howe, 1897).

J H Porter, 'Industrial Peace in the Cotton Trade, 1875-1913' *Yorkshire Bulletin of Economic and Social Research* 19 (1967).

'Raw Cotton to Finished Garment: Activities of the House of Bannerman' *Empire Mail* June 1925.

'Sir Charles Wright Macara, Bart' in *Reign of George V: Representative Subjects of the King* (Dod's Peerage Publishers, 1916).

Textile Mercury 5 Jan 1929.

Times 3 Jan, 5 Apr 1929.

Oliver Warner, *The Life-Boat Service. A History of the Royal National Life-Boat Institution 1824-1974* (Cassell, 1974).

WWW.

McCRINDLE, John Ronald

(1894-1977)

Airline executive

John Ronald McCrindle was born at the Grange, Middlesbrough, Yorkshire, on 29 November 1894, the son of James Robert Ronald McCrindle, a Scottish physician and surgeon, and his wife, Elizabeth Pullan née Kelabow.

Ronald McCrindle was brought up in Kingston, Jamaica, where his father was in practice. He was educated first at Jamaica College and then at Glasgow University, where he studied medicine, but he had not yet qualified when the First World War began.

In August 1914 McCrindle was gazetted a 2nd lieutenant in the Territorial Brigade of the Gordon Highlanders from the Glasgow OTC. From there, in November 1914, he was seconded to the Royal Flying Corps. During the next four years McCrindle served as a pilot in the RFC in France, Mesopotamia, Egypt, Palestine and then again in France. He ended the war as a major, was mentioned in dispatches three times and was awarded the Military Cross.

Between December 1918 and October 1919 McCrindle commanded No 1 Communications Squadron RAF, part of a Wing which flew the first London-Paris air services, during the Versailles Peace Conference. Afterwards he was attached to the British Delegation in Paris, and then became RAF Delegate on Marshal Foch's Aeronautical Advisory Committee. Subsequently Foch invited McCrindle, who spoke French fluently, to join his staff, an honour he declined.

During his time in France, McCrindle met a young American, Odette Feder, daughter of Joseph Fuller Feder, a New York banker. They were married in New York on 26 December 1921. In the following spring, McCrindle elected to retire from the RAF to study at Harvard Business School, graduating in 1924.

Returning to England, McCrindle read law, was called to the Bar at Lincolns Inn in 1927, and practised at the Chancery Bar for the next six years. He did not, however, give up his interest in aviation, but joined the London Aeroplane Club at Stag Lane and acquired a DH Cirrus Moth. In 1932, McCrindle was appointed legal adviser to Edward Hillman (qv), who had formed the independent Hillman's Airways Ltd in November 1931, and started a London (Maylands)-Paris (Le Bourget) air service on 1 April 1933. Edward Hillman died on 31 December 1934, and in April 1935 McCrindle was appointed managing director of the airline.

Hillman had been backed by Leo d'Erlanger (qv), partner in Erlangers Ltd, the merchant bankers. During the next few months, at d'Erlanger's instigation and in collaboration with the Hon Clive Pearson, chairman of Whitehall Securities (which had a holding in United Airways and Spartan Air Lines), a merger was effected between those two airlines and Hillman

Airways to form first, 'Allied British Airways' (registered by Whitehall Securities on 30 September 1935) and then, from 29 October 1935, British Airways Ltd with McCrindle as managing director and its head office at Terminal House in Grosvenor Gardens, London W1. In this way, under the chairmanship of W D L Roberts, McCrindle was back in the operation of the London-Paris air route, on which British Airways Ltd flew at first between Gatwick and Le Bourget and then from Heston to Le Bourget (after a short spell from Croydon when Gatwick was flooded by winter rain and became unusable).

British Airways Ltd absorbed the privately-owned British Continental Airways in August 1936 so that the enlarged company became, substantially, a 'Second Force' in British air transport after the state-supported Imperial Airways. By this time, British Airways Ltd had become McCrindle's pride and joy and his consuming interest.

A further fillip came in December 1936, when an old friend and distinguished airman, Alan Campbell Orde, AFC, was appointed operations manager in charge of flying and engineering at British Airways. Campbell Orde had been in McCrindle's squadron on the London-Paris air route in 1919, and subsequently had been one of the pioneer pilots of the first London-Paris commercial air service operated by Aircraft Transport & Travel Ltd during 1919 and 1920, later becoming one of Britain's leading test pilots. Together McCrindle and Campbell Orde were to form a highly professional team.

Throughout its twelve years of existence, Imperial Airways had bought and operated only British aircraft. In 1936, however, the board of British Airways Ltd determined to develop their air services with the best equipment available anywhere in the world. In December 1936 they received government permission to buy seven of the new Lockheed 10A Electra ten-passenger aircraft, the first twin-engined, all-metal, low-wing monoplane with a retractable undercarriage and variable pitch propellors to be put into service with any British airline company. The British Airways Electras began services on the London-Paris air route on April 1937 with an eighty minute schedule, at £4 10s a single fare, which eclipsed the Imperial airways service scheduled at two-and-a-quarter hours. Later that month, a seven-and-a-quarter hour service between London and Stockholm was opened by Electras, and then the first scheduled night services to Paris.

All this — together with Imperial Airways' disputes with their flying staff and an unwise declaration of an increased (9 per cent) dividend paid out of subsidy — brought about an inquiry into the operation of British air transport under Lord Cadman (qv). The Cadman Report of February 1938 was highly critical of Imperial Airways. It recommended that British Airways should be allocated a major role in the development of British air services into Europe and the pioneering of services to South America, with receipt of subsidy. Imperial Airways would concentrate primarily on the development of Empire air routes.

Discussions were started on a London-Lisbon air service as the first sector of a future South American air route, for which British Airways was working closely with the Fairey Aviation Co on a projected four-engined 22-passenger aircraft, the FC-1. By the end of 1938, Imperial Airways, spurred by these achievements of British Airways, had cut their flying times on the London-Paris air route to one hour exactly, achieved by the introduction of the new de Havilland DH 91 Albatross aircraft. Talks between British Airways and Imperial Airways, in which the Government was also involved, then led to a joint service by the two airlines from 16 April 1939 on the London-Paris air route, flying eight services a day on DH 91 aircraft with a seventy-minute schedule.

By the summer of 1939, British Airways's route network included routes to Berlin, Brussels, Budapest, Copenhagen, Frankfurt, Hamburg and Warsaw, and from 9 August, a London-Berlin night-mail service, flown by Junkers JU52 aircraft jointly with Deutsche Luft Hansa, thereby establishing a link through Berlin to South America.

A merger between the two British airlines was now seen by the Government as desirable. The Bill merging Imperial Airways and British Airways into a new state-owned airways corporation British Overseas Airways Corporation (BOAC) modelled on the BBC and with Sir John Reith (qv), formerly Director-General of the BBC, as chairman received the Royal Assent on 4 August 1939, with the intention that BOAC should be brought into being from 1 April 1940. In the circumstances of the time, McCrindle accepted the merger, even though with regret at the eclipse of his own company.

Ronald McCrindle was appointed deputy director-general of the new BOAC, with Alan Campbell Orde as operations director. Those who had led British Airways were thus in key positions in the new corporation.

With his pleasant personality, his obvious competence and his clear views, McCrindle was soon on good terms with his BOAC associates. McCrindle and Gerard d'Erlanger were the only two members of the original BOAC board not to resign in 1943 as a result of differences with the Air Ministry. From 1947 to 1958 McCrindle, as BOAC's managing director for external affairs (1947-49) and then as the company's advisor on international affairs (1948-58), took a leading part in the negotiations of many international agreements on air transport which followed the war. He acted as the foremost British airline advisor to the British Government Delegation at the Chicago Civil Aviation Conference in 1944 and at the Anglo-American Air Transport Agreement, signed in Bermuda in February 1946.

In 1945 he became a founder member of the executive committee of the International Air Transport Association (IATA) where his knowledge, wisdom, sense of humour, gift for languages and his invariable patience made a major contribution to the progress of air transport throughout the world during the next twelve years. Travelling frequently across the Atlantic to and from IATA's headquarters in Montreal and to meetings in other parts of the world, he always had command of his facts, he rarely missed an important occasion and he always kept his word.

Ronald McCrindle remained on the board of BOAC until 1958, although increasingly handicapped by deafness which he gallantly struggled to overcome. In 1959 he was invited to become chairman of IATA's 'Breaches Commissions', which were formed to examine allegations of malpractice on the part of member airlines. In this capacity, his legal knowledge, readiness to listen attentively, courtesy, sense of fair play and his knowledge of the business was recognised everywhere (including his goodhumoured gesture of turning off his hearing aid when repetition ceased to contribute usefully to discussion). His rulings were clear, firm and never challenged. When he handed over this arduous assignment in 1969 his colleagues in IATA presented him with a bound volume of his findings, a desk and a clock — a gesture which touched him deeply.

McCrindle's perceptive unravelling of complicated problems into simple solutions, combined with his universal goodwill and his enjoyment in entertaining those whose company he cherished, made for him a wide circle of friends, shared by his wife, throughout the world. His wife also shared his enjoyment of books, painting, opera and ballet. He enjoyed tennis and swam whenever he could, but was also a connoisseur of wine, cigars and Stilton cheese. He specially relished the countryside, most of all around his country house, Lossenham Manor, Newenden, Hawkhurst, in Kent. There, a leading American diplomat described him as a British gentleman of the first order, a fitting tribute.

In addition to his MC, awarded in 1918, an OBE in 1919 and the CMG in 1948, McCrindle had several foreign honours. He was created an Officer of the Crown of Belgium, a Commander of the Order of Orange Nassau, an Officer of the Légion d'Honneur and a Member of the Swedish Order of Vasa.

His first marriage, from which there was one son, ended in divorce, and in 1932 he married the writer, Susan Ertz, daughter of Charles Ertz, oil merchant. There were no children of the second marriage, which was a very happy one.

Ronald McCrindle died at his home in Kent on 12 March 1977 at the age of eighty-two, leaving £50,147 gross.

PETER G MASEFIELD

Sources:

Unpublished

BCe.

MCe.

PrC.

Information from Sir William Holden, Sir Robert Maxwell, Alan Campbell Orde, Mrs Ronald McCrindle (Susan Ertz).

Published

Aeroplane 49 (1935), 50 (1936).

John Stroud, *Annals of British Commonwealth Air Transport* (Putnam, 1962).

WWW.

Lord McFadzean (courtesy of BICC).

McFADZEAN, William Hunter

Lord McFadzean of Woldingham

(1903-)

Cable manufacturer

William Hunter McFadzean was born at Stranraer, Wigtownshire, on 17 December 1903, the second of the three sons of Henry McFadzean (1864-1918), a farmer and later a grain merchant, and his wife Agnes Wylie (d 1960), daughter of William Hunter of Garthland Mains, Stranraer. The McFadzeans were a family of farmers who had held land for some generations. William was educated at Stranraer Academy and High School, and Glasgow University. After serving articles with McLay, McAllister & McGibbon, chartered accountants in Glasgow, he qualified as a chartered accountant in 1927. He then joined Chalmers Wade & Co, where he was responsible for auditing the accounts of the British Insulated Cables Ltd of Prescot, Lancashire. In 1932 he became the accountant for that company and subsequently was appointed financial secretary in 1937 and executive manager in 1942.

During this period he became closely associated with Sir Alexander Roger (qv), another Scot, who became chairman of British Insulated Cables in 1930. Roger and McFadzean had a vision of an international electric cable group, and in the years up to the Second World War worked to achieve a merger with other leading cable manufacturers including Callender's Cable & Construction Co Ltd. However, nothing came of these attempts until 1942, when negotiations were re-opened with Callenders. McFadzean was closely involved in these negotiations and acted as the main intermediary between the two companies in the extended discussions that led to their merger as British Insulated Callender's Cables Ltd (BICC) on 29 June 1945. On the formation of the new company, which had an issued capital of £11.2 million and 40,000 employees, Roger became chairman with McFadzean as an executive director. Two years later McFadzean became deputy chairman while still only forty-three years old, the youngest man ever to hold this position in either of the two founding companies of BICC in fifty years. In 1950 he became chief executive as well as deputy chairman of the company, and on the retirement of Roger in 1954 he succeeded him as chairman, an office which he combined with that of managing director. In that year, BICC had an issued capital of £14.3 million, and made a pre-tax profit of £5.9 million.

McFadzean was an incessant traveller, devoting at least a quarter of the year to overseas visits to build up the company's interests around the world, seeking new opportunities and maintaining contact with the management and employees of the overseas companies, ensuring he was up-to-date with affairs in these countries and 'showing the flag' for both Britain and BICC.

A most important contribution to the growth of BICC's overseas manufacturing resources was his recognition that their long term success could only be assured by partnership with local interests and a full appreciation of local aspirations. Largely due to his foresight, these resources have been little affected by the growth of nationalism throughout the world and particularly in those countries which have gained their independence in more recent times. Nevertheless, he did not neglect the older Commonwealth countries and Canada, Australia and South Africa are now (1984) the company's main areas of investment outside Britain.

McFadzean was one of the first of the new generation of accountant managers that emerged in the period following the Second World War and did a great deal to bring financial control to what was a very traditional part of British industry, electric cable making. However as well as financial control, he also brought a sense of purpose, a sense of direction, and a strong belief in the value of teamwork, and to this end he developed a management structure that brought together the skills of engineers, accountants, and other disciplines, to develop and expand the company. He retired as managing director in 1960, continuing as chairman until 1973. He was essentially a 'statesman', presenting himself as a man of style whose well-tailored suits were always adorned by a red carnation.

Between 1945 and 1973 BICC became a major international group, with manufacturing resources in more than 17 countries, a workforce of over 50,000, and annual sales that grew from £30 million to almost £500 million. On his retirement from the chair, McFadzean was appointed honorary president of the company.

Outside BICC and its subsidiaries, McFadzean was also a director of the Midland Bank, 1959-81 (deputy chairman, 1968-77); chairman of the Standard Broadcasting Corporation (UK) Ltd, 1972-79, of Home Oil (UK) Ltd, 1972-78, and of Canada Life Unit Trusts Managers Ltd, 1971–84; deputy chairman of RTZ/BICC Aluminium Holdings Ltd, 1967-73, of the National Nuclear Corporation, 1973-80, and of the Canada Life Assurance Co of Great Britain, from 1971; and a director of the Midland Bank Executor & Trustee Co, 1959-67, the English Electric Co, 1966-68, the Steel Co of Wales Ltd, 1966-67, Anglesey Aluminium Ltd, 1968-73, and the Canadian Imperial Bank of Commerce, 1967-74. He was a member of the Council of the Institute of Directors, 1954-76.

McFadzean contributed much to Britain's export drive as president of the Federation of British Industries (later CBI) from 1959 to 1961, as founder chairman, 1960-64, and later honorary president (1964) of the Export Council of Europe, as chairman of the Commonwealth Export Council, 1964-66, and as founder chairman, 1964-66, and president, 1966-68, of the British National Export Council.

His work for British industry at home and overseas was rewarded by a knighthood in 1960 and a life peerage in 1966. He also received the relatively rare distinction of being a Knight of the Thistle, a particular honour for a son of Scotland; Denmark made him a Grand Knight Commander of the Order of the Dannebrog, and Portugal, a Grande Oficial da Ordem do Infante Dom Henrique, a rare honour for a foreigner.

McFadzean married in 1933 Eileen, daughter of Arthur Gordon, a timber merchant of Blundellsands in Lancashire. They have one son and two daughters, one of whom was adopted.

ROBERT M MORGAN

Writings:

'Development and Organisation of British Insulated Callender's Cables Ltd' in R S Edwards and H Townsend (eds), *Business Growth* (Macmillan, 1966).

Sources:

Unpublished

MCe.

Published

Burke's Peerage and Baronetage.

Robert M Morgan, *Callender's, 1882-1945* (Prescot: BICC PLC, 1982).

WW 1982.

McGOWAN, Harry Duncan

1st Lord McGowan of Ardeer

(1874-1961)

Chemical manufacturer

Sir Harry McGowan, 1928 from the Orpen painting (courtesy of ICI plc).

Harry Duncan McGowan was born in Glasgow on 3 June 1874, son of Henry McGowan and his wife Agnes (d 1937), daughter of Richard Wilson. His father was a master flesher and brass finisher, who left £93 in 1926. McGowan was educated in 1887-89 at Allen Glen's School in Glasgow, and entered the Glaswegian office of Nobel's Explosives Co as an office boy earning 5s a week in 1894. A shrewd judge of character, he became assistant general manager of the company under F J Shand in 1909, and his skill in bargaining was recognised when he was made responsible for Nobel's business diplomacy with German and US explosives manufacturers, including du Pont.

In 1910-11 McGowan had his first outstanding success for Nobel in negotiating with du Pont the amalgamation of numerous Canadian explosives companies into the unified Canadian Explosives Co, of which he became a director in 1911. His methods at this time have been described:

> Having decided that a deal was worth making, he never drove too hard a bargain, preferring a willing seller to a resentful opponent. He was well aware of the importance of personal popularity, particularly with the contractors who bought explosives. He allied himself with popular men and took care to cultivate popularity himself {Reader (1970) 209-10}.

McGowan was elected as chairman of the High Explosives Trade Association in 1910, joined the Nobel board in February 1915, and reached overall ascendancy in the company during the First World War.

After the outbreak of war, the Anglo-German explosives ring, as represented by the cosmopolitan Nobel Dynamite Trust, was dismantled. In Britain Nobel's Explosives, which in the past had absorbed several competitors, began consolidating the British explosives industry under their control. They foresaw that with the onset of peace, there would be a severe contraction of demand for explosives, and perceived that major rationalisation was necessary. After his experience in Canada, McGowan was 'expert in the mechanics and politics' of mergers and held 'the largest ideas of what might be achieved' by cartels {ibid, 254}. He masterminded Nobels' absorption in November 1918 by a new combine, Explosives Trades Ltd (ET), with issued capital of £16 million. ET was a holding company, the main subsidiaries of which were Nobel's Explosives, Kynoch Ltd (explosives, ammunition and metals), Curtis & Harvey (general explosives), Eley Brothers (shotgun cartridges) and Bickford Smith (safety fuses).

McGowan's strategy was, however, more ambitious, and as chairman he pushed ET into a bolder diversification. Rather than try to develop explosives capacity, he determined to reduce the commitment to explosives and broaden the group's industrial base. His personal enthusiasms, and his taste for high-level industrial finance and business diplomacy, dominated the subsequent development of ET, the name of which was altered in September 1920 to Nobel Industries Ltd. In 1918 Nobels took a large shareholding in Dunlop Rubber and its related Tyre Investment Trust, which at that time was undergoing a reckless inflation of its capital under the chairmanship of Sir Arthur du Cros (qv): indeed in 1920-25 it was only saved from bankruptcy by the financial reconstruction of F A Szarvasy and the chairmanship of Sir Eric Geddes (qqv). In 1919 ET also made a series of investments in motor component and motor-cycle companies designed to bring collaboration with ET's metal interests (pre-eminently the old Kynoch factory in Birmingham). Finally, influenced by du Pont, during the boom of May 1920, Nobels bought 609,425 shares, with a book value of £3,460,900, in the General Motors Corporation of USA. To cover this and other investments in subsidiaries, Nobels in October 1920 issued 8 per cent seven-year notes worth £3 million.

McGowan was a director from 1918 of Britain's leading dyestuffs manufacturers, Levinstein Ltd, and of the British Dyestuffs Corporation from 1919. He was also chairman of British Celanese for some years until March 1925, when he was succeeded by Guy Dawnay (qv).

In October 1926 McGowan and Alfred Mond (qv) conceived the merger of their companies, Nobel Industries and Brunner Mond, together with United Alkali of Sir Max Muspratt (qv) and the British Dyestuffs Corporation, to form Imperial Chemical Industries Ltd. This was a defensive response to the German formation in 1925 of IG Farben. Both the British and du Pont were apprehensive of this new combine, while Alfred Mond badly wanted access to their hydrogenation technology, particularly oil-from-coal. McGowan remained chairman and managing director of Nobel Industries after the formation of ICI, but was unanimously elected chairman and sole managing director of ICI in December 1930, following Mond's death. The emoluments paid to him in these posts rose to £64,410 for 1937. During 1930-37 he was supreme in ICI's policy-making. He elaborated its cartel system, coming to terms with IG Farbenindustrie about their mutual over-capacity in nitrogenous fertilisers (1930) and extending the world nitrogen cartel thereafter; in 1931 ICI joined the coal-oil hydrogenation patents pool with IG Farben, Royal Dutch Shell and Standard Oil; and in 1932 they entered a cartel with Swiss and German interests in dyestuffs. McGowan also launched ICI on a policy of founding joint overseas companies with the US chemical manufacturers, du Pont, who were also closely interested in the General Motors Corporation. This again required all his diplomatic ability and financial dexterity.

McGowan's other great achievement was in rescuing ICI from the imbroglio of their Billingham investment. Brunner Mond had begun developing the advanced technology of ammonia synthesis at Billingham in 1919, before ICI's formation, but later, under Alfred Mond's influence, high hopes were pinned on nitrogenous fertilizers and oil from coal; in 1927 an investment programme for Billingham totalling £20 million was agreed. Here McGowan was content to follow Mond's leadership. Already by 1929, before Mond's death, it was evident that the predictions for the world nitrogen market, on which this investment decision was based, were awry; the impact of the Slump worsened the position. McGowan in turn presided over the painful reorganisation of Billingham, from whose fertiliser plant £5.11 million was written off as late as 1937.

McGowan's despotism was curbed by his co-directors after 1937. He had long indulged in speculation on his family's behalf, and in April of that year he enjoyed credit from brokers of £1.9 million, supported by securities and commodities on open account: his commitments for stocks, shares and commodities (chiefly rubber) comprised £1.7 million. These operations disintegrated during the course of the year, and by November he was only saved from bankruptcy by a bank guarantee of £60,000 from Lord Camrose (qv), a fellow member of the Other Club, and by other desperate shifts. News of this débâcle, and of colourable transactions by McGowan in General Motors and International Nickel shares, led to a revolt of his co-directors, and he would certainly have been dismissed if his chosen usurper, the Second Lord Melchett (qv), had not fallen seriously ill at a late stage in the revolt. Instead, McGowan survived as chairman both of ICI and its new Management Board. However, he ceased to be managing director and executive power devolved on the Management Board, backed by eight executive committees with managerial or co-ordination responsibilities. This Management Board introduced a new layer of ICI control in the form of non-executive deputy chairmen: men whom he soon cleverly turned into his own inner cabinet. By 1943 he had recovered much of his effectual power.

Apart from his war production responsibilities, McGowan chaired an ICI post-war planning committee from April 1942. The 1940s saw ICI develop several new lines of business. With effect from 1944 ICI was divided into six groups (heavy chemicals, including alkali, lime and salt divisions; dyestuffs and pharmaceuticals; ammonia and agriculture; metals; explosives; paint and plastics, including a leathercloth division). In the case of the second group, the interests of the dyestuffs division completely overwhelmed those of pharmaceuticals until after McGowan's period. In 1935 ICI's activities in plastics were auspiciously inaugurated with their discovery of polyethylene, which they began marketing in 1939 and which enjoyed a great wartime demand for use in radar sets. War also increased demand for Perspex as a glazing material for aircraft. ICI and Courtaulds had agreed in 1928 to abstain from invading the respective areas of their traditional business, and in 1939 formed a joint company to manufacture and develop nylon yarn, under du Pont's patents. However, their joint subsidiary, British Nylon Spinners, the troubled child of an unhappy marriage, suffered considerable difficulties in obtaining adequate plant and raw materials until 1949. Another synthetic fibre, Ardil, intended to compete with wool, was delayed in its launch until 1951 and having missed the opportunity of a period of high wool prices, was abandoned in 1957. ICI's development of Terylene, from 1944, although also tardy, was ultimately a commercial success. To cover the large capital expenditure entailed by these and other projects, ICI raised £20 million on the market in 1948 and another £20 million, privately placed, in 1950. McGowan took an interest in all these matters, although he spent much of the final years of his chairmanship 'travelling round the outposts of ICI ... in semi-regal splendour, meeting Heads of State on terms not far short of equality'. Although he never recovered his pre-1937 dictatorial powers at ICI, 'there were few who would withstand the old despot in person' {Reader (1975) 445}, and his co-directors waited until he was in South Africa before informing him that they would not extend his service contract beyond 1950. He ceased to be chairman on 31 December, although thereafter he was styled honorary president of ICI.

McGowan took a close interest in the Lake Magadi Soda Co in the 1920s, when it was dogged by scandal involving A W Tait (qv), and became its chairman in 1931. He was additionally a director of the Midland Bank from May 1927 until December 1954, and of numerous other companies including General Motors, the International Nickel Co and London & Lancashire Insurance. He was also on the governing council of the British Overseas Bank formed in 1919.

McGowan was a member of the government committee on telegraph services (1927) and chaired the committee on electrical distribution in 1935-36. The latter's report tried to increase private enterprise's role in the national grid system and has been criticised for its 'facile equation of "large" with "efficient" and of "small" with "inefficient"' {Hannah (1979) 250}. He was president of the Society of Chemical Industries (1931), the Institute of Fuel (1934), the British Standards Institute and the National Safety First Association; he was also honorary colonel of the 52nd

The Winnington works of ICI at Northwich, Cheshire, with the research block in the foreground (courtesy of ICI).

(Lowland) Divisional Signals, Royal Corps of Signals, 1934-39. From 1928 he was vice-president of the London Homoeopathic Hospital, and he received the Messel memorial medal in 1934. He went on an industrial mission to Australia in 1928, and delighted in travelling all over the world in great state. He was made honorary LLD by Glasgow and Birmingham universities in 1934, and DCL by Oxford in 1938. He was created KBE in 1918 and a baron in 1937. Politically he was 'a twentieth century industrial Tory' who believed in 'technical and managerial revolution' and supported 'imperialism as the most advanced stage of monopoly capitalism — a stage at which finance capital has merged with industrial and political power in the creation of vast economic estates under unified private control' {*Observer* 23 Jan 1944}. Before the Second World War he flirted with National Socialism, and his visit to the Nuremberg Rally of 1938 was later exploited by British and American enemies of ICI's cartel system. That system was put under heavy strains by the war (which severed relations with IG Farben), and by the US Government's anti-trust litigation against du Pont and ICI, begun in 1944. This forced the two companies to cancel their Patents and Processes Agreement in 1948. Judgement was eventually given in the US Government's favour in 1952, by which time ICI greatly missed their previous interchange of technical information with du Pont.

McGowan advised Winston Churchill on his electrical and American share investments after 1929, and for some years made money for Churchill with speculative purchases on margin. In 1930 he was elected to the Other Club, a convivial dining club with a strong but not predominant political flavour, formed in 1911 by Churchill and F E Smith. He was himself a lavish host, who invited a large and mixed range of celebrities (from business, politics, the Services and drama) to his table.

> He might have served as a model for a painting of 'Success'. Florid of countenance, sanguine in expression, he dressed soberly, as became his position, yet with a sufficient hint, chiefly in his accessories, of opulence. He was fond of good living, which one painter has symbolised by giving him a large cigar, and of company, especially of the great, whom he could entertain with outrageous stories. At the same time he took care to cultivate opinion in the factories, where he could astonish the men by his grasp of their idiom. This rather coarse heartiness served the purpose of a powerful mind and a dictatorial personality {Reader (1970) 380}.

McGowan was an autocrat who was ruthless, purposive and resolute. He never pretended to technical understanding, but was an expert commercial man, very strong-minded and full of self-confidence, with a flair for negotiation and finance.

In 1903 McGowan married, at Paisley Town Hall, Renfrewshire, Jean Boyle Young (d 1952); they had two sons and two daughters. He died in hospital in Paddington on 13 July 1961, leaving £207,453 and some confusion for his executors.

R P T DAVENPORT-HINES

Writings:

letters on oil from hydrogenated coal *Times* 22 May, 11 Aug 1931.

letter on capital and labour *ibid* 20 Nov 1931.

letter on labour welfare *ibid* 11 Oct 1934.

letter on British Industries Fair *ibid* 14 Jan 1935.

letter on coalmining *ibid* 14 Nov 1936.

Report of the Committee on Electricity Distribution (Ministry of Transport, 1936) (chairman).

letter on food supplies and straw *Times* 29 Mar, 2 Apr 1940.

One Hundred Years of Chemistry (Seventh Dalton Lecture) (Royal Institute of Chemistry, 1951).

Sources:

Unpublished

Bodleian Library, Oxford, diary of Earl of Woolton, 30 Sept 1940, 13 May, 19 July 1943.

PRO, papers of Foreign Office and Ministry of Munitions.

Published

Complete Peerage.

Sir Colin R C Coote, *The Other Club* (Sidgwick, 1971).

DNB.

Martin Gilbert (ed), *Winston S Churchill: The Wilderness Years 1929-1935* (Heinemann, 1981).

Leslie Hannah, *Electricity Before Nationalisation* (Macmillan, 1979).

Geoffrey G Jones, 'The Growth and Performance of British Multinational Firms before 1939: The Case of Dunlop' *Economic History Review* 2nd ser 37 (1984).

Observer 23 Jan 1944.

William J Reader, *Imperial Chemical Industries* (2 vols, Oxford University Press, 1970-75).

—, 'Imperial Chemical Industries and the State 1926-1945', in Barry E Supple (ed), *Essays in British Business History* (Oxford University Press, 1977).

Peter Richardson, 'Nobels and the Australian Mining Industry 1907-25' *Business History* 26 (1984).

Times 14, 20 July 1961.

WWW.

MACKAY, James Lyle

1st Earl of Inchcape

(1852-1932)

Shipping company chairman

James Mackay, Lord Inchcape (courtesy of P & O Group Information).

James Lyle Mackay was born in Arbroath, Scotland, on 11 September 1852, the second son and fourth child of James Mackay of Arbroath, a master mariner and shipowner, and his wife Deborah née Lyle, of Canada. He went to school at Arbroath Academy until the death of his father in 1862, after which he continued his education at the Elgin Academy. His father was drowned, lost overboard from his own full-rigged ship, the *Seafield*, and his son's patrimony of £2,000, invested in three East Indian barques, stood him in good stead in his lean years. Mackay's first post, as a 'scrivener' or copier in a local lawyer's office, lasted only a year, after which he was apprenticed to a firm of rope and canvas makers, with the customary pittance of £5 for the first year, increasing by £5 yearly.

His next move was the start of his career in shipping; it was to London, to work for the shipping agency of Gellatly, Hankey, Sewell & Co, at a starting salary of £50 a year. After some months at the bill of lading desk, he was appointed customs clerk. This post, which entailed clearing consignments through customs, as well as entering and clearing inward- and outward-bound ships, brought Mackay into contact with the shipping operation, and many of the captains whom he met were afterwards associated with him in India.

In 1874 he was offered — and immediately accepted — his first overseas posting, as an assistant in the Calcutta firm of Mackinnon, Mackenzie & Co, managers of the British India Steam Navigation Co. He was then aged twenty-two.

Like most expatriates of the time, Mackay shared a bachelor 'chummery' in Calcutta with other young men in similar posts. From his biographer one gets the impression of a man abounding in energy, with a lively sense of humour and a zest not only for his routine work, far more demanding but at the same time more attractive than in a similar job in Britain, but also for the many social and sporting activities offered by a close-knit gregarious society.

James Mackay soon made himself indispensable to the Mackinnons: his first opportunity to distinguish himself came when British India's Bombay agents, William Nicol & Co, were hit hard financially by the suspension of the City of Glasgow Bank in 1878. Mackay was sent to Bombay to restore the position and to transfer the agency to Mackinnons. It is a measure of his success that he was created a partner that same year, at the age of twenty-six.

Returning to England in 1881, to recuperate from a bout of typhoid fever, James met and fell in love with a neighbourhood friend of his sister Annie, Jean (Janie) Shanks, whose father owned a prosperous engineering works; two years later the couple were married at Roseley, the Shanks' home near Arbroath. They had one son and three daughters.

The British India Steam Navigation Co which James Lyle Mackay joined in 1874 was founded as the Calcutta & Burmah Co in 1856. From Burma, its mail steamers served Penang and Singapore, and there was a service up and down the Persian Gulf and to China from 1868. The opening of the Suez Canal in 1869 lead to the establishment of the 'Home' services from the United Kingdom: a mail contract was arranged with the Queensland Government in 1881 and the formation of the (unsuccessful) Imperial British East Africa Co in 1887 was followed by the introduction of the London to Zanzibar service, via Mombasa, in 1890. Apart from the mail services, the 'BI' ships carried a great number of troops on various punitive expeditions during the Boxer Rebellion of 1900. In addition there were the 'coolie contracts' for carrying contracted Indian labour from India to Burma, the Malay Straits and Mauritius. Although there is little written record of Mackay's activities from his arrival in Calcutta until he left in 1893, there is no doubt that he was totally involved in this exciting period of expansion. By the time he left Calcutta he was a senior partner in Mackinnon, Mackenzie & Co. His reorganisation of Binny & Co of Madras had extended his activities to jute, tea and coal in Bengal, and cotton and wool in Madras. He had also founded the Australian firm of Macdonald, Hamilton & Co.

Public recognition of James Mackay's ability soon followed. President of the Bengal Chamber of Commerce, 1889-93, he was a member of the Calcutta Port Commission for nine years and in 1891 was elected Sheriff of

Lord Inchcape presents the King's medal and other prizes to cadets of Thames Nautical training college HMS Worcester *at Greenhithe (courtesy of P & O Group Information).*

Calcutta. His appointment in that year as a member of the Legislative Council of the Viceroy (Lord Lansdowne) set him on the road which was to lead to an earldom and a shipping empire of enormous commercial significance. In the short term it earned him a CIE in recognition of his contribution to the extension of commercial relations between England and India. Promotion to Knight Commander of the Indian Empire came in 1894 as the result of his efforts on behalf of Indian currency reform (chairman of Indian Currency Association, 1892). After nearly twenty years' service in India, the death of Sir William Mackinnon in 1893 meant the recall of Mackay to Britain. He was the mainstay of the caretaker administration of James Macalister Hall, 1893-94, and eventually became managing director under the chairmanship of Duncan Mackinnon, 1894-1913, whom he succeeded as chairman of British India.

It is difficult to deal briefly with the multifarious public activities of Sir James: a member of the Council of India at Whitehall, 1897-1911, and a member of most Government Committees dealing with Indian affairs, he found time, in addition to his onerous work for British India, to serve on a committee for increasing the commercial intelligence provided by the Board of Trade in 1898 and to travel to China, as Special Commissioner and Plenipotentiary of the British Government, to negotiate with his European and Japanese colleagues a revised Customs Tariff in 1901-2. For this service he was awarded the GCMG. In 1903, while serving as president of the Chamber of Shipping of the United Kingdom, he also served on a Government Committee for improving the Consular Service. His public life brought further honours: a second knighthood (KCSI) in 1910 and a barony (Inchcape of Strathnaver) in 1911, the latter to mark his retirement from the India Council.

Just before his China expedition, Sir James made an eight months' tour of inspection in Australia in 1900-1, during which he planned the reorganisation of the BI associated company, the Australasian United Steam Navigation Co, and of BI's affairs on the Queensland coast. He was instrumental in the formation of a pool with the other lines serving the trade to avoid cut-throat competition.

His commercial 'outreach' matched the scope of his governmental functions; his directorships included the Suez Canal Co (1904), the Chartered Bank of India and the East Indian Railway Co.

Just before the outbreak of the First World War, negotiations which had been going on between Lord Inchcape and Sir Thomas Sutherland, the chairman of P & O, came to fruition, and the two companies amalgamated by means of an exchange of stock; to effect this arrangement P & O's capital was increased by £1,388,133. Sir Thomas retired shortly after the merger, and his place was taken by Inchcape, who continued also as chairman of British India. Never bitter competitors, co-operation between the two companies had grown with the years, and a fusion of interests was a logical step. In many ways, however, the two companies enjoyed almost complete autonomy until 1971, when a single identity emerged under the P & O aegis.

During the war, when Inchcape was the shipowners' spokesman and negotiator with the Government on such matters as war risk insurance and rates of hire for requisitioned vessels, he extended the P & O's geographical trading limits by acquiring the New Zealand Shipping Co and its associate, the Federal Steam Navigation Co in 1916. The Union Steam Ship Co of New Zealand was taken over in 1917, when P & O and British India jointly assumed control of the Hain and Nourse Lines. In the immediate post-war period a large holding in the Orient Line was added to the P & O, which also entered the sphere of short-sea trading by buying a three-quarters interest in the old-established General Steam Navigation Co in 1920. The group's losses during the First World War amounted to about 7 per cent of national ship losses (518,316 as against 7,750,000 tons). This has to be seen in the perspective of the very large tonnage owned by the group, 1.5 million for P & O, BI, New Zealand and Federal in 1916, 7.7 per cent of the national tonnage.

One of Inchcape's most notable achievements was the sale, on behalf of the Government, of 196 standard steamers (built by the Government in anticipation of war losses during the First World War to a small number of standardised designs, to make best use of scarce resources in time and materials) of more than a million tons, which realised almost £24 million at a cost to the country of a few hundreds. This was followed up in 1920, when he took over the sale of the British share of ex-German tonnage; this involved 418 vessels, and realised over £20 million.

Meanwhile, in addition to his work in the shipping industry, Inchcape had gradually acquired a network of shareholdings in a variety of companies, which had previously been held by the Mackinnon family. Initially acting as the senior working partner in India, he succeeded to the Mackinnon family interests in London on the death of Sir William. (These holdings were later to form the foundations of the Inchcape Group of Companies, an international trading firm launched by his grandson, the Third Earl, in 1958.) In India, these companies included the shipping agency firm of Mackinnon, Mackenzie & Co, the managing agents of the BI in Calcutta, and the merchant house and textile firm of Binny & Co in Madras, which he rescued from bankruptcy in 1906. In 1915, Lord Inchcape acquired the entire UK and India interests of Barry & Co (managers of tea estates and jute mills) and Macneil & Co (agents for the Rivers Steam Navigation Co and the Equitable Coal Co among others). In the Gulf, Lord Inchcape played an important part in the formation of the Mesopotamia Persia Corporation in 1920, an amalgamation of two shipping agency and trading companies, Gray Mackenzie & Co and Lynch Bros. In London, Lord Inchcape had served as a director of Gray Dawes & Co since the end of the nineteenth century. As well as holding the London agency for the BI, this partnership, who acted as a confirming house with its bills accepted as bank bills, was recognised as a merchant bank for the purpose of sharing brokers' commissions on new issues in 1915. In 1918, Lord Inchcape acquired Delmege, Forsyth & Co, coaling and shipping agents in Ceylon, who were also involved in importing sugar and flour. These and many other investments were to form the main business interests of the Inchcape family in the years to come.

In the last decade of his life his energy was unabated, and public demands on his time and expertise increased. Whether wielding the 'axe' with Eric Geddes (qv) on the Committee on National Expenditure, 1922, or organising India's finances as chairman of the Indian Retrenchment Committee, 1922-23, he did not neglect his own vast complex of undertakings, masterminding the reconstruction of the fleet (130 ships were built in the inter-war years — 700,000 tons), while insisting on seeing, and having a few words with, every one of his commanders when their ships docked in the United Kingdom. It was this blend of immensely wide vision and an almost obsessive attention to detail which made him a financial and commercial overlord of the first significance. He was created Viscount Glenapp of Strathnaver in 1924 and Earl Inchcape in 1929. The most unusual recognition of his prominence came in 1921, when he was offered the Crown of Albania by representatives of British business interests in the Balkans on behalf of the Albanian Foreign Minister and parliament: he was told that 'the new king would be expected to do all in his power financially and politically to help in the construction of Railways, Roads, Schools and Public Buildings throughout the country'. Lord Inchcape turned down the offer with the brief statement that 'it is not in my line' {Bolitho (1936) 161-63}.

The loss of his third daughter, Elsie, while flying the Atlantic in 1928 must have been a great shock, and could possibly have contributed to the pessimistic world view which characterised his last years. He died suddenly and quietly on board his yacht *Rover* at Monaco on 23 May 1932. His total estate was £2,124,707 (£552,808 in the UK). Even on the last day of his life, 'the daily mail-bag still arrived from Leadenhall Street: the affairs of the company were still tightly clenched in his hands' {*ibid*, 252}.

GEOFFREY STOW

MACKAY James Lyle

Sources:

Unpublished

National Maritime Museum, British India Collection, BIS/8/4-7, Lord Inchcape's letters 1912-22, 1927-29, 1929-32; P & O Collection, P&O/20/9 et seq, sundry letters and memoranda.

SSRC Elites Data.

Information from Dr Stephanie Jones, archivist, Inchcape PLC.

Published

'Agreement ... Respecting the New Chinese Customs Tariff' *British and Foreign State Papers* 97 (HMSO, 1908).

George Blake, *B I Centenary 1856-1956* (Collins, 1956).

Henry Hector Bolitho, *James Lyle Mackay, First Earl of Inchcape* (John Murray, 1936).

Boyd Cable, *A Hundred Year History of the P & O: Peninsular and Oriental Steam Navigation Company — 1837-1937* (Nicholson & Watson, 1937).

David Divine, *These Splendid Ships: The Story of the Peninsular and Oriental Line* (Frederick Muller, 1960).

DNB.

Sir Percival Griffiths, *A History of the Inchcape Group* (1977).

PP, Committee on Indian Currency (1893-94) C 7060.

PP, Committee on Dissemination of Commercial Information (1898) C 8962.

PP, Constitution of the Consular Service (1903) Cd 1634.

PP, Committee on Status and Working of Board of Trade and Local Government Board (1904) Cd 2121.

PP, National Guarantee for the War Risks of Shipping (1908) Cd 4161.

PP, Insurance of British Shipping in Time of War (1914) Cd 7650.

PP, Committee on Food Production (1914-16) Cd 8048.

PP, Committee on Currency and Foreign Exchanges After the War (1918) Cd 9182.

PP, Committee on Gold Production (1919) Cmd 11.

PP, Advisory Committee on Civil Aviation (1919) Cmd 449.

PP, Committee on National Expenditure (1922) Cmd 1581.

WWW.

McKENNA, Reginald

(1863-1943)

Banker

Reginald McKenna, 1934 a portrait sketch by James Gunn (courtesy of the Midland Bank plc).

Reginald McKenna was born in Kensington, Middlesex, on 6 July 1863, the youngest of the eight children of William Columban McKenna, a 'Crown surveyor' {BCe} and his wife Emma née Hanby. Emigrating from Ireland in 1838, William McKenna had entered the Inland Revenue service but was financially ruined by the Overend Gurney failure of 1866. His younger children were brought up in Brittany, and Reginald was educated at St Malo (until 1874) and Ebersdorf (until 1877). By 1877 the family's finances allowed them to return to England and Reginald completed his education at King's College School. He won a scholarship to Trinity Hall, Cambridge, took a degree in mathematics, and was called to the Bar by the Inner Temple in 1887.

Reginald McKenna's political achievements were completed in little more than twenty years. In 1895 he was returned as Liberal MP for North Monmouthshire, a constituency he continued to represent until he unsuccessfully contested the new Pontypool division in 1918. Originally a protégé of Sir Charles Dilke, he came to prominence in the House of Commons during Lloyd George's campaign against the 1902 Education Bill. When the Liberals won power in 1905, he was appointed First Secretary to the Treasury, serving under Asquith. He was promoted to Cabinet rank as President of the Board of Education in 1907 and, when Asquith succeeded Campbell-Bannerman as Prime Minister in 1908, McKenna was appointed First Lord of the Admiralty. In harness with Sir John Fisher, the First Sea Lord, in 1909 he carried through the bitterly-fought programme for building eight Dreadnought battleships and successfully defended Admiralty policy against the attacks of Lord Charles Beresford. In an exchange of office with Churchill, he moved to the Home Office in 1911. His four years there were dominated by disputes over the Welsh Church Bill and the women's suffrage movement, although his achievements included the Mental Deficiency Act (1913) and the Criminal Justice Administration Act (1914).

In May 1915 McKenna succeeded Lloyd George as Chancellor of the Exchequer in Asquith's new Liberal Coalition Government. In this role he adopted the principle that the servicing of all the country's new wartime borrowing should be paid out of new taxation, a novel principle which 'raised a standard of finance which was far higher than that of any European Power' {*Times* 7 Sept 1943}. New measures included the £600 million 4.5 per cent War Loan, Excess Profits Duty, the so-called 'McKenna duties' which conferred substantial protection on certain new industries in the name of import savings, and the development of the War Savings schemes initiated by Lloyd George: War Savings raised £40 million during their first year. He also agreed to the first of the major

He was also committed to the development of the Bank's overseas links; the Midland's foreign 'correspondent' banks multiplied from about 650 in 1919 to 1,200 by 1929. Control of most of the Bank's UK business was left to Hyde and the other general managers, but McKenna was directly involved in reconstruction schemes affecting some of the Bank's major corporate customers, notably at Vickers in 1926 and in the Harland & Wolff section of the Royal Mail shipping group between 1930 and 1944. He remained chairman of the Midland until his death.

McKenna's other business interests comprised the chairmanship of the Midland Bank Executor & Trustee Co, directorships of the Clydesdale Bank (a Midland subsidiary), the Canadian Pacific Railway and the Société Financière des Transports et d'Enterprises Industrielles (Sofina). He was also chairman of the Tobacco Securities Trust but he resigned in 1936 when it emerged that one of the Trust's subsidiaries had invested in James & Shakespeare, a commodity firm which had collapsed during the 'pepper crisis' of 1935-36.

McKenna married Pamela, daughter of Sir Herbert Jekyll and Agnes, Lady Jekyll in 1908. They had two sons, of whom the elder, Michael, died in 1931. Through Pamela's aunt Gertrude Jekyll he was introduced to Edwin Lutyens (qv), who built no less than three houses for the McKenna family; Lutyens was subsequently commissioned by McKenna to design the head office and three major branches of the Midland Bank. McKenna was devoted to music and served on the Council of the Royal College of Music from 1929 until his death (latterly as honorary treasurer). As a young man he was an oarsman, rowing bow in the winning Cambridge Eight in 1887, and in middle age he became an expert bridge player. He died at his flat above the Midland Bank's Pall Mall branch on 6 September 1943. His wife Pamela (twenty-six years his junior) died only two months later. His estate was valued at £89,448.

EDWIN GREEN

Writings:

Midland Bank Review speeches to annual general meetings 1920-1939.

International Exchange address to University of Manchester (pp, 1920).

International Debts address to Institute of Chartered Accountants (pp, 1921).

Reparations and International Debts address to American Bankers' Association (pp, 1922).

Trade Prospects address to Worsted Spinners' Federation (pp, 1922).

Address before the Belfast Chamber of Commerce (pp, 1923).

'Banking' *Guildhouse Monthly* May 1928.

Monetary Policy (BBC, 1931).

'What is Banking?' *Bankers' Magazine* Dec 1942.

Sources:

Unpublished

Churchill College, Cambridge, McKenna papers.

Midland Bank, archives.

Newcastle University Library, Runciman papers.

BCe.

MCe.

PrC.

Published

Michael and Eleanor Brock (eds), *H H Asquith. Letters to Venetia Stanley* (Oxford University Press, 1982).

John Campbell, *Lloyd George. The Goat in the Wilderness, 1922-31* (Cape, 1977).

DNB.

Paul Einzig, 'Reginald McKenna. An Appreciation' *Financial News* 7 Sept 1943.

—, 'Death of a Great Banker' *Banker* Oct 1943.

Financial News 7 Sept 1943.

Financial Times 7 Sept 1943.

Roy F Harrod, *The Life of John Maynard Keynes* (Macmillan, 1951).

Roy Jenkins, *Asquith* (Collins, 1964, 2nd ed 1978).

'K' (John Maynard Keynes), 'Mr R McKenna. An Appreciation' *Times* 15 Sept 1943.

Stephen McKenna, *Reginald McKenna 1863-1943. A Memoir* (Eyre & Spottiswoode, 1948).

Ellis T Powell, 'Master Minds in Business' *Business Organization and Management* Jan 1921.

Richard S Sayers, *The Bank of England, 1840-1944* (3 vols, Cambridge: Cambridge University Press, 1976).

Scotsman 7 Sept 1943.

Statist 10 Sept 1943.

Times 7 Sept 1943.

W A Wills and A A Saunders, 'Money and the Gold Standard' *Gold Mining Record* June 1936.

WWMP.

WWW.

MACKIE, James

(1864-1943)

Manufacturer of textile machinery

James Mackie was born in Belfast in 1864 into a Presbyterian family. He was the eldest of the two sons and one daughter of James Mackie (b 1820), a manufacturer of linen machinery, who had come to Ireland from Forfar in 1845 to install a steam engine in a linen mill in Drogheda. His work so impressed the foreman, James Scrimgeour, that when the latter decided to set up his own foundry and engineering works in Belfast, he appointed Mackie as manager. Later Scrimgeour offered him a partnership which he declined, deciding simply to invest money in the business; the result was that when the firm went bankrupt in 1858, Mackie was not liable for its debts. Although he lost some of his money, he still managed to purchase the firm's Albert Street premises and some of its equipment and began in a small way repairing machinery. With the cotton famine of the 1860s there was a great increase in linen production and consequent rise in demand not only for new machines but also for the servicing of existing stock. Thus James Mackie Jr was born at a time when his father's business was making steady progress. However, when the linen boom ended in the 1870s, the survival of the firm was ensured only by rigid economies.

The younger James was given only an elementary education, at the Belfast Model School on the Falls Road. He entered the business in 1874, continuing his education at Queen Street Working Men's Institute (later to become Belfast College of Technology). At this stage the firm was still small, specialising in mill machinery renovations, fluting rollers, turning spindles and accepting contracts for dismantling and re-erecting textile plants. James travelled widely in Britain and on the Continent selling the firm's products. In 1884 he became a junior partner in the firm, and soon after married Elisabeth née Pringle, by whom he had five sons and a daughter.

During the 1870s and 1880s the firm increasingly moved away from repair work towards the production of textile machinery and received its first European order from the firm of J A Fuge of Trautenau, Bohemia. This was the first of many contracts in Central Europe and from 1895, after a visit by James, the firm began to export to the Russian market. When his father died in 1887, James succeeded with his brother Thomas (1870-1956), who was primarily responsible for production. The same year the partnership had a stroke of luck which considerably improved its financial position. The firm's main boiler was condemned as unsafe and a new one ordered, which was damaged in transit. The insurers paid up. When the boiler arrived, however, it was found still to be in working order and was used for several years.

In 1893, after building up a substantial export trade, Mackies acquired a four-acre site on Belfast's Springfield Road which, although greatly

James Mackie & Co, flax or hemp hackling machine fitted to an automatic spreader (from W E Coe, The Engineering Industry of the North of Ireland).

enlarged after 1919, remains (1984) the company's location. The business expanded steadily, producing 100 wet spinning frames a year and also, under licence, the flax-preparing machinery patented by Brooks & Doxey of Manchester, notably cutters, bundling presses and twisting frames. (George Shaw of Brooks & Doxey was brought in as foreman.) In 1897 Mackies became a limited company and in 1902 it took over the Clonard Foundry and brought in John Horner, the previous owner, to the board. Together the Mackies and Horner developed the Horner-Mackie hackling machine, embodying a differential drive and grouping of metal pins to comb the flax.

In the pre-war boom the firm expanded rapidly. In 1907 it was one of the first firms in the city to electrify and in 1911, together with Sir Otto Jaffé (1846-1929), linen merchant and ex-Lord Mayor of Belfast, diversified by acquiring McTears' spinning works in East Belfast. Later this, as the Strand Spinning Co Ltd, became wholly owned by the Mackie family. (Jaffé, who was German consul in Belfast, was interned during the war as an alien.) At this time the firm was employing around 350 men. After 1914 the company went over to making munitions; its labour force nearly doubled to 650 and the factory premises were greatly extended. From 1920 the linen industry entered into a period of long term decline and the business looked to other markets. It began to experiment in the production of jute machinery, evolving a high speed doffing frame incorporating, under licence, the Longworth automatic screwing device, which greatly improved the rate at which the finished yarn could be produced. The company also built a mill on its Springfield Road site where the products could be tested, which provided a useful additional source of income as 20 tons of yarn were annually exported to Scotland. By 1929 jute manufacturing equipment had become the firm's most important product.

The business was almost wholly export-oriented; by the end of the 1930s its overseas staff totalled 110, out of a workforce of 2,000, and covered 52 countries. Mackies were by this stage one of the world's leading suppliers of sisal and hard fibre spinning machinery and were pioneers in the development of a complete range of products for processing jute, including looms. The company were also among the first to adopt the package arrangement for the establishment of factories overseas, taking responsibility for planning, supplying and installing the equipment, and starting up the production process.

The Second World War, like the First, saw a movement in the firm over towards munitions, such as armour-piercing shells, hand grenades, breech rings and aircraft parts. In certain specialised projectiles 9 per cent of national requirements came from Mackies. The firm expanded enormously. By the time of James's death, the labour force, hitherto almost exclusively male, had increased to 12,000, 7,200 of them women; a further 8,000 were employed in associated Mackie organisations. That year the company's nominal capital was still only £156,000, a figure which bore no relation to the firm's true value.

Throughout its development the firm remained a private company, controlled almost wholly by James and Thomas Mackie and their sons. The precise individual contribution of the two brothers is impossible to determine; James remained managing director until his death, although it is clear that by the Second World War Thomas Mackie (awarded the CBE in 1942) was primarily responsible for the day-to-day running of the firm. The success of the business was based on a mixture of technical awareness and prudent finance. The brothers lived frugally (their sons, for example, received their further education at Belfast Technical College rather than at university), and must have ploughed a considerable proportion of their profits back into the firm. The company's finances would also appear to have benefited greatly from the two world wars, in both of which it expanded rapidly. During the post-war period, the business continued to prosper with markets in both the communist and non-communist areas, moving away from jute towards machinery used for wool and man-made fibres. It has also remained a private company, entirely controlled by the family, and still, as it has less than fifty shareholders, produces no financial details publicly.

James Mackie had many outside business interests, though his public offices were few: DL for the city of Belfast, a JP for Co Antrim, for six years a member of the Belfast Harbour Board, and founder of the Workingmen's Committee for the Royal Victoria Hospital. He was chairman of the Strand Spinning Co Ltd, a director of the Whitehouse Spinning Co Ltd, Robert McCalmont & Sons Ltd, the Ulster Spinning Co Ltd, Dromona & Maine Ltd, and the Rosebank Weaving Co Ltd, and a member of the Board of Supervisors of the Belfast Banking Co Ltd. He was succeeded as managing director by his brother Thomas, and his sons James and John. James Mackie died on 12 April 1943, leaving an estate of £111,555 gross.

DAVID S JOHNSON

Sources:

Unpublished

Belfast City Library, A S Moore Collection, G1, A S Moore, 'A History of the Belfast Engineering Firm of Jas Mackie & Sons Ltd, Written to Celebrate Its Centenary', 1946 (typescript).

PrC.

Published

Belfast Newsletter 13 Apr 1943.

Belfast and Ulster Directories 1897-1943.

W E Coe, *The Engineering Industry of the North of Ireland* (Newton Abbot: David & Charles, 1969).

Manchester Guardian Commercial Supplement 10 Dec 1937.

Northern Whig 13 Apr 1943.

Barrie Whyte, 'Mackies the Myth and the Millions' *Belfast Telegraph* 15 Dec 1976.

MACKINTOSH, Harold Vincent

1st Viscount Mackintosh of Halifax

(1891-1964)

Confectionery manufacturer

Harold Mackintosh from W H Beable The Romance of Great Businesses.

Harold Vincent Mackintosh was born over a small pastry-cook shop in King Cross Street, Halifax, on 8 June 1891, the eldest of the three sons of John Mackintosh (qv), then a textile mill hand, and his wife Violet née Taylor, daughter of a carpet weaver. His parents developed their toffee-making business during Harold's infancy, though his mother evidently withdrew by the time his father set up his first toffee factory in the mid 1890s.

Harold was raised in an atmosphere of piety, the family being stalwart members of Queen's Road Methodist (New Connexion before 1907 and United Methodist thereafter) Church and he later recalled that 'the Sunday School was my university' {Mackintosh (1966) 37}. Meantime he attended an ineffectual Dame's School, then a Board School and lastly Halifax New School, a private school not far from the family's home in Park Terrace, where he became head boy and captain of cricket and hockey.

At eighteen Harold started in the family business and was sent by his father to Crefeld, near Cologne in the Rhineland, where John Mackintosh had set up a toffee factory ca 1906. Here Harold learned the manufacturing side and the language, and gained experience selling toffee throughout Germany. He returned to Halifax in 1911, spent two more years mastering the business and, soon after reaching his majority, was made a director of the firm. He remained with his father during the early part of the First World War but when his younger brother John Douglas Victor (1897-1981) was repatriated in the first batch of POWs (having lost a leg in the trenches) in 1917, Harold joined up as a sub-lieutenant in the RNVR and served as a lieutenant in anti-submarine patrols until early in 1919. While the family business was 'much curtailed but not seriously impoverished' {Mackintosh (1966) 52} by the war, his father's health was seriously impaired and within a year of Harold's return to Halifax John Mackintosh was dead.

Harold became company chairman and managing director with his brother Douglas and his father's two associates, John Esdon Henderson and John William Greenwood (the sons' uncle), as directors, and immediately pushed forward plans for a major expansion that had been suspended in 1914. Record net profits (exclusive of excess profits and corporation taxes) in 1919 of £358,616 confirmed that the time had come for investment. Harold decided to go to the capital market for finance and in March 1921 John Mackintosh & Sons Ltd was floated as a public company with an authorised capital of £750,000. The private firm of John Mackintosh Ltd was sold to the public company for £588,962 (£289,746 in cash and £299,216 in £1 ordinary shares) leaving the family safely in control. The balance of the 300,000 issued ordinary shares and the 300,000 issued 10 per cent cumulative £1 preference shares were all subscribed (at par) within forty-eight hours. Between 1921 and 1927 the firm's fixed assets were increased by 72 per cent, from £143,056 to £246,620 and by 1925-26 the firm's labour force was double its pre-war level, totalling nearly 2,000 people. In 1921 even before the new investment at Halifax, the firm claimed an output capacity of 50 million pieces of toffee a week.

Like his father, Sir Harold Mackintosh (he was knighted in 1922 for public services but really to honour his father) kept two objectives in mind, and did so throughout his career: 'first, quality, second, publicity' {*ibid*, 58}. Quality was preserved by the continued application of scientific methods to quality control; in 1925 the firm had three or four full time chemists in its works laboratory. Publicity was rapidly developed, new investment starting with front page advertisements, one a month for six months (October 1921-March 1922), in the *Daily Mail*, the *Daily Express*, the *Daily News*, the *Daily Mirror*, the *Daily Sketch* and several leading provincial papers, all for an outlay of £25,000. The advertisements comprised a succession of illustrations on the theme of Toffee Town drawn by leading comic artists, including Heath Robinson, Charles Harrison, Mabel Lucie Attwell, Bruce Bairnsfather, George Morrow and H M Bateman.

The investment programme of 1921 was checked by the severe slump of 1921-22 and the difficult years of the 1920s. The year 1926-27 was particularly bad, with net profits of only £12,426, compared to £90,313 in

'The Story of Toffee Town' pictures by famous artists, 1922 (courtesy of Rowntree Mackintosh plc).

1925-26 and £60,126 in 1924-25. Sales picked up again and by the mid-1930s, growth resumed. In 1936 with all the £750,000 authorised capital now issued, fixed assets stood at £292,762 and net profit at £73,665. However the fixed assets figure excluded investment in subsidiary companies (a figure given as £107,626 after writing off), chief of which was Caleys.

The opportunity to get into chocolate markets came in 1932, when D'Arcy Cooper (qv), chairman of Unilever, offered his faltering subsidiary, A J Caley & Son Ltd of Norwich, to Mackintoshs. Sir Harold paid £137,788 for the Caley business. One motive for purchasing it was to provide his youngest brother Eric with a major managerial challenge. Under Eric Mackintosh (1906-78), Caleys was pushed into the quality market by a combination of organisational and technical and marketing tactics: by centralising controls over foremen and operations; by installing Praletta chocolate moulding machines, the latest technology available, under a royalty arrangement with Monheim Bros of Germany; by purchasing higher quality cocoa beans than the old firm had done; by numerous improvements in social conditions in the factory (like air-conditioning; improved electric lighting and public music via loudspeakers, all in 1934); and by a series of new confectionery product lines (in addition to reinvigorating Caleys' line in Christmas crackers). The most notable of these new lines were Double Six and, also launched in 1936, the moulded chocolate pieces in Quality Street — 18 varieties of toffees and chocolates which sold under the Mackintosh name, and in an attractive packaging designed by Caley artists, at 6d a quarter — Rolo (a soft toffee coated with chocolate) introduced in 1937 and a Milk Tray block, marketed in 1939. Caley's sales showed an eight-fold increase between 1933 and 1938. Eventually so much production of combinations of toffee and chocolate was being undertaken at Norwich that in 1939

Mackintosh and Caley were completely amalgamated. In 1939 John Mackintoshs' net profits were £203,440, which placed it not far behind Rowntrees, whose net revenue that year was £247,148 (in turn well under a fifth of the level of Cadbury profits).

On the labour side the most important change introduced by Sir Harold Mackintosh between the wars was a profit sharing scheme. Commenced in 1922 it provided an annual bonus at the same rate as that paid in annual dividends on the ordinary share capital — an attempt to reward labour and capital equally. He publicly recorded his commitment to co-partnership but in 1925 felt it should be confined to a welfare department (which the firm had) and profit sharing, rather than sharing management. In addition Mackintosh set up worker insurance arrangements in his firm in the early 1920s.

During the Second World War the firm again suffered from being a producer of luxury goods partly made from foreign raw materials. The sugar quota imposed on manufacturers by the Ministry of Food was based on pre-war consumption and confectionery was rationed, with the pre-war per capita weekly consumption of sweets being reduced from seven to three ounces. Many of the firm's employees were drafted into the Services and the Mackintosh workforce fell from 1,400 in 1939 to 800 during the war. However, the hardest blow to the firm came on 29 April 1942 when a German air raid on Norwich destroyed the Caley factories. No lives were lost but the plant and buildings were razed to the ground. Through the mediation of the Cocoa, Chocolate and Confectionery (War-time) Association competitors helped (with personnel, machinery, raw materials) and production was gradually transferred to Halifax where there was plenty of spare machine capacity.

After 1945 the major task facing Mackintoshs was the rebuilding of the Caley factories at Norwich. This became an opportunity to re-equip with the most modern plant available, a task completed in 1955. At the same time the firm's administration was moved to Norwich. Among the new products launched under Harold Mackintosh's chairmanship were Week-End and Munchies (both 1957), Caramac (1959) and Good News (1960) — a chocolate assortment the name of which brashly linked the chairman's faith and business. By 1956 John Mackintosh & Sons Ltd and its subsidiaries had attained trading profits of £1,328,000, and profits after tax of £617,000, on sales of £12,536,000; fixed assets were then valued at £2,338,000; employees numbered well over 4,000.

Outside the Mackintosh business Sir Harold held other directorships which in 1939 he listed as the Halifax Building Society — the Equitable which he joined in 1921 having been amalgamated with the Permanent under the chairmanship of Sir Enoch Hill (qv) in 1928 — Martins Bank Ltd (Leeds and District board), Alliance Assurance Co Ltd (Yorkshire and Derbyshire area board), House Property & Investment Co Ltd (deputy chairman) and Methodist Publications Ltd. In 1961 he was director of First Hethersett Investment Co Ltd, Martins Bank, Methodist Publications Ltd, Ranks and Second Hethersett Investment Co Ltd.

After the First World War Harold Mackintosh first made an impact as a public figure when he assumed many of the interests and offices of his father in the Halifax area — as secretary of Queen's Road United Methodist Church, chairman of Halifax YMCA, vice-president of the

Press launch, 1936 (courtesy of Rowntree Mackintosh, plc).

national YMCA, president of King Cross Band, and director of the Equitable Building Society & Bank. He was also a freemason, having joined Probity lodge, No 61, before entering the RNVR in the First World War. Throughout the 1920s his business activities and connections helped to draw him into national prominence.

Wider service and further national recognition came with his involvement in the Sunday School movement and the Methodist Church. In 1924 he was elected president of the Sunday School Union, which then represented 6.5 million children and 240,000 teachers in Great Britain (more than in the elementary day schools). In 1928, at its Los Angeles convention, he was elected president of the World's Sunday School Association; shortly after he retired as president in 1958 the WSSA covered 53 countries and an enrolment of over 65 million pupils and teachers. He was also an honorary treasurer of the WSSA. Sunday Schools, he believed, gave children 'a strata [sic] of moral conscience, which helps more than anything else to keep the national life sound and steady' {Mackintosh (1925)}, an opinion he held throughout his life. For his Sunday School work Sir Harold was made a baronet in 1935.

Within Methodism he was a strong advocate of the union of the Wesleyan, Primitive and United Methodists which occurred in 1932 (when he chaired its first Youth Rally held in the Albert Hall), and welcomed the spirit of the ecumenical movement, though he doubted it would lead to a single united church. He was a governor for more than thirty years of Ashville College, Harrogate, a Methodist school. One of his highest denominational posts was that of joint treasurer of the Home Missionary Committee of the Methodist Church, which he held with J Arthur Rank (qv) from the 1930s when Rank was also on the national committee of the WSSA (and through Rank he joined the Joseph Rank Charity Trusts in 1953). In 1960 Mackintosh was appointed chairman of the Council of the Methodist Church and president of the Central Finance Board, bodies set up by act of parliament, and with Lord Rank was joint chairman of the Methodist Central Buying Association. After moving to the Norwich area in 1947 Sir Harold Mackintosh became a regular worshipper at Park Lane Methodist Church, Norwich.

One other public movement into which Sir Harold threw himself was the British Empire Cancer Campaign. Mackintosh came to it through Sir Berkeley Moynihan (later Lord Moynihan and surgeon to the Royal Family) who had removed Harold's appendix in 1912. Yorkshire started its autonomous branch and in Mackintosh it had a master of advertising techniques who quickly became adept at fund raising, in association with Lord Lascelles (later Lord Harewood) and Lord Moynihan. The first campaign in Yorkshire raised £200,000 and by 1964 the Yorkshire Cancer Campaign, of which Sir Harold became chairman in 1936, had raised nearly £2 million.

Voluntary work — in the National Savings Movement — eventually took Sir Harold Mackintosh to his greatest prominence and though separate from his Methodist, Sunday School, Cancer Campaign and business activities, it was not unrelated to them. His flair for publicity and fund raising found their fullest expression in work for the National Savings Movement whilst his puritan ethic discovered in it the opportunity to promote thrift on the grandest scale. In 1940 he joined the Halifax War Savings Campaign Committee and sharpened the war savings effort by collecting for specific items (three destroyers in the first instance) and by instigating an inter-town competitive spirit. In one week the Halifax effort raised £2,077,000 and Mackintosh was soon helping to organise the efforts of other Yorkshire towns. In 1941 he was elected to the National Savings

Committee whose president Lord Kindersley (qv) asked him to become a vice-chairman in charge of publicity. Between 1941 and 1945 War Savings brought in £2,777 million, largely attributable to the two promotional techniques developed under Mackintosh's leadership: a massive recruitment of voluntary helpers, whose savings groups grew from about 40,000 in 1939 to 275,000 by 1945; and, more powerfully, a series of national War Savings Weeks of which 'Salute the Soldier' held in spring 1944 prior to D-Day was the most successful, raising £628 million. Mackintosh became chairman of the National Savings Movement in 1943 and succeeded Lord Kindersley as president in 1946, holding both positions until his death. In peacetime he continued his promotional campaigns and the total amount in National Savings rose from under £3,000 million to over £8,000 million by 1964-65. 'In producing close on £1 million a day [the Savings Movement] has undoubtedly reduced the country's taxation bill by a considerable amount. Little wonder that few Budget speeches have passed without an acknowledgment of his efforts' {*Times* 29 Dec 1964}. He periodically expressed dissatisfaction with the range of facilities offered by the Savings Movement and sought fresh incentives for people to save. His most controversial innovation was the introduction of Premium Savings Bonds in 1956, which caused ripples in the churches and brought a mild snub from the Archbishop of Canterbury. Mackintosh, a member of the Churches' Committee on Gambling whose views were well known, retorted 'I know it is the business of the Churches to save sinners, but I didn't know it was their duty to stop sinners saving' {Mackintosh (1966) 133}, arguing that people were gambling away not their money, only its interest. The numbers of the winning premium bonds were chosen by ERNIE (Electronic Random Number Indicator Equipment), a novel piece of electronic equipment designed by the Post Office's engineers. At the time of his death Mackintosh was discussing with James Callaghan, Chancellor of the Exchequer, a scheme to establish a national unit trust in which the country's 30 million National Savings savers would enjoy a higher yield.

For his work with the National Savings Movement Harold Mackintosh was made Baron Mackintosh of Halifax in 1948 and Viscount Mackintosh of Halifax in 1957. Never involved in party politics (but with Liberal inclinations in his early career), he was made a DL for the West Riding of Yorkshire, a JP, an honorary LLD of Leeds University and honorary freeman of the County Borough of Halifax.

Lord Mackintosh had several hobbies: building a significant collection of English paintings particularly of the Norwich School, some of which decorated his office in the 1920s (an instructive contrast to his father's preference for company advertisements and toffee tins); collecting pottery and researching it in his typically thorough manner (his Toby Jugs were a rarely matched collection, sold after his death); a life-long, and typically for a Yorkshireman, passionate interest in cricket; and cattle breeding. At Connyngham Hall near Knaresborough (to which he moved from 'Greystones', Halifax in 1925) he bred prize-winning Jerseys and at Thickthorn Hall near Norwich (to which he moved in 1947), Herefords.

In Norfolk Viscount Mackintosh's national stature marked him out as a potentially powerful sponsor of the University of East Anglia. Its foundation was proposed by a small group of local citizens in 1958, in response to the national discussions on the expansion of further education which produced the Crowther Report of 1959. Lord Mackintosh gave it his wholehearted support, as chairman of the promotion, executive and appeal committees (which under his leadership raised almost £1.4 million). Characteristically he challenged the University of York Appeal to beat the UEA Appeal target for the prize of a heifer from his Hereford stud — a challenge UEA lost. Lord Mackintosh was elected first Chancellor of the University of East Anglia but died five months before the ceremonial installation. At the first meeting of the University Court after Viscount Mackintosh's death, the first Vice-Chancellor, Professor Frank Thistlethwaite, recalled his intelligence, imagination and courage, concluding that, in a word, he was 'magnanimous' {Mackintosh (1966) 290}.

Harold Mackintosh met his wife on a holiday in Switzerland in 1912. Constance Stoneham, second daughter of Edgar Cooper Stoneham, a civil servant (chief accountant to the Board of Trade when he retired), was then also celebrating her coming of age, sharing the same birth date as Harold. They were married on their twenty-fifth birthday in 1916 and had one son, John (1921-80) and one daughter, Mary (b 1927).

Viscount Mackintosh suddenly died of a stroke at Thickthorn Hall, shortly after celebrating one of his typically jolly family Christmases, on 27 December 1964. He left £218,404 gross. He was survived by Viscountess Mackintosh, his son (who succeeded to the title) and his daughter.

DAVID J JEREMY

Writings:

'The Moral Conscience and Other Matters' *Yorkshire Weekly Post* 30 May 1925.

Early English Figure Pottery. A Collection of Ralph Wood and Contemporary Pottery (Chapman & Hall, 1938).

By Faith and Work. The Autobiography of the Rt Hon the First Viscount Mackintosh of Halifax (Hutchinson, 1966).

Sources:

Unpublished

Rowntree Mackintosh PLC York, Archives, papers of John Mackintosh & Sons Ltd: abridgement of company prospectus 24 Mar 1921; annual company reports for 1936 and 1965.

BCe.

PrC.

Information from Kingsley Johnson and Professor Frank Thistlethwaite.

Published

William H Beable, *Romance of Great Businesses* (2 vols, Heath Cranton, 1926) 2.

Confectionery Journal 12 Jan 1928, 10 Jan 1934, 29 Mar, 26 Apr 1939.

Daily Mail 13 Mar 1920, 29 Dec 1964.

DD 1923, 1939, 1946, 1961.

DNB.

Financial Times 29 Dec 1964.

Guardian 29 Dec 1964.

Halifax Daily Courier and Guardian 29 Jan 1922.

Eric D Mackintosh, *Norwich Adventure. An Account of Events at Chapel Field Works, 1932-1942* (pp, 1947).

MC (John Mackintosh & Sons Ltd house journal) Apr 1965.

Methodist Times & Leader 1933.

Stock Exchange Year Book 1922.

Times 29 Mar 1964.

Who's Who in Methodism, 1933.

WWW.

Yorkshire Evening Post 28 Dec 1964.

Yorkshire Weekly Post 30 May 1925.

John Mackintosh, in 1909 (courtesy of Rowntree Mackintosh plc).

MACKINTOSH, John

(1868-1920)

Toffee manufacturer

John Mackintosh was born in Dukinfield, Cheshire, across the River Tame from Ashton-under-Lyne, on 7 July 1868, the second and oldest surviving child of the three sons and five daughters born to Joseph Mackintosh, a cotton spinner, and his wife Mary Jane (d 1912) daughter of Henry Burgess, master of the British School in Dukinfield. A few months after John was born, the family moved to Halifax, Yorkshire, where Joseph Mackintosh took an overseer's position with Bowman Bros, cotton spinners — a position he owed to an older brother who had become manager of Bowmans' new Halifax mill.

Strong Nonconformist traditions shaped John's background: his mother had belonged to Albion Congregational Church and his father to the Methodist New Connexion Church, both in Ashton. After John's parents married, the family became attached to the Methodist New Connexion. In Halifax they at first belonged to the Salem Church in North Parade, Halifax. When Joseph was promoted, taking charge of three rooms in Bowman's second mill in Pellon Lane, the Mackintosh family moved to the west side of the town and joined Salem's daughter school-church in Hanson Lane, a congregation whose church in Queen's Road was built in 1877. In mill, church and home Joseph Mackintosh was a stern and resolute figure, over-strict perhaps; in contrast, John's mother, who had taught in her own father's school, exercised her influence by a gentle, more lenient, disposition. Educated by his mother and in the New Connexion Sunday School, John Mackintosh started at the age of ten, as a 'half-timer', labouring half a day, six days a week, in Bowman Bros' mill. At thirteen he was a full timer, minding a pair of 'twiners' or doubling machines, twisting yarn into thread.

Soon after he reached his majority three events occurred which set him on a business career. Firstly his father Joseph Mackintosh developed cancer from an old injury to the roof of his mouth and died in April 1891 (leaving a personal estate of £125). Thereafter John had to support not only a widowed mother, five sisters and a younger brother in ministerial training but also a wife. John's marriage in September 1890 was a second turning point. His wife Violet Taylor (d 1932), daughter of James Taylor, a carpet weaver, also belonged to Queen's Road Church and was a 'Confectioners Assistant' {MCe}. Then, thirdly, the young couple, shortly after settling into their new home in King Cross Street, Halifax, decided to use their joint savings of £100 to open a pastry cook's shop. While John went to the mill Violet made and sold 'meat pies, fruit pies, Madeira cakes, Eccles cakes, sponge loaves' and tarts and cheesecakes and much else. {Crutchley (1921) 32} A few months later they cast around for a speciality, in order to develop a new and more vigorous market than the pastries which were in demand chiefly on Saturday afternoons, the only commercial half holiday of the week. They chose toffee. English toffee was then very hard and brittle but by 1890 soft caramels were being imported from America. As John Mackintosh recalled, '*Then came the great idea*! Why not blend the English "Butter Scotch" and the American caramel. Experiments were made and an article produced which was named "Mackintosh's Celebrated Toffee".' {*Daily Mail* 13 Mar 1920} The original toffee recipe which Mrs Mackintosh recorded in 1890 and guarded to the end of her life was deceptively simple: '4 lbs moist sugar; a small handfull of salt; two cupfulls of water; 12 oz butter; boil very quickly without the butter, about 20 minutes, taking of the skum, then drop in the butter, and boil about 10 minites, till it thickens, take off before too brown.' (original spellings) {Mackintosh (1966) 48}

John Mackintosh put out an advertisement offering free samples of the new toffee. Hundreds came and that Saturday supplies were exhausted long before closing time. The following Monday a second advertisement appeared: 'On Saturday last you were eating Mackintosh's toffee at our expense. Next Saturday pay us a visit and eat it at your own expense.' {Crutchley (1921) 33}

The toffee business was such a success that in mid-1891, after his father died, John Mackintosh gave up his mill job to work full time in making and selling toffee. At first it was made by his wife, with the assistance of one girl, in batches of ten pounds which were boiled in a ten pound brass pan and cooled in tin trays. John fitted a number of trays into a tin trunk and took them to Halifax market where he broke up the toffee with a hammer and sold it at a stall. Within a year of taking over the shop, John Mackintosh decided to move from the retail to the wholesale side, which meant increasing his scale of production.

In 1894 he rented a small warehouse in Bond Street and a year later took a larger warehouse in Hope Street. Here he set up his 'Steam Confectionery Works' and personally supervised operations which in 1895-96 were described thus:

> a corner building of stone, which contains admirable appliances for boiling, cutting, and packing the various sweetmeats. Brierley's steam boiling pans are perhaps the best in the trade, and are in use at this establishment, and the boiling department, as well as all others, presents a very animated and busy appearance. Many vans are kept constantly delivering in Halifax and the immediate neighbourhood, and a large trade is done by rail. He [John Mackintosh] has appointed agents in almost every county in England, and also in Ireland and Wales. Several travellers are constantly engaged in calling upon customers in the North and Midlands. To achieve this amount of success in five years is an undoubted record, and it is only a matter of time for "Mackintosh's Toffee" to be known throughout the British Isles. As a proof of the estimation in which his goods are held, we may mention that they were awarded a diploma and gold medal at the Leeds International Exposition, 1895. {*Illustrated Account of Halifax* (1895-96) 18}.

The growing demand for toffee persuaded Mackintosh to find and equip a much larger manufacturing facility. To finance it the business in 1899 was converted into a limited liability company, John Mackintosh Ltd, with an authorised capital of £23,000. The site and buildings in Queen's Road, Halifax, reputedly cost £15,000 and when the capital was insufficiently subscribed Mackintosh had to borrow (reportedly) £4,000 from a reluctant bank manager who told him 'if you made all the toffee that the United Kingdom could consume, you could never employ £15,000. I call it fool-hardy.' {Beable (1926) I, 147} A company balance sheet dated 31 December 1899 shows that £18,765 of capital had been issued and after payment of interest on the preference shares and debentures a profit of £865 19s 5d was available for dividend on the 6,000 £1 ordinary shares. However, no dividends were distributed for many years. The firm intermittently suffered from a shortage of working capital and trade deteriorated at the end of the Boer War when the Government imposed a tax on sugar, which forced up confectionery prices and checked demand. The absence of firm records denies a clear view of Mackintosh's business tactics and strategies in this situation, beyond his policy of ploughing all profits back into the firm. Apparently he exhibited unshakeable determination to start again, if the business should fail, so convinced was he of its potential and his own ability to succeed. The loyalty and competence of two managerial henchmen — his wife's brother-in-law, John William Greenwood, and John Esdon Henderson — helped to sustain the business through the difficult times of these early years.

A nasty setback occurred on 29 October 1909 when the Queen's Road factory burned down. It was insured for £20,000 and John Mackintosh took the opportunity to relocate at a more advantageous site, the empty Albion Mills, adjacent to the Calder & Hebble Navigation Co canal and the Old Station which was served by the Lancashire & Yorkshire and the Great Northern railways. The head office (all that survived the Queen's Road fire) and another part of the manufacturing operation, at Brunswick Mills, were moved to Albion Mills. In 1912 these comprised a general office (employing at least 20 clerks and typists), a large manufacturing shed and two mills (one of five storeys, the other of four), besides workshops (where John Mackintosh and his works manager invented and developed some of their own special equipment), stables, boilerhouse and yard, all enclosed within the site's boundary walls. The employees numbered hundreds — by 1920 the firm had nearly 1,000 employees at Halifax and in its various depots. Production operations required many more women and girls than men, with men performing the initial stages of boiling and cutting toffee and the final packing and despatch, 'the girls' and womens' work being solely wrapping, boxing, labelling, and finishing.' {*Confectioners' Union* 15 Nov 1912} Mackintosh relied on piece rates, pleasant working conditions and his own benevolent paternalism to motivate his employees — who (as a group) were otherwise provided with dining rooms (one for women and one for men), and a bonus at the end of the First World War. During the war the firm paid £10,000 to the dependents of employees on active service.

Mackintosh's rapid success derived partly from the fact that he was first in the field; it was also due to the quality and variety of his product. By the mid-1890s he packaged his toffee in colourful printed one pound, four pound and seven pound tins, free from torn or dirty labels, which made an attractive display in shop windows. And his toffee, even as early as 1896, came in a wide range of flavours: Creamery Toffee, Broken Scotch, Yorkshire Dairy, Yorkshire Buttercups, Aniseed Toffee, King of all Toffee, Invalid Toffee, Cream of Malt Toffee, Sherbet Toffee, Caramel Toffee, Everton Toffee, Honey and Butter Toffee. By 1914 his 'toffee de luxe' was advertised as 'the Foundation stone of Public Favour' {*Daily Mail* 8 Dec 1914} but there were then other sorts: Egg and Milk Toffee, Creamy Bits, Creamy Milk, Vienna Toffee, Tipperary Toffee, Golden Pats and Allies Toffee.

Much of Mackintosh's success sprang from his penchant for publicity. Within four years his aggressive advertising propelled him and his product to the forefront of the confectionery trade, though he was, in size, far behind the chocolate manufacturers like Cadbury, Fry and Rowntree. As early as 1896 he advertised his product with a portrait of himself over the caption 'Mackintosh the toffee king at your service' {*Confectionery* 12 Mar 1896} and he was soon vigorously exploiting what have since been identified as 'pull' and 'push' techniques. From the very start he appealed directly to the ultimate consumer (the 'pull' marketing effect) by using local newspaper advertising and handbills. Cognisant of the ingenious sales promotions of Alfred Harmsworth and Arthur Pearson (qqv), the newspaper publishers, Mackintosh also launched several competitions. One offered a model cottage or £250 to the person collecting the most toffee packet coupons. This left so many disappointed entrants that

"MACKINTOSH,"
THE TOFFEE KING,
AT YOUR SERVICE.

His AMBASSADOR ("CONFECTIONERY") IS BEFORE YOU.
Your Orders will be Esteemed.

THE TOFFEE MILLS, HALIFAX.

*Mackintosh's 'Toffee King',
advertisement 1896 (courtesy of
Rowntree Mackintosh).*

Mackintosh devised a more egalitarian competition, this time shrewdly aimed at children and parents. The top prizes in Mackintosh's Scholarship Competition were two three-year scholarships, each worth £30 a year, for a short essay telling exactly what the child thought of Mackintosh's toffee, but there were other prizes and every one of the 10,000 entrants received an inscribed certificate.

Mackintosh's practice of giving away free samples was extended in the 1900s by specially-equipped caravans, for touring villages and towns, which distributed samples to the public and trial quantities to potential agents. The practice was given a fresh twist in February 1905 when Mackintosh sent a tin of toffee to each of the 670 MPs reassembling after the winter recess, with the suggestion that they might like to open an account with the firm.

In his drive to capture a national market Mackintosh sent advertisements to schools and had others placed on the railways. By 1914 he had 500 posters on the railways (where a complete national coverage was estimated at 20,000 signs) but the war prevented an extension of this pull marketing method. While John Mackintosh prided himself on giving his personal attention to the drafting of his advertisements and producing advertisements that 'were direct and honest, with natural and homely appeals by picture and text ... [and were not] ... mere displays of cleverness' {Crutchley (1921) 61}, he took professional advice. From early in the 1890s, Edgar Osborne, Manchester representative of the London firm of advertising agents, T B Browne Ltd, advised Mackintosh to place advertisements in national magazines, starting in 1898 with the *Strand* magazine. By 1903 Mackintoshs were taking full-page pictorial advertisements in the *Daily Mail* and even front page adverts — which, at £350 each and with sales of one million newspapers, were much cheaper than printing and posting a million individual advertisements (estimated to cost £4,200).

John Mackintosh also worked hard on 'push' forms of marketing, starting at first by supplying Halifax shopkeepers, then by setting up agencies and depots in the North of England and then the Midlands. Within five years he was exhibiting at the London International Confectionery Exhibition of which the trade journal commented 'the show would be incomplete without the appearance of Mr Mackintosh of Halifax' {*Confectionery* 12 Sept 1896}. He offered two cwts of toffee free to the wholesaler whose order was opened first each Monday morning — weekly for three months in autumn 1897. Breaking into the London market was less easy because of the resistance of wholesalers. Mackintosh thereupon (at a date unspecified) hired 15 commission salesmen who took parcels of toffee out from the London depot directly to the retail shops in the City and achieved high sales. The wholesalers then submitted and willingly 'pushed' Mackintosh toffee. Push and pull methods were complementary and a base in the London market was essential to both.

Mackintosh also developed agencies overseas after first touring Northern Europe in 1902 (a tour intended to explore the Russian butter market). A factory was established at Crefeld near Düsseldorf ca 1906, following which he established retail outlets in Germany. Mackintosh himself personally developed the German market, although he did not speak the language (with an eye to future developments he sent his eldest son Harold (qv), when he was eighteen, to Germany for this purpose, as well as to serve his managerial apprenticeship). Imperial markets were also built up, with factories in Canada and Australia before 1914. At that date Mackintosh toffee went to 40 countries and a third of the output of English factories was exported. Mackintosh entered the American market in 1903 when he first toured the USA, signing a contract on his first day there with J Walter Thompson, the advertising agent, 'to spend £100,000 in the first two years of business in America' {Crutchley (1921) 32}. The following year he went back and found a suitable factory at Asbury Park,

O-o-oh! Isn't he lucky!

A whole tin of Mackintosh's! Mackintosh's has delight in every bite, a power to dispel all momentary gloom—in the home or the trenches—and is the purest, most wholesome toffee it's possible to produce: made from butter, sugar, and thick, rich cream in the inimitable Mackintosh Way.

MACKINTOSH'S TOFFEE DE LUXE

Secure a tin at once from the nearest confectioners. 5/- per 4lb. tin, or 1/4 per lb. Also in 1/- tins.

Mackintosh's Toffee de Luxe, advertisement, 1915 (courtesy of Rowntree Mackintosh plc).

on the New Jersey coast within 50 miles of New York City, America's eastern entrepôt. However, within a few years it closed, and Mackintosh lost 'almost all the money he had made in England' {*ibid*, 33} because the heat of American summers reduced the hard Halifax toffee to treacle. Only after the toffee was wrapped and packaged in small pieces did the firm get a secure foothold in the American market.

Expansion was severely checked by the First World War. Sugar, butter and milk were strictly rationed, eventually to 20 per cent of manufacturers' pre-war levels. Employees went into the Services or into munitions work so that the workforce fell from nearly 1,000 to 250. The Germans sequestrated the factory at Crefeld. Two of John Mackintosh's three sons, Harold and Douglas, went into the Navy and Army respectively (Eric (b 1906) was too young to volunteer). And John Mackintosh himself, appointed to the Board of Trade advisory committee (under the Trades Board Act) on confectionary trades, suffered increasingly from a heart condition as well as gout. When wartime controls increased his costs, compelling him to raise his prices, he met the wholesalers' resistance by resorting to large national newspaper advertisements (as in the *Daily Mail* of 8 December 1914) explaining his policy. These 'splashes' {Fletcher (1920) 6} proved very effective in sustaining demand throughout the war years. The post-war boom revived the Mackintosh business and by 1921 the company employed over 1,000 people, its output was sixty times that of 1899, it had net assets of £350,512 (in September 1920) and average profits for the three years 1918-20 of £220,863 (before Excess Profits Duty of 60 per cent and Corporation Profits Tax of 5 per cent).

Outside his firm John Mackintosh was vice-chairman of the Equitable Bank of Halifax and of the Equitable Building Society, doing 'much to help in the cause of public thrift which he so strongly advocated' {*Halifax Weekly Courier* 28 Jan 1920}.

Throughout his life John Mackintosh remained an active member of the Queen's Road Methodist Chapel (New Connexion until 1907 and thereafter United Methodist), serving as a long-time secretary to the chapel trustees and teacher, secretary and superintendent in the Sunday School. He was also the circuit treasurer steward. He was frequently a delegate to his denomination's annual conferences and took a special interest in foreign missions. He was also a moderate temperance reformer. He held, among other religious offices, a vice-presidency of the YMCA.

In the Halifax locality Mackintosh became renowned as a philanthropist whose 'benefactions were too numerous to record' {*ibid*}, the beneficiaries ranging from local churches and the hospital, and in the war years various soldiers' and sailors' funds, to individuals (employees or any needy cases he heard about, often via his Queen's Road church minister). Indeed he was characterised by his local obituarist as 'a man whose chief study seemed to be how best he could help' {*ibid*}.

While his religious and philanthropic activities clearly occupied most of John Mackintosh's career outside his business, he was eventually persuaded to enter politics. A Liberal, in 1913 he was elected to the Halifax Town Council; in his election address he declared 'while I have my political and religious opinions, I am a moderate man, and can "live and let live", looking for the best and not the worst in everyone'. {Crutchley (1921) 165} In 1918 he became a borough magistrate.

The president of several local sports clubs and himself a physically big man who enjoyed exercise in his youth, John Mackintosh took a keen interest in bowling, football and cricket. He lived in Halifax nearly all his life, after 1895 in Park Terrace and in his last years at Greystones, the middle in a block of three large terraced houses on the edge of Savile Moor. He died suddenly at Greystones on 27 January 1920 at the relatively young age of fifty-one, leaving a widow and three sons. His estate was proved at £254,564 gross.

DAVID J JEREMY

Sources:

Unpublished

Rowntree Mackintosh PLC, York, Archives, John Mackintosh Ltd balance sheet 31 Dec 1899, abridgement of company prospectus for John Mackintosh & Sons Ltd 24 Mar 1921.

BCe.

MCe.

PrC.

Information from Kingsley Johnson.

Published

William H Beable, *Romance of Great Businesses* (2 vols, Heath Cranton, 1926) 2.

Confectioners' Union 15 Nov 1912.

Confectionery Mar, Apr, June, Sept, Oct 1896-97, Oct-Nov 1909.

Confectionery Journal Jan 1920.

George W Crutchley, *John Mackintosh. A Biography* (Hodder & Stoughton, 1921).

Daily Mail 8 Dec 1914, 13 Mar 1920.

E L Fletcher, 'The Advertising Genius of John Mackintosh' *Advertising World* Mar 1920.

Halifax Weekly Courier 28 Jan 1920.

An Illustrated Account of Halifax and District (Brighton: W T Pike & Co, 1895/96).

In Memoriam. John Mackintosh of Halifax (pp, Halifax, 1920).

Harold V Mackintosh, *By Faith and Work. The Autobiography of the Rt Hon the First Viscount Mackintosh of Halifax* (Hutchinson, 1966).

Times 28 Jan 1920.

George P Wadsworth (ed), *Halifax. A Commercial and Industrial Centre* (Sells Ltd, 1915).

C B B McLaren, 1st Lord Aberconway (from Sir Allan Grant, Steel and Ships *Michael Joseph, 1950).*

McLAREN, Charles Benjamin Bright

1st Lord Aberconway of Bodnant

(1850-1934)

Shipbuilding, iron and coal companies chairman

Charles Benjamin Bright McLaren was born in Edinburgh on 12 May 1850, the third son of Duncan McLaren (1800-86), later (1865-80) MP for Edinburgh, and of Priscilla née Bright, sister of John Bright, MP, the Anti-Corn Law leader. It was a background of Liberal and Radical thinking. He was educated at Edinburgh University where he gained Hamilton and Fergusson scholarships, and a first-class degree in philosophy, and also studied at the universities of Bonn and Heidelberg. After a brief spell of journalism he was called to the Bar at Lincoln's Inn in 1874 and then practised as a Chancery lawyer, specialising mainly in company and mercantile law. He became a Queen's Counsel in 1897 but in the same year he ceased legal practice to devote himself to industrial affairs.

The transition from the Bar to industry was a consequence of the commercial nature of his legal practice and of connections made by his marriage. In 1877 McLaren married Laura, only daughter of Henry Davis Pochin, a chemical manufacturer with an estate at Bodnant in Denbighshire. Pochin was described as an 'advanced radical' {*Times* 24 Jan 1934} and his wife Agnes wrote *The Right of Women to Exercise the Elective Franchise* in 1855. Laura Pochin was herself a passionate advocate of women's rights throughout her life, even if she did not support the more violent actions of the suffragettes in the years before the First World War. Pochin's death in 1895 left Laura the heir of her father's fortune since her brother was cut out of the will.

With such connections, it was natural for McLaren to enter parliament as a Liberal. He was elected MP for Stafford in 1880 and was an active member (and a founder of the National Liberal Club in 1882), but lost his seat in 1886 over Home Rule. During a second, and longer, term as MP for the Bosworth Division of Leicestershire (1892-1910), parliament took up less of his attention. He took an interest in both Irish and Scottish affairs, supported the Channel Tunnel project in 1884, and in 1886 moved that the Government ought to consider the desirability of appointing properly qualified diplomatic agents in foreign capitals for the express purpose of promoting the extension of British commerce.

Pochin's wide interests in industry included directorships of John Brown & Co, Palmer's Shipbuilding & Iron Co, the Sheepbridge Coal & Iron Co, Tredegar Iron & Coal Co, Bolckow Vaughan and Staveley Coal & Iron Co as well as the Metropolitan Railway. Charles McLaren was to be involved with nearly all these companies in the course of his long industrial career. In 1895, the year of Pochin's death, he became chairman of Tredegar Iron & Coal Co, a post which he held for thirty-nine years. In 1904 he became chairman of the Metropolitan Railway Co and held that position until the Metropolitan's absorption in the London Passenger Transport Board in 1933. Other chairmanships included Palmers Shipbuilding & Iron Co of Jarrow (until 1910) and the Sheepbridge Coal & Iron Co.

McLaren's most important industrial connection, however, was with John Brown & Co. He became a director of John Brown, in 1882, under the chairmanship of John Devonshire Ellis (qv) and made sufficient impression to become deputy chairman in 1897, an appointment that probably led to his retirement from the Bar. On the death of J D Ellis in 1906 he became chairman, a post he held until 1934. His services to industry and politics were amply recognised: he was created a baronet in 1902, a Privy Counsellor in 1908 and a baron, with the title of Lord Aberconway of Bodnant, in 1911.

During his long period of chairmanship John Browns' fortunes varied considerably. The period up to 1914 was notable for the building of the *Lusitania* and *Aquitania* as large passenger ships and of the warships *Inflexible* and *Bristol*. During the First World War the warships *Tiger*, *Barham*, *Repulse* and *Hood* were completed, along with the passenger liner *Ormonde*. Shipping construction was undertaken at Clydebank but there was much activity in steel-making and munitions production at Sheffield, with John Browns' establishments in both places being brought under government control in accordance with the Munitions of War Act of 1915.

HMS Hood *built by John Brown &*
*Co Ltd (*Brassey's Naval Annual
William Clowes & Sons Ltd).

After the war the general economic problems associated with the 1920s brought unemployment and lower levels of activity, notably to the collieries in South Yorkshire. In 1921 Lord Aberconway was one of those critical of the situation of the iron and steel industry, saying at John Browns' annual meeting at the end of June that the country had spent the last two years in 'a perfect orgy of extravagance, inflated prices and idleness' {Carr and Taplin (1962) 364}. Another burden which he deplored was the cost of local authority rates, observing at the annual meeting in 1923 that Sheffield rates amounted to an impost of at least £2 a ton on materials at the Atlas Works and that other districts in the country were less heavily assessed. Aberconway was still chairman of John Browns when the firm in December 1930 won the Cunard contract to build no 534, the 81,200 ton *Queen Mary* (launched September 1934 and introduced into service in 1936), a contract worth £3.27 million.

Overall, Aberconway's role in the running of John Browns seem to have been mainly supervisory and financial, as was probably the case in his chairmanship of other companies as well. For example, during his chairmanship of the Metropolitan Railway Co, the dominant figure for much of the time (1908-30) was R H Selbie (qv), the general manager. Two episodes in which Aberconway was involved were an agreement made in October 1904 with the Great Central Railway over sharing of track in the north-west London suburbs and negotiations in 1930-31 for the inclusion of the Metropolitan Railway and the Underground in the London Passenger Transport Board. In that episode there were suggestions that, in endeavouring to raise the value of the company's shares, Aberconway was pressing for better terms than the Minister of Transport, Herbert Morrison, was willing to agree and that Morrison was irritated by hints that Aberconway could make trouble for the proposed London Transport Bill in the House of Lords.

Similarly, as chairman of Tredegar Iron & Coal Co he left day-to-day management very much in the hands of the general manager, with his activity being limited to occasional visits to South Wales and to regular attendance at board meetings. Nevertheless, there is evidence that coal was the one industry in which he took more interest than any other. At John Browns during the First World War, when owing to wartime pressure separate management committees were set up for Sheffield, Clydebank and the collieries, Aberconway chaired the Collieries Committee. He was closely involved in the negotiations which resulted in the formation of Yorkshire Amalgamated Collieries Ltd, registered on 7 March 1927 and involving Denaby, Cadeby Main, Dinnington Main, Maltby and Rossington Main collieries in which Sheepbridge Iron & Coal Co and John Browns had important interests. Aberconway himself became chairman of the new company. In general, he was sympathetic with the tendency to amalgamation in the coal industry and in 1933 he condemned the attempts of some coalowners to circumvent the provisions of the Coal Mines Act of 1930. For him it was still not too late for the industry to reap the advantages of closer co-operation, which would result in more economic prices for coal to the advantage of owners and workers alike. He was in favour of voluntary schemes of amalgamation, such as that suggested by West Yorkshire coalowners, rather than compulsory schemes promoted by politicians. His general tone of moderation as a coalowner was reflected in his comments on miners. He characterised Yorkshire miners as 'attractive men' as a class. The Yorkshire miner he said, 'is sober, steady and attentive to his work'. Equally, he thought 'there is ... no better miner than a Welshman. He is, it is true, hot headed, impulsive and difficult to lead. Sentiment appeals to him more powerfully than reason which, to some extent, accounts for the development of Communistic ideas among his class ... [Yet] the courage of the Welsh miner is unbounded ... No danger, however menacing, ever deters him; and there are no finer pages in history than those which record the devotion of the Welsh miner to his comrades in the darkness of the mine' {Aberconway (1927) 26, 254-55}. He identified 'the root of the trouble in our recent labour disputes' as 'inflated wages during the War [which] were the product of an abnormal period which can never recur' {ibid, 347}. His interest in miners was shown in his board membership of the Industrial Housing Association, a body which he was instrumental in forming in 1922 with Charles Markham (qv) of the Stanton & Staveley Co.

His pragmatic approach to business problems may explain in part why he was acceptable as chairman of so many companies over a long period. He was regarded as something of an authority on general industrial problems, partly because his chairman's address at John Browns' annual general meetings usually included a survey of the current state of the heavy industries. As Sir Charles McLaren he wrote articles on 'The Financial Aspects of Engineering and some Allied Industries' in the Engineering Supplement of the *Times*. Possessed of considerable charm, he, and his wife, enjoyed entertaining fairly frequently at their London home. On the occasion of his golden wedding he advised the pursuit of interesting activities and mixing as much as possible with young people. He was a man blessed with an abundant energy.

His hobbies included shooting, forestry, and photography. Although the gardens at his homes at Bodnant and at Cap d'Antibes were famous among horticulturalists, their creation and care were much more due to his wife and to his son, Henry Duncan McLaren, than to himself. Aberconway was a magistrate for Denbighshire, Flintshire, Middlesex and Surrey. His wife

Laura predeceased him in 1933, leaving an estate of £750,000 gross. There were two sons and two daughters of their marriage, but one son was killed during the First World War. Lord Aberconway died on 23 January 1934, leaving £15,043 gross.

Just before Aberconway's death in 1934 his son, Henry Duncan McLaren (qv), became chairman of John Browns, retaining this position until 1953 when he was succeeded by his son, Charles Melville McLaren, who retired from the chairmanship in 1978 but continued as president of the company. Since the McLarens neither founded John Browns nor had a controlling financial interest such a long period of high office by one family is remarkable.

GRAEME HOLMES

Writings:

'The Coal Trade' in Sir Swire Smith (ed), *Protection and Industry* (Methuen & Co, 1904).

'Prospects of Iron and Steel Investments' *Financial Review of Reviews* Oct 1906.

'Labour Exchanges and Compulsory Insurance' *ibid* June 1909.

PP, Interim and Final Reports on Scheme of Out-of-Work Donation (1919) Cmd 196, 305 (chairman).

The Basic Industries of Great Britain (Benn, 1927).

Guide to the Garden at Bodnant (Edinburgh, 1928).

'The British Coal Industry in 1933' *Iron and Coal Trades Review* 26 Jan 1934.

Sources:

Unpublished

Bristol University, National Liberal Club records.

PrC.

Interviews with 3rd Lord Aberconway of Bodnant.

Information from Glasgow University archives.

Published

Theodore C Barker and Michael Robbins, *A History of London Transport* (2 vols, George Allen & Unwin, 1963-74).

James C Carr and Walter Taplin, *A History of the British Steel Industry* (Oxford: Blackwell, 1962).

Stanley D Chapman, *Stanton and Staveley* (Cambridge: Woodhead-Faulkner, 1981).

DNB.

Charlotte J Erickson, *British Industrialists: Steel and Hosiery, 1850-1950* (Cambridge: Cambridge University Press, 1959).

Sir Allan Grant, *Steel and Ships: The History of John Browns* (Michael Joseph, 1950).

Francis E Hyde, *Cunard and the North Atlantic 1840-1973* (Macmillan, 1975).

Iron and Coal Trades Review 26 Jan 1934.

Eric Mensforth, *Family Engineers* (Ward Lock, 1981).

Times 24 Jan 1934.

Western Mail 24 Jan 1934.

WWMP.

WWW.

H D McLaren, 2nd Lord Aberconway (from Sir Allan Grant, Steel and Ships *Michael Joseph, 1950).*

McLAREN, Henry Duncan

2nd Lord Aberconway of Bodnant

(1879-1953)

Industrialist

Henry Duncan McLaren was born at Barnes, Surrey, on 16 April 1879, the eldest child of Charles Benjamin Bright McLaren (qv) and his wife Laura Elizabeth, daughter of Henry James Pochin. After education at Eton, where he was captain of the Oppidans, he read history at Balliol College, Oxford, graduating with second class honours in 1902. He travelled for a year or two and then in 1905 was called to the Bar but never practised.

Until early middle age Henry McLaren combined an interest in politics with some activity in business, as his father had done, and then business interests became his main concern. His family background brought him naturally into contact with Liberals and in 1906 he was elected Liberal MP for West Staffordshire, soon becoming parliamentary private secretary to Lloyd George, whom he served both at the Board of Trade and at the Exchequer. After defeat in the January election of 1910 he was returned in the December election for the Bosworth division of Leicestershire which he represented until defeat in 1922; thereafter he did not seek re-election. Had he devoted more time to politics, he would probably have had a distinguished political career, but even if Lloyd George appreciated his abilities, his other interests intruded too much on his political activity.

Paramount among his other concerns were the industrial companies associated with his father and with his maternal grandfather. Unlike his father, he was soon involved in the family concern, H D Pochin & Co, and so came to acquire extensive knowledge of the china clay industry. As chairman of Pochins from before 1914 he took a major part, together with H Stanley Pochin, in forming English Clays Lovering Pochin & Co Ltd (ECLP) in 1932. It was essentially a merger of three china clay producing companies (English China Clays Ltd, Lovering China Clays Ltd and H D Pochin & Co Ltd). McLaren was not a director of English China Clays Ltd (ECC) but he became the first chairman of ECLP and had considerable influence on its management until his death. The 1930s were a difficult period for the china clay industry and in 1939 the chairman of ECC, R Martin, and McLaren as chairman of ECLP, each drew attention to depression in America, to international trading problems and to the burden of increased coal prices. The Second World War brought even greater problems and by 1941 the industry was working on approximately a third of the 1939 output. Only a bare profit could be expected. ECLP achieved it, maintaining a steady but low dividend of 1 per cent throughout the war. By 1949 Aberconway's (he had succeeded his father in 1934) report to ECLP's annual general meeting noted that overall trade for the company had recovered to 86 per cent of that of 1939; general trading conditions improved in the 1950s.

In spite of his arts background, McLaren developed an insight into industrial techniques, perhaps an inheritance from his Pochin grandfather. This capacity for understanding the problems of production, coupled with his business and political background, was a factor in his appointment as Deputy Director of Area Organisation at the Ministry of Munitions during the First World War, for which McLaren was made CBE in 1918. During the 1920s his business interests increased and he became a director of John Browns, Bolckow Vaughan, Palmers Shipbuilding and Tredegar Iron & Coal Co Ltd. He made sufficient impression in the enterprises with which he was associated for him to be regarded as a natural successor to his father. For example, he took a prominent part in the merger forming Firth Brown in 1931. This merger of John Browns' steelworks and Firth steelworks made commercial sense because of the geographical interconnections of the two firms. John Browns held 83 per cent of the equity and McLaren was chairman of Firth Brown until steel nationalisation in 1949. He succeeded also to his father's chairmanships, including John Browns, Sheepbridge, Cortonwood, Yorkshire Amalgamated Collieries and Tredegar. His wide interests meant that, like his father, his role was largely supervisory, but he could delegate responsibility successfully. These chairmanships involved much time spent on problems of organisation during the Second World War and on the transition to a new order after the war, not least, in the case of the colliery companies, with the negotiations concerned with nationalisation. He was also a director of the National Provincial Bank and of London Assurance.

In business he was interested in trying to promote technical advancement. For example, an approach by Sir Kingsley Wood to Lord Aberconway in the late 1930s to interest John Browns in acquiring an aircraft business, resulted in the acquisition, in association with Associated Electrical Industries, of Westland Aircraft, with Aberconway becoming chairman of the new board. When, in 1947, a new model electron microscope became available, Aberconway promptly ordered the next two models for English China Clays and for Firth Brown.

Yet the spread of his many interests evidently reduced his effectiveness as a businessman. 'Lord Aberconway had many interests: politics, shipbuilding, steel, engineering, china clay, banking, insurance and quarrying, and was an expert on rhododendrons. To many, he appeared autocratic, and it was not easy to oppose him, but he respected any sound argument. I believe that he made some decisions without investigation in depth ... He devoted little time to annual meetings and his colleagues did not know of the contents of his Chairman's statement until they heard it read to the shareholders' {Mensforth (1981) 82}. All observers comment on his abundant energy and on his capacity to initiate and to think creatively. He did not suffer gladly either the foolish or the incompetent, and if he drove himself hard he could drive others hard also.

Outside business, Aberconway was a good shot, enjoyed travelling, collected antiques and owned a succession of open Rolls-Royce motor cars. He was a conscientious JP and a chairman of Denbighshire quarter sessions. Nevertheless, his great personal interest lay in the development of the gardens at Bodnant. Encouraged by his mother Laura, he created a famed array of plants, especially in the planting and hybridisation of rhododendrons. In 1949, the gardens were given to the National Trust, together with a generous endowment for their upkeep. It was his expertise in gardening which made him a well-known and successful president of the Royal Horticultural Society from 1931 until his death in 1953.

He married in 1910 Christabel Mary Melville, younger daughter of Sir Melville Macnaghten, chief of the Criminal Investigation Department. There were two daughters and three sons of this exceptionally happy marriage. The second son, John Francis, a barrister who joined John Brown as an executive in 1949, died tragically in March 1953. Lord Aberconway himself died at Bodnant on 23 May 1953, leaving an estate of £242,252 gross (excluding settled land) and £23,525 in settled land. He was succeeded in the title by his eldest son, Charles Melville McLaren (b 1913) who also distinguished himself in business.

GRAEME HOLMES

Sources:

Unpublished

PrC.

Interviews with the Third Lord Aberconway of Bodnant.

Published

Lord Aberconway, *Basic Industries of Great Britain* (Benn, 1927).

DNB.

Sir Allan Grant, *Steel and Ships: The History of John Browns* (Michael Joseph, 1950).

Kenneth Hudson, *The History of English China Clays* (Newton Abbot: David & Charles, 1968).

Eric Mensforth, *Family Engineers* (Ward Lock, 1981).

WWMP.

WWW.

McLEAN, Sir Robert

(1884-1964)

Railway and aviation company manager

Robert McLean was born in Claremont, Alloa, near Stirling in Central Scotland, on 3 February 1884, son of Rev D McLean, a Presbyterian minister, and his wife Annie née Younger. He was educated at Edinburgh Academy, 1897-1901, where he showed unusual ability at an early age, notably winning awards in mathematics. In 1901 he went to Edinburgh University, where in 1904 he took a science degree in engineering.

In 1905 McLean joined the Indian public works department as an assistant engineer. He was posted to the state railways and was soon engaged in the operation and maintenance of existing railways and in the survey and construction of new lines. By 1914 he was with the North-Western Railway.

In the First World War, McLean was a captain in the Railway Corps of the Indian Army, from 1915, first in India, and then with the Aden Field Force. Later he transferred to the Royal Engineers, serving in India and with the Expeditionary Force in Mesopotamia. In 1916, he returned to India where he was made assistant secretary of the newly-formed Railway Board. However, in 1917 he went home to the UK and served in the Royal Engineers on the Western Front in France.

After demobilisation in 1919 he returned once again to India and became Secretary of the Railway Board. In 1920 he was loaned to the Great Indian Peninsular Railway where he was deputy agent and, from 1922, general manager. In the latter capacity, he introduced the first railway electrification scheme in India — first of the Bombay suburban lines and then of a main line scheme, initially extending over a distance of 240 miles. McLean was elected president of the Indian Railway Companies' Association in 1925 and became a trustee of the Port of Bombay, 1922-27. He was knighted in 1926 for services in India and then retired, returning to the UK in 1927.

In that year McLean was elected to the board of Vickers Ltd, thus beginning at the age of forty-three the most important part of his career, in a field which contrasted sharply with his previous experience of over twenty years of government service in India. The year after he joined Vickers, the company was completely re-organised. On 29 June 1928 the aircraft works at Weybridge became Vickers (Aviation) Ltd, and McLean was appointed its chairman and managing director on 4 July. Five months later, largely at McLean's instigation, Vickers acquired the Supermarine Aviation Works Ltd at Southampton and he became chairman of this new subsidiary as well.

The ten years which followed, with McLean as head of Vickers' aviation activities, have been the subject of much controversy. By nature, the new chairman was a strong, austere, independent and sometimes uncommunicative individual of immense capacity, who expected and was allowed a large measure of freedom in running his companies. For most of this period he was, in fact, subject only to general guidance by the parent Vickers board which was headed by Sir Herbert A Lawrence (qv), a remarkable soldier-banker, who believed in delegating as much authority as possible to his selected lieutenants. McLean was, at the same time, effectively quite independent of the rest of the Vickers organisation.

During 1928-37, McLean's forceful and imaginative leadership of Vickers (Aviation) and of Supermarine, shown in such matters as the British winning of the Schneider Trophy and in the complete rebuilding and modernisation of the Weybridge factory, established the companies as leaders in the industry. He later played a major role in launching development of the Wellington bomber and Spitfire fighter (he is said to have chosen the latter's name). Unfortunately, at the same time, his independence antagonised Sir Charles Craven and some other members of Vickers's main board. He was not an easy man to get on with and, over the years, he also had disagreements with a number of his senior managers who left the company as a result. Others, more able or more amenable, survived, and were strongly supported and promoted.

McLean was sometimes openly critical of his principal customer, the Air Ministry, and also took many important decisions without adequate reference to the Vickers main board, exciting criticism and resentment both in the Ministry and at Vickers. Notable controversial issues during his regime included his outright refusal to accept an Air Ministry order for the G 4/31 biplane, his insistence that the monoplane Wellesley be substituted, his direct dealings with Lord Swinton and the Air Staff over policy matters, his decisions — with the support of Sir Arthur Sidgreaves (qv) at Rolls Royce — to develop the Spitfire as a private venture instead of a derivative of the unsatisfactory F 7/30 official specification, and his advice to the Air Ministry against continuation of the four-engine Supermarine bomber.

Sir Herbert Lawrence was succeeded as chairman of the parent Vickers company by another banker, Archibald Jamieson, in April 1937. At the same time, at least partly because of Air Ministry pressure, Craven was appointed chairman of Vickers (Aviation) and of Supermarine, in addition to his duties as chairman of Vickers-Armstrongs, while McLean was relegated to managing director of the aviation companies. After Craven's appointment, when problems arose in bringing the Spitfire and

Wellington into production, it was not surprising that McLean should find his position untenable and he resigned on 14 October 1938, just before the two aviation companies were absorbed into Vickers-Armstrongs.

McLean's disagreements with the Air Ministry and with some of the Vickers directors were unfortunate but most of his policies — except perhaps that to develop geodetic structures — were to be proved sound by subsequent events. His strong presence at the head of Vickers's aviation interests until 1938 was of great benefit to the RAF and prevented Craven, the rising power in Vickers and no great believer in air power, from adopting policies which might have reduced the effectiveness of Britain's preparations for war.

After he left Vickers, McLean was retained for a short time as an adviser but that same year became managing director of Electrical & Musical Industries Ltd. During the Second World War, he led EMI as it played a distinguished part in the development, production and bringing into operational service of another vital war product, radar. He retired in 1943.

McLean was chairman of the Society of British Aircraft Constructors, 1935-37, sometime president of the Institution of Production Engineers and vice-president of the Royal Society of Arts. He was a freeman of the City of London.

After his retirement he took up farming near Galashiels, Selkirkshire, in Scotland. In 1908 he married Evelyn Noel, daughter of H E Girard of Calcutta; they had two daughters.

Sir Robert McLean died at Clovenfords near Galashiels on 9 April 1964 at the age of eighty.

PETER W BROOKS

Sources:

Unpublished

Edinburgh Academy biographical schedule completed by Sir Robert McLean, 6 February 1950.

Correspondence with Sir George Edwards, 16 Dec 1980, 13 Jan 1981.

BCe (Scots).

Published

Edinburgh Academy Register 1914.

Edinburgh Academy Register Supplement 1921.

Flight 16 Apr 1964.

John D Scott, *Vickers. A History* (Weidenfeld & Nicholson, 1962).

Times 11 Apr 1964.

University of Edinburgh Journal 1964.

WWW.

McLINTOCK, Sir William

(1873-1947)

Accountant

Sir William McLintock (from E Green and M Moss, A Business of National Importance *Methuen, 1982).*

William McLintock was born in Glasgow on 26 September 1873, the eldest son of Thomson McLintock, chartered accountant, by his first wife, Jeanne née Marshall, the daughter of a merchant seaman. William's mother died when he was a child and his father subsequently married Mary née McKinnell, by whom he had two sons and three daughters. All three of Thomson McLintock's sons were to enter the accounting practice which he founded in Glasgow and which is now (1984) one of the ten largest in the United Kingdom.

William McLintock was educated at Dumfries Academy and Glasgow High School and became apprenticed to his father. He was admitted to membership of the Glasgow Institute of Accountants and Actuaries in 1896, although only after several failures in the final examination, and in 1901 became a partner in his father's practice, which was well-established in Glasgow but not elsewhere. The opportunity to expand out of Glasgow came in 1914 when Thomson McLintock was appointed liquidator of Northern Equitable Insurance, a company founded in Glasgow which had moved its head office to London, with William McLintock supervising the work of his youngest brother, Charles, who moved to London to run the new office. The firm thus became one of the first Scottish firms of chartered accountants to move into England, although its expansion was to be based not on auditing but on the growth of McLintock's reputation as a tax expert and as an adviser on the amalgamation and reconstruction of companies; in this latter field McLintock was to play a pre-eminent role in the inter-war period.

McLintock's first major tax commission came in 1914 when he negotiated for the Lanarkshire coal owners with the Inland Revenue to secure uniform rates of depreciation on coal wagons. His performance was impressive enough for the Treasury to invite him in 1916 to become a member of the Board of Referees which had been set up under the excess profits duty legislation of 1915 to tax war profits. The Board was both an appeal body for taxpayers and responsible for fixing profit standards for each trade and industry. McLintock was thus brought into close contact with the Inland Revenue, the Government, and the many trade associations involved in negotiating the standards, and he established a reputation as a man of outstanding character and ability. The first of the major amalgamations in which McLintock was involved began in 1916 when McLintocks and W B Peat & Co engaged in the long series of negotiations and investigations with 35 companies that culminated in 1918 with the merger of the whole of the explosives industry into Explosives Trades Ltd. The moving force behind the merger, and probably the source of the work for McLintock, was Harry McGowan (qv) of Nobels, a friend of McLintock. The firm became the joint auditors of the new company with Peats and were engaged in a considerable amount of tax work amongst the constituent companies in the group. The connection with McGowan also brought the firm work from other companies in which Nobels had investments. Thus the firm became auditors to the firm of Henry Dreyfus (qv) — later renamed British Celanese — when it was founded in 1916 and McLintocks was responsible for the investigation leading to the creation by merger of the British Dyestuffs Corporation, an assignment which led to McLintocks opening an office in Manchester in 1919. As Nobels expanded in the post-war period, McLintocks received more work investigating target companies. In some ways McLintocks' role was more comparable to that of a merchant bank and including acting as underwriters to an 8 per cent note issued in 1920. When Nobels, BDC, UAC and Brunner Mond merged in 1926 to create Imperial Chemical Industries, McLintocks became joint auditors of the new company with Price Waterhouse; ICI remains (1984) the firm's largest audit client.

The immediate post-war period was a time of vigorous expansion for the firm and also saw the emergence of McLintock as a public figure. The firm became secretary to various trade associations in the lead industry, auditors to the major firm of Goodlass Wall & Lead Industries, and accountants to the Mining Association of Great Britain, which would lead to the firm developing one of the foremost practices in the coal industry, culminating in their appointment as auditors to the National Coal Board. Although for the purposes of the International White Lead Convention the firm had an office in Paris for a short time, there does not seem to have been any real attempt to create an international practice. McLintock turned down an offer by William Plender (qv) of Deloittes to co-operate in a South American practice, probably because of the lack of control he could have over the work. A small Birmingham firm, Charles Baker & Co, was acquired in 1921 and with it came some important audits in the motor industry, including Standard Motors and Triumph Motorcycles. Within the practice, however, McLintock had recognised the importance of taxation as a growth area for those firms able to master it, by appointing F J Cooksey, a tax inspector from the Chief Inspector's Office of the Inland Revenue, as manager of the firm's tax department in 1920. It is indicative of the importance of such work to the firm, in contrast to auditing, that it was not until 1929 that an audit manager was appointed. McLintock's own reputation as a tax expert was recognised in his appointment to a number of government committees on taxation: the Committee on Financial Risks in 1918, the Royal Commission on Income Tax in 1919, the Committee on the Simplification of Income Tax and Surtax Forms and the Committee on National Debt and Taxation in 1924. His knighthood and the CVO were awarded in 1922 for his work on advising on the reorganisation of the finances of the Royal Household; the GBE was added in 1929 and he became a baronet in 1934.

One unexpected result of McLintock's service on the Royal Commission on Income Tax was his appointment as accountant to the Persian Government. A fellow member of the Royal Commission, Sir Sydney Armitage-Smith, had become financial adviser to the Persian Government, which wanted revisions made to the method of calculating royalties under the terms of the concession granted to the Anglo-Persian Oil Co.

Armitage-Smith realised that an accountant would need to examine the computation of royalties and recommended McLintock as 'one of the leading gentlemen in his profession' {Ferrier (1982) 366}. In his initial report of 1920, made within a few months of appointment, McLintock had exposed errors and omissions resulting in underpayment of royalties. Apart from the importance of his report in the subsequent negotiations, it also became an annual task for McLintocks to check the accuracy of the royalty calculations. McLintock was awarded the Order of the Lion and the Sun by the Shah of Persia in 1921 in recognition of his service and the unexpected degree of independence he had shown in challenging the basic assumptions of the Anglo-Persian Oil Co. It was perhaps particularly notable in that there were family connections with the company. McLintock's sister was married to William Milligan Fraser (qv), a director of Anglo-Persian who later became the company's chairman.

McLintock was involved in many of the reconstructions of companies in Britain's older industries which were badly affected by the collapse of the post-war boom. His own position was always to be constructive in such operations, by attempting to persuade creditors that the best way to preserve the value of their security was to make new arrangements to continue trading rather than by realising the assets for what they were worth. He was not, however, always successful in persuading creditors that this was the most effective course of action. Beardmores, the Scottish heavy engineering firm which was becoming dangerously illiquid, asked McLintock to examine the financial position of the company in 1926, but the scheme he produced was not acceptable to the banks or to the Treasury and the company was later saved only by the reluctant intervention of the Bank of England. More successful was the firm's involvement with the amalgamation of over 20 collieries into Manchester Collieries in 1929, and the merger and reorganisations creating the Wigan Coal & Iron Co in 1930. The firm was also responsible for the work involved in merging a number of private collieries into Hargreaves Collieries in 1932.

In addition to his work in coal and steel, McLintock was also involved in the problems of other industries. Together with Sir Otto Niemeyer, he was appointed financial adviser to the Imperial Cable Conference of 1928, which had been called to decide what to do with the Empire cable telegraph system, whose economic viability had been badly affected by the advent of radio. Eastern Telegraph and Marconi Wireless Telegraph had agreed to merge if an agreement could be reached with the various government systems; McLintock and Niemeyer were responsible for negotiating the terms by which these government cables, the Post Office radio system and the companies were brought together into one large new company, Cable & Wireless in 1929. On a more domestic level McLintock was asked by Ranks and Spillers in 1929 to work out the quota agreement administered by the Millers' Mutual Association, which regulated output and closed down redundant capacity in the milling trade, ensuring that the remaining millers entered a period of prosperity when the economic depression set in.

The great amount of work that Sir William was bringing into the firm was naturally reflected in a large increase in the fee income of the London office, which rose from £13,000 in 1919 to £102,000 in 1927. After the death of Thomson McLintock in 1920, a new partnership agreement had been written which increased the partnership capital from £1,200 to £18,600 and the number of partners from four to seven, with Sir William receiving a salary of £3,000 a year and 43.5 per cent of the profits. His brother, Thomas Liddell McLintock, was effectively in charge of the Glasgow office but relations between the two offices were deteriorating. Glasgow by 1927 had become the minor part of the practice, its fee income having risen in the same period from £28,000 to only £45,000.

Despite the increasing amount of business, Sir William found time for an impressive amount of public service: a member of the Industrial Arbitration Court and the Racecourse Betting Control Board, both from 1928 to 1935; a member of the Economic Advisory Council in 1929, serving on the sub-committee enquiring into the cotton industry; and membership of several government commissions, including the Unemployment Insurance Committee, 1927, the Public Utilities Advisory Committee, 1930, the Committee on Main Line Electrification, 1931, and, notably, the 1925 Committee on Company Law Amendment. Although the work of this committee, embodied in the 1929 Companies' Act, did result in some extensions to disclosure requirements in companies' accounts, it became apparent in the failure of the Royal Mail Group in 1930 that they had failed to deal with the problems posed by holding company accounts. As auditor to Nobels and British Dyestuffs Corporation, McLintock was the only one of the three accountants on the committee who had any experience of consolidated balance sheets, and his views on their desirability clearly emerged when the evidence was taken, in which process he played a major part. The committee as a whole, however, was clearly impressed by the weight of professional opinion, which was not then in favour of this innovation.

McLintock's involvement with the affairs of the Royal Mail Group was probably the most important, certainly the most prominent, work that he engaged in. The group of companies built up by the Philipps brothers (qqv) controlled nearly 15 per cent of the British shipping fleet through a complex structure of cross-holdings of shares in companies including Royal Mail, Elder Dempster, African Steam, Union-Castle, Lamport & Holt, and White Star. The numerous other interests included the Harland & Wolff Shipyards, and Colvilles, the steel company. These companies, apparently successful from their published accounts, were actually seriously illiquid and unable to make repayments on loans made under the Trade Facilities Act of 1921. Plender, chairman of the advisory committee under the Act, proposed to the Treasury that McLintock should be appointed to investigate the finances of the Royal Mail Group. By March 1930, within a few months of appointment, McLintock had prepared an initial report, disclosing that the group had made large trading losses since 1921, disguised in the accounts by transfers from hidden reserves and funded by bank overdrafts not disclosed in the balance sheets. He estimated the total liabilities of the companies at over £30 million and recommended that the principal creditors should meet, be told the facts, and be asked to agree a moratorium so that a reconstruction could be made. These proposals were accepted after a series of meetings with the banks and discount houses involved and McLintock was selected as one of three Voting Trustees, appointed to protect the lenders' interests and exercise voting control over the Group's companies, so that a reorganisation could be accomplished. It soon became apparent that this could not be done quickly, and the moratorium was extended. In February 1931 a meeting had to be called of the preference shareholders of Royal Mail and White Star to get permission for the Voting Trustees to cancel the next dividend payments. At this meeting McLintock explained the group's position and, for the first time, made public the trading losses which had occurred. The response was sensational. Widely reported in the press, questions were asked in parliament, with suggestions of fraud being made. In May 1931 Kylsant (the chairman of the group) with H J Morland, the company's auditor, was charged under the Larceny Act with publishing a false statement of accounts. Kylsant was also charged separately with issuing a false prospectus.

At the trial McLintock was one of the principal witnesses for the prosecution. It was widely felt at the time that Kylsant, as a leading businessman, and Morland, a chartered accountant and partner in the esteemed firm of Price Waterhouse, were on trial for engaging in and approving of the then widespread business practice of using hidden reserves to maintain a façade of profitability. McLintock was in the difficult position of not wanting to say anything which would prejudice the ability of the Voting Trustees to rescue the group companies, but the unsought-for prominence of his role made him a target for criticism both by defence counsel at the trial and within his own profession. Although Kylsant and Morland were acquitted of the charge of publishing false accounts, Kylsant was convicted and imprisoned on the charge of publishing a false prospectus. One of the effects of the trial was that some leading accountants, including McLintock, urged their fellows to act in advance of the changes in company law which the trial had exposed as necessary, and to take an extra-legal view of their duties and responsibilities to shareholders. McLintock himself caused a crisis at ICI in 1931 when he objected to the value at which the board proposed to take the huge but over-valued Billingham plant into the balance sheet and, partly at his prompting, ICI began a programme of writing-off its value.

The trial of Kylsant and Morland had virtually suspended the work of the Voting Trustees; they had managed to sell off some of the company's interests but had not yet dealt with the major companies in the group, beyond a long series of fruitless negotiations which had been held with Cunard to take over White Star. Late in 1931, however, the trustees managed to reorganise the assets of a number of the companies into two new operating companies, Royal Mail Lines and Elder Dempster Lines, and over the next two years, with the added involvement of the Bank of England and the Government, the amalgamation of White Star and Cunard was eventually settled. Since the Voting Trustees had freed over half of the group's tonnage from the burden of debt and successfully preserved the value of the fleets as going concerns, the trust was wound up. The future of the remaining companies would be solved by McLintock and his fellow-trustee, Brigadier General Sir Arthur Maxwell (managing partner of Glyn, Mills Bank), going on to the boards of the companies involved to represent the creditors' interests. A complex series of proposals was then formulated to set up realisation companies which would hold the shares of the main companies until their shares could be sold. The sale of most of these companies was successfully completed by 1936.

Because of the group's ownership, through Harland & Wolff, of Colvilles, McLintock had, simultaneously with his work with the shipping companies, been closely involved with plans to rationalise the Scottish steelmakers. With the Bank of England's support, he advised on a merger between the five main companies, including Colvilles. His proposals foundered in prolonged discussions with the companies involved over the share their respective enterprises should have in the new company. With McLintock's support John Craig, the chairman of Colvilles, over the next six years virtually accomplished the rationalisation of the industry by his own efforts, and the flotation of Colvilles in 1936 made possible a capital reconstruction of Harland & Wolff in 1937. The reconstructions of the Royal Mail group's companies as a whole realised over £25 million through asset sales, and a further £20 million was distributed in shares in the new companies. The total loss to original investors and unsecured creditors had been estimated at £50 million, but if the Group had gone into liquidation the loss might have been more than double this amount, with incalculable effects on the British shipping industry.

Despite the demands on the practice's resources generated by the prolonged involvement with the Royal Mail companies, other aspects of the firm's business also continued to expand. By 1933 the gross fee income had risen to £159,000, while that of the Glasgow office had fallen to £37,000, and McLintock decided that, instead of the two offices being run independently but as a single practice, as had been the case since 1927, a complete separation should be made, although he remained a partner in the Glasgow practice. The firm was still acquiring new clients, notably the George Weston/Associated British Foods group, whose takeover activities in the food industry provided much work. Other projects included the receivership of Gamages in 1931, acting as financial advisor to the Government in the complex negotiations which resulted in the creation of the London Passenger Transport Board in 1933, the reconstruction of the Lancashire Cotton Corporation in 1936, and involvement in a curious echo of the Kylsant case. In 1935 McLintock was appointed liquidator to the Bishirgian companies which had been involved in unsuccessful speculation, especially in pepper futures, financed with the aid of the issue of a fraudulent prospectus. Three directors of the companies were tried, convicted and imprisoned for issuing the prospectus, although McLintock did not in this case have to give evidence personally. In 1937 he was involved in another unsavoury, if less public, matter when he investigated the private financial affairs of McGowan at the instigation of the board of ICI. He found evidence of share speculation on an extensive scale, which had led to McGowan's near bankruptcy, and recommended that the board should cease to give their support to him. The board's plans to replace McGowan as chairman came to nothing, however, when his intended replacement, Henry Mond (qv), had a sudden heart attack.

Not all of McLintock's ventures were entirely successful. In common with a number of other accountants at the time, the firm had founded several investment trusts: the Grange Trust, established in 1926, and Ailsa, established in 1927, had not been very successful, Grange paying no dividend from 1932-33 to 1934-35. McLintock was also a director of a number of other investment trusts and of National Mutual Insurance from 1926 to 1931, while J M Keynes (qv) was chairman, but generally he did not accept directorships. By the mid-1930s McLintock's prodigious appetite for work was obviously affecting his health: already a sufferer from chronic bronchitis, he also had a kidney removed in 1934 and was unable to accept a commission from the South African Government to inquire into the financial position of the country's harbours. By 1936, however, he was well enough to agree to help negotiate the outstanding questions on contract costing which had arisen during the prolonged negotiations between the Air Ministry and the Society of British Aircraft Constructors, the firm having become auditors to some of the society's members (Boulton & Paul and Bristol Aeroplane). The first 'McLintock Agreement' proved to be unsatisfactory in practice, with the firms making very high profits, and in 1939 a second agreement was negotiated, but for most of the war individual contracts were negotiated outside the formulas of the agreement. McLintock's last acts of public service were to accept the chairmanship of a commission to inquire into the workings of the Northern Ireland Road Transport Board in 1938, and membership of the Committee on Cement Production in 1940-41.

McLintock's great energy and practical ability had enabled him to create a major accounting practice and to develop a public reputation as one of the foremost accountants of the inter-war period. The development of the practice was aided by some outstanding staff but the separation of the firm into two partnerships and McLintock's reluctance to engage in any international undertakings were to create problems for his successors and to ensure that their solution would give the modern firm a unique structure. Although he was unable in London to take part in the professional activities of the Glasgow Institute, he made time to give some excellent lectures to students, despite his dislike of public speaking, and these form the basis of most of his publications. He was also president of the Association of Scottish Chartered Accountants in London in 1926-27 and 1930-31.

Fond of music to the extent that, as a young man, he apparently wished to be a singer, he also enjoyed tennis, golf, shooting and running the farm he acquired in the mid-1930s. McLintock remained a member of the Church of Scotland and contributed generously to the rebuilding of St Columba's Church in London.

In 1901 he married Margaret, daughter of Henry Lyons of Sligo, by whom he had three daughters and one son, Thomson McLintock, who qualified as a chartered accountant and entered the firm for a time. Sir William McLintock died in Bournemouth on 8 May 1947, leaving an estate worth £430,005 gross.

MICHAEL BYWATER

Writings:

'Income Tax' *The Accountant* 20, 27 Nov 1915.

'Liquidations' *The Accountants Magazine* Apr 1926.

Speech at the Annual Dinner of the Birmingham Chartered Accountants Student Society *The Accountant* 11 Apr 1931.

'Company Reconstruction Schemes' *The Accountants Magazine* Feb 1932.

Some Aspects of Income Tax (Gee & Co, 1933).

'Creditors Voluntary Liquidations' *The Accountants Magazine* Apr 1936.

Sources:

Unpublished

PrC.

Published

The Accountant 24 May 1947.

William Ashworth, *Contracts and Finance* (HMSO and Longmans Green, 1953).

Ronald W Ferrier, *History of British Petroleum: The Developing Years 1901-32* (Cambridge: Cambridge University Press, 1982).

M P Fogarty (ed), *Further Studies in Industrial Organisation* (Methuen, 1948).

Edwin Green and Michael Moss, *A Business of National Importance: The Royal Mail Shipping Group, 1902-37* (Methuen, 1982).

John R Hume and Michael S Moss, *Beardmore, the History of a Scottish Industrial Giant* (Heinemann, 1979).

J Harry Jones, *Josiah Stamp, Public Servant* (Pitman, 1964).

Hugh Barty King, *Girdle Round the World* (Heinemann, 1979).

Peter L Payne, *Colvilles and the Scottish Steel Industry* (Oxford: Clarendon Press, 1979).

William J Reader, *Imperial Chemical Industries, a History* (2 vols, Oxford University Press, 1970-75).

R S Sayers, *The Bank of England, 1891-1944* (3 vols, Cambridge: Cambridge University Press, 1976).

Stock Exchange Official Year-Book 1932-40.

Times 9 May 1947.

Rex Winsbury, *Thomson McLintock & Co — the First Hundred Years* (Glasgow: pp for Thomson McLintock, 1977).

WWW.

Sir Frederick Macmillan (courtesy of Macmillans).

MACMILLAN, Sir Frederick Orridge

(1851-1936)

Publisher

Frederick Orridge Macmillan was born in Cambridge on 5 October 1851, the eldest son of the publisher and bookseller Daniel Macmillan and his wife Frances, daughter of Charles Orridge, a Cambridge chemist. After Daniel's death in 1857, his widow and children went to live with his brother Alexander, who had been his partner. Frederick was educated at Uppingham, and then joined the family firm. Since 1867 Alexander Macmillan had published from Bedford Street in London, while the Cambridge bookshop, then called Macmillan & Bowes, was run by Robert Bowes. Frederick learned about retail bookselling under Bowes, and about printing at the Oxford University Press (his uncle was printer to the University from 1863 to 1881), before working his way through the various departments of the Bedford Street publishing house. In 1871 he went to America, spending five years working with Macmillans' agent in New York, George Brett. In 1874, the year he was admitted to a partnership in the firm, Frederick married Georgiana Warrin of Long Island, returning to England two years later to settle in London.

By 1890, when Alexander more or less retired from the business, there were three young Macmillans in the firm: Frederick, his brother Maurice and his cousin George. In 1896, following the death of Alexander Macmillan, a limited company was formed, with a capital of £240,000; Frederick was its first chairman. The American branch was incorporated as the Macmillan Co of New York under the presidency of George Platt Brett, the son of George Brett.

The American business was one of Frederick's special responsibilities, together with the Toronto branch set up in 1905. (Macmillans were also setting up branches in India, the Far East and Australia before the First World War.) His main responsibility was for the general literature list, of fiction, poetry and 'art' books. H G Wells's characterisation of Macmillans as 'solid and sound and sane' {Morgan (1943) 147} could well be applied to Frederick's choice of books for this list. He disliked extremes of style or content, did not want to publish indecent books, nor be bound by the prejudices of professional guardians of literary morality like St Loe Strachey. He was aware of the need for '*new blood* which it is always important to infuse into our publishing veins' {BM Add 54,788, f 66}, and was ready to publish works of distinction which did not promise a large profit, or any profit at all, both because it pleased him to publish such works, and because he felt that 'Anything reasonable that we get to increase our turnover is all to the good. We have a large and expensive machinery and must keep it going' {ibid, f 38}.

The creation of this 'large and expensive machinery' owed much to Frederick's combination of sound taste, wide knowledge of all the technical aspects of the book trade, and astute business sense. During his years with the firm Macmillans became a major international publisher with several branches overseas and an international reputation. At his death, the nominal capital of the company stood at £740,000, following capitalisation of £480,000 of reserves in 1928.

However, Frederick Macmillan's major contribution to publishing, one which greatly benefited the entire trade, was in the initiation of the Net Book Agreement. This Agreement, still in force today (1984), though in a modified form, united publishers and booksellers against the practice of offering large discounts (sometimes over 25 per cent) on the retail price of newly-published books. So widespread had this practice become that it was difficult for booksellers not to follow suit, even if this meant it was almost impossible to make a living from the sale of new books alone. Frederick Macmillan's solution, proposed in a letter to *The Bookseller* in February 1890, was that publishers should refuse to supply books to retailers who would not undertake to sell them at the marked, 'net', price. He was not the first to propose this solution to a problem that had bedevilled the trade for decades. 'Net' prices had been fixed earlier by Macmillans, and other publishers, for very expensive books of limited appeal. But he was the first publisher to be willing to test it systematically in practice with books which might expect a wide sale. From 1890, an increasing proportion of Macmillan's books were issued at 'net' prices, and gradually, with the increasing support of the retail trade, other publishers followed. The protracted negotiations and discussions aroused within the trade resulted not only in the Net Book Agreement, which came into operation on 1 January 1900, but also in the setting-up of the Booksellers' Association of Great Britain and Ireland in 1895, and the Publishers' Association in 1896. By making the retailing of new books profitable once more, the Net Book Agreement 'quietly revolutionised the trade both in this country and America' { *Times* 2 June 1936}.

Frederick Macmillan was a prominent member of the Publishers' Association from its inception and served as its president in 1900-1 and 1911-12. He was one of the most authoritative and influential figures in the trade, playing a part in the settlement of the 'Times Book War' of 1906-8, when the Times Book Club tried to bypass and discredit the Net Book Agreement, and in the framing of the Copyright Act of 1911. There were limits to his belief in the virtues of collective action. He did not want the Publishers' Association to turn into a 'Trades Union' {BM, Add 54,788, ff 182-83} and he resented what he interpreted as an attempt by other members of the PA to interfere with the management of Macmillans' affairs over the issue of 7d novels in 1909. Nor was he wholly in favour of the moves towards closer co-operation within the trade championed by Stanley Unwin (qv), though he was prepared to admit he might be mistaken in this judgement.

To his friends, Macmillan was a jolly, unpriggish man who loved a good cigar. In the office, he was a firm but just disciplinarian, remote, like the other partners, from the ordinary staff, but able to unbend at office functions. So soundly-based was the organisation of Macmillans that when, following a fall while doing his morning exercises in the bathroom, Frederick Macmillan died on 1 June 1936 within three months of the deaths of George on 3 March and Maurice on 30 March, the business ran smoothly on, as their place was taken by Maurice's sons Daniel and Harold. Frederick himself had no children.

Besides his work through the Publishers' Association, Frederick Macmillan served as a trustee of the Booksellers' Provident Institution and a member of the council of the Royal Literary Fund. He was chairman of the Board of Management of the National Hospital for Paralysis, and was knighted in 1909 on the occasion of the opening of a new building there. He was a member of the Royal Commission on Paper in 1916, and served as a JP and DL for Hertfordshire. In 1920 he was made a Commander of the Royal Victorian Order. He left £202,224 gross.

CHRISTINE SHAW

Writings:

letter on net prices for books *The Bookseller* 24 Feb 1890.

The Net Book Agreement, 1899 and The Book War, 1906-1908 (Glasgow: pp, 1924).

Sources:

Unpublished

British Library, Macmillan Archive, Add MSS 54,887, 54,788.

C Reg: Macmillan Ltd (46,694).

PrC.

Information from Mr R Johns.

Published

The Bookseller 6 Mar 1890, 4 June 1936.

DNB.

C W Guillebaud, 'The Marshall-Macmillan Correspondence over the Net Book System' *Economic Journal* 75 (1965).

R J L Kingsford, *The Publishers Association, 1896-1946, With an Epilogue* (Cambridge: Cambridge University Press, 1970).

Charles Morgan, *The House of Macmillan 1843-1943* (Macmillan & Co, 1943).

Publishers' Circular 6 June 1936.

Times 2 June 1936.

WWW.

MAGGS, Joseph Herbert

(1875-1964)

Dairy company chairman

Joseph Herbert Maggs was born at Melksham, Wiltshire, on 22 July 1875, one of the eleven children of Charles Maggs, a rope and twine manufacturer, and his wife Charlotte Elizabeth née Stratton. In 1889 Charles Maggs started a butter factory and Joseph with his brother Leonard (qv) followed his father into the dairy trade.

After education at Wycliffe College, Stonehouse in Gloucestershire, Joseph started work at his father's factory in 1889, at the age of fourteen, and learned about the trade through the eyes of the rural producer and manufacturer. In 1896 his father became the first chairman and a principal shareholder in a newly-formed wholesale firm, Wilts United Dairies. He died in 1898, however, (leaving £31,103) and responsibility for the family's shares fell to Joseph Maggs. In 1901 a small wholesale business was acquired at the Great Western Railway's Paddington terminus in London, and Joseph was asked by the Wilts United Dairies managing director, Reginald Butler (qv), to become the company's representative in the London milk trade. Experience had shown that butter factories, creameries and condenseries could profit from the high prices paid by retailers in London for 'accommodation milk' in times of shortage of supply or increased consumer demand.

Joseph was an outstanding success and in 1911 the London wholesale operation was expanded with the acquisition of Freeth & Pocock Ltd. Circumstances were favourable, with 40 per cent growth in the quantity of railway milk imported into London in the period 1901-11, but a poorly organised and inefficient trade structure. Wilts United Dairies were able to increase their share of the market, and after the outbreak of the First World War became the core of a large new dairy combine formed in 1915 as United Dairies Ltd. United Dairies started with an authorised capital of £1 million; initially concerned exclusively with the wholesale trade, by 1917 it had acquired some of the largest retail organisations in the country, mostly based in London. In that year the capital was increased to £4 million. In 1920, by acquisitions and share exchanges, United Dairies had a controlling interest in 13 companies. Joseph Maggs became chairman in 1922. The next ten years were a period of dramatic growth for the group. In 1930 United Dairies (Wholesale) Ltd controlled 32 subsidiary companies and through them operated over 700 shops and over 50 condenseries and creameries in England and Wales and two in Normandy. By 1939 two more companies had been acquired but rationalisation was taking place and only 40 creameries were now operated. Joseph Maggs retired from the chair in 1942, when he was succeeded by his brother Leonard, but remained on the board until 1956.

Despite his naturally retiring disposition, Joseph Maggs became a dominant personality. His standards were strict and his unrivalled knowledge of the intricacies of the dairy industry was based upon personal experience of the production, manufacturing, wholesale and retail sectors of the milk trade. He farmed on a large scale in Wiltshire and was involved in trade organisations as president of the National Dairymen's Benevolent Institution, 1912-13, the first chairman of the Central Milk Distributive Committee, and a member of the National Milk Publicity Council, 1938-39.

Joseph Maggs married in 1902 Ada Fry (d 1963); they had no children. Maggs's main recreation was fishing. He died on 1 February 1964, leaving an estate proved at £93,553.

P J ATKINS

Writings:

Milk marketing scheme *Milk Industry* 14 (1934).

Dairying history *Journal of the Society of Dairy Technology* 1956.

Sources:

Unpublished

BCe.

Published

Dairy Engineering 81 (1964).

Dairy Industries 29 (1964).

Milk Industry 54 (1964).

Stock Exchange Official Year-Book 1939.

Stock Exchange Year-Book 1916, 1918, 1920, 1930.

Times 5 Feb 1964.

United Dairies Notebook 44 (1964).

WWW.

MAGGS, Leonard

(1890-1959)

Dairy company chairman

Leonard Maggs was born at Melksham, Wiltshire, on 27 May 1890, the youngest of the eleven children of Charles Maggs, a hemp manufacturer and his wife Charlotte Elizabeth Stratton. Charles Maggs started a butter factory there in 1889, and Leonard, with his brother Joseph (qv), followed their father into the dairy trade.

Leonard was educated at Wycliffe College, Stonehouse in Gloucestershire, and went on to the British Dairy Institute at University College, Reading. Afterwards he spent a year in Normandy learning French and French cheesemaking, and on his return joined a retail milk business at Willesden in North West London. After some time as an employee, 'LM', as he became known, decided to practise in his own right, and started a retail milk business at Gerrards Cross, Buckinghamshire. In 1912, however, he sold out and joined his brother Joseph at the London premises of Wilts United Dairies, acting as a representative for this wholesale firm which his father had helped to create in 1896.

During the First World War Leonard Maggs acted as a lorry driver with the Army Service Corps, and on his return from France became an inspector in Dorset of the farms that supplied milk to the new combine, United Dairies Ltd, which had been formed in 1915 during his war service. With the purchase of the Salisbury, Semley and Gillingham dairies in 1920, he was given responsibility for the Salisbury area, and soon afterwards became an assistant to Percy Butler, the then managing director of Wilts United Dairies at Trowbridge, whom he succeeded in 1923. In 1925 Leonard was elected to the board of United Dairies Ltd and succeeded his brother Joseph as its chairman in 1942.

During the early years of his chairmanship, there was a fall in the number of retail outlets. By 1950 there were about 60 shops, still mainly in London and the suburbs, and 40 creameries and condenseries in England, Scotland and Wales were being operated. In 1959 negotiations took place with Cow & Gate Ltd, another large firm with complementary interests in the dairy trade. Cow & Gate were stronger in processed milk products, such as powdered milk. In March that year United Dairies (authorised capital £12 million) acquired Cow & Gate (authorised capital £5 million) and Unigate Ltd was registered with an authorised capital of £30 million. Leonard Maggs became the first chairman of Unigate Ltd and died in office in the same year. The company has since become one of the largest food corporations in the world.

Leonard Maggs was modest and unassuming with a humane personality that endeared him both to his employees and his customers. He was a partriarch who had a gift for friendly relations and the ability to remember the Christian names and faces of staff he had not seen for years. He was also a sportsman and a practical farmer who was willing to roll up his sleeves and help with the haymaking. His keen business sense was based upon a vast experience of the dairy trade in all aspects of its operations and a close attention to detail.

Leonard Maggs died on 23 August 1959, leaving £288,129.

P J ATKINS

Sources:

Unpublished

BCe.

PrC.

Published

Dairy Industries 24 (1959).

Milk Industry 45 (1959).

Times 25 Aug 1959.

Unigate Ltd, *The Cow & Gate Story* (1959).

United Dairies Notebook 39 (1959).

MALCOLM, George William

(1870-1933)

Salt manufacturer

George William Malcolm was born in London on 5 May 1870, the eldest son of William Malcolm, a merchant of Twickenham and Japan, and his wife Elizabeth, daughter of William Just of Eastham, Cheshire. He was educated at St Paul's School. At the age of eighteen he undertook an apprenticeship as a mechanical engineer with J & H Gwynne of Hammersmith and in 1891-92 with the Pacific Steam Navigation Co of which his grandfather, William Just, was chairman. He subsequently worked for the Royal Naval Armament & Construction Co at Barrow-in-Furness.

In 1892 Malcolm entered the sugar refining industry by obtaining his first appointment, in Mauritius, as chief engineer to Anglo-Ceylon & General Estates Ltd. Nine years later he became manager and engineer to Forges et Fonderies de Maurice. Here he became familiar with the multiple effect vacuum evaporation process for sugar crystallisation which he later adapted for the production of salt. His most notable contribution to the sugar industry in Mauritius was in applying his engineering skills to installing a light railway system, thus replacing animal-drawn transport of sugar cane which was being disrupted by tsetse fly. By the time Malcolm left Mauritius he had become a member of the Institution of Mechanical Engineers and of the Institution of Electrical Engineers.

In 1908 Malcolm accepted an invitation from the Salt Union Ltd to become their chief engineer. This UK company had been formed in 1888 by the amalgamation of over 60 salt properties and works in Cheshire, Worcestershire, the North East and Ireland. Lack of sound technical management and inept commercial practices had, almost since its formation, left the company virtually unprofitable. In 1908 it made a profit of £50,000, employing capital assets of £2,890,000. Malcolm arrived at a propitious moment. With money obtained from the sale of some of its properties the Salt Union was planning to erect a multiple effect evaporation salt plant at its works at Weston Point in Cheshire. Malcolm took over the project and, adapting his experience in the sugar industry, ensured its successful construction and start up. More importantly, he conceived the idea of raising the large volume of steam required for salt evaporation in conjunction with a power generation plant which could sell its electricity profitably to local authorities. This was a turning point in the fortunes of the Salt Union. In 1913 a grateful board appointed Malcolm managing director and he became chairman of the Mersey Power Co Ltd, formed and owned by the Salt Union to manage its electricity business at Weston Point.

For his services during the First World War, when the Salt Union undertook the manufacture of munitions, Malcolm was awarded the MBE. His resourcefulness and skill in labour management during the war years when employment conditions were difficult were crucial to the Salt Union's success in meeting its government contracts and further enhanced the growing viability of the company.

After the war, Malcolm's main efforts were devoted to rationalisation and modernisation of the industry by closing down small, inefficient plants and concentrating Salt Union manufacture in some half-dozen main centres, such as Merseyside, Winsford in Cheshire, and Staffordshire. His rescue of the Salt Union from disorganisation was accomplished against a background of steadily declining demand for UK evaporated salt due to a fall in exports, as local manufacture got under way in many important overseas markets, and to replacement of salt brine in the UK chemical industry in, for example, the manufacture of alkali. Consequently, no dramatic financial results were achieved though there was some improvement in profitability — profits for 1923, for example, were £237,000 though by 1933, the year of Malcolm's death, they had declined to £166,000.

Outside the Salt Union companies, Malcolm was a director of the British Power & Light Corporation Ltd, of the North Wales Power Co Ltd, and of Electricity Distribution of North Wales.

Despite his heavy involvement as chairman or member of professional committees, Malcolm was governor of Sir John Deane's Grammar School, Northwich, chairman of the Mid-Cheshire Boy Scout Association and a magistrate for the county. In 1896 he married Adelaide Marian, daughter of William Maclachlan. They had three sons, Kenneth Just, Ian Colquhoun, and Alan Alexander, who was killed during the war while serving with the Royal Flying Corps. Still at work, Malcolm died on 4 March 1933 at his home in Davenham, Cheshire, leaving an estate of £16,891 gross.

FRANCIS DICK

Sources:

Unpublished

Chester RO, records of the Salt Union Ltd, DIC/SU3/1.

PrC.

Published

Albert F Calvert, *A History of the Salt Union. A Record of 25 Years of Disunion and Depreciation* (Effingham Wilson, 1913).

—, *Salt in Cheshire* (E & F N Spon, 1915).

WWW.

MALLABY-DEELEY, Sir Harry C

(1863-1937)

Property dealer

Harry C Mallaby Deeley, who assumed the surname of Mallaby-Deeley and was later confirmed in it by Royal Licence in 1922, was born in London on 27 October 1863, second son of William Clarke Deeley, of Curzon Park, Chester, by Elizabeth (1837/9-1924), daughter of I Wilson Mallaby, of Bebington, Cheshire. He was educated at Shrewsbury, and in 1882 went to Trinity College, Cambridge (BA 1885; LLB 1885; MA 1891; LLM 1891). He was called to the Inner Temple, but did not practise and was for a time assistant secretary to Henry (later Lord) Chaplin, leader of the Tory Squires in the House of Commons.

In the Edwardian period Mallaby-Deeley emerged as a bold and distinctive property dealer who attracted celebrity and riches by his acquisition of large or ducal properties in Central London. He acted alone in his deals, moving more quickly and flexibly than a property speculator encumbered with partners, or a syndicate of developers; the original source of his money is unclear. In 1909 he bought the Piccadilly Hotel for £500,000, and the following year he bought the eight large blocks of flats comprising St James's Court in Buckingham Gate, Westminster, for a reported £250,000. At that time St James's Court had an annual rent-roll of over £30,000, with an estimated further potential rental value of £8,000.

In July 1913 Mallaby-Deeley agreed to buy the site of St George's Hospital for £460,000, but withdrew the offer in December after disagreements among the hospital trustees. Many of his deals were conducted privately, and his gentlemanly social tone coupled with a punctilious personal appearance was undoubtedly an asset. His most famous coup was his purchase, as a private investment, of 19 acres of the Covent Garden estate in Central London from the Duke of Bedford for £2 million, in November 1913. One-third of this price was payable in four instalments to March 1917, with the residue remaining on mortgage to the Duke at 4.5 per cent for up to twelve years. It was unprecedented for such a large, compact area to be sold in Central London; the estate included Covent Garden Market, the Waldorf Hotel, the Royal Opera House, and the Aldwych, Drury Lane and Strand theatres. Mallaby-Deeley preferred direct negotiations with vendors, and once a particular scheme interested him, would seek a personal interview with the owner. Usually, if the latter was willing to sell, Mallaby-Deeley left the meeting with the deal recorded on a half-sheet of notepaper. He dispensed with detailed professional valuations or legal investigations of his purchases, and this habit led to fatal complications in the Covent Garden deal. Mallaby-Deeley and Bedford began disputing the boundaries of the 19 acres, and in May 1914 he opened legal proceedings against the Duke for non-performance of the contract. In June, therefore, Mallaby-Deeley sold his option to purchase the Covent Garden Estate to the drug manufacturer Sir Joseph Beecham (qv) for £250,000 and in July the latter reached agreement with the Duke.

Mallaby-Deeley was later involved in acquiring another large London estate. In 1924 56 acres of Bloomsbury owned by the Foundling Hospital were bought for £1.65 million by the Dunlop Pneumatic Tyre Co of Sir Arthur du Cros (qv), which company changed its name in 1925 to the Parent Trust & Finance Co. This huge property had an annual rental (excluding its squares and the nine-acre site of the Foundling Hospital itself) of £44,500, which was expected to rise to £109,000 per annum by 1940. Mallaby-Deeley, however, bought control of Foundling Estates Ltd from PT & F Co in 1933. His main purpose seems to have been investment. Reputedly he was averse, even before the Landlord and Tenant Act of 1927, from interfering with the tenure of sitting tenants, and seems to have been content with taking the rental income without undertaking major redevelopment.

By another adept bargain, Mallaby-Deeley gained control of the Leinster ducal estates. In 1919 Lord Edward FitzGerald, the profligate young heir to the dukedom, went bankrupt, and Mallaby-Deeley advanced him £60,000 to cancel the debts in return for the sale of FitzGerald's reversionary life interest in the Leinster estates. The contract contained a clause which enabled Mallaby-Deeley to prevent FitzGerald from risking his life and thus reduce the term in which Mallaby-Deeley and his heirs legally owned the ducal estates, which in 1923 had an annual income of £80,000. In that year FitzGerald succeeded to the dukedom, and the Mallaby-Deeley family to the income from the Leinster settled estates, which they continued to enjoy until the suicide of FitzGerald (the seventh Duke of Leinster) in 1976. The Duke's trustees sought to buy back the life interest for £250,000, but Mallaby-Deeley refused to sell for under £400,000 and made a voluntary gift of £1,000 per annum to the Duke instead.

Mallaby-Deeley held other business interests. He was a London director of Norwich Union Life Insurance around 1900, and his own passion for being faultlessly attired led him in 1920 into a cut-price tailoring venture. Declaring a campaign for cheap men's clothes, he opened a shop at 112 Strand, which by March 1920 was receiving 800 orders daily given in person at the shop, and 10,000 applications daily by post. He had received a total of some 100,000 enquiries by 10 March, and in April his shop window was smashed by an aggrieved tailor. This phenomenal demand far outstripped Mallaby-Deeley's maximum weekly supplies of 5,000 suits, and after serious organisational difficulties, the scheme seems to have been abandoned around 1923 leaving Mallaby-Deeley with a personal loss of £60,000. There was a taint of showmanship in him, a characteristic shared with his younger brother, who under the name of Frank Curzon (1868-1927) was an impresario managing at one time nine West End theatres simultaneously. After Curzon's death, Mallaby-Deeley paid his executors £60,000 to buy his Derby winner *Call Boy* to prevent it being sold abroad. At the end of the 1927 season the horse was retired to stud at a fee of 400 guineas, but its foals were only moderately successful. In 1920 Mallaby-Deeley also bought the china clay works at Ivybridge in South Devon for £47,000.

Mallaby-Deeley lived at Mitcham in Surrey, where he was chairman of Mitcham Common Conservators for twenty-five years until 1931. At Mitcham he bought the Prince's Golf Club from Hippisley Cox, and subsequently promoted and was chairman of Prince's Golf Club at Sandwich. The Mitcham club was on common land, and there was local controversy over the terms and low rental that Mallaby-Deeley arranged his club should pay the Conservators.

In January 1910 Mallaby-Deeley was elected Conservative and tariff reformer MP for Harrow, sensationally capturing the seat against the national trend of the general election. He was seldom seen in parliament, but in 1913 promoted the contentious Northern Junction Railway Bill there. This proposed to build a railway from Brentford to Wood Green, with connections at Hanwell, Wembley and Ealing; Mallaby-Deeley pledged himself before the Parliamentary Select Committee on the Bill to find the £2 million capital needed for the scheme. The proposed railway traversed his constituency, and was hotly opposed by residents (especially in Hampstead Garden Suburb) for its adverse effect on local amenities. The Bill was defeated in 1913, and the Northern Junction Railway was therefore abandoned.

During War Weapons Week in 1918, Mallaby-Deeley capped £150,000 subscribed by both Willesden and Birmingham for war bonds with two equal sums, and also capped the war bond subscriptions of Leyton, Poplar, Shrewsbury and other towns. He was succeeded as Conservative MP for Harrow by Oswald Mosley in 1918, and was Conservative MP for East Willesden from 1918 until his resignation through illness in February 1923. His baronetcy of 1922 doubtless acknowledged his contribution to party funds.

Mallaby-Deeley was a patron of five Anglican livings, and lord of the manors of Ravensbury, Biggin in Derbyshire and Tamworth, Staffordshire. For some years he sat on the committee of the Royal Female Orphan Asylum. Among his charitable donations were gifts of £16,000 to Westminster Hospital in 1924, £15,000 to the London Hospital in 1927 and £36,000 towards providing the Foundling Hospital with a new site. He paid the cost of providing the Carlton Club with a new front, and gave £32,500 to support publication of the *Complete Peerage* in 1926-34.

He married first, in 1890, at Whitchurch, Shropshire, Julia Jane Parson ('Joan') (1864-1933), third daughter of John Parson Smith of Shrewsbury, and had one son. He married secondly, in 1935, at Southwark, Edith Maud ('Bridget'), daughter of W J G Shoebridge of West Wickham, Kent. Latterly he lived on the French Riviera, where he was active in medical charities, captain of Mandelieu golf club and vice-president of Grane golf course. He died of kidney disease on 5 February 1937 at his French home, Château des Fayères at Cannes, leaving unsettled estate in Britain worth £488,863 gross.

R P T DAVENPORT-HINES

Sources:

Unpublished

MCe.

Published

Sir Thomas Beecham, *A Mingled Chime* (Hutchinson, 1944).

Burke's Peerage 1949.

Sir Percy A Harris, *Forty Years In and Out of Parliament* (Andrew Melrose, 1947).

Alan Jefferson, *Sir Thomas Beecham* (MacDonald & James, 1979).

Brian Masters, *The Dukes* (Blond & Briggs, 1977).

F H W Sheppard (ed), *Survey of London:* vol 36 *The Parish of St Paul Covent Garden* (Athlone Press, 1970).

Times Dec 1913, 10 Mar 1920, 6 Feb 1937.

WWMP.

WWW.

MALLINSON, Sir Stuart Sidney

(1888-1981)

Timber merchant

Sir Stuart Mallinson (courtesy Mallinson & Denny Mott Ltd).

Stuart Sidney Mallinson was born at Clapton, London, on 24 April 1888, the third son of William (later Sir William) Mallinson (1854-1936), owner of a timber merchant's concern in the East End of London, and his wife Amelia Louise née Tucker. Brought up in a large Methodist family of four sons and six daughters, Stuart was educated at Ashville College, Harrogate, and the Leys School, Cambridge. He entered the family firm in 1907 and in January 1914 was appointed a director, having been trained in practical matters by his father who sent him out on the road as a traveller. The outbreak of war, however, interrupted his business career and he found himself on active service with the Royal Artillery in France. He returned to England after the war, having reached the rank of lieutenant-colonel with an MC and DSO. At the age of thirty he resumed his place in the family firm.

The family business, William Mallinson & Sons Ltd, had been founded by Stuart's father in February 1877 when he opened a small warehouse and shop for veneer-cutting in the furniture-making district of Shoreditch, East London. The foundation of a prosperous business was laid in the 1880s as the firm turned to the production of hardwood lumber and began importing and machining softwood. In the 1890s, as the enterprise expanded, setting up workshops, warehouses and woodyards in the surrounding areas of Hackney and Bethnal Green, it became one of the pioneers in the production of plywood.

The company's early success had depended very much on the work of partners, notably James Richardson, but it was the intention of the founder to make it a family concern. On 16 January 1913 the new private company of William Mallinson & Sons Ltd was registered with an issued share capital of £160,004. From this date William James Mallinson (qv), Stuart's eldest brother increasingly directed operations, especially after 1923 when their father resigned.

The firm went public in 1937 with an issued ordinary share capital of £300,000 and £250,000 preference shares which were taken up by the Kenterne Trust Ltd. (Stuart Mallinson was assistant managing director with a salary of £2,000 a year, exclusive of directors' fees.) By the time of his death in 1944, William James Mallinson had developed a single merchanting business into a public company with two subsidiaries, extensive interests in France, Belgium and Holland, and a technical lead in the development of plywood.

Stuart Mallinson succeeded his brother as chairman and managing director. Initially, he relied much upon the experience of the assistant managing director, Dan Drysdale, who had been with the firm as a director since 1937. A number of important steps were taken toward securing timber supplies: a subsidiary company was established in North

Queensland; in East Africa a link was established with two brothers, W and D Hickman; and a woodland estate was acquired at Lilford, near Peterborough. Manufacturing activities were set up at Crayford; and J & A Stewart Ltd of Glasgow, an established member of the hardwood trade, was taken over.

In 1953 Drysdale became joint-managing director with Mallinson, who was frequently abroad. The partnership presided over an unhappy period in the firm's history. In Kenya there were management and political problems; manufacturing at Crayford incurred persistent losses; and trading problems developed in Australia. In the words of one director it was soon plain 'that the company's expertise in manufacture fell a long way short of that on the merchanting side, on which the fortunes of the company had been built' {Mackie (1977) 74}. Net profits before tax declined steadily from £347,000 in 1951 to £120,000 in 1962, leaving out of account the profit contribution brought in by Bloomer-Holt Ltd of Manchester in 1961, one of the firm's few successful take-overs in this period.

By this time Mallinson was over seventy and he reluctantly came to accept the view that it was necessary for him to stand down. He became honorary president in June 1962. The chairmanship was taken over by his nephew Sir Paul Mallinson, a non-executive director, and the management team was the first to be drawn from outside the family. From 1963 onwards losses decreased. The growth of large groupings in the timber trade encouraged a merger with Denny Mott & Dickinson to form William Mallinson & Denny Mott Ltd in 1969.

Mallinson was president of the Timber Research and Development Association, 1963-73 and served as president of the Commonwealth Forestry Association. In 1954 he was a member of the Eastern Electricity Board. He was honorary president of the Magnet Building Society and of the Town & Country Building Society.

Alongside his business activities, Mallinson was very prominent in religious and public affairs. Like other members of the family he was committed to the furtherance of the interests of the Methodist Church and was secretary of Shernhall Methodist Institute Sunday School, 1907-35, president of the National Sunday School Union in 1923, and chairman of a number of religious organisations. He was heavily involved in public voluntary work, and was president and chairman of several Essex charitable and welfare organisations. He was made High Sheriff of Essex in 1939, a county in which he was also DL and JP and became DL for Greater London, 1966-76. He was a governor of four schools and retained his links with various military organisations. His presidency of several athletic, cricket and football clubs in Essex reflected his enthusiasm for sport, which he believed had the capacity to cut across racial and class barriers. He was president of the Walthamstow Liberal Party, 1910-25. Upon retirement he devoted himself to the promotion of Anglo-American relations, which was an extension of his half-century of work for the English Speaking Union. A large garden party was held every year at the White House, his residence in Woodford, to further this aim. Stuart's ability to communicate readily and relate to people of all ages, particularly with the young, and with special concern for ESU scholars, was said to have been perhaps his greatest gift.

He was awarded the CBE in 1938 and knighted in 1954. In 1916 he married Marjorie, daughter of Rev Alfred Soothill; she was also awarded the CBE. They had three sons, one of whom was killed in action in 1944. Lady Mallinson died in 1969; Sir Stuart on 31 October 1981, leaving an estate proved at £121,728 gross.

GEOFFREY TWEEDALE

Sources:

Unpublished

PrC.

Information from Mr T S Mallinson.

Published

Edward Bryan Latham, *History of the Timber Trade Federation of the United Kingdom. The First Seventy Years* (Ernest Benn, 1965).

W Euan Mackie, *The Mallinson Story 1877-1977* (William Mallinson & Denny Mott Ltd, 1977).

Sir William Mallinson, *A Sketch of My Life* (Epworth Press, 1936).

J L Oliver, *The Development and Structure of the Furniture Industry* (Pergamon Press, 1966).

W C Potter, *The House of Mallinson, 1877-1947* (Southern Editorial Syndicate, 1947).

Times 3, 6, 14 Nov 1981.

Times *Prospectuses* 94 (1937).

WW 1979.

MALLINSON, Sir William James

(1879-1944)

Timber merchant

William James Mallinson was born in Clapton, London on 28 July 1879, the eldest son of William (later Sir William) Mallinson (1854-1936), a timber trader in London's East End, and his wife Amelia Louise née

Sir W J Mallinson from W Euan Mackie The Mallinson Story.

Tucker. Brought up in a strict Methodist household, which eventually included three other sons and six daughters, William James ('WJ' as he became known) was educated at a private school at Park House, Gravesend, run by his uncle James. Afterwards his father sent him to Paris for a year, and then on a year's world tour, to complete his education and broaden his outlook. In 1898 he was brought into the family business.

The family firm had been founded by WJ's father in 1877, when he set up in business as a veneer merchant in Shoreditch. Mallinson soon turned to the production of hardwood lumber, the importing and machining of softwood, and pioneering attempts at the manufacture of plywood. Due to the efforts of James Richardson, who was admitted as senior partner when William Mallinson & Co was formed in 1893, trading links for the import of timber were established with the USA.

WJ received his practical training at one of the firm's East End wharves, but soon devoted himself to selling and the supervision of the firm's travellers. He became convinced that here lay the key to the overall success of the enterprise and it gave him the chance to assert his dominant personality. In 1904 he was received into the partnership, which was then capitalised at £32,000 (William Mallinson's share was £23,000, James Richardson's £8,000, and WJ's £1,000). Within only three years a number of factors — WJ's desire to seize control of the business, coupled with his incompatibility in temperament with Richardson, and the desire of his father to devote himself to other matters, such as the Methodist Church — led to Richardson's departure and the formation of William Mallinson & Son. For the next few years WJ increasingly took control, with his father playing a consultative role.

WJ Mallinson soon focused his attention on Europe. In 1910 the firm's first overseas timber and veneer cutting branch was established in Rotterdam, under a Dutchman, E Verveer. Due to the founder's wariness of foreign ventures, the capital was privately subscribed by members of the family, and not by the London partnership. The success of the Dutch venture led to the establishment of another Mallinson trading branch, in Paris in 1912. In January 1913 William Mallinson & Sons Ltd was incorporated, with an issued share capital of £160,004. The founder accepted the position of governing director (a post he retained until 1923) with WJ as managing director. Though father and son still conferred, and though the board also included William Mallinson's other sons, including Stuart (qv), WJ was now in effective control.

The First World War gave the company the opportunity to utilise its pioneering work in plywood. Whilst WJ and Stanley Mallinson devoted themselves to the timber merchanting side of the business, their father concerned himself with meeting the wartime demands for aircraft plywood at premises in Kingsland Road, Shoreditch. Plywood manufacturing was also extended in France, where Mallinson's French interests became centred in Nantes under the style Etablissements William Mallinson. Shortages of timber necessitated the purchase of a family business, Whitmores Timber Co, of Bury St Edmunds, in 1918 (capital £15,000). Though purchased outside the London business, Whitmores eventually became, in 1929, the first wholly-owned Mallinson subsidiary.

The period 1923-36 was a difficult one. Nevertheless, Mallinsons' growth was slow but steady. In 1926 WJ attempted to gain a foothold in

HARDWOODS FOR AEROPLANES.

UNEQUALLED FACILITIES FOR SUPPLYING PERFECT TIMBER.
SPECIAL SKILL AND GREAT EXPERIENCE DEVOTED TO ORDERS FOR AEROPLANE WOODS.
ALL KINDS OF HARDWOODS IN PLANKS, OR CUT AND PLANED TO SIZE.
DRESSED SPARS AND STRUTS OF ALL TYPES.

Testimonials from successful Aviators.

WILLIAM MALLINSON & SONS,

TIMBER & VENEER MERCHANTS (Direct Importers & Exporters).

130-138, Hackney Road, LONDON, N.E.

Telegrams: "ALMONER," LONDON.

Telephone: 4770 LONDON WALL (2 Lines)
P.O. 3854 CENTRAL.

CORRESPONDENCE IN ANY LANGUAGE.

1910 Mallinson advertisement in Jane's All the World's Air Ships.

the US market: J H Smith Veneers was incorporated in Chicago with a capital of £100,000, but bad management on the US side led to its liquidation in 1937 after persistent losses. In 1927 another plywood firm, the Tucker Armoured Plywood Co Ltd of Crayford, Kent, was purchased. In 1923 record sales of £348,549 gave profits before tax of £50,210; in 1936 sales were £309,237, with net profits before tax of £45,688.

Early in 1937 the firm was converted into a public company with an issued ordinary share capital of £300,000, £250,000 5.5 per cent cumulative preference shares, which were taken up by the Kenterne Trust Ltd and total net assets, exclusive of goodwill, of £521,000. Also included was the issued capital of a hardwood trading company, R M Turner & Hunters Ltd, which had been acquired privately by the family in 1919. The board included, besides WJ, Stanley and Stuart Mallinson, Walter Potter, and Daniel Drysdale. Drysdale, a young Scottish rubber company executive, was appointed by WJ, the first recruit from outside the family to top management since Richardson's time.

During the Second World War WJ Mallinson became Senior Deputy Controller and Financial Adviser to the Timber Control Board of the Ministry of Supply located in Bristol, and the running of the business was left largely to Drysdale. Under his guidance Mallinsons was closely involved with the war effort, especially in the production of aircraft plywood through its Aeronautical & Panel Plywood Co Ltd. To augment urgently-needed supplies of plywood, with the help of the Ministry of Aircraft Production, a factory at Lydney, Gloucestershire, was erected in 1941 with WJ Mallinson as director.

It was in the midst of his wartime activities that WJ Mallinson died suddenly in his sleep on 26 February 1944 at his temporary home, Bruinwood, Wraxall, near Bristol. To him must largely go the credit for developing a family-based business, with a market mainly in the UK, into a public company with numerous domestic and foreign subsidiaries and world-wide trading links, supplying the important home markets of architecture, the railways, motor manufacturers, and shipbuilders. This was achieved by a strong but not very endearing personality. A colleague wrote:

> The strength of his personality was evident wherever he went and within his own business his dominance was complete. His robust and sometimes slightly cruel sense of humour, frequently exercised at the expense of an inferior, was not always appreciated by the unfortunate recipient. He was unable to conceal his contempt for any who showed fear of him, or toadied to him, but he liked and respected those who demonstrated spirit enough to stand up to him, albeit with a proper degree of deference {Mackie (1977) 43, 45}.

A gift for entertaining visitors and customers, a capacity for hard work, a deep concern for the Methodist Church, and an interest in the general prosperity of the timber trade as a whole, were said to be his other characteristics.

W J Mallinson succeeded his father as second baronet in 1936, and was also a JP and DL of Surrey. In 1905 he married Mabel, daughter of J W Rush, of Tunbridge Wells; they had one son, William Paul, who was born in 1909. Mallinson left an estate of £197,273 gross.

GEOFFREY TWEEDALE

Sources:

Unpublished

PrC.

Published

Edward Bryan Latham, *History of the Timber Trade Federation of the United Kingdom. The First Seventy Years* (Ernest Benn, 1965).

W Euan Mackie, *The Mallinson Story 1877-1977* (William Mallinson & Denny Mott Ltd, 1977).

Sir William Mallinson, *A Sketch of My Life* (Epworth Press, 1936).

J L Oliver, *The Development and Structure of the Furniture Industry* (Pergamon Press, 1966).

Walter C Potter, *The House of Mallinson, 1877-1947* (Southern Editorial Syndicate, 1947).

Times 28 Feb, 1 Mar, 18 Oct 1944.

Times *Prospectuses* 94 (1937).

WWW.

MANFIELD, Sir Moses Philip

(1819-1899)

Shoe manufacturer, wholesaler and retailer

Moses Philip Manfield was born at Bristol on 26 July 1819, a son of Moses Philip Manfield, a Unitarian cordwainer (perhaps formerly a shoe manufacturer). His paternal grandfather had been a Bristol barber.

His early life was shaped by the strong character and Unitarian faith of his mother, who taught him reading, writing and arithmetic at home (he also received instruction at the Bristol Unitarian Sunday School), and by the poverty endured by the family as a result of his father's paralysis, contracted when Philip was an infant. The family made an inadequate and precarious living from a second-hand bookstall and after Philip's seventh birthday he did many jobs in order to supplement his mother's earnings, including being a barber's boy and a stage-hand at the Bristol Theatre. At the age of twelve, with the sovereign he had saved by writing window cards for local shopkeepers, he bound himself apprentice to a Mr Harris, a boot closer of Bristol.

When he was sixteen, Philip Manfield went to London as a journeyman closer for a short while, to gain experience of making and retailing best quality work, before returning to Bristol. Here he quickly rose to the position of manager of Messrs Brightman's shoe factory; unusually for a man of his background, he had already purchased his own house. In 1843 he migrated to Northampton to take up the position of manager at Messrs Swann's boot and shoe warehouse in King Street. Within six months this business had failed. A Miss Carpenter, of the celebrated Unitarian family of Caleb, whom Manfield had met while in London, provided him with letters of introduction to the Northampton Unitarian community who now offered to assist him. Manfield refused the offer of a partnership with Swann's brother-in-law, Henry Harday (later one of the town's largest wholesale manufacturers), and instead, in 1844 committed his savings of £150 to setting himself up in business.

From these inauspicious beginnings, Manfield developed one of the dominant footwear manufacturing and distribution firms in both Britain and Europe. He can be regarded as '... one of the great [Victorian] captains of this industry ...' {Adkins (1893) 59}.

The progress of the firm under Manfield can be divided into three periods, 1844-58, 1858-85, and 1885-99. During the first, the formative, period, Manfield initially traded from small warehouse premises in Silver Street, then, from 1846, larger premises in Broad Lane. In 1849, another removal was made to premises in Regent Street. Like all wholesale manufacturers at this time, he organised production upon a purely outwork basis, and he traded mainly in cheaper grades of footwear for colonial markets and government military contracts. Soon he became one of Northampton's largest government contractors. The early success of

Manfield's enterprise was reflected in his improved social circumstances. By 1854 he was resident at 8 Royal Terrace, Northampton, a locality much favoured by the town's growing commercial and business class. While one obituary claims that Manfield was married before he arrived in Northampton, no trace of this marriage or of a son (who apparently died young) have been found. After 1843 he married twice; in 1845 to Elizabeth Cambridge Newman of Surrey, daughter of Henry Newman, a commercial clerk, and after her death at the age of thirty-three in 1852, in 1854 to Margaret Milne, then aged thirty-three, a daughter of James Milne, the Northampton borough surveyor. While his former marriage was celebrated in an Anglican church near his wife's home, this one took place at South Place Unitarian Chapel in the City of London. At the time Margaret was employed in a 'Ladies Shoe Warehouse' in London. Philip and Margaret Manfield had two sons, Harry (b 1855) and James (b 1856).

The years 1858-85 witnessed a further substantial growth in trading, during which time Manfields established its British and European multiple chain, and became one of the largest producers of footwear in the country. This second phase was signalled by the move to a purpose-built factory in Fleetwood Terrace, Campbell Square: the first proper factory erected for the Northampton shoe trade. It was built '... on the pretentious scale of the in working system in the days when most shoemakers worked in their own homes and most manufacturers' premises were but warehouses, flush with mean dwelling houses ...' {Burnham (1936)}. The completion of a building of such radical design, after just fifteen years' trading, is a reflection both of Manfield's early business success and of his progressive outlook. Between its opening in 1858 and 1892, when the firm vacated the premises, it was one of the town's model factories.

It was first occupied at a time when capital and labour were engaged in a bitter two-year dispute over the introduction of the trade's first machines: local shoemakers regarded the coincidence of such an innovation and the commissioning of this and another similarly-designed factory, as a radical threat to their control over the work process. Already Manfield had emerged as a leading figure at periodic manufacturers' meetings, convened to decide matters of mutual interest, mainly prices. From this time until his death he was at the centre of trade and labour relations matters within the industry. He was a founder of the re-vamped Northampton Chamber of Commerce in 1867 and the local manufacturers' association in 1879, of which he was president during the town's momentous strike in 1887. Largely as a result of Manfield's intervention, part of the settlement agreement enabled the establishment of conciliation and arbitration machinery, despite the opposition of more extreme employers. Similar Boards were established in other main shoe centres, and Manfield was credited with responsibility 'for the introduction of arbitration in the settlement of trade disputes in the shoe trade' {*Times* 1 Aug 1899}. A moderate, he gave much time to the establishment of conciliatory labour relations policies in the public's consciousness, and played a significant role, as an arbitrator and umpire, in settling wages questions in Northamptonshire and other shoe centres, including a bitter dispute in Bristol in 1890.

In fact the trade's transition to full factory production was a relatively slow, discontinuous process, not completed until the 1890s. In the interim, a transitional phase, incorporating organisational elements of both the old and the new order persisted in the trade: Manfields' development in this second phase must be judged against this background. It rested upon three related elements. First was Philip Manfield's commitment to modern techniques. He was in the vanguard of those manufacturers who increasingly centralised production. By the 1880s, the firm's rate of investment in machinery began to increase, with more factory workers being taken on; steam power was probably introduced a decade earlier. Hand workers were accommodated in nearby rented warehouses, whilst new machinery was erected in adjacent houses which were purchased and adapted for use as workshops. Within the main factory, power-driven leather presses and machines to sew and otherwise attach the sole to the boot top were installed; such work had previously been done by sub-contractors, known locally as 'sewers to the trade'. Only in 1888, when further extensions of this kind became impracticable, did a major extension to the factory take place. The apparent delay in committing large sums to capital projects was not uncommon in the industry: 'many of the factories seem to have been built room by room, as the necessity for extensions became too pressing to be further disregarded' {*Boot and Shoe Trades Journal* 23 Oct 1886}.

Of Manfield's 900 employees, 500 still worked outside in 1888, and were to do so until the new factory was occupied in 1892, when the factory workforce increased to 1,100. Manfields had their better-quality work made up by Northampton shoemakers, whilst cheaper grades were made by outworkers under the control of agents in surrounding villages, particularly Abthorpe. Later, this work was consolidated into rural branch factories at Ascote, Pattishall and Harpole. Amongst Northampton shoemakers, increasing numbers were labouring in their own workshops, rather than their homes, and Manfield evidently gave these outworkers financial assistance to erect these workshops. In the trade he was widely known for the assistance and advice he gave to young manufacturers.

The decade after 1885 witnessed the crucial introduction of mechanised production in 'best practice' firms, both in Northampton and throughout the industry. Not only had engineers developed machines to perform the processes formerly difficult to mechanise — welt-sewing, lasting, finishing — but, from this time, the industry began to experience the continuous disturbance of new techniques and an endless flow of modifications and improvements to existing machines. The influence of Manfield's hand can be clearly seen in this process. In 1888, he was the leading figure in a syndicate of one Stafford and six Northampton manufacturers, who set up the Northampton Shoe Machinery Co Ltd to market and later manufacture the Chase lasting machine under licence from the Shoe Lasting Machine Co of Boston, USA. The company was influential in determining the pace of machine adoption in Northampton during the early-1890s and within a short period agreements to market the machines of other American companies were secured. Manfield was for a time the company's managing director, and his son James a director.

Manfield was also in the vanguard of those manufacturers adopting American systems of production and management. In 1892, the firm moved to a four-acre green-field site at Wellingborough Road, Northampton, where a one storey 'American-style' factory, equipped with electricity, a telephone system and an 80 hp steam engine, was built. The factory was regarded as a model for the whole trade.

The second element in Manfield's success during 1858-85 was the foundation of a multiple chain. Philip Manfield's younger son, James, initiated and was responsible for the early development of this new departure. Between 1878 and 1883 three shops were opened in London under the name Cash & Co. Within a year the office staff was increased from six to 11 persons and by 1895 a further 29 people had joined it. Following wholesalers and retailers of other goods, in 1882 Manfields started to produce men's branded footwear at a uniform price. The firm also sought to strengthen its prestige by securing Exhibition awards and won prizes at Cape Town (1877), Sydney (1879), Melbourne (1880) and Paris (1889). From 1884, the family name was used, and the British chain began with premises in Manchester, followed by Liverpool, Glasgow and Birmingham. By 1889 there were 16 branches, by 1895, 21 and by 1900, 30. Manfield's marketing policy appears to have rested upon the quality and depth of service given at each branch, rather than opening as many branches as possible.

By the early 1890s a slump in exports caused Manfields to devote production to supplying the growing needs of their branches. Initially production sagged, 100 shoemakers were discharged, and many more placed on short time. Partly to restore full-time working and to lessen seasonal fluctuations in production, and partly to ensure supplies to branches, an in-stock system was inaugurated. By 1893 a stock of 200,000 pairs was maintained, with annual production running at over 350,000 pairs as compared with 250,000 pairs twenty-five years earlier. Making wholesale goods for export was not resumed until 1910; however, trading outside Britain did not entirely cease. In 1898 a retail establishment was opened in Paris; and in the years that followed shops were opened in provincial France, in Belgium, in Holland and in Germany. (By 1916 there were 23 shops in mainland Europe.)

Manfield's other outside business interests included directorships in local firms, such as the Northampton Turkish Baths Co and Smiths Timber Co Ltd. Prominent in the trade from the mid-century, Philip Manfield emerged as a leading public figure in Northamptonshire from the 1860s. After his sons had been taken into partnership in 1878 he became much more involved in public affairs. By 1885, he had practically relinquished all active involvement in the management of the firm and he formally retired in 1890, although he remained a partner.

A Liberal member of the Northampton Borough Council, 1866 to 1877, and again from 1882 to 1892, Manfield served two terms as an alderman, 1871-77 and 1886-92, and was elected mayor, 1882-85. He became a JP for Northampton in November 1886. His first election was fought under the auspices of the newly-established Northampton Reform League. Both he and his fellow Liberal candidate, Richard Turner, another prominent shoe manufacturer, stood in the town's Conservative-dominated East Ward, yet were returned with substantial majorities. With similar results in the town's West Ward this election was considered to have 'changed the face of Northampton politics' {*Northampton Mercury* 4 Aug 1899}, re-establishing the Liberals as a political force in the borough. Within three years, the party dominated the town council and elected their first mayor for fourteen years. The movement to extend working class freehold house ownership then became an important weapon with which to consolidate the Liberal vote, and in this Manfield played a prominent part. He was successively the president of the Northampton Town & Country Benefit Building Society, and president and chairman of the Northampton Freehold Land Society.

Educational matters absorbed much of his political time. He was vice-president and a council member of the National Educational Association, and was a prominent member of the Northamptonshire Education League. He supported the aim to establish a national system of non-denominational schools. In 1871, he unsuccessfully stood for the local School Board as an 'Unsectarian Liberal', although his wife was to be a Board member for a number of years. In later years he was a governor of both the Northampton and County Modern and Technical School and of the local Grammar School. In 1898 he helped to form the Northampton Committee of the Liberation Society. He also displayed much interest in adult education schemes, leading a local campaign for evening lectures in the mid-century. As president of the local Working Men's Club, he consistently fostered educational developments there.

Several biographical sketches and obituaries of Manfield suggest that he was an advanced Liberal throughout his life. In fact, his ideological position within the party shifted several times. As a young man, in the 1840s, he espoused the Chartist cause and was a supporter of G J Holyoake's views on co-operation. In his early years as a town councillor he was the leader of the moderate Northampton Liberal Association. Manfield initially opposed Bradlaugh's parliamentary candidature for the borough, and consequently supporters of Bradlaugh, the newly-formed Northampton Radical Association (NRA), unseated Manfield at the 1877 municipal elections. Within three years, however, increased Radical support for Bradlaugh led moderate Liberals like Manfield to recognise the need to accept his candidature if parliamentary representation locally were not to remain in Conservative hands.

From this time, Manfield's political views became more radical. He joined the NRA, serving as its vice-president, and he was re-elected as Radical member for the town's East Ward. In this period he also gave assistance to the Hon C R Spencer MP in county hustings and meetings, and for a time filled important positions in the South and Mid Northamptonshire Liberal Associations. Following Bradlaugh's death in 1891, Manfield was elected an MP for Northampton in February 1891. He fully endorsed Gladstone's Home Rule policy. He was again elected in 1892, but retired in 1895, because of his 'advanced age and weak heart' {Adkins (1893) 59}.

Manfield brought to politics those qualities of ability, energy and perseverance which, it was stated, had underpinned his business success. Politically adroit, he regularly attended debates. For many years he was the speaker of the Northampton Debating Society.

Manfield's mature years were marked by many acts of private charity and public philanthropy — several contemporaries remarked that his personal wealth was considerably reduced by his open-handed benevolence. He served as president of the National Thrift Society; chairman of the Northampton Town Domestic Mission and the East End

Domestic Mission; vice-president of the Northampton Nursing Institution, the Northampton and Artisan Labour Friendly Society, and the Northampton Corps of the St John Ambulance Brigade; a trustee of the Municipal General Charities; and a committee member of the Northampton Royal Victoria Dispensary, the Northampton Branch of the NSPCC, and the Northampton Poor Children's Christmas Dinner Fund from 1882. In addition, he devoted much time to the Northampton General Hospital, and from 1886 was the treasurer of the Hospital Week Fund Committee.

These attitudes of benevolence infused his relations with employees. By nature, he was an autocratic paternalist. It was widely accepted that he made financial provision for employees and their families during trade depression, strikes and on their retirement. During the 1887 strike he provided funds for the dependents of all strikers. His firm became one of the very first in the town to endorse the current ideals of the industrial welfare movement. Many sporting, social and welfare societies were formed within the firm, and an increasing emphasis was placed upon the ideal of the Manfield community. Philip Manfield himself was at one time president of the Northampton and County Amateur Athletic Association, which did much to foster inter-firm sporting links in the period. Much of this philanthropic effort was fired by religious conviction. He was a life-long Unitarian, and gave active support to that denomination locally. In 1897, he bore the whole cost — in excess of £6,000 — for the erection of Kettering Road Free Church and schools. He had the Unitarian's love of the intellectual, being something of a bibliophile. His library was reputed to be one of the best local private collections at this time.

Despite a full and active life, he found time to indulge in a personal interest in horticulture; he was a president of both the Northamptonshire Horticultural Society and the Northamptonshire Chrysanthemum Society.

Towards the end of his life many public honours and rewards were bestowed upon him. He was knighted in May 1894 in recognition of his public services, and in July 1899 was made the first honorary freeman of the County Borough of Northampton.

Sir Philip Manfield died at his Northampton home, 'Redlands', Cliftonville — he also had a London home, Bloomfield House, London Wall — on 31 July 1899, aged eighty. His two sons survived him, but his wife, who had been such a strong force in his life, and an active worker for the Sunday School Movement and the British and Foreign Unitarian Association, predeceased him by two weeks, leaving personal effects to the value of £1,216 9s 5d. Sir Philip left an estate valued at £68,334 gross.

KEITH BROOKER

Sources:

Unpublished

Manfield & Sons Ltd, Wellingborough Road, Northampton, archives, correspondence, 1891-92.

MANFIELD Sir Moses Philip

Northamptonshire Public Libraries, W E Burnham 'A Century of Shoemaking 1844-1944' (unpublished MS, ca 1944).

Northamptonshire RO, YZ 720, YZ 9627-29, Box 200, Box X1665, Box X1752, P2289-98.

PRO, BT 31/4025/25654.

C Reg: Manfield & Sons Ltd (164,082).

PrC.

Published

W R D Adkins, *Our County 1893* (Elliot Stock, 1893).

Black and White 21 Feb 1891.

H B Bonner, *Charles Bradlaugh* (T Fisher Unwin, 1908).

Boot and Shoe Trades Journal 23 Oct 1886, 16 Aug 1890, 5 Aug 1899, 25 June 1909.

E W Burnham, *In the Service of a Famous Firm* (Northampton: pp, 1936).

F A Channing, *Memories of Midland Politics* (1918).

'The GOM of Northampton, Sir Philip Manfield' *Manfield Magazine* Jan 1930.

Victor A Hartley, 'Monsters in Campbell Square!' *Northamptonshire Past and Present* 4 part 1 (1966-67).

Kelly's Handbook 1897.

Kettering Evening Telegraph 1 Aug 1899.

The Making of the Shoe as the Duke (of York) Saw It (Northampton, 1931).

'Messrs Manfield & Sons New Premises' *Boot and Shoe Trades Journal* 20 Aug 1892.

A Nichols, 'Reminiscenses of 1875' *Manfield Magazine* Jan 1930.

Northampton Chronicle 11, 13, 27 July 1899.

Northampton Daily Reporter 27, 31 July, 1, 4 Aug 1899.

Northampton Herald 29 July 1899.

Northampton Independent 20 May, 5 Sept 1908.

Northampton Mercury 14 July, 4 Aug 1899.

Edward Royle, 'Charles Bradlaugh, Freethought, and Northampton' *Northamptonshire Past and Present* 6 part 3 (1980).

'Sir Philip Manfield — A Romance in the Leather World' *Fortunes Made in Business* (3 vols, Sampson, Low & Co, 1905).

The Story of a British Industry — Manfield & Sons (Northampton: Joseph Rogers, 1908).

'The Story of Our Firm' *Manfield Magazine* Feb, Mar, Apr, June 1930.

W L Terhune, 'How Europe is Shod: England — Northampton' *Boot and Shoe Recorder* 9 Dec 1891.

Algar Thorold, *The Life of Henry Labouchere* (Constable, 1913).

Times 13 July, 1 Aug 1899.

VCH Northamptonshire.

WWMP.

WWW.

G N C Mann (courtesy of Mann Egerton).

MANN, Gerard Noel Cornwallis

(1872-1941)

Motor vehicle distributor and manufacturer

Gerard Noel Cornwallis Mann was born at Falmouth, Cornwall, on 28 October 1872, the younger son of Rev Charles Noel Mann, Vicar of St Issey, Cornwall, and his wife Emily May née Grylls. He was educated at Marlborough and Trinity College, Oxford, where he read engineering and graduated in 1894. He then became a pupil with the Brush Electrical Co at Loughborough where he trained as an electrical engineer.

Mann set up his own business in Norwich in 1898. He purchased the electrical contracting side of a Norwich firm, Lawrence & Scott, and opened premises at Redwell Street, Norwich, and later at Bank Plain in the city. Initially he specialised in installing electric lighting in country houses.

It soon became clear to him that East Anglia and the Fens, good touring country centred on the wealthy city of Norwich, offered a promising market for the new motorcars which agents like Letts and Rolls (qqv) were importing from the USA and the Continent. In 1900 he went into partnership with Hubert Wingfield Egerton, a motoring enthusiast and engineer who earlier that year had driven a De Dion Bouton from Land's End to John O'Groats.

They formed a limited company, Mann, Egerton & Co Ltd, which was converted into a private company in 1908. Building specialist car bodies, together with vehicle maintenance and repairs, comprised the firm's primary motor vehicle activity, designed to serve the clerics, doctors, bankers and gentry of Norwich and East Anglia. In 1906 a firm publication described how 'their Norwich establishment possessed a gentleman's waiting room, "replete with every possible convenience", with leather armchairs, newspapers, writing materials, and a coal fire, while the ladies' room contained "every requisite from a long scissors to a pair of curling tongs."' {Richardson (1977) 217} In thirteen months in 1907-8 the firm sold 80 cars, new and second-hand, of various makes: De Dion, Singer,

Kenneth Richardson, *The British Motor Industry, 1896-1939* (Macmillan, 1977).

Times 22 Dec 1926, 15 Dec 1927, 15 Dec 1928, 12 Dec 1934, 13 Dec 1935, 11 Dec 1936, 8 Dec 1937, 7 Dec 1938, 4 Dec 1939, 6 Dec 1940, 12 Dec 1941.

Times *Prospectuses* 58 (1919).

MANN, Reginald William

(1898-)

Mining electrical engineer

Reginald Mann (courtesy of the Central Library, Newcastle upon Tyne).

Reginald William Mann was born in Birmingham on 30 November 1898, the son of William Mann, a master tailor who owned a small clothing factory and four tailor's shops making bespoke men's clothes. He was educated at Birmingham Grammar School and at the age of sixteen became a professional apprentice at the Electrical & Ordnance Accessories Co Ltd, a Birmingham subsidiary of Vickers Ltd, continuing his formal education part-time at Birmingham College of Technology. After two years he volunteered for the army but the managing director of the firm insisted that he enter the navy, which he did, as an electrical artificer. On demobilisation in 1919 Mann discovered that the Birmingham subsidiary was being closed and he was transferred to Metropolitan Vickers Ltd at Manchester. There he was introduced to the work of all departments and, in particular, paid attention to time and motion study. However, he decided to specialise as a mining electrical engineer, so successfully that in 1924 he was appointed as Vickers's mining engineer in the North East, responsible for all the company's sales in the Northumberland and Durham coalfield. From that date he settled on Tyneside.

During the 1920s Mann designed much underground electrical equipment for Metropolitan Vickers, including electric drills to replace existing compressed air drills. The new drills did not, however, prove satisfactory until, during a visit to BTH Co of Rugby (which had been taken over by Vickers), he was introduced to high speed electric motors fed by frequency changers. A new drill was designed but Metropolitan Vickers was not interested in commencing production. In the meantime Mann got to know Harold B Crofton, who had taken over his father's mining engineering agency on Tyneside. In July 1929 the two men set up Charles Crofton & Co (Engineers) Ltd, using the title of the old agency, to develop production of the improved drill. With an initial contribution to capital of £50 each, they rented office premises at St Peter's, Newcastle, from British

Engines Ltd, who were to manufacture the new firm's products. From 1931 the new drills were patented and began to be marketed under the trade name 'Victor'. Together with the introduction of a new drilling bit, they began to challenge the dominance of German imports. In addition to drills, flameproof plugs and sockets were developed for underground use. Capital issued increased to £1,500 and by the financial year 1934-35 turnover had reached £40,000, net profit was £3,300 and there was a total staff of 30. In 1935 premises were taken at Wallsend, and some production commenced there; by 1937 turnover was £90,000 and employment had almost doubled. During this period Mann continued to be employed by Vickers, being responsible for the design and installation of electrical equipment for many collieries and acting merely as design consultant for the new firm. In 1937, however, a crisis occurred when British Engines decided that it would not continue to manufacture for the company and, as a result, Crofton felt that he could no longer run it on his own. Mann therefore resigned from Vickers and joined the company full-time from 1 January 1938, taking responsibility for commercial management and design, while Crofton was responsible for the factory. A loan of £25,000 was raised from the Nuffield Trust, the banks having refused to make a loan, and within a year employment reached 127.

Not everything went smoothly, however. There were severe problems when customers discovered that spare parts would not fit because of the failure to manufacture to adequate tolerances. At the end of the 1930s Mann drew up a works production system, controlling all output, costed efficiently, with standard production times on piece rates. The idea of piece rates was abhorrent to a labour force drawn mainly from ex-shipyard workers, and 'shadow' earnings figures, based on the piece rates, were given on pay slips. In almost all cases these were seen to be above time earnings and piece rates came to be accepted with a considerable increase in labour productivity.

During the Second World War, although mining drilling equipment was on the essential list, other production was run down and replaced by government contracts for war supplies. At this time Crofton began to act as consultant to the Ministry of Supply and left the running of the business more and more to Mann, who finally bought out Crofton's share in 1944. In July of that year the name of the company was changed to Victor Products (Wallsend) Ltd. Now in complete control of the company, Mann could develop it as he wished. In 1943 a London agent was appointed, a first step towards developing export sales. Subsequently numerous overseas agents were appointed and large overseas orders began to be obtained from 1945. The range of products expanded, especially into coal-face lighting, and new manufacturing departments were opened to make components which had previously been bought in. By 1950 authorised capital had been increased to £100,000, turnover had reached £500,000 and there were 375 employees. As output increased there came further diversification, to the manufacture of flameproof and weatherproof lighting systems for industries such as oil and petro-chemicals. By 1958, when Mann was awarded the OBE for services to industry in the North East, authorised capital was £500,000, turnover £1 million and there were 500 employees. In the 1960s petrol pump lighting (of which the company is the chief UK producer) and electrical control equipment became

An original coal drill (courtesy of the Central Library, Newcastle upon Tyne).

significant areas of production. In 1965 Mann ceased to be managing director, being replaced by his nephew, Roy Mann, who had joined the company in 1955, after taking a degree in electrical engineering at the University of Birmingham and working for Pye Ltd. Mann resigned as chairman in 1972 and was appointed president, a position he still (1984) retains. By the end of the 1970s the company had £5 million capital employed, turnover of £10 million, net profit of £1 million and 750 employees.

Much of the success of the firm is due to Mann's recognition of the necessity to involve employees in company affairs. Beginning in the war years, a Works Committee was established, with a representative from each department, meeting monthly in the board-room to discuss the company's position. At the same time a suggestions scheme was introduced. In the late 1940s Mann issued a questionnaire to all employees, asking what they most wanted from the company. The leading requests were security and a sense of belonging. As a result, from 1948 employees were encouraged to buy shares in the company at a discount of 10 per cent, and in 1950 a non-contributory pension scheme was introduced for all employees over the age of twenty-five; back-dating was obtained for those with existing service from that age by means of a contribution by Mann of £70,000 to the fund. In 1950 a bonus scheme was also introduced, which from 1956 became based on profits in order to avoid the implication of paternalism. In addition a social club was developed with many sports sections, while a house journal and information sheets kept the employees well informed and in 1954 long service awards were introduced for employees completing twenty-five years service. Annual holidays in excess of national agreements were given. Recognition by Mann of the mutual relationship between management and employees and close attention to labour relations through consultation with shop stewards and union officials has meant that the company never experienced a strike apart from national engineering disputes. The firm became a closed shop at the end of the war and all staff were recommended to join a union.

At the end of the war Mann was asked by Mark (later Sir Mark) Hodgson, who had been charged by the Government to find means of increasing industrial output, to take responsibility for this matter on Tyneside. The result was the formation of the Tyneside Productivity Association, of which Mann was chairman for a number of years and through which he did a great deal of work to persuade other local employers to adopt methods similar to his own. In recognition of his services the Association, on his retirement, established an annual lecture on industrial matters which is still given each year at the University of Newcastle upon Tyne. He was awarded the honorary degree of DCL by the University of Newcastle in 1983. He was also a member of the Tyneside council of the FBI. Mann's other major interest has been in the support of a wide range of local charities, especially at Wallsend and Whitley Bay. In 1955, recognising that death duties would necessitate the sale of the firm when he died (with potential risk to the security of the employees), he decided to give away 75 per cent of his then holding in the company (he had previously given the pension fund 25 per cent of the total ordinary share capital). Part of this holding went to the establishment of the R W Mann Charitable Trust, set up to make donations to a wide range of charitable activities on Tyneside; it now has total assets exceeding £1 million. Mann is patron, after being president for many years, of Whitley Bay Council of Social Service and is also president of the local YMCA, Sea Cadets and Red Cross branch.

In 1925 Mann married Margaret Cicely Gratrix, daughter of a Manchester law-writer. They had no children. Mann's leisure activities were chiefly sporting and social, especially golf and bridge.

D J ROWE

Sources:

Unpublished

Interview with R W Mann, Mar 1982.

Published

Industrial Tyneside Jan 1952.

Victor: The First Fifty Years 1929-1979 (Wallsend: Victor Products (Wallsend) Ltd, 1979).

Victor Views (company house journal).

MANTON, 1st Lord Manton
see WATSON, Joseph

MANVILLE, Sir Edward

(1862-1933)

Electrical engineer and motorcar manufacturer

Edward Mosely was born at Upper Westbourne Terrace, Paddington, on 27 September 1862, son of Benjamin Ephraim Mosely (1835-96) of Maida Vale, and Adeline (1841-1934), daughter of Benjamin Hyam, draper, of Broughton, near Salford, by his wife, formerly Kate Levy. His father, who took the surname of Manville for his family instead of Mosely in the 1870s, was a dental surgeon with practices in Mayfair and Bath. Edward Manville's grandfather Ephraim Mosely, also a distinguished dental surgeon in London, Bath and Newcastle upon Tyne, was enriched by his patent chemical preparation of white india rubber to make false teeth, gums and palates. Other members of the Mosely family, such as Simeon, Lewin, Isaac and Benjamin, were dentists with fashionable practices in mid-nineteenth century London, and as late as 1901 there were six members of the family listed in the *Dentists' Register*. Ephraim Mosely, who seems to have owned an oil and Italian warehouse in Leadenhall Street and a coal business in Fenchurch Street, was an elder of the congregation of the Western Synagogue off Haymarket in the 1850s. Benjamin Manville left £343 in 1896. On his mother's side Edward

Manville was first cousin of two brothers engaged until the First World War in importing grain from Romania, Sir Sigismund Mendl and Sir Charles Mendl, later British press attaché at Paris, 1926-40. Other maternal cousins made a fortune as clothing wholesalers: Lieutenant Colonel Ernest Samuel Halford, formerly Hyam, died in 1932 aged fifty-nine leaving £619,441; Frank Louis Halford was general manager of Shell Mex BP until his death in 1945; and Sir Edmund Davis (qv) was also a cousin.

Edward Manville was educated in 1874-78 at his father's old school, University College School, which had many Jewish pupils and a progressive reputation. As an adult he does not however seem to have practised Judaism, and his racial antecedents, disguised by his father's anglicized surname, were not widely known. The first electrical exhibition at Paris in 1878, and subsequent demonstrations at Crystal Palace in 1882, attracted Manville's youthful curiosity. After technical training in the 1880s, he became joint managing director of the United Electrical Engineering Co of Albert Embankment, Lambeth. This was formed in 1885 as the Jablochkoff & General Electricity Co to exploit the patents of Jablochkoff's electric arc light system which had first illuminated the Paris Opera House in 1882. Its name was changed in 1888; other directors included W G Ainslie, Conservative MP and Lancashire iron and steel manufacturer; but the expectation of Osborne O'Hagan (qv) that the company 'would fall as flat as a pancake' proved correct {O'Hagan (1929) I, 122}.

Next Manville became partner in the Westminster electrical engineering consultancy of Dawson, Kincaid, Waller & Manville, headed by Sir Philip Dawson (1867-1938). Among other works, this firm designed the original electrification of the London, Brighton & South Coast Railway. Manville advised many local authorities and companies on electrical undertakings, designed the Buenos Aires electric tram system, and was involved in overseas contracting before 1914.

After Harry Lawson (qv) and his fellow speculators in the British Motor Syndicate had been dislodged from control of the Daimler Motor Car Co, Manville joined the board in 1902. He and George Flett (1855-1910) soon emerged as the financial experts among the Daimler directors. After the company's reconstruction in November 1904, on issued capital of £142,568, it earned profits of £83,167 in 1905 and £213,469 in 1906. Showing profits of 110 per cent on invested capital, Flett and Manville in October 1906 extracted a maximum bank overdraft limit for Daimler of £150,000, which Sir Edward Holden (qv) stipulated 'was not to go into bricks and mortar, but into machines for Stock' {MBA, Holden diary 31 Oct 1906}. In the event Daimler only availed themselves of £36,000 overdraft in 1906-7, and the limit was reduced to £100,000 in May 1907; but it was evidence of the confidence which Flett and Manville engendered.

Flett was also a consulting electrical engineer, who had done major works in Japan and the Far East and was managing director of Dick, Kerr and other electrical companies. Like Henry Royce (qv), Flett and Manville were innovators who found the challenge and novelty of motorcar development as exciting and rewarding as those of electrical engineering. In autumn 1910, shortly after Flett became the first British motor car manufacturer to be crushed to death by one of his own models, Daimler was bought by Birmingham Small Arms for over £600,000. Manville became deputy chairman of BSA and chairman of Daimler. Under the terms of the deal Daimler was obliged to make a series of large annual payments to BSA (such as £150,000 in July 1914) which left the former company short of working capital to invest in development.

Manville had other business interests in motoring. He was one of the earliest directors, and chairman from 1907 until his death, of Car & General Insurance, which was probably the first insurance company specialising in motorists' risks. Formed in 1903 with authorised capital of £100,000, Car & General made a profit to November 1904 of £1,875, which after promotion expenses of £1,751, left £123 carried forward. In another innovation of motoring business, Manville served for over a decade on the board of the Gearless Motor Omnibus Co, initially as chairman and latterly as a director. This company was formed in 1906 to run motor buses in London and its suburbs, with issued capital of £43,040. During the First World War Manville was also a director of the British Motor Spirit Syndicate Ltd.

Manville held other positions in the Edwardian period. He was an original director of the Corporation of Western Egypt Ltd which was formed in 1904 to exploit a concession of thirty years' duration granted by the Egyptian Government to irrigate and re-sell 600,000 feddans (over 600,000 acres) of land at a rate not exceeding 20,000 feddans annually. The Corporation also received a seventy-year railway concession to connect the Nile to the Oases, together with mineral concessions and a railway monopoly around the Libyan desert oases. A railway opened by the Corporation in January 1908 was transferred to the Egyptian Government in May 1909 for £128,105. The 1904 concession was cancelled in 1909, and a new one granted which confined the Corporation's activities to the Khargeh oasis area. In 1913, after Manville had left the board, the Corporation had £498,168 issued capital: its debit to general development, reclamation and irrigation was £93,548 and its general expenditure debit was £25,326. It was a fine example of stock-jobbing imperialism which only enriched company promoters.

Manville was a director from its foundation in 1907 until its reconstruction in 1909 of the Aluminium Corporation, which held various hydro-electric rights in which Manville was interested. Like the Egyptian Corporation, no dividends were paid during his association with it. He was briefly on the board of British West Indies Copra Ltd during the World War.

According to a writer in 1907, 'Manville is a characteristic type of the jovial-natured, sportsmanlike Englishman who loves a fair field and no favour ... he has never thrust himself into public view ... But among a wide circle of friends ... is an immensely popular figure. A keen-minded man of affairs Mr Manville impresses his personality on those about him' {*Birmingham Gazette* 11 Dec 1907}. To the Minister of Reconstruction, Manville was 'very helpful and suggestive' {Bodleian Library, Addison diary 23 May 1918}. Later an obituarist called him 'a likeable character' with 'a knowledge of men and affairs [and] a tactful, conciliatory manner' {*Times* 20 Mar 1933}.

He was a member of the Institution of Civil Engineers and of the

Institution of Electrical Engineers, a magistrate and active in trade organisations. He was president of the Society of Motor Manufacturers and Traders in 1907-13 (set up to lobby for a protective tariff on imported cars), first president of the Motor Trades Association in 1911-12 and again in 1924-30, president of the Motor and Cycle Trades Benevolent Fund in 1908, vice-president of the Institute of Motor Trades from 1931, and patron of the Industrial Transport Association. Together with Hugo Hirst (qv) he sat on the Empire Trade and Industry Committee of the Royal Colonial Institute; this committee in turn spawned in 1919 'the Britannic Industrial Alliance' {*United Empire* (1919) 501}. He was Coventry Chamber of Commerce's representative on the Council of the Association of British Chambers of Commerce from 1915, and in 1917 the ABCC nominated him to the Foreign Office committee to select candidates as commercial attachés and consuls. He was president of ABCC in 1918-20 and was their spokesman in governmental discussions of reconstruction problems. He criticised the financial facilities available to British exporters, drawing the attention of the Chambers of Commerce in March 1916 'to our large interests abroad and to the impossibility of our Bankers, under the existing system, rendering financial assistance upon a large scale to new enterprise'. Manville wanted British bankers to offer 'business [facilities] now done by the Deutsche Bank and similar German establishments', and particularly advocated 'tied loans' whereby foreign loans issued in London were conditional that 'orders given for material in respect thereof should be placed in England' {PRO, BT 55/32/FFT 2, Lord Faringdon's summary of Manville's views, 1916}. He was vice-president of the ninth British Imperial Council of Commerce at Toronto in 1920, and in 1923 became chairman of the British Imperial Council of Commerce. He was sometime president of the British & Latin American Chamber of Commerce Inc. He represented BSA on the executive committee of the National Alliance of Employers and Employed from 1917, and was a leader of the National Industrial Alliance in the 1920s. As an employer he participated in the Turner-Mond Industrial Conference on labour relations in 1928-29. He was a founding vice-president and council member of the Federation of British Industries (1916), and in 1918 was their nominee to the Lord Chancellor's committee to revise the Rules of Court concerning the service of writs in England on foreign defendants. He was appointed to the Board of Referees on Excess Profits Duty in January 1916, the Income Tax Commission in March 1919 and government committees on bank amalgamations (March 1918) and uniformity in commercial law (April 1918). He was Master of the Coachmakers' Company in 1929-30.

Manville supported attempts by the Business Leagues of Dudley Docker (qv) to increase the influence of Midlands industrialists on Government by establishing a 'business party' in the House of Commons. League sympathisers financed much of the Unionist organisation in Coventry, where Manville was adopted as Unionist candidate in June 1911. In the general election of 1918, after receiving the Coalition Coupon and an expenses subsidy from the British Commonwealth Union, he defeated the sitting Radical MP. Herbert Austin's biographer is thus wrong to claim that the latter 'was the only motor manufacturer to become an MP' {Church (1979) 170}, especially as Manville was elected chairman of the House of Commons' Industrial Group in 1923. He was knighted in the same year, but lost Coventry in the election of December 1923 and did not stand again.

After the war his business interests diversified. From December 1921 until his death he was a director of Royal Exchange Assurance, and in February 1925 he also became a director of State Assurance Ltd. He remained chairman of Car & General, and was also chairman of the Reinsurance Corporation formed in 1919 to operate in all reinsurance except life and bond investment.

Some of his interests were speculative. In the 1920s he was a director of Porcupine Goldfields Development & Finance Ltd which owned some worthless mines in Ontario and was the subject of litigation. From 1928 he was chairman of Latifiyah (Iraq) Estates Ltd which held a cotton concession of 60,000 acres in Iraq, but paid no dividend during the five years of his chairmanship. He also briefly chaired the British Acetate Silk Corporation in the mid-1920s.

From July 1926 until his death Manville was an active director of the Metropolitan Railway, associated with the Docker group on the board, and served on its Chiltern Court committee.

Another post which he held until his death was the chairmanship of Phoenix Oil & Transport Ltd. This company was formed in 1920 to acquire Anglo-Continental Oil Ltd and the Masterson Roumanian Oil Syndicate Ltd, which held oilfields at Unirea. Phoenix also came to control Beciu (Roumanian) Oilfields Ltd, Traian Roumanian Oil Ltd, the Anglo-Roumanian Petroleum Company, Stavropoleo Moreni (Roumanian) Oil Properties Ltd, Orio SA de Petrol, and Roumanian Consolidated Oilfields Ltd. Manville was chairman, deputy-chairman or a director of all these subsidiaries. Phoenix developed new fields at Gura Ocnitei in 1924-25, which with 114 wells working in December 1930 was Romania's third largest oil producer: although by the onset of Manville's final illness, it had fallen to fourth place with 87 wells working on 1 January 1933. Manville was invested as Grand Officer of the Crown of Romania in 1927.

Throughout 1910 to 1928 he continued as chairman of Daimler, deputy-chairman of BSA, and chaired such subsidiaries as Daimler Hire Ltd and William Jessops & Sons Ltd. During the 1920s the BSA board was invertebrate and unenterprising: a reckless deal of 1919-20 between Manville's friend and executor Percy Martin (qv) and George Holt Thomas (qv) triggered a long financial crisis and a succession of bad results in most departments except motor-cycles. Manville was made chairman of the group in 1928, but he failed to make reforms and its decline continued. While it had a bank balance credit of £275,000 in November 1929, this had turned into an overdraft of £515,000 by February 1931 (reduced to £95,000, October 1932). In July 1932 Manville was replaced as chairman by Arthur Pollen (qv), while remaining a director.

In the final pioneering work of his life, Manville was chairman in 1927-30 of the new Baird Television Development Ltd which handled the sole Baird rights for the British Empire. Baird's mechanical television set, later known as the 'disc televisor', produced flickering and shadowy pictures: although technically over-complex and commercially otiose, its development was not abandoned until 1937. Manville was thus among the first in Britain to recognise the commercial possibilities of electricity, and half a century later those of television. His relations with Baird were, however, strained. The inventor 'resented the old gentleman', and later complained of Manville, 'He boomed at me, through a cloud of cigar smoke, innumerable pointless questions and, what was worse, he made impossible suggestions. When I tried to explain that they were impossible, his booming became angry and ominous' {Moseley (1952) 104}.

Manville first married, in August 1894, at Newport, Maud Elizabeth, daughter of Colonel Charles Thomas Wallis, VD, JP, DL (1841-1918), of Chesterholme, Stow Park, Monmouthshire and Plas Isa, Porthcawl, Glamorganshire, who had served as a special constable in the Indian Mutiny and was subsequently active in the Welsh volunteer and territorial armies. She apparently died in 1909 and he re-married in 1911, at Westminster, Jane Rachel Violet (1879-1940), daughter of John Holmes, a civil engineer of Calcutta. Both marriages were childless. After several months illness he died at midnight on 18 March 1933 after an operation in a nursing home in Beaumont Street, Marylebone. He left £47,277, bequeathing £1,000 to Coventry & Warwickshire Hospital, and £5,000 each to the Institutions of Electrical Engineers and Automobile Engineers to found scholarships.

R P T DAVENPORT-HINES

Writings:

letter on proposed Ford motor car factory at Cork *Times* 23 Mar 1917.

letter on industrial unrest *ibid* 21 Sept 1918.

letter on National Alliance of Employers and Employed *ibid* 21 Mar 1923.

letter on trusts and combines *ibid* 12 Oct 1923.

letter on McKenna duties on motor cars *ibid* 26 Apr 1924.

letter on Steel-Maitland's proposed industrial truce *ibid* 3 Oct 1924.

letter on British industry and inter-Allied debts *ibid* 10 Jan 1925.

article on Motor Insurance *ibid* (British Motor Number) 26 Apr 1932.

Sources:

Unpublished

Bodleian Library, Oxford, diaries of Viscount Addison.

Cambridge University Library, papers of Earl Baldwin of Bewdley (vols 30, 76 and 140).

Coventry City RO, Broadgate, Coventry, papers of Daimler Motors.

Greater London RO, papers of Metropolitan Railway.

Guildhall Library, London, papers of Association of British Chambers of Commerce.

House of Lords RO, papers of Sir Patrick Hannon.

MANVILLE Sir Edward

Midland Bank Archives, diary of Sir Edward Holden.

PRO, Board of Trade and Foreign Office papers.

University of Warwick, Modern Records Centre, Coventry, papers of Birmingham Small Arms and Federation of British Industries.

BCe.

PrC; Will.

Information from Judge Mendl.

Published

Anthony Bird and Francis Hutton-Stott, *Lanchester Motor Cars* (Cassell, 1965).

Birmingham Gazette and Express 11 Dec 1907.

Bernard L P Caillard, 'British Cars for Dominions' *Times* 19 Apr 1928.

Roy Church, *Herbert Austin* (Europa, 1979).

Richard Davenport-Hines, *Dudley Docker* (Cambridge University Press, 1984).

Dentists' Register (Spottiswoode, 1901).

Electrical Engineering passim.

George H Frost, *Munitions of War: The Record of the BSA and Daimler Companies 1914-18* (Birmingham: BSA, 1921).

Globe 17 Mar 1915, 24 Feb 1916.

Maurice Millioud, *The Ruling Caste and Frenzied Trade in Germany* (Constable, 1916).

Sydney Moseley, *John Baird* (Odhams, 1952).

H Osborne O'Hagan, *Leaves from My Life* (2 vols, John Lane, 1929).

Maurice Pearton, *Oil and the Roumanian State 1895-1948* (Oxford University Press, 1971).

Kenneth Richardson, *British Motor Industry 1896-1939* (Macmillan, 1977).

Cecil Roth, *Records of the Western Synagogue 1761-1932* (Goldston, 1932).

S B Saul, 'The Motor Industry in Britain to 1914' *Business History* 5 (1962).

Times 4 Apr 1906, 9 Nov 1907, 12 Nov 1908, 20 Mar, 11 Nov 1909, 1 Nov 1911, 16 Jan, 28 Mar, 16 Apr, 21 June, 3 July, 23 Aug, 30 Oct, 1, 22 Nov 1919, 9, 22 Jan, 7 Feb, 8, 9 Mar, 22, 24 Apr 1920, 5 Feb, 12 Mar, 16 July, 10 Sept 1921, 3, 4 Feb, 29 Apr, 10 June, 7 Nov 1922, 30 Apr, 2 July, 12, 20 Nov 1924, 5 Feb, 13 May, 11 June 1925, 1 July 1926, 5 Apr, 27 May, 13-15 June 1927, 6 July 1928, 20 Feb, 26 Apr, 12 Oct 1929, 8, 11 Apr 1930, 18, 20 Mar 1933.

United Empire 10 (1919).

John F Wilson, 'A Strategy of Expansion and Combination: Dick Kerr & Company 1897-1914' *Business History* 27 (1985).

WWMP.

WWW.

X, 'A Plea for Cinderella' *United Empire* 8 (1917).

Sir Frederick T Mappin (from A W Chapman The Story of a Modern University *Oxford University Press, 1955).*

MAPPIN, Sir Frederick Thorpe

(1821-1910)

Cutlery and steel manufacturer and utility company chairman

Frederick Thorpe Mappin was born at Sheffield on 16 May 1821, the eldest son of Joseph Mappin and his wife Mary, the daughter of Thomas Thorpe, a Bedfordshire land agent and surveyor. The family had for several generations been involved in the cutlery trades and the Radical politics of Sheffield; if, as some have claimed, 'Sheffield provides the largest example of Mass Heredity in an English town' {Abercrombie (1924) 10}, Mappin was, in both respects, a prime model. Crucial to Mappin's business career was the success of the cutlery firm established by his father in 1825, which soon acquired a reputation for its ingenious sportsmen's knives. By 1840 it employed about 100 workers, placing it near the top of an industrial hierarchy which rested on a broad bottom of small workshops. Educated at Mr Wright's School, Sheffield, Mappin joined the family firm at the age of fourteen on the retirement of his father's partner, Arundel. This early experience was vital, for Joseph Mappin died in 1841 leaving the youthful Frederick in charge both of the firm and of three younger brothers who were to be introduced into it.

The rapid progress of Mappin Bros over the next two decades owed much to the ability of Frederick in the context of a period of general expansion in the Sheffield light trades. In 1845 W Sampson & Co, Sheffield cutlers, were taken over, and by the late 1850s the firm's workforce had grown five-fold. This expansion of productive capacity, marked by the opening of the Queen's Cutlery Works in 1851, was matched by Mappin's cultivation of marketing opportunities. Rather than rely on London factors, he purchased a London shop in 1845, the success of which led in 1856 to the acquisition of a warehouse. By 1860 this could claim to be London's largest cutlery warehouse. From their northern manufacturing base, Mappin Bros were thus able to reach the affluent metropolitan and provincial middle class market, to whom it supplied, inter alia, knives and razors, picnic boxes and travelling bags, (electro-plated) claret jugs and asparagus tongs. At the same time, a large export trade was built up, with Mappin himself travelling in Europe and America, and with a number of agencies in America, Canada, Australia and elsewhere. Reputedly the youngest Master Cutler in 1855, Mappin had established himself in the forefront of the cutlery trades, with a business characterised by its large scale, its wide range of high-class products, and its merchanting capacity. This firm would eventually (in 1908) become part of Mappin & Webb but the creation of the latter was the achievement of Frederick's youngest brother John Newton Mappin (1836-1913).

Frederick himself retired from Mappin Bros in 1859 after a partnership dispute, and in 1860 entered the heavy steel industry by purchasing for £76,066 the firm of Thomas Turton & Sons, in partnership (until 1868) with W A Matthews. In this transition from cutlery to steel, signalled by his joining the Institution of Mechanical Engineers in 1862, and that of Civil Engineers in 1865, Mappin was typical of his generation, which included men such as John Brown and Charles Cammell (qqv). Turtons were among the largest of pre-Bessemer steel firms, with (in 1852) 11 converting furnaces and 48 melting furnaces; for the Great Exhibition of 1851 they had produced a monster ingot of 24 cwt, the largest ever mass of crucible steel. But Turtons had also in 1839 taken over the well-known file and edge-tool firm of William Greaves & Sons, whose Sheaf Works had in 1823 been the first large-scale factory created in the Sheffield cutlery industry 'embracing all the essential processes from the production of steel to the completion of the perfect article' {Lloyd (1913) 182}. By 1860, the steel industry was on the verge of revolution and the next twenty years saw the emergence of giant firms with large work-forces (2,000-4,000) and very substantial amounts of capital (Browns and Cammells were capitalised at £1 million in 1864). Turtons was not to match these in size (only 1,000 workers in 1865) or capital (of the nominal capital of £100,000 only £75,000 was called up by 1886). But in two specialised areas, those of the manufacture of files and railway springs, the firm could claim leadership.

The basis of Turtons' reputation lay in its excellent quality steel, evinced by awards at international exhibitions, as in 1862. Under Mappin, however, Turtons also became pioneers of mechanisation in the cutlery trades, a development seen as crucial if Sheffield were to hold back European and American competition. Mappin in 1865 introduced the first grinding machine for file-cutting in Sheffield, challenging the hold of the handicraft unions (the more extreme of whose activities came at the same time under the scrutiny of the Sheffield Outrages Enquiry) and precipitated a major strike in the file trade in 1866. This dispute began over wages but the underlying issue was the introduction of machinery. A lock-out by the employers (who formed a File Manufacturers' Association which Mappin was later to head) was, after sixteen weeks, successful. Nevertheless, the extension of mechanisation was slow, the employers agreed to put only skilled men on machine work, and into the 1890s Turtons themselves continued to employ much hand-labour although still in the forefront of machine methods. Turtons' leadership in this traditional but changing trade was complemented by their expertise in the modern sector of railway-spring manufacture (mechanised in the 1860s and 1870s), the branch of the railway goods market in which Sheffield specialised. Possibly this was the more profitable branch of Turtons' activities, with depots in London, Paris and New York. In 1886 Turtons became a private limited company, with Mappin as chairman, a post he held until his death. However, he retired from an active managerial role in favour of his sons Frank (1846-1920) and Wilson (1848-1925), who now also became the firm's leading shareholders and the architects of its continued expansion in the late nineteenth century.

After 1885, Frederick Mappin's key business interests lay in railways and gas. In 1869 he had joined the board of the Midland Railway and remained a working director until 1903. More importantly, the Sheffield Gas & Light Co became Mappin's favourite business child. A director since 1863, Mappin was to be chairman between 1873 and 1908, in which year the company was the second largest private provincial gas undertaking, with an annual output of 3,238 million cubic feet. Under Mappin's guidance, the capital of the company had more than doubled, while financial and technical efficiency provided probably the cheapest gas in the country. This boon to domestic and industrial consumers, which owed much to the astute management of Hanbury Thomas, was matched by regular 10 per cent dividends to the shareholders (the maximum permissible) which left Mappin a confident advocate of private enterprise against municipal trading and a complacent defender of gas rather than electric power. Earlier, and less happily, Mappin had been associated with the Sheffield Water Co at the time of the flood disaster in 1864, the result, many felt, of the directors' negligence. He was also a director of the Bridgewater Navigation.

Mappin the businessman defended cheap gas as a public benefit but as a politician and philanthropist, he was also to further the welfare of Sheffield. Above all, perhaps, he was the leading advocate of technical education in the town, and largely responsible for the establishment of its Technical School in 1884. He continued to oversee this institution, which evolved into the department of technology of the University of Sheffield, of which Mappin became a Charter Pro-Chancellor in 1905. However heavy-handed Mappin's approach in educational affairs, his contribution was vital, less perhaps in terms of his financial gifts (in toto, over £14,000) than in arousing the support of his fellow-industrialists, few of whom expected to benefit directly from educational initiatives. The suspicion that Mappin's interest in technical education lay 'in the development of a system of training in engineering and metallurgy that would wrest control over the formation of the attitudes and practices of the skilled labour force away from the trade societies' {Smith (1982) 223} lacks direct evidence; more plausibly, Mappin's support reflected widespread business fears that Britain was facing increasing foreign competition and that technical education, rather than protection, provided the solution.

Like other local industrialists, Mappin served on the town council (1854-57, 1876-83, Mayor 1877-78). He took a noted interest in schemes of financial management and reform but was increasingly contemptuous of his colleagues, 'so many contractors, speculators and such like' 'unable to grapple with large affairs' {Sheffield UL, Mundella papers, Mappin to Robert Leader 20 Mar 1882}. He was also for thirty-five years one of the Town Trustees (from 1871) and from 1893, Town Collector. Sheffield benefited in several ways from his doctrine of wealth as a trust: physically, by his support for public parks and the erection of a coffee house, culturally by his donations to, and organising role in setting up, the Mappin Art Gallery (the benefaction of his uncle, J N Mappin (1800-83)); spiritually, by his generous support of all churches after he abandoned the Congregationalism of his forebears for the Anglican church. The granting to Mappin of the Freedom of the City in 1900 recognised his close identification with the town, where he had resided all his life, unlike many of his fellow steel magnates who had sought the solace of county society and the joys of rural life. Mappin's own recreations were restricted to cricket, the Volunteers (1861-72) and picture-collecting. He was, however, a JP and DL of the West Riding, and in 1878 was awarded the Légion d'Honneur as a juror at the Paris International Exhibition.

Mappin's wider ambitions were, by and large, political. In the 1860s he

directly under Geoffrey Marks, went on, in turn, to fill positions of the highest rank in other important life offices.) Before his retirement, Marks had Nicholas Davenport, a City man and financial journalist, brought on to the board, because, he told Davenport, 'I want someone on this blasted board who can answer Keynes back' {*ibid*, 31}.

Recognition of Geoffrey Marks's great abilities went far beyond the bounds of the National Mutual. He was elected president of the Institute of Actuaries, 1918-20, a period when his strong guiding hand meant much in the reconstitution of the functions of the Institute in a new era. It was during his term of office that the decision was taken — revolutionary as it then seemed — to admit women to membership. He was chairman of the Life Offices' Association, 1914-16, and chairman of the British Insurance Association in 1926 (although not unique, it is very unusual for the BIA to appoint a chairman from an office the business of which is devoted solely to life assurance). He was also chairman of the Joint Board Administrating Special Scheme of Unemployment Insurance to the Insurance Industry from its formation in 1921 until 1937 (the board was set up under the Unemployment Insurance Act of 1920, which permitted any industry to provide benefit for employees more advantageous than those laid down by the Act to set up its own scheme).

His skill and experience in the management of assets made Geoffrey Marks known and respected outside the purely insurance world. He was finance officer of the Metropolitan Special Constabulary, 1914-16; personal assistant to the controller, Navy and Army Canteen Board, 1917-19; member of the Advisory Committee of Insurance Offices and Trust Companies on Mobilisation of Dollar Securities; chairman of Miss Holman's Home and Club for Disabled Officers; a governor of the Prince of Wales General Hospital, Tottenham; member of council of the Royal Patriotic Fund Corporation, 1918-20; and a member of the Royal Commission on Decimal Coinage, 1918-19; and the Royal Commission on the Income Tax, 1919-20. He was made a CBE in 1920.

As well as continuing as a director of the National Mutual after his retirement, Geoffrey Marks was chairman of Clitheroe Estate Co Ltd, a director of Coal & Iron Trades Insurance Co Ltd and a director of Beyer Peacock & Co Ltd.

Marks married Alys Mary Bridges (d 1930); there were no children of the marriage. He lived at Nateley Scures, near Basingstoke. Geoffrey Marks died on 25 August 1938, aged seventy-four, leaving an estate of £26,570 gross.

ERIC E G STREET

Sources:

Unpublished

BCe.

PrC.

Published

Robert Finch and Alfred Roberts, *The History of the National Mutual Life Assurance Society, 1830-1930* (pp, the Society, 1930).

George H Recknell, 'Geoffrey Marks' *Journal of the Institute of Actuaries* 69 (1938).

Eric Street and Richard Glenn, *The National Mutual Life Assurance Society, 1830-1980* (pp, the Society, 1980).

WWW.

H H Marks from Vanity Fair *1889.*

MARKS, Harry Hananel

(1855-1916)

Newspaper proprietor

Harry Hananel Marks was born in Marylebone, London, on 10 April 1855, the son of David Woolf Marks, head of the Reformed Congregation of British Jews, and his wife Cecilia née Woolf, daughter of a Liverpool merchant. Educated at University College School and at the Athenée Royale, Brussels, Marks began his career in newspapers at sixteen, leaving England to seek 'the roughest and most thorough literary training which America offered' {*Financial News* 27 Dec 1916}. From 1871 to 1873, he worked as a reporter with the *New Orleans Picayune*, and from 1873 to 1880, as a reporter and night editor with the *New York World*. The house style of the *Financial News*, particularly what Marks defined as its 'rough and ready boldness' {*ibid* 23 Jan 1904} owed much to his American apprenticeship.

After appointment as editor of the *Daily Mining News* in 1880, Marks speculated profitably on the New York stock market, accumulating the funds with which he started the *Financial News* when personal circumstances persuaded him to return to London in 1884. The *News*, London's first financial daily, pre-dating the *Financial Times* by four years, provided a news service and an international coverage which existing City weeklies could not match. Its stylistic affinities with the contemporary 'new journalism' enhanced its appeal to small investors, thus ensuring a substantial income from new company advertising. Under Marks's direction, Financial News Ltd experienced continuous growth and consistent profitability, paying an average of 17 per cent to ordinary shareholders for the twenty years before his retirement after a stroke in 1909. Marks's other newspaper interests included the *Evening Post*, launched in 1887 but absorbed by the *Evening News* in 1889; the *Eastern*

Post, bought in 1892 to improve his prospects as a parliamentary candidate; and the *Sun*, through his connection with E T Hooley's (qv) London & County Newspaper Syndicate after 1898. From its establishment in 1886, he chaired the Argus Printing Co, printers of the *Financial News* and specialists in company circulars.

A Conservative, noted for his advocacy of protection and the restriction of immigration, Marks served on London County Council from 1889 and as MP for St George's in the East, 1895-1900, and Thanet, 1904-10. His political career was blighted by persistent and well-founded allegations that he used the *Financial News* to fleece investors, 'puffing' dubious enterprises in which his own interest was concealed and accepting payments from unscrupulous company promotors. The reputation which the *News* had earned as 'the trusted guide of the investing public' {*Sell's* (1889) 166-67} was seriously compromised.

Harry Marks was married in 1882 to Annie Estelle Benjamin and had two children. He died in London on 22 December 1916, leaving £30,933 gross.

DILWYN PORTER

Writings:

Small Change: Or Lights and Shades of New York (New York: Standard Publishing Co, 1882).

Down with the Jews! A Meeting of the Society for Suppressing the Jewish Race (New York, 1882).

The Metropolitan Board of Works: A Brief Account of the Disclosures Which Have Led to the Appointment of a Royal Commission to Investigate the Charges Brought Against It (Argus Printing Co, 1888).

The Case for Tariff Reform (1905).

Sources:

Unpublished

British Museum, Balfour papers, Add MSS 49,762, 49,9771.

Northumberland RO, Ridley (Blagdon) papers, ZRI 25/100.

Quex Park, Birchington, Kent, Powell-Cotton papers.

BCe.

PrC.

J J Bennett, 'East End Newspaper Opinion and Jewish Immigration, 1885-1905' (Sheffield M Phil, 1979).

Published

Broadstairs and St Peter's Mail 4 Mar 1904.

Financial News 23 Jan 1884, 23 Jan 1904, 27 Dec 1916.

Alfred G Gardiner, *John Benn and the Progressive Movement* (E Benn, 1925).

Henry Hess, *'The Critic' Black Book* (British and Colonial Publications, 1901).

Isle of Thanet Gazette 30 Dec 1916.

Jewish World 27 Dec 1916.

Kentish Express 18 June 1904.

Stephen Koss, *The Rise and Fall of the Political Press in Britain* vol 1 (Hamish Hamilton, 1981).

Newspaper World 30 Dec 1916.

Henry Osborne O'Hagan, *Leaves from My Life* (John Lane, 1929).

Cornelius O'Leary, *The Elimination of Corrupt Practices in British Elections 1868-1911* (Oxford: Clarendon Press, 1962).

Temple Orme, *University College School, London; Alphabetical and Chronological Register for 1831-1891* (H Walton Lawrence, 1892).

William T Pike, 'Contemporary Biographies' in T B Jones (ed), *Kent at the Opening of the Twentieth Century* (Brighton: W T Pike, 1904).

The Representation of Thanet (Margate: Thanet Conservative and Unionist League, 1905).

Sell's Dictionary of the World's Press (H Sell, 1889).

Harry Simonis, *The Street of Ink: An Intimate History* (Cassell, 1917).

Times 16 Mar 1909, 10 Mar 1910, 19 Jan 1911.

L H West, 'Newspaper Companies as Investments' *Sell's Dictionary of the World's Press* (H Sell, 1898).

Who's Who in Kent, Surrey and Sussex (Horace Cox, 1911).

WWMP.

WWW.

MARKS, Michael

(1859-1907)

Chain store founder

Michael Marks was born in Slonim, Russia, in June 1859, the youngest child of Mordecai Marks, a tailor, and his wife Rebecca. Michael's mother died in childbirth, and he was brought up by his elder sister. Little is

Michael Marks (courtesy of Marks & Spencer plc).

known of his early life, except that the family was poor, suffering the social and political disadvantages of the oppressed Russian Jewish community. When a new wave of violent anti-semitism followed the assassination of Tsar Alexander II in 1881, Michael Marks was one of the many thousands of Jews who fled to Western Europe and the USA, although the exact year in which he emigrated is not known. He arrived in North-East England, with no money, and knowing nothing of the language.

Marks came to Leeds looking for the firm of Barran clothing manufacturers, founded by John Barran (qv), whose generosity in employing refugees was known even in Eastern Europe. While trying to find them he met Isaac Dewhirst, a wholesaler who sold supplies to itinerant pedlars. Dewhirst befriended him, and offered to lend him £5, which Marks used to buy goods from Dewhirst's warehouse. Physically frail, Marks was ill-suited to the life of an itinerant peddlar, but soon, in 1884, he opened a stall in the open market at Kirkgate in Leeds. Since this market only operated on Tuesdays and Saturdays, Marks also opened stalls in nearby Castleford and Wakefield, which had different market days. All his merchandise was displayed in open baskets, with the prices clearly marked, and could be freely inspected by customers.

Soon Marks moved his stall in Leeds from the outdoor to the covered market, which was open all week. Here he divided his goods into two sections, separating all those goods costing a penny from the rest. Above the penny section he hung a notice 'Don't ask the price, it's a penny'. This idea proved so popular that soon Marks only sold goods costing a penny. This simplified his calculations, for he kept no written accounts, but also meant he had to search constantly for good quality merchandise which could be sold at a penny. With such a low selling price and consequent small margins, he had perforce to rely on a large turnover, but he was able to deal in a wide variety of goods, ranging from haberdashery, earthenware, hardware and household goods to toys and stationery. The move to the covered market at Leeds brought changes in the organisation of the business, for Marks could no longer attend all his stalls personally, and assistants were appointed to take charge of them under his supervision. Marks concentrated on buying in stock and distributing it to the stalls. It was not long before he moved across the Pennines to reach the promising markets represented by the still expanding cotton textile districts. New 'Penny Bazaars' were opened in Warrington in 1887, and in Birkenhead in 1890. In 1891 Marks opened a stall in the market hall of Wigan and as this was a geographically more convenient centre for the supervision of his business, moved there with his wife and family. He had married Hannah Cohen in 1886; their first (living) child Simon (qv) was born in 1888, and they had four other children, all daughters.

Establishing a warehouse in Wigan as a centre of distribution, Marks opened another penny bazaar in Bolton market hall in 1892, and, in 1894, a shop in Cheetham Hill, Manchester. The business was becoming too large for one man to handle alone, so Marks sought a partner. He first approached Isaac Dewhirst, but Dewhirst declined. Instead, Marks entered into partnership with Thomas Spencer, Dewhirst's cashier, and a friend of Marks. Spencer 'had little imagination or enterprise, but was something of an organiser, with an eye to small economies; he had some experience of buying and through Dewhirst's had useful connections in

Some of the last minutes signed by Michael Marks and Thomas Spencer (courtesy of Marks & Spencer plc).

Subscription to the articles of Association 1903, signed by Michael Marks and Thomas Spencer (courtesy of Marks & Spencer plc).

the trade, which enabled him to put Michael Marks in direct touch with manufacturers'. {Rees (1969) 10}

The firm of Marks & Spencer was formed in September 1894, with Spencer paying £300 for a half-share in the business. Marks's own capital in the firm was at first £453 15s 11d but this was reduced to £300 during the first six months, as Marks withdrew the surplus. Spencer saw to the warehouse and the dispatch of goods to the bazaars, while Marks was responsible for buying and for visiting branches and looking out for potential new ones.

On the formation of the partnership, Marks moved to Manchester, where he established his family home above the penny bazaar in Cheetham Hill. The headquarters of the firm was moved to Manchester in 1897, and a warehouse leased in Robert Street. In 1901 the warehouse was moved to Derby Street, to the first building to be specially constructed for the firm. By 1903 there were 40 penny bazaars, still largely in the North of England, and mostly in covered market halls, though there were now a dozen or more shops, some in London. The great variety of goods sold in the Penny Bazaars contrasted with the strategy adopted by other growing chains of stores catering to working-class customers, such as those of George Beale, George Watson and Thomas Lipton (qqv), who usually dealt in a deliberately restricted range of food and drink.

In that year a limited company, Marks & Spencer Ltd, was formed, with a capital of 30,000 £1 shares. Michael Marks and Thomas Spencer were each allotted 14,995 shares, and both became directors of the company. However, Spencer retired soon after the formation of the company; he died in 1905. William Chapman, a handkerchief manufacturer, was appointed to represent Spencer family interests. There were further small issues of shares, bringing the capital up to £33,000 in 1907; the shares went to members of the Marks and the Spencer families, and to employees of the firm.

Spencer's retirement and death greatly increased Marks's burden of work, not least because he continued to expand the business, even more rapidly than before. There were over 60 branches by 1907, only a third now in market halls and arcades, sites which gave little scope for alteration and expansion. The formula of open display and self-selection (features well in advance of the retailing methods prevailing at the time) coupled with a fixed price and consistent efforts to supply a wide range of quality goods within that price restriction, was understandably popular with Marks's working-class customers, and the bazaars prospered; profits in 1907 were £9,000. But the increased work and responsibility took their toll, and contributed to Michael Marks's early death on 31 December 1907; he left an estate of £27,256.

The principles on which Marks founded and ran his business, principles derived from an instinctive understanding of his market rather than abstract theories of retailing, strongly influenced the later distinctive development of the firm. Concern that his customers should have a fair deal was as much an expression of his humanitarian temperament as was his concern for the welfare of his staff. His benevolence was expressed outside his business too — his son-in-law, Isaac Sieff (qv), remembered watching him 'giving away half-sovereigns to the needy down at the Working Men's club in Manchester' {*ibid*, 245}. Another son-in-law,

Harry Sacher, recalled 'He inspired confidence and affection in even casual acquaintances; he never quarrelled; and he never lost a friend.' {*ibid*, 10} His partner, Spencer, had been a friend, and remained one, despite the contrast between Spencer's narrow horizons and conservative attitude, and Marks's dynamic approach to the development of the business. It is, therefore, ironic, and a little sad, that Marks's son, Simon, had to engage in a prolonged and sometimes bitter battle to win control of the firm from the representatives of the Spencer family, before he could proceed with the development of the business in accordance with the spirit of his father's principles.

CHRISTINE SHAW

Sources:

Unpublished

Information from Marks & Spencer plc archives.

PrC.

Published

Goronwy Rees, *St Michael; A History of Marks & Spencer* (Weidenfeld & Nicolson, 1969).

Israel Sieff, *Memoirs* (Weidenfeld & Nicolson, 1920).

Simon Marks (courtesy of Marks and Spencer plc).

MARKS, Simon

1st Lord Marks of Broughton

(1888-1964)

Chain store chairman

Simon Marks was born in Leeds on 9 July 1888, the only son and eldest child of Michael Marks (qv) and his wife Hannah née Cohen (d 1917). Michael Marks was just beginning to build up his chain of penny bazaars. As the business developed, the family moved first to Wigan, in 1891, and then in 1894 to Manchester. The Jewish community in Manchester was large, about 30,000, with traditions of tolerance, charity and culture; Simon Marks was greatly influenced in later life by one of the leading members of that community, Chaim Weizmann (later President of the State of Israel). Simon attended Manchester Grammar School (which he enjoyed, though he was not academically inclined) from 1901-1905. It was there he met Israel Sieff (qv), who became a lifelong friend and an important collaborator in the development of Marks & Spencer. He then went abroad to learn French and German and got to know some of his father's business contacts on the Continent. He particularly enjoyed his stay in Paris, and his family had some difficulty in persuading him to come back to England.

Just after Simon returned from Paris and joined Marks & Spencer, by then a chain of over 60 penny bazaars, his father died in December 1907. The only surviving director of the company was William Chapman, a handkerchief manufacturer, who had been appointed in 1905 to represent the interests of the family of Thomas Spencer, Michael Marks's former partner, who had died in that year. Spencer's son, also called Thomas, had already worked for the firm for several years, but was neither able nor willing to assume control. Simon Marks himself was too young and inexperienced to take charge. In January 1908, Bernard Steel, a jeweller, and one of Michael Marks's executors, was appointed a director to represent the interests of the Marks family, and it was he and Chapman who assumed direction of Marks & Spencer.

Soon battle was joined for control of the company. Chapman had his own business to attend to, but had a constant ally in Thomas Spencer Jr, whom he dominated. Steel could give all his time to the company, but Chapman was determined to have the decisive voice. Simon Marks was appointed editor of the Marks & Spencer *Annual*, published as a publicity venture from 1909 to 1915 (just one of a number of publications for children and condensed popular novels published by the firm at this time but abandoned when it became clear they were not profitable). He was also largely responsible for buying both at home and overseas, particularly in France and Germany; Chapman complained he was buying too much. 'Chapman, having no sentimental or family ties to Marks and Spencer, was always ready to sell out to a bigger organisation if the terms were right. Simon on the other hand, was already passionately involved in the life of the business his father had founded, and regarded it as his filial duty to build it up' {Sieff (1970) 63}.

In 1909 Simon Marks successfully opposed a proposal by Chapman and Steel to increase the share capital of the company to £100,000, a proposal probably made with the intention of securing control of the company themselves, for neither the Marks nor Spencer interests could take up this suggested issue. Marks and Thomas Spencer Jr both joined the board in December 1911, and were to be responsible for buying and other duties assigned to them 'as necessity arose and time permitted' {Rees (1969) 36}. The following year Chapman forced Steel to resign. When Marks proposed the election of Alexander Isaacs, a trustee of Michael Marks's estate, as a replacement at the AGM in February 1913 and secured, by a small margin, a majority of votes in favour, Chapman ruled the appointment of a director required a three-quarters majority. Faced by Chapman's evident determination to wrest the company from the Marks's interests, Simon Marks slowly acquired more shares, often at high prices, as they became available, helped by his mother, his uncle Ephraim, Israel Sieff and Sieff's father. Chapman retaliated by refusing to register the transfer of shares, or accept perpetual proxies for them in favour of Marks.

When exactly the same number of votes as in 1913 were cast at the 1915 AGM in favour of appointing Isaacs and Israel Sieff as directors, Chapman again declared the resolution defeated, and then at a board meeting the same day, elected, with Spencer, a long-serving employee of the company, W F Norris, to the board, offering to appoint Israel Sieff to complete the quota of directors allowed under the articles of association. Marks took the dispute to court, and won his case in the Court of Chancery, and the appeal in January 1916. The new board — Chapman, Spencer, Marks, Isaacs and Sieff — was no more united, with Chapman complaining of ruinous over-buying, and Isaacs and Sieff proposing the dismissal of Spencer for neglect of his duties. Marks replaced Chapman as chairman in April 1916, and in June 1917, following an emergency general meeting called to remove the still disruptive Chapman from the board, both Chapman and Spencer retired. Spencer, whose health had been failing, died the following month. The two new directors representing the Spencer Trust, A Davis and J Luther Green (a relative of Agnes Spencer, Thomas Spencer's step-mother, who had always been fond of Simon Marks) worked amicably with their colleagues.

During the struggle between Marks and Chapman for control of the company, Marks & Spencer had continued to expand. By the beginning of the war, there were 140 branches, and, since under 10 per cent of them were in market halls and arcades, the typical branch was now a shop. Rival chains of penny bazaars had been acquired; the most important being the London Penny Bazaar Co, bought in 1914 for £15,000, which established Marks & Spencer in the London area. There had been experiments — with advertising, with selling goods above 1d in part of certain stores — but they had not proved successful, and Marks felt that the company, though it continued to be profitable, would lose out to competitors if a more dynamic approach were not adopted.

An open-fronted shop, Stratford, London, 1910 (courtesy of Marks & Spencer plc).

However, soon after he became chairman he was called up for military service with the Royal Artillery in May 1917; Sieff took his place as chairman during his absence. After a couple of months Marks was transferred to London, and resumed chairmanship of the company. In July 1917 Marks signed a fourteen-year contract, stipulating a salary of £1,700 a year as well as director's fees of £300 a year, plus 5 per cent of profits over £35,000. He was seconded from the army to set up and run political headquarters for Chaim Weizmann in London; Sieff also assisted Weizmann at the time.

Difficulties of supply and inflation caused by the war forced the company to abandon its penny price limit; leaving it without a clear merchandising policy and threatening its distinctive identity in the minds of the public. It was some years after the war before Simon Marks, who in 1920 had moved to London, worked out a new strategy. It was not particularly original and owed much to the example of US variety chain stores like Woolworths, whose progress in Britain Simon Marks watched with apprehension. 'I was conscious of my own shortcomings and ignorance. I had never worked in a shop. I had no training in the business, other than that which I was to acquire by trial and error. I felt that somehow I had to expand my experience, learn from other people how to face up to the competition' of Woolworths {Sieff (1970) 141}. He travelled widely in the USA in 1924, paying particular attention to chain stores. 'I

*Early Marks & Spencer logo, 1932
(courtesy of Marks & Spencer plc).*

learned the value of more imposing, commodious premises, modern methods of administration and the statistical control of stocks in relation to sales'. He learned how new accounting machines could speed up the flow of information. 'Hitherto, we had always been behind hand in our information, which was a formidable handicap'. He learned the value of 'counter footage, that is, that each counter foot of space had to pay wages, rent, overhead expenses and earn a profit'. He decided that Marks & Spencer had to study more exhaustively the goods they were selling, and the needs of the public, and to retrain their staff. {*ibid*, 142}

Thus Marks himself summed up the fruits of his American journey, though Sieff felt that 'what he had seen and heard only confirmed what he had thought out for himself. But the visit had been essential: it cemented his confidence in his own vision of what his policy should be' {*ibid*}. He also came back from the USA 'more than ever imbued with a general sense of the moral basis on which modern business should be conducted, so that all participants, management, employee and public, could benefit' {*ibid*, 143}.

In order to raise the capital to realise his ideas, the company had to be made public. The annual profits after tax of about £40,000 in the early 1920s were not sufficient to buy the freehold premises required for carrying out the policy of improving the stores, their position and layout. An approach in 1924 to an issuing house, the British Foreign & Colonial Corporation, met with a cool response, but in 1926, with the support of the Prudential Assurance Co (whose association with Marks & Spencer proved permanent), a public company was formed in 1926. The new public company of Marks & Spencer Ltd had an issued capital of £330,000 in 10s ordinary shares and £350,000 in 7 per cent cumulative participating preference shares. (Most of the Spencer family chose to sell their shares, part of which were taken up by the Marks family interests and the rest by the Prudential, and the Industrial Finance Investment Corporation.)

For many years Marks & Spencer have been widely regarded as something of a phenomenon in British business; arguably the most consistently successful of all British companies, a household name which relies on its reputation with shoppers rather than advertisements to fill its stores; an example of efficient and humane administration which has evoked admiration and much study by journalists, academics, other business leaders and politicians and Governments at home and abroad. It was Simon Marks whose ideas and ideals shaped the development of the company and whose energy and enthusiasm so fired those who worked with him that the company ethos he created survives twenty years after his death. He himself sometimes found it difficult to believe how completely his ideas had come to fruition. To him, the large, bright, airy stores, clean enough to satisfy even his obsession with hygiene, seemed like 'fairyland' {Rees (1969) 147}. He was delighted at the reputation Marks & Spencer goods enjoyed for consistent quality (one of his favourite cartoons showed a board of directors gloomily contemplating a chart showing their plummeting sales, as the chairman said, 'This may sound radical, gentlemen, but as we've tried everything else, why not try making a decent product?') and low prices. To help keep prices low, distribution of goods to the stores was made as simple as possible with manufacturers supplying goods directly to the individual shops. The relations established with their

of business, but was also expected to think about the business as a whole. Formal board meetings took place every six months, but the directors, departmental heads and store managers, met constantly. Simon Marks remained the undisputed head of the firm, though Sieff was his constant adviser, confidant and adjutant. Throughout Marks's career, Sieff was indispensable to him, and when in the early 1920s Sieff was based in Manchester and Marks in London, although they were in frequent contact, Marks became unhappy and, feeling the lack of his friend with whom he could discuss all his problems and ideas, declared he could not go on. Once Sieff became a full-time director of Marks & Spencer, and moved to London in 1926, Marks recovered his characteristic optimism and enthusiasm for the business.

Indeed, his 'whole life was bound up with the business. It was not that he could not relax or give himself to other interests, but that he saw Marks & Spencer as an integration of human life. He had a sense of harmony and essential human experience which he groped for in his daily life, sensing when enjoying the perfection of philosophy and art how far his work was falling short of his ideal' {*ibid*, 188-89}. Naturally dominating, aggressive by instinct, 'From the beginning ... desperate to show he could succeed' {*ibid*, 204} and taking intense pride in his achievements and the success of Marks & Spencer, Marks so 'tamed and controlled all this by a strict sense of duty' {*ibid*, 38}, that to those who did not know him intimately, he appeared 'to an extraordinary degree modest and unassuming'. {Rees (1961) 65} He could be impatient and high-handed to those around him, but never with his employees. He never lost his habit of visiting the shopfloors and storerooms of the branches, of seeing for himself that all was well. No detail of the business, he claimed, bored him.

To the end of his life he took intense interest in the design and quality of all the new lines that came into the stores, wishing to see and approve everthing personally. However he never lost sight of strategic goals in his attention to detail. He combined

> 'the instincts of the merchant with the flair of the financier and the ability to inspire men; he has spent much time in the stores and knows their personnel and the temper of the public; he has kept his finger on the pulse of every separate activity of the firm and yet at all times he has seen the business as an organic whole; he has known how to select able assistants and subordinates and he has worked harder than any of them. In short, during Sir Simon's career, the planning and coordinating functions of the firm have been successful largely because of the diverse and human qualities of this man. Lacking such a person, the history of the firm might have been quite different' {Dimock (1960) 166}.

As a consequence of the success of Simon Marks's policy of providing quality goods at the lowest possible price, Marks & Spencer, particularly in the 1950s, was seen as having brought about a minor social revolution. By making it possible for a shopgirl (so the comparison usually ran) to be dressed just as well (well, almost as well) as a duchess, the firm had helped to reduce class differences, and raise the self-esteem of the working classes. As Sir Leon Bagrit put it, he 'educated not only his suppliers but his customers to expect quality. Had there been no Simon Marks the likelihood is that the shoddy would have been equated with the cheap. He brought quality to vast masses and with it the elevation and self-respect that access to quality gives' {*Observer* 13 Dec 1964}. Again, his emphasis on the importance of integrating scientific research and a scientific approach into commercial processes was perceived as having consequences far outside the confines of his firm. When Marks was made an honorary fellow of the Royal College of Surgeons, Sir Archibald McIndoe, the plastic surgeon, said of him 'He is among the leaders who have brought the technician from the back room to the front room. He has built up a great firm not as a simple distributing agency for other people's goods but as a highly scientific organisation which is a model for all such industries in the world today. In this, his own field, he has provided a social revolution entirely due to his scientific outlook' {Rees (1961) 54-55}. The *Times* obituarist described Marks as 'one of the great formative influences in the social and economic life of England during the past generation' {*Times* 9 Dec 1964}. His contribution to the country was recognised by a barony in 1961, when he took the title of Lord Marks of Broughton. A distinction he was given the following year, the Tobe award for the most distinguished retailer, pleased him as much, particularly as it was the first time it had been awarded outside the USA.

Marks was made an honorary fellow of the Royal College of Surgeons, a rare distinction, in 1950, following gifts of over £150,000 to the College. His numerous charitable donations also included over £150,000 to University College, London — an honorary DSc (Economics) from the University of London in 1939 gave him 'transports of delight' {Sieff (1970) 40} — and £50,000 to Manchester Grammar School for new science laboratories. (He also received honorary LLDs from Manchester and Leeds Universities.) In 1963 he organised gifts totalling over £200,000 for the British Heart Foundation; he refused to accept the credit for this, saying he had merely acted as an agent. 'Rich men', he said, 'run away when they see me coming' {*Financial Times* 9 Dec 1964}, for he was convinced the rich should be generous and told them so. He himself enjoyed giving money away more than making it.

He was generous too in donations to institutions in the new state of Israel, for his commitment to Zionism was his principal interest in life, after his firm. He was made an honorary fellow of the Weizmann Institute of Science in Israel, and given an honorary PhD of the Hebrew University in Jerusalem. However, his British patriotism was as intense; he had a passionate conviction that British textiles were the best in the world, and was proud of the fact that almost all the goods sold in Marks & Spencer's stores were British made. His religion and his family were very important to him. His principal relaxations were the theatre, music, and his collection of Impressionist paintings, and he loved parties.

Marks married in 1915 Miriam, daughter of Ephraim Sieff and sister of Israel Sieff. They had one son, Michael, who joined Marks & Spencer for a short time only, and a daughter, Hannah. Lord Marks of Broughton died at Marks & Spencer's head office (it was said while examining a new line of merchandise) on 8 December 1964, leaving £1,830,935 gross.

CHRISTINE SHAW

MARKS Simon

Sources:

Unpublished

Marks & Spencer plc, archives, collection of press obituaries of Lord Marks.

PrC.

Published

Marshall E Dimock, *Administrative Vitality: The Conflict with Bureaucracy* (Routledge & Kegan Paul, 1960).

DNB.

Financial Times 9 Dec 1964.

Observer 13 Dec 1964.

Goronwy Rees, *The Multi-Millionaires: Six Studies in Wealth* (Chatto & Windus, 1961).

—, *St Michael: A History of Marks & Spencer* (Weidenfeld & Nicolson, 1969).

Israel Sieff, *Memoirs* (Weidenfeld & Nicolson, 1970).

Sunday Times Magazine 7, 14, 21 Oct 1984.

Times 9 Dec 1964.

K K Tse, *Marks & Spencer: Anatomy of Britain's Most Efficiently Managed Company* (Pergamon Press, 1985).

Chaim Weizmann, *Trial and Error* (Hamish Hamilton, 1949).

Margaret Wray, *The Women's Outerwear Industry* (Duckworth, 1957).

WWW.

Woodrow Wyatt, *Distinguished for Talent: Some Men of Influence and Enterprise* (Hutchinson, 1958).

MARQUIS, Frederick James

1st Earl of Woolton

(1883-1964)

Department store manager

Frederick James Marquis was born in Salford on 23 August 1883, the only son of Thomas Robert Marquis, a saddler, and his wife Margaret Ormerod. He had a thoroughly Mancunian education at Ardwick Higher

Grade School, Manchester Grammar School, of which he was later to become a governor, and Manchester University, where he studied mathematics, physics, chemistry and psychology (he would become Chancellor of the university in 1944). He obtained his BSc in 1906, but could not afford to accept the offer of a research fellowship in sociology, a burgeoning subject, at London University. Instead he became senior mathematics master at Burnley Grammar School and in 1908 assistant general secretary of the Co-operative Holidays Association, which had its headquarters at Colne. Taking up this second appointment he later described as the one wrong decision in his life. Fortunately for Marquis he found a more convenient niche for himself in Liverpool's dockland at the David Lewis Hotel and Club Association, part of a cluster of charitable organisations set up by the David Lewis Trust; and he soon added to this responsibility the wardenship of the University Settlement. In 1910 he was made a research fellow in economics at Manchester University and in 1912 obtained his MA. In the same year he married Maud, daughter of Thomas Smith, a mechanical engineer; she shared his enthusiasm for the settlement movement and worked closely with him in all his settlement activities.

Marquis was always practical rather than theoretical in his outlook, although he was deeply interested in the causes and consequences of poverty, including bad nutrition and infant mortality. He became a member of the Fabian Society, but resigned in 1917, following a change of views due to his wartime experience as a civil servant. Marquis was unfit for military service in 1914, and after a number of civil service jobs became Secretary of the Leather Control Board and later Civilian Boot Controller. This provided him with his first experience both of a large-scale organisation and of a control system. Yet, 'as the war went on, I became aware of the power exercised by civil servants and found it alarming. It seemed to me that they were living in a world apart from the rest of the country' {Marquis (1959) 47}. Marquis came to the conclusion that, with more abundant supplies, the control system was against the public interest, and resigned his post, at the same time resigning from the Fabian Society. Thereafter he was to put his trust in business as the great lever not only of economic but of social progress. There would be more boots — and cheaper boots — if there were no Civilian Boot Controller.

Having resigned, Marquis planned to return to the Liverpool Settlement, where his wife was still working. The then honorary secretary of the David Lewis Club, Rex D Cohen, a retailer, invited him instead to join Lewis's, the highly successful retail organisation founded by David Lewis (qv), which had several provincial branches. Marquis preferred, however, to stay with the boot industry and became secretary of a newly-founded federation of the industry, which had been formed with the purpose of maintaining internal goodwill between capital and labour and enhancing the external reputation of the industry. Already he was drawn to the service of what came to be called 'welfare capitalism'.

It was not until 1920, however, that Marquis became a practising businessman in the Lewis's organisation, and later in life he liked to tell the story of how he became the first non-Jew and the first non-member of the family to participate in the decision-making of what was already a thriving retail concern. He had already decided to visit the United States on behalf of the boot industry, when Rex Cohen invited him to accompany him on a series of business visits to American factories and retail stores; and at the end of the journey it was Marquis, not Cohen, who wrote the report for Lewis's. The day that he returned to Liverpool, Rex's father, Louis Cohen, a Liverpool alderman as well as head of Lewis's, repeated Rex's invitation to him to join the firm. 'This is the first time', he told him, 'that I have ever invited anybody not of my family and not of my faith [Marquis was a Unitarian] to join me' {*ibid*, 63}. At first, Marquis refused, but when he was satisfied that the younger members of the family would accept him, he agreed — for a limited period and on his own terms. He became a member of the board at the age of thirty-seven, and when the limited period, a period not without toils, was over, he stayed on in the business. By then Louis Cohen was dead, and his son Harold Cohen had become chairman.

Marquis brought to Lewis's — and to retailing — a social conscience, an immense capacity for work and outstanding qualities as an organiser. He proved also, once in the job, to have a keen financial brain. Even before the end of the short period of trial on which he had insisted, he had controversially changed pricing policy to reduce stocks and had been vindicated in his decision only after the end of the first quarter, for initially there was a heavy loss and Cohen had told his sons that Marquis would ruin the business. Marquis, however, won their confidence. Equally important, he won the confidence of a growing staff. He knew how to communicate and how to delegate and he knew also how to make the most of extended welfare schemes. Managers he chose himself; they included men of great ability, like R I McAlpine, who was to join the board in 1928, F C Hooper (qv), who was to move first into public life, then into other branches of business, John Tringham and S H Leake.

Below this level there was also a changed approach. General managers, key figures in the organisation, were given special training, specialists were appointed in such services as transport and food hygiene, and new assistants of every grade were fully informed about the maze of departments in which they found themselves and the basic principles on which Lewis's operated, some of them laid down by David Lewis himself in the nineteenth century. They were all told clearly that 'to enable you to know where you fit in relation to the other members of the staff you must first understand the main operation of this business organisation. The underlying idea is to bring the Producer and Consumer into the closest possible relationship' {Briggs (1956) 153}.

With a persisting interest in consumers as well as in shopkeeping, a product of his sociological concern and imagination, Marquis saw their relationship as a changing one. Retailing had to be brought up to date, both in its environment and in its range of goods and services; and in the vanguard had to be 'a new Lewis's'. A central publicity organisation was created in 1922, an interesting first step, and a year later a central buying office was set up in London, the first time that Lewis's had moved to the capital city.

To make further progress, there had to be structural reorganisation; and at the end of 1924 Lewis's was converted into a public company with an authorised, issued capital of £1,675,000 divided into cumulative preference shares and deferred ordinary shares, the latter remaining in the hands of the Cohen family.

Harold Cohen became chairman and remained so until his death in 1936, but it was Marquis who now provided the managerial drive. It was he, too, who insisted that additional capital, hitherto never sought outside the business, was required to finance an expansion of the enterprise. Beginning with a public issue in 1924 of £1.5 million of 5 per cent debentures, he did not hesitate to appeal to the public, and through this new source of funding it was possible to open new stores at Glasgow (1929), Leeds (1932), Hanley (1934), and Leicester (1936). In 1929, on the death of Rex Cohen, a holding company, the Lewis's Investment Trust, was set up in what now became an elaborate but effective institutionalised financial structure very different in style from the family housekeeping of David Lewis or the close, uncommunicative financial management of Lewis Cohen.

The new stores were as different internally and externally from the old Lewis's stores as was the new finance from the old. In Leeds the new store was a feature of a new Headrow building scheme, while in Glasgow the new store was located on a historic site, Anderson's Royal Polytechnic, with an even longer history than Lewis's in Liverpool. The Leicester store was smaller than the others, but more daring in its design. Marquis was proud of the fact that in a period of economic depression consumer expenditures in these stores, all of them centrally located, was rising and that, in his own words, the luxuries of yesterday were becoming the necessities of today. Some of the necessities bore brand names, another feature of what has been called a 'retail revolution': most had standard specifications. There were also new lines. Thus, bulbs, rose trees, and garden-ware became highly popular lines during the house building (and garden) boom which helped to pull Britain through the Depression. At the same time, in a quite different line of business, ladies' hairdressing — at far lower prices than in private salons — was introduced. There was also an expansion of food and catering services.

Marquis became joint managing director of Lewis's in 1928 and in 1936 he succeeded Harold Cohen as chairman. Meanwhile, he had become a member of a large number of national committees, showing a marked aptitude for business statesmanship. An active and effective president of the Retail Distributors' Association from 1930 to 1933 during the worst years of the Depression, he became chairman in 1934. In that year he joined the boards of the Royal Insurance Co, the Liverpool & Globe Insurance Co and Martin's Bank. He became Commissioner for Lancashire and the South East — one of three such statutory appointments for special areas of distress — and was a member of several important government committees during the 1930s. These included the influential committee on civil aviation chaired by Cadman (qv) and the Hailey committee on deep shelters and through this work he became well-known to politicians as well as to civil servants. In 1935 he was knighted, and four years later was given a barony, taking the title Lord Woolton.

The Second World War was to have an even bigger influence on Woolton's life than the First. In April 1939 he had been made honorary adviser on Army clothing, what he described as one of the most difficult of all his assignments, and in September 1939 he was appointed Director General of Equipment and Stores in the Ministry of Supply. Already he was being thought of for ministerial office, and in April 1940 he accepted

Prime Minister Neville Chamberlain's invitation to become Minister of Food, a difficult and challenging job which he retained under Churchill, when the supply position further deteriorated. It was in this capacity that he became known to his fellow countrymen, 'Uncle Fred' at his avuncular best. 'We not only cope' ran a motto over his door, 'we care'. Woolton's retailing experience was invaluable to him, although he was now coping with scarcity rather than with plenty and with control rather than with competition; and he forged a crucially effective relationship with his senior civil servant, Sir Henry French. He enjoyed communicating with the public, and would have preferred not to have been moved to the Ministry of Reconstruction in November 1943 and the War Cabinet in May 1945.

Although Woolton moved back to Lewis's at the end of the war and was chairman and managing director in 1951 when the company acquired its first London store, the famous Selfridges, it was through politics that he remained best known, serving in various posts in the Churchill Government of 1951-55 and ending as Minister of Supply (and Chancellor of the Duchy of Lancaster) by congenially winding up his own ministry. In 1945 he had joined the Conservative Party and for the next ten years served as its chairman. He saw his task as much that of increasing confidence as of oiling the machine, and he was rewarded by its return to power. Woolton had been made a CH in 1942, became a viscount in 1953 and an earl in 1956. He took all these honours in his stride. Yet it was always business which mattered to him most.

After the death of his first wife in 1961, he married in 1962, Dr Margaret Eluned Thomas. He had a son and a daughter from his first marriage. Lord Woolton died on 14 December 1964, leaving an estate of £407,790 gross.

ASA BRIGGS

Writings:

The Adventures of Reconstruction: Peace, Expansion and Reform. Selected Speeches (Cassell & Co, 1945).

Trade is Frustrated (reprinted from *Sunday Times*, 1945).

The Modern Conservative (Conservative and Unionist Central Office, 1948).

The Political Scene (Margate: Thanet Press, 1949).

The Memoirs of the Rt Hon the Earl of Woolton (Cassell, 1959).

Sources:

Unpublished

MCe.

PrC.

Personal knowledge.

Published

Asa Briggs, *Friends of the People. The Centenary History of Lewis's* (B T Batsford, 1956).

DD.

DNB.

Richard J Hammond, *Food* (HMSO, 1951).

Times 15 Dec 1964.

WWW.

Sir James Marr (courtesy of Mr J F Clarke).

MARR, Sir James

(1854-1932)

Shipbuilder

James Marr was born in Newcastle upon Tyne on 9 September 1854, the son of Christopher Hall Marr, and his wife Ellen (d 1906), the daughter of Archibald Bell, manager of the Ford Paper Works. One of James's brothers worked in a foundry and another in a shipyard as a bricklayer. At the age of fourteen James, after an elementary schooling, entered the pioneering iron shipbuilding yard of T R Oswald. In 1876, at the depth of the depression that finally closed Oswald's yard, Marr went to J L Thompson's shipyard, which had only begun iron shipbuilding five years earlier. Six years later Marr was appointed general manager, a tribute to his ability in what was very much a family shipyard.

In that year, 1882, the yard launched almost 28,000 tons of shipping, the highest on the River Wear. Output increased by 10 per cent in the next year and the yard maintained a leading position for many years. In 1887 James Marr, with other members of the shipyard as partners, purchased a forge at Pallion and established the successful Sunderland Forge & Engineering Co. In 1912 this works added the manufacture of electrical machinery to its activities. In 1894 Marr was appointed to the board of the shipyard, when J L Thompson & Sons became a limited liability company. Seven years later, in 1901, he became chairman and managing director. During the years 1904-7 Thompsons' annual ouput averaged about 46,000 tons. His success in the North East led to an invitation in 1909 to join the board of Laings, the famous Deptford shipyard. Laings was then in some difficulty, no ships being launched that year. His efforts to restore the

General view of the new Greenwell Dry Dock at Sunderland (courtesy of Mr J F Clarke).

company's fortunes resulted in an output of almost 26,000 tons in 1912, the year he was made chairman.

Marr played an important part in the organisation of shipbuilding production during the First World War, when he served on the Advisory Committee of the Ministry of Shipping; later he became a member of the Shipbuilding Council of the Admiralty. He helped to introduce the programme of building standard type ships. During the war years Laings completed almost 133,000 tons of shipping, including 12 oil tankers, and at Thompsons output exceeded 82,000 tons (only Doxfords had a higher output on the River Wear).

The onset of depression in shipbuilding was to test all Marr's managerial skills. Although in 1922 Laings launched 30,382 tons, the two ships built by Thompsons (12,196 tons) were well below half the yard's capacity. In the following year Thompsons built no ships and Laing's yard a mere 3,832 tons. Marr tried to support his allied companies, and his confidence was such that he built a large graving dock on the Wear for his repair company, T W Greenwell & Co Ltd, the electrical machinery being supplied by the Sunderland Forge Co. The same year, 1925, he set up the Silver Line Ltd, with a capital of £500,000, and very soon afterwards this company placed the largest order ever on the River Wear up to that time, for six motor cargo vessels costing £1 million. The order was divided equally between Laings and Thompsons for the ships, the Sunderland

Forge Co supplying the auxiliary plant and the engines being purchased from Doxfords. Even with orders from this new shipping line, in his later years Marr had to face no output from Laings in 1929, 1931 and 1932 and none from Thompsons in 1931 and 1932. There was, however, enough of a base created for the yards to restore their output when trade improved in the late 1930s.

In addition to the chairmanships already noted, he was chairman of the Wolsingham Steel Co Ltd and a director of the Wearmouth Foundry Co Ltd.

Marr was a very active member of the Wear Shipbuilders Association, of which he was chairman from 1912 to 1919. From the outset he represented Wearside on the national Federation of Shipbuilding Employers and played an important role in modifying local practices to suit a national policy. He normally took a tough line on labour relations matters. Marr joined the North East Coast Institution of Engineers and Shipbuilders in the year of its formation, 1884, and was elected to its Council in 1903; he was later a vice-president and fellow of the Institution. 'The first complete welfare scheme ... in the Sunderland district' {*Sunderland Echo* 24 Nov 1932} was established by him in 1922, with the opening of a recreation ground and institute for the apprentices in all his companies.

Created a CBE in 1918, James Marr became a baronet in 1919. He was an associate of the Institute of Naval Architects, a member of the Worshipful Company of Shipwrights and served on the management committee of Lloyd's. He was also a freeman of the City of London. Marr served as a JP in the County of Durham and was vice-president of the Sunderland Incorporated Chamber of Commerce. He was a Conservative in politics.

James Marr married Mary Abigail Ann (1855-1943), daughter of John Lynn, a papermaker of Hylton, Sunderland, in 1876; they had two sons and a daughter, Ellen. Their first son John Lynn died in September 1931, and John's son Leslie succeeded to the baronetcy. James Marr's younger son William Bell (b 1881) later became chairman of Sir James Laing & Co Ltd. Sir James Marr died on 24 November 1932, leaving an estate of £189,730 gross.

J F CLARKE

Sources:

Unpublished

Sunderland Public Library, Corder MSS.

Tyne and Wear Archives, records of the Wear Shipbuilders Association, J L Thompson & Sons Ltd, and Greenwell Dry Dock Co.

BCe.

MCe.

PrC.

Published

Shipbuilder 1932.

Victoria Embankment, 1906, the first major asphalt surfacing contract in the country, carried out by Trinidad Lake Asphalt Paving Co Ltd (courtesy of Wells (Trinidad Lake Asphalt) Ltd).

Marriott was also deeply involved in the technical requirements of using asphalt for building work, particularly roofing, flooring and damp-proofing. New problems were presented by airfield construction in the Second World War with the need to ensure suitable wearing surfaces for heavy bombers. Later he was able to supply electrically conductive flooring for hospitals to reduce the risks of explosion from flammable gases and static electricity. He was prominent in the establishment of the Asphalt Roads Association and especially in seeking to foster co-operation to raise standards of technical control.

Although many of the competing firms supplying coated macadam had built up close links with aggregate suppliers, Marriott's company disregarded their own sources of supply and even failed to take advantage of opportunities which presented themselves. In consequence they found themselves at a disadvantage in negotiations with suppliers, many of whom had developed their own coated macadam business.

The authorised capital of the Limmer & Trinidad Lake Co was increased from £200,000 in 1916 to £350,000 in 1920, increased again in 1924, 1939 and in 1951 to £1 million. In 1951 the chairman of the company, Lord Courtauld Thomson, who himself had been a director of the old Limmer Co, was able to report, 'This is the seventy-ninth successive year in which we have paid a dividend out of the profits earned in each of those years' {*Economist* 9 June 1951}. The company's undoubted success over many years no doubt brought about an element of complacency. Marriott, for example, refused, until forced by the success of his competitors, to use mechanical road finishers, preferring the spreading of asphalt by hand. When one of his plant supervisors asked for a mechanical shovel Marriott asked, 'What do you want that for?' {Oral, D C Broome}. On the other hand, he was able to inspire his staff by his knowledge and example.

Marriott was forced by ill-health to retire in 1954 after sixty years' service with the company. In the same year Bond died and the company also lost Lord Courtauld Thomson, who had been a director for fifty years and chairman for thirty-two. In 1971 the company was taken over by Tarmac (now, 1984, Tarmac PLC).

Marriott married in 1909, in the Strand Register Office, Gertrié Annette, daughter of Edwin John Jones 'of independent means' {MCe} and had one son and two daughters. Very little is known about his private life except that he was a generous benefactor of charities, particularly for the elderly. He was Master of the Worshipful Company of Paviors in 1936. Apart from his directorships of the Limmer & Trinidad Lake Asphalt Co and subsidiary asphalt companies, Marriott was also chairman of British Rototherm, Hutchinson Instrument Co, the Insulated Concrete Pipe Co, Roadways Equipment 1938 Ltd and a director of Safeway Products Ltd. He died on 26 July 1956 at Putney Hill, aged seventy-eight, leaving £86,790 gross.

FRANCIS GOODALL

Sources:

Unpublished

MCe.

PrC.

DCe.

Interview with D C Broome, June 1984.

Published

DD 1955.

J B F Earle, *Black Top. A History of the British Flexible Roads Industry* (Oxford: Basil Blackwell, 1974).

Economist 9 June 1951.

Stock Exchange Official Year-Book 1952.

Stock Exchange Year-Book 1921.

F C Marshall (courtesy of Swan Hunter Shipbuilders Ltd).

MARSHALL, Francis Carr

(1831-1903)

Marine engine designer and builder

Francis Carr Marshall was born at Bedlington, Northumberland, on 25 April 1831, the son of Joseph and Elizabeth Marshall; his family had for many generations worked a smithy and farriery near Felton. His father worked as a blacksmith at the Bedlington iron works of Michael Longridge & Co, but left there when Francis Carr was seven and moved to Newcastle upon Tyne, where he worked for the engineers R & W Hawthorn. After seven years at the Westgate Academy, run by a Methodist, Francis entered the Forth Banks Works of Hawthorns as an apprentice. Five years were spent in passing through the various workshops until his uncle George, formerly boiler yard manager at Forth Banks, paid the premium necessary for him to enter the drawing office, where design engineering was learned at this time. His wages were then 6s, having started at 2s. Marshall progressed well under the chief draughtsman R Morrison, who later established his own firm. During an illness of Morrison's successor J S Bell, Marshall took charge of the drawing office.

The death of his father in 1854 left Francis Marshall with responsibility for four sisters and a brother. Not long afterwards he moved to the post of chief draughtsman at the Spring Gardens Engine Works of Thompson & Wood (later Thompson & Boyd). His success there led in 1860 to the post of manager of the Marine Engine Works of Palmers at Jarrow, where the workforce was to increase substantially under his direction, reaching more than 900 by 1865. Marshall reorganised and equipped the works; the engine output included powerful engines for transatlantic liners. During 1866 he had to deal with a dispute linked with a demand for a nine-hour day, but it was Charles Palmer (qv) the owner who made the decisions and did not always support his manager.

When B C Browne (qv) was negotiating to buy Hawthorns in 1870, he sought Marshall as a partner to manage the design and building of marine engines, on the very attractive terms of £1,000 a year salary and a quarter share of the profits (after 5 per cent was paid on capital), to build up a holding of a quarter of the capital in the new company that was taking over the Forth Banks works. Marshall quickly displayed his value by securing 18 marine engine orders in the last six months of 1870. His efforts to increase efficiency by managerial changes led to labour troubles early in 1871 and later that year there was the Nine Hours Strike which seriously affected the new partnership. Marshall seems to have been unwilling to yield during this dispute; in later years Browne was always insistent that he himself should deal with labour matters, perhaps indicative of his realisation of Marshall's uncompromising stance on such issues.

Marshall's marine engine activity was based in the newly-erected and -equipped St Peter's Works. During the first five years an output of 9,320

Compound engine with Marshall valve gear (courtesy of Mr J F Clarke).

nominal horse power of engines, costing £461,600, resulted in an overall loss. However, after 1876 marine engine output was the main source of company profits, averaging more than £11,000 a year in the period 1876-80 and more than £26,000 in the years 1881-85, when marine engine turnover had nearly doubled. His capital holding in 1884 was £16,200.

It was Marshall who, during the summer of 1885, responded to the efforts of Arthur Coote of the Hebburn Shipyard of Andrew Leslie & Co to establish a limited liability company; together they sketched out a draft agreement and Marshall consulted the bankers. In the new public company R & W Hawthorn, Leslie & Co Ltd, which had an authorised capital of £600,000, Marshall was allocated 571 of the 5,400 £100 shares issued and was paid a salary of £3,200 a year. The relative size of this salary may be judged by the fact that the St Peter's Works averaged a balance on its profit and loss account of £18,600 for the years 1886-98. Apart from his role in leading design and production control, Marshall spent long periods in Russia negotiating orders, which were vital for the company's success.

Warship engines became a speciality of the St Peter's Works; one of the biggest customers was Armstrongs' shipyard. Marshall was instrumental in the formation of Società Industriale Napoletana Hawthorn Guppy, a company based in Naples which used designs prepared at St Peter's; Marshall was a director. In 1894 the output of the St Peter's works of 48,650 hp was the highest of any marine engine company in the UK.

Marshall became one of the leading marine engineers of his day, highly regarded for his originality, though he took out only three patents (the principal one was concerned with valve gear). He was an early and strong advocate of 'forced draught' as well as high-speed marine engines. He was particularly skilful at selecting able young men to work under him and took great care with their development as engineers.

Marshall joined the Institution of Mechanical Engineers in 1865, serving on its council twice, and the Institution of Civil Engineers in 1866. A member of the Institution of Naval Architects, he was elected to its council in 1885 and was a very regular contributor to their discussions. With W Boyd (1839-1919) he played a key role in establishing the North East Coast Institution of Engineers and Shipbuilders (the title was his proposal) in 1884 and served for many years on its council, being president, 1888-90. In 1882 he was the principal promoter of the North East Coast Exhibition of Naval Architecture and Marine Engineering.

Although he shared a Reform platform with his leading craftsmen while manager at Jarrow, he did not devote his energies to public life, but always described himself as 'a staunch radical'. He was a life-long Nonconformist, being described as one of the pillars of the Congregational Church at Tynemouth. He married Jane Alice Rowell. His only son Frank Theodore (b 1866) survived his father by just two years; two of his daughters married leading naval architects of the day. Marshall became seriously ill in 1896 and although he returned to work, he retired as a director in 1899 and was succeeded by his son, who already had charge of St Peter's Works. Francis Marshall died on 24 February 1903, and left an estate valued at £25,141.

J F CLARKE

Writings:

'Progress and Development of the Marine Engine' *Proceedings of the Institution of Mechanical Engineers* 1881.

(with R L Weighton) 'On High Speed Engines' *Transactions of the North East Coast Institution of Engineers and Shipbuilders* 2 (1885-86).

Presidential address in *ibid*, 1888-89.

British Patents:

1867 (2,278) (with H Stewart)
1879 (2,138)
1880 (4,185).

Sources:

Unpublished

Tyne and Wear RO, records of Hawthorn Leslie, and North East Coast Institution of Engineers and Shipbuilders.

Published

Edward Allen, Joseph F Clarke, N McCord and David J Rowe, *The North East Coast Engineers' Strike of 1871* (Newcastle upon Tyne: Frank Graham, 1971).

Joseph F Clarke, *Power on Land and Sea. A History of R & W Hawthorn Leslie* (Clark Hawthorn Ltd, 1979).

The Engineer 94 (1903).

Engineering 75 (1903).

Newcastle Chronicle 25 Feb 1903.

'The Jubilee of a Tyneside Engineer' *Newcastle Daily Leader* 17 July 1895.

Proceedings of the Institution of Mechanical Engineers 1903.

Times 26 Feb 1903.

Transactions of the Institution of Naval Architects 24-37 (1883-96), 45 (1903).

Transactions of the North East Coast Institution of Engineers and Shipbuilders 1884-1903-4.

Cecil Martin (courtesy of Mr J B F Earle).

MARTIN, Cecil

(1888-1985)

Road materials manufacturer

Cecil Martin was born at Huddersfield on 10 June 1888, the son of Fred Martin, a partner in a firm of fine worsted cloth manufacturers, and his wife Janet Louisa née Hanson, the daughter of an architect; his relations with them were always excellent. He was educated at Cheltenham College.

In 1908 he became a trainee with the Jermyn Street Motor Co, a car hire and motor repair firm. Martin worked in the motor repair shops in Stacey Street off the Charing Cross Road, where about a dozen men were employed. For the first six months he received no pay; for the second six months 10s a week. By 1914 he had advanced to being manager of a small London car firm, the LA Co Ltd of West London, which sold cars, including Hupmobile cars, imported from the USA. Here he earned £400 a year. In 1914 he married Isabel Katherine, the daughter of Victor Hickman, a member of the important West Midlands family of iron manufacturers. They had acquired the control of Tarmac Ltd in 1905 from its founder, E P Hooley, the county surveyor of Nottinghamshire, in order to find an outlet for their production of blast furnace slag at Bilston in Hooley's patent road-surfacing material, 'Tarmac'.

During the First World War, Martin joined the army with a commission in 1915 and was soon sent to France as a Motor Transport Workshop Officer. Shortly after the Armistice in November 1918, D G Comyn, the managing director of Tarmac Ltd, offered him a job as his assistant at a salary of between £500 and £600 a year. Martin's demobilisation was quickly arranged and he joined Tarmac Ltd (then quite a small company, with an issued capital of £136,000) early in 1919.

Tarmac Ltd flourished in the years immediately after the war. The profit, after tax, in 1918 was only £16,295 but by 1922 it was £84,261. In that year Martin, who had become general works manager, was congratulated on record outputs. The following year, he was appointed to the board.

Trouble, however, was right ahead. Prices were falling and the price of tar, largely as a result of the occupation of the Ruhr, was becoming very high. Comyn, relying on his undoubted skills as a salesman, would not increase prices, hoping to beat Tarmac's competition down. But profits tumbled, so that 1926 was the only year, in over seventy years of history, in which Tarmac Ltd suffered a loss (of £49,576). Comyn was, in fact, ill and in March 1926 he resigned. In April 1926 the board appointed Martin managing director, a position he was to hold for thirty-two years.

Martin's first step as managing director was to institute a policy of retrenchment; among other measures, directors' fees were halved and head office staff costs reduced by 20 per cent. The next year, despite continuing fierce competition in the tarmacadam trade, profits recovered, to £44,231;

average annual profits after tax for the years 1929-34 were about £45,000.

During these years, three important developments took place, in which Martin played a large part. In 1929 he convinced the board of the need to buy road transport for delivering Tarmac, instead of relying largely on rail, as hitherto. The new policy of road haulage was to a considerable extent financed by gradually selling off railway wagons, and culminated in 1936 in a decision to abandon a plan to build a rail-side plant at Brent to distribute coated slag from Corby in London and to buy instead 60 light lorries and deliver direct. The second policy was the adoption in the early 1930s of bitumen derived from petroleum refining as a binder for road material, a policy Martin encouraged. Thirdly, Martin was a leading figure in the development of price co-operation in the trade, a policy which his predecessor Comyn had always opposed. Once these developments were well under way, Tarmac's profits began to increase; the average annual profit after tax for 1935-39 was about £68,000.

During the Second World War coated macadam was much in demand, especially for airfield construction, and Tarmac was well equipped in the size and distribution of its works to benefit fully from the opportunity; average profits before tax, 1940-45, were about £235,000.

After the war, the board decided upon an ambitious policy of works reconstruction to cope with the anticipated increase in demand. New plants were built at Ettingshall and Acklam in 1949, the Corby plant was completely rebuilt and a new plant built at Scunthorpe in 1950. By 1953 over £2 million had been spent on reconstruction and mechanisation of existing works, and the acquisition of new contracting plant, while the transport fleet had been almost entirely renewed, and greatly enlarged. Profits before tax for 1946-52 averaged about £293,000. Much work was done for the Air Ministry in the rearmament programme from 1950. In 1954, Martin negotiated a major deal with Dorman Long, who proposed to construct two very large new furnaces at Teesport. He persuaded an initially reluctant Dorman Long to accept an offer from Tarmac for the whole slag output of their furnaces, having consulted major customers to ensure their orders would be forthcoming. New works were built to process the slag, together with a wharf which could take ships of up to 3,000 tons capacity. Profit during these final years of Martin's direction of the company averaged £681,000. Martin retired at the beginning of 1958.

Martin's period of office was not one of great expansion of road construction; that did not come until the first motorway was opened in 1959. His success was not due to luck nor, though it gave him his start, to his connection with the Hickman family. It was based on his character, coupled with a sound engineering background. Not particularly brilliant, he was immensely industrious. He was authoritarian, though he backed his chosen subordinates loyally, and no detail escaped him. In the industry he was respected and admired. His patience in negotiation was remarkable, especially in the early days of price associations, in which he strongly believed. His integrity was of a rare quality, and it enabled him to come to terms with hostile competitors, who by upbringing and training were ready to suspect everybody. Moreover, he would not let himself be diverted from his aims. The highest remuneration he received was about £27,000 a year, much being commission on profits.

Martin's outside directorships were in Hickman family businesses, including Haunchwood Collieries Ltd, of which he was joint managing director.

He has always been a very enthusiastic philatelist and ornithologist but also enjoyed field sports and other open-air recreations. He occasionally contributed to *The Field*.

Martin's wife died in 1953. They had four sons, of whom one, Robin G Martin, became chairman and chief executive of Tarmac in 1971. Cecil Martin died on 15 April 1985, aged ninety-six.

J B F EARLE

Writings:

Occasional contributions to *The Field*.

Sources:

Unpublished

BCe.

MCe.

Information from Cecil Martin.

Published

J B F Earle, *A Century of Road Materials: The History of the Roadstone Division of Tarmac Ltd* (Oxford: Basil Blackwell, 1971).

—, *Black Top: A History of the British Flexible Roads Industry* (Oxford: Basil Blackwell, 1974).

Times 22 Apr 1985.

MARTIN, Sir James

(1893-1981)

Aircraft ejection seat designer and manufacturer

James Martin was born at Crossgar, County Down, Ireland, on 11 September 1893, the only son of Thomas Martin, a farmer, and his wife Sarah. His father, an inventive man who designed farm implements and a bicycle, died when James was two years old and he was brought up with his only sister by his mother.

As a boy James was known for his inventiveness and as a young man he designed a three-wheel motor car. An interview at Queen's University in Belfast convinced him that he already knew more about engineering than he was likely to learn there, and so he joined his sister in London. By 1925 he had established his own vehicle-fabricating business at Acton. He began to race a Salmson car, surviving a crash in an Ulster Tourist Trophy race. In 1929 Martin formed a private company, the Martin Aircraft Co and moved to new premises in Denham, aiming to build simpler, safer, cheaper aeroplanes, which could be more easily produced. His staff consisted of two boy mechanics.

Between 1929 and 1946 five prototypes were constructed, but none went into production. Like F G Miles (qv), Martin's problem was that he was a radical and unorthodox designer who defied the bureaucracy and the profession. His first design, a monoplane, was never completed, for after three months the cash ran out. With new backing from a friend Martin built the less radical MB-1 which was successfully test-flown in 1935. Meanwhile in 1934 Captain Valentine Henry Baker joined the company as chief test pilot after teaching Martin to fly at the London Aeroplane Club before 1931; the company became Martin-Baker Aircraft Co Ltd. As the war approached, Martin designed the MB-2 fighter. First flown by Baker in August 1938 it was as fast as the Hurricane and simpler and cheaper to produce as well as easier to maintain. But it was not bought because the Martin-Baker Co was not a member of the Air Ministry approved list of firms, known as 'the Ring'. A fresh design, the MB-3, was developed, but on 12 September 1942 its engine failed just after take-off and Baker was killed. This deeply affected Martin, who began to search for a means of reducing pilot losses.

In 1940 he had begun supplying the RAF with the barrage balloon cable cutter, an explosive device fitted to the wings of bomber aircraft, enabling them to sever the cables of barrage balloons protecting enemy targets. During the Battle of Britain he developed a simple mechanism to enable pilots to jettison the cockpit canopies of disabled Spitfire aircraft so they could climb out and parachute safely. For use against the night Blitz bombers, Martin designed a special nose for the Douglas Havoc which carried 12 machine-guns, thus tripling the aircraft's firepower.

In 1944, he designed an ejector seat, again operated by an explosive device, which was successfully tested in flight in May 1945. By 24 July 1946 work had progressed so successfully that a live ejection was made from a Meteor doing 420 mph at 12,000 feet. Shortly after this, representatives of the US Navy visited Denham and before the end of the year an order was placed for Martin-Baker ejection seats for US Navy fighters. In June 1947 the decision was made to fit Martin-Baker ejection seats to British military aircraft and the company at last moved into production.

The earliest seat only ejected the aircrew member, who then had to release the seat and pull the ripcord of his parachute. It soon became evident that this was not adequate and Martin set to work on a fully-automatic seat in which the parachute was an integral part. In 1956, after a successful demonstration of ejection during take-off, the US Navy fitted all their carrier aircraft with British-made Martin-Baker ejection seats to save lives being lost at low level. Once the seats were installed there was a significant decrease in the fatality rate and a corresponding rise in the psychological health of carrier aircrew. At the same time, NATO air forces also decided to switch from unsatisfactory US-built ejection seats to Martin-Baker designs. Later developments included the successful evolution by 1960 of rearward-facing ejection seats, and a demonstration on 1 April 1961 of an ejection from a stationary aircraft on the ground.

For his work, Martin was awarded the Wakefield gold medal of the Royal Aeronautical Society in 1951, the Laura Taber Barbour Air Safety Award in 1958 (the first non-American to be so honoured), an OBE in 1950, CBE in 1957, the Cumberbatch Air Safety Trophy in 1959, and the Royal Aero Club gold medal in 1964. He was knighted in 1965, elected a liveryman of the Guild of Air Pilots and Air Navigators in 1966, awarded a DSc by Queen's University, Belfast, and made a fellow of the Institute of Science and Technology of the University of Manchester. He joined the Royal Aeronautical Society as a fellow in 1951 and was awarded an honorary fellowship in 1973.

Friendly and forthright, Martin got on well with his workforce. Though he frequently quoted from the Bible, he was not a churchgoer. He married in 1942 Muriel Haines; they had two sons and two daughters. A devoted family-man, Martin hated to be away from their home in Denham and never took a holiday. Sir James Martin died on 5 January 1981, leaving £815,493 gross.

ROBIN HIGHAM

Sources:

Unpublished

PrC.

Published

Bill Bedford, letter *Flight International* 12 Mar 1983.

Daily Telegraph 6 Jan 1981.

John Jewell, 'The Life and Work of Sir James Martin' *Aerospace* May-June 1982.

Times 6, 10 Jan 1981.

WW 1979.

MARTIN, Percy

(1871-1958)

Motorcar manufacturer

Percy Martin was born in Columbus, Ohio, USA, on 19 June 1871. He graduated at Ohio State University, Columbus, as a mechanical engineer (in electrical engineering) in 1892. He was president of the Class of '92, a staff officer in the OSU Cadets and an active member of Phi Kappa Psi, his fraternity. His involvement with the British motor industry began virtually by accident, when he was on holiday in England on his way back to the USA in 1901, after working as an engineer for General Electric in Milan and Berlin. In London he met H F L Orcutt, who had been asked by Sir Edward Jenkinson, chairman of Daimlers, to look for a suitable candidate as works manager at Daimlers, following the departure of J S Critchley for Brush. After an interview, Martin was appointed from October 1901 and continued with Daimlers and the amalgamated Daimler/BSA concern until his retirement in 1934. He became a naturalised English citizen.

Within a year of his appointment, the company had been turned round with a more rational model policy, Martin having designed and built new 12 and 22 hp cars. The financial reconstruction as the Daimler Motor Co (1904) Ltd was accompanied by continued royal patronage, the introduction of larger models, and competitive successes (Martin himself driving a Daimler into third position in the first Shelsley Walsh Hill Climb in 1905). By November 1906 Martin had become managing director, a position he retained for more than two decades. He was chairman of Daimlers from January 1934 to October 1935, retaining his seat on the board after retirement.

During the First World War the group's factories were all given over to military production, notably staff cars, lorries, tank and aero engines, and aeroplanes. Martin was made Deputy Controller of Petrol Engine Supply at the Ministry of Munitions early in February 1917 and given a seat on the Air Board. Later that month he was appointed Controller of Mechanical Transport, an office he held until departmental reorganisation in November of the same year. His role was advisory and allocatory, but his drive and engineering expertise found their scope in munitions manufacture in general, and engine production in particular, over the years 1915-18.

There were three major landmarks in Martin's career with Daimler/BSA, two of them drawing on his technical as well as his managerial skill and judgement. The first involved a fellow countryman, Charles Y Knight of Wisconsin, whose sliding or sleeve valve engine took the interest of Daimlers and was developed by them, much of the work being undertaken by F W Lanchester. The 'Silent Knight' engine which emerged and was marketed first in 1909 was more expensive to build and maintain than the poppet valve type, but it had the advantages of being smoother and quieter in operation, until engine design and fuel improvements removed its advantages by the early 1930s. Daimlers acquired the rights to exclusive manufacture in the United Kingdom and to export. Bird and Huttons Stott regard the adoption of the sleeve valve engine as a drain on Daimlers' resources, which therefore made the second landmark, the merger with BSA in 1910, something of a rescue operation for Daimlers. In contrast, St John Nixon considered that 1910 was an extraordinarily successful year for Daimlers, so that they merged with BSA from a position of strength. Daimlers certainly had something to offer BSA as car manufacturers and it is significant that Percy Martin became managing director of the reconstituted Daimler concern and one of three Daimler directors on the BSA board.

The third landmark in his career was a technical one, like the first. In 1929 Daimler/BSA acquired manufacturing rights in the Föttinger Hydraulic Coupling (Hermann Föttinger (1877-1945) was an engineer and hydraulics specialist): this gave rise to the Daimler fluid flywheel. Martin is credited with the adoption of the epicyclic (Wilson) gearbox in conjunction with the fluid flywheel, which for a short period had been introduced with the cone clutch and normal gearbox. According to his daughter, Martin was particularly proud of his part in the development and introduction of this technical improvement. It came near the end of a long and significant career in the British motor industry in which, as his daughter confirmed, work was the whole of his life.

Outside his firm, he was a member of the Ancient Fellowship of Cappers and Feltmakers of Coventry. In his personal life, Martin was one of a select number of Midland industrialists, including Siddeley and Dudley Docker (qqv), who chose to live in Kenilworth, conveniently situated five miles from Coventry. He bought Spring Farm in 1910, later adding the adjoining Camp Farm. When he retired in 1935, he devoted much of his time to improving his pedigree Guernsey herd. The estate remains in family ownership. Martin married in July 1902 a fellow American, Alice Helen Heublein of Hartford, Connecticut, whom he had met in Berlin while she was there on holiday; they had a son, John, and a daughter, Helen. Percy Martin died on 10 November 1958.

RICHARD STOREY

Sources:

Unpublished

Interview with Miss H Martin.

Information supplied by Ohio State University Archives.

Published

A Bird and F Hutton-Stott, *Lanchester Motor Cars* (Cassell, 1965).

Coventry Evening Telegraph 11, 17 Nov 1958, 16 Feb 1959.

Coventry Standard 23 Dec 1954.

St John C Nixon, *Daimler 1896-1946* (Foulis, 1946).

John Prioleau, *Forty Years of Progress* (Coventry: Daimler Co Ltd, 1936).

John B Rae, *The American Automobile. A Brief History* (Chicago: University of Chicago Press, 1965).

Brian E Smith, *The Daimler Tradition* (Transport Bookman Publications, 1972).

MARTIN, Sir Richard Biddulph

(1838-1916)

Banker

Sir Richard Biddulph Martin (from the Institute of Bankers 1879–1929 *Blades, East & Blades Ltd, 1929).*

Richard Biddulph Martin was born in London on 12 May 1838. His father Robert Martin (1808-97) was one of the fourth generation of Martins in the banking business at the Sign of the Grasshopper in Lombard Street, a business that traced its beginnings to Sir Thomas Gresham. His mother, Mary Ann Biddulph, was the daughter of John Biddulph, of Cocks, Biddulph & Co, a bank that was to merge with Martins in 1919.

Martin was educated first at a private school at Hardenhuish, a school of which in later life he did not think very highly. Thence he went on to Harrow and Exeter College, Oxford. He joined the family bank in 1861, and became senior partner in 1878.

In 1891, after an alarming involvement in the Baring crisis resulting from a widespread but quite unfounded rumour that Martins were in trouble too, the partners overcame their long-standing reluctance to accept limited liability, and Martin became the first chairman of the limited company, a position which he held until his death in 1916. As a limited company the bank's rate of growth increased, but, remaining still essentially a London bank, its expansion did not match that of the larger joint stock banks, which were extending their national branch networks. Thus, in the twenty years before Martin's death their deposits increased from £2.1 million to £4.3 million; in the same period Barclay & Co Ltd, with a comparable private bank ancestry, increased theirs from £26 million to £94 million. Two years after Martin's death the bank sought wider coverage through a merger with the Bank of Liverpool Ltd. (Many years later, in 1969, Martins were to merge with Barclays.)

Martin is remembered in banking history not so much for his chairmanship of the family bank as for his leadership of the movement for an Institute of Bankers. In 1877 he chaired the meeting of bankers that resulted in its foundation in 1879. His subsequent influence in shaping the new body was considerable. In particular, while fully recognising the importance of the professional qualification that its examinations would provide, he strongly and successfully resisted the suggestion that examinations should be the Institute's sole purpose: he urged that it should be for senior as well as junior bank staffs, and from the outset lectures and the presentation of papers, and the provision of a library, accompanied the setting of examinations as the Institute's objects.

The sympathetic interest of Sir John Lubbock (qv), probably the most influential banker of his time, was enlisted, and Lubbock became the first president when the Institute was established in 1879. He wanted to see the Institute adopt a broadly academic syllabus, but Martin supported the view, which in the event prevailed, that it should be technically based. Martin was first treasurer of the Institute, and held the office again from 1897 to his death. His great contribution was recognised in his election as Lubbock's successor as president, 1883-85.

Martin was a fellow of the Royal Geographic Society and of the Anthropological Institute (his brother recorded that two customers closed their accounts with the bank when Richard attended Darwin's funeral!); and he took a particular interest in the Royal Statistical Society, of which he was treasurer and, in 1906, president.

Active in public life, Martin was an MP for seventeen years, first as a Liberal, 1880-85, for Tewkesbury (a constituency for which the Martins had periodically provided members since 1741; the family home, Overbury Court, was there), and from 1892 to 1905 as a Liberal Unionist for Droitwich. He was a Lieutenant of the City of London and a JP for Kent, Worcestershire and Gloucestershire. He was an active member, and twice Prime Warden, of the Fishmongers Company, and as its representative served on the executive committee of the City and Guilds of London. He was created baronet in 1905.

His business interests included membership of the Council of Foreign Bondholders and directorships of the Sun Insurance Office, the Sun Life Assurance Society and the Notting Hill Electric Lighting Co. He was chairman of the Debenture Corporation, the Anglo-American Debenture Corporation, the Assets Realisation Co and the British Borneo Co.

His recreations were photography, of which he was an early master, archery and sketching. His work for charity included the treasurership of St Mark's Hospital for Fistula, the Royal Orthopaedic Hospital, the Childhood Society and the Association for Promoting the Welfare of the Feebleminded. He was honorary secretary of the Metropolitan Hospital-Sunday Fund.

Martin married in 1864 Mary Francis, only daughter of Admiral Richard Crozier, of West Hill, Yarmouth, Isle of Wight. He died on 23 August 1916, leaving no heir to his baronetcy, and an estate proved at £331,065 gross.

P E SMART

Sources:

Unpublished

SSRC Elites data.

MCe.

PrC.

Published

Edwin Green, *Debtors to their Profession. A History of the Institute of Bankers, 1879-1929* (Methuen, 1979).

Institute of Bankers, *The First Fifty Years of the Institute of Bankers 1879-1929* (Blades, East & Blades, 1929).

Times 24 Aug 1916.

WWMP.

WWW.

MASEFIELD, Sir Peter Gordon

(1914-)

Airline executive

Sir Peter Masefield (courtesy of Sir Peter Masefield).

Peter Gordon Masefield was born at Trentham, North Staffordshire, on 19 March 1914, the eldest of three sons of Dr William Gordon Masefield, CBE, MRCS, LRCP and his wife Marian née Lloyd-Owen. A physician and surgeon, Dr Masefield was then in general medical practice at Trentham and Stone, Staffordshire, but he later moved to Essex. Peter was educated at Homewood House Preparatory School near Colchester, Essex (1921-25), Brentwood School, Essex (1925-27), Westminster School (1928-29), Chillon College, Switzerland (1929-32) and Jesus College, Cambridge (1932-35) where he took an honours degree in engineering.

Peter Masefield began his career in the design engineering department of the Fairey Aviation Co Ltd at Hayes and Heath Row, Middlesex where he worked on the design of the Swordfish, Battle and Albacore aircraft. However, he stayed at Faireys for only eighteen months and in January 1937 joined the editorial staff of *The Aeroplane* where he came under the influence of the formidable C G Grey, an outstanding veteran journalist whose astringent writing had contributed much to aviation policy since its earliest days. He also learned to fly at this time and obtained a private pilot's 'A' licence in 1937. He was to keep this current for the next thirty-three years, during which his experience included flying with the RAF and the 96th Bombardment Group of the United States Eighth Air Force during the Second World War, participating in the London-New Zealand Air Race in 1953 and coming third in the King's Cup Air Race of 1964.

Following the outbreak of war in 1939, Masefield became technical editor of *The Aeroplane*. In 1940 he also took on the job of air correspondent of the *Sunday Times* and, in 1942-43, of the BBC. Later, as a war correspondent, he covered RAF and United States Army Air Force operations from the United Kingdom. He played a major role during the war years in convincing the Services of the importance of proper training in aircraft recognition. In the process, he founded and edited two widely-read journals — the private *Aeroplane Spotter* and the official Ministry of Aircraft Production *Inter-Services Journal on Aircraft Recognition*, of which he remained editorial committee chairman until the end of the war.

In 1943 Masefield gave up full-time journalism and became personal advisor on air transport to Lord Beaverbrook (qv) who, as Lord Privy Seal, had Cabinet responsibility for planning the United Kingdom's future civil aviation policy. As part of this job, Masefield was, until 1945, secretary of a War Cabinet Committee on post-war civil air transport. He was also secretary of the steering committee for British participation in the Chicago International Air Conference of 1944. He was appointed civil air attaché at the British Embassy in Washington at the end of the war, the first time such an appointment had been made. Late in 1945 he went from his new post to Bermuda to make arrangements for the crucial Bermuda Conference which was to set the pattern for the international regulation of air transport for the following thirty-five years. After discussing the Conference agenda with leaders of the British delegation who had arrived there, he returned to Washington to agree it with the State Department. Subsequently, as a member of the British delegation at the conference, he was a signatory of the historic agreement of 1946. In that year he also joined the United Kingdom delegation to the inaugural meeting in Montreal of the Provisional International Civil Aviation Organisation which later became ICAO, the United Nations' civil aviation body. In 1947 he returned to the United Kingdom to a senior planning appointment as Director General of Long Term Planning at the recently-formed Ministry of Civil Aviation. During this period, in addition to leading the UK delegation to the South Pacific Air Transport Conference and serving on several internal committees, he was chairman of the Ministry of Civil Aviation/Royal Aero Club Light Aircraft Committee (1947-48).

Two years later Masefield joined the state-owned British European Airways and, in October 1949, was appointed to the board and made chief executive under the full-time chairman, Lord Douglas of Kirtleside (qv). BEA had been formed three years earlier as a short-haul offshoot of British Overseas Airways Corporation, incorporating European services of RAF Transport Command and United Kingdom domestic services of several small private airlines. At this time, BEA badly need to be pulled together, rationalised and given a sense of purpose. Douglas and Masefield achieved this during the next six years, with the result that a loss of £2.75 million in 1949 had been turned into a profit in 1955, by which time BEA had established itself as Europe's dominant airline. The improvement was soundly based because profitable operations and BEA's strong competitive position were sustained for the following six years. Equally significant was that this was done while operating a succession of British aircraft developed and put into production largely at BEA's instigation. These include the Vickers Viscount — the world's first turboprop airliner and Britain's biggest civil aircraft export success.

Masefield left BEA in 1955 and joined Bristol Aircraft Ltd as managing director. Bristol at this time was hoping to repeat the success of the Viscount with its Britannia, the world's first long-haul turboprop transport. It failed for reasons of timing. The programme was late being launched and engine problems delayed development. Its potential useful life was, in any case, curtailed by the world's airlines' decision in the late 1950s to opt for jet propulsion. This was becoming economically viable, particularly on longer hauls, partly because of marked and sustained reductions in the price of fuel (in constant terms) which continued until the early 1970s.

By 1960, when Masefield left Bristol, moves were afoot under government pressure to consolidate the numerous United Kingdom aircraft manufacturers into two large groups. Masefield pursuaded the board of Pressed Steel Co Ltd, prosperous car body manufacturers of Cowley, who were at this time keen to diversify, that they should similarly consolidate manufacture of light aircraft which had been lagging seriously in Britain since the war, despite the country's earlier pre-eminence in this field. Masefield joined the Pressed Steel board and became managing director of a new subsidiary, Beagle Aircraft Ltd, formed out of an amalgamation of two existing United Kingdom light aircraft companies, Auster and Miles (founded by Frederick Miles (qv)). This attempt to launch a range of British light aircraft was terminated in 1970 after ten years of struggle against continuing losses, perhaps largely because a promised RAF order did not materialise, although the takeover of Pressed Steel in the motorcar industry and government retrenchment in the aircraft industry also played their parts.

In 1965 while still with Beagle, of which he became chairman in 1968, Masefield returned part-time to the public sector when he became first chairman of the new British Airports Authority. BAA was formed to take over from the Civil Service the running of United Kingdom airports. In this task, Masefield was faced with problems similar to those which he had tackled effectively in BEA twenty years before. His success during six years at BAA was recognised in 1972 with a knighthood. In 1971 he became chairman of Project Management Ltd and a director of Worldwide Estates Ltd and in 1973 he joined the boards of London Transport Executive and the Nationwide Building Society.

Masefield returned to aviation in 1975 when he joined the board of Caledonian Airways Ltd, the holding company of British Caledonian Airways and of a number of associated companies. As the largest private enterprise airline in the United Kingdom, British Caledonian is the designated British flag carrier on a worldwide route network. Masefield became joint deputy chairman of Caledonian Airways in 1977 and deputy chairman of the Caledonian Aviation Group plc in 1981 — where he played a major part in the discussions which led to the Government's White

Paper and policy decisions on a new deal for British air transport in 1984.

In 1980, after eight years on the board, Masefield was appointed full-time chairman and chief executive of London Transport. There was a good deal of public criticism of its board at that time and staff morale was low. Masefield accepted the job on a short-term basis, but by the time he handed over in 1982 he had pulled the organisation together and had significantly improved its finances, its morale and efficiency. In that year he became a non-executive member of London Transport International.

Throughout his career, Masefield was unusually active in support of professional and learned societies and similar institutions. His honorary appointments included presidency of the Aircraft Recognition Society, 1947-55, Institute of Transport, 1955-56, Royal Aeronautical Society, 1959-60, Ultra-Light Aircraft/Popular Flying Association, 1948-54, Institute of Travel Managers, 1967-70, Association of British Aviation Consultants from 1973 and Institute of Road Transport Engineers, 1979-82. He was chairman of the National Joint Council for Civil Air Transport, 1950-51, of the Aviation Committee of the Royal Aero Club, 1959-65, of the Club itself, 1968-71, of the Royal Society of Arts, 1977-79, of the Board of Trustees of the Imperial War Museum, 1977-78 and of the board of governors of Reigate Grammar School from 1979.

In addition, he was a member of several important committees including the Transport Aircraft Requirements Committee, 1951-55, Aeronautical Research Council, 1958-61, Cairns Committee on aircraft accident investigation, 1960, Council of the Business Aircraft Users' Association, 1961-70, Council of the Society of British Aerospace Companies, 1962-69, Cambridge University Appointments Board, 1976-79, and *HMS Belfast* Trust from 1978. He is a liveryman of the Guild of Air Pilots and Air Navigators and a freeman of the City of London. In 1977, he was awarded honorary doctorates by the Cranfield Institute of Technology and Loughborough University of Technology.

Although ceasing to be a full-time journalist during the war, Masefield has written and published innumerable articles, papers, reports, lectures and one book, *To Ride the Storm*, a full length historical study of the 1924-30 British airship programme. As one would expect, his writings have been mainly on aviation but have also, in some depth, covered the subjects of transport, management and the First World War.

During a remarkably diversified career, most of which has been spent in aviation in both private and public sectors in aircraft design and manufacture, in government service and in the airline industry, Masefield has displayed exceptional imagination, energy, enthusiasm, application and willingness to accept new challenges. An effective leader, he has a flair for getting on with people. Some of his undertakings were more successful than others. He contributed significantly towards getting world air transport organised on realistic lines immediately after the Second World War. His partnership with Lord Douglas in British European Airways demonstrated that a state-owned airline, using exclusively British equipment, could be profitable and competitive. His support for the Viscount contributed to the launch and large exports of Britain's most successful airliner. Bristol Aircraft and the Britannia were less successful for reasons mainly beyond his control. Beagle was a gallant failure in which imagination and enthusiasm proved a handicap rather than a help. However, determination and tenacity did keep the struggle going for more than ten years in the face of overwhelming difficulties. British Airports was a success to which his BEA experience probably contributed materially — as it was to do once again, on a wider canvas, with London Transport.

Few indeed played a larger or more diverse role in British aviation than Peter Masefield during the quarter century following the Second World War. Moreover, as a technical journalist with ideas which he could lucidly express and explain and in such posts as chairman of the Graduates and Students Section of the Royal Aeronautical Society, he started from an early age in the 1930s to influence the course of British aviation. That influence has now been sustained for more than fifty years so that in the 1980s, as an 'elder statesman', he still contributes much valuable forward thinking to his wide range of aviation and other interests.

In 1936 Sir Peter married Patricia Doreen, third daughter of Percy H Rooney, a company director, of Wallington in Surrey. They have a daughter and three sons, eleven grandchildren, and three great-grandchildren.

PETER W BROOKS

Writings:

A full list of Sir Peter Masefield's publications is held in the *Dictionary of Business Biography* files.

To Ride the Storm—The Story of the Airship R101 (William Kimber & Co, 1982).

Sources:

Unpublished

BCe.

MCe.

Private information.

Published

Flight Directory of British Aviation 1983.

WW 1984.

MASHAM, Lord Masham of Swinton
see LISTER, Samuel Cunliffe

Hugh Mason (courtesy of Mr E A Rose).

MASON, Hugh

(1817-1886)

Cotton manufacturer

Hugh Mason was born at Stalybridge, Cheshire, on 30 January 1817, the third and youngest son of Thomas Mason and his wife Mary Woolley née Holden. Some four or five years later, Thomas took advantage of a boom in the cotton industry to begin cotton spinning in nearby Ashton-under-Lyne; he was familiar with this trade, having worked in a cotton factory as a child. From very small beginnings, financed probably from the profits of his wife's smallware shop, Thomas built up a prosperous concern in which his sons took their place as they reached maturity. As a child, Hugh worked a thirteen-hour day with his father in the factory and then spent two or three years at a private school in Ashton before entering a local bank at the age of fourteen. In 1838 he joined the family business and soon became the dominant influence, as a result of his immense energy, enthusiasm and, it must be said, domineering personality, which made him reluctant to work side by side with others. Characteristically, in McLachlan's picture of the Cotton Famine Relief Committee, he is shown perusing papers, aloof from the remainder of the board. 'The father was industrious but he did not possess his son's enterprising spirit. Thomas was inclined to cling to old fashioned ideas, whereas Hugh was never many weeks behind adopting the most improved and serviceable machinery' {*Ashton Reporter* 6 Feb 1886}.

Consequently it seems likely that Hugh Mason was the leading spirit in the firm's decision to abandon rented premises and build both mills and houses in Oxford, a district in the west end of Ashton-under-Lyne, alongside the Manchester-Ashton canal. The two Oxford Mills were built in 1845 and 1851, and a colony of workers' houses started in 1845 which was extended at intervals over the next fifty years until a total of 150 houses had been built around the mills. His brothers retired in 1848 and 1853 and so Hugh became sole proprietor on the retirement of his father in 1860. During the next twenty-five years he proved to be a most successful cotton spinner, often during times of great economic difficulty. No short time was worked during the cotton depression of the 1870s and 1880s and still more remarkable, Masons was one of a handful of concerns which worked full time throughout the cotton famine of 1861-65, the only one to do so in the Ashton area: '... when all others had ceased, his mill still worked on, when the solitary black wreath round the chimney top ... proclaimed the forethought and the kindness of the man who kept peace and plenty in the cottage homes that nestle at its base' {Ashmore and Bolton (1975) 46}.

Spindleage grew steadily, from ca 20,000 in 1846 to 75,000 by 1887. Some expansion of the workforce took place in the early phases of this growth, but by 1861 it levelled out at about 375 to 400. Thereafter growth was achieved by the introduction of self-acting mules and more efficient

Oxford Mills, Ashton-under-Lyne (courtesy of Mr E A Rose).

machinery which was reflected in an increase in the ratio of spindles to employee. Much but not all the firm's output was for sewing thread.

Mason's approach to his workforce was strongly paternalistic, expressed chiefly through the provisions made at the Oxford colony. The site was well drained and carefully laid out with high quality housing graded in size and external ornament. In 1860 a library and reading room was erected, superseded in 1868 by a larger Institute, complete with swimming bath and followed in 1870 by a recreation ground and children's playground. Social provisions included sewing classes, lectures and a band making the Oxford Mills 'the centre of a higher civilisation than prevails generally in the Ashton and Stalybridge district' {*City Jackdaw* 3 Dec 1875}. Wages were higher than in neighbouring mills and advances were generally unsolicited. Although Mason had not approved of the Ten Hours Act, he later came to favour shorter hours and in January 1871 was the first local employer to close his mill at noon on Saturdays. It was said he would not employ a man who was unfaithful to his wife. This paternalism produced a stable, high quality workforce, bound together by a strong sense of loyalty to their employer — an important factor in enabling the firm to hold off emerging competition from the Oldham district limited companies.

Mason's energy also found expression in wider fields. As chairman of the Manchester Cotton Co set up in September 1860 to encourage the use of Indian cotton, he was a bitter and outspoken critic of the India Office, while for three years (1871-74) he was president of the Manchester Chamber of Commerce, where his pugnacious self-righteousness made him unpopular with other cotton employers, particularly those less efficient than himself. His moralistic tendency came out again in his chairmanship of the Steam Users' Association, where he implied that every boiler owner outside its membership was morally responsible for manslaughter. In addition to his cotton interests, he was chairman of the Society for Promoting Scientific Industry, a director of the Bridgewater Navigation, director of the Midland Railway, a member of the Mersey Dock Board and chairman of the Nantyglo & Blaina Ironworks & Coal Co.

His parents were convinced Nonconformists and Hugh attended Methodist New Connexion Sunday Schools in Stalybridge and Ashton-under-Lyne, a background which gave him early training in public speaking in addition to contributing to a markedly puritanical outlook. In 1846 he joined Albion Congregational Church, Ashton-under-Lyne, which numbered among its congregation several millowners, one of whose daughters he married in the same year. Thereafter he remained a faithful member, holding office as deacon and treasurer until his death. Such a background led naturally to a Liberal alignment in politics. Mason dominated the Ashton-under-Lyne Borough Council during the period 1856-74, when there was a permanent Liberal majority, and served a three-year term as mayor in 1857-60. The local Liberal Association was in his pocket and from 1880 to 1885 he served as MP for Ashton-under-Lyne, one of a small group of extreme radicals, and spokesman for part of that time for the Women's Suffrage Association. A founder member of the Manchester Reform Club, the two principal streets of his factory colony were named after Liberal politicians: John Bright and Milner Gibson. He gave generously to a wide variety of Nonconformist chapels and causes, notably to the Liberation Society, formed to secure disestablishment of the church, and the United Kingdom Alliance, the spearhead of the temperance movement.

Hugh Mason was married three times: first in 1846 to Sarah Buckley (1823-52), a daughter of Abel Buckley of Ryecroft Mills, Ashton-under-Lyne; secondly in 1853 or 1854 to Betsey (1830-61), his deceased wife's younger sister; and thirdly in 1864 to Anne Ashworth (1821-1901), whose father George Ashworth, was a leading woollen manufacturer of Rochdale and principal backer of the *Rochdale Observer*. Only the four children of the second marriage survived their father, the two sons, Rupert and Sidney, assuming control of the firm. Hugh Mason died at his home, Groby Hall, Ashton-under-Lyne, on 2 February 1886, leaving a personal estate valued at £290,933.

E A ROSE

Sources:

Unpublished

PrC.

Published

Owen Ashmore and Trevor Bolton, 'Hugh Mason and the Oxford Mills and Community' *Transactions of the Lancashire and Cheshire Antiquarian Society* 78 (1975).

Ashton Reporter 6 Feb 1886.

Winifred M Bowman, *England in Ashton-under-Lyne* (Altrincham, Cheshire: John Sherratt & Son, 1960).

City Jackdaw 3 Dec 1875.

William H Mills, *Grey Pastures* (Chatto & Windus, 1924). In this collection of essays Henry Stonor of Granite Hall is based on Hugh Mason.

—, *The Manchester Reform Club 1871-1921* (Manchester: pp for the Manchester Reform Club, 1922).

Nonconformist 4 Feb 1886.

WWMP.

MASON, Sir Josiah

(1795-1881)

Pen manufacturer

Sir Josiah Mason (from Hand and Heart. Church Herald and Review *24 June 1881).*

Josiah Mason was born at Kidderminster, Worcestershire, on 23 February 1795, the second son among three sons and one daughter of Josiah Mason Sr, a carpet weaver, and his wife Elizabeth née Griffiths. His elder brother William was a chronic invalid and to augment the family income Josiah Jr in his early years went round the town selling cakes and bread made by his mother and a local baker. By the time he was fifteen he was also selling fruit and vegetables door-to-door. He then sought regular employment permitting him to stay at home to look after his elder brother. He tried shoe-making and, in turn, shopkeeping, baking, carpentering, blacksmith's work, house-painting and eventually in 1814 his father's trade of carpet weaving. Meantime he attended the Unitarian Sunday School at Kidderminster Old Meeting (Richard Baxter's chapel in the seventeenth century) and afterwards the Wesleyan Sunday School where he learned to write and gained a reputation as a 'mender' of quill pens.

Finding carpet weaving wages depressed, after two years he visited Birmingham where his uncle, Richard Griffiths, a clerk in Gibbins's glassworks, had a small gilt toy (fancy imitation jewellery) business. Josiah fell in love with his cousin, Anne Griffiths, married her at Aston Church on 18 August 1817 and, after living in his uncle's house for a while, managed Griffiths's gilt toy business in Legge Street. After six years, in which Josiah's craft, skills and salesmanship enabled the business to flourish, it was sold in 1822 without Josiah's knowledge, to get his uncle out of 'difficulties with a working partner' in the glassworks. {*Birmingham Daily Post* 17 June 1881}

Josiah refused to serve the new owner. He had been expecting a partnership with his uncle. Almost immediately Heeley (member of an old Birmingham family, leading Wesleyan, and attender at Belmont Row Wesleyan Chapel where Josiah taught in the Sunday School) introduced him to Samuel Harrison (d 1833) who had a business in Lancaster Street where he made split steel rings. Harrison, shortly to retire, was looking for someone to take over his business. Mason, then with savings of £20, moved into his house and twelve months later in 1824 bought the business for £500, in five £100 instalments paid between August 1823 and May 1824. He devised machinery for bevelling hoop rings which gained him £1,000 from increased production in 1825.

Some of the earliest steel pens had been made by Samuel Harrison for his fellow Unitarian Dr Joseph Priestley but were hand-made and produced with difficulty. By the late 1820s about half-a-dozen manufacturers of steel pens existed in Birmingham, all using manual techniques. Split rings and steel pens had one common feature, a slit in metal. Josiah Mason spotted this in 1829 when he saw a card of steel pens on sale in a Birmingham bookshop window and took a sample home to copy. The manufacturer of the steel pen, James Perry of Red Lion Square, London (formerly of Manchester), made his pen slits by cracking the steel with a hammer. Josiah Mason (and at about the same time Joseph Gillott and John Mitchell) applied machinery using the press-and-die method of cutting the slit. Mason sent a sample pen to Perry and immediately became Perry's supplier, the pens being sold under Perry's name. In 1829 Mason was despatching 20 or 30 gross at a time and employed 12 people in his Lancaster Street works making split rings and pens. In 1831 he produced £1,421 of pens for Perry. Over the next fifty years the extension of educational opportunity by state-aided denominational school societies (though limited), together with the growth of popular literature, the Penny Post and the record-keeping demands of industrial society, were the major components in creating demand for writing pens. By 1850 'the best barrel pens, which had once cost 5s each, could be sold wholesale for a penny, and the best nibs for six a penny'. {Gill and Briggs (1952) 302}

In the 1850s Isaac and William Smith (Mason's nephews) joined the firm, developed new pens and marketed Mason pens through A Somerville & Co in Europe. In 1858 the firm was making over 50 million pens a year. By 1874 the firm was rolling over 150 tons of steel a year to produce 225 million pens, and employed nearly 1,000 people: the largest penmaking business in the world. In the interests of his employees and their efficiency Mason paid particular attention to organisation and working conditions: 'in his works large, lofty, well-ventilated, and well-lighted shops were provided, so that no injury might be caused to the health of the thousand people — men, women and children — who worked in the pen factory. Cleanliness was enforced: each department had its special washing places and other conveniences; good order was secured, not only by careful superintendence but by particular arrangments for such seemingly trivial matters as the hanging up of the clothes of the workers, and the provision of cooking places' {Bunce (1890) 249}. His factory worked like a hive with Mason aiming at excellence and industry: '"I will have no drones" was a favourite maxim with him' {*ibid*, 251}.

Between 1842 and 1856 Mason was also a partner with the brothers George Richards Elkington (1801-65) and Henry Elkington (1810-52) who, with J Skirrow, developed a process for the electro-plating of copper with gold and silver. Mason injected capital into the enterprise and supervised the construction of showrooms and workshops in Newhall Street and a factory for plated spoons and forks in Brearley Street. Warehouses and showrooms were later set up in London and Liverpool, with agencies covering country districts. Mason and George Richards Elkington vertically integrated by establishing a copper smelting works at Pembrey, Carmarthenshire in South Wales (where Mason set up a school for several hundred children) to work a patent taken out by Alexander Parkes (1813-91) the chemist and metallurgist. By 1860 Elkingtons employed 800 people and was firmly established as the leading EPNS and silverware company in the country. Mason also established a nickel refining business.

Mason sold his pen and split ring making business to the limited liability company, Perry & Co, formed in 1875 with an authorised share capital of £500,000 (£210,865 issued by 1880) and debenture capital of £60,000; dividends paid 1876-80 were $7\frac{1}{2}$ per cent annually.

Josiah Mason had no business interests outside his firm except the chairmanship of the Birmingham Banking Co, formed in 1866, which he reluctantly took in order to erase the failure of a former company.

The self-effacement Josiah Mason practised in business — his pens were never marketed under his name — he continued as a philanthropist. Genuinely fond of children but childless, and mindful of his crippled brother, Josiah Mason in late middle age decided to set up an orphanage. In 1858 he built at Erdington (where he had taught in the Wesleyan Sunday School) an almshouse for 30 women and an orphanage for 30 girls. This only whetted his appetite and he planned a bigger project. In view of sectarian differences among the clergy he set up a non-sectarian institution and carried out the scheme almost unaided. The second orphanage, also at Erdington, was started in 1860 and opened in 1868, eventually at his death accommodating 300 girls, 150 boys, and 50 infants, without restriction of locality, class, creed or legitimate birth. (Among the early orphans was Horatio Bottomley (qv).) It cost £60,000 to build and Mason endowed it with £200,000. In recognition of this princely philanthropic gesture Josiah Mason was knighted in 1872.

With the orphanage open, he decided to employ the rest of his wealth in creating some appropriate educational institution. His legal adviser, G J Johnson, and several others suggested a Science College, to match those of Manchester and Liverpool in the federated Victoria University launched by industrialists spurred by foreign competition. Mason founded the college 'being deeply convinced from his long and varied experience ... in different branches of manufacture of the necessity and benefit through systematic scientific instruction specially adapted to the practical mechanised and industrial pursuits of the Midland district'. {Sanderson (1972) 69, quoting the foundation deed of 12 Dec 1870} The college was built between 1875 and 1880 (and became the first independent civic university in 1900 through the work of Joseph Chamberlain (qv)). Mason met the £60,000 costs of the building and the total amount of his foundation came to £200,000.

In private life Mason was frugal and unblighted by a sectarian spirit. He held no public office. Sir Josiah Mason died on 16 June 1881 and was buried under the mausoleum erected in the Orphanage grounds in memory of his wife, who died in 1870. He left a personal estate valued at £56,729. Management of his great institutions passed to the Birmingham Town Council (both buildings are now demolished).

DAVID J JEREMY

Sources:

Unpublished

PrC.

Information from Mrs Barbara M D Smith.

British Patents:

Joseph Gillot 1831 (6,169), John Mitchell 1842 (9,514), James Perry 1830 (5,933), 1832 (6,215), Alexander Parkes 1850 (13,118).

Published

Birmingham Daily Mail 17 June 1881.

Birmingham Daily Post 17, 27 June, 9 July, 4 Aug, 1 Sept 1881.

John T Bunce, *Josiah Mason. A Biography* (W & R Chambers, 1890).

Burdett's Official Intelligence 1882.

DNB.

Conrad Gill and Asa Briggs, *History of Birmingham* (2 vols, Oxford University Press, 1952).

David Owen, *English Philanthropy, 1660-1960* (Cambridge, Massachusetts: Belknap Press of Harvard University Press, 1965).

Michael Sanderson, *The Universities and British Industry, 1850-1970* (Routledge & Kegan Paul, 1972).

VCH Warwickshire 7.

MATHER, Sir William

(1838-1920)

Mechanical and electrical engineering company chairman

William Mather was born in Manchester on 15 July 1838, the son of William Mather, a Salford machine maker (whose father, Colin Mather, had come to Manchester from Montrose and set up as a machine maker) and his wife Amelia, daughter of James Tidswell of Manchester. He attended a private day school near Salford until the age of twelve, when he was apprenticed at his own request for three years at the Salford Iron Works, part of which were leased by his uncle, Colin Mather. By 1852,

Sir William Mather (courtesy of Dr H E Coles).

Colin Mather had entered into partnership with William Platt, whose family owned the Salford Iron Works.

After following the rigid discipline of the works apprenticeship, at the age of fifteen William Mather returned to boarding school in Accrington, and was later tutored in Germany. He returned from Germany in 1855 to complete his works apprenticeship while continuing his theoretical studies at night classes.

In 1858 William Mather became assistant manager at the works which manufactured boilers, pumps and textile printing machines. He made business trips abroad to Holland, Belgium, Germany and Austria, laying the ground work for his eventual partnership with his uncle, Colin Mather and William W Platt in 1863. His first visit to Russia was in 1860, and in ensuing years he built up a very prosperous outlet for textile equipment. A competent engineer (he became a member of the Institution of Mechanical Engineers in 1867) he invented many pieces of equipment for textile finishing, notably the Mather-Kier, a chamber for the bleaching of fabrics, and was an authority on artesian well-boring for water supplies.

William Mather's other interest as a very young man was education. On assuming the responsibilities of the employer of a large engineering workforce, he determined to make the education of the people one of his prime concerns in his public life. The firm had a record of concern for technical instruction: Mather & Platt was one of the subscribers to the new building of the Salford Mechanics' Institute in 1852, and William Wilkinson Platt and Colin Mather were both active in the committee of the organisation; Colin was vice-president. In 1866, William Mather started a Mutual Improvement Society for his apprentices; and in 1873 started the Salford Iron Works Evening Science School for them. This proved to be successful, and other subjects were added to the course. The works' school was established at a time when few private institutions of its kind existed in this country; it continued until 1969.

Electrical equipment manufacture by Mather & Platt was introduced by William Mather following a visit to the United States of America in 1883 and after he had made an arrangment with Thomas A Edison to build and market the Edison dynamo in Britain. Mather & Platt was the first firm of mechanical engineers to expand into the new electrical industry. In 1894 Dr Edward Hopkinson joined the firm from Siemens and took charge of electrical-machine manufacture. It was under his direction that the application of electricity in industry and traction was pioneered.

In 1889, Mather & Platt undertook the contract for the electrical equipment for the City & South London underground railway. This was then the deepest railway system in London, built with the use of the tunnelling shield of J H Greathead (qv) and after it was equipped with electric traction and opened in December 1890 it became the first electric 'tube' railway in the world in the sense of having a line with defined stations and a signalling system.

Mather & Platt developed the steam-ager (1876-79) and the chain-merceriser (1898). It diversified its interests and manufactured a very wide range of products such as pumps, electrical motors, textile machinery, food manufacturing machinery and fire engineering equipment (the latter after Mather met Frederick Grinnell, who agreed to let the company manufacture his sprinkler from 1883), yet over the years it gained an

Advertisement showing Mather & Platt's productions, made for use at the Manchester Exhibition.

international reputation and sustained business success. The number of employees increased from 300 in 1863 and 600 in 1873 to about 4,000 in the early 1900s. The firm became a private limited company in 1892 and was amalgamated with Dowson, Taylor Co Ltd, in 1899 with a capital of £800,000. Outside the company, Mather founded the Chloride Electrical Storage Co Ltd in 1891 and promoted the Castner-Kellner Co Ltd in 1895.

William Mather continued to be interested in technical education. He accepted the position of special commissioner of the Royal Commission on Technical Education set up in 1881, agreeing to make investigations in the United States of America and Russia at his own personal expense. He donated prizes, equipment and workshops in educational institutions for manual training. Mather published a number of pamphlets on technical education and labour relations.

Mather recommended his employees to join trade unions and as a result the firm maintained good industrial relations. (The company never joined the employers' organisation.) Consultation with the works' employees took place before changes were effected in conditions of employment. Mather &

Platt was a family firm which tended to be paternalistic. During the industrial conflict of the 1890s over the eight-hour day it was William Mather who considered that the shorter working day was just, and could be made to be efficient. He devised a scheme for a forty-eight hour working week on a year's trial in 1893. In 1897 Mather acted as mediator in the engineers' national dispute over the eight-hour day and opposition to more efficient manufacturing practices. He created a workpeople's holiday fund based on a trust in memory of his son Ernest who died tragically in 1899, and many welfare and sports facilities were instigated by Mather for his employees.

William Mather was an active member of the Court of Governors of Owens College during 1889, and was a member of the College Council in 1895. His interest in the College persisted when it became Manchester University; he made many benefactions to it, and helped to found the department of Russian language and literature (there is now a Sir William Mather Chair of Russian). He was awarded an honorary LLD by the University in 1908.

When the Association of Technical Institutions was formed in 1894, Mather was invited to become its first president. He organised an education exhibition at his own cost, which displayed a whole range of British education lectures and demonstrations. The profits went to French and British charities. In the Sudan, which he visited in 1902, he donated engineering workshops and equipment to the Gordon College at Khartoum. Actively associated with the Union of Lancashire and Cheshire Institutes for over fifty years, he served as president from 1908 to 1918, and donated many of its scholarships and exhibitions. He was third president of the Textile Institute in 1915 and suggested that it should create for itself an institution; on his retirement from the Institute in 1918 he made a large donation towards the fund for the foundations of an institution.

A Liberal, Mather sat as MP for the Southern division of Salford, 1885-86, for the Gorton division of Lancashire, 1889-95, and for the Rossendale division of Lancashire, 1900-4. As MP for Gorton, he was influential in the passing of the Technical Instruction Act of 1889 and the Local Taxation (Customs and Excise) Act of 1890 which raised money made available to local authorities for subsidising technical education. In religion he was a Swedenborgian. He was knighted in 1902 as a Liberal MP on the recommendation of A J Balfour, the Conservative Prime Minister, for his services in the reorganisation of the War Office during the Boer War, and retired from active political life in 1904. On the recommendation of H H Asquith, the Liberal Prime Minister, he was sworn of the Privy Council in 1910.

Mather married in 1863 Emma Jane, daughter of Thomas Watson of Highbury; they had nine children. After Sir William's death, his son Loris Emerson assumed management of the company, and his grandson, Sir William Loris Mather, was managing director until his retirement in 1978.

Sir William Mather died on 18 September 1920, leaving an estate of £405,841 gross.

HOWARD COLES

MATHER Sir William

Writings:

'Well Boring and Pumping Machinery' *Proceedings of the Institution of Mechanical Engineers* 1869.

PP, RC on Technical Instruction: Report on Technical Education in the USA and Canada (1884) C 3981-I.

The Relation of Technical Instruction to the Progress of the Engineering and Kindred Trades in the Future, Address to the Manchester Association of Employers, Foremen and Draughtsmen (Manchester: pp, 1885).

The Bearing of the Technical Instruction Act on Education and Industrial Progress (Manchester: National Education Association, 1889).

'Labour and the Hours of Labour' *Contemporary Review* Nov 1892.

Trade Unions and the Hours of Labour (Manchester: Guardian Printing Works, 1892).

'Report on the Forty-Eight Hours Week' *Times* 31 May 1894.

The Forty Eight Hour Week: A Year's Experiment and Its Results at the Salford Iron Works, Manchester (Mather & Platt) (Manchester: Guardian Printing Works, 1894).

'The Education Bill' *Manchester Guardian* 16 Sept 1902.

Education and Duty (Manchester University Education Society, 1908).

'Cotton Growing in the Sudan' *Times* 14 Oct 1910.

Presidential address *Proceedings of the Textile Institute* 6 (1915).

'Ways to Industrial Peace' *The Nineteenth Century* Feb 1917.

Sources:

Unpublished

Hawarden Reference Library, Hawarden, Clwyd, file of letters of the Rt Hon William E Gladstone.

Mather & Platt, Park Works, Manchester, records.

PrC.

Published

J Aiken, *Description of the Country Round Manchester* (repr, Newton Abbot: David & Charles, 1975).

Peter W Kingsford, 'Sir William Mather, 1838-1920' *The Manager* June 1957.

Lancashire Leaders: Social and Political (Exeter: Pollard, 1897).

Manchester Guardian 10, 21 July, 22 Aug 1852, 15, 16 Sept 1897, 20 Sept 1920.

Loris E Mather, *Sir William Mather, 1838-1920* (Richard Cobden-Sanderson, 1926).

F Scholefield, 'Sir William Mather: His Contribution to the Textile Industry' *Journal of the Textile Institute* 41 (1950).

WWMP.

WWW.

MATHESON, Hugh Mackay

(1821-1898)

Overseas trader and head of international mining company

Hugh Mackay Matheson was born in Edinburgh on 23 April 1821, the second son of Duncan Matheson, an advocate, and his wife, Annabella née Farquaharson. His mother died when Hugh was eight years old and he and his two brothers and two sisters were raised by their father at Leith. The family lived contentedly, despite its sad loss. Duncan Matheson worked as a presiding magistrate and the children attended local day schools. In their free time the children enjoyed outdoor activities like swimming, golf and walking and with their father would often read literature and the Bible. Visits to relatives in and around Edinburgh formed a major part of their wider social life.

The religious and moral thinking of his father and relatives made a deep impression on the young Matheson. He became convinced at a very early age of the need to seek God's guidance in all matters through prayer and detailed reading of the Scriptures. As a corollary he accepted that as a Christian he should behave in a modest and trustworthy fashion whilst working hard not only to improve his own life but also those of others. Even as a schoolboy, at Edinburgh High School and later at Cunningham's Academy, he was seen as a quiet, purposeful individual with an exceptional interest in Christian teachings. He retained this interest with undiminished intensity throughout his life.

Hugh Matheson began his business career at fifteen years of age when, following the sudden death of his cousin, John Matheson, in 1836, he was asked to replace John as junior clerk in the Glasgow merchant house of James Ewing & Co. The opening must have seemed a fair one: the business was very prosperous and both Ewing and his managing partner, William Mathieson, were men of substance and good repute. Ewing was MP for Glasgow and a former Lord Provost of the city; he was also an associate of Hugh's uncle, James Matheson, partner in the China trade merchants Jardine-Matheson & Co. It is possible that even then Hugh had been singled out for a job with Jardine-Matheson, once suitably trained by Ewings.

Matheson spent the next seven years learning his trade and establishing his personal independence. His working life was generally tedious and his labours brought him little reward: his annual salary rose from £10 in the first year to £20 in the third. Money was needed from his father to supplement this meagre income. Nevertheless, Hugh diligently applied himself to learning the intricacies of international commerce, and, out of personal interest, attended classes at the University of Glasgow in logic and moral philosophy. His main pleasure was the local church, St Enoch's, where he made many good friends and became an active member of the Sabbath School Society.

His years in Glasgow, though generally happy, were not free from personal difficulty. He suffered a severe bout of typhoid fever early in 1838, and his father, after bringing Hugh home to Edinburgh, caught the disease too and died a few weeks later. At the time his elder brother, Donald, was away in China with Jardine-Matheson, and Hugh, although in poor health, was obliged to take on many family responsibilities. The strain proved too much and in 1839 he was forced into convalescence. He returned to Glasgow in 1840 and resumed his career and former interests with fervour, wholly in the spirit of his father's advice that he should lead an active, useful life and conduct himself with 'a high tone of honour and integrity' {Matheson (1899) 4}. Increasingly, he impressed his friends and colleagues with his dependability, maturity of outlook and soundness of judgement. His uncle James was also impressed: in 1843 Hugh was invited to join Jardine-Matheson & Co as an agent in China with the prospect of a 'great position and large fortune' {*ibid*, 15}.

After much soul-searching Matheson declined the offer. Jardine-Matheson was heavily involved in the opium trade and he could not reconcile his Christian conscience with this. Instead he accepted a clerical position with Jardine-Matheson's corresponding agents in London, Magniac-Jardine & Co, quickly settled down to work in a friendly office largely staffed by fellow Scots and within weeks was involved with the local Presbyterian church. In the course of the next two years he made many friends who were his main support during the frequent periods of ill-health he suffered during his first years in London.

However, Matheson's work was routine and rather dull and he felt that his career prospects were restricted by a lack of first-hand knowledge of overseas trading. Consequently, in October 1845 he took leave of absence from Magniac-Jardine and set out on an eighteen-month tour of the East with the intention of making new business connections and studying how British trade with that part of the world was conducted. The tour had an enduring influence on Matheson's life. As he travelled through India, Ceylon and China he became friendly with many of the leading merchants of the day, like the Indian tea and opium magnate, Sir Jamsetjee Jeejeebhoy and the partners in Jardine-Matheson & Co. Even more significantly, what he saw of life in these exotic lands and his long conversations with diplomats and missionaries sharpened his intellectual focus and increased his sense of social purpose. Essentially, he came to believe that the European nations stood higher on the scale of human civilisation because of the Christian religion and the acceptance in society of Christian values. The only way forward for the 'decadent' societies of the East, he concluded, was through the spread of Christian ideas — indirectly with the growth of capitalist interests and directly through the missionary effort. Ideally, trade and the Bible should be hand in hand to further God's work on earth.

When he returned to England Matheson was soon presented with the opportunity to exploit his newly-acquired commercial knowledge and connections. During his absence Magniac-Jardine & Co had run into severe financial difficulties and by 1847 was on the point of liquidation. Under the direction of Jardine-Matheson, the old partnership was dissolved and in 1848 the firm was reconstituted as Matheson & Co, with Hugh as managing partner. The firm grew steadily over the course of the next few decades to become one of the leading merchant houses in London. Initially, its main business was the importation of China tea and silk on behalf of Jardine-Matheson. But progressively Matheson & Co's activities became more diverse, as it exported a range of British manufactures to China and secured a large share of the Lancashire cotton piece-goods trade. A further boost to business came towards the end of the 1850s when the firm became the corresponding agent of Jardine-Skinner & Co of Calcutta. Within a few years the firm was importing sufficient Indian goods to justify the leasing of specially constructed warehouses at Hay's wharf, London. Subsequently, the scope of its activities was widened still further with the establishment of specialist chartering and insurance departments.

The demands of business did not lessen Matheson's commitment to the Presbyterian church. As soon as he returned from the East he became involved in establishing its China mission and he promoted the mission's work for half-a-century, first as treasurer and then as convenor. He also served the church devotedly through various other activities: encouraging theological debate by the founding of Presbyterian newspapers and journals, establishing a Presbyterian college, raising funds for many new churches and offering advice on important matters of church finance, organisation and doctrine. In all these activities he had the full support of his wife, Agnes née McFarlen, whom he married in 1855. The couple lived contentedly in Hampstead throughout their married life, raising two daughters and a son. Their home was always open to visiting churchmen and missionaries, of whom many became close friends. At holiday times they would retreat to Elswick House, their beloved country home at Strathpeffer in the Scottish Highlands, purchased by Matheson in 1858.

As family man and church elder Hugh Matheson was thoroughly conservative: indeed after his death one clergyman remarked that 'during the half century of his residence in London Scotland changed more than he did' {*ibid*, vii}. However, this conservatism was not evident in his business life. As the financial power and reputation of Matheson & Co grew, his attention turned to ever more ambitious schemes. In the early 1860s Matheson & Co and Jardine-Skinner & Co became joint managers of various Indian tea estates. Later in the decade Matheson helped Jardine-Matheson to promote the construction of railways and cotton mills in China. Other large projects followed and by the early 1870s Matheson was known as one of the most adventurous capitalists of Europe.

At this time he became involved in two particularly noteworthy projects. The first sprang from the remarkable concession granted in 1872 by the Shah of Persia to Baron Julius de Reuter (qv) for the economic development of his country. Under this Reuter was granted the exclusive right to build and operate all Persian railways, tramways and canals and exploit virtually all the natural resources of the country for a period of seventy years. It was Matheson who laid the financial plans to take advantage of the concession. He proposed the formation of a limited company in Britain with an authorised share capital of £6 million and various subsidiaries to take charge of specific projects. In the event, however, the scheme came to nothing.

The second Matheson project also required great skill and large amounts of money to develop the natural resources of an economically backward and politically troubled land. In 1871 the financially-beleaguered Spanish Government put up for sale the state-owned Rio Tinto mines, containing the most extensive deposits of cupreous pyrites in Europe. The proposal aroused little interest on account of Spain's political troubles and the vast amount of capital needed to purchase and develop the mines. Matheson took a more positive view. He reasoned that Spain's political problems were not deep-seated and that the rising European demand for the sulphur and copper of Rio Tinto made the mines a rich potential source of profit. Early in 1873 he formed an international consortium to purchase the mines for £3.68 million and in the following May, with Hugh Matheson at its head, the Rio Tinto Co was launched to work the concession. For the next twenty-five years Rio Tinto was Matheson's main preoccupation in the world of business.

The early years of the Rio Tinto Co's existence were fraught with difficulties. Frequent appeals to bankers were needed to finance the massive construction programme undertaken in Spain and the chemical companies which bought Iberian pyrites had to be won over to Rio Tinto against fierce opposition from existing suppliers. With these and many other problems Matheson took the lead in finding solutions, displaying a flair for public relations as he carefully built up confidence in the future of the enterprise. Under his leadership the company soon emerged as the biggest supplier of sulphur and copper in the world. From then on Matheson did not hesitate to use the strong market position of the firm to increase its profitability or to use its financial muscle to overcome opposition to its activities in Spain or elsewhere. By the 1890s the Rio Tinto Co was famed in mining and financial circles for its technological achievements, market leadership and high profitability.

In advancing the fortunes of the Rio Tinto Co Hugh Matheson was generally tough-minded and occasionally ruthless in his business dealings. Yet he retained the image throughout of a quiet, courteous and benign individual. This was partly because of his church work and advocacy of liberal political values and partly because of his practical commitment to improving the lot of the 10,000 or so workmen and their families living in the villages surrounding the Rio Tinto mines. From the start Matheson considered the material and moral well-being of company employees to be his responsibility as a Christian. Through the provision of comfortable houses, churches, schools, stores, recreation facilities, pensions and a medical service, paternalism was carried to the limit at Rio Tinto. Hugh Matheson took a personal interest in every detail, from the school curriculum to design of the cottages. Though the company certainly gained from the system, there is no reason to doubt the sincerity or depth of Matheson's concern for the welfare of the mining community. This was recognised by the King of Spain who, following a visit to Rio Tinto in 1882, made Matheson a Knight Grand Cross of the the Order of Isabella the Catholic. He was one of the few foreigners, apart from heads of government or ambassadors, to receive this special mark of distinction.

The powerful position occupied by Hugh Matheson as a leading figure in the City and chairman of the Rio Tinto Co did not lead him to seek admission to the inner ranks of the establishment. As an ardent supporter of the Liberal party and reformist thinking he despised the 'exclusiveness and selfishness which is found so difficult to eradicate from our national habit and national laws' {*ibid*, 197}. He could not abide power-seeking through social means and, whilst serving his party as president of the Hampstead Liberal and Radical Association, he was not disposed to seek political office, six times declining offers from constituencies to stand as a parliamentary candidate. His inclination was to perform his public duty in relatively modest capacities, as a JP and as chairman of the China and East India section of the London Chamber of Commerce.

Hugh Matheson died on 8 February 1898, at the age of seventy-six. He worked hard at his church and business papers virtually until the end. Following his death tributes from all over the world expressed a common sentiment: that his passing was a sad loss, not simply because of his wisdom and energy, but because of his humanity and care for those with whom he had dealings. He was survived by his wife and three children. He left an estate valued at £88,895 gross.

CHARLES HARVEY

Writings:

(A Matheson ed), *Memorials of Hugh Mackay Matheson* with a prefatory note by J Oswald Dykes (Hodder & Stoughton, 1899).

Sources:

Unpublished

Cambridge University Library, Jardine-Matheson archive; Jardine-Skinner archive.

The Rio Tinto Zinc Corporation Ltd, London, papers.

PrC.

Published

David Avery, *Not on Queen Victoria's Birthday: The Story of the Rio Tinto Mines* (Collins, 1974).

Edward Bond, *Working His Purpose Out: The History of the English Presbyterian Mission 1847-1947* (Publishing Office of the Presbyterian Church of England, 1948).

Sydney G Checkland, *The Mines of Tharsis* (George Allen & Unwin, 1967).

Charles E Harvey, *The Rio Tinto Company: An Economic History of a Leading International Mining Concern* (Penzance: Alison Hodge, 1981).

Jardine-Matheson & Co Ltd, *Jardine Matheson and Company: An Historical Sketch* (Hongkong: pp, 1969).

PD, 3rd ser 217 (1873) cols 290-301.

A P Thornton, 'British Policy in Persia 1858-1890' *English Historical Review* 69 (1954).

Times 10 Feb 1898.

George Matthey (courtesy of Johnson Matthey).

MATTHEY, George

(1825-1913)

Refiner of precious metals

George Matthey was born on 8 May 1825, the third son of John Matthey, a wealthy London stock broker whose father, Simon, had left his home town of Le Locle in Switzerland in about 1790. He was educated at a private school in Twickenham. In 1838, at the age of thirteen, he was apprenticed to Percival Norton Johnson of Hatton Garden, a leading refiner of gold and platinum who had concluded an agreement with the boy's father whereby, in return for an injection of new capital, two of his sons should enter Johnson's business, established in 1817.

At first George was a junior assistant under instruction but his special interest soon became the chemistry and metallurgy of the platinum metals. Thus in 1845 he was put in charge of their refining and quickly began to prepare larger and more malleable ingots of platinum and to improve the methods of separating the other platinum group metals.

When the Great Exhibition of 1851 was proposed Johnson, like many other industrialists, was unwilling to take part. George Matthey, however, realised the opportunity the Exhibition presented and finally persuaded his employer to exhibit a number of platinum articles together with specimens of palladium, iridium and rhodium, a small display which earned a prize medal. Matthey now resolved to become pre-eminent in the platinum business and, seeking a more assured supply of raw material, he made an arrangement with some mine owners in the newly-discovered platinum source in the Ural Mountains in Russia. These two achievements prompted Johnson to take the young man into partnership in 1851, the name of the firm then becoming Johnson & Matthey.

Shortly afterwards Johnson began to relinquish control, leaving Matthey virtually in charge of the business. Up to this time the only means of producing platinum in malleable form was the powder metallurgy method of pressing the sponge in a mould and hot-forging. While a number of scientists had succeeded in melting small samples, the resulting metal was nearly always brittle because of contamination by carbon or refractory materials. A major advance resulted from a visit by George Matthey to the Paris Exhibition in 1855. He became friendly with Paul Morin, who was associated with the Société d'Aluminium, an enterprise founded by Henri Sainte-Claire Deville, Professor of Chemistry at the École Normale in Paris, to exploit his process for producing aluminium by the reduction of aluminium chloride with sodium. This work led him to investigate the melting of metals that had so far proved to be difficult. To this end he employed a mixture of coal gas and oxygen, and with his assistant Jules Henri Debray he devised a simple piece of equipment consisting of two large blocks of lime, each hollowed out and then placed one over the other, in which they could melt platinum in considerable quantity.

French and British patents were filed for this process in the name of Debray, and George Matthey was offered the English rights in the process in August 1857. Matthey promptly accepted and the new process was put in hand in Hatton Garden. Simultaneously new industrial applications for the metal were sought, one being large platinum boilers for the concentration of sulphuric acid.

When the international Metric Commission was set up in 1870 in Paris George Matthey played an important part, supplying the platinum and iridium for the proposed alloy from which the standard metre and kilogram were made, making a great many large castings and machining the bars. For this purpose he turned to a new method of refining, involving preliminary alloying with an excess of lead to facilitate the removal of rhodium and iridium, and it was this process that he described in a paper read to the Royal Society in 1879. He was elected an FRS two months later.

By 1880 the platinum business had developed into a prosperous activity and George Matthey, while continuing to supervise the refining and melting, turned his attention, charm and business sense to maintaining and extending his contacts with the scientific community. He had been a member of the Chemical Society since 1871, and he joined the Royal Society of Arts in 1881, serving as vice-president, 1884-86 and 1889-91. He was also a member of the Royal Institution, and became vice-president, 1896-97. At a meeting there in 1895 to hear a lecture by Roberts-Austen on rarer metals Matthey supported the lecturer with a display of melted and rolled iridium, large specimens of rhodium and osmium and a large mass of palladium valued then at £2.5 million.

Matthey was for many years a leading figure in the Worshipful Company of Goldsmiths. Elected to the Livery in 1853, and to the Court in 1865, he became Prime Warden in 1872 and again in 1894. His advice on questions of assaying was of great assistance to the Company, and on their behalf he played an important part in establishing the City and Guilds Colleges in Finsbury and South Kensington, serving for many years on their governing bodies.

Friendship with a great number of scientists of his time was of mutual benefit, as he was always ready with encouragement and the provision of the platinum metals without charge to those studying their properties and applications.

In 1891 Johnson, Matthey was incorporated as a limited company and George Matthey, now aged sixty-six, became chairman, retaining supervision of the platinum refining. He finally retired in 1909, but a year earlier he had been nominated by the newly-formed Institute of Metals as their first honorary member 'in view of his wonderful record in the science of metallurgy' {*Journal of the Institute of Metals* 1 (1909) 37}.

Beginning on a laboratory scale, platinum refining and fabrication developed under his creative guidance and determination and his keen eye for new applications. The earliest recorded figures show sales of around 15,000 ounces in 1860, increasing to some 75,000 ounces a year in the 1880s compared to over a million ounces today (1984).

George Matthey died at his home at Eastbourne on 14 February 1913, at the age of eighty-seven, leaving £315,003.

L B HUNT

Writings:

'The Preparation in a State of Purity of the Group of Metals Known as the Platinum Series and Notes upon the Manufacture of Iridio-Platinum' *Proceedings of the Royal Society* 28 (1879).

Sources:

Unpublished

PrC.

Published

Leslie B Hunt, 'George Matthey and the Building of the Platinum Industry' *Platinum Metals Review* 1979.

Journal of the Institute of Metals 1 (1909).

D McDonald and Leslie B Hunt, *A History of Platinum and Its Allied Metals* (Johnson Matthey, 1983).

WWW.

MATTISON, Francis Charles

(1860-1944)

Photographic equipment manufacturing company chairman

Francis Charles Mattison was born in Alnwick, Northumberland, on 6 May 1860, the son of John Mattison, a house painter, and his wife Mary Ann née Alder. Little is known of his early life except that he became a bank manager and that this led to an encounter with a Kodak Ltd director which resulted in his appointment as an assistant manager of the firm. Kodak Ltd, the British subsidiary of Eastman Kodak of New Jersey, had had problems with managers more interested in the technical aspects of the production of photographic materials than with the financial and commercial aspects of the business.

George Eastman, the inventor of the amateur roll-film and the eponymous Kodak camera, opened a branch of the Eastman Co in Soho Square, London, employing about six people in 1885, and forming the Eastman Photographic Materials Co Ltd in 1889 with a nominal capital of £150,000. A factory was built at Wealdstone, Middlesex, in 1890 to manufacture film and photographic paper, as well as to process exposed film. In 1898 Kodak Ltd was incorporated as a public company in London with an authorised capital of £1.6 million. This company took over the business of the Eastman Photographic Materials Co Ltd, acquired all the British and foreign business (except in the USA), and 98 per cent of the shares of the Eastman Kodak Co. In 1902, however, because of increased taxation in Britain resulting from the Boer War, the Eastman Kodak Co took over the territories outside Great Britain and the capital of the British company was consequently reduced to £250,000, all held by the American company.

The fortunes of the British company improved after poor performance in the 1890s. Film production was stopped around 1900 because improved film made by continuous-process manufacture was imported from the United States. In the years before the First World War Kodak acquired several small photographic concerns for their plant and technical knowledge. Some companies, notably Ilford Ltd founded by Alfred Harman (qv), rejected Kodak's advances. The expertise gained helped Kodak Ltd to become a major supplier to the Royal Flying Corps.

Mattison became secretary in 1903, joined the board of Kodak Ltd in 1911, and in 1919 became joint managing director, a post he retained until he was appointed chairman of Kodak Ltd in 1927. In close contact with George Eastman, he played an important part in Eastman Kodak's acquisitions in Europe in the 1920s. Kodak-Pathé was established in 1927 to take over Charles Pathé's company in order to eliminate competition in the motion picture field. A base-making plant at Köpenick near Berlin was acquired under Kodak AG, and soon manufactured film, while in Hungary a photographic paper plant was brought into operation. Kodak Ltd was responsible for supplying the British market, parts of Europe and the Empire.

In Britain Kodak Ltd dominated the motion picture field and had an increasing share of the amateur market. Film production restarted in the 1920s and cameras were assembled. The workforce expanded from about 1,400 in 1918 to 4,400 in 1938. In the late 1920s Kodak acquired a controlling interest in a number of photofinishing firms, still known as 'B' companies, which were required to use Kodak products exclusively.

Mattison was not particularly interested in the manufacturing side of the business, and only visited the Harrow factory on the rare occasions when George Eastman visited. The Harrow factory was run by an American, Walter G Bent, who became chairman for a while during the Second World War. At Bent's suggestion a research laboratory was established in 1928, partly because scientific workers were cheaper in Britain than in the United States. This laboratory was one of the first to be established overseas by an American multinational, and grew considerably in the 1930s and 1940s.

In 1931 Mattison was elected to the board of Eastman Kodak. He remained chairman of Kodak Ltd until 1943, even though in his later years he was confined to a wheelchair. He died one year later, on 14 December 1944, in Bournemouth, at the age of eighty-four, leaving £227,658 gross.

D E H EDGERTON

Sources:

Unpublished

Information from Geoffrey Bawcutt, archivist, Kodak Ltd, and Ernest Amor, chairman, Kodak Ltd, 1966-69.

E E Blake, 'The Growth and Development of Kodak' (Edwards Seminar Paper 88, 30 Jan 1951).

BCe.

PrC.

Published

Carl W Ackerman, *George Eastman* (Boston and New York: Houghton Mifflin Co, 1930).

British Journal of Photography 12 May 1911, 16 Jan 1920, 29 Dec 1944.

Burdett's Official Intelligence 1891.

Monopolies Commission, *Report on Colour Film* (HMSO, 1966).

MAUDSLAY, Reginald Walter

(1871-1934)

Motor vehicle manufacturer

Reginald Walter Maudslay was born in Kensington, London, on 1 September 1871, the son of Athol Edward Maudslay and his wife Kate Golder née Lucas. His great-grandfather was Henry Maudslay, the machine builder and marine engineer, and his maternal grandfather was Thomas Lucas, founder of a large firm of building contractors. After education at Marlborough, Maudslay followed family tradition and began his career in engineering, initially as an apprentice, and later as an employee, with Sir John Wolfe Barry's (qv) London firm of civil engineers. This gave Maudslay valuable commercial and technical experience; but in addition Wolfe Barry provided him with the capital (reputed to be £3,000) to establish his own business when he left the firm in 1902. Two more of Barry's pupils in the 1890s, Alexander Gibb (qv) and Rustat Blake, later became major shareholders in Maudslay's firm, Standard Motor Co, and were among Maudslay's closest confidants. Why Maudslay decided to abandon his civil engineering career is uncertain, though according to Gibb 'his heart was always in motor cars' {*Times* 19

Dec 1934}. However, in 1902 his cousin, Cyril Maudslay, became managing director of the Coventry-based and newly-formed Maudslay Motor Co, and it may have been this which precipitated Reginald's move from London. Apart from personal considerations, Coventry was an obvious choice for Maudslay to locate his own motor company, since the city enjoyed a number of resource and other advantages as the principal centre of the new industry.

After leasing a small Coventry workshop in 1902 for experimental purposes, Maudslay moved in the following year to larger premises in Much Park Street where he established the Standard Motor Co. Between 1907 and 1912 the firm was under the control of Charles Friswell (qv), whose well-known motor distributing agency became sole agent for Standard cars, but for most of the period from its inception until Maudslay's death in 1934 Standard was under the direct leadership of its founder. Like most other Coventry motor firms, the company was handicapped in its early years by limited financial resources, and even when it went public in 1914 its capital only amounted to the comparatively modest sum of £50,000. However, production expanded quite rapidly in the pre-war period. By 1913 the firm's annual output reached 750 vehicles, making it one of the larger Coventry producers, though small by comparison with Ford, the market leader.

During the First World War Standard turned to the manufacture of military equipment, including aero engines and airframes, for which a new site was purchased at Canley, subsequently the company's principal manufacturing base. A difficult time was experienced during the latter part of the 1920s, with heavy losses and a six-year period without dividends. This was reversed in the following decade when car production increased sharply, reaching about 53,000 units by 1939, or nearly 13 per cent of the total output of the six largest producers, compared with 5.1 per cent at the start of the decade. By 1939 Standard was Coventry's leading volume producer of motor cars and firmly established as one of the industry's 'Big Six'. Maudslay's personal contribution to the development of the company is difficult to assess. He relied heavily upon the engineering skills of John Budge, who joined the firm in 1905 after working for the Triumph Cycle Co and Climax Motors. When Budge retired in 1929 John Black was recruited from Rootes Bros as Maudslay's assistant and it was Black who reorganised production methods in the 1930s and was regarded within the company as responsible for the improved growth performance of that decade. As the firm grew, Maudslay delegated responsibility for technical development, but the board retained close control of production, pricing and financial policies.

Maudslay's entrepreneurial strengths and weaknesses are illustrated by two key business decisions with which he was personally associated. During the period when Friswell was the company's chairman Maudslay pressed for the mass production of a small car for the popular end of the market. Friswell rejected this advice, preferring a limited output of high-powered expensive vehicles, a policy which resulted in a formal protest by the directors being recorded in the company's minutes. After Friswell's departure, Maudslay successfully introduced the company's first volume car, the 9.5 hp Model 'S', which, had it been introduced earlier, could well have placed the company in a much stronger position by 1913. Maudslay was also personally anxious to extend the company's sales abroad and by 1932 Standard cars were sold in 33 countries. This policy contained many pitfalls as well as potential advantages: it appears that Maudslay's enthusiasm overcame his sound judgement when in 1927 he allowed the company's production arrangements to be dominated by one Australian order which, when it collapsed, left the firm with heavy losses and contributed eventually to John Black's appointment.

Maudslay was a designer of considerable ability, reputedly inventing the side entrance car body in place of the tonneau, but his most significant contributions to the development of the Standard Co were the importance he attached to volume production, the acquisition of the Canley site at a bargain price in 1916 and the recruitment of John Black in 1929. Maudslay's life appears to have been dominated by a consuming interest in the motor industry, but sadly he missed perhaps the greatest days of the company he had pioneered.

Maudslay married in 1908 Gwendoline Susan, daughter of John Herbert; they had three children. He died on 14 December 1934, leaving £216,284 gross.

DAVID W THOMS

Sources:

Unpublished

British Motor Industry Heritage Trust.

University of Warwick, Modern Records Centre, records of the Standard Motor Co.

BCe.

MCe.

PrC.

Published

John R Davy, *The Standard Car 1903-1963* (Coventry: Sherbourne Press, 1967).

Times 19 Dec 1934.

MAXWELL, John

(1877-1940)

Film production and exhibition company chairman

John Maxwell was born in 1877. Nothing is known about his parents, upbringing, or schooling. He was trained as a solicitor and established himself in Glasgow. In 1912 he entered the cinema business, acquiring an interest in a small Glasgow picture house. In 1918 he began his long collaboration with Arthur Dent when they formed a distribution company called Waverley Films Ltd. The firm prospered and in 1923 they took over Harry Hibbert's Wardour Films Ltd, the London-based firm with which they were associated. Dent became managing director, Maxwell chairman, though it was not until 1925 that Maxwell moved to London.

Like Isidore Ostrer (qv) at Gaumont, Maxwell was determined to grasp the opportunities offered by the forthcoming Film Quota Act. In 1926 he acquired the Alliance Studios at St Margaret's, Twickenham and formed a production company with the film director, Maurice Elvey (M E Productions). St Margaret's was small and old-fashioned though, and Elvey left to join the Gaumont Co.

Maxwell's real break into the production side of the industry came early in 1927 when discord among the directors of British National Pictures Ltd threatened to jeopardise the opening of Britain's first large and modern studio complex. Maxwell stepped in, provided the requisite amount of finance, and within three months had gained control of British National and its Elstree studios. In April 1927 British International Pictures was formed as a private company with a nominal capital of £100,000 to acquire the assets of British National. In November a public issue of £312,000 was made and in February the following year the issued capital of the company was increased to £750,000.

Maxwell launched an ambitious production programme, although BIP, like the rest of the British film industry, was rather thrown out of gear by the coming of sound to the cinema. Maxwell coped better than most; by April 1929 the Elstree Studios had been equipped with RCA recording equipment and the first sound film produced by BIP, Alfred Hitchcock's *Blackmail*, proved a resounding success. Subsequent productions failed to live up to this early promise and Maxwell soon came to the conclusion that film production was inherently risky and was best offset by interests in exhibition. In November 1928 Associated British Cinemas had been registered as a public company with an authorised capital of £1 million; BIP held a controlling interest. While other exhibitors hesitated over what to do about sound, Maxwell rapidly bought up a large number of cinemas and equipped them with RCA sound apparatus.

By July 1929 the circuit consisted of 80 cinemas and over the next eighteen months doubled in size to reach 160 by the end of 1931. To undertake rapid expansion during a period of acute economic depression was not without its dangers. Ralph Bromhead, who became assistant general manager of ABC, recollected that the company was extremely short of cash and had to rely on very large overdrafts from the National Provincial Bank. Increases in income tax, cuts in unemployment benefit, and from September 1931 an increased Entertainment Tax naturally had an adverse effect on cinema attendance, though the novelty of the sound film and the general cheapness of the cinema as a form of entertainment shielded the box office from the worst effects of the Depression. Nevertheless Maxwell was cautious enough to prepare for the worst and in 1930 Bromhead was given 'the unpleasant task of cutting the wage — already very low — of every worker at every cinema, from manager to part-time cleaner'. {Bromhead (1981)}

In September 1933 ABC, BIP and Wardour Films were consolidated into a single company, Associated British Picture Corporation Ltd. ABPC had only one serious rival for the leadership of the British film industry, the Ostrer Brothers' Gaumont-British Picture Corporation. In September 1934 Maxwell attempted a take-over bid, despite the fact that Gaumont-British had an issued capital of £6.25 million compared to ABPC's £3 million. The bid was unsuccessful, but the ramshackle Gaumont-British empire seemed to exercise an irresistible attraction on him and in October 1936, just when it seemed that Gaumont-British was to pass into American hands, Maxwell announced the successful conclusion of a deal by which the Ostrer brothers would sell to ABPC their shares in Metropolis & Bradford, the holding company which controlled Gaumont-British. However, although Maxwell had acquired the 250,000 non-voting 'B' shares in Metropolis & Bradford (for £620,000), his option on the crucial 5,100 'A' voting shares, by which the Ostrers controlled the Corporation, could only be exercised with the consent of 20th Century Fox, the holder of the remaining shares in Metropolis & Bradford. Maxwell failed to reach an agreement with the Americans. The normally astute Maxwell had landed himself in a difficult position.

ABPC now had a substantial interest in the ailing Gaumont-British Corporation with no power to re-order its affairs. A chance did occur in April 1937 when dissident shareholders combined with the American and ABPC interests in attempting to wrest control from the Ostrers. There were good reasons for supposing that the Corporation would be unable to pay the interim dividend on the preference shares — which would entitle their holders to voting rights. An overnight agreement between the Ostrers and their former managing director, C M Woolf (qv), the head of the successful General Film Distributors, relieved Gaumont-British of the liability of their production and distribution facilities and the preference dividend was paid.

Maxwell himself began legal proceedings against the Ostrers for 'fraudulent misrepresentation'. The action was brought before Mr Justice Goddard in October 1938 but a deal was reached, and the hearing lasted only a couple of hours. By this time Maxwell had resigned his directorship of Gaumont-British and a full-scale Board of Trade inquiry into the Corporation commenced the following January. The ABPC shares in Metropolis & Bradford were eventually sold in 1941 to J Arthur Rank (qv), who took up Maxwell's expired option on the voting shares, won over the Americans, and secured control of Gaumont-British.

There is evidence to suggest that the Gaumont-British affair took a heavy strain on Maxwell's physical and possibly his mental capacities. He was already a diabetic and the long months of stressful infighting and the frustration of his ambitions can hardly have improved his health. However, ABPC continued to perform satisfactorily and in October 1937 he acquired the 168 cinemas of the Union Circuit, making ABPC the biggest exhibitor in the country with 493 cinemas.

ABPC also planned to expand its film production activities. Maxwell had been one of the first to warn of the folly of spending lavishly on films in the hope that (like Alexander Korda's (qv) *Private Life of Henry the Eighth*) they would prove an international success. Production at Elstree had remained cautious and cost-conscious and consequently had hardly been affected by the 1937 slump which had driven many of the newer production companies into bankruptcy. Consequently, by 1938 Maxwell was in a good position to fill the gap left by these numerous casualties. He began commissioning major directors and actors such as Erich Pommer and Charles Laughton, and also made a bid for the neighbouring Amalgamated Studios. The Second World War, and J Arthur Rank, curtailed Maxwell's ambitions in this direction. In 1939 both the BIP and Amalgamated Studios (acquired by Rank and later sold to MGM) were requisitioned by the Government.

Maxwell was always highly regarded for his financial acumen and in contrast to the unhappy relations between directors and shareholders which troubled Gaumont-British, and several other film companies, he was considered to be the shareholder's friend. ABPC and its predecessor companies performed adequately, if not brilliantly, through all the vicissitudes of the 1930s. The amount earned on the ordinary share capital between 1931-41 averaged 15 per cent (a peak of 48.9 per cent in 1937) though Maxwell's caution kept the amount actually paid in dividends down to 5.8 per cent (nearer 20 per cent, 1937-39).

Legitimate reservations might be expressed about the type of film produced by BIP, a studio which seemed adept only at producing what was bland and mediocre. Alfred Hitchcock, who worked there between 1928 and 1932, seemed stifled by its atmosphere, and even within the Maxwell empire the films were not very highly regarded. Ralph Bromhead recalled that 'the exhibiting side was not helped in its work by the output from Elstree, rather the reverse' {ibid}. On the other hand, Maxwell's determination to avoid the extravagant excesses of more adventurous film producers did at least ensure that Elstree provided a useful training ground for directors, technicians, and script-writers to whom, unlike most studios, it was able to offer continuous employment. Between 1929 and 1939 almost 200 films were produced at Elstree, a total far greater than that of any other British production company. Though the output of BIP did little to encourage the belief in the cultural standards of the British film industry, the consistent profits Maxwell managed to achieve showed that it did not have to be a graveyard for investors.

John Maxwell was a shrewd businessman with a good financial mind rather than an impresario or showman. According to Ralph Bromhead, 'he could look at a very complicated balance sheet or set of figures for a few minutes only, and master it completely. quoting the figures months afterwards from memory in great detail' {ibid}. As the head of a vertically-integrated combine which straddled the conflicting interests of production, distribution and exhibition, his position was not always easy. That in giving evidence to the government commission set up to make recommendations for a second Films Act in 1938 he chose to represent the American-dominated Kinematograph Renters Society rather than the Film Producers' Group of the Federation of British Industries indicates that Maxwell's record of success was based on a very firm sense of realism.

John Maxwell died on 2 October 1940, aged sixty-three. Ironically in view of the success with which he had kept ABPC free of American interests, half of his controlling share in the company was bought by Warner Brothers; Sir Philip Warter, Maxwell's son-in-law, succeeded him as chairman.

ROBERT MURPHY

Sources:

Unpublished

C Reg: Associated British Picture Corporation (321,978).

Typewritten notes from and interview with Mr Ralph Bromhead, 1981.

Published

Adrian Brunel, *Nice Work. The Story of Thirty Years in British Film Production* (Forbes Robertson, 1949).

Economist 24 Sept 1932, 7 Oct 1933, 6 Oct 1934.

Investors Chronicle 17, 24 Oct, 12 Dec 1936.

Kinematograph Weekly 13 Jan 1927, 12 July 1934.

Rachael Low, *The History of the British Film 1914-1918* (George Allen & Unwin, 1950).

—, *The History of the British Film 1918-1929* (George Allen & Unwin, 1971).

Political and Economic Planning, *The British Film Industry* (PEP, 1952).

Times 4 Oct 1940.

Alan Wood, *Mr Rank. A Study of J Arthur Rank and British Films* (Hodder & Stoughton, 1952).

MAY, George Ernest

1st Lord May of Weybridge

(1871-1946)

Insurance company executive

George Ernest May was born at Cheshunt, Hertfordshire, on 20 June 1871, the son of William May, a grocer and wine merchant, and his wife Julia Ann née Mole. He was educated at Cranleigh School. After entering the Prudential Assurance Co Ltd in May 1887 as a junior clerk in the cashier's department, May qualified in eight years as a fellow of the Institute of Actuaries and was transferred in 1902 from the actuarial department to the investment department. With his flair for finance, he quickly gained a series of promotions from principal clerk in 1905, to deputy controller and controller in 1907 and 1910 respectively.

Whilst in the investment department, May was largely responsible for a policy of earning higher yields on the company's immense holdings, by a wider distribution of funds. In a paper to the Institute of Actuaries in 1912 he revealed the thinking behind his investment policy at the Prudential. The investment of life assurance funds, he argued, had been severely restricted by a lack of expertise and knowledge. A knowledge of, and an investigation into, potential investments were key elements in taking decisions on investment. Outside information on an investment had to be used with caution and chiefly as a means of confirmation. May did not agree with the oft-quoted principle that an insurance company should never sell its investments but believed securities should be sold if the price increased to a level where the company was no longer justified in holding them. In 1862, A H Bailey had laid down five canons for investment, to which May suggested a sixth be added, namely, that in order to minimise the result of temporary fluctuations and to secure the safety of the capital in the best way possible it was desirable to spread these investments over as large a geographical area as possible. He also argued that more investment should be undertaken in higher-yielding securities.

In 1915 May became company secretary of the Prudential. In this capacity he suggested to the Government in 1915 that, in order to provide funds in the United States to meet Britain's growing purchase of munitions, foods and other wartime necessities, the UK Government ought to take over and sell or pledge in the USA the Prudential's American rail and other securities, said to amount to £10 million. The offer was accepted, the Prudential's American securities were put at the Treasury's disposal at a fair price and May himself, appointed manager of the new US Dollar Securities Commission, was asked to arrange the collection of all similar securities held by other British companies so that they could be used for the same purpose. The City regarded his work in this field between 1916 and 1918 as one of the best pieces of finance work executed during the war. During the war, May also served as Deputy Quartermaster

General of the Navy and Army Canteens Board. He was awarded a KBE in 1918.

On returning to the Prudential Assurance Co after the First World War, May was threatened by blindness and, despite several operations, was almost completely blind for a considerable period. This prompted him to develop his memory to an extraordinary degree and he became even more efficient as company secretary. During the period when May held this office, 1915-31, the company's assets in all branches increased from £94,794,798 to £255,793,860 and the interest and dividend and rents in all branches increased from £3,677,558 to £12,765,892. In 1919, May appeared as a witness before the Board of Trade Industrial Life Assurance Committee and gave evidence on the management expenses involved in carrying on the business of industrial assurance.

May was a tall, slender man with an air of slightly supercilious courtesy which tended to be emphasised by his use of a monocle. He was capable of succeeding in any task to which he thoroughly applied himself but was rarely able to devote his whole attention to one matter. This was evident in his work at the Prudential, where he attacked any new problem or idea with the utmost zest for a few days, never allowing himself the slightest rest until, with the fundamentals of the subject mastered, his interest would cool and he would hand it on to someone else to complete or revise. However, May never tried to find a scapegoat and always took responsibility for an error made by one of his staff at the Prudential. His versatility exemplified the old maxim: 'Know something of everything and everything of something'. May's quickness of mind and commanding personality ensured that his ideas were usually accepted, although he avoided formal meetings of the insurance world as he realised that his ability to express himself at appropriate length, either in speech or in writing, was limited.

In 1931, May was given a baronetcy. In that year, at the age of sixty, he retired from the Prudential Assurance Co to become chairman of the Government's Economy Committee. This committee was composed of eminent banking figures from the fields of insurance and industry: Lord Plender (qv), Arthur Pugh, Sir Thomas Royden, Charles Latham, Sir Mark Webster Jenkinson (qv) and P Ashley Cooper. The Labour Government established the committee in the face of strong demands from the Conservatives for some restrictions to be placed on public expenditure in order to restore confidence and to promote employment. Until the publication of the May Report on 1 August 1931, Britain's economic problems had been viewed in essence as a technical crisis of confidence, the drain of sterling being attributed to the individual economic troubles of the withdrawing countries. The publication of the Report, with its savage indictment of the policies of the Labour Government, sent tremors into every corner of the financial world.

The Report calculated a budget deficit of £120 million (which was later revised upwards to £170 million) and May and his business colleagues rebuked the Government for embarking on an inflationary path. The Economy Committee argued that borrowing money for the jobless must cease and advocated a cut in unemployment benefit of £67 million, and other economies saving a further £30 million. The findings reflected the orthodoxy of the banking world: a budget deficit of this magnitude was inflationary and could not be reduced by increasing general taxation as this would damage business confidence. Consequently, the only solution in the eyes of the May Committee was to decrease expenditure on the unemployed. The May Report, with its underlying suggestion that London was not a secure depository for overseas interests because the Government was bent on inflationary policies, intensified the flight from sterling. Influential Liberals and Tories and the majority of newspapers used the Report to bludgeon the Government into cutting social services and indeed, as the drain on sterling continued and the Government awaited responses from Paris and New York to its applications for credit, the Labour administration itself looked fragile. When nine Ministers opposed a 10 per cent cut in unemployment benefit the collapse of the Labour Government and the formation of a National Government became inevitable. However, the May Report's effects on the British economy did not cease with the resignation of the Labour Government and, following the withdrawal of £20 million from London on one day alone, Britain left the Gold Standard on 21 September 1931. May was a distinguished actuary, but he possessed no qualifications as an economist or as an expert in public finance and the May Report, in retrospect, was generally condemned as unsound and thought to be alarmist in its wording, which was intended to make a strong impression on the politicians the members regarded as spendthrift. J M Keynes referred to the Report as 'the most foolish document I have ever had the misfortune to read' {Cross (1966) 279}. Yet some blame for the Report's disruptive effects must lie with Labour politicians who, failing to foresee how it would be received, published the Report without any commentary or declaration of policy.

May's services were called upon by the Government again in 1932 when he was made chairman of the newly-appointed Import Duties Advisory Committee (a position he retained until his death). Other members of the Committee included Sir Sydney Chapman and Sir G A Powell, with Percy Ashley as secretary. Once the decision had been taken by the Government to experiment with protective tariffs, it had to be decided which industries were to be protected and to what extent. Such deliberations were open to misunderstanding and a confusion of interests if brought into the political arena, so there was an obvious advantage in entrusting the task to an independent body. As chairman, May was impartial, yet possessed a good knowledge of British industry. He was particularly concerned with the difficulties of the iron and steel industry which had suffered from a reduced demand for its products and dumping by other countries. Undaunted by the fact that the Act outlining the Committee's terms of reference did not authorise it to enter this field, May believed that reorganisation of the industry could not be divorced from the issue of tariffs and set about formulating a scheme for establishing machinery to carry out such a reorganisation. May addressed himself to the problems confronting the iron and steel industry in a memorandum in 1932. Dumping could be checked by the establishment of an organisation in Britain with the power to negotiate production arrangements with other countries. Certain problems were present in the industry itself: it was burdened with a backward organisation, old-fashioned production methods and a lack of rationalisation. May proposed the existing machinery of Trade Associations and the National Federation of Iron and

Steel Manufacturers be grouped together to form effective instruments of control over production. These in turn would be co-ordinated by a new organisation, the Iron and Steel Corporation of Great Britain. This new corporation would promote the setting-up of approved associations and encourage the rationalisation of existing ones by assisting amalgamation and preventing the duplication of plant.

In the event protective tariffs were imposed in 1932 on the understanding that the industry would reorganise itself. However, hopes of reorganisation remained substantially unfulfilled, especially with regard to trade association reform, regional mergers and the elimination of inefficient plant. May himself did not markedly persist with his efforts in this field, leaving much of the initiative to his able colleague on the committee, Sir Alfred Hurst. On the other hand, a new central organisation for the industry, which emerged by 1935, did produce genuine successes in international bargaining, price and investment supervision, and the then-fashionable pursuit of cartelisation, as well as laying the foundations for an efficient organisation of iron and steel during the Second World War. Much of this success rubbed off on the Import Duties Advisory Committee and on May. Winston Churchill recognised the value of May's impartiality when, referring to the work of the Committee, he said, 'I do not think we could have had a better, more competent, more honourable, or more disinterested Committee than the one which has been set up' {Hutchinson (1965) 34}. In recognition of his services to this and the other Committees, Sir George May was given a barony in 1935, taking the title May of Weybridge.

In 1903, May had married Lily Julia, daughter of G Strauss, a merchant; they had two sons and one daughter. Lily May was later awarded an OBE. In earlier years, May excelled at lacrosse and tennis and had a natural aptitude for any ball game. He took up golf late in his career at the Prudential and soon reduced his handicap. Lord May died on 10 April 1946, leaving an estate valued at £195,902 gross.

SARAH SILCOX

Writings:

'The Investment of Life Assurance Funds' *The Journal of the Institute of Actuaries* 46, part 2 (Apr 1912).

PP, Board of Trade Industrial Life Assurance Committee (1920) Cmd 618.

Memorandum on the Reorganisation of the Iron and Steel Industry in *Iron and Steel Re-Organisation Scheme — Correspondence Between the National Committee for the Iron and Steel Industry and the Import Duties Advisory Committee* (HMSO, 1933).

Sources:

Unpublished

Prudential Assurance Co Ltd, annual reports.

BCe.

MCe.

PrC.

Published

Colin Cross, *Philip Snowden* (Barrie & Rockliff, 1966).

DNB.

Sir Herbert Hutchinson, *Tariff Making and Industrial Reconstruction* (George Harrap & Co, 1965).

Ibis Magazine (Journal of the Ibis Society) Apr 1931, May 1946.

Journal of the Institute of Actuaries 72 (1944-46).

PP, Report of Committee on National Expenditure (1930-31) Cmd 3920.

Prudential Bulletin Apr 1931.

Robert Skidelsky, *Politicians and the Slump: The Labour Government 1929-1931* (Macmillan & Co, 1967).

Times 16 Apr 1946.

WWW.

Sir Basil Mayhew (courtesy of Ernst & Whinney).

MAYHEW, Sir Basil Edgar

(1883-1966)

Accountant

Basil Edgar Mayhew was born at Ipswich on 9 November 1883, the elder son of Thomas Edgar Mayhew (d 1931), a chartered accountant in practice at Ipswich, and his wife Amelia Turner née Rainer. He served his articles with his father, qualifying in January 1905. Moving to London, he joined Price, Waterhouse & Co in that year; there he met another young accountant, Harold Barton (qv), who had recently left his native Hull. It soon became apparent that they would not be made partners for some years and they decided, with the approval of their employers, to leave to set up on their own. As Barton, Mayhew & Co, their first office was situated on the third floor of 26 Great St Helens, London, EC3. Each had been allowed to take one client from Price, Waterhouse as the basis for the practice; Barton took the audit of Griffiths & Co, a building contractor, and Mayhew the retailing interests of Van den Berghs, which included a substantial share in the Meadow Dairy Co of George Beale (qv). In 1909, Van den Berghs arranged for Meadow Dairy to take over the Keeloma Dairy, in which they also had an important shareholding. Considering it prudent to appoint another director to Meadow's board to safeguard their increased holding, Van den Berghs selected Basil Mayhew to perform this role. Meadow's growth, financed by Van den Berghs (who increased their holding to obtain formal control of the company in 1912), had been too fast for its own good and Mayhew was entrusted with representing the preference shareholders' capital. His advice was clearly appreciated, as in December 1913 the board of Van den Berghs, dissatisfied with the financial management of another subsidiary, Pearks, consulted him over the revitalisation of the ailing company.

During the First World War, it was decided that Mayhew, who had married in 1911, should stay in the City to run the firm, while Barton would volunteer for military service. Mayhew had, in fact, married Dorothea Mary Paget, the daughter of Stephen Paget, a consultant surgeon at the Middlesex Hospital, and this connection resulted in Barton, Mayhew & Co obtaining a number of medical and charitable clients, including the Croydon Nursing Homes, United Nursing Services Club, Queen Alexandra's Hospital, the Royal College of Nursing and the RAF Benevolent Fund. In this period Mayhew served as secretary to the joint financial committee of the British Red Cross and the Order of St John of Jerusalem. For this work he was awarded a KBE in 1920.

Mayhew's financial expertise and City connections meant that he was in demand as a business consultant throughout the 1920s. In January 1926 Blackburns, Barton, Mayhew & Co (the name changed in 1919 following a short-lived merger with H W & J Blackburn) were appointed auditors to Bowaters, who had been brought to the point of collapse by a scheme to build a new paper mill at Northfleet. Sir Basil Mayhew's suggestion that a new company, W V Bowater & Sons (1926) Ltd, be formed to take over the old merchant business and raise fresh preferred capital on the stock market was accepted by Eric Bowater (qv). Given the uncertain situation this was not easy and the strategy only succeeded when a friend of Harold Barton, John Keeling of the London & Yorkshire Trust, agreed to underwrite the issue. Mayhew was instrumental in negotiating with Armstrongs, the mill contractors, the financial arrangements for the much delayed and partially completed buildings. The survival of Bowaters depended on both the final sum and the method of payment. Sir Gilbert Garnsey (qv) of Price, Waterhouse had been called to represent Armstrongs and together they agreed that a further £175,000 should be paid in cash, the remainder in securities. At the same time Mayhew was responsible for devising a general reconstruction scheme for Bowaters, which resulted in the division and centralisation of head office functions.

Mayhew's friendships throughout industry and Government resulted in his firm obtaining a number of special commissions. In 1930, for example, Sir David Milne-Watson (qv), governor of the Gas Light & Coke Co, requested advice on a coke-order scheme and subsequently on a two-part method of charging domestic consumers which would involve a standing charge and 'half-price gas'. In 1934, when the contracted term expired, the partner, A E (later Sir Edgar) Sylvester, who had been entrusted with the work, was invited to become the Gas Light & Coke Co's comptroller responsible for financial policy. He left Barton, Mayhew to form a budget and audit department and overhauled the cost accounting systems. In 1941 Sylvester became the general manager and served as the governor from 1945-46.

Mayhew developed a considerable experience of committee work, beginning with his secretaryship of the Joint War Finance Committee, 1915-36. In 1918-20 he was secretary to the Central Demobilisation Board. Subsequent appointments were particularly concerned with farming, and included his service from 1921 as a trustee of the Rural Industries Bureau, of which he was chairman in 1952-62. Mayhew was a member of Lord Linlithgow's Departmental Committee of 1923 to investigate the disparity in price of agricultural and kindred produce. He was a member of the standing committee to advise on grants to assist agricultural co-operation or credit (1924) and served on the committee of inquiry into the Co-operative Bacon Factory Industry in 1925. In the following year he was on the standing committee (agricultural section) to consider the Merchandise Marks Act. In 1931 Mayhew sat on the Economic Advisory Council Committee on Centralised Slaughtering and in 1933 was appointed chairman of the British Industries Fair Site and Buildings Committee. Mayhew also served on the joint committee set up by the British and Argentine Governments to inquire into the conditions of their meat trade and in 1947 on the Agricultural Marketing Committee (the Lucas Committee). This work and his links with the National Farmers Union brought Barton, Mayhew & Co the audit of the first marketing boards, for hops (1931), pigs (1933), milk (1933) and potatoes (1934). His appointment as a receiver of Southern Roadways in 1932 ultimately led to the firm becoming auditors of British Road Services.

In 1935 Mayhew accepted a directorship of J & J Colman Ltd. He had encountered the Colman family through the audit of their newspapers, the *East Anglian Daily Times* and the *Norfolk News*. On the death of his first wife in 1931, he married Beryl Caroline Rees, younger daughter of Russell J Colman, in the following year. When two board members died unexpectedly in 1936, Mayhew accepted an invitation to join the company on a full-time basis, leaving Barton, Mayhew in September. During the period of his partnership the firm's fee income had risen from around £1,200 in 1908 to £39,121 in 1928 and reached £66,891 by 1935.

Originally Mayhew's responsibilities were for the Carrow factory at Norwich and in 1943 he became chairman of J & J Colman, the company that operated this mustard and starch works — a post which he retained until 1947. In addition, he was a member of the main board (Reckitt & Colman Ltd) from 1938 until 1954, being the vice-chairman from 1945. He was also the first chairman of MPP (Products) Ltd and a director of a number of Reckitt & Colman subsidiaries. Latterly, he served as a non-executive director of Reckitt & Colman Holdings from its formation in 1953 until his retirement in 1962. His role throughout was that of financial expert drawing on an accumulated experience of company operation.

Mayhew was not particularly active as a member of the Institute of Chartered Accountants in England and Wales, though he served in 1930 as chairman of the London Members Committee. His standing in the profession was such that in 1929 he was called as an expert witness for the prosecution in the case against Clarence Hatry (qv), whose company, Austin Friars Trust, had delayed the publication of its annual report to conceal its grave financial condition from the investing public.

By his first marriage to Dorothea Paget, Mayhew had two sons (one being killed in 1942) and three daughters. His eldest son, Christopher (b 1915), was the Labour Minister of Defence (RN), 1964-66, and was subsequently given a life peerage as Lord Mayhew. Sir Basil Mayhew died on 2 November 1966, aged eighty-two and left £136,398 gross.

EDGAR JONES

Sources:

Unpublished

BCe.

MCe.

PrC.

Information from Reckitt & Colman, and Colman's of Norwich.

Published

Accountant 95, no 3218 (6 Aug 1936), 155, no 4795 (12 Nov 1966).

Carrow Works Magazine 29 (Jan 1936).

Stirling Everard, *The History of the Gas Light & Coke Company 1812-1949* (Ernest Benn, 1949).

Edgar Jones, *Accountancy and the British Economy 1840-1980, The Evolution of Ernst & Whinney* (Batsford, 1981).

Peter Mathias, *Retailing Revolution: A History of Multiple Retailing in the Food Trades Based upon the Allied Suppliers Group of Companies* (Longmans, 1967).

William J Reader, *Bowater, A History* (Cambridge: Cambridge University Press, 1981).

WWW.

MELCHETT, 1st Lord Melchett
see MOND, Alfred Moritz

MELCHETT, 2nd Lord Melchett
see MOND, Henry Ludwig

MELCHETT, 3rd Lord Melchett
see MOND, Julian Alfred Edward

MENELAUS, William

(1818-1882)

Iron and steel firm manager

William Menelaus (courtesy of L J Williams).

William Menelaus was born in Edinburgh in 1818 and was apprenticed as a millwright, which at the time implied a seven-year training in practical engineering. In 1844, at the age of twenty-six, he was sent by a London engineering firm to re-model a corn mill at the Hensol Castle estate of the South Wales ironmaster, Rowland Fothergill. He stayed on in South Wales for the rest of his working life and became one of the most outstanding of the large number of men from Scotland and the North of England who contributed to the Welsh iron and coal trades. He first joined the staff of Fothergill's Abernant ironworks in the Aberdare valley where he became manager, leaving in 1850 to take up a post as blast furnace manager at the Dowlais Iron Works. It was his last change of firm: when he died thirty-two years later he was still an employee of the Dowlais Iron Co.

The importance of William Menelaus lies in the crucial part he played in reviving, nurturing and sustaining this great iron firm. As its general manager for over a quarter of a century he was one of the major early figures of the emerging breed of professional managers who played the innovative and entrepreneurial roles previously associated with owner-capitalists.

When Menelaus arrived at Dowlais it was still deep in the long crisis precipitated by bitter discussions connected with the renewal of the lease in 1848, and intensified by the death of its sole owner, Sir John Guest, in 1852. In 1856 overall control of the firm fell into the hands of one of the trustees appointed under Sir John's will, George T Clark (qv). Clark maintained and exercised ultimate control throughout Menelaus's reign and beyond, an important consideration in making any assessment of the part played by Menelaus. Nevertheless, Clark left the active management to Menelaus, who also provided wide-ranging advice and guidance.

Menelaus was appointed as general manager at Dowlais in 1856, perhaps the most crucial of the general strategic decisions taken by Clark. The significance of the appointment can be indicated by a few specific points. Thus, Menelaus efficiently operated a modern system of management, requiring from each department weekly reports on a few centrally-determined strategic statistics, such as output, costs and hours, and himself giving similar summaries to Clark. In addition, besides informative annual statements (Dowlais remained throughout this time a partnership), he gave perceptive special reports from time to time. The major recommendations of these reports determined the main Dowlais strategies. He defined the Dowlais problems in 1857, in the masterly 'Report ... on the General State of the Dowlais Works': 'Dowlais is standing still instead of taking the lead as from her size and position she ought, and is quietly falling into the rear' {Glamorgan RO, Dowlais MSS}; the rest of his life he spent in successfully reversing this position and re-establishing Dowlais as the dominant firm in the South Wales iron and steel trade.

Menelaus proposed and implemented all main policy changes. A long-standing coal shortage was solved by purchasing the coal taking of the Penydarren Iron Co and by an extensive programme of new sinkings. The decisions were based on careful detailed costings and embodied calculations based not on short-run profit maximisation but on long-term requirements. He launched Dowlais into the sale-coal trade on the grounds that the extra production would give the ironworks an insurance against shortages, would enable economies of scale in coal working, and would provide additional profit. The likelihood of profit was enhanced by Menelaus's introduction of a process which allowed Dowlais to use the small coal in iron production. This effectively reduced the cost of producing large steam coal at Dowlais since, for the Welsh colliery companies, small coal was a waste product.

It was Menelaus, moreover, who set up the famous early experiments on the Bessemer process at Dowlais in 1856. He also later visited English works which were starting steel-making and generally sustained enthusiasm and confidence that steel would ultimately be profitable. The first Dowlais steel rails were rolled on 10 June 1865, although no orders for them existed and the expansion remained very slow until 1870. Menelaus conducted the complicated negotiations with Bessemer (qv) between 1863 and 1865. His cost analyses also highlighted the increasing difficulties over supplies of iron ore and it was he who went to Spain in October 1871 to negotiate an agreement on ore supplies, conducting the detailed financial and legal negotiations with the Consett Iron Co, Krupps of Essen and the Ybarra family of Spain that led, in July 1873, to the formation of the jointly-owned Orconera Iron Ore Co. Menelaus was also acutely aware of the significance of transport costs to a company like Dowlais, dependent on the movement of large amounts of low value, heavy, bulky materials, such as coal, iron ore, and limestone, and spent much time and effort on ensuring that rail and dock companies provided adequate facilities. He was able to do so, as he told the Select Committee on Railway and Canal Charges in 1881, because 'We are strong enough to fight the railway companies ourselves; we appeal to their selfishness ...' {*PP, HC* 1881 (394) XIII 623}.

Menelaus was also entrepreneurial in a more directly innovative sense. He designed a huge new rolling mill, the Boat Mill, which incorporated a two-directional mill and a number of mechanical handling devices of his own invention. More important, he was quick to see the value of other people's innovations. Compressed air for underground haulage in collieries was first used in South Wales at Dowlais; the waste gases were used to heat the furnaces; the Dowlais works was probably, in 1870, the first in Britain to use the waste gases from the coking ovens; as already indicated, he introduced the use of small coal in the furnaces; and his careful calculations exposed old mythologies about the virtues of keeping blast furnaces going for long 'campaigns' by showing that 'old worn out furnaces are merely vehicles for destroying fuel' {*PP*, (1871) C 435-I, B8}.

William Menelaus not only became general manager when the Dowlais firm was already in difficulty, but his reign coincided with a period of acute crisis for the Welsh iron trade generally. Many firms — even the Crawshays of Cyfarthfa — failed, or slid into decline. The Dowlais record is, by comparison, one of considerable success based on bold and substantial capital expenditure. It could not have been achieved if decisions had been determined by short-run profitability. In the six years from 1857 to 1862 capital expenditure on new works totalled £175,442 (an average of £25,240) and total profit was £73,135 (an average of £12,139). But over the rest of the period from 1863 to 1882 profits totalled £2,384,628 (an average of £119,231) and new capital expenditure totalled £548,232 (an average of £27,411).

Menelaus was the leading figure behind the founding of the South Wales Institute of Engineers in 1857, becoming its first president; he was an active promoter of engineering and industrial activities in the region. He was also a founder member of the Iron and Steel Institute of Great Britain in 1869, and its president from 1875 to 1877. He was a regular contributor to debates at the Institute, and was awarded the Bessemer medal in 1881. He was a member of the Institution of Mechanical Engineers, serving as vice-president in 1874, and as a member of the council in 1878.

William Menelaus married in 1852 Margaret Rhys, whose family owned the Llwydcoed ironworks, but his wife died a few months later. Menelaus brought up two boys, who may have been related to him, William and Charles Darling. They both went into the law: William became a judge; Charles an MP, and later a baron. William Menelaus died whilst on holiday in Tenby on 30 March 1882, leaving £193,290 gross. Amongst his bequests, he left his art collection to the Cardiff Free Library, while the bulk of his fortune went to the Darlings.

L J WILLIAMS

Writings:

'Improved Machinery for Rolling Rails' *Journal of the Iron and Steel Institute* 1869.

PP, RC on the Coal Trade (1871) C 435-I.

Presidential address *Journal of the Iron and Steel Institute* 1875.

PP, *HC* 1881 (374) XIII, SC on Charges for Conveyance of Goods on Railways and Canals.

Sources:

Unpublished

Glamorgan RO, Dowlais MSS.

National Library of Wales, Clark MSS.

Erickson workcards.

PrC.

M J Lewis, 'G T Clark and the Dowlais Iron Company, an Entrepreneurial Study' (University of Wales MSc (Econ), 1983).

Published

Cardiff and Merthyr Guardian 4 Sept 1852.

John H Morris and Lawrence J Williams, *The South Wales Coal Industry, 1841-1875* (Cardiff: Cardiff University Press, 1958).

John A Owen, *The History of the Dowlais Iron Works 1759-1970* (Risca, Gwent: Starling Press, 1977).

PP, *HC* 1873 (313) X, SC on Present Dearness and Scarcity of Coal.

Western Mail 31 Mar 1882.

Charles Wilkins, *The History of the Iron, Steel, Tinplate and Other Trades of Wales* (Merthyr: Joseph Williams, 1903).

MENSFORTH, Sir Holberry

(1871-1951)

Engineering company manager

Holberry Mensforth was born at Snow Hill, Bradford, Yorkshire, on 1 May 1871, the second son of Edward Mensforth and his wife Dorcas née Harrison. His mother's family were engineers, of Crabtree Harrison,

Sir Holberry Mensforth (courtesy of Sir Eric Mensforth).

general machine makers of Bradford. His father was a painter and decorator, though in a much smaller way than Holberry's grandfather, Thomas. Thomas Mensforth had been influenced by Robert Owen, the famous socialist leader, and this may have led to the name 'Holberry', after the well-known Chartist leader, Samuel Holberry.

Holberry attended Christ Church Day School in Bradford until about the age of twelve, gaining an 'excellent' in geometry in 1881, and in freehand drawing in 1882. After a few months as a lawyer's office boy, a job he disliked, he became a millwright's apprentice at S Clayton & Co, St Thomas Engine Works, the makers of the Bradford gas engine. Before completing his time he acted as foreman. Further technical instruction followed at evening classes at the Mechanics Institute, enabling him to secure in 1893 a second class in the National Department of Science and Art examination in steam, and in 1894 a second in applied mechanics and a first in machine construction. In 1896-97 he was an instructor in metalwork at the Hull Municipal Technical School under Dr Riley. Mensforth emerged as a versatile mechanic and toolmaker and head of Clayton's engineering shop and proudly became a full member of the Amalgamated Society of Engineers.

After briefly going into business under the style of Mensforth & Warburton, Gear Cutters to the Trade, he joined B H Thwaite's heavy engineering firm, in Westminster, London, which specialised in blast furnace gas engines and blowers, involving large dimensions because of the low calorific value of the fuel. Holberry was particularly interested in the gas engine's application to blast furnaces, thereby acquiring a useful knowledge of iron and steel works' plant. He erected pioneer installations at Barrow, Seaton Carew, Clay Cross, Sheepbridge, and in Germany and France.

At about this time the American firm Westinghouse was establishing a large British subsidiary at the Trafford Park works in Manchester (later to become the Metropolitan Vickers Co) to produce gas engines, steam turbines and a complete range of electrical equipment. Mensforth was introduced to the firm by Charles Paxton Markham (qv), a prominent engineer and Westinghouse customer, and in 1903 he joined the Westinghouse engine department as a technical engineer. He made rapid progress with the firm, and in 1909 he was appointed superintendent of the engineering department. In 1917 he became general manager, a post which revealed not only his engineering ability, but also his capacity to administer successfully a large business organisation. To combat the disruptive effects on factory labour caused by the First World War, he set up in 1917, nine months before Whitley Councils, a works committee and staff committee. The original works committee included 14 trade union officials and two management representatives, with a superintendent and two foremen in attendance. The management members alongside Mensforth were G E Bailey (later chairman of AEI) and M A McLean. Such joint consultation was also pioneered in the Manchester area at about the same time by Charles Renold (qv). Mensforth also recognised the importance of research and development, approving in October 1917 plans drawn up by Arthur P M Fleming (qv) to systematise development and set up a general research organisation. He appreciated the value of a university training and the need to attract graduates to his works as apprentices. Ex-Westinghouse apprentices were subsequently to be found in many parts of the world and through their goodwill contributed to the commercial success of Westinghouse.

During the First World War Mensforth became a founder member and chairman of the Manchester and Districts Armaments Committee. Comprised of leading firms such as Westinghouse, Crossley Bros, W G Armstrong Whitworth, and Mather & Platt, it was principally designed to ensure a continuous supply of shells. ' ... Perhaps because of his Yorkshire pertinacity, [Mensforth was] particularly successful in handling wartime labour difficulties and increasing the output of munitions in the district' {Dummelow (1949) 75}. His management philosophy was later summarised in 1920 in a paper read before the Manchester Association of Engineers, in which he emphasised that the success of an undertaking rested on the 'human considerations' involved. Mensforth's chairmanship brought him into contact with Henry D McLaren, later Second Lord Aberconway (qv), and also earned him a CBE. In recognition of his work on education, which included the use of wartime 'profits' from the Committee's operations to endow engineering scholarships, he was awarded an honorary MSc by Manchester College of Technology in 1919.

After the war Sir Eric Geddes (qv) recruited Mensforth to put the munitions establishments on an economic peace-time basis. As Director General of Factories in 1920-26 he was involved in the drastic reduction of the numbers involved and the closure of some works, the reorganisation of others for normal production, the introduction of modern costing and managerial methods, the securing of the goodwill of the trade unions, and the provision of alternative employment by making new products such as locomotives. As he was an industrialist, it was felt that he would introduce reforms more in keeping with commercial practice. This he did; for instance, the practice followed for two centuries of invariably filling superintendent posts at Ordnance Factories at Woolwich with serving officers was abolished. In 1923 he was created a KCB. But Mensforth was less successful in 1925 as a member of the Biles Sub-Committee, an offshoot of a committee on Fighting Services Economy, chaired by Lord Colwyn. The Biles, or Dockyard Committee, named after its chairman, Sir John Biles, a consultant naval architect, was appointed to investigate the Royal Dockyards and their administration. The appointment of Mensforth and the other board members, such as Sir James Lithgow, the Clyde shipbuilder, and Lithgow's replacement, William L Hichens (qv), reflected the Treasury's view that the dockyards should also benefit from the expertise of businessmen. The final report was highly critical, but the Admiralty successfully deflected most of its proposals.

On completion of his duties Mensforth was invited through McLaren to become managing director of Bolckow Vaughan & Co Ltd, an ailing coal, iron, steel, and chemical producer in the North-East, and to assist in its modernisation and reorganisation. He introduced new methods, drastically cut managerial extravagances, and, characteristically, instituted joint consultation to improve labour relations. In 1931 he negotiated the merger with another large and declining iron and steel producer, Dorman Long. Whilst continuing for two years as a non-executive director of the latter company, he and McLaren became unhappy at the way Dormans was run, and resigned.

In 1930 Mensforth accepted the chairmanship of the English Electric Co Ltd, in succession to William L Hichens. EE had steadily declined in the 1920s under P J Pybus (qv), and was reorganised in 1930 under an American syndicate. Mensforth took two vital executive decisions: he negotiated a comprehensive technical and commercial agreement with Westinghouse in 1931 and, to run the business, appointed as managing director one of his apprentices from his Westinghouse days, George H Nelson, later First Lord Nelson (qv). Mensforth then accepted the chairmanship of Edmundsons Electricity Corporation, an electricity supply holding company with about 50 subsidiaries throughout England and Wales, linked with one of EE's financial backers, the Chicago Utilities Power & Light Co. In 1932 Edmundsons supplied 143,900 consumers, but by 1935, the year Mensforth resigned from the company, the figure had risen to 758,728. This expansion partly reflected Mensforth's imaginative idea of extending hire-purchase facilities to allow poorer people to buy appliances. Edmundsons was more profitable than EE and Mensforth, having installed Harry Towers from Bolckow Vaughan in the purchasing department, used it as a business ally to place favoured but strictly competitive orders with EE for transformers, switchgear, and, increasingly, domestic appliances. Mensforth handed over the chairmanship of EE in 1933 to Nelson, who continued as managing director.

In 1933 McLaren invited Mensforth to join the board of John Brown & Co, on which he served as a non-executive director, a close associate of the chairman. He particularly concerned himself with the engineering aspects of the collieries, steelworks, and shipyard, including work on the *Queen Mary* and *Queen Elizabeth* passenger liners. He also took the chair of a number of subsidiaries, including Nasmyth Wilson of Manchester and Cravens Railway Carriage & Wagon Works, Sheffield. Mensforth was to make three particular contributions to Browns: the development of the Firth Brown Engineers' Tool Department for the manufacture of high-quality cutting tools, which was the practical expression of his obsession with precision work; the modernisation of the Clydebank facilities and Sheffield heavy machine shops; and the purchase in 1936 of Markham & Co Ltd of Chesterfield for £50,000, which, after an increase in capitalisation to £150,000, strengthened Brown's position in the heavy engineering field. Mensforth also welcomed a refugee from Nazi Germany, Ludwig M Loewy, whose designs for aluminium extrusion presses enabled John Brown & Co to close a dangerous gap in British aircraft production facilities. Mensforth remained on the John Brown board until his retirement in 1945. He was also a board member of the Tredegar Iron & Coal Co Ltd until his death.

A vice-president of the British Electrical & Allied Manufacturers Association, Mensforth was also a member of the Institution of Civil Engineers and the Institution of Mechanical Engineers, and contributed occasionally to debates. He was a member of the executive council of the National Union of Manufacturers, and in 1928 was part of a deputation received by Stanley Baldwin, calling for the safeguarding of British industries. In 1931 he gave evidence to the Royal Commission on the Civil Service, when he suggested that since the basis of the Service was clerical it should not undertake any technical work which could be done more efficiently outside. ' ... It would be better if the State encouraged outside firms to do armament and aeronautic work. When a prominent person was sick, he did not go to the Ministry of Health — he went to the medical profession' {*Times* 25 Feb 1931}. In 1932 he attended a three-day conference arranged by the League of Nations at the London School of Economics on the effect of disarmament on unemployment, where he emphasised that pressure from the armed forces was an important spur to metallurgical innovation.

He was remembered as a 'hard taskmaster, ruthless when he had made up his mind on a particular course of action, and he could, on occasion, express himself with a gruffness which lent some colour to the belief; but he was quick to appreciate the need for teamwork in any large organisation ...' {*Engineer* 14 Sept 1951}. His son paid tribute to his 'practical skill, his firmness but fairness and integrity in dealing with men and unions, and his intuitive design feel ... [though] ... he was very cautious as to novel design' {Mensforth (1981) 55}. He was not committed to any political party and served willingly either Labour or Conservative. He played the violin and sang, but in his later life his main hobby and relaxation was to work in his precision workshop at home. In notes made just before his death he referred to his life as 'sixty years a mechanic'. Throughout he was a keen motorist, enjoying tinkering with his car and touring.

He married at Shipley in 1900 Alice Maud (d 1948), third daughter of William Jennings, of Rossington Grange Farm, near Doncaster, and Emmie Temperley. They had one daughter, Muriel (b 1911), and two sons, Thomas (b 1901), and Eric (later Sir Eric, b 1906). Both sons became distinguished engineers, Tom in steelworks plant, underground machinery and electrical power generators, Sir Eric with steelmaking and general engineering, including pioneering work on helicopters, hovercraft, and high altitude environmental control.

Sir Holberry Mensforth died on 5 September 1951 at his home, The Red House, Hazlemere, Buckinghamshire, leaving £6,207 gross.

GEOFFREY TWEEDALE

Writings:

'Some Phases of Works Management' *Proceedings of the Manchester Association of Engineers* 1919-20.

letter on coal research *Times* 8 Apr 1926.

Minutes of Evidence Taken before the Royal Commission on the Civil Service (1929-31) (HMSO, 1931).

Sources:

Unpublished

PRO, Adm/116/2374, Biles Sub-Committee Report.

PrC.

Information from Sir Eric Mensforth (letter of 13 Aug 1984) and Dr R P T Davenport-Hines.

Published

J Bissett, *History of the Board of Management of the Manchester & District Armaments Output Committee 1915-1919* (Manchester: Holiday, Taylor & Co for private circulation, 1919).

Jonathan Boswell, *Business Policies in the Making: Three Steel Companies Compared* (George Allen & Unwin, 1983).

John Dummelow, *1899-1949* (Manchester: Metropolitan Vickers Co Ltd, 1949).

Engineer 192 (14 Sept 1951).

Engineering 172 (14 Sept 1951).

Sir Allan Grant, *Steel and Ships: The Story of John Brown's* (Michael Joseph, 1950).

Oliver F G Hogg, *The Royal Arsenal* (2 vols, Oxford University Press, 1963).

Robert Jones and Oliver Marriott, *Anatomy of a Merger: A History of GEC, AEI, and General Electric* (Cape, 1970).

Sir Eric Mensforth, *Family Engineers* (Ward, Lock, 1981).

Proceedings of the Institution of Mechanical Engineers 166 (1952).

Stephen Roskill, *Naval Policy between the Wars. I: The Period of Anglo-American Antagonism 1919-1929* (Collins, 1968).

Times 12 June 1928, 25 Feb 1931, 2 Mar 1932, 6 Sept 1951.

WWW.

MERCER, Thomas

(1822-1900)

Chronometer manufacturer

Thomas Mercer was born in Liverpool in 1822. After apprenticeship with his grandfather, a watch movement maker in St Helens, he secured employment in 1843 with Russells, a Liverpool firm of nautical opticians. Brought up by his grandparents, who were Nonconformists, Mercer sympathised with radical views and was an ardent follower of Cobden and Bright. In 1854 he went to London and bought a single passage to the United States, intending to emigrate. At the last moment he changed his mind and stayed on in London as a springer and finisher for John Fletcher, chronometer manufacturer, of Leadenhall Street.

Thomas Mercer (courtesy of Mr Alun Davies).

Within four years he set up as an independent chronometer maker in the Clerkenwell area, firstly in Newton Street, then in Goswell Road and finally in Spence Street. He established contacts with a network of over 150 nautical opticians and retailers of chronometers, some in the North of England, others in areas of Europe not supplied by his main competitor, Victor Kullberg (qv). In 1874 for reasons of ill-health he moved his manufacturing base to St Albans, where his workshop employed between a dozen and 16 men and produced an annual output of about 150 instruments. In 1863, four years after the founding of the British Horological Institute, Mercer was elected to its Council, and served as secretary, 1875-95. At the Institute's debates he supported those who were unsuccessfully trying to change the industry's conservative, pre-industrial method of production, and he advocated the adoption of standard and interchangeable parts, on Swiss and American lines.

He died on 22 September 1900, en route to Paris to judge at the International Exhibition. His gross personal estate was valued at £14,948, his gross real estate (22 houses) at £10,805, and his stock in trade, machinery, fixtures and fittings were valued at £2,507. The firm passed to his sons, Tom (1876-1935) and Frank (1882-1970), who successfully restructured it. They adopted new methods of manufacture, bought Swiss and American machinery, and reorganised production on self-sufficient lines. The firm gradually diversified into the manufacture of synchronised ships' clock systems and other specialised engineering products, enabling it to survive the depression that crushed the rest of the industry after the First World War. Mercers is the only remaining chronometer manufacturer in the UK (1984).

ALUN C DAVIES

Sources:

Unpublished

PrC.

Published

Alun C Davies, 'The Life and Death of a Scientific Instrument: The Marine Chronometer, 1770-1920' *Annals of Society* 35 (1978).

—, 'The Rise and Decline of Chronometer Manufacturing' *Antiquarian Horology* 12 (1980).

Tony Mercer, *Mercer Chronometers* (Ashford: Brant Wright Associates, 1978).

MERTHYR, 1st Lord Merthyr
see LEWIS, William Thomas

MERZ, Charles Hesterman

(1874-1940)

Consulting engineer

Charles Merz (from John Rowland, Progress in Power *Newman Neame, 1960).*

Charles Hesterman Merz was born in Gateshead, Durham, on 5 October 1874, the son of John Theodore Merz (1840-1922) and his wife Alice Mary née Richardson. John Merz, an industrialist with interests in chemicals and other local industries, was also a gentleman-philosopher: his four-volume *History of European Thought* was a worthy and unusual attempt to unite the two cultures of science and the arts. Unusually for the time, science as well as business was a regular topic of conversation in the Merz household, and the young Charles grew up in a cultured environment which owed as much to his father's German education as to English influences. His mother was the sister of Wigham Richardson (qv), a leading Tyneside shipbuilder, thus providing access to the Quaker community of the North East, and Charles remained a Friend throughout his life. His uncle, Spence Watson, was a prominent local Liberal, and Charles's sympathies also remained with the Liberal party, though he was not active politically.

Charles went to Bootham a Quaker public school in York, and then to Armstrong College, Newcastle (at that time part of Durham University). He had already decided to become an engineer, and he left college soon afterwards without completing the course. These were exciting times in the North East, with a vigorous and expanding industrial base in coal, iron and shipbuilding, and developments in engineering such as Parsons's (qv) steam turbine with its application in traditional fields and new ones such as power generation. Several new electrical undertakings were established by local industrialists and in 1892, at the age of eighteen, Charles became an indentured pupil of Pandon Dene generating station to learn engineering on the job with the American-owned British Thomson-Houston Co, of which his father was later to become a director. The regime was very stiff, with work beginning at 6.00 am and wages low, but his father's allowance permitted him to live at the respectable level of £120 per annum.

Merz was able over the years to build up a fund of engineering and electrical experience, with the BTH Co, including some exchanges with London and Lincoln firms and, in 1896-98, a spell at Croydon helping to build a new power station designed by Sir Alexander Kennedy. He was subsequently appointed as manager and engineer at Croydon, responsible for operating the plant and developing sales of electricity, but wanted wider experience, for example, in the developing market for electric traction. This came in Cork — a posting which he at first found profoundly unattractive — but he had a greater responsibility when he went there in 1898 to develop an undertaking to supply electricity for lighting, traction and power. It was here that he met many of his future colleagues and worked out with them the fundamental principles of interconnected operations of electric power systems to supply lighting, industrial and traction needs on a large scale: these principles were to be the cornerstone of his later success.

His first opportunity to develop his ideas independently came, like his apprenticeship with BTH, through family influence. His uncle, Wigham Richardson, decided to apply for the franchise to supply electricity on the north bank of the Tyne and to the east of Newcastle, and Merz advised on and improved the consulting engineer's plans. He also appeared as an expert witness before the parliamentary select committee which examined the proposal and accepted it in 1899. His uncle's company wanted Merz as their chief engineer, but he decided he wished to retain his freedom as a consultant, and he was employed by the company on this basis. He left the employ of BTH, much to the latter company's regret, though he was very soon acting as a consultant for them also. His new freedom enabled him to visit the USA to survey developments there, and his consultancy prospered. On 1 January 1902, when he had about 20 salaried employees, he took a partner, William McLellan. William McLellan (1874-1934) had met Merz when they were both working for the Cork Electric Tramways & Lighting Co, Merz as the engineer and manager, McLellan as a mains engineer, and he had also been associated with Merz on Tyneside in the electric power undertaking of the Walker & Wallsend Gas Co, before joining him in the consultancy, originally as an assistant. In 1909 the name of the practice was changed from Charles H Merz to Merz & McLellan, the name it retained from then on.

Merz & McLellan's primary achievement in the pre-war years was the development of the Newcastle (later North-Eastern) Electricity Supply Co (NESCo) group, which grew from his uncle's initiative and in the first decade of the century was the largest and among the more efficient electricity undertakings in Europe and the Empire. Although the group had an able set of managers, the ideas on which it was built were fundamentally those of its consulting engineers. Merz introduced the modern three-phase AC system with large scale generation and widespread interconnection of power stations and load centres in the North Eastern area. His family connections with local industry were an enormous help, but the sheer competitive power of cheap electricity won NESCo more business than less efficient electricity undertakings in other parts of Britain. The threat from electric trams led George Gibb (qv) to electrify parts of the North Eastern railway system; new electro-chemical industries were attracted to the North East by cheap power; and industries already established in the area like coal, iron and shipbuilding were among the leaders in electrification. Merz's classic paper on power station design (written with his partner McLellan) was read before the Institution of Electrical Engineers in April 1904, and laid the basis of modern large-scale economical design from their own experience in developing Carville power station. While it was Sebastian de Ferranti (qv) who was lionised as the archetypal electrical innovator in the contemporary press and by historians, it is to Merz that the title 'the British Edison' justly belongs. While Ferranti's Deptford station was a magnificent failure, Merz proved the effective pioneer of modern interconnected large-scale power generation and the expansion of a cheap and reliable power system.

The Merz & McLellan partnership developed apace at home and abroad and by 1913 was employing 73 staff. The early recruits recalled an imaginative and stimulating working atmosphere. Where manufacturers could not design adequate equipment they used German equipment, or developed their own, as with the Merz-Price switchgear and overhead protection, which was widely used in this country and abroad. There were consultancy contracts with railways, electrical and tramway undertakings. In 1905 an attempt to develop efficient electricity supply in London met with some political obstruction, condemning London to an inadequate electricity service for several decades, but providing Merz with some experience of politics, and some useful contacts with the City. These proved valuable in developing overseas contracts, but already a large proportion of the firm's consulting was abroad. Their London office (in Victoria Street, along with many other Northern firms) specialised in the overseas contracts (though drawings and specifications were handled in the Newcastle office) and business with South Africa, Australia and America was brisk. In addition to much work on the design of power stations and transmission systems, the firm had, by 1914, advised on more than 4,500 miles of railway electrification throughout the world. Merz travelled abroad on many of these contracts, particularly to Australia and America, but also to Argentina and India. In middle age, in 1913, he capitalised on some of the Irish social contacts of his youth and married Stella, the daughter of Edmond de Satur of Dublin, an artist. They had twins, a son and a daughter.

During the First World War, Merz and three members of the staff were drafted by Sir Eric Geddes (qv) into the Admiralty to take charge of experiments and research. Although they met resentment from the insiders at first, they were successful in cutting through an unwieldy bureaucracy and bringing in outside talent from the universities and industry. This had little immediate impact, but it brought valuable long-run results for anti-submarine work. McLellan, who joined the Northumberland Fusiliers as second lieutenant in 1914, was also drafted by Geddes into the Ministry of Munitions, to help with the task of providing an adequate supply of power for munition work. He spent two years on the work, becoming Director of Electric Power Supply, and being given the rank of lieutenant-colonel. In 1918 he accompanied diplomatic naval missions to the USA and Italy, and was awarded the CBE in 1919.

The firm's electrical work continued, with advanced design work on the North Tees power station (which later caused many enquiries from overseas), though Merz himself was increasingly concerned with national policy-making. The report of the Electricity Subcommittee of the Cabinet's Reconstruction Committee on Coal Conservation was largely written by him. It proposed the wider adoption and development of the design philosophy which he had already actualised in NESCo and abroad, suggesting that the 600 electricity districts in Britain should be reduced to only 16 if they were to gain the benefits of economies of scale and interconnection. These ideas were mulled over in Whitehall and Westminster for several years but met political opposition because of their implications for existing vested interests and for the debate on municipal versus private ownership. The establishment of an Electricity Commission to promote voluntary co-operation between the existing undertakings was a pale shadow of what Merz had proposed, and he was undoubtedly wise to turn down the chairmanship of the Commission which Geddes offered to him. He also turned down an honour for his war-work (for which he refused payment), declining to profit from a war which troubled his Quaker leanings. (He continued to refuse all political honours, as well as the presidency of the Institution of Electrical Engineers, though in 1932 he accepted the Faraday medal of the Institution and an honorary DSc from his old university, Durham.) While shunning direct involvement in Government, he nonetheless used his reputation to press for movement along the lines he had advocated during the war. His firm's design, in which McLellan had a large part, for the County of London Co Barking station (opened in 1924) was a partial step towards an integrated power supply for London, and a continuing relationship with that company represented a long-run pay-off from the firm's unsuccessful pre-war adventure in London. He gave evidence against railway companies who wished to set up their own independent, small-scale power stations. By the mid-1920s, he was advising Lloyd George on electricity policy, and when the Conservative Government was driven by criticism from industrialists to intervene to secure a more efficient and integrated electricity supply system, he was influential both in preparing technical data for Lord Weir's (qv) report recommending the establishment of a National Grid, and for the later planning and design of large sections of the Grid. As a member of the Individualist Society, which opposed collectivism, he found that some of his friends criticised these initiatives, which required the creation of a state enterprise, the Central Electricity Board, but the technical logic of the situation did, he felt, demand it and he refused to adopt a dogmatic laissez-faire attitude. He admired the integration of industry, science and the state in Germany, feeling it was fully compatible with the personal freedom that he valued in Britain and felt the Individualist Society should promote. He defended a Socialist member of his staff, against the criticism of his more right-wing business clients. He, more than anyone, deserves the credit for the development of a nationally co-ordinated and efficient system of electricity supply in Britain in the inter-war years. On the economies of the Grid his judgement certainly proved more accurate than that of Sir John Snell, chairman of the Electricity Commission.

His interests were not by any means confined to Britain: indeed much of his work on the Grid was based on his experiences abroad, where longer transmission distances had already required the development of more advanced high-voltage transmission practice. In South Africa, where Merz formed a friendship with the Prime Minister, Smuts, he applied the same principles of electrical development to his advice on industrial and railway electrification, leading, as in Britain, to large-scale development with state involvement. The Electricity Supply Commission of South Africa 'is as much the creation of Merz wishing to sell British technology as it is the creation of South African industrialists' {Christie (1979) 145}. He was also involved in India, Australia and the USA, particularly in the latter country with the Commonwealth Edison Co of Chicago. Working with the US consultants Sargent & Lundy, Merz & McLellan were better able to develop the work they had begun on the re-heat generating sets at North Tees, which proved more suitable for development in the American market than the British.

By the inter-war years, Merz & McLellan were clearly established as the premier British electrical engineering consultants, with only Kennedy & Donkin as serious rivals on the national and international scale. The firm had expanded rapidly on the basis of the growing reputation of its principals. From the late 1920s, Merz and his partner admitted other employees as major partners, or partners in related organisations (Merz & Partners specialised in electric traction and Indian work and McLellan & Partners in industrial and mining work). By 1939, five other colleagues had been admitted to the main partnership. Others had left to form their own businesses or to join other organisations: one index of the quality of the firm is their role in producing many of the leading engineers of the next generation such as Sir John Hacking (qv). By 1939 the Group employed some 200 people. Merz himself remained a shy man, happier with the smaller scale and personal relationships of earlier days. He generally shunned public speaking and preferred his arguments to win over red tape and political obstruction on their merits. His brief embroilments left him with no taste for bureaucracy or politics, and he left it to others to take his ideas over these vital hurdles. There can be little doubt that in opting out of this field, he was exploiting his comparative advantage as a brilliant engineer.

The profession of consulting engineer has in general received a bad press from historians. It is alleged, for example, that they encouraged an undue proliferation of design. This, however, was never fairly said of Merz, who was a pioneer in the development of standardised, interconnected systems. As their prestige grew, Merz & McLellan were also criticised for over-elaborate design: an elephant, the electrical industry proverb ran, is a mouse designed by Merz & McLellan. There was something in this: for example, the firm's design for distribution systems in the 1930s was arguably over-expensive; and their South African contracts were criticised for over-elaborate design for local conditions and under-estimation of costs. Yet Merz's personal contribution, especially in the early years, was consistently biased in the direction of economy in design. His power stations in the North East were a monument not only to creative, economical engineering but also to the beauty which clean, economical lines could produce: and this was an age which indulged in expensive architectural monstrosities such as London's Battersea power station. The temptations of the top firm to capitalise on past reputation and to design extravagantly rather than on an optimal basis are well known in all the consulting professions (whose fees are often proportional to the money they spend): it is to his credit that Merz was, perhaps, better than most at resisting it.

On 15 October 1940, shortly after his sixty-sixth birthday, as he was yet again to be drafted into the Government's wartime planning, he, his two children and some of his household staff were killed instantly by a direct hit on his Kensington home. Family trusts make it difficult to assess the personal wealth he created in his lifetime, but he left £200,480 gross, rather more than the £18,980 his father had left. The beneficiaries of charitable bequests included the National Council of Social Service, the British & Foreign Bible Society, his old university, and various electrical charities.

LESLIE HANNAH

Writings:
(with W McLellan) 'Use of Electricity on the North Eastern Railway and upon Tyneside' *Proceedings of the British Association* (Cambridge, 1904).

(with W McLellan) 'Power Station Design' *Journal of the Institution of Electrical Engineers* 33 (1904).

'Power Supply and its Effects on the Industries of the North-East Coast' *Journal of the Iron and Steel Institute* 1908.

'Electric Power Distribution' *Proceedings of the British Association* (Newcastle, 1916).

(principal author of collective report) *PP*, Interim Report on Electric Power Supply in Great Britain (1917-18) Cd 8880.

'The Transmission and Distribution of Electrical Energy' in *Transactions of the First World Power Conference* (5 vols, Lund & Humphries, 1924) 3.

'The National Scheme of Electricity Supply in Great Britain' *Proceedings of the British Association* (Johannesburg, 1929).

(with F Lydall) 'The Economical Operation of Electrified Railways' in *Transactions of the Second World Power Conference* (2 vols, Berlin: VDI Verlag, 1930).

There were also many privately printed reports by Merz and his colleagues produced for clients of the consultancy.

Sources:

Unpublished

The Electricity Council, Millbank, London, papers.

Merz & McLellan, biographical notes on William McLellan; C H Merz, typescript memoirs (1936).

North Eastern Electricity Board, Newcastle, papers.

Tyne & Wear Archives, Merz & McLellan papers.

BCe.

MCe.

PrC; Will.

Interview with E R Wilkinson, former colleague of Merz, 1974.

Renfrew Christie, 'The Electrification of South Africa 1905-1975' (Oxford D Phil, 1979).

Published

Ian C R Byatt, *The British Electrical Industry 1875-1914* (Oxford: Clarendon Press, 1979).

DNB.

Leslie Hannah, *Electricity Before Nationalisation* (Macmillan, 1979).

Thomas P Hughes, *Networks of Power: Electrification in Western Society, 1880-1930* (Baltimore: Johns Hopkins University Press, 1983).

John Rowland, *Progress in Power: The Contribution of Charles Merz and His Assistants to Sixty Years of Electrical Development 1899-1959* (Newman Neame for Merz & McLellan, 1960).

WWW.

METHUEN, Sir Algernon Methuen Marshall

(1856-1924)

Publisher

Algernon Methuen Marshall Stedman (who later changed his surname to Methuen) was born in Southwark, London, on 23 February 1856, the third son of John Buck Stedman, a doctor, and his wife Jane Elizabeth née Marshall. He was educated at Berkhamsted School and Wadham College, Oxford. On leaving Oxford in 1878 he worked as a tutor in a coaching establishment, until in 1880 he opened his own school at Milford in Surrey.

While a schoolmaster, he wrote many Latin, Greek and French textbooks which were very successful. At first he marketed them himself from the school, then through the publishers George Bell & Sons. The persistent demand for his own works may have encouraged him to realise an ambition of starting his own publishing firm, which he had first thought of soon after leaving Oxford. He consulted various authors, and after he had obtained promises of books from two of the more popular authors of the day, Edna Lyall and Rev S Baring-Gould, he opened a publisher's office in a room off a bookshop in Bury Street, near the British Museum, in June 1889. The owner of the shop, W W Gibbins, acted as his trade manager. Later in the year Stedman took over the publication of his own books from George Bell; but he called his publishing firm Methuen & Co because he wished to keep his publishing and teaching activities separate. Business was very difficult for about three years, until the publication of Kipling's *Barrack-Room Ballads* in 1892 began to establish the prosperity and reputation of the firm. By 1894 annual sales had reached £18,178, with a profit of £1,721, on a list of about 70 titles. In that year larger offices in Essex Street were taken, but it was not until 1895 that Methuen gave up his school to concentrate on publishing. In 1899 he identified himself even more closely with his business by formally adopting Methuen as his surname. By the following year, his list had grown to 546 titles, whose sales that year totalled £50,584, yielding a profit of £7,366.

Although, from 1892, he enjoyed the services of an excellent manager, George Webster (who had been with Kegan, Paul, Trench & Co for sixteen years), and had in E V Lucas one of the best-known literary advisers of the day, Methuen always supervised the details of his business closely. Even when, after he became chronically ill in 1907, his visits to London from his home in Haslemere, Surrey, became much less frequent, daily letters with lists of queries were sent to him, to which he replied by return of post.

Methuen was not an innovative publisher, either in the works he published or in his choice of their format. His strength lay in the consistent astuteness with which he selected authors and books or backed the judgement of his staff over a wide range of fields, building up a long, comprehensive and profitable list. By 1906 this list was generating sales of £135,220, and a profit of £19,714. His single most profitable venture was probably the publication of several of the novels of Marie Corelli, for she was among the half-dozen best-selling novelists who dominated the fiction market at the turn of the century: the first edition of her novel *Temporal Power* (1892) was of 120,000 copies. Methuen was prepared to foster comparatively unknown authors in the hopes that they might become profitable later. Among those he was prepared to back when other publishers refused to take a risk were Henry James and Joseph Conrad; neither proved particularly remunerative for him. But he was not willing to take legal risks. When D H Lawrence's *The Rainbow* was prosecuted for obscenity, Methuen, who had offered Lawrence a contract on the strength of a recommendation from the literary agent J B Pinker, did not attempt to defend the work.

A limited liability company was formed in 1910, with George Webster as managing director. The business continued to grow, though apparently at a rather slower rate than in the first years of the century. In the year of Methuen's death, 1924, sales totalled £194,392, from a list of 2,121 titles.

Methuen's main interests outside publishing were his garden at Haslemere, and politics. He was chairman of the Haslemere Liberal Association, and was an unsuccessful Liberal candidate for Guildford in the general election of 1910; he also wrote several political pamphlets. He was created a baronet in July 1916.

His wife, whom he married in 1884, was Emily Caroline, the daughter of Edwin Bedford, a London solicitor. They had no children. Methuen died on 20 September 1924, leaving £386,056 gross. The main beneficiaries of his will, apart from his wife who had a life interest in the bulk of his property, were his old school and college, and the staff of Methuen & Co.

CHRISTINE SHAW

Writings:

Peace or War in South Africa (Methuen & Co, 1901).

The Tragedy of South Africa (Methuen & Co, 1905).

England's Ruin (Methuen & Co, 1905).

A Simple Plan for a New House of Lords (Methuen & Co, 1911).

An Anthology of Modern Verse (Methuen & Co, 1921).

Shakespeare to Hardy: An Anthology of English Lyrics (Methuen & Co, 1922).

An Alpine A B C and List of Easy Rock Plants (Methuen & Co, 1922).

Methuen also wrote a large number of school textbooks.

Sources:

Unpublished

BCe.

MCe.

PrC.

Published

Alton Mail 13 Nov 1909, 27 Sept 1924.

Paul Delany, *D H Lawrence's Nightmare: The Writer and His Circle in the Years of the Great War* (Hassocks: Harvester Press, 1979).

DNB.

Farnham, Haslemere and Hindhead Herald 13 Nov 1909.

Guildford and Godalming Free Press 13 Nov 1909.

James Hepburn (ed), *Letters of Arnold Bennett* (Oxford: Oxford University Press, 1966).

Brian Masters, *Now Barabbas Was a Rotter: The Extraordinary Life of Marie Corelli* (Hamilton, 1978).

Sir Algernon Methuen, Baronet: A Memoir (pp, 1925).

Methuen's Gazette and Literary Notes, then *A Book Gazette and Notes on Works Published by Methuen and Company* Apr 1894-Oct 1899.

Public Opinion 29 Apr 1904.

Frank Swinnerton, *Background With Chorus: A Footnote to Changes in English Literary Fashion between 1901 and 1917* (Hutchinson, 1956).

—, *Figures in the Foreground: Literary Reminiscences 1917-1940* (Hutchinson, 1963).

Times 21 Sept, 20 Nov 1924.

WWW.

F G Miles, pictured in a wartime photograph (courtesy of Adwest PLC).

MILES, Frederick George

(1903-1976)

Light aircraft manufacturer and designer

Frederick George Miles was born at Worthing, Sussex, on 22 March 1903, the eldest of four sons of Frederick Miles, a Sussex laundry proprietor, and his wife Esther née Wicks. He displayed characteristic independence by leaving his Brighton school at the age of thirteen to start his own business. Between 1916 and 1928 he acquired a wide knowledge of most aspects of engineering in a number of jobs. In the same period he also learned higher mathematics, became a skilful aviator and showed noticeable potential as an aircraft designer.

His interest in flying was first stimulated in 1922 when he made a brief 5s joy-ride in an old Avro 504 from a local field. Shortly after, with a few friends, he designed and built his first aeroplane, the Gnat. Although this was never intended to fly, its completion provided Miles with valuable experience and also led to a meeting with the early aviation pioneer and experienced RFC pilot, Cecil Pashley. Miles's infectious enthusiasm persuaded Pashley to provide an aircraft and form a business partnership with him in 1928. The result was the Gnat Aero Co Ltd, which shortly became two related companies, the Southern Aero Club Ltd and Southern Aircraft Ltd. Initially the former was merely a joy-riding and flying school concern, but before long Pashley had taught Miles to fly — in fact Miles was actually giving instruction and joy-rides the day after his first solo — and soon the latter firm also undertook aircraft overhaul, reconstruction and repair work. In typical fashion Miles personally combined the roles of flying instructor, joy-ride pilot, test pilot, and licensed ground engineer and inspector. In 1929, the first of six Southern Martlet biplane aircraft was flown, Miles having played a major part in its construction and design. In summer 1931, Miles left Southern Aircraft Ltd, intending to emigrate to South Africa, but as soon as he reached Cape Town, he decided to return to England. In 1932 he married Maxine (usually known as Blossom) daughter of Sir Johnston Forbes-Robertson, the London actor-manager. He had taught her to fly two years earlier; now she became her husband's business partner, and keenest critic.

F G Miles with the Secretary of State for Air, Sir Kingsley Wood and a Miles Monarch at the official opening of factory extensions (courtesy of Adwest PLC).

While temporarily living in rented accomodation in Sevenoaks, they designed the elegant Miles M1 Satyr, the first true Miles aeroplane; this diminutive one-off aerobatic biplane was built by Parnall Aircraft of Yate, Gloucestershire and first flew in September 1932. Already Miles was planning the design of a low-wing monoplane which could be mass-produced cheaply enough for private owners and flying clubs; his chief problem was to find a manufacturer. However, in September 1932 Miles and his wife visited Reading Aerodrome, and so convinced Charles Powis, the aerodrome owner and managing director of Phillips & Powis Aircraft

(Reading) Ltd, of the merits of their ideas that he offered them part of a hangar in which to design and build their new monoplane.

The M2 Hawk prototype with a Cirrus engine was test flown on 29 March 1933, and performed well. The Hawk had attractive lines, and an attractive price, £395 — then almost half the cost of an equivalent biplane. About 30 Hawks were built in the first year of production by Phillips & Powis. Approximately 20 different variants were built, both to suit individual owners' specifications and for experimental and research purposes. The most significant of these variants was the M2F Hawk Major which was put into production as the Hawk Trainer, and became the first low-wing monoplane trainer to be used by the RAF. This aircraft was also notable for its wooden construction at a time when most other manufacturers used metal, and for being the first British aircraft to be equipped with split trailing-edge flaps as a standard fitting.

In 1935 the company and Miles achieved great success in the Kings Cup Air Race. Miles won a speed prize in his new M5 Sparrowhawk and Phillips & Powis aircraft took first, second, third and fifth places overall: the first and only time that the first three winning aircraft in this annual event had been designed and built by a single company. This success aroused far greater interest in the firm world-wide, and was partly responsible for the conversion of the firm into a public company in 1935, renamed Phillips & Powis Aircraft Ltd, with Rolls Royce providing the majority of outside share capital. Charles Powis was succeeded as chairman and managing director by a Rolls Royce representative, Miles was himself appointed technical director and the company began major expansion as a manufacturer of mainly military aircraft to meet future requirements of the RAF.

Miles was now generally acknowledged to be one of Britain's most progressive aircraft designers and his future projects were to benefit the company still further. In 1936 he produced his first twin engined all-wood cabin monoplane, the M8 Peregrine, and also built the prestigious Miles M12 Mohawk, which was a unique long-range cabin monoplane designed for Charles Lindbergh, the Atlantic pioneer. Miles became managing director of the company later that year but still carried out much of the design work, with much technical assistance provided by his wife Blossom. Over the following twelve years, their company was responsible for a prodigious number of designs and projects, some of them only experimental prototypes or never constructed, yet many others were built in quantity for the armed forces in the Second World War, such as the Magister, the Master and the Martinet. The Air Ministry placed a £2 million order with the company for the Miles Master in June 1938, then the largest single order ever placed for a training aircraft.

Many more technical and aeronautical advances were made by the company during the war; their designs varied from target-towing aircraft, twin-engined fighters and medium bombers to troop-carrying gliders. Their ultimate design, the Miles M52 Supersonic Project, was summarily cancelled by the Government in 1946 before final completion of the prototype. Through their cancellation the UK lost the chance of being the first country to achieve manned supersonic flight.

When Rolls Royce ceased to be involved with Phillips & Powis in 1941, Miles bought their financial interests in the firm with the assistance of his

The first production Miles M94 Master I (N7408); this aircraft first flew on 31 March 1939 and final production of this model reached 898 (courtesy of Adwest Group PLC).

immediate family, and became chairman and managing director on the new board. A year later the firm's achievements were formally recognised when it was elected to full membership of the Society of British Aircraft Constructors (SBAC), and in October 1943 the name of the company was changed to Miles Aircraft Ltd. Miles had now fulfilled an earlier ambition, to obtain full control of the company he had done so much to create. At its peak during the Second World War, Miles Aircraft Ltd employed over 6,000 people and was noted for its enthusiasm, inventiveness and friendly organisation.

However, in the early post-war era, for a variety of reasons, the firm unfortunately became the victim of its own success. Unlike most other major aircraft manufacturers, Miles Aircraft Ltd was only a young company and hence heavy wartime restrictions on the amount of profit they could make prevented them from investing sufficiently in industrial plant and machinery (the majority of this still being government property in 1948), and also led to a lack of financial reserves for the company. Perhaps F G Miles himself can be criticised for continuing to employ too large a workforce after the war's end, at a time when the post-war British civil aircraft market was in a very poor state. Despite diversifying production to many new peacetime products (such as the 'Biro' ballpoint pen), there was insufficient work for the employees but Miles also seems to have persisted with wartime management levels. This situation was made far worse in 1947 by cancellations and a lack of orders for Miles's new civil aircraft types, a bad winter and associated power cuts of that same year (which affected the storage of raw materials as well as working conditions), interference from politicians and Government, and inevitably an increasing overdraft. Eventually, with a £600,000 overdraft, incessant demands for repayments of debts to creditors, and an apparent refusal from the bank to increase overdraft facilities, Miles was forced to call in a receiver and faced voluntary liquidation. By the middle of 1948, the firm had ceased to manufacture aircraft, but was beginning a recovery based on the production of other engineering products — although by this time Miles himself had left.

Miles never again experienced such success in his later business activities, although he remained within the aircraft industry. In 1949 he formed a new company at Shoreham known as F G Miles Engineering Ltd, of which he was chairman and managing director until 1961, when it was amalgamated with several other aircraft companies to form the Beagle Group (whose managing director was Peter Masefield (qv)). The financial collapse of Beagle in 1969 was largely due to earlier government intervention and marked the end of an era in light aircraft manufacturing in Britain. By this time, Miles had begun to specialise in flight simulators, aircraft instrumentation, and early applications of electronics in aviation. In the early 1970s he served as chairman and managing director of both Miles-Dufon Ltd and Miles Hivolt Ltd and was also chairman of Miles Nautical Instruments Ltd and Hivolt Ltd.

Frederick and Blossom Miles (d 1984) had two children, a daughter Mary (who pre-deceased him) and a son, Jeremy, who served in the Fleet Air Arm. Miles had few hobbies. He enjoyed cinematography and yachting but had little time for either. Frederick Miles died on 15 August 1976, leaving £224,761 gross.

JULIAN C TEMPLE

Sources:

Unpublished

PrC.

Published

Philip Birtles, 'Learning from the Student' *Aeroplane Monthly* 3 (May 1975).

Don L Brown, *Miles Aircraft Since 1925* (Putnam, 1970).

—, 'Wings Over Sussex Part 2' *Aeroplane Monthly* 7 (Oct 1979).

Flight 9 Sept 1937.

A H Lukins (ed D A Russell), *The Book of Miles Aircraft* (Leicester: Harborough Publishing Co Ltd, 1946).

Midland Counties Aviation Research Group, 'Beagle Aircraft. A Production History' (Hinckley: Midland Counties Publications, 1974).

Miles Aircraft Ltd, *Milestones Nineteen Hundred and Forty Six* (pp, the Company, 1946).

Gordon Riley, 'Blossom Miles' *Vintage Aircraft* 31 (July-Sept 1984).

WWW.

Sir Humphrey Milford (courtesy of Oxford University Press).

MILFORD, Sir Humphrey Sumner

(1877-1952)

Publisher

Humphrey Sumner Milford was born at East Knoyle, Wiltshire, on 8 February 1877, the youngest of ten children of Rev Newman Milford, the Rector of East Knoyle, and his wife Emily Sarah Frances, daughter of Charles Richard Skinner, Bishop of Winchester.

Milford was a scholar of Winchester and New College, Oxford, where he took a first in 'Greats' in 1900. He thereupon joined the University Press in Oxford and for six years worked closely with, and acquired a great attachment to, the Secretary of the Delegates of the Press, Charles Cannan. He was, however, always destined for the London office of the press. Henry Frowde was the London publisher; he had started his career as a warehouseman, distributing Oxford Bibles, but emerged in the course of time as a publisher in his own right. When Milford joined him in 1906 on a salary of £700 a year (Frowde earned £1,800) the way was open for further expansion — and Milford appeared the ideal man to shake off a reputation for academic fustiness and cramped pedantry. He succeeded Frowde as Publisher to the University in 1913, and thereafter his name became famous as it appeared on the title pages of all OUP books published from London.

From the time he arrived to help Frowde, hardly a year went by without some striking innovation. In 1906 the Press acquired 66 volumes of World's Classics from the bankrupt publisher Grant Richards. Milford cherished this series for the rest of his time with the Press: it once and for all established Oxford in general publishing. In 1907 he entered into a form of partnership with Ernest Hodder Williams of Hodder & Stoughton to launch a new series of medical publications, under the guidance of Sir William Osler, Regius Professor of Medicine at Oxford. The arrangement lasted until 1923 when OUP bought out Hodder and enjoyed the full fruits of a lucrative and highly distinguished series. A similar arrangement brought into being another semi-autonomous department, for juvenile books. After the First World War Milford created a music department under the eccentric genius Hubert Foss: he allowed it to lose money for many years, but it finally established Oxford as one of the outstanding music publishers in the country and contributed greatly to the prosperity of the Press. Perhaps the most far-reaching of Milford's innovations was the establishment of a department for overseas education. This led in due course to the setting-up of branches throughout the world, and turned the Press into a genuinely international publishing house.

Milford appeared to have unlimited confidence in his ability to achieve his aims, and he expected his appointed managers to follow his example. He allowed a great measure of independence, and was often reluctant to interfere except on the rare occasions when a rescue operation might be necessary. He was with the Press throughout his working life, from 1900 to retirement in 1945.

He had a high reputation among his fellow publishers in London. President of the Publishers' Association in 1919-21, he was awarded an honorary D Litt by Oxford University in 1928, and was knighted in 1935.

In 1902 he married Marion Louisa (d 1940), daughter of Horace Smith, a magistrate, and in 1947 Rose Caroline Wilson (d 1966). There were two sons and one daughter by the first marriage. Sir Humphrey Milford died on 6 September 1952, leaving £12,197 gross.

PETER SUTCLIFFE

Writings:

(ed), *Selected Modern English Essays* (Oxford University Press, 1925).

(ed), *The Oxford Book of Regency Verse* (Oxford University Press, 1928).

(ed), *Selected English Short Stories* (Oxford University Press, 1930).

(ed), *The Oxford Book of English Verse of the Romantic Period* (Oxford University Press, 1951).

Milford also edited the works of Borrow, Browning, Clough, Cowper and Leigh Hunt.

Sources:

Unpublished

Oxford University Press, Oxford, files and letter-books.

MCe.

PrC.

Published

DNB.

Peter Sutcliffe, *The Oxford University Press: An Informal History* (Oxford: Clarendon Press, 1978).

WWW.

MILLBANK, 1st Lord Millbank
see DUVEEN, Joseph

Bertram Mills (courtesy of Mr Bernard Mills).

MILLS, Bertram Wagstaff

(1873-1938)

Circus proprietor

Bertram Wagstaff Mills was born in Finsbury, London, on 11 August 1873, the son of Lewis Halford Lupton Mills, then a joint-stock company secretary, and his wife, Mary Fenn née Wagstaff. His father owned a coach-building works at Paddington and also two farms in the country, at Smarden in Kent and at Chalfont St Giles in Buckinghamshire, where the horses were rested. Bertram spent much of his childhood on these farms, where he learned to ride and developed a passion for working with horses.

He attended the Philological School, Marylebone (later Marylebone Grammar School), leaving at the age of fifteen to join his father's business. For the next twenty-five years he worked with coaches and horses, and travelled around the horse-shows in England, the Continent and America, exhibiting his vehicles. With the advent of the motor car in the 1890s, the firm, in addition to coach, carriage and harness making, built car bodies and much later imported American automobiles. Bertram Mills retained his first love for horses and became a breeder and an international judge and exhibitor of hackney harness horses. He also invented and manufactured the Mills Horse Show Wagon. At the outbreak of war in 1914 he joined the Royal Army Service Corps and was demobilised at the end of the war with the rank of captain.

Mills returned home in 1919 to find diminished opportunities for coach-building. After watching a rather indifferent circus performance in the Grand Hall at Olympia he opined, under some pressure from two of his friends (both Olympia directors) that 'If I couldn't do better I'd eat my hat' {Mills (1967) 15}. Reginald Heaton, the managing director of Olympia, seized the chance to complete the coming season's tenancies and Sir Gilbert Greenall Bt, the other Olympia director, persuaded Mills on a bet to present a circus at Olympia over the winter of 1920-21. At the time the popularity of circuses was at a low ebb. They were regarded as second-rate entertainment and since the Olympia exhibition hall first opened in 1886 there had been only 13 Christmas shows of which just five were circuses, and none of these had been sufficiently profitable to be staged a successive season. Bertram Mills decided to bring the spectacular American three-ring circus of Ringling, Barnum & Bailey to London. Apparent disaster struck when John Ringling informed him in June 1920 that he was unable to obtain shipping space to bring his circus across the Atlantic. Mills faced the alternatives of either breaking his contract or of organising his own circus. Characteristically he chose the latter. Over the next six months he toured the major circuses of Europe and assembled a programme of turns for a single ring (eventually playing to 7,000 people) performance to run for five weeks. The result was a highly acclaimed run for 'The Great International Circus,' hailed in the press as 'Best show in London for many years' {*ibid*, 20} and for which some 350,000 tickets were printed and sold.

Heartened by his success, Bertram Mills took the Olympia lease for a second season, recruiting performers from Europe, like Rastelli the unsurpassed juggler. Thereafter Mills presented a circus at Olympia each December until his death. From autumn 1922 it was known as 'Bertram Mills Circus' and a visit to it increasingly became part of the social calendar of all classes. To overcome upper class prejudice against circuses Mills sedulously cultivated their patronage. Colonel Hugh Cecil Lowther, Fifth Earl of Lonsdale (1857-1944), an old friend of Mills, became honorary president of the circus in 1921. From the beginning Mills commenced each season with a press and society luncheon which effectively helped to change the circus image. By the mid-1930s over 1,300 guests attended and those in 1937 included 63 peers, three bishops, and 14 MPs, as well as the Lord Mayor of London and numerous other dignitaries. The Prince of Wales visited the circus (incognito) in 1926 and other members of the Royal Family followed, though a reigning monarch did not attend until 1952.

Between the wars the Bertram Mills circus presented many of the world's leading artistes at its indoor site in the Grand Hall at Olympia. They included Captain Alfred and his 70 lions from the Nouveau Cirque in Paris; Schaeffers' troupe of 30 midgets; Koringa 'the only female fakir in the world' {*ibid*, 87}; the acrobat-comic, Charlie Rivels, recruited in Spain, who is still working to this day (1983); and, most famous of all, Coco the clown, who first performed for Mills in 1929. Showmanship and sheer spectacle, for which Bertram Mills and his son Cyril travelled 50,000 miles in 1937 alone (to recruit new turns), was not the only explanation of his success. Right at the start he chose a very capable man to head his executive team and take care of organisational details: J Russell Pickering, a chartered accountant and an old army friend who had been his senior officer in the RASC. Mills himself took several steps to protect his market advantage, besides the reshaping of the circus's social image. Since his circus occupied only about a third of the Grand Hall at Olympia, he sublet the remainder to people who operated rides, games and sideshows, which provided a funfair that complemented rather than competed with his circus; one showman who started there was Sir Billy Butlin (qv). When in 1923 the National Hall was added to the Olympia site, Mills secured the advertising rights on its main road frontage and arranged for it to be converted into a gigantic ballroom, providing space for 5,000 dancers, with its bands playing after the evening's circus show had ended.

Throughout his eighteen years as a circus proprietor Bertram Mills was acutely conscious that 'he was an amateur amongst professionals' {Smith (1939) 175} and remained intensely reserved with his performers. For their part, they liked and respected him, despite his policy of cutting down their time in the ring, to give the audience rapid changes of laughter, excitement and thrills. He always said 'Keep them hungry: never give them all they want to see' {Information from B N Mills}. Although Mills had not been brought up in the circus he had encountered it many times while attending international horse shows, particularly on the Continent, before the war. In addition

He possessed, it is true, one great asset in this new profession; his knowledge of horseflesh was profound; he was the equal of any gypsy horse-wizard. Perhaps that is why the Bertram Mills liberty horses are the finest that have ever been seen in the ring. {Smith (1939) 173}

Within and beyond his business activities Bertram Mills was a straight dealer who kept his word and never hesitated to expose crooked dealings, as at first emerged in the Olympia fun-fair for example. To the circus world he was known as 'the Guv'nor':

> The Guv'nor was a short, stocky man with a bald head, a ruddy, pugnacious face, a grey moustache, and twinkling, shrewd blue eyes. His eyes were as blue as the cornflower he invariably wore in his button-hole. He would have looked undressed without that cornflower. {*ibid*, 172}

In 1925 Bertram Mills brought his two sons into the firm but after three seasons it was clear that there was insufficient business to occupy them and their father, especially during the spring and summer months. Furthermore three other circuses had been launched in London in the late 1920s, representing a threat to their market dominance. To resolve the situation Bertram's two sons persuaded their father to start a tenting circus: this would absorb their energies during the summer months and counterbalance any diminution in Olympia earnings. The tenting circus took to the road in April 1930 at Luton. By 1937 the tenting season saw the Bertram Mills circus perform in 47 towns, attracting 829,000 attendances, compared to 393,000 attendances (plus 44,000 at the fun-fair) during the indoor Olympia season of 1937-38. Net profits for the whole Bertram W Mills business, before income tax, fluctuated between £35,000 and £44,600 per annum, 1935-37.

Outside the circus Bertram Mills was a prominent member of the Hackney Horse Society, of which he was president in the late 1920s. To the end of his life he rode to hounds and, as a hobby, avidly indulged his interest in road coaching; his coaches ran between London and such provincial points as Brighton, Boxhill and Oxford. He was a member of the Coaching Club (which still exists) and he was also a member of the British Horse Society. In defence of responsible animal trainers and against cruelty towards animals, Mills worked tirelessly for a new code of laws which was incorporated in the Performing Animals (Regulation) Act of 1925.

Bertram Mills sat on the London County Council, representing East Fulham, 1928-34, and the Clapham Division, 1934-38. A member of the dominant Municipal Reform Party (Conservatives), he chaired a number of committees and subcommittees including those on Entertainment Licensing, Inspection of Films, and Sunday Entertainment. He was also a member of the Special Consultative Committee of Experts to the British Board of Film Censors, 1934-38, and president of the Showmans' Guild of Great Britain and Ireland, 1934-38.

Bertram Mills in 1901 married Ethel Kate, daughter of William Notley, a farmer of Thorndon, Suffolk. They had two sons, Cyril Bertram, who went to Harrow and then graduated at Corpus Christi College, Cambridge, and Bernard Notley, who was at Jesus College but did not graduate. They succeeded their father and continued to run the circus until 1965.

Bertram Mills died of pneumonia at the age of sixty-four on 16 April 1938, leaving £131,012 gross.

DAVID J JEREMY

Sources:

Unpublished

BCe.

MCe.

PrC.

Information from Bernard N Mills.

Published

DNB.

Frank Foster, *Clowning Through* (Heath Cranton, 1937).

—, *Pink Coat, Spangles and Sawdust. Reminiscences of Circus Life with Sangers's, Bertram Mills and Other Circuses* (Stanley Paul & Co, 1948).

W Eric Jackson, *Achievement. A Short History of the London County Council* (Longmans, 1965).

Cyril Bertram Mills, *Bertram Mills Circus: Its Story* (Hutchinson, 1967).

Eleanor Smith, *Life's a Circus* (Longmans, Green & Co, 1939).

Times *Prospectuses* 77 (1929), 101 (1947).

WWW.

MILNE, Sir James

(1883-1958)

Railway manager

James Milne was born in Dublin on 4 May 1883, the younger child of Joseph Milne, JP, of Clondillure, Palmerston Park, Dublin. His father, a Scottish Presbyterian, had come from Aberdeen to Dublin in the 1870s, becoming a director of W H M Goulding, the fertiliser manufacturers.

James (or 'Jimmy' as he was known generally) was educated at the High School, Dublin then, following his brother, John William, at Campbell College, Belfast, a school with a Presbyterian foundation. He was at Campbell College between 1896 and 1900 after which he attended the Victoria University, Manchester, where he took a BSc (engineering) degree. After graduating, at the age of twenty-one he joined the Great Western Railway as a pupil in the locomotive department under the chief mechanical engineer, G J Churchward. He became a member of the Institution of Civil Engineers in 1909.

After passing through the Swindon workshops, mechanical laboratory and drawing office he transferred to the company's headquarters at Paddington and began an unusually rapid ascent up the promotion ladder. He had experience in the office of the superintendent of the line, then in the general manager's office. The general manager of the time, Sir James Inglis (qv), built up a small office where men of ability could show their worth. Milne worked in the statistical and Board of Trade sections, where he demonstrated his flair with figures and understanding of financial matters, abilities which were to play an important part in the later development of his career. However, in 1912 he returned to the office of the superintendent of the line, Charles Aldington, and took charge of the running department at the exceptionally young age of twenty-nine. His experience of everyday operations was further increased two years later when he was appointed chief clerk to the divisional superintendent at Pontypool Road and was for a short time the acting divisional superintendent at Swansea. In 1917 he became assistant divisional superintendent at Plymouth. Thus by the age of thirty-five Milne had reached the ranks of middle management.

In September 1919 he left the GWR and entered Whitehall. Sir Eric Geddes (qv) appointed Milne to the position of director of statistics in the recently-established Ministry of Transport. Here, under the Director General of Finance and Statistics, he had responsibility for the collection of the extraordinarily detailed statistics and returns which transport undertakings were required to supply to the Minister each year. Subsequently he was selected to assist the Committee on National Expenditure which Lloyd George appointed in 1921. The committee, which was chaired by Geddes, was charged with the task of identifying all the possible reductions in supply services that could be made in order to reduce current expenditure. It sat until February 1922. Although Geddes refused to be associated with the subsequent stringent policies of deflation that came to be linked with his name (the 'Geddes Axe'), and resigned from the Commons and political life in March 1922, for Milne the Geddes committee provided a further opportunity for public service, and public recognition.

Meanwhile, the death of one general manager, Frank Potter, and the early retirement of his successor, Charles Aldington, had opened up the prospects for promotion into the higher management of the GWR. On 1 January 1922 Milne became assistant to the newly-appointed general manager, Felix Pole (qv), his former colleague in the general manager's office before the First World War. In April 1922 Milne became the principal assistant to the general manager.

Later in the same year his services were loaned by the company to the

Indian Retrenchment Committee. Apparently he was selected by Lord Inchcape (qv), who, as a member of the Geddes Committee, had been impressed with Milne's mastery of financial and fiscal matters. Inchcape was also a director of the GWR (1918-33) and may have watched Milne's advancement within the company. Milne accompanied Inchcape to India and was one of the co-signatories to the Committee's report. He returned to Paddington in April 1923 and soon after was made a Companion of the Order of the Star of India in recognition of his services. In 1924 he was promoted once more, becoming assistant general manager: in effect Pole's deputy and heir apparent. His salary of £3,075 a year was raised to £4,250 three years later.

Milne succeeded Pole, who left to become the executive chairman of AEI, in July 1929. His starting salary of £7,000 was increased to £8,000 in 1932 and to £10,000 in 1937. There is little doubt that Pole's departure gave Milne the post much sooner and with the prospect of a much longer tenure than he could have expected, for only six years separated the ages of the two men. Milne was forty-six at the time of his appointment. While his promotion reflected the company tradition of the internal recruitment of chief executives, in Milne's case it was neither an insular nor a conservative appointment. For he brought an unusual breadth of knowledge and experience to the task of managing this gigantic concern with its issued capital of £147 million, its labour force of 106,429 workers and operations over 3,749 miles of running road. Not only did he have a direct knowledge from the early part of his career of the company's two largest departments (locomotive and traffic), and later of decision-making at the highest levels, but also of the inner workings of the machinery of central government. This last was invaluable in a period when the hand of government touched many of the company's decisions and defined many of its options.

In the year that Milne took over (1929), the GWR came within 3.5 per cent of earning the 'standard revenue' which had been fixed the year before by the Railway Rates Tribunal. It was never to come that close again. The ability of the company to maintain its income was limited by the persistent problems of the staple industries of South Wales and the loss of traffic to road competitors, both major considerations in the development of company policy. Net revenue in the 1930s was highly volatile and followed the general movement of the economy, reaching a low of £4.46 million in 1932 and a peak of £6.9 million in 1937. However, the rate of return on revenue account expenditure held up much better, because under Milne costs were carefully controlled and improvements were achieved in efficiency. The key technical indicator of efficiency, the average net ton-miles per engine hour, improved.

Although a number of improvements in practice could be made within the limits of the existing provision of capital, there were many others, such as the modernisation of the South Wales docks and their appliances to take 20 ton wagons, the remodelling of the great marshalling yards at Banbury, Severn Tunnel Junction and Rogerstone, and the extension of automatic train control — all accomplished in the period — which plainly could not. In cases such as these, Milne was severely limited by the poor stock market valuation of the company and the top heavy capital structure which it had carried since the 1921 Railways Act. Nevertheless, some progress was made through an extensive programme of development works in co-operation with the Government, using the financial provisions of the Development (Loans, Guarantees and Grants) Act (1929). The financial assistance given by the Government took the form of annual grants of interest on the company's capital expenditure, at varying rates up to 5 per cent for periods of from five to fifteen years. Between 1929 and 1935 just over 60 per cent of the company's expenditure on capital account was devoted to projects connected with this scheme.

Milne, an indefatigable worker without the slightest regard for time, expected and usually got the same commitment from his management team. He pressed the heads of department to prepare investment plans as soon as possible. These he then skilfully presented to the government committee that considered applications, the Public Utility Advisory Committee, and by October 1931 40 GWR proposals had been approved. In 1935, together with the leaders of the other mainline railways, Milne was involved in discussions with the Treasury about the possibilities of further financial assistance. The outcome, modelled closely on the provision made for London Transport earlier in the year, was the Railways (Agreement) Act (1935). The Railway Finance Corporation was established to raise new capital on behalf of the mainline companies at low rates of interest and with a guarantee of interest and principal by the Government. Within a matter of months, the company was ready with plans to spend £5.5 million on a wide range of projects, including the adaption of certain lines for use by heavier trains, the doubling of other lines and the enlargement and improvement of certain important stations. The cumulative effect of these and the projects undertaken earlier was quite considerable. They were the visible expression of Milne's great pertinacity in the face of an unpromising economic and financial climate.

His energies were also devoted to the daunting task of finding ways to combat competition. Despite the vast increase of concentration in the railway industry after the 1921 Act, in the early 1930s there still remained a considerable amount of inter-company competition as the mainline railways struggled to protect their incomes in the face of the Depression. After prolonged negotiations involving Milne and the other general managers, comprehensive pooling arrangements were drawn up and given Ministry of Transport approval in 1933. Naturally enough Milne added his voice to the railway demand that road interests should make a fair contribution to the costs of their 'permanent way', to bring parity with the operating conditions facing the railways. Some recognition of this point of view was given in the Road and Rail Traffic Act (1933), which promised some relief to the railways by causing road transport costs to rise.

Meanwhile the railways used powers granted in 1928 to acquire a financial stake in existing road firms and to exert their influence from the boardroom. In this way the GWR became involved in a number of bus companies and also acquired, with the other mainline railways, a controlling interest in several important road haulage firms. Its total investment in road firms between 1929 and 1934 was £2.9 million. Milne played a major part in the negotiations with Carter Paterson and Pickfords, which were conducted in an atmosphere of mutual suspicion between the railway managers. Eventually the Hay's Wharf Cartage Co, Pickfords and Carter Paterson became the joint property of the four mainline companies in 1933. The general managers joined all three boards and Milne chaired Carter Paterson.

While the railway's participation in road haulage was far too limited to curtail outside competition, at least the subsidiaries paid their way, something which their air transport interests generally failed to do. Like Pole, who possibly was the first railway manager to show a serious interest in air transport, Milne was apparently attracted by the commercial potential and prestige value of a railway airline. He was good at delegating, and it seems that his assistant general manager, K W C Grand, was very active in pursuing the venture. The GWR put on the first effective railway air service in April 1933 and a year later participated with the other railways and Imperial Airways in the formation of Railway Air Services Ltd. By the late 1930s the railways had secured a semi-monopoly of air services within Great Britain.

Milne's preoccupation with external relations may have deflected him from making a thorough appraisal of the company's management structure. Pole had made some progress in modifying the strongly departmental system that had been inherited from the nineteenth century, but it still remained the formal basis of the organisation. It is clear though that the system was not so rigid and inhibiting as might be supposed, for it did generate a flood of worthwhile investment projects. Milne was accessible to his senior managers and tried to create a team spirit.

Perhaps its weakness was more apparent when the company came to consider a change in the technological basis of its operations, such as electrification, although even here managerial conservatism cannot fully explain the decision not to go ahead. The problems of raising capital, the high cost of peak demand for electric current and the limited scope for suburban electrification must also be considered. Any internal resistance, at Swindon for example, must, however, have been encouraged by the report of Messrs Merz & McLellan, the consulting electrical engineers, who were commissioned in 1938 to re-examine the feasibility of electrifying the Taunton to Penzance main line, a study first undertaken by Sir Philip Dawson in 1925-27. Merz & McLellan found that an investment of £4.5 million over four years would produce a return of only 0.75 per cent a year. The choice of this route in preference to busier parts of the network where electrification could have been applied more efficiently may well have prejudiced the outcome.

Milne was a member of the Railway Executive Committee from its inception and its deputy chairman, 1941-47. He played a leading part in the protracted negotiations from 1937 to 1940 which established the basis of the Government's guarantee of the net receipts of the railways and the London Passenger Transport Board during the Second World War. The REC initially consisted of the general managers of the mainline companies and the chairman of the LPTB. It had an elaborate organisation of its own and a staff of experts drawn from the railway companies. In the first two years of the war it is plain that the unified control which the REC was supposed to effect, was not altogether apparent; indeed a national railway crisis existed in 1940-41. There were strong differences within the REC on matters of policy; moreover it was impossible for the chairman, Sir Ralph Wedgwood (qv), to represent to the Minister of War Transport the complexity of the problems and needs of the individual companies. At

Paddington Milne was confronted with many crises, for the GWR bore the brunt of the burden of increased war traffic, especially in South Wales, where lines had been laid out primarily to deal with exports, not to serve inland destinations. Milne's regular reports to the board during the war vividly captured the daily difficulties that the company faced but still offered a cool, analytical appraisal of the situation and of the available options. According to Grand 'All through the raids — and there were many — he appeared quite unruffled and inspired a quiet confidence' {*Railway Gazette* 11 Apr 1958}. Yet, apart from the company and the REC, he was chairman of the General Managers Conference of the Railway Clearing House for six successive years until 1944 — a record tenure.

To these enormous responsibilities was added another in August 1941. The REC was reorganised so that a direct link was established between the Committee and the Ministry. Sir Alan Anderson (qv), a former director of the LMS, became the chairman but also held the post of controller of railways in the Ministry. Milne was made deputy chairman and in effect was the senior representative of the railways on the Committee. Administrative improvements followed and contributed towards the movement of a greatly enlarged volume of traffic without an effective increase in capacity. Shortly before he assumed this new position, Milne had been elected to a seat on the board of the GWR, the intention being to combine this with his executive duties. This unprecedented step in the history of the company, requiring a special act of parliament to change its nineteenth-century constitution which prohibited officials from becoming directors, provides an indication of the high regard in which Milne was held by the board. In the event he decided not to take up the directorship. This was done in deference to the wishes of the Minister of War Transport, who could not accept him as a director of a railway company — serving the interests of its shareholders — while he continued to serve on the REC. The Minister was obviously keen for Milne to stay on the Committee; indeed within two months of resigning from the board he was made its vice-chairman.

Milne resigned from the general managership of the GWR in August 1947 before, as he put it 'our beloved company is vested in the British Transport Commission' {PRO, RAIL 1014/33 21 Aug 1947}. He was sixty-four years of age. It seems that he was offered but declined the chairmanship of the Railway Executive of the BTC. Accustomed to the exercise of considerable autonomy as the general manager of the GWR, he may have felt that he would not enjoy a similar freedom of action within the confines of the Railway Executive.

The following years saw the continued involvement of Milne in transport affairs. For example, in 1948 at the invitation of the Eireann Minister for Industry and Commerce he undertook an inquiry into the transport position of that country, refusing to take the substantial fee offered to him and asking that the report might be seen as his contribution to the advancement of transport in the country of his birth. Members of his family still lived in Dublin; indeed his brother was managing director of W H M Goulding, the firm with which his father had been associated. At the time of his death he was chairman of the Ship Mortgage Finance Co Ltd, and a director of nine other companies connected with transport: the

Belfast Steamship Co Ltd, the British & Irish Steam Packet Co Ltd, the Central Africa Railway Co Ltd, Coast Lines Ltd, Nyasaland Railway Ltd, Thos Cook & Son Ltd, Thos Cook & Son (Continental & Overseas) Ltd, the Trans-Zambesia Railway Co Ltd, and the Tyne-Tees Steam Shipping Co Ltd. He also held directorships in Bedford General Insurance Ltd, Bentworth Trust Ltd, and British Holiday Estates Ltd.

Apart from the CSI Milne received a number of other public honours. He was knighted in 1932 and created KCVO in 1936. He was a member of council and sometime vice-president of the Institute of Transport.

Milne's personal life remains less visible than his public career, for he was a very private man. In 1912 he married Norah Rebecca, the daughter of Levi L Morse, Liberal MP for the Wilton division of Wiltshire, 1906-10, and member of Swindon Town Council. Milne died on 1 April 1958, survived by his wife and two sons. His estate was valued at £80,858 gross. In an appreciation, K W C G Grand, then the general manager of the Western Region of British Railways, who had been close to Milne for thirty years, wrote of Milne's sense of 'humour, human understanding and love for his family' {*Railway Gazette* 11 Apr 1958} — characteristics which sadly are not, and probably cannot be, revealed in the minute books and memoranda.

GEOFFREY CHANNON

Writings:

(with Sir Felix J C Pole), 'The Economics of Passenger Transport' in *Modern Railway Administration: A Practical Treatise by Leading Railway Experts* (Gresham, 1925) 2.

PP, Report on the Efficiency and Adequacy of the Coast-Watching Organisation (1931) Cmd 3918.

Conference on Rail and Road Transport (Ministry of Transport, 1932).

Report on Transport in Ireland (Dublin: Stationery Office, 1948).

Sources:

Unpublished

PRO, Kew, Great Western Railway: reports, minutes, letters and memoranda; in particular: Minutes of Chief Officers Conference, RAIL 250/253, 254; Papers on Development Works, RAIL 1005/196; Secretarial papers on the Electrification of the Taunton to Penzance Section, RAIL 258/274; General manager's reports to the board during the war (1939-45), RAIL 250/776; Misc papers RAIL 1014/33; Treasury: minutes of the Development (Public Utility) Advisory Committee, T 1919/3.

GWR, annual reports and accounts.

MCe.

PrC.

Communications from Mr William Joseph Callcott Milne, son of John William Milne (James Milne's brother) and Mr Brian Wilson, Headmaster Campbell College, Belfast, dated 3 Dec and 23 Nov 1984 respectively.

Published

Derek H Aldcroft, *Studies in British Transport History 1870-1970* (Newton Abbot: David & Charles, 1974).

—, *British Transport since 1914. An Economic History* (Newton Abbot: David & Charles, 1975).

Michael R Bonavia, *The Organisation of British Railways* (Shepperton: Ian Allan, 1971).

—, *Railway Policy between the Wars* (Manchester: Manchester University Press, 1981).

—, *The Birth of British Rail* (Allen & Unwin, 1979).

Great Western Magazine 31 (1919), 34 (1924), 41 (1929), 43 (1931).

John Hibbs, *The History of British Bus Services* (Newton Abbot: David & Charles, 1968).

Railway Gazette 20 Sept 1940, 21 Mar 1941, 24 Dec 1948, 11 Apr 1958.

Railway Returns.

Christopher I Savage, *History of the Second World War: Inland Transport* (HMSO, 1957).

Times 3 Apr 1958.

Gerard L Turnbull, *Traffic and Transport. An Economic History of Pickfords* (Allen & Unwin, 1979).

Gilbert Walker, *Road and Rail. An Enquiry into the Economics of Competition and State Control* (Allen & Unwin, 1947 ed).

WWW.

MILNE-WATSON, Sir David

(1869-1945)

Gas company executive

David Milne-Watson was born in Edinburgh on 10 March 1869, the only surviving son of elderly and wealthy parents, David Watson and Anne Carnegie née Milne. He was given a broad education at Merchiston Castle School and thereafter at the universities of Edinburgh, Paris, and Marburg and at Balliol College, Oxford. He became a barrister at the Middle Temple in 1896 and unsuccessfully contested South East Essex as a

Liberal in the election of 1895. Thereafter his life was devoted to the gas industry.

Finding life as a young barrister hard and impecunious, Milne-Watson answered an advertisement in 1897 for the post of assistant to the secretary and general manager of the Gas Light & Coke Co. It was specifically noted in the terms of appointment that the post did not carry any right to the chief appointment in the event of its becoming vacant. Nonetheless, so able did the young Milne-Watson prove, that when in 1903 the company decided to separate the posts of secretary and general manager, he was appointed general manager in charge of a wide range of company affairs including tariffs, coal buying and the sales of by-products. In 1916, on re-organisation following the death of the governor, Sir Corbet Woodall (qv), he became managing director (a new appointment) with a seat on the court of directors. At the beginning of 1919 he became governor of the company, combining this post with that of managing director.

David Milne-Watson remained governor of the Gas Light & Coke Co until 1945. Until 1929, when R W Foot was appointed as general manager, Milne-Watson personally directed all aspects of the company's affairs. Thereafter he concerned himself more with questions of broad policy, although continuing to take a direct interest in coal buying, the design of each new showroom, welfare activities and a host of other matters. It was only during the Second World War years that ill-health forced him gradually to lay down some of his responsibilities. He was, therefore, head and chief executive of the Gas Light & Coke Co in the critical period between the wars; a time when the gas industry was fighting a rearguard action against the rise of competitive fuels and sources of energy, above all electricity.

During these years, the Gas Light & Coke Co became the outstanding gas undertaking, both in size and technical efficiency, in the United Kingdom. It was indeed the largest gas company in the world, producing by 1938 one-eighth of the entire amount of gas in the country. Milne-Watson himself achieved the leadership of the whole gas industry, for his energies were devoted also to setting up various national bodies in order to strengthen the co-operation among the 1,000 or so separate undertakings which at that time comprised Britain's gas industry.

As far as the Gas Light & Coke Co was concerned the expansion under David Milne-Watson's leadership was the result of a series of amalgamations which saw the territory of the company expand from 67 square miles in 1909 to 134 square miles in 1925 and to 547 square miles in 1933. Particularly significant was the absorption of the old-established Brentford Gas Co in 1926. By these amalgamations the Gas Light & Coke Co expanded east and west from its inner London base, forming eventually the territory from Southend to Old Windsor which substantially became that of the North Thames Gas Board upon nationalisation in 1949. Increasing size brought increasing problems of internal organisation. Indeed, during the depression years of the early 1930s the company faced a period of crisis and a drastic overhaul of its organisational machinery was necessary. This Milne-Watson carried out with the aid of Edgar Sylvester, later to succeed Milne-Watson as governor of the company and also to become the first chairman of the Gas Council in 1949. Although the company did not undertake any more amalgamations after 1932 it did promote a new holding company in 1934, the South-Eastern Gas Corporation. Sir David was chairman of the Corporation, and by 1938 the Gas Light & Coke Co managed the affairs of eight gas undertakings through its majority share holdings. The holding company movement, which grew significantly among gas undertakings in the 1930s, was one means whereby large and efficient undertakings could rationalise and improve the management of other concerns without outright ownership.

Milne-Watson was actively interested in every measure to enable the company to withstand the growing inroads from its competitors. New research laboratories were set up and a group of Oxford-trained scientists was employed at the company's laboratories in Fulham. In 1926 the company established a major research centre at Watson House, named in honour of the governor. Milne-Watson was also concerned with promoting the sales and service organisation of the company and a notable contribution was the emphasis placed by him on sales of appliances through company showrooms and authorised dealers as a way of boosting competition. Competition from electricity brought with it the threat of the 'all-electric household' with no place for gas. On Milne-Watson's initiative the Gas Light & Coke Co successfully pressed for legislation (obtained in 1934) which gave gas companies the duty to supply gas to consumers who desired it.

In his handling of company affairs Milne-Watson was essentially autocratic and paternalistic. He was, in the words of Stirling Everard, brusque and uncompromising and did not take kindly to opposition. He was, nonetheless, genuinely concerned with employees' welfare (the Gas Light & Coke employed over 25,000 by the 1930s). He was devoted to the company's co-partnership scheme, which he had helped to set up in 1909 and of which he remained chairman until 1944, and he took a personal interest in schemes to improve medical and sports facilities, hold annual camps for apprentices and numerous other welfare schemes. He instituted a special chairman's hardship fund. He was an unfailing attender at the great annual gatherings held at the company sports grounds and which attracted many employees and their families.

Outside the company Milne-Watson devoted his energies to improving co-operation and integration within the still fragmented industry. He was knighted for his services to the gas industry in 1927 and received a baronetcy in 1937. He helped set up and became the chairman of the National Gas Council, 1919-43, and of the National Joint Industrial Council for the Gas Industry, 1919-44. He was also chairman of the Federation of Gas Suppliers and president of the British Gas Federation. He was a member of various public bodies, including the Advisory Council of the Department of Scientific and Industrial Research and the National Fuel and Power Committee, and was chairman of the government Market Supply Committee, but his single-minded devotion to the gas industry meant that he did not pursue so active a part in public life as that which industrialists of comparable stature have sometimes come to play.

Milne-Watson married in 1899 Olga Cicely (d 1952), daughter of Rev George Herbert; they had two sons. His main recreations were fishing, shooting and gardening.

During the Second World War Sir David's health began to fail. In 1942

Sylvester was appointed joint managing director and subsequently became sole managing director in 1944. In April 1945 Sir David announced his retirement from the governorship and on 3 October that year he died, aged seventy-six, leaving £84,740 gross. His younger son, Michael (who was knighted in 1969), joined the Gas Light & Coke Co in 1933, becoming governor of the company in 1946, and the first chairman of the new North Thames Gas Board in 1949. For six decades, therefore, a Milne-Watson held high office in the nation's leading gas undertaking, a striking record in a major industry.

MALCOLM FALKUS

Sources:

Unpublished

Information from Sir Michael Milne-Watson.

PrC.

Published

Burke's Peerage and Baronetage.

Co-Partners' Magazine (house magazine of the Gas Light & Coke Co) 1911-45.

DNB.

Stirling Everard, *The History of the Gas Light and Coke Company 1812-1949* (Benn, 1949).

WWW.

MILWARD, Sir Anthony Horace

(1905-1981)

Airline executive

Anthony Horace Milward was born in Feckenham, near Worcester, on 2 March 1905, the son of Henry Tomsom Milward and his wife Elsie née Newton. Anthony's father was a needle manufacturer; the firm of Milwards Needles had been founded in 1730. After education at Rugby and Clare College, Cambridge, where he took a BA, Milward eschewed

Sir Anthony Milward (courtesy of Historical Aviation Service).

easy entry into the family business and joined the textile merchanting firm of Glazebrook Steel & Co Ltd in Manchester in November 1926. The following year he was sent to the Bombay Co Ltd in India, working for a year in Calcutta followed by short spells in Madras, Bombay and Karachi. In 1929 he was recalled to Manchester, becoming a director of Glazebrook Steel in 1930.

During the mid-1930s he began to take an interest in flying and joined the newly-formed Civil Air Guard, where he eventually acquired his 'A' pilot's licence in 1939. At the age of thirty-four he was not, at first, accepted for flying duties by the services in the war. Despite every endeavour it was not until late 1940 that he could join the Fleet Air Arm. He became one of the few pilots to remain on flying duties until the war ended. His conversion training was at Eastleigh, in Hampshire, then he went on to Lee-on-Solent and Arbroath where he flew observers on training. When training was transferred, he was appointed to the Royal Naval Air Station at Piarco, Trinidad, where, in addition to training duties he flew anti-submarine patrols and convoy escorts. In 1943 he was promoted lieutenant-commander (A) RNVR and given charge of the Naval Section at the Radar Experimental airfield at Defford, Worcestershire. Here he test-flew airborne radar and experimental night-flying equipment. In 1945 he was awarded the OBE.

The experience gained during the war changed Milward's outlook and he decided to relinquish his directorships in the textile world and begin a fresh career in civil aviation. In January 1946 he joined the British Overseas Airways Corporation, transferring to the newly-formed British European Airways (BEA) in April as general services manager. A few months later he was appointed the first general manager of Continental Services. His characteristic energy and enthusiasm were apparent as he tackled the early post-war problems in Europe with an ever-growing network of services. During this steady build-up of business Milward became controller of operations in 1952 and he was appointed chief executive in 1956 under the chairmanship of Lord Douglas of Kirtleside (qv). Up to this time he was relatively unknown outside the industry, but, though unobtrusive, he was a man of strong character, with an awareness of other people's views yet with strongly-held convictions regarding the future of BEA and the British aircraft industry. The deputy chairman of British Airways, Roy Watts, found him 'always easy and relaxed and good company; abstemious yet always convivial; a listener, yet to be listened to. Not over-numerate, but a true leader' {*British Airways News* 22 May 1981}. In 1960 Milward was made a CBE. He was a determined fighter, not only for what he believed to be right for BEA, but also on behalf of his staff. They knew they would have his backing and so gave him their affection and respect.

Leadership and dedication to the airline were to become two of his greatest assets when he succeeded Lord Douglas as chairman of BEA in 1964. His main pre-occupation was for BEA to succeed in being in charge of its own affairs, decisions and future. The late 1960s were bedevilled by government interference in the nationalised industries and their performance. Milward was much exercised about what he believed to be lack of clear-cut modern aviation policy in Britain. In reply to an article which stated 'a nationalised business cannot be allowed to choose a course of action solely on a basis of its own prospective profitability', he wrote, 'You thus announce in three lines one of the most important dictums about nationalised industries which I have ever heard, and one which is totally at variance with my own views and those of everyone in BEA ... it seems to destroy in one sentence the basis on which I believe nationalisation was founded, ie, to run in public ownership, a commercial enterprise' {*Flight International* 29 Sept 1966}.

Milward was also concerned with the number of Ministers whom the industry had to 'educate' before they moved on after a short period, to say nothing of the officials who were involved in major airline decisions. Intervention in internal matters was particularly galling: 'We are not free to follow our own commercial dictates and it tends to make a mockery of the dictum "BEA will operate as a commercial undertaking"' he wrote {*BEA Magazine* June 1967}. He was a strong proponent of the International Air Transport Association, not because of its monopolistic powers, but because it gave a world-wide forum for discussion. Similarly he was sanguine concerning the Common Market, saying 'Nobody need expect our business will begin immediately to expand because entry into the Common Market is going to be a slow and painful process but, in the long-term, intra-European trade must grow and we [BEA] will grow with it' {*ibid*, May 1967}.

Straightforwardness and plain talking was the essence of his approach towards the airline and associated industries. He always bore in mind his duty of public accountability, and often referred to the open recording of all the airline's business in its annual Report and Accounts. He was acutely aware of the future aircraft requirements of the airline and he spared no effort in pushing the 'Buy British' policy of BEA. When his efforts to persuade the Government to invest in the BAC 211 with Rolls Royce RB211 engines failed, he was concerned for the financial viability of the airline, and of the aircraft manufacturing firms. Had his advice been taken, the European joint airbus construction would not have begun.

Milward retired from the chairmanship of BEA in 1970. He took up the chairmanship of the London Tourist Board in 1971, a post he held until 1976 when he was appointed president. He was knighted in 1966.

He married in 1931 Frieda Elizabeth Anne, daughter of Gustav Adolf von der Becke, a merchant. Sir Anthony Milward died on 12 May 1981, survived by his wife, one son and one daughter, and leaving £100,765 gross.

RONALD WILSON

Writings:

'Wasted Seats in Air Transport' (Institute of Transport 23rd Brancker Memorial Lecture, 14 Feb 1966) *Journal of the Institute of Transport* Mar 1966.

letter to the editor *Flight International* 29 Sept 1966.

'The Development and Future of Air Cargo' (Royal Aeronautical Society's 24th British Commonwealth Lecture, 3 Oct 1968) *Journal of the Royal Aeronautical Society* Nov 1968.

As chairman, he made a monthly contribution to *BEA Magazine*.

Sources:

Unpublished

BCe.

MCe.

PrC.

Sir Anthony Milward, 'British European Airways — Five Years On' (Edwards Seminar paper 375, 22 Nov 1966).

Published

BEA Magazine May-July 1967.

British Airways News 22 May 1981.

Charles Gardner, *British Aircraft Corporation: A History* (B T Batsford, 1981).

WW 1979.

MISSENDEN, Sir Eustace James

(1886-1973)

British railways chairman

Sir Eustace Missenden (courtesy of the National Railway Museum).

Eustace James Missenden was born at Deptford, London on 3 March 1886, the son of James Missenden, a railway station master and his wife Lucy née Alcock. He was educated at Folkestone, but his formal education ended at the age of thirteen when he became a booking clerk on the South Eastern & Chatham Railway. Thereafter his rise in the railway service was almost uninterrupted. In 1920, at the age of thirty-four, he became a district traffic superintendent of the SECR; three years later, on the formation of the Southern Railway, he became a divisional operating superintendent of the Southern. In 1930 he was appointed assistant superintendent of operations, and three years later, docks and marine manager. After only three years in that post he was appointed traffic manager. In 1937 he was awarded the OBE.

It is probably the case that up to 1939 the Southern board had regarded him as a highly competent departmental officer rather than as a future general manager. However, the general manager of the Southern Railway, Sir Herbert Walker (qv) had retired in 1937 and his successor, Gilbert Szlumper, was called to the War Office on the outbreak of the war in 1939 to become Director-General of Transportation and Movements, with the rank of major-general. When Szlumper was given leave of absence by the Southern Railway board, the general managership became vacant at a highly critical time. The board decided to invite Missenden to fulfill the duties of the post until Szlumper's return. Missenden declined to accept an 'acting' appointment, facing the directors with a dilemma. Eventually they accepted Missenden's terms and appointed him general manager, leaving the anomaly of Szlumper's position to be sorted out later.

Szlumper's release from his government appointment towards the end of 1942 presented the board with the problem of whom to confirm as general manager and whom to retire. John Elliot (qv), at that time deputy general manager, was consulted privately about the difficult choice by the Southern Railway chairman, Robert Holland-Martin, and the deputy chairman, Eric Gore-Browne. His opinion was that Missenden's qualities were those most required by the railway, a view accepted by the board. Szlumper accordingly retired and Missenden was confirmed as general manager.

During the war Missenden represented the Southern Railway on the Ministry of War Transport's Railway Executive Committee, and he was knighted in 1944. But the post-war prospect of nationalisation and the passage of the Transport Act, 1947, for a time made his future uncertain. Sir James Milne (qv) of the Great Western Railway was invited by the Minister, Alfred Barnes, to become chairman of the new Railway Executive. Milne considered accepting the RE position, despite his dislike of nationalisation, but insisted upon being permitted to retain some outside company directorships. This was refused by Barnes and Milne thereupon lost interest in the post. The question of Missenden's future was thus simplified; as the only general manager still available (his counterparts on the LMS and the LNER having moved to the British Transport Commission), his claim to lead the RE was strong and he took office in the 'shadow' Executive in September 1947, pending its incorporation on 1 January 1948.

The position of first chairman of the unified British Railways might have seemed a dazzling culmination to a professional railwayman's career. Missenden, however, was unsympathetic to nationalisation and loyal to the traditions of the Southern Railway. In addition, the post had two great disadvantages. First of all, his relationship with the functional members of the Railway Executive was not that of a general manager with his departmental officers; he was simply primus inter pares and a spokesman on policy matters. Secondly, and more important, was the existence of a nominally superior body, the British Transport Commission, which constantly demanded information and sought, in Missenden's view, to influence railway policy unduly. Consequently his exchanges with Sir Cyril Hurcomb (qv), chairman of the Commission, tended to be acerbic; the two men were temperamentally poles apart. This was a major factor in Missenden's decision to retire at the end of March 1951 when his appointment still had more than two years to run.

His departure enabled him to score a final point against Hurcomb. The

Minister was required under the Transport Act to consult the Commission before making appointments to the Executives. Hurcomb put forward the name of F A Pope, a BTC member and career railwayman, to succeed Missenden. Barnes however — unusually, for he had a high regard for Hurcomb's judgement — consulted Missenden, who strongly urged the selection of John Elliot, then chief regional officer of the London Midland Region. Barnes accepted Missenden's recommendation and appointed Elliot, which initially much displeased Hurcomb although he later came to appreciate Elliot's managerial qualities.

Missenden was a career railwayman with few outside interests. As general manager at Waterloo he was not an innovator; he was respected by his departmental officers for his keen professional competence but he was not seen as a leader in the Herbert Walker mould. Unlike Herbert Walker and John Elliot he had little rapport with his opposite numbers on foreign railways — he had no knowledge of other languages. He tolerated a degree of independence, especially on the part of his brilliant but wayward chief mechanical engineer, O V S Bulleid, that Walker would scarcely have admitted.

Later, as chairman of the Railway Executive he felt unable to question R A Riddles's policy of building new standard steam locomotives, though his experience with the Southern Railway had convinced him of the advantages of electrification, with subsidiary diesel traction, as the motive power of the future. This led him into perhaps the most significant of his many clashes with the Transport Commission.

Missenden's lack of formal education made him rather chary of the written word apart from the use of standard railway phraseology: policy papers were always prepared for him by his staff. His personality struck many as cold, but he appreciated loyal and efficient service, and took care to reward it. He delegated effectively and declined to work outside normal office hours. Once, during a crisis which was greatly exercising the Transport Commission, Hurcomb asked Missenden to return from holiday, to speak for the Railway Executive; but Missenden flatly refused, insisting that he had an effective deputy in whose hands he would leave the matter.

Missenden married in 1912 Lilian Adeline (d 1959), daughter of Henry Gent, a builder. She was an elegant woman, but her timidity in company with others was a bar to the expansion of Missenden's outside interests. There were no children of the marriage. Sir Eustace Missenden died on 30 January 1973 at the age of eighty-four, leaving £87,764 gross.

MICHAEL BONAVIA

Sources:

Unpublished

PRO, MT 74/141, 76/41 (Southern Railway Board Minutes; Railway Executive Minutes).

BCe.

MCe.

PrC.

Information from Mr J L Harrington.

Published

Michael R Bonavia, 'Seven Chairmen' *Modern Railways* May 1976.

—, *The Birth of British Rail* (Allen & Unwin, 1979).

—, *British Rail: The First 25 Years* (Newton Abbot: David & Charles, 1981).

Sir John Elliot, *On and Off the Rails* (Allen & Unwin, 1982).

A J Pearson, *Man of the Rail* (George Allen & Unwin, 1967).

Times 2 Feb 1973.

WWW.

MITCHELL, Sir Godfrey Way

(1891-1982)

Builder and civil engineering contractor

Godfrey Way Mitchell was born at Peckham, London, on 31 October 1891, the younger son of Christopher Mitchell and Margaret née Way. At the time of his birth, his father was a clerk of works employed by London County Council, having moved to the metropolis from Dorset where he had managed a Portland stone quarry. His quarrying expertise took him into a partnership with Matthew Ascot Rowe: Rowe, having made a fortune in the USA, put up the capital and supervised granite quarries in Alderney while Christopher Mitchell, in London, saw to the shipment of the stone and its sale to London boroughs for road surfacing.

Between 1902 and 1907, Godfrey Mitchell attended Haberdashers' Aske's School at Hatcham; he shone at mathematics and science, but his inability to spell caused many a dire report.

On leaving school at sixteen, Godfrey Mitchell went straight into his father's firm, in charge of the partners' office at London Bridge. Besides advancing his metropolitan connections, the work taught him the elements of accounting and office management, the structure of the London market for roadstone and, most importantly, the intricacies of tendering and chartering. The First World War and illness brought this commercial experience to an abrupt end. Tuberculosis, contracted in 1914, prevented Mitchell from passing an army medical for two years; eventually he was offered a commission with the Royal Engineers, from which he was discharged in 1919 with the rank of captain. He spent most of the war running quarries in the Pas de Calais using German prisoners of war; war service also gave him a useful contact with Sir Henry Maybury, Director General of Roads and Quarries.

The enormous wartime increase in shipping rates and the death of their partner Rowe compelled the Mitchells to sell the business. Godfrey Mitchell's father, suffering from ill-health, retired but supported his son's search for a new venture. On the advice of his uncle, George Mitchell, Godfrey settled on the well-established firm of building contractors at Hammersmith founded by George Wimpey in 1880. Wimpey had died in 1913 and three of his four sons had gone off to the war. At its end they found themselves short of working capital and disinclined to continue as contractors. Mitchell bought their firm in June 1919 for £3,000 (£2,500 for stock in trade and £500 for goodwill), a sum which he raised from his post-war gratuity and the sale of 1,000 shares in the Limmer & Trinidad Asphalt Co, of which his uncle was joint managing director. For working capital, his father lent him £3,000, part of the amount realised from the sale of Rowe & Mitchell.

Godfrey Mitchell's first action was to turn the business into a limited company in June 1919 with a nominal capital of £10,000 in £1 ordinary shares — an action designed to limit his father's risk, Mitchell recalled. At Hammersmith he found an ill-organised business. There was no regular bookkeeping system and no profit and loss account. But there was a core of experienced contractors' staff; to these Mitchell added his old firm's secretary and soon reformed Wimpey office procedures.

During the 1920s Mitchell developed Wimpey's previous activities, chiefly paving and roadworks, not least because the growth of suburban London occasioned plenty of this kind of work. When, in 1921, he won a contract to build the Dartford to Erith road, he learned from Maybury, now an adviser in the new Ministry of Transport, about asphalt made from clinker. This brought two unexpected repercussions for Mitchell. At Sheffield, which he visited for discussions about clinker asphalt with a local authority engineer, the sight of masses of unemployed in the 1920-21 slump fired him with the determination to use his firm as a weapon against unemployment. Clinker asphalt also brought into Wimpey Lionel Daniel Lewis (d 1950), a trained borough engineer from South Wales who served under Maybury in France and in the Ministry of Transport. Lewis took over the asphalt side of the business and proved so able a manager that Mitchell felt free later to move into housebuilding.

Wimpey under Godfrey Mitchell grew appreciably during the 1920s. Turnover rose from under £25,000 in 1921 to nearly £140,000 in 1925. Like John Laing (qv), he eschewed loan capital to finance the firm's expansion; instead he ploughed back profits, amounting to £51,500 in the 1920s. Control of the firm remained securely with Godfrey Mitchell and his father who, in 1927, equally shared 60,000 of the 63,000 issued ordinary shares. But if Wimpey fortunes rose in the 1920s, they shot up in the 1930s when Mitchell was able to plough back £306,000 from profits. The achievement rested on his move into housebuilding.

MITCHELL Sir Godfrey Way

When, in 1928, Godfrey Mitchell made an experimental investment in a housing estate at Greenford Park, Middlesex, housebuilding had been state-subsidised for nearly a decade while population concentration and family formation gave the South East and the Midlands the fastest growing suburbs in the country. Within a year of building 12 houses at Greenford Park, Mitchell hired his first house designer. He had discovered the way to make speculative building pay: by controlling and undertaking within the firm all the phases of estate building, from roads and sewers to house construction, legal conveyancing and advertising. During the 1930s the firm built and sold an average of 1,200 houses a year, then a market share of less than 0.5 per cent. Mitchell took advantage of economies of scale and mechanisation, importing equipment, from the USA for example, when necessary. Early in the 1930s, too, he reorganised Wimpey, breaking it into eight departments (main road jobs; streets, south of the Thames; streets, north of the Thames; asphalt; housebuilding; bridges; plant and transport; and research, of an applied kind). Purchasing, wages and accounts remained at the head office. A ninth department, a regional office at Edinburgh (1931), represented his response to asphalt competitors whom he decided to fight on their home ground. The success of these policies, in a market of falling building costs and rising white-collar demand for semi-detached ownership, became clear in 1933 when ordinary dividends of 20 per cent, recorded in 1931 and 1932, were raised to 30 per cent. Prospects looked so bright that new sources of capital had to be tapped. To this end Mitchell turned Wimpey into a public company in March 1934 with a nominal capital of £350,000, composed of 200,000 £1 ordinary shares and 150,000 6 per cent cumulative preference shares. Of the 150,000 ordinary shares issued, Godfrey Mitchell and his father held nearly 57 per cent. The prospectus showed that over the previous five years the company's profits had risen from £53,099 in 1929 to £95,355 in 1931; then they slipped to £77,554 in 1932 but had moved back to £81,396 in 1933.

While housebuilding pre-occupied Mitchell throughout the 1930s, he welcomed the chance to move into civil engineering works. The first of these was the Team Valley Trading Estate, Gateshead; another was the Wimbledon Flyover for the Southern Railway (a contract worth £500,000). Rearmament after 1936 brought still larger contracts. Among these was the Royal Ordnance Factory at Bishopton outside Glasgow, started in October 1937 and valued at £2.8 million, one of the largest of the explosives factories.

War brought new challenges for both Mitchell and his firm. Like other leading contractors, Wimpey competed for government contracts throughout the war years. Altogether, the firm constructed 93 aerodromes, out of 577 built for the RAF and the USAAF during the war; coastal defences; an underground ammunition dump at Corsham; Prince's Pier at Greenock for berthing the *Queen Mary* and *Queen Elizabeth*; and a chemical plant for ICI. So successful was Roy Chalcraft, the Wimpey estimator, in winning government contracts, that the newspapers raised suspicions of corruption, even alleging that Churchill had a stake in the company. Mitchell requested an official investigation into the allegations. Conducted by J L Clyde, KC, the investigation completely exonerated Wimpey.

Although his overriding involvement was with Wimpey, Mitchell still

Sir Godfrey Mitchell with Harold Macmillan viewing 'No Fives' houses at Eastcote, Middlesex in 1953 (courtesy of Wimpey News).

found time to develop other interests and commitments. During the Second World War, he was a member of several government committees, including the advisory committee of the Defence Ministry on scientific research, the Labour Ministry's Hankey Committee assessing the likely staffing requirements at higher levels in industry after the war and how to meet them, the advisory council to the Ministry of Works and the Economic Planning Board. For a time, he was Controller of Building Materials at the Ministry of Works, and served on the National Coal Board for over two years.

In 1948 he was knighted in recognition of his public services. He continued to serve on a number of committees and commissions, including the Civil Engineering Scholarship Trust, the 1954 Court of Enquiry into the docks dispute and the Restrictive Practices Court in 1956. He was chairman of the Federation of Civil Engineering Contractors in 1948-49 and of the Export Group for the Constructional Industries from 1949 to 1951. For nearly thirty years he was a member of the Standing Joint Committee of the Institution of Civil Engineers and the Federation of Civil Engineering Contractors for the practical training of young engineers with contracts.

The vast increase in scale of operations needed to meet the demands of war and its aftermath led Mitchell into a progressive restructuring of Wimpey. Early in the war, he broke up Department 2 (street works south of the Thames) under Ernest S Yarwood and his deputy, Walter Barr, into four geographically-based units and placed them under the able engineers Yarwood and Barr had recruited in the 1930s. In 1945 the prospect of a crowd of veterans returning home to claim their old jobs, together with the certain demand for post-war building, prompted Mitchell to extend his regional structure further. Departments based on Cardiff, Newcastle, Manchester, Nottingham and Birmingham, each became a major contracting organisation, all served by central departments at Hammersmith covering estimating, accounts, plant, transport and research.

When the wartime scarcity of labour and building materials revived the search for non-traditional housebuilding methods, Mitchell, with other builders, favoured concrete and, like Laing, opted for in situ, rather than pre-cast, formation of walls. He heard about a 'no-fines' (no sand) method used in Norway and directed his architect Eric Collins, his head of research Dr Len Murdock and his building manager F W McLeod to develop it. Prototypes were built at Eastcote, Middlesex, in 1947. Until restrictions on private building were lifted in 1954, Wimpey employed 'no fines' to gain local authority contracts for council estates and by the early 1950s the firm was building 18,000 local authority houses a year out of an estimated 200,000: a market share of nearly 10 per cent.

At the same time, Mitchell kept the firm in civil engineering where a major achievement was the construction of Heathrow Airport during and immediately after the war: a £13 million project which employed 1,900 at its peak. Wimpey Department 1 also won an £8.5 million contract to build a new steelworks at Port Talbot. By 1950 the company had a turnover of nearly £27 million, compared to £6.7 million in 1939, and now ranked as the top firm in the construction industry.

Wartime concerns turned Mitchell's attention to overseas markets. He deputed Philip G Hudson (previously a deputy director at the Air Ministry) and Magnus Pearce (who served under Yarwood and Barr) to investigate construction opportunities in the Middle and Far East. Their efforts coincided with the discovery of oil in Kuwait, which Mitchell visited in summer 1947. Before the end of the year the company had won a £10 million contract to build a coastal oil town and supporting oil storage and docking facilities. This success decided Mitchell to start, in 1947, a new department (Department 19) to handle overseas work. In the 1950s and 1960s, the company moved into Australia, Canada and Africa where it formed subsidiaries to handle its work.

Mitchell remained in the chair at Wimpey until 1973, when he handed over this office to R H Gane who had been with the company all his working life, and became executive director. From 1979 until his death he was life president. The discovery of North Sea oil in 1969 took the company into the much larger contracts and complex work of designing and constructing drilling rigs and services. On the eve of Sir Godfrey's retirement Wimpey and its 26 subsidiaries (13 in the UK) had a turnover of more than £240 million and a net profit of £8.5 million (1972), making it an industry leader. At this date the Group's overseas operations accounted for 21 per cent of its turnover.

Sir Godfrey Mitchell's achievement rested on a variety of skills and qualities: the ability to perceive market possibilities and to design a firm structure through which they could be seized; success in choosing able subordinates and the capacity to inspire confidence in himself and his firm (he was always affectionately known in the firm as GWM); a willingness to divorce himself from detail (even before 1939 he gave up attending departmental tendering meetings, though he always wanted to know why contracts had been missed); and financial skill, especially before the Second World War, in shaping his firm's capital structure.

In 1955, he established a charitable trust, Tudor Trust, to which he transferred almost the whole of his personal shareholding and private estate. The trust in 1980 had a shareholding in Wimpey equivalent to 49.9 per cent of the issued share capital and, since 1955, had made payments totalling over £10 million to charities, particularly to those concerned with education, old age and mental and physical handicap. This arrangement helped to protect the company from takeover as well as diverting half the distributed profits of Wimpey to charitable causes.

Sir Godfrey Mitchell was highly respected in the construction industry, as evidenced by his honorary fellowships of the Institution of Civil Engineers (1968) and of the Institute of Building (1971). He was a member of the Worshipful Company of Paviors, 1924-73, and served as Master in 1948. He always shunned publicity and consistently adopted a modest life style. Notwithstanding his modesty, he was always thoroughly fearless in his opinions and uninhibited in expressing them.

In 1929 Mitchell married Doreen Lilian Mitchell (1902-53) by whom he had two daughters.

Sir Godfrey Mitchell died on 9 December 1982, aged ninety-one, leaving £693,822 gross.

DAVID J JEREMY

Sources:

Unpublished

C Reg: Wimpey Construction UK Ltd (156,617).

BCe.

MCe.

PrC.

Jack Pizzey, filmed interview with Sir Godfrey W Mitchell (1974).

Interviews with Sir Godfrey W Mitchell 4 Sept 1980 and D R W Watts 11 Sept 1980.

Information supplied by Sir Godfrey's daughter and by D R W Watts.

Published

Marian Bowley, *The British Building Industry: Four Studies in Response and Resistance to Change* (Cambridge: Cambridge University Press, 1966).

Harry W Richardson and Derek H Aldcroft, *Building in the British Economy Between the Wars* (George Allen & Unwin, 1968).

Times 10 Dec 1982.

Times *Prospectuses* 87 (1934).

Valerie White, *Wimpey, the First Hundred Years, 1880-1980* (Wimpey News, 1980).

Wimpey News Nov-Dec 1981, Jan-Feb 1983.

WWW.

MITCHELL, Sir Henry

(1824-1898)

Woollen textile merchant

Sir Henry Mitchell (courtesy of Dr D Jenkins).

Henry Mitchell was born at Esholt near Bradford, Yorkshire, in 1824. His father, Matthew Harper Mitchell, was a small textile manufacturer. Henry received an elementary education locally and went into his father's mill at fourteen, learning the basic principles of textile manufacture. Within a few years he was taken on by the worsted firm of William Fison & Co, which had been founded in Bradford by William Fison and W E Forster but later moved to Burley in Wharfedale. In 1848 Henry Mitchell was recruited by A & S Henry as a buyer at their Bradford branch.

By 1848, the firm of A & S Henry was one of the major mercantile houses in the transatlantic textile trade. It was being run by John Snowden Henry and Mitchell Henry (1826-1910), the two sons of Alexander Henry II (d 1862), who founded the firm at Manchester in 1804 and who later opened branch warehouses at Leeds, Huddersfield, Bradford, Belfast and Glasgow. From the 1840s it would seem that the different branches of the business of A & S Henry gained a degree of autonomy in their operations.

In the following two decades the Leeds and Bradford branches were managed by John Mitchell, who was unrelated to the Henry family. He became a prominent member of Bradford Town Council, an alderman and an active promoter of free trade, helping to represent Bradford's interests during the negotiations for the 1860 Anglo-French Treaty of Commerce. John Mitchell moved to the Manchester branch of the firm in 1868 and the operation of the Bradford branch became the responsibility of Henry Mitchell. He was not related to the Henry family, nor to the manager of the branch, John Mitchell. He appears to have attained immediately considerable success in the branch. Within four years, at the age of twenty-eight, he was made a local partner. He travelled regularly to America for the firm and became widely respected as an able and influential merchant, developing Bradford as the main branch of the Henry business.

By the 1870s Henry Mitchell was widely recognised, with Jacob Behrens (qv), as one of the chief authorities on the worsted trade and was consulted regularly on many aspects of the trade both at home and abroad. He worked hard for Bradford Chamber of Commerce, which was very active in representing the trade's interest. He was made president of the Chamber in 1878, and filled that post in five later years. In 1876 he was appointed a judge for woollen and silk goods at the important Philadelphia Centennial Exhibition. Many merchants and manufacturers in West Yorkshire boycotted that exhibition because of the protectionist policies of the United States, but Henry Mitchell learned a lot about the development of the United States' wool textile trades as a result of his attendance. Two years later, Mitchell was appointed vice-president of the jurors for worsted yarns and fabrics at the Paris International Exhibition. He helped organise a party of local artisans to visit the exhibition and published a well-received report. As a result of what he learned at Paris he attempted to promote the manufacture of all-wool worsted in Bradford, a branch of the industry in which the French had gained considerable pre-eminence. He also opened a 'French Department' of his business.

When the Royal Commission on the Depression in Trade and Industry enquired into the progress and problems of the Bradford worsted trade in 1886, Mitchell was one of the main witnesses, providing much information on the size and value of the industry, and the content and direction of its trade. He was outspokenly critical of some aspects of Bradford manufacturing and argued about the inefficiencies of technical education, the consular service and rail transport.

Henry Mitchell was not a supporter of the free trade movement. He was often described as a 'fair trader', arguing for reciprocity in trade and at times urging the adoption of measures of commercial retaliation, for example in relation to the proposed new French tariff in 1890.

The firm of Henrys was converted to a limited liability company in 1889, with a capital of about £1 million. Henry Mitchell presented shares in the concern to all the workpeople in his Bradford warehouse. Half the shareholders of the company were engaged in the firm's business.

Mitchell's business activities outside his own firm included the offices of director of the Bradford Old Bank and president and trustee of the East Morley & Bradford Investment Savings Bank.

The promotion of technical education became a major personal cause for Mitchell. He was strongly convinced that Continental superiority in that area had provided great benefits for the development of Continental textiles, and he became active in many aspects of the development of education in Bradford. He was one of the founders of Bradford Technical

College between 1878 and 1882, making substantial financial donations to the College. He was a governor of Bradford Grammar School, a member of the Bradford School Board and a vice-president of the Bradford Mechanics Institute. He was knighted for his services to education in 1887.

Henry Mitchell also served Bradford well in other respects. In 1870 he was elected to Bradford Town Council and soon made an alderman. He became Mayor of Bradford in 1874-75 and served as chief magistrate. In spite of attempts to persuade him to stand for parliament he kept out of national politics. He was described as a 'moderate conservative' and at one time was vice-president of the Bradford Conservative Association. Although brought up as an Anglican, Henry Mitchell was converted to Wesleyanism and became a staunch local supporter of that church, subscribing to local Wesleyan chapels and schools and campaigning for the abolition of pew rents. Overall Mitchell is reputed to have donated over £100,000 to Bradford philanthropic purposes during his lifetime. In 1898, a few days before his death, Mitchell was made Bradford's first freeman as a result of his local activities. Both his business and public activities give the impression that Mitchell was basically a modest man and in no way a self-publicist. He appears to have carried out his business and philanthropic activities in a quiet, efficient manner.

In 1851 Mitchell married Annie, daughter of Rev D W Gordon of Earlston in Scotland. They had three sons, Gordon, Henry and Samuel. The eldest, Gordon, suffered from a weak chest and emigrated to the warmer climate of South Africa where he became a successful merchant. He died in Algiers in about 1893. Henry became a surgeon-major in the Guards. Annie died in 1886 after a long period of mental illness. Sir Henry Mitchell himself died on 27 April 1898, leaving £144,436 gross.

D T JENKINS

Writings:

Report of Henry Mitchell upon the Paris Exhibition, Together with the Report of the Artisans (Bradford, 1878).

PP, RC Depression of Trade and Industry (1886) C 4715.

Sources:

Unpublished

PrC.

Published

J R Beckett (ed), *Bradford Portraits of Influential Citizens* (Bradford: M Field & Sons, 1892).

Bradford Observer 28 Apr 1898.

Fortunes Made in Business (3 vols, Sampson Low, Marston, Searle & Rivington, 1887) 3.

Rev W J Heaton, *Bradford's First Freeman: Sir Henry Mitchell* (Francis Griffiths, 1913).

David T Jenkins and Kenneth G Ponting, *The British Wool Textile Industry, 1770-1914* (Heinemann, 1982).

Eric M Sigsworth, *Black Dyke Mills, a History* (Liverpool: Liverpool University Press, 1958).

Times 28 Apr 1898.

WWW.

MITCHELL, John Thomas Whitehead

(1828-1895)

Co-operative wholesale society executive

John T W Mitchell (courtesy of the Co-operative Union Library, Manchester).

John Thomas Whitehead Mitchell was born in the 'Mount' district of Rochdale on 18 October 1828, the son of a working-class mother and no acknowledged father. At the time of John's birth his mother was in domestic service; later she kept a beerhouse. It is clear that she was strongly attached to her son and, determined to give him as good a start as her position allowed, refused to send him to work in the mills, sending him instead to the Red Cross Street National School to gain a rudimentary education. This maternal dedication so influenced Mitchell in later years that Sir William Maxwell remarked, 'I used to think it strange to hear an elderly man speaking of his mother with such affection' {Redfern (1923) 13}.

On leaving school at the age of eleven, Mitchell began to work as a piecer in the Townhead Cotton Mill, Rochdale. Employed for long hours and with few holidays his only relief came on Sundays when he attended classes in secular subjects. His education was further broadened in 1846 when he was encouraged to join the congregation of the Providence Independent Chapel by J T Pagan, an important flannel manufacturer and teacher of the young men's class. This introduction to new religious and political opinions led him to embrace a broad Christian faith and belief in human possibilities and persuaded him to go against his mother's wishes in signing a pledge of total abstinence.

Mitchell accepted Pagan's offer of a place in the warehouse of his flannel mill at 16s a week, and remained with the firm of Pagan & Stewart until 1867, rising to the managership of the warehouse.

In 1852 Mitchell joined the Rochdale Society of Equitable Pioneers, and although this was not his first introduction to co-operation (his grandfather had been associated with the fledgling co-operative in Toad Lane in 1833) it represented his first formal participation in the co-operative movement. It also brought Mitchell new friendship with a young married man and fellow co-operator, Abraham Howard, and it was with the Howards that he found a second home after the death of his mother on 11 June 1855. By 1856 he had risen to some prominence in the Rochdale Society and early in January 1857 he was elected to the post of part-time secretary to the committee — at a time when membership was dramatically on the increase — and was also appointed to the important library committee.

In 1869 Mitchell was one of the Rochdale delegates to the first of the modern series of Co-operative Congresses. Although his role in this pioneering co-operative gathering was somewhat limited, on 20 November he was elected to the directorate of the Co-operative Wholesale Society 'for one year'. This marked the beginning of Mitchell's major contribution to the development of the CWS. The nature of that contribution, however, is disputed: some commentators say he simply 'lent to the movement the talents of an exceptionally good Victorian businessman', a contribution which 'was in no sense creative' {Backstrom (1974) 110}, while others have described him as 'perhaps the only prophet produced by the modern movement' {Carr-Saunders (1938) 38}.

In 1870 the Wholesale Society was no more than six years old, at a vital stage in its development and in need of forceful management. According to the minutes of the CWS it was Mitchell who emerged as a leader, supervised the extension of operations into the production of footwear and drapery and looked towards CWS involvement in banking. His determination and confidence in promoting co-operative manufacturing was no doubt fuelled by the economic 'boom' triggered by the outbreak of the Franco-Prussian war. Yet it is apparent that Mitchell intended to capitalise fully on the opportunities that election to the board were to offer him and he was seen to rise 'like a lion' {Redfern (1938) 41} at official meetings in support of his ideas.

In May 1874, six days after the official retirement of the chairman of the CWS, Mitchell was elected to succeed him. Capital stood at £196,000, sales at £1,637,000 and individual co-operative retail society membership of the Wholesale Society at 199. Mitchell brought to the post a confirmed belief in the integration of religious observance with secular practice, and a considerable talent for handling committees:

> Being a surefooted parliamentary tactician he would often, when opposed to a particular policy, manoeuvre the delegates into deadlock, thus postponing the question ostensibly for further investigation, until it lost its timeliness and died a natural death. {Backstrom (1974) 162}

Mitchell was always inspired by one objective: the enlargement and increased power of the organisation of which he was the head. His concept of expansion, moreover, was not limited to Britain and his vigorous support for the Manchester Ship Canal project reflected his desire to consolidate CWS overseas trading. This support for growth was tempered only by his business prudence. Development and production had to be preceded by organisation and testing of the market. If, thereafter, profits

CWS Premises at Balloon Street, Manchester, built 1906–10, Corporation Street frontage (courtesy of the Co-operative Union Library, Manchester).

were forthcoming, capital had to be depreciated and reserves built up (a policy which was to prove valuable to the movement long after his death). The combination of innovative spirit and keen business sense contributed greatly to the considerable growth of the CWS in the latter half of the 1870s and by 1880 annual sales had reached £3.34 million. Growth, however, was accompanied by a widening theoretical division within the co-operative movement as a whole and the ensuing debate, in which Mitchell played a telling role, shaped the future course of co-operative development.

From 1854 onwards the Christian Socialists had promoted the concept of co-operative co-partnership in industry, and as late as 1868 two of their members, Ludlow and Hughes, were requested to bring their knowledge and experience to bear upon the 'vital subject of division of profits in co-operative industrial partnerships for production' {*Co-operator* 8 (1868) 313}. It was this question of profit-sharing which was central to the controversy. In 1872 when the Wholesale Society decided to establish factories of its own the Christian Socialists were not in immediate opposition because a 'bonus to labour' scheme was to be operated. However, when this scheme was swept away after a trial period of three years they viewed it as a massive defeat: 'they believed sincerely that the Wholesale, in denying participation and co-partnership, was relapsing into joint-stock capitalism' {Binyon (1931) 92}. This defeat was reinforced over the next twenty years as Mitchell provided a theoretical justification for the expansion of the CWS as a 'normal' business rather than as an organisation committed to worker participation. Mitchell was the consumers' advocate, unmoving in his belief that the rewards of production should be returned to the consumer:

> So far as I am concerned all my labour and my efforts and the power of my voice will be in favour of making consumption the basis of the growth of all co-operative organisation {*Co-operative News* 23 (1892) 610}.

His conception of the consumer's role thus supplied a logical programme of expansion: 'step by step, own distribution eliminating middlemen's profit, production for use replacing production for sale, mutual financing and mutual insurance in the large and secure frame of federalism'. {Fay (1939) 19}

Mitchell clearly saw that it was conducive to business to retain the profits from manufacturing even though it might not be 'conducive to co-operative honour' {Holyoake (1906) 668}. As the debate within the movement continued, Mitchell discovered his greatest ally in the young Beatrice Potter, later Mrs Sydney Webb. Despite the fact that she often talked of him in less than glowing terms — 'Unfortunately he was not only intellectually inarticulate but also a megalomaniac about his subject' {Webb (1929) 386} — she was instrumental in gaining converts to the Mitchell approach, while being critical of the leaders of the Christian Socialists for encouraging 'appeal to the desire for personal independence and personal gain among the workers' {Webb (1907) 154}. Their combined arguments ensured the defeat of those promoting worker self-government within the CWS and conversely ensured the success of the consumer cause. This ideological shift was to have an enormous impact on the pattern of co-operative growth in that it gave emphasis to retail co-operatives at the expense of other forms of co-operative enterprise — an emphasis which was in evidence at the Co-operative Congress at Lincoln in 1891 when Mitchell protested vehemently against the subscribing of funds to aid emergent agricultural co-operatives in Ireland.

Once Mitchell had fully comprehended the economic potential inherent in consumers' co-operation he was vociferous in its favour until his death. But despite his unquestioned business acumen (by 1895 CWS annual sales had reached £10 million, retail society membership stood at 1,035 and the foundation for success over the next seventy-five years had been firmly laid), he was little concerned for his own financial position, being content to live on the exiguous fees allowed to board members for attendance at meetings, never amounting to more than £150 a year. Indeed, his dedication to the CWS was matched only by his faithfulness to the Sunday School at the Milton Church (founded after a disagreement amongst the congregation of the Providence church in 1850 over the appointment of a new minister). Mitchell taught in the Sunday School from 1854, and later became superintendent until his death; he returned week after week throughout his career, regardless of the travelling distance involved.

Mitchell never married, but from the early 1870s found companionship with a neighbour, Thomas Butterworth. Butterworth had been imprisoned for theft from the local co-operative store and had been ostracised by the Rochdale community. Sympathetic to his plight, Mitchell placed his trust in Thomas, who became first his devoted servant and, after inheriting some property, his landlord and constant companion for over twenty years. Following an abnormally harsh winter and a round of gruelling engagements, Mitchell succumbed to a long-standing bronchial complaint and died on 16 March 1895. Thomas Butterworth, who had also fallen ill, survived his friend by less than three days.

Despite rumours to the contrary, Mitchell had not amassed great wealth during his lifetime and his total estate was returned at £350 17s 8d. As the Webbs commented, 'no private fortune has ever been made out of co-operative administration' {Webb (1921) 389} and certainly personal monetary reward was not a stimulant to Mitchell. He summed up his own faith in his presidential address to the Co-operative Congress in Rochdale in 1892: 'The three great forces for the improvement of mankind are religion, temperance and co-operation; and as a commercial force, supported and sustained by the other two, co-operation is the grandest, noblest and most likely to be successful in the redemption of the industrious classes' {*Report of the Annual Co-operative Congresses* 1892}.

STEPHEN LAWRENCE

Writings:

Minutes of Evidence Given by Proponents and Opponents of the Manchester Ship Canal Bill (6 vols, pp by Waterlow & Sons, 1883-85) copy in Greater Manchester CRO, Manchester Ship Canal Co archives.

PP, RC on Labour (1893) C 7063.

Considerable reference is made to the speeches of Mitchell in the *Report of the Annual Co-operative Congresses* 1872-94 and in editions of *Co-operative News* during the period of his chairmanship of the CWS.

Sources:

Unpublished

PrC.

Published

Philip N Backstrom, *Christian Socialism and Co-operation in Victorian England* (Croom Helm, 1974).

Gilbert C Binyon, *The Christian Socialist Movement in England: An Introduction to the Study of its History* (The Society for Promoting Christian Knowledge, 1931).

Thomas Blandford, *Co-operative Workshops in Great Britain* (Manchester: Co-operative Union, 1896).

MITCHELL John Thomas Whitehead

Alexander M Carr-Saunders et al, *Consumers Co-operation in Great Britain: An Examination of the British Co-operative Movement* (George Allen & Unwin, 1938).

George D H Cole, *A Century of Co-operation* (George Allen & Unwin, 1947).

Co-operative News 3 (1873), 20 (1889), 23 (1892).

Co-operator 3 (1862-63), 5 (1865), 8 (1868).

CWS Annual 1880-92.

Charles R Fay, *Co-operation at Home and Abroad: A Description and Analysis* (2 vols, P S King & Son, 1939).

George J Holyoake, *The History of Co-operation* (T Fisher Unwin, 1906).

Benjamin Jones, *Co-operative Production* (Oxford: Clarendon Press, 1894).

Percy Redfern, *The Story of the CWS: The Jubilee History of the Co-operative Wholesale Society Limited, 1863-1913* (Manchester: CWS, 1913).

—, *John T W Mitchell* (Manchester: Co-operative Union, 1923).

—, *A New History of the CWS* (J M Dent & Sons, 1938).

Report of the Annual Co-operative Congresses 1869-77, 1879-93.

Beatrice Webb, *The Co-operative Movement in Great Britain* (Swan Sonnenschein, 1907).

—, *My Apprenticeship* (Longmans, 1929).

Beatrice and Sydney Webb, *The Consumers Co-operative Movement* (Longmans, 1921).

Alfred Mond 1st Lord Melchett (courtesy of ICI).

MOND, Alfred Moritz

1st Lord Melchett of Landford

(1868-1930)

Chemical manufacturer and industrialist

Alfred Moritz Mond was born at Farnworth near Widnes, Cheshire, on 23 October 1868, the second son of Ludwig Mond (qv) and his wife Frederike (Frida) née Lowenthal. He was educated at Cheltenham College and St John's College, Cambridge, where he read natural sciences but was lazy and failed his final degree examination. Partly influenced by John Brunner (qv) he decided to enter politics and in preparation for this studied law at Edinburgh University. He was called to the Bar at the Inner Temple in 1894 and briefly practised on the North Wales and Cheshire circuit. In the same year he married Violet, daughter of James Goetze, a coffee merchant of Mincing Lane; they had one son, Henry Ludwig (qv) and three daughters.

In order to provide legal expertise for his father's firm, Brunner, Mond, Alfred Mond was elected to the company's board in 1895 and shortly afterwards he became a managing director. However, his attention was increasingly taken up with the development of the Mond nickel process in collaboration with his father, brother Robert (qv) and Dr Carl Langer. The Mond Nickel Co was formed in September 1900 and the shares offered on the Stock Exchange in May of the following year but in 1902 problems arose at the Clydach works. A strike took place early in 1902 and in November three workmen died of nickel carbonyl poisoning. As a result Ludwig retired from the company leaving Alfred in charge of managing the works and paying the preference dividend from his own pocket as no profit had been made in the first year. Within three years Alfred's financial astuteness brought the company round and moderate profits were made. He also instigated a search for new markets for nickel products as there was a real danger of world overcapacity.

Alfred Mond had stood as the Liberal candidate for Salford in the election of 1900; inexperienced and opposed to the popular Boer War he went down to heavy defeat. The campaign to win Chester for the Liberals in the next election was more carefully conducted. His wife set up a mission for the Welsh immigrants at Hoole, north-east of Chester, in 1904 and became president of the newly-formed Hoole and Newton Liberal Association. Supported by a visit from Lloyd George, Mond won the seat in the 1906 election by a very narrow margin. In the Commons he was best known for his defence of Free Trade, attacks on the Conservatives' financial policies and for his views on industrial questions such as the fuel problem. He was also anxious to reform the House of Lords and introduce women's suffrage. While he was respected by Asquith, he was not considered suitable for ministerial office. In 1910 Mond was elected for Swansea where the Clydach works were situated. That year he was made a baronet and in 1913 was sworn of the Privy Council.

At the outbreak of the First World War, being of German descent, Mond was the subject of much abuse and he was twice forced to take his slanderers to court to obtain redress. In actual fact, such insinuations were wide of the mark; rejection by his fellow pupils at Cheltenham had made Alfred Mond 'more British than the British'. From the start he threw his energies and experience into the war effort. He advised the Government on industrial and technical matters and was a leading supporter of 'total war' policy, calling for conscription and prohibition of alcohol. He founded the group which favoured the replacement of Asquith by the more dynamic Lloyd George, a loyalty rewarded by Mond's appointment as First Commissioner of Works in 1916. In this key post he was responsible for the colossal building programme that was necessary for new factories, new government offices, new Service headquarters and so on. After the war he was also responsible for overseeing the erection of war memorials and War Graves Commission cemeteries and for establishing the Imperial War Museum. In the post-war coalition, Mond became Minister of Health, 1921-22, and used his wartime experience to establish the national housing programme on a firm footing.

At the beginning of 1922 Mond's political career appeared assured. He was a close colleague of the Prime Minister and was rising through the Cabinet while gaining reputation as an administrator. All this was lost by the fall of the Coalition in 1922 and Lloyd George's subsequent drift towards the left. Mond was always a pro-capitalist, right-wing Liberal and he never hesitated in the post-1922 period to attack the Labour party's socialist policies or Lloyd George's pale imitation as exemplified by his proposals in 1925 for a national land policy. This was the proximate cause of Alfred (and Henry) Mond's defection to the Conservative party in January 1926. He had narrowly lost his Swansea seat to Labour in 1923 and was returned for Carmarthen in 1924, supported by both the Liberal and Conservative constituency associations. On this ground he did not feel obliged to seek re-election after joining the Conservatives. However, his political career was now effectively finished and his peerage was at least partly a result of his embarrassing position in the Commons.

From being a prominent politician, Alfred Mond came to be regarded by the general public as a 'rationaliser' of industry, in the sense of amalgamation followed by the cutting out of surplus capacity with the aim of stabilising prices. His own definition, solicited from him by the editor of Nuttall's *Standard Dictionary* in 1929, was more oblique:

> The application of scientific organisation to industry, by the unification of the processes of production and distribution with the object of approximating supply to demand {Bolitho (1933) 290}.

He defended the need for rationalisation in terms of the inevitable march of progress:

> The trend of all modern industry is towards greater units, greater co-ordination for the more effective use of resources. This process is taking place in all countries of the world, and it therefore becomes clear ... that the industries of Great Britain cannot stand aloof {Mond (1927) 9}.

The fruits of amalgamation, he argued in 1927, were 'progress, economy, strength, prosperity'. Apart from Imperial Chemical Industries, Mond was involved in three other rationalisation schemes. As MP for Swansea, he had been concerned about the fragmented state of the South Wales anthracite industry. As a result of approaches from some of the leading anthracite colliery owners, he sponsored the formation of Amalgamated Anthracite Collieries in 1923 and he became its chairman. Five years later, he reached an agreement with Lord Buckland and Sir David Llewellyn (qqv) which gave his company control over 85 per cent of the Welsh anthracite industry.

Mond's early industrial career had been associated with Mond Nickel, rather than Brunner, Mond, and it was this company to which he returned as chairman in 1923 and which was his main business interest up to the end of 1925. Even after becoming chairman of ICI the following year, Mond was closely involved with Mond Nickel management. In the 1920s it became clear that Mond Nickel could not hope to surpass the large International Nickel Co of New Jersey and that the future of the Canadian industry lay in the efficient exploration of the new mine at Frood, Ontario, which was then being developed in parallel by the two companies. In the autumn of 1928, International Nickel's attorney, J Foster Dulles, presented him with a plan of amalgamation. The Dulles plan was accepted after negotiations in New York had produced significant alterations suggested by Melchett (he was raised to the peerage as First Baron Melchett of Landford in June 1928). Both firms were worried by increasing nationalism in Canada, and partly for this reason the amalgamation took the form of a takeover of the two companies by a former subsidiary of the International Nickel Co, the International Nickel Co of Canada. Although warmly supported by Melchett, Henry Mond and Lord Weir (qv), the merger was opposed by some of the Mond family and smaller shareholders as an effective takeover of Mond Nickel by the Americans.

At the same time, Lord Melchett brought about the formation of an Anglo-American finance house, the Finance Corporation of Great Britain & America Ltd. He was also a director of the Westminster Bank.

Although he resumed his Brunner, Mond directorship which he had resigned in 1916, Mond took no active part in the management of the firm, which was under the control of a triumvirate, Roscoe Brunner, J H Gold and J G Nicholson from 1923 to 1925, when Mond's political future lay in the balance. With the fall of Roscoe Brunner (in the wake of the settlement with Lever Bros) and the formation of the German IG Farbenindustrie in the winter of 1925, Mond suddenly found himself chairman of a company in a difficult situation. However, he relished nothing better than difficult situations and sought to solve the question of Brunner, Mond's position in the new order by reaching a far-ranging agreement with IG Farben. As a rationaliser of the South Wales coal industry, he was particularly anxious to become associated with the oil-from-coal process which the Germans were developing.

In March 1926, shortly after Alfred Mond became chairman of Brunner Mond, Carl Bosch of IG Farben offered the British company comprehensive information about high-pressure processes in return for a large minority shareholding. Mond met Bosch in Brussels between 9 and 11 August, and produced a scheme for a new British company consisting of at least Brunner, Mond and British Dyestuffs, and possibly United Alkali and Nobel Industries. This concern would then combine with IG, Solvay, Allied Chemicals and possibly du Pont to exploit the oil-from-coal process.

This grandiose plan came to grief on the rock of the implacable opposition of Orlando Weber of Allied Chemicals to any international agreements: an opposition which appeared during negotiations held in America in September. A bipartite agreement between Brunner Mond and IG was still possible but at this point Harry McGowan (qv) of Nobels arrived in New York. He put his plan for a purely British combine to Mond over lunch; it had been proposed and rejected earlier. This time Mond agreed. On 6 October 1926 McGowan and Mond left New York on the *Aquitania*; by the time they reached England they had drafted plans for the formation of Imperial Chemical Industries. Although the more experienced businessman, McGowan deferred to Alfred Mond's public reputation and agreed that Mond should become chairman while he himself became president and vice-chairman. Needless to say, Alfred Mond's determination that ICI should become a shining example of rationalisation in operation was strongly supported by McGowan. The rationalisation was carried out by the system of committees used for restructuring Nobels in the early 1920s. Steps were also taken to give the

ICI board complete control of the four merging companies (Brunner, Mond; Nobel Industries; United Alkali Co; and British Dyestuffs Corporation) to prevent the formation of a loose federation. The legal independence of the subsidiary companies was abolished in 1927 and power lay in the hands of the president, chairman and a small group of executive directors. The interests of the subsidiary companies were completely ignored; what mattered was the benefit to ICI as a whole.

The implications of this restructuring had the greatest impact on the alkali operations. Many United Alkali works which had struggled on since 1890 were closed down. They included the last two works on Tyneside, Tennants and Allhusens, and the Weston works. This in effect created the final victory of Brunner, Mond over the older Leblanc manufacturers. Nearly 2,000 employees were displaced by the rationalisation but most were pensioned off or transferred to other works.

Inspired by his father's example, Alfred Mond vigorously promoted pure research. As early as November 1926 he had persuaded Sir Frederick Keeble, the Sherardian Professor of Botany at Oxford, to 'devote himself to Research and Propaganda in fertilisers' {Reader (1975) 81} and in the autumn of 1927 he set up a Research Council so the ICI research department heads could have discussions with eminent scientists. The two most prominent academics were Professor F A Lindemann (later Lord Cherwell) and Professor Robert Robinson. A grant of £14,000 was given to promote the academic research suggested by the Research Council. Mond wanted high priority to be given to organic chemicals such as fusel oil and acetylene, fertilisers and above all, fuel research. This was his most cherished topic, one related to Amalgamated Anthracite Collieries and South Staffordshire Mond Gas as well as ICI, and one to which he had devoted much attention during his political career. It was the basis of three papers in his book, *Industry and Politics*. He saw fuel as one of the problems of the future and regarded hydrogenation of both coal and oil (to petrol) and low temperature carbonisation of coal and the more efficient use of fuel as the way forward. From this vision of the future sprang the negotiations with IG Farben and the financial disaster of Billingham.

In contrast to McGowan's preference for links with du Pont, Mond still favoured an agreement with IG Farben. A meeting was held in Paris in January 1927. Bosch suggested an exchange of shares and a profit pool. ICI for their part merely wanted to give IG some shares in exchange for technical information. At a second meeting, held in London in April, Carl Bosch sought an IG holding of 50 per cent in British Dyestuffs and Synthetic Ammonia & Nitrates (Billingham) — an idea flatly rejected by Mond and McGowan. They were more concerned with setting-up a joint ICI-IG merger to develop the oil-from-coal process in Britain. This misunderstanding between the two sides continued during the summer of 1927. When, at the fourth meeting held in London on 21-22 June, the tireless Bosch put forward a plan for a 'Super Board of Control' which would oversee most of the European chemical industry, the ICI team fell into disarray. While united in their rejection of the 'Super Board', Mond and McGowan differed over the form of ownership linkages, Mond favouring an exchange of shares, McGowan a profit pool. Having reached a favourable agreement with Standard Oil of New Jersey during August and doubting ICI's ability, in the face of governmental disapproval, to

PEEPS INTO THE WONDERFUL FUTURE

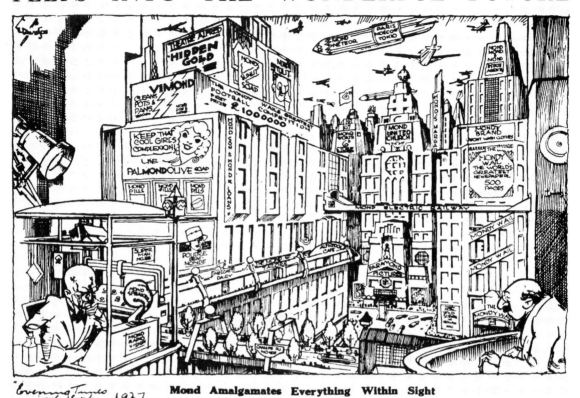

Mond Amalgamates Everything Within Sight

Mond cartoon which appeared in the Evening Times *19 Sept 1927 (courtesy of ICI).*

deliver the goods they wanted, the Germans went on the offensive. When a low-level team from ICI visited Frankfurt at the beginning of September the IG sales director, Georg von Schnitzler, presented a savage review of British Dyestuff's capabilities and made unacceptable demands. The following month the Germans similarly requested that Billingham should be halted: ICI refused.

As a former poker player, Alfred Mond realised that he needed one last card which might force IG to moderate their demands. Drawing on his political connections, he wrote to Philip Cunliffe Lister, President of the Board of Trade, at the end of October:

> It has occurred to me that it would be of very great assistance to me — and would enable me to deal with these difficult negotiations — if you would write me — for my use at my discretion — a letter giving me the reaction either of the Government, or yourself as President of the Board of Trade ... Such a letter would, of course, remain entirely confidential but its possession would strengthen my hand very much indeed ... I have taken the liberty of drafting the kind of letter which would be extremely valuable for me to have in my hands {ICI, Melchett papers, Board of Trade file}.

When Bosch wrote to reiterate the IG's various demands, Mond had received Cunliffe Lister's reply — almost word-for-word the letter drafted by himself — and was thus enabled to reach new heights of righteous indignation. Thereafter, Mond's idea of a grand alliance faded and while limited agreements were reached between the two companies, ICI came to be associated with du Pont, not IG Farben.

The main reason for an international alliance from Mond's point of view was the technical aid and commercial protection that such an agreement could give to ICI's infant synthetic ammonia plant at Billingham. This synthetic ammonia plant, started by the Government in 1918, had eventually been taken over by Brunner, Mond. Although the profits were only £105,000 in 1925, Mond anticipated an annual profit of £1,235,000 by 1928 and insisted that allowance should be made for such profits in the capitalisation of ICI. This was done on the basis of deferred shares which only paid dividends if the ordinary dividend was 7 per cent. The grounds of Billingham's projected prosperity were large increases forecast in the sale of nitrogenous fertiliser to farmers in Great Britain and the British Empire. Such hopes appeared well-founded; between 1922 and 1926, world nitrogen consumption had grown by an annual rate of 12 per cent. Even a modest rate of growth, say 7 per cent, was sufficient to justify spending £15-20 million on Billingham between 1927 and 1932. Yet ICI knew little about fertilisers and even less about the needs of the farmers. Nevertheless, the plant worked well, and furthermore there was grave danger that the expanding fertiliser markets in the Empire could be captured by IG Farben. The prospect was unbearable for an imperialist like Mond.

Problems, however, soon mounted. The fertiliser sellers showed themselves to be a formidable bottleneck in the sale of ICI fertilisers to farmers and the English sellers refused to allow themselves to be taken over. Even in Scotland, where ICI formed Scottish Agricultural Industries by amalgamating the various small firms, the result was not to ICI's benefit. Far more serious was the growth of the world capacity of the nitrogen industry. Not only was IG increasing capacity at Oppau and Leuna but other Governments were encouraging native synthetic ammonia industries. As early as November 1927, Mond wondered if the optimistic forecasts had been properly checked, and in May 1929 debated if it would be better to restrict output and maintain prices or to try and obtain full output at the cost of allowing the price to continue falling.

The Wall Street crash of October 1929 left ICI with no option but to restrict severely output at Billingham. Some relief was obtained by the signing of a nitrogen sales agreement with IG Farben, in February 1930, which gave ICI 19.5 per cent of their joint world sales. Even so, £20 million had been spent on plant which in all probability would never be used.

ICI ordinary shares fell sharply from the price of 33s 6d, at which they had been used to raise capital for Billingham in May 1929, to 9s 10½d in 1931. Production at Billingham was severely curtailed, men were laid off, about 6,000 in 1929 alone, and capital spending was cut from £8.3 million in 1929 to £1.7 million the following year. The return on capital employed was a mere 0.29 per cent in 1931. The imperial vision turned into a financial nightmare.

Alfred Mond's critics have roundly condemned his technical judgement, citing his preoccupation with the nitrogen-fixation and synthetic petrol programmes, and his relative neglect of organic chemicals. Alfred's technical judgement was governed by the optimistic maxim, shared with his father, that sound chemical reactions were usually good commercial propositions. Yet his father's disastrous involvement with the Bischof white lead process should have been a salutary lesson. That it failed to be, arose from Alfred's lack of technical training. His background was neither the chemical education of a Ludwig Mond nor the commercial training of a McGowan. His lack of academic success at Cambridge created an excessive respect for the views of eminent scientists, and especially academics like Sir Frederick Keeble, and an awe of IG Farben's battalions of chemistry PhDs which would have been scorned by his heterodox father.

Alfred Mond additionally failed to appreciate the future importance of petrochemicals and thermoplastics. In this respect, his critics are right, but it was far from clear in the 1920s that the future of the chemical industry lay with the United States and with Union Carbide in particular. Few indeed, would have been incautious enough to have predicted that the shape of the industry was being forged, not in the advanced laboratories on the banks of the Main and Rhine, but by a small team of chemists made redundant by the Mellon Institute, working in the backwoods of West Virginia.

Alfred Mond's belief in the Empire developing independently of America and Europe had grown since the First World War. In 1900 he had been an anti-imperialist, a keen free-trader. This stance was understandable given his European background and the success of his father's firm under free-trade conditions. Not only did the behaviour of Germany in 1914 weaken his belief in European co-operation, but he also saw how important, in economic terms, the British Empire was to the defence of the mother country. This impression was strongly reinforced by the evidence presented to the Balfour Committee on Post-War Trade, of which he was a member before joining the Government in 1916. After the war, Mond presented plans to the Coalition Government for greater Imperial economic unity but it was left to the Baldwin administration to implement them, and then only in part.

Mond's passion for an Imperial economic union rested on one basic principle: the Empire counter-balanced the short-comings of the mother country. Britain was small, overpopulated, over-industrialised, had too small a home market and insufficient natural resources. The Empire was extremely large, underpopulated, under-industrialised, had a potentially enormous reserve of natural resources, and provided a large and rapidly growing market for finished goods. Mond criticised, in a speech to Conservative MPs in 1927, the lack of inter-Imperial trade before the war. The Empire took 43.75 per cent of British exports in manufactured goods in 1923 and the mother country took 39.5 per cent of its raw materials from British possessions. He felt that both proportions could be increased, but particularly the volume of British imports from its colonies. To achieve the kind of economic co-operation and rationalisation he sought, Mond recommended the setting-up of an Imperial body with the power to set quotas and compensation levels.

Having failed to achieve victory while in Government, Mond supported Baldwin's efforts, which he regarded as halfhearted, and worked for Lord Beaverbrook's (qv) campaign for Empire Free Trade, in 1929-30. He set up the Empire Economic Union and enrolled as an 'Empire Crusader' as well as going on a lecture tour of South Africa. However, it was chiefly as chairman of ICI that Mond was able to give practical effect to his ideas.

The Empire was important to ICI not so much as a source of raw materials but as a market for their goods, such as fertilisers, alkali and dyestuffs. As a concession to local opinion and as part of the economic development of the colonies, ICI were also reluctantly willing to consider erecting small chemical plants in the Dominions. In return for this monopoly in Imperial markets, Mond was willing to see ICI's share of other markets reduced but not eliminated altogether. The theory was not so much one of self-sufficiency but that the Empire would form a firm basis for an assault on external markets. Of all Mond's ideas, the Imperial markets concept was perhaps the most successful, despite Billingham. The Empire was to a large extent safeguarded against American and German penetration. Furthermore, ICI carried on a large and expanding export trade with the colonies and helped to develop the chemical industries of South Africa, Canada and Australia.

Alfred Mond was also very much concerned with labour relations at the national level. Brunner, Mond had an enviable record and in this area Alfred was therefore determined that this would remain the case at ICI. Nevertheless, and perhaps to avoid conflict with his political efforts, Alfred Mond largely delegated ICI's labour policy to his son, Henry Mond, and ICI's chief labour officer, Richard Lloyd Roberts. Alfred's main concern lay with the works councils set up at the local level and rising through the General Works Council to the Central Works Council, presided over by Alfred Mond himself. He was also very enthusiastic about the ICI Workers' Shareholding Scheme, whereby workers could buy ICI shares at a discount and pay by instalments. There was also a certain number of free shares related to pay. In this way Mond hoped to link the workers to the company's fortunes and also increase their savings.

These measures and to a greater extent the Staff Grade scheme, which gave staff type benefits to long-serving and reliable workers, were seen by the unions as a threat to themselves and working class solidarity. Senior union leaders, wary of the Central Labour Department, attempted to deal with Alfred Mond directly. It appears that in the aftermath of the Mond-Turner talks, Mond was more favourably inclined towards the unions than his son, but not to the extent that he was willing to change ICI's policy.

In the period of the General Strike, the membership of the trade unions was falling and this strengthened the hand of the moderates who included Ernest Bevin. Lord Weir (qv), a non-executive director of Mond Nickel, saw an opportunity for the two sides of industry to discuss matters of mutual interest in what he regarded as a new air of realism. The result of his approach to Bevin was the Mond-Turner conference at the beginning of 1928 between several important employers, including Mond, Weir and McGowan, and the General Council of the TUC headed by its chairman, Ben Turner. Mond played a leading role in breaking down the suspicions of the union leaders and therefore in making the conference relatively successful. At the end of the conference, a statement was issued urging the recognition of trade unions as the appropriate machinery for discussion and negotiations of labour questions, but the only practical result was a reduction of the hostility generated before and during the General Strike. Ernest Bevin, himself a pragmatist, was sufficiently impressed by Mond's sincerity to say after the latter's death that:

> It might have been better for industry and for himself and the well-being of the nation had the whole of his life been devoted to industrial reorganisation and development rather than to politics {*In Memory of Alfred, Baron Melchett* (1931) 27}.

For the last decade of his life, Alfred Mond was closely associated with the Zionist movement. As a young man, he had not shown any interest in Judaism or incipient Zionism, and was an agnostic in outlook. The key year appears to have been 1917. In April he spoke in protest about the treatment of the Jews in Russia and following the Balfour Declaration on 2 November 1917 he wrote to a Zionist meeting in Swansea, recording that:

> The dignity and importance of our whole race will be enhanced by the existence of a national home where those of our people who have been compelled to live under less favourable conditions than we enjoy will be able to establish themselves on the soil of their ancestors {Bolitho (1933) opp 359}.

He was later introduced to Chaim Weizmann by Simon Marks (qv) and they soon became close friends not least because of their joint interest in industrial chemistry. Afterwards, Mond contributed large sums to the cause and at the beginning of 1922 he visited Palestine.

Following this visit Mond became president of the Economic Board and founded his own kibbutz, Tel-Mond, at Migdal on the Sea of Galilee. He went on to become president of the English Zionist Federation and joint chairman of the Jewish Agency. Melchett's most prominent action towards the end of his life was the defence of the Jewish National Home against the hostility of the British authorities following the riots of 1929. Lord Passfield, the Colonial Secretary, published a White Paper recommending limitations on Jewish immigration, land development and the role of the Jewish Agency. In protest Mond and Weizmann resigned from the Jewish Agency on 21 October 1930 but as early as 3 November progress towards a mutual settlement was in sight. Mond died before it was achieved.

Alfred Mond was elected FRS in 1930. He also received honorary degrees from the universities of St Andrews, Manchester, Durham, Oxford and Paris. Alfred Mond, First Lord Melchett, weighed down by the problems posed by Passfield and at Billingham, died at his home, Melchett Court in Hampshire, on 27 December 1930, from phlebitis and heart disease. He left £1,044,174 gross.

PETER MORRIS

Writings:

'The Nationalisation of the Railways' *Financial Review of Reviews* Apr 1908.

Questions of Today and Tomorrow (Methuen, 1912).

Industry and Politics (Macmillan, 1927).

Imperial Economic Unity (George Harrap, 1930).

Sources:

Unpublished

ICI Millbank, London, Melchett papers.

PrC.

Published

Hector Bolitho, *Alfred Mond, First Lord Melchett* (Martin Secker, 1933).

John M Cohen, *The Life of Ludwig Mond* (Methuen, 1956).

DNB.

Jean Goodman, *The Mond Legacy* (Weidenfeld & Nicolson, 1982).

In Memory of Alfred, Baron Melchett of Landford 1868-1930 (ICI Magazine Supplement, 1931).

George W McDonald and Howard F Gospel, 'The Mond-Turner Talks, 1927-1933: A Study in Industrial Cooperation' *Historical Journal* 16 (1973).

William J Reader, *Imperial Chemical Industries. A History* (2 vols, Oxford University Press, 1970-75).

WWMP.

WWW.

MOND, Henry Ludwig

2nd Lord Melchett of Landford

(1898-1949)

Chemicals industrialist

Henry Ludwig Mond was born in Chelsea, London, on 10 May 1898, the son of Alfred Mond (qv) and his wife, Violet née Goetze. Educated at Winchester, Henry Mond served with the South Wales Borderers during the First World War and was severely wounded in May 1916. He was Liberal MP for the Isle of Ely in 1923-24 and, after joining the

Conservative Party with his father in 1926, MP for Liverpool, East Toxteth, 1929-31. He succeeded to the title of Baron Melchett on his father's death at the end of 1930.

Henry Mond was made a director of Brunner, Mond in 1925, and a year later was elected to the founding board of Imperial Chemical Industries (ICI). He became the first labour director in 1927 and labour relations remained his main interest for many years. He was relatively progressive on labour matters and took part with his father in the Mond-Turner talks with the trade unions. In 1931, he opposed the proposal made by the Yorkshire section of the Chemical and Allied Employers' Federation to cut wage rates by 10 per cent. Henry Mond also served on ICI's commercial, financial and overseas executive committees and took an interest in ICI's dealings with foreign companies. He was a supporter of closer links with IG Farben in contrast to Harry McGowan's (qv) preference for co-operation with du Pont.

As an MP, Henry Mond was in a position to help ICI in political matters, such as the extension of the Dyestuff Acts, which controlled dyestuff imports, in the face of opposition from the textile trade in 1930. Later, as a peer, he kept sympathetic colleagues in the House in touch with developments within ICI, in collaboration with his sister's father-in-law and fellow ICI director, the Marquess of Reading (Rufus Isaacs).

This familiarity with the corridors of power, and his popularity, made Melchett the obvious figurehead for the anti-McGowan group of directors led by H J Mitchell which arose in the mid-1930s. As well as being one of McGowan's few friends, Melchett was in any case a reluctant industrialist and had only recently succeeded in reorganising his own family's finances. He was not, therefore, inclined to act against the chairman, but an investigation of McGowan's private financial dealings at the end of 1937 (carried out by Sir William McLintock (qv)) revealed speculation in the shares of General Motors and International Nickel. Not only was bankruptcy a possibility but there was a clear conflict of interest between McGowan's private shareholdings and ICI's substantial interest in the same companies. A meeting of the rebel directors was held in Lord Weir's (qv) flat on 9 December. They decided that McGowan would have to go and agreed that Melchett was the only acceptable successor. However, on Christmas Day Melchett suffered a heart attack which put him out of active life for a year and the anti-McGowan coup collapsed.

As a compromise, McGowan was retained as chairman but was restrained, at least in theory, by the creation of a new management board with which he would share power. Naturally, Melchett was a member of this committee until it was disbanded at the end of 1943. At the beginning of 1940, McGowan proposed the creation of deputy chairmanships, which were intended to 'form a rallying point for the maintenance of the company's affairs' {Reader (1975) 271}, but which also undermined the management board. Melchett, dogged as he was by ill-health, was not inclined to disagree and a deputy chairmanship was as much responsibility as he could bear, if not more. During the war he worked on the Blacker Bombard and other weapons developed by ICI. He was also the board's main contact with the atomic bomb project, because he had helped some of the scientists associated with the programme when they became exiles from Germany. In 1944, Sir Henry Tizard attacked ICI for its inability to open up new fields of research. Melchett responded by encouraging the setting up of ICI fellowships to promote research in universities.

Towards the end of the war, Melchett became a member of the Post-War Committee, formed to consider post-war policy, and of the Public Relations Committee, despite his heavy commitments in the political sphere. In November 1944, McGowan wrote a private letter to Melchett, nominating him as his successor as chairman after his death, as long as Melchett's health permitted it. This pledge, although probably sincere, was never particularly meaningful as McGowan had no legal right to nominate a successor, and in any case Melchett's health grew steadily worse, until he was forced to retire from the ICI board in 1947 at the age of forty-nine.

Henry Mond strongly supported the Federation of British Industries and served on the Grand Council between 1928 and 1938.

After his father's death, Melchett's political activities were increasingly taken up with Zionism. He visited Palestine in 1932, was very impressed by the Maccabi sports festival held in Tel Aviv, and was thereafter a firm supporter of the movement. Although baptised an Anglican and brought up by a devout mother, Melchett became interested in Judaism and was particularly attracted to the Liberal form. As a result he was received into the Liberal Synagogue in July 1933 and later wrote a book entitled *Thy Neighbour* about the Jews, Judaism and Zionism. He also gave help to Jewish scientists exiled from Germany and in the immediate pre-war period passed reports from contacts within Germany to the Foreign Office. As a member of the House of Lords, Lord Melchett acted as an intermediary between Chaim Weizmann and the British Government, was chairman of the Jewish Agency, and set up a Parliamentary Palestine Committee. During the war this work became increasingly heavy and tragic, when he was also under strain at ICI.

Apart from his poetry and *Thy Neighbour*, Melchett also published a pamphlet, *Why the Crisis?* and a book, *Modern Money* about the economic crisis in the early 1930s. Neither work was of particular merit and while they received good reviews, they had no practical impact on the situation.

Henry Mond married Amy Gwen, an author, daughter of Edward John Wilson, a consulting engineer, of Klerksdorp, Transvaal in January 1920; they had two sons and a daughter. His elder son, Derek, died on active service in 1945 and the younger, Julian, succeeded to the title.

Lord Melchett died in Miami Beach, Florida, from heart disease on 22 January 1949, leaving an estate proved at £96,968.

PETER MORRIS

Writings:

Poems of Dawn and the Night (Chapman & Hall, 1919).

Why the Crisis? An Analysis of the Present Depression (Victor Gollancz, 1931).

Modern Money. A Treatise on the Reform of the Theory and Practice of Political Economy (Martin Secker, 1932).

Thy Neighbour (Frederick Muller, 1936).

Sources:

Unpublished

ICI, Millbank, London, Melchett papers.

BCe.

MCe.

PrC.

Published

Jean Goodman, *The Mond Legacy* (Weidenfeld & Nicolson, 1982).

ICI Magazine Mar 1949.

William J Reader, *Imperial Chemical Industries: A History* (2 vols, Oxford University Press, 1970-75) 2.

WWMP.

WWW.

MOND, Julian Edward Alfred

3rd Lord Melchett of Landford

(1925-1973)

Nationalised steel industry chairman

Julian Mond 3rd Lord Melchett (courtesy of the British Steel Corporation).

Julian Edward Alfred Mond was born in London on 9 January 1925, the second son of Henry Ludwig Mond, and grandson of Alfred Mond, First Lord Melchett, founder of ICI (qqv). His mother was Amy Gwen née Wilson of Klerksdorp, Transvaal, a friend of Augustus John and, before her marriage to Mond, a mistress of the novelist Gilbert Cannan.

Julian was educated at Eton before joining the Royal Navy in 1942 as a Fleet Air Arm pilot. At the end of the Second World War he tried his hand at farming in Bedfordshire, but his various schemes had mixed success, and a deteriorating relationship with his dying father and with his mother led to his moving to London. Newly-married and soon to inherit the Melchett title on his father's death in 1949, he embarked upon a career in the City.

In 1947 Mond was invited to join the merchant banking firm of M Samuel & Co by its chairman, Lord Bearsted, who placed him in charge of

Air Contractors Ltd, a small air charter company. It was not a commercial success but Samuels were sufficiently impressed with his abilities to agree to back one of his agricultural schemes for grass-drying, British Field Products Ltd. He became a director of Samuels, then a director of the Guardian Assurance Co, and also through Samuels, a director of the Bermuda-based Anglo-American Shipping Co Ltd.

During his period at Samuels Melchett forged ambitious links with the First National City Bank of New York. Alongside Sir Kenneth Keith, he also negotiated in 1965 the merger of Samuels with Philip Hill, Higginson, Erlangers Ltd to form the world's largest merchant bank with assets of well over £200 million. Melchett became director of Hill, Samuel's banking and overseas department, with Keith as deputy chairman. But personality clashes developed and Melchett left to devote himself to farming. He still held on to his various directorships, however, and membership of the British Transport Docks Board from 1963 to 1966 gave him his first practical experience of the workings of a nationalised industry. About this time he was a member of the Advisory Council of the Export Credits Guarantee Department and served on the Council of Administration of Malta Dockyard.

In 1966 Richard Marsh, then Minister of Power, was drawing up a short-list of candidates for the post of chairman of the organising committee established in September 1966 to plan the transfer of the bulk of the British steel industry to public ownership. Melchett was suggested by Marsh's City contacts and a meeting was arranged; it led to Melchett's appointment on 1 October 1966. Melchett was virtually unknown to the public at this time and the move seemed likely to be unpopular with both Labour and Conservative MPs. As Richard Crossman commented: '... if he wasn't the son of Lord Melchett no one would dream of this appointment' {Crossman (1976-77) II, 49}. But Marsh was impressed by Melchett's 'total sincerity' and found him 'an incredibly tough individual ... almost to the point of fanatical stubbornness' {Marsh (1978) 76, 78}, clearly important assets in the coming political battles. For Melchett the post offered the opportunity to shrug off a disappointing banking career and to run an organisation that was as impressive as anything associated with his illustrious forebears.

The difficulties were immense. Formal establishment of the organising committee gave Melchett less than a year to organise the take-over and merger of 14 manufacturing companies and over 200 of their subsidiaries. At vesting day on 28 July 1967 these companies had a total capital of £1,400 million, a turnover of £1,000 million per annum, a labour force of 270,000, and a theoretical annual capacity of 30 million tonnes. It was the biggest industrial merger that the world had seen and created a steel giant in the West that was second only to the US Steel Corporation. But the constituent firms of the new BSC were neither highly profitable nor very productive, especially in comparison with their foreign rivals. At headquarters many of the chairman's colleagues were former chief executives of the privately-owned steel companies and were deeply antagonistic to the idea of nationalisation. Melchett was also acutely conscious of his own lack of knowledge of the industry, something he attempted to make good by spending a great deal of time and energy touring steelworks both in Britain and abroad.

Nevertheless, Melchett moved quickly and decisively to create the new Corporation with methods 'aimed at building a unified business entity that can achieve — first through cost reduction and later through optimum capital investment policies and the most effective marketing operations — an increasingly competitive position in the world steel industry' {BSC, *Report on Organisation* (1967) 20}. Melchett's determination in dealing with Whitehall and Westminster was shown when he secured from the Government annual salaries for the board ranging up to £24,000 (he himself agreed to serve for £16,000), at a time when the salaries in nationalised industries rarely exceeded £10,000.

Thereafter the BSC was seldom away from the headlines. The events of Melchett's chairmanship are not easily summarised, but they include: a major internal reorganisation of the BSC; two further Acts of Parliament relating to the financing of the Corporation; a continuous turnover in the personnel of the boardroom; a lengthy examination of investment alternatives; five changes of minister with statutory responsibility for the BSC (and a change of Government); a major policy of plant closures and redundancies; debates over the adoption of steel technologies; adjustment to the membership of the EEC; and constant intervention by the Government of the day in the pricing policies of the Corporation. Melchett himself suffered a serious heart attack in January 1968, which kept him out of action for nearly six months.

After his recovery, the single most important political development for the future of the BSC was the return of a Conservative Government in June 1970. Amongst the plans outlined by the Secretary of State for Trade and Industry, John Davies, were the sale into private hands of some of the BSC's most profitable activities, such as the special steels division, and the division of the remainder (bulk iron and steelmaking) into two separate corporations that would be in competition with each other as well as with the private sector and foreign producers. Melchett was violently opposed to these measures, which would effectively destroy his painful reorganisation, and also to the imposition of a Joint Steering Committee, which was appointed in 1971 to review the BSC's progress. The struggle between Melchett and the Government lasted throughout 1971 and 1972 and was bitter enough to lead one BSC man to conclude that 'Melchett must be the biggest masochist in Britain to be so eager to hang on to such a painful job' {*New Statesman* 17 Sept 1971}.

Eventually Melchett's views prevailed. In December 1972 the Government outlined a £3,000 million programme of expansion, later published as the 'Ten-Year Development Strategy' White Paper, which aimed to increase the BSC's annual steelmaking capacity to 36-38 millions tonnes by 1983. Investment was to be concentrated at major sites at Port Talbot, Llanwern, Scunthorpe, Lackenby and Ravenscraig, and in addition a new development was to be instituted at Teesside, where nearly £1,000 million was to be spent to provide an annual capacity of about 12 million tonnes.

For a time the prospects for running the BSC on a commercial basis looked more promising. After net losses of £108 million during 1967-72, a small net profit of £3 million was reported in 1972-73. However, on 15 June 1973 Melchett died suddenly from a second heart attack whilst holidaying in Majorca (his main relaxation apart from flying and art collecting). He was remembered as a 'tough and courageous fighter, who sought neither to capitalise on his family's name and prestige nor to retire when the going became difficult' {*Times* 16 June 1973}, but it was also said that it would be some time before his work could be fully evaluated. In retrospect, the timing of Melchett's reorganisation was unfortunate. His expansionist strategy, also pursued by his deputy and successor Dr H M Finniston, foundered after his death when the gravest depression since the 1930s hit the world's steel industry. The BSC's performance after 1975 made a nonsense of any plans to run it profitably: losses totalled £545 million in 1979-80; the labour force declined from 220,000 in 1975 to 138,000 in 1980; and an attempt to delay a wage increase in 1980 precipitated a traumatic national strike.

Julian Mond married on 16 April 1947, Sonia (b 1925), daughter of Lieutenant-Colonel Roland Harris Graham. They had one son, Peter Robert Henry Mond (b 1948), who inherited the title, and two daughters, Kerena and Pandora. Lord Melchett left £310,500 gross.

GEOFFREY TWEEDALE

Writings:

PD, Lords 5th ser 261, cols 173-7 (5 Nov 1964), 276, cols 993-9 (28 July 1966), 324, cols 906-10 (28 Oct 1971).

letter on employees on Steel Boards *Times* 23 May 1967.

PP, BSC Report on Organisation (1967) Cmnd 3362.

PP, *HC* 1968-69 (163) XXXV, BSC Second Report on Organisation.

PP, *HC* 1969-70 (60) XVI, BSC Third Report on Organisation.

letter on British Steel Corporation *Times* 17 May 1971.

PP, *HC* 1972-73 (141) XXV, SC on Nationalised Industries: British Steel Corporation.

Sources:

Unpublished

PrC.

Lord Melchett, 'The British Steel Corporation. Its Tasks and Problems' (Edwards Seminar paper 407, 6 May 1969).

Published

R A Bryer, T J Brignall and A R Maunders, *Accounting for British Steel. A Financial Analysis of the Failure of the British Steel Corporation and Who Was to Blame* (Aldershot: Gower Publishing Co, 1982).

Will Camp, 'The Battle For Steel' *New Statesman* 17 Sept 1971.

Elizabeth Cottrell, *The Giant with Feet of Clay: The British Steel Industry 1945-1981* (Centre for Policy Studies, 1981).

Richard Crossman, *The Diaries of a Cabinet Minister* (3 vols, Hamish Hamilton & Jonathan Cape, 1976-77).

Jean Goodman, *The Mond Legacy* (Weidenfeld & Nicolson, 1982).

Richard Marsh, *Off the Rails* (Weidenfeld & Nicolson, 1978).

Janet Morgan (ed), *The Backbench Diaries of Richard Crossman* (Hamish Hamilton & Jonathan Cape, 1981).

Keith Ovenden, *The Politics of Steel* (Macmillan, 1978).

PP, British Steel Corporation: Ten Year Development Strategy (1973) Cmnd 5226.

Times 16 June 1973.

John Vaizey, *The History of British Steel* (Weidenfeld & Nicolson, 1974).

WWW.

MOND, Ludwig

(1839-1909)

Chemical manufacturer

Ludwig Mond (courtesy of ICI).

Ludwig Mond was born in Cassel on 7 March 1839, the second and oldest surviving son of Meyer Baer ('Moritz') Mond and his wife Henriette née Levinsohn. Moritz Mond (1811-91) worked for his father-in-law, Aaron Levinsohn, and then as a textile merchant on his own account. Ludwig Mond's grandfather, Baer Meyer (d 1820), a merchant of Ziegenhain near Cassel, took the surname of Mond when surnames became compulsory for Jews in the Napoleonic period. Ludwig was educated at the Realschule and Polytechnic in Cassel. He then studied chemistry under Hermann Kolbe at Marburg (1855-56) and under R W Bunsen at Heidelberg. Burdened by debts, he left without taking his doctorate. Ludwig Mond married his cousin, Frederike (Frida) Loewenthal of Cologne in October 1866. They had two sons, Robert Ludwig and Alfred Moritz (qqv).

Ludwig Mond's premature departure from Heidelberg was in part the result of his belief that chemistry was a means rather than an end. He was impatient to apply his chemical knowledge and natural abilities to solving problems in chemical manufacture. The common view that Mond was primarily interested in these problems as a scientist does not bear examination. While he was clearly aware of the value of a scientific training and scientific research in the rapidly developing chemical industry, Mond saw himself as a new type of entrepreneur. The old class of businessmen had made their fortunes by exploiting commercial openings, Ludwig Mond intended to make his by developing technological possibilities. From the beginning he looked at the commercial prospects of the plants he managed and at the savings which could be made. For he was not so much interested in slow methodical research, as in gaining relatively rapid profits and then moving on. Although his judgement was usually sound, Mond was often over-optimistic about the financial gains that could be made. While he was developing the ammonia-soda process, Mond looked forward to reaping the fruits of his present labour, and after success was assured, he moved into new areas such as gas distribution, nickel purification, the gas battery and even electric light. Seen from this perspective, his career falls into three periods.

In the first period of his career, 1859-71, Mond held several posts in the chemical industry and attempted to exploit various new processes, culminating in his sulphur recovery process. At first he worked in his future father-in-law's electrochemical works, but realising that Adolf Loewenthal was a poor businessman, became technical manager of a wood-alcohol plant at Mombach near Mainz, and then of another at Hachenburg in Nassau. In June 1860 Mond was offered a more satisfactory, if poorly-paid, position in the laboratory of a Leblanc soda-works at Ringenkuhl near Cassel. After a brief interlude at a leather factory at Ehrenfeld near Cologne, he returned to Ringenkuhl to test a new process he had developed partly in the laboratory and partly in his own time. This recovered the sulphur formerly thrown away by the Leblanc soda manufacturers as 'galligu' waste. Mond then erected a pyrites-burning plant for the Dutch firm of P Smits en Zoon. There was a disagreement with the partners about the performance of the plant and he left with only £15 and not the promised £50.

Ludwig Mond then visited England to see the 1862 Exhibition and also sought to interest the English Leblanc soda manufacturers in his process. Through his contacts in Manchester, Mond was introduced to John Hutchinson of Widnes who offered to employ him as a consulting chemist for £300 a year; this was later increased to £1,000 a year. In return Mond was to develop the sulphur recovery process to enable Hutchinson to gain an annual profit of £450. However, the process was found to be uneconomic in England, because the original sulphuric acid was produced from cheap Irish pyrites and labour costs were higher than on the Continent. There were also disagreements about the division of the expected licence income between Hutchinson and Mond. Meanwhile, his old Dutch employers, now called Smits & de Wolff, invited him to erect a Leblanc factory for them at Utrecht. Between July 1863 and his marriage in 1866, Mond spent most of his time at Utrecht and made only occasional visits to England. While Richard Powell was in charge in the Hutchinson works, progress on the agreement to develop his process was slow, but when Henry Brunner took over in October 1865, matters took a new turn. Hutchinsons now began to employ the sulphur recovery process in earnest.

Between 1867 and 1872, Mond attempted to persuade the British and French Leblanc manufacturers to use the process. He erected a plant for Charles Tennant in 1867 and for the Netham Chemical Co at Bristol in

1870. There was also the hope that new anti-pollution measures would force manufacturers to use the recovery process and in this connection, Mond and Henry Brunner testified before the River Pollution Committee in May 1869. When the passing of a River Pollution Act looked likely in May 1870, Mond proposed the setting-up of a joint concern by all Leblanc manufacturers to exploit his process. The scheme proved abortive, partly because of the fierce competition between manufacturers but also because at least two other sulphur-recovery processes were in the field. While Mond enjoyed a total income of £5,000 from his patents between 1863 and 1876 (leaving a profit of £2,240 after deducting his expenses and salary), it soon became clear that his attempts to make the application of his process universal in Britain and France were doomed to failure. Licences were still granted after 1871 but no further effort was given to the development of the sulphur recovery process.

About 1870 John Brunner (qv), the chief clerk at Hutchinsons, and brother of Henry Brunner, approached Mond with a proposal for a partnership. Brunner was a commercial man and needed a technical expert to collaborate with him. His brother, although an engineer, was less forceful and satisfied with his position at Hutchinsons. A relative of Mond, Philip Goldschmidt of Manchester, was a possible source of financial help and Brunner was able to get money from his father and well-to-do mother-in-law. After the collapse of the joint sulphur recovery scheme, Mond considered several possibilities. He could buy galligu and recover the sulphur, go into the French Leblanc industry, enter the chlorine industry or perhaps manufacture fertilisers, a popular activity in this period in the London area. Had it not been for the rumours of a new soda process being developed in Belgium, it is likely that Brunner and Mond would have entered the Leblanc industry and used their efficiency to undercut their competitors.

Mond's notebooks for 1871 contain notes and calculations about the ammonia-soda process. The basic process had been patented by Harrison G Dyar and John Hemming in 1838 but their pioneer plant at Whitechapel was dogged by technical difficulties and failed. Later attempts by James Muspratt and Henry Deacon of Holbrook Gaskell suffered the same fate. The most successful plant in Britain, at Hunslet near Leeds, existed for about a decade but also failed in the early 1860s. Meanwhile, Ernest Solvay, a self-taught chemist who worked in his uncle's gas-works in Belgium, developed his own process and in 1863 began, in conjunction with his brother Alfred, to build up a plant at Couillet, near Charleroi, which was turning out three tons of soda a day in 1869. This was small compared to England's Leblanc production and offered no realistic cost advantage. For these reasons, the Solvay brothers did not try to introduce their process into Britain. Mond, however, had heard of their work through his French contacts and in April 1872 went to Belgium to persuade Ernest Solvay to grant a licence. Solvay was happy enough to give them the opportunity and an agreement was signed whereby the English partners had to bring their factory in operation within two years and to pay a royalty of 8s a ton of soda. In return the Solvays would give them the technical 'know-how' obtained from the construction of Couillet.

While the new process was cheaper, less toxic and more efficient than the Leblanc process, at least on paper, no-one had succeeded with it in the commercially hostile conditions of the English industry. For the next four years it appeared to be more than likely that Brunner and Mond would simply be the latest and most spectacular of the eminent failures. The initial problem was finance. Between them the partners (the partnership was legally formed in February 1873) had £5,000 but they needed at least twice as much. Goldschmidt refused to help and an advertisement in the *Times* produced no worthwhile results. Eventually John Brunner persuaded Charles Holland, the son of a Liverpool merchant and a well-off civil engineer with a penchant for investments in risky railway shares, to lend them £5,000 at 5 per cent with a right to a third of the profits up to a maximum of 25 per cent of his capital. The partners were also fortunate in their bank (Parr's of Warrington) who gave them a generous overdraft and advice. After much negotiation, they bought the Winnington Hall estate near Northwich from the eccentric Moslem peer, the Third Lord Stanley of Alderley, for the excessive figure of £16,108 in March 1873.

While John Brunner looked after the commercial and financial side of the new business, Ludwig Mond was in charge of the construction, production and other technical matters. That is not to say that he had nothing to do with financial matters. Mond used costing techniques during the construction, he never understood Solvay's ad hoc attitude to costs, and had a sound understanding of business cycles and the economics of the alkali market.

Brunner had many worries in the early years about the finances of Brunner, Mond & Co, but the technical problems were truly daunting. The Solvay process involved many difficulties, such as the encrustation of pipes, clogging of the filter with the very fine sodium bicarbonate, and most of all, the loss from the system of the expensive ammonia. Added to these anticipated difficulties, Mond was also troubled by poor plant and delayed supplies. This was not so much due to the newness of the process, as to the complacency of the late-nineteenth century English machinery manufacturers. Local firms were probably also worried about the adverse reaction of the Leblanc manufacturers. From December 1873 to September 1874, a series of mechanical breakdowns and delays in the repairs kept the plant in and out of production. This sensitivity to mechanical breakdowns was a consequence of the Solvay process breaking new ground as a continuous process in contrast to the batch processes of the Leblanc system.

According to John Brunner, 'Everything that could break down, did break down, and everything that could burst did burst' {Cohen (1956) 145}. The delays caused by the incompetence of Neill & Son, the manufacturer of the blowing engines, forced Brunner, Mond to claim and obtain damages at arbitration. There were also serious problems with the boilers, and one man died as a result of an explosion, although Mond claimed that their boilers were being asked to do nothing more than any normal boiler. By contrast, the ammonia towers, in which ammoniated brine reacted with carbon dioxide to form sodium bicarbonate, were a new type of chemical plant and the operating difficulties were solved in conjunction with the Solvays. Charles Holland was also able to give advice and put them in touch with consulting engineers.

Mond was able to solve these problems with his wide experience in the construction of chemical plant, his knowledge of both chemistry and engineering, and not least, by having an indomitable determination to succeed. To erring suppliers he was invariably polite, helpful and inflexible in his insistence that they had to supply sound materials in good time. He was equally benevolent but unbending towards his staff and demanded their total commitment to the project. Eventually, he despaired of them, even Mebus the German works chemist, and worked day and night for weeks on end.

Production finally got under way in August 1874, only just in time to meet the deadline set by Solvay, and 800 tons of soda were made in the second half of the year. Not surprisingly, a loss of £4,300 was made in 1874, but this was turned into a profit of £2,405 in 1875; £1 for every ton of soda produced. By 1877, Brunner, Mond & Co, were able to double the size of the Winnington plant in order to produce 8,000 tons of soda a year. While there were occasionally financial difficulties, such as Holland's threat to withdraw his money in August 1878, the company had now turned the technical and financial corner.

This development took place against a background of decreasing soda prices and fierce competition. Home sales were always healthy, because of the strength and purity of Brunner, Mond's ash, and from 1875, American sales were also important although Brunner, Mond complained to their American agents of 'starvation prices' {Cheshire RO, DIC/BM/7/23/3, Brunner, Mond to B Wyn & Evans}. Some firms, such as Reid & Hall of Newcastle, were reluctant to act as agents because of threats from Leblanc soda producers, and Brunner, Mond's agents often lost their former custom from Leblanc firms.

An irritating and possibly dangerous competitor was the Sandbach firm of Richards, Kearne & Gascoigne whch was founded in 1874. Solvay had licensed this company as a hedge against the possible, even probable, failure of Brunner, Mond. However, because of the agreement between Solvay and Mond, the new firm had to pay a royalty of 20s a ton against Brunner, Mond's 8s. The Sandbach works were mismanaged and the partners were glad to sell out to Brunner, Mond at the beginning of 1878.

By 1880, Brunner and Mond wanted to gather the fruits of their labour, and to seek new capital for the rebuilding of the Winnington works. On 1 January 1881, they sold the works at Winnington and Sandbach to a limited company, Brunner, Mond & Co Ltd, with a nominal capital of £600,000, of which £360,000 was issued. Brunner and Mond were created managing directors for life by the articles of association and were allotted two-thirds of the 18,000 £10 ordinary shares issued, as payment for their business. The first half-year's profits were £12,957 and by the end of 1882, the half-year profits reached £52,428 — a result of the new Winnington works running at full capacity. The ammonia-soda process had at long last beome a commercial success; Mond commented 'We are no longer making chemicals, we are making money' {Cohen (1956) 155}.

At this time, Ludwig Mond was also involved in setting up the Society of Chemical Industry, a national organisation of industrial chemists. In November 1879, John Hargreaves of Widnes proposed the formation of a South Lancashire Chemical Society along the lines of the successful Newcastle Chemical Society. In this task, he was supported by Mond and Professor Henry Roscoe of Manchester. In April 1880, Eustace Carey, with the backing of Roscoe, suggested the formation of a national society, which was set up a year later. Mond originally favoured a local society, but soon appreciated the value of a national society for the promotion of applied chemistry. Mond drew up the plans for the society's journal and underwrote the cost until it became self-supporting. With his knowledge of languages and the continental industry, he served as the foreign secretary until his election as president in 1888–89. Towards the end of his life, in 1906, Ludwig Mond was awarded the Society's medal for his services to the British chemical industry.

With the ammonia soda process running smoothly, Ludwig Mond turned his attention to the production of cheap ammonia, and the recovery of the chlorine lost in the Solvay process. Much of the research was done by young British and German chemists and Mond only spent part of his time in the laboratory. He failed in his attempts to recover the lost chlorine, but mention must be made of those aspects which became of industrial significance.

Having come close to anticipating the Frank-Caro process of nitrogen fixation in 1879, Mond went on to develop a new form of ammonia-rich producer-gas (Mond gas). A full-scale plant was erected at Winnington and the product used as fuel, after the ammonia had been recovered. It had a low calorific value but Mond was able to demonstrate that it was nevertheless suitable for the production of Siemens steel. The Power Gas Corporation was set up to exploit the process by issuing licences and giving technical advice. This was only for the factories of industrial manufacturers but Mond sought to make Mond gas more readily available in the Black Country as it was suitable for small foundries and smokeless. Despite strenuous legal opposition from existing gas companies, he was successful in setting up the South Staffordshire Mond Gas Co, which continued to supply factories and homes until nationalisation. Both companies were floated in 1901, probably because Mond needed cash for ventures with nickel and white lead. As a means of overcoming the low calorific value of the gas, Mond worked on a gas battery based on the Grove battery, and on gas turbines, but neither became a commercial proposition.

The action of carbon monoxide on nickel was of interest for the gas battery and chlorine recovery. Mond and his colleague, Dr Carl Langer, discovered in 1889 that nickel could reversibly form a volatile compound with carbon monoxide. Furthermore, this nickel carbonyl could be used as the basis for nickel purification. Initially, Mond intended simply to sell his patents, but failing to obtain a buyer, set his own plant up in Wiggin's works at Smethwick in 1892. The decade that followed was spent in developing the process and securing a guaranteed supply of Canadian nickel, Mond himself putting £250,000 of his own money into the enterprise. In conjunction with his sons and Dr Langer he formed the Mond Nickel Co in September 1900 and erected full-scale works at Clydach near Swansea. The flotation of the company in May 1901 raised £600,000; Mond received £325,000 for the business, properties and patents. Although Ludwig Mond remained chairman until his death, the control of the business passed into the hands of his younger son, Alfred. A very pure form of zinc was also produced at Winnington as a spin-off from the research into the recovery of chlorine, but never became commercially significant.

His nickel research brought Mond the scientific honours he ardently desired, although he made only a minor contribution. He was elected an FRS in 1891, and was given honorary doctorates by the universities of Padua in 1892 and Heidelberg (his alma mater) in 1896.

Apart from Mond gas and Mond nickel, which were loosely associated with the Solvay process, Ludwig Mond was also commercially involved with the development of electric light, using Bernstein's lamps, during the 1880s. This was obviously associated with his work with the gas-battery, but again nothing came of it.

The search for new outlets for Mond-gas, and his early research into pigments, explains Mond's expensive and ultimately fruitless involvement with the Bischof white lead process. The Bischof White Lead Syndicate had been set up in 1893 to develop a new process patented by Professor Gustav Bischof, which was safer and more rapid than traditional methods of white lead manufacture. One step in the process involved the use of water gas which could be replaced by Mond-gas: hence Ludwig Mond's interest, which began in the late 1890s. The business was offered to the public in 1900 as the Bischof White Lead Corporation (1900) Ltd, with a heavy capitalisation of £350,000. Even with Mond's backing, the flotation was unpopular with the investing public and a large part of the stock (57 per cent of the preference shares and 27.5 per cent of the ordinary) was taken by the Commercial Development Corporation Ltd. This company was also associated with Ludwig Mond, who was forced to give financial guarantees when it went bankrupt in 1902. Mond was not on the board of the Bischof company himself, but was represented by his elder son and nephew.

Bischof was dismissed in July 1902 after coming into conflict with the new manager of the company's experimental plant at Willesden. At the same time, a site for a full-sized factory was found at Brimsdown on the Lee Navigation Canal in Hertfordshire, and after Bischof's death in January 1903, the company was renamed the Brimsdown Lead Co. The financial problems mounted and Mond continued to pour money into the ailing company. It went into liquidation in 1905, which permitted the writing-down of the capital by £141,000. By 1906, all the original directors had left the board, but the Mond interest remained in the company. Only in the First World War, after Ludwig Mond's death, did the firm start to make even modest profits. Its unhappy existence ended when it was merged with Associated Lead Manufacturers in 1925.

Ludwig Mond never published any books or articles on his business life or his business philosophy. As a chemist, he produced a large number of scientific papers and patents, some of which were of a general and retrospective nature. His address as president of the Society of Chemical Industry in 1889 has remained his memorial. It was chiefly concerned with the development of Mond gas but Mond concluded with a characteristic passage which attempted to cover his own career with a more disinterested lustre than it truly deserved:

> The statement is frequently made that 'Necessity is the mother of Invention'. If this has been the case in the past, I think it is no longer so in our days, since science has made us acquainted with the correlation of forces, teaching us what amount of energy we utilise, and how much we waste in our various methods for attaining certain objects, and indicating to

us where and in what direction, and how far, improvement is possible; and since the increase in our knowledge of the properties of matter enables us to form an opinion beforehand as to the substances we have available for obtaining a desired result. We can now foresee, in most cases, in what direction progress in technology will move, and, in consequence, the inventor is now frequently in advance of the wants of his time. He may create new wants, to my mind a distinct step in the development of human culture. It can then no longer be stated that 'Necessity is the mother of Invention'; but I think it may truly be said that the steady methodical investigation of natural phenomena is the father of industrial progress {*Journal of the Society of Chemical Industry* 7 (1889) 510}.

After the flotation of Brunner, Mond, Ludwig Mond spent comparatively little time at Winnington, although he remained managing director until his death, keeping in touch with John Brunner and company officials by correspondence. This was clearly unsatisfactory, and from about 1889 Brunner often felt obliged to take urgent decisions on his own. (After Ludwig Mond's death, Alfred Mond thanked Brunner for taking the management of the business out of his father's hands without hurting his feelings.) Ludwig Mond's time was now divided between London and Italy where he spent his winters. He bought 'The Poplars' in St John's Wood in 1884 and leased the Palazzo Zuccari in Rome in 1889, eventually buying it for a family friend. Mond met the art historian J P Richter in 1883 and began to build up an impressive collection of paintings, most of which were bequeathed to the National Gallery. He also gave money generously to various scientific institutions, notably the Royal Institution, which he presented with the Davy-Faraday laboratory.

As a young man in Germany Mond had been a liberal and a republican. After coming to Britain, he supported the Liberal Party and Liberal organisations such as the Free Land League. However, Mond was never an active politician in contrast to his partner, John Brunner, and late in life he became a moderate Conservative. Similarly, he was reconciled with Judaism shortly before his death, after being a life-long agnostic despite coming from an orthodox Jewish family.

The decade before his death in 1909 was filled with financial and other worries caused by the Mond Nickel Co, and the Brimsdown Lead Co, family problems and illness; he suffered from insomnia, exhaustion and an increasingly weak heart. He had a heart attack in December 1902, partly as a result of the death of some Clydach workers from gas poisoning and the collapse of the Commercial Development Corporation, but he made a partial recovery. The death of his daughter-in-law from an accidental drug overdose in 1905 affected him greatly, but with his great strength Mond lived to see his seventieth birthday and died from heart failure on 11 December 1909. He left an estate of £1,422,075 gross.

PETER MORRIS

Writings:

On the Recovery of Sulphur from Alkali Waste (Liverpool: W B Jones, 1868).

PP, RC Pollution of Rivers: Mersey and Ribble Basins (1870) C 109.

'On the Origin of the Ammonia-Soda Process' *Journal of the Society of Chemical Industry* 4 (1885).

Presidential address *ibid* 7 (1889).

'The History of the Process of Nickel Extraction' *ibid* 14 (1895).

The papers cited are only the most notable of his scientific papers.

Sources:

Unpublished

Cheshire RO, Chester, Brunner-Mond papers, D/IC/BM.

ICI Millbank, Melchett papers, Mond papers.

PrC.

J Lischka, 'Ludwig Mond and the British Alkali Industry: A Study in the Interrelation of Science, Engineering, Industry and Government' (Duke University PhD, 1970).

Published

Hector Bolitho, *Alfred Mond, First Lord Melchett* (Martin Secker, 1933).

D W Broad, *Centennial History of the Liverpool Section Society of Chemical Industry 1881-1981* (Society for Chemical Industry, 1981).

John M Cohen, *The Life of Ludwig Mond* (Methuen, 1956).

W F L Dick, *A Hundred Years of Alkali in Cheshire* (Winnington, ICI Mond Division, 1973).

DNB.

Jean Goodman, *The Mond Legacy* (Weidenfeld & Nicolson, 1982).

Stephen E Koss, *Sir John Brunner: Radical Plutocrat 1842-1919* (Cambridge: Cambridge University Press, 1970).

William J Reader, *Imperial Chemical Industries: A History* (2 vols, Oxford University Press, 1970-75).

David J Rowe, *Lead Manufacturing in Britain: A History* (Beckenham: Croom Helm, 1983).

Kenneth Warren, *Chemical Foundations: The Alkali Industry in Britain to 1926* (Oxford: Clarendon Press, 1980).

John I Watts, *The First Fifty Years of Brunner Mond and Co* (Brunner Mond, 1923).

—, 'Ludwig Mond' *Transactions of the Chemical Society* 118 (1918).

WWW.

Sir Robert L Mond (from Obituary Notices of Fellows of the Royal Society 1936–1938 *Harrison & Sons Ltd, 1939).*

MOND, Sir Robert Ludwig

(1867-1938)

Chemical and non-ferrous metals company executive

Robert Ludwig Mond was born at Farnworth near Widnes, Cheshire, on 9 September 1867, the elder son of Ludwig Mond (qv) and his wife Frederike (Frida) née Lowenthal. Educated by a Prussian schoolmaster at a weekly boarding school until he was thirteen and then at Cheltenham College, he graduated in natural sciences from Peterhouse, Cambridge, in 1888; afterwards he attended, for a year each, Zurich Polytechnicum, Edinburgh University and Glasgow University (where he worked under Lord Kelvin). In contrast to his gauche brother Alfred (qv) he developed his youthful neatness, quietness and persistence into an easy charm and a cosmopolitan lifestyle which made him at home in England and France.

Lacking his father's industrial ambitions and 'for want of a more exciting alternative' {Goodman (1982) 74} he joined the research team at Brunner, Mond & Co Ltd, the alkali firm based at Winnington, Cheshire, and founded by his father and John Brunner (qv). He became especially concerned in the Mond Nickel Co, formed in 1900 by his father and Dr Carl Langer, who had discovered in 1889 a way of producing nickel carbonyl which could then be used as the basis for nickel purification. This drastically cheapened production of pure nickel and became of great interest to the handful of major manufacturers in the world. Robert Mond carried out research into metallic carbonyl and investigated the production of zinc by electrolysis of zinc chloride. By 1914 he was a director of Brunner, Mond & Co Ltd, Mond Nickel Co Ltd, Natal Ammonium Ltd and deputy chairman of South Staffordshire Mond Gas (Power & Heating) Co — all his father's creations. Robert Mond was chairman of Mond Nickel, 1919-23. He yielded the chair to Alfred after Alfred's political prospects suffered from the collapse of the Lloyd George coalition. By the early 1930s Robert was still a director of four major companies, including the International Nickel Co of Canada, created in 1928 by a merger between Mond Nickel and the International Nickel Co of New Jersey, the two leading firms in the industry. In none of his companies was he the prime mover. His strength was as 'the administrator, in which capacity his earlier practical experience combined with his shrewd knowledge of men.' {Thorpe (1938) 627} From the 1890s onwards he harboured interests outside business which grew with age.

For a while after his father's death in 1910 he took up scientific farming at Combe Bank, Sevenoaks, a large estate purchased by his father and staffed with over 50 servants. He made his mark in the world of science primarily as a participating benefactor of the Royal Institution (equipping the Davy-Faraday research laboratory given by his father and contributing large sums for its reconstruction in 1931) and of the French chemical societies. From the 1890s he developed an equally abiding interest in archaeology — as field worker, organiser of expeditions and financial backer of digs, antiquities' preservation and research publication. His personal participations ranged from Thebes to Palestine (where his support achieved the establishment of the British School for Archaeology in Jerusalem) and Brittany. Robert Mond's large benefactions to the universities of Liverpool and Toronto were recognised by honorary doctorates of laws. He was knighted in 1932 and elected FRS in 1938. He was also a Commander of the Légion d'Honneur.

Mond was twice married: firstly, in 1898 to Helen Edith (d 1905), third and orphaned daughter of Julius Levis, a Jewish German (they had two daughters, one of whom married Herbert Brackley (qv)); secondly, in 1922 to Marie Louise, daughter of Guillaume Jean Le Manach of Belle-Isle-en-Terre, Brittany, and widow of Simon Guggenheim.

Sir Robert Mond died in Paris on 22 October 1938, leaving £381,959 gross.

DAVID J JEREMY

Writings:

Report of Work in the Necropolis of Thebes During the Winter of 1903-04 (Cairo: Institut Français d'Archéologie Orientale, *Annales du service des Antiquités de l'Egypte* 6, 1905).

Michael Faraday (Aberdeen: Aberdeen University Press, 1931).

(with Oliver H Myers) *The Bucheum* (Egypt Exploration Society, 1934).

—, *Cemeteries of Armant* (Egypt Exploration Society, 1937–40).

Catalogue of the Collection of Drawings by the Old Masters formed by Sir Robert Mond (Eyre & Spottiswoode, 1937).

(with Oliver H Myers) *Temples of Armant. A Preliminary Survey* (Egypt Exploration Fund, 1940).

Sources:

Unpublished

PrC.

Published

DD 1914, 1931.

DNB.

Jean Goodman, *The Mond Legacy. A Family Saga* (Weidenfeld & Nicolson, 1982).

History of Henry Wiggin & Co Ltd, 1835-1935. Centenary Publication (pp, 1935).

A C Sturney, *The Story of Mond Nickel* (pp, 1951).

J F Thorpe, 'Sir Robert Mond' *Obituary Notices of Fellows of the Royal Society of London* 2 (1936-38).

Venn, *Alumni Cantabrigienses*.

WWW.

MONTAGU, Samuel

1st Lord Swaythling

(1832-1911)

Merchant banker

Montagu Samuel was born in Liverpool on 21 December 1832, the second son of Louis Samuel (1794-1859) and his wife Henrietta née Israel. The Samuel family had emigrated from Mecklenburg-Strelitz in northern Germany in the mid-eighteenth century. Louis had established himself as a watchmaker and silversmith in Liverpool in the 1820s, while his brother Moses (1796-1860) became a translator and subsequently editor of the *Cup of Salvation*, the Jewish literary magazine.

Montagu's parents altered his given name of Montagu Samuel to Samuel Montagu as soon as he completed his education at the Mechanics' Institution (later the Liverpool Institute). The remainder of the family kept the name of Samuel. After Louis Samuel retired from business in 1847, the family moved to London, where Montagu joined the money-changing firm of his brother-in-law Adam Spielmann. In 1850 or 1851 he was appointed London manager of V Monteaux & Co, a private bank in Paris, but in 1852 he asked his father to finance his own business. Louis Samuel agreed to provide £5,000 on condition that Montagu (who was not yet twenty-one) ran the business in partnership with Montagu's elder brother Edwin Samuel, who was already a banker and bullion merchant in Liverpool. On this basis the firm of Samuel & Montagu was established at 142 Leadenhall Street in February 1853. The firm took over Monteaux's lease at 21 Cornhill in 1862 and moved to its present (1984) address in Old Broad Street in 1865.

Advertisements issued by the new firm emphasised bullion and exchange services and also offered bill collection and bankers' draft services. Montagu's experience and expertise in bullion and foreign exchange were the key elements in these operations. Within two decades the firm had 'assumed an undisputed lead in the silver market' {*Jewish Chronicle* 20 Jan 1911}, alongside older-established concerns such as Mocatta & Goldsmid, Pixley & Abell and Sharps & Wilkins. His skills in foreign exchange, especially in the use of fine margins, gave him the reputation of founding a fortune on 'the quarter pfennig and the half-centime' {Franklin (1967) 4}.

Edwin Samuel played a relatively small part in the development of the new firm, remaining in Liverpool until he wound up his own bank in 1872. Montagu's principal ally was Ellis Abraham Franklin, the firm's first employee. Franklin married Montagu's sister Adelaide in 1856 and, by an agreement made in 1853, he became a partner when Montagu married in 1862. The firm was then renamed Samuel, Montagu & Co (the comma was dropped when Edwin died in 1877). Even at this early stage of the firm's history, this structure created a succession problem. Edwin, Montagu, and

Ellis Franklin each had four sons, who would normally be expected to enter the firm. In 1868 Montagu tackled this potential overcrowding by establishing a separate bank under the management of his two senior clerks, Assur Keyser and Gustav Bitter. The new firm, known as A Keyser & Co, was installed at 21 Cornhill, and the partners of Samuel Montagu & Co were each permitted to nominate two sons to partnerships at Keyser and two at Samuel Montagu & Co. Keyser & Co (subsequently part of Keyser Ullmann, now absorbed into the Charterhouse RIT Group), remained under Samuel Montagu & Co's control until 1908.

Although Montagu's reputation was based on his expertise in bullion and foreign exchange, by the 1870s he had also brought the firm into the market for foreign loans and bills. These interests were cultivated by frequent visits to Western Europe, where, in his wife's words, he acted as 'the bank's courier' from the 1870s onwards {Montagu (1913) 61}. By 1896 his international contacts led to the firm's appointment as the issuing house for the Belgian Government's £1 million 3 per cent loan.

The financial progress of the firm in Montagu's lifetime is not recorded in any detail. In the mid-1890s, however, Henry Smith, manager of the London & Westminster Bank's Lothbury branch, reported that Samuel Montagu & Co 'gave particulars of their capital to the Bank of England a few years ago showing that they had £700,000 but that amount must have been increased considerably since'. Montagu himself admitted in 1896 that 'we have a capital of at least £1,000,000. Some people give us credit for having more than this'. 'For practical purposes', advised one London banker in 1896, 'they are as good as Rothschilds' {Midland Bank Archives, M153/44}.

Throughout his career, Montagu insisted upon simple and narrow methods of control over the firm. In particular, procurations were not granted to any members of staff until Montagu retired from active business life in 1909. As a result, for the first fifty years of the firm's existence it was necessary for either Montagu or Franklin to sign every letter and every cheque issued by the bank. As a corollary to this reluctance to delegate, he was sharply impatient with staff and customers who would not accept instructions and advice. The firm remained private until 1951. In 1982 ownership was shared between Midland Bank plc (60 per cent) and Ætna Life & Casualty Co (40 per cent).

Montagu was elected Liberal MP for the Whitechapel Division of Tower Hamlets in 1885. He was 'far from being a brilliant speaker' {Montagu (1913) 67}, but he was a popular member in his East End constituency and in the Commons. A devoted follower of Gladstone, he was active as a Home Ruler (he contributed to the Parnell Expenses Fund) and as an advocate of free trade. In economic affairs he advocated bi-metallism as the basis for foreign exchange stability, and he argued in favour of decimalisation, the reduction of Stamp Duties, and the reform of legislation affecting bills of lading. He was responsible for ensuring the exemption of works of art from death duties in the Finance Act of 1894. A member of the Gold and Silver Commission of 1887-90, he was frequently consulted on financial questions by Treasury ministers of both Liberal and Unionist Governments; this advisory work continued even after his retirement from the Commons in 1900. He also gave valuable evidence on the British banking system to the US National Monetary Commission of

1908-12, which led to the formation of the Federal Reserve System in 1913. He was created a baronet in recognition of public services in 1894 and raised to the peerage as Lord Swaythling in 1907 (taking his title from a village near his country home in Hampshire). He was DL for the County of London and JP in both London and Southampton.

Montagu was strictly orthodox in religion and he played an extremely active role in Jewish affairs. He became a member of the Board of Deputies in 1862 and he was also a member of the Board of Guardians and the Select Committee on Alien Immigration. He founded the Jewish Working Men's Club at Aldgate in 1870 and he subsequently gave £10,000 for the Tottenham Housing Scheme. A seat-holder at no less than 40 synagogues, he founded the synagogues at Brighton, St John's Wood and was the first warden at New West End, London; he was a 'synagogue opener par excellence' {*Jewish Chronicle* 13 Jan 1911}. He visited Russia in 1882 and took part in the organisation of emigration following the persecutions of Russian Jews. Although expelled from Russia during another visit in 1886, he remained prominent in the affairs of the Mansion House Fund (later the Russo-Jewish Committee, of which he was president between 1896 and 1909).

Montagu married Ellen, the youngest daughter of Louis Cohen, a merchant, in 1862. They had ten children, including Edwin Montagu (1879-1924), who became Asquith's private secretary and later Minister of Munitions (1916) and Secretary of State for India (1917-22). Montagu, whose country home was South Stoneham House, Hampshire, was a keen horseman and an expert fly-fisher. Over several decades he amassed a large and celebrated collection of antique silver and a notable collection of English paintings (including works by Reynolds, Turner and Morland); he was elected a fellow of the Society of Arts in 1897. He was a contributor to *Palgrave's Dictionary of Political Economy*, *Encyclopaedia Britannica*, and the *Jewish Chronicle*. He died on 12 January 1911, leaving an estate with gross probate value of £1,150,000. Most of his fortune was left in trust for his children with the proviso that they should not leave or marry outside the Jewish faith.

EDWIN GREEN

Writings:

Contributions to:

Encyclopaedia Britannica.

Jewish Chronicle.

Palgrave's Dictionary of Political Economy.

US Congress Senate, National Monetary Commission, Senate Report 405, 2nd Session, 61st Congress (1909-10).

Sources:

Unpublished

Midland Bank Archives, London.

Samuel Montagu & Co Ltd, London, archives.

S E Franklin, 'Samuel Montagu & Co. A Brief Account of the Development of the firm' (unpublished memoir, at Samuel Montagu & Co Ltd, 1967).

MCe.

PrC.

Published

DNB.

K Grunwald, *Studies in the History of the German Jews in Global Banking* (Jerusalem, 1980).

Jewish Chronicle 13, 20 Jan 1911.

Lilian H Montagu, *Montagu, Baron Swaythling. A Character Sketch* (Truslove & Hanson, 1913).

The Samuel Family of Liverpool and London (Routledge & Kegan Paul, 1958).

Times 13 Jan 1911.

WWMP.

WWW.

MOON, Sir Richard

(1814-1899)

Railway manager

Sir Richard Moon (courtesy of the National Railway Museum).

Richard Moon was born in Liverpool on 23 September 1814, the elder son of Richard Moon, a Liverpool merchant, and his wife Elizabeth, daughter of William B Frodsham. Richard Moon's sister, Eliza Ann, married Ralph Brocklebank (qv) of the well-known shipping family in 1836; Richard himself married Ralph Brocklebank's half-sister Eleanor on 27 August 1840. He had originally intended to take Holy Orders, but this was opposed by his father, so after studying at St Andrews University (where he did not take a degree) Richard entered the family firm. His father died in 1842, leaving five daughters as well as Richard and his younger brother Robert, who was educated at Cambridge and became a barrister in 1844.

The Moon family were early railway shareholders, and Richard Moon, who had retired from business before 1851 and was by then living in

Birmingham, was in February 1851 elected to the board of the London &
North Western Railway. This was a result of the recommendations of a
committee of shareholders appointed to investigate new management
arrangements for the company following the phasing-out of the
transitional local boards which had supervised the constituent sections of
the London & North Western Railway since its formation by
amalgamation in 1846. Among the committee's recommendations was the
proposal that the main board of the company be enlarged to 30 and 'new
blood' recruited. Moon quickly became identified with the reformist
group of directors on the LNWR board, and acquired a reputation for
challenging the executive management of the company under Mark
Huish, general manager of the company since its formation. In 1855,
following a series of defalcations and resignations by staff, Moon headed a
committee of investigation which led to the establishment of a small
executive committee of 13 directors to supervise traffic operations. In 1858
he was responsible for a further reorganisation and reduction of board
committees, to six, and in the same year Huish, who had become
increasingly isolated, resigned and was replaced by William Cawkwell,
goods manager of the Lancashire & Yorkshire Railway.

Moon's opposition to Huish and his management style is well-
documented: the London & North Western Railway had reached a crisis in
its affairs by the mid-1850s, and while this was partly due to the
development of competing trunk routes which eroded some of the
LNWR's traffic base, a share of the company's difficulties can be ascribed
to Huish's attempts to protect traffic by extensions, cartels, and aggressive
railway diplomacy, much of which proved in the long run to be counter-
productive. However, Huish was supported in his policies by successive
chairmen, and the Marquis of Chandos, chairman since 1853, continued
with similar strategies. In 1861, however, Chandos was driven to resign
when, against his opposition, the entire board supported a scheme agreed
between Cawkwell and his opposite numbers from the Great Northern and
Manchester, Sheffield & Lincolnshire railways for a joint lease of the latter
by the Great Northern and LNWR.

Chandos was briefly succeeded by Admiral Constantine Richard
Moorsom, who had started his railway career in 1831 as joint secretary of
the London & Birmingham Railway; Moon was appointed as deputy
chairman. Moorsom died on 26 May 1861, and Moon was elected
chairman by his fellow-directors early in June. At the first of the half-
yearly general meetings at which he presided, on 23 August 1861, he had
the task of recommending the lowest half-yearly dividend in the company's
history, equivalent to an annual rate of 3.75 per cent. For the next thirty
years, however, he directed the company's affairs with such assiduity and
singleness of purpose that when he retired on health grounds on 20
February 1891 the difficult circumstances in which he took over were all
but forgotten and the *Times* leader was able to comment that he had 'so
impressed the management of that great company with his individual
character that to name the North-Western is to call up his image in the
minds of all who are in any degree conversant with railway business'
{*Times* 21 Feb 1891}.

When Moon took over the chair, the LNWR was already the largest
British railway company with the most mature network. His chairmanship

was a period of consolidation and conservatism, during which the LNWR followed rather than led in service development, and Moon himself, in his addresses to the company's shareholders and in his dealings with Government, both on behalf of his company and through the Railway Companies Association, showed himself to be opposed to any extension of state intervention in matters of railway safety, labour relations, and commercial policy. His frugality was a byword, and this was reflected in his attitudes to matters such as train speeds or the extension of third-class passenger facilities. He discouraged the development of commuter services, so that at a time when other main-line companies serving London were encouraging the development of suburbs the LNWR sector of London's hinterland remained relatively underdeveloped. His strongly-held religious views also led him to oppose the extension of Sunday train services.

But Moon's influence on the LNWR during his long chairmanship was far from negative and restrictive. The company's network grew from 1,030 to 1,830 miles; traffic development beyond this network was fostered by the judicious promotion of joint lines and running powers; agency functions were brought under the company's direct control; locomotive and rolling stock manufacture was concentrated and rationalised; major technological improvements were initiated, such as the installation of a Bessemer steel plant at Crewe works in 1864 or the introduction of gravitational goods marshalling at Edge Hill in 1873; Euston and other major stations were modernised; facilities for Irish and transatlantic traffic were improved and the company's own Irish shipping operations expanded. Some developments, particularly in express passenger operations, were undoubtedly stimulated by competition; in some of its practices the LNWR clung perhaps too doggedly to its own systems: braking was an obvious example, where the LNWR ultimately paid a heavy price for its persistence first with the chain brake and then with the simple vacuum system. But the LNWR was prepared to learn by example as well as to promote innovations developed by its own staff: a party from the board visited the USA and Canada in 1881 to study railway operations there, an officer was sent on a further transatlantic tour of inspection in 1884, and Moon himself quoted French practice as an example to his own company. Moon's guiding principle was to adopt what he saw as best for the company and its shareholders, and of course the financial criterion was one of the clearest indications of this. In these terms, the success of Moon's long term of office can be best judged by the fact that in the year he took over the company returned its second lowest annual dividend, 4.25 per cent, and when he retired the dividend stood at 7.25 per cent. While opinions differed on Moon's policies and administration, contemporaries were unanimous in their acknowlegement of the probity and soundness of the company's finances under his chairmanship, and it is perhaps characteristic of his approach that one of the major measures carried through during his period of office was the consolidation of the preferred and guaranteed stocks of the company in 1878.

Moon remained an advocate of strong central control of the management and policies of the company by the board of directors. Indeed, when Cawkwell retired in 1874 Moon publicly questioned whether one executive could effectively control the entire working of the system, and a group of four directors including Moon himself and Cawkwell, who had been elected to the board on retirement, were given special executive responsibilities. George Findlay (qv), who succeeded Cawkwell as chief executive officer, was given the designation of chief traffic manager; in 1880, however, he was appointed general manager. While Moon before and during his chairmanship was instrumental in rationalising both board structures and the company's divisional management, in formal terms the management structure of the company remained largely unchanged during his period of office. Changes in management practice seem largely to have reflected the extent to which the general manager of the day had had time to establish himself in the confidence of the board and its chairman, and Moon seems to have worked well and harmoniously with both Cawkwell and Findlay. The former ultimately became deputy chairman to Moon and to his successor; the latter was canvassed as a successor to Moon himself in 1891.

Moon's contribution was not so much a particular theory or style of chairmanship and relations with executive officers, but rather the time, commitment and singlemindedness he brought to ensuring that the chairman of the elected board of the largest British joint-stock company was able to control the concern in the same fashion as the senior partner or sole proprietor of a commercial or manufacturing undertaking. That Moon saw this as a full-time commitment was never in doubt: he missed only one half-yearly general meeting throughout his chairmanship, and he refused all other positions apart from directorships of subsidiary companies controlled by the LNWR. However, he distinguished his role from that of a salaried employee of the company, accepting an annual fee of only £2,000 compared with the £5,000 salary Sir George Findlay ultimately received as general manager. Revealingly, Moon is claimed to have said that at such a fee the shareholders were his servants, whereas if he accepted more he might become theirs. Characteristically, he also refused any financial testimonial on his retirement.

Moon's singlemindedness and devotion to the interests of his company was seen by some contemporary and subsequent commentators as a weakness, hindering progress and adaptation and stultifying the development of other views within the LNWR. Even some friendly commentators remarked that Moon, by then in his late seventies, would have had difficulty in adapting to the changed railway environment of the 1890s. Some of this criticism was a reflection of Moon's character; he was a Victorian among Victorians; a man of old-fashioned principles and attitudes, which reflected themselves in deeply-held religious belief, an abhorrence of personal publicity, fixed views and a stern attitude to colleagues and employees. He had, however, a high view of the responsibility of an employer for his employees, and despite his reputation for autocracy was accessible and available to colleagues and staff, who regarded him with loyalty and respect. Had Moon's term of office been shorter he would undoubtedly have been regarded as a reforming chairman, but it became the longest in the company's history, and coincided with a long period of continuity among the senior officers of the LNWR and a financial stewardship which gave shareholders little reason to seek change. Much of the criticism of the company during Moon's later chairmanship was perhaps inevitable: a reflection of the success of policies which, by raising the LNWR to a pre-eminent position, made it an obvious standard for comparison. Individual innovations by other lines were contrasted in isolation with LNWR practice, and the company was often cast in a representative role when British and foreign railway operations were compared. Though the LNWR suffered in some of these comparisons, it remained a progressive company, prepared to innovate and improve according to its priorities. Moon's place in British railway life was recognised by a baronetcy in the Jubilee honours of 1887; in the same year, he became the first freeman of Crewe, which celebrated its own jubilee as a railway town in 1887.

Politically Moon was a Conservative; he was once approached to stand as a Conservative candidate for Liverpool but declined. An Anglican of liberal sympathies, he contributed generously to religious and philanthropic charities, though refusing to allow his name to appear on subscription lists. After his resignation Moon lived quietly at his house, Copsewood Grange, near Coventry; he suffered a serious illness in 1897, and, though recovering, remained almost an invalid until his death on 17 November 1899 at the age of eighty-five. He left £395,844 gross.

Sir Richard's wife had died on 31 January 1891 just before his retirement; his eldest son, Edward, died on 12 April 1893. He was succeeded in the baronetcy by his grandson Cecil Ernest, Edward's eldest son. Two of the Moons' six children had died in childhood, and Sir Richard was survived by two sons and a daughter. Ernest Robert, the younger of the two surviving sons, had followed his uncle Robert as a barrister, and served on several government committees dealing with railway matters; he was knighted in 1919. The elder surviving son, Richard, settled in Shropshire, and as the second baronet died without direct male heirs the baronetcy passed ultimately to this line of the Moon family.

M C REED

Sources:

Unpublished

MCe.

PrC.

Published

Geoffrey Alderman, *The Railway Interest* (Leicester: Leicester University Press, 1973).

Bradshaw's Railway Manual, Shareholder's Guide and Directory.

Burke's Peerage and Baronetage.

Sir George Findlay, *The Working and Management of an English Railway* (6th ed, Whittaker & Co, 1899).

Terence R Gourvish, *Mark Huish and the London & North Western Railway: A Study of Management* (Leicester: Leicester University Press, 1972).

Herapath's Railway and Commercial Journal 13 (1851), 23 (1861), 53 (1891), 61 (1899).

George P Neele, *Railway Reminiscences* (McCorquodale & Co, 1904).

Railway News 21 (1874), 55 (1891), 66 (1899).

Railway Times 24 (1861), 59 (1891), 76 (1899), 77 (1900).

Wilfred L Steel, *The History of the London & North Western Railway* (Railway & Travel Monthly, 1914).

Times 20, 21 Feb 1891, 18, 21, 22 Nov 1899, 16 Feb 1900.

WWW.

Sir John Moores (courtesy of the Littlewood Organisation).

MOORES, Sir John

(1896-)

Football pool promoter and retailer

John Moores was born in Eccles, Lancashire, on 25 January 1896, the eldest son of the four sons and four daughters of John William Moores and his wife Louise née Fethney. After education at a higher elementary school, he started work at the age of fourteen as a messenger boy with the Post Office in Manchester. In his spare time he studied telegraphy at the Post Office School of Telegraphy and then, at sixteen, joined the Commercial Cable Co as a junior operator. A year later he was made an operator and transferred to Bradford.

In 1916 he joined the Royal Navy as a wireless telegraphist and was posted to a shore station in Aberdeen. On demobilisation in 1919 he returned to the Commercial Cable Co, this time in Liverpool. In 1921 John Moores was transferred to the company's cable station in Waterville, County Kerry, handling transatlantic cables and it was there that in his spare time he started his first business.

The station was a remote one and he and three companions conceived the idea of supplying colleagues and members of the local golf club with equipment. This led to John Moores forming a small company, the Waterville Supplies Co, to supply general goods, including books and stationery; he operated it entirely in his spare time.

After eighteen months at Waterville John Moores was moved back to Liverpool by his firm. The urge to be in business on his own account was still a strong one and in 1923, at the beginning of the 1923-24 football season, John Moores and two partners started a football pool. The name of Littlewoods was chosen because the three original partners were all employees of the cable company and did not wish to reveal their spare-time business activity. Littlewood was the original family name of one of the partners and was chosen as being unlikely to be connected with them. Like the Waterville Supplies Co, it was a spare time enterprise and the very first dividend paid was just £2 12s. Initially the venture lost money and the partners withdrew, John Moores buying them out. With the help of a girl assistant and one of his sisters at weekends, John Moores persevered with Littlewoods Pools during the 1924-25 season. Gradually the business picked up, his brother, Cecil Moores, came in as manager and at one time three of his sisters were also helping.

After three years John Moores was able to give up telegraphy and become fully involved in the pools firm. By 1932 he had made his first million pounds and with capital available he looked to other fields in which to exploit his entrepreneurial flair. He turned back to the shopping club idea which he had first explored with his supplies company in Ireland and in 1932 founded Littlewoods Mail Order Stores. Started in a small office in Whitechapel, Liverpool, the mail order business expanded steadily and within a few years had grown into a large organisation.

Littlewoods Mail Order Stores Ltd was launched with an initial capital of £20,000, and operated on the 'club' system which characterised most mail order businesses before the Second World War. A £1 club consisted of 20 members, each of whom paid 1s a week for 20 weeks, the amounts being collected by a club organiser who enrolled members and received a goods or cash commission on payments. There were also £2 clubs and £3 clubs, but the principle was the same. By means of a draw it was arranged that one member received his £1 worth of goods from Littlewoods after the first weekly payment and so on. Thus, unlike catalogue mail order today, the business in its early days was a cash one. Of vital importance from the outset was the catalogue. The first one was sent out in January 1932, and consisted of 167 pages printed in sepiatone. Organisers were initially recruited from the lists of pools 'subscribers' which the parent company held.

With his mail order operation prospering, John Moores again looked around for a new field for his energies and in 1936 he started Littlewoods' Chain Stores, the first store being opened in Blackpool the following year. By 1939 there were 24 chain stores in various parts of the country.

With the outbreak of war Moores placed his entire organisation at the service of the nation and Littlewoods subsequently became a vital cog in the war machine. Various buildings in the North-West of England which had been part of the pools, mail order and chain store business turned over to producing munitions, barrage balloons, parachutes and other safety equipment for the Forces. Expansion of the company's war effort was rapid and dramatic. In 1939 it consisted of one pools building which had been handed over for government censorship work and another which had been requisitioned for the first products, parachutes. By 1944 there were more than 16 factories, laid out and equipped in the most modern way, working around the clock. Typewriter mechanics and watch repairers became skilled armourers, pools and mail order girls turned out balloons, parachutes and emergency food packs. At one stage of the war Littlewoods' output was so much higher than that of Government-sponsored factories that top officials were despatched from London to

The J M Centre, Liverpool headquarters of the Littlewood Organisation (courtesy of the Littlewood Organisation).

Liverpool to find out why and Littlewoods' methods were subsequently adopted in many other munitions operations. Littlewood's war output was remarkable: 11.75 million shells, 6 million fuses, 5 million parachutes, nearly 50,000 rubber dinghies, 20,000 barrage balloons and 700 Wellington bomber fuselages.

After this war effort John Moores resumed development of his retailing empire. However, in the post-war years progress was not easy. Building controls did not allow the construction of new stores and the country was combed for existing premises which could be adapted. Of necessity, these were a mixed bag. They did not help the long-term Littlewoods image in the nation's High Street and this was not really put right until the development of the stores division in the 1970s. However, as controls were relaxed in the 1950s there was a weeding out of poorer stores, redevelopment of others and the building of new stores. By 1954 there were 52 stores, by 1959, 56, and by the mid-1960s more than 70. Today (1984) there are 108 stores.

In the post-war mail order field, John Moores recognised the imminent arrival of the credit buying society and while Littlewoods Mail Order Stores continued on the 'club' principle, he laid plans to launch his first credit mail order business. This was Burlington (originally known as Burlington Warehouses), started in Manchester in 1952, with agents instead of organisers and goods being delivered before even one payment had been made.

Credit mail order developed fast and in 1953 John Moores opened a third mail order firm, Brian Mills, based in a modern building at Sunderland. In 1959 the original mail order operation, Littlewoods Mail Order Stores, was re-named John Moores Home Shopping Service. A year later a fourth mail order company, the third trading on credit, Littlewoods Warehouses, was opened in Liverpool. The market, and the Littlewoods Group, now known in its entirety as Littlewoods Mail Order Stores, continued to grow and in 1964 a fifth company, Janet Frazer, opened at the same Sunderland site as Brian Mills. In 1968 a sixth mail order firm, Peter Craig, was launched.

In 1960 John Moores relinquished his association with his first major enterprise, the pools, when he became a director of Everton Football Club, but his interest and involvement in the affairs of Littlewoods Mail Order Stores — to be renamed the Littlewoods Organisation in 1973 — continued unabated. By 1980 there were six companies in the mail order division, one of the largest mail order businesses in Britain and more than 110 stores throughout the country. The Littlewoods Organisation ceased to be a private company, in the technical sense determined by the Companies Acts, in December 1979, but it is still wholly owned by members of the Moores family and related family trusts. In all its wide-ranging activities, Littlewoods employs some 36,000 people. The headquarters of the Organisation has remained in Liverpool. Moores announced his retirement as chairman of the Littlewoods Organisation Ltd in October 1977, but remained on the group's board, returning for a further term as chairman from October 1980 to March 1982. He was made life president of the company in June 1982.

John Moores had two spells as chairman of Everton Football Club, 1960-65 and 1972-73, and until his retirement in July 1977 remained a very active member of the Everton board. He is still the club's biggest shareholder. Keenly interested in most other sports, he served as a steward of the British Boxing Board of Control and a patron of the British Olympic Association. As chairman of the Liverpool Motorists' Annual Outing for Physically-Handicapped Children, he organises a seaside trip for some 1,000 children from special schools in Liverpool each year. Active in the promotion of road safety, to stimulate interest in the problem he provides road safety shields for competitions in cities and towns throughout Britain. He has also become recognised as a leading patron of the arts and biennially, since 1957, in conjunction with Liverpool's Walker Art Gallery, he holds a national painting competition, for which he contributes substantial prize money; the prize-winning entries are exhibited at the gallery.

Some of his main contributions to charity included covenants providing £20,000 a year for seven years to the Liverpool Boys' Association and £12,000 a year for seven years to assist in the creation of a new school of business management at Liverpool University. He also endowed sports scholarships worth £5,000 a year at the universities of Liverpool and Bath. His keen interest in young people was reflected in his firm's enthusiastic participation in the Government's Youth Opportunities Programme. Littlewoods was one of the first organisations to pledge support, and one of the largest participants. Other schemes include short industrial courses and special provisions for the educationally sub-normal.

In 1970, John Moores was made a freeman of the City of Liverpool, and in the Birthday Honours of 1972 he was made a CBE in recognition of his charitable work for youth and the arts on Merseyside. In 1973 an honorary doctorate of laws was conferred on him by the University of Liverpool. In 1978 he was the first recipient of the Merseyside gold medal for achievement, inaugurated by Radio City and the Liverpool Publicity Association. He was knighted in 1980.

In 1923, shortly after his return to Merseyside from Ireland, John Moores married Ruby Knowles, the daughter of a Liverpool shipping clerk. Until her death in September 1965, they enjoyed a happy married life, during which Mrs Moores supported and encouraged her husband through all his business ventures and wide-ranging activities in public life. They had two sons, John and Peter, and two daughters, Lady Grantchester and Mrs Janatha Stubbs. His two sons and one of his daughters (Lady Grantchester) as well as his brother, Cecil, are directors of the Littlewoods Organisation. Sir John lives in a modest four-bedroomed house in Formby, Lancashire. His hobbies include painting, modern languages and sport.

BRIAN WEST

Writings:

(with Cecil Moores) 'How to Become a Millionaire' *Empire News* 9, 16, 23, 30 Oct, 6, 13 Nov 1955.

'Littlewoods' in *Effective Management on Merseyside* (Liverpool: Merseyside Industrial Development Office, 1972).

Sources:

Unpublished

Littlewoods Organisation Ltd, Liverpool, records.

BCe.

MCe.

Published

WW 1982.

MOREING, Charles Algernon

(1855-1942)

Mining engineer and financier

Charles Algernon Moreing was born in Braidwood, New South Wales, Australia in 1855 where his father was a Gold Commissioner; Charles Moreing received his education in England from 1866, completing it at King's College, London. In 1874 he was articled to Thomas J Bewick, a member of the Institution of Civil Engineers whose mining engineering practice extended throughout the mineral producing world. This enabled the young Moreing to gain wide experience as a manager, surveyor and consultant, including taking charge of the foreign mining department of Sir Francis Bolton's business. In this capacity he controlled metalliferous mines in Portugal, Algeria, France and Germany.

On becoming an associate member of the Institution of Civil Engineers, Moreing set up on his own account, and in 1881 went to South Africa as manager of the Compagnie Français des Mines des Diamants du Cap. He became a keen advocate of the amalgamation of the Kimberley mines, but clashed with the Central Diamond Co, and thus failed to effect the change later achieved by Cecil Rhodes. Resigning on health grounds in 1885, he went into partnership with his old master to form the Bewick Moreing Co.

The 1890s were years of rapid expansion of the company and of growing eminence in mining circles for Charles Moreing. He was actively involved in the International Exhibition of Mining, held at Crystal Palace in 1890, following which he played a major part in founding the Institution of Mining and Metallurgy in 1892. As the *Mining Journal* commented, Bewick Moreing had done

> more than most of their contemporaries — to maintain and advance the character and importance of mining engineering during times when ... it had too often suffered detriment. {*Mining Journal* 9 Jan 1892}

During this period Moreing first became involved in the Cornish mining industry which was to provide him with a permanent base, and his firm with much of their British business. The rigours of international competition had brought crisis to Cornish mining, with the urgent need to attract development capital. Indeed, the massive capital investment needed to sink and develop metalliferous mines everywhere, not simply in Cornwall, led by the 1890s to the growth of the mining houses of which Rhodes' Consolidated Goldfields was perhaps the prime example. Moreing himself had been engaged by the South African Trust & Finance Co Ltd and by the Mexican Investment Corporation, as well as being a director of two London-based mining finance houses, the Australian & Commonwealth Trust and the Western Australian Exploration Co Ltd. In the Cornish context he chiefly confined himself to the directorships in those companies where Bewick Moreing had a managerial interest, notably East Pool and Agar Mines Ltd.

MOREING Charles Algernon

In the early 1890s Charles Moreing travelled widely prospecting mining areas and ventures. In 1890 he set out for Kara Sea and the mouth of the Yenisei river in Siberia, but a recurrence of ill-health forced his return. In 1891 as London agent for the Mozambique Co of Lisbon he brought an action against the British South Africa Co following the invasion by forces of that company of the mines in Mancia territory. A branch office of the company was maintained both in San Francisco and Salt Lake City, and in 1899 Moreing became president of the St Lawrence Power Co, then constructing facilities at Massena, New York. Increasingly, however, Charles Moreing's interest focused on Western Australia where a severe depression had revived gold mining on a considerable scale and where there was a severe shortage of skilled engineers and metallurgists. To take advantage of this shortage, Bewick Moreing employed a young mining engineer named Herbert Hoover (the future President of the USA), and in 1897 sent him to Kalgoorlie.

Hoover's great capacity as an organiser and mining engineer did much to establish technical efficiency in the Western Australian goldfields. Possibly his greatest success was the reorganisation of the Sons of Gwalia Mine, which he superintended whilst adding other ventures to the Bewick Moreing group. His methods did, however, bring clashes with labour, and the growing number of mines coming under control or management by Bewick Moreing caused increasingly adverse comment. The Royal Commission of 1904 examined allegations of bribery and inside dealing by the company in connection with the Great Boulder Perseverance Mine, and the election campaign in Australia that year was fought with slogans against Bewick Moreing.

Although the company did not technically own a monopoly, their structure of dominant firm and its 'group' of managed mines did represent a new scale of mining organisation — a close alliance of technical expertise and investment capital enthusiastically hailed by Hoover. He estimated that in 1904-5 Bewick Moreing controlled or managed enterprises with a market value of over $70 million, mostly in Western Australia. Hoover's services to Bewick Moreing were recognised in 1901 when, on the retirement of Thomas Bewick (son of the founding partner), Charles Moreing invited Hoover to become a partner. The reconstituted firm consisted of four men with Moreing, who was to take 50 per cent of the profits, as the senior partner.

As the senior and richest partner, Moreing was in charge of mining finance, raising money and persuading stockbrokers to recommend investment in the Bewick Moreing mines. Hoover, who was to take 20 per cent of the profits, supervised the operation of the mines, while the two other partners, A Stanley Rowe, an accountant (who also took 20 per cent of profits) and Thomas Wellsted, a mechanical engineer (who had 10 per cent) looked after administration in London. Bewick Moreing undertook to supply resident mine superintendents, engineering staff and lawyers for various foreign miines, to provide facilities for stock transfers and to handle business arising from the mining companies being registered in London.

The period after 1901 was the high point of the company's fortunes. By 1907 45 mining concerns were affiliated to the firm, and £895,000 was distributed annually in wages throughout the world. In Western Australia 'company mining' had become almost synonymous with Bewick Moreing.

Yet at the same time all was far from well. The activities of the Chinese Engineering & Mining Co provided an example of one of the cruder episodes of British and Belgian expropriation in post-Boxer China. This resulted in a Chinese mandarin, Chang Yen Mao, director general of Mines for Chilli and Jehol, bringing an action in the British couurts against Moreing and others involved in the company, including Colonel Albert Thys, leading financial adviser to King Leopold of the Belgians. Hoover appeared to have felt strongly that Moreing dishonoured promises made by Hoover to Chang.

Furthermore, in 1902 A S Rowe, one of the four partners, was discovereed to have used company funds to speculate, recouping his losses by the issue of forged share certificates in Great Fingalls Consolidated Mine, Western Australia. Although not legally liable, Moreing (who hastened home from China in January 1903 when the scandal erupted) and his partners accepted liability to save their firm's reputation. Hoover lost $125,000, Moreing as senior partner presumably lost more heavily. Increasingly, there was friction between Hoover and Moreing, and in July 1907, having freed himself of the debts incurred by the Rowe débâcle, Hoover resigned. He later stated that he had found Moreing a wholly impossible partner.

From then on there was increasing tension between those companies in which Hoover was involved and Bewick Moreing. Moreing felt strongly that Hoover had squeezed him out of business he himself had generated in the Baku oil fields in Russia in 1908-9. Yet, despite their differences of personality the two men shared the aim of transforming the structure of international mining, and during their partnership laid the foundations of notable concerns today. The immense silver lead deposits at Bawdwin, Burma (subsequently Burmah Mines) was one such enterprise started by Bewick Moreing. Perhaps their most famous successor is the Rio Tinto Zinc Corporation. It was Hoover and Moreing's support of new treatment processes for tailings at Broken Hill, Australia, that led to their taking over the Zinc Corporation in 1905.

Despite Moreing's important interests in China, Burma and elsewhere, the focus of his business was in Western Australia, where by 1906 existing mines were declining in value and few new mines of any potential were being discovered. Between 1904 and 1906 Bewick Moreing examined hundreds of mining propositions, but found only two worthy of adoption. From 1909 to 1912 Moreing was active in the illusory Russian oil boom centred in Maikop, but by 1912 most of his ventures were unsuccessful.

However, Moreing continued to play an active part in British metal mining. He helped found the Cornish Chamber of Mines in 1917. The following year, together with Charles Thomas and Oliver Wethered, he formed Tehidy Minerals Ltd, the company which subsequently purchased the mineral rights of the Basset and Lanhydrock Estates and thus of almost the whole of the major mining districts. The triumvirate thus owned the leasing rights for such important producers as Carn Brea and Tincroft Ltd, Dolcoath and South Crofty as well as Moreing's East Pool and Agar.

Despite increasing age, Charles Algernon Moreing continued to expand his interests. After the First World his firm took over the management of the Von Donnersmark estates in Silesia, and subsequently the Bergwerks Union mines at Mezica, Yugoslavia and the Raibl zinc mines, which finally fell to Italy during the Second World War. By the late 1930s Bewick Moreing were connected with the Tanami Syndicate in Australia, and with concerns like the Dominion Reefs, Rosterman and Borderland Syndicate in Southern and Central Africa.

Politically, Moreing was a supporter of Joseph Chamberlain (qv), and stood unsuccessfully as parliamentary candidate for Gainsborough in the 1906 election. In addition, he was inventor, in 1896, of the Moreing and Neals telegraphic code for mines; was a fellow of the Royal Geological Society; a keen mountaineer and member of the Alpine Club.

Moreing married Helena Marian, daughter of Edward Harcourt Longden of the East India Company; they had two sons, Algernon (b 1889) and Adrian (b 1892), both of whom became partners in Bewick Moreing and sat in the Commons as Conservative MPs, though Algernon was initially a Liberal. Charles Moreing died on 5 September 1942, leaving £19,525 gross.

GILL BURKE

Sources:

Unpublished

Charter Consolidated Ltd, archives of Tehidy Minerals Ltd.

Hoover Archives, West Branch, Iowa, USA, Bewick Moreing Co files.

PrC.

Gill Burke, 'The Cornish Miner and the Cornish Mining Industry 1870-1921' (London PhD, 1982).

Published

Gill Burke and P Richardson, 'The Decline and Fall of the Cost Book System in the Cornish Mining Industry 1895-1914' *Business History* 23 (1981).

Mining Journal 18 Apr 1891, 9 Jan 1892, 12 Sept 1942.

Mining Manual 1892, 1899, 1902, 1908, 1919, 1938.

George H Nash, *The Life of Herbert Hoover* vol 1 *The Mining Engineer 1874-1914* (New York: Norton, 1983).

Times 10 Sept 1942.

WWMP.

WWW.

MORGAN, David

(1833-1919)

Draper and department store retailer

David Morgan from The First Hundred Years. David Morgan Ltd.

David Morgan was born at Cae Crwn, a small farm just northwest of Brecon, on 28 October 1833, the eldest of the six children of David and Anne Morgan. After rudimentary schooling until he was twelve, he went to work for a shopkeeper in Rhymney and was then apprenticed to a draper in Newport.

He next worked in London for a wholesale firm in St Paul's Churchyard at the time of the Great Exhibition of 1851 and also worked in Birmingham, where he is said to have spotted a site for his future shop. But the prosperity of Rhymney with its thriving iron works and direct railway link to Cardiff Docks as well as his mother's wish that he should look for a business nearer home, led him to go into partnership there. After a disagreement with his partner he put his share of their stock of fabrics on a handcart and pushed it to Cwn Shon Mathew Square, where he opened a shop of his own in 1858.

In the same year he opened a second shop in Pontlottyn, competing directly against the company store run by the iron works company. He went on to open another in Abertillery, which is still trading there as Morgan & Francis. In Pontlottyn in 1868 he married Margaret, the daughter of John Llewellyn, a local butcher, but she died only three years later, after bearing their only child, John Llewellyn Morgan. By 1874 he had acquired sufficient resources to buy the farm at Llanbrynean of which his father had become the tenant.

But his big step was taken in 1879. Unlike some of his fellow-countrymen who were attracted by the possibilities of retail trade in London, David Morgan saw that Cardiff Docks, from which Welsh coal

Opened the Shop at 5 P.m Friday Oct 31. 1879 first sale on Tuesday the 28th 2/7 & sold goods every day up to day & including this Evening making the total receipts — 7 3 7¾

David Morgan

Diary entry by David Morgan, from The First Hundred Years. David Morgan Ltd was being shipped all over the world, were bringing great prosperity to the city, and decided, as he wrote to his bank at the time, 'to take a shop in Cardiff' {Morgan (1979) David Morgan to the Bristol & West of England Bank, 9 Sept 1879}. Like all the successful pioneers of retailing, he knew instinctively what constituted a first-class location. The one he chose was on the Hayes, a main thoroughfare running parallel to St Mary's Street in the heart of the city. Although the area between the two streets was a maze of narrow alleys, small courts and squalid hovels, there was lively and growing customer traffic on all sides. The trams from Roath to the Docks passed two railway stations on their way and stopped outside his shop, while the Royal Arcade nearby led not only to St Mary's Street but also to the Great Western Railway station (now Cardiff Central).

From the beginning, the Morgan shop flourished and its owner was able to pursue a policy of expansion which he continued for over thirty years, acquiring new land and new premises, negotiating and bargaining, and going, when necessary, to litigation. In 1884 the first buildings between his shop and the Royal Arcade were bought; in 1898 he opened a shop on St Mary's Street and in the years immediately afterwards completed the Morgan Arcade between the two main streets; in 1904 he acquired other shops and two public houses to give for the first time a continuous front along the Hayes; over this whole period there was scarcely a year in which he was not planning something new or implementing something already planned. Not only did he thus ensure the growth of his own business but he also thwarted the plans of his rival James Howell (whose store is now

Morgan & Co, the Hayes, Cardiff, 1879 from The First Hundred Years. David Morgan Ltd.

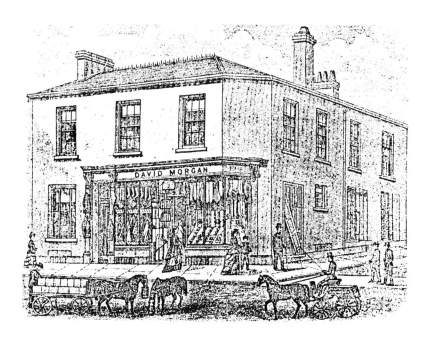

The Pontlottyn Shop from The First Hundred Years. David Morgan Ltd.

(1984) part of the House of Fraser), who had bought up some of the land in the area in a bid to keep Morgan off St Mary's Street. The struggle between the two was resolved in an exchange of parcels of land.

By 1904 'Morgans The Hayes' was one of the largest stores in Wales and its founder's ambitions had been largely fulfilled. But it must be said that the complex of buildings he had put together had resulted in a store of a very awkward shape with many operating problems. Upper floors were on different levels, the premises were traversed by three public throughfares, selling space was divided up by too many interior walls, there were far too many entrances and exits, and in fact the buildings were too big for the trade the firm was doing. Many of these shortcomings were put right by David Morgan's son and his eldest grandson, Bernard, who also made the final purchase of the last remaining site between the two streets in 1930.

David Morgan was concerned not only about his own premises but also about their environment and the improvements that could be made in the city around them. He believed, for example, that the only effective way of installing and maintaining all the pipes and cables necessary for modern urban living was to house them in a single specially-constructed tunnel, accessible through man-holes, under each street. When the Cardiff city authorities refused to allow him to put his idea into practice under the street, he installed a sample tunnel under the Morgan Arcade which he had just completed alongside the store.

But Morgan was not just a real estate developer. He was a master draper who understood and put into practice, often ahead of others, the principles of modern retailing which were just being developed. Like Boucicaut of the Bon Marché in Paris, his simple principle was 'one price, plain figures, no discounts'. In his shop there was no bargaining, the staff and customers understood that the marked price was the only price. He carried this policy to the extreme of refusing to hold clearance sales with temporarily reduced prices. He believed in a small but quick return on each article sold, which was made possible only by strict control of costs. Much of this cost control was exercised by him personally; it was said of him that his prosperity was due not so much to what he made as to what he saved.

As a manager he enjoyed good relations with his employees, was opposed on their behalf to long opening hours and insisted on good living-in conditions in the days when all shop employees lived in or over the shop premises. He himself lived in until 1893. In 1913 he was disturbed to find that his male employees were demanding an end to living-in and were prepared to strike to get the practice stopped. He settled the dispute by allowing senior male employeees to live out, while female and junior employees were still required to live in. Living-in finally came to an end at Morgans in 1935.

Morgan & Co became a private limited liability company with £40,000 capital in 1916. David Morgan attended to business every day until just before he died on 21 April 1919, leaving £245,112 gross.

DEREK KNEE

Sources:

Unpublished

MCe.

PrC.

Published

Aubrey Niel Morgan, *David Morgan 1933-1919: The Life and Times of a Master Draper in South Wales* (Risca: Starling Press, 1977).

David Morgan Ltd, *The First Hundred Years* (pp, 1979).

Samuel Morley, from a portrait in Vanity Fair *15 June 1872*

MORLEY, Samuel

(1809-1886)

Hosiery merchant and manufacturer

Samuel Morley was born in Homerton, London, on 15 October 1809, the third son and youngest child of John Morley (1768-1848). His father had continued the family's farming activities at Sneinton Manor House and hosiery manufacturing in Nottingham in partnership with his brothers Samuel (who died in 1797) and Richard (1775-1855), but about 1796 moved to London to set up a branch of the family business there. The brothers took into partnership William Wilson (1769-1833), a Nottingham retailer and fellow Congregationalist who became their brother-in-law. The business was carried on under the name of Chambers, Wilson & Morley for a time and then as Morley, Wilson & Morley from about 1800 to 1820, from which date it traded under the style of I & R Morley.

Samuel Morley was educated at Nonconformist boarding schools at Melbourn in Cambridgeshire and Southampton until the age of sixteen, but the main influence on his early life was that of his pious and earnest family. His parents' home at Hackney was a centre of Nonconformist activity, while his uncle, Alderman Wilson, spearheaded evangelical Nonconformist activity in Nottingham.

In its early years the Morley business was evidently very modest, for the Nottingham warehouse was described as 'a long, narrow room up a yard, with a length of counter and a few racks at one end, and a counting house at the other; an attic overhead, with a dozen or so of hand [stocking] frames would represent the home department of machinery' {Hine (1876) 34-35}. Most of the manufacturing was done by a corps of domestic framework knitters who were dispersed in workshops in the town or villages round about. The future course of development and prosperity of the business was, however, inaugurated about 1796, when John Morley opened a warehouse for the firm at 18 Wood Street in the City of London. Nottingham merchant hosiers had kept stock in rooms in the inns of this part of the City from the early part of the eighteenth century, and a few had London agents, but it was still unusual to have a partner permanently stationed in the metropolis. The move was made at a time when the hosiery industry, stimulated by the steep decline in the price of machine-spun cotton, was growing rapidly, and Nottingham was also benefiting from its success with various forms of machine-made lace. At the end of the Napoleonic Wars more than half of the 44 hosiery and lace warehouses listed in Johnstone's *London Commercial Guide* can be linked with Nottingham and Leicester.

There are scarcely any business records relating to the Morleys but it is possible to discern some reasons for their early success. Hard work appears in a letter from John Morley in 1807: 'I come to town every day $\frac{1}{2}$ past 8 and stop till 8 at night and often 9 o'clock (except only the day we had our

child baptised) ... my business is my chief enjoyment of a worldly nature'
{Nottinghamshire RO, Wilson of Radford MSS}. Another reason is that I
& R Morley always insisted on the very best craftmanship; at the
Nottingham warehouse if the stockings 'were not absolutely perfect, the
workmen were in for a very bad time!' Thirdly, the Morleys were closely
connected for generations with religious Nonconformity, and familiarity
with other manufacturing families of the same persuasion suggests that
this brought a network of marketing connections, and perhaps also of
credit.

When Samuel Morley entered the family business in 1825 as a clerk in
the counting house in Wood Street, it seems that these features of the
business were already established practice, and for the next thirty years or
so he built on them. Samuel proved to be much the most able of the three
brothers. By degrees his control of the accounts led him to a general
oversight of every department of the London warehouse, and he was quick
to discover and correct any weakness in the organisation. He particularly
prided himself on his financial acumen: 'He knew how to turn the capital
of the firm to the best account, never keeping larger balances than were
absolutely needful lying idle, and taking advantage of every favourable
change in the money market to gain by his discounts' {Hodder (1887) 25}.
His father, uncle and brothers retired in turn, leaving Samuel Morley in
sole charge of the London business in 1855, and the Nottingham one in

I & R Morley's factory at Golden Lane, London (courtesy of Dr Stanley Chapman).

1860. He was always identified as a firm disciplinarian, and from this time became the autocrat of the business.

The first public sign of new growth at I & R Morley came in 1848-50, when a five-storey warehouse block was built in Wood Street on the site of six houses, and the payroll increased from 30 to 100. According to Bank of England and popular opinion, the project 'absorbed more available capital than it was quite prudent to do' {Bank of England, Leicester Agent's Letter Books, I, 71}. The principal aim of policy at this period appears to have been to increase the range and turnover of hosiery goods; a price list of 1835 shows that sales were limited to cotton hose and some lace, but in the course of the next generation this was extended to include underwear, gloves and socks in all the varieties known to fashion. The domestic market was served by a growing corps of travelling salesmen, while an export business was gradually built up.

In the 1840s the Morleys were prominent among the hereditary leadership of the hosiery industry that resisted the advent of the factory system, nor did they appear among the innovators of the 1850s. Their first factory was built in Nottingham in 1866, and from this time Samuel Morley pushed ahead a programme of factory building in the town and satellite manufacturing villages, though this was not completed before his death in 1886. The policy was evidently to absorb the younger knitters into the factories while employing the older generation to their retirement. The transition was a long one, for in 1900 I & R Morley's payroll still included 3,950 domestic workers, a figure that must be compared with 3,173 factory hands working in the seven factories and 1,241 staff in the Wood Street and Nottingham warehouses. The manufacturing end of the business retained a momentum of its own, and the managers met the Wood Street buyers only on rare occasions. Samples were sent up to London, but it was left largely to the Nottingham managers to decide the quantities to be made in the various lines.

Much of the success of the business must have been due to the Nottingham partner, Thomas Hill, who, it was said, had an unrivalled knowledge of hosiery machine technology and its development. According to Morley's Victorian biographer, 'Morley's factories were the best in the North Midlands; special attention was given to cleanliness, light and ventilation, and, above all, the fullest and freest fraternity was established between capital and labour, between master and workmen, merchant and clerks ...' {Hodder (1887) 142}. Morley's personal ideology can be identified in the claim of a contemporary journalist that the young men at Wood Street 'are not merely as much as possible preserved from the perils of London life, but they are stimulated to Christian life and activity in many ways' {Ritchie (1869) 221}.

John Morley had gradually withdrawn from his business from 1840 to devote his time to Nonconformist charities and politics, and Samuel Morley followed a similar course. A Liberal, he sat for Nottingham from July 1865, but was unseated on petition in 1866, and did not stand at the subsequent election. In 1868 he became Liberal MP for Bristol. In Parliament he emerged as the leading figure in a coterie who appointed themselves to represent the Nonconformist conscience and interest, being particularly concerned with education, temperance, housing, industrial relations and the condition of the working classes generally. Morley was also regarded as an authority on all questions connected with trade. His interest in these areas is surveyed in Hodder's *Life*. He retired from the Commons in 1885.

When Samuel Morley entered the family firm, the largest wholesale hosiers in London were George Brettle & Co, whose manufacturing operations were based on Belper. However, Brettle died in 1835, and shortly afterwards his firm languished, I & R Morley taking the lead. The drive that Samuel Morley gave to it generated continuous growth. In 1830 sales were little more than £100,000, but in 1848 they exceeded £500,000, £1 million in 1859, and over £2 million in 1871. Morley's move into politics and later retirement to Hall Place scarcely restrained this growth; sales were £2.8 million in the year of his death. Unfortunately no record of the firm's capital appears to have survived.

In early life Morley became a member of the King's Weigh House Chapel in the City of London, where Rev Thomas Binney's congregation included merchants who still lived as well as worked at the centre of British commerce and finance. Binney was an uncompromising opponent of the Church of England, and it was no doubt under his influence that Morley took the lead in 1847 in launching the Dissenters' Parliamentary Committee to promote the return of Nonconformists in the House of Commons. From this period Morley became increasingly involved in Nonconformist affairs but not always in a narrow denominational way. He gave strong financial backing to General William Booth's 'rescue work' with the Salvation Army in London, to the evangelical campaigns of Moody and Sankey, and to the YMCA. In 1868 he resigned from the Society for the Liberation of Religion, the Nonconformist group fighting for disestablishment of the Church of England, so acquiring the fuller support of his Bristol electorate. Among many religious causes, temperance 'claimed his attention more than any other' in his later years {Hodder (1887) 315}.

Morley's health began to fail in 1880, and he increasingly withdrew to the country house and estate, Hall Place, Leigh, near Tonbridge, Kent, that he had bought in 1871. He enjoyed being a country squire, JP and local philanthropist, but declined a peerage offered by Gladstone. In later years Morley became the leading benefactor of Nonconformity in Britain. 'There is hardly a chapel built to which he is not a subscriber ... A great revival of home missionary efforts has been the result' {Ritchie (1869) 224}. At his death on 20 November 1886 he owned the biggest hosiery manufacturing and wholesale enterprise in Britain, and left £484,291 (well over £500,000 if his 1,400-acre estate is included).

Samuel Morley married in 1841 Rebekah Maria, daughter of Samuel Hope, a banker. The eldest of their five sons, Samuel Hope Morley (1845-1929), was for many years senior partner of I & R Morley, became a director of the Bank of England and Governor, 1903-5, and was created Lord Hollenden in 1912. The second son, Howard (1846-1920), devoted his career to I & R Morley. The third son, Charles (1847-1917), retired as a partner in I & R Morley in 1888, was honorary secretary of the Royal College of Music, 1882-1917, and MP for Brecknockshire, 1898-1906. The fourth son, Arnold, was MP for Nottingham, 1880-95, Chief Liberal Whip, 1886-92, and Postmaster General, 1892-95, and created a Privy Councillor. The sons added a shirt, tie and umbrella making factory in

Golden Lane, London, and a manufactory of gloves in Grenoble to the business, but otherwise do not appear to have changed its structure or style; it remained a partnership until after the First World War. The second generation's London sales peaked at £6.7 million in 1919, then fell away during the inter-war years.

STANLEY D CHAPMAN

Sources:

Unpublished

Bank of England Archives, Leicester Agent's Letter Books.

Hall Place Estate Office, Leigh, Tonbridge, records of Lord Hollenden.

Nottinghamshire RO, Wilson of Radford MSS.

MCe.

PrC.

N B Harte, 'A History of George Brettle & Co Ltd 1801-1964' (Courtaulds plc, typescript).

Published

DNB.

Charlotte J Erickson, *British Industrialists: Steel and Hosiery 1850-1950* (Cambridge: Cambridge University Press, 1959).

Thomas C Hine, *Nottingham Castle* (Nottingham, 1876).

Edwin Hodder, *Life of Samuel Morley* (Hodder & Stoughton, 1887).

Nottingham Review 1 Nov 1833.

James E Ritchie, *British Senators* (1869).

Frederick M Thomas, *I & R Morley, a Record of a Hundred Years* (pp, 1900).

Threads (house magazine of I & R Morley) includes 'A Short History of the Firm' (Oct 1925) and an 1835 price list (Apr 1935).

WWMP.

MORPHY, Donal William

(1901-1975)

Electrical appliance manufacturer

Donal William Morphy, the son of Arthur Morphy was born in 1901. Very little is known about his birth or early education. He was educated at Imperial College, London, where he distinguished himself as an oarsman and his father presented a cup to be competed for annually to encourage rowing in the College.

On leaving college he was apprenticed to Metropolitan Vickers at Manchester, then worked successively for the Cox Cavendish Electric Co and the General Radio Co Ltd in London. He tried setting up his own business, making radio components, but failed.

Success came in 1936 when Morphy entered into partnership with Charles Frederick Richards (b 1900). They began in a former oast house in Kent, assembling electric fires. Their initial capital was £1,000, partly subscribed by a third individual. Electric fires proved to be a seasonal business, and within months they added electric irons to their range. By 1939 they were producing 5,000 thermostatically controlled irons a week and had 20 per cent of the UK market. Although irons were by far their best known and most successful product, they also produced 'pop-up' toasters and refrigerators.

Morphy was the inventive half of the partnership, with a talent for designing graceful-looking products and organising their production. He preferred to collaborate with his suppliers and buy in components designed to his specification and at a mutually agreed price, rather than to buy competitively. He was concerned for the welfare of the employees, and industrial relations. Richards was responsible for marketing their products. In 1960 EMI bought out Morphy-Richards after a takeover battle, and Morphy retired. Richards did not stay long with EMI and joined GEC as joint managing director of its appliance division. Richards, who was married with two sons, died on 15 November 1964 leaving £151,765 gross. Morphy moved from Chislehurst, in Kent, to Petworth, Sussex. He was married, with one daughter. Donal William Morphy died on 25 May 1975 leaving £280,669 gross, including a bequest of £10,000 to the parish church at Petworth, half for 'religious purposes' and half for the poor of the parish.

BRIAN BOWERS

Sources:

Unpublished

Imperial College, Archives.

PrC.

Published

T A B Corley, *Domestic Electrical Appliances* (Jonathan Cape, 1966).

Electrical Times 1960.

Electrical Who's Who various dates.

Times 17 Nov 1964, 5 Feb 1965, 27 May, 30 July 1975.

Herbert Morris (from D Wainwright Cranes and Craftsmen. The Story of Herbert Morris Limited *Hutchinson Benham Ltd, 1974).*

MORRIS, Herbert

(1864-1931)

Crane manufacturer

Herbert Morris was born at Dalston, London, on 26 February 1864, the son of John Stuart Crosbie Morris, a publisher, and his wife Caroline née Bennett. His father had become wealthy as a trading entrepreneur in France and Germany; Herbert accompanied him on his business trips.

At the age of twenty-one, Herbert Morris quarrelled with his father. Having observed the expansion of the German engineering industry, he borrowed £100 from an uncle, and set up business at 211 Upper Thames Street, London, with the agency for a German worm-geared pulley block of advanced design. He also became agent for Shardlows, lifting gear manufacturers of Sheffield. When the senior partner died in 1889 Morris raised £1,000 to buy the lifting gear part of the company, and began to manufacture at the Ealing Works, Attercliffe, Sheffield. His works manager in Sheffield was a German-born engineer, Frank Bastert. Morris patented the Herbert Morris & Bastert patent brake in 1892, and began to manufacture travelling hoists and cranes, selling to the Admiralty, the War Office, the Crown Agents, the Royal Ordnance factories and the Royal Dockyards.

In 1897, having carefully examined the map of England for a town with available labour and transport (canals and railways), and readily accessible to major industrial centres, he built the Empress Works in Moor Lane, Loughborough, between the Midland and Great Northern railway lines, and linked with the Grand Union Canal.

Herbert Morris & Bastert became a limited company in 1900 with a capital of £250,000. They began to manufacture electric cranes, the first (delivered on 2 July 1901) for the Central Electricity Supply Co of London, for Marylebone power station. In 1908 a scale model of a Morris electric crane was deposited in the Science Museum, as representing 'most

Dockside crane built for Arcos, buying agent for the USSR, at the North Works, 1931 (from D Wainwright Cranes and Craftsmen. The Story of Herbert Morris Limited Hutchinson Benham Ltd, 1974).

perfectly the highest state of knowledge of this subject at the present time' {HM Board of Education citation}. Before 1914 the company had sales offices throughout Britain, in Paris and in Toronto. Exports were sent to China, Japan, New Zealand, India, Burma, Egypt, South America, and throughout Europe. The company provided lifting gear for Shackleton's Trans-Antarctic Expedition of 1914. Salesmen were backed by detailed illustrated catalogues and multilingual literature.

Bastert left the company in 1911 and in the following year its name was changed to Herbert Morris Ltd. The company continued to prosper under the chairmanship of Walter Henry Purnell, for long Morris's aide, though

Morris's youngest son Frank became a director in 1928, and eventually chairman, and then president. Subsequently Herbert Morris Ltd proved its strength by acquiring a number of rival companies during the 1930s — the crane division of Craven Brothers (Manchester), the Vaughan Crane Co of Manchester, and Royce Ltd (the creation of Sir Henry Royce (qv)) of Trafford Park.

Between 1929 and 1933 the company made some 50 cranes to the order of Arcos, the USSR buying company. They were intended for shipyards in Estonia, and were still to be seen on the docksides long after the Second World War. The business risk — at a time of tension between Britain and the Soviet state — was considerable, but proved profitable. After 1945 the company diversified into container handling systems, linear motors and retail security systems. In 1977 Herbert Morris Ltd was taken over by the American conglomerate, Davy International.

Morris married in 1891 Eva Margaret Caroline, daughter of Edmund Walter Weller, confectioner; they had four daughters and three sons.

Herbert Morris died at Nice, where he had long been in retirement, on 25 April 1931, leaving £101,629 gross.

DAVID H E WAINWRIGHT

Sources:

Unpublished

BCe.

MCe.

PrC.

Published

David Wainwright, *Cranes and Craftsmen: The Story of Herbert Morris Ltd* (Hutchinson Benham Ltd, 1974).

John Morris (courtesy of Ashurst, Morris Crisp & Co).

MORRIS, John

(1823-1905)

Solicitor and promoter of railways and public utilities

John Morris was born in the small Devon town of South Molton in 1823. Nothing is known of his family background, except that his paternal grandfather, also called John Morris, may have been a successful builder in Devon. Nor is anything known of his education before, at the age of fifteen, he began work as a clerk in the office of Gilberd Pearse, a local solicitor. Three years later he secured a similar post in the London firm of William Ashurst, where he later served his articles and became a partner in 1854.

A free-thinker and a radical, Ashurst had long been active, both privately and professionally, in the great liberal campaigns of the day. Naturally, Ashurst had shaped the practice in ways that would be felt by any successor, but in addition his influence was to be felt by Morris in two quite particular respects.

First, it had been because of shared views and a mutual acquaintance with Robert Owen that the wealthy haberdasher and Radical MP, James Morrison, had entrusted his legal affairs to Ashurst from 1818. As the fortunes of the Morrison family grew, so did the need for litigation and delegation, and it was as the chief lieutenant to Charles Morrison (qv), eldest son of James, that Morris would pass the greater part of his career.

Secondly, the important part played by the Ashursts, father and son, in the campaign for a penny post, led to the appointment of William Ashurst Jr as solicitor to the Post Office in 1862. This appointment obliged him to retire from the firm, bequeathing to Morris the thriving company business which had grown up around the core provided by the investments of the Morrisons and which, up to this time, had been handled almost exclusively by the younger Ashurst.

Not yet forty, and with little knowledge of company law, Morris found himself plunged into the affairs of some of the largest concerns of the time. James Morrison had diversified into general trading and merchant banking in North Atlantic markets in the 1830s, and thence into North American railways, and it may have been at the instigation of Charles Morrison that Morris was retained by the principal shareholders of the Grand Trunk Railway Co of Canada, working with Edward Watkin (qv) on the reconstruction which culminated in the Grand Trunk Arrangement Act of 1863. Shortly afterwards Morris was concerned in the promotion of the District Railway between Westminster and Kensington, the first of a long succession of urban utilities in London and abroad with which he would be connected.

In the aftermath of the Overend Gurney crisis of 1866 Morris was active in the liquidation of the Albert Life Office and in salvaging the Great Eastern Railway, the Consolidated Bank, and the Agra & Masterman's Bank. Following the crash of 1873, his connections with Morrison and Sir

Edward Watkin brought Morris into contact with the affairs of a number of ailing US railways, notably the Erie, the Wabash, and the Baltimore & Ohio.

During a long career, terminating in partial retirement only at the close of the century when he was in his late seventies, Morris consistently pursued these early interests in American railroads and London utilities, playing a part in the introduction of tramways to London in 1868 and in the unsuccessful attempt by the County of London Tramways syndicate to amalgamate the tramways of the metropolis almost thirty years later. He was also active in the introduction of the telephone to Britain at the end of the 1870s. At the same time, however, he diversified in a number of directions, organising a syndicate to buy the liberal *Daily News* in 1868 and make it into a penny daily, and sitting on the boards of various companies that ran public utilities in Saratov, Beirut, and Recife, hotels in Rumania and the South of France, sugar factories in Brazil, and mines in Cornwall.

The most significant diversification, however, and one in which he certainly followed his wealthy client Charles Morrison, was into the River Plate republics of Argentina and Uruguay. A new company, the River Plate Trust, Loan & Agency, was set up in 1881 to acquire the assets of the Mercantile Bank. Morris was elected to the board of the River Plate Trust, Loan & Agency in 1883 and the following year he became chairman, a position he was to fill for more than twenty years. The Trust company was to prove one of the most profitable of all Anglo-Latin American ventures, yielding a nominal annual average return to the investor of 16.5 per cent over the years 1881-1905. More than this, it became the core of a substantial group of Anglo-River Plate railway, utility, financial, and land companies, many of which were also clients of Ashurst, Morris, Crisp.

The prime concern of the Trust was to lend sterling on mortgage, usually for a term of four years, to the wealthy pastoralists of the established Argentine provinces of Buenos Aires, Entre Rios, and Santa Fé and the choicest parts of Uruguay. In addition, however, the firm gradually acquired shares in a number of new Anglo-River Plate ventures, and provided a wide range of management services in London and South America, from issuing bonds to bribing politicians, for associate companies tied to it by overlapping directors and major investors.

Morris interested himself in the detailed general management of more than two dozen ventures during his chairmanship, working closely with his London general manager, James Anderson. Following his British and North American experience, Morris paid the closest attention to utilities and railways, including successive companies formed to construct and operate the water supply and drainage systems of Rosario, Paraná, and Montevideo, as well as the Buenos Aires and Belgrano Tramways and the River Plate Electricity Co Ltd. Underpinning these interests was the *South American Journal*, a specialist financial weekly, acquired in 1888 by a syndicate of Anglo-South American capitalists including Morris and the railway contractor, J G Meiggs.

Morris was no mere manager or lieutenant for Charles Morrison and his other wealthy clients. By the 1880s he had himself become a substantial capitalist and, by about 1895, with little short of £100,000 invested in equities of eight companies, he was rather more heavily committed to the River Plate in proportion to his total wealth than was Morrison.

Although Morris visited the City infrequently after 1898 and spent more time at his country house near Folkestone, Kent, he continued to take an interest in the affairs of the Trust company and its affiliates up to his death.

Nothing is·known of Morris's interests or activities outside his business. Presumably he shared the political views of his partners and major clients, most of whom were Radicals or Liberals, but he is not known to have taken any active part in politics.

John Morris married in 1854. He had at least three sons, one of whom joined the army, while another became a partner in his father's firm, and one, perhaps two, daughters. John Morris died on 25 March 1905, at his London home in Hyde Park Square, leaving a gross estate of £370,480.

CHARLES A JONES

Writings:

Argentine Republic: The Forced Currency and Gold Contracts (Effingham Wilson, 1886).

Two Lectures on the Jurisdiction and Practice of the High Court of Admiralty of England Delivered Before the Incorporated Law Society ... London, on the 14th and 21st December 1859 (Hepburn & Sons Ltd, 1904).

Sources:

Unpublished

Mandatos y Agencias del Rio de la Plata, Buenos Aires, Argentina, archives. (These records have been destroyed, but detailed notes are to be published shortly.)

C Reg: Mortgage Co of the River Plate (26,562); River Plate Trust, Loan & Agency (15,740); River Plate & General Investment Trust (26,355).

PrC.

Charles A Jones, 'British Financial Institutions in Argentina, 1860-1914' (Cambridge PhD, 1973).

Published

DD.

Charles A Jones, 'Commercial Banks and Mortgage Companies' in Desmond C M Platt (ed), *Business Imperialism, 1840-1930: An Inquiry Based on British Experience in Latin America* (Oxford: Clarendon Press, 1977).

Linda and Charles A Jones and Robert Greenhill, 'Public Utility Companies' *ibid*.

Charles A Jones, 'Great Capitalists and the Direction of British Overseas Investment in the Late Nineteenth Century: The Case of Argentina' *Business History* 22 (July 1980).

Report of the Proceedings at the Golden Wedding Presentations to Mr and Mrs John Morris, at the Whitehall Rooms, Hotel Metropole, London, on Mr Morris' Eighty-First Birthday, the 12th December 1904 (pp, 1904).

James Fred Rippy, *British Investments in Latin America, 1922-1949: A Case Study in the Operations of Private Enterprise in Retarded Regions* (Minneapolis: University of Minnesota Press, 1959).

South American Journal 25 Mar, 6 May 1905.

MORRIS, William

(1834-1896)

Soft furnishings designer and manufacturer

William Morris (courtesy of Victoria & Albert Museum).

William Morris was born at Clay Hill, Walthamstow, a village east of London, on 24 March 1834. His father, also called William, was a partner in a firm of discount brokers whose successful speculation in a Devon copper mine saw the market value of his 272 shares rise from £1 to £800 each. This increased wealth enabled the family to move first to Woodford Hall and then, in 1848, to the Water House, Walthamstow (now the William Morris Gallery).

The third of nine children, Morris was educated at Marlborough and Exeter College, Oxford, where he read divinity. With four fellow students he developed a passion for all things medieval, not only in design and decoration but for the high ideals and principles of chivalrous life. They read Thomas Carlyle, John Ruskin and Charles Kingsley, all critical of Victorian society, and the strong impressions made on the young Morris influenced his work throughout his life, as writer, manufacturer and political activist.

Before leaving Oxford, Morris had abandoned ideas of entering the Church and instead, with his great friend, Edward Burne-Jones, decided 'to begin a life of art' {Mackail (1899) I, 2}. Having inherited an annual income of £900 on reaching his majority, Morris joined the office of G E Street, a leading Gothic-revivalist architect, but he soon found that his work as an apprentice, which involved copying plans and drawings, was not to his liking. His private income enabled him to join Burne-Jones in rooms in London and the two began to design and make furnishings for their new home, finding nothing suitable available in the London shops.

In 1859 Morris married Jane, the daughter of Robert Burden, an Oxford stableman, and commissioned the building of the Red House, Bexleyheath. The furnishings and decoration of this house by Morris and friends led to the formation of Morris, Marshall, Faulkner & Co on 11 April 1861. The initial capital for the firm was provided by £1 shares subscribed by the eight partners, with an unsecured loan of £100 from

A view of the Menton Abbey Works of Morris & Co (courtesy of Victoria & Albert Museum).

Morris's mother. Premises were taken, initially at Red Lion Square (later moved to Queen Square), and the company's first products were mural decorations, architectural carvings, stained glass, metalwork and furniture. At the International Exhibition of 1862 they exhibited stained glass, furniture and embroidery in the Medieval Court, sold £150 worth of goods and were awarded two gold medals by the jurors.

As managing partner, Morris was the inspirational and artistic force behind the company but the success of this and the subsequent firm was also due, in part, to two managers, George Warrington Taylor and, later, George Wardle, whose efficient direction of financial matters allowed Morris to concentrate on the artistic output. The original partners gradually dropped out of active participation in the firm's affairs, leaving Morris to dissolve the partnership on 25 March 1875, reorganising it as Morris & Co under his sole proprietorship. In 1877 the shop was moved to Oxford Street and became the focal point of the fashionable interior decorating trade.

For the next few years Morris concentrated on the production of printed and woven textiles and carpet weaving and revived a number of natural dyeing techniques at the Hencroft Works, Leek with Thomas Wardle (qv). In 1881 he acquired a factory on the River Wandle between Merton and Wandsworth and here set up a stained glass studio, block-printing tables and looms for the manufacture of tapestries and carpets and furnishing fabrics of silk, cotton, wool, linen and mohair, all patterned with Morris's characteristic designs.

Morris's aim to improve industrial design was coupled with a strong desire to recreate the guild principles of the Middle Ages, when, he believed, the status of the craftsman was recognised and good working conditions made work enjoyable. With contemporary conditions in large Northern factories in mind, he defined his ideal:

> That the workman shall take pleasure in his work, that decent conditions of light and breathing space and cleanliness shall surround him, that he shall be made to feel himself not the brainless "hand" but the intelligent cooperator, the *friend* of the man who directs his labour, that his honest toil shall inevitably win fair and comfortable wages ... {Lazarus (1886).}.

Profit-sharing at the works involved managers and foremen but, as the nature of printing and weaving necessitated piece work, was not extended to all staff. Instead, wages were fixed above normal rates and bonuses were paid. The workers, many of whom were past retirement age, were encouraged to take as much free time as they wished and could afford, without affecting the completion of orders.

Morris's prolific career as a poet, writer, lecturer, designer, typographer and active socialist (helping to found the Socialist League in 1884), had few equals. He became the inspiration of idealists and hard-headed industrialists alike, affecting the design of fabrics and industrial practices throughout the British textile industry at the end of the nineteenth century.

Morris died at his London home, Kelmscott House, on 3 October 1896, survived by his wife and two daughters, and leaving an estate valued at £62,118 gross. Morris & Co was left in the hands of F and R Smith, partners in the firm since 1890, who had previously acted as managers on George Wardle's retirement, and J H Dearle, Morris's assistant and manager of the Merton Abbey Works. In 1905 the firm was registered as a private company under a board of eight directors with a nominal capital of £45,000 in £1 shares. Variations in title and directorship occurred throughout the period 1905-30 and by the start of the Second World War, with a dwindling workforce, shortages of raw materials and a changing market, it was clear that the firm could not survive; it was wound up on 21 May 1940.

LINDA PARRY

Writings:

(May Morris ed), *The Collected Works of William Morris* (24 vols, Longmans & Co, 1910-15).

—, *William Morris, Artist, Writer, Socialist* (2 vols, Oxford: Basil Blackwell, 1936).

Sources:

Unpublished

MCe.

PrC.

Published

Philip Henderson, *William Morris: His Life, Work and Friends* (Thames & Hudson, 1967).

Emma Lazarus, 'A Day in Surrey with William Morris' *Century Illustrated Magazine* 22 (1886).

John W Mackail, *The Life of William Morris* (2 vols, Longmans & Co, 1899).

Morris & Company 1861-1940 (exhibition catalogue, Arts Council, 1961).

Linda Parry, *William Morris Textiles* (Viking Press, 1983).

Paul Thompson, *The Work of William Morris* (Heinemann, 1967).

William R Morris, Lord Nuffield (from Graham Turner, The Leyland Papers *Eyre & Spottiswoode, 1971).*

MORRIS, William Richard

Viscount Nuffield of Nuffield

(1877-1963)

Motor vehicle manufacturer

William Richard Morris was born in Worcester on 10 October 1877, the son of Frederick Morris, an assistant to a draper in Worcester, and his wife Emily Ann, daughter of Richard Pether, a farmer of Headington, Oxfordshire. There were seven children, but only William and a sister survived childhood. Frederick Morris, who came from Oxfordshire, returned to Oxford to farm when William was aged three. William attended the local school in Cowley. His upbringing was overshadowed by his father's ill-health, which compelled him to leave school at fifteen to earn money for the family. He was briefly apprenticed to a bicycle trader, but had no formal technical training apart from an engineering evening class that he attended only twice. 'From that date', Morris later wrote, 'the work-shop appeared to me infinitely more attractive than the schoolroom' {Morris (1933) 252}. At the age of sixteen, he set himself up in his parental home with £4 capital as a bicycle repairer, graduating from that to actually making bicycles to order with parts acquired from the blossoming Midlands cycle industry. By 1896 he was able to advertise himself as a 'cycle-maker', and by 1901 he was established in Oxford at 48 High Street. A year later, in partnership with Joseph Cooper, he set out to manufacture motor-cycles as well, made from components and castings bought from outside. The partnership broke up over disagreements on risk-taking a year later, and in 1903 Morris became independent again. At 100 Holywell Street he set up a motor repair and motor cycle business and gradually began to work with motor-cars, repairing, servicing and garaging them. In 1909 bicycles were finally abandoned and Morris rechristened the business the 'Morris Garage', offering his services as a 'motor car engineer'. He became the local agent for a number of popular car models, and began to hire out cars as well. In 1913 the whole business was consolidated and renamed 'Morris Garages (W R Morris Proprietor)'. Sales rose from £2,000 in 1906 to £32,000 in 1912, by which time total annual profits were £1,200. His was a successful and popular local business, but small in scale. By 1912 Morris employed about 20-30 workers at four shops and workshops scattered around Oxford.

It was a small step to move to the actual production of motorcars. Using components and engines bought in from other suppliers, Morris designed his own small car with a view to large-scale manufacture. Work began on the design in 1910-11, when, Morris later said, he was 'convinced that there was going to be a big demand for a popularly priced car' {Morris (1924) 73}. By 1913 the first Morris Oxford cars were ready at a price of £175 and within a year he was producing at the rate of 1,000 cars a year, something that very few British car-makers had yet achieved. Though the new enterprise was interrupted by the coming of the First World War, during which Morris provided a variety of military equipment though few vehicles, it continued to expand after 1919. At the end of the war Morris began to assemble cars again from the parts left over from his earlier production. The firm was now housed in a disused military academy at Cowley, which Morris had first rented and then bought. In 1919 the Cowley works produced 387 cars, by 1923 20,048. The workforce rose from 200 to 5,000 over the same period, and net profits from £45,000 in 1920 to £852,000 three years later. In the course of a decade Morris had established himself as one of the major British producers, catering for a new mass demand for small family cars.

There were a number of reasons for Morris's early success. First of all he was convinced that motoring would soon become a mass pursuit, and that the demand for cheap, small cars would be more important than the luxury, small-scale production of the pre-1914 industry. 'From the first', he later wrote, 'I set out to cater for the man-in-the-street — the potentially large class of enthusiastic but not too well-off owner-drivers' {Morris (1933) 252-53}. The question of price was crucial here, and Morris aimed from the start to produce cars at as low a price as possible. The gamble that he took in 1921 with the coming of deflation, to cut prices dramatically at a stroke, helped him to gain a considerable proportion of the vigorous post-war demand. The second factor was his policy of buying in components at highly competitive prices and assembling them as efficiently and cheaply as current factory practice would permit. He had visited the United States in 1914 and was impressed with the buying-in and assembly methods that he saw there, and the attention to standardisation which was common practice. He recognised that he could not design and make the whole car himself — he lacked the technical skills and the money — and instead spread the financial risk among his suppliers (of which there were over 200 by 1923), as well as obtaining high-quality standard parts quickly and cheaply. Morris thus avoided the burden of excessive capitalisation at a point where the car market was still very unstable and investors very wary. This system also allowed Morris to keep a careful eye on costs and reflected his view that sound finances and close managerial supervision were essential ingredients for success. He preferred self-financing, and apart from a small bank loan in 1904 and £4,000 put up by the Earl of Macclesfield in 1913 (both of which were quickly repaid) Morris's business grew only as fast as his turnover would allow. 'I've always believed in economy', he claimed, 'I've always believed in putting profits back into the business'. {BBC interview, Nuffield (1951) 3} His strength was in careful commercial practice and costing policy and vigorous marketing rather than engineering skills, and in a good eye for intelligent imitation of factory practice and selling techniques elsewhere.

During the 1920s Morris emerged as the foremost British car manufacturer. He was helped by a favourable set of market conditions. Ford's pre-eminence declined after the war because of commitment to out-dated models, while American import competition was restricted by tariffs and the high horse-power tax which favoured the smaller British cars. Morris was fortunate in being able to fill a large demand in the mid-1920s before more American capital came into the industry and before his major rivals woke up to the opportunities. High levels of output then reinforced this lead by encouraging further rationalisation and lower prices. By 1927 Morris cars were half the price of their leading rivals in the field. In that year Morris produced 61,000 of the 164,000 cars produced in Britain, while total sales of all the Morris businesses had risen from £216,000 in 1919 to £14.4 million in 1928. Net profits reached £1 million in the same year, with assets of £5.5 million. During the course of this expansion Morris bought up subsidiary businesses, including the Hotchkiss firm that had produced his early engine, because the scale of demand for parts and components required greater control by the assembly firm. He also diversified, with rather less success, into producing other vehicles, lorries, vans, taxis and luxury cars, including the MG range of sports cars. In 1926 all the different businesses were consolidated into Morris Motors (1926) Ltd, and converted into a public company with an issued capital of 3 million £1, 7.5 per cent cumulative preference shares and 2 million £1 ordinary shares, all of which were held by Morris. He also bought up other, less successful firms, Wolseley in 1927, and Riley in 1938; and he helped to found the Pressed Steel plant at Oxford which pioneered the production of steel sheet mouldings for British cars.

As the firm grew bigger, success was harder to maintain. The risks involved in selecting the right models and in production innovation on a large scale grew with increases in firm size, and became greater still as the car industry gradually eliminated the weaker businesses and became concentrated around six major producers. During the Depression Morris's sales began to decline at a faster rate than total trade, and in 1933 had fallen to 44,000 out of the industry's output of 220,000. Other manufacturers were competing more effectively on price, had offered good small capacity cars sooner than Morris, and in the case of Ford were prepared to put substantial money into adopting the most modern American flow-production methods. The situation for Morris Motors was exacerbated by Morris's insistence on maintaining tight personal control over the firm's policy. He still took most of the major decisions, even though the amount of time that he could devote to increasingly complex managerial tasks was limited by his growing pre-occupation with activities outside the firm or with particular aspects of the business at the expense of others.

Morris reacted to the decline in his business fortunes by delegating more responsibility, particularly to the energetic engineer Leonard Lord (qv), by streamlining product policy and producing new smaller capacity cars (the Morris 8 was the most successful), but most of all by a large injection of capital into new plant and factories at Cowley where full conveyor-belt production was introduced. The new factory was the most up-to-date in Europe, with a capacity of 100,000 cars a year. With the new methods a car left the production line every two minutes. They were cheaper, and of better quality, and quickly captured the public's enthusiasm at a time when model and service competition was as important as price. By 1938 Morris was producing 90,000 cars a year, a smaller proportion than in the 1920s but still greater than that of any rival producer. Net assets were £11.4 million in the same year, against £5.5 million a decade before, and profits reached over £2 million by 1936, at which time Morris began to release his ordinary shares for sale to the public.

During the Second World War Morris businesses turned out large quantities of military equipment, both in the car and components plants and in the so-called 'shadow factories'. After the war civilian production was restarted slowly, and with less success than in other companies. Morris found the combination of government restrictions, poor financial performance and American competition a threat sufficient to encourage the search for a merger with other firms. In 1951, after a number of years of exploratory talks and inter-company standardisation, Austin and Morris came together to form the British Motor Corporation, an organisation of which Morris became the first president. After 1945 he had taken less direct interest in the firm and although his ideas could not be ignored, product policy, sales and finance were conducted more or less independently of Morris. The organisation was rationalised to meet the needs of a large corporate structure which, by 1951, employed over 20,000 people and had profits of £8.7 million.

Morris's success as an entrepreneur came from his sense of where demand lay, something which was still largely a product of intuition and business imagination in the early part of the century. He was also a keen imitator. He was able to exploit ideas, techniques, production methods pioneered by others, in such a way that he could offer better, cheaper products to larger numbers of customers. There was no special secret to his success. His financial caution and his commitment to salesmanship were not unique to Morris. It was the combination of all these factors, in a climate favourable to rapid growth, that singled Morris out. He was also an indefatigable worker, prepared to put everything into the business and expecting the same enthusiasm not only from other managers but from his workers as well. Any money that he made went straight back into the business until the 1930s when he sold off his shares to take up charity work.

Of all these factors, salesmanship was perhaps the most important. Morris, who had been a car agent himself before the First World War, recognised how important it was to develop a network of sales outlets with reliable agents who would provide good after-sales service. 'The satisfied owner', Morris wrote, 'is one of the best possible selling media in this trade ... Only by service after purchase can you keep the owner satisfied' {Morris (1924) 76}. He insisted that his agents operate standard service charges, and carry a large stock of spare parts. He built up a large network of concessionaires in the early 1920s, well before many of his rivals. He was also one of the first car makers to recognise the importance of hire purchase and to extend the facility on a nationwide basis, with funds made available by Morris himself. By 1926 half of all car sales were on credit terms. Advertising was also very important. Morris was an instinctive salesman and publicist. He promoted his cars in the press, through special advertising gimmicks, and through the pages of the *Morris Owner*, a magazine founded in 1924 to provide regular information and advertisement for the company. He appointed a full-time sales director in 1923. Though there were weaknesses on the side of design and product selection throughout Morris's time with the business, they were offset by the tradition of successful product information. Yet even this success was qualified. When Morris looked for sales outside Britain he was faced with a string of failures, such as an abortive production venture at Le Mans in France, or the poorly-designed 'Empire' car. When exports of Morris cars expanded in the 1930s it was with the help of protected Imperial markets.

Morris was also an early convert to Taylorism. A visit to the United States in 1914, and further visits in the 1920s, convinced him that the only way to produce a cheap car was to use the most modern production techniques and an efficient division of tasks both among the workforce and between the assembly plant and its main suppliers. At Morris Engines an attempt was made to introduce a completely mechanised assembly line in the 1920s, though the attempt failed because the specifications for the equipment were too advanced. Morris also insisted that his major suppliers adopt the same factory practice or lose his orders. Where they could not do so, he bought them up and reorganised production himself. As the firm grew larger there was sufficient money to ensure that Morris could stay ahead of his major competitors both in production technology and in the modernisation of the product. This lead was gradually eroded, particularly after the Second World War, but by 1939 Morris still had one of the largest flow-production factories in Europe. He was always committed to large-scale production, which brought its own economies with it. Though still small by US standards, Morris was one of the few British producers to think in terms of large production units from the outset. This in itself gave added strength to his competitive position.

Only in his attitude to management did Morris exhibit any real weaknesses, more obvious as the firm became larger and its organisation more complex. The chief problem was Morris's reluctance to forgo control of the firm. 'I continue', he said in 1951, 'because I've created such a great responsibility. It is not easy to drop the reins suddenly without a thought for the people who work in the organisation' {BBC interview, Nuffield (1951) 5}. But in practice Morris was less and less involved in the day-to-day running of the firm from the late 1920s onwards, though still insisting on his right to take the major decisions and to interfere in any areas of managerial responsibility, even where he knew very little about what was going on. His attitude to management was old-fashioned and autocratic, difficult to adapt to the needs of a large corporation. As decisions became more complex, his rough-and-ready judgements, which he regarded as a virtue, became more damaging to the firm: while his lack of self-doubt turned increasingly into intolerance and even arrogance.

Nor were the men that he selected for high office in the firm always the best choice, reflecting Morris's preference to be surrounded by people like himself. He distrusted formal educational qualifications and the tradition of non-graduate management survived right down to the time of his death and beyond. He also disliked formal committee and paper work, and always encouraged his managers to be out on the shop floor, getting on with production rather than with the more important tasks of corporate planning, sales and finance. As a result the Morris business fluctuated during the 1930s and 1940s between efforts to decentralise responsibility and to centralise it excessively. But as long as Morris remained in the chair it proved impossible to set up a permanent and successful corporate structure. After 1945 the weaknesses in managerial competence and in the links between the different parts of the business slowed down the revival of the firm, leaving it well behind the performance of Austin or Ford. Miles Thomas (qv), managing director after the war, complained that 'Although W R had said long before that he was going to leave running of the business to the Board, he still persisted in exercising what was inappropriately, if undeniably, his right of destructive criticism' {Thomas (1964) 250}. Gradually Morris himself came to terms with this weakness and the final merger with Austin was acknowledgement that his long period of direct entrepreneurial activity had come to an end.

There were problems too in his attitude to labour, although for much of his business career they remained subdued by his conviction that high wages made for a contented workforce. 'A low wage', he wrote, 'is the most expensive method of producing. A moderately high wage gives a man an interest in life. Men are only going to work if they are going to earn more comforts, hobbies, amusements' {Morris (1924) 74}. For most of the period after 1919 Morris paid well above union rates for the job, working on a bonus system. He also tried in the 1930s to iron out the irregularities of work, brought about by the seasonal nature of car demand, by introducing longer-running car models which could be produced on a year-round basis. Nevertheless, job security was not good, and Morris expected full co-operation and hard work from his men, and made little allowance for the stress caused by the progressive introduction of new work methods. Men could be hired and fired at will, and Morris obstructed the coming of unions into his business for as long as he could. 'I never allow trade unions to interfere with me', he said in 1927. 'Much has been said and written about welfare schemes for workers. I do not believe in over-doing it.' {Whiting (1983) 37} In 1951 he blamed post-war industrial difficulties on the fact that 'so many people [were] doing as little work as possible for the highest pay in the shortest possible time' {BBC interview, Nuffield (1951) 6}. He was a Conservative by conviction, a firm believer in free enterprise and a strong opponent of socialism. While this mattered little in the context of the inter-war years, it made it more difficult to establish a proper framework for the conduct of labour relations thereafter.

Morris devoted his whole life to his business. He had modest personal ambitions, and ran an unostentatious household. He retained the same small office throughout his business career and disliked outward display. He married an Oxford schoolteacher, Elizabeth, daughter of William J Anstey, a furrier, in 1904, but the marriage was childless, something which Morris greatly regretted. He was not much interested in religion, enjoyed travelling abroad, and took a sporadic interest in politics. He was an inactive chairman of Cowley Conservative Party, and in the early 1930s flirted with Oswald Mosley's New Party, to which he gave £50,000. His only active interventions in national politics concerned the industry: in 1924 when he campaigned against the repeal of the McKenna duties on cars, in the mid-1930s over the scale and planning of rearmament for the motor industry and after the 1945 election in the campaign against controls over industry. His other major interest was charity. From the mid-1930s onwards he released his ordinary shares to the public and used the proceeds to establish a wide number of medical, academic and social benefactions, most notable of which were Nuffield College in Oxford, the Nuffield Foundation and the British United Provident Association scheme set up in 1947. His donations totalled £30 million and had some considerable influence both on policy for the depressed areas in the 1930s and on the development of the health system.

When asked in 1951 what he thought were the main ingredients for successful entrepreneurship he replied: 'Enthusiasm for your work. Being on the spot ready to seize opportunities as they present themselves. Foresight and determination, and get right out of your mind that you can get there on luck, for you're sure to have many setbacks to overcome, and above all, avoid getting a swollen head ...' {ibid, 4}. Morris displayed all these virtues and some of the vices of the world of great Victorian businessmen into which he was born. But unlike many of his contemporaries he had a shrewd grasp of the importance of salesmanship and a positive attraction to modern factory practice. As a result he neatly straddled the age of individualism and the age of the corporation.

His business and his charity earned him high status, something whch interested him perhaps more than money itself. He was given an OBE in 1917, became a baronet in 1929, a baron in 1934 and in 1938 became Viscount Nuffield, a name taken from the village in which he lived and to which he had moved from Cowley after his peerage. He was awarded numerous honorary degrees, and became a fellow of the Royal Society in 1939. In 1949 he was made an honorary fellow of the Royal College of Surgeons, fulfilling in a roundabout way his early ambition to be a doctor. At Nuffield, he pursued an interest in golf (which included buying the Huntercombe Golf Club). He was a very fit man, winning cups for cycle racing in his youth; and he was possessed of an enormous energy and inner drive which kept him actively at his desk until his death on 22 August 1963. He left an estate proved at £3,252,764 gross.

William Morris was almost certainly the most successful and wealthiest industrialist of his age. He was Britain's Henry Ford, for years a household name both through the cars that made him rich and the generosity with which he gave those riches away. He began working life as a bicycle repairer and ended it as chairman of Britain's largest motor company. From the early 1920s Morris dominated the motor industry and contributed substantially to the way in which it developed in Britain. As an example of a self-made multi-millionaire, he plays an important part in any wider discussion of the nature of entrepreneurship.

R J OVERY

Writings:

'Policies that Built the Morris Motor Business' *System* 45 (1924).

'How We Made a £6,000,000 Turnover Last Year' *ibid*.

'Motor Industry' in Hugh J Schonfield (ed), *Book of British Industries* (Dennis Archer, 1933).

Sources:

Unpublished

Oxford Central Library, Morris collection (newspaper cuttings and advertising material).

Transcript, BBC Radio interview with Lord Nuffield, October 1951.

There is a small collection of private papers at Nuffield College, Oxford, which is closed to researchers.

PrC.

Published

Philip Andrews and Elizabeth Brunner, *The Life of Lord Nuffield: A Study in Enterprise and Benevolence* (Oxford: Basil Blackwell, 1954).

Roy Church and M Miller, 'The Big Three: Competition, Management, and Marketing in the British Motor Industry' in Barry Supple (ed), *Essays in British Business History* (Oxford: Clarendon Press, 1977).

DNB.

Robert Jackson, *The Nuffield Story* (Frederick Muller, 1964).

Richard J Overy, *William Morris, Viscount Nuffield* (Europa, 1976).

William Miles Thomas, *Out on a Wing: An Autobiography* (Michael Joseph, 1964).

Times *Prospectuses* 72 (1926).

R C Whiting, *The View from Cowley* (Oxford: Clarendon Press, 1983).

WWW.

Charles Morrison (courtesy of Dr Charles Jones).

MORRISON, Charles

(1817-1909)

Merchant banker

Charles Morrison was born in London, in 1817, the eldest of the seven sons and four daughters of James Morrison and Mary Ann née Todd. Although James Morrison was then not yet thirty, he had already risen from a rural middle-class background in Hampshire to manage the London warehouse of Messrs Todd & Co, with an annual turnover of more than £650,000 in haberdashery and drapery. He married Mary Ann Todd, the daughter of his employer in 1814, receiving a partnership as dowry; by 1818 his control of the business was undisputed; and by 1830 he was a MP and a JP, with a country seat at Fonthill, near Salisbury, and a considerable range of mercantile and financial interests besides the Fore Street warehouse.

Unlike his younger brothers, who went to Eton, Charles was educated at private schools in London and Geneva (1826-27) until the age of fifteen, before spending three years each at the University of Edinburgh and

Trinity College, Cambridge. At Fonthill the family mixed freely with old-established local families. At the same time, the Morrison circle included many bankers and businessmen and, because of the Radical leanings of James Morrison, a fair sprinkling of political economists, European liberals in exile, and leading English Radical politicians.

The fear of James Mill that Cambridge might spoil Charles for commerce proved unfounded. In 1841 he joined his father and his younger brother Alfred in a new firm, Morrison, Sons & Co, of 62 Moorgate Street, which took over management of the varied investments outside the Fore Street warehouse which James had been developing over the previous decade. These included a substantial mortgage business, in which large sums had been lent to Lord Headfort, the Duke of Buckingham and Chandos, the Duke of Sussex, and other landowners. In addition, Morrison had developed a large merchant banking business centred on North America, which survived the crash of 1837 only through a loan of £325,000 from the Bank of England. Even after the crisis, the Morrisons remained encumbered with an extensive portfolio of American stocks that had been deposited as security by the Bank of the United States before it went into liquidation in 1841.

It was in connection with the realisation of the assets of the Bank of the United States that Charles Morrison made his business debut in 1842, travelling widely in the Eastern and Southern States. With his brother Alfred he succeeded in unravelling the complicated relations between their firm and the Bank by the middle of 1843. But not all the assets were liquidated. The Morrisons held on to a nucleus with good long-term prospects to which they added substantially in subsequent years. At his death James held over £800,000 in US securities.

The firm's attention in the 1840s was much taken up with railways, including the Philadelphia, Wilmington & Baltimore line, the Camden & Amboy, and the Philadelphia & Reading in the USA, and, with Sir John Easthope, the lines from Paris to Rouen, Paris to Strasbourg, Orléans to Cherbourg, and Lyons to Orléans. As in the American liquidations of 1841-43, Charles and Alfred travelled widely and were responsible for most of the detailed negotiation, while their ageing father remained in the background, preoccupied with his campaign for stricter state regulation and control of the British railway system and the adoption of a railway clearing-house.

When James Morrison died in 1857, Charles inherited substantial estates in Scotland and Berkshire, the town house in Upper Harley Street, and about £1 million in cash and securities. The partnership of James Morrison & Sons had already been broken up, and while Charles had continued its business on his sole responsibility as well as remaining a partner in the Fore Street warehouse until it was sold in 1864, Alfred found the life of a country gentleman more congenial and settled at Fonthill. There was no pressing reason why Charles should not have followed the example of Alfred and played the laird at Islay or the connoisseur at Basildon, or, like his brother Walter, have entered parliament. Instead, he devoted himself principally to business.

The reason for this is to be sought partly in disposition, and partly in Charles's observation, as a young man, of the way in which so many fortunes built up in commerce by men like his father had subsequently been squandered. As early as 1842 he set out his recipe for success to his father in a letter from the United States:

> The rich men in this country (I mean all those who succeed in continuing rich) make a business of their investments — have an office, keep accounts, become directors in a company whenever they invest in its stock, spend the hours of business in Wall Street and such places, know of everything which is stirring, and as far as possible do everything themselves. In this way Boston capitalists have preserved themselves through all the bad times, and are now thriving — while genteel families of Philadelphia, who invested their money in companies which they left to be managed by others, have lost everything and have disappeared by scores in obscurity and beggary. A capitalist who will submit to these conditions may invest his money in US as safely as in Europe, and at a much higher rate of interest. One who will not, will have his very eyes picked out of his head by the vultures who are always ready to pounce on everything which is left unwatched and unprotected. It depends on each one's circumstances whether it is worth his while to incur the trouble for the sake of profit. In our case I believe it is ... Our partners must feel that there is constantly in the counting house a mind as well acquainted as themselves with everything that is going on there ... in short, the rule must be that one of us shall be in the counting house every day and work there with only short and accidental exceptions ... we have seen the fate of all sleeping partners, or sleeping principals of Yankees. {Gatty (1976) 219-20}

Having once made up his mind, Charles adjusted his life accordingly, remaining a bachelor, and keeping regular office hours, when in town, until well into his eighties.

Destruction of business records in the family office in Coleman Street by enemy action has left so little evidence of Charles Morrison's half-century of one-man merchant banking that much diligent primary research will be required before a balanced assessment of his range of interests can be made. The problem is made worse by the very quiet way in which Morrison conducted himself. Noted as a shy and delicate man from his youth, he generally worked through lieutenants, seldom sitting on the boards of companies himself. His ideal of the businessman as set out in his very competent *Essay on Labour and Capital* of 1854 was almost certainly a self-portrait. The man of business, he wrote, should be:

> ... a man sparing of words — close in disposition — often intuitively seeing what is best to be done without being fluent in explaining to others his reasons for doing it — wary in his choice of men — cautious and balanced in his opinions — careful never to promise as much as he expected to perform — innovating only in a gradual, practical, and tentative manner — averse to tumult and verbal contention — willing to work in obscurity for a result only to be realised after years of patience — instinctively distrustful of everything showy and popular — and punctiliously correct in the minutest pecuniary detail. {Morrison (1854) 126}

In spite of his shyness, Morrison did sit on the boards of the Netherlands Land Enclosure Co, the Swedish Central Railway Co, and, as chairman or deputy-chairman, the Trust & Loan Co of Canada, the Hounslow & Metropolitan Railway Co, and the North British & Mercantile Insurance Co. His strategy appears to have been to continue in high class mortgage business, railways, and utilities, but to move on to new frontiers as rates of interest on European and US investments fell in the last third of the century.

One important episode in the later business career of Charles Morrison is sufficiently well understood to serve as some indication of the way he managed his investments, and that is his move into River Plate securities. In the mid-1870s, when overseas securities were very depressed, Morrison began to buy up the shares of the ailing Mercantile Bank of the River Plate, which had been set up in 1872 at the peak of the foreign investment boom to draw British capital into the old-established Buenos Aires firm of Lumb, Wanklyn & Co. By 1880 Morrison was the second largest shareholder. The following year a new company, the River Plate Trust, Loan & Agency Co, was formed to take over the assets of the Bank, and once again Morrison was prominent. Two years later the chair of the Trust company was taken by John Morris (qv), senior partner in Ashurst, Morris & Co, the solicitors who had acted for the Morrison family since 1818.

The Trust company under Morris became the centre of a network of Anglo-River Plate mortgage, investment, utility, and railway companies employing a total capital in excess of £10 million, and linked by directorships, common management services, and overlapping investment patterns. No evidence exists to indicate how far Morris was principal in this business, and how far he was an agent for Morrison, but it may be inferred that Morrison took an active interest in River Plate affairs, since he initiated the business before Morris had anything to do with it, and he continued, in the 1890s, to hold more than £500,000 paid-up ordinary and preference shares of British registered Anglo-River Plate companies.

The Times obituary of Morrison suggests that his move into River Plate securities in the depressed 1870s may have been typical of his methods. Here, Morrison was said to have exerted a beneficial contracyclical influence on the stock market by buying up securities of sound companies which had fallen disproportionately at times of general panic. Whether this was so must remain a question for future research, as too must the matter of whether management structures similar to the River Plate Trust Co existed to supervise Morrison investment elsewhere, the extent to which the corporate clientele of Ashurst, Morris, Crisp & Co reflected Morrison interests, the degree to which Morrison may have worked formally with other City men such as Alexander Henderson (qv) in syndication of new issues, and the part he may have played — as a very interested party — in the Overend Gurney crisis of 1866 and the Baring crisis of 1890.

Morrison was very retiring, partly because he suffered from chronic cystitis throughout his life. He appears, within this limit, to have taken on the minimal public duties imposed by the ownership of property in a conscientious manner, especially in Islay, where, for example, he ran a steamer service for several years at an annual loss of over £6,000 to get his tenants' stock to market. This he saw not as philanthropy, but as rational self-interest operating to protect the capital value of the estate. He was a DL for Berkshire and Argyll. A member of the Church of England, he probably remained Liberal to 1886 at least, though inclined to the policies of Sir Robert Peel. He did not share the collectivist views of his father's more radical Liberalism. He had a fine collection of paintings, including works by Turner and Rembrandt, part of which he inherited from his father.

Charles Morrison died on 25 May 1909, leaving an estate worth well over £10 million (£10,939,298 gross).

CHARLES A JONES

Writings:

Letters on America *Morning Chronicle* 1842.

An Essay on the Relations between Labour and Capital (Longmans, 1854).

Sources:

Unpublished

Berkshire RO, D/EMo, manorial documents of the Basildon Park and other estates of the Morrison family, 1775-1938.

Guildhall Library, London, records of Morrison, Cryder & Co.

Islay Estate Office, records of the Islay Estate.

PrC.

Published

John Bateman, *The Acre-Ocracy of England* (B M Pickering, 1876).

DD 1885, 1900.

Richard Gatty, *Portrait of a Merchant Prince: James Morrison 1789-1857* (Northallerton: pp, 1977).

Charles Jones, 'Great Capitalists and the Direction of British Overseas Investment in the Late Nineteenth Century: The Case of Argentina' *Business History* 22 (July 1980).

William D Rubinstein, 'The Victorian Middle Classes: Wealth, Occupation, and Geography' *Economic History Review* 2nd ser, 30 (Nov 1977).

Times 11 Feb 1858, 27 May, 5 June 1909.

WWMP.

MORSON, Sir Thomas

(1825-1908)

Pharmaceutical manufacturer

Sir Thomas Morson, from The Chemist and Druggist *29 Jan 1916 (courtesy of the Pharmaceutical Society).*

Thomas Morson was born in London in 1825, the son of Thomas Newborn Robert Morson (1800-74), a pharmaceuticals entrepreneur. Thomas attended University College School and then, following in his father's footsteps, went to Paris where he studied with some of the leading French pharmacists of the day. He returned to join his father's growing business and in 1857 married Mme Dagomet, daughter of a Boulogne pharmacist. They first lived above the pharmacy in Southampton Row, London, and later in Queen Square, nearby. Their two sons, Thomas Pierre and Albert Robert, both followed in the business.

TNR Morson had established his pharmacy in 1821 and maintained a prominent position in the British chemical and pharmaceutical world, becoming a founder member of both the Pharmaceutical Society and the Chemical Society. After having studied alkaloid chemistry in Paris, he gained a quick lead with quinine imports and marketing upon his return to London. Expanding from six products in 1821 to over 50 by 1825, he could offer a variety of fine chemicals, dyes, perfumes, and drugs. He operated as an importer and wholesaler in addition to running the retail business, thriving particularly on the quinine trade and other alkaloids, including morphia. These medicines were regarded as among the most effective of their time, quinine being used to reduce fevers while morphia and other alkaloids were used to dull pain. Although TNR Morson built the firm, it was Thomas who made the company a significant force in the slowly expanding British pharmaceutical industry.

Thomas had been centrally involved in the business of the firm for two decades before his father's death in 1874, especially as his father devoted considerable efforts to his gentlemanly scientific pursuits. Thomas effected a change in the orientation of the firm from gentlemanly to commercial science by hiring Robert Taubman, a skilled chemist who, from 1891 until his death in 1905, served as a partner. In this way Thomas Morson distinguished the company from their rivals in emphasising the place of the laboratory in the firm. Though the laboratory was mainly concerned with routine testing, Taubman and Morson brought it beyond that in a number of cases. One most interesting connection the firm maintained was with the pioneering surgeon, Joseph Lister (1827-1912). Taubman was consulted in 1889 by Lister about the possibility of using zinc cyanide and double salt as antiseptics, and about the production of sterile catgut as a suture material. This led to the marketing of 'Lister's cyanide', one of a handful of products the firm developed as a result of consultations with leading medical scientists of the time. There was also some considerable correspondence relating to the use of Perkin's (qv) mauvine as an antiseptic, which brought the firm into contact with synthetic dye makers, but led to no new products. Although there was considerable chemical skill on hand, the further step of organising the laboratory for product development never took place.

The laboratory was near the retail pharmacy on Southampton Row, the offices of the firm in Queen Square, and also a number of the most important medical institutions and hospitals. The Southampton Row pharmacy was closed in 1900, and by 1904 new offices and warehouses were established at 14 Elm Street, Gray's Inn Road. The manufacturing was concentrated at that time on several acres at Summerfield Works, Ponder's End, Middlesex, where the firm continued to grow through the inter-war period. It became a private limited company in 1915, and was later acquired by Merck, Sharp & Dohme.

Morson is said to have taken no part in public or philanthropic work, but cultivated artistic friends and accumulated a respectable collection of contemporary paintings. In addition to the local and national pharmaceutical societies, Morson maintained membership in the Chemical Society, the Geological Society, and the Zoological Society, preserving in that way his father's sort of gentlemanly pursuits. He died on 5 February 1908, leaving £4,947 gross in his will, and a thriving business.

JONATHAN LIEBENAU

Sources:

Unpublished

Royal College of Surgeons, Clifford Morson deposit, Joseph Lister papers.

Morson business and family papers, held by A F Morson, Hadley Wood, Hertfordshire.

Correspondence with A F Morson, 1981.

PrC.

Published

Boase.

Chemist and Druggist 14 May 1870, 8 Feb, 28 Mar 1908, 29 June 1916.

A C Morson and B C Morson, 'Memories of Lord Lister' *Proceedings of the Royal Society of Medicine* 64 (1971).

Pharmaceutical Journal 7 Mar 1874, 8, 15 Feb 1908, 18 Apr 1981.

Red Book of Commerce 1936.

MORTIMER, William Egerton

(1878-1940)

City solicitor

William Egerton Mortimer was born on 9 August 1878, the son of Rev Christian Mortimer, Canon Resident of Lichfield Cathedral, and his wife Lucy Sarah Hannah née Scholfield. He was educated at Shrewsbury School and Christ Church College, Oxford where he held the Careswell and Boulter Exhibitions.

He was admitted a solicitor in October 1904 and for the next eight years practised alone from 21 Cannon Street. On 1 January 1912 he joined, as a partner, the firm of Slaughter & May. It was a young and growing firm, founded some years earlier by William Slaughter (qv) and William May who had left the well-known solicitors Ashurst Morris Crisp & Co, to establish themselves separately.

The firm flourished in the 1920s and 1930s for, despite and sometimes because of the economic depression, there was a growing volume of commercial work for city solicitors. Rothschilds was a client of Slaughter & May and Mortimer became well-known there for his forthright manner. In 1932 he became senior partner and in the eight years he held that position Slaughter & May grew to become one of the largest and most active legal firms in the City. The number of partners increased from four to ten by the outbreak of the Second World War.

Mortimer became a member of the Council of the Law Society in 1924; his services to his profession included sitting on the Company Law Amendment Committee and the Law Revision Committee.

He married in 1938 at Holy Trinity, Brompton, Cicely Eleanor, daughter of the late Prebendary William Melville Pigot of Ipswich and widow of Major-General Neville-White. The marriage was, however, short-lived for Mortimer died on 3 December 1940 at the age of sixty-two, leaving £87,372 gross.

JUDY SLINN

Sources

Unpublished

BCe.

PrC.

Information from Slaughter & May and the Law Society Records Department.

Published

The Law Lists.

R Palin, *Rothschild Relish* (Cassell, 1970).

Times 8 Aug 1938, 10 Dec 1940.

WWW.

*Sir James Morton (courtesy of
Morton Sundour Fabrics Ltd).*

MORTON, Sir James

(1867-1943)

Textile manufacturer

James Morton was born in Darvel, Ayrshire, on 24 March 1867, the third of the nine children of Alexander Morton and his wife, Jean née Wiseman. His parents, like most adults in his own and the neighbouring villages, were handloom weavers of 'madras' muslin, the work being farmed out to them by Glasgow merchants. By the time James was born, his father had organised the selling of the local product direct to retailers throughout the UK, and the partnership Alexander Morton & Co (Alexander, a brother and a cousin) had 400 weavers executing their orders. The firm was soon to start the production (first by hand, then by machine) of the heavier types of decorative fabrics and the large-scale manufacture of curtain lace on the Nottingham lace machine.

James went to his village school and Ayr Academy, leaving the latter at the age of sixteen, to be a technical apprentice in the firm. He was soon engaged in the styling of the firm's various ranges (by now also including machine-woven carpets) in which he was deeply influenced by the Arts and Crafts movement started by William Morris (qv) and others. Styling and selling, both at home, on the Continent and in the USA, occupied his energies until 1902. At the end of this period he and his elder brother, Guy, set up a large factory in Carlisle.

In 1902 he was shocked to see one of his firm's fabrics, carefully coloured by himself, badly faded after a week's exposure in the windows of Liberty's of London, and decided there and then what radical improvement in performance was called for. Three years of intensive study of the selection and application of suitable dye-stuffs, in collaboration with John Christie of the United Turkey Red Co (near Glasgow), made it possible to issue, in 1905, the first fabrics ever to be sold with a guarantee that 'any goods fading or failing to stand ordinary laundry wash will be replaced'. Extensive advertising under the brand name 'Sundour' adopted in 1906 ('dour' being an old Gaelic word for water and also meaning stubborn or hard to move) met a ready response.

In spite of the considerably higher prices necessitated by the dyestuffs and processes involved in their production, within four years the Sundour ranges were producing half Alexander Morton & Co's total profits of £16,500, and within seven years three times the profits of all the firm's other activities together, £21,250 and £7,000 respectively. At this point, 1913, it was decided to split the firm into two separate companies, Alexander Morton & Co concentrating on lace at Darvel and a new company, Morton Sundour Fabrics Ltd, producing and merchanting the other fabrics at Carlisle, with James Morton its governing director and holder of nearly all the equity, but with Alexander Morton himself remaining chairman of both.

The complex dyestuffs needed for Sundour fabrics were made almost exclusively in Germany. The outbreak of war in 1914 could, therefore, have proved a disastrous blow. However, up to five months' stock of the most essential dyestuffs gave a little breathing space. Before the stocks were exhausted, under Morton's leadership and helped by co-operative engineers able to devise the bare minimum of high-performance chemical plant required, the firm's chemical technicians were producing adequate supplies for the firm's own requirements. By 1918 the firm produced a range of dyestuffs available for other United Kingdom users, justifying the formation of a special branch, Solway Dyes Ltd, which also licensed the processes involved to dyestuff makers in the USA.

The demand for supplies from outside users and the prospects of successful further research led to the development of a new site at Grangemouth, near Edinburgh. Scottish Dyes Ltd was set up in 1919 as a separate company with a capital of £300,000, half of the new money coming from outside. The research led, among other things, to the discovery of Caledon Jade Green, the fastest dyestuff so far produced, for which the post-war German dyestuff makers found themselves driven to seek a licence. But as dyestuff making was extraneous to his main interest, James Morton sold Scottish Dyes Ltd in 1923 to the British Dyestuffs Corporation, which was shortly to be absorbed in Imperial Chemical Industries. He served on the Dyestuff Division Board of ICI until his death. Meanwhile, Morton had become the first recipient of the gold medal struck to celebrate the Faraday Benzene Centenary, and was eventually, in 1936, knighted for service to the dye and colour industries.

In addition to the major diversion of his energies to dyestuff-making, he also found time during the First World War to serve very actively on the Ministry of Reconstruction's Committee on Adult Education, and helped in the formation of the Design and Industries Association. In 1931 he served on the Government's Committee on New Industrial Development.

Having shed personal responsibility for Scottish Dyes Ltd, Morton turned to the active development of ideas, long maturing in his mind, for machinery which could, in his view, largely replace the age-old methods of using loom and shuttle to construct most textiles, combining a radical improvement in warp-knitting technique with a completely novel method of inserting continuous wefts. Prototype machines were operating by 1935, which he showed to Samuel Courtauld (qv), chairman of Courtaulds Ltd and himself a very knowledgeable and imaginative textile expert.

A joint company, FNF Ltd (the initials of 'fly-needle frame', Morton's description of the new machines), was formed to exploit the technique.

Courtaulds were allotted 60 per cent of the equity in return for supplying the necessary working capital and also paid £250,000 for a quarter of the equity in Morton Sundour Fabrics Ltd; Morton Sundour took the remaining 40 per cent of the equity of the new company. FNF Ltd failed to fulfill James Morton's and Samuel Courtauld's high hopes during Morton's life-time, but a year after his death in 1943, FNF Ltd was able to give a full-scale demonstration to the trade of a machine (using only the improved warp-knitting element) running between three and four times the speed of the conventional warp-knitting machine, and FNF machines were immediately put into commercial production for world-wide sale.

The chance of such a deal with Courtaulds, which also included the issue to them of a special class of preference shares and the placing of a nominee of Courtaulds on the Morton Sundour board, had been welcomed by James Morton because, after a highly successful period of trading in Sundour and other decorative textiles in the 1920s, profits since the 1929-30 slump had recovered only slowly. His own difficulties had been aggravated, partly by the diversion of his energies into the dyestuff enterprise and the development of the new machinery, still more by the untimely loss of his chief commercial executive, who had been enticed to join one of the firm's biggest customers, itself even more heavily hit by the slump. Morton only started to receive substantial help, to compensate for this loss, during the late 1930s when he was joined by his elder son Alastair (eventually to become a Royal Designer for Industry) and his son-in-law Lieutenant Commander R S E Hannay RN in the styling and factory sides of the business respectively. Both made great contributions to the firm in the post-war years.

Morton married in 1901 Beatrice Fagan, a teacher trained by Charlotte Mason, imbued with the same artistic ideals as himself. They had six children. Sir James Morton died on 22 August 1943.

JOCELYN W F MORTON

Writings:

History of Lace (Lecture at Glasgow Weaving College, 1900).

William Morris: An Appreciation paper read to the XL Club (pp, by Chiswick Press, 1901).

Notes on Industry and Education (paper written and printed for circulation to members of Ministry of Reconstruction's Committee on Adult Education, 1917).

The Dyes Question: An Open Letter to My Friends the Free Trade Members of Parliament (pp, 1921 or 1922).

To Young Weavers speech at annual distribution of prizes at the Textile Institute (S Phillips & Co, 1927).

Fast Dyeing and Dyes lecture at Royal Society of Arts (Edinburgh: T & A Constable, 1929).

Dyes and Textiles in Britain lecture to British Association (Edinburgh: T & A Constable, 1930).

Miscellaneous speeches, articles, letters printed in the local or national press included in the Morton of Darvel Muniments at the Scottish RO, Edinburgh.

Sources:

Unpublished

Science Museum, London, business and other records and files (including all matters dealing with patents); experimental trials; correspondence etc, dealing specifically with chemical and technical mechanical matters.

Scottish RO, Edinburgh, Morton of Darvel Muniments, correspondence, business records and memoranda, photographs.

Victoria and Albert Museum, London, examples of Morton textile products of most periods, paper designs for textiles, correspondence with or about specific designers and artists.

Published

Jocelyn Morton, *Three Generations in a Family Textile Firm* (Routledge & Kegan Paul, 1971).

WWW.

MOSS, Harry Neville

(1895-1982)

Draper

Harry Moss was born in Kensington, London, on 25 October 1895, the younger son of George Frederick Moss (1855–1910), a master tailor, and his wife Lucie Phoebe Amy née Campbell. His grandfather Moses Moss was a bespoke tailor and itinerant second hand clothes dealer who on occasion travelled as far as Scotland to obtain good quality stock. Moses first took premises in Covent Garden not far from the present (1984) shop in 1860. There were five sons but only two, George, the eldest (Harry's father) and Alfred (1862-1937), enjoyed their father's confidence; these two were set up in business in a shop on the present Covent Garden site in 1881. George, a practical tailor and cutter built a fine quality ready-to-wear suit business but Alfred was in overall charge of the shop and business, buying best quality misfit clothing from dealers and tailor's shops.

Three years after his father's death, Harry, aged thirteen, left school and following his elder brother (who was killed in the First World War), went to help his uncle in the family business at a starting wage of 10s a week. Here he tidied up cloth in the cutting room and was put to work in different departments to learn the business. In the war he was commissioned and served at Salonika.

Meanwhile, in 1914, the business was converted into a private limited company with a capital of £10,000 under the direction of Alfred Moss, who held the great majority of the shares. By this time it had become established as a military outfitters, and a showroom, and later a shop, were opened at Camberley, selling military uniforms to the Sandhurst cadets, which proved a great success. During the war the firm's ability to produce high quality ready-to-wear uniforms at short notice stood them in good stead, and from this service grew a large clientele that came back after the war to buy civilian wear.

Meantime Harry, back in the business, had won the confidence of his uncle Alfred (who had married late in life and had a very young family) and in 1921 was made a company director. The second-hand and misfit establishment slowly became the menswear store and saddlery, shoes, hats and hosiery departments were added. At this time the hiring of clothes by Moss Bros & Co developed considerably, for the cost of buying suits and morning clothes after the war was very high. This also prompted demand for the hire of velvet court suits, diplomatic uniforms and full dress uniforms for the Army, Navy and Air Force. Moss Bros' service was never advertised but became known by word of mouth. By 1934 the business employed about 100 people, and turnover was £224,000 a year. That year Harry took over as managing director, and after his uncle died in 1937 he ran the business almost single-handed until the early 1950s; thereafter younger members of the family joined him.

With the outbreak of the Second World War the sale of civilian clothes and the morning and evening hire business almost ceased. However, in 1938-39 Moss Bros & Co managed to assemble a considerable stock of uniforms and uniform cloth which, with their civilian stock, was moved from Covent Garden to a disused bus station at Dorking in rural Surrey. Harry Moss also decided to 'go provincial', opening branches in Manchester and in Bristol, as well as many other small depots where there were concentrations of troops.

As soon as the war ended, Moss initiated an intensive publicity and advertising campaign, representing a new approach for the company, whose business had previously been gained through word of mouth. Ironically, later advertisements emphasised that Moss Bros actually sold clothes as well as hiring them. He was also advocating a policy of greater expansion, producing more ready-to-wear civilian clothing and later diversifying into women's wear (hiring out wedding and evening gowns) and sports equipment.

In 1947 the business was converted into a public company, with an authorised capital of £190,000. A quarter of the ordinary shares of 4s nominal value were offered for sale at 41s 3d. Profits before tax in 1946 were £108,000. In 1958 the company's name was changed to Moss Bros.

The company continued to expand and diversify under Harry Moss's leadership and drive and in the 1970s its 'One Up' shop for the 'young of heart' was a great success. By 1971 it had 32 branches (two of them in Paris), and it had two large workshops. Total staff numbered 1,350 and annual turnover was £3.5 million. Harry Moss, no longer managing director, though still chairman, continued to visit one branch a week, holding weekly dress parades in London to check out new designs and stylings. The issued capital in this year was £350,000 ordinary stock, with over 56 per cent owned or controlled by directors and their families and family trusts. Despite its considerable growth, the business still, in fact, remained very much a family one, with promotion generally coming from within the firm, and today (1984) there are still six Mosses in the business.

Outside his work Harry Moss enjoyed sport — cricket and golf — and he encouraged his firm in sponsoring and contributing to sports events such as show jumping, skiing and golf. He also had a keen interest in young people and in the underprivileged. He served the Park House Approved School at Peper Harrow as honorary treasurer for some twenty years. He was governor, and treasurer from 1957, of the Lucas Tooth Gymnasium Trust, president of the Master Tailors' Benevolent Association and joint president of the Boys Club Movement.

He married Sophia Ida Woolf in 1920, at the Jewish Synagogue in Marylebone, West London. Their son, Monty Moss, became chairman of the company. Harry Moss died on 11 May 1982, leaving £190,477 gross.

ALEXANDRA KIDNER *and* FRANCIS GOODALL

Sources:

Unpublished

BCe.

MCe.

PrC.

Information from Mr M Moss.

Published

Times 17 May 1982.

Warren Tute, *The Grey Top Hat: The Story of Moss Bros of Covent Garden* (Cassell, 1961).

MOTT, Sir Basil

(1859-1938)

Consulting civil engineer

Sir Basil Mott (courtesy of Mr T M Megaw).

Basil Mott was born at Leicester on 16 September 1859, the youngest of three sons of Frederick Thompson Mott, a wine merchant, of Birstall Hall, near Leicester, and his first wife, Elizabeth Ann née Dobell. He was educated at Leicester Grammar School, International College, Isleworth, and at Solothurn, Switzerland. For two years he was a pupil of a mining engineer called Harrison of Whitwick, Leicester. In 1876-79 he studied at the Royal School of Mines in South Kensington, being awarded the Murchison medal for his final year. He then entered into engineering pupilage, from 1880 to 1882, with J H Wood, a Sheffield mining engineer, and subsequently worked for several collieries, including three years at the Neston Colliery in Cheshire.

In 1886 his uncle, Charles Grey Mott, a director of the Great Western Railway, became chairman of the City & South London Railway from Monument to Stockwell, having been instrumental in finding finance for its construction. The consulting engineer J H Greathead (qv), a notable pioneer of the tunnelling shield, engaged Basil Mott and promoted him to resident engineer in 1887 at the age of twenty-eight. The railway was the prototype of London's deep level 'tubes', and was the proving ground for many new ideas and techniques, in the development of which Mott took an important part. Unlike earlier 'cut and cover' underground lines of the 1860s and 1870s, the City of London & Southwark Subway, originally so named, was designed to be built as a bored tunnel, using the techniques of the Tower Subway of 1869. The ground was given immediate support during excavation by a Greathead shield, and permanently lined with circular cast iron rings, through which grout was injected. A major benefit during construction was that, while following public rights of way beneath streets, there was little disturbance at the surface, except at stations and at shafts.

Most of the route was planned through London clay, an excellent material for shield tunnelling, but at one spot in Swan Lane, near the start in the City, the top of one tunnel emerged from the clay into waterbearing gravel. To overcome the inflow of water the novel technique of tunnelling in compressed air in conjunction with the shield was adopted. Waterbearing gravel was similarly encountered for a considerable length near the end of the line at Stockwell. Operation of the railway by cable traction was originally proposed, but C G Mott was not satisfied with the principle and, at a late stage, electric locomotive traction was adopted as feasible, its first use in Britain, though electric traction with combined motor and passenger cars had been used in Brighton in 1883. The necessary design modifications, including provision of a power station, were effected. So impressive was Basil Mott's part in the construction and

EX LIBRIS
SIR BASIL MOTT
BART·C·B

commissioning up to the Royal opening in 1890 that he was asked to take charge, as engineer, of the initial years of operation.

The success of this tube railway pointed the way to many competing promoters, some thirty different schemes being proposed, and mostly rejected, but the next to concern Mott was the Central London Railway from the Bank to Shepherds Bush, which was opened in 1900 as 'The Tuppenny Tube'. Sir Benjamin Baker (qv), was consulting engineer for the project and on the death of J H Greathead, his partner and Mott's friend and mentor, took Mott into partnership for the construction in 1896.

In 1902 Mott formed a partnership with David Hay (d 1938), who also had worked on the City & South London Railway, for the contractor and later for Baker, and had been resident engineer at the Blackwall Tunnel. This partnership acted as consulting engineers to both tube railways after the death of Sir Benjamin Baker in 1907. They continued in partnership throughout their lives, the firm becoming Mott, Hay & Anderson in 1920, when David Anderson was taken into partnership. The firm is still (1984) in existence, having expanded into a world-wide consultancy with an interlocking structure of companies.

A connection with the City of London was established in 1906 when Baker was appointed engineer for the widening of Blackfriars Bridge but, owing to ill-health, handed over his work to his partner, Mott. More bridge work followed, including reports on rebuilding Kingston upon Thames Bridge, and on Southwark Bridge. The Central London Railway was extended to Liverpool Street where escalators were installed in 1912, following a report by Mott on a visit to the USA in 1910.

During the First World War Mott served on various government committees, advising on defence schemes, and visiting France and India to

Mersey Tunnel at the time of its opening in 1934 (courtesy of Mr T M Megaw).

report and give advice. He was appointed CB for his services. Over the next twenty years Mott and his partners were the engineers for many important structures throughout the country. There were extensions and improvements to the London tube railways, including a remarkable enlargement of the City & South London Railway. Among varied bridge works were Southwark Bridge reconstruction, Queensferry Bridge (Chester), Tyne Bridge (Newcastle), Tees (Newport) vertical lift bridge at Middlesbrough, approached by the first all-welded bridge over the London & North Eastern Railway, and reports on bridges over the Forth, Tay, and Severn, and at Charing Cross. Mott also gave advice on the Channel Tunnel in 1930, was a member of the Severn Barrage committee and took part in the planning of the Dartford Tunnel. Of particular importance and personal interest was Mott's work on the structural strengthening of St Paul's Cathedral, and in the driving of the Mersey Queensway Road Tunnel.

Signs of deterioration in the structure of St Paul's Cathedral had given cause for concern from 1907, and in 1921 Mott was consulted. He advised the setting-up of a commission of architects and engineers, which in 1925 formed a works committee with Mott as chairman to execute effective remedial measures. They found no evidence of any failure in the foundations. The main piers, of dressed Portland Stone with a rubble core set in lime mortar, had cracked, due to differential strains; they were strengthened by controlled injection of cement grout and insertion of reinforcing steel through holes drilled in from the face. The structure carrying the dome showed signs of spreading, probably due to movement caused by seasonal changes of temperature. Stainless steel bars forming an enclosing chain below the outer dome, and a lattice structure of bars grouted into the brick drums carrying the dome and lantern, effected the necessary restraint. The Cathedral, on which a 'dangerous structure notice' had been served, was made structurally secure by 1930.

The Mersey road tunnel between Liverpool and Birkenhead was the subject of a report in 1923 by Mott, together with Sir Maurice Fitzmaurice and John A Brodie, which recommended the construction of a tunnel in preference to a bridge. The report was accepted, and the tunnel, then the largest subaqueous tunnel in the world, carrying a four-lane highway between the two city centres, was built under Mott's direction and was opened in 1934 by King George V. Mott continued as a senior partner of Mott, Hay & Anderson until his death in 1938, the firm's practice being principally in major tunnel and bridge projects within the UK.

A member of the Institution of Civil Engineers since 1895, Basil Mott became a vice-president in 1920 and president in 1924. His presidential address emphasised his lifetime interest in the improvement of passenger transport in London, including cross-river communication. He reviewed the growth of public transport from the introduction of the cab in 1820, described some of the problems of tube construction, and discussed the road bridges across the Thames. He commented on the lack of new bridges and on the unsatisfactory piecemeal planning of the tube railway system, resulting from excessively narrowly-based competition for the most profitable lengths and routes.

Basil Mott was made a baronet, of Ditchling in Sussex, in 1930, in recognition of his many services to engineering. He was elected an FRS in 1932, and a fellow of Imperial College in 1933. He was also an associate of the Royal School of Mines, and a member of the Société des Ingénieurs Civils de France.

In 1887 Mott married Florence Harmer Parker, daughter of William Parker, by whom he had two sons.

Sir Basil Mott died on 7 September 1938, leaving £43,959 gross.

T M MEGAW

Writings:

(with D Hay) 'Underground Railways in Great Britain' *Transactions of the American Society of Civil Engineers* 1905.

Presidential address *Proceedings of the Institution of Civil Engineers* 219 (1924-25).

Sources:

Unpublished

BCe.

PrC.

Published

DNB (entry written by Mott's partner, David Anderson).

J E Drower, 'St Paul's' *Transactions of the Chartered Surveyors Institution* 63 (1930-31).

Journal of the Institution of Civil Engineers 10 (Nov 1938).

Obituary Notices of Fellows of the Royal Society of London 3 (1939–41).

C S Peach and W G Allen, 'The Preservation of St Paul's Cathedral' *Journal of the Royal Institute of British Architects* 37 (1930).

WWW.

Stephen Moulton (courtesy of the late Mr Ken Ponting).

MOULTON, Stephen

(1794-1880)

Rubber manufacturer

Stephen Moulton was born at Whorlton, County Durham, on 7 July 1794, the youngest of three sons of Stephen Moulton, a law stationer who resided in the parish of St Dunstan in the West, West London, and his wife Catherine née Bellamy. Little else is known of his early life. He married Elizabeth Hales (d 1888) at St George's Church, Hanover Square, London in 1826 and later emigrated to New York where he was first recorded as a broker in 1839.

In the USA Moulton encountered Charles Goodyear (1800-60), who was searching for a method of preventing indiarubber from melting, sticking and decomposing in heat. In the midst of a long series of experiments with sulphur (which commenced in 1838 and eventually led to Goodyear's American patent for vulcanisation in 1844), the impoverished Goodyear sent Stephen Moulton to England with samples of his improved rubber. Moulton, who had instructions to sell the invention for £50,000, visited England in 1842 and 1843, leaving his samples with Messrs Macintosh & Co. They contacted Thomas Hancock (1786-1865), who had also been experimenting with rubber and in 1844 Hancock, a prolific inventor,

359

patented in England his own version of vulcanisation. In the litigation that followed, Hancock's patent was upheld by the English courts.

Moulton visited England again in 1847. He took out a British patent for a new vulcanisation process, using hydrosulphide of lead instead of free sulphur, and with the financial backing of William, Emery and John Rider (three American rubber manufacturers of New York) he set up a plant to manufacture rubber under his patent. The machinery, originally imported from the USA, was installed in Kingston Mill, Bradford-on-Avon, where Moulton also found a family home, The Hall, and a further £5,000 of investment from Captain Septimus Palairet of Woolley Grange. Manufacturing began in October 1848 when 21 males and two females were employed. At least one key workman, a Mr Frost, was recruited from America (from the Vulcan Iron Works, New York) in 1848; he stayed for six years in a supervisory capacity. Ownership, shared between Moulton and the Rider brothers from 1850 to 1853, then passed to Stephen Moulton and his son Alexander, who together managed the concern. Their progress was impeded by Hancock and Macintosh & Co, who in 1852 successfully sued Moulton for infringing Hancock's vulcanisation patent. Until the Hancock patent expired after 1858 the Moultons were forced to manufacture under licence.

In the early years Moulton produced a range of products, from clothing and sheeting to air cushions and water beds. Moulton rubber, superior in quality to that of its half-dozen competitors and sold at a price 10 per cent lower, acquired a growing reputation. George Spencer (qv), holder of a number of important patents for rubber components in railway buffers, springs and bearings, began to use it in 1858, being dissatisfied with the quality of the rubber supplied by Charles Macintosh & Co of Manchester, the industry's leading firm. Moultons quickly became Spencer's major supplier, making 80 per cent of Spencer's requirements by 1866; this then represented 35 per cent of Moulton's total sales. Moulton's output of rubber for mechanical purposes rose between 1858 and 1880 from 57 per cent to 98 per cent of total sales, which nearly tripled up to £48,392 a year. Stephen Moulton and George Spencer were on good terms and discussed a joint partnership in 1879. After Stephen Moulton's death the two firms eventually amalgamated in 1891, largely because Spencers moved into a monopolist position, which in turn was made possible by the relative managerial inertia of Stephen Moulton's successors, his sons Alexander and Horatio.

As well as Alexander and Horatio, Henry and George, two others of Stephen Moulton's seven sons (he also had two daughters), assisted their father in the business. Henry directed the London office until he returned to the USA in 1851. On his departure, this responsibility passed to George, who in 1861 became a broker on his own behalf in Mincing Lane. Alexander and Horatio assisted their father in Bradford. Alexander was manager of the Kingston Mill from 1861 until his death in 1885, then management passed to Horatio, who outlived him by eight years. Thenceforth John, the youngest son, remained chairman of Spencer-Moulton until his death in 1925.

Outside his business Stephen Moulton devoted much of his time and money to restoring The Hall into the wonderful house and garden it had been in the seventeenth century.

At his death on 26 April 1880 Stephen Moulton left an estate proved at £90,000 gross.

K G PONTING

Sources:

Unpublished

PrC.

Information from Dr Alex Moulton and his private papers.

Published

A Moulton, 'Innovation' *Journal of the Royal Society for the Encouragement of Arts and Manufactures* 1980.

Spencer Moulton, *1848-1948. A Hundred Years of Rubber Manufacture* (1948).

Peter L Payne, *Railways and Rubber in the Nineteenth Century. A Study of the Spencer Papers* (Liverpool: Liverpool University Press, 1961).

W Woodruff, *The Rise of the British Rubber Industry During the Nineteenth Century* (Liverpool: Liverpool University Press, 1958).

—, 'India Rubber' *VCH Wiltshire* 4.

MOUNTAIN, Sir Edward Mortimer

(1872-1948)

Insurance underwriter

Sir Edward Mountain (courtesy of Eagle Star Group).

Edward Mortimer Mountain was born on 24 November 1872, the second son of Henry Stanford Mountain, a prosperous Southwark hop merchant who lived in Dulwich, and his wife Louisa, daughter of Henry Eve. His father died at a relatively early age in 1890, leaving a modest fortune of £18,653. Mountain, after education at Dulwich College, began his career in a Lloyd's insurance broker's office. Around the turn of the century, he joined with others, including his elder brother, Henry Stanford Mountain Jr, to found Hawley, Mountain & Co, to undertake insurance broking.

In 1902 this firm merged with Robert Gardner & Co, managed by Frederick Hall (later Sir Frederick, MP for Dulwich, 1910-32), to form

Robert Gardner Mountain & Co. Apparently the Mountains invested in steamship companies in order to influence the placing of insurance and specialised particularly in Norwegian hull business. Mountain did not become an underwriting member of Lloyd's, disliking the principle of unlimited liability. When he began to underwrite a small office account the Committee of Lloyd's asked him to decide between underwriting and broking. In consequence, in 1904 Gardner Mountain took over the marine account of the recently-formed British Dominions to float the British Dominions Marine Insurance Co, with some £100,000 paid up capital. Edward Mountain became its managing underwriter. The corporate form provided him with limited liability and allowed some policy holders to take an interest in the results of the underwriting of their vessels. The company had a substantial connection from the start, writing a net premium income of £127,132 in its first fifteen months of operation. In the following decade it expanded steadily, to underwrite £324,091 by 1913.

As a result, Mountain became an increasingly important figure in the marine insurance market. He played a central role in efforts made in the Edwardian period to stabilise competition, becoming the first chairman in 1910 of the Joint Hull Committee, which brought together Lloyd's and company underwriters. Between 1908 and 1914 negotiations led to the standardisation of the previously disparate policy terms offered by different underwriters. The principal underwriters also began to exercise influence over premium rate movements in the face of trade recession and the major accessions of capacity as British and American general insurance companies entered the market as part of the diversification characteristic of the period.

Mountain played a leading role in these discussions for many years, despite his important commitments elsewhere. When he eventually retired from the chair of the Joint Hull Committee in 1920, the *Times* commented that the ' ... market is very much alive to the value of the services rendered to the underwriting community for many years by Sir Edward ...' {*Times* 9 Dec 1920}. Lloyds paid him the special honour of electing him their first company underwriting member. His reputation was enhanced by the knowledge that his intuition had made him the one prominent underwriter who had declined to accept the *Titanic*.

Throughout these years, however, the main thrust of Mountain's energies was directed towards the expansion of British Dominions. In 1911 a fire insurance department was opened and the company's name changed to the British Dominions General Insurance Co. At first business grew slowly and the company was best known to the general public for encouraging motor insurance. However, in 1914 Mountain purchased the North-Western Insurance Co, a small non-tariff fire office that had run into difficulties in American insurance, but which had a good core of domestic business, a modest branch organisation, and an excellent manager, S A Bennett. This provided a foundation for subsequent development in general insurance.

Dramatic purchases to secure good connections or talented management were to be Mountain's hallmark in the following years. The war had a profound effect on marine insurance, inflating revenues and profits. By 1913 British Dominions's marine premium income placed it among the larger British marine insurance companies. This position was consolidated

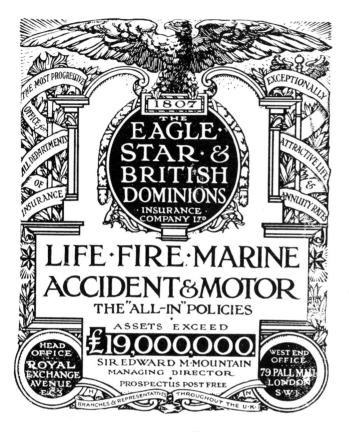

All Classes of Insurance Business Transacted

Annuities—Boiler—Burglary—Contingency—Disease and Sickness—Engine Insurance — Employers' Liability — Electrical and other Machinery—Fidelity Guarantee—Fire—Gas Plants —Indemnity—Leasehold Redemption —Life — Lifts — Live Stock—Loss of Profits—Licence—Marine—Marriage—Motor Car—Personal Accident—Plate Glass—Public Liability—Securities in Transit—Sprinkler Leakage—Tractor.

"All-In" Policy for Householders, House Owners. Special Insurances for Women. Special Insurances for Farmers. Provision for Children. "Pluvius" Weather Policies.

The policy, 23 July 1921 (courtesy of Eagle Star Group).

by Mountain's willingness to write marine war risks from the outbreak of hostilities, when the rest of the market held back. Marine market buoyancy had a disproportionate effect on the company's profitability, especially as this was not discounted by a heavy involvement in other markets that were less favourably affected by the war. By 1917 the company wrote a marine premium income of £1,909,792, some six times the substantial pre-war figure. This made the possibility of a share in its equity highly attractive to other companies, notably specialist life offices that had been hit by investment depreciation and the initial wartime slump in sales of new policies.

As a result, when the marine market reached its peak Mountain was able, in a notable coup, to take over three life companies within ten months. In December 1916 he purchased the Eagle, in May 1917 the Sceptre and in September 1917, the Star. All were long-established concerns with solid connections, able staff, and a substantial business, albeit temporarily inhibited by the war. These moves placed the combined company, renamed the Eagle Star & British Dominions Insurance Co, among the dozen largest British life offices in 1918. By 1917 Mountain had become chairman and managing director of the enlarged company.

While other, more modest concerns were subsequently purchased, expansion was not only produced in this way. Mountain's well-chosen staff produced a steady flow of innovatory schemes. These were often as noted for their general publicity value as for their direct impact on underwriting. The company quickly established itself in the public eye by extensive advertising and press comment. A J Shepherd, Mountain's publicity manager, revolutionised insurance marketing with brilliant visual work aimed directly at the public, calling its attention to the hazards against which insurance could protect them.

At the beginning of 1916, in an important technical advance, the British Dominions offered the first policy covering all the usual householder's requirements in one contract for one inclusive premium. This 'All-In' policy enabled the Eagle Star to make considerable inroads into the profitable non-hazardous insurance market. When the Government launched a drive to raise funds for a War Loan in 1917, the Eagle Star devised a scheme whereby purchases could be financed by an endowment assurance policy over five, ten or fifteen years. Although other companies offered similar arrangements, Eagle Star obtained the lion's share of publicity and the response was described by Mountain as 'fantastic' {*Times* 24 May 1918}. The company purchased £5 million of War Loan stock entirely financed by this means, which gave its new combined life business an excellent start. In 1920 Mountain purchased the 'Pluvius' weather underwriting business from C E Heath (qv) and ensured that this continued to obtain maximum publicity for the company. At about the same time, a department was established entirely staffed by women to deal with the special insurance problems faced by their sex. In this and many other ways, the Eagle Star developed a reputation which prompted the *Times* to comment, '... probably no composite insurance office has adopted more enterprising methods' {*ibid* 23 May 1917}. Between 1913 and 1919 the company's fire and general premium income rose from £40,416 to £1,214,688. In 1919 its £3 paid up shares peaked at £20 and they never fell below £12.

The Eagle Star's competitive edge, including its innovatory policies, was in large measure dependent on remaining outside the tariff agreements in fire and accident insurance. Yet, perhaps for this very reason, Mountain was never anti-tariff. His experience in the marine market had shown him the benefits of co-operation and this, combined with the Eagle Star's growth, encouraged him to take the lead in matters of general concern to independent offices. The most important example of this came in 1917 when he obtained their support for the formation of the British Insurance Association, which became the organ representing insurance companies of all types.

The end of the war brought important changes for Mountain. In 1921 he and his brother purchased Gardner Mountain's shares in Eagle Star and in 1923 Edward Mountain sold his interest in Gardner Mountain. The decision must have been easy. Quite apart from the burgeoning success of Eagle Star, the collapse in marine business that Mountain had frequently predicted during the wartime boom transpired. The early 1920s saw falling revenues and below-cost underwriting. In response the Eagle Star cut its marine underwriting business in order to limit underwriting losses. These difficulties continued throughout the inter-war period and by the late

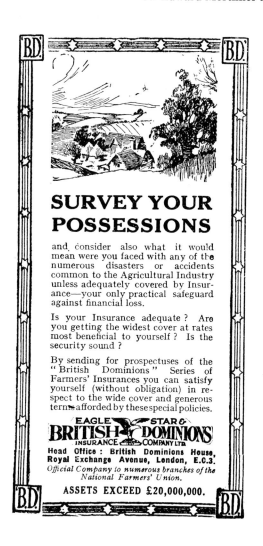

Advertisement which appeared in Farmer & Stockbreeder *July 1923 (courtesy of Eagle Star Group).*

1930s the conservative policy the company pursued had so reduced its premium income that it was no longer a leading marine company.

Compensation came from motor insurance. In this rapidly expanding market it was not difficult for those who had been involved in the business from an early stage and who kept clear of the rating agreements of the tariff companies, to collect large revenues. From 1911, A L Royle had written motor insurance for the company and created a reputation for it of being a flexible and competitive underwriter. By 1938 it was the sixth largest British motor insurer with some 80 per cent of their motor insurance business in the British Isles. The account generated a premium income of £1,607,232, one-third of the company's total premium income.

Though generating revenue and reserve funds, motor insurance was not highly profitable, partly because of the need to provide a substantially greater local service than had been necessary in traditional branches of insurance. In the 1920s, therefore, much of the company's efforts were directed towards the creation of a branch office network. In the war the company had had some dozen offices; by 1922 the number had risen to 39; by the mid-1930s it was directly represented in some 75 British towns. While a necessary component of success in motor insurance, this development helped the marketing of all types of business. Concomitantly, S A Bennett built up a remarkably influential set of local boards of professional and business men: 'The strength which this has given to the Eagle Star is beyond calculation' {*Post Magazine* 25 Dec 1937}.

The life market also offered scope for growth. Among a range of new policies, the Eagle Star pioneered the new potential of 'group' policies providing companies with pensions provisions for employees. After recovery from the depression of the early 1930s this business grew at an astounding rate, in some years by as much as 70 per cent.

By 1938 the company's continued growth had generated a premium income of nearly £5 million and assets of over £27 million. This placed Mountain in control of substantial investment funds. In the early 1920s he supported Gibson Jarvie in the establishment of the United Dominions Trust, which provided credit finance for car purchase, doubtless to the advantage of the Eagle Star's motor account. In the late 1920s Mountain became associated with the financier Philip Hill (qv), who joined the Eagle Star board in 1929. Subsequently, Mountain and Eagle Star played an increasingly important role in providing finance for schemes with which Hill was associated. This led to an involvement with Beechams, the associated Covent Garden Properties and the creation of Second Covent Garden in 1933 to take advantage of lower interest rates and expand investment in property. A similar arrangement led to Mountain joining the board of Olympia. Hill also created a collaboration with Oscar Deutsch (qv), in which Eagle Star assisted in the finance of the Odeon cinema chain in the 1930s. The association was so close that Edward Mountain became a vice-chairman of Philip Hill & Partners and, after the death of Philip Hill in 1944, chairman of that concern and of the Philip Hill Investment Trust. Through Eagle Star investments, Mountain became chairman of United Drapery Stores in the late 1930s and was for a while deputy chairman of Mosul Oilfields. Behind these more prominent connections lay a host of smaller commitments, especially in property, but above all the insurance of industrial concerns created a steady flow of investment opportunities that were attractive in their own right and cemented premium income.

Edward Mountain was physically a small man but with an authoritative manner and an immense, exuberant energy which spread itself in many directions with equal facility and success. His management routine between the wars was to meet with his senior staff every morning at 9.30 am, by which time they were expected to be able to answer all his questions and put all problems to him. He seems to have combined the apparently incompatible characteristics of the Lloyd's underwriter and the company general manager. He was undoubtedly a brilliant individualist whose intuitive qualities as an underwriter made him not only a leading marine underwriter in his younger days, but encouraged him to write independently in the new markets he entered later. Yet at the same time, his contemporaries were struck by the way in which he was able to select outstanding managers — S A Bennett, his general manager, Spencer, who managed the company's finances, Merriman, the marine underwriter, A L

Royle, in the motor department, and the Simmons brothers whose partnership handled all legal affairs — and weld them together into a successful team to build a large organisation. His achievements as a force for co-operative action at Lloyd's were an important measure of his capacity to secure agreement between large numbers of often idiosyncratic individuals with very disparate interests.

Mountain's energy also allowed him to engage in an enormous range of interests outside business. From an early age he bred homing pigeons and retained the interest at least into late middle age. He enjoyed his country homes, Oare Manor, near Brendon, North Devon, and Dunkeld House in Perthshire, becoming closely and directly involved in the management of their grounds, gardens and conservatories, in which he grew notable orchids. He studied painting and made a collection of both old masters and modern work. He enjoyed sport, owning and sailing yachts and playing golf. In his later years, even when confined to a wheelchair, he became an enthusiastic fisherman on waters he owned on the Spey and Tay, near his Perthshire home. In 1934 he attracted national interest by organising a careful watch to try to obtain evidence of the existence of the Loch Ness monster. He was knighted in 1918, and created a baronet in 1922.

In 1897 Mountain married Evelyn Ellen Regina, daughter of August Siegle, a bookseller; they had one child, Brian Edward Stanley. He remained actively at the head of Eagle Star as chairman and managing director until the year before his death, when his son became general manager. Sir Edward Mountain died on 22 June 1948, leaving £582,824 gross.

OLIVER M WESTALL

Sources:

Unpublished

Information supplied by the Eagle Star Group and J M Keyworth.

MCe.

PrC.

Published

Stanley D Chapman, 'Hogg Robinson: The Rise of a Lloyds Broker' in Oliver M Westall (ed), *The Historian and the Business of Insurance* (Manchester: Manchester University Press, 1984).

DD 1914, 1921, 1926, 1931, 1935, 1939, 1947.

Insurance Shareholders Guide 1920-21.

Lloyd's List 25 June 1948.

Post Magazine 1 Jan 1916, 25 Dec 1937, 3 July 1948 and passim.

Times 23 May 1917, 24 May 1918, 9 Dec 1920, 24 June 1948 and passim.

WWW.

Charles Edward Mudie from W H Beable, The Romance of Great Businesses.

MUDIE, Charles Edward

(1818-1890)

Circulating library proprietor

Charles Edward Mudie was born in Chelsea, London, on 18 October 1818. He was the youngest son of Thomas Mudie, who kept a newspaper and stationery shop, with a small circulating library from which books were loaned at a penny a volume. All that is known of his education is that it was, in his own words, 'properly cared for' {Curwen (1873) 424}.

In 1840 Mudie opened his own newspaper and stationery business in Upper King Street (now Southampton Row) in Bloomsbury. Unable to afford all the books he wanted for his personal reading, or to satisfy his serious interests in existing lending libraries, in 1842 he began to form a collection of 'progressive' theological and philosophical works which he lent at the rate of a guinea a year for one exchangeable volume to provide a service for young men like himself. His library — much frequented by students from the new London University — soon expanded to cater for customers with more general interests as well, and gradually Mudie concentrated on this aspect of his business to the exclusion of the others.

Mudie's guinea rate became as famous as the Library itself. It was well below the four to ten guineas charged by his competitors in the 1840s, and even when they reduced their rates to match his, a subscription to Mudie's Library was always a bargain when a newly-published work often cost a guinea or more. He also made a point of making new works available to his subscribers immediately on publication, in quantities large enough to meet their demands promptly. However, one of the most important reasons for the success of Mudie's Select Library with the respectable Victorian middle-class reader was not commercial. As well as providing the best in non-fiction, he supplied only *selected* novels, excluding any of a dubious moral tone, and as Mudie himself wrote in 1860, the public knew this and subscribed 'accordingly and increasingly. They are evidently willing to have a barrier of some kind between themselves and the lower floods of literature.' {*Athenaeum* 6 Oct 1860, 451}

In 1852 the Library moved to larger quarters at the corner of New Oxford Street and Museum Street. Between 1853 and 1862 almost 960,000 volumes were added, with the number of books bought each year rising from over 100,000 volumes to over 180,000 between 1858 and 1861. In December 1860 a large new hall and library were added. 16,000 books were shelved in the Great Hall alone; on the higher floors books in less frequent demand, including foreign and standard works, were kept. One contemporary estimated that Mudie would need a building twice the size of the British Museum if all the volumes on loan were to be returned to stock at once, but Mudie considered it impossible to estimate their numbers as the stock varied so much through the sale of old and the purchase of new books. Soon branches were established elsewhere in

Mudie's library, Oxford Street from W H Beable, The Romance of Great Businesses.

London as well as in Birmingham and Manchester. Arrangements were made to supply book societies and clubs and provincial libraries as well as individual subscribers in the country. Volumes were shipped abroad in special tin-lined boxes to the Continent, Africa and Asia. Most subscribers wanted novels, but Mudie took pains to keep up a collection of books for students and the more serious-minded readers.

This expansion was more rapid than his capital could sustain, and in 1864 Mudie formed a limited liability company, Mudie's Select Library Ltd. This had a nominal capital of £150,000 (a figure which remained unchanged until the winding-up of the firm in 1937), but only 4,378 of the nominal 7,500 shares were taken up during Mudie's lifetime. Of these Mudie himself held 2,246, and he remained sole manager, with a salary of £1,000 a year. He maintained tight control over the company, deciding its policies as well as supervising the day-to-day running of the business. He was often to be seen in the Great Hall, dealing personally with subscribers' orders, and handing favoured patrons out to their carriages. His elder son, Charles Henry, entered the firm when he came of age in 1871, and was groomed to assume control. When he died in 1879 Mudie was grief-stricken, and never really recovered from this blow. He took progressively less interest in the business and in 1884 handed over control of the Library to his younger son, Arthur.

Even in the 1850s, novelists noted sales of their works to Mudie as a measure of their success. By the 1860s, as the owner of by far the largest circulating library in the country, Mudie's commercial influence on book-publishing, particularly the publishing of fiction, was such that his preferences could determine not only the price of a book and the numbers to be printed, but also its appearance, and even the title and the plot. 'Mudie paid the piper, and on behalf of his large clientele he called the tune' {Altick (1957) 296}. However, by the time he retired the great days of Mudie's Select Library were already drawing to an end. The three-volume novel, which had been the mainstay of the Library, became less and less remunerative as too many novels of low quality, for which demand was very short-lived, poured out of the publishing-houses and popularly-priced reprints threatened the sales of surplus library stock which had been a profitable and useful adjunct to the business.

Mudie's selection of books on moral grounds was based on a strong sense of his duty to the public, stemming from his deep religious faith. He occasionally preached in a small Nonconformist chapel, and worked in the slums of Westminster; he was elected from Westminster to serve on the first London School Board, 1870-73. In 1872 he published *Stray Leaves*, a collection of poetry which included some hymns. He was a director of the London Missionary Society and a fellow of the Royal Geographical Society.

In 1847 he married Mary Kingsford Pawling, the daughter of Rev Henry Pawling of Lenham in Kent. They had eight children.

Charles Mudie died on 28 October 1890, leaving £60,000; all his interests in the Library were left to his son Arthur.

CHRISTINE SHAW

Writings:

letter on his criteria for selecting books *Athenaeum* 6 Oct 1860.

Stray Leaves (pp, 1872).

Sources:

Unpublished

PRO, BT 31/31743/1499: Mudie's Select Library Ltd.

MCe.

PrC.

Published

Richard D Altick, *The English Common Reader: A Social History of the Mass Reading Public 1800-1900* (Chicago: University of Chicago Press, 1957).

Athenaeum 1 Nov 1890.

Amy Cruse, *The Victorians and Their Books* (Allen & Unwin, 1935).

Henry Curwen, *A History of Booksellers, the Old and the New* (Chatto & Windus, 1873).

DNB.

Francis Espinasse, *Literary Recollections and Sketches* (Hodder & Stoughton, 1893).

Guinevere L Griest, *Mudie's Circulating Library and the Victorian Novel* (Bloomington: Indiana University Press, 1970).

C J Pomponio, 'Charles Edward Mudie' *International Library Review* 4 (1972).

Times 30 Oct 1890.

A Wynter, 'Mudie's Circulating Library' *Once a Week* 1861.

MUIRHEAD, Alexander

(1848-1920)

Electrical instrument designer and manufacturer

Alexander Muirhead was born on 26 May 1848, at Barley Mill, Saltoun, in East Lothian, the second son of John Muirhead, a farmer, who also practised as an architect, and his wife Margaret, youngest daughter of Alexander Lander of St Clement Wells. Alexander at the age of three was injured when his nurse fell with him. He received a blow on the head which left him permanently, though only partially, deaf. As a child he was thought rather stupid because he wished to know the reason for everything before doing it. An experiment recorded against him was the planting of a toy spade in order to grow a larger one. Soon after 1850 his father abandoned farming and architecture and brought his young family to London where he worked for the Electric Telegraph Co as a superintendent.

Initially the family lived near Kennington Oval and then close to Waterloo Station at the same address as the Electric Telegraph Co's stores. Finally they went to Lauder Cottage, a pleasant house adjoining the Electric Telegraph Co's factory in Gloucester Road, now Gloucester Avenue, where his father was superintendent. Alexander was thus brought up from a very early age in an engineering environment. There is no evidence that he had much education in Scotland and when brought to London he spoke such broad Scots that he was not understood. He went to a private tutor until he was fifteen, when he was sent to University College School, chosen because no corporal punishment was allowed there. His deafness was a handicap but nevertheless he did extremely well, particularly in mathematics and the sciences, in which fields he carried off the principal prizes.

He then went on to University College, where he was taught mathematics by Dr Morgan who imbued in him a spirit of accuracy which dominated his whole life. He graduated BSc with honours in chemistry in 1869 and would have liked to go on to read medicine, but his father thought his deafness would be too great a handicap and sent him to study chemistry under Dr Mathieson at St Bartholomew's Hospital. In spite of this Alexander made attempts to study biology and for one term his mother paid his fees.

His wife wrote of one experiment he made during this period. One afternoon he carried 'wires to the bedside of a patient at St Barts who was very ill, and he secured attachments to the wrist at one end of the wire and affixed the other end to Thomson's Recorder [an ink writing siphon recorder] which had just been invented. The nurse had strict injunctions that the connection was not to be broken. During the early hours of the morning the heart beats became very violent — the patient was delirious then — but a good record was taken' {Muirhead (1926)}. This must have been the first electrocardiogram and with a continuous ink record on paper tape it was fifty years before its time.

In spite of his interest in medicine Alexander had to stay with the natural sciences and in 1872 obtained his DSc. (At that time a doctorate was obtained by written and oral examination and not by thesis or published work.) His studies had been interrupted by his father's partner, Josiah Latimer Clark, who persuaded Alexander to work on his 'standard element', one of the first cells developed for use as a standard of electromotive force. Although this was later largely superseded by the Weston Standard Cell, successive Muirhead companies continued to make the Clark cell for nearly a century.

After obtaining his doctorate, Muirhead was appointed scientific adviser to his father's firm of telegraph engineers formed about 1869-70, Warden Muirhead & Clark (later Latimer Clark, Muirhead & Co), where his laboratory was an old cottage covered with a vine in Regent Street (now Regency Street), Westminster. Alexander Muirhead's laboratory work here was in two interlinking fields: methods and equipment for signalling over submarine telegraph cables, particularly 'duplexing', which virtually doubled the traffic capacity of a telegraph link; and precision electrical measurements of resistance and capacity.

Up to 1885 he travelled abroad for Warden Muirhead & Clark (in 1874 he was in Bombay) presumably installing Muirhead equipment. He joined forces with his brother John and with H A Taylor to solve the problem of cable duplexing, that is, arranging terminal apparatus so that traffic could be handled simultaneously in both directions. The key patent was taken out jointly with H A Taylor in 1875 and the whole system tried out on the Marseilles-Bona cable. By January 1877 the whole circuit to India was duplexed and by the end of that year the first Atlantic cable was too.

This work involved the development of manufacturing techniques for waxed paper and foil capacitors. Condensers and resistances were made up in artificial line boxes, each corresponding to about 60 miles of cable and each occupying about 2 cubic feet of space. The cable companies bought the hardware and paid annual royalties to the patentees to use them in their systems.

Alexander Muirhead continued to work for his father's firm and when it became Latimer Clark, Muirhead & Co Ltd, he and his elder brother John became directors. Apparently he and John did not get on together and in 1882 Alexander set up as an independent consultant, though he still advised his old firm when necessary. After his father's death in 1885, however, under pressure by the cable companies, he started manufacturing separately, under the name Muirhead & Co. Latimer Clark, Muirhead & Co Ltd, was wound up in 1894 and what was left of the business was taken over by Muirhead & Co. In 1895 Muirhead built a new instrument factory at Beckenham, Kent, and in 1899 he bought Nalder Bros & Co Ltd, an instrument-making firm with a very high reputation for precision electrical measuring equipment.

In addition to his work in the fields of cable telegraphy and electrical measurement, Muirhead had become very actively involved with the new field of wireless. In 1894 he attended a lecture at the Royal Institution given by his friend Dr Oliver (later Sir Oliver) Lodge on Hertzian waves. His wife recalls that 'that night he could not sleep, for the new idea had gripped him and the next day he went to Lodge with the suggestion that messages could be sent by use of these waves to feed cables. The two agreed to co-operate' {Muirhead (1926)}. Lodge and Muirhead had worked together before on the design of lightning protectors and it was this work which led to Lodge's interest in the work of Hertz. Lodge's great contribution was his understanding and development of the idea of tuning and all it meant in the separation of one transmission from another, simultaneous, one. Muirhead brought practical instrument experience and its application, particularly to the wheel coherer, in making wireless reliable. The Lodge-Muirhead Wireless Telegraphy Syndicate Ltd was formed in 1901.

Three years later Muirhead & Co became a limited liability company with two of Alexander's brothers on the board; the younger one, Frank, remained managing director until Alexander died in 1920. Alexander's progress, however, received a severe setback. He embarked on litigation with two very able engineers, Sydney Brown (qv) and Dearlove, in spite of a warning from his brother Frank, a barrister, supported by counsel's opinion, that his case had no merits. Muirheads lost and the costs crippled the company's and the family's finances for a decade.

Professionally, though, Alexander prospered. In 1904 the company took up production of the Heurtley Magnifier, probably the best of the pre-electronic amplifiers to be adopted generally by the cable companies. He saw his work with Lodge on 'wireless' vindicated by court decision against Marconi in 1911. With the coming of war in 1914 his factory was flooded with government work. In 1920 the government arbitrator decided that the Admiralty had infringed the Lodge Muirhead patents when it installed wireless in naval vessels long before the war.

As well as telegraphy and wireless, Muirhead was interested in arc lamps, on which he worked with John Hopkinson (qv), dynamos, the telephone, and insulating compounds.

Muirhead married in 1893 Mary Elizabeth Blomfield, who survived him. They had no children. From 1905, Muirhead was increasingly incapacitated by ill-health. He died on 13 December 1920, leaving £105,807 gross.

WILLIAM C LISTER

Writings:

'Chloride of Silver Element as a Standard of Electro-Motive Force' *Journal of the Institution of Electrical Engineers* 7 (1878).

'Muirheads' Duplex System' *Telegraph Journal* 7 (1879).

'Notes on the Constancy of Capacity of Certain Accumulators' *Reports of the British Association* 1879.

'New Form of Standards of EMF' *Electrician* 17 (1886).

'Note on the Use of Saunders Capacity Key in Comparing Capacities'

(with Sir Oliver Lodge), 'Syntonic Wireless Telegraphy: With Specimens of Large-Scale Measurements' *Proceedings of the Royal Society* A 82 (1909).

Sources:

Unpublished

PrC.

Published

Journal of the Institution of Electrical Engineers 59 (1921).

[Mary Muirhead], *Alexander Muirhead* (pp, Oxford: Basil Blackwell, 1926).

Nature 1921.

Proceedings of the Royal Society A 100 (1922).

MULHOLLAND, John

1st Lord Dunleath of Ballywalter, Co Down

(1819-1895)

Linen manufacturer

John Mulholland was born in Belfast on 16 December 1819, the only son among the five children of Andrew Mulholland (d 1866) and his wife Elizabeth née MacDonnell. He was educated at the Belfast Royal Academy. Andrew Mulholland and his elder brother Thomas (d 1830) had been partners in building the first wet spinning flax mill in Belfast, after their cotton mill had been destroyed by fire in 1828. This change from cotton to flax spinning made commercial sense for several reasons: the tariff barrier protecting Irish cotton yarn had been lifted in 1824; in that year James Kay of Preston patented his wet spinning process for spinning fine linen yarns, a process successfully adapted for commercial purposes by Marshalls of Leeds, the main flax spinning firm in Britain by 1828; from 1826 the UK cotton industry had been sliding into a deep recession; and finally, the cost of machine spinning flax was about half that of hand spinning, while flax was still widely handspun in Ireland.

The Mulholland brothers' flax spinning mill began working in 1830, but Thomas died later that year leaving Andrew as the sole proprietor of the firm. The venture was an immediate success, so much so that many other businessmen (particularly linen bleachers and cotton spinners) followed suit. By 1840 there were 38 wet spinning mills in Ireland running almost 250,000 spindles.

In that year Andrew took John into partnership in the firm and for six years trained him to take over its management. During this period John showed 'that keen aptitude for business and those sterling qualities which so eminently fitted him for playing a prominent part in the commercial life of a thriving city like Belfast' {*Belfast Newsletter* 13 Dec 1895}. Andrew retired in 1846 to Springvale Estate in County Down leaving John as sole proprietor of the firm.

John Mulholland took on Nicholas de la Cherois Crommelin of Carrowdore, the husband of one of his sisters, as a managing partner. With Crommelin dealing with the day-to-day running of the firm Mulholland concentrated his attention on overseas marketing. Since the mechanisation of flax spinning the Irish linen industry had become increasingly dependent on overseas markets, especially the USA and, to a lesser extent, Europe and the prospering temperate colonies like Canada and Australia. The export of Irish linen had at the beginning of the nineteenth century been generally carried on through merchants in British ports. However, industrialisation with its concentration of capital in the hands of a few firms encouraged the Irish linen producers to export their goods directly to overseas markets, by selling through established agencies. Mulholland realised that the interests of these agents were not necessarily the same as those of the manufacturers, particularly as an agent might well be acting for a number of Irish linen firms. Mulholland pioneered the forging of direct trading links between Irish linen firms and overseas customers by establishing branches of the firm overseas. By 1882 the firm had opened branches in Paris (1870), New York (1871), London (1874), Berlin (1876) and Melbourne (1882).

In 1860 Crommelin retired as managing partner of the firm (which had been re-named the York Street Flax Spinning Co in 1851), and was succeeded by Ogilvy Blair Graham, a native of Belfast who had acquired a fortune in New Orleans. The fortunes of the York Street Flax Spinning Co and the rest of the Irish linen industry were greatly enhanced by the outbreak of the American Civil War in 1861, when the Northern States' blockade of the Southern States' ports virtually cut off the supply of raw cotton to Britain, bringing the cotton industry to a virtual standstill but boosting the demand for linen. Between 1861 and 1864 (the height of the Cotton Famine) output of Irish linen yarn and cloth almost trebled, while prices increased 30-40 per cent.

Mulholland, who nursed social and political aspirations, took the opportunity of this boom to float the firm as a limited liability company in 1865, selling off a sizeable portion of his holding in it to raise money to buy a landed estate. The York Street Flax Spinning Co Ltd was one of the first joint stock companies in the Irish linen industry, and one of the most highly capitalised, with a nominal share value at the time of incorporation of £500,000 (although not all the shares were called up). John Mulholland, although retaining a large holding in the firm, received £164,250 for the shares he sold. With this money he bought Southwell Estate in Downpatrick, and from this beginning he eventually became an extensive landowner throughout the counties of Down and Tyrone. As a major landowner of Downpatrick he later built the town hall there (this was destroyed in a fire in 1982).

The incorporation of the York Street Flax Spinning Co in 1865 was beneficial for the company for two reasons. Firstly, the uncalled shares

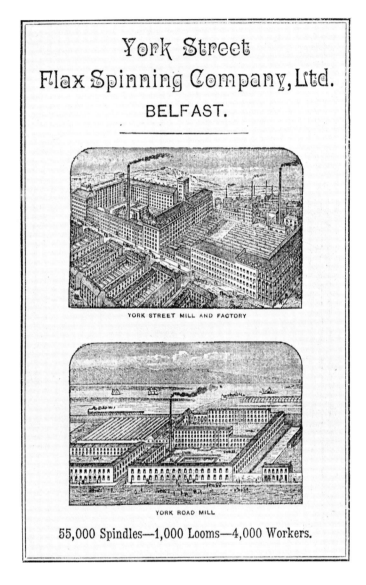

York Street
Flax Spinning Company, Ltd.
BELFAST.

YORK STREET MILL AND FACTORY

YORK ROAD MILL

55,000 Spindles—1,000 Looms—4,000 Workers.

*Advertisement for York Street Flax Spinning Co Ltd (*Irish Textile Journal Directory 1881*).*

provided the York Street Flax Spinning Co Ltd with a ready source of capital on which it could depend to expand and develop its activities, and the new board of directors ensured that the firm had a well chosen team of professional managers, including R H Reade and William (later Sir William) Crawford (qv). The expertise of these men and the solid financial backing of the firm facilitated its success and expansion in the last third of the nineteenth century, despite the generally depressed state of the Irish linen industry, which was suffering severely from over-expansion during the American Civil War, growing competition from overseas producers, and the increasing use of cotton in products traditionally made from linen. The firm's continued success after the boom of the American Civil War period also owed much to the re-organisation of its overseas outlets, which

John Mulholland had initiated. The prosperity of the York Street Flax Spinning Co in these years can be gauged from the expansion of its plant. In the late-1860s new spinning mills and a powerloom weaving factory were built at York Street. The firm also purchased Lepper's Dam close by, to supply the mills with water. In 1879 it bought Milewater Mill, a short distance away from York Street, for £28,000 and in 1883 it added Muckamore Bleachworks near Antrim to its plant, also at the cost of £28,000. By 1892 the York Street Flax Spinning Co was the largest integrated flax spinning, weaving and marketing concern in the world.

After the firm's incorporation, although Mulholland continued to take an interest in the business he became increasingly involved in politics. A Conservative, he stood unsuccessfully for parliament for Belfast in 1866, but was elected MP for Downpatrick in 1872, a seat he retained until 1885. As an extensive landowner he was particularly interested in the controversial Irish land question. Like almost all other Irish industrialists, he was adamantly opposed to Home Rule. In the late 1870s he sat on the Royal Commission of Inquiry into the advisability of the state purchasing the Irish railways.

Apart from his interest in the land and in politics Mulholland's major abiding interest was the Church of Ireland. When it was disestablished in 1869, he took a major role in reorganising it and putting it on a sound financial footing. He was a member of the general synod, as well as the diocesan synods of Down and Connor and of Dromore, and gave generous donations to the Church of Ireland's Young Men's Society. Mulholland was raised to the peerage in 1892, taking as his title Lord Dunleath..

In 1851 Mulholland married Frances Louise Lyle, daughter of Hugh Lyle of Knocktana, County Derry. The couple had three sons, one of whom died before his father.

After some years of failing health, Dunleath died on 11 December 1895 in his town house in Euston Square, London, at the age of seventy-six. His effects left in Ireland were valued at over £65,000, but the gross valuation of his personalty was £583,266. He had also been a considerable landowner, but a year before his death he had divided this property between his two surviving sons so that they would not have to pay death duty on it after he died. He was succeeded to the title by his son, Herbert Lyle Mulholland, former MP for Derry.

EMILY BOYLE

Sources:

Unpublished

Emily Boyle, 'The Economic Development of the Irish Linen Industry 1825-1913' (Queens University, Belfast PhD, 1979).

Published

Belfast Newsletter 13 Dec 1895.

Fibres and Fabrics Aug, Sept 1943.

WWMP.

S R Mullard (courtesy of Mullards Ltd).

MULLARD, Stanley Robert

(1883-1979)

Valve manufacturer

Stanley Robert Mullard was born in Bermondsey, London, on 1 November 1883, the third of the five children of Robert Mullard (d ca 1918) and his wife Ann née Ludford. By the time that Stanley Mullard left school at the age of fourteen, Edison & Swan's master patents for electric lamps were beginning to expire, and the way was clear for competitors to enter the field. One was the small firm of Mackey, Mackey & Co, wholesale and export chemists and druggists by whom Stanley Mullard's father was employed in the City of London.

In 1898 the firm moved to Bermondsey and a separate company, Mackey's Electric Lamp Co Ltd, was incorporated in August 1898 with a nominal capital of £2,000 in £1 shares, of which 1,994 were held by John Mackey, the chairman. Robert Mullard held a single £1 share.

In 1899 Stanley Mullard joined his father in the lamp factory as assistant to the manager and at the age of twenty-three he was made a director. Over the next few years he gained invaluable experience, not only in the practical art of glass-blowing, but also in wider aspects of management and salesmanship. By 1908, however, technical developments in the industry, especially the substitution of metallic for the early carbon filaments and the importation of low-priced lamps from the Continent, were creating difficulties with which the little company could not compete and in 1909 it was put into liquidation.

After a brief spell with the Paris lamp factory of Julius Pintsch, which gave him an insight into the production methods of a German-owned firm, Mullard returned to England and joined Ediswan at Ponders End, where he was placed in charge of their lamp laboratory.

During the First World War he was released to take up a commission as a lieutenant in the Royal Naval Air Service and in 1916 to take charge, under the Royal Naval Signal School, of a laboratory in South Kensington for the testing and development of wireless valves in co-operation with the various manufacturers.

After demobilisation early in 1919, Mullard took up an appointment as managing director of a small lamp manufacturer at Southfields, the 'Z' Electric Lamp Manufacturing Co, but with an arrangement with the owners of the company that he could manufacture wireless valves on the company's premises under his own name. In conjunction with the Royal Naval Signal School, he continued with the development of the silica transmitting valve and, on 17 September 1920, on the basis of an order from the Admiralty for 250 silica valves, he formed the Mullard Radio Valve Co. It had a nominal capital of £30,000. In the event, only 26,000 of the £1 shares were issued, of which 5,000 were allotted to Mullard and his wife, credited as 'fully paid' in recognition of the knowledge and experience he was contributing to the new company.

Mullard established his new company with only 20 employees in the premises of a disused laundry in Hammersmith. In parallel with the manufacture of the silica valves for the Royal Navy, he designed a new pattern of receiving valve to which he gave the trade name 'ORA' and which, in the autumn of 1921, he placed upon the market at a price of only 15s as compared with an average price of 30s charged by other manufacturers for their receiving valves. The ORA valve quickly established a reputation for consistent reliability and, with demand encouraged by the lower price, production had to be increased almost ten-fold within only eighteen months. The establishment of the British Broadcasting Company (as it was then called) in 1921 also gave rise to a greatly increased demand and made imperative a move to larger premises in Balham in 1923. By the end of that year the firm employed about 250 people; and by late 1924 production was running at an annual rate of 2.5 million valves.

While possessing very wide experience and capability in all the practical aspects of electric lamp and wireless valve manufacture, Mullard was conscious of the growing need for access to a wide range of research facilities. With this need in mind he began in 1923-24 to make tentative overtures to a number of established concerns and eventually he persuaded his fellow-directors and shareholders, of whom there were only 14, to agree secretly in January 1925 to the sale of 50 per cent of their holdings to the n v Philips' Gloeilampenfabrieken of Eindhoven in Holland, a long-established and leading manufacturer of electric lamps, X-ray tubes, wireless valves and allied products. The object of the sale was to gain access to the work of Philips's research department and to the use of Philips's patents.

The purchase of the second half of the equity by Philips was completed in January 1927, from which time the Mullard Co has been a wholly-owned subsidiary of Philips. For the acquisition of the Mullard Co, Philips paid only £226,000. For three years Mullard continued to direct the company as managing director at a salary of £1,500 per annum with additional emoluments totalling a further £1,500 for entertainment and other purposes.

It seems doubtful whether Mullard himself realised at the time that the change in ownership of the company would be likely to render untenable his own position as managing director and chief executive. Prior to 1925, Mullard had in effect been personally responsible for every aspect of the company's activities, but from 1927 onwards it was inevitable that the new owners of the company would insist on their right to determine matters of policy and management. In 1930 he was succeeded by S S Eriks (qv). Although he continued to hold an appointment as a director — until 1970 when he formally retired — Mullard held no executive authority after 1930 and his duties were purely nominal: a courteous recognition by Philips of his early work in establishing the company and leading it through its early years.

Mullard married Emmie Gladys Winifred, daughter of George Walter Hole, an estate agent, in 1908; they had five children. He died on 1 September 1979, leaving £48,994 gross.

G R M GARRATT *and* IAN NICHOLSON

Sources:

Unpublished

Mullard Ltd, London, archives.

BCe.

MCe.

PrC.

Published

Daily Telegraph 3 Sept 1979.

MUNDELLA, Anthony John

(1825-1897)

Hosiery manufacturer and industrial statesman

Anthony John Mundella was born at Leicester on 28 March 1825, the first child of Antonio Mundella, a teacher of modern langauges and a refugee from Como in Northern Italy who had escaped to England after an unsuccessful rising against the Austrians, and his wife Rebecca née Allsop, a lady of Welsh descent who owned some property. Although his father was a Roman Catholic, A J Mundella was sent to a Church of England school, St Nicholas National School, which he left at the age of nine. He spent nearly two years as a printer's devil and was then apprenticed to a stockinger, William Kempson of Albion Street, Leicester.

In the 1830s and 1840s conditions in the hosiery trade were wretched, largely due to the flooding of the domestic industry with cheap rural labour in a period in which fashion change (notably men's stockings being superseded by trousers) restrained demand. The problem was exacerbated by exploitation of workers, by the spread of frame renting and the rise of middlemen. Wage rates were being forced down and at times of trade depression whole families starved. Women and children seamed the flat hosiery knitted on the manually-operated stocking frames and were therefore thrown out of work along with the knitters. Faced with the New Poor Law, the knitters readily turned to Chartism. In these harsh and turbulent times the adolescent A J Mundella was deeply influenced first and foremost by Thomas Cooper (1805-92), the Leicester schoolmaster and Chartist agitator, and then Richard Cobden, the Anti-Corn Law crusader.

Relief came through technical rather than political change. In this industrial renewal A J Mundella played a crucial role by bringing technological advance to commercial fruition and by harmonising relations between factory masters and the new workforce.

When Mundella entered the industry, the technical possibilities for applying power to the knitting frame had been known for several years, Marc I Brunel having patented a rotary machine in 1816. For the most part, invention in hosiery technology had been left to the craft knitter familiar with his individual machine. Merchant hosiers showed little interest in concentrating these improvements and applying power in order to effect a transition to the factory system such as had occurred in cotton spinning seventy years earlier. Until the mid-1840s they were sceptical that power-driven machinery could be designed to put fashioning into stockings and at a speed that would match hand-powered machines. However in 1845 Thomas Collins collected a number of rotary frames into a factory in Barkby Lane, Leicester, and drove them by steam power. Mundella entered the stream of change when, that year, he left Kempsons and became an overseer in one of two large warehouses set up by Harris & Hamel, merchant hosiers. Harris, the senior partner, had in 1844 taken out two patents to cover improvements in the manufacture of fancy hosiery which increased average earnings to £1 a week or twice the average rate. Mundella received £200 per annum plus a commission on profits and in an atmosphere of reawakening technical advance learned the business of the merchant hosier in a house whose head shared his Chartist sympathies. When Richard Harris was elected MP for Leicester and the Chartist movement collapsed in 1848, Mundella accepted the offer of a partnership from Jonathan Hine of Nottingham who, with his son Benjamin Hornbuckle Hine and grandson John Hine, was about to build a large new factory. Hines had been a small firm of merchant hosiers, established half-a-century earlier, and like other hereditary leaders of the Nottingham hosiery industry appear to have lacked both the incentive and the financial means to undertake technical innovation. The reason for their sudden change of interest has never been explained, but may well be connected with John Hines's marriage to the daughter of a partner in Overend, Gurney & Co, enterprising London merchant bankers. John Hine retired from the family partnership but left £30,000 in it, and by 1854 B H Hine and A J Mundella were contributing £15,000 each. The total capital, £60,000, was already in excess of that of the two best known firms of merchant hosiers in Nottingham, Heard & Hurst with £40,000 and I & R Morley with an estimated £55,000.

The Hines were determined to beat the large steam hosiery factories of Chemnitz, Saxony, which marketed for 2s 6d articles that sold in Nottingham for 10s. Hine & Mundella decided to adapt the new circular frame knitting machine developed by Peter Claussen of Brussels, who patented it in England in 1846 and 1847 and then exhibited it in Nottingham. In September 1851 Hine & Mundella's new steam-driven factory built opposite the Midland Railway Station was opened. Mundella then hunted for technical improvements by which the flat frame producing fully-fashioned work might be given rotary motion and so be power-driven. A key improvement was secured from a poor but ingenious knitter, Luke Barton. Throughout the 1850s Hine & Mundella repeated this tactic of finding inventions among craftsmen, covering them with a patent held jointly by the firm and the craftsman-inventor, and rewarding the inventor. Although Hine & Mundella's future rivals, I & R Morley, headed by Samuel Morley (qv), eventually secured rights to the perfected powered flat-frame patented by William Cotton in the 1860s, Morleys did not start factory production until 1866.

By 1857 Hine & Mundella employed some 4,000 workers, 10 per cent of them in the new factory and warehouse, the others no doubt as domestic framework knitters and helpers. Turnover mounted from £20,000 to £200,000 in the 1850s; in the same decade I & R Morley's sales rose from £700,000 to £1 million a year, still higher than Hine & Mundella but a much lower rate of growth. Factory wages were high, ranging on average from £1 to £3 and working conditions were clean and well-lighted. The working day was reduced to nine hours without the half-time labour of children. All of this established Mundella as one of the most advanced employers of mid-Victorian Britain. A major setback, however, occurred on 1 February 1859 when the hosiery factory was destroyed by fire, accidentally started. The cost of replacing the machinery alone was estimated at £35,000. At the London Exhibition of 1862, Hine & Mundella won the only gold medal awarded for hosiery made on power-driven machines. The citation commended their machinery 'which narrows or widens [stockings] without stopping, giving the public a better and much cheaper article' {*Reports by the Juries* Class XXVII, 8}.

Meanwhile Mundella had become a spokesman for the hosiery trade. As chairman of the Nottingham Chamber of Commerce, he went to Paris for a month in 1860 with the delegation, headed by Richard Cobden, which negotiated the Anglo-French Treaty of Commerce, and secured a new market for British stockings. Mundella became prominent too as an industrial arbitrator. In 1860 when the accelerating transition from handwork to factory production triggered four strikes among the framework knitters in the still-depressed outwork industry, he counselled conciliation rather than confrontation. While over 1,000 framework knitters were on strike, representatives of employers and operatives held a round-table conference in September and Mundella broke the impasse by persuading the employers to grant the wage increase demanded and to set up a board of arbitration for the industry. The idea had been suggested fifteen years earlier by William Felkin who had read about the Conseils des Prudhommes in France in the 1830s. 'It was Mundella's flair, however, that translated Felkin's idea into a fact' {Armytage (1951) 33}. Comprising six employers and six operatives, with Mundella elected as president, the Arbitration Board first met in December 1860 and established Mundella's reputation as the champion of the trade unions. Between 1860 and 1867 the services of the Arbitration Board were rarely needed and in the six years of its existence 'no strike or lock-out has taken place, no personal attacks have been made, and no inflammatory handbills circulated' {Felkin (1867) 486}. The Hosiery Arbitration Board was replicated in other industries, first in Leicester for hosiery (1866), then in the Nottingham lace trade (1867) and by 1896 there were 64 boards of arbitration in a wide range of industries. Mundella himself arbitrated in strikes called by the Lancashire colliers in 1867 and by Newcastle engineers in 1871 (when he failed to convince Lord Armstrong (qv)).

Mundella suffered a nervous breakdown in 1863 and went to Italy to recuperate. During, and perhaps because of, Mundella's illness, the partnership of G H Hine, Mundella & Co was converted in July 1864 into a limited liability company, the Nottingham Manufacturing Co Ltd. Its capital of £200,000 in £20 shares was three-quarters subscribed in summer 1864 and Mundella became a director. At the same time the company entered an agreement to buy the straight bar machines for making fashioned garments patented by William Cotton. The Nottingham Manufacturing Co absorbed the old merchant firm of J J & J Wilson with interests in Nottingham and Saxony and further interests were acquired in Boston to gain access to American markets.

Mundella recovered by spring 1865 and in 1868 he was elected MP for Sheffield (which he represented until his death), having been Liberal leader in Nottingham during the 1850s and 1860s when his Tory opponents conjured all kinds of innuendos around his large black beard, hooked nose and foreign extraction. In the Commons Mundella drafted and piloted a moderate trade union bill which in 1869 protected union funds, following the *Hornby v Close* decision of 1867. He also strongly supported W E Forster's Education Bill of 1870, securing the clause requiring secret ballot in School Board elections. Mundella's and George Leeman's Borough Funds Act of 1872 permitted corporations to run their own public utilities, a measure which unleashed municipal trading whose model became Joseph Chamberlain's (qv) Birmingham. He fought against child labour and for the adoption of the nine-hour day. This came in 1874 under the Conservatives, as did the legalisation of trade unions, and Mundella received a share of the credit for each.

Having visited America in 1870 and Europe on many occasions and with his knowledge of the international hosiery trade, Mundella concluded that the state would have to provide a system of technical education if British industrialists were to keep up with their competitors. In Gladstone's second ministry, he was sworn of the Privy Council and as Vice-President of the Committee of Council on Education, 1880-85, he immediately threw himself into major educational reform. Under his direct influence the Mundella Act of 1880 finally made school attendance compulsory for children aged ten or under. Secondly, he reorganised technical education. He set up the Normal School of Science which consolidated all the science schools at Kensington and amalgamated them with the Royal School of Mines in 1881. He appointed a committee to investigate higher education in Wales and in 1881 a Royal Commission under his ally Bernhard Samuelson (qv) was appointed to compare technical education abroad with that in Britain.

As President of the Board of Trade, 1886 and then 1892-94, he was much concerned with the problem of high railway rates, which had the effect of restraining trade. He imposed a reduced schedule of railway rates and charges, against fierce opposition from the railway interest, which became effective in 1893 and statutorily fixed the following year. Among other reforms affecting business he set up a statistical department within the Board of Trade in 1886 and a labour department in 1893.

Mundella's parliamentary career was ruined in 1894 after the affairs of the New Zealand Loan & Mercantile Agency, of which he was a director between 1869 and 1892, became public. The Agency had started in 1865 with a capital of £500,000 and by 1894 had a capital of £4.5 million. In 1893 a number of Australian banks failed and the New Zealand Agency suspended payments. When the reports of the Board of Trade Receiver were delayed Mr Justice Vaughan Williams in the Court of Chancery ordered a public examination of the directors. Mundella was accused of trying to cover up and with suggestions of conflict of interest he had no choice but to resign from office.

A J Mundella married in 1846 Mary Smith of Leicester who loyally supported him in his business and political careers until her death in 1890. They had one daughter, Maria Theresa.

His precipitate departure from office denied Mundella the honours he richly deserved. In Nottingham he served as Sheriff, Alderman and JP and was also a JP of Middlesex. He was elected to the exclusive Political Economy Club in 1874, was a juror at the Paris Exhibition in 1878, and was an FRS and FSS. He was an Anglican and in 1884 was president of the Sunday School Union.

A J Mundella died on 21 July 1897, leaving £42,620 gross.

DAVID J JEREMY *and* S D CHAPMAN

Writings:

Arbitration as a Means of Preventing Strikes (Bradford, 1868).

A Royal Commissioner on the Contagious Diseases Acts speech 11 Nov 1874 (1874).

The Proposals for the Revision of the Educational Code (Newcastle and Darlington: North of England School Furnishing Co, Jarrold & Sons, 1881?).

Secular and Religious Education (pp, 1884).

PP, HC 1896 (311) XII, SC on Petroleum 1896.

British Patents:

1853 (1,967)
1854 (325,365)
1857 (1,448)
1861 (2,899).

Sources:

Unpublished

Bank of England Archives, Leicester Agent's Letter Books, I and II. I & R Morley's capital has been estimated from that given for Heard & Hurst on the basis of the numbers of stocking frames employed by the two firms.

PrC.

Published

Walter H G Armytage, *A J Mundella, 1825-1897. The Liberal Background to the Labour Movement* (Ernest Benn, 1951).

Stanley D Chapman, 'Enterprise and Innovation in the British Hosiery Industry, 1750-1850' *Textile History* 5 (1974).

DNB.

Charlotte Erickson, *British Industrialists. Steel and Hosiery, 1850-1950* (Cambridge: Cambridge University Press, 1959).

William Felkin, *History of the Machine-Wrought Hosiery and Lace Manufacturers* (1867; repr with introduction by Stanley D Chapman, Newton Abbot: David & Charles, 1967).

J F C Harrison, 'Chartism in Leicester' in Asa Briggs (ed), *Chartist Studies* (Macmillan, 1959).

International Exhibition, 1862. Reports by the Juries (1863).

F A Wells, 'The Textile Industry: Hosiery and Lace' in Singer, *History of Technology*, 5 (1958).

—, *The British Hosiery and Knitwear Industry: Its History and Organisation* (Newton Abbot: David & Charles, 1972).

WWMP.

MURPHY, Frank

(1889-1955)

Radio manufacturer

Frank Murphy was born in London on 16 June 1889, the sixth child of John Murphy, a headmaster, and his wife Annie née Leggo. At the age of four, Frank attended the Whittington School in Kentish Town and then probably attended the High Street Plumstead Board School (after his father became headmaster there in 1897), winning a scholarship to the City and Guilds. Excelling in mathematics, Frank won a scholarship to the East London Technical College (now Queen Mary College), where he took a degree in electrical engineering when only nineteen. Too poor to take up a scholarship at Oxford, he entered the research section of the General Post Office, having come first out of 300 candidates in the 1910 Civil Service Entrance examinations. In the evenings after work he continued post-graduate studies at East London Technical College on the cathode ray tube.

When the First World War broke out, he was at first in a reserved occupation, but in 1917 he was released from the Post Office and joined the

"F.M."

Frank Murphy (courtesy of Mrs Joan Long).

Army's new Royal Flying Corps as a wireless operator. After eight months in France, he was recalled to reorganise a school for wireless officers at Farnborough. He also used his technical knowledge to great effect in improving the ground-to-air communication link between Dover and the Occupation Forces in Cologne in 1919.

Once demobilised, he determined to set up in business rather than return to his old job, and with a friend, Charles Rupert Casson, started an advertising agency, the Engineering Publicity Service, in Kingsway, London. After some years of struggle, the company was successful, numbering among its clients such names as Mullard, Belling, Ediswan, and Vickers-Armstrong.

At this time Frank Murphy was impressed by the ideas of Henry Ford, particularly his high wages policy, and was keen to try them out in a company in England. He therefore left the advertising agency in 1928 and started Murphy Radio Ltd with Edward J Power, another radio enthusiast. After eighteen months of research in a tiny factory in Welwyn Garden City, the first Murphy sets were produced for sale in July 1930 and offered, like Ford cars, through specially selected dealers chosen for integrity and competence.

With the help of his old partner Casson, Murphy ran a striking series of full-page advertisements in the *Radio Times*, using direct, down-to-earth language to describe his sets and his policy. The craggy features of 'The Man With the Pipe' soon became nationally known. In the space of only five years the sales rose from a single set in the first month to 80,000 a year in 1935, with a company turnover of £1,025,000.

The reasons for success were clear. The Murphy sets were excellent value for money and far more reliable than most of their competitors; and they were renowned for their technical innovations, the first example being automatic volume control in 1932. The Murphy dealers worked tirelessly under Frank Murphy's leadership, with the market rapidly expanding as radio became a standard piece of household equipment rather than a rich man's toy.

However, the radio trade was in those days very seasonal. Business was slack through spring and summer, but quickened with the shorter days of autumn, and reached a peak just before Christmas. Consequently, manufacturers were forced to lay off hundreds of workers during the slack summer months. Deeply disturbed by this, Frank Murphy ran an expensive summer advertising campaign on the theme 'Buy Your Murphy Now' and also introduced his new models at the beginning of the year. This had significant results in providing steady employment for the majority of his workers, and for those in other companies too.

There were other examples of Murphy's 'square-deal' policy. As well as paying higher than average wages, even in the depression years, the company made a point of employing handicapped people, and providing a works canteen, welfare services, holidays with pay and sick-pay schemes, long before these were general in Britain. Pleasant living and working conditions were ensured in the Garden City. Staff and dealers were encouraged to express their opinions freely in the lively house magazine *Murphy News*.

Despite the success of the limited dealership scheme, Frank Murphy felt that retailing was far less efficient than manufacturing. He began to

NOW THE D24 FOR USE ON D.C. MAINS

ALL ELECTRIC SUPERHETERODYNE RECEIVER,
fitted with self-contained moving coil speaker. Cabinet finished
in Walnut inlaid with beautifully-grained Birdseye Maple. Single
tuning control. Illuminated wavelength dial. Automatic volume
control. Fitted with gramophone jack and extra loud-speaker
sockets. Will receive British and many Continental stations
and has very beautiful reproduction.

Cash Price

£14.10ˢ

Also A24 for use on A.C.
Mains. Specification and price
as above.

Hire Purchase Terms Available.
This price does not apply in I.F.S.

"...*the longer you look
at it the more you like it!*"

HERE is a big disagreement of opinion about the A.24 Cabinet design, and quite a lot of people think we ought to change it and give
you "something that everybody will like."
Well, I'm not going to change it, but I do think you are entitled to know why.
First of all, we are not making either wireless sets or cabinets with the
main idea of selling as many as possible. We are trying to make them as
good as we can. So far as the set is concerned, it is a plain fact that
Murphy technique is now definitely leading the industry. And it does so
chiefly because our Chief Engineer—Mr. Power—and his staff are trying
to make fine sets, not "sellable" sets.
But when we come to beauty of design we are on very difficult and
dangerous ground. Most of us will admit that we cannot lay down laws
on how to achieve beauty. I certainly can't. So we did the obvious thing.
We put our cabinet design in the hands of Gordon Russell, who give their
life to trying to find and build beauty in the design of furniture. And if
you could see their works in Worcestershire, or their showrooms in
London, you would agree that they succeed.
Beauty in machine-made furniture is so rare that most of us do not
recognise it when we see it. And many of us are not even willing to try!
Meanwhile, in 3 weeks thousands of people have bought the A.24 and
they know that what I say is true.
The longer you look at it the more you like it.

Frank Murphy

MURPHY

MURPHY RADIO LIMITED, WELWYN GARDEN CITY, HERTS.   TELEPHONE: WELWYN GARDEN 82

*1934 Murphy advertisement,
showing the A24, whose cabinet design
marked a breakthrough in the radio
industry (courtesy of Mrs Joan Long).*

develop his own theories about the true function of a shop-keeper, who, he
considered, should ideally be the consumer's adviser rather than a
manufacturer's agent. He also realised that security of employment and
reasonable working conditions for the average worker depended ultimately
on the benevolence of his employer, whose terms of reference in the
normal limited liability company were primarily to make money for
shareholders. Eventually, in January 1937, he saw that he could no longer
work within the existing system, resigned his chairmanship and severed all
connections with Murphy Radio.

He founded a new furniture manufacturing company, Frank Murphy
Ltd, to be run on the lines of his 'New Conception of Business'. Murphy
retained the framework of the limited liability company, but changed its
terms of reference from pure profit-seeking to 'applying knowledge with
integrity' and allowing all to 'express their individuality in the service of

society' {'A New Conception of Business'}. The basic rights and obligations of workers, management, shareholders and the honorary board of trustees who were to fulfil the role of a board of directors were safeguarded in a detailed constitution which embodied the 'Rule of Law'. Each new employee undertook to sign an agreement to abide by these principles, and once permanently appointed, could be dismissed only for 'lack of integrity', at the decision of a panel of work-mates.

The furniture produced by Frank Murphy Ltd was also unusual. Using market research technique (then in its infancy), the designers first established what were the basic uses for tables, chairs, sideboards and wardrobes, and then proceeded to design what was needed, using the best quality oak and walnut available for mass production, unstained but covered with an effective clear protective polish. In this Frank Murphy was undoubtedly influenced by his years of association with Sir Gordon Russell (qv), a pioneer in this country of fine furniture designed on simple lines, whom Murphy had persuaded in 1931 to design the distinctive cabinets for Murphy radio sets.

Unfortunately the plans to go into full production and establish a chain of showrooms were defeated by the outbreak of the Second World War in 1939, and the company reluctantly went into liquidation in 1940. A broadly pacifist outlook prevented Frank Murphy from undertaking any significant war work, and after the war his desperate attempts to start a fresh business in this country were frustrated by lack of capital and government restrictions on supply of raw materials such as timber. In 1947 he emigrated to Canada, hoping to re-establish his 'New Conception of Business' in a country where individual initiative was less hampered by planning regulations. However, this proved an uphill task, since he was unknown in Toronto, and without capital of his own. Eventually, after various stop-gap jobs he returned to his first love, mathematics, and became a teacher in a Toronto high school. On 23 January 1955 he collapsed with a serious heart attack and died shortly after being admitted to hospital.

Murphy was survived by his ex-wife, Hilda Constance, daughter of Charles Howe, an insurance agent (they had married in 1912, and divorced in 1946), by a son, Frank Maurice, and a daughter, Joan. His political opinions were broadly socialist, but he was not aligned to any particular party; though he remained aware of the debt he owed to his Christian upbringing and his Baptist affiliations as a young man; in later years he was a humanist rather than a religious believer.

In 1936 Murphy had crossed the Atlantic in the *Queen Mary* as chairman of a nationally famous radio firm; when he died, his only valuable possession was a gold watch given to him by some of his former Murphy dealers as a mark of their respect and affection.

JOAN LONG

Writings:

Some Thoughts on Retailing and Distribution (Murphy Radio Ltd, 1935).

Some Arguments on Advertising (Murphy Radio Ltd, 1935).

Making Peace Simple (Welwyn Garden City: pp, Frank Murphy, 1945).

The Root of the Matter (Toronto: pp, Frank Murphy, 1950).

A Short Autobiography (Toronto: pp, Frank Murphy, 1953).

Sources:

Unpublished

MCe.

Personal information (the author is the subject's daughter).

Frank Murphy, 'A New Conception of Business' (in the possession of the author).

Published

Making Wireless Simple (1930).

Murphy News (house organ of Murphy Radio Ltd) 1-8 (1933-37).

Murphy Review (house magazine of Frank Murphy Ltd) Sept 1938-Dec 1939.

MURPHY, William Martin

(1844-1919)

Dublin financier

William Martin Murphy, a portrait by William Orpen.

William Martin Murphy was born in Bantry, County Cork, on 21 November 1844, the eldest son of Denis William Murphy, who came from small farming stock in West Cork, and his wife Mary Anne, daughter of James Martin of Castletown Bere, County Cork. Denis moved in 1846 to Bantry, where he became a successful building contractor and owner of a sawmill and timber yard.

William attended the local National School in Bantry. It was decided that he should become an architect and he was sent to the prestigious Belvedere College in Dublin, which was run by the Jesuit order. In Dublin, he was befriended by the Sullivan family from Bantry. A M Sullivan worked on the nationalist paper *The Nation*, and William Murphy was a regular visitor to the paper.

After leaving school, Murphy was apprenticed to the architect, John J Lyons, the proprietor of the *Irish Builder*. On occasions, he acted as a subeditor and contributed notes and articles to that journal.

signatories conditions which are contrary to individual liberty and which no workman or body of workmen would reasonably be expected to accept.' {Wright (1914) 270-71} Whether Murphy was largely responsible for the harshness of the employers' tactics during the lock-out, is impossible to say on the basis of available sources, but it would appear that, as the leader of the employers, he lost his sense of proportion. Although he won the gratitude of the members of the Dublin commercial community, his inflexibility alienated many influential members of the Irish middle classes.

In appearance, Murphy looked like a 'typical family solicitor of the old school — the man who is the repository of many secrets and who blends the milk of human kindness with an unswerving rectitude of conduct.' {*ibid*, 78} A tall spare man, he wore a black coat, had a neatly-cut beard, and grey hair swept on the side. Like many of his fellow Irish employers, William Martin Murphy was in no sense a man of high culture. He earned the reputation of a 'philistine' because of his opposition to the building of a gallery in Dublin to house the famous Sir Hugh Lane art collection. But if he had little interest in painting, he had less in sport. He resolutely refused to learn how to play golf. For leisure, he enjoyed sailing his yacht — the *Myth* — off the south coast of Ireland. At the time of his death, the *Daily Express* wrote that Murphy's personality was 'a case of the iron hand in the velvet glove. Behind the blue-eye dwelt the soul of iron' {*Independent* 28 June 1919}.

William Murphy married in 1870 Mary Julia (d 1900), the daughter of James Fitzgerald Lombard, JP, of South Hill, County Dublin. They had three sons and three daughters.

William Murphy died in Dublin on 25 June 1919. In his will Murphy left a personal estate of £264,005 on which death duty was £36,185. William Murphy also left £19,175 in England. A sum of £2,000 was left for charity and £200 to be spent on Masses. His typist got one year's salary; his housekeeper received £70; his butler was left £50, the gardener got £25 and a pension of £1 a week and each of his domestics received three months wages.

DERMOT KEOGH

Writings:

The Irish Industrial Question a lecture delivered for the Wood-quay National Registration Club, 10 Jan 1887 (Dublin: M H Gill & Son, 1887).

The Home Rule Act 1914 Exposed (Dublin, 1917).

Sources:

Unpublished

National Library of Ireland, papers of William O'Brien MP.

PRO Dublin, Dublin Chamber of Commerce (DCC) Minutes 1911.

PrC.

PrC (Ireland).

Published

Dublin United Tramways Company (1896) Ltd, Meeting of Motormen, Conductors, Antient Concert Rooms, 19 July 1913 (1913).

Leslie Hannah, *Electricity before Nationalisation: A Study of the Development of the Electricity Supply Industry in Britain to 1948* (Macmillan, 1979).

Independent 28 June 1919.

Irish Worker 1912-13.

Dermot Keogh, *The Rise of the Irish Working Class: The Dublin Trade Union Movement and Labour Leadership 1819-1914* (Belfast: Appleton Press, 1982).

Robert B McDowell, *The Irish Convention 1917-1918* (Routledge & Kegan Paul, 1970).

William Lombard Murphy, address on William Martin Murphy, 29 June 1941, in *Souvenir of Presentation by the Staff of Independent Newspapers Ltd, to Dr William Lombard Murphy* on the completion of twenty-one years as chairman of the company (Dublin: pp, 1941).

Patrick J Walsh, *William J Walsh, Archbishop of Dublin* (Dublin: Talbot Press, 1928).

Arnold Wright, *Disturbed Dublin* (Longmans & Co, 1914). This was commissioned by the Dublin employers following the 1913 lock-out.

WWMP.

WWW.

MURRANT, Sir Ernest Henry

(1889-1974)

Shipping executive

Ernest Henry Murrant was born at Brixton, London, on 15 July 1889, the son of Henry John Murrant, a grocer's assistant, and later a self-employed builder in South London, and his wife Minna Augusta Schultz. His education cut short by family circumstances, Murrant joined Furness

Sir Ernest Murrant (courtesy of the Furness Withy Group).

Withy's London branch as an office-boy at £20 a year on 3 November 1902, following an introduction secured by his father. He would remain there, apart from wartime interruptions, for over fifty-six years. His outstanding shorthand skills soon brought him to the notice of his superiors and, when a vacancy arose as secretary to Frederick Lewis (qv), later deputy chairman, Murrant was appointed. At the outbreak of war in 1914 he joined the Board of Trade as a member of the Shipping Control Committee, advising upon the collection and distribution to Allied owners of neutral and captured enemy tonnage, work for which he was awarded the MBE.

Sir Frederick Lewis, Murrant's friend and sponsor, became chairman of Furness Withy in 1919 when the company was reorganised to buy out the Furness family interest. Murrant, in the right place at the right time, now worked closely with Lewis not just as personal secretary but with responsibility for seeing through his chairman's ideas. When the Danube Navigation Co was formed to acquire German and Austro-Hungarian holdings in river navigation under Furness Withy's management, Murrant became secretary and Lewis chairman. In 1924 Murrant was elected a director of Furness Withy and in 1935 deputy chairman. By then Furness Withy had become a highly-diversified multinational company which not only operated on its own account but had acquired control (partly or wholly) of 30 or more concerns, ranging from other shipping companies like Houlder Brothers and Royal Mail lines to hotel and tourist facilities in Bermuda, stevedoring, port agencies and a financial trust. Perhaps exploiting his acquired experience of Balkan shipping, Murrant was in 1941 designated by the Minister of War Transport as Special Representative in the Near East, responsible for co-ordinating Allied tonnage, liaising with friendly Governments and advising the Middle East Supply Centre, services recognised by the award of the KCMG in 1945. Upon the death of Sir Frederick Lewis (then Lord Essendon) in 1944, Sir Ernest Murrant returned home to be appointed Furness Withy's chairman.

Sir Ernest's chairmanship was uncontroversial. Despite spiralling working costs, flags of convenience and the new regulatory framework of exchange controls, the post-war period was not all gloom. Furness Withy emerged with large cash balances while freight rates (boosted by the Korean War and the Suez Crisis) remained high until the end of the 1950s, apart from the slump of 1953-54. A conservative board restrained dividends (even when the Government relaxed corporate regulations), heavily wrote down asset values and accumulated reserves of some £23 million by 1959. Consequently, new tonnage and American liberty ships were gradually acquired to replace war losses and extend the group's fleets by some 500,000 tons of modern shipping, even though construction costs were two or three times above pre-war levels. Under Murrant's chairmanship (1945-59) Furness Withy doubled its own fleet from 85,000 to 167,000 tons and raised its fixed assets from £9.5 million to over £17 million largely by investing profits. Passenger and cargo routes lost to neutral or American tonnage were re-entered, new ones opened in South Africa and the Far East, and the less successful abandoned — in Roumania which Soviet tonnage dominated, in Newfoundland where air services replaced shipping, and on the United States-River Plate route, from which the cross-traders were excluded. The damage to North Pacific cargoes of a devalued pound was offset by expanding earnings from the American tourist trade to Bermuda. Furness Withy also diversified into new complementary operations, Furness (Canada) Ltd and Airwork, developed by a consortium of shipowners.

Murrant's personal style of leadership was probably more in tune with that of autocratic chief executives epitomised by Lord Essendon, than with the decentralised managerial system that followed. The benefit of hindsight, then, rather suggests that Furness Withy and Sir Ernest missed the post-war winds of economic change. Administrator rather than innovator, Murrant conceived his task as the preservation of Furness Withy's independence, gathering up the pre-war threads and ensuring efficient fleet operation. He, like so many British shipowners, looked back rather than forward to the new challenges of giant tankers, containers and roll-on, roll-off facilities, which were largely ignored until the 1960s. To this misallocation of resources was added the group's honourable but ultimately dangerous reluctance to rationalise services fully and abandon those that did not pay. The traditional pricing policy of what the market would bear still prevailed over one based on actual costs, which might have upset shippers. Project appraisal thus remained rule of thumb, guided by 'feel' rather than by discounted cash-flow techniques. Murrant was a competent, if conventional, chairman, for under his stewardship untangling the wartime muddle to retrieve the company's 1939 position took precedence. It may be true that the post-war freight market did not return to 'normal' until the end of the 1950s, by which time it was too late. In any event Murrant did not have to grapple with these new problems, since ill-health forced his retirement in March 1959.

Beyond his many City directorships in shipping, banking (Barclays Bank), finance and insurance, Sir Ernest's public career reflected his position and his own keen interest in the welfare of seafarers, which remained active even after he left business. He became president of the Chamber of Shipping, 1947-48, but he was also chairman of the Committee of Management of the Seamen's Hospital Society for over twenty years until 1967, honorary treasurer of the Royal Alfred Merchant Seamen's Society and vice-chairman of the Committee of Management of the Thames Nautical Training College (HMS *Worcester*). In addition to serving upon official investigations of the shipping industry and port efficiency, he was a member both of the Company of Master Mariners and the Worshipful Company of Shipwrights, of which he was prime warden in 1957.

To his business colleagues Sir Ernest may have appeared rather cold, perhaps autocratic, and certainly a determined man with a ferocious capacity for work even in the heat of Cairo. Lord Essendon, whose own standards were exemplary, admired his protégé's keen mind, poise and bureaucratic skills. To his family, he was a devoted husband and kindly father who in his last years preferred the quiet of home to the bustle of society.

Murrant married May, the youngest daughter of John Archer of Belfast, on 1 August 1914; they had two children, one of whom died in infancy. His wife's death in 1973 sapped his will to live. After increasing ill-health Sir Ernest Murrant died on 29 March 1974, survived by an elder sister and his son Geoffrey, who subsequently became deputy-chairman of Furness Withy. Sir Ernest left £325,279 gross.

ROBERT G GREENHILL

Writings:

letter *Times* 19 Apr 1947.

Sources:

Unpublished

PRO, MT 59.

C Reg: Furness Withy (34,810).

BCe.

PrC.

Interview with Geoffrey Stow, former director of Prince Line, 27 Feb 1984.

Interview with Geoffrey Murrant (son), 14 Mar 1984.

Published

Fairplay Annual Survey of British Shipping Finance.

Log May-June 1959, Winter 1974.

PP, Committee of Inquiry into Shipping (Rochdale Report) (1970) Cmnd 4337.

Times 30 Mar 1974.

WWW.

MURRAY, Sir George Evelyn Pemberton

(1880-1947)

Post office administrator

George Evelyn Pemberton Murray was born in London on 25 July 1880, the only son of George Herbert Murray and his wife Mary, daughter of John Mulholland, later First Lord Dunleath (qv). The Murrays were on

Sir Evelyn Murray (a 'Crown Copyright').

the fringes of the aristocracy, and both father and son were at times heir presumptive to the Dukedom of Atholl; Evelyn's grandson indeed succeeded as Tenth Duke in 1957. The family had, however, followed the typical path of junior branches of aristocratic families into the Church. George Herbert Murray (1849-1936) was the son of a clergyman and fellow of All Souls, and after an education at Harrow and Christ Church, Oxford, he entered the Foreign Office in 1873. He transferred to the Treasury in 1880, and in 1897 he was appointed chairman of the Inland Revenue. From 1899 (when he was knighted) until 1903 he was Secretary to the Post Office, and then returned to the Treasury in 1903 as joint Permanent Secretary and, from 1907 until his retirement in 1911, sole Permanent Secretary. After his departure from public office he held directorships of the Westminster Bank and Southern Railway.

Evelyn Murray was therefore born into a family which was intimately connected with the world of politics and public service, and his career developed along similar lines to his father's. He was educated at Eton and Christ Church, Oxford, and he joined the Civil Service in 1903. His first appointment was private secretary to the President of the Board of Education, and his subsequent career progressed rapidly with his promotion to Commissioner of Customs and Excise in 1912, and Secretary of the Post Office in 1914. Evelyn Murray was a member of that administrative élite of classically educated offspring of the professional upper middle class which staffed the higher reaches of Whitehall and the Empire, and he found himself in the possibly anomalous position of running a civil service department which was in many ways a business concern. By 1914, the Post Office employed 250,000 and had an annual revenue of £32.6 million; it had moved beyond its traditional mail services to add such ventures as the Post Office Savings Bank in 1861, and had acquired the private telegraph companies in 1870 and telephone companies in 1912. How well suited was Murray to administer what was arguably the largest business in Britain?

D O Lumley, who was Murray's private secretary from 1922 to 1927, has provided an insight into his working methods. His office hours did not follow the normal habits of St Martin's le Grand, for he arrived a little before noon and remained until 8pm, a pattern which is symptomatic of his apparent avoidance of contact with the rest of the Department. Murray, according to Lumley, 'said very little as a rule, his instructions were laconic and he disliked going into explanations or answering any but the most essential questions' {Post Office archives, Lumley}. When a decision was to be taken, Murray was punctilious about acquiring facts even at the expense of delay, and he would summon officials to supply information. What he would not do was arrange a meeting to discuss an issue; he would also consult the Postmaster General and Treasury alone. This is not to say that all power was retained in his hands, for anything relating to labour relations was left to a subordinate. The general impression of Murray is that he was an aloof, patrician figure who saw his role as assuring that the administrative machinery functioned smoothly, and this produced a deep-rooted caution in the face of change. He certainly had an abiding horror of practices which smacked of business rather than the Civil Service. Viscount Wolmer, reflecting on his term as Assistant Postmaster General, commented in 1932 that 'the Post Office is a great business which is organised not as a business but as a Government Department' {Wolmer (1932) 249}, and Murray's approach would certainly support his contention.

It should be admitted that Murray faced a difficult task when he joined the Department, for the First World War disrupted its functioning. Staff shortages, the dislocation of transport, mounting costs, the need to adjust tariffs and curtail services, dominated his first five years at St Martin's le Grand. After the war, he had to face conflicting pressures for the restoration of pre-war services and the Penny Post on the one hand, and on the other the imperative to recover the financial position of the Department, which had lurched from a surplus of £5.2 million in 1913-14 to a deficit of £6.7 million in 1920-21. It is not surprising that the Post Office was concerned with immediate and pressing issues such as negotiating contracts with railway companies; reducing the cost of road services, in part by replacing outside contracts with 'official' motor services; reabsorbing men after demobilisation; adjusting to the new structure of the Whitley councils and the need for consultation with the staff; and economising on labour costs. There can be no doubt that Murray faced extreme problems of wartime dislocation and post-war reconstruction, and it was no mean achievement to avoid a breakdown in services and to build up the surplus from £4.5 million in 1922-23 to £12.3 million in 1933-34. Murray did help the Department to weather the problems of war, but his administrative strengths were to prove a liability when attention turned to the reform of the structure of the Department.

When Murray joined the Post Office in 1914 there had been a long debate over the need to devolve executive power to the regions, which would permit the Secretary's office in London to concentrate upon the major issues of policy. The overcentralisation of the administration created a bottleneck which was all the more apparent when the telephone companies were nationalised. There was general agreement that devolution of power was necessary, but there had been a marked difference between Murray's immediate predecessors about the best means to this end. The result was stalemate and minimal change, so that the telephone companies were brought into a system which was already considered to be inadequate for the mail service. Sir George Murray, commenting on events from the Treasury, remarked that the highly centralised system had been breaking down for years and that matters could not continue much longer as they were. But the prospect that his son would produce a workable scheme was frustrated by the war. The Select Committee on Telephones after the war did suggest the creation of two distinct organisations for posts and telecommunications and, although this was rejected, in 1922 two new offices were created below the Secretary — the Director of Postal Services and Director of Telegraphs and Telephones. This did nothing, however, to reduce the centralisation of executive power in the hands of the secretariat in London, and pressure was building up in the late 1920s and early 1930s for a fundamental reform. Demands in the Commons eventually led to a committee of enquiry under the chairmanship of Lord Bridgeman which reported in 1932 in favour of a new regional structure with responsibility for executing policy, leaving the headquarters in London to concentrate on the formulation of policy. At the same time, the autocratic position of the Secretary as the sole co-ordinating figure at the head of the hierarchy should be replaced by a functional Board with a Director-General as primus inter pares. These proposals were anathema to Murray, and in his view they were 'based on incomplete knowledge and a misconception of the position, eg they assume that wide delegation would become practicable whereas there is little left to delegate'. The existing system had, in his view, proved its worth and 'it would be safer to mend it rather than to scrap it'. He admitted that 'my own inclination by temperament is to the conservative side' {PO Archives, Post 33/5529, M8566/1940}, and it is not surprising that he departed from the Post Office when the reforms were implemented in 1934. The opinion of Lumley was that 'chinks in the palpably top heavy structure of the Post Office did not show themselves earlier, solely because of the immense administrative ability and experience which Murray brought to its management' {Post Office archives, Lumley}, and this is a fair assessment. Murray was an administrator who could keep a large government department operating on existing lines, but who was loath to make changes.

Evelyn Murray was both the youngest and the longest serving of the Secretaries of the Post Office since the introduction of the Penny Postage in 1840. He and his father were indeed representative figures of the civil service as transformed by the Northcote-Trevelyan report with its rejection of patronage and its emphasis upon entry through success in literary examinations. This was not, of course, to say that a career in the upper echelons of the civil service was open to all talent, for the method by which merit was tested implied a long period of public school and university education. So far as the Post Office was concerned, one result was to remove the chance of rising to the secretaryship by long service within the Department, as had been the case with John Tilley or Frank Ives Scudamore (qv), both of whom came from less elevated social backgrounds.

When Murray left the Post Office he returned to Customs and Excise as chairman, remaining there until his retirement in 1940. He was knighted (KCB) in 1919.

Evelyn Murray married in 1906 Muriel Mildred Elizabeth, daughter of Philip Beresford Hope of Bedgebury Park, Kent; they had a son George Anthony (b 1907), who was killed in command of an artillery regiment in Italy in 1945; his son, George Iain, succeeded as Tenth Duke of Atholl in 1957. Sir Evelyn Murray died on 30 March 1947, leaving £40,415 gross.

M J DAUNTON

Writings:

The Post Office (G P Putnam's & Sons, 1927).

Sources:

Unpublished

Post Office Archives, D O Lumley, 'The Last Secretary to the Post Office', unpublished typescript; Post 33/5529, M8566/1940.

BCe.

PrC.

Published

Burke's Peerage and Baronetage.

M J Daunton, *Royal Mail: The Post Office since 1840* (Athlone, 1985).

DNB.

PP, HC 1922 (54, 54 Ind) VI, SC on Telephone Service.

PP, Committee on Post Office (1931-32) Cmd 4149.

Times 6 Apr 1936, 31 Mar 1947.

Viscount Wolmer, *Post Office Reform: Its Importance and Practicability* (Ivor Nicholson & Watson, 1932).

WWW.

MUSGRAVE, John

(1820-1889)

Engineer

John Musgrave was born at Bolton, Lancashire, on 3 September 1820, the third of four sons of John Musgrave, and his wife Hannah née Brook. His father had come to Bolton in 1804 and with his eldest son Joseph, established the business of John Musgrave & Son, engineers, in 1839 at Globe Ironworks, Kay Street, Bolton.

Little is recorded of his early background except that the family was brought up in the Wesleyan Methodist tradition. It is clear that in due course John was employed in his father's business, and together with his brothers went into partnership with his father in 1852 under the title John Musgrave & Sons, engineers and millwrights.

At this time the Globe Ironworks was conducting general engineering and millwrighting work, particularly for local cotton mills, and since 1841 had also been making stationary steam engines, mostly beam engines of between 20 and 50 nominal horsepower. The engine-making side of the business developed gradually, despite the trade recession of 1847-48, and output increased notably from 1849 onwards. By 1850 a total of 85 engines, totalling approximately 8,405 indicated horsepower (2,788 nominal horse-

Horizontal single cylinder corliss engine by J Musgrave & Sons, Bolton, 1880s, 250 ihp for a cotton weaving mill. From 'Catalogue of Engines' J Musgrave & Sons, ca 1892.

Horizontal tandem compound corliss engine by J Musgrave & Sons, Bolton, for Union Spinning Mills, Bolton 1884, 1250 ihp. It powered 83,000 spindles. From 'Catalogue of Engines' J Musgrave & Sons, ca 1892.

power), had been produced by Musgraves; at that time the Globe Ironworks occupied over two-and-a-half acres. The majority of these engines were built for local cotton mills and, to a lesser extent, local collieries. In 1862 John Musgrave & Sons diversified their interests by taking over the Atlas Mill, Bolton, and this was soon built up into a very extensive cotton spinning business. The engineering business was largely managed by John Musgrave Sr until his death in 1864, together with Joseph and John Jr; Joseph became the senior partner upon his father's death.

John Musgrave became an accomplished engineer and businessman, and travelled abroad extensively for the firm. He visited Russia on many occasions and built up a considerable business with cotton mills in and around Moscow. From the late 1850s and until the early twentieth century, the firm exported mill engines, gearing, and boilers to Russia, which was their single most important export market until the 1890s. Their busiest period in this market was between 1871 and 1880 when at least 100 engines aggregating approximately 20,313 indicated horsepower were built by Musgraves for Russia, mostly for the cotton mills of Moscow and St Petersburg. Between 1858 and 1890 a total of at least 213 Musgrave engines aggregating 53,258 indicated horsepower were constructed by the firm for this market.

During the lifetime of John Musgrave Jr, the Globe Ironworks expanded considerably, covering over eight acres and employing about 1,000 workers by 1894. Between 1841 and 1890, the firm built some 900 engines totalling around 200,000 indicated horsepower; about one-quarter of this output was exported to Russia.

John Musgrave played a leading role in the development of the firm's export trade and was greatly assisted by his older brother Joseph, who in addition to running the engineering business after his father's death, was

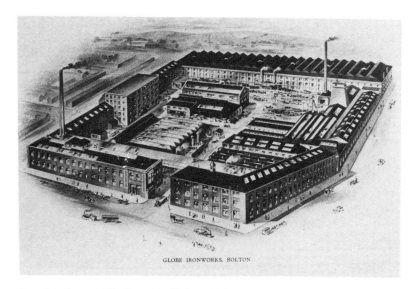

Globe Ironworks, Bolton of John Musgrave & Sons, early 1900. From 'Catalogue of Engines' J Musgrave & Sons, 1913.

also a leading public figure in Bolton. John Musgrave took little active part in the public life of his native Bolton, although he was associated with several charitable institutions and took an interest in the running of the Infirmary. He was a strong Wesleyan Methodist and a Conservative, following the family tradition, but he held no office at the Park Street Church he attended, nor in politics. He married but had no children. In his later life he handed over some of the foreign business of the firm to his favourite nephew, Herbert Musgrave, and, after a long illness, died on 3 April 1889, leaving £116,777 gross.

D A COLLIER

Sources:

Unpublished

Hick, Hargreaves & Co Ltd, Bolton, engine records of John Musgrave & Sons.

PrC.

Published

Bolton Chronicle 6 Apr, 18 May 1889.

Engineer 12 Apr 1889.

'Pioneers of the Cotton Trade: The Musgrave Family' *Bolton Journal and Guardian* 16 June 1933.

Sir Max Muspratt (courtesy of CBI).

MUSPRATT, Sir Max

(1872-1934)

Industrialist

Max Muspratt was born at Seaforth Hall, Litherland, north of Liverpool, on 3 February 1872. He was the fifth of eight children born to Edmund Knowles Muspratt and his wife Frances Jane née Baines. The origin of the Muspratt family is not clear, but Max's grandfather, James Muspratt, came to Liverpool from Dublin in 1821 and was responsible for erecting one of the largest alkali works for producing soda by the Leblanc process. Because of the difficulty of operating these large works (due to the obnoxious by-products) James was forced to move his works to St. Helens, Newton-le-Willows and Widnes. His sons, James Sheridan, Frederick, Richard, as well as Edmund Knowles, were all involved to a greater or lesser extent in the running of the family's chemical works.

After his early education at Hemel Hempstead and Clifton College, Max followed his grandfather and uncles into chemistry and was sent to the Zurich Polytechnic in Switzerland. There in 1892, he became the first Englishman to win the Swiss Government's Diploma in Industrial Chemistry. He began working at the family's works in Widnes, Lancashire, gaining knowledge and experience of all aspects of the alkali trade. In 1891 the Muspratts together with most of the other alkali manufacturers using the Leblanc process, formed themselves into the United Alkali Co in an effort to unite against the competition provided by Brunner, Mond & Co Ltd, who were producing cheaper soda by the Solvay process.

The UAC, with a subscribed capital of £8.2 million, was the largest chemical business in the world. Size was no measure of efficiency, however. A cumbersome board of 27 members (representing the family interests of constituent firms like the Tennants, Gaskells and Gambles) stifled much chance of achieving vigorous management for the UAC's 48 factories in Lancashire, the North East and Glasgow. By 1893 the UAC's profits were falling behind those of Brunner, Mond. Clinging to outdated technology (not least because of the conservative attitudes of its head of research, a Swiss), the UAC sought survival through price and output agreements with Brunner, Mond and smaller competitors (in 1895 and 1907). Well before 1913, when the UAC's profits were the worst in its history and its capital was reduced from £8,853,670 to £6,367,368, the United Alkali Co was recognised as the dying giant of the industry.

Max Muspratt made little impact in reversing the UAC's long term decline. Elected a director in 1901 with special responsibility for the technical side he failed to reverse the UAC's stubborn rejection of electrolysis and the possibilities of electro chemistry. After he became chairman of UAC in succession to his father in 1914 the 'accident of war' gave the illusion of revival. Without wartime demands for picric acid,

ammonium nitrate, ammonium perchlorate, chlorine and mustard gas —
for explosives and gas warfare — the UAC, Muspratt admitted in 1916,
'would by then have been in "a condition ... of considerable financial
difficulty"' {Reader (1970) 289}. During the war Muspratt himself was
consulted constantly by the Ministry of Munitions about chemical matters
and it was largely in recognition of these services that he was created a
baronet in 1922.

With a management characterised by nepotism and exhaustion and
clinging to obsolete technology, the UAC board was not even consulted
when Alfred Mond and Harry McGowan (qqv), troubled by German and
American competition, in October 1926 agreed upon a major defensive
merger in the British chemical industry. The UAC, proud of departed
glory, at first resisted the projected merger which formed Imperial
Chemical Industries. As respective heads of Brunner, Mond & Co Ltd and
Nobel Industries Ltd, Mond and McGowan evidently made it clear to Sir
Max Muspratt that they 'were determined to go ahead whether or not
UAC came in' {ibid, 464}. The UAC did not join Brunner, Mond, Nobel
Industries and the British Dyestuffs Corporation in signing the share
exchange agreement of 21 October 1926. However, Muspratt persuaded
his board to participate in the merger and the UAC gained two seats on the
ICI board instead of the one originally proposed. Sir Max Muspratt
became one of the first ICI directors, apparently with responsibility for the
Liverpool activities of his firm, holding his seat until his death.

As a result of his standing in the chemical industry he became deputy
chairman of the Sulphuric Acid Association, chairman of the Association
of British Chemical Manufacturers in 1924 and, in 1926, president of the
Federation of British Industries. He was also vice-president of the Society
of Chemical Industry, and chairman of the Liverpool Section of that
Society. His other business activities included a directorship of the
International Automatic Telephone Co; in 1926 Muspratt was appointed
by the Ministry of Transport as its nominee to the board of the Mersey
Docks & Harbour Board. He was a freeman of the Worshipful Company of
Patten Makers and of the Dyers Company.

Muspratt played a prominent part in local political life. Liberalism, like
chemistry, was a family tradition and Muspratt became a Radical and a
Free Trader like his father and grandfather. From 1895 he engaged in
political activity at Widnes and between 1903 and 1934 he sat almost
continuously on Liverpool City Council, representing the Princess Park
ward and (after 1908) Vauxhall ward. Able and much respected, he was
Lord Mayor of Liverpool in 1916-17. In 1918 he succeeded Sir William
Bowring as Liberal leader on the Liverpool council and afterwards
continued to support the coalition led by Lloyd George, but when it fell
'he found the atmosphere of the orthodox Liberal camp too chilly,
especially for a Free Trader with reservations' {Liverpolitan Oct 1932}. In
1926 he joined the Conservatives in the Council Chamber and was
chairman of the powerful Finance Committee at the time of his death.
From 1907 he was a JP for Lancashire, and a member of the Council of
Liverpool University. Briefly he was Liberal MP for the Exchange
division of Liverpool, January-December 1910. After losing the Bootle
division to Bonart Law in March 1911 he abandoned his attempts to get
into the House of Commons.

Max Muspratt married in 1896 Helena, daughter of T W Ainsworth of Blackburn; they had two sons, Rudolph and Terence, and two daughters, Frances and Vanda. Lady Muspratt was also very active in political and social work. The two sons predeceased their father.

Sir Max Muspratt died on 20 April 1934 at his home The Grange, Fulwood Park, Liverpool following an operation. He left £208,045 gross.

PETER N REED

Sources:

Unpublished

BCe.

PrC.

Published

Chemistry and Industry 27 Apr 1934.

Kelly's Handbook to the Titled, Landed and Official Classes 1931.

Liverpolitan Oct 1932.

E K Muspratt, *My Life and Work* (John Lane, 1917).

William T Pike (ed), *Liverpool and Birkenhead in the Twentieth Century — Contemporary Biographies* (Brighton: W T Pike & Co, 1911).

William J Reader, *Imperial Chemical Industries. A History* (2 vols, Oxford University Press, 1970-75).

M D Stephens and G W Roderick, 'The Muspratts of Liverpool' *Annals of Science* 29 (1972).

Times 21 Apr 1934.

WWMP.

WWW.

N

NAPIER, Montague Stanley

(1870-1931)

Car manufacturer and aero-engine designer

Montague Stanley Napier was born at 68 York Road, Lambeth, South London, on 14 April 1870, the fourth son of James Murdoch Napier and his wife Fanny Jemima née Mackenzie. He came from a family of Scottish engineers descended from Robert Napier (1726-1805), a Dunbartonshire blacksmith, and his wife Jean Denny (1722-1800). Montague Napier's grandfather David (1790?-1873), a pupil of Henry Maudslay, moved from the Clyde in the 1830s and by 1836 founded in York Road, Lambeth, a business which specialised in printing machinery for the expanding newspaper industry of the day. David's younger son James Murdoch Napier, though a competent, even brilliant, engineer and inventor, was an opinionated eccentric who cared little for commercial success. He built precision machinery for arsenals, banks and mints which in its day had a high reputation but by the time he died, in 1895, the business of D Napier & Son had faded almost to extinction.

Nothing is known about Montague's education — he was very secretive about many things — but he was 'introduced into the practical side of the business at an early age' {*Times* 28 Jan 1931} and on his father's death he bought the family business from the executors. Like many other mechanical engineers, Montague Napier turned his attention to motor cars, and about 1899 he was introduced to S F Edge (qv), a brilliant salesman seeking to turn his talents to account in the infant motor industry. Napier's engineering ability seemed to Edge exactly what he needed as a complement to his own marketing flair, and with financial backing from Harvey du Cros (qv) Edge set up the Motor Vehicle Co which contracted with Napier to buy all the cars he could make. The arrangement did not go unremarked by another aggressive motor car salesman in search of an engineer, and about five years later the Honourable C S Rolls (qv) came to terms in rather the same way with Henry Royce (qv).

In 1902 Napiers's works were moved from Lambeth to a roomier site at Acton. Success, over the years that followed, was founded on a combination of advanced engineering — in 1904 Napiers launched the first commercially successful six-cylinder engine — and strenuous goggles-and-dust promotion by Edge in tests, trials and racing, and the partners aimed right at the top of the market. They also took advantage of less glamorous opportunities. Four-cylinder and even two-cylinder cars were built, so were taxis — more than 1,000 in 1909 and 1910 — and 'business vehicles'. By 1906 Napiers had assets of £216,373 and employed 1,000 people at Acton.

Edge's and Napier's business, as it developed, was extending towards workaday vehicles, but at its height its strength lay in large, powerful, hand-built cars in which the personal quirks of the buyer were given the freest possible rein, at an appropriate price. The competition was with Rolls-Royce, not with Ford or Morris (qv), and mass-production did not enter into Napier's scheme of things. Between 1906 and 1924, when the last Napiers were made, the firm made 8,582 vehicles of all kinds, of which only 4,258 were cars, whereas Morris's output for 1924 alone was 5,000.

The partnership between Edge and Napier broke up in acrimony, in the face of competition from Rolls-Royce and others, in 1912. Edge thought Napier's quality control was growing slack: Napier thought Edge was too greedy in his mark-up. Napier bought Edge out and set up a new public company, D Napier & Son Ltd, with a share capital of £650,000 and £100,000 5.5 per cent first mortgage debenture stock, which embarked on plans for a range of cars very different from any that the firm had put on the market before.

These plans were frustrated by the outbreak of war in 1914. Napiers went on making motor vehicles, in decreasing numbers, but Montague Napier's attention was diverted towards aero-engines. After experience at Acton of making engines designed elsewhere, Napier undertook to develop an engine at his own expense, on the understanding that if it were successful he should have his money back from the company and royalties when production started. He came to an agreement with the authorities in July 1916 and began to work on ideas which took shape, just before the end of the war, in the Lion, a water-cooled engine with 12 cylinders arranged in the form of a broad arrow, developing 450 hp at 2,000 rpm and weighing a little less than 850 lb.

In 1924 Jane's *All the World's Aircraft* showed 73 types of British aircraft flying, of which 35 might be fitted with Napier's engines, nearly all Lions. The only British competitors were Rolls-Royce, making engines for 16 types, Armstrong-Siddeley (11) and Bristol (6). By 1927 Napiers were employing about 1,600 men and turning out about 50 engines a month, for British and foreign customers.

With Series VII, especially designed for racing, the Lion was spectacularly successful in Schneider Cup air races and in speed record attempts in the air, on the water and on land. In other forms, culminating in Series XI (540 hp), it gave good service over long distances. At one time it was advisable to carry chewing gum for running repairs, but as early as 1926 Imperial Airways' Lions had flown more than two million miles, and the engine had established a reputation for reliability.

In 1915 Montague Napier's health broke down. In 1917 he withdrew permanently to Cannes, where he set up a design office. He remained a large shareholder in D Napier & Son and his personality was strong enough, when he wished, to have a decisive effect on decisions of policy, but his formal relationship with the business became that of a designer on a very lucrative agreement, and in theory there was nothing to stop him from making similar agreements with other aero-engine makers. In 1928, when the Lion was approaching obsolescence, the firm entered into an agreement with F B Halford (qv), one of the most eminent engine-designers of his day, but the link with Montague Napier was preserved.

Napier was a figure of the very early days of the aircraft industry, when it was feasible for one man to contemplate the development of an aero-engine virtually from his own resources, with nothing in the way of elaborate research and development facilities or immense financial reserves to back him up. With only one customer to rely on — the Air Ministry — the risk was high, and when the Cub, Napier's intended 1,000 hp successor to the Lion, was rejected by the Ministry, after initial encouragement and a promising start, Napier had nothing to put in its place. The individualist's day had passed.

Montague Napier's career was blighted by ill-health from the age of forty-seven onward: what he might otherwise have made of his business we shall never know. He had two very great successes: the pre-1914 Napier cars and the Lion engine, but in each of his chosen fields he was eventually outstripped by Rolls-Royce, a firm with a much keener cutting edge of commercial acumen and a related willingness to face the necessity of large-scale organisation which success implied. Had Montague Napier been a fit man, the story might have been different.

Montague Napier died at the age of sixty, on 22 January 1931. He was by then very rich, for he left £1,200,208 net personalty (£1,267,662 gross). His nurse and reputed mistress, Norah Fryer, was well provided for, but in his will there is no mention of his wife and his bequests to his children are hedged with the threat that any child who challenged the provisions of the will should forfeit all interest thereunder. The residue of the estate, after Mrs Fryer's death, was to go to cancer research. He left no related successor in the business, and after a distant cousin, I P R Napier, ceased to be a director in 1942, when D Napier & Son was taken over by English Electric, the family connection was broken.

W J READER

Sources:

Unpublished

BCe.

PrC.

Published

Selwyn F Edge, *My Motoring Reminiscences* (G T Foulis & Co, 1934).

St John Cousins Nixon, *The Antique Automobile* (Cassells, 1956).

David Scott-Moncrieff, *Veteran and Edwardian Motor Cars* (B T Batsford, 1963).

Times 28 Jan 1931.

Charles H Wilson and William J Reader, *Men and Machines, A History of D Napier & Son Engineers Ltd 1808-1958* (Weidenfeld & Nicolson, 1958).

NEALE, Edward Vansittart

(1810-1892)

Christian socialist and organiser of the Co-operative movement

Edward Vansittart Neale was born at Bath, on 2 April 1810, the son of Rev Edward Neale, LLB, an Evangelical and Rector of Taplow, Buckinghamshire, and his second wife, Anne, the second surviving daughter of Isaac Spooner, of Elmdon, near Birmingham.

Initially he was educated solely by his father, a strict disciplinarian, but was later taught at a private school in Hitcham before going up to Oriel College, Oxford, at the age of seventeen. The period at Oxford was an important one, not so much for his intellectual achievements — a third class in Classics and a second in mathematics — but for his friendship with a young fellow of Oriel, John Henry Newman, the Tractarian and future cardinal. Newman's rejection of fervent Evangelicalism together with his belief that true happiness could only be found by the sublimating of one's own interests in the needs of others furnished the major foundation of Neale's philosophy of life.

Contrary to his father's wishes, instead of becoming a clergyman, he entered Lincoln's Inn in 1832 and was called to the Bar five years later, becoming a Chancery barrister almost immediately. At law he was conscientious and moderately successful, but the work was unsatisfactory, and he devoted his leisure to reading authors who sought a progressive social message in the Christian gospel. In the 1840s he began to study utopian socialism, met occasionally with the Odd Fellows, and joined forces with the Law Amendment Society.

In 1850 Neale was attracted to the Society for Promoting Working Men's Associations, which brought him into the world of the Christian Socialists, his wealth and social position inevitably bringing him membership of its governing Council of Promoters. Hence Neale became aware of the northern co-operative stores which had followed the successful example set by the Rochdale Equitable Pioneers in 1844. Soon converted to a belief in co-operation, in October 1850 Neale opened his own experimental co-operative store at 76 Charlotte Street, Fitzroy Square, London, on the site of an old Owenite centre. Prominent Christian Socialists such as Thomas Hughes, Jules Lechevalier and Lloyd Jones, alongside an expert in the grocery business, Joseph Woodin, were recruited to run what was essentially a wholesaling organisation, though it could also function as an exchange agency for goods made by societies of producers. This was expanded in 1851 into the Central Co-operative Agency, which, to some extent, anticipated the later Co-operative Wholesale Society, though some of the Christian Socialists strongly disapproved of it.

Neale determined to create a new organisation which could accommodate his own ideals, and those of his fellow Christian Socialists, while being catholic enough to include Owenites, secularists and anyone else who cared to join. In 1852, therefore, he founded the Co-operative League, largely as an educational centre, where papers could be read by members as well as other prominent co-operators and social theorists. He also attempted to marshal all independent co-operative activities under common operating procedures and rules, publishing a number of guides, such as *Suggestions to Aid in the Formation of a Legal Constitution for Working Men's Associations* (1852). The League soon expired, though it had brought Neale into contact with the foremost leaders of English and French socialism.

During the great engineers' strike in 1852 Neale lent both moral and financial support to the Amalgamated Society of Engineers. Besides appearing at a meeting of the metropolitan trades he also wrote *May I Not Do What I Will with My Own?* (1852). When the men were defeated, Neale purchased the Atlas Ironworks, Southwark, where he established the leading engineers in a productive association. But skilled workers proved unable to manage it and the scheme was a total failure. Neale's other scheme, the Central Co-operative Agency, also ran into difficulties at this time and it was finally forced to close its doors in 1857. Since the backing for these ventures came entirely from Neale's own pocket, the failures brought him a severe financial loss, which he later estimated at £40,000. Despite these problems and setbacks he had 'worked out a practical mechanics for implementing [his co-operative] principles and in doing so laid the foundation for the modern Co-operative Movement' {Backstrom (1974) 44}. At a short series of Christian Socialist conferences in the 1850s he mapped out much of the future direction of the co-operative movement: he inspired the Rochdale Pioneers to establish a Wholesale Department; initiated a co-operative banking society; founded a short-lived newspaper, the *Co-operative Commercial Circular*; and in the Industrial and Provident Societies Union provided a central headquarters.

Meanwhile, he gave evidence before the Select Committee on the Savings of the Middle and Working Classes, which reported in 1850. When the resulting Industrial and Provident Societies Act (1852) legalised co-operatives and led to a great expansion of the movement, Neale closely associated himself with the northern co-operators, though this did not prevent him keeping in touch with the Society of Promoters (now merged in the Working Men's College). He was particularly active as a legal adviser, usually charging an extremely modest fee (for his extensive involvement with the Industrial and Provident Societies Bill of 1862 his fee to the Rochdale Pioneers was only 7 guineas). He prepared, wholly or in part, all the amendments proposed in the Act of 1852; and the

Consolidation Act (1862) and the Industrial and Provident Societies Act (1876) were mainly due to his efforts. His other 'unofficial' work on behalf of the co-operators included a prolific outpouring of pamphlets, articles, published advice, and a major statement of his Christian Socialist views, *The Analogy of Thought and Nature Investigated* (1863).

In 1863 he drafted the rules for registration of the North of England Co-operative Wholesale Agency & Depot Ltd, which, as the Co-operative Wholesale Society (CWS), was to become the great success story of the co-operative movement with a membership by the end of the decade approaching a quarter of a million and a turnover of nearly £2 million. Neale was also one of the founders of the Cobden Memorial Mills in 1866, and of the Agricultural and Horticultural Association in 1867, which aimed to extend co-operation into agriculture.

In the 1860s and 1870s there was a revival of interest in co-operative production, partly due to the publicity accorded the work of Edward Owen Greening in founding a number of industrial partnerships. Despite Neale's antipathy to trade unions, no doubt stimulated by his past failures with workingmen's associations, he was drawn into the movement. In 1867 Greening called for an Industrial Partnerships Conference which Neale attended: this led in 1869 to the First Co-operative Congress in London, out of which grew Neale's long-awaited Co-operative Union. Neale became one of the most active promoters of the annual co-operative congress. After 1873 he took on both the secretarial duties of the union (initially at £250 a year) and its legal business, for which he received no pay. His untiring efforts as legal adviser, organiser and propagandist, alongside his official duties, made him an almost indispensable element in the co-operative movement.

For seventeen years Neale was a director of the Co-operative Insurance Co, and for sixteen years a member of the committee of the Co-operative Newspaper Society. He fostered international links in co-operation by corresponding with foreign members and attending Continental congresses. In 1875 he founded the Mississippi Valley Trading Co, a scheme for international co-operation between the American Patrons of Husbandry (the Grangers) and British co-operators. A disillusioning trip to America in 1875, however, convinced Neale that his ambitious scheme of exporting cotton from New Orleans and linking the fortunes of the British movement with those of the fragmented Grangers was not economically viable. Nevertheless, Neale drew up co-operative plans for the Grange which were later of great benefit during the agricultural depression.

Neale retired from the secretaryship on 11 September 1891 at the age of eighty-one, though this meant no reduction in his legal duties for such organisations as the Labour Association and the Guild of Co-operators. At the end of his life, in an address to the Birmingham conference 'The True Objects of Co-operative Production', Neale reiterated his central tenets of co-operation and warned against the enormous development of consumer co-operative societies on the one hand and the spread of socialist panacea on the other. Although Neale regarded it as important that the working classes became their own shopkeepers, his main object was to raise their condition as producers. However, he failed to convince the wholesale society of the need for this course, and so shortly before his death he abandoned the Consumers' Movement which he had supported for more than forty years and turned his attention to the creation of an entirely new union.

In 1892 he retired to his country estate, Bisham Abbey, which he had inherited in 1885. He died in London on 16 September 1892, leaving £14,534 gross. He had married in 1847 Frances Sarah, eldest daughter of Sir James William Farrer, Bt, Master in Chancery. The marriage, which produced two sons and three daughters, was an unfortunate one since Neale's wife shared none of his views and for most of his life they met only occasionally.

GEOFFREY TWEEDALE

Writings:

The following is only a selection of Neale's output: for a fuller listing see Backstrom, below.

May I Not Do What I Will With My Own? (1852).

Suggestions to Aid in the Formation of a Legal Constitution for Working Men's Associations (J J Bezer, 1852).

The Co-operator's Hand-Book, Containing the Laws Relating to a Company of Limited Liability (1861).

The Analogy of Thought and Nature Investigated (Hertford, 1863).

The 'Co-operative News' and Why Co-operators Should Support It (Manchester: Co-operative Printing Society, 1878).

The Economics of Co-operation (Manchester: Co-operative Printing Society, 1885).

The Common Sense of Co-operation (Manchester: Central Co-operative Board, 1886).

Sources:

Unpublished

Neale's papers are in the possession of the family, Bisham Grange, Marlow, Buckinghamshire. For the various locations of Neale's voluminous correspondence, consult Backstrom, below.

PrC.

Published

Philip N Backstrom, *Christian Socialism and Co-operation in Victorian England: Edward Vansittart Neale and the Co-operative Movement* (Croom Helm, 1974).

Torben Christensen, *Origin and History of Christian Socialism 1845-54* (Aarhus, 1962).

DLB.

DNB.

George J Holyoake, *The History of Co-operation* (2 vols, T Fisher Unwin, 1906).

Thomas Hughes, 'Edward Vansittart Neale as Christian Socialist' *Economic Review* 3 (1893).

NELSON, Sir Amos

(1860-1947)

Textile manufacturer

Amos Nelson (from Nelsons of Nelson The story of James Nelson Ltd, 1881-1951).

Amos Nelson was born at Winewall Bridge, Colne, Lancashire, on 31 January 1860, the son of James Nelson, a powerloom overlooker, and his wife Mary Ann née Hartley. His ancestors were handloom weavers, and his father, James Nelson (1831-1912), who started work at the age of eleven, became a powerloom weaver and rose to the position of manager at Christopher Armstrong's mill in 1867. When this mill closed in 1881, James Nelson, accompanied by his wife and six children, moved to Nelson then becoming a major centre for the production of fine cotton fabrics. With savings of £1,200, he purchased 100 looms and rented 'room and power' in a mill. His eldest son, Amos Nelson, who started work as a full-time twister at thirteen and became an apprentice weaver in 1876, had saved £200 by the time he was twenty-one and became a partner in the venture.

In the next forty years James Nelson & Son grew into one of the largest weaving firms in the country. Within fifteen years the partners had 748 looms in six mills weaving strong lustrous cotton cloth for the China market. In 1894-95, they erected the large Valley Mills, starting with 1,200 looms, and four years later added a doubling mill where yarn was gassed in secrecy for venetian fabrics which were used as a lining cloth. A nearby firm with a further 400 looms was acquired in 1907 to increase the output of this fabric. After 1909, the Nelsons made poplins for dresses and skirting. In 1912 they ran 3,000 looms and employed 2,000 hands in their doubling and weaving mills together. Their annual output of 20 million yards was further increased by government requirements during the First World War. To secure their yarn production, the firm purchased a controlling interest in spinning and doubling firms, and at the end of the war had eight mills producing yarn and cloth. After James Nelson's death, a private limited company was formed in 1914, and Amos Nelson presided over a board dominated by the third generation for the next thirty-three years.

At the end of the war, the company encountered its first serious setback.

Its mills were closed for three months in 1921. An intensive marketing campaign in the United States brought a temporary respite. Realising the inevitability of a long-run decline in the industry's export trade, Nelson invested in the production of rayon fabrics and organised a world-wide marketing network through associated companies. A subsidiary, Lustrafil Ltd, produced viscose yarn at the Valley Mills in 1924, introduced pot-spinning in 1929 and subsequently pioneered a system of continuous spinning. From 1929, Nelson Silk Ltd made acetate yarn at Lancaster. As the company moved into the manufacture of elaborate rayon fabrics, it modified its marketing system. Instead of selling cloth to merchant converters, Nelson acquired five subsidiaries in Manchester and Bradford which specialised in finishing and selling the company's branded fabrics in both popular and high-class markets at home, and in regional markets overseas.

Nelson's interest in production and product innovation in spinning and weaving contrasted sharply with the poor record of Brookes & Doxey (1920) Ltd, textile machinery makers of Manchester and Todmorden of which he was chairman, 1920-47. Brookes & Doxey joined the Textile Machinery Makers Ltd when it was formed in 1931 with Sir George Bullough (qv) as chairman but Amos Nelson himself was pointedly excluded from the board, the only chairman of a constituent firm of TMM to be so black-balled. In the 1930s, perhaps in reaction to his personal exclusion from TMM, Amos Nelson directed his manufacturing companies to pursue technical change in the synthetic fibre field. One of his companies was developing a new process for the continuous spinning of viscose rayon yarn, when war broke out, halting development in 1939.

Within his own firm Nelson introduced a number of welfare provisions. In 1909 he proposed a profit-sharing scheme which was rejected by the workforce. During the First World War, he paid a weekly allowance to dependents of employees on active service, and as a war memorial provided sports facilities and a social club for employees.

The prominence of James Nelson & Son in Nelson (by 1914 they were the town's largest employers of labour) made Amos Nelson a major figure in the industrial relations of the industry. The Nelson Weavers Association was in the inter-war years the most politically radical and industrially militant of all the Lancashire cotton-trade unions. In 1928 conflict locally between the union and employers came to a head in a town lock-out over the issue of a 1s fine of an operative, a vice-president of the union. The lock-out lasted for seven weeks and Amos Nelson feared that the town would lose its trade as a consequence, Nelson being more prosperous than most Lancashire cotton towns in the 1920s.

He intervened with the help of the town's Labour mayor, Andrew (later Sir Andrew) Smith and tried to bring the two sides together, offering to employ the weaver, who had been first fined and then dismissed, himself. When this was not successful he attempted to persuade a number of fellow employers in the town to suspend the practice of fining operatives for an experimental period of a year. This so infuriated his fellow employers that their organisation, the Cotton Spinners and Manufacturers Association, threatened to take action against him if he did not withdraw.

Despite his unsuccessful attempts as mediator, Sir Amos Nelson (he was knighted in 1922) became known throughout Lancashire as an industrial statesman. This reputation was strengthened during the 'more looms' question in Lancashire in the early 1930s when he achieved an agreement with the trade unions where other employers had failed. Contemporaries found it particularly baffling that this agreement was made with the very union that was the most bitter in its opposition to the proposed new changes! Fellow employers were particularly angry at his ability to work with the unions, afraid that it would give James Nelson & Son a competitive advantage. The 'more looms' experiment was an attempt to alter working practices in the industry: weavers were to mind eight looms rather than the traditional four. The experiment had been first tried in Burnley, where Sir Amos was chairman of the Chamber of Commerce, but soon after the experiment had begun it met growing union hostility which produced two industry-wide disputes, the 1931 weaving lock-out and the 1932 weaving strike. Sir Amos began negotiations in 1930 towards an agreement with the local Nelson Weavers Association and the county's Amalgamated Weavers Association to introduce a 'more looms' system into his own factories. He, however, offered much higher wages of 60s compared with 50s in Burnley plus fall back pay and a minimum wage. These were the very measures that his fellow employers were not prepared to grant to the union. Even more threatening as far as other employers were concerned was that he was introducing the system with semi-automatic looms which required increased investment.

The provisional agreement of 1930 so outraged his fellow employers that the Cotton Spinners and Manufacturers Association again intervened forcing Sir Amos to end negotiations. The deepening of the economic crisis in 1931 led Sir Amos to defy his fellow manufacturers and re-negotiate the previous year's agreement which was now put into effect. The working of the new 'more looms' system was investigated by the Shirley Institute in Manchester which confirmed its success especially for the operatives. The contrast between Sir Amos's success and the bitter and disastrous history of industrial relations in the cotton industry, especially in its weaving section, could not be more marked. That this was achieved in a town noted nationally for its trade union strength was even more remarkable.

In 1894 Amos was elected to the Nelson town council serving as mayor 1904-6. Originally a Liberal, in 1910 he changed his allegiance to the Conservatives following his conviction that Tariff Reform was crucial to Britain's continued economic strength. His change of allegiance and the campaign he waged in support of the Conservative candidate, a working man, caused considerable public controversy and it led to Nelson's retirement from the town council. However, he remained active in local politics standing as the Conservative candidate for Nelson and Colne at the 1923 general election, when Tariff Reform was again the major issue; despite his local popularity he was defeated by Arthur Greenwood, the Labour candidate.

In 1922 he purchased the Gledstone estate at Skipton where Sir Edwin Lutyens (qv) constructed one of the most magnificent residences in Yorkshire between 1925 and 1927.

Sir Amos Nelson turned his family firm into a public company, James Nelson Ltd in 1946. The firm was capitalised at £1.2 million (£883,475 issued). It comprised a manufacturing and merchanting group of two spinning companies (with a viscose yarn mill and an acetate yarn mill — 20,752 creping spindles and 24,934 doubling spindles), three rayon weaving and doubling companies (4,243 looms) and seven merchanting companies. In addition it contained two property-owning companies which let 'room and power' to the other companies in the group. It employed 2,600 workpeople in November 1946, as compared to the normal complement of 3,050 {Times *Prospectuses* (1946) 242}. Between 1936 and 1946 the group's combined gross profits rose from £125,961 to £448,381 with a wartime peak of £534,357; net profits before tax rose from £97,387 to £420,969, peaking again in 1943 at £505,360.

The public flotation caused some controversy which largely arose from a misunderstanding as the shares were offered to the public by a London finance company, the Whitehead Industrial Trust. It was initially assumed the firm was being taken over by the Trust which aroused memories of the post-1918 speculation in the industry. The trade raised the question with the President of the Board of Trade, Sir Stafford Cripps, but nothing came of the protest.

Amos Nelson married twice: firstly in 1879 to Mary Driver (1861-1931) daughter of Henry Driver, a shoemaker of Nelson; they had three sons and two daughters. Secondly in 1931 he married Harriet, daughter of William Hargreaves, an estate agent of West Marton near Barnoldswick, Yorkshire; they had one son. Sir Amos Nelson died on 13 August 1947 at Gledstone Hall, an estate of 40 farms and 6,000 acres. The gross value of his estate was £444,246 — a measure of his great success in comparison with his father who left £38,875 in 1912.

W GORDON RIMMER *and* ALAN FOWLER

Sources:

Unpublished

BCe.

MCe.

PrC.

Published

Country Life 77.

Douglas A Farnie, *The English Cotton Industry and the World Market, 1815-96* (Oxford: Clarendon Press, 1979).

Alan and Lesley Fowler, *A History of the Nelson Weavers Association* (Nelson, 1984).

Mark Girouard, *Life in the English Country House* (Harmondsworth, 1980).

Nelson Leader 4 Oct 1912, 15 Aug 1947.

Nelsons of Nelson: The Story of James Nelson Ltd, 1881-1951 (Harvey Publishing Co Ltd, 1951).

Times 14, 15 Aug 1947.

Times *Prospectuses* (1946).

George Horatio Nelson, the 1st Baron Nelson of Stafford (courtesy of the General Electric Company, plc).

NELSON, George Horatio

1st Lord Nelson of Stafford

(1887-1962)

Heavy electrical equipment manufacturer

George Horatio Nelson was born at Islington, London, on 26 October 1887, the son of George Nelson, a warehouseman, and his wife Emily Walsh née Lewis. Originally the Nelsons were a Leicestershire textile family. He had a comfortable if not wealthy upbringing. His education was of a technical nature, and he may in later life have regretted its exclusivity because he always advocated a better balance between the arts and the sciences. Educated at the London City and Guilds Technical College, in the same class as Handley Page (qv), he studied under Professor Sylvanus Thompson, an expert in electricity and magnetism. Before he was eighteen years old he had taken his City and Guilds diploma and won the Mitchell Exhibition as well as obtaining a postgraduate Brush studentship which enabled him to work at the Brush Electrical Engineering Co in Loughborough. There he worked in the drawing office and on the shop floor and gained a good grounding in both mechanical and electrical engineering. By the age of twenty-two, he was already their chief outside engineer.

However, in 1912, he moved to British Westinghouse, Trafford Park, Manchester, being made chief superintendent two years later. It was here that he worked under Holberry Mensforth (qv) whom he must have impressed quite significantly for it was Sir Holberry who was to ask him to join English Electric fifteen years later. In 1919, British Westinghouse merged with Vickers's electrical interests to form Metropolitan-Vickers, and Nelson was promoted to the management of the Metropolitan Vickers Electrical Co at Sheffield in 1920. As he had during his time at Manchester, Nelson established many contacts in the Sheffield area which later proved helpful to him. He also began to play an important local part within the Institution of Electrical Engineers, an institution he had joined as early as 1905 as a student member.

The turning point in Nelson's career came when he joined English Electric. The English Electric Co had been formed by a wartime group of electrical manufacturers based on Dick Kerr & Co of Preston. They acquired the Coventry Ordnance Works from a consortium of shipbuilders and after incorporation with a capital of £5 million in 1919, they bought the former Siemens Dynamo Works at Stafford for £1 million. The firm's first years showed a very poor profit record, especially in comparison with GEC headed by Hugo Hirst (qv). Other American interests, however, wanted to develop a British base, and Westinghouse, together with the Chicago utility magnate Harley Clarke, apparently acting through

Lazards, gained control of English Electric. They asked Holberry Mensforth to become chairman and he in turn asked Nelson to become managing director in 1922. Surprisingly — for English Electric's prestige was at a low ebb — Nelson accepted.

English Electric's competitive position was a weak one, but Mensforth and Nelson developed a new strategy based on tightening their control of the market. Nelson was a strong supporter of price rings and monopoly power, which he felt particularly necessary where large resources were required (as for R&D). He also believed they were the best means of improving the standard of living of the workers. His strategy, however, was in many respects constrained by the situation he inherited. He bitterly regretted English Electric's agreements with Siemens under which they had sold their profitable lamp interests (the lamp cartel was among the most profitable) and were effectively barred from telecommunications, thus being restricted to the heavier side of electrical engineering. The agreements he had negotiated with Westinghouse and the Harley Clarke interest, however, provided a sound basis for growth, the first keeping Westinghouse out of English Electric's European and North America markets, in return for technical support and royalties, while Harley Clarke's British electric utility subsidiaries (the Edmundsons Group) provided a guarantee of orders.

Throughout the 1930s, Nelson gave all his energies to restructuring English Electric — cutting out waste and paying close attention to costs while, at the same time, investing heavily in R&D. He himself moved to Stafford in 1930, though the firm's head office remained in London, and the firm took over the former Siemens works which it had earlier acquired and Nelson engaged initially on retrenchment — not a happy task for one so dedicated to maintaining and expanding employment. In 1933 Mensforth retired and Nelson took on the joint role of chairman and managing director. In the 1930s English Electric slowly became more prosperous. Nelson won an important contract for part of the electrification of the Southern Railway (the total cost of electrification was £11.5 million over the period 1926-35); he also arranged the finance and negotiated with the Polish Government for a contract worth £2 million for the electrification of railways around Warsaw. Just before the Second World War, English Electric began construction of research laboratories at Stafford and simultaneously moved into a new field of production, aircraft manufacture, obtaining a contract from the Air Ministry for 75 Hampden bombers (designed by Handley Page). In 1938 English Electric first paid a dividend on its ordinary shares: profitability, if not excessive, was at least restored.

During the war years, English Electric concentrated heavily on war production such as tanks and aircraft. The Handley Page Halifax bomber was built in large quantities at the company's Preston works and Napiers, a major producer of aero-engines, were acquired. Nelson himself served on the United Kingdom Tank Commission to America and Canada in 1942 and was a member of the Heavy Bomber Group Committee of the Air Ministry between 1939 and 1945. Sir George Nelson (he was knighted in 1943) also served as president of the Federation of British Industries during the latter part of the war (1943-45). During his presidency he made speeches in which he looked to the future of manufacturing in post-war

Sir G H Nelson (left) and Mr J R Sully, General Manager, Stafford works, discussing points of manufacture in one of the heavy plant shops (courtesy of the General Electric Company, plc).

Britain. Towards the end of the war he became a member of the Reconstruction Joint Advisory Council.

In the post-war world Nelson came into his own as a public man and also pursued some of his cherished social ambitions for his workforce and his company. The changeover to domestic production was hampered by shortages of raw materials and skilled men. Partly in response to the need to encourage craftsmen, technicians and engineers to move to Stafford, and partly in response to a desire to improve living standards, Nelson formed a housing association, which was to complete 1,300 houses by March 1952. The need for qualified men was increased by the extension and completion of the Nelson Research Laboratories, which were opened in November 1949 by Harold Wilson, then President of the Board of Trade.

Even before the war ended, Nelson had been planning for peace-time, attempting to fill the gap in the order books that would naturally occur and to reduce his company's dependence on public corporation orders. The restrictive agreement with Siemens was due to expire in 1944 and, partly because of the ties with the company and his own admiration for Siemens's founders, he attempted to take over British Siemens. This would have given English Electric a foothold in the light engineering markets, but the company went to AEI. He was, however, successful in the take-over of Marconi in 1946 against competition from EMI. With the Marconi company, English Electric entered the radio, radar and television markets, and ultimately space technology.

English Electric may now have felt it no longer needed Westinghouse technology, and with the nationalisation of Edmundsons, Harley Clarke's interests in British manufacturing must have waned. Whatever the reasons, the withdrawal of American interests in English Electric probably took place over a period of time in the late 1940s and in those years the Westinghouse technology agreements broke down. It was reported at the Annual General Meeting of English Electric shareholders on 30 March 1949 that the company stock was very widely held and there was no outstanding large holder among the 12,500 ordinary shareholders. In 1950 English Electric bought a controlling interest in a Canadian firm and was active in the North American markets, suggesting that the restriction on English Electric had been removed. However, contact was maintained with Westinghouse, and they continued to exchange information on research, design and manufacture.

The post-war development of the company was still tied to heavy engineering — particularly turbine-generators, hydroelectric power and railways. In addition, Nelson had decided to stay in the aircraft business and a design team was established at Preston which produced the record-breaking Canberra jet bomber and the UK's first supersonic fighter the Lightning. Soon after, government pressure soon built up for rationalisation in the aircraft industry. It declined to give the TSR2 project to either Vickers or English Electric individually. In 1960 they merged their interests into the newly-formed British Aircraft Corporation, in which English Electric held only 40 per cent later to become 50 per cent; and Napiers aero-engines were sold to Rolls Royce.

During this period more public offices and honours came to Sir George. In 1945 he chaired the Census of Production Committee. He received a large number of honorary academic awards, reflecting his participation in university affairs. Between 1950 and 1953 he was president of the British Electrical and Allied Manufacturers' Association (BEAMA), on whose Council he had long served, and he headed many other electrical bodies. A baronetcy was conferred in 1955, the same year that he became president of the Institution of Electrical Engineers. In 1960 he was raised to the peerage. Other honours included the presidency of the Institution of Mechanical Engineers, and he became a freeman of the Borough of Stafford. Throughout the post-war period he continued to serve on public bodies — the Committee on Future Scientific Policy, the General Board and the Executive Committee of the National Physical Laboratory (1945-51), the Heavy Electrical Plant Consultative Committee, 1952, the Overseas Activity Committee, 1956-60.

Nelson's expansion of English Electric led to substantially increased employment: from 4,000 in 1932 to 35,000 in 1949, and 80,000 by 1960, when the company had a turnover of £200 million. Nelson had established a pension fund for staff in 1937 and subsequently an augmentation of the National Insurance Pension for long-service shop-floor workers. The company also introduced life insurance for both staff and work people and various benevolent funds. Provision was made for workers who required convalescence with the opening by Lady Nelson of Hampsfield Grange in Furness in 1946. In addition, the company introduced dental clinics, sun-ray clinics and baths. Each plant had both Works and Staff Committees and numerous sports and social clubs for employees and their families.

In all this, education was not forgotten; it could not be since Lord Nelson was dedicated to improving the amount and quality of education both nationally and at company level. English Electric maintained large intakes of apprentice craftsmen and technicians and graduate engineers (in 1951 they had 2,000 people in training). They fostered links with the local technical colleges, and English Electric supplied the Stafford College with equipment for its engineering laboratories on permanent loan (eventually making it a gift). Lord Nelson's dedication to education can be seen not only by his associations with Queen Mary College and Imperial College, London, Manchester University and Cambridge University (where he was a member of the Appointments Board, 1946-51), by his membership of the Higher Technological Education Committee (1944-45), the Council of the City and Guilds of London Institute, 1958 (and its vice-presidency) and by his chairmanship of the Union of Educational Institutions (1946-47), but also by his appointment of C P Snow as executive director of English Electric. Snow had special resonsibility for training and research. He instigated the appointment of education officers at plant level and encouraged expenditure on R&D.

Constantly seeking to improve standards, cut costs and find new markets, Lord Nelson worked on Sundays (despite being a religious man). He encouraged the formation of a Christian Fellowship at the Stafford branch of English Electric in 1948, stating it would encourage the members to live up to the principles and ethics of Christian teaching. His rule was autocratic, although his power did not come from a large holding of shares but from the force of his personality and the regard both employees and shareholders had for him as an engineer and businessman. He commanded great respect, possibly verging on fear, among his associates and subordinates.

It was not until 1956 that he gave up the post of managing director, appointing his son, Henry George (qv), to take his place, but remaining an active executive chairman. His later years were marked by the opening of prestigious London headquarters in the Strand and by his failure to achieve a merger with GEC. The latter might have taken him into the more profitable lighter sides of electrical engineering, but he was unwilling to be drawn into a stock market battle for control.

Nelson in 1913 married Florence Mabel Howe, the daughter of Henry Howe, JP, a merchant, also from Leicestershire. They had two children, Margaret Joan (b 1915) and Henry George. Lord Nelson died at the age of seventy-four on 16 July 1962, at work in the Stafford offices. He left £78,350 gross. He was not one of those leaders who simply fade away — he worked for English Electric to the very end. Whoever provided the capital, it was Nelson who rescued English Electric and it was his vision and dedication that ensured the company a place among the major electrical manufacturing firms.

PATRICIA A DUTTON

Writings:

'Works Production' *Journal of the Institution of Electrical Engineers* 61 (1923).

'Road to Recovery' *The Electrician* 108 (1932).

Industry and the Future: Post-War Prospects and the Place of Private Enterprise (Federation of British Industries, 1943).

'Industry's Achievement in Four Years of War' *British Industries* 28 (Oct 1943).

'Britain and the Future of Exports' *ibid* 29 (Mar 1944).

'Post-War Objectives for Industry' *ibid* 30 (May 1945).

'The Electrical Manufacturing Industry' BBC Series *Reconversion of Britain's Principal Industries* broadcast 15 Oct 1946.

'Technical Education and Human Personality' Presidential address given to the Union of Educational Institutions on 26 Oct, at the 51st Annual Meeting, 1946 *Annual Report of the Union of Educational Institutions* (Birmingham, 1946).

'Industrial Administration' *Proceedings of the Institution of Mechanical Engineers* 157 (1947).

'Electrical Engineering in World Trade' *Proceedings of the British Electric Power Convention* 1954.

Inaugural Address *Proceedings of the Institution of Electrical Engineers* 103 (Jan 1956).

'Electricity and World Progress — Britain's Contribution' *Proceedings of the British Electric Power Convention* 1958.

Presidential Address *Proceedings of the Institution of Mechanical Engineers* 172 (1958).

Sources:

Unpublished

BCe.

MCe.

PrC; Will.

Information from the Second Lord Nelson of Stafford.

P A Dutton, 'The Employment Effects of Mergers: A Case Study of GEC, AEI and English Electric' (Warwick PhD, 1980).

Published

W J Baker, *A History of the Marconi Company* (Methuen, 1970).

Chartered Mechanical Engineer Sept 1962.

English Electric and Its People 1-8 (1946-58).

Leslie Hannah, *Electricity Before Nationalisation: A Study of the Development of the Electricity Supply Industry in Britain to 1948* (Macmillan, 1979).

Robert Jones and Oliver Marriott, *Anatomy of a Merger. A History of GEC, AEI and English Electric* (Jonathan Cape, 1970).

Journal of the British Electrical and Allied Manufacturers' Association 1956, 1960.

Journal of the Institution of Electrical Engineers 8 Nov 1962.

Proceedings of the Institution of Mechanical Engineers May 1957.

Railway Magazine 44 (Apr 1929).

J D Scott, *Vickers: A History* (Weidenfeld and Nicolson, 1962).

Stafford Advertiser 19 July 1962.

Stafford Newsletter 21 July 1962.

WWW.

NELSON, Henry George

2nd Lord Nelson of Stafford

(1917-)

Industrialist

Henry George Nelson, 2nd Baron Nelson of Stafford (courtesy of the General Electric Co plc).

Henry George Nelson was born in Stretford, Manchester, on 2 January 1917, the only son of (Lord) George Horatio Nelson (qv) and his wife Florence Mabel née Howe. He was educated at Oundle and at King's College, Cambridge, where he was an exhibitioner in 1935, graduating in mechanical engineering with a BA honours degree in 1937. Before going up to Cambridge he did a spell in the Stafford workshops of the English Electric Co Ltd, of which his father was chairman and managing director, and later spent two years gaining further practical experience at Renault in France and Sulzers and Brown Boveri in Switzerland, where he also acquired a useful knowledge of French and German.

As the only son, George Nelson was groomed to follow in his father's footsteps. He joined EE Co's Preston works in 1939 as a superintendent, and by 1942 had risen to the post of deputy works manager, by which time the factory had switched from locomotive to aircraft manufacture. By 1945 a record number of 3,000 Handley Page Hampden and Halifax bombers

423

had been made at Preston, and George Nelson had contributed to this achievement by solving many problems related to production planning. The Preston factory later established its own design and development centre in which he played a leading part. This team produced Britain's first jet-bomber, the record-breaking Canberra, and later Britain's first supersonic fighter, the Lightning.

In 1942, George Nelson was appointed managing director of the Napier aero-engine company, then a new member of EE Co, where he was responsible for the development and production of the Napier Sabre, the world's most powerful reciprocating aero-engine, which powered the Typhoon and Tempest fighters. Four years later he also became an executive director of the Marconi Co Ltd, which had become another EE Co subsidiary following its purchase from Cable & Wireless. In October 1949 he was brought into head office and made deputy managing director, in which capacity he was responsible for EE Co's successful aviation business and, using his experience at Napiers and Marconis, he played a leading part in the reorganisation of the company's activities to meet the many changes required in the immediate post-war period. He was very much involved in developments of new products and the introduction of new technology. This included the establishment of the company's new guided-weapon business and its nuclear power business through a consortium, the Atomic Power Construction Co Ltd, involving Babcock & Wilcox and Taylor Woodrow.

George Nelson became managing director in 1956, his father remaining chairman. They worked closely together on the continuing expansion of the business, the latter now spending more time overseas promoting the company's growing export activities, though he remained a dominant force at EE Co until his death in his Stafford office in 1962 at the age of seventy-four. The Second Lord Nelson was appointed chairman and chief executive. By this time he himself was playing an active part in developing the company's overseas activities. In 1958 he went to South and Central Africa, in 1959 to India, Pakistan and Ceylon, and in 1960 to the Sudan and the Middle East. He also led official UK trade missions to the United Arab Republic in 1960 and to Iraq in 1961.

To meet the changing needs of the period, following his father's death, the Second Lord Nelson began rationalising the company's management structure, helped in 1965 by the management consultants McKinsey & Co. This reorganisation, which gave more authority to the line executive, enabled EE Co to expand its overseas manufacture and to play an important role in the rationalisation of the home electrical industry, both of which he saw to be a growing necessity if the company's competitiveness in world markets was to be retained. EE Co acquired Dormans and Ruston Paxmans to become one of the country's two major diesel engine manufacturers. Rationalisation in the electrical and electronics industry also included the purchase of a number of electrical companies, such as Hackbridge & Hewittic and the Elliott Automation Group, the acquisition of which, when combined with the company's Marconi interests, gave EE Co a leading position in the electronics field. EE Co's turnover rose from £200 million in 1962 to over £400 million in 1967, with pre-tax profits rising from £10 million to nearly £30 million over the same period.

In 1967 the GEC, under its new aggressive management led by Arnold (later Lord Arnold) Weinstock, sensing the need for future change and rationalisation of the electrical industry, made a successful take-over bid for AEI (formerly Metropolitan Vickers and British Thomson Houston). This strengthening of the GEC position, particularly in the electronics and telephone business, prompted the Plessey Co the following year to make a £260 million take-over bid for EE Co with a particular eye on its Marconi/Elliott electronics interests. Lord Nelson and his colleagues rejected this approach but, advised by their merchant bankers Lazards and supported by the Government, they opened discussions on a merger with GEC. Nelson increasingly favoured some kind of agreement with Weinstock, whose business record he admired. By 1968 Nelson was aware of the need for stronger managing directors at the centre of EE Co and both he and Weinstock believed in decentralised management and the creation of large units as an answer to the problems of the electrical manufacturing industry. (As early as 1960 advanced discussions had taken place with a view to merging EE Co and the GEC but financial terms could not be agreed and the proposition was dropped although Lord Nelson favoured the move.)

On 6 September 1968 Nelson and Weinstock announced a merger of EE Co and the GEC. The latter name was retained, with Nelson as chairman of the new group, and Weinstock as managing director. The combination of Weinstock's hard-headed attention to financial detail and Nelson's knowledge of the industry and its customers proved exceptionally successful. In 1968 the GEC had sales of £257 million and pre-tax profits of £18.6 million; by 1984 sales had reached £5.6 billion, with pre-tax profits of £671 million, and the company had acquired a formidable cash reserve position. It had become Britain's largest electrical, engineering, electronics and telecommunications group. According to Lord Weinstock:

> 'Lord Nelson played a crucial part in bringing about the merger, and in the subsequent development of the Group. He moulded the job to his own style, handling the internal problems which are an inevitable aftermath of all mergers with humanity, kindness and skill, while outside GEC he patiently explained to apprehensive customers, suppliers and various official bodies the benefits and opportunities made possible by the merger. Equally at home with important customers and on the factory floor, his engineering ability and his warm personality have gained George Nelson universal respect and esteem' {Weinstock (1983) 28-29}.

Nelson recognised the importance of the export business and its dependence on personal knowledge and contacts and he travelled extensively in pursuit of overseas orders. He took a particular interest in the possibilities of the Chinese market, which he visited many times as chairman of the GEC and as president of the Sino-British Trade Council from 1973 to 1982. He also led a London Chamber of Commerce Trade Mission to the Argentine in 1978.

Lord Nelson occupied a number of other executive posts. He co-operated with the Government in the merging of EE Co's aircraft interests with those of Vickers to form the British Aircraft Corporation of which he was deputy chairman, 1960-77. He 'remained a pillar of strength in BAC for all of its seventeen years of existence' {Gardner (1981) 34}, supporting Lord Portal and Sir George Edwards (qqv) in their fight against the negative views of the report prepared by Lord Plowden (qv) and a frequently hostile Government. In 1961 he became a director of the Bank of England: he also joined the boards of Royal Worcester (as chairman), the International Nickel Co of Canada, the London Board of Advice of the National Bank of Australia Ltd, and International Computer (Holdings) Ltd, formed from the merger he negotiated of the System 4 computer interests of EE Co with International Computors & Tabulators (ICT).

Lord Nelson has been associated with many technical societies and Government advisory bodies (listed fully in *Who's Who*) and has been awarded numerous fellowships and honorary degrees. He was, for example, president of the British Electrical and Allied Manfacturers Association in 1966, and president of the Institution of Electrical Engineers in its centenary year, 1970-71. He served on the Advisory Council of the Ministry of Technology, 1964-70, and was chairman of the National Defence Industries Council, 1971-77: both bodies were broadly aimed at rationalising and improving the efficiency of British industry. He also continued his links with higher education, lecturing on industrial management at the University of Cambridge, 1947-49, and was chancellor of the University of Aston in Birmingham, 1966-79. The application of scientific methods to business is a subject close to his heart and he has stated his belief that, although 'a large area of management is essentially an art ... there is much in management that is a science' {Nelson (18 Nov 1964) 622-23} — a view which led him to head an appeal which raised £5 million for the foundation of the London and Manchester Business Schools. The need for Britain to raise productivity, to increase exports, and to adopt a more satisfactory basis for industrial relations has also engaged his attention.

His close associate described him as: 'basically a shy man who readily laughs at a joke but makes few jokes himself. He gets on well with everyone because his innate decency shines through everything he says and does. His devotion to his job is a major influence in his life, and he expects the same attitude from others. He can be critical, but always fair and always kind' {Weinstock (1983) 29}.

Lord Nelson married on 8 June 1940 Pamela Roy, daughter of Ernest Roy Bird, formerly MP for Skipton, Yorkshire. They have two sons, Henry Roy George (b 1943) and James Jonathan (b 1947), and two daughters, Caroline Jane (b 1942), and Sally Louise (b 1955).

Lord Nelson retired from the chairmanship of the GEC in 1983 at the age of sixty-six when he was succeeded by Lord Carrington, though he continues to serve as an active director. He became prime warden of the Goldsmiths Company 1983-84 (a position held by his father in 1960-61) and is a member of the Lords Committee on Science and Technology.

GEOFFREY TWEEDALE

Writings:

speech on scientific policy and manpower *PD*, Lords, 5th ser 256, cols 448-54 (11 Mar 1964).

speech on education for business and management *ibid* 5th ser 261, cols 622-27 (18 Nov 1964).

speech on Cabora Bassa and Rhodesian sanctions *ibid* 5th ser 306, cols 937-39 (15 Dec 1969).

speech on the British aerospace industry *ibid* 5th ser 309, cols 480-5 (15 Apr 1970).

'The Impact of Advanced Technology on the Electrical Industry' presidential address *Proceedings of the Institution of Electrical Engineers* 118 (1971).

speech on Latin America and the United Kingdom *PD*, Lords, 5th ser 327, cols 369-77 (26 Jan 1972).

speech on Code of Industrial Relations Practice *ibid* cols 1349-50 (10 Feb 1972).

PP, *HC* 1973-74 (21-I) VIII, Wages and Conditions of African Workers Employed by British Firms in South Africa.

speech on the economic situation and industry *PD*, Lords 5th ser 354, cols 1275-83 (26 Nov 1974).

letter on trade with China *Times* 14 Mar 1975.

letter on electricity power plant suppliers *ibid* 19 May 1977.

letter on Sea Wolf *Sunday Times* 12 Sept 1982.

'Export Competitiveness — A Factor of Management and/or Design' Institution of Electrical Engineers: First Lord Nelson of Stafford lecture 26 Apr 1984 (in press).

speech on industrial health and hygiene *PD*, Lords 5th ser 457, cols 447-50 (15 Nov 1984).

Sources:

Unpublished

English Electric Co Ltd, Reports and Accounts 1967.

General Electric Co Ltd, Annual Reports and Accounts, 1968-84.

BCe.

MCe.

Pat A Dutton, 'The Employment Effects of Mergers: A Case Study of GEC, AEI and English Electric' (Warwick PhD, 1981).

Second Lord Nelson, 'The Development and Organisation of English Electric Co Ltd' (Edwards seminar paper 334, 5 May 1964).

Interview with the Second Lord Nelson, 14 Nov 1984, and information from Peter Gillibrand, GEC plc.

Published

W J Baker, *A History of the Marconi Company* (Methuen, 1970).

Burke's Baronetage and Peerage 1980.

Charles Gardner, *British Aircraft Corporation. A History* (Batsford, 1981).

Robert Jones and Oliver Marriot, *Anatomy of a Merger: A History of GEC, AEI, and English Electric* (Cape, 1970).

Anthony Sampson, *The Changing Anatomy of Britain* (Hodder & Stoughton, 1982).

Times 3, 12 Mar, 23 June, 19 Nov 1964, 7 Jan 1965, 30 Aug 1968, 16 Dec 1969, 16 Apr 1970, 27 Jan 1972, 17 May 1973, 27 Nov 1974.

Lord Arnold Weinstock, 'Born with a Silver Spanner' *Staffordshire Life* Apr 1983.

Charles Wilson and William J Reader, *Men and Machines. A History of D Napier & Son, Engineers, Ltd 1808-1958* (Weidenfeld & Nicolson, 1958).

WW 1984.

NETTLEFOLD, Joseph Henry

(1827-1881)

Woodscrew manufacturer

Joseph Henry Nettlefold (courtesy of Guest Keen & Nettlefolds plc).

Joseph Henry Nettlefold was born on 19 September 1827 and baptised at St George's parish church, Bloomsbury, London, on 26 April 1828. He was the second son of John Sutton Nettlefold (1792-1866), the owner of a brass founders and ironmongery business based at 8 Red Lion Street, Holborn, and his first wife, Martha née Chamberlain (1794-1866). The firm flourished and his father moved to new premises at 54 High Holborn. Shortly after the Great Exhibition of 1851, J S Nettlefold, having discovered the existence of an American patent for the manufacture of woodscrews by self-acting machinery, decided to establish a modern works in Birmingham. The cost of the plant, together with the UK patent rights, amounted to £30,000. Accordingly, he asked his brother-in-law, Joseph Chamberlain Sr, a wholesale bootmaker, to invest in the project. The latter agreed and a partnership was formed in 1854. The factory, erected in Heath Street, Smethwick (designed by the London architect, Thomas Chatfeild Clarke), was run initially by J S Nettlefold's eldest son, Edward John (1820-78), and the younger Joseph Chamberlain (qv) who handled the commercial side of the business. Nettlefold & Chamberlain was so successful that when Joseph Chamberlain and his two brothers sold their interest in 1874 they left with more than £60,000.

After a private education at a Nonconformist academy in London, J H Nettlefold gave early proof of a mastery in mathematics that was to distinguish him in later life. On leaving school he joined his father's hardware firm in Holborn but soon visited Birmingham to learn more of screwmaking at the family works. As these trips became increasingly regular, J H Nettlefold decided to move to Birmingham. Although he had received no formal training in mechanical engineering, he acquired the necessary practical skills and became responsible for much of the planning

A late nineteenth century exhibition stand showing the range of Nettlefold's screw and fastener products (courtesy of Guest Keen & Nettlefolds plc).

required to extend the mills at Heath Street (in 1860 he was elected a member of the Institution of Mechanical Engineers). When Chamberlain retired in 1874 Nettlefold's responsibilities at the works greatly increased. On the death of his father in 1866 Edward Nettlefold became chairman of both Nettlefold & Chamberlain and J S Nettlefold & Sons and on Edward's death in 1878 J H Nettlefold succeeded as chairman of the Smethwick screw works.

J H Nettlefold was the prime mover in the promotion of Messrs Nettlefolds as a public company. The flotation was timed to coincide with the acquisition of the plant and machinery of a number of rival screwmakers. Achieved in 1880, this strategy resulted in the takeover of their neighbours, the Birmingham Screw Co (valued at £143,000), the Manchester Steel Screw Co (£50,000), situated in the Bradford district of that city, Messrs Lloyd & Harrisons's Stourport Works (£21,000) together with the wire manufacturer, John Cornforth, Berkley Street, Birmingham (£24,000). Both the Manchester and Stourport enterprises were swiftly closed and only the St George's works of the former Birmingham Screw Co was preserved as a major adjunct to Heath Street. At the time of the company promotion Messrs Nettlefolds's business (valued at £786,000) comprised the screw mills at Smethwick and King's Norton (acquired in 1866 from James & Avery), the nut and bolt works (Imperial Mills, also at Smethwick, but purchased in 1869 from the Patent File Co Ltd of Sheffield), the Castle Iron Works at Hadley, a leasehold colliery at Ketley, Shropshire and a wire works in Princip Street, Birmingham.

The success of the company in the period leading up to the flotation and for the remainder of the nineteenth century was achieved by a combination of technical innovation and determined marketing. Rivals within the UK, as before in Chamberlain's period of management, were either taken over or brought to financial difficulties by price-cutting competition; in this way, for example, they had been able to purchase the Birmingham Screw Co and subsequently, after J H Nettlefold's death, buy the British Screw Co at Leeds in 1898. Various cartel agreements ensured that there was little interference in home markets from the Continent or America and they were free to exploit the opportunities created by the Empire. Screwmaking machinery was of the latest design and was up-dated by the company's engineers, being guarded by patents, whilst any requests to buy overseas rights were flatly refused. Profits were high and consistent: £64,204 in 1881, £72,759 in 1882 and £74,824 in 1883.

J H Nettlefold's decision to acquire the Manchester Steel Screw Co had not solely aimed at protecting their virtual monopoly of UK screw production. He perceived a future growth in demand for steel and was concerned to exploit any technical advantage Nettlefolds gained. He concluded that the steel wire they were using was of insufficient quality to make uniformly good screws and resolved the problem by vertical integration. In 1881 Siemens furnaces for experimental purposes and costing no more than £15,000, were to be installed at their Castle Works, Hadley (until then it had comprised puddling furnaces for wrought iron). In the event the works proved too remote from supplies of coal and iron ore to be profitable on a large-scale so in 1886 Nettlefolds transferred their steelworks to a green-field site at Rogerstone, near Newport. There two acid Bessemer converters were erected together with plant for the rolling of billets, rod, hoops and wire.

When J H Nettlefold died in 1881 his fellow directors acknowledged that his 'great business capacity' had been a chief cause of their current profitable position {GKN Minute Book, 6 Dec 1881}. He was succeeded in the chairmanship by his younger brother, Frederick Nettlefold (1835-1913) and his nephew Edward Nettlefold (1856-1909) was elected to the board. Although the former remained with the company until the 1890s, he became increasingly involved with the running of Samuel Courtaulds & Co (a connection resulting from his marriage to Mary Warren a member of the Courtauld family) and he eventually served as their chairman (1904-10). Edward remained committed to Nettlefolds and was its deputy chairman from 1894 until the merger in 1902 with Guest, Keen & Co. Arthur Keen (qv) became the new chairman though Edward Nettlefold also served on the board of GKN until his death.

J H Nettlefold married Mary Maria (1835-1881), the only daughter of John Seaborne of Birmingham in March 1867 at the Unity Church, Islington. They had three daughters, Florence, Winifred and Maud. John Sutton Nettlefold was the first member of the family to become a Unitarian, a faith to which he had probably been introduced by his first wife as the Chamberlains were members of that denomination; J H Nettlefold remained a Unitarian throughout his life.

He died on 22 November 1881, aged fifty-four, at his Highland residence, Allean House, near Pitlochry, after an apoplectic seizure. J H Nettlefold left £287,887 gross but had already presented his fine collection of pictures by David Cox (reputedly then worth £40,000) to the City of Birmingham in October 1881.

EDGAR JONES

Sources:

Unpublished

GKN, Nettlefolds Ltd, Directors Minute Book No 1, Mar 1880-Aug 1886. Nettlefolds Ltd, prospectus and balance sheets.

PrC.

Published

Donald C Coleman, *Courtalds. An Economic and Social History* (3 vols, Oxford: Clarendon Press, 1969-80) 1 and 2.

C Anthony Crofton, *The Nettlefolds, A Genealogical Account of the Family Nettlefold* (Lewes: pp, 1963).

Engineer 14 July 1865, 16 Apr 1909.

Proceedings of the Institution of Mechanical Engineers 33 (1882).

NEVILE, Sir Sydney Oswald

(1873-1969)

Brewer

Sydney Oswald Nevile was born at Thorney, Nottinghamshire, on 12 July 1873, the thirteenth in a family of 15 of Rev Christopher Nevile (1806-77), landowner and rector, and his third wife, Mary Anne (d 1919), daughter of Robert Tooth, who had interests in hop-growing, brewing and banking. The Neviles had owned Thorney lands since the sixteenth century. Sydney Nevile's widowed mother brought him up under reduced

Sir Sydney O Nevile (from S O Nevile, 70 Rolling Years.

circumstances in Brighton and Bognor, where he attended the preparatory school of Mr Travers.

Early in 1888, when Nevile was fourteen, his mother paid a premium for him to be articled as a pupil at the brewery of E Robins & Son, in Hove. Later, he was briefly a pupil at Brandon's Putney Brewery Ltd, where he started as assistant brewer in July 1890. In 1896 he became head brewer, probably the youngest one in England. As Brandons had a large off-licence trade, Nevile experimented with supplying the bottling stores with beer in tank wagons and studied bottling plants in the United States. He developed valuable business connections during the First World War while representing the drink trade with the Government. In 1919 he became a director of Whitbreads where he played a large role in public relations. He retired from day-to-day work in 1946 and as director in 1968 when he was appointed chief consultant.

Nevile built his reputation by serving the brewing trade as a whole. Before the First World War he attracted attention as an advocate of a constructive policy of 'sobriety plus good service' or public house improvement, as contrasted with mere resistance to temperance attacks. During the war he entered 'the inner cabinet of trade politics' {Nevile (1958) 12}. After Nevile had suggested that public houses could assist in war savings, Lord d'Abernon arranged for his appointment to the Central Control Board (Liquor Traffic), on which he served during 1917-21. When Lloyd George asked the Brewers' Society to discuss the financial details of State Purchase with Lord Milner in 1917, Nevile represented the London brewers. From later that year he also worked with trade leaders such as Sir Richard Garton (qv), Edward Giffard, and Cecil Lubbock on the post-war reform of the drink trade and helped draft the private members' bills introduced on 2 March 1920 and 18 February 1921 which influenced the Licensing Act of 1921.

Nevile served the Home Office, on the Council of State Management Districts, 1921-55, and the Morris Committee, 1942-44, on bombed licensed property; the Ministry of Agriculture, on the Hop Control Committee, 1917-23; and the Ministry of Food, as chairman of the Advisory Committee on the Brewing Industry, 1940-46. He was knighted in 1942. As a prominent figure in the brewing trade, he was president of the Institute of Brewing, 1919-21; master of the Brewers' Company, 1929-30; chairman of the Brewers' Society, 1938-40; chairman of the National Trade Defence Association, 1946-48; and vice-president of the Federation of British Industries in 1958. In 1930 he testified before the Royal Commission on Licensing and in 1933 he advocated controversial ('beer is best') collective advertising.

Nevile preferred to negotiate over dinner, ordinarily at Oddenino's in Regent Street. An active rower in his younger days, he later became a salt water sailor. In 1946 he married Madeleine de Lacy, a member of a prominent Anglo-Irish family and daughter of Dr C A Wickham of Willesborough, Kent. Nevile was a member of the Church of England. Sir Sydney Nevile died on 3 September 1969, leaving an estate valued at £49,409. His home was in Worthing, Sussex.

DAVID M FAHEY

Writings:

PP, RC on Licensing (1931-32) Cmd 3988 (1932).

Seventy Rolling Years (Faber & Faber, 1958).

Nevile also wrote a number of technical papers on the brewing and allied industries.

Sources:

Unpublished

BCe.

MCe.

PrC.

Published

Burke's Landed Gentry 1965.

Times 4, 12 Sept 1969.

WWW.

NEWALL, Robert Stirling

(1812-1889)

Wire rope inventor and chemical manufacturer

Robert Stirling Newall was born in Dundee on 27 May 1812, the son of Walter Newall, a merchant. After a short time in a mercantile office there he moved to London to join the merchant firm of Robert M'Calmont, concerned with rapid production of steam. After visiting America as M'Calmont's agent he patented in 1840 an invention for wire rope manufacture by machine and established a works for the process at Gateshead, a long-established centre for making hemp ropes. His partners were initially Lewis Gordon and Charles Liddell, young associates of I K Brunel and George Stephenson respectively, but after disagreement the firm was re-established as R S Newall & Son. Unlike the wire ropes developed in the previous two decades, Newall's cables avoided twisting the individual wires and were far stronger than their hemp counterparts on a weight-for-weight basis. And, of course, they could also carry an electric current. Faced very soon with the prospect of taking an electric telegraph wire across a river, Newall conceived the idea of covering it with gutta percha (of which he had just received one of the first samples from Borneo), and surrounding that insulator with strong wires. Thus was made practical the idea of telegraphic cables under the sea, the first to be successfully laid being that between Dover and Calais in 1851. Other submarine cables, manufactured by his firm, were soon laid across the North Sea, the Irish Sea and the Red Sea. In 1853 he introduced a drum-brake for laying cables at great depths. His firm manufactured half the cable first used to cross the Atlantic successfully (though briefly) in 1858. Newall was often personally involved in the laying as well as the manufacture of the submarine cables, showing great courage and coolness in the many crises which then occurred: a lost cable might be worth many thousands of pounds. The last cable whose laying he personally supervised was from Newbiggin in Northumberland to Ringkjobing in Denmark in 1868.

In 1849 Newall married Mary, youngest daughter of Hugh Lee Pattinson, inventor of a process for de-silvering lead and a chemical manufacturer with works at Felling and Washington near Gateshead. During the 1860s Newall joined his father-in-law's Washington Chemical Co and bought the firm in 1872. His own son Frederick Stirling Newall (1855-1930) joined them in 1875 as manager, becoming managing director after his father's death. The firm later concentrated on the production of magnesium carbonate and magnesium oxide from the immense deposits of dolomite in the vicinity of Gateshead. The discovery that magnesium carbonate, mixed with asbestos, formed a strong insulating material with totally non-inflammable properties led to the formation and development, under F S Newall, of, successively, Magnesia Coverings Ltd in 1903, Newalls Insulation Co Ltd in 1908 and Turner & Newall Ltd in 1920. F S Newall was chairman of the first two until 1920 and of Turner & Newall, 1924-29; at his death in 1930 he left £807,384.

Another of R S Newall's children, his daughter Phoebe, allied the family to the Cooksons (qqv), the lead manufacturers, with her marriage to N C Cookson. His second son followed R S Newall along a different path: Hugh Frank Newall (1857-1954) became professor of astrophysics at Cambridge, in a field where his early interest was inspired by his father's 25-inch refracting telescope, installed in the family home at Gateshead.

Robert Stirling Newall flourished in an area and at a time when science was an important element in local culture. A member of the prestigious Newcastle Literary and Philosophical Society, he was also a founding member of the Newcastle Chemical Society and belonged to the North of England Institute of Mining and Mechanical Engineers. He served as vice-president of both the Natural History Society and the Field Club in the area. He became an FRS and a member of the Institution of Mechanical Engineers and was also a fellow of the Royal Astronomical Society. A philanthropist on a considerable scale in the area, he was also a notable patron of the arts, with a collection of paintings. He was a JP and twice mayor of Gateshead.

R S Newall died after a short illness on 21 April 1889, leaving £166,981 gross.

C A RUSSELL

Writings:

letter on Submarine Telegraph Cables *Times* 12 Nov 1852.

Observations on the Present Condition of Telegraphs in the Levant (1860).

Facts and Observations Relating to the Invention of the Submarine Cable and to the Manufacture and Laying of the First Cable between Dover and Calais in 1851 (E & F N Spon, 1882).

British Patents:

1840 (8,594)
1841 (9,160)
1843 (9,656)
1847 (11,582)
1848 (12,274)
1854 (2,308)

Sources:

Unpublished

MCe.

PrC.

Published

DNB.

Nature 16 May 1889.

Newcastle Daily Leader 23 Apr 1889.

Proceedings of the Institution of Mechanical Engineers 1889.

Proceedings of the Royal Society 46 (1890).

Times 25 Apr 1889.

NEWNES, Sir George

(1851-1910)

Periodical and newspaper proprietor

Sir George Newnes from W H Beable, The Romance of Great Businesses.

George Newnes was born at Matlock in Derbyshire on 13 March 1851, the youngest of the six children of Thomas Mold Newnes, the Congregational minister of Glenorchy Chapel, and Sarah, the daughter of Daniel Urquhart of Dundee. He was educated at Silcoates, a school in Yorkshire for the sons of Congregational ministers. He was not a particularly outstanding schoolboy, except for his facility in arithmetic, and his parents decided that he would not be suited for the ministry as they had hoped. After a few terms at the City of London School, he was apprenticed, at the age of sixteen, to a firm of fancy goods wholesalers in the City. After five years, he was sent to Manchester to open a branch warehouse there for another London firm of fancy goods merchants.

It was in Manchester that he conceived the idea of composing a magazine entirely from the stories and snippets of trivial information that had fascinated him from childhood. (George Newnes had no illusions about his own tastes or intellectual qualities: 'I *am* the average man. I am not merely putting myself into his place. That is why I know what he wants.' {Friedrichs (1911) 188}) He made up a dummy paper but failed to convince the rich merchant, or the Manchester publishing firm, that he approached for the capital he needed. Unable to borrow the capital, he set about earning it, starting a vegetarian restaurant to cater for office workers (though Newnes himself could be found lunching off steak in a nearby eating-house) and within a year could sell the business for a sum which enabled him to launch his projected magazine — *Tit-Bits* — in October 1881.

The combination of his flair for what the 'average man' (or woman) wanted to read for entertainment and his sound commercial sense made *Tit-Bits* an immediate success. He was the first to tap the huge potential market at all social levels for light, but unexceptionable, reading which was not satisfied by the sentimental moralising of the magazines produced for the 'home circle', often by religious bodies or associations, and the sporting magazines which were often rather raffish in tone and considered disreputable. For the first few years the magazine was largely compiled from material culled from other publications, but then more original material was submitted to, or commissioned by, *Tit-Bits*.

From the first, Newnes's promotion of *Tit-Bits* was characterised by striking advertising stunts. The first issue was advertised by 100 members of the Manchester Boys Brigade, wearing bands reading *Tit-Bits* in large letters on their caps, marching up Market Street. Newnes was the originator of many ploys to advertise his magazine and to promote its circulation which became part of the standard repertoire of popular journalism — prize competitions, buried treasure hunts, with clues hidden in stories in the magazine, and free insurance schemes which meant that each copy of *Tit-Bits* carried by a passenger killed in a railway accident constituted an insurance policy. These schemes and competitions were expensive to run, but Newnes only embarked on them after careful calculations, and they gave excellent returns. The free insurance scheme, for example, helped to take the circulation to 700,000, for the price of 20 to 30 sums of £100 paid out in Newnes's lifetime. Raising the circulation was the principal aim of these competitions, although Newnes also claimed they attracted readers from the sporting papers and helped cultivate a taste for the more wholesome reading he offered in his magazine. For years the competitions were the nearest approach to advertising Newnes permitted to appear in *Tit-Bits*, until, as the circulation rose and the offers of advertising agents became more tempting, he agreed to add a four-page cover devoted entirely to advertisements.

It was shortly after the famous offer in November 1883 of a house, Tit-Bits Villa, as the first prize in a short story competition (which helped to boost the circulation from what was then a steady 200,000) that Newnes moved his publishing-office to London. Another competition, with a situation in the *Tit-Bits* office as first prize, brought C Arthur Pearson (qv), another pioneer of the 'new journalism', into publishing in 1884. Alfred Harmsworth (qv) got the idea for his own immensely successful magazine *Answers* from the *Tit-Bits* feature 'Answers to Correspondents', to which Harmsworth was a frequent contributor at one time. Indirectly Newnes can also be credited with wide influence on popular newspaper journalism, for the principles behind *Tit-Bits*, 'that of finding the kind of things that people are interested in rather than the kind of things they ought to be interested in, and of making a feature of it ... was in truth the basis of the success of the first halfpenny papers' {*Daily Graphic* 10 June 1910}. Newnes himself attributed his own success to his inclination 'to do things differently from, rather than in the same way as, other people, and I have always struck while the iron was hot'. {Friedrichs (1911) 144} His readiness to experiment in journalism is of a piece with his enthusiasm for the technical innovations of his lifetime such as the telephone, electricity, and motorcars.

George Newnes also published several other magazines, including the *Strand Magazine*, started in 1891, which combined popular literary matter with a picture on every page, *Country Life* (1897) and two women's journals, *Ladies' Field* and *Woman's Life*. In 1896 he introduced the Penny Library of Famous Books, publishing the unabridged texts of favourite tales and novels in closely printed volumes of 80-120 pages. He was not the first, nor in 1896 the only, publisher in this field, but there was still a substantial market for these cheapest of cheap books: sales in the first year averaged nearly 100,000 a week. He had his failures, notably the *Daily Courier*, an unsuccessful attempt to launch a society gossip journal.

Newnes's principal venture into newspaper proprietorship was not a great commercial success either, but he had probably not expected it to be. When the Liberal evening newspaper the *Pall Mall Gazette* changed hands and politics in late 1892, Newnes (who had been a Liberal MP since 1885) engaged all the journalists and literary staff who had lost their jobs and in January 1893 started the *Westminster Gazette*. Newnes succeeded in giving the paper financial stability, although its circulation never rose above 20,000 and it cost him £100,000 before he surrendered the responsibility to another Liberal, Sir Weetman Pearson (qv), in 1908. Newnes took much less direct personal interest in his newspaper than in his magazines, particularly *Tit-Bits* and the *Strand Magazine*, for which he read nearly all the copy personally for many years. No doubt he recognised that the kind of journalism at which he excelled was not suited to a London evening paper seeking to exert a serious political influence, although he did allow himself the discreet advertising ploy of printing the *Westminster Gazette* on pale green paper, ostensibly because it was more restful on the eyes of commuters in suburban trains, but in fact to stimulate talk about the new journal. Although Newnes was an MP for twenty years, sitting for Newmarket from 1885 to 1895 and for Swansea from 1900 to 1910, he rarely spoke in the House. He described himself as 'a quiet member', though 'perhaps a useful one in many ways' {Koss (1984) 83}. His proprietorship of the *Westminster Gazette*, and his saving of the *Cambria Daily Leader* for the Liberal Party were his most notable political contributions.

His retirement from parliament in 1895 (when he was created a baronet) was voluntary, for he wished at that time to concentrate on his business, which was enjoying its period of most rapid growth in the 1890s. He had formed a company, George Newnes Ltd, in 1891, with a nominal capital of £400,000. Newnes took £250,000 of the £1 shares in return for the assets he made over to the company (he also received £150,000 cash to bring the total price paid to him up to £400,000) and took a further 60,000 shares; the rest were distributed among many small shareholders, largely booksellers, newsagents, and stationers. George Newnes was to be governing director for life, with power to appoint or remove all other directors. By 1897 Newnes had disposed of about 70,000 of his shares, but in that year (when profits were £66,698) the company was reorganised with an increased nominal capital of £1 million. Newnes was to be the permanent governing director so long as he held at least £200,000 of the company's capital.

In 1875 he married Priscilla, the daughter of a Nonconformist minister, Rev James Hillyard of Leicester. They had two sons; the younger, Arthur, died in childhood, and Newnes was succeeded in the business by his elder son, Frank. Sir George Newnes died on 10 June 1910, having been ill for some time with diabetes; he had also had a drink problem for some years. He left £173,362 gross.

CHRISTINE SHAW

Sources:

Unpublished

PRO, BT31/5097/34316 George Newnes Ltd.

C Reg: IPC Magazines Ltd (53,626).

PrC.

Published

Robert D Altick, *The English Common Reader: A Social History of the Mass Reading Public 1800-1900* (Chicago: University of Chicago Press, 1957).

Daily Graphic 10 June 1910.

DNB.

Thomas H S Escott, *Masters of English Journalism: A Study of Personal Forces* (T Fisher Unwin, 1911).

Hulda Friederichs, *The Life of Sir George Newnes, Bart* (Hodder & Stoughton, 1911).

Stephen Koss, *The Rise and Fall of the Political Press in Britain* (2 vols, Hamish Hamilton, 1981-84).

Reginald Pound and Geoffrey Harmsworth, *Northcliffe* (Cassell, 1959).

Times 10 June 1910.

Tit-Bits 25 June 1910.

Westminster Gazette 9 June 1910.

WWMP.

WWW.

NICKALLS, Thomas

(1828-1899)

Stock jobber

Thomas (always known as Tom) Nickalls was born in 1828. Little is known about his background and early life, apart from the fact that as a boy he accompanied his father on a visit to Chicago. He entered the London Stock Exchange in 1845, becoming a jobber; and there he achieved his fame in the American railroad market, which, in the wake of the Civil War and the establishment of a regular exchange of prices across the Atlantic, became during the 1870s and 1880s the most active and largely dealt-in department of the Stock Exchange. He was popularly known as the 'Erie King', as he specialised in that favourite speculative counter of the period, following a protracted battle in the late 1860s and early 1870s between London and New York for control of the Erie stock.

> In ousting [Jay] Gould, shares had to be bought by tens of thousands and shipped over to New York to be voted on. The Erie King was frequently

seen on pay day half buried in bundles of stock. Mr Nickalls had sometimes so many Eries to receive that they had to be piled on tables or heaped on the floor. A carelessly dropped match might on one of those exciting pay days have annihilated a fourth part of the Erie capital. {Duguid (1901) 249-50}

There exist various descriptions of Nickalls in action as the undisputed leader of his market, or certainly the non-arbitrage part of it. The journalist J H Richardson, in his youth in the 1870s a jobber's clerk, recalled 'a great, burly man with the voice of the "bull of Bashan"', whose 'habit was to come into the market and bellow "I buy Eries", and the small fry of jobbers would gather around him and the price of that time was pulled up and down as Tom Nickalls dictated' {Richardson (1927) 51}. One of his main qualities seems to have been an apparently incorrigible optimism, as years later a Stock Exchange columnist recalled about the death of Vanderbilt in 1877:

> I remember when 'the Commodore' died, what excitement there was in the American market at the opening on the following morning, and about the only man who stuck to his guns was Mr Tom Nickalls, and very well it paid him, as when the turn came, as it speedily did, the arbitrage dealers were all caught short, and he made Messrs Leon & Co dance to a merry tune for a time. {*Citizen* 18 July 1896}

His fellow-members admired also his impulsive expansiveness, always taking the large, if not exactly scientific view, as another Stock Exchange columnist recorded in 1891:

> He had — and still has — any amount of pluck, taking a view and acting on it, sublimely disregarding the minute calculations on which smaller speculators pin their faith. It is no use talking to him about figures or dividends. 'Who is buying?' or 'Who is selling?' he asks, and then makes up his mind what to do. {*Financial Times* 20 July 1891}

By the 1890s, however, the American market was on the wane, and Nickalls spent most of that decade in semi-retirement, fulfilling his duties as master of the Surrey staghounds. He still made occasional appearances in Capel Court, in 1894 even taking his pitch in the thriving South African market, known as the Kaffir Circus. He died on 10 May 1899 at his home, Pattison Court, near Redhill, leaving £135,815 gross. He was remembered with affection on the Stock Exchange 'He was always "Tom" to everybody, and no better sportsman ever entered Gorgonzola Hall [the Stock Exchange]. He was a true friend to anyone in trouble' {*Citizen* 13 May 1899}.

DAVID T A KYNASTON

Sources:

Unpublished

PrC.

Published

Citizen 18 July 1896, 13 May 1899.

Charles Duguid, *The Story of the Stock Exchange* (Grant Richards, 1901).

Financial Times 20 July 1891.

Guy Nickalls, *Life's a Pudding* (Faber & Faber, 1939).

Vivian Nickalls, *Oars, Wars and Horses* (Hurst & Blackett, 1932).

Joseph Hall Richardson, *From the City to Fleet Street* (Stanley Paul & Co, 1927).

NIXON, John

(1815-1899)

Coal-owner

John Nixon (courtesy of L J Williams).

John Nixon was born at Barlow, near Newcastle upon Tyne, on 10 May 1815, the son of a tenant farmer. After being educated up to the age of fourteen at Dr Bruce's Academy in Newcastle he worked on the farm for two years. Nixon was then apprenticed to Joseph Gray, a prominent mining engineer and chief mining agent for the Marquis of Bute in the North of England, and on completion of his apprenticeship worked for two years as an over-man (colliery official) at Garesfield.

Nixon went to South Wales in 1839, when he was twenty-four, in response to an advertisement by Crawshay Bailey for a manager at the Nantyglo Ironworks, but the job was restricted to the company's collieries, which were too small to offer an attractive career. However, his connection with Joseph Gray helped to secure him a temporary post to conduct a survey for Lord Bute of the Dowlais collieries; Nixon's report condemned wasteful working methods there. He was then commissioned to report for an English company on the possibility of setting up an ironworks in France.

Nixon successfully linked these brief excursions to Wales and France by opening a market for Welsh steam coal in France. He arranged with Thomas Powell, whose Aberdare collieries formed the nucleus for the later Powell Duffryn Co, to get a royalty on each ton sold. Perhaps because Powell reneged on the agreement, Nixon soon decided to open his own coal-mine at Werfa in the Aberdare valley in 1845. In 1855 he went into partnership with William Cory and Hugh Taylor, and had already in 1855 begun the sinking of the Navigation Colliery (opened in 1860) in the Aberdare valley. A year later, the partners bought, in the same valley, the Deep Duffryn colliery. Between 1869 and 1875 Nixon sank the Merthyr Vale colliery in the Taff valley, an undertaking involving such risk and cost (£250,000), because of the depth of the pit, that his partners at first did not join in this enterprise. The firm was known as Nixon, Taylor & Cory until it was converted into a limited liability concern in 1882 under the title of Nixon's Navigation Co Ltd, with a total capital of £780,000. John Nixon held 2,340 of the £100 shares. The Cwm Cynon colliery in the Aberdare valley was added in 1896. By 1897 the annual output of Nixon's group of mines was 1.25 million tons.

The contributions made by John Nixon to the business life of South Wales can be divided into three rough categories — entrepreneurial, innovative and organisational. At several stages Nixon displayed substantial entreprenerial flair in identifying and pioneering new business opportunities. He saw the huge potential for the special steam-raising qualities of Welsh coal and took the risk of shipping a cargo to France. Starting with the owner of a sugar-refining plant in Nantes he persuaded many industrialists to try the fuel and also secured its use by the French navy well before its adoption by the Royal Navy, though that too was a campaign in which he later played an active part. He was also one of the earliest men to move into coal ownership deliberately and specifically to exploit the emerging market for steam coal. He was early to recognise the necessity to sink 'to the deep' to win the steam coal and demonstrated this at both Navigation and Merthyr Vale.

His innovative qualities were clearly demonstrated in his introduction of the long-wall system of mining into South Wales (a claim also made by Richard Bedlington, manager of Rhymney Iron Works). Despite strong opposition from the colliers he pressed through the change by persuasion, guile and use of the law (successfully withholding, in 1862 and 1863, wages from miners who left without notice because they objected to the substitution of long-wall for pillar-and-stall working). He was similarly adamant about forcing through the associated change from single-shift to double-shift working, where he again led the way amongst the coalowners of South Wales. These were changes which fundamentally altered the working practices, and the social life, of Welsh miners. Similarly far-reaching and pervasive was his invention of a machine, the 'Billy Playfair', which would separate the large from the small coal, and accurately weigh the large, the only coal for which the miners of South Wales received payment. Previously this had been done by the judgement of a colliery official, the 'cropper', a practice which led to continual and acrimonious disputes. Nixon also invented a winding engine and a spiral winding drum and a ventilating machine. This he installed in his Navigation colliery in 1861; at the time it was the deepest pit in South Wales. This was a period when there were numerous explosions caused by the gas and pressure associated with the steam-coal seams, but although Navigation was potentially one of the most dangerous collieries it did not experience any major disasters.

His organisational contributions were not made at the level of the firm, and he does not appear to have initiated any changes in managerial structure or methods. He was, however, active at the industry level. He was chairman of the meeting at the Windsor Hotel, Cardiff, at which the Aberdare Steam Collieries Association was formed in 1864 and continued to play a positive role as it came to represent all the coalowners of South Wales. From the outset its main function, as its carefully worded Deed of

Association made clear, was in the field of industrial relations. Alexander Dalziel, an employee of Nixon, was secretary of this Association from 1864 to 1883, when he was succeeded by his son. Nixon also served the industry by giving evidence at a number of parliamentary committees dealing with railways, docks and mines.

John Nixon reaped a substantial reward for his entrepreneurial talents and business success. The enterprise was highly profitable: perhaps more remarkably, for a fluctuating industry like mining, it was persistently profitable. Nixon told his board of directors in 1893 that the firm had paid a dividend every quarter, with one strike-bound exception, for over thirty years. He himself left over £1 million. This was also a tribute to his frugality: even his commissioned laudatory biographer noted that Nixon's life was not based on 'altruistic principles' but was lived 'in pursuit of his own interests for his own sake' {Vincent (1900) 3}. He was a long-time friend of Sir William Lewis, later Lord Merthyr (qv), whose general attitudes he shared. Although from the mid-1870s he lived mostly in London and Brighton, Nixon continued, in a general way, to manage the collieries until 1894, when he was succeeded by his nephew H E Gray.

Nixon was much more interested in sport than in either politics (he was a Conservative) or religion (he was a member of the Church of England) and, as the *Times* obituary noted, still carried a gun on his own moors in his eighties.

Nixon married late in life, to Elsie (otherwise unidentified). They had no children. John Nixon died in Brighton on 3 June 1899, leaving £1,179,128 gross and was buried at Aberffrwd cemetery in Mountain Ash where a year later a reredos was placed in the church as a memorial. His widow inherited the Brighton house, £50,000, and an annuity of £5,000 as long as she remained a widow: the bulk of the estate went to nephews and grand-nephews, especially H E Gray and C L Gray, who assumed the colliery interest.

L J WILLIAMS

Writings:

Speech on opening of Navigation Colliery *Merthyr Guardian* 12 May 1860.

Ferndale Colliery Explosion. The 'Single Shift' System of Working Collieries as Practised in Wales (Cardiff: 'Chronicle' Office, 1867).

The Single Shift System: The Cause of Double the Loss of Life (Cardiff, 1867).

PP, RC Accidents in Mines (1886) C 4699.

Sources:

Unpublished
PrC.

Published
Colliery Guardian 8 Nov 1862.

DNB.

Merthyr Guardian 30 Oct 1858, 24 Jan 1863.

John H Morris and Lawrence J Williams, *The South Wales Coal Industry 1841-75* (Cardiff: University of Wales Press, 1958).

South Wales Daily News 5 June, 29 July 1899, 3 Nov 1900.

Times 5 June 1899.

James E Vincent, *John Nixon, Pioneer of the Steam Coal Trade in South Wales* (J Murray, 1900).

Charles Wilkins, *The South Wales Coal Trade and its Allied Industries, from the Earliest Days to the Present Time* (Cardiff: Owen & Co, 1888).

NOBLE, Sir Andrew

(1831-1915)

Arms manufacturer

Andrew Noble was born in Greenock, Scotland, on 13 September 1831, the third son of George Noble, at one a time a lieutenant in the Royal Navy, and his wife Georgiana, only daughter of Andrew Donald Moore of Virginia, USA. He was educated at Edinburgh Academy and the Royal Military Academy at Woolwich, which he entered as a cadet in 1847. He joined the Royal Artillery in 1849, and attained the rank of captain in 1855. Most of his military career was spent abroad.

Employed initially on magnetic survey work at the Cape of Good Hope, Noble in 1857 was made Secretary to the Royal Artillery Institution. In 1858 he was appointed Secretary to the Committee on Rifled Cannon and in 1859 to that on Plates and Guns. The most controversial issue of that time for military men was the merit of the new guns designed by W G Armstrong (qv). Before their adoption by the Government, it was necessary to compare the accuracy of their shooting with that of the smooth bored weapons which it was proposed they displace. A plan by which this could be effected was devised by Noble. He was appointed Assistant Inspector of Artillery in the proofing department of the Woolwich Arsenal in 1859 and the following year became assistant member of the Ordnance Select Committee, commencing shortly after long service as a member of the government committee on explosives. Noble's obvious talent as a gunnery officer was complemented by assiduous cultivation of the scientific side of his work.

In 1860 Noble left the Royal Artillery, being recruited by William Armstrong to become joint manager, with the engineer George Rendel, of the Elswick Ordnance Co's Works at Newcastle upon Tyne. Noble commenced research into ballistics as soon as he joined Armstrong. His first experiments ascertained the maximum pressure produced by ignited powder in the bore of the largest guns of the period, and in 1867 he carried out the first electro-ballistic investigations in the United Kingdom, inventing in the process the Noble chronoscope for determining the velocity of a projectile in the barrel of a gun. In subsequent years he undertook (with Abel) a long series of experiments on fired gunpowder which became acknowledged as classics in the history of explosives. Later, when the era of smokeless powders arrived, Noble experimented with the new cordite, testing adaptability and safety in large guns, determining the pressure to which they gave rise in the bore and investigating the advantage to be gained by increasing the length of the barrel of the gun. He succeeded in greatly increasing muzzle velocity and penetration capacity.

Noble's great ability in the science of explosives was recognised in 1870 with an FRS and again in 1880 with the award of its gold medal. In the work of convincing military authorities of the necessity for improving weaponry he played a large part, and in recognition of his services he was appointed a CB in 1881, a KCB in 1883 and a baronet in 1902 as well as an honorary DSc of the University of Oxford, ScD of Cambridge and DCL of Newcastle.

As well as technical mastery, Noble displayed a fanatical capacity for work, great ambition, tenacity, perservance and a choleric personality. His initial status as a salaried employee of Armstrong was soon replaced by a partnership in the business and by the early 1880s he had emerged as the undoubted successor to Armstrong as head of the firm. Increasingly he devoted his attention to the whole range of output at Armstrongs, playing an important role in the ascent of the company to its position as the country's principal arms manufacturer of the 1890s. He was deeply involved in the absorption by Armstrongs of the Tyneside shipbuilders Charles Mitchell & Co in 1882, in the establishment of a branch arsenal in Italy, and in the acquisition of the Manchester armourers, Sir Joseph Whitworth & Co, in 1897. In 1900 he succeeded Armstrong as chairman of Sir W G Armstrong, Whitworth & Co Ltd.

As a limited company from 1883, Armstrongs exhibited great profitability which reached record levels under Noble's chairmanship. The company enjoyed also a fine reputation for investment in research and development. Despite this, Armstrong, Whitworth's supremacy as Britain's leading arms manufacturer was eroded after 1900 by Vickers. Contemporary directors of Armstrongs, and subsequent historians of the arms industry, have been heavily critical of the ageing Noble's dynastically-based direction of the firm, to the extent that his managerial style is held up now as an example of capricious autocracy, sterilising debate, and stifled innovation and management development, together responsible for the relative decline of the company. At a time of heavy world demand for arms, however, the decline was only relative and to the end of Noble's active management of the firm in 1911 (he remained chairman until his death), the financial strength of Armstrongs was impressive. Employing over 20,000 persons on Tyneside alone, the business had great significance for the condition of the local economy and Noble figured prominently in the commercial life of the region, serving as a JP and president of the North East Coast Institute of Engineering and Shipbuilding as well as featuring on the governing bodies of several of the great professional institutions. As a major exporter of arms, Noble was showered with awards by overseas governments, particularly when, like the Japanese in 1905, their British-built navies were successful in battle.

Noble married in 1854 Margery Durham, daughter of Archibald Campbell, a notary of Quebec. They had four sons and two daughters; two of his sons followed Sir Andrew into top management posts with Armstrongs. His recreations were shooting and tennis.

Sir Andrew Noble died on 22 October 1915 in his native Scotland, leaving £734,418 gross.

R J IRVING

Writings:

Internal Ballistics (W P Griffith & Sons, 1892).

Artillery Progress since 1850 (W Clowes & Son, 1909).

Artillery and Explosives (1906).

Sources:

Unpublished

BLPES, Tariff Commission papers, TC 31/309, evidence of Sir Andrew Noble, 9 Nov 1905.

Tyne and Wear RO, Newcastle upon Tyne, papers of Lord Rendel and Armstrong Whitworth.

PrC.

Published

Burke's Peerage and Baronetage.

DNB.

The Engineer 29 Oct 1915.

Frederick E Hamer, *The Personal Papers of Lord Rendel* (Ernest Benn, 1931).

Robert J Irving, 'New Industries for Old? Some Investment Decisions of Sir W G Armstrong, Whitworth & Company Limited, 1900-1914' *Business History* 17 (1975).

John D Scott, *Vickers: A History* (Weidenfeld & Nicholson, 1961).

Times 23 Oct 1915.

Clive Trebilcock, *The Vickers Brothers: Armaments and Enterprise, 1854-1914* (Europa, 1977).

WWW.

NORMAN, Montagu Collet

Lord Norman of St Clare

(1871-1950)

Central banker

Montagu Collet Norman was born at Kensington, Middlesex on 6 September 1871, the son of Frederick Henry Norman and Lina Susan Penelope, only daughter of Mark W Collet, a partner in the London accepting house, Brown Shipley & Co. Collet was elected to the Court of the Bank of England in 1866 and served as Deputy Governor, 1885-87, and Governor, 1887-89. The Norman family had been involved in London commerce since the beginning of the eighteenth century, when they founded a prosperous Norwegian timber importing business. George Warde Norman, Montagu's grandfather, had been elected to the Court of the Bank in 1821 and remained an influential member for almost fifty years. His ideas helped to shape the Bank Act of 1844. He married Sibella, one of the three daughters and co-heirs of Henry Stone, a partner in the country bankers Stone & Martin (later Martin & Co). Their son, F H Norman, started life as a barrister but in 1881 became a partner in Martin & Co, followed by his youngest brother in 1884. Their eldest brother, Charles Loyd, was a partner in Baring Bros.

Montagu Norman had an unhappy schooling at Eton where he resented the rules and found little to excite his intellect. In 1889 he went up to King's College, Cambridge, but left after a year. He then moved to Dresden to develop his German and travelled widely in Germany and Austria, shifting to Switzerland to improve his French. He spent two years on the Continent before entering Martin's Bank in October 1892. Early in 1894 he was commissioned into a Militia Regiment, the 4th Battalion of the Bedfordshire and Hertfordshire Regiment, and later in the year joined his grandfather Collet's firm, Brown Shipley & Co. This was a natural choice. He had always been closer to his grandparents than his own parents and Brown Shipley were badly in need of young men to handle their overseas business particularly the connection with their sister house, Brown Bros of New York. In the autumn of 1895 as part of his apprenticeship, he was sent to work at Brown Bros in New York to learn American business methods and see something of the country. He made long tours right across the country and was fascinated by what he saw of American commerce and industry, particularly the railroads. He began to develop a keen interest in the relationship between the fixed assets he saw on the ground and the capital that supported them. His work at Brown Bros gave him first-hand knowledge of American attitudes towards the financing of the commodity trade with Europe. He was also fortunate to witness the wave of mergers that was sweeping the country, arranged by New York and Boston bankers, which created out of private companies and partnerships giant corporations like American Bicycle Co, Central

Foundry Co, and New England Cotton Yarn Co. He returned to London in the summer of 1898 and was given power to sign for Brown Shipley & Co on 1 January 1899. At the end of the year he was back in America on a fact-finding expedition.

Norman returned in time to sail with his regiment to the Boer War. He enjoyed active service in its combination of outdoor life and administrative duties. In April 1901 he took command of the Mounted Infantry at Mafeking and in the next few months participated in a number of skirmishes against the Boers. Much to his surprise he was awarded a DSO. Early in October his health broke down due to the strain and the recurrence of a nervous disorder that, contrary to some assertions, was not an affliction of manhood but one he had suffered since infancy. He was invalided home. It was not until the end of the year that he was fit enough to resume work with Brown Shipley, of which he had become a partner in 1900 just after joining his regiment.

Back in harness in the City, he brought a new blend of talents to merchant banking which had the reputation of being parochial. His own firm had been criticised by Brown Bros for its failure to keep itself well informed about events in America. In the depressed trading conditions in the opening decade of the century, Norman recognised the value of strong ties with the United States at a time when a large proportion of the country's external trade was still financed by sterling credits. He visited the country regularly. He rapidly developed an uncanny instinct for business, knowing almost intuitively whose bills to accept and whose to reject. His work fascinated him. He came to understand by careful analysis of the firm's ledgers that Britain depended for her prosperity on international trade and not as popularly imagined just on trade with the Empire. By 1906 he dominated the firm, working long hours with few outside interests and in October 1907 his skill and dedication were recognised when he was elected to the Court of the Bank of England. During 1904 he had purchased Thorpe Lodge on Campden Hill and lavished much money and effort on converting it to his own tastes, even helping make some of the fittings himself. He took to walking, rather than using transport, ruminating on the business of the day and jotting down notes on slips of paper he kept in his pockets. By the end of the decade he found himself becoming gradually distanced from his partners at Brown Shipley, who found his pace too fast for their liking. In 1911 he refused to countenance the firm becoming involved in overseas land mortgages, taking the view that an accepting house must keep most of its resources in readily realisable assets. Coming from a family of bankers, who had witnessed all the major financial catastrophes of the nineteenth century, he knew all too well the perils of tying up a bank's funds in mortgages. These strained relations told on his health and contributed to a breakdown in 1911, from which he took two years to recover. Much of his trouble centred around his disagreement with his partners and his inability to devise a career for himself in the work which he loved.

When he returned to business in the autumn of 1913 he became further estranged from his partners. In May and June 1914 he was in America visiting Brown Bros, returning in time to witness the massive dislocation of the world financial system in the month before the outbreak of the war and the efforts of the Governor of the Bank of England to deal with the crisis. He was appalled at the total lack of preparation by the Government for the finance of a long campaign and the failure of the Governor, Walter Cunliffe (qv), to discuss measures fully with the Court. After the outbreak of war Norman found more and more of his time taken up at the Bank of England where his knowledge of the American money market was invaluable. In April 1915 he was appointed a financial adviser to the War Office and in June chairman of the Aircraft Insurance Expert Committee. By the end of the year his advice was being sought by a number of committees and departments. His war work left him no time for the affairs of Brown Shipley and at the end of the year he retired from the partnership. In January 1916 he was appointed 'devil' to the Deputy Governor, Brien Cokayne, who had taken over many of the Governor's duties in Cunliffe's enforced absence due to ill-health. Norman enjoyed his new position, making a firm friend of Ben Strong, Governor of the Federal Reserve Bank. In March he was appointed a member of the Committee of Treasury, largely composed of former Governors. He quickly found that the Governor had failed to win the confidence of the Committee through regular consultation. There were growing doubts about the wisdom of the Bank's endorsement of the massive borrowings by the Government from the United States which Norman believed would have serious implications for the exchange rate in the future. The Governors also took Norman on their visits to the Treasury, whose officials he found unimpressive and dispiriting. In the summer of 1917 Cunliffe's failure to consult his colleagues on the Committee of the Treasury precipitated a crisis when it became known that he had agreed to place gold held by the Bank in Canada at the disposal of J P Morgan & Co to meet a call on a Treasury loan in the Bank's name. Norman, as Cunliffe's chief critic, found himself the spearhead of the opposition. Skirmishes continued into the autumn of 1917 and reached a climax over the nominations for the post of Governor and Deputy Governor. In November Cokayne was elected Governor and Norman, Deputy Governor.

Norman took office in March 1918 and was immediately plunged into the problems of creating a policy for dealing with the effect of the huge war debts on the exchanges and interest rates in the coming peace. One of his first duties was to draft the Bank's evidence to the Cunliffe Committee on Currency and Foreign Exchanges after the war. The Committee of Treasury agreed that a return to the pre-war Gold Standard was essential, which could only be achieved by the Government exercising severe financial discipline and reaching terms for the payment of war debts; but it refused to endorse Norman's suggestion that imports should be restricted and capital exports prohibited. Immediately after the Armistice Cokayne and Norman geared the Bank up for an early return to gold. They were to be disappointed; the post-war boom, fuelled in part by the inability of the Treasury to persuade the Government to dampen the economy by calling in arrears in excess profits duty and tax, forced the New York exchange rate down to $3.20 by February 1920. Norman's answer to these problems had been to propose in April 1919 that the Government should put its house in order by raising a compulsory loan of £1,000 million from taxpayers to cover the floating debt. Although such an unorthodox measure would have gone to the heart of the problem, the Treasury instead issued Voluntary Victory Bonds which raised only three-quarters of the sum required. Norman continued to press the Government for deflationary fiscal measures as an alternative to raising interest rates which had to be put up in the winter to protect the exchanges. This was new territory for the Bank since the Government, under the National Assistance measures introduced before the war, had far greater commitments in pension, welfare and benefit payments, quite apart from the gigantic war debt.

Norman was elected Governor at the end of March 1920 for the first of twenty-four successive one-year terms. He at once began to reform the organisation of the Bank, introducing a modern registry system on the lines of those that he had seen established in Government departments during the war and making arrangements for the Bank's senior officials to be informed of Bank policy. He was determined that his authority as Governor should derive from the Committee of Treasury and the Court and he would only act with their consent. As a result of the report of the Revelstoke Committee of 1918 on the membership of the Court of Directors and Committee of Treasury, he could call on a much wider body of expertise to advise him. He believed that the central bank should not jeopardise its fiduciary position by taking political decisions. If the Bank were required to act as surrogate for the Treasury then he would only do so at the invitation of the Chancellor of the Exchequer.

These principles were clearly evinced in the lengthy task of taking Britain back on to the Gold Standard in 1925. Although Norman and his colleagues at the Bank were committed to the policy, he considered the decision to be political and in dealing with successive Governments he took pains to allow the politicians to reach their own conclusions about exchanges and price levels. However he battered away at the Treasury and the Chancellors over the level of government expenditure and debt and interest rates. His own attitude to the Gold Standard changed. At first he saw it as a means of rapidly re-establishing the pre-war pattern of world trade and later as an anchor in the uncharted waters of the depressed conditions of the 1920s. He could see all too clearly the perils of a floating exchange, particularly when a Government might choose to depress the exchange rate by using low interest rates to ease the funding of its own debts with little concern for the effect on trade and industry. His experience in the pre-war commodity trade convinced him that high fixed exchanges would benefit the economy by holding down the price levels of imported raw materials. At this time he did not regard short-term movements in interest rates as critical for the economy as a whole. Moreover a strengthening pound would attract deposits to London, enabling the London money markets to lend overseas to help finance reconstruction especially in Central Europe.

On his appointment Norman was greatly troubled by the financial chaos in Central Europe. Unlike most politicians who knew little of Europe, Norman understood how important Central European markets had been in the pre-war economy. He was irritated that the Government had failed to consult the Bank over the question of German reparations and the technical problem of how the Reichsbank was expected to fund them. Of more concern were the financial problems of Austria and the newly independent countries which had formed part of the old Habsburg empire. For the next five years much of Norman's time was occupied with these issues and with endless discussions over reparations and the Dawes Plan. He saw the League of Nations with its Finance Committee and League-endorsed reconstruction loans as hopeful beacons in a very confused and disturbed sea where few, except those like Norman who had first-hand knowledge of the transatlantic trade, could comprehend the reason for the urgency of restructuring the economy of enemy countries. With the help of the London merchant bankers who had extensive European business, Norman managed to achieve a monetary reconstruction in Central Europe by 1925 with the establishment of central banks wedded to the Gold Standard and sound money. Between 1925 and 1928 Norman dominated the world financial community. His opinion was respected by both Americans and Europeans. Such dissent as there was centred around the Bank of France who distrusted his willingness to help the Germans and his reliance on advisers of German origin. In the winter of 1928-29 Norman gave much of his time to the Young Committee, set up at the end of the Dawes Plan's first five years to review the system of international settlements. This led to the formation in 1929 of the Bank for International Settlements which Norman was determined should serve not merely as a mechanism for settling outstanding reparation questions but as a neutral international forum for central bankers.

At home the years 1925 to 1931 were a grave disappointment to Norman who summed them up in a phrase 'continuously under the harrow' {Sayers (1978) 221}. Following the return to the Gold Standard the world economy failed to respond in the way he and Ben Strong at the Federal Reserve Bank had hoped. In holding the fixed exchange Norman had to maintain a constant watch on reserves and interest rates which had to be altered three times in 1925 before settling at 5 per cent. He could not bring the rate down to 4.5 per cent until 1927. Despite a deterioration in the reserves and terms of trade, the rate was held until early 1929 following the speculative boom on Wall Street. By this time Norman had begun to discover part of the reasons for the sluggish behaviour of the British economy.

In the 1920s one of the Bank of England's most important private customers was the Tyneside armaments and shipbuilding firm of Armstrong Whitworth & Co. After the war the Bank had made large advances to the company to allow it to diversify away from armaments into other industries like locomotive building and civil engineering and invest in a newsprint complex in Newfoundland. By 1925 the company was in serious financial difficulties. Norman, with the help of Edward Peacock (qv) of Baring Bros and Frater Taylor (qv), a company 'doctor' from Canada, began the task of unravelling the company's accounts which were in total disarray. In many ways Armstrong, Whitworth's problems mirrored those of the Central European countries Norman had done so much to help. There was a large amount of unfunded debt, some of which belonged to the Government, and any semblance of financial control had totally vanished. No sooner had Norman become enmeshed in the problems of Armstrong, Whitworth than he found himself drawn into the difficulties of the Lancashire cotton industry, the Glasgow armaments and shipbuilding firm of William Beardmore & Co and the shipbuilding industry as a whole. He realised that the Bank lacked the expertise to deal with such problems and he began to build up under Frater Taylor's leadership a powerful group of advisers to give professional technical, accounting and legal advice. This group eventually found formal identity in the formation in 1929 of Securities Management Trust as a subsidiary of the Bank with Frater Taylor and then Charles Bruce-Gardner (qv) as managing directors. SMT and the Bankers' Industrial Development Corporation (formed in the spring of 1930 as a co-operative venture with the clearing banks to assist industrial reconstruction) quickly outlined schemes, often in considerable detail, for rebuilding nearly all Britain's basic industries, along with proposals for generating investment in newer industries.

Although these industrial problems were not properly the concern of a central banker, Norman realised that as the failure of the companies and industries that were referred to him could jeopardise the financial system he had gone to such lengths to protect, he had no alternative but to use his fiduciary position to act more or less as a receiver for much of British industry in the absence of any official agency. He took enormous trouble to monitor various rationalisation schemes, interviewing senior industrialists to assess their qualities and win their support and going through capital reorganisation proposals with a fine tooth comb. He insisted the SMT and BIDC should carry out penetrating investigations of the firms that it had under review, gathering vast quantities of financial and technical reports. He found time, even when he was otherwise heavily occupied, to work through most of these papers including those on complex technical matters, making marginal jottings in pencil throughout the accounts and reports. He displayed an astonishing aptitude for interpreting accounts and a shrewd judgement in assessing market reaction. By the spring of 1930 he was privy to the innermost secrets of a great number of concerns and the level of their commitments to the financial institutions and the clearing banks. He knew that the plight of British industry was so grave that simple solutions like lowering the exchange rate and protection could offer little succour. Moreover, he was aware that the huge Royal Mail Shipping Group was technically bankrupt with vast liabilities and that if this news became public a stock market collapse and retreat from gold would be inevitable.

In March 1930 Norman was called to give evidence to the Macmillan Committee on Finance and Industry. His recent industrial reconstruction experience had left him with little sympathy with the view that credit restrictions were responsible for Britain's ills. On the contrary he suspected that the banks, especially the clearers, had thrown good money after bad and that the Government had acted irresponsibly in not clearing up the credits given to industry out of the wartime emergency taxes. He made a bad witness, answering the questions put by the committee, especially by Reginald McKenna (qv) from the Midland Bank and Keynes (qv), in a perfunctory fashion. He made no attempt to disguise his personal dislike of some of the members of the committee and gave the impression that his mind was on other things. Unknown to the committee he was deeply troubled by the developing Royal Mail crisis which threatened to destroy many months of patient work in rebuilding the steel and shipbuilding industries. He also knew far too much to be able to reply frankly to questions about the Bank's recent activities. If he had told the committee that he thought much of the management of British industry

was incompetent and was to blame for its problems, he would have destroyed the trust that he had managed to build up with the business world.

Throughout 1930 Norman was preoccupied by the sharp decline in the world economy and the high level of unemployment. When the Bank's gold reserve came under severe pressure, Norman counselled that monetary measures alone could do little to reflate the economy but he pushed the bank rate down to 3.5 per cent in March. Towards the end of the year there was a growing distrust of sterling and gold drained away to France which had chosen to undervalue the franc at the time of stabilisation. In January 1931 Norman had urgent discussions to hammer out a policy should gold reserves fall further. He knew how damaging a rise in interest rates would be to the fragile recovery and for the first half of the year made every effort to hold bank rates. On 14 May the rate was actually cut to 2.5 per cent in an attempt to relieve the enormous problems of debtor countries. This it failed to do. Three days earlier the Austrian Credit-Anstalt bank had crashed precipitating a massive crisis in Central Europe which aggravated the Bank of England's position by freezing London's short-term claims. In checking the crisis Norman believed that prices in Britain needed to be brought into line with those of foreign competitors by cutting wages and pushing up productivity and at the same time drastically pruning Government expenditure. His critics believed a floating exchange rate would be sufficient. Norman, who perhaps better than any other, knew the appalling state of much of British manufacturing industry — the linchpin in a sustained recovery — was sceptical. Throughout June he was preoccupied with the negotiations leading up to the announcement of the standstill agreement on German and Austrian loans made in mid-July.

On 13 July the crisis deepened when one of Germany's biggest banks closed its doors and the Macmillan Committee published its report which stated that sterling was over-valued by 10 per cent. The Bank of England immediately began to lose gold and the sterling exchanges slipped below parity. It is difficult to discern Norman's view of the crisis as after weeks of long hours and nervous strain his health collapsed on 29 July. He had belatedly on 23 July raised Bank Rate by 1 per cent as he had come to the conclusion that the solution was for politicians, not for the bankers. Although he would have preferred the mainstay of the Gold Standard, he probably realised it was no longer tenable and as in 1925 he looked to the politicians to fix the rules. He must have feared that a sudden depreciation in sterling, coupled with some measure of protection, would destroy all his painstaking efforts to reform large sections of Britain's basic industries and to impose financial discipline on other countries. He was absent on sick leave until almost the end of September, leaving his deputy Sir Ernest Harvey and Edward Peacock of Barings to carry the Bank through the centre of the storm. On his return he was profoundly depressed to learn that the Gold Standard had been abandoned. A floating exchange in an unpredictable market was an unpleasant surprise at a time when he was still grappling with industrial problems where raw material import prices were critical.

During his absence Norman's close group of supporters led by Harvey, Peacock, Kindersley (qv) from Lazards Bros, and the economist Henry

Clay, had come to appreciate the colossal strain the Governor had borne almost single-handed since 1920. The need to monitor the exchange rate by maintaining close contact with the market gave them an opportunity to lighten the burden through a series of committees. Norman adjusted remarkably quickly to the new situation. He was immediately faced with the giant problem of navigating a path for the wrecked Royal Mail Group which was barely afloat and if it foundered would make the problems of July seem merely a local difficulty. His skill was also badly needed in shaping a long-term policy for the German standstill agreements. As solutions were found to these difficult questions he had time to turn his attention to the exchange rate policy. He was certain that sudden movements in the exchanges were harmful to manufacturing industry which he had discovered lacked the accounting skills to determine its own costs even in a stable market. However, he realised the Bank had insufficient gold resources to maintain any semblance of a policy and it could not buy gold without increasing the money supply. The only weapons were high interest rates and strict control of government expenditure at a time when the market was awash with unfunded debt. Norman found it hard to maintain these massive deflationary policies as the economy slumped in the winter and pressure grew for reflation. He was in too close a contact with industry to believe that a dash for growth could be successful and from a careful scrutiny of the loans sanctioned by the new financial intermediaries had no faith in the new industries as engines for recovery. He believed in a steady and carefully implemented lowering of interest rates to a platform that could be held for several years. He and his advisers knew that this could only be achieved if some mechanism were found for stabilising the exchange. As a result in the 1932 Budget the Exchange Equalisation Account was established by the Treasury out of the Consolidated Fund and, operated by the Bank, was to stabilise the rate of exchange in the short run as far as practicable. This would insulate domestic credit from the effects of arbitrary movements in the exchanges. At the same time Harvey, with Norman's encouragement, piloted the gigantic scheme of converting the 5 per cent War Loan to 3.5 per cent. These two manoeuvres allowed the Bank to push interest rates down to a 2 per cent plateau which was sustained to the eve of the war.

Norman was alive to the dangers of this policy. He was concerned that low interest rates would lead to a stock market boom and avoided the temptation to expand credit. Throughout the next two years he maintained a firm grasp on the monetary tiller, refusing to alter course in response to fashionable demands for imperial monetary union made at the Ottawa conference in 1932 and pressing for a reformed gold standard at the World Economic Conference in 1933. The collapse of the Conference, following the election of President Roosevelt who was committed to more nationalistic policies, saddened Norman. Immediately, his worst fears were confirmed as funds began to flow into London, pushing up the money supply which, if not controlled, would tend to be inflationary. He was angry that the world had made no progress towards monetary stability which he believed was essential for sustained recovery. In October in this despondent mood, he made his famous remark at the Mansion House: 'The dogs may bark but the caravan moves on' {*Times* 4 Oct 1933}. In this much criticised statement he was speaking not only for himself but for his small band of supporters who had worked incredibly hard to provide a framework for recovery and had been repeatedly thwarted by the myopic attitude of many British businessmen and foreign bankers who completely failed to grasp the reality of their position. At home he was locked in frustrating negotiations with Sir Percy Bates to bring about an agreement between Cunard and White Star which would allow work to begin again on the *Queen Mary* then standing seemingly as a monument to the depression on the ways at Clydebank.

By early 1934 Norman could begin to see the fruit of his efforts to nurse the assets of much of British industry and to protect some financial institutions like Lazards from annihilation. The exchanges were settling and Norman could look kindly on some increase in Government borrowing to fund unemployment relief. He resisted calls for a return to gold for fear that fixed rates in the absence of any general agreement on the world monetary system would force an upward movement in interest rates which in some ways had replaced gold as the main component in his monetary strategy. Instead he encouraged the negotiations which led up to the Tripartite Monetary Agreement of 1936. Meanwhile, Norman had been striving to find some solution to the problems associated with the standstill agreements declaring that a writing down of debts was inevitable. Although the Hungarian debt was limited, the question of the bigger German deficit remained outstanding until the following year. By this time the shadow of war was beginning to stretch across Europe.

Throughout the 1930s Norman and his band of advisers continued to struggle to reshape the structure of British industry. In approaching this task Norman had always behaved correctly as the 'lender of last resort' demanding prior liens for any new money supplied by the Bank and imposing stiff conditions. He was able to note in 1945 that of all the money advanced 'not a bob seems to have been lost' {Bank of England archives, Norman to Niemeyer 20 June 1945}. He had never intervened without consulting the Committee of Treasury and in the case of the Royal Mail Group had only acted at the invitation of the Chancellor of the Exchequer since the Treasury represented one of the Group's largest creditors. As the economy began to recover the need for the Bank to be involved in rationalisation plans subsided and gradually SMT was converted to other purposes and BIDC wound up. Norman, however, remained willing in his fiduciary position to veto plans and to chair crucial meetings. He was anxious that the merchant banks and the clearing banks should take over the Bank's duties and learn from its experience in monitoring the affairs of large borrowers. With the introduction of the tariff he felt the Treasury and Board of Trade should accept responsibility for industrial and commercial policy.

By the late 1930s Norman was becoming increasingly preoccupied with preparations for war. He was determined that orderly arrangements should be made to finance the coming conflict and that there should be no repetition of the chaos of 1914 on which he blamed most of the problems of the inter-war years. The international crisis of August-September 1938 provided a dress rehearsal for the following year. Norman considered that draconian measures to prevent the flight of sterling, including the introduction of exchange control, would be necessary in the event of war, and urged this policy on a reluctant Treasury. As 1939 unfolded he gradually allowed the Treasury to take control of the exchanges and money market. He discouraged foreign loans and persuaded the Chancellor to forbid forward dealings in exchange. At the outbreak of war Norman was fully prepared to restrain monetary growth and prevent the massive inflation that had taken place under Cunliffe in the First World War. He used his power in tandem with Keynes to fight the war at 3 per cent, more or less, forcing the Government to hold down prices of war materials and to impose efficient management on inefficient producers. He saw himself as a bridge between Whitehall and the City and by implication all the concerns that used its services to finance production. In order to achieve his goal of minimising the cost of the war, Norman had to manage the market with great care, establishing the Capital Issues Committee for this purpose. He instigated the system of Treasury Deposit Receipts in July 1940 to absorb surplus funds in the banks and was behind efforts to channel small savings into the National Savings scheme.

As the war progressed he became anxious about the future of British industry after the war. Early in 1943 he and Sir Harold Hartley (qv) looked hard at the importance of industrial research and advocated widely the stepping up of research initiatives. In March he established a committee within the Bank to consider post-war financial needs, especially effective co-operation between the Government and the financial institutions. This led to the recommendation to form an Industrial Development Corporation. The gigantic strain of the war, with Norman often spending three nights a week sleeping at the Bank, told on his health and early in 1944, under doctor's orders, he was obliged to stand down. After much pressure from his friends he agreed to accept a peerage which had been first offered some twenty years before. In retirement, increasing ill health prevented him from taking part in public affairs.

Norman will always remain a controversial figure. He did little to meet his critics during his lifetime. In conversations and at meetings he tended to dramatise events, a trick he found useful in forcing through the Bank's policy and persuading individuals to tell him more than they intended. His theatrical behaviour often gave the impression to the unwary that decisions were taken on a whim. They would have been surprised to see the vast array of well-referenced files containing information on every subject that crossed his desk which he had amassed as a basis for decision-taking. Contrary to general belief his policy was rarely personal and nearly always hammered out after prolonged and tense discussions with his advisers, particularly Sir Edward Peacock, Sir Ernest Harvey, Vivian Hugh Smith (qv) of Morgan Grenfell, Sir Warren Fisher, Sir Richard Hopkins, Sir Robert Kindersley, Sir Guy Granet (qv), Sir Andrew Duncan (qv), Sir Henry Clay, Sir William McLintock (qv), Sir James Lithgow, Sir Charles Bruce-Gardner, and his private secretary, E H D Skinner. These men who were close to him respected his judgement and always accepted his veto as absolute. He was from first to last a man of the market. He trusted its judgement and framed all his plans with market reaction in mind, skilfully testing proposals before launching a scheme. He realised that his fiduciary position in the market gave him unique powers which he was careful never to jeopardise by partisan operations. This led him to eschew public statements that might compromise him. However he listened to the Press as an indication of market opinion, collecting and filing press cuttings on every subject in which the Bank was interested. He was renowned for his secretiveness, but this stemmed from the delicacy of many of the negotiations to which he was privy and his respect for the market and those who sought his confidence. Commentators tried to cast him in roles but he detested play-acting, preferring the cold cutting edge of the accountant's figures. He enjoyed harmless fun, calling himself Plodgerite (a nickname derived from his home, Thorpe Lodge) in telegrams, but this was a way of keeping spirits up in the difficult tasks that he had set the Bank. It is hardly surprising that his health broke down on several occasions; most lesser men could not have encompassed the sheer weight of business that passed through his office.

It is hard to judge whether he stayed too long. He had considered going in the late 1920s but there was no-one with his knowledge to take his place. His long rule gave a remarkable consistency to economic policy in the 1920s and 1930s, particularly in tackling long-term problems like war debt, industrial reconstruction and the standstill agreements.

In 1933 he married Priscilla Cecilia née Reyntiens, divorced wife of Alexander Louis Wynand-Koch Worsthorne; the security she offered took away much of the stress that had troubled him since childhood.

Lord Norman died on 4 February 1950, leaving £253,316 gross.

MICHAEL MOSS

Writings:

PP, Finance and Industry, 1929-31 (1931) Cmd 3897.

Sources:

Unpublished

Bank of England Archives.

BCe.

MCe.

PrC.

Published

Andrew Boyle, *Montagu Norman* (Cassell, 1967).

Henry Clay, *Lord Norman* (Macmillan, 1957).

DNB.

Edwin Green and Michael S Moss, *A Business of National Importance — The Royal Mail Shipping Group, 1902-1937* (Methuen, 1982).

Susan Howson, *Domestic Monetary Management in Britain 1919-1938* (Cambridge: Cambridge University Press, 1975).

Donald E Moggridge, *The Return to Gold 1925* (Cambridge: Cambridge University Press, 1969).

Richard Sayers, *The Bank of England* (3 vols, Cambridge: Cambridge University Press, 1976).

Times 4 Oct 1933.

WWW.

NORTH, Sir Jonathan

(1855-1939)

Shoe manufacturer and retailer

Jonathan North was born at Rothley, Leicestershire on 3 January 1855, the son of William North, an ostler, and his wife Ann née Ashby. When he was still very young his family migrated to Leicester, where his father entered the wholesale boot trade, newly founded in the town.

After being privately educated, he also entered the industry, being trained as a shoemaker by his father. In the mid-1870s he joined James Leavesley, a prominent Leicester boot manufacturer and public figure, in partnership, as Leavesley & North, footwear manufacturers, of Erskine Street, Leicester. Here North's administrative and managerial abilities were nurtured and developed. The firm did a varied trade in medium and best grade ladies' and children's shoes, developing extensive British, South African, and Australasian markets. In a period of rapid technological and organisational change within the industry, the firm was one of the first in the town to use machine welted techniques, which were designed for quality footwear. The principals' ability and energy ensured continued success and growth; and by the end of the century they were in the front rank of Leicester footwear concerns. Unfortunately, as is so often the case in the shoe industry, no records of the firm are extant, but the following description gives some notion of the firm's position at this time:

> Messrs Leavesley & North's factory ... consists of a large and substantial building containing three spacious floors and basement. The mechanical equipment throughout is of a highly efficient and well-organised character, and the proprietors have certainly surrounded themselves with every known and approved resource of their industry and called in requisition every facility obtainable for the economising of labour and for the improvement of production. Altogether a staff of about three hundred is busily engaged in the various departments under the expert management of specialists. {*Men of the Period* (1897) 117}

At least part of this success was based upon manufacturing for large factoring houses, which were an important feature of Leicester's Victorian industry. In particular Leavesleys developed a close working relationship with Freeman Hardy & Willis Ltd which was underscored by North joining the board of the latter, as joint managing director with Robert Hyslop in 1903. Ten years later North became chairman of the board in succession to Sir Edward Wood (qv); his eldest son, W A North, joined the board at this time, replacing Hyslop, who retired. Freemans acquired a third of the share capital in Leavesley & North Ltd when it was formed in 1919 and in 1926 took it over entirely.

The two Norths' retirement in 1929 was precipitated when Messrs Sears & Co (True-Form Boot Co) Ltd, founded by John George Sears (qv), acquired a controlling interest in Freeman Hardy & Willis. North's years at Freemans span the most influential of his business career. And it was recorded that his shrewdness, ability and business aptitude made him '... one of the leaders of the shoe industry who placed Leicester in the van of the country's shoe production centres ...' {*Times* 14 Nov 1939}.

North also held other local directorships, including those of the Leicester Temperance & General Permanent Building Society, and the local board of the Commercial Union Assurance Co Ltd.

Despite these considerable business activities, however, he devoted much of his time and energy to local government and community service. Initially a member of the School Board of the Belgrave District of Leicester, he served as a Leicester Poor Law Guardian from 1888 to 1897, for two years as chairman. Regarded as the natural, talented leader of a rising group of radical Guardians, he was prominently concerned in the anti-vaccination movement which engulfed the country and Leicester in particular. He also did much to alleviate distress caused by technological unemployment in the industry. A Liberal, he was elected to the Town (later City) Council in 1897 representing the Spinney Hill Ward: he had unsuccessfully contested the Charnwood Ward a year earlier. He was elected an alderman in 1909, served as mayor of Leicester during the First World War, and remained on the Council until 1937 by which time he was an elder statesman of considerable influence. He was appointed a JP in 1907 and DL for Leicester in 1931. Hand in hand with ardent Liberalism went his Nonconformist faith. Active in the work of the Independent Christian Meeting House in Grafton Street, Leicester, he was a Sunday School teacher from the mid-1870s. During the First World War, as mayor he inaugurated a fund which raised £10,600 to relieve local hardship, partly by establishing the Leicester Frith House of Recovery (the country's second neurasthenic hospital) and the Oadby Homes (a small garden suburb with social facilities to house ex-servicemen's families). In recognition of his wartime services North was made an honorary freeman of the city of Leicester and an honorary lieutenant colonel in 1919; that year too he was knighted for those services.

For some thirty years from 1904 he was a powerful and influential chairman of Leicester's Education Committee. He was also the chairman of the governors of the Wyggeston schools. He lent his support to founding the Leicester University College (later Leicester University) in 1921, and was chairman of the College's Council until 1939. He was also a member of the Council of Birmingham University. In 1925 he endowed an education trust to provide higher education for local people at the University College and in 1938 the Sir Jonathan North Educational Endowment Scheme was inaugurated.

He was a generous benefactor to the city and its institutions, and '... in his lifetime devoted scores of thousands of pounds to charity and gifts to his native city ...' {*Times* 13 Nov 1939}. Besides donating most of the money for the Victoria Park War Memorial by Sir Edwin Lutyens (qv) in 1933, he was principally responsible for the erection of the city's premier concert hall, De Montfort Hall. He was also a popular and energetic president of the local Poor Boys' and Girls' Summer Camp and Institute: he provided £3,000 to fund a holiday home at Mablethorpe.

North in 1879 married Kate Eliza Trott, the only daughter of Mark King Trott, a plumber of Taunton: she predeceased him in 1930. They had two sons and a daughter, his elder son, W A North JP, being High Sheriff of Leicestershire in 1935. Latterly North resided at Brackendale, Stoneygate, Leicester.

Sir Jonathan North died at his home, Glebe Mount, Oadby, Leicester, on 12 November 1939, and was accorded a public funeral service at Leicester Cathedral. He left £390,912 gross.

KEITH BROOKER

Sources:

Unpublished

Leicestershire RO, British Shoe Corporation Archive (ref DE 2357).

BCe.

MCe.

PrC.

Published

Colin D B Ellis, *Catalogue of Local Portraits* (Leicester: Leicester Museums and Art Gallery, 1956).

DD 1914-39.

'Freeman, Hardy & Willis' *Leicestershire Survey (Part One); Histories of Famous Firms: 1956.*

H Hartopp (comp), *Roll of Mayors of the Borough and Lords Mayor of the City of Leicester, 1209-1935* (Leicester, 1935).

Kelly's Directories of Leicester.

Leicester Mercury 13 Nov 1939.

Men of the Period (Biographical Publishing Co, 1896).

'Jonathan North, Chairman of the Board of Guardians' *Wyvern* 15 June 1894.

W T Pike (ed), *Leicester and Rutland Contemporary Biographies* (Brighton: Pike, 1902).

Times 13, 14, 16 Nov 1939.

WWW.

NORTH, John Dudley

(1893-1968)

Aircraft manufacturer

John Dudley North was born at Upper Sydenham, Surrey, on 2 January 1893, the only child of Dudley North, a solicitor, and his wife Marian née Felgate. He went to Bedford School where he did well in mathematics and gained an honours in the London Matriculation examinations. At the age of seventeen, in 1910, his father died and he left school to be apprenticed by his grandfather to Sir W G Armstrong Whitworth & Co Ltd at Elswick, Newcastle upon Tyne at 3s a week.

At Bedford School, however, North had begun to take an interest in the new aviation. He avidly read the two weekly aviation papers, *Flight* (first published January 1909 and edited by Stanley Spooner) and *The Aero* (first published March 1909 and edited by C G Grey). After he won a competition in *The Aero* to test general knowledge of the pioneer aircraft of those days, North received a congratulatory letter from C G Grey which led to a correspondence and encouragement from Grey for him to consider a career in aeronautics. As a direct result, his grandfather allowed John North in 1911 to join Horatio Barber's Aeronautical Syndicate Ltd of Hendon — the builders of Valkyrie monoplanes.

Shortly after, the Aeronautical Syndicate was wound up and sold to Claude Graham-White at Hendon. John D North joined the Graham-White Aviation Co Ltd as chief engineer where, at the age of nineteen he completed his first design — a small, cheap, simple-to-build, two-seat, tandem sesquiplane powered with a 35 hp Anzani, three-cylinder engine, a design which owed its original layout to Horatio Barber. Named the Graham-White Type 7 'Popular', the aircraft was flown in January 1913, followed by a larger variant — the Graham-White Type 6 which carried a Colt machine-gun, one of the first applications of armament to an aeroplane. Thus, the young, tall, bespectacled and deep-voiced John D North came into the forefront of pioneering aircraft design. In summer 1913 he followed his initial success by designing the Graham-White Type 10 Charabanc or Aerobus, the largest British aeroplane built up to that time. It flew well and set up a world record in October 1913, when Louis Noel flew for twenty minutes with nine passengers, one of whom was John North.

North left the Graham-White Co after a sharp disagreement with F H Paine, the production manager, in May 1915. He went to the Austin Motor Co at Longbridge as aircraft production manager and superintendent of the Austin Aviation Department, then in production with the Royal Aircraft Factory's RE8 artillery spotter aeroplane for the Royal Flying Corps.

He moved again in August 1917 when he became chief engineer of the aircraft department of Boulton & Paul Ltd of Norwich, originally furniture makers who had entered the aircraft business in 1915 to produce the Royal Aircraft Factory's FE2B fighter-reconnaissance aircraft for the RFC. The aircraft department of Boulton & Paul Ltd had been set up initially in the cavalry drill hall adjoining Mousehold Heath at Norwich under J D Dawson Paul and, shortly after John North joined the company, turned over to the production of Sopwith Camel fighters at its Rose Lane works. North stayed with Boulton & Paul for the rest of his career, in due course becoming a director, and in 1934, chairman and managing director.

While concentrating upon the production of Sopwith Camels, John North began the design of a Camel replacement, flown in 1918 as the Boulton & Paul P3 'Bobolink' single-seat fighter, with the 230 hp Bentley BR2 rotary engine. Although the Bobolink's performance was rather better than the competing Sopwith Snipe, and its flying characteristics were excellent, its narrow-track undercarriage made it difficult to land and the production contract went to the Snipe.

By the early 1920s North had completed some pioneering work on metal aircraft structures as a replacement for the wood universally used at that time. In 1922 he produced the P15 Bolton three-seat, day bomber, the structure of which was wholly of steel strip construction, the first successful all-metal design to be flown. It was first shown at the Paris Aero Show at the Grand Palace and was patented. In 1923, North further developed the Bolton into the P25 Bugle and then, in 1926, into the P29 Sidestrand with two 425 hp Bristol Jupiter engines, a wholly stainless steel tube structure, a top speed of 144 mph and remarkable aerobatic characteristics.

The Sidestrand entered Royal Air Force service in March 1929, and remained for some years the fastest twin-engined aeroplane in the Service. The BP Sidestrand was succeeded in No 101 Squadron RAF in January 1935, by a developed version, the P75 Overstrand which, for the first time, brought into service a power-operated gun turret. Some 24 Overstrands were built, the last delivered late in 1936.

North, however, was not only a bomber designer and manufacturer. In 1927, he produced the remarkably advanced P31 Bittern single-seat, twin engine, monoplane fighter, too much ahead of its day to be ordered in quantity, and in 1928, the BP33 Partridge single-seat, all-metal fighter biplane, which narrowly lost the Air Ministry competition to the Hawker Fury.

During this time North used his skill and experience as the leading designer and manufacturer of metal aircraft structures in Britain to make a major contribution to the advanced stainless steel and duralumin structure of the British airship R101. Structural components of the R101 were designed and fabricated by Boulton & Paul at Norwich and delivered to Cardington for assembly there by the Royal Airship Works for the first flight in October 1929.

In 1934, Boulton Paul Aircraft Ltd with a capital of £250,000 was formed from the former Aircraft Department of Boulton & Paul Ltd and the new company was moved to Wolverhampton in August 1936. At this stage, the early phase of rearmament, the Air Ministry conducted a management survey of aircraft manufacturing companies and Boulton & Paul were numbered among those not to be entrusted with orders for complete machines. Air Ministry investigators in 1937 reported that

Boulton & Paul management had undergone drastic changes including the appointment of a new general manager from the Ford Motor Co and production had improved.

With the expansion of the Royal Air Force, North produced to a Royal Air Force requirement for a two-seat fighter, the P82 Defiant, a single-engine, all-metal, monoplane of much the same size as the Hurricane and Spitfire but with a four-gun power-operated turret behind the pilot. The Defiant, which made its first flight in August 1937 was employed on nightflying duties during the Second World War when 1,064 Defiants were built.

By 1938, power-operated gun turrets had become a major part of the Boulton Paul business and J D North began to specialise in power-controls for aircraft, marine use and motor cars, using power-controls as an extension of human muscles and moving on from that to operational research.

While this work occupied much of his time, Boulton Paul continued to produce new aircraft types, including, in 1954, the BP-108 Balliol Advanced Trainer for the RAF and, in 1950, a single-seat, research Delta Jet. The firm also undertook sub-contract work on a substantial scale, including the building of wings for the Beagle B206 series of light, twin-engine aircraft.

In 1961, Boulton Paul Aircraft Ltd became a member of the Dowty Group, founded by Sir George Dowty (qv) and its name was changed to Dowty Boulton Paul Ltd in January 1970. John North remained on the board until his death.

J D North was a member of the Council of the Society of British Aircraft Constructors from 1931 to 1962 and was appointed a member of the Council of the Air Registration Board and of the governing body of the College of Aeronautics at Cranfield, to both of which he contributed much wisdom and valuable experience. He was honoured with a CBE in 1962 and an honorary DSc from Birmingham University in 1967. Nor were his talents confined to engineering aspects and the mathematics of which he was a master. He delighted in an almost professional knowledge of horticulture (particularly Alpine plants) and of cooking. With all this, he was a man of confirmed modesty who never pressed his own talents upon others.

In 1922 North married Phyllis Margaret Huggins, daughter of Edward James Ward Huggins, clerk to the Norwich Board of Guardians, and his wife Jeanette. The Norths had two daughters. J D North died at his home in Bridgnorth, Shropshire, on 11 January 1968, leaving £70,103 gross.

Sir PETER G MASEFIELD

Writings:

'Manual Control as a Stochastic Process' *Ergonomics* 6 (1963).

Sources:

Unpublished

PrC.

John D North, 'The Rational Behaviour of Mechanically Extended Man' (paper to conference at Royal Military Academy of Science, 1954).

Personal knowledge.

Information from Peter Fearon.

Published

DNB.

Peter Fearon, 'Aircraft Manufacturing' in Neil K Buxton and Derek H Aldcroft (eds), *British Industry between the Wars. Instability and Industrial Development, 1919-1939* (Scolar Press, 1979).

Flight International 7 Oct 1965.

Journal of the Royal Aeronautical Society Dec 1968.

Harald Penrose, *British Aviation. The Pioneer Years 1908-14* (Cassell, 1980).

Times *Prospectuses* 88 (1934).

WWW.

NORTHCLIFFE, 1st Viscount Northcliffe
see HARMSWORTH, Alfred Charles William

NORTHUMBERLAND, 8th Duke of Northumberland
see PERCY, Alan Ian

NORTON-GRIFFITHS
see GRIFFITHS, Sir John Norton

NUFFIELD, 1st Viscount Nuffield
see MORRIS, William Richard

NUGENT, Sir Roland Thomas

(1886-1962)

First Director of the Federation of British Industries

Sir Roland Nugent (courtesy of CBI).

Rowland Thomas Nugent, who in adult life spelt his forename Roland, was born at 12, South Eaton Place, Belgravia, London, on 19 June 1886, only surviving child of Edmond Henry Stuart Nugent (1849-1935), and his wife Grace Mary (1862-1925), ninth and youngest daughter of Edward Nathaniel Conant (1820-1901), DL, JP, of Lyndon Hall, Rutland, a barrister who in 1879 owned some 5,063 acres in Rutland and Lincolnshire producing about £9,683 annually, and whose personalty was sworn in 1903 at £474,731. Nugent's father was called to the Bar at Lincoln's Inn in 1872, and practised as an equity draughtsman and conveyancer until 1914, when he succeeded to family estates in Northern Ireland. In 1879 these had comprised 4,638 acres in County Down and 2,137 in Westmeath worth respectively £7,675 and £1,670 per annum. The Nugent family had been settled at Portaferry in Down since the early seventeenth century: E H S Nugent returned there, becoming a magistrate and in 1923 High Sheriff of County Down; he left English property worth £22,974 in 1935.

Roland Nugent was educated at Eton in 1899-1904 and at Trinity College, Cambridge, where he was a minor scholar in history and had a special interest in economics. Destined for a diplomatic career, he next studied at the University of Bonn, and passed a competitive examination for the diplomatic service in September 1910. He became a third secretary in September 1912, and having passed an examination in public law in December of that year, transferred to the Foreign Office as a junior clerk in April 1913. He took particular interest in commercial policy, and around 1915 became head of the Foreign Office's Foreign Trade Department and secretary of an interdepartmental committee on capturing German trade. Later, in association with Sir Alexander Henderson (qv), Sir Victor Wellesley and others, he took a lead in reorganising the consular service, and establishing the Department of Overseas Trade during 1916-17. These reforms were part of the institutional preparations for the Anglo-German trade war which was then expected to erupt when military hostilities ended.

One of the businessmen in the 'trade warriors' movement was Dudley Docker (qv), who in 1916 launched the Federation of British Industries with a view to its becoming a 'Business Parliament' expressing the opinions of the industrial community on tariff protection, labour relations and legislation affecting businessmen generally. Docker and his closest supporters, such as Sir Vincent Caillard and Sir Edward Manville (qqv), attached importance to FBI liaison with the Foreign Office in organising and co-ordinating the post-war exports campaign against German manufactures. It was chiefly for this reason that Nugent (a diplomat with an interest in trade policy, an administrator with knowledge of law and languages) was recruited by Docker as Director of the FBI in 1916 at the lavish annual salary of £1,500. He had leave of absence to serve as a second lieutenant in the Grenadier Guards in 1917-18, but formally retired from the Foreign Office in April 1918, and remained as FBI Director until April 1932. As such, he had overall charge of the Federation's general policy, as determined by its presidents (elected annually), together with the executive council. The work was divided into two departments, Home and Overseas, which initially were headed by two enthusiastic young men, Charles (later Sir Charles) Tennyson (1879-1977), formerly of the Colonial Office, and Guy Locock (qv), late of the Foreign Office and Department of Overseas Trade. Nugent 'was well qualified' for 'big bow-wow stuff' with Government and major industrialists, 'for in spite of his youth, blue eyes and fair hair, his tall, slightly stooping figure and deliberate speech gave him an authority beyond his years' {Tennyson (1957) 143}. In all matters he showed 'initiative, astuteness and persistence'; energetic, tactful, and keen, his success as FBI Director derived from 'his strong grasp of policy, his remarkable skill in draughtsmanship and his loyalty and consideration as a colleague and chief' {Tennyson (1962) 10}.

In his first years at the FBI, Nugent gave much attention to settling its organisation and structure, including the industrial classification of member companies into 17 categories, and the institution of specialist sections and sub-committees. He also had to harmonise conflicting interests, for Docker's views on the need for tariff protection, a business party in the House of Commons and a progressive labour policy all provoked opposition. The Lancashire cotton men, and other free-traders, prevented unanimity on fiscal policy, and in order to avoid a complete split, the subject was avoided until Neville Chamberlain's introduction of protection in the 1932 Budget. Other members, led by Sir Peter Rylands (qv), opposed the FBI becoming active in parliamentary politics, and proponents of this view instead directed their hopes and money into the British Commonwealth Union, originally founded by Sir Trevor Dawson (qv). Finally, in 1918, Sir Allan Smith (qv) and the Engineering Employers Federation threatened to withdraw from the FBI unless the latter undertook to eschew labour policy, except through the National Confederation of Employers Organisations formed in 1919. The FBI met more success in its early years in its work on overseas trade policy, although the impetus of this was lost after Germany's economic collapse in 1919-20. The FBI were concerned in the formation of foreign trade banks by men such as Lord Faringdon, Godfrey Isaacs (qv) and George Manzi-

Fé, and were involved in the export credit guarantees system introduced by the Government in 1920-21.

In the post-war reconstruction period, Nugent was active in modifying government proposals on transport, fuel and power policies (1919-22), and campaigned publicly and privately against both threatened industrial nationalisation and the peacetime continuation of Excess Profits Duty, which was finally abolished in 1921. Monetary and fiscal policy, and the problems of German reparations and Russian indebtedness, were of keen interest to Nugent and the FBI throughout the 1920s; and at different times he gave special attention to specific problems of individual industries, such as rolling-stock in 1919-20 or films after 1925. Technical education was another perennial interest. During the coal strike of 1920, the General Strike of 1926, and other periods of industrial dislocation, the FBI acted as an intermediary between its district organisations, manufacturers and the central Government. It was much involved too in discussions on the location and commercial organisation of industry. Nugent was also a member of the Civil Aviation Consultative Committee in the late 1920s.

The FBI passed through three stages during Nugent's directorship. In the first, during the convulsion of war and crisis of post-war reconstruction in 1916-19, the Federation was at its most ambitious, militant and turbulent, producing ideas that were fertile, contentious and risky. During the second period of 1920-25, Nugent and his staff consolidated the FBI's position, establishing peacetime recognition of its role as the authorised representative of British industry. But increasingly after 1925, the FBI's work tended to fall into automatic routines, and to be concerned with the minutiae of technical questions rather than the sweep of high national policy: there was a certain flatness in its activities until the onset of rearmament during the presidency of Hugo Hirst (qv) in 1936-38. In personal terms, Nugent was at his happiest with Sir Peter Rylands, president in 1919-21, whose intellectual virtuosity was delightful, and in 1925-26 with Vernon Willey (qv), who had been Nugent's contemporary at Eton. Some presidents, such as Sir Richard Vassar-Smith (qv) in 1917 or Colonel O C Armstrong in 1921-22, seem to have been mere cyphers, while others such as Docker in 1916-17 or Sir Eric Geddes (qv) in 1923-25 were domineering.

Nugent had leave of absence from the FBI through illness in January 1931, and although he returned to work, retired as Director in April 1932 to take charge of his family estates at Portaferry. He was then made vice-president of the Federation. He afterwards became active in Ulster politics as a magistrate from 1934, Senator for Northern Ireland from 1936, and Lord Lieutenant for County Down after 1959. He was appointed major (local lieutenant colonel) in the Grenadier Guards in 1942. He was Leader of the Ulster Senate in 1944-50, unpaid Minister without Portfolio in 1944-45, Minister of Commerce in 1945-49, Minister in the Senate during 1949 and Speaker of the Northern Ireland Senate in 1950-61. Knighted for his industrial work in 1929, he was sworn of the Privy Council of Northern Ireland in 1944, and was created a baronet on his political retirement in 1961. He received an honorary LLD from Queen's University, Belfast, in 1958.

Nugent married, in 1917, at Mayfair, Cynthia Maud (b 1891), eldest daughter of Frederick William Ramsden (1864-1928), of Willinghurst, Guildford, and grand-daughter of the Third Marquess Conyngham. Her brother Charles Frederick Ingram Ramsden (1888-1958), who served as a diplomat in Spain, Persia, Romania and Russia in 1910-19, joined the FBI in 1919, and was its Overseas Director during 1929-52. Nugent had two sons, who were both killed in the Second World War, and a daughter. He died on 18 August 1962 at Portaferry, when his baronetcy became extinct. He left estate in England worth £77,723.

R P T DAVENPORT-HINES

Writings:

(with Sir Ernest Fitzjohn Oldham), *Reconstruction and the Future of British Trade, Industry and Labour* (Pamphlet for private circulation July 1916. Copy in Steel-Maitland papers GD 193/568).

letter on postwar employment *Times* 12 Dec 1916.

letter on Federation of British Industries *ibid* 8 Sept 1917.

letter on future control of industry *ibid* 8 Aug 1919.

letter on proposed congress of British manufacturers *ibid* 13 Jan 1920.

letter on Excess Profits Duty *ibid* 30 Apr 1920.

letter on London headquarters of FBI's overseas organisation *Times* Trade Supplement 9 Oct 1920.

letters on exports credit scheme *Times* 21, 25 Oct 1920.

interview on Lloyd George and retrenchment *ibid* 2 Dec 1920.

letter quoted on Post Office rates and services *ibid* 3 Feb 1922.

letter on briquetting machinery *ibid* 15 Feb 1922

letter on surcharge of Poplar Borough Council for excess wages payments *ibid* 16 June 1923.

letter on fixed date for Easter *ibid* 5 Nov 1926.

letters quoted on rating relief *ibid* 18, 19 June 1928.

letter on trade with Denmark *ibid* 21 Oct 1930.

letter quoted on tariff truce *ibid* 14 Nov 1930.

letter on building regulations *ibid* 29 Nov 1930.

letter on gold and prices *ibid* 30 May 1931.

letter on customers' demands *ibid* 18 Dec 1931.

Sources:

Unpublished

House of Lords RO, papers of Andrew Bonar Law (eg BL 98/8/6, Austen Chamberlain on FBI delegation on Excess Profits Duty, Mar 1920).

PRO, papers of Board of Trade (Evidence with Sir V Caillard and E F Oldham on behalf of FBI to Lord Balfour of Burleigh's committee on trade policy after the war, 16 Feb 1917, PRO BT 55/10), Foreign Office and Ministry of Munitions.

Scottish RO, papers of Sir Arthur Steel-Maitland.

University of Warwick, Modern Records Centre, papers of Federation of British Industries.

BCe.

MCe.

PrC.

Information from Lord Barnby.

Peter Mathias, 'The History of the Federation of British Industries' (np, 1980).

Published

Edward F Benson, *Deutschland Uber Allah* (Hodder & Stoughton, 1917).

Stephen Blank, *Industry and Government in Britain* (Farnborough: Saxon House, 1973).

Burke's Landed Gentry of Ireland (Burke, 1958) (*sub* Nugent of Portaferry).

Burke's Peerage (*sub* Conant and Ramsden).

Ian D Colvin, *The Safety of the Nation: Showing How Our Security Rests upon Our Industries* (John Murray, 1919).

Richard Davenport-Hines, *Dudley Docker* (Cambridge University Press, 1984).

Federation of British Industries Bulletin.

German Business and German Aggression (T Fisher Unwin, 1917).

W H Hooker, *The Handicap of British Trade with Special Regard to East Africa* (John Murray, 1916).

Labour Research Department, *Studies in Labour and Capital no 5: The Federation of British Industries* (Labour Research Department, 1923).

Robert Keith Middlemas, *Politics in Industrial Society* (Deutsch, 1979).

Spectator 28 Dec 1918.

Sir Charles B L Tennyson, *Stars and Markets* (Chatto and Windus, 1957).

—, *Times* tribute 23 Aug 1962.

Times 28 Sept, 8 Oct, 22 Nov 1920, 5 Feb, 28 June 1921, 17 Mar 1922, 20 Feb 1929, 15 May 1931.

Times Trade Supplement 13 Dec 1919.

John A Turner (ed), *Businessmen and Politics, 1900-1945* (Heinemann, 1984).

WWW.

OAKLEY, Sir Henry

(1823-1912)

Railway manager

Henry Oakley was born on 12 November 1823, the second son of Herbert Oakley of Nottingham Place, Marylebone, London. Little is known of his parental background or early formative years. His father, an officer in the British army, secured for him a Civil Service position as a clerk in the Library of the House of Commons. There his work attracted the attention of E B Denison, the first chairman of the Great Northern Railway. All railway companies needed to obtain private acts of parliament to authorise their operations, and Denison was doubtless anxious to acquire the services of a young and trustworthy man of ability who could superintend this important aspect of the Great Northern's activities. He offered Oakley employment with the company, and on 13 July 1850 Oakley joined the Great Northern; the following year he was nominated chief clerk to the then secretary, J R Mowatt.

Oakley's rise within the company was rapid and spectacular. In 1854 he became the company's assistant secretary and, four years later, following his part in the successful detection of the frauds perpetrated by the Great Northern's infamous chief registrar, Leopold Redpath, he was promoted company secretary. In this position he mastered every aspect of the company's operations. In 1870 he succeeded Seymour Clarke as general manager at a salary of £2,500, a post he held for the following twenty-eight years.

Oakley's secretaryship and management of the Great Northern thus covered the period of nearly half a century during which it became one of the most efficient, competitive and prestigious British railway enterprises. He was a painstaking and methodical worker, with a fine grasp of the administrative detail, an eye for the main chance, and sound business sense. When he joined the company its lines, stretching southwards from Yorkshire, the East Midlands and the East Coast, had not yet reached London. As secretary, he was chiefly responsible for the growth of its London suburban routes and for the expansion of facilities for the export by rail of manufactured goods from Yorkshire throughout the United

Kingdom. In 1862 he was one of the moving spirits behind a fierce price-cutting war between the Great Northern and the London & North Western Railway, which resulted in passenger fares from Lancashire to London being offered at 2s 6d return. As general manager his competitive instincts grew. He increased the company's mileage from 544 to over 800, and its paid-up capital doubled under his stewardship of the company's affairs. In the 1870s he sustained a battle with the Midland Railway for the South Yorkshire coal trade, reducing carriage costs for this traffic by two-thirds. Later he concentrated on the improvement of facilities, especially journey times and passenger comfort. He also paid particular attention to the development of holiday traffic, and in 1895 was one of the instigators of the 'race' to Aberdeen between the Great Northern and its east-coast partners, and the London & North Western and other companies operating the west-coast route.

By this time Oakley had become a national industrial figure, the 'Grand Old Man' of British railways. But his public reputation did not in fact rest upon his activities as secretary and general manager of the Great Northern. In 1867 he had agreed to become honorary secretary of the United Railway Companies' Committee, which changed its name to the Railway Companies Association in 1870. The association was, and remained, the sole representative organisation of the British railway companies, trying on the one hand to maintain a united front in the face of creeping government control of railway regulation in the later nineteenth century and, on the other, to help successive Governments, and a variety of commercial and industrial pressure groups, to understand the problems railway companies faced. As honorary secretary from 1867 to 1900 Oakley found himself the chief intermediary between the companies and the Board of Trade in the many delicate and difficult negotiations concerning such matters as railway safety and railway charging powers. Here his early parliamentary experience proved invaluable. He gained easy access to the corridors of Westminster Palace and Whitehall; he was on friendly terms with bureaucrats and politicians. Government and parliament alike relied on his expert knowledge in framing their own views of railway questions.

But Oakley was not blind to political realities. His realism in this regard showed itself in sharp contrast to the over-strident and headstrong attitudes of some of his fellow railway administrators. He counselled in vain against the massive increase in railway rates which led to the unprecedented statutory freezing of these charges in 1894, and which signalled the end of laissez-faire as far as British railway regulation was concerned. Nonetheless, his personal efforts in this as in many other matters of railway regulation, were widely appreciated in political and governmental circles. His knighthood, in 1891, though intended to mark the completion of twenty-one years as general manager of the Great Northern, was in reality a token of national gratitude for the many hours of work he had devoted, unpaid, to assisting government regulation of railways and in preparing and giving evidence to almost every major parliamentary inquiry into the railway system in the late nineteenth century.

Oakley did not court publicity and he does not appear to have entertained any political ambition. He saw himself as a railway administrator rather than as an entrepreneur, and his control of Great

Northern affairs was strongly paternalistic. He was an active chairman of the Railway Benevolent Institution, of which he was one of the founders, and a colonel in the Railway Engineer and Volunteer Staff Corps. He shared the deep antipathy of most of his colleagues in the railway world towards trade unions in general and the Amalgamated Society of Railway Servants in particular. One of his major policy decisions as general manager of the Great Northern was to signify the adherence of the company to an anti-strike agreement which all the leading companies, except the North Eastern Railway, entered into in December 1897; the agreement was first used during the Taff Vale strike in 1900.

In March 1898 Oakley retired as general manager of the Great Northern; he was awarded a £1,000 pension and immediately elected a director of the company, a position he retained until his death. He became chairman of the Central London Railway Co in 1898, retiring in 1911. He lived long enough to witness the first national railway strike (August 1911) and the destruction of the 1897 agreement he had helped draw up. He was an associate member of the Institution of Civil Engineers and was a Chevalier of the Légion d'Honneur.

Of his private life little information has survived. He appears to have been a devout Anglican. He married twice: firstly, in 1850, to Fanny, daughter of Francis Thompson who had been been in the service of the Honourable East India Company and secondly, in 1863, to Caroline Lillias Mary, eldest daughter of F E Thompson. Sir Henry Oakley died in London on 8 February 1912. He was survived by a daughter and two sons, and his estate was sworn at £30,889.

GEOFFREY ALDERMAN

Writings:

PP, HC 1876 (312) XIII, Railway Passengers' Duty.

PP, HC 1877 (285) X, Employers' Liability.

PP, HC 1890–91 (394) XIV and XV, Railway Rates and Charges.

PP, HC 1893–94 (385) XIV, Railway Rates and Charges.

Sources:

Unpublished

PrC.

Published

Geoffrey Alderman, *The Railway Interest* (Leicester: Leicester University Press, 1973).

Burke's Peerage, Baronetage and Knightage 1907.

C H Grinling, *The History of the Great Northern Railway 1845-1902* (1902).

Lodge's Peerage, Baronetage, Knightage and Companionage of the British Empire for 1912 (2 vols, Kelly's Directories, 1911-12).

Railway Gazette 16 Feb 1912.

Railway News 6 June 1891, 10 Feb 1912.

Times 9 Feb, 9 Mar 1912.

WWW.

George Odey (courtesy of George Odey).

ODEY, George William

(1900-)

Leather manufacturer

George William Odey was born at Colney near Norwich on 21 April 1900, two months after the death of his father, also George William Odey, a warrant officer and engineer in the Royal Navy. An only child, strong willed by nature, he was brought up by a determined mother, Mary née Mathew, with considerable assistance from his grandfather, George Odey of Gillingham, Kent, with whom George and his widowed mother lived during his early childhood.

At the age of eight he was sent as a boarder to Faversham Grammar School, Kent. He went in 1917 to University College, London and took a second class honours degree in history in 1921. He was president of the UCL Union Society in 1921-22 and president of the University of London Union Society in 1922. Between 1922 and 1925 he was assistant secretary of the University of London Appointments Board. He was diverted into the leather industry when Frederick Marquis (qv) introduced him to William A Posnett, then chairman of a newly-organised leather company, Barrow Hepburn & Gale Ltd.

This had been formed in 1920 by a merger between Hepburn, Gale & Ross Ltd and Samuel Barrow & Bro Ltd. The former was one of the largest, and one of the few vertically integrated, firms in the industry (and one of the largest contractors of leather goods to the British Army by the mid-1890s) with a tanning business in Grange Road, Bermondsey, South East London (registered as a limited company in 1895). Samuel Barrow & Bro Ltd, (registered as a limited company in 1890), had both a tannery in Bermondsey (the Grange Tannery) and a merchanting business with offices in London, Leicester, Kettering and Northampton. On the crest of the post-war boom of 1920 the firm sought further growth by purchasing Richard Hodgson & Sons of Beverley, Yorkshire, later that year. The timing of this large vertically integrated amalgamation proved disastrous, for wartime price controls ended in 1920 and in the post-boom collapse hide prices almost immediately fell from 20d to 2d a pound and hides became subject to wide price fluctuations. The effects were exacerbated by the time lag (nine or ten months) between purchase of hides and sale of finished leather which involved heavy losses on hides bought at pre-boom prices. Values of manufactured leather exports fell from £11 million in 1920 to £3.8 million in 1921, recovering somewhat to between £6 million and £7 million in 1923-25. These losses forced Barrow, Hepburn & Gale into a capital reconstruction in 1923. Authorised capital was written down from £2.5 million (in 1.5 million £1 ordinary shares and 1 million 7.5 per cent cumulative preference shares) to £1.8 million and their paid-up capital from £2.3 million to £1.6 million (by writing 10s off each paid-up £1 ordinary share and reducing fixed dividend on preference shares to 6 per cent). In compensation preference share holders were given voting rights. The crisis was intensified by internal conflicts between W A Posnett and Sir Samuel Barrow, heads of the two merged firms. It was at this point that George Odey came into the firm, initially as Posnett's private secretary but soon as one of two management trainees, one of whom Posnett hoped would be his successor.

At the outset Odey had little understanding of the product, the market, or the commercial world and, for his first three years in Barrow, Hepburn & Gale, he trained in all departments of the business, first at Bermondsey, later at Beverley. This on-the-job training gave him an understanding of all aspects of the business while his own robust personality won the support of the workforce. He was quickly promoted, being appointed a manager of Richard Hodgson & Sons in 1928.

His swift rise was not without its complications, especially because he was an outsider in a family business, in which there were quarrels at the top. He was appointed to the board in 1929 when, following two years of trading losses, four directors resigned. There followed a second scheme of capital reconstruction (with the value of ordinary shares being cut from 10s to 5s and the cancellation of dividend arrears on preference capital) and a thorough internal reorganisation of the business in 1930. A somewhat more stable period followed with earnings sufficient to pay the preference dividend, but only once before 1938 was an ordinary dividend paid (3 per cent in 1933).

Despite the difficulties of the 1930s, when the value of British leather output stagnated (1930-35) and that of UK leather exports halved, George Odey took command at Barrow, Hepburn & Gale, becoming managing director in 1934 and chairman in 1937. Under his guidance, family support and control were discarded and the firm turned instead to the City for capital requirements. It was no coincidence that his chairmanship saw two important changes in the leather industry, firstly a drive to rationalise the tanning operation to dominate an increasingly international market and, secondly, a movement to stabilise the price of hides in that market with an international understanding amongst tanners. These two objectives were uppermost in his mind as he drove the company through a series of acquisitions which reduced competition and by 1974, when he retired, made Barrow, Hepburn & Gale the largest tanners in the UK.

The first acquisition was G Appleyard & Co Ltd, in 1933; then came Thomas Holmes & Sons of Sculcoates, Hull (three tanneries) in 1935;

Split hide and dressing hide tanyard of Richard Hodgson & Sons Ltd, Beverley (from Dennis Bardens Everything in Leather The Story of Barrow, Hepburn & Gale Limited).

Grange Tanning Co Ltd in 1936; Blackman Leather Goods Co Ltd in 1937; and J Mullins & Co, manufacturers of fibre goods in 1939. To safeguard his raw material sources, and avoid sharp price changes, Odey in the 1930s began to form overseas subsidiaries, starting in 1939 with the Hodgson Extract Co (Pty) of Merebank, Natal, South Africa, for producing mimosa tanning extract on a scale sufficient for the Barrow, Hepburn & Gale tanneries and also for sale to other tanners.

The outbreak of war in 1939 again brought wartime controls and the hide price stabilisation that the tanners wanted. The industry, still characterised by a large number of small firms covering the three main sectors of fellmongery, tanning and dressing, and harness leathers, came under the Leather Control headed by Dr E C Snow, previously manager and director of the United Tanners' Federation. Under the exigencies of war the leather and shoe industries produced over 70 million pairs of boots for the men's services, of over 150 types, achieving this with a much-slimmed workforce (reduced by 34 per cent in the shoe industries) and a 25 per cent increase in productivity. At Barrow, Hepburn & Gale the wartime workforce rose from 2,300 to 5,000 (while nearly 580 of the peacetime staff left for wartime service) and the group made over 35.5 million articles worth £20 million, including 6.5 milllion pairs of cut soles.

ODEY George William

Butt yard showing overhead travelling crane, Richard Hodgson & Sons Ltd, Beverley (from Dennis Bardens Everything in Leather The Story of Barrow, Hepburn & Gale Limited).

In the face of a sharp drop in exports Odey seized the chance to raise the level of co-operation within the industry still further. In November 1940 he was instrumental in forming the Leather, Footwear and Allied Industries Export Corporation — representing factors, tanners, curriers and belting, footwear and leather goods manufacturers — which was designed to increase the export trade of members through jointly-funded advertising and export servicing arrangements. He chaired the Corporation 1940-46 and was its president from 1947. In 1941 he represented the Ministry of Supply in a Leather Mission to Washington to negotiate a joint purchase of hides with American producers. In 1943, he similarly participated in a joint Anglo-American Mission on Hides and Leather to South America. In recognition of his wartime work he was made CBE in 1945. After the war he went into politics as Conservative MP for the Howdenshire division of Yorkshire, 1947-50, and then for Beverley, 1950-55. He played a major part in the drafting and passage of the Leather Charges Order, which protected tanners from exchange fluctuations when decontrol came in 1954, but at a time when Barrow, Hepburn & Gale needed to grow he found himself spending too little time in the office and therefore retired from parliament in 1955.

After the war, still convinced of the advantages attending increased scale and rationalisation, George Odey resumed his acquisition strategy, and in the 1950s moved into chrome upper leather tanning while maintaining full participation in the sole leather industry. By 1954 Barrow, Hepburn & Gale Ltd had 18 subsidiaries with current assets of £2,845,320 (progressively, George Odey adopted consolidated accounts in the late 1930s before these became statutory under company law); by 1964 it had 32 subsidiaries with current assets of £3,678,595; and in 1973 it had nearly 50 subsidiaries with current assets of £21,670,060. Its final acquisition under his chairmanship, the Harvey Group, a leading firm of sole and leather tanners, made the Barrow, Hepburn & Gale Group Ltd (renamed in 1971) the largest tanners in the UK. In 1973 it had a turnover of £150 million, a 10 per cent share of the international market, and, in the UK, a 50 per cent share of the sole leather market and a 30 per cent share of the upper leather market. In 1964 its main factories were at Bermondsey and Mitcham in

London, with branches at Kettering, Leeds, Leicester, Northampton and Norwich; it then had 11 overseas companies, in France, the USA, Canada, Australia and East Africa. By 1974 the Barrow, Hepburn & Gale Group had moved its head office from Bermondsey to the West End of London and had its main factories at Battersea, Beverley, Hull, Leeds, Bolton and Grantham. By 1973 its foreign subsidiaries were augmented with branches in Italy and New Zealand. It long remained a vertically integrated business confined to the leather industry, specialising in tanning and manufacturing tanning extracts, glue, gelatine, luggage, belting, bags and cartons, as well as merchanting hide skins. However, three threats to traditional leather markets forced George Odey to begin diversification in the 1960s.

One threat came from foreign imports. During the mid-1950s Odey campaigned against cheap leather from India and the Far East, observing in a letter to the *Times* that

> In 1948 and 1949 the full chrome upper leather industry supplied over 90 per cent of the 90m sq ft of this type of leather used by footwear manufacturers in this country in addition to exporting 10 to 15m sq ft. Since then imports have grown steadily year by year, and in 1954 accounted for 27 per cent of the total consumption of the United Kingdom ... Approximately three-quarters of the imports came from the Commonwealth countries, India is by far the largest supplier, having trebled her exports since 1948 ... Unless some change of policy takes place, not only the cotton industry and the leather industry but many others will be faced with a constantly contracting home market, rapidly diminishing exports and substantial unemployment. { *Times* 28 June 1955}

A second threat came from leather substitutes. George Odey, as president of the International Council of Tanners, sounded warnings both in Britain and on an American tour in 1955. Synthetics for soles first swept the USA and then Europe; British manufacturers resisted longest. In 1955 80 per cent of soles made in Italy were synthetic, compared to 46 per cent of those made in Britain. Between 1956 and 1959 20 out of 100 tanneries in the UK went out of business in the face of competition from rubber, crepe and plastic sole manufacturers.

The third threat came from a persistent rise in the price of raw hides, aggravated by large-scale purchases in international markets by Russia, China and Japan. This led to a further contraction of the industry in the late 1950s, with Barrow, Hepburn & Gale closing their Grange Tannery in Bermondsey (120 employees and a capacity of 3,500 hides a week) in March 1959.

Against these threats both to his firm and his industry, George Odey fought back in various ways. As an MP in 1955 he urged the Government to impose controls on cheap imported footwear. He campaigned for a leather mark, to distinguish leather from its substitutes, which is widely used today. He promoted a publicity campaign to improve the public image of leather goods. And he was prominent in developing industrial training through the National Leathersellers' College. Within Barrow, Hepburn & Gale, he not only rationalised, by removing less profitable units such as the Grange Tannery, but he strengthened the Group by take-over growth in which small units were closed and larger ones strengthened; by investing in research and development (£60,000 was invested in new laboratories, with a staff of 40, for the group in Beverley in 1957); and by diversification into chemicals. This last step came in the 1960s with the acquisition of Colloids Inc of Newark, New Jersey, an American chemical company manufacturing synthetic adhesives for the production of yarn for the textile industries. Reflecting the group's new direction was the appointment to the board in 1973 of Professor Roland Smith, a management specialist, who succeeded George Odey as chairman in 1974.

Within the post-war leather industry George Odey's abilities were widely recognised and utilised. He was chairman of the United Tanners' Federation in 1951 and president of the International Tanners' Council, 1954-67; president of the British Leather Federation, 1965, of the Federation of Gelatine and Glue Manufacturers, 1955-57, and of the British Gelatine and Glue Research Association in 1950. He was a member of the Western Hemisphere Exports Council from 1960 to 1964, on the Committee for Exports to the United States in 1964, and took a great deal of interest in the affairs of the Leathersellers' Company, being a liveryman from 1939 and 4th Warden in 1965-66, and was chairman of the governors of the National Leathersellers' College, 1951-77. He is also a member of Lloyd's. He was elected a fellow of University College, London in 1953 and was made an honorary freeman of Beverley in 1977 and a DL of Humberside the same year.

His recreations include farming (he now oversees his 300-acre farm in Yorkshire) and yachting (he has been a member of the Royal Yorkshire, Lloyds, Scarborough and House of Commons Yacht Clubs). An Evangelical Anglican, he has recently spent his time successfully raising £850,000 needed to restore Beverley Minster.

George Odey married firstly, in 1926, Dorothy Christian, daughter of James Frederick William Moir, an engineer. They had one son, George Richard Odey, who went to Harrow and Queen's College, Oxford and was commissioned in the King's Dragoon Guards before joining his father's firm in 1950, becoming chief executive in 1974. After George Odey's first wife's death in 1975, he married secondly, in 1976, Mrs Doris Harrison-Broadley, a widow of his own age who died of a painful illness in January 1981. In November 1981 he married his present wife, widow of Sir Richard Barwick Bt, and lives at Keldgate Manor, Cottingham, near Hull, his home since the Second World War.

DAVID J JEREMY

Writings:

'British Hide Values' *The Shoe and Leather News* 28 Oct 1954.

letter on leather from India *Times* 28 June 1955.

Sources:

Unpublished

Barrow, Hepburn Group Ltd annual report and accounts 1976.

BCe.

MCe.

Mr George Odey's correspondence and press cuttings albums 1954-59, 1976-81.

Information from George William Odey, George Richard Odey and from University College, London, Registry.

Published

Helen Pearl Adam, *British Leather: A Record of Achievement* (Batsford, 1946).

Dennis Bardens, *Everything in Leather. The Story of Barrow, Hepburn & Gale Ltd* (pp, F H Beatley Ltd, 1948).

DD 1931, 1933, 1936, 1939, 1943, 1946, 1953, 1963, 1973.

Leadership of British Footwear No 2 (ca 1945-46).

Leather Trades Review 6 July, Oct 1955, 26 June 1957, 26 Mar 1959.

Leather Trades Year Book 1938.

Leather World 3 Nov 1955.

Brian R Mitchell and Phyllis Deane, *Abstract of British Historical Statistics* (Cambridge: Cambridge University Press, 1962).

The Recorder 1 Mar 1958.

The Shoe and Leather News 28 Apr, 17 Nov, Dec 1955, 20 Feb 1958.

The Shoe and Leather Record 14 May 1959.

Stock Exchange Year Book 1920, 1921, 1929-30, 1933.

Stock Exchange Official Year Book 1934-39, 1945-46, 1954, 1964, 1973-75.

Times 6 May 1959.

WW 1982.

WWMP.

O'HAGAN, Henry Osborne

(1853-1930)

Company promoter

Henry Osborne O'Hagan was born at Blackburn, Lancashire, on 13 March 1853, the son of Henry O'Hagan, and his wife, Emily née Buckaman. His father, a civil engineer from Ulster, was related to Thomas (later Lord)

479

O'HAGAN Henry Osborne

H Osborne O'Hagan (from H Osborne O'Hagan, Leaves from My Life *John Lane, the Bodley Head Ltd, 1929).*

O'Hagan, Lord Chancellor of Ireland, 1868-74 and 1880-82. He was educated at Rochester Grammar School, and privately in Streatham, but his schooling was terminated by his father's entanglement in the Overend Gurney crash of 1866 and subsequent death while working as a railway engineer in Honduras.

At the age of fifteen O'Hagan became a junior clerk at 10s a week with a City firm involved in the promotion of acts of parliament and Board of Trade Provisional Orders authorising the construction of railways, tramways, and other public works. He also undertook an intensive course of self-education, abandoned novel-reading and began a lifetime's habit of devoting at least two hours daily to scrutinising the *Times*: 'I was not after the news, but the wealth of knowledge it diffused' {O'Hagan (1929) I, 19}. By the mid-1870s he had set himself up as an independent company promoter, with three successive specialities in the following two decades: tramways (in Croydon, Birmingham, Manchester, the Potteries, and even Berlin); collieries, including the Newbiggin and Hatfield Main companies controlled by Emerson Bainbridge (qv); and English breweries, including Daniell & Sons (1886-87), Northampton Brewery (1886-87), Hull Brewery (1887-88), Springwell Brewery (1888), Taylor's Eagle Brewery of Manchester (1888), Lovibond of Greenwich and Salisbury, Flint's Canterbury Brewery, Barnsley Brewery (1888), Manchester Brewery (1888) and Threlfall's Breweries (1888), Parker's Burslem Brewery (1889), Plymouth Breweries (1889), Massey's Burnley Brewery (1889), Edinburgh United Breweries (1889), Nottingham Breweries (1890), Newcastle Breweries (1890); and American breweries. It was through the Hull and Canterbury companies that he first became involved with Sir John Ellerman (qv), who also chaired the Milwaukee & Chicago Breweries Ltd (1890-91).

In 1882 Osborne O'Hagan founded the City of London Contract Corporation to take over the business of Messrs Charles Phillips as public works contractors. With O'Hagan as chairman and his brother Thomas as managing director, the board comprised L Bishop, the novelist Sir William Magnay and Major General Sir J Phillips. Included in issued capital of £198,500 were 13 founder's shares of £100 each which did not rank for dividend until ordinary shareholders had received 15 per cent per annum, whereupon the founders received half of the distributable balance, the other half passing to the ordinary shareholders. The City of London Contract Corporation paid annual dividends varying from 15 to 60 per cent and was the vehicle for most of O'Hagan's promotions. In 1890 he also formed the London & Chicago Contract Corporation with issued capital of £315,160 ordinary and £3,176 founders shares. Its published figures suggest that it was less successful at company promotion than the City of London Contract Corporation. O'Hagan also sat briefly on the board of North Staffordshire Tramways in the mid-1880s. He was a London director of the Equitable Insurance Society of the United States, but resigned over the rates of return on their tontine policies.

In the wake of the limited liability legislation of 1855-62, Osborne O'Hagan appears to have pursued a much more ambitious range of activities than that attempted by earlier company promoters, notably David Chadwick and Albert ('Baron') Grant (qqv); while in comparison with Ernest Terah Hooley and Horatio Bottomley (qqv), the two other

Oliver married in 1893 his cousin Katharine Augusta, eldest daughter of Lord M'Laren, Senator of the College of Justice in Scotland. They had two sons and a daughter. He contracted consumption (which he had long feared) around 1906, and this increased his fastidious and somewhat precious manner which proved so valuable as a high-class draper. He died at Edgerston on 3 June 1934.

R P T DAVENPORT-HINES

Writings:

'Tradesmen and Tariff Reform' *St James's Gazette* Jan 1904.

[as John Draper] *The Statesman and the Bishop* (Constable, 1904).

Alexander Hamilton, an Essay on the American Union (Constable, 1906).

'Whiggism' *National Review* 52 (1908).

'The Nature of a Whig' *ibid*.

'From Empire to Union' special supplement to *ibid* 53 (Mar 1909).

letters on fiscal policy *Times* 5 Jan, 26 Apr 1910.

'Tactics and Ideas' *National Review* 56 (1911).

The Alternatives to Civil War (Murray, 1913).

What Federalism Is Not (Murray, 1914).

letters on Irish crisis *Times* 27 Mar, 14 May, 23 July 1914.

Ordeal by Battle (Macmillan, 1915).

Ordeal by Marriage: An Eclogue (R Clay, 1915).

Ireland and the Imperial Conference (Macmillan, 1917).

'What We Fight For: A Reply to Woodrow Wilson' *Times* 4 Jan 1917.

(with Earl of Selborne) *A Method of Constitutional Cooperation* (1918).

The Endless Adventure: A Study of Walpole and the Politics of his Age (3 vols, Macmillan, 1930-35).

Sources:

Unpublished

Birmingham University Library, papers of Sir Austen Chamberlain.

Bodleian Library, Oxford, papers of Lionel Curtis, Viscount Milner, Earl of Selborne and Round Table Movement.

British Library, papers of Viscount Cecil of Chelwood (Add MS 51090), of Macmillan, the publishers (Add MSS 55027-55028), and of Walter Shaw Sparrow (Add MSS 48203, 48207).

House of Lords RO, papers of Andrew Bonar Law.

National Library of Scotland, Edinburgh, papers of F S Oliver.

OLIVER Frederick Scott

Plunkett Foundation for Cooperative Studies, Oxford, papers of Sir Horace Plunkett.

PRO of Northern Ireland, papers of Lord Carson.

Scottish RO, Edinburgh, papers of Marquess of Lothian and Sir Arthur Steel-Maitland.

West Sussex RO, Chichester, papers of Leo Maxse.

Published

D G Boyce and J O Stubbs, 'F S Oliver, Lord Selborne and Federalism' *Journal of Imperial and Commonwealth History* 5 (1976).

Maurice Corina, *Fine Silks and Oak Counters* (Hutchinson Benham, 1978).

Duncan Crow, *A Man of Push and Go* (Hart-Davis, 1965).

Empire Review 29 (1915).

A M Gollin, *The Observer and J L Garvin 1908-1914* (Oxford University Press, 1960).

—, *Proconsul in Politics* (Anthony Blond, 1964).

Stephen Gwynn, *The Anvil of War* (Macmillan, 1936).

John E Kendle, *The Round Table and Imperial Union* (Toronto: Toronto University Press, 1975).

Paul Kennedy and Anthony Nicholls (eds), *Nationalist and Racialist Movements in Britain and Germany before 1914* (Macmillan, 1981).

M Robertson [pseudonym 'Roland'] *The Future of Militarism: An Examination of F S Oliver's Ordeal by Battle* (T Fisher Unwin, 1916).

Lord Tweedsmuir, *Memory Hold the Door* (Hodder & Stoughton, 1940).

OSTRER, Isidore

(1889-1975)

Film maker and distributor and cinema owner

Isidore Ostrer was born in Poland in 1889, the eldest child of Nathan Ostrer, a shoemaker and his wife Sonia. Early in his childhood the family emigrated to England and settled in Bow, East London, where Nathan seems to have prospered as a shoe-maker. Little is known about Isidore's upbringing and schooling, except that he had four younger brothers and a sister and that his parents both died in 1932.

Apparently he started work as a stockbroker's clerk where his career gained a fillip when he succeeded in impressing one of his employer's clients. He first appears in the records as one of the two directors of the Lothbury Investment Corporation — a banking and underwriting concern — in 1919. By this time he was a stockbroker and living in Hampstead. He was now obviously in a position to undertake ambitious schemes. In 1921 the Ostrer Bros Merchant Bank was formed by Isidore with his brothers, Maurice and Mark, and after protracted negotiations they managed to buy out the French interests in the Gaumont Co, which had hitherto acted as a distribution agency for the films of Leon Gaumont (December 1922). The newly-autonomous company continued to be run by the brothers AC and RC Bromhead, and the fact that in 1923 Isidore became a director of the large textile combine, Illingworth-Morris, indicates that the Ostrers were by no means irretrievably committed to the film industry. However, the situation was radically changed by the prospect of a Film Quota Act which would make the showing of a percentage of British films compulsory. In March 1927 the Ostrers organised a syndicate to float a £2 million merger between Gaumont and two important film distribution agencies (W & F and Ideal) and the Biocolour chain of cinemas. Little over a year later the new Gaumont British Picture Corporation had expanded its chain of cinemas to nearly 200 and incorporated Michael Balcon's (qv) Gainsborough Studios into its group. In December 1928 Isidore persuaded Lord Beaverbrook (qv) to accept £2 million for his Provincial Cinematograph Theatres, thus adding another 116 cinemas to the Gaumont British circuit.

With total assets of around £11 million the Corporation had reached an unprecedented size for a British film concern. However, the effects of the Film Quota Act (which became law in November 1927) were not quite as beneficial as had been expected, and the situation was further complicated by the coming of sound to the cinema. In July 1929 the Ostrers paid over £1.5 million for the remaining £1.25 million 10s ordinary shares of GBPC as yet unissued; the capital was needed for re-equipping the 300 odd cinemas for sound and a public issue would have been unlikely to have been successful, as the stock-market was now wary of investment in the film industry. This was not, however, a wholly altruistic move. Despite repeated denials rumours persisted that some sort of deal with the American Fox Co was in the offing. In September AC and RC Bromhead resigned their posts as respectively chairman and managing director, insisting that shareholders pass a resolution removing voting rights from foreign holders of ordinary shares before they did so. Isidore became chairman, Mark Ostrer vice-chairman and C M Woolf and Maurice Ostrer joint managing directors. Subsequent events are shrouded in myth and mystery but early in 1930, when the mist dispersed a little it emerged that the shares held by the Ostrers had been invested in a holding company called Metropolis & Bradford, which with 53 per cent of Gaumont's ordinary capital controlled the GBPC. The share capital of M & B was divided into one million £1 non-voting 'B' shares — 750,000 held by the Fox Corporation, 250,000 held by the Ostrers, and 10,000 'A' voting shares of which the Ostrers had managed to retain a narrow majority and thus control. William Fox had paid virtually £4 million for his shares, undoubtedly under the illusion that he was buying control. Fox's subsequent overthrow and bankruptcy put him in a weak position to press his claim.

There are signs that having created the biggest film company in the country, having survived the coming of sound, and having outwitted the Americans, Isidore was getting bored. As his daughter Pamela Mason later commented:

> He liked to play chess with companies: he wasn't particularly interested in what they did. When he ran two film studios he didn't visit them. {*Daily Mail* 24 May 1976}

The day-to-day running of the company was left to Mark and Maurice — and such able subordinates as Michael Balcon and C M Woolf. In June 1931, after an unsuccessful attempt to involve Ramsay Macdonald's Government in the company, Isidore created the post of president for himself, resigning the chairmanship in favour of Mark (described in a newspaper report as 'one of the three best businessmen in Wardour Street, and in a class of his own as a company chairman'. {*Daily Express* Jan 1938}). Though refraining from active political activity Isidore had strong opinions about economics and his acquisition of the *Sunday Referee* in September 1931 can be seen partly as an attempt to gain a platform from which to propagate Keynesian ideas. In 1932 he published *The Conquest of Gold*, a bold if unrigorous diatribe against the prevailing economic orthodoxy.

It is difficult to estimate how much Isidore's radical views impinged on the running of the company. The film technicians' union, the Association of Cinematograph Technicians (ACT), was able first to establish itself at Gaumont's Shepherds Bush Studios, but this probably had as much to do with Balcon, a staunch socialist, as with the Ostrers. More directly attributable to Isidore Ostrer is the development of the corporation into a conglomerate which spanned not only the three main branches of the film industry — production, distribution and exhibition — but such peripheral fields as the manufacture of projectors and cinema seating. He had a keen awareness of the potential of new technology and invested heavily in Bush Radio, the British Acoustic Co and Baird Television, all of which became subsidiaries of Gaumont British.

Unfortunately the rather remote control Isidore wielded over GBPC, the lack of any machinery of centralised co-ordination, its organisation as a collection of semi-autonomous companies, made it difficult to ensure that far-sighted investments were followed up by vigorous development and marketing operations. Both Baird TV and the British Acoustic sound film apparatus lost their early market leads to competitors with more thorough and ambitious research and development programmes.

In 1936 began the long struggle for power which five years later led to Isidore selling control of Gaumont-British to J Arthur Rank (qv). Briefly, a deal between the Ostrers and the brothers Joseph and Nicholas Schenck, the heads respectively of 20th century Fox and Metro-Goldwyn-Mayer (MGM), was interrupted by a counter bid by John Maxwell (qv) of Associated British Picture Co (ABPC). The 250,000 non-voting shares which the Ostrers held in Metropolis & Bradford were sold to Maxwell for £600,000 in October 1936, but Fox, disgruntled at the frustration of their own bid for control, vetoed the sale of the crucial voting shares. Thus as the British film industry moved into another period of crisis, the Gaumont British board was divided into three mutually hostile factions. No sooner had Maxwell admitted defeat and resigned his directorship, than dissident shareholders appealed successfully in January 1939 for a Board of Trade Inquiry into the company. Its report, though critical, exonerated the Ostrers from the charges of fraud and financial malpractice which had been levelled against them.

In the Press there was much criticism of the Ostrers for the tiny financial basis of their control of Gaumont British, but there is little indication that Isidore had any wish to retain power. When in 1941 Maxwell's (vetoed) option on the Ostrer voting shares ran out, an agreement with Rank was quickly reached. Rank was able to mollify the Americans, relieve ABPC of its non-voting shares (at £150,000 discount), and for the price of £750,000 acquire those elusive 5,100 voting shares through which the Ostrers had controlled Gaumont British.

Mark and Maurice retained their executive posts but Isidore cut his links with the film industry completely. His gains were invested via the Lothbury Investment Corporation in the Illingworth Morris Co, turning what had been a minor interest into a controlling one. It was reported in 1981 that Isidore held 60 per cent of the Lothbury and Maurice 40 per cent while Lothbury's sole investment was a 27 per cent stake in Illingworth Morris; in addition Isidore reportedly held a further 19 per cent in Illingworth Morris directly while other members of the Ostrer family held another 10 per cent.

> Over the 1950s, 1960s and early 1970s, Isidore bought companies and assets — always for perishable cash borrowed from the banks — in the most uninhibited manner. When he died in 1975, Illingworth had borrowings as high as its shareholders' funds.
>
> Isidore's grand plan had been to build the world's biggest wool textile company and dominate the industry. In some measure he succeeded, though his most ambitious scheme — to take Illingworth beyond woollens by a reverse takeover of Courtaulds — was thwarted.
>
> One or two of his later acquisitions failed to live up to their promise. Yet Isidore never visited prospective acquisitions; he just concentrated on reading the balance sheets. But when wrinkles subsequently appeared he fought tooth and nail to prevent closures. He was acutely conscious of his responsibilities as an employer. And he rarely disposed of assets. If someone was prepared to match the asking price, he reasoned, then the asking price was too low. Always a buyer, never a seller, Isidore died leaving Illingworth in hock to the bankers. {*Sunday Times* 11 Oct 1981}

For the last thirty years of his life Isidore Ostrer exercised his control of Illingworth Morris at a distance, rarely visiting the Bradford base of the company which employed 5,000.

After the Second World War he developed an obsession for healthy living. He fasted frequently, sometimes for thirty days. He seriously believed he could live to be one hundred-and-thirty. And as for the pursuit of money, he told members of his family, it was important only in as much as 'it permitted him to write books or poems, or to paint' {*ibid*}. He and his brother Maurice spent up to four months a year in a rented flat at Cannes (from whence they sent directives to Illingworth Morris, without secretarial help) but Isidore never became a tax exile, not least because of his socialist convictions.

Isidore Ostrer in 1914 married Helen Dorothy, daughter of Lloyd Spear-Morgan, a solicitor; their daughter Pamela became a Hollywood film star whose second husband was the actor James Mason.

Isidore Ostrer died on 3 September 1975, leaving £1,492,435 gross. Described as both a crook and a genius, Isidore Ostrer remains one of the most enigmatic of twentieth century business figures.

ROBERT MURPHY

Writings:

A New International Company (1921).

The Conquest of Gold (Jonathan Cape, 1932).

Sources:

Unpublished

PRO, BT 64/86.

MCe.

PrC.

Published

Daily Express Jan 1938.

Daily Mail 24 May 1976.

Sunday Times 11 Oct 1981.

WWW.

OVERSTONE, 1st Lord Overstone
see LOYD, Samuel Jones

OWEN, Sir Alfred George Beech

(1908-1975)

Manufacturer of engineering components

Sir Alfred G B Owen (courtesy of Lady Owen).

Alfred George Beech Owen was born at Streetly, Staffordshire, on 8 April 1908, eldest of the two sons and daughter of Alfred Ernest Owen (1869-1929) and his wife Florence Lucy née Beech. Alfred Ernest Owen had come to Darlaston from North Wales in 1893, having completed an engineering apprenticeship, (in Messrs Taylors Engineering Works, Sandycroft, near Chester), to become partner of John T Rubery in Rubery & Co, following the withdrawal of John's brother, Thomas Rubery. The Ruberys, who had started the firm in 1884, employed about 30 people in their Victoria Ironworks, The Green, Darlaston, trading as 'blacksmiths and manufacturers of fencing, gates, roofing, light bridge work, and general fabrications in sheet and rolled sections'. {Owen (1965) 1} After Alfred Ernest Owen arrived the firm moved into the manufacturing of structural steel for the construction industry and (in 1896) chassis frames for the infant motor industry. From 1900 new power presses were installed to make improved chassis types. In 1905 the firm was renamed Rubery, Owen & Co and in 1910 John T Rubery retired leaving Alfred Ernest Owen the sole proprietor. Turnover rose from £29,000 in 1904 to £137,000 in 1913 and £382,000 in 1917. The firm became a privately-owned limited company in 1920, with a nominal capital of £1 million. By the end of 1929, when Alfred Ernest died suddenly, Rubery Owen & Co Ltd had a turnover of about £580,000, employed 1,750 and was well-established as a motor vehicle components supplier. The firm then consisted of five departments: motor frame, producing car chassis and pressed components; structural, making steel work for buildings; aviation, manufacturing components turned from the bar for aircraft and also nuts and bolts for cars; the motor wheel department, making disc and wire wheels; and the metal aircraft department, which pressed sheet metal components for aircraft.

Alfred Owen came into the family business precipitately. From Lickey Hill Preparatory School he was sent to Oundle School and then in 1927 went up to Emmanuel College, Cambridge, to read engineering. At Cambridge his Anglican upbringing was revitalised through the Cambridge Inter Collegiate Christian Union and he made a personal commitment to Christ. 'Soon after his conversion he met La Maréchale, General Booth's daughter, who asked him 'What are you doing for the Lord?' This question spurred him on to reconsider his whole life as an act of service to God'. {Service of Thanksgiving (1975) 3} He contemplated training for the Anglican ministry. On the death of his father, however, he left Cambridge and returned home to take charge of the family firm, shortly after his twenty-first birthday.

He was soon joined as joint managing director by his younger brother Ernest (1910–1967) and despite the economic depression of the 1930s the

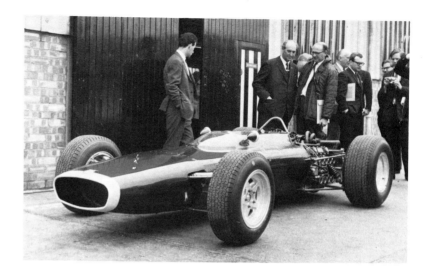

Alfred Owen viewing the BRM H16 engined 3 litre Formula 1 car at Bourne, Lincolnshire in 1966 (courtesy of the Rubery, Owen Group).

business grew with the building boom and then the expansion of the motor industry. Rubery Owen secured large structural steel contracts for, inter alia, Wolverhampton Civic Hall, flats and shops around Marble Arch, London, and framework for the Rugby Union headquarters at Twickenham and football stands for Wolverhampton Wanderers, Manchester United, Derby County, Milwall and Reading. To this and to motor vehicle components Alfred Owen added metal storage equipment (the department opened in 1932). When rearmament started in 1936 three new departments were formed: armour plate in 1937, airframe parts in 1939 and a department for 'the machining and assembly of aircraft components and hydraulic mechanisms' {Owen (1965) 3} also in 1939. With the spread of unit construction of motorcar chassis and body, Rubery Owen's chassis building capacity was increasingly directed towards heavy commercial vehicles in the 1930s. During the Second World War the company's fabricating and presswork departments were employed in a wide range of products, from lifeboats to aircraft propeller hubs. The latter involved the technique of flashwelding two heavy steel pressings and after 1945 it was successfully applied to axle case production for commercial vehicles.

Soon after the end of the war, when Rubery Owen employed 16,000 (December 1946), Alfred Owen sought growth by taking over smaller metal-working and motor vehicle components firms. As a conscious long-term policy no dividends were paid to shareholders; instead profits were invested in new ventures or plant replacement. This pattern of expansion by acquisition was reflected in the number of Alfred Owen's directorships which rose from 10 in 1939 to 24 in 1946, 31 in 1950, 73 in 1961, 88 in 1965 and 97 in 1969. The number of the Rubery Owen & Co group's subsidiaries rose from 14 (all in the UK) in 1945 to 66 based in the UK and 18 subsidiaries overseas in 1969.

At Darlaston in the mid-1950s the parent company's loose structure of manufacturing departments 'each operating and negotiating with customers in its own way' {ibid, 4} was replaced by a divisional structure of six divisions, each responsible for design, manufacture and sales, with central control exercised over finance, purchasing, research, personnel and engineering plant and maintenance services. Meetings between divisional managers and heads of the functional departments were regularly held under the chairmanship of Alfred or Ernest. 'Financial control is based on standard costing throughout the works ... Each year divisional managers submit to the board for approval their budgets in which sales are forecast and estimates of capital expenditure outlined; and monthly operating statements are produced for each department which highlight variances from standard.' {ibid, 4} In 1965 the six divisions at Darlaston comprised the structural (design and fabrication of steel work for buildings); motor (car components, particularly chassis frames, presswork, wheels, axle cases and fuel tanks); bolt and nut; contracts (manufacture of earthmoving equipment and cranes for sub-contract); metal assemblies (deep-drawn presswork, particularly for vehicle brake cylinders, compresser shells for refrigerators, and gas bottles); and metal equipment (steel shelving, pallets, containers). In 1969, when Alfred Owen retired, the company employed approximately 6,000 people at Darlaston where the turnover was around £25 million per annum.

By the early 1960s the Rubery Owen Group consisted of some 50 companies whose activities extended to many fields — mechanical handling equipment, aircraft landing gear, motor vehicle components, cab assemblies and specialist car bodies, steel buildings, automation equipment, kitchen equipment, office furniture, petrol pumps, central heating, plant hire as well as the retailing of cars throughout Staffordshire and Shropshire and agricultural equipment throughout Shropshire. To handle these diverse activities, Rubery Owen & Co Ltd was formed into a holding company (Rubery Owen Holdings Ltd) in 1965 and the main manufacturing company at Darlaston was then merely the largest of the group's many subsidiary companies. At that time, the remainder of the group's subsidiaries employed approximately 10,000 people and the total group turnover was around £80 million per annum. Outside Darlaston the main subsidiary company was Electro Hydraulics Ltd, a public company based at Warrington, which manufactured aircraft landing gear, hydraulic mining equipment and fork lift trucks. The other subsidiary companies were mostly in the West Midlands but also at Sheffield, Wrexham, Leeds, Coventry and South Wales. Overseas subsidiaries were established in South Africa, India and Australia. During their latter years Alfred and Ernest Owen controlled the subsidiary companies by regular attendance at the subsidiaries' board meetings. Decisions were taken independently at those meetings with Alfred and Ernest Owen providing the common link with the rest of the group. A substantial head office team covering commercial and financial activities enabled them to provide additional support for the subsidiaries as well as a measure of financial control. The general philosophy, however, was for the subsidiary companies to be autonomous under the overall guidance and control of Alfred and Ernest Owen. In practice, the degree of autonomy varied to some extent depending upon the strength and capabilities of the managing directors concerned.

Under Alfred Owen the company had a good labour relations record until the mid-1960s. Inflation in the economy thereafter exposed the

A minute proportion of the day's Mini wheel build rolling towards the Rubery Owen inspection and paint shop ready for despatch, 1965 (courtesy of the Rubery, Owen Group).

group's regional and, at Darlaston departmental, wage differentials. However, the task of sorting these out fell to the third generation in the family firm.

Besides its size as the largest private manufacturing business in the Black Country, Rubery Owen was unusual for its tone which came directly from Alfred Owen's Christian commitment. When Alfred took over his father's desk on 6 January 1930 he told his executives that in future the firm would be run by him as a Christian business. 'Nothing would be permitted which could not be done with a clear conscience. I was told I would ruin the business' {Blythe (1959)}. Genial and enthusiastic, Alfred Owen chose a personal life style which carried conviction when he applied his Christian principles in industry — he lived in a six-bedroomed villa in Sutton Coldfield for most of his married life and did not smoke or drink (in four years he removed the works canteen liquor licence by so heavily subsidising lemonade that it entirely displaced alcohol).

The company earned a high reputation in the Black Country for its welfare provisions even before the First World War. In 1912 Alfred Ernest

Owen provided a canteen, works institute, bowling greens, tennis courts and meeting hall. Alfred augmented these. Between the 1930s and 1950s he introduced a sports and social club; a hostel and a youth club for apprentices (by the 1950s the firm took 50-60 apprentices per annum on five-year courses); a medical centre; a nursery (open to the Darlaston community also); subsidised housing for employees; a savings bank; a staff pension scheme; a convalescent home near Barmouth (1946-60s); and an innovative retirement scheme, the Sons of Rest Workshop (1949), with courses on preparing for retirement and the opportunity for light jobs in workshops away from the factory site.

Beyond Rubery Owen, A G B Owen's business activities included the deputy chairmanship of the Development Corporation for Wales in 1967 and a leading role in the BRM (British Racing Motors) project where he happily combined his passion for speed, his pride in British engineering and his strong belief in private enterprise. Alfred Owen was one of the first businessmen to promise financial assistance when Raymond Mays conceived a plan to raise finance to build a British grand prix racing car in 1945. He took a leading part in the BRM project and in the formation of the British Motor Racing Research Trust in 1947. The first BRM racing car was demonstrated at Folkingham, near Bourne, Lincolnshire (where it was built), in 1949 but then severe technical and financial troubles delayed its few successes on international circuits. In 1952 the BRM trust decided to wind up the company and sell its assets. A G B Owen purchased the company and made it a department of Rubery Owen & Co Ltd. Characteristically, Owen refused to change the name of the cars to 'Owens' and persisted with their development. In 1959 the Swedish driver, Jo Bonnier, gave a BRM its first victory in a Formula I world championship event by winning the Dutch Grand Prix. 'Three years later Owen was present when Graham Hill won the South African Grand Prix in a BRM, securing the 1962 Drivers' World Championship and the Manufacturers' Cup as well' { *Times* 30 Oct 1975}. For similar reasons he backed Donald Malcolm Campbell's attempt at breaking the world land speed record. Campbell's racing car *Bluebird* was built by Motor Panels Ltd of Coventry, a subsidiary of Rubery Owen, with assistance in specialist machining from the parent firm's R & D staff at Darlaston and in hydraulics technology from Electrohydraulics. No-one was more delighted than A G B Owen when Campbell reached a new record speed of 403 mph (attaining a maximum of 429 mph) at Lake Eyre, South Australia, on 17 July 1964.

Despite these heavy business involvements Alfred Owen assumed numerous, and at times demanding, duties in the spheres of local government, social service and Christian work. In local government he started in 1934 with his election as a Conservative (with independent tendencies) to the Darlaston Urban District Council, of which he was chairman, 1942-46 and 1952-54. In his home town of Sutton Coldfield he was elected to the Borough Council in 1937 and served as mayor in 1951. Through his membership of Staffordshire County Council, 1949-66, of which he was chairman 1955-62, he became a member of the Council of the University College of North Staffordshire and after the College gained its charter, Pro-Chancellor of Keele University, 1962-70. He was also a member of Birmingham University Council.

Rubery, Owen structural steel work for Birmingham Technical College, 1952 (courtesy of Rubery, Owen Group).

In the field of social service he was acting chairman of Dr Barnardo's Homes, 1949-50, and then chairman, 1950-70; chairman of the National Road Safety Advisory Council, 1965-67 (despite several convictions for exceeding the speed limits); vice-chairman of the National Savings Movement, 1960-73; president of the St John Ambulance Association for Staffordshire; chairman of the governors of Bishop Vesey's Grammar School, Sutton Coldfield; and, in Darlaston, president of the Old People's Welfare Committee, the Sons of Rest, the Darlaston and District Social Services, the Garden and Allotments Association and the Fellowship for the Disabled. Rather differently, he was also a director of Walsall Football Club.

From the day he was converted at Cambridge, A G B Owen threw himself into all sorts of Christian work. An Anglican lay reader, 'On most Sundays he could be found preaching, taking a service or helping with a Bible class' {*ibid*}, preaching in Nonconformist chapels as well as parish churches. He acted as sidesman in his parish church (St John's Walmley near Sutton Coldfield) and was patron of the living of Bucknall-cum-Bagnall near Stoke on Trent. With his wife in the 1930s he ran a children's service at Sutton Coldfield parish church (moved during the war to another hall known, from its roof, as the 'Tin Tab'). He was a Crusader leader all his active life; president of the West Midlands Boys Brigade, accompanying them on summer camps for many years; chairman of the National Sunday School Union; and a trustee of the Grubb Institute. When the American evangelist Billy Graham first came to England in 1946-47, A G B Owen, like John Laing (qv), sponsored the early crusades, acting as treasurer of the London crusade in 1954. The Owens became long-time friends with Billy Graham and his wife and members of his team. As a result of this influence A G B Owen helped to establish and became treasurer of Birmingham Youth for Christ.

A G B Owen's services were recognised variously. He was made an OBE in 1946, CBE in 1954 and knighted in 1961. Keele University made him an honorary DSc in 1965. His achievements in motor racing brought him the Ferodo Gold Trophy in 1962 and a British Automobile Racing Club gold medal in 1963. He was made a DL for Warwickshire in 1967 and a freeman (the last, it so happened) of the borough of Sutton Coldfield in 1970.

Alfred Owen in 1932 married Eileen Kathleen Genevieve ('Viva') McMullan, daughter of Captain A McMullan, an army officer. They had three sons and two daughters. Sir Alfred Owen 'mixed easily with national figures and indeed with members of the Royal Family but was perhaps most at home in his beloved Black Country. With scant regard for his best suit, he would snatch a few minutes to pick raspberries in his garden before rushing off to a civic function and then, in the small hours of the morning, would return to the factory to patrol the night shift' {Service of Thanksgiving (1975) 7}.

Running one of the largest family businesses in the country and engaging in all his other local government, social service and Christian interests took their toll. 'For many years he worked an eighteen-hour day and drove himself in his long-suffering Bentley up to 50,000 miles a year. On 22 October 1969, while waiting to preach at St Matthew's Church, Walsall, he suffered a serious stroke from which he was never fully to recover. To such an active man the physical limitations caused by his illness must have been frustrating but he amazed those closest to him by the stoic patience with which he faced them right up to the last' {ibid}. Sir Alfred Owen died on 29 October 1975, leaving £224,220 gross.

DAVID J JEREMY

Sources:

Unpublished

BCe.

PrC.

Alfred G B Owen, 'The Development and Organisation of Rubery Owen & Co Ltd' (Edwards Seminar paper 349, 9 Mar 1965).

'A Service of Thanksgiving for the Life of Alfred George Beech Owen, 5 Dec 1975, Darlaston Parish Church' (pp, Darlaston, 1975).

Information from the family of Sir Alfred Owen and Mrs Barbara M D Smith.

Published

George C Allen, *The Industrial Development of Birmingham and the Black Country* (George Allen & Unwin, 1929).

Birmingham Mail 13 Mar 1982.

Susan Blythe, 'The Man Who Doesn't Want to be a Millionaire' *Daily Mail* 15 Jan 1959.

DD 1939, 1946, 1950, 1961, 1965, 1969, 1975.

Evening Mail 3 Oct 1975.

The Goodwill (Rubery Owen house magazine, Christmas 1946, Spring and Summer 1947).

Opportunity: Training, Educational and Welfare Facilities at the Rubery Owen Group of Companies (company brochure, 1963).

Samuel B Saul, 'The Motor Industry in Britain to 1914' *Business History* 5 (1962).

Sunday Times 7 Sept 1969.

Times 7 Jan 1969, 30 Oct 1975.

Graham Turner, *The Carmakers* (Harmondsworth: Penguin Books, 1964).

Who's Who in the Motor Industry 1955.

WWW.

OWEN, Owen

(1847-1910)

Department store owner

Owen Owen was born near Machynlleth, Montgomeryshire, on 13 October 1847, the first son of Owen Owen, a tenant farmer, and his second wife Esther Elizabeth (d 1855), daughter of William Evans a Wesleyan Methodist minister who had retired to Machynlleth. His maternal uncle Samuel, a linen draper in Bath, financially assisted the education of his nephews at the Wesleyan College, Taunton, and took three of them, Thomas, Owen and William successively, as his apprentices at Bath. By 1863 Thomas had become a partner with his uncle in the Bath drapery business which was expanding rapidly.

Owen Owen was determined to set up on his own account and in 1867 decided to move to Liverpool where a paternal uncle, Robert (d 1856), had had a successful drapery business. At Liverpool his first act was to write out a code of rules to guide his behaviour and business life.

> 1. Rise very early, and live very well and very cheaply. 2. Be honest to my customers and just to my creditors — this will give confidence. 3. Pay debts as soon as possible so as to owe no man; and give no credit to anyone for longer period than two months; this can't be thought of at first. 4. Work myself and be as much as possible in the shop. Help hands, for I have no

lands. 5. Be civil, to everyone. 6. Time being money, waste none; for now is the time to work, read and make a fortune. 7. Do not frequent theatres, music halls, or anything to neglect the business. {Davies (1984) 20}

Within a couple of months he rented suitable premises in London Road, only a few doors from his late uncle's business, and in May 1868 single-handed he opened his shop. His policy of low profit margins on high turnover of goods, clear labelling and accurate stock and financial controls helped his business to flourish; within five years he was employing 120 people and he was occupying several adjoining shops with a frontage of 120 feet. By 1876 he purchased his shop premises, paying £5,500 down and the balance of £8,000 in one payment ten years later. Over the next few years he purchased many more adjacent houses; this enabled him both to enlarge his shop premises and also to provide supervised hostels for his apprentices and his female staff, many of whom like himself came from a Welsh Methodist background.

While presiding over the rapid expansion and profitable development of his Liverpool store, Owen Owen looked for areas into which he could diversify. In the 1880s he invested over £10,000 in railway shares, particularly in North America and subsequently substantially more. Rather than setting up more stores in his own name, Owen assisted other members of his family to get into or expand similar businesses. His elder brother Thomas was now heavily involved in paper mills as well as the Bath drapery business; when the latter was formed into a separate limited company in 1889, Owen took £5,000 of shares and became a director. From the 1870s he lent substantial sums and became involved heavily in the business his brother William had set up in Bayswater, West London, opposite William Whiteley (qv). When the business was converted into a limited liability company in 1903 Owen's investment was valued at £53,000. R O Davies, Owen's brother-in-law, had also established a drapery business in Bayswater and Owen invested in this too. Owen became a frequent commuter between Liverpool and London. At the London homes of his relatives Owen met other London Welshmen including Lloyd George and D H Evans, a young draper whose success had been as spectacular as his own; and also his future wife Ellen who was working at Gorringes, another large drapery store.

Following his marriage in 1891 Owen set up home in London. More and more his interests turned to the Metropolis. He made substantial investments and became a director in the Bon Marché, Brixton and John Barnes in the Finchley Road, both department stores in prime suburban locations rather than in central London. He also invested heavily in central shopping sites, in many cases undertaking the development himself. His property company Owen Owen Estate Ltd, formed just before his death, had an issued capital of £249,993. Meantime he continued to develop his Liverpool business and improve the premises. He advertised extensively and held regular sales; his store was one of the biggest and most respected in the North of England. It was also very prosperous; from 1902-3 until 1905-6 a dividend of 12 per cent was paid and thereafter until Owen's death the dividend was 16 per cent. The business had been formed into a limited liability company in 1899 with an issued share capital of £260,000 of which Owen held around 45 per cent and for the balance he received over £140,000 cash. Despite this organisational change, Owen remained a dominant influence in the direction of the Liverpool business. In 1906 he made a trip to study American stores and their administration. It is perhaps an indication of his failing health that whilst he was impressed with some aspects of American practice, he felt the stimulation of the visit had come too late for him to act upon the lessons he learned.

Owen became a keen early cyclist starting with a tricycle in 1884 and then graduating to a bicycle after a course of lessons in 1897. This interest subsequently extended to motorcars and he purchased the Burlington Carriage Co in 1907; this company imported French cars and sold them from one of Owen's London properties.

Owen Owen's close involvement with Wesleyan Methodism gradually weakened and in the 1880s he began to worship as a Unitarian. He supported generously Methodist and other charities, particularly those connected with the drapery trade and with Welsh education, until the end of his life. He was also closely interested in the Welsh Societies in Liverpool and London and in the Eisteddfod. Concerned for the welfare of his employees, he was prominent in the movement for shorter working hours and his was the first Liverpool store to introduce a weekly half-holiday. In 1900 he set up the Owen Owen Trust for staff. Owen became a magistrate in North Wales around 1906 — ten years earlier he had bought an estate in Penmaenmawr (whence he sent employees in need of convalescence) — and that year acquired an estate near Machynlleth.

Owen Owen married in 1891 Ellen Maria Richards, daughter of George Richards; they had two sons and two daughters. Owen had made no alternative arrangements for succession hoping that one of his sons would take over. The elder (1895-1921), who was only fifteen when Owen died, was killed in a railway accident and the younger (b 1902) became interested in the estate company rather than the drapery business. In the years following Owen's death the store's success began to falter. Only after his son-in-law, Duncan Norman, who married Owen's younger daughter, took over in 1925 did the business begin to flourish again, and even then for a period in the 1930s the business of Owen Owen Ltd was financially controlled by Owen Owen Estate Ltd.

Owen Owen died on 27 March 1910 after a period of failing health. He left £477,800 gross.

FRANCIS GOODALL

Sources:

Unpublished

MCe.

PrC.

Published

Alison Adburgham, *Shops and Shopping 1800-1914* (Allen & Unwin, 1964).

David Wyn Davies, *Owen Owen: Victorian Draper* (Aberystwyth: Gwasg Cambria, 1984).

Stock Exchange Official Year Book 1934.

Stock Exchange Year Book 1911, 1921, 1930.

Times 31 Mar 1910.

OWEN, William Barry

(1860-1914)

Gramophone company executive

William Barry Owen (courtesy of Raymond R Wile).

William Barry Owen was born at Vineyard Haven, Massachusetts, on the island of Martha's Vineyard, on 15 April 1860, the elder of the two children of Leander C Owen, a whaling captain, and his wife June née Luce. William was educated in a mainland preparatory school and afterwards entered Amherst College with the intention of pursuing a career at law. Abandoning this course, he took a position with the McPhail Piano Co, but the company failed, despite efforts on the part of Owen's friends to rescue it. He then became the manager of the autoharp department of Albert Dodge.

On 22 February 1887 he married a local Vineyard Haven girl, Mary M Robinson. Two children were born of the marriage, Paul (b 1891) and Knight (b 1893).

In September 1895 Emile Berliner, who had been attempting to market his invention, the gramophone, through the small Washington-based United States Gramophone Co, managed to interest a promoter, William C Jones, in his product. Jones was able to gather a group of Philadelphia businessmen to organise a new company, the Berliner Gramophone Co, to take over the tools and stock in trade of US Gramophone, which henceforth would be a patent holding company. They hoped to market the gramophone through a series of regional companies. Only two such were organised, a New England Gramophone Co and the New York Gramophone Co, organised by Frank Seaman, an advertising agency executive, and two associates in February 1896. Owen, who had become an associate of Seaman some time before, was placed in charge of the operation. The invention itself was crude and unless improved seemed destined for failure. An earlier European marketing scheme launched in 1890 had already become dormant.

Seaman and Owen soon began to advertise the product extensively and arranged for coverage in the *Scientific American* of 16 May 1896. They also urged the Berliner Co to continue in its efforts to have Eldridge R

Continent to arrange contracts for coal and coke. He also promoted, and the partnership owned, the West India Dock Railway, which was fully operational early in 1852, to speed conveyance of its coals in London. The partnership also owned extensive railway networks in Northumberland and Durham. By the early 1890s, shortly before Palmer's retirement, his coal interests employed about 6,000 men and had an annual output of about two million tons. All of this was achieved on credit (the partnership had borrowings of £180,000 in 1855) largely achieved on the name of John Bowes but due to Palmer's financial acumen, which got the partnership through the 1857 crisis which would have destroyed a lesser man faced with the same problems. In 1871 the partnership was minimally valued at £1 million and at £2 million in 1875 (after a fall from a higher figure at the peak of the coal famine). In 1866 Palmer's holding increased to one-third after the death of Nicholas Wood and from 1883 he was joint partner after the death of Sir William Hutt. He became chairman and managing director (at a salary of £3,000 per annum) of the limited company which was formed in 1886 after the death of John Bowes. He retired from these positions in 1895 and was succeeded as managing director by his second son, Alfred.

From his coal interests Palmer moved into shipbuilding. By the end of the 1840s the railways began to bring significant amounts of coal to London from inland coalfields. Faced with this competition, coalowners in the Great Northern Coalfield sought reductions in transport costs incurred in reaching the London market. Palmer succeeded by developing a steam-powered, water-ballast, iron collier, *John Bowes*, built in 1852. Yet the existing wooden vessel shipyard at Jarrow, which Palmer and his brother George took over in 1851 as Palmer Bros & Co, produced as its first vessel an iron-built steam tug, the *Northumberland*. It is, therefore, less than clear that the venture into shipbuilding had as its original aim the solving of the coal transport problem. Nevertheless, Palmer must be credited for the solution as well as for pioneering iron shipbuilding on any scale on the Tyne. To overcome the doubts of the existing shippers of coal in wooden sailing colliers, Palmer set up in 1852 the General Iron Screw Collier Co, of which he was managing director, with a capital of £250,000 in £5 shares raised chiefly from London sources, to offer steam colliers on charter in order to develop the coal shipping trade. In addition he had hydraulic machinery devised for the rapid unloading of the vessels (the higher capital investment in iron steamships could not be left to the delays of the coal whippers) and made special arrangements with the London railway companies for the rapid distribution of the coal in the metropolis. The results of his ships' voyages were spectacularly successful and output of screw colliers, the progenitor of the cargo steamer, reached the point where the standard joke was that Palmers built them by the mile and then chopped them up to the required length.

In 1856 Palmer achieved another spectacular triumph, contracting for the building of the ironclad floating battery, the *Terror*, for the Government for use in the Crimean War. It was remarkable that such a newly-established firm should have obtained a government contract but it was won by the fame of Palmer's colliers and his offer of a three month completion date. In order to try to meet this date (the vessel was actually completed in three-and-a-half months), Palmer instituted the first

The works of Palmers shipbuilding Co Ltd, Jarrow-on-Tyne ca 1890 (courtesy of the Central Library, Newcastle upon Tyne).

successful use of rolled iron plates, a quicker process than the traditional forging. Although not his own invention, the technique became known as 'Palmer's rolled plates' throughout the industry.

The *Terror* was to be the first of many warships built for the Admiralty as well as for many foreign navies and Palmer's yards (in 1860 Palmer took over a yard at Howdon on the north bank of the Tyne from Coutts) subsequently built many cargo vessels, including oil tankers and passenger vessels. In order to increase orders for the latter Palmer was actively involved in establishing and developing a number of shipping lines which purchased vessels from his yards. They included the Guion, National and Union Lines of transatlantic steamers; an arrangement with the Italian Government to work a line of steamers between Italy and Egypt; and the amalgamation in 1864 of several Tyneside shipping companies to form the Tyne Steam Shipping Co Ltd, of which Palmer became chairman.

Expansion of shipbuilding capacity undoubtedly caused Palmer problems with the supply of materials and led him into backward integration which was to make the Jarrow firm a classic example of total integration from raw materials to finished ships and other iron products. In 1856, at the time that he purchased the bankrupt Wallsend iron works, he took a lease on ironstone workings at Hinderwell on the North Yorkshire Moors near Staithes and at a cost estimated at £30,000-40,000 erected a harbour, to be called Port Mulgrave, at which his own ships could load the ore. At Jarrow three blast furnaces were erected (there were eventually to be five, augmented in 1882 with Siemens-Martin steel plant) and by 1859 forges and rolling mills were added. It was estimated that the works could deal with 2,500 tons of ore weekly and were capable of producing 1,000 tons of wrought iron. By 1870 the output of shipping was averaging 20,000 tons per annum and many of the ships were engined by Palmers engine works (which also built stationary engines) and, if in need of subsequent repair, they could be accommodated in the firm's large graving dock completed in 1865.

That year the Jarrow works became one of the first large companies to be sold to the public, and also part of the largest vertical combine then organised in Britain. Charles's brother had retired in 1862 and it would seem that Charles wished to reduce some of his responsibilities for the iron and shipbuilding activities and provide the scope for diversification for his restless abilities. It is also probable that extra capital was needed to maintain the firm's expansion. The new concern, set up as Palmer's Iron & Shipbuilding Co Ltd, was largely owned by a group of Manchester men who paid about £700,000 for the old firm, together with a further sum for stocks, a promotion organised by David Chadwick (qv). Palmer became chairman (a position he was to hold until 1893) and managing director at an annual salary of £3,000. Expansion of the firm continued and peak outputs of more than 60,000 tons of shipping in several years in the 1880s made it the country's leading shipbuilder with an annual wage bill of more than £500,000. By the time of Palmer's final withdrawal from the company in 1893 it had launched a total of nearly one million tons of shipping, 'Palmer's town' of Jarrow had grown from 4,000 to 40,000 in population and the works covered 100 acres with a river frontage of three-quarters of a mile and a labour force of 7,500.

From the late 1860s, however, Palmer's involvement with the company was lessened as he spent more time on other matters (he was by this time senior partner in the family firm, now called Palmer, Hall & Co) and especially on politics. In 1868 he unsuccessfully contested South Shields as a Liberal and almost certainly with political motivation he took the largest share in the Tyne Plate Glass Co, set up to take over the South Shields works of R W Swinburne (qv). Because of its old-fashioned production methods, this previously important factory was succumbing to fierce competition from Belgium and elsewhere in Britain. The new company proved a considerable drain on Palmer's own finances and then on those of John Bowes & Partners, from which Palmer drew increasingly, eventually causing a financial crisis in the colliery concern. It is noticeable that in this period in the 1870s the coal partnership lost ground to its rivals while Palmer's attention was on other matters and he was spending very little time on the colliery concern. In 1879, a year of deep depression in the country, Palmer became sole owner of the glassworks and commenced strenuous efforts to turn the company round by seeking new management and installing modern equipment. In 1886 the firm went public but it could not withstand the intensification of competition and was wound up only five years later having lost the whole of its capital, £89,000.

Palmer became president of the British Plate Glass Association. He was also a member of the North of England Institute of Mining Engineers and an original member of the Iron and Steel Institute. In 1872 he set up the Durham Coal Owners Association and chaired its inaugural meeting. He was chairman of the Tyneside Shipbuilders Association, president of the North of England Steamship Owners Association, president of the Newcastle and Gateshead Chamber of Commerce and chairman of the Committee of Northern Ironmasters at the time of the lock-out in the iron trades in 1865. Although his role in that dispute has received much criticism, he appears in general to have been a fair employer who adopted a moderate approach and had his employees' interests at heart. He astutely kept his works going during the 1871 engineering strike, and avoided the opprobrium which hit his rival, W G Armstrong (qv), by promising to grant the nine-hour day when other employers did so (and he kept his promise). Although the development of Jarrow was left largely to private enterprise, Palmer was responsible for the building of some houses for his employees but, more importantly, a works' building society was set up in the early 1860s which led to nearly half of the town's houses being owner-occupied: a remarkable phenomenon for any nineteenth century town, let alone an almost entirely working-class one. He made benefactions to the Jarrow Mechanics' Institute (and was several times president of the Northern Union of Mechanics' Institutes) and to schools, churches and chapels in Jarrow and on his Yorkshire estate, while in 1870 he had a hospital built at Jarrow as a memorial to his first wife. It is clear that Palmer was much respected by working men, as much by trade union leaders such as John Kane with whom he negotiated, as by his employees who in 1904 erected a bronze statue to him (a project they initiated and to whose cost of over £2,000 they largely contributed).

In 1874 Palmer became Liberal MP for North Durham, a seat he retained until the creation of the Jarrow constituency in 1885, which seat he then held until his death, a tenure he probably owed to his unique role in the creation of the town of Jarrow. He was an active member on trade and industrial matters and was a member of the Royal Commission on the Depression of Trade and Industry of 1884-86. He was also a director of the Suez Canal Co, as a representative of British shipowners, and played a major part in the arrangement of the company's charges.

Palmer was undoubtedly one of the 'larger-than-life' entrepreneurs of the nineteenth century, a great showman and advertiser, regarded by contemporaries as a remarkable man with boundless energy, always anxious to expand his empire and reduce his dependence on others. For example, he formed the Bede Metal Co at Jarrow to manufacture non-ferrous metals for parts for his ships. He was a highly capable organiser who worried everyone for technological or administrative solutions to problems which he perceived and he was always ready to try out new ideas. His association with Jarrow was absolute. When it became a borough in 1875, despite his other activities, he became its first mayor and, although handing over the duties soon after taking office, he remained an alderman until his death and retained a considerable interest in the town which he frequently visited.

His fortune made, Palmer purchased the estate of Grinkle Park in the North Riding of Yorkshire, near his ironstone leases, with 2,664 acres of land in 1876 and nearly 4,000 by his death. There he became lord of the manor of Easington, built model cottages for his agricultural workers and replaced the old mansion with Grinkle Hall to the design of Alfred Waterhouse (qv).

He was created baronet in 1886 and was made Commander of the Order of St Maurice and St Lazarus of Italy in 1892. He was a DL and JP for both the North Riding of Yorkshire and County Durham, and a lieutenant colonel of the Jarrow Engineer Volunteers. His leisure activities included shooting and driving (he was a member of the committee of the Coaching Club) and he was a member of Brooks and the Reform Clubs.

Palmer was three times married: firstly in 1846 to Jane, daughter of Ebenezer Robson, a draper of Newcastle, by whom he had two sons; after her death in 1865 he married in 1867 Augusta Mary, daughter of Albert Lambert of Paris, by whom he also had two sons; and after her death in 1875 he married thirdly in 1877 Gertrude, daughter of James Montgomery, DL, JP of Cranford, Middlesex, by whom he had a son and a daughter.

As well as Grinkle Hall, he owned a house in Newcastle and one at 37 Curzon Street, London, where he died on 4 June 1907, leaving an estate of only £15,226.

D J ROWE

Writings:

'On the Construction of Iron Ships and the Progress of Iron Shipbuilding' in Sir W G Armstrong (ed), *The Industrial Resources of the Three Northern Rivers, the Tyne, Wear and Tees* (Longman & Co, 1864).

PP, RC Depression of Trade and Industry (1886) C 4715.

Sources:

Unpublished

MCe.

PrC.

Colin E Mountford, 'The History of John Bowes & Partners up to 1914' (Durham MA, 1967).

Catherine Ross, 'The Development of the Glass Industry on the Rivers Tyne and Wear 1700-1900' (Newcastle upon Tyne PhD, 1982).

Published

Edward Allen et al, *The North East Engineers' Strike of 1871* (Newcastle upon Tyne, 1971).

Bateman.

S Keith Chapman, 'Port Mulgrave Ironstone Workings' *Bulletin of the North East Industrial Archaeology Group* 5 (March 1968).

John F Davidson, *From Collier to Battleships: Palmers of Jarrow 1852-1933* (Durham, 1946).

Malcolm Dillon (comp), *Some Account of the Works of Palmers Shipbuilding & Iron Co Ltd* (Newcastle upon Tyne: W E Franklin, 1900).

DNB.

The Durham Thirteen. Biographical Sketches of the Members of Parliament returned for the City Borough and County of Durham at the General Election of 1874 (Darlington: J H Bell, 1874) repr from the *Northern Echo*.

Jarrow Guardian 7 June 1907.

James S Jeans, *Pioneers of the Cleveland Iron Trade* (Middlesborough-on-Tees: 'Gazette' Publishing Offices, 1875).

Evan R Jones, *Heroes of Industry. Biographical Sketches* (Sampson Low & Co, 1886).

William D Lawson, *Tyneside Celebrities. Sketches of the Lives and Labours of Famous Men of the North* (Newcastle upon Tyne: W D Lawson, 1873).

Mark Noble, *Short Sketches of Eminent Men of the North of England* (Newcastle upon Tyne, 1885).

The Palmer Record (house journal) 1-4 (1902-7), especially 'the Late Sir Charles Mark Palmer, Bart, MP' 4 (1907).

Henry Pelling, *Popular Politics and Society in Late Victorian Britain* (Macmillan, 1968).

Sidney Pollard and Paul Robertson, *The British Shipbuilding Industry 1870-1914* (Cambridge, Massachusetts: Harvard University Press, 1979).

Vincent Rea (comp), *Palmer's Yard and the Town of Jarrow* (Jarrow, 1975).

Ellen Wilkinson, *The Town that Was Murdered. The Life-story of Jarrow* (Victor Gollancz, 1939).

WWMP.

WWW.

PALMER, George

(1818-1897)

Biscuit manufacturer

George Palmer (courtesy of Mr T A B Corley).

George Palmer was born at Long Sutton, Somerset, on 18 January 1818, the eldest son of William Palmer (1788-1826), a farmer, and his wife Mary (1786-1880), daughter of William Isaac, a Dorset tanner. The yeoman Palmers, devout Quakers since 1720, had few distinctive characteristics, but Mary Isaac by her marriage clearly introduced a new and vigorous strain into the family. Her mother had been one of the talented Clarks of Somerset, also Quakers, and her own first cousins were Cyrus and James Clark, who founded the shoemaking firm of C & J Clark of Street, Somerset, which was run by James's son, William Stephens Clark (qv), in the later nineteenth century.

William Palmer died prematurely in 1826, and his resourceful widow decided to forsake the land and have her three sons trained for various trades and professions. George was educated at Sidcot School, a Quaker establishment near Weston-super-Mare, and at the age of fourteen was apprenticed to one of his uncles as a miller and confectioner. In 1841 he

Mixing and stamping out biscuits, Huntley & Palmers' new factory, 1861 (courtesy of Mr T A B Corley).

moved to Reading to become a partner with his cousin by marriage, Thomas Huntley (1803-57), contributing half the £1,000 capital.

The Huntley biscuit firm, founded in 1822, enjoyed a reputation for quality, selling hand-made biscuits over a wide area of Southern England. Turnover in 1841 was £2,700 but profits were negligible. George Palmer's intention was to mechanise biscuit production. With the assistance of the highly skilled engineer, William Exall (1808-81) of Barrett Exall & Andrewes, later the Reading Iron Works Ltd, by 1846 he had devised the first continuously-running biscuit machinery in the world. That year Messrs Huntley & Palmer opened a factory at Kings Road, Reading. When Thomas Huntley died in 1857, turnover was £125,000 and profits £18,000; some 2,500 tons of biscuits were being turned out annually.

On the marketing side, George Palmer set up a network of commission agents who between them covered the whole of the British Isles. As early as 1847 he had on his books over 700 retailers in nearly 400 different localities. From the outset he aimed his biscuits, which were expensive, at the carriage trade; he therefore created a team of the firm's travellers (who replaced the agents) and provided novelties (such as one lb individual tins) and advertising, such as showcards for the family groceries which sold the bulk of his output. In 1850 he married Elizabeth Meteyard (1825-94), daughter of a Quaker druggist who sold the firm's biscuits; they had seven children. On Thomas Huntley's death he bought out the Huntley interests and took into partnership his younger brothers, Samuel (1820-1903) and William Isaac (1824-93); the firm became Huntley & Palmers. William Isaac ran the production side, while Samuel — whose commercial gifts matched those of his eldest brother — resided in London, responsible both for the substantial sales in the Metropolis and for exports.

Growth thereafter was spectacular both at home and abroad. By 1874-75 turnover approached £920,000 and net profits £120,000, while nearly 14,000 tons of biscuits were produced: Huntley & Palmers claimed to be

Travelling oven discharging biscuits (from The Working Man *2 June 1866).*

the largest biscuit firm in the world. Exports had hardly existed in the 1850s but topped £300,000 by the late 1870s, when turnover for the first time exceeded £1 million. Its global reputation was enhanced by its consistently winning medals at international exhibitions from the Paris exhibition of 1867 to that of 1878, and by the two gold medals it won in the 1900 Paris exhibition.

Between 1874 and 1892 three of George Palmer's four sons and four sons of Samuel Palmer became partners, each responsible for a department of the firm in Reading or London. George Palmer was then able to devote more time to outside activities. He had been a very active councillor, in the Liberal cause, for Reading since 1850, taking a special interest in public health and education, and served as mayor in 1857-58. He started to become an important landowner in Berkshire and adjacent counties from the 1870s onwards, learning to his dismay that absentee farming rarely paid. While owning a country home, he continued to live in a fairly modest residence close to the factory. In 1878, on the insistence of his Quaker friend, John Bright, he stood for Reading and was elected MP. His maiden speech was in support of a bill to give women the vote (he later changed his mind on this issue), but thereafter he rarely contributed to debates; however, he was often consulted by fellow politicians on industrial questions. After a defeat in 1885 he did not stand for parliament again.

In 1891, the golden jubilee of his partnership, he was made a freeman of Reading and a statue of him was erected in the town's main shopping street. However, that year proved to be the last of his fully active life. To declining health and deteriorating eyesight was added the jolt of his wife's death in 1894. William Isaac Palmer had died the previous year and

Samuel Palmer was incurably ill. The second generation of Palmers was therefore in full charge of the firm. Soon after George Palmer died in 1897 the firm was turned into a limited company, becoming Huntley & Palmers Ltd in 1898. Annual turnover then exceeded £1,275,000, over one-third being sold overseas, while profits were £163,000; output came to 23,000 tons of biscuits.

Of no more than middle height, George Palmer was an impressive man. With a bushy, white beard, far-seeing eyes and a tight-lipped expression inherited from his formidable mother, he might have been a retired sea-captain and he ran his factory as tightly as any seagoing vessel of the time. He once threatened to throw out of his office two employees who rashly demanded a wage rise, and his temper was liable to flare up on any occasion. Yet he was a generous man. To the people of Reading, he presented the 49-acre Palmer Park and the Thameside King's Meadow, and donated money to Reading University College, Reading School, the Royal Berkshire Hospital and — less predictably — to several Anglican churches: while remaining a committed Quaker, he was not narrow in his religious views. Within the firm he established a sick club, with a part-time factory doctor, in 1849, and for a time had a schoolmaster for the boy employees. The firm and the Palmer brothers personally made many benefactions, such as paying for the funerals of employees who died in the firm's service and helping families in distress. George Palmer's readiness to bestow half-crowns indiscriminately is said to have turned Reading in his lifetime into the haunt of beggars from all over the kingdom. At the same time, as the largest employer in the town — with a total of about 7,000 employees — he paid no more than subsistence wages to unskilled workers, so that there was an unduly high incidence of primary poverty there by the early twentieth century.

George Palmer often claimed to have created an 'industry' in Britain, by bringing about the successful mechanisation of biscuit-making. He won for himself ample rewards in his lifetime: he was almost a millionaire; he was offered a baronetcy, which he refused; and about the time that it received a royal warrant, in 1884, his firm became almost a national institution, being featured in a *Times* leader (3 October 1883) and a *Punch* cartoon (13 October 1883) after a local bishop had commended its biscuits for conveying 'a savour of the quiet fireside and the social board', while the phrase 'take the biscuit' was adapted by those who could not afford its products into 'take the Huntley and Palmer' {Corley (1972) 138-39}.

George Palmer died in Reading on 19 August 1897, leaving £969,373 gross. He was not to see the relative decline of the company under his three sons: George William (1851-1913), also mayor and Liberal MP for Reading who was made a Privy Counsellor in 1906; Alfred (1852-1936) who declined a knighthood; and Sir Walter (1858-1910), Conservative MP for Salisbury whose wife was one of the great London hostesses of the day and who was made a baronet in 1904. Rival firms, such as Peek Frean under Arthur Carr (qv) and the Scottish manufacturers who opened plants in England round about the turn of the century, displayed more vigorous entrepreneurship and a livelier appreciation of changing public tastes at home in biscuits; by 1939 Huntley & Palmers produced less than 8 per cent of the country's total biscuit output. In 1982 the company, which had earlier amalgamated with Peek Frean and Jacobs in The Associated Biscuit

Manufacturers Ltd (later Huntley & Palmer Foods plc) was acquired by Nabisco Brands Inc of the United States.

T A B CORLEY

Sources:

Unpublished

Reading University Library, archives of Huntley & Palmers.

PrC.

Published

Sir Arthur Lyon Bowley and Alexander R Burnett-Hurst, *Livelihood and Poverty* (G Bell & Sons Ltd, 1915).

Christian World 26 Aug 1897.

T A B Corley, 'Nutrition, Technology and the Growth of the British Biscuit Industry 1820-1900' in Derek Oddy and Derek Miller (eds), *The Making of the Modern British Diet* (Croom Helm, 1976).

—, 'The Palmer Family and the University of Reading' *Staff Journal* (University of Reading) 6 Nov 1968.

—, *Quaker Enterprise in Biscuits: Huntley & Palmers of Reading 1822-1972* (Hutchinson, 1972).

Daily Mail 20 Aug 1897.

DNB.

Reading Mercury 7 Nov 1891, 21 Aug 1897.

Reading Observer 7 Nov 1891, 21 Aug 1897.

Times 20 Aug 1897.

WWMP.

PANMURE-GORDON

see **GORDON, Harry Panmure**

Major Albert Pam (from Mea Allan, E A Bowles. His Garden at Myddelton House *Faber & Faber, 1973).*

PAM, Albert Samuel

(1875-1955)

Merchant banker

Albert Samuel Pam (known familarly as 'Pamski') was born at Clapham Park, Surrey, on 26 June 1875, eldest of the three sons of Leopold Pam (1838-1909), of Bohemia Villa, Clapham, and his wife Philippine née Firth (1851-1938). His father was a merchant who left £29,853 in 1909 (at which time he was a shareholder in Marmite, and two South African mining companies, Village Deep and Consolidated Bulfontein); he had a strict and peevish temperament, with no interests except his business. Albert's brother Edgar (1882-1945) was president of the Mine Managers Association in 1915 and of the Institute of Mining and Metallurgy, 1944-45; with special knowledge of goldmining, later associated with Mond Nickel Co, he left £68,887. Albert was possibly a nephew of Julius Pam, a diamond merchant of Holborn, who in the 1890s was chairman of British Lomagunda Development Co, and director of Anglo-Australian Exploration Ltd, British West Charterland Co, Free State Mines Ltd, and Gallymont Goldfields Ltd.

Albert Pam was educated at City of London School in 1889-92 and then spent two years at a gymnasium at Frankfurt-on-Main and a year at Ouchy near Lausanne perfecting his German and French. Beginning his career with a Mincing Lane sugar merchant, without pay, after six months Pam was awarded an annual salary of £160. He joined a voluntary brigade of the Royal Fusiliers, which he commanded at both the Diamond Jubilee and funeral of Queen Victoria. Pam subsequently formed the International Mercantile Co. From an early age he developed a keen, systematic and tenacious interest in ornithology, zoology and horticulture. He first visited South America in 1900 with his uncle Otto H Fuerth, a widely-travelled polyglot of Austrian extraction, based in Paris but with Amazon business interests near Pará. This was the first of many visits to South America, especially the southern half of the continent, in which Pam combined business with the study of natural history. By his early thirties he was recognised as one of Britain's outstanding authorities on the plants, birds and animals of South America, and kept a distinguished collection of specimens at his English home. Similarly few men in the City of London knew Southern America more intimately, from a business standpoint, than Pam.

In the early Edwardian period he became a member of the Ethelburga Syndicate, whose other members included Otto Fuerth, a prominent city solicitor Francis (later Sir Francis) Voules, Arthur (later Sir Arthur) Stanley MP (son of the Earl of Derby), Henry Mauborget of Paris, T M C Steuart, and the Pam family. This syndicate (with nominal capital of only £20,000) was described by the Controller of Commercial Affairs at the Foreign Office as 'a highly speculative organisation', whose members were always able to carry out their financial engagements {PRO FO 368/580, Sir Algernon Law minute of July 1911}; in his view the syndicate 'seem to like risky business and can be left to look after themselves' {PRO FO 368/444, Law minute of Apr 1910}.

Pam's first major coups were in Venezuela. Salt was a government monopoly there, with mining licenses sold by the detested regime of General Cipriano Castro, who was described by Pam as

> completely uneducated, despotic and cruel, and had managed to retain his position by killing or incarcerating anyone who opposed him politically. He had never been outside Venezuela, but seemed to possess a crude instinct for business; he acquired by sheer robbery a substantial interest in many enterprises, farming lands, and coffee plantations. He was addicted to many vices, and was altogether an unpleasant individual {Pam (1945) 13}.

In 1905 overtures about the salt monopoly were made by Venezuela's second vice-president, General J A Velutini, to Otto Fuerth, as a result of which Albert Pam went to Caracas for the first time. In October 1905 he was personally granted a monopoly on salt in Venezuela, which in November he transferred to the Ethelburga Syndicate's Venezuela Salt Monopoly Co. Pam agreed that his company would pay an annual rental four times the maximum which the Government had encashed under previous arrangements, and gave Castro personally some 30 per cent of the English company's shares. There was popular indignation at this deal, but Pam was undaunted.

Industrialisation had scarcely advanced beyond the handicraft stage in these smaller American republics: the only opportunities for factory or workshop manufacturing were in simple mass consumer goods such as matches, cigarettes, candles and footwear. As early as 1899 the principle of a national match monopoly had been approved by Venezuela's parliament; in 1904 a twenty-five year monopoly for the exclusive manufacture and sale of all matches in the republic was granted to a man of straw, Manuel Tejera, who formed the highly over-capitalised Companhia Anonima Fabrica Nacional de Fosforos. This transaction was 'a bare-faced sham based on a misconstruction of the law' {PRO FO 368/66, commercial despatch 50 of Outram Bax-Ironside, 23 May 1906}, and led to a flourishing contraband trade in matches, to the detriment of Tejera's factory. Subsequently Velutini approached the Ethelburga Syndicate about the match concession, and while Pam was in Caracas during the summer of 1905, he investigated the Fosforos business. He reported that it held a sound commercial basis, but had exorbitant expenses and delinquent management. Later in 1905 his syndicate registered Venezuela Match Monopoly Ltd in London and bought the Fosforos concession. Hugo Aaron Paul Pam (1880-1930), his brother, was set to reform Fosforos' bookkeeping, and soon discovered that the accounts were fictitious. Charles Rennie, assistant Liverpool manager of Bryant & May, was recruited to run the national factory in Venezuela, and soon had it working efficiently. Employees were paid well and regularly, in return for which they were required to be scrupulously honest. The Ethelburga Syndicate however was not welcomed by British diplomats, who had seen the Castro régime sequester most profitable foreign enterprises such as the Bermudez

Asphalt Co or the Orinoco Steamship Co. As Sir Outram Bax-Ironside reported from Caracas, the Ethelburga Syndicate

> have gone into this business with their eyes open, and prepared to take the great risks involved in these monopolies. If successful, their profits will be enormous; but, in case of failure, they will doubtless turn for assistance to His Majesty's Government. Their position is, however, totally different to that of the English enterprises and other old-established concerns in this country {PRO FO 368/66, commercial despatch 46, 8 May 1906}.

Two years later, in January 1908, while Albert Pam was visiting Caracas, Generals Castro and Velutini abruptly cancelled both monopolies, on the pretext of bad match quality and decreased revenue. They may have been incited to this by Frederico E Schemel, a German ex-director of Tejera's company, who wanted to open a rival match factory at Maracaibo.

British diplomats declined to intervene until the syndicate had exhausted legal remedies in Venezuela, but the only lawyer willing to act against Castro's Government, Dr Bance, had to go into hiding shortly afterwards. In the subsequent manoeuvres, the London company's name was altered in 1909 to the National Match Factory of Venezuela Ltd. Albert Pam visited the USA to engage American politicians and financiers in his syndicate's cause, and in 1910 successfully coerced the Venezuelans into a settlement. The Caracas Government found that the New York market had been turned against them over the cancelled monopolies, and were apprehensive that it would ruin the London market's attitude to a Venezuelan national bank scheme then mooted with the Philipps Group of Viscount St Davids (qv). Early in 1911 Castro confirmed his acceptance of Fosforos' 1904 concession to Pam's company, which thereafter prospered.

Pam also obtained a Bolivian match monopoly for the syndicate. The Government in La Paz in 1907 granted a national monopoly to manufacture and sell matches, and the National Match Factory of Bolivia Ltd was registered in London, again with Pam as a director. Under the terms of the concession, the Bolivian Government received half of this company's net profits: the sale of matches began in 1910, and the monopoly ran for twenty years from that date, expiring in May 1929. As in Venezuela, the Bolivian factory was well-administered and produced matches of adequate quality. Shrewdly, in 1927, the Ethelburga Syndicate sold its interests to the Swedish Match trust masterminded by Ivan Kreuger, the subsequently disgraced financier. Swedish Match was ruthless in trying to extort an extension of the concession beyond 1929, but to no avail: the decision of the Ethelburga Syndicate to sell out in 1927 was vindicated in its timing and commercial judgment.

Pam's other activities on behalf of his syndicate are not all traceable. In 1908 his Caribbean Anglo-Colombian Cable Co acted in collaboration with the Direct West Indian Cable Co in a scheme to link Venezuela's telegraph cable system to the new cable joining Jamaica to Savanilla in Colombia. This would have linked Britain by cable directly to Venezuela, but the idea was aborted during General Castro's feud with Pam in 1908-10. In April 1910 the Ethelburga Syndicate signed a contract to loan £500,000 to the Bolivian Government at 90 per cent bearing 5.5 per cent interest plus 1 per cent for a sinking fund. Most of the loan was to have been placed by Fuerth and Mauborget in France, and the proceeds were to have been spent on sanitation schemes and a new Bolivian national bank; but the contract seems not to have been ratified, for in June 1910 the same loan was discussed by the Bolivians with the London merchant banking house of Schroder. In that same year Pam, representing Lord Howard de Walden's syndicate and Count Vitali's Régie Générale des Chemins de Fer et des Travaux Publics, ousted Arthur Grenfell (qv) from a contract worth over £4 million to construct the Chilian Longitudinal Railway, which in consequence was built by Norton Griffiths (qv). In subsequent years as a director of Societé de Travaux Publiques au Chili he was much involved in trying to solve the problems which arose under this 'very unfortunate contract' {Pam (1945) 51}. Early in 1911 the Ethelburga Syndicate tendered to float a Belgrade municipal loan worth £1 million; but despite careful preparations, their tender was defeated by local bribery. In this Serbian case, the syndicate was backed by Baron d'Erlanger's London financial house, which may have been involved in their other activities. Later in December 1912 and January 1913 the syndicate contracted to loan £500,000 for forty years to the provincial government of Pechili in China, secured on wine and tobacco taxes. However the British Government had only weeks earlier made clear its implacable opposition to the Chinese loan of Birch Crisp (qv), or to any British lending to China not put through the Hong Kong & Shanghai Bank. Whitehall therefore refused to record the transaction, or countenance it officially in any form.

Another business in which Pam was active for many years was the Marmite Food Extract Co. It was formed in 1901-2 to exploit a process which made a yeast extract closely resembling a meat extract by Fred Wissler, a friend of Pam, who joined the board. 'After heart-rending difficulties during its first few years', the Marmite Co succeeded {Pam (1945) 116}. It opened a factory at Burton-on-Trent, Pam acting as managing director for a time. When Marmite suffered a financial crisis shortly after the Armistice, Pam became chairman. Issued capital was increased in 1924.

Pam also joined the board of Sena Sugar Factory Ltd which began business in 1906 and was registered in 1910 as sugar refiners and planters in Portuguese East Africa, with 12,747 acres under cultivation by 1915. The Sena company was dominated by John Peter Hornung's family, and in 1920 it merged with Hornung's private company (which had been doing business in Mozambique since 1890) to form Sena Sugar Estates Ltd. This bought the Zambesi Navigation Co in 1921, and was increasingly involved in the Zambesi River Bridge, Beira port and other transportation schemes conceived by the energetic Anglo-Belgian financier, Libert Oury, who was also a director of Sena Sugar Estates. In the 1920s the company owned four cane mills and sugar factories at Mopea, Caia, Marromen and Luabo. The estates covered 290 square miles by 1925, with 65 square miles cultivated, serviced by 200 miles of private light railways. The company also held labour concessions over certain districts which exercised the Anti-Slavery Society, and a sugar refinery on the Tagus at Lisbon. In many respects it was a private principality of the Hornung family, who in 1934 controlled 245,000 acres of Portuguese East Africa (45,700 acres under cultivation).

In December 1914 Pam was sent to Chile, at two days notice, by the Director of Naval Intelligence to trace the German cruiser *Dresden* which was hiding after the Battle of the Falklands. He was recommended for this job by Colonel Herman Le Roy-Lewis a co-director of the French company which financed the Chilean railway and British military attaché in Paris. The *Dresden,* however, was scuttled just as he reached Santiago. Instead he pursued confidential enquiries in Chile and Bolivia, 'without the knowledge of the British diplomatic and consular officers', covering 'the activities of Germans on the coast, their clubs, their papers, their trade'; the First Secretary in La Paz, who disliked Pam for racial reasons, suspected he was 'grinding some private axe' {PRO FO 368/1493, Sir Godfrey D N Haggard to Sir Algernon Law, 11 March 1916}. Subsequently, in 1916-18, Pam served in France on the headquarters staff of the Third Army. He reached the rank of major, which thereafter he bore in business life, was thrice mentioned in despatches and received the OBE. He was also decorated with the Belgian Croix de Guerre and Crown of Belgium, and the French Légion d'Honneur. From November 1918 until April 1919 he was a member of the British Mission to the Permanent International Armistice Commission at Spa, and participated in the slow and wearisome negotiation of the exact terms of the German surrender of material and equipment. His linguistic ability was invaluable. He was acting chief of staff to General Sir Richard Haking in January 1919.

After the war, Pam's career was modified. As a young man he was described as 'a keen business man, used to fishing in troubled waters' who 'does not hesitate to push his own interests by any means that may come to hand' but who 'acted quite frankly in his dealings' {PRO FO 368/241, Sir Vincent Corbett to Sir Arthur Hardinge, 2 May 1908}. He had spent much of his life in a hard business environment, where both the risks and rewards were high, and although his personal honesty was never questioned, more fastidious spirits shrank from the bold and ruthless strokes of the Ethelburga Syndicate. After 1918, however, he spent less time among the ruffian politicians of southern America and more in the solid environs of the City of London where, as a merchant banker with Schroders, he was soon recognised as a creative and innovative industrial financier of extensive influence.

The merchant banking firm of J Henry Schroder had been founded in 1804 by Johann Heinrich Schroder (1784-1883), who became a naturalised British subject in 1864 and was created a Prussian baron in 1868. Under J H Schroder and his eldest son Sir John Henry William Schroder the firm developed into perhaps the most prominent acceptance house in the City. Its relations, through Hamburg, with the Central and South American republics (especially Peru) were particularly prosperous. The London partnership, which was allied with J Henry Schroder Banking Corporation of New York, was deeply involved in German business, and suffered a major eclipse after the outbreak of war in 1914. Pam's first contact with Schroders came when they and Sir Walpole Greenwell organised the English financial backing for the Chilean Longitudinal Railway. Subsequently Pam helped Schroders solve several difficulties with which they were confronted; and they appointed him to various boards where his services were useful. While at Spa in 1919 he was recruited by Frank Tiarks to become a junior partner earning a percentage of the profits but with no stake in the ownership. Pam and Tiarks then considered that Schroders's prospects were poor, both because of the firm's German name, and because their issue business (which had been very important) seemed unlikely to revive for a decade. In fact this prediction was wrong, for Schroders's first post-war issue, for the State of São Paulo, in conjunction with Barings and Rothschilds, in 1921, was followed by many others. With Baron Bruno Schroder and Tiarks (a director of the Bank of England 1912-45) as its senior partners, Schroders enjoyed a revival in the 1920s, becoming with Higginsons (in which Sir Guy Granet (qv) was a partner) the first established London issuing houses to handle domestic industrial issues. This was a major innovation of British institutional finance, in which Pam had a pre-eminent part. He was for many years the most important force in Schroders's investment department, to whom indeed the firm owed much for its survival.

Pam, however, made further contributions. Following the collapse in 1926 of Armstrong, Whitworth, the Bank of England became involved in trying to unravel the complexities left by Sir Glynn West (qv). They wanted to merge two of Armstrongs' subsidiaries, Pearson & Knowles and the Partington steelworks, both associated with Sir W Peter Rylands (qv), into the Wigan Iron & Steel Co, another Lancashire company with similar problems. Pam was asked to arrange the amalgamation by Montagu Norman (qv), and after studying the industrial structure, conceived a scheme and secured the participation of issuing houses and other City interests. Pam's scheme was one of the most solid achievements of the rationalisation movement of the late 1920s. The moderate-sized Lancashire Steel Corporation was floated, and the merger completed, early in 1930: its success was a tribute to the tact and judgement of Pam. After LSC was securely established, with a substantial Bank of England holding, Pam urged that the arrangements which the Bank had obtained from the City over LSC should be preserved: his suggestion led to the formation of the Bankers Industrial Development Corporation under Charles Bruce Gardner (qv). This again was a major advance in British institutional finance.

In a related development, Schroders in 1935 formed Leadenhall Securities Corporation to finance those medium and small British industrial companies whose needs the City of London's existing machinery failed to meet. Leadenhall Securities (unlike BIDC) supported businesses with prospects, rather than lame ducks in declining staple industries; its usual method was to invest in redeemable preference shares, and take some ordinary shares for a fixed term after which they were bought back by the client company. This innovation bore Pam's influence too. He was also chairman of the London United Trust, a private company formed in 1929, whose other directors were Sir Arthur Guinness, partner in the merchant bankers Guinness Mahon of London and New York, John Hugh Smith of Hambros, and Robert G Simpson, an accountant who was a director of several other financial trusts.

Pam was of course busy in other areas of Schroders's business. They were for example active in eastern Europe and the Balkans, especially Romania. In 1922-23 Frank Tiarks and Pam represented Schroders in unsuccessful negotiations with Sir Robert Williams, Sir James Dunn (qv) and Alfred Loewenstein concerning a proposed debenture issue of £5 million for Tanganyika Concessions Ltd to secure the future of the Benguela Railway. Also in 1922-23 Pam was actively involved when Schroders led a consortium including Rothschilds, joint-stock bankers

PAM Albert Samuel

Sources:

Unpublished

PRO, BT 55/32, evidence of 5 July 1916 by Frank Tiarks to Lord Faringdon's committee on financial facilities for trade.

PRO, papers of Foreign Office, commercial (FO 368) and political (FO 371) files.

Schroder archives, London, manuscript autobiographical notes by Pam of 1955.

BCe.

MCe.

PrC.

Information from Lt Col D C Venning, Dr Richard Roberts and John Armstrong.

Published

Mea Allan, *E A Bowles and His Garden at Myddelton House, 1865-1954* (Faber, 1973).

Philip W S Andrews and Elizabeth Brunner, *The Life of Lord Nuffield* (Oxford: Blackwell, 1955).

Financial Times 10 Apr 1908.

Miriam Hood, *Gunboat Diplomacy 1895-1905: Great Power Pressure in Venezuela* (Allen & Unwin, 1975).

Simon E Katzenellenbogen, *Railways and the Copper Mines of Katanga* (Oxford: Clarendon Press, 1973).

Percy F Martin, *Through Five Republics: A Critical Description of Argentina, Brazil, Chile, Uruguay and Venezuela in 1905* (Heinemann, 1905).

James W Moir, *The Harrow School Register 1885-1949* (Rivingtons, 1951).

Richard J Overy, *William Morris, Viscount Nuffield* (Europa, 1976).

Richard S Sayers, *The Bank of England 1891-1944* (3 vols, Cambridge: Cambridge University Press, 1976).

Times 5 Sept 1955.

R C Whiting, *The View from Cowley* (Oxford: Oxford University Press, 1983).

WWW.

534

*Sir Albert Lindsay Parkinson
(courtesy of S M Gaskell).*

PARKINSON, Sir Albert Lindsay

(1870-1936)

Builder and contractor

Albert Lindsay (known as Lindsay later in his life) Parkinson was born at Lytham, Lancashire, on 24 February 1870, the third of the four sons and three daughters of Jacob Parkinson, a joiner, and his wife Mary Anne née Hall. The family moved to neighbouring Blackpool when he was three, and here Albert Parkinson lived for the rest of his life.

In 1876 his father began operating on a small scale as a builder and contractor. Based in a joiner's workshop in Kent Road, Blackpool, the firm was registered in 1877 as Jacob Parkinson & Co. Behind the development of the business was clearly the driving force and character of Mrs Parkinson who helped keep the family going by running a boarding house called 'Parkinson's Eating House'. Eventually all four sons entered the firm. In 1884, at the age of fourteen, Albert Parkinson joined his father in what was then essentially a two-man operation. Together they expanded the joinery business and along with it a flourishing trade as builders in the Blackpool area, which was then rapidly developing, with the population rising from 14,229 in 1881 to 50,000 in 1900. The firm moved in 1896 to new premises which included a saw-mill and joinery works for supplying the timber work for their building operations. In the same year Albert Parkinson took control. Over the next decade he established the firm's reputation for 'getting jobs done quickly and well' {Parkinson (1955) 7}. In doing this he took advantage of the prevailing structure and organisation of the building industry, in which the various trades and specialisms were held together by the general builder with a mixture of direct employment and sub-contracting. The weakness of this system was, however, the lack of overall control and organisation of the supplies of labour and materials. Together with the architects' practice of nominating sub-contractors, this generally served to diminish the building contractors' control of the building process and caused uncertainties over costs and completion dates. Albert Parkinson exploited this situation and built up an organisation which reached new levels of efficiency and reliability.

On this basis the firm established its reputation at a time when the dramatic growth of Blackpool as a popular resort created a demand for the rapid completion of hotels and places of entertainment. Parkinsons completed, for example, the Talbot Hotel within seven weeks. In the process Albert Parkinson transformed the firm into one which undertook large-scale contracts in several districts. Ability to meet a deadline earned them the contract for the Theatre Royal in Newcastle upon Tyne — to meet its six month time limit joiners were sent from Blackpool. Subsequently the firm established an office in Newcastle and was responsible for several buildings in the area, 1902-7. Using this experience, the firm won contracts for building theatres in many towns in the North and Midlands, as well as skating rinks (including one in Paris), during the 1900s. The firm built the Prince's Theatre and re-built the interior of the Lyceum, each under six months, in London in 1905. Also that year Parkinson opened a London office, signalling his intention to compete in the national market.

Parkinson transformed the business from a small scale operation into a large scale enterprise. After the death of Jacob Parkinson in 1902 the business was turned into a limited company with Lindsay Parkinson as managing director. Its issued share capital was £241,000 (in 1,000 preference shares, 90,000 second preference shares and 150,000 ordinary shares). The directors included two of Lindsay Parkinson's brothers, and Robert Jackson Singleton, a corporation official. William Parkinson was responsible for the day-to-day running of the business and for the workshop, while Lindsay Parkinson, in the decade before the First World War, negotiated increasingly ambitious contracts, exploiting economies of scale and utilising new materials. The award of the £1 million contract for the Lancashire County Council Asylum at Whalley in 1911 marked this new direction. Its completion in 1914 placed Parkinsons in the country's small group of big contractors.

Besides moving into large-scale contracting, Lindsay Parkinson developed the company's interest and later specialisation in reinforced concrete construction. His first scheme involving this material was Blackpool racecourse, undertaken in 1905. The experience gained was of great importance for the firm during the First World War when there was a pressing demand for new aerodromes, of which Lindsay Parkinson was especially aware because of his own personal interest in aviation. A pioneer motorist, he later took up flying and in 1908 was a prime mover in the organisation of the country's first aviation meeting at Blackpool. He realised the potential in the development of Squires Gate Aerodrome in Blackpool. By 1914 his firm had the capacity to build new aerodromes and he constructed two, estimated at £800,000 and £900,000 respectively, and also extended other airfields. All its wartime contracts — on railway depots and military establishments as well as aerodromes — consolidated the firm's reputation for speedy and efficient work. Lindsay Parkinson was directly responsible for this achievement through his development of more effective mechanisation and through close attention to the flow of materials. The company purchased its first mechanical excavator in 1918 and evolved an early type of pre-fabricated house of reinforced concrete in conjunction with the Trussed Concrete Steel Co. In this, the columns and beams of the basic structure were precast in reinforced concrete, erected by crane, and clad with concrete slabs externally and breeze slabs internally.

Parkinson exploited wartime opportunities for shrewd commercial ends. The Blackpool works were converted into a war factory turning out shell-boxes and War Department joinery. More importantly, by 1918 the firm undertook large-scale contracts in the face of changing architectural and engineering requirements. They put up several large housing estates in Lancashire and the North East, developing the Parkinson-Kahn reinforced concrete house as an early type of prefab, aimed at overcoming the post-war shortage of skilled labour and at meeting the pent-up demand for housing. The firm now started taking on work on large-scale structures in London. It used steel frame construction in Aldwych House, an office block costing £400,000 in 1920. It built the reinforced concrete Poland Street Garage, with the first circular ramp for cars, in 1924. In 1936 the firm completed the White House near Regent's Park at a cost of £500 per flat. Advances in the technical capacity of the firm were reflected in its increasing involvement through the 1920s and 1930s with industrial buildings such as the new fish dock at Grimsby (1930-34) or the grain silos at Avonmouth Dock (1937). Similar work was undertaken overseas in the colonies, as well as for the War Office and the Royal Air Force. The company, under Lindsay Parkinson's direction, was steadily extending its civil engineering connections. In the mid-1920s contracts were secured for sections of the Western Avenue and Barnet By-pass in Middlesex, while in 1929 the firm's tender of £2,147,000 was accepted for the East Lancashire Road covering the 25 miles between Manchester and Liverpool. This latter scheme involved some 3,000 workers and was the largest completed contract the firm undertook between the wars, and it was here that Parkinson pioneered, in this country, the use of heavy mechanised methods of excavation and construction.

At Lindsay Parkinson's death in 1936 the firm was one of the leading civil engineering contractors in the country (with an annual turnover of £1,626,969 in 1937), characterised by the continuing diversity of its undertakings: housing and flats, schools and public buildings, aerodromes and army camps, roads and sewers, docks and stations. Despite the vast increase in the scale of its operations and its London headquarters, the firm nevertheless retained its base in Blackpool. Here it was responsible for numerous public and private buildings: a presence reflecting Lindsay Parkinson's personal activity in his home town. He was Mayor of Blackpool, 1916-19, Honorary Freeman of the Borough and in 1918-22 sat as Coalition Unionist MP for Blackpool. As mayor he was responsible for the equitable and efficient distribution of food supplies during the war when the town was more generally characterised by profiteering. As a town councillor he substantially reduced the final bill for the construction of Blackpool promenade. In 1926 he cut through the arguments as to whether the town needed a public park, when he procured most of the land for the future Stanley Park and offered it to the Council at cost price on condition it was laid out as a park. At the same time his business benefited from Blackpool's municipal development. Early investment in such a venture as the Raikes Hall Pleasure Gardens enabled him to sell the land profitably in the post-war building boom; similarly the Blackpool & Fleetwood Tramroad, which he had bought before the war, he was able to sell to the Corporation in 1919 when the system was flourishing and demand for it increasing. In later years he maintained an interest in several local businesses related to the holiday and leisure activities of Blackpool, and at the same time, in conjunction with his brother George, extended his interests in other concerns such as breweries and hotels in other parts of the country. This divergence of activities was reflected in the reorganisation of the company in 1927 when he formed two separate companies dealing respectively with the building and contracting operations, and the property ownership and management concerns. Property holdings included Oddenino's Hotel, London, taken over when the owner could not pay for it; Louis Tussaud's Waxworks in Blackpool; and the Wentworth Estate, Virginia Water, Surrey.

Lindsay Parkinson had thus followed in the tradition of the great nineteenth century contractors in transforming a small local jobbing business into a major national and international firm. In this he stood out in an industry where the size of firms remained predominantly small. The Census of Production of 1935 indicated that only 78 out of 67,450 firms in the building and contracting industry employed 500 people or more. In 1937 Parkinson's firm had an annual turnover of £1.6 million.

Outside his business, his main interest and activity lay in sport. As a young man he played for the South Shore Football Club which in 1899 amalgamated to form the Blackpool Football Club. Later as an amateur he played for Blackburn Rovers and had several offers from leading clubs to sign up as a professional. From 1890 onwards he played cricket for Blackpool. In the 1920s he took up the new interest in greyhound racing and 'Alby' Parkinson (as he was known on the circuit) was a successful owner and racer of greyhounds until his death. He was also a racehorse owner, with rather less success. Wins included the Manchester Gold Cup, but according to family tradition he lost £60,000 on horses in the last year of his life. In the inter-war period he was a supporter and benefactor of sporting activities in Blackpool. With his brother William, he gave the town the cricket ground and pavilion which was later to become the county ground. At the time of his death he was chairman of Blackpool Football Club and president of the Cricket Club. Apart from these sporting connections, Lindsay Parkinson was a considerable art collector, but like many other businessmen his interest seems to have been primarily in the scale of acquisition rather then the detail, purchasing as a totality the 'Romanoff Imperial Russian Art Collection'. Though the collection included paintings by Correggio, Poussin and Rembrandt, among others, as well as valuable groups of ceramics, ivories and icons, his own taste seems to have been reflected more in the various curios which he added to it.

Parkinson was knighted in 1922 in recognition of his public services and it was then that the company took the title of Sir Lindsay Parkinson & Co Ltd. He was offered a baronetcy in 1934, but declined it after consultation with his eldest son, Robert. Lindsay Parkinson married twice. His first wife died some time around 1908. In 1911 he married Margaret, daughter of Robert Jackson Singleton, a corporation official and one of Parkinson's partners.

Sir Albert Lindsay Parkinson died on 3 February 1936, leaving £112,151 gross. He had, at times, been considerably wealthier but lost heavily on racehorses and in speculations on the Manchester Cotton Exchange; unfortunately he died just before the big expansion of the later 1930s. He was succeeded by his brother William, who in turn was succeeded by his son, A E Parkinson. From about 1940 only one of Sir Lindsay's sons played a significant role in running the business. After the war, its management seemed to lack some of Sir Lindsay's talent for creative innovation and the firm gradually lost its leading position, being sold in the early 1970s to Leonard Fairclough & Co for a very small sum.

S MARTIN GASKELL

Sources:

Unpublished

BCe.

MCe.

PrC.

Information from P G L Parkinson.

Published

Richard Ainsworth, *A History of the Parkinson Family of Lancashire* (Accrington: Wardleworths, 1936).

Architect and Building News 14 Feb 1936.

Blackpool Evening Gazette 13 Sept 1963.

Blackpool Gazette and News 7 Mar 1929, 25 Aug 1934.

Builder 150 (1936).

Charles Allen Clarke, *The Story of Blackpool* (Blackpool: Palatine Book Co, 1923).

Kathleen Eyre, *Seven Golden Miles: The Fantastic Story of Blackpool* (Clapham, N Yorkshire: Dalesman, 1975).

Illustrated Catalogue of the ... Art Collection Known as the Romanoff Imperial Russian Art Collection Purchased and Enlarged by the late Sir Lindsay Parkinson (Birmingham: Edwards Son & Bigwood & Mathew, 1953).

Sir Lindsay Parkinson & Co, *This Way Forward: A Resumé and a Record of Building and Civil Engineering Construction during 75 Eventful Years* (pp, Sir Lindsay Parkinson & Co, 1955).

Times 4 Feb 1936.

WWMP.

WWW.

PARSONS, The Honourable Sir Charles Algernon

(1854-1931)

Turbine and engineering equipment manufacturer

The Honourable Charles Algernon Parsons was born in London on 13 June 1854, the sixth and youngest son of William Parsons, the Third Earl

*The Honourable Sir Charles A
Parsons (courtesy of Mr J F Clarke).*

of Rosse (1800-1867), and his wife Mary (d 1885), elder daughter and coheiress of John Wilmer Field of Heaton Hall, Yorkshire. There was a family tradition in scientific activity: Parsons's grandfather, the Second Earl Lawrence (1758-1841) was a vice-president of the Royal Society and his father, an astronomer of international distinction, was its president in 1849-54.

On his father's insistence Charles, like his brothers (of whom two died in childhood), was educated at home and by such distinguished tutors as the astronomer Robert (later Sir Robert) S Ball (1840-1913). The family seat of Birr Castle, County Offaly, Ireland, had fine workshops (where the Earl of Rosse built a 72-inch telescope) and in these as a boy Charles developed his first engineering talents. Although his father died when he was only thirteen, it was from him that Parsons later declared he 'learnt the first principles of mechanical construction and engineering' {Parsons (1915)}. His mother continued to show great interest in her son's skills as a model maker demonstrated when, at the age of fifteen and with his brothers, he built a steam road carriage.

After his father's death the family toured Switzerland or northern Italy each year. Formal education began when at seventeen he went to Trinity College, Dublin, and after two years he proceeded to St John's College, Cambridge. In 1877 he passed out as eleventh wrangler in the mathematics tripos; Parsons also attended lectures on mechanisms and applied mechanics as there was no formal course in engineering then available at Cambridge.

Next Charles Parsons went to Tyneside and served a four-year premium engineering apprenticeship at the great Elswick works of Sir William Armstrong (qv). Here he learned the essentials of production engineering, as well as the research and development techniques of Armstrong and his staff, while enhancing his own manual craft skills. The Elswick Works provided useful future business contacts including William Cross, later managing director of Hawthorn's Forth Bank locomotive works. Parsons took out three patents in this period; one in 1878 for a rotary steam engine, which was the development of ideas and a model constructed while he was still at Cambridge; another patent was shared with Cross. After completing his apprenticeship, Parsons worked for the distinguished Leeds engineering firm of Kitson & Co, 1881-83, joining his brother Richard Clere Parsons (1851-1923) who had gone to Leeds after a spell at the Kent engineering works of Easton & Anderson.

At Leeds Parsons experimented with the rocket propulsion of torpedoes, gas engines and the development of his four-cylinder engine, sharing the costs with Sir James Kitson (qv). His four-cylinder engine was aimed at providing the higher speeds needed for the satisfactory generation of electricity and a number were made and received notice in the engineering press at the Inventions Convention of 1885.

Following his marriage in January 1883 Parsons acquired a junior partnership in the Gateshead engineering company of Clarke, Chapman & Co (founded 1864); his £20,000 share formed one-eighth of the capital structure. The new junior partner took charge of a newly-formed electrical department, particularly developing electricity generation for ships' lighting (Clarke, Chapman being established suppliers of ships' auxiliary equipment). Within a few months the key patents for the steam turbine and its associated generator were taken out (April 1884); these and the numerous others that followed were described as opening 'up a new era in the production and application of power' {Ewing (1931) v }. This first generator produced $7\frac{1}{2}$ kW and within a year provided light on the SS *Earl Percy*. Parsons quickly propagated the merits of his new machinery through technical papers; in November 1885 he spoke in discussion at the Institution of Civil Engineers on his turbine, while two years later in Newcastle at the North East Coast Institution he read the first of his 74 technical papers, in which he explained the principles of his compound steam turbine and reported on it to the Institution of Mechanical Engineers at Dublin three years later. However, the machine, with a rotational speed of 18,000 revolutions per minute was not readily accepted. Parsons was also experimenting at the Gateshead works with the production of carbon rods and filaments for both arc lamps and incandescent lamps, produced in a joint venture with Clarke-Chapman — the Sunbeam Lamp Co. These lamps were successfully marketed and in 1887 the Marine Engineering Exhibition on Tyneside was lighted with them, powered by Parsons's turbines and generators, a success achieved with the help of the principal of the Durham College of Science, D W Garnett. By 1889 some 300 turbines had been produced at Clarke, Chapman's Gateshead works and the largest single unit was 75 KW. Parsons, however, was not satisfied. His bounding ambition fostered a growing impatience with his partners and in June 1889 he parted from Clarke-Chapman and set up on his own.

A two-acre site at the Newcastle suburb of Heaton was chosen by Charles Parsons for a new works, operated initially by a staff of 48. He brought with him from Gateshead about 12 men, including R Williams, works manager, J B Willis, chief draughtsman, J A Armstrong, foreman in the armature shop and G Stoney, a future FRS and son of another family tutor. Perhaps unexpectedly Parsons found himself without his patents, which were the property of his former partners' company. Undaunted, he proceeded to publicise his new firm and to produce a new design of turbine, the radial type. Such turbines were supplied for central power stations at Newcastle upon Tyne, Scarborough and Cambridge; Parsons backed his products by personal investment and management participation in these supply companies. Tests carried out by Professor J A Ewing FRS on the Cambridge equipment silenced many sceptics but it was still a struggle to build markets. Parsons and his assistants worked relentlessly to improve the design and performance of the new type of turbine, investing significantly in research and development — he believed a company should devote from 1.5 to 3 per cent of its turnover to R&D. On the production side Parsons's brother, Richard Clere, was in charge as manager. By 1892 the company not only quoted for generating equipment but also for a whole station and a basic supply system, following their success in equipping the Newcastle & District Electric Light Co. Matters greatly improved for Charles Parsons when in 1894 he recovered the use of his basic patents after arbitration proceedings for the modest sum of £1,500. Also in 1894 his turbine design was adopted by the Metropolitan Electric Supply Co to replace steam reciprocating engines when, because of the noise levels of its Manchester Square station, London, it faced a court injunction. This case encouraged many more customers and hastened the

Parsons's 1,000 kilowatt Turbo-alternator, as erected for the trials at the Heaton works, Newcastle-on-Tyne for Elberfeld (courtesy of Mr J F Clarke).

ultimate establishment of the steam turbine as the standard prime mover for central power stations using heat engines.

Financial success was still limited; at the end of 1897 Parsons told his brother that for the £25,000 put in 'what has been drawn out has been approximately 3 per cent per annum the whole time plus about £3,000 invested in Cambridge, Newcastle and Scarborough' {Appleyard (1933) 135-36}. In 1895 General Electric Co in the USA sent a three–man team to Newcastle with a view to acquiring a manufacturing licence but electrical engineer-scientist G P Steinmetz (1865-1923) dissuaded them; however George Westinghouse (1846-1914) sent his vice-president, E E Keller, with powers to act and by the end of 1895 Parsons had begun what was to be a liberal international licensing policy. Westinghouse bought sales rights in the USA for £10,000 but were required to build a minimum Kw of output during that time. Intermittently stormy, the relationship between Parsons and Westinghouse provided Westinghouse with their chief turbine engineer, Frank Hodgkinson (1867-1949). Hodgkinson was one of the original twelve from the Clarke, Chapman & Co and he took the first Parsons turbine to America. In August 1899 a special company with a capital of £60,000 was created to handle the foreign licences, under the executive management of S F Prest (1859-1931), who negotiated the Westinghouse deal and frequently played the role of peacemaker in Parsons's disputes. This company was a particularly profitable venture, particularly after the installation of the 1,000 Kw generating set at Elberfeld in 1900 which led many Continental companies to buy manufacturing licences.

A few years earlier Parsons's business colleague and friend, the coal owner J B Simpson (1837-1926), instigated the application of the turbine for ship propulsion. A private company with a capital of £24,000 was formed in 1894 and three years later in July 1897 it was floated as a public company, The Parsons Marine Steam Turbine Co, with a nominal capital of £500,000 and an issued capital of £208,000. A new 21-acre site was purchased at Wallsend, buildings erected and plant and machinery installed costing more than £70,000. The most extensive research and model trials were conducted by Parsons's firm before the experimental 100 foot vessel *Turbinia* demonstrated at the 1897 Spithead Naval Review the high speeds which the new means of propulsion made possible. With the Anglo-German naval race gathering momentum, demand for marine turbines emerged.

In the merchant marine Cunards first adopted turbines in 1905 when their 30,000 ton *Carmania* was fitted with them, as were their larger liners *Mauretania* and *Lusitania* in 1906. *Mauretania* held the record for the fastest Atlantic liner for more than twenty years. Following the success of direct drive turbines for both high speed passenger and naval vessels, Parsons made strenuous efforts to adapt his innovations to the needs of smaller merchant vessels, firstly by linking a turbine with the exhaust steam of the triple expansion engines used by Denny's SS *Otaki* (1908) and much more fundamentally by developing the application of gearing to reduce the very high turbine speed to the rotation rate appropriate for propellers: this was, of course, also highly important for naval vessels. To demonstrate the viability of this application to shipowners he formed a company to buy the SS *Vespasian*, refurbishing her existing engines and carrying out trial trips before replacing the engines with geared turbines and then reporting the successful results in technical papers. To overcome difficulties in producing accurate gears Parsons (who was always closely concerned with production problems) applied himself to machine tool design and by developing the 'creep' table assured a future for geared power transmission.

The Heaton works had expanded considerably by 1900. In the previous year about 8 acres was added to the site area, with new workshops 385 feet long and a new office block. However, the turbine generating plant constructed had only reached 33,113 kW. Output then massively increased to reach 358,244 kW by 1910, a tenfold increase on the previous decade. Parsons's research effort, personnel selection and general management had finally paid off. As the generation of electricity increased throughout the world so did the output of Parsons steam turbines, with a further half million kilowatts of capacity manufactured in the decade to 1920. Accumulated output reached 2,613,3737 kW before Parsons's death. This output penetrated the very heartland of the industrial USA when the Chicago Fisk station purchased a 25,000 kW plant in 1911 and followed this with an order for a 50,000 kW plant in 1922. Design and construction advances increased thermal efficiency from the 15.5 per cent at Elberfeld to 36.8 per cent at the Dunston power station in 1930.

The early years had not been easy. Director Christopher J Leyland, stood guarantor for £100,000 for the first Admiralty contract in case of failure. The tragic loss (not through any turbine fault) of the first two destroyers, *Viper* and *Cobra*, and the research and development costs which reached £10,439 in 1900-1, might have unnerved others, but not Charles Parsons. Eventually in 1904 the first dividend was paid and by

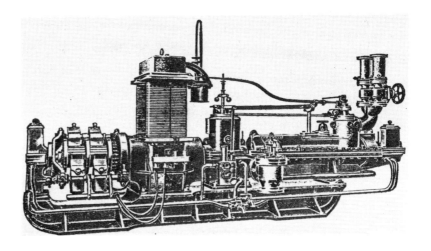

Parsons's Turbo-generator, 75 kilo-watts output, from C A Parsons' catalogue, 1897.

1911 the accumulated dividends paid reached 115 per cent. During the First World War and for two years afterwards dividends of 25 per cent were distributed. Inevitably the shipbuilding depression and the virtual elimination of naval contracts made Parsons's marine turbines unprofitable in trading terms and it may be Parsons underestimated the need to establish the double reduction drive system his company had begun. During the 1920s a judicious investment of early profits in gilt-edged securities enabled modest dividends to continue. Property and assets stood at £610,000 in June 1930. In the world as a whole the value of marine turbines built was approaching £90 million in value.

With his family background it is not surprising that Charles Parsons had a life-long interest in optics and glass production. As soon as he established his own turbine business he began to work on developing a parabolic searchlight which, with both naval applications and use in the Suez Canal, formed a not unimportant part of the output from Heaton. However, it was in the 1920s that he invested heavily in other fields of glass and optical production. Firstly in January 1921 he acquired a controlling interest in the London-based Ross Ltd, who manufactured binoculars, and later that year he purchased the Derby Crown Glass Co and so helped to sustain a competitive element in the scientific glass industry. The Parsons Optical Glass Co produced about 100 different kinds of glass for optical purposes. After purchasing Sir Howard Grubb & Sons, makers of large astronomical telescopes, Parsons gained a new international reputation for the high quality glass which included two 74-inch reflectors for Toronto and Pretoria. A new works was opened at Walkergate, adjacent to the Heaton turbine works.

The range of Charles Parsons's interests was indicated by the £30,000 he spent on attempting to produce artificial diamonds and his invention of the 'auxetophone', a device for the amplification of the sound of stringed instruments, which was used at the Queen's Hall in 1906. Altogether Parsons took out more than 300 patents. If he had a weakness it was an excessive pursuit of novelty — regardless of the costs of over-diversifying. This, the quest for fresh applications of scientific knowledge, rather than profits, appeared to be the dominant motive in Parsons as he created almost a new industry, steam turbine production for power generation and ship propulsion.

Charles Parsons held his skilled craftsmen in high regard (he preferred the word artisan to workman); probably the interesting nature of the work and perhaps above-average wages kept his plant free from local labour problems. The wage bill at Heaton rose from £67,511 in 1904 to £94,569 in 1907, when the firm reached fifth among the engineering works on the North-East coast. A year earlier the Marine Turbine Works paid £41,342 in wages but the vagaries of shipbuilding cut this to £25,912 in 1907. By 1914 the firm employed 1,200 and at Parsons's death about 1,800. A management subordinate of Parsons described him 'as advanced in his treatment of staff and work people as in his technical outlook' {Gibb (1947) 213}. Parsons set up a sick benefit fund for employees to which they could subscribe. He later developed a share scheme for employees, in which he retained a personal right to repurchase. He was concerned to see the establishment of adequate educational provision for a skilled workforce at both graduate and craft levels, and he formed an apprentice school at Heaton in 1919.

Parsons had the ability to identify and promote talent. S S Cook was speedily put in charge of turbine blade design and later C D Gibb (qv) was made technical director. Although Parsons's Celtic temper clashed for a time with Stoney, they were reconciled and the company must have been for a time the only engineering works with three fellows of the Royal Society on its permanent staff. He was chairman of the Board of Trade committee on the Electrical Trades in 1915; member of the Advisory Council for Scientific and Industrial Research and member of the Fuel Research Board in 1916; afterwards he served as chairman of the Scientific Instruments Research Association in 1920. His local directorships included the Newcastle & District Electric Lighting Co, Cambridge Electric Supply Co Ltd and Scarborough Electric Light Supply Co Ltd.

Although he was for a year president of the Tyneside Unionist Association and a member of the Carlton Club, the view of his close colleague Claude Gibb is no doubt correct: 'Parsons displayed only a minor interest in politics and there appears to be no record of his having expressed views on any of the political questions of his time' {*ibid*, 213-14} He was, however, vice-president of the Tariff Reform League and a member of the Tariff Reform Commission in 1904.

Parsons was widely recognised for his achievements: he was appointed CB in 1904 and KCB in 1911, and was admitted to the Order of Merit in 1927 (the first engineer to be so honoured). Elected FRS in 1898, he later served on the Royal Society's council and was a vice-president in 1908; he received both its Rumford (1902) and Copley medals (1928). From the Institution of Civil Engineers, which he joined as a student in January 1879, he received the Kelvin medal in 1926; he was a council member of the Institution for eight years. An honorary member of the French, American and German Institutions of Mechanical Engineers, he received the Grashof medal, the highest award of the German Institution, in 1904. The Royal Society of Arts awarded him the Albert medal in 1911 and in 1920 he received the Franklin medal from the Franklin Institute of America in Philadelphia. From the new universities of Liverpool and Sheffield he received doctorates in engineering, while the Scottish universities of Glasgow and Edinburgh awarded the degree LLD and finally Oxford, Cambridge, Dublin and Durham awarded him honorary DScs. He participated in nearly all the engineering Institutions, joining the Institution of Mechanical Engineers in 1880 (becoming an honorary life member in 1925) and the Institution of Naval Architects in 1899 (serving on its Council for twenty-seven years); he was president of the Junior Institution of Engineers in 1899-1900 and held the same office in the Institute of Marine Engineers in 1905-6 and in the North East Coast Institution of Engineers and Shipbuilders in 1912-14. In 1909 he was elected an honorary member of the Institution of Electrical Engineers. He was president of the British Academy in 1919 and also a past president of the Institute of Physics and the British Association. He received the freedom of the City of Newcastle in 1914. He was a JP of Northumberland and that county's High Sheriff in 1898.

'Shy, self-contained, inexpressive' was how Sir Alfred Ewing described Charles Parsons: 'even in the universal celebrity of his riper years, he kept an air of self-effacement, an exaggerated though natural modesty which puzzled strangers as much as it endeared him to his friends'. {Ewing (1931) viii} Such comments may understate the power of his personality and the great determination behind his success. He was always actively involved at all levels from the highest managerial decisions to matters on the workshop floor. Long hours on his current experimental work always gave him the greatest satisfaction and at such times he was apt to forget most other matters as he worked late into the night. His interest in sport remained with him throughout his life; he rowed at Cambridge and was a keen shot, enjoyed fishing (especially trout), and delighted in cycling. An enthusiastic motorist, he took a keen interest in air flight, being active in the Northern Aero Club; he made his own sketches of airship designs.

Parsons married in 1883 Katherine (1859-1933), daughter of William Frogatt Bethell of Rise Park, Hull; she provided unswerving support for her husband, accepting the many early morning excursions which were characteristic of the early years of his professional work, and was active in advancing the cause of women in engineering, and also the Conservative Party's north east women's group. In 1919 Lady Parsons was the first woman to address the North East Coast Institution of Engineers and Shipbuilders — her subject, women's work in engineering and shipbuilding during the war. A founder member of the Women's Engineering Society in 1920 she assisted eight girls to establish an engineering company. The Parsons's only daughter Rachel (1885-1956) graduated from the engineering school at Cambridge and their only son Major A G Parsons, RA was killed in action in 1918 aged thirty-one. At his death Parsons owned several properties: 6 Windsor Terrace, Newcastle upon Tyne; Ray Estate, Kirkwhelpington, Northumberland; and 1 Upper Brook Street, Mayfair, London. Earlier he also owned Holeyn Hall, Wylam, Northumberland.

Sir Charles Parsons died on board the *Duchess of Richmond* at Kingston, Jamaica, on 11 February 1931, leaving £1,214,355 gross.

J F CLARKE

Writings:

'The Compound Steam Turbine and Its Theory as Applied to the Working of Dynamo Electric Machines' *Transactions of the North East Coast Institution of Engineers and Shipbuilders* 4 (1887).

'Electricity' in Wigham Richardson (ed), *Official Local Guide — British Association Newcastle upon Tyne* (Newcastle upon Tyne: Andrew Reid, 1889).

'Application of the Compound Steam Turbine to the Purpose of Marine Propulsion' *Transactions of the Institution of Naval Architects* 38 (1897).

(with R J Walker), 'The Combination System of Reciprocating Engines and Steam Turbines' *ibid* 49 (1908).

'The Application of the Marine Steam Turbine and Mechanical Gearing to Merchant Ships' *ibid* 51 (1910).

'Presidential Address' *Transactions of the North East Coast Institution of Engineers and Shipbuilders* 29 (1912).

'Presidential Address' *ibid* 30 (1913).

'Reply on Receiving the Freedom of Newcastle upon Tyne' *ibid*.

speech *Transactions of North East Coast Institution of Engineers and Shipbuilders* 30 (1915).

The Scientific Papers of William Parsons, Third Earl of Rosse 1800-1867 (P Lund Humphries & Co, 1926).

(G L Parsons ed), *Scientific Papers and Addresses of the Honourable Sir Charles A Parsons* (Cambridge: Cambridge University Press, 1934). This contains a large bibliography of Sir Charles's papers.

Patents too numerous to list beginning with 1878 (4,266).

Sources:

Unpublished

Newcastle upon Tyne City Library: R W Martin, 'The Honourable Sir C A Parsons 1854-1931' (scrapbook, nd); R W Martin 'Parsons scrapbook 1890-1970' (nd).

Science Museum, London, papers of Sir Charles Parsons.

Tyne and Wear Archives, papers of the North East Coast Institution of Engineers and Shipbuilders.

BCe.

MCe.

PrC.

Published

Rollo Appleyard, *Charles Parsons, His Life and Work* (Constable, 1933).

Aubrey F Burstall, 'The Place of Sir Charles Parsons in the History of Mechanical Engineering' *Heaton Works Journal* Summer 1954.

E Kitson Clark, 'Sir Charles Parsons and Marine Propulsion' in Very Rev W R Inge (ed), *The Post Victorians* (Nicholson & Watson, 1933).

PARSONS The Honourable Sir Charles Algernon

J F Clarke, *An Almost Unknown Great Man — Charles A Parsons and the Significance of the Patents of 1884* (Newcastle: Newcastle upon Tyne Polytechnic, 1984).

—, *A Century of Service to Engineering and Shipbuilding* (North East Coast Institution of Engineers and Shipbuilders, forthcoming).

Stanley S Cook, 'Sir Charles Parsons and Marine Propulsion' *Proceedings of the Institution of Mechanical Engineers* 1938.

John Cutler (ed), *Reports of Patent, Design, and Trade-Mark Cases. In the Matter of Parsons' Patent* (HMSO, 1898).

A W Davis, 'Eighty Years with the Marine Turbine' *Transactions of the Institute of Marine Engineers* 87 (1975).

DNB.

S F Dorey, 'Reduction Gearing for Marine Steam Turbines' *Transactions of the Institute of Marine Engineers* 54 (1942).

R Dowson, 'George Gerald Stoney' *Obituary Notices of the Fellows of the Royal Society* 4 (1942).

Engineer 20 Feb 1931.

Engineering 1931.

Sir Alfred Ewing, 'The Hon Sir Charles Parsons, OM, KCB — 1854-1931' *Proceedings of the Royal Society* 131 (1931).

Sir Claude Gibb, 'Parsons — The Man and his Work' *Journal of the Institution of Mechanical Engineers* 156 (1947).

Heaton Works Journal (pp, Newcastle upon Tyne, 1933-39) 1-3.

Nature obituaries 28 Feb 1931 (G Stoney; R T Glazebrook; H F Heath).

Robert H Parson, *The Development of the Parsons Steam Turbine* (Constable, 1936).

—, *The Early Days of the Power Station Industry* (Cambridge: Cambridge University Press, 1940).

C A Parsons & Co, catalogues from 1897.

—, *History of the Development of the Heaton Works, 1889-1926* (pp, 1927).

Harold D Passer, *The Electrical Manufacturers 1875-1900* (Cambridge, Massachusetts: Harvard University Press, 1953).

Sir Alexander Richardson, 'The Evolution of the Parsons Steam Turbine' *Engineering* 1911.

William Richardson, *History of the Parish of Wallsend* (Newcastle upon Tyne, Northumberland Press, 1923).

'Stanley Smith Cook' in *Obituary Notices of the Fellows of the Royal Society* 8 (1952).

E V Telfer, 'Sir Charles Parsons and the Naval Architect' *Royal Institution of Naval Architects* 108 (1965).

Times 13 Feb 1931.

Transactions of the Institution of Naval Architects 73 (1931).

Transactions of the North East Coast Institution of Engineers and Shipbuilders 47 (1930-31).

WWW.

successful businessmen he distrusted politicians and civil servants. He considered that the more they left business alone, the better. He had great sympathy with the history of the German-speaking section of Bohemia, but this did not lead him in any way to support what Hitler was doing in Central Europe. The Second World War obviously caused a complete break. Eric Pasold and his brother Rolf, who had become British subjects in 1936 and 1937 respectively, were able to retain certain rights in the Fleissen business, but with the complete Communist takeover in 1948 the long story of Pasolds as textile manufacturers in Bohemia came finally to an end.

The early years at Langley were difficult. In the 1930s trade was not good and the type of garment it was hoped could be manufactured would not sell. New fabrics and garments had to be designed, notably a ripple cloth which involved a number of technical problems. It was also necessary to enter the fancy and fashion trade which was against Eric Pasold's original intention. His ideal of maximum efficiency was to make one garment in one size and in one colour.

There were also difficulties with the dyeing which was done on commission, but so badly that it was decided to build the firm's own dyehouse. By dint of hard work and with great emphasis on technical know-how and marketing, the business slowly became profitable and by the outbreak of the Second World War there were 300 employees, turnover had risen to £120,000 and profits were £15,330.

The way in which the company's expansion was financed deserves attention. The Pasolds had reasonable capital in Czechoslovakia but it is difficult to state accurately how much. After the war, following much study and deliberation, the Foreign Compensation Commission in London informed Eric Pasold and his brother Rolf, that the value of their nationalised Czechoslovak possessions had been assessed at £588,706 and in due course they received a dividend of 9 per cent or £53,000 in total settlement of their claim. However, it remains difficult to convert this figure of estimated assets which belonged to the two brothers into one of total assets before the war. The problem was that none of this could be transferred legitimately to England and Eric Pasold overcame this in various ways. Some useful transfers were made via Switzerland using numbered accounts already at that time well known on the Continent. A certain amount of money was smuggled across Europe from the Leibitschgrund factory. But early expansion was largely financed out of profits. The war years were difficult but the entity of the factory was retained under the Concentration of Industries Scheme and during these years Eric Pasold began to play a leading part in the national hosiery trade associations. He had clearly foreseen that in the world of the future the isolated businessman was going to have a more difficult time than previously.

Expansion came after the Second World War, with turnover climbing from £194,484 in 1945 to £679,161 in 1950. Profits grew similarly, rising from £49,000 in 1945 to £172,500 in 1950. Between 1955 (when Pasolds became a public company) and 1968 sales grew from £1.68 million to £16.178 million on which profits were £305,000 and £2.12 million respectively.

This expansion could only be obtained first by building additional

PASOLD Sir Eric Walter

factories on the large site at Langley, so wisely purchased in 1932. After
that, expansion was maintained by a policy of takeovers, including the
long-established firm of Chilprufe Ltd, manufacturers of children's wear
at Leicester, and the well-known Scottish hosiery firm of Donaldson
Textiles Ltd, perhaps better known at Donbros. It is noticeable that
profits increased more quickly when expansion was confined to Langley as
compared to the later period when the takeover of other businesses
occurred. Eric Pasold's experience in Czechoslovakia had confirmed his
belief in brand marketing and the trademark 'Ladybird', which was
registered in 1938, was a stroke of genius. Ladybird became a household
name not only in this country, but in the majority of export markets in the
western world, mainly because of the superb value offered, but also helped
by Eric Pasold's own delight in writing successful advertising matter
which appealed to the young. There was a great demand for textiles of all
kinds in the years following the war, firms like Marks & Spencer and
Woolworths would willingly have bought almost all of Pasold's
production, but this was contrary to Eric Pasold's conviction that brand
merchanting was the key to an expansion policy. He established a series of
agencies throughout Britain, with shops in all important towns as
designated Ladybird stockists. This policy was excellently suited to the
period when Eric Pasold was controlling the fortunes of the company.
With the ending of Resale Price Maintenance in 1964 and a tendency for
big firms like Marks & Spencers to acquire an even larger hold on
consumer sales, it would have needed changing, perhaps to the ownership
of more and more retail outlets. It was in fact the hope that this could be
done in collaboration with Coats Paton that led him to push forward with
this takeover. For reasons that can hardly be dealt with here, this in fact
did not happen.

As the business expanded, Eric Pasold was much concerned with
problems of management. Until the mid-1950s, he and his brother Rolf
were well able to keep everything under their personal control and
direction. Udo Geipel, Eric's cousin, who had played a leading part in the
Czechoslovak business, joined the board in 1954. In 1957 Pasolds Ltd, by
this time the largest children's wear manufacturers in Britain, became a
public company and for a number of years were very much a glamour
share; an investment of £100 in 1957 became worth £1,500 within the short
span of only four years; though profits did not expand at anything like this
rate.

In the mid-1960s Eric Pasold foresaw that textiles in Britain had reached a peak and that decline was more likely than expansion. He decided that a link with a major textile group would best ensure the future of the business he and his brother had established. These were the days when take-overs were much in the air and Eric Pasold has given his own account of his negotiations with Prouvost, the well-known Continental textile group, with Courtaulds and finally with Coats Patons. As a result in 1965 Coats Patons bought 54 per cent of the total equity of Pasolds Ltd, and he himself became a director of CPB; but serving on the board of a great public comapny did not appeal to him and perhaps his individual approach to problems was not really fitted for it. During these three years his health deteriorated, and on doctor's advice, he resigned on 31 December 1968 and retired to Switzerland. The remainder of the Pasolds equity was sold to Coats Patons in 1971.

Eric Pasold was one of the most successful entrepreneurs in the British hosiery industry of his generation. His family background brought the attributes of hereditary leadership, together with capital and a sound technical training, but such advantages could easily have been lost or dissipated in the difficult economic conditions of twentieth-century Europe. In Britain his greatest assets proved to be his unorthodox approach to problems, his far-sightedness and feeling for market potential, complemented by a sound knowledge of engineering. He was a man who sought challenges, an autocratic bachelor who lived over his work — his flat was literally a few steps from his office at Langley. He pressed all his varied talents into creating his vision of an efficient, vertically-integrated factory, free from the traditions and prejudices of the old industry. His success at communication played a major part in this achievement.

During the Second World War, Pasold was chairman of the South of England Knitting Industries Association, a member of the council of the National Hosiery Manufacturers' Federation and served on the War Emergency Committee and the Post-War Reconstruction Committee. He sat on the Grand Council of the Federation of British Industries and its overseas policy committee. In 1946 as a member of the Combined Intelligence Objectives Subcommittee he investigated and reported on the textile industry in Germany.

He had wide interests outside the business and during the 1950s and 1960s built up a fine antique collection, which included paintings, guns, coins and Bohemian woodwork from Egerland, his old and much-loved home country. He was a pioneer in the use of private aeroplanes — a pilot himself who owned a series of aircraft. He played a leading part in the formation of Crawley New Town and founded the Pasold Research Fund with the object of financing research in textile history, particularly on his much-admired William Lee, the great English inventor of the stocking frame in Queen Elizabeth I's reign.

During his years of retirement in Switzerland he continued to collect and to write his autobiography published under the title *Ladybird Ladybird*. He had intended to write a detailed account of the post-war years, but failing health made it clear that this could not be done and consequently the last two or three chapters of the book are rather condensed. The appreciative reviews that appeared gave him much pleasure during the last months of his life. Meanwhile he had received several well-deserved honours, including the OBE in 1961 for services to export (he was vice-chairman of the Hosiery and Knitwear Export Group) and the honorary degree of MA from Nottingham University in 1977.

Eric Pasold died at Lucerne, Switzerland, on 5 January 1978.

K G PONTING

Writings:

Ladybird Ladybird, A Story of Private Enterprise (Manchester: Manchester University Press, 1977).

'In Search of William Lee' *Textile History* 6 (1975).

Sources:

Unpublished

Pasolds' Ltd, annual accounts, 1954-70.

Information from Eric Pasold.

Published

Times 12 Jan 1978.

PATERSON, John Craig

(1881-1955)

Tanner

John Craig Paterson was born in Hamilton, Lanarkshire, Scotland on 3 March 1881, the son of William Paterson, a quarry owner, and his wife Mary née Craig. After attending Hamilton Academy, Paterson joined the firm of Martin & Millar, leather manufacturers at Glasgow, of which his uncle John Millar was head. During his time here Paterson was sent for a few months to America to gain experience with the firm of Beggs & Cobb.

Some time after Paterson joined Martin & Millar the partners separated, the Millars remaining in heavy leather manufacturing and the Martins going into upper leather manufacture. Paterson remained with his uncle but after Millar died he had a disagreement with Millar's son who now headed the firm. After this Paterson, aged twenty-five, moved south to Birkenhead, bought a small tannery and founded the British Leather Co Ltd; this developed into one of the largest producers of rough tanned leather in the country. In 1934 he acquired the Litherland Tannery Co Ltd which had previously been associated with British Tanneries. In view of a recently imposed additional duty on imported calf leather, he converted the Litherland Tannery from producing sole leather to calf leather.

The single most important factor in the growth of the company was the demand for motorcar upholstery. With Connolly Brothers of London, the British Leather Co became major suppliers of leather to the British motor trade. An indication of the growth of the business comes from average annual profits. From £4,000 per annum in its first decade, these mounted to between £13,000 and £14,000 per annum in the next two decades (1916-35); they then rose to £45,000 in the decade spanning the Second World War and then doubled to £118,000 per annum for the years 1946-55 with the appearance of mass markets for the motorcar. The company's workforce rose from 40 people in 1910 to around 400 in 1955 and over the period the number of hides processed per week went up from 150 to 7,000.

Paterson took an active part in trade associations, and especially the United Tanners' Federation from its inception in 1908. He was chairman of the UTF in 1931-32 and at the time of his death its honorary president. He was also chairman of both the Master Tanners' Association and of the Hide and Allied Trades Improvement Society, where his 'broad outlook and mature judgement were greatly appreciated' {*Leather World* 8 Dec 1955}. He was also closely involved with the trade benevolent association and had contributed to the extension of the National Leathersellers' College.

In private life he was a lifelong lover of horses, steeplechasing and riding to hounds. He hunted with both the Wirral Harriers and the Cheshire Fox Hounds of which he was a joint master, 1946-49.

Paterson married in 1912 Katherine Louise, the daughter of Alfred Dobell, well known in the Liverpool timber trade. They had four children, one of whom A D Paterson succeeded his father as chairman of the British Leather Co Ltd.

J C Paterson died while out hunting on 3 December 1955. He left £62,072 gross.

FRANCIS GOODALL

Sources:

Unpublished

MCe.

PrC.

Biographical information supplied by A D Paterson in letters dated 22 Dec 1980, 27 Feb 1981.

PATERSON John Craig

Published

Birkenhead News 7 Dec 1955.

Leather Trades Review 7 Dec 1955.

Leather World 8 Dec 1955.

Stock Exchange Year Book 1929-34.

A Paton (from the Liverpool Courier).

PATON, Alexander Allan

(1874-1934)

Cotton broker

Alexander Allan Paton was born in 1874, the only son of five children of Alexander Allan Paton, who was born in Newmilns, Ayrshire in 1837, but emigrated to the United States just before the Civil War. He married Marie, daughter of John Crowshaw, in New York and in the Civil War worked for the US Military RR. After the war he became general freight agent of the Memphis & Louisville RR. He entered the cotton trade in 1868 in partnership with S M Anderson and established branches in St Louis, Memphis and New Orleans. His headquarters were in St Louis, but he was also one of the founder members of the Memphis Cotton Exchange in 1873. Anderson purchased cotton and Paton used his connections in England to sell it. In 1868 he visited Liverpool and founded with his elder brother, Andrew Brown Paton (1833-1913), the cotton importing firm of A B Paton & Co. Paton's younger brother, J R Paton, also joined the partnership but later established his own cotton broking firm. According to Dun & Bradstreet in 1880, Paton, 'a scheming and calculating man', was, after some difficulties in the 1870s, worth in America not less than $150,000-200,000, and his firm was 'good, safe and reliable' {Harvard Baker Library, Dun & Bradstreet 29 p 5}. In 1889, A B Paton & Co divided, A A Paton establishing his own firm of Paton McLaren & Co in Liverpool, with George S McLaren as partner in Memphis.

Alexander Allan Paton Jr, was therefore born into a well-established Liverpool cotton importing business with good connections in the United States. He was educated at the Leys School, Cambridge, and joined his father's firm in 1892. In 1898 he became a partner and in 1899 he was sent out to take charge of the Memphis branch and for several years spent much time in the Southern states. A A Paton Sr died in 1904 leaving an estate in England worth about £45,000 to his five children. A A Paton was the only boy and became senior partner. There are no internal records of the business, but directories show that in 1911 the firm had branches in Memphis, Tennessee, and Dallas, Hillsboro and Sulphur Springs, Texas, thus following the Cotton Belt westwards. There was also in 1911 a firm of Baker, Paton & Co, established in 1900, in New Orleans, but it is not clear if this was related. In 1910 most of the foreign buyers in the South were English, representing Liverpool and Manchester firms. Such firms purchased cotton in very large volumes from factors and country merchants, arranged transport on through bills of lading across the Atlantic, sold in Liverpool to mill buying brokers, and hedged their transactions on the New York and Liverpool Cotton Exchanges.

The head office of the firm remained in Liverpool and Paton rapidly became prominent in the trade and in the city. He was a director of the Liverpool Cotton Association from 1907 to 1910, serving on many committees. He was on the Council of the British Cotton Growing Association. He also began to gain membership of Liverpool companies. In 1910 he joined the board of the Royal Insurance Co, and in 1924 became deputy chairman, and in 1930 chairman. He was also chairman of the Liverpool & London & Globe Insurance Co, and a director of the Thames & Mersey, the British Foreign & Marine and the Legal Insurance companies. When war broke out in August 1914, just as the cotton season was about to start, the Bank of Liverpool which had a strong interest in the cotton trade appointed two cotton directors, of whom Paton was one, to help restore confidence in the trade. During the war Paton served in the British Embassy in Washington as a representative of the Contraband Department of the Ministry of Blockade, and in 1917 he was appointed to the Balfour Mission to the United States as an adviser on the Blockade. He was offered an OBE in 1918, but refused appointment. He served as establishment officer, 'in charge of the establishment at the Hotel Majestic', at the Paris Peace Conference, for which he was made a CB in 1920.

Paton returned to the cotton trade after the war. During the war American firms had taken over the international marketing of cotton and it is likely that Paton's firm was restricted to the domestic marketing of American cotton after 1918. In 1925 he served as vice-president of the Liverpool Cotton Association and in 1926 as president. He was also a member of the New York Cotton Exchange. He became deputy chairman of the Bank of Liverpool in 1922 and chairman 1929-34. During his tenure the Bank opened a new head office and reformed its system of management. Paton had many other public interests. He served on the Liverpool City Council before the war. On the council he was treasurer of the Unemployed Fund, and president of the Labour Enquiry Sub-Committee which investigated unemployment. He was also an active member of the Voluntary Hospitals in Liverpool, president of the Royal Southern Hospital and a member of the board of management of the Liverpool Hospital for Consumption. He played cricket and golf and was a member of the Royal Clyde Yacht Club. In 1928 he purchased *Lulworth* a well known racing cutter with which on one occasion he was able to defeat Sir Thomas Lipton's (qv) *Shamrock V*.

Paton was an unostentatious but efficient man. He was described in 1911 when he won his position on the City Council as a man of quiet tastes but a very painstaking and efficient worker, and an unidentified friend recalled that while his reputation in Liverpool was gained by 'distinguished and disinterested public service, the place he held in the heart of his friends was due to personal qualities of a most outstanding order. Under a somewhat sardonic and impassive exterior he concealed a heart of gold and many a shaken soul in Liverpool could testify to his charity and generosity' {*Times* 7 July 1934}. He did not marry and his firm vanished from the Liverpool trade directories with his death.

Alexander Allan Paton died on 27 June 1934 leaving £436,418 gross in England and also left assets in America. After small bequests to friends and servants, the remainder of his estate was left to his sisters and their descendants.

JOHN R KILLICK

Sources:

Unpublished

Harvard University, Graduate School of Business Administration, Baker Library, Dun & Bradstreet Credit Registers (R G Dun & Co Collection).

Liverpool City Libraries, Liverpool Cotton Association Records; newspaper cuttings, Liverpool worthies, vols 6, 9, 14, 17-18, 22, 23, 27, 31.

Memphis Cotton Exchange, Memphis, Tennessee, Memphis Cotton Exchange Records.

PrC.

Published

Annual Cotton Shippers' Book 1910-11 (Savannah, Georgia, 1910).

George Chandler, *Four Centuries of Banking* (2 vols, B T Batsford, 1964).

Liverpool Trade Directories.

Times 8 May 1917, 7 July 1934.

WWW.

Sir Edward Peacock (courtesy of Mr John Orbell).

PEACOCK, Sir Edward Robert

(1871-1962)

Merchant and central banker

Edward Robert Peacock was born at Kenyon Township, Glengarry, Ontario, Canada, on 2 August 1871, the son of Rev W M Peacock, the local Congregational minister. After his father died in 1883, his mother Jane McDougall, in straitened circumstances, took the children to Almonte where Edward attended Almonte High School. He quickly overcame the disadvantage of not being able to read or write (his father had not sent him to primary school). In 1891 he entered Queen's University, Kingston, Ontario, one of the oldest and most prestigious of Canada's universities, where he read English and philosophy, graduating magna cum laude in 1894.

That year he entered the School of Pedagogy in Toronto and afterwards accepted a teaching post at Upper Canada College, one of the best-known of Canada's public schools, then under the headship of Sir George Parkin. Parkin, like Peacock's old principal at Queen's, G M Grant, and his mentor, Adam Shortt, was an apostle of imperial unity and the influence of the three sharply moulded Peacock's views.

Peacock's choice of profession was by no means unusual. His *Canada* describes teaching in Canada as a 'stepping stone' to other more lucrative careers, and assures readers that 'many of the best known public men began life as teachers' {Peacock (1900) 27}. Within two years at Upper Canada College he was a senior housemaster but an interest in financial affairs was already evident. His 1898 article 'Trusts, Combines and Monopolies' acknowledged a need for public regulation and education concerning 'big business', which he saw as inevitable given the capitalisation and organisation required by modern manufacturing technology.

In 1902 he became personal assistant to E R Wood, a leading financier in Canada who had recently established Dominion Securities Corporation (DSC) of Toronto run by G H Wood and Harry Gundy. This company held a leading position in the marketing of securities of Canadian business and when it was discovered that Peacock 'knew important people all over Canada' {Queen's University Archives (QUA), Peacock Papers, 2170 1 16} he joined DSC's staff as a bond salesman. His rise through the ranks was meteoric. When Wood and Gundy left to set up Wood, Gundy & Co, Peacock was made manager of DSC and in 1907 opened a European office in London. Europe, especially England, was the major supplier of Canada's long-term capital, and a London office marked a major expansion of DSC's business. In 1909 he came to live in London permanently. He quickly built on the connections he had already established in Canada and appears to have become acquainted with such leading public figures as Lord Milner and Arthur Steel-Maitland. In this way he may have been assisted through his connection with the Round Table movement, an important group formed at the turn of the century and concerned with imperial affairs, in which apparently he assumed the role of a leading 'eminence grise'. Of longer term importance, in 1907 he met and became a very close friend of Montagu Norman (qv), then a partner of Brown Shipley.

Peacock's proving came in 1915. Amongst the interests of DSC were important holdings in a series of public utility companies promoted by Dr F S Pearson and backed by Canadian capital. They included the Brazilian Traction, Light & Power Co Ltd, which controlled the Barcelona Traction, Light & Power Co Ltd and the Mexican Tramways, Light & Power Co Ltd. When Pearson drowned in the *Lusitania* disaster of 1915, Peacock was quickly installed as vice-president of the prosperous Brazilian company with responsibility for finance, and was also appointed president of the other two companies which were in difficulties. He became preoccupied with their affairs, rearranging finance, rebuilding credit, and in Spain and Mexico carrying out an extensive investment programme, although his lack of languages was 'a serious handicap' {ibid}. London financiers were impressed. Gaspard Farrer, the second partner of the eminent London merchant bankers, Baring Brothers, and an expert on the American securities business, had corresponded with Peacock since at least 1918. In 1922 he urged Robert Winsor, head of the leading Boston banking house of Kidder Peabody, who was then crossing the Atlantic in the same steamer as Peacock, 'to make tracks for him. He is well worth knowing. He took up Dr Pearson's interests ... all in the same state of utter impecuniosity and brought them through in a wonderful way' {Baring Brothers Archives (BBA) DEP 33.21}.

Farrer had already introduced Peacock to Barings' senior partner, Lord Revelstoke (qv), and by 1922 the two were participating in investments jointly. However, Barings' formal link with Peacock, in his capacity as president of the Barcelona Traction, Light & Power Co Ltd, came in 1920 with the underwriting of an issue of that company's debentures. Deeply impressed, Revelstoke, a senior director of the Bank of England, supported Montagu Norman, by then Governor of the Bank, in obtaining Peacock's election to the Bank's Court in 1921. Revelstoke had a natural ally in the Governor who was ever anxious to improve the calibre of directors, extend the concept of central banking to the Dominions, and ensure the continuation of the important sterling balances built up by Dominion Governments during the war years which were crucial in obtaining an early return to a gold standard. As early as 1922 Peacock's standing was such that he joined the Bank's key Committee of Treasury, and attended the Paris conference on Mexican debts and the important International Economic Conference at Genoa.

Revelstoke and Farrer had other reasons for promoting Peacock. Farrer, who had given outstanding service as Revelstoke's deputy since 1902, was rapidly approaching retirement age while Revelstoke was almost sixty. In Barings' partners room premature deaths had left a team either too old or too inexperienced to lead the house in the middle term, so Revelstoke, ever mindful that the Baring Crisis of 1890 had been caused through the mismanagement of partners with poor judgement, invited Peacock to join Barings as a director. Peacock agreed, albeit after considerable soul searching, as it meant having to resign his directorship of the Bank since tradition dictated that no house could provide more than one director. Initially he had declined but relented a year later, having been influenced by the Governor. His compensation was surely more than enough. His appointment as senior director of perhaps the most influential and prestigious City merchant bank provided a platform from which he could become deeply enmeshed in British financial and industrial affairs. This was an opportunity which would not have been available to him at his old company. For Barings it was a brave decision and its announcement caused a mild sensation in the City. It prompted Gaspard Farrer to explain to Robert Winsor that 'of course [he] has a different upbringing from any of us here ... but the set of his mind and all his ways are on the same lines as ours' {ibid, DEP 33.22}. In a letter to a closer friend, the head of Hope & Co of Amsterdam, Farrer wrote more frankly: 'he is absolutely straight, and without any pretence to special brilliance, has one of the wisest heads I know' {ibid}.

Peacock's arrival at Barings in 1924 came at a time of great change in the affairs of London merchant banks. The shrunken, although still important, role of sterling in international finance after 1918; the various embargoes placed on the issue of foreign loans in the London market; and the desperate plight of many leading companies in British industry closed as many doors to merchant banks as they opened. Peacock, arriving at the time of this watershed, was responsible for the immensely successful transition of Barings from a house that had specialised in the issue of securities of foreign Governments and business organisations to one which became skilled in the reorganisation and financing of British business. He was in his element. In 1927, in reporting to Lord Revelstoke talks with his weekend guest, Montagu Norman, he went almost unnecessarily far out of his way to stress his viewpoint to this banker nurtured in a different age. Norman 'is full of plans and problems' he began,

> and spoke particularly of the importance of bringing about closer relationships and a much better understanding between the City of London and the great industries of England, particularly iron, steel, coal and textiles. On this subject he found a sympathetic listener, because I feel that it is a matter of vital importance to this country that there should be a much better understanding and more active intervention by the financial people, not merely the rather passive assistance afforded in the form of overdrafts by joint stock banks {ibid, PF 38A}.

He was hardly at his desk at Barings before he became deeply enmeshed in one of the major company reconstructions undertaken between the wars. The great armaments manufacturers, Armstrong, Whitworth, had become hopelessly lost in post-war diversification, not least through the ambitious yet poorly planned projects of their Newfoundland Power & Paper Corporation subsidiary. Their bankers, the Bank of England, were already providing vital support and doubtless under pressure from Norman, the company appointed Barings as financial advisers. As Armstrongs' plight went from bad to worse as the 1920s wore on, Peacock, working closely with Norman who was equally concerned for the national interest, arranged a succession of reconstructions; brought in urgently-needed new management in the form of company 'doctor' Frater Taylor (qv); played a leading role in disposing of the Newfoundland interests; and then handled the merger of many of Armstrongs' interests into Vickers Armstrong and the Lancashire Steel Corporation. It was work poles apart from that undertaken by pre-war merchant bankers.

In 1928 Peacock became equally involved in the setting up of the Lancashire Cotton Corporation, perhaps the most ambitious scheme of industrial reorganisation carried out between the wars. By 1933 well over 100 mills had been combined into the new company. The industry had suffered from intense overseas competition and had responded badly because of poor senior management. Moreover one or two clearing banks that had financed the industry were in danger of being dragged under as the industry's fortunes declined. Once again Peacock worked closely with Norman in devising the initial scheme that was introduced in the early months of 1929, although Barings' role was only partially formalised in mid-1929 by the appointment of A C Tod, Liverpool Agent, to the board of the new Corporation. The bank was subsequently appointed Trustees of the debenture holders. The onset of the slump soon meant that the ambitions set were not being realised so that further 'nursing' became essential. Further schemes of reconstruction were devised and underpinning these, new management was injected. In early 1931, for example, at Peacock's request, Sir Eric Geddes (qv) undertook an investigation of the Corporation and made recommendations for improving efficiency. This resulted in wholesale change of senior management, Frank Platt (qv) being brought in at this point.

Although Armstrong Whitworth and the Lancashire Cotton Corporation were perhaps the two most significant projects with which Peacock became involved, his work at Barings was much more broadly based. On Revelstoke's death he 'took over general direction of the firm, and particularly the control of policy and dealing with confidential accounts' {QUA 2170 I 16}. His senior partners, by virtue of years of service, acknowledged that he stood 'some eight or ten years nearer to the starting line' {BBA Cecil Baring to Lord Stamfordham 21 May 1929}. By the end of 1929 his interest in the partnership of Baring Brothers & Co, which effectively controlled the bank, was made equal to that of the other seniors. In 1933 he strengthened Barings' management by bringing in as a director, C H G Millis ('My Millis') of Slaughter & May, the City solicitors. As leader he oversaw the commercial credit business in the difficult years of the 1930s but he was not concerned with its day-to-day direction. Indeed, he joined Barings with no experience of accepting and persuaded Farrer to stay on for a year in order 'to initiate me into the mysteries of Barings' business' {QUA 2170 I 16}. In international finance his role was more energetic. In the 1920s Barings, invariably as part of a syndicate including N M Rothschild & Sons and J Henry Schroder & Co, made numerous bond issues for continental Governments, provinces and municipalities to finance reconstruction of capital infrastructure or to stabilise their currencies. They were equally involved in the issue of South American securities, especially those of the Brazilian Government and the State of São Paulo, while Barings retained their reputation in London as unchallenged experts in Argentine finance. When the world's economy faltered in the late-1920s, Barings became party to schemes to facilitate debt payments. Most notable of these was the creation of the Anglo

Argentine Convention Trust and the conversion of a substantial proportion of Argentine long-term debt held in Britain.

Apart from the reconstruction of staple industries, Barings, under Peacock's leadership, played an active role in the financing of the so-called 'new industries'. In 1926 Barings were appointed financial agents to the Underground Electric Railways Co of London Ltd which held controlling interests in a considerable number of underground, tram and omnibus companies in the capital. Later in 1926 Peacock joined the board (until 1929), and in his two capacities played a central role in the company's capital reorganisation and in its issue of new capital to finance extension of the Underground network. In the 1930s he also oversaw issues for such companies as North Metropolitan Power Station Co Ltd; Charing Cross Electricity Supply Co Ltd; British Tanker Co Ltd; and Goodyear Tyre & Rubber (Great Britain 1927) Ltd. When the Royal Mail group of shipping companies crashed in 1931, Barings, working closely with the Bank of England, arranged for the assets of the important component, Elder Dempster, to be acquired by Ocean Steamship Co Ltd.

Peacock's return to the Bank's Court and the Committee of Treasury almost immediately after Revelstoke's death in 1929 enabled him to resume his official role in the Bank's monetary and industrial policy. In reality, since 1924 he had never been far from the Governor's side; there was scarcely a day when he did not cover the 200 yards from Barings to the Governor's office. The two worked extremely closely and on more than one occasion Peacock forced the pace. He later explained that 'I was the favourite of the Governor and it came to be recognised that if things were to be got through with the Governor I had better make the approach, and that happened very often' {ibid 2170 1 16}. The activities of the Bank of England, many of which were pioneering as it completed its metamorphosis into a fully fledged central bank, are well described in the entry on Montagu Norman. It is sufficient here to indicate the profound influence exercised by Peacock in its affairs. When Norman fell ill between July and September 1931, it was Peacock who appeared alongside the Deputy Governor as the natural leader of the Bank, and steered it through the crisis which led to the fall of the Government and forced the country from the Gold Standard. Over a two-month period he and the Deputy Governor were in conference with the Prime Minister and Chancellor almost every day and kept the two other Party leaders informed. When the Governor took the unprecedented step of calling a press conference in 1930 to explain the formation of the Bankers' Industrial Development Corporation as a vehicle to assist industrial reconstruction it was Peacock who sat at his side. In 1932 he was made party to the deliberations of the tiny 'Hush Hush Committee', which planned the War Loan Conversion as a step to cheaper money. The Peacock Committee, formed in 1931 under his chairmanship, investigated the Bank's organisation in order to reduce the direct burden falling on the Governor by the creation of a more broadly-based Executive. He retired from the Bank of England in 1946 but in 1952 was asked by the Governor to examine the question of establishing a financial concern to finance projects in the Dominions and Colonies. Out of this was born the Commonwealth Development Finance Co Ltd of which Peacock was a director from its inception in 1953 until 1959. He had reluctantly accepted this task, realising the great disparity between the needs of the Commonwealth and the resources which Britain could provide.

Peacock was a valued adviser to successive British Governments and to politicians. He was especially friendly with Treasury officials Sir Warren Fisher and Sir Richard Hopkins. His most notable appointment was as a Treasury Representative concerned with the wartime disposal of direct British investments in the United States. In early 1941 Britain's dollar and gold reserves began to run dangerously low at a time when the Neutrality Acts ruled out any Government-to-Government dollar loans. Moreover, a powerful lobby in the United States was far from convinced that Britain had done everything she could to finance her war effort through the liquidation of her assets. In these difficult and unpleasant circumstances Peacock oversaw the rushed and controversial sale of Britain's most valuable asset in North America, Courtauld's American Viscose Corporation, for $62 million. Subsequently, through an effective series of delaying tactics and relying heavily on old friends, he was able to negotiate loans totalling $425 million against the collateral of remaining British direct assets thus preventing their enforced sale at inevitable bargain prices. In 1943 the Chancellor of the Exchequer and the Governor called on his services again and sent him on a top secret information-gathering mission to Canada. As Commander Royal and aged well over seventy, he flew out to Toronto in the belly of a bomber aircraft, laying on floor boards and packed like a sardine with fellow passengers.

In March 1929 the Prime Minister invited him to take up the chairmanship of the Channel Tunnel Committee and, pressed by Revelstoke who was anxious to help Baldwin in the run-up to the general election, agreed to do so. Its Report, presented to parliament in 1930 and favouring the building of rail tunnels, was not acted upon. With this responsibility on his hands, he declined the new Labour Government's invitation in mid-1929 to join a Consultative Committee to consider Government-aided schemes to reduce unemployment. In 1934 he was appointed a member of the Royal Commission on Tithes. Only occasional glimpses of his connections with politicians can be obtained. He was well known to the senior Labour Minister, J H Thomas, and was a source of advice for him on emigration to Canada, a favourite subject of Peacock. In March 1929, at the invitation of the Minister of Labour and his old friend Sir Arthur Steel-Maitland, he sketched out some arguments which the Conservative Party could put before the electorate on the vexed question of rising unemployment. On the one hand he pointed to foundations laid for future prosperity through the recent initiation of industrial rationalisation schemes — 'rationalisation means higher wages and a higher standard of living in spite of the fact that there may be short intervals of less employment' {BBA, PF 38 A}. On the other, he urged the creation of jobs through the modernisation of the docks, the extension of land drainage schemes, and the clearing of slums.

Peacock's knowledge of finance and the securities market made him a valued adviser to charitable bodies. Notwithstanding the enormous workload of his daily responsibilities he was involved with many such bodies, participating fully in general policy as much as in finance. At the behest of the Prince of Wales he took a prominent part in the foundation of the National Council of Social Service, being an active chairman from

1940 until 1953 of the General Purposes Committee which agreed policy. He was especially important in determining the continuation and development of the Citizens' Advice Bureau Service when its future was in doubt on the conclusion of the war. In succession to Revelstoke, he became treasurer to King Edward's Hospital Fund and chairman of its Finance Committee in 1929, continuing as treasurer until 1954 and as a member of the General Council until 1961. Between the wars the Fund became a mainstay of voluntary hospitals in London and after the introduction of the National Health Service used its resources to fill gaps in the new Service and raise standards of care generally. Until his death he was chairman of the Trustees of the Imperial War Graves Commission to which he had been appointed in 1926; chairman of the Board of Management of the Royal Commission for the Exhibition of 1851; and a Trustee of King George's Jubilee Fund from its creation in 1935. From 1925 until his death he was a Rhodes Trustee and in the early years of his appointment worked very closely with Lord Lothian.

Throughout his life he maintained close links with Canada. On the business side he was European director of the Canadian Pacific Railway Co from 1926 until his death, while also in 1926 he was appointed to the Grand Truck Pacific Railway Advisory Committee on Debenture Stock. From 1931 until 1952 he was on the board of the Hudson Bay Company. He also continued as a board member of the Brazilian Traction Light & Power Co Ltd, although he resigned from the Barcelona Co in 1925 and from the Mexican Co in 1927. As such he played a central role in the formation of the Société Internationale d'Energie Hydro-Electrique (SIDRO) by the Belgian financiers Dannie Heineman and Alfred Loewenstein, which gained control of the Barcelona Co, and also in preventing the controversial and flamboyant Loewenstein from gaining control of Brazilian Traction. As chairman of the wartime Overseas Committee of Canadian National Service Fund Advisory Board, he helped supervise the finances of all welfare agencies for Canadian Forces abroad. He was active in the creation of several vehicles to invest in Canadian securities. Most notable of these was Harris & Partners in 1952 when Barings joined with Morgan Grenfell and Canadian interests to form a company to issue, underwrite and deal in securities in the Canadian market. Peacock was its first chairman. He was a generous benefactor in Canada, in particular to his old university, Queen's, of which he was a member of the Board of Trustees from 1912 until 1947. He endowed two chairs.

Peacock succeeded Revelstoke to many of his offices. Most notable was the Receivership General of the Duchy of Cornwall, an important role in the management of the Royal Family's finances, which he took up in July 1929. Revelstoke, a close friend of George V, had presumably groomed Peacock for the task, but his emergence as an intimate adviser on a whole range of matters was astonishingly swift. When the economic and political crisis of 1931 reached its climax it was Peacock with whom the King chose to dine on the Sunday evening that Ramsay Macdonald was invited to form a National Government on tendering his resignation as Prime Minister. Following this audience Peacock drove the Prime Minister back to Downing Street, entering by the back gate in order to avoid the Press, and encouraged acceptance of the King's wish as the opposition leaders arrived for preliminary discussions. At the time of the Abdication, Peacock, while not condoning Edward VIII's decision, was at his side for long hours in the weeks leading up to the crisis offering advice, in the most delicate of circumstances, well beyond financial matters. He had already come to know the King 'exceptionally well' {QUA 2170.1.16}. His skill at maintaining the middle ground enabled him to play a key role in the subsequent financial negotiations. Certainly at one difficult lawyers' meeting, the new King found Peacock to be 'a very great help' {Donaldson (1974) 292}. He held office as Receiver General until 1961 having served four sovereigns.

In 1934 the King appointed him a GCVO in recognition of his services to the Royal Family. He was a Lieutenant of the City of London and received honorary degrees from Oxford (1932), Edinburgh (1938) and Queen's.

Sir Edward retired from Barings at the end of 1954 at the age of eighty-three. He had laid secure foundations for Barings' growing corporate finance business although it is probable he had remained for too long in a key executive position. Despite his distinguished role in finance and his many charitable interests, he kept well from the public eye. His public utterances were few, and after his departure from Upper Canada College he did not publish. A tall, handsome and dignified man with clear eyes and firm features, he possessed great presence. He was as reassuring as he was self-confident but the hallmark of his qualities was clarity of thought. Contemporaries described him as wise rather than clever, and doubtless it was a faculty that underpinned his work as a successful mediator. Above all, his contemporaries remember him as a self-effacing and humble man. Towards the end of his life he dismissed 'I have fought the good fight' as too arrogant by far — and doubtless too final! — as his motto. He chose instead 'It is always time to be doing good'.

In 1912 he married Katherine, daughter of John Coates of Ottawa and they brought up two adopted daughters. Sir Edward Peacock died on 19 November 1962, aged ninety-one, universally recognised throughout the City of London as 'The Elder Statesman of Finance'. He left £133,440 gross.

JOHN ORBELL

Writings:

'Trusts, Combines and Monopolies' *Queen's Quarterly* 1898.

Canada, A Descriptive Text-Book (Toronto, 1900).

PP, Report of the Channel Tunnel Committee (1929-30) Cmd 3513 (chairman).

Sources:

Unpublished

Baring Brothers, London, archives.

Queen's University Archives, Kingston, Ontario, Canada. Peacock Papers, presented by Professor G S Graham, Rhodes Professor of Imperial History, Emeritus, University of London.

Rhodes Trust Annual Report, Dec 1926.

Information from Professor G S Graham.

Published

Sir Henry Clay, *Lord Norman* (Macmillan, 1957).

DNB.

Frances Donaldson, *Edward VIII* (Weidenfeld & Nicolson, 1974).

H P Gundy, 'Sir Edward Peacock' *Douglas Library Notes* Queen's University, 12,1 (1963).

John E Kendle, *The Round Table Movement and Imperial Union* (Toronto: University of Toronto Press, 1975).

Arthur W Kiddy, 'Sir Edward Peacock' *The Banker* Oct 1941.

Richard S Sayers, *The Bank of England 1891-1944* (3 vols, Cambridge: Cambridge University Press, 1976).

Times 20 Nov 1962.

WWW.

PEACOCK, John Atkins

(1898-1979)

Egg and provisions wholesaler

Jack Peacock (from Katherine Baker, Nurdin and Peacock Ltd: A History 1810–1977).

John (Jack) Atkins Peacock was born in London on 8 September 1898, the second son of Thomas Peacock and his second wife Maude née Atkins, the daughter of a Suffolk doctor. Jack's father was a partner in the London provisions merchants Nurdin & Peacock which at that time traded mainly in imported eggs. His parents divorced when he was eleven.

Nurdin & Peacock had developed from a small egg wholesaling business founded by a Frenchman, Paul Nurdin, in London around 1810. In the 1820s Nurdin employed John Peacock, Jack's great-grandfather, and the men became close friends. In 1842, Nurdin made Peacock a partner and on his death twelve years later left him his share of the business. Ownership and control of the business thereafter resided with the Peacock family.

PEACOCK John Atkins

Jack's father, Thomas, extended the range of the company's interests. In 1910 he set up an agency called Peacock & Co to import eggs, butter and cheese. He also purchased Newman & Guardia, a firm manufacturing photographic and scientific equipment. In 1919 Nurdin & Peacock Ltd was formed with a capital of £100,000 to take over the constituent businesses. Whilst still in his early twenties, Jack was given responsibility for managing Newman & Guardia and in 1923 he took over management of Peacock & Co from his elder brother, Ronald, who left to set up his own business which failed some years later. In 1924, at the age of twenty-six, he was appointed a director of Nurdin & Peacock and undertook a major assignment in 1925, travelling to South Africa to arrange the purchase and shipment of eggs for the British market.

In the inter-war period progress was steady; new sources of supply for eggs were established, pickled eggs from Italy, tinned eggs from China, frozen eggs from Australia and shell eggs from South Africa. Butter and cheese were imported especially from Australia and New Zealand and the firm was the first in England to use butter packing machinery (imported from Germany) which established the $\frac{1}{2}$lb pack as the standard. At the same time, direct importing was gradually reduced and more purchases were made through other importers. Peacock & Co in Tooley Street by the London docks handled this aspect of dealing.

Jack Peacock was appointed chairman of the London Egg Exchange in 1939, though he held this post for only a few months, until war broke out. He then became Director of the Imported Eggs Division of the Ministry of Food and the following year had his field of responsibility extended to include home-produced eggs. He had the formidable task of organising the collection, production and distribution of eggs in England and arranging for the importation of eggs, mainly from Canada and the USA. Jack Peacock's major innovation at the Ministry of Food during the Second World War was the development of dried eggs for domestic and commercial use; this made a significant saving of shipping tonnage needed for imports. For this important wartime work he was awarded the CMG in 1949. Jack remained with the Ministry of Food until 1954 and during this period organised the formation of the Egg Marketing Board. With the death of his father in 1949, he took control of Nurdin & Peacock as executive chairman, a post he held until his death.

Problems of deliveries to and from the warehouse just off Oxford Circus forced the firm to consider an alternative location and the move to Raynes Park, completed in 1960 only a few weeks before parking restrictions were imposed in Central London, gave them a 2.5 acre site with excellent road access. The employment of a cashier to deal with customers who wished to collect their own purchases from the warehouse and rising transport costs persuaded the company to make the change to cash-and-carry, which was also preferred by customers. The first two wholesale cash-and-carry warehouses were opened that year to serve the retail grocery trade which was to come under increasing pressure from the multiple grocery chains such as Sainsburys and Tesco. Turnover in 1960 was just over £5 million before the cash-and-carry warehouses opened and the profit record was variable. By 1968 there were 17 cash-and-carry branches with a turnover of £15.7 million while the turnover of the other activities was only £100,000. Profits had increased steadily from the early 1960s to £326,000 after tax. When the company went public in 1968 with an offer of 2s shares by tender (which sold at a striking price of 15s) control of the majority of shares still rested with the family interests. By 1977 sales had increased to £214 million, profits to £2.6 million after tax. Computer control had been introduced into the 25 warehouses which were nearly all located in the South-East, the newest and most outlying branches being at Avonmouth and Nottingham.

Jack in 1925 married Phyllis, daughter of Edwin Horace Jones, an engineer; they had two sons and a daughter. The second of his sons, William Michael, succeeded him as chairman. Jack Peacock died on 24 October 1979, leaving £973,077 gross.

ALAN C McKINNON

Sources:

Unpublished

C Reg: Nurdin & Peacock (158,287).

BCe.

MCe.

PrC.

Published

Katherine Baker, *Nurdin & Peacock Ltd: A History 1810-1977* (pp, Nurdin & Peacock, 1979).

Stock Exchange Official Year Book 1976-77.

WWW.

Sir Kenneth Peacock, chairman of GKN from 1953-1965 (courtesy of Guest Keen & Nettlefolds PLC).

PEACOCK, Sir Kenneth Swift

(1902-1968)

Steel engineering manufacturer

Kenneth Swift Peacock was born at Walsall, Staffordshire, on 19 February 1902, the only son of Tom Swift Peacock (d 1946) and his wife Elizabeth Amy née Richards. He was educated at Oundle School and on leaving there in May 1920 entered the GKN group where his father had risen to high office. In 1892 T S Peacock had joined F W Cotterill Ltd, manufacturers of nuts and bolts at Darlaston, as their company secretary. He became general manager in the following year and the managing director in 1900. When, in 1919, GKN, who already had large screw interests, decided to extend their fastener business and acquired Cotterills, T S Peacock was appointed a director of the main board. In the following year, under the reorganisation inspired by the merger with John Lysaght Ltd, he rose to joint managing director of GKN. From July 1933 T S Peacock also served as their deputy chairman, a post he held until retirement in July 1941.

Kenneth Peacock first worked in GKN's Heath Street factory where they manufactured Nettlefold woodscrews. Apart from the steelworks, this was the company's largest operating plant and the source of most of its profits. There, under T Z Lloyd, Peacock learned about the business in its various aspects but eventually specialised in sales and marketing. Success in this crucial part of the group resulted in Peacock's promotion to the main board in July 1933. He then set about recruiting able young graduates or professionals to become managers. In January 1936, when still in his early thirties, Peacock became a joint managing director of GKN. Peacock took responsibility, then and afterwards, for negotiating the important trade agreements with Continental screwmakers which helped to ensure that GKN remained the leading manufacturer in Britain. He played a leading part in guiding GKN through the vicissitudes of the Second World War and established himself by his knowledge of its widespread interests thoughout the world, taking a special interest in the fastener, steel and re-rolling sides.

From August 1950 Peacock combined the roles of deputy chairman and managing director, an indication that he had been selected for the principal executive office. Peacock succeed J H Jolly (qv) as chairman in July 1953. Although relinquishing the post of managing director in January 1964, he retained the chairmanship of GKN until his retirement in August 1965 when R P Brookes (qv) became the chief executive. To recognise his long service, Sir Kenneth Peacock was elected to the honorary office of president of the company.

As GKN's steelworks had been nationalised in 1951, one of Peacock's earliest actions on becoming chairman was to re-acquire them from the Iron & Steel Holding and Realisation Agency. He had, in fact, already moved his office from the Heath Street works to head office and in 1948 under the threat of state ownership he had been responsible for the formation of GKN (Midlands) Ltd and GKN (South Wales) Ltd to remove the group's re-rolling and fastener plant from acquisition. The medium-sized steelworks at East Moors, Cardiff, formerly owned jointly with Baldwins Ltd was purchased outright in 1954 and re-named Guest, Keen Iron & Steel Co, while the adjacent rolling mills and wire-drawing and nailmaking plants, GKN South Wales, were also recovered in the same year. In 1955 GKN bought back Normanby Park and Brymbo steelworks, the latter having been acquired largely at Peacock's suggestion in 1948 to provide special steels for the group's forging companies. This policy was determined by the necessity of obtaining steel in regular quantities and standard quality. Steel for the engineering side of the group (particularly for screws and fasteners) could only be guaranteed in time of shortages by vertical integration. Sales to outside customers were considered of secondary importance and as a means of allowing plant to operate at an optimum rate. However, with the exception of the East Moors plant which had been extensively rebuilt in 1934-36 at a cost of £3 million, these works were not modern (both Brymbo and Normanby Park had been opened before the First World War) and they required further heavy capital spending. Accordingly, in 1957, Peacock initiated a major programme of reinvestment in steel. Some £13.25 million were to be spent at Normanby Park on new coke ovens, a sinter plant, blast furnace and additional rolling mills, while a further £1.75 would provide Brymbo with new electric furnaces. Capital was repeatedly ploughed into the company's steelmaking plants: £7.9 million in 1958, £7.8 million in 1959, £6 million in 1960, £8.9 million in 1961 and £9.6 million in 1962. Despite these various schemes for modernisation, the surplus on trading from the steelworks gradually declined: £8.6 million, £10.6 million, £11.8 million, £6.4 million and £4.9 million per annum from 1958 to 1962. However, these figures are not wholly accurate records of performance as high rates of depreciation had been charged each year to pay for the reinvestment programme, a policy urged upon the steelmakers by the BSIF.

The engineering side of the GKN group was not neglected as capital reinvestment there followed: £6.1 million, £5.3 million, £7 million, £7.5 million and £6.3 million per annum respectively between 1958 and 1962. These figures obscure the real expansion which was chiefly secured by acquisition. The surplus on trading was nevertheless at a higher level than in steel — £9.4 million, £9.4 million, £11.4 million, £10.4 million and £9.2 million per annum, respectively.

For the group as a whole, profits before tax rose consistently during the 1950s as markets recovered and shortages were overcome. Climbing from £7.7 million in 1953 to £24.9 million in 1958, they attained a peak of £31.62 million in 1960. In the following year profits fell to £22.76 million and remained at this level until the last year of Peacock's chairmanship: £22.3 in 1962, £24.5 million in 1963 and £31.74 in 1964. This occurred despite the fact that worldwide turnover grew strongly throughout the period of his office, rising from £84.7 million in 1953, to £251.5 million in 1960 and £338.1 million in 1964.

The expansion of GKN from the time that Peacock became managing director resulted in various organisational problems. In 1948 the GKN group comprised 32 operating companies within the UK; by 1953 the number had reached 40, by 1960 was 48 and in 1964 had grown to 65. Appreciating the strain this imposed on the existing holding-subsidiary company relationship, in 1963 Peacock and his colleagues commissioned Production-Engineering Ltd, management consultants, to consider the structure of the group. This led to the formation of 'sub-groups', though the full implementation of their report, published in November 1964, followed under Brookes, his successor. Under this scheme head office functions were concentrated but a degree of responsibility delegated to the sub-groups whose chairmen were each represented on the main board. Some steps, had, in fact, already been taken to reorganise the running of the group and the principles on which it was to be operated had been outlined. In January 1961 GKN Steel was formed to oversee the three steelworks and to co-ordinate policy between them. At the same time as the acquisition of the Acton Bolt group from Pearson in December 1962, moves were made to concentrate GKN's screw and fastener operations; in that year both GKN Bolts & Nuts and GKN Screws & Fasteners were formed. The creation of GKN Forgings & Castings in January 1964, embracing eight subsidiary companies, also followed this trend. Peacock, in retrospect, considered that the purchase of the Acton Bolt group, which operated in a market that was shortly to be eclipsed, was a retrograde step.

Kenneth Peacock was knighted in 1963. His outside directorships included Lloyds Bank (1949-66), the United Steel Cos Ltd (1955-66), and the Steel Co of Wales Ltd (1957-66). He was a member of the Council and Executive Committee of the British Iron and Steel Federation.

In his youth Sir Kenneth Peacock had been a keen amateur racing driver and in 1929-34 competed in the RAC Tourist Trophy races in Ireland and the 24-hour competition at Le Mans often as a member of the Lea-Francis, Riley and Aston Martin teams. He won the Rudge-Whitworth Cup and was awarded the 'Index of Performance' at Le Mans in 1934. An enthusiastic horse rider, he hunted with the North Cotswold Hounds, the Devon and Somerset Stag Hounds and the Exmoor Foxhounds.

His first marriage was in 1925 to Hilaria (d 1926), daughter of Sir Geoffrey Syme of Melbourne, by whom they had a daughter. In 1934 Peacock married Norma Rigby; they had two sons.

Unlike his father, who had the reputation of being a tough disciplinarian of an autocratic nature, Sir Kenneth Peacock was a manager of kindness, sensitivity and modesty, who was regarded affectionately at all levels. He possessed an imaginative mind, a compendious memory and sound business judgement; he had a profound knowledge of the group and the inter-relationships between its constituent parts, whilst maintaining a commitment to long-term investment and prudent financial policy. A concern for employees resulted in a good industrial relations record. During Peacock's chairmanship, GKN, already a major manufacturing group with strong overseas elements, continued to grow consistently and successfully. Sir Kenneth Peacock died aged sixty-six on 6 September 1968, leaving £76,405 gross.

EDGAR JONES

Sources:

Unpublished

Information from various GKN Departments and Sir Anthony Bowlby, W W Fea, J F Howard, S Lloyd and F C Rowbottom.

GKN Annual Reports 1953-64.

PrC.

Published

Nettlefolds News Aug 1963.

Times 9 Sept 1968.

WWW.

Andrew Pears (from W H Beable, The Romance of Great Businesses Heath Cranton, 1926).

PEARS, Andrew

(1846-1909)

Soap manufacturer

Andrew Pears was born at 55 Wells Street, off Oxford Street, London on 21 January 1846, the son of Francis Pears and his wife Mary née Williams. His great-grandfather Andrew Pears (d 1838), the son of a Cornish farmer, had started making soap for his barber's shop in Gerrard Street, Soho, London in 1789. He developed a toilet soap whose transparency was regarded as indicative of its purity and to prevent unscrupulous imitations Andrew Pears Sr autographed each package of soap. Andrew Pears Sr, now based in a shop at 55 Wells Street, London, in 1835 took his grandson, Francis, into partnership, the business taking the name of A & F Pears. By 1860 Pears and Knights were the largest manufacturers in the toilet soap trade. Pears expanded after 1864 when the energetic and aggressive Thomas J Barratt (qv) joined the firm.

Little is known about Andrew Pears's early career. He entered the family soap business before he was nineteen. After Barratt married Andrew's sister Mary in 1865, the firm was reorganised with a total capital of £7,000 and with Andrew, his father and Barratt as joint partners. While Barratt took responsibility for the London shop (with one assistant) in Great Russell Street and for marketing, Andrew, still a minor, took charge of production at the firm's soap works (built in 1862) at Isleworth, Middlesex.

Francis Pears, who regarded Barratt's expenditures as reckless, retired in 1875, though he left £4,000 in the firm. Thereafter Barratt increased advertising investments and the demand which this created, in a society enjoying a rising standard of living, was met by a growth in productive capacity supervised by Andrew Pears. In 1864 the Isleworth 'factory' worked one pan three times a week and employed very few hands. Andrew Pears lived in a house next door to the works. By 1892 the works at Isleworth comprised two factory complexes, the Lanadron Works and the Orchard Works, warehouses, offices, manager's house and stabling, all held freehold and valued at £121,191.

The partnership between manufacturer and salesman or the combination of their skills in one individual, increasingly evident in other businesses producing luxury goods, led in the case of Pears to the ascendancy of the salesman: in 1891, profits amounted to £176,950, 'before deducting costs of advertisments' {Times *Prospectuses* (1892) 54} which were £103,956 — net profits being calculated as £72,994. When the firm went public the following year Barratt became chairman while Pears became a director.

Locally Andrew Pears was regarded as model employer, being the first to introduce the 48-hour week without a reduction in wages and, it was reported, found no fall in production despite reduced hours. He gave $3\frac{1}{2}$ acres to the Pears Athletic Club (of which he was president) for playing fields, and other property to the County Schools. An active leader of the local Liberal party, he supported Home Rule for Ireland but declined offers to stand for parliament because of his business commitments. In addition he was a JP for Middlesex, one of the first county aldermen, school governor, chairman of the Isleworth Board of Charity Trustees, and a freemason. A keen sportsman, he enjoyed shooting, rowing and, later, motoring.

Andrew Pears died on 10 February 1909 at his home, 'Mevagissey', St John's Road, Isleworth (once a part of Sir Joseph Banks's estate). He left £123,433 and was survived by his wife, six sons and three daughters, his son Andrew Pears Jr having predeceased him by a few weeks.

DAVID J JEREMY

Sources:

Unpublished

BCe.

PrC.

Published

William Henry Beable, *Romance of Great Businesses* (2 vols, Heath Cranton Ltd, 1926).

Middlesex Chronicle 16 Feb 1909.

Clement K Shorter, 'The Romance of the House of Pears' *Pears Cyclopaedia* 19th ed (1915).

Times 11, 13 Feb 1909.

Times *Prospectuses* 3 (1892).

Charles A Wilson, *The History of Uniliver. A Study in Economic Growth and Social Change* (2 vols, Cassell, 1954).

Sir C A Pearson (from S Dark, The Life of Sir Arthur Pearson).

PEARSON, Sir Cyril Arthur

(1866-1921)

Newspaper proprietor

Cyril Arthur Pearson was born at Wookey, Somerset, on 24 February 1866, the only son of Rev Arthur Cyril Pearson, Rector of Springfield, Essex, and his wife Philippa née Maxwell Lyte, a grand-daughter of the hymn writer, Henry Francis Lyte. He was educated at Eagle House, Wimbledon, and, briefly, at Winchester, an experience he regarded as 'a waste of time and money' {Fraser (1961) 24}. George Newnes's (qv) *Tit-bits*, where he secured a post as a clerk in 1884 by winning first prize in one of its competitions, was a more important formative influence.

Prodigious energy and precocious managerial skill ensured rapid advancement. In six years with Newnes, Pearson's annual salary rose from £100 to £350 in recognition of his appointment as manager of *Tit-bits* in 1885 and, additionally, as business manager of the *Review of Reviews* in 1889. Though he was able to supplement this income by freelance journalism, family responsibilities encouraged him to seek greater rewards. Refused a rise in 1890, he broke with Newnes, raised a private loan of £3,000 and started *Pearson's Weekly*, a publication differing from *Tit-bits* only in that it was 'a bigger pennyworth and offered larger and more attractive prizes in its competitions' {*Sell's* (1901) 153}.

Adaptation of the successful formula developed by Newnes and Alfred Harmsworth (qv), combined with vigorous and often ingenious sales promotions, raised the circulation of *Pearson's Weekly* to a peak of 1,250,000 in 1897 and secured a major share of the expanding market for cheap magazines. It was the first of a series of weeklies which, as one Pearson editor explained, contrived to be 'just what the average person wants to read' {*Newspaper Owner and Manager* 12 Oct 1898}. In 1896, on the formation of C Arthur Pearson Ltd, the business, of which Pearson owned 51 per cent, was valued at £360,000.

As a daily newspaper proprietor, Pearson was less successful than as a weekly proprietor. Though his assessment of the 'practically illimitable' market for a new halfpenny daily proved sound, the *Daily Express*, launched in 1900, recovered slowly from substantial early losses and was 'inadvertently neglected' between 1903 and 1905 while Pearson directed the operations of the Tariff Reform League as executive chairman and served as vice-chairman of the Tariff Commission {Blumenfeld (1933) 192}. His protectionist inclinations led to an unhappy connection with the *Standard*, bought in 1904 on behalf of a Chamberlainite syndicate and sold in 1910, with the modestly profitable *Evening Standard*, when Pearson had despaired of 'a publication which showed no signs of becoming a genuine financial proposition' {Dark (1922) 125}. Pearson's projected Crewe-based network of provincial dailies foundered on the persistent unprofitability of such properties as the *Birmingham Gazette and Express*; his hopes of controlling the *Times* evaporated when he was dramatically out-manouevred by Northcliffe in 1908.

When Pearson's sight failed in 1912, he sold his newspaper interests, devoting himself to the welfare of the blind. His fund-raising rescued the National Institute for the Blind from near bankruptcy (he carried its income from £8,010 in 1913 to £358,174 in 1921) and supported, after 1915, the St Dunstan's hostels for blinded ex-servicemen, 'the biggest single business I ever conducted' {Pearson (1919) 32}. He continued, also, to work for the Fresh Air Fund, which he had established in 1892 to provide country holidays for East End children.

In 1916 he was created a baronet and in 1917 received the GBE. Pearson married twice: firstly in 1887 to Isobel Sarah, daughter of Rev F Bennett of Salisbury, by whom he had three daughters who survived him; secondly in 1897 to Ethel Maude (created OBE, 1920), daughter of W J Fraser of Herne Bay (their only child, Neville Arthur (b 1898) succeeded to the baronetcy). Sir Arthur Pearson died after an accident in his bath in London on 9 December 1921. He left £93,927 gross.

DILWYN PORTER

Writings:

'Blinded in Battle' *National Review* 67 (Mar 1916).

Victory Over Blindness: How It Was Won by the Men of St Dunstan's and How Others May Win It (Hodder & Stoughton, 1919).

The Conquest of Blindness (Hodder & Stoughton, 1921).

Sources:

Unpublished

BL, Northcliffe papers, Add MSS 62172.

BLPES, Brittain papers; Tariff Commission papers, TC 6 1/26.

House of Lords RO, Blumenfeld papers.

Sheffield University Library, Hewins papers.

BCe.

MCe.

PrC.

Published

Ralph D Blumenfeld, *RDB's Diary* (Heinemann, 1930).

—, *All in a Lifetime* (E Benn, 1931).

—, *The Press in My Time* (Rich & Cowen, 1933).

—, *RDB's Procession* (Nicholson & Watson, 1935).

Harry Brittain, *Pilgrims and Pioneers* (Hutchinson, 1946).

Viscount Camrose, *British Newspapers and Their Controllers* (Cassell, 1947).

Daily Express 10 Dec 1921.

Sidney Dark, *The Life of Sir Arthur Pearson* (Hodder & Stoughton, 1922).

DNB.

Thomas H S Escott, *Masters of English Journalism: A Study of Personal Forces* (T Fisher Unwin, 1911).

Lord Fraser of Lonsdale, *Whereas I Was Blind* (Hodder & Stoughton, 1942).-

—, *My Story of St Dunstan's* (Harrap, 1961).

M T Gammage, 'The Birmingham Daily Gazette: A Case Study of the Conservative Provincial Press' *West Midland Studies* 13 (1980).

The History of the Times (Times Publishing Co, 1947).

Stephen Koss, *The Rise and Fall of the Political Press in Britain* (2 vols, Hamish Hamilton, 1981-84).

Alan J Lee, *The Origins of the Popular Press in England 1855-1914* (Croom Helm, 1976).

Maurice Milne, *Newspapers of Northumberland and Durham* (Newcastle upon Tyne: Frank Graham, 1972).

Newspaper Owner and Manager 12 Oct 1898.

Newspaper Owner and Modern Printer 7 Mar 1900.

Newspaper World 16 Dec 1916, 17 Dec 1921.

Dilwyn Porter, 'A Newspaper Owner in Politics: Arthur Pearson and the Tariff Reform League' *Moirae: Journal of the School of Politics, Philosophy and History, Ulster Polytechnic* 5 (1980).

Reginald Pound and G Harmsworth, *Northcliffe* (Cassell, 1959).

Public Opinion 11 Nov 1904.

Sell's Dictionary of the World's Press (H Sell, 1901).

John D Symon, *The Press and Its Story* (Seeley, Service & Co, 1914).

Mary G Thomas, *The Royal National Institute for the Blind* (Brighton: *Brighton Herald* Ltd, 1958).

Times 10 Dec 1921.

John B Wainewright, *Winchester College 1836-1906: A Register* (Winchester, 1907).

Leonard H West, 'Newspaper Companies as Investments' *Sells Dictionary of the World's Press* (H Sell, 1898).

Who's Who in Kent, Surrey and Sussex (Horace Cox, 1911).

WWW.

PEARSON, Sir James Reginald

(1897-1984)

Motor vehicle manufacturer

Sir Reginald Pearson (courtesy of Vauxhall Motors Ltd).

James Reginald Pearson was born at Dudley, Worcestershire, on 17 November 1897, the son of George Henry Pearson, a fender moulder, and his wife Annie née Stringer. After a period in the local infants school he moved to the Park Demonstration School and later to Dudley Higher Elementary School. He left school at fifteen but continued evening classes at a local technical college.

His working life began with a machining apprenticeship with the firm of Bullers Ltd of Tipton which he pursued from 1913 until joining the Royal Flying Corps for a brief spell in 1914. He was recalled to civilian duties and continued his training at the National Projectile Factory in the Black Country. In 1919 Pearson travelled to Luton hoping to secure a job with a local machine-tool company. However, when he arrived the vacancy had been filled, so the young Pearson applied for a job at Vauxhall. He began work with Vauxhall in September 1919 as a centre-lathe turner in the machine shop. Thus began, almost by accident, a career with Vauxhall that was to span forty-three years and that took the young Black Country man from shop floor to boardroom.

Promotion for Pearson really began in 1927 when he became a foreman. Two years later he was made an area manager and in 1934 he became assistant production manager under Charles Bartlett (qv), the managing director. In the crucial year of 1939 Pearson became production manager, and was thus deeply involved in the changeover to wartime production — at first mainly Bedford trucks for the armed services, later Churchill tanks and a wide array of other war matériel.

Both as assistant and production manager, Pearson was closely in contact with the men on the shop floor. A skilled shop floor worker himself, he understood and appreciated the problems which faced the men. He always felt that it was essential for managers to retain a close

The Vauxhall 'Cadet'. The first mass-production car produced by Vauxhall Motors which rolled off the assembly lines in 1930 (courtesy of Vauxhall Motors Ltd).

involvement with the workforce to enable smooth industrial relations which became the hallmark of Vauxhall during most of his management career.

It was he who was largely responsible for the operation of the group bonus system in Vauxhall from the later 1920s until the late 1950s. His aim was always to make time and motion measured operations comfortable for the men and to ensure a reasonable bonus within each group of workers.

In 1942 Pearson was made factory manager, an even more demanding appointment in a plant that was working under great pressure to produce vehicles and other items under government contract. The Luton plant was

1937 Vauxhall 10 (courtesy of Vauxhall Motors Ltd).

1954 Vauxhall Cresta E-type (courtesy of Vauxhall Motors Ltd).

damaged twice by enemy bombers, the worst occasion being in August 1940, but the effect on production was minimal. As the man with major responsibility for keeping the plant in full production, Pearson's contribution to the war effort was very considerable.

During the war he was chairman of the Luton district committee of the Institute of Production Engineers, and also of the Bedfordshire committee of the Eastern Regional Board for Industry.

In 1946 he was appointed a director of Vauxhall Motors, and in 1950 was awarded the OBE. In 1953 he was appointed executive assistant to the managing director, and in 1958 he became deputy chairman. A year later, in 1959, Pearson's contribution to the British motor industry, in peace and war, was further recognised when he was knighted. He retired from Vauxhall Motors in December 1962 and lived in Harpenden, Hertfordshire — near enough to the Luton plant to keep in fairly close touch with his many friends at Vauxhall, until his death.

From 1963 to 1968 Sir Reg, as he was now known to his friends, acted as chairman of the Dawley New Town Corporation in the Midlands, a job to which he brought local knowledge as a Black Country boy himself. For a time he was also a vice-president of the Royal Society for the Prevention of Accidents.

The wide spread and diversity of Sir Reg's other interests can be gauged from his membership of the Glyndebourne Festival Society, the English Speaking Union, and his fellowship of the Royal Horticultural Society. After his retirement he retained close connections with Vauxhall Motors, and was seen at a number of social and recreational events in the Luton area. He was life president of the Vauxhall Motors Recreation Club.

In 1925 he married Nellie Rose (d 1977), daughter of William Scardon Vittery, a draper; they had one daughter. Sir Reginald Pearson died on 17 March 1984, leaving £290,354 gross.

LEN HOLDEN

Writings:

'From Group Bonus to Straight Time Pay' *Journal of Industrial Economics* 1960.

Sources:

Unpublished

BCe.

MCe.

PrC.

Interview with Sir Reginald Pearson 1979.

Published

Philip W Copelin, 'Development and Organisation of Vauxhall Motors Limited' in Ronald S Edwards and Harry Townsend (eds), *Studies in Business Organisation* (Macmillan, 1961).

L D Derbyshire, *The Story of Vauxhall 1857-1946* (Luton, 1946).

L T Holden, 'Think of Me Simply as the Skipper: Industrial Relations at Vauxhall 1920 to 1950' *Oral History* 9 (1981).

Maurice Platt, *An Addiction to Automobiles* (Warne, 1980).

Michael Sedgwick, *Vauxhall* (Beaulieu: National Motor Museum, 1981).

W J Seymour, *An Account of Our Stewardship* (Luton: Vauxhall Motors Ltd, 1946).

Graham Turner, *The Car Makers* (Eyre & Spottiswoode, 1963).

Kenneth Ullyett, *The Vauxhall Companion* (Stanley Paul, 1971).

WW 1982.

Weetman Pearson, 1st Viscount Cowdray (courtesy of Lord Cowdray).

PEARSON, Weetman Dickinson

1st Viscount Cowdray

(1856-1927)

Contractor and builder

Weetman Dickinson Pearson was born at Woodfield House, Kirkburton, near Huddersfield on 15 July 1856, eldest son among the eight children of George Pearson (d 1899) and his wife Sarah Weetman née Dickinson (d 1911). The family firm of builders and contractors, S Pearson & Son, was founded in the year of Weetman's birth when his grandfather Samuel Pearson (d 1884, leaving £20,000), a farmer of Scholes who had gone into partnership with a Huddersfield builder and contractor in 1844, took his eldest son George into partnership. The firm had a brickworks on the Whitehall Road, Cleckheaton, and in the late 1850s undertook railway and water supply contracts in the West Riding. The location of the contracts led Samuel Pearson to move the business to Bradford whence George moved his family.

George Pearson took business lightly and pleasure seriously. While his father held the firm together, his wife dominated the home. She imbued Weetman with a strong will and the determination to resist adversity. Weetman attended a private school, Hallfield, in Bowling, Bradford and then at thirteen was sent to Pannal College, a boarding school at Harrogate. In summer 1872 he returned to his parents at Bradford and at sixteen went straight into the family firm, learning surveying and brickmaking and taking charge of contracts in the absence of his father. In 1874 he was placed in control of the brickworks and the following year his father sent him on a tour of the USA to seek new business, especially orders for bricks, glazed tiles and sanitary piping, which now comprised a major activity of the firm. That tour gave Weetman Pearson his first glimpses of the contours of the international market in building and contracting. 'I returned home with an intense admiration for the Americans ... Some of their methods of work were instructive, their energy and ambition infectious,' he recalled at the end of his life. {Spender (1930) 301}.

Afterwards he was entrusted with the personal superintendence of one of the most important contracts undertaken by the firm, that for the construction of a new main drainage system for the town of Southport, Lancashire, valued at £70,000 gross. A difficult contract, because of the waterlogged, shifting subsoil, it took nearly three years but taught him how to manage a workforce in disagreeable conditions. He was rewarded with a tour of Italy, Greece, Palestine and Constantinople in spring 1879 and, later that year, when his grandfather retired, with the perceptive founder's share of the business. Weetman soon discovered that the firm had an overdraft with its bankers far beyond that warranted by its assets or prospects, partly the result of his father's easygoing optimism. Two contracts, skilfully managed by the new partner pulled the firm out of danger: one worth £60,000 for the main drainage system at Ipswich (carried out in 1879), the second worth £105,000 (the largest to date) for a dock at King's Lynn (1879-84). Weetman took personal charge of both.

At this point Weetman Pearson made two decisions that he thereafter regarded as momentous. In 1881 he married Annie, the eighteen-year-old daughter of Sir John Cass (1832-98), a Bradford millowner. They settled briefly at King's Lynn, and subsequently had a family of three sons and a daughter: Weetman Harold Miller (1882-1933), Bernard Clive (1887-1965), Geoffrey (1891-1914), who was killed in the battle of the Marne, and Gertrude Mary (1884-1954), later wife of the Third Lord Denman. Annie gave unstinted support to her husband, and even accompanied him on one railway contract to Spain (1890) where she arranged for 'hot food and dry sheets ... at the end of the day's march or ride' {*ibid*, 16}. In later years, as a lavish London hostess (who also supported the suffragettes), she displayed the social ambitions he distrusted. Secondly in 1882 Weetman decided to enter the London market. That year he secured from the Metropolitan Board of Works the contract for the construction of the Deptford storm outfall sewer. Though worth only £34,000 it enabled him to move beyond the limited horizons of Yorkshire and the Eastern Counties. In 1884, when the firm's net assets were no more than £30,000, he transferred his headquarters from Bradford to London, taking offices in Delahay Street, Westminster, a location favoured by engineers and contractors. By 1888 the firm moved to 10 Victoria Street and in 1906 added a large office at 47 Parliament Street (formerly the Whitehall Club). Simultaneously Weetman settled his family into a house on Campden Hill, leaving his father in Bradford to run that end of the business. After the move to London Weetman effectively took over the firm and in December 1894 became sole partner. Within two years of his move to London Pearson claimed to be one of the country's leading contractors.

According to J A Spender, between 1880 and 1889 the firm's contracts totalled £4.076 million (for contracts started but not necessarily finished in these years); in 1890-99, £22,153,400; in 1900-9, £12,411,000; in the five years 1910-14, £4,283,600; and in the last decade of Weetman Pearson's life, 1917-27, £8,549,600. Until the late 1880s Pearson was winning large British or imperial contracts, primarily for dock construction at Milford Haven (1885-90), Halifax, Nova Scotia (1886), and Southampton (the Empress Dock 1886-91), besides the Portsea Torpedo Range (1887). In the late 1880s he began to seek business abroad more regularly, starting in 1888 with the Avila to Salamanca railway (which cut 65 miles off the Madrid-Lisbon line) for the Madrid & Portugal Direct Railway Ltd. Then in 1889 Pearson won two contracts which placed him, although he was still in his early thirties, alongside Britain's large imperial contractors like John Aird and John Jackson (qqv). Firstly he secured the contract for the Hudson River Tunnel connecting New York with Jersey City, a project worth £235,000, for which the consulting engineers were Sir John Fowler and Benjamin Baker (qqv) who already had experience of deep-level tunnelling for London's underground railways. Secondly he secured the contract to build the Grand Canal, a huge scheme for draining the 7,000 foot high and 2,220 square mile plateau on which stood Mexico City amid lakes and swamps. After hard and perilous work on the Hudson Tunnel in October and November 1889 Weetman Pearson and his wife had taken the Montezuma Express from New York to Mexico City, partly to recuperate (he had suffered a severe attack of the bends in the tunnelling shield), partly in response to an official invitation from Porfirio Diaz, President of Mexico, to consider tendering for the Grand Canal contract, a copy of which Pearson had received earlier in the year. Pearson made his surveys and followed an earlier plan to take a 29.5 mile long drainage canal north through a mountain tunnel and hence into a river system draining into the Gulf of Mexico. The contract took six years to complete and was worth £2 million, much of which was paid in silver.

The 1890s were clearly the most expansive decade for S Pearson & Son. The firm's net assets stood at £290,000 in 1892 but only six years later had soared to £869,000. In 1898 profit was £130,000 on a turnover of over £1.5 million. The previous year the business was registered as a limited company, S Pearson & Son Ltd, with a capital of £1.5 million (one million £1 ordinary shares, half being issued, and 500,000 £1 preference shares). The step was taken so that the firm could compete for government contracts, Weetman then being an MP. Of the firm's £22 million worth of contracts started during the 1890s, £10.3 million or 47 per cent came from the Mexican Government or Mexican companies — the Vera Cruz Harbour Works, the country's major Atlantic port undertaken in 1895-1902, worth £3 million; the Coatzacoalcos Port Works, 1896-1909, worth £1.4 million; the Tehuantepec National Railway, 190 miles long and linking Coatzacoalcos on the Atlantic and Salina Cruz on the Pacific coast, which employed 5,000 labourers at one time and was built, 1898-1906, worth £2.5 million; and the Salina Cruz Harbour and Docks, 1899-1907, worth £3.3 million, his largest Mexican contract.

Among his largest domestic contracts in the 1890s were three sections of the Lancashire, Derbyshire & East Coast Railway, from Chesterfield to Lincoln, to serve the new Derbyshire and Nottinghamshire coalfields, built 1892-97 and worth £1,035,000; the 33.5 mile loop line from Wootton Bassett near Swindon to Patchway on the South Wales line between Bristol and Newport, built for the GWR 1898-1904 and worth £1.3 million but which involved a loss of nearly £500,000 over which Weetman unsuccessfully fought in the Courts and thereafter never tendered for the GWR; the Great Northern & City Railway Co's line from Finsbury Park to Finsbury Pavement, a distance of three-and-a-half miles, to facilitate the commuter's journey from the north to the City and Bank, built 1898-1906, and worth £2,457,000; and the Admiralty Harbour at Dover, built 1898-1909, and worth £3,365,000; following his experience in New York, Pearson constructed the Blackwall Tunnel then the fourth under the Thames, for London County Council in 1891-97, a contract valued at £870,000.

Between 1900 and the First World War, when the firm won over £16 million of contracts, five out of the 33 contracts were over £1 million: the four East River Tunnels, connecting New York with Long Island, for the Pennsylvania, New York & Long Island Railroad Co, worth £3.5 million and completed 1904-9; Para Port Works, Brazil, worth £2.1 million and completed 1906-11; Hull Joint Dock, worth £1.334 million and built 1906-16; the Royal Albert Dock Extension (South) for the Port of London

Authority, worth £1.398 million and constructed 1912-18; and Valparaiso Port Works, for the Chilean Government, worth £2.71 million and completed 1912-24.

Any explanation for the pattern of Weetman Pearson's success before the First World War, by which time the firm was the leading contractor in the country, must take account of his skills at financial, organisational, labour and technical levels, besides his personal qualities and changes in the international contracting and building market. Early in his career Pearson realised that he needed relatively little finance for undertaking large contracts, providing he could meet two conditions. Firstly he needed accommodation from his bankers. By the late 1880s, when he had contracts in hand worth over £1 million, he was extending his overdraft limits (then £35,000) with the Yorkshire Banking Co by using clients' stocks and shares as collateral. (In 1901 the Midland Bank took over the Yorkshire Banking Co and inherited their Pearson account at the City Square, Leeds, branch.) After 1892, he had a London account with Messrs Williams Deacons Co. In 1900 he opened an account with the Capital & Counties Bank, recording that his contracts in hand were then worth more than £9 million, that his turnover exceeded £1.5 million per annum, and that he needed an overdraft of £100,000 in addition to the two overdrafts for £150,000 each he already had from his two other bankers. In 1900 he used a cement works company as collateral. In effect Pearson's phenomenal expansion was mounted on bank overdrafts as little as 3 to 5 per cent of the value of his current contracts, and since he used his clients' securities as collateral, was self-financing (work done being paid for on a monthly basis).

Secondly, in order to make the majority of his contracts profitable and thereby to sustain his bankers' confidence, Pearson had to get his costings just right: 'A too cautious man would have lost contracts by leaving himself too much margin, and a less prudent one have landed himself in trouble by underestimating his costs and risk.' {*ibid*, 29} Weetman therefore took enormous pains, as his voluminous notebooks show, over his contract specifications: 'He takes nothing for granted, sanctions no method and uses no machinery which he does not thoroughly understand, and not infrequently works out estimates of his own, independently of those of his staff, and not until all this is done, and done again if needs be, does he let his tender go forward.' {*ibid* 30} Most of the contracts he undertook were of the 'measure and value' type in which the work was detailed in the specification and the contractor named his price for each item. He generally opposed the prime cost plus percentage-for-profit contract, on the grounds that it placed the contractor under suspicion of increasing costs to augment profits. Rarely Pearson took on the third type of contract, the lump sum contract, in which he was required to bear all the risk, including the expense of design faults and unforeseen costs.

In the early days everything in the preparation and supervision of contracts fell on Weetman Pearson himself, and throughout his working career he initiated, supervised and financed every contract undertaken by his firm. However, as the business grew and several contracts were being undertaken simultaneously he was forced to rely more and more on lieutenants and on effective organisational structure. By the late 1880s he was giving his most trusted engineers charge of individual projects. Ernest

Admiralty Harbour, Dover, construction of a pier staging looking seaward, 1902 (Pearson papers, courtesy of Science Museum Library, London).

(later Sir Ernest) Moir, for example, was transferred from Benjamin Baker's staff in 1889 to join Pearson in completing supervision of the Hudson Tunnel contract and a decade later was in sole charge for much of the Admiralty Harbour project at Dover. Among other project engineers and managers whom Pearson appointed were Edward (later Sir Edward) Ernest Pearson (1874-1925), his brother, John B Body (his most trusted lieutenant in Mexico), and Frederick (later Sir Frederick) Thomas Hopkinson (1863-1947). Clarendon (later Sir Clarendon) Golding Hyde (1858-1934), a barrister who joined the firm in 1887-88 and later became a Liberal MP, gave Weetman legal and financial advice in drafting contracts while J H Macdonald, a chartered accountant, managed the firm's accounts. When the firm was registered as a limited company in 1897, Hyde and three of the managers (E E Pearson, Moir and B C Cass) were made directors.

Retaining his core of managers on salaries (rather than dismissing them at the end of each contract, as was common), Pearson placed each in charge of a project, and then treated each contract as if it were a separate entity —

'obtaining its own material and labour, keeping its own accounts, and in the end making up its own balance sheet' {*ibid*, 37}. In this way he could quickly identify his profitable or unremunerative undertakings and pinpoint financial and management problems.

Unlike other contractors Pearson took opportunities to integrate forwards and often promoted or operated the enterprises whose capital construction was undertaken by S Pearson & Son. 'On the Tehuantepec railway [his firm] not only reconstructed the railway and built the ports at both ends, but ran the railway and shared the profits with the Mexican Government. In the case of the Great Northern & City Railway it promoted the company and raised the capital and ran the railway for three years' {*ibid*, 49}. In the interests of securing the best available constructional expertise he demonstrated organisational flexibility and, for example, in the case of steel bridges, sublet part of his work to specialist steel contractors.

Good labour relations were essential to Pearson. On every contract he paid the standard rate of wages and frequently added bonuses for good and quick work. The only strike he suffered, on the Royal Albert Dock Extension in October 1913, arose from an inter-union dispute. Because he regarded his men's stoppage as involuntary he continued to pay long-serving (over three years) men 10s a week if single and 20s if married. A number of his foremen served for twenty years or more and Pearson took some trouble to keep them. He generously supported the Navvies Mission Society (and the work of Mrs Elizabeth Garnett who established it in 1877 to evangelise, educate and provide refreshment among navvies) and the Aged Pension Fund.

Pearson's achievements relied too on his technical familiarity with the possibilities and limits of traditional constructional materials, and his willingness to modify the available technology to meet a particular project's requirements. On his first visit to the USA in 1875 he encountered a newly-patented brick kiln, contacted the inventor and wanted to purchase rights for its use. On the Hudson and Blackwall Tunnel works in the early 1890s Pearson worked with his engineer, Ernest Moir, to improve the tunnelling shield popularised by James Greathead (qv) and in 1891 took out a British patent (with his father and on behalf of the firm) for these improvements. For the Mexico City Grand Canal scheme, Weetman Pearson and his future brother-in-law, Frederick (later Sir Frederick) Lobnitz (1863-1932), of Lobnitz & Co of Renfrew, dredger specialists, in 1890 devised five custom-built dredgers, the largest of which went down 50 feet and deposited the sludge 200 feet from the centre of the dredger to the bank. Weetman turned to Lobnitz again in 1893 to build an ocean-going dredger for deepening and enlarging Bermuda Harbour.

Finally, any explanation of Pearson's success must include those personal qualities which informed and infused his business relationships and skills. O'Hagan (qv), the company promoter, was impressed by his fair mindedness, generosity and willingness to heed advice, as evidenced in disputes relating to the Wouldham Cement Co (which Pearson formed to supply cement to his Dover Harbour work). Randall Davidson, the Archbishop of Canterbury, who met him in his later years, glimpsed 'through the veil of his modesty to see how widely and persistently his generosity had been shown long before he had as a very rich man reached

Dredger General Diaz *(port side) in dry dock, May 1909 (Pearson papers, courtesy of Science Museum Library, London).*

the position in which he could make his munificent gifts effective' {*ibid*, 282}. While he constantly had to take risks his were made on the basis of heavily-researched calculations. Indeed he detested gambling (which he never permitted in his house) and always denied he had ever 'gambled in oil'. {*ibid* 171} At the end of his life he recorded the sense of creativity awakened when he first visited Sir Titus Salt's (qv) Saltaire in the 1880s:

> to beautify one's surroundings, to introduce order and method and cleanliness where such things are not became to me an end in themselves, apart from the joy of creating them, or from the pleasure and happiness the public derives from their existence. {ibid, 300}

Integrity and generosity, together with those familiar entrepreneurial qualities of willingness to keep long hours, hard work, persistence and frugality, all inspired by a sense of creativity, would help to carry him through the most trying period in his career, the years of his Mexican involvement. A contemporary glimpse of Pearson came from Sir James Kitson (qv) of Leeds who confidentially informed Edward Holden (qv) of the Midland Bank in 1902 that:

> he had been to Pearson's house twice, and he was impressed with the enormous amount of expenditure going on there, that Pearson gives dances and parties, which, in his opinion, were altogether unwise. Yet at the same time, it must be admitted that Pearson was a hard-working man, and thoroughly understood his business. In some contracts, he made money, and in some contracts he lost money. It was well known that he had lost money in the Great Western Contract {Midland Bank Archives, Holden Diaries (26/3) 27 May 1902}.

For over thirty years Weetman Pearson's contract work — confined to drainage and sewerage works, reservoirs, docks, railways and tunnels — typified that of earlier Victorian contractors, with the scale and organisation of his works differing only in degree from theirs. Oil in Mexico, however, took him into a new technology and new markets. Returning from Mexico in April 1901 he stopped at Laredo in Texas and found it wild with excitement about a Spindle Top oil gusher. The scene reminded him of a surveyor's report of an oil seepage in Mexico and he immediately cabled J B Body to secure all the land he could near Tehuantepec. By 1906 Pearson owned 600,000 acres of land in Mexican oil country and royalty leases for 300,000 acres more. He recalled two years later, 'I entered lightly into the enterprise, not realising its many problems, but only feeling that oil meant a fortune and that hard work and application would bring satisfactory results' {Spender (1930) 155}. Between 1902 and 1912 the oil business took him to Mexico for three months in every year, often accompanied by his wife and younger son, Clive. He expected to get good returns on an investment of £1.5 million but expended twice that sum before his drilling crews moved northwards to the littoral between Vera Cruz and Tampico and on 27 December 1910 struck Potrero No 4 well which gushed at the rate of 100,000 barrels a day and took sixty days to bring under control. The find retrieved Pearson's fortunes in a vexing and then vicious oil war with the Waters Pierce Oil Co (WPO). For thirty years Henry Clay Pierce had monopolised the supply of oil to Mexico, marketing for the Standard Oil Co which subsequently purchased a two-thirds share of his firm. When Pearson and Pierce failed to agree arrangments for partitioning the Mexican market Pearson, at considerable risk, in 1908 launched into oil marketing in competition with WPO. The oil strike at Potrero placed Pearson in a commanding position. He created a vertically integrated business, controlling production, refining, distribution and selling, operated by three companies: Compania Mexicana de Petroleo El Aguila SA, known as the Aguila (Mexican Eagle) Oil Co (registered in Mexico in 1909 with a capital of $Mexican 30 million), which ran the production and refining operations; Eagle Oil Transport Co (registered in the UK in 1912 with a capital of £1 million, soon increased to £3 million) which immediately ordered 20 tank steamers and took charge of oil distribution; and Anglo-Mexican Petroleum Co (registered in the UK in 1912) which soon employed 800 in Finsbury Circus House, London, becoming 'the model of a well-run company' {Jones (1981) 70}, and handled the marketing of Pearson's oil in all countries except Mexico. Confronted by tumbling oil prices and his usurpation by Pearson, Pierce turned dirty. He ran stories in Mexican, American, French and English newspapers alleging that Pearson was making losses; that Pearson was bribing and corrupting President Diaz of Mexico (and, after he was overthrown in May 1911, that successive presidents were likewise corrupted); and that Pearson was using his position (first in the Commons and then after July 1910, when he was made Baron Cowdray of Midhurst, in the Lords) to influence the British Government in his firm's interests. (Cowdray lent some appearance to these charges when he sent the Master of Elibank, a well-known Liberal political negotiator, to South America in January 1913 to negotiate oil contracts — much to the dismay of North Americans.) Shadowed by detectives; his telegrams intercepted and read; his geological adviser, Dr Charles Willard Hayes (a top American geologist who later ran Cowdray's oil business in Mexico until his death in 1916), tempted with other contracts — Cowdray pressed on. He discovered in 1910-11 that Pierce, not Standard Oil, was behind the villification and harassment. In 1912 the Standard Oil Co directors including John D Rockefeller Jr gave Cowdray a reconciling dinner at New York and, more gratifying for Cowdray, Standard Oil began buying Aguila (Mexican Eagle) oil. By 1914 the Mexican oil output of 15,695,000 barrels represented 5 per cent of world production.

Where American oil interests failed, Mexican political turmoil and the British Government's mishandling succeeded. Between 1911 and 1917 five coups and as many presidents threatened not only the Aguila Co's operations but also Cowdray's titles to oil lands (under President Carranza's decree of 1915). With war in Europe, oil became a strategic commodity and Cowdray secured a fuel oil contract in July 1915 for supplying the British Admiralty with 200,000 tons of Mexican oil per annum. However the British Government's peacetime resignation of Mexican oil interests to the USA's sphere of influence turned in wartime to positive restraint of Cowdray's oil activities. His attempts to withdraw from Mexico brought the threat of the Defence of the Realm Act. By the end of the First World War, however, Cowdray determined to withdraw fom Mexico, not least because the oil business was not as profitable as expected (his agent in Mexico, J B Body, recorded that no ordinary dividend was distributed until 1915 when 8 per cent was declared). In 1919 Cowdray sold his Mexican oil interests to the Royal Dutch Shell Group headed by Henri Deterding: on 26 March 1919 S Pearson & Son Ltd sold 1.5 million of the 4,225,519 issued $10 (Mexican) ordinary shares in the Aguila Co for £7.35 million sterling and 375,000 of the 750,000 issued £1 ordinary shares in the Anglo-Mexican Petroleum Co Ltd for £375,000 sterling to the Royal Dutch Shell Co (which bore 60 per cent of the cost) and the Shell Transport & Trading Co Ltd (40 per cent of cost).

The other new business which Cowdray developed in Mexico was electricity undertakings. He commenced in 1902 after the completion of the Vera Cruz Harbour work when President Diaz invited him to take over and electrify the local tramway system. He recruited a Canadian electrical engineer, A E Worswick, who had just completed a 100-mile electric tramway system for Mexico City, and together they launched a series of electric power, light and tramway companies, one each for the cities of Vera Cruz, Puebla, Orizaba, Cordoba and Tampico. Cowdray promoted further electrical investments after 1916 in Santiago and Valparaiso, Chile.

During the First World War Cowdray played an active part in the war effort. The 17 vessels (215,000 deadweight tons) of his Eagle Oil Transport Co carried 3 million tons of oil in four years despite the sinking of three of them and damage to five more. In just over eighteen months (1915-17) S Pearson & Son built the munitions town of Gretna near Carlisle, which housed 20,000 workers and had an annual output of 40,000 tons of munitions; for supervising this work Edward Pearson received a knighthood. Submarine defences at Dover Harbour and the mouths of the Thames and the Humber together with a tank factory at Châteauroux in France (capable of producing 1,500 tanks a month) comprised the other major contracts executed by Pearsons. In October 1914 Cowdray ordered his geologists to explore for oil in Britain and in 1919, shortly after S Pearson & Son were appointed Petroleum Development Managers to the Ministry of Munitions, his drillers struck high-quality oil at Hardstoft, Derbyshire. Cowdray himself was made President of the Air Board early in 1917, with the object of improving Britain's performance in the air war. His directives raised the output of machines from 2,000 to 5,000 a quarter and he prepared the way for creating a separate Air Ministry. He resigned in November 1917 on learning, to his dismay, that Lloyd George had offered the new Air Ministry to Northcliffe (qv).

After the First World War, Cowdray, now sixty-two years old, reorganised his business which now spanned contracting, oil, electrical and financial activities. In 1919 he constituted S Pearson & Son (Contracting Dept) Ltd to manage his contracting interests, leaving S Pearson & Son Ltd as a holding company; Whitehall Petroleum Corporation Ltd was formed to handle oil interests outside Mexico; Whitehall Trust Ltd was formed as a finance and issuing house; soon after S Pearson & Son acquired an equal interest with Lazard Frères of Paris in the London House of Lazard Bros & Co; and in 1922 Whitehall Electric Investments Ltd was formed to manage Pearsons' electric light, power and tramway undertakings in Mexico and Chile. In 1919 he formed the Amerada Petroleum Corporation, with Thomas Ryder, former head of Mexican Eagle, as the company's president. Cowdray retained a controlling interest in Amerada until 1926 by which time it was a successful oil prospecting organisation, having drilled in Oklahoma, Kansas, Louisiana, Arkansas and Texas.

In the 1920s three projects preoccupied Cowdray. Firstly he, like Arthur Burr (qv), believed that Kent had an industrial future and that coal and steel could be produced without polluting the atmosphere or disfiguring the landscape. He formed a partnership between Dorman, Long & Co, who already had investments in the Kent coalfield, and Whitehall Securities Corporation Ltd (registered in 1907 to take over Pearson's non-contracting interests) and put up £1.5 million, half the partnership's investment. Pearson & Dorman Long Ltd then developed Betteshanger Colliery near Deal (contract for £140,000, performed 1922-25) and Snowdown Colliery between Dover and Canterbury. Mineral and surface rights were acquired and further development followed Cowdray's death.

Secondly in the 1920s Cowdray returned to an earlier interest, newspapers. In 1908 he had joined a syndicate of ten which acquired the

The Sennar Dam (from J A Spender Weetman Pearson 1st Viscount Cowdray *Cassell & Co Ltd, 1930).*

Liberal evening *Westminster Gazette* from Sir George Newnes (qv). In the face of spiralling costs after 1918, when he was bearing the brunt of the loss, Cowdray decided that a new morning paper in the Liberal interest would increase circulation figures. In the event Cowdray joined forces with the *Daily News* though, more accustomed to the contractor's certainties in estimating and forecasting, he never adjusted to the unpredictability of the business, arising from the whims of public opinion.

Cowdray's last major contracting project was the Sennar Dam in the Sudan, designed to irrigate the 300,000-acre Gezira Plain in the triangle between the Blue and White Niles south of Khartoum. In 1922 Pearsons won the contract worth £3,864,000, against five other leading British firms (on a fixed rate basis), to complete the dam on which an earlier company had started preliminary work but then stopped when it proved too costly. Cowdray appointed Frederick Hopkinson director in charge; though he himself never went to the Sudan his hand was on every detail of the specification, the execution of which he watched closely. The huge project — the dam was two miles long and 128 feet high from a base 90 feet broad — was completed just ahead of time in three seasons, between the annual four-month long floods. Employing 20,000 men at its busiest time in 1924, the project was a test of contracting ability on the grandest scale. Simultaneously 585 miles of irrigation canals were completed.

Weetman Pearson ventured into national life with some reluctance, preferring the contractor's world to the public gaze. He was elected Liberal MP for Colchester in 1895, after losing in 1892, and retired in 1910. A Liberal Imperialist, he supported Rosebery and was a close friend of Asquith and Sir Edward Grey who valued his integrity, generosity to the party and lack of political ambition. To the end he remained a silent member and found the House of Commons, as he told his wife, 'a weary business for a man of business who has work waiting for him at every hour of the day' {*ibid* 34}. He was frequently absent, causing his critics to dub him the 'Member for Mexico'. Beyond his presidency of the Air Board, his only other public office was that of Lord Rector of Aberdeen University, to which he was elected in 1920. In his rectorial address he advocated the goal of an 'ideal wage' (comprising the elements of a minimum wage, piece work and a bonus on profits) which he believed could only be attained through forms of co-partnership.

Cowdray gave away more than £1 million in addition to a steady flow of private benefactions of which no record was kept. In the First World War the King Edward VII Sanatorium at Midhurst and restoration of St George's Chapel, Windsor, received his substantial support. In two or three years after the war he gave nearly £325,000 to establish the Royal Air Force Club in Park Lane, £100,000 to the Cowdray Hospital, Mexico City (established before the war); £50,000 each to the League of Nations Union, Cambridge University Chemical Department and the Royal Infirmary, Aberdeen; £25,000 to Birmingham University School of Mining; £20,000 each to University College, London, for Engineering Buildings, and Aberdeen Art Museum. For his various services Cowdray was made a baronet in 1894, raised to the peerage in 1910, sworn of the Privy Council and promoted to a viscountcy in 1917, and created GCVO in 1925. He was made High Steward of Colchester in 1909 and later became a DL of Aberdeenshire.

He bought his first country estate, the 6,000-acre Paddockhurst, in 1894, and in 1908 for £340,000 purchased Cowdray House and Park near Midhurst, also in Sussex. Eventually he had 25,000 acres of land in England. From 1906 he accumulated 28,000 acres in Aberdeenshire and Kincardineshire, and improved the conditions of those living on his property. For lighting his own house at Dunecht he built a hydro-electric plant on Loch Skene and made other constructional and engineering changes of the kind that he enjoyed instigating on his Sussex estates. In 1919 he gave Cowdray Park to his son and moved with his wife to Dunecht in Aberdeenshire, keeping Carlton House Terrace as his London residence and Paddockhurst as his English country home.

Viscount Cowdray, the greatest late Victorian and Edwardian contractor (and certainly the most honoured), died on 1 May 1927, leaving £4 million gross, the largest estate left by a builder and contractor.

DAVID J JEREMY

Writings:

'Labour: Its Problems and the Ideal Wage' (1920) in Spender, *Weetman Pearson* Appendix II.

British Patents:

1891 (18,267)

Sources:

Unpublished

Midland Bank Archives, Holden diaries, 26/3 and 26/11.

Science Museum, London, S Pearson & Son Ltd papers, a huge collection searched only for company reports, the 1919 agreement with the Royal Dutch-Shell Group and illustrations of Pearson's technology.

PrC.

Published

Burke's Peerage and Baronetage 1980.

DNB.

Geoffrey G Jones, *The State and the Emergence of the British Oil Industry* (Macmillan, 1981).

Robert K Middlemas, *The Master Builders* (Hutchinson, 1963).

Henry Osborne O'Hagan, *Leaves from My Life* (2 vols, John Lane, Bodley Head, 1929).

John Alfred Spender, *Weetman Pearson. First Viscount Cowdray, 1856-1927* (Cassell, 1930).

WWMP.

WWW.

Desmond Young, *Member for Mexico. A Biography of Weetman Pearson, First Viscount Cowdray* (Cassell, 1966).

PEASE, John William Beaumont

1st Lord Wardington of Alnmouth in the county of Northumberland

(1869-1950)

Clearing banker

John William Beaumont Pease was born at Westgate, Newcastle upon Tyne, on 4 July 1869, the son of John William Pease, JP, DL, and his wife Helen Maria née Fox. He was educated at Marlborough College and New College, Oxford, graduating in 1891 with a third class honours degree in modern history. On leaving Oxford, Pease became a partner in the old-established and prosperous private bank of Hodgkin, Barnett, Pease, Spence & Co of Newcastle upon Tyne, in which his father was a partner.

In 1903 this firm, with its extensive branch network, amalgamated with Lloyds Bank Ltd, to whose board Pease was then elected. Pease already had a link with Lloyds Bank through his mother: she was a direct descendant of Sampson Lloyd II, one of the four partners who, in 1765, established the banking business of Taylors & Lloyds to which Lloyds Bank owes its origin. In 1909 Pease became deputy chairman of Lloyds and chairman in 1922 on the death of Sir Richard Vassar-Smith (qv). He joined the board of the London & River Plate Bank when it was acquired in 1918 and became its chairman in 1921. In 1923 it merged with the London & Brazilian Bank to form the Bank of London & South America. Pease continued as chairman of Lloyds until 1945 and of BOLSA until 1948. He was also alternate chairman of Lloyds & National Provincial Foreign Bank (afterwards Lloyds Bank Europe) and a director of Alliance Assurance Co Ltd. Pease served four separate terms as chairman of the Committee of London Clearing Bankers and as president of the British Bankers' Association.

Pease was a conservative banker with orthodox views on monetary and financial questions: in the 1920s, for example, he strongly supported the return to the Gold Standard and later, on how to meet the onset of depression, declared that 'what is really required is old-fashioned and has no imaginative appeal. The humdrum virtues of patience and economy are out of date ...' {Annual statement, 1931}. He also held firmly to the belief that the banks were able to run their own affairs without outside supervision. Pease was essentially a good 'partnership banker' in the old tradition. However, the attitudes which he had inherited and methods of conducting business in which he had been trained as a private banker were not always suitable for a nation-wide clearing bank. Board meetings tended to be cut-and-dried affairs, with little opportunity for or encouragement given to directors to discuss or question, while a tight rein was also kept on branch managers.

Even so, during Pease's chairmanship the bank achieved a solid, but uneven, increase in business. The 1920s saw a marked growth in lending and an expansion of the branch network but the subsequent slump of the early 1930s was reflected in a sharp contraction in advances and a decline in profitability, while the Second World War brought special problems of a renewed cut-back in lending, greatly increased liquidity, closure of branches and call-up of staff. Over the whole period, deposits rose over two and a half times, from £331 million in 1922 to £868 million in 1945, although in real terms deposits just doubled over these twenty-three years, and in relation to the deposits of all the London Clearing Banks, Lloyds' share fell slightly, from just over 19 per cent in 1922 to not quite 18 per cent in 1945; while total accounts nearly doubled in number, from nearly 1.3 million in 1922 to 2.3 million in 1945. The increase in the number of branches, on balance, was quite small, from 1,610 in 1922 to 1,670 in 1945; although the expansion of the 1920s raised the total to nearly 1,950 in 1931, branch closures followed during the depression and, more particularly, during the war years.

Pease was a considerable sportsman, with marked ability in hunting, golf, shooting and lawn tennis; he represented Oxford at golf and tennis and England at golf and was Master of the Percy Foxhounds 1906-30.

In 1923 he married the Honorable Mrs Dorothy Charlotte Lubbock, widow of the Honourable Harold Lubbock and elder daughter of the First Lord Forster. There were two sons of the marriage.

PEASE John William Beaumont

In 1936 he was created Baron Wardington of Alnmouth in the County of Northumberland. He remained on Lloyds' board after 1945 until his death at Wardington Manor, Banbury, on 7 August 1950. He left £83,264 gross.

J R WINTON

Writings:

PP, Committee on Finance and Industry (Macmillan Committee) 1929-1931 Cmd 3897.

Sources:

Unpublished

BCe.

MCe.

PrC.

Information from Lord Runciman (former director, Lloyds Bank), the late A H Ensor (former chief general manager, Lloyds Bank) and the late Sir Henry Lawson (former deputy chief general manager, Lloyds Bank).

Published

David Joslin, *A Century of Banking in Latin America* (Oxford University Press, 1963).

Maurice W Kirby, *Men of Business and Politics: The Rise and Fall of the Quaker Pease Dynasty of North-East England, 1700-1943* (George Allen & Unwin, 1984).

Richard S Sayers, *Lloyds Bank in the History of English Banking* (Oxford University Press, 1957).

Times 8 Aug 1950.

WWW.

Joseph Albert Pease, 1st Baron Gainford of Headlam (courtesy of Lord Gainford).

PEASE, Joseph Albert

1st Lord Gainford of Headlam, County Durham

(1860-1943)

Industrialist

Joseph Albert ('Jack') Pease was born at Darlington, County Durham, on 17 January 1860. He was the younger son of Joseph Whitwell Pease (1828-1903), a senior Liberal backbencher in the House of Commons, the first Quaker to accept an honour from the Crown (a baronetcy in 1882) and one of the most prominent industrialists in the North East of England. His mother, Mary, also a Quaker, was the daughter of Alfred Fox, shipping agent of Falmouth.

At the time of Pease's birth his family's industrial fortunes were growing rapidly. His great-grandfather, Edward Pease (1767-1858), had been a woollen manufacturer by trade but he is best remembered as being the principal sponsor of the Stockton & Darlington Railway in the early 1820s. Edward's son, Joseph (1799-1872), the first Quaker MP, diversified into coal, ironstone and limestone mining, acted as treasurer to the Stockton & Darlington Railway and founded the port of Middlesbrough in the 1830s. Joseph also invested in ironmaking and locomotive construction and rationalised the family's financial affairs, both personal and business, by establishing a private banking firm in Darlington. Jack Pease was thus born into a prosperous Quaker family, linked by marriage, either directly or indirectly, with other leading Quaker families in the world of business such as the Backhouses, Gurneys, Barclays and Frys.

Pease was educated at Tottenham Grove House, a Quaker school, and after leaving Trinity College, Cambridge in 1881 he entered the colliery department of the family business. By this time, however, the family was deeply involved in local and national politics and it was not long before Pease made his mark. In 1889 he served as Mayor of Darlington, the youngest mayor in England, and in 1892 he entered parliament for the first time. By 1908 he had risen to the position of Liberal chief whip and in 1910 Pease entered the Asquith Cabinet as Chancellor of the Duchy of Lancaster. Thereafter, he served as President of the Board of Education and in 1916 received his final ministerial appointment as Postmaster-General, a position which he held until the fall of Asquith's coalition cabinet.

During the period in which Pease was increasing in stature as a politician he was involved in a deeply traumatic business failure — that of the family bank, J & J W Pease, in 1902 — a failure due, in the last analysis, to his father's imprudence and inflexibility. Jack was a partner in the bank, together with his father and elder brother, and bankruptcy proceedings were avoided only on the receipt of generous financial support from other members of the family, Quaker business associates and Sir Christopher

Furness (qv), and an arrangement whereby the whole of the transferable assets of the partners were realised except for certain personal effects.

The 1902 crisis marked the end of an era for the Pease family. In 1892 the various mining and metallurgical interests had been merged together in the form of a partnership and in 1898 Pease & Partners had become a public company. The family bank thus owed its significance to the fact that it was the last concern to be wholly-owned by the Peases. Sir Joseph Whitwell Pease died in 1903 and in the same year his elder son, Alfred, was grateful to accept the position of Resident Magistrate in the Transvaal. Jack devoted himself to politics but retained an active interest in business affairs. In 1904, two years after he had been obliged to vacate his directorship of Pease & Partners Ltd, he was re-elected to the board, a move which was made possible by the fact that Pease's business reputation had survived the collapse of the bank intact. It was generally acknowledged that both he and his brother were not responsible for the failure: they had been partners in name only.

At the end of 1916 Pease's political career was terminated when he failed to achieve office in the Lloyd George coalition cabinet. In the following year he was raised to the peerage as Baron Gainford of Headlam in the County of Durham. By then Pease was nearly sixty but a new lease of life awaited him. The background of Quakerism, his days as a senior Liberal politician, the acquisition of a peerage and the possession of a genial personality — all of these in combination were to equip him with a number of useful attributes for the role of an 'elder statesman' of industry in the inter-war Britain. It is significant that in 1919 he was chosen by the Mining Association of Great Britain to be its principal witness before the controversial Coal Industry (Sankey) Commission. The Sankey Commission ultimately proved to be a successful attempt by Lloyd George to neutralise the miners' strong bargaining position inherited from the war, but during the course of the proceedings the latter were able to use the Commission as an effective vehicle for advancing their case for the nationalisation of the coalmining industry. Thus, much of the burden of defending the private enterprise system in mining fell on Pease. It is generally agreed that the miners were far more effective in presenting their case than the employers. Pease's evidence, although tempered by the desire for conciliation, is chiefly remembered for its uncompromising rejection of public ownership. In his final report recommending nationalisation Mr Justice Sankey made effective use of Pease's pronouncement that he was authorised to say on behalf of the Mining Association 'that if owners are not to be left complete executive control they will decline to accept the responsibility of carrying on the industry, and though they regard nationalisation as disastrous to the country, they feel they would in such event be driven to the only alternative — nationalisation on fair terms' {*PP*, (1919) Cmd 210, 11-12}. This statement is significant for its rejection not only of nationalisation but also of the miners' case for joint control of the pits as an alternative to public ownership. The public stance of the Mining Association, as expressed by Pease, therefore appeared to be negative and intransigent.

Behind the scenes, however, matters were entirely different. In February 1919, one month before the Commission began its proceedings, the Mining Association had circulated to its members, largely at the instigation of

Pease, a draft scheme for the cartelisation of the industry, together with a plan for the establishment of a national organisation to co-ordinate the export of coal. To Pease's disappointment these proposals — which were never published — were rejected, but in the aftermath of the Sankey Commission he was able to persuade the central council of the Mining Association that he should be permitted to enter into negotiations with the Government for the reorganisation of the industry on the basis of private initiative. Pease's new proposal was that if colliery owners failed to reorganise within a four-year period then the state would be empowered to impose 'unification', ie amalgamation of colliery concerns by statute. In the event the Mining Association was not put to the test because nothing came of this proposal. The Government refused to nationalise the industry and after a suitable interval of time quietly abandoned its own scheme of district unification. It would be interesting to speculate on the subsequent course of events if these private initiatives had gone further. As it was, they foundered on the fact that the proceedings of the Sankey Commission were a politically-charged event. By introducing nationalisation as one of their post-war objectives the miners reinforced the existing conservatism of the Mining Association. Henceforth, 'unification' was anathema to the majority of colliery owners: statutory amalgamations in particular would prepare the way for public ownership. Conscious of the need to respond in some way to the miners' demand, it is a tribute to Pease's powers of persuasion that he was able to secure the consent of suspicious and sceptical colleagues to a surprisingly radical scheme of reorganisation.

In 1925 Pease participated once more as a witness before a Royal Commission on the coalmining industry (the Samuel Commission). By then his influence in the Mining Association was waning and he appeared this time as principal witness for the National Association of Coke and By-Product Plant Owners. In 1927-28, following the General Strike and miners' lockout, he held office as president of the Federation of British Industries. His term of office coincided with the emergence of 'Mondism' — the desire on the part of a group of employers led by Sir Alfred Mond (qv) for a rapprochement with the trade union movement. Pease's reaction to Mond's initiative was hostile but he was undoubtedly constrained in his response by his close links with the Mining Association's central council, one of the principal sources of opposition to national negotiations with the TUC. At the same time Pease renewed his interest in industrial reorganisation. He became a firm advocate of marketing schemes in the coalmining industry. Pease & Partners Ltd was a Durham-based concern and although his own coalfield, unlike a number of others, failed to produce a voluntary scheme it was in response to promptings from Pease and his fellow North East colliery owners that the Mining Association, late in 1928, decided to appoint a central marketing committee charged with the task of preparing a national scheme for the marketing of coal. Negotiations between the district colliery owners' associations were protracted but by the time of the advent of the second Labour Government substantial progress had been made. The North East initiative thus paved the way for the industry's acceptance of the new Government's own proposals for the marketing of coal. These were eventually incorporated in part I of the Coal Mines Act, 1930.

Pease's final contribution to the reorganisation of the coalmining industry was his campaign, launched in 1934, for the creation of a central body to administer mineral royalties. The royalties system provided a fund of grievances for colliery owners, particularly in a period of great trading difficulty. Quite apart from the burden on costs of production, there were many mining districts where the large number of separate leases impeded effective exploitation of the coal measures. Furthermore, the royalties system as a whole was a major obstacle in the way of reorganisation by means of amalgamations. The Coal Mines Reorganisation Commission, a body established under part II of the 1930 Coal Mines Act to bring about amalgamations by compulsion if necessary, had repeatedly drawn attention to the disadvantages of the royalties system. Whilst Pease was firmly opposed to statutory amalgamations he went as far as to advocate the nationalisation of mineral royalties. His speeches on this theme were widely quoted by government spokesmen in the years after 1935 in order to placate Conservative backbench opposition to the Cabinet's decision to enact a measure of nationalisation. In 1938 mineral royalties were nationalised and their administration handed to the Coal Commission, the successor to the Reorganisation Commission. The former was endowed with far more effective powers for bringing about amalgamations, not the least of which was the selective granting of mineral leases.

In surveying Pease's role as a leader of business opinion it is clear that although he was a member of the senior hierarchy of the Mining Association he nevertheless identified himself with progressive elements in the industry, particularly with regard to matters concerning reorganisation. His activities in this respect, in an industry which had seemed to represent the essence of individualistic free enterprise in the heyday of its prosperity before 1914, contributed in no small measure to the growth of 'business collectivism' in inter-war Britain.

In 1922 Pease had accepted an invitation to become chairman of the newly-established British Broadcasting Company and after its incorporation in 1926 he was appointed vice-chairman of the BBC. He held this office until 1932. Three years later he became president of the Radio Manufacturers' Association. Other offices held by Pease after 1919 included the following: chairman of the National Confederation of Employers' Organisations (in 1932); deputy chairman of the Durham Coalowners' Association; vice-chairman of the Durham Coke Owners; chairman of the South London Electricity Supply Co; chairman of Cast Steel Foundry Ltd; chairman of the Tees Fishery Board; chairman of the trustees of the Bowes Museum; member of the advisory committee to the Board of Education on the Victoria and Albert Museum. Of all his business activities the one which gave Pease the greatest satisfaction was his continuing association with Pease & Partners Ltd. It was a poignant moment for him when in 1927, following the death of his cousin, Sir Arthur Pease, he was elected chairman of the company — twenty-five years after he had been obliged temporarily to vacate his directorship due to the failure of the family bank.

Throughout his life Pease was an active sportsman. As a young man he had excelled at cricket and he remained a keen fisherman, rider to hounds and a first-class shot well into old age.

In 1886 Pease married Ethel, the only daughter of Lieutenant General Sir Henry Marsham Havelock-Allen Bt, VC, GCB, MP, and herself a non-

Quaker. They had one son, Joseph, and two daughters, Miriam and Faith.

Lord Gainford died on 15 February 1943. His last public service had been to act as arbitrator for the Ministry of Labour and National Service in assessing cases for exemption from military service. His private estate was valued at the modest sum of £26,878 gross.

M W KIRBY

Writings:

PP, RC on the Coal Industry (1919) Cmd 210.

PP, RC on the Coal Industry (1919) Cmd 360.

PP, RC on the Coal Industry (1925) 2 Minutes of Evidence (1926) Cmd 2600.

Sources:

Unpublished

Nuffield College, Oxford, Pease Papers.

BCe.

MCe.

PrC.

Published

Complete Peerage.

DNB.

M W Kirby, *The British Coalmining Industry 1870-1946: A Political and Economic History* (Macmillan, 1977).

—, *Men of Business and Politics. The Rise and Fall of the Quaker Pease Dynasty of North-East England, 1700-1943* (George Allen & Unwin, 1984).

Times 16 Feb, 11 June 1943.

WWW.

PEAT, Sir William Barclay

(1852-1936)

Accountant

Sir William Peat (courtesy of Peat, Marwick, Mitchell & Co).

William Barclay Peat was born in Forebank, Kincardineshire, on 15 February 1852, the second son of James Peat, a farmer, and his wife Margaret née Barclay. He was educated at Montrose Academy and on leaving school was apprenticed to a solicitor in Montrose. In 1870, for reasons unknown, he abandoned the study of Scots law and at the age of eighteen made his way (according to legend walking to conserve his capital of £20) to London where he had the good fortune to be engaged as a junior clerk by Robert Fletcher.

Fletcher, one of the founders in 1867 of the Society of Accountants in Aberdeen, had moved to London shortly afterwards to assist in the reorganisation of the London, Chatham & Dover Railway. There he established the firm of Robert Fletcher & Co in which he had as a partner Roderick Mackay. The firm was also active in the North of England, Fletcher's 'bonhomie making him a great favourite with the northern ironmasters, with whom he had large business relations' {*Aberdeen Free Press* 23 June 1883}.

To serve this connection Peat was sent to Middlesbrough in 1876, attaining a partnership the following year. In 1879 he became an associate of the Institute of Accountants which was merged into the Institute of Chartered Accountants in England and Wales in 1880 with Roderick Mackay as a member of its first council. Peat became a fellow of the new Institute in 1882.

Fletcher died in 1883 and the firm's name was changed to R Mackay & Co. Eight years later in 1891 Mackay died in Monte Carlo at the relatively early age of forty-seven, leaving substantial private debts behind him. Peat, who was well-established in Middlesbrough, had to make a choice. He decided to move to London to take over the office there and to make sure that Mackay's debts (for which he was in no way responsible) were repaid. The firm was renamed W B Peat & Co. There were three other partners at this date: Francis McBain and G B Nancarrow in Middlesbrough and J A Forster in Barrow-in-Furness. The distribution of offices reflected the firm's involvement in the iron and steel industry.

Peat's abilities were recognised by his election as a member of the English Institute's council in 1894 and then his election as president in 1906. Popular, genial, kind and hardworking, he was re-elected for a second term. He was forthright in his public support of English chartered accountancy, deprecating competition from unqualified accountants and supporting state registration of all qualified accountants. Although proud of his Scottish ancestry, he was very much an English chartered accountant, remarking in jest during his presidency that 'Much as he admired and respected their Scottish friends, he did not want to put "CA" after his name, so that anyone might be misled as to his being a member of their Scottish brethren' {*The Accountant* 4 May 1907}.

The firm grew mainly through audit work, Peat or his firm acting as auditors for many banks and railway companies and especially iron and steel companies in the North of England. An acknowledged authority on the industry, he was secretary of the National Federation of Iron and Steel Manufacturers from its formation in 1918 until 1925. He also advised on many amalgamations in the iron and steel trade and carried through large liquidations and receiverships. Peat in 1902 was called in by Barclays (prospective purchasers) to examine the accounts of the Darlington bank of J & J W Pease, as the result of an internal quarrel among members of the Pease family. Peat pronounced the bank insolvent, an opinion which precipitated the collapse of Pease & Partners, the great Quaker dynasty of North-East England, and the humiliating failure of Sir Joseph Pease, father of Joseph Albert Pease (qv), its head. Peat was auditor of the private accounts of the Sovereign, an appointment which has remained in the Peat family through five reigns.

The First World War brought closer connections with the Government. From 1917 to 1920 Peat was Financial Secretary to the Ministry of Food and was responsible for the introduction of the costings system, under which controlled prices for various articles of food were fixed. Should such controls be continued in peacetime? The majority view of the Royal Commission on Agriculture, 1919-20, of which Peat was chairman, was that they should. The Government accepted this recommendation and legislated accordingly but later reversed the policy. In 1925 Peat sat on the Royal Commission on Food Prices.

Whilst travelling to New York on the Cunard liner *Berengaria* in 1911, Peat met James Marwick, a Scottish chartered accountant practising in North America. From this meeting developed, in the USA, Canada and France, the firm of Marwick, Mitchell, Peat & Co. The UK firm remained as W B Peat & Co until 1925 when the name Peat, Marwick, Mitchell & Co was adopted for the UK, continental Europe and North America. Peat retired in 1923 after fifty-three years with his firm, forty-six as a partner and thirty-two as senior partner.

He was an active supporter of the Chartered Accountants' Benevolent Association over which he presided for twenty years and to which he made several gifts. His interest in students was demonstrated by his establishment of a Robert Fletcher prize, in memory of the founder of the firm, and a W B Peat gold medal and prize.

Peat was knighted in 1912, made a CVO in 1921 and received a number of foreign honours including Chevalier of the Légion d'Honneur.

Peat married in 1873 Edith, only daughter of Henry Roberts, a solicitor of Usk in Monmouthshire. There were six children of the marriage, three of whom (Sir Harry, Roderick and Charles) became partners in his firm, two of them serving as senior partners. Charles carried on the Teesside connection and was MP for Darlington, 1930-45. He was president of the Institute, 1959-60. Although Peat, Marwick, Mitchell & Co has long ceased to be a family firm, members of the family have continued to serve it.

Sir William Barclay Peat died on 24 January 1936, leaving £604,644 gross.

R H PARKER

Writings:

PP, RC on Agriculture (1919-20) Cmd 345, 365, 391, 445, 473, 665 (chairman).

PP, RC on Food Prices, Sub-committee on Night Baking (1924-25) Cmd 239 (chairman).

Sources:

Unpublished

MCe.

PrC.

Information from Mr Gerrard Peat, June 1981.

Published

Aberdeen Free Press 23 June 1883.

The Accountant 94 (1936), 101 (1939).

M W Kirby, *Men of Business and Politics. The Rise and Fall of the Quaker Pease Dynasty of North-East England, 1700-1943* (George Allen & Unwin, 1984).

K Morrison, 'PMM in the Past. The Founders' *Platform* (quarterly journal of Peat, Marwick, Mitchell & Co, UK firm) summer 1980.

—, 'PMM in the Past. W B Peat' *ibid* autumn 1980.

—, 'PMM in the Past. The First PMM Office' *ibid* spring 1981.

Robert H Parker, *British Accountants. A Biographical Sourcebook* (New York: Arno Press, 1980) sv Peat and Fletcher.

James C Stewart, *Pioneers of a Profession: Chartered Accountants to 1879, Being Biographical Notes on the Members of the Scottish Chartered Societies 1854-1879* (Edinburgh: Institute of Chartered Accountants of Scotland, 1977).

Times 25 Jan 1936.

WWW.

PEDDIE, James Mortimer

Lord Peddie of the City and County of Kingston upon Hull

(1905-1978)

Co-operative executive

James (Jim as he was known) Mortimer Peddie was born in Hull on 4 April 1905. He was one of six sons of Crofton Peddie, a colour works labourer, and his wife Ethel née Whisker. He was educated at St Paul's School, Hull, and Hull Municipal Technical College before going to the London School of Economics in 1927-28 when he took both day and evening classes on the general course, supporting himself by part-time night work. He returned to Hull to become a lecturer in economics at Hull Technical College, and then, from 1928 until 1939, was lecturer in economics and industrial administration at Hull College of Commerce. During these years he was involved in the local Labour movement, both as chairman of his constituency Labour Party and as publicity manager and then director of the Hull Co-operative Society Ltd. Sir William Richardson, who knew him then, later recalled that Peddie 'was already known in the city of strong personalities as a youthful and outspoken radical, a student and teacher of politics and economics, whose ideas frequently ruffled the feathers of an older generation' {*Co-operative News* 19 Apr 1978}.

At Hull he had been successful in both the trading and the political sides of the local Co-operative movement. The Second World War provided him with administrative experience at the national level. He worked for the Ministries of Food and Information, 1940-45, and received an MBE in 1944.

In 1945 Peddie became a director of the CWS Ltd, the Co-operative Insurance Society Ltd, and the Co-operative Permanent Building Society; he became vice-chairman of the board in 1961, holding his Co-operative posts until 1965. The CWS expanded rapidly during these years which included a boom in consumer spending in the 1950s and early 1960s. In the financial year ending in 1946 the CWS's sales figures were £182,750,000. These had grown to £488,500,000 by the year ending in January 1965. During Jim Peddie's time on the CWS board the banking business also grew rapidly. Peddie's area of expertise on the CWS board was finance. He served on the board's finance committee from the time of his appointment in 1945; and he was vice-chairman of the Co-operative Insurance Society's board. At CWS divisional meetings Peddie frequently dealt with members' financial questions. He took an interest in the growth of the Co-operative's banking activities. During his time on the CWS board the banking business's annual turnover rose from £1,162 millions in 1945 to £7,951 millions in 1965. Also, as a CWS director he was directly involved in wage negotiations with the trade unions representing the CWS's workforce of 55,000 (early 1960s). He gained a reputation as a shrewd and tough businessman. An obituarist observed of him, 'a tough and seemingly aggressive negotiator, both in trade and political matters, Lord Peddie was involved in many critical decisions in the difficult post-war adjustment by the Co-op to the new High Street trading conditions' {*Times* 14 Apr 1978}. Sir William Richardson recalled, 'He never hesitated to initiate or take up a challenge. On the CWS board he was fertile of ideas and at times impatient that the federation was not making a greater impact on the nation and the co-operative movement' {*Co-operative News* 19 Apr 1978}.

Peddie preached Co-operative movement ideals to businessmen and business efficiency to the political activists of the Co-operative movement. For him the two elements were indivisible. He was a firm believer that the Co-operative movement needed to be involved in politics. Thus, he told the Co-operative Party Conference in 1961:

> Today large scale business in a variety of ways takes its politics seriously and, aided by considerable expenditure, endeavours to exert political pressure. Yet there are still a number of people both outside and inside the Movement who believe that organised co-operators should be content to be the passive victims of political decisions made by other people. Such people ignore the facts of life. Co-operative societies at every point of their operation and development are affected by political policy or enactment {*ibid*, 8 Apr 1961}.

Jim Peddie's career as a Co-operative businessman was intimately linked with his involvement in Co-operative and wider Labour movement politics. Peddie was to be chairman of the Co-operative Party during its most influential period. When he was elected chairman in 1957 it was widely commented that it was the first time in the Party's forty-year history that one of the movement's businessmen had occupied that position. Peddie told a press conference, 'My primary interest is in the trade of the co-operative movement, but I realise the necessity for political participation on grounds of defence' and added that his appointment was 'a demonstration of the solidarity between the trading and political sides of the movement' {*ibid*, 13 July 1957}.

During his eight years as Co-operative Party chairman, Peddie became a national political figure. He supported Hugh Gaitskell in the Labour Party and, even though Co-operative Party conferences supported CND, Peddie bluntly told political audiences that he was 'a supporter of multilateral disarmament and could not support the unilateralist point of view' {*ibid*, 4 Mar 1961}. During these years he was a major figure at Labour movement meetings, speaking with figures such as Harold Wilson, George Brown and Denis Healey. His time as chairman of the Co-operative Party also coincided with a time of crisis in relations between the Labour and Co-operative parties. In February 1957 the National Executive Committee of the Labour Party informed the Co-operative Union that it wanted to limit the number of Co-operative-sponsored candidates. Peddie gained wide respect within the Co-operative movement for his firmness in the ensuing negotiations and in his success in late 1958 in reaching an agreement which was acceptable to the Co-operative movement.

Peddie was also president of the Co-operative Union at an important time. In 1958 he chaired not only the annual congress in May but also a special one in November which considered the report of the independent Commission of Inquiry into 'the whole field of co-operative production and marketing', a commission chaired by Hugh Gaitskell. Peddie was a strong advocate of the need of the Co-op to respond rapidly to new approaches in retailing. As president when the movement discussed Gaitskell's report, Peddie was unambiguous in pointing the way forward. Thus at the Special Conference in 1958 he urged:

> I have always believed that the principles upon which our Movement is based and the social purpose which has provided its inspiration are not deterrents to progress, but let us guard against respect for these principles being offered as an alternative to efficiency and progressive management. In recent years we have seen the emergence of modern business conditions which have stimulated the powerful competition which we have to face. This challenge demands from us an enthusiastic urge for ever increasing strength and efficiency {The Co-operative Union, *The Special National Congress 1958: Report of the Proceedings* (1959) 2-3}.

Seven years later Peddie was to be one of the CWS representatives on a review of the relationship between the CWS and the co-operative retail societies. The Joint Reorganisation Committee brought about greater co-ordination of the Co-operative movement's buying power — with the emphasis changing from the CWS selling to retail societies to it buying for them.

After the death of Hugh Gaitskell in 1963, Peddie became known as 'a George Brown man'. When George Brown, as Minister of Economic Affairs, set up the National Prices and Incomes Board in 1965, Peddie became one of its full-time members, relinquishing both his CWS directorship and the chair of the Co-operative Party. At the 1965 Co-operative Party conference he informed delegates that 'for fourteen days he had stood out against the combined pressure of the Prime Minister and George Brown to take on the post but when he received the assurance that this new post dealing with prices and incomes was basic to the strength and continuity of the Labour Government it was impossible to refuse' {*Co-operative News* 24 Apr 1965}. Peddie was the Co-operative Movement representative on the board, just as Hilary Marquand was there as a former Labour Minister and Robert Willis as a member of the TUC Council. In late October 1970 he succeeded Aubrey Jones as its chairman for the few months until it was abolished on 31 March 1971. During his time as chairman the Board completed work on ten matters referred to it, including low pay, solicitors' remuneration, London Transport's fares and the prices, profits and cost of food distribution.

As one of the Labour movement's financial experts, Lord Peddie was consulted over the Stonehouse affair in 1975, figuring John Thomson Stonehouse. When Stonehouse, former Labour Co-operative MP for Walsall South, Privy Councillor and Labour Minister of State for Technology, was brought back from Australia in 1975 (having disappeared, apparently drowned) and charged with fraud, Peddie was appointed one of the two caretaker directors to look after the affairs of London Capital Securities, Stonehouse's secondary bank.

Peddie was always a vigorous advocate of consumer interests. 'One of his major contributions was the development of consumer protection legislation and he served in the 1960s on the former Government-aided

Consumer Council which passed many of the reforms now taken for granted by shoppers' {*Times* 14 Apr 1978}. He was also well-known for his vigorous chairmanship of the Post Office Users' National Council. Sir William Richardson observed, 'In some nationalised industries consumer councils have degenerated into little more than channels for passing on complaints. Under Jim Peddie's leadership POUNC developed a philosophy and a practical policy for combining participation in the development of a great national service to a strong, independent assertion of consumer rights' {*Co-operative News* 19 Apr 1978}.

Peddie was made a life peer in 1961 and led joint parliamentary delegations to Sweden (1965) and Finland (1968). He served as a member of the Council of Europe in 1974 and of the Joint Parliamentary Statutory Instruments Committee of 1973. 'Peddie is a character about whom few people can be neutral — one cither admires him considerably or dislikes him intensely' {Carbery (1969) 53}. His life-long friend, Sir William Richardson, recalled him as 'a bonny fighter for policies and principles that he believed in and he fought to win' {*Co-operative News* 14 Apr 1978}. He was a capable chairman of business meetings and of public meetings, and, whilst he was well-known for being abrasive, he was also well-known for his wry sense of humour. He was deeply committed to co-operative principles. It is interesting to note that his brother, Arthur Peddie, was also deeply involved in the Co-operative movement, being the chief executive of United Co-operative Dairies before his retirement in 1969. Jim Peddie received various honours besides his peerage, including an LLD from Manchester University (1966) and the honorary citizenship of Fort Worth, Texas (1963). He was made a freeman of the City of London in 1972. His recreation was golf 'as an excuse for walking' {*WWW*}.

During his career he held a number of directorships; these included (pre-1965) the West Norfolk Fertiliser Co, British Luma Lamp Co, Travco Hotels Ltd, and (after 1973) Education Services Ltd, Technical Laboratory Services Ltd (1974) and Ena Ion Plastics. Peddie was also governor of the British Film Institute, 1948-54, and was Industrial Arbitrator for the film industry in 1964.

Jim Peddie in 1931 married Hilda Mary Alice daughter of J E Bull, a fish merchant; they had one son and two daughters; one daughter pre-deceased him. Lord Peddie died on 13 April 1978, leaving £183,783 gross. Roy Hattersley gave the address at his memorial service on 24 May 1978.

CHRIS WRIGLEY

Writings:

Pricing in the Public Sector (1975).

Lord Peddie was also author of articles on economic and political subjects in Co-operative and other journals.

Sources:

Unpublished

London School of Economics and Political Science, Registry, file F/27/516S.

University of Warwick, Modern Records Centre, Labour Party East Midlands Regional Organisers' Reports, MSS 9/3/18 and 19.

BCe.

MCe.

PrC.

Published

Thomas E Carbery, *Consumers in Politics: A History and General Review of the Co-operative Party* (Manchester: Manchester University Press, 1969).

Alan Clinton, *Post Office Workers: A Trade Union and Social History* (George Allen & Unwin, 1984).

Co-operative Congress Reports.

Co-operative News 1945-78 including obituary and tribute by Sir William Richardson, 19 Apr 1978.

Daily Telegraph 14 Apr 1978.

Guardian 14 Apr 1978.

Geoffrey W Rhodes, *Co-operative-Labour Relations 1900-1962: Co-operative College Papers, No 8* (Manchester: Co-operative Union, 1962).

Sir William Richardson, *The CWS in War and Peace 1938-1976: The Co-operative Wholesale Society Ltd in the Second World War and Post-War Years* (CWS, 1977).

Times 1965-78 including obituary 14 Apr 1978.

WWW.

PENDER, Sir John

(1816-1896)

Telegraph and cable company chairman

John Pender was born at Vale of Leven, Dumbarton, Scotland on 10 September 1816, the son of James Pender and his wife Marion née Mason. His father belonged to 'the Scotch Lowland and middle class' {*City News* 11 July 1896}. He was educated at Vale of Leven parish school and Glasgow High School.

Little is known about his early career except that he became a cotton merchant in Glasgow and then in Manchester. As a Manchester cotton merchant during the 'Cotton Famine' created by the American Civil War 'he not only kept on his workmen, but was one of the foremost in organising relief and in chivalrously extending the helping hand of charity to all the sufferers.' {*Lancashire Leaders* 2 (1897) 13} By 1851, the year the world's first submarine telegraph was laid between Dover and Calais, he had amassed a fortune and was looking for new investment opportunities. His first involvement in submarine telegraphy was as shareholder and director of the English & Irish Magnetic Telegraph Co (capital £300,000) formed by John Watkins Brett (1805-63), a Bristol engineer, in 1852 to establish a telegraph between London and Dublin. By 1855 it was operating 2,200 miles of telegraph out of a world total of 8,000 miles.

When Cyrus W Field (1819-92), a wealthy American paper manufacturer, acquired the fifty-year charter which Frederick N Gisborne had been given by the Newfoundland legislature to build an overland telegraph to that remote territory from New York, he decided to extend the line under the Atlantic to Britain. Failing to induce his American friends to help him finance what they considered a mad-cap scheme, he came to England and persuaded John Pender and some 300 other English investors to join him in founding the Atlantic Telegraph Co, of which Pender was elected a director in 1856. After the first attempt to lay a transatlantic cable failed in August 1857, Pender risked unpopularity by supporting Field in his insistence that the company should try again. The cable laid in June-July 1858 succeeded in establishing communication between Britain and America — but only for four weeks. To make the 2,500 mile cable which the *Great Eastern* was to lay for the third attempt, Pender amalgamated the two cable manufacturers, the Gutta Percha Co and Glass, Elliot & Co, to form (in 1864) the Telegraph Construction & Maintenance Co (Telcon) with a capital of £1 million. They contracted to make it and lay it for £837,000. In mid-Atlantic in August 1865 the third cable broke, and there was no equipment in existence capable of raising it. The exasperated directors of the Atlantic Telegraph Co threatened to sue Telcon, which to Pender, as a director of both companies, was somewhat of an embarrassment.

He at once offered to make and lay a fourth cable, and to recover the 1865 cable, for £500,000. When few of the public shareholders wanted to risk further money on a scheme they were now convinced was totally impractical, John Pender put down £10,000, Daniel Gooch (qv) £20,000 and Thomas Brassey £60,000 to finance it. To mollify his fellow directors at Telcon, who also flinched at becoming involved in an enterprise which would further damage their reputation, Pender guaranteed the firm £250,000 of his own and his wife's money. The gamble was a 25 per cent return on their capital if the 1866 cable could be made to work (and stay in communication) and nothing if once more the project had to be abandoned. Between 13 and 27 July 1866 the *Great Eastern* not only succeeded in laying a cable which conveyed signals from Ireland (Valentia) to Newfoundland (Heart's Content), but managed to raise the end of the 1865 cable. By 8 September 1866 there were two operating Atlantic cables.

When all the privately-operated inland electric telegraph companies were bought out by the British Government in 1868 and entrusted to the Post Office to run as an integrated national service, some £8 million was repaid to shareholders and became available for reinvestment. The English

& Irish Magnetic Telegraph Co was among those nationalised and John Pender used his compensation money to help finance a grand scheme he had long been considering: the amalgamation of all existing links and the creation of new ones to link Britain by submarine cable to India, Britain's source of raw cotton. In 1869 he launched the British-Indian Submarine Telegraph Co, to link Bombay with Aden, and the Falmouth Gibraltar & Malta Telegraph Co, to link Malta with England (in the event, not Falmouth but Porthcurno). The Red Sea line between Bombay and London, of which these cables were sections, was opened on 23 June 1870. With his formation of the British-India Extension Telegraph Co (Madras to Singapore), in October 1869 and the British-Australian Telegraph Co (Singapore to Port Darwin) in January 1870, he established a submarine telegraph between Britain and Australia. In Britain the first message from Port Darwin was heard on 16 November 1871, and from Adelaide on 23 June 1872. The official opening of the All-Sea Australia to England Telegraph was 21 October 1872. To manage the main section of the line John Pender merged four companies to form the Eastern Telegraph Co registered on 1 June 1872 with an authorised capital of £3,800,000.

In order to extend the line to the Far East he formed the China Submarine Co (Singapore to Hong Kong) and in 1873 he amalgamated all his Far East companies into the Eastern Extension Australasian & China Telegraph Co which, with the Eastern Telegraph Co, formed the nucleus of his great submarine telegraph empire, owning a third of the total cable mileage of the world. This giant, the Eastern & Associated Telegraph Co, had its headquarters in Old Broad Street, London. To enable the public to spread their investment over individual operating companies, in 1873 he created the Globe Telegraph & Trust Co which held shares in other telegraph companies but mainly Pender's Eastern Telegraph group and Anglo-American which ran the North Atlantic Telegraph. The intention of merging into one company all the principal submarine telegraph companies, and submarine and land lines, did not meet with public support and the Globe became purely a trust company.

Pender's cables reached other quarters of the globe also. He formed the Eastern & South African Telegraph Co in 1879 to lay a cable to the Cape of Good Hope; and in South America he merged the Brazilian Submarine and Western & Brazilian into the Pacific & European Telegraph Co.

John Pender was for ever striving to reconcile the instincts of an idealist who favoured a system of world communications unfettered by commercial considerations with his responsibilities to the shareholders of a public company. He was determined to keep his companies buoyant without heavy borrowing, and refused to pay large dividends, annually adding up his reserves to pay for the continual cable breaks and for the duplicate lines which would mitigate their effects. In Africa his ambitions were threatened by Cecil Rhodes, in the Mediterranean by the French Government, in Egypt by Arabi Pasha, in the Middle East by the Government of India. His financial calculations were upset by the Government's Posts and Telegraphs Departments who fixed cable rates at international conferences from which he was excluded; and his ocean telegraphy monopoly was undermined by the national aspirations of Canada and Australia.

He took no interest in submarine telephony; he opposed the plan of the

Canadian and Colonial Governments conceived by Sir Sandford Fleming of the Canadian Pacific Railway to lay their own Pacific Cable (eventually opened in 1902); and he affected to see no threat to his cable companies from the wireless telegraph of Guglielmo Marconi who took out his English patent in 1896. His communications empire operated over 50,000 nautical miles of submarine cable, carried two million messages a year and employed 1,800 of whom some 650 crewed the fleet of ten cable repair ships. The Group was the largest and most successful international telegraph business of its day. Sir John was also chairman of the Metropolitan Electric Supply Co.

Herbert Herkomer's unsmiling portrait of Sir John Pender now in the board room of Electra House, Victoria Embankment, London, gives little hint of his personality. He seems to have had few outside interests. 'I do not hunt, I do not shoot, I do a little bit of yachting' he told Eastern Telegraph shareholders at the meeting of 25 January 1894, 'but the greatest pleasure of my life is to attend to the interests and duties devolving on me as your chairman ... I have made submarine telegraphy to a great extent my hobby' {Cable & Wireless Archives, Report of AGM, 25 Jan 1894}.

Pender was elected unopposed Liberal MP for Totnes in 1862; but after a Commons Committee upheld allegations of bribery during the election, he was unseated in 1866. He had two more spells in the House as MP for Wick Burghs 1872-85 and 1892-96. He unsuccessfully contested Linlithgowshire in 1868, Stirling in 1886 and Govan in 1889. He moved to London in the 1860s; bought 18 Arlington Street off Piccadilly where his wife Emma, a friend of John Millais, held a reception every year before the Royal Academy Exhibition. Pender had little influence as a member of the House of Commons; whatever political power he wielded was behind the scenes. 'The news you will find in the papers of the purchase by our Government of the Khedive's Suez Canal shares' wrote Emma Pender to her son-in-law, Sir William des Voeux, on 28 November 1875,

> will astonish you as it has done the country generally. We knew that the French were in some difficulties as to finding the £4,000,000, and Mr Pender urged, through Lady Derby, that we should go in for them. Then on Tuesday the Rothschilds telegraphed the Foreign Office that they could be had. And on Thursday morning the bargain was concluded. I understand Mr Pender's letter, but without his name being given, was read at the Cabinet council and at least did a great deal towards influencing the decision. {Cable & Wireless Archives}

Pender received numerous honours. He became a JP for the counties of Kent, Middlesex, Lancashire, Denbigh, Argyle and Linlithgow; a DL for Lancashire; he was created KCMG in 1888 and advanced to GCMG in 1892. He was an Officer of the Légion d'Honneur and held numerous foreign decorations, from Turkey, Greece, Portugal and Italy. He was an FRS, a fellow of the Imperial Institute, the Royal Society of Scotland, the Royal Geographical Society of Scotland, and the Society of Antiquaries of Scotland.

Pender married twice, firstly to Marion Cearns of Glasgow on 28 November 1840; she died on 16 December 1841; their son James (later Sir James Pender Bt) (1841-1921), was Tory MP for mid-Northamptonshire,

1895-1900, and chairman of Kodak Ltd, 1898-1913. Secondly, he married in 1851 Emma, daughter of Henry Denison, a conveyancer of Nottingham; they had two sons, Henry Denison-Pender (1852-78) and John (later Sir John) Denison-Pender (1855-1929), managing director of the Eastern Telegraph Co from 1893 and chairman from 1917; and two daughters, Marion (Lady des Voeux) and Anne.

Sir John Pender died on 7 July 1896, leaving £337,180 gross.

The Pender cable companies were fused with the Marconi Co by the Imperial Telegraphs Act of 1929 as the Imperial & International Communications Co, the name of which was changed to Cable and Wireless Ltd in 1934; in 1946 it was transferred to public ownership.

HUGH BARTY-KING

Writings:

Statistics of Trade of the United Kingdom from 1840 (1869).

Sources:

Unpublished

Cable and Wireless Ltd, London, archives: letters of Emma, Lady Pender to her daughter Marion (Lady des Voeux) and others, 1875-88; letters from the Superintendent, Porthcurno Cable Station to the Eastern Telegraph Co's head office, London, 1876-93.

William (Dan) Cleaver, 'A History of Porthcurno' (1953).

F H C Farver, 'The Associated Cable Companies in South America 1866-1922' (1934).

J E Packer, 'Cornish Cable Communcations' (1974).

—, 'PK Notebook' 1974.

MCe.

PrC.

Published

K C Baglehole, *A Century of Service, Cable and Wireless Ltd 1868-1968* (Cable and Wireless, 1969).

Hugh Barty-King, *Girdle Round the Earth* (Heinemann, 1979).

Charles Bright, *Submarine Telegraphs: Their History, Construction and Working* (Crosby Lockwood, 1898).

City News 11 July 1896.

Vary T Coates and Bernard Finn, *A Retrospective Technology Assessment: Submarine Telegraphy. The Transatlantic Cable of 1866* (San Francisco: San Francisco Press Inc, 1979).

DNB.

Lancashire Leaders 2 (1897).

G L and L R Nicholson (eds), *The Telcon Story* (pp, 1950).

WWMP.

PENRHYN, 2nd Lord Penrhyn
see DOUGLAS-PENNANT, George Sholto Gordon

Sir L Peppiat (courtesy of Ms J Slinn).

PEPPIATT, Sir Leslie Ernest

(1891-1968)

Solicitor to the Bank of England

Leslie Ernest Peppiatt was born at West Hackney, London, on 7 November 1891, the eldest son of William Peppiatt, a mercantile clerk, and his wife Emily Elizabeth née Giles. He was educated at Bancroft's School, Woodford, Essex until he was sixteen, when he was articled to Mr Charles Price. He was admitted as a solicitor in July 1913, and took a position with the firm of Ince, Colt, Ince & Roscoe. On the outbreak of the First World War he joined the 7th London Regiment, with which he served until 1918, reaching the rank of major. His war record was distinguished — he was twice mentioned in dispatches and was awarded the MC and Bar.

On his return to civilian life, Peppiatt went back to Ince, Colt, Ince & Roscoe for a brief period and then, in 1921 he joined the British-American Tobacco Co as a solicitor. In 1935 he was invited, doubtless through an introduction from his brother Kenneth, then Chief Cashier of the Bank of England, to join the firm of Freshfields, Leese & Munns. Partners of the firm had, since the early eighteenth century, held the appointment of Solicitor of the Bank of England. By 1935 there was no longer any member of the Freshfield family in the firm and the then senior partner, Sir William Leese (qv) was aged sixty-seven. Peppiatt accepted the offer to become heir apparent to Sir William, who died suddenly two years later.

The outbreak of war in 1939 led to the departure on active service of several of the younger partners and staff. Although the volume of work was reduced, particularly on the commercial side, since mergers, capital reconstructions and issues were suspended by Government Order for the duration of the war, the business had to be kept going in difficult war-time conditions. These were exacerbated in 1944 by the destruction by bombing of the firm's offices in Old Jewry. After ten months in temporary accommodation in the Bank of England, the firm moved into Bank Buildings where it remained throughout Peppiatt's time (except during the reconstruction of the block between 1959 and 1963).

In the years immediately after the war Freshfields was a comfortable close-knit partnership; with seven partners it was considerably smaller than other major City firms at that time. Family clients still formed the backbone of the practice and the firm's reputation in the City rested mainly on the appointment as solicitors to the Bank of England. In these years control was to all intents and purposes in the hands of Leslie Peppiatt as the two more senior partners were both in poor health. Peppiatt became senior partner in name as well as fact in 1953 and for the next nine years under his 'benevolent autocracy' the firm embarked on the first stage of the growth which was to transform it, by 1983, into a leading international law practice with 50 partners, over 400 staff and overseas offices in New York, Paris and Singapore.

Peppiatt's work for the Bank of England concerned him, in 1957, on the Bank's behalf with the Bank Rate Tribunal, whose enquiry, under Sir Hubert Parker, exonerated all those who could have leaked information.

He was also responsilbe for an extension of the firm's financial and commercial practice. As merchant banks and accountants moved into competition with solicitors in the City Peppiatt warned his professional colleagues of the challenge. When American investment in the sterling area increased in the late 1950s Peppiatt developed useful connections for Freshfields in the United States.

His personal charm and interest in other people led to a relaxation of formality in the office and a fostering of more social contacts between partners and staff. He was an active member of two legal dining Clubs — The Justinians and the City Law Club. He was a member of the Council of the Law Society from 1940 and president of the Society, 1958-59, being awarded a knighthood, by then customary for holders of that office, in 1959.

Peppiatt believed that solicitors should play an active part in public affairs. He served on the Departmental (Spens) Committee on the Remuneration of Medical Specialists and of Dental Practitioners in 1947; from 1949 to 1955 he was chairman of the disciplinary committee of the Architects' Registration Council: in 1960 he was chairman of the Departmental Committee on Betting on Horse-Racing. Among the charities with which he was connected were the George VI Memorial Fund, the 1930 Fund for the Benefit of Trained District Nurses and the Solicitors' Benevolent Association. He acted on a number of occasions for the Lord Mayor of London's Appeal Fund.

In his spare time he was an avid fisherman. He married Cicely Mallyn, daughter of Edward Howse, a company director, in 1927 and had two sons, one of whom Hugh, became senior partner of Freshfields in 1982.

Sir Leslie retired from Freshfields in 1962 and died on 15 November 1968, leaving £145,545 gross.

JUDY SLINN

Sources:

Unpublished

MCe.

PrC.

Information from Hugh Peppiatt.

Published

DNB.

Judy Slinn, *A History of Freshfields* (pp, 1984).

WWW.

PERCY, Alan Ian

8th Duke of Northumberland

(1880-1930)

Coal owner and newspaper proprietor

A I Percy (from Gavin Maxwell, The House of Elrig Longmans, 1965).

Alan Ian Percy (whose second forename was registered as Ion) was born in central London on 17 April 1880, fourth son of Henry George Percy (1846-1918), Seventh Duke of Northumberland, PC (later KG), by Edith (1849-1913), eldest daughter of the Eighth Duke of Argyll, KG, KT, PC, and grand-daughter of the Second Duke of Sutherland, KG. His family were adherents of the evangelical sect founded by Edward Irving (1792-1834), later known as the Catholic Apostolic Church, which believed in the restoration of the Twelve Apostles and the imminence of the Second Coming. The Irvingites for a time met in the Owenite Socialist headquarters in Gray's Inn Road, but had many prosperous members. The thirteen Percy children were reared with a strong sense of duty and discipline, but as one recalled, 'Whatever privileges my generation enjoyed in its youth, a sense of security was not one of them. It was ... overshadowed by premonitions of catastrophe ... I remember no time ... when a European war did not seem to me the most probable of prospects, or when I forgot my first ugly taste of public disaster in the Black Week of Colenso and Magersfontein, which had darkened the Christmas school holidays of 1899' {Percy (1958) 11}.

Alan Percy was educated at Eton (1893-97) and Christ Church, Oxford. He joined the Grenadier Guards in 1900, and served (1901-2) in the Boer War in Cape and Orange River Colonies (winning the Queen's medal with four clasps). He served in Egypt in 1907-10, and fought in operations at Jebel Nyima district, Southern Kordofan, in the Sudan, for which he was awarded the Egyptian medal with clasp (1908). He was promoted lieutenant in 1903 and captain in 1908. His prospects were however transformed by the death in December 1909 of his eldest brother, a Conservative politician of rare character and intelligence: Alan Percy became heir to the dukedom and assumed the courtesy title of Earl Percy. In 1910-11 he was an extra ADC to a Northumberland neighbour, Earl Grey, who was Governor General of Canada. While in the Dominion, Percy won popularity by walking in remarkable time from Montreal to Ottawa, at sub-zero temperatures, in mid-winter. This adventure was the outcome of a wager (which he won by minutes only), but typified his forceful, stubborn and combative character.

Percy, who was elected a fellow of the Royal Colonial Institute in 1912, was a strong imperialist and advocate of compulsory military service. A political sympathiser of Leo Maxse, the refractory editor of the right-wing *National Review*, he contributed 38 articles to that monthly magazine between 1909 and 1926: these were chiefly on military and defence topics, and varied between the reflectively analytical and the bellicose or trite. During the First World War, he served in France (1914-15) and in the War Office Intelligence department (1915-18). He was mentioned in despatches. His other decorations were the Turkish Order of Medjidieh, 4th class (1910), Légion d'Honneur (5th class) of France, and the Order of St Anne of Russia (3rd class). In 1919 he was created CBE and MVO. 'One of the quietest and most unassuming of men', according to an admirer, 'of all [Britain's] unused men of talent he was the straightest, whitest and most far-sighted patriot' {Croft (1949) 121-22}.

By the death of his father in May 1918, he succeeded as Eighth Duke of Northumberland. The family estates in 1883 had comprised a total of 186,397 acres worth £176,048 per annum (a rental income that was third largest among British landowners after the Dukes of Buccleuch and Devonshire). On his succession to the dukedom, Northumberland inherited estates totalling 169,000 acres on the surface: his acreage of proved mineral rights underground amounted to about 244,500, with an average annual coal output (1913-18) of 1,950,444 tons yielding an average annual income after tax (1913-18) of £69,195. Testifying to Lord Sankey's Royal Commission on the Coal Industry in May 1919, Northumberland stated that his gross income from coal royalties in the previous year was £82,450, but that after deduction of £16,407 for Excess Mineral Rights

Duty and of £42,153 for income tax, mineral rights duty and supertax, he was left with £23,890. The average coal royalty per ton received by the Seventh and Eighth Dukes of Northumberland in 1913-18 was 6.77d (9.25d gross in 1918; 3.4d after tax). Northumberland, who did not work any of the collieries himself, owned by far the largest acreage of mineral rights in Britain. The nearest magnates in North-East England to approach him were Lord Londonderry (mineral rights for 5,808 acres in Durham) and Lord Durham (coal under 12,411 acres yielding gross royalties and rents of £58,911 in 1913 and £40,523 in 1918; Durham had sold his own workings to Lord Joicey (qv) in 1896). Elsewhere, the Welsh collieries whose mineral rights were held by Lord Dunraven and Mountearl may have had greater proportionate output (17,602 acres yielded in 1918 2,318,248 tons, royalties of £58,854 and wayleaves of £5,516), while 48,878 acres of Glamorganshire with mineral rights belonging to Lord Bute produced an average annual income (1913-18) of £109,277 royalties and £6,495 wayleaves; but Northumberland was by far the best known coal owner. To the Sankey Commission, whose members included Arthur Balfour, Sir Arthur Duckham and Sir Allan Smith (qqv), Northumberland denounced the proposed nationalisation of coalmines as revolutionary preparations for the confiscation of all private land; in journalism and on public platforms, he was equally fervent and uncompromising in his defence of property from Socialism and Bolshevism.

Northumberland was the leading critic of Lloyd George's sale of honours, and his damning attacks on the peerages given in 1922 to William Vestey (qv), Samuel Waring (qv) and others undoubtedly hastened the fall of the Coalition Government in October that year. He gave evidence to the Royal Commission on Honours in November 1922. The Irish settlement of 1921, the subsequent difficulties of loyalists in the Irish Free State, and the Anglo-Soviet diplomatic rapprochement of 1924 were other bêtes-noires of the Duke. He deplored the dangerous sentimentalism of the League of Nations ideals, and maintained his interest in the coal industry and its labour unrest. He testified to the Royal Commission on Coalmining in December 1925. His fiery and militant polemical style made him the most politically controversial of dukes.

In April 1924 Northumberland bought the *Morning Post* from Lady Bathurst, daughter of Algernon Borthwick, Lord Glenesk, its editor (1853-72) and proprietor (1877-1908). Founded in 1772 by Sir Henry Bate Dudley, it was a daily newspaper published in London with a right-wing middle and upper class readership: its readers subscribed £28,000 for Brigadier R E H Dyer after his troops had shot 379 Indians at Amritsar in 1919. Its editor, H A Gwynne, described himself as 'a high old Tory' who 'always believed that the aristocracy of this country were more patriotic, more unselfish and more honourable in public affairs than the ordinary politician' {Bodleian, Gwynne 22, Gwynne to Lord Derby 18 April 1918}. Northumberland took an active part in the management of the *Morning Post*, and was a frequent contributor to its columns, as well as to those of a fringe periodical, the *Patriot*. After Northumberland's death, many of his shares were bought by Sir Percy Bates of Cunard and he was succeeded as chairman of the newspaper board by Major J S Courtauld: the *Post* was sold in July 1937 to Lord Camrose (qv), who closed it in September 1937 to end its competition with his *Daily Telegraph*.

Northumberland's family had strong scientific interests. He was the third successive duke of his line to be president of the Royal Institution (1918-30); he was also president of the Congress of the Royal Sanitary Institute (1919), president of the Institution of Naval Architects for six years, joint president of the Irish Unionist Alliance (1920), president of the Central Landowners Association (1920), the Newcastle committee of the Royal Agricultural Show (1922) and the National Unionist Association (1923). He was a member of the council of the Royal United Services Institution in the 1920s, and vice-president of the Royal Society of Arts, 1926-27. Northumberland chaired the Southern Irish Loyalists Relief Association from 1923 and the Newcastle Diocese Commission from 1926. He was elected to the committee of the Somme Battlefield Memorial in 1923. Honorary colonel of the Electrical Engineers Regiment, and of territorial reserves in Surrey and Northumberland, he succeeded his father as Lord Lieutenant of Northumberland in 1918. He was made LLD by Cambridge University in 1927, and DCL by Durham shortly before his election as Chancellor of that university in 1929.

Northumberland was a shy man, with fastidious tastes, but without a tinge of pride or exclusiveness. Conscientious and with a high sense of duty, he had a zest for controversy and political chiliasm. In addition to his scientific pursuits, he was interested in antiquarian and archaeological subjects. 'He was slight and wiry, red-haired and red-moustached, with a curious lift to the outermost corner of his lower eyelids, which contrived to give him both a far-sighted and slightly aggressive expression' {Maxwell (1965) 114}; 'His Grace, perhaps, was not quite a tiger, but he had at least the appearance and the ferocity of a large and articulate ferret' {Janitor (1928) 131}.

He married in 1911, Lady Helen Magdalen Gordon-Lennox (1886-1965), fourth daughter of the Seventh Duke of Richmond and Gordon, KG, GVCO. She was Mistress of the Robes to Queen Elizabeth the Queen Mother (1937-64), and a woman of 'extraordinary, porcelain beauty of face and of figure' {Maxwell (1965) 114}. They had four sons and two daughters. The Duke died of a perforated duodenal ulcer on 23 August 1930 at his house in Kensington, leaving £400,000 (excluding settled land) and land to the value of £2,110,000 gross.

R P T DAVENPORT-HINES

Writings:

A complete list of Percy's *National Review* articles 1909-26 is in the *DBB* files.

(pseudonym of Daniel) *The Writing on the Wall* (1911).

'The Military Disadvantages of Home Rule,' essay in S Rosenbaum, *Against Home Rule* (Frederick Warne, 1912).

'The Real Meaning of Nationalisation' *National Review* 74 (1919).

PP, RC on the Coal Industry (1919) Cmd 360.

International Revolutionary Propaganda: The Situation in Ireland (Reconstruction Society, 1920).

PERCY Alan Ian

'Nationalisation' *National Review* 75 (1920).

(with Henry M Hyndman) *The Cause of Industrial Unrest* (G W Patterson, 1921).

PP, RC on Honours (1922) Cmd 1789.

PP, RC on Coal Industry (1925) Cmd 2600.

The Shadow on the Moor (Blackwood, 1931).

'*La Salamandre': The Story of a Vivandière* (Blackwood, 1934).

Sources:

Unpublished

Bodleian Library, Oxford, papers of Howell Gwynne.

West Sussex CRO Office, Chichester, papers of Leo Maxse.

PrC.

Published

Leopold C M S Amery, *Diaries 1896-1929* (Hutchinson, 1980).

Complete Peerage.

Henry Page Croft (Lord Croft), *My Life of Strife* (Hutchinson 1949).

DNB.

Robert M H Dobson, *Final Night, a Record of the Last Days of the Morning Post* (Uxbridge: King & Hutchings, 1938).

Wilfrid H Hindle, *The Morning Post 1772-1937* (Routledge, 1937).

Janitor (pseudonym of J G Lockhart and Mary Lyttelton (Lady Craik)), *The Feet of the Young Men* (Duckworth, 1928).

J S M, 'Lord Percy' *National Review* 54 (Feb 1910).

Gavin Maxwell, *The House of Elrig* (Longmans, 1965).

Lord Eustace S C Percy, *Some Memories* (Eyre & Spottiswoode, 1958).

Times 25, 27 Aug 1930.

WWW.

Sir W H Perkin in 1860 (from W H Perkin Jubilee of the Discovery of Mauve and the Foundation of the Coal-tar Colour Industry).

PERKIN, Sir William Henry

(1838-1907)

Dyestuff manufacturer

William Henry Perkin was born at Shadwell, London, on 12 March 1838, the third son of George Fowler Perkin, a boat-builder and carpenter, and his wife Sarah née Cuthbert. He was educated at the City of London School and attended extra-curricular lectures in chemistry. His father had hoped that his son would study architecture but with the encouragement of his teacher, Thomas Hall, Perkin enrolled at the Royal College of Chemistry at the age of fifteen. He carried out research under the guidance of Professor A W Hofmann, becoming his honorary assistant in 1857.

A private laboratory had been set up at his parents' home in 1854 and two years later he produced the first fast synthetic dye, aniline purple, while working on the synthesis of quinine. Having received a favourable report on the new dye from Pullars of Perth, Perkin then threw himself into its production with the help of his father and elder brother, Thomas, who was a builder. They formed the firm of Perkin & Sons and the family savings were used to erect a factory at Greenford Green, then just west of London. Perkin not only used his chemical training to develop a new industrial route to aniline from coal-tar benzene but also investigated the nature of the dyeing process. The industrial production of aniline purple, inaccurately dubbed 'Tyrian Purple', began in 1858.

Unfortunately Perkin's French patent was declared invalid and the French industry produced the dye in competition with Perkin under the now familar name of mauve. They also made a commercial success of magenta, an aniline dye which had been rejected by Perkin as being too fugitive. Its manufacture in Britain was undertaken by Simpson, Maule & Nicholson who had been refused a licence for aniline purple. While Perkin still made various advances in the creation of dyestuffs (he discovered Britannia Violet in 1864) he inevitably suffered competition from new dyes developed by rivals in Britain, France, and latterly Germany. They included his old teacher Hofmann, who had initially disapproved of Perkin's industrial activities. Perkin also took pains to develop new dyeing techniques and carried out a search for mordants for the dyeing of cotton.

In 1868, two students of Adolf Baeyer in Munich, C Graebe and C T Liebermann, patented a synthetic route to the madder dye, alizarin, but this initial route was uneconomic. Recalling his research at the Royal College of Chemistry, Perkin soon discovered a cheaper method, but was beaten to the Patent Office by Heinrich Caro of BASF, by the space of a day. Undaunted, Perkin went on to develop a more satisfactory process in November 1869. BASF thereupon agreed to collaborate with Perkin and gave him a licence for alizarin manufacture in Britain. This was a considerable, if often unappreciated, achievement on Perkin's part as alizarin manufacture soon became of considerable commercial importance.

The Greenford factory was turning out 220 tons of artifical alizarin as early as 1871 and this rose to 435 tons in 1873.

Alizarin was so profitable that the German members of the Alizarin Convention were paying dividends of 30 per cent in the 1880s and by 1900 controlled 80 per cent of the world dyestuff industry. Perkin, on the other hand, had 'a natural dislike of business' and had long wished to devote himself to pure chemistry. As soon as he was satisfied that the technical hurdles to large-scale production of alizarin had been overcome, he sought to sell his works and patents. The firm of Simpson, Maule & Nicholson, who had been supplying Perkin & Sons for some time with nitrobenzene, a dyestuff intermediate, were the obvious buyers and under their new designation of Brooke, Simpson & Spiller took over the Greenford factory in 1873. Perkin made a personal profit of around £100,000.

Perkin now retired to nearby Sudbury, Middlesex, and lived there for another thirty-four years. His old house on the site was converted into a private laboratory and he passed his time studying the newly-established physical organic chemistry and attending meetings of scientific societies, notably the Chemical Society. Perkin had been elected FRS at the early age of twenty-eight, and was awarded the Royal Society's gold medal in 1898. He was president of the Chemical Society in 1883-85, and president of the Society of Chemical Industry in 1884-85. Perkin was knighted in 1906, when there were world-wide celebrations in honour of the golden anniversary of the discovery of mauve, and he travelled widely, including an extended visit to the United States.

W H Perkin was a total abstainer from alcohol and a rigid vegetarian; he was also a devout Evangelical Anglican. He took little interest in politics, preferring photography, music (all the Perkin family were musical) and cycling.

Perkin in 1859 married his cousin, Jemima Harriott, daughter of John Lissett, a mathematical instrument maker. The two sons born before Jemima died in 1862, William Henry Jr (1860-1929) and Arthur George (1861-1937), became distinguished professors of chemistry. He married secondly in 1866, Alexandrine Caroline, daughter of Ivan Hermann Mollwo, a Pole; they had another son Frederick Mollwo (1869-1928), who was later a famous electrochemist, and four daughters. Sir William Perkin died on 14 July 1907, leaving £86,231 gross.

PETER MORRIS

Sources:

Unpublished

BCe.

MCe.

PrC.

Published

James G Crowther, 'William Henry Perkin' *British Scientists of the Nineteenth Century* (Harmondsworth: Penguin Books, 1941) 2.

DNB.

David W F Hardie and J Davidson Pratt, *A History of the Modern Chemical Industry* (Oxford: Pergamon Press, 1966).

Raphael Meldola, *Transactions of the Chemical Society* 93 (1908).

Raphael Meldola, A G Green and J C Cain (eds), *Jubilee of the Discovery of Mauve and the Foundations of the Coal-Tar Colour Industry by Sir W H Perkin* (George Edward Wright, 1907).

Alfred von Nagel, *Fuchsin, Alizarin, Indigo* (Ludwigshafen: BASF AG, 1970).

WWW.

PERKINS, Francis Arthur

(1889-1967)

Diesel engine manufacturer

Frank Perkins ca 1950 (courtesy of Mr J C Thompson).

Francis (known as Frank) Arthur Perkins was born at Clifton Villa, Park Road, Peterborough, on 26 February 1889, the second son of John Edward S Perkins and his wife Margaret Charlotte née Long.

His grandfather, Thomas Perkins, had set up as an ironmonger and agricultural machine-maker in Hitchin, Hertfordshire. He took out a number of patents for improvements to agricultural machinery and in 1865 became a partner in the Peterborough firm of Amies, Barford & Co, which in 1872 became Barford & Perkins. Thomas Perkins became head of the company when William Barford died in 1898. Francis's father, J E S Perkins, in turn joined Barford & Perkins in 1884 after graduating at King's College, London and training in Manchester; eventually he became managing director of Barford & Perkins.

At the age of nine, Frank spent a year at the King's Grammar School, Peterborough, before going to Lindley Lodge Preparatory School in Staffordshire as a boarder. At thirteen he entered Rugby School but the spartan regime overtaxed his health and he was removed after one year to complete his schooling at Gresham's, Holt (1904-7) where the Norfolk air was considered beneficial and where his younger brother, Christopher, had already started. Neither boy was outstanding at school. Christopher trained as an artist at the Slade School in London. Frank went up to Emmanuel College, Cambridge in 1907, graduating in 1910 with a third class degree in engineering.

After Cambridge Frank went into farming, starting as a farm pupil and next taking a rented farm in Hertfordshire. War interrupted his career. Volunteering in 1914, he was commissioned in the army and served in the 34th Divisional Company of the Royal Engineers in the Dardanelles, Palestine and Egypt until demobilised in 1918 with the rank of major.

After leaving the army at the age of twenty-nine he moved to a 400-acre farm at Leintwardine, Herefordshire, but after a few years, now married and with two children, he joined his father in Peterborough at the Queen Street Ironworks of Barford & Perkins where John Perkins was joint managing director. By then the family firm had joined the Agricultural & General Engineers (AGE), a holding group which embraced old-established family-run companies such as Garretts of Leiston (Steam Road Locomotives), Aveling & Porter of Rochester (Steam Road Rollers), Paxmans of Colchester, Blackstones of Stamford (both of the latter making oil engines), and of which Barford & Perkins of Peterborough was one of the smaller units.

At that time Barford & Perkins were making a variety of agricultural machines and also hand lawn rollers and mowing machines and machinery for the local brickmaking industry. They were, however, pioneering the manufacture of motor rollers powered by petrol engines and used for both sports grounds and road construction purposes. Frank was 'put through the works' and gained experience fast.

By 1929 Frank had become works director of Aveling & Porter at Rochester, another firm in the AGE Group, which had gained worldwide fame as manufacturers of steam rollers and steam traction engines. They too were converting the motive power of their products to oil engines and were using a heavy single-cylinder horizontal oil engine made by Blackstones (another AGE subsidiary) mounted on top of a dummy boiler. Oil engines had the advantages of running without a load of coal and, more importantly, without regular visits to the village duck pond or ditch for water to raise and keep the old steam traction engine in steam. Frank was developing a high speed (so called) diesel engine to power an agricultural tractor made by Garretts of Leiston, an associated company. A four-cylinder version for the tractor had successfully gone through a thousand hours of tests and a six-cylinder version of 90 hp (designed by Charles W Chapman and intended for a Garrett lorry) had just under gone a two-month prototype stage. However the economic situation halted the project. Under the circumstances created by the economic crisis of 1931 Aveling & Porter Ltd and Barford & Perkins Ltd agreed to rationalise production. The two companies' products were to be made at Aveling's Rochester works as of 1 January 1932, and the Barford works at Peterborough to be closed. In February 1932 Barclays Bank Ltd petitioned for a receiver for AGE Ltd who subsequently decided to sell off the constituent companies individually rather than market the group as a whole. As Aveling and Barford were so closely interlinked, they were purchased together through the strenuous efforts of Edward Barford (qv), with financial assistance from Ransomes, Sims & Jefferies Ltd, Ruston & Hornsby Ltd and R A Lister & Co Ltd. The new business of Aveling-Barford Ltd then moved to a new site at Grantham in October 1933 — February 1934.

At the age of forty-three Frank found himself out of a job for the second

Aerial view of Perkins plant at Peterborough, 1982: with an area of 1,403,000 square feet, it was the largest diesel plant in the world (courtesy of Mr J C Thompson).

time in his life. He could not return to his family firm for, like Avelings, Barford & Perkins at Peterborough were finished too. Frank Perkins and Charles Chapman decided to start again from scratch, Frank believing he could raise the £10,000 needed to get going. Chapman, who had previous engine experience with Beardmores of Manchester and Petters at Ipswich (where he had been personal assistant to Sir Ernest Petter (qv)), began the task of designing an engine while Frank set up an office in a rented house in Peterborough.

The directors of the company consisted of Frank Perkins, chairman and managing director, A J M Richardson, vice-chairman (a landowner and Frank's brother-in-law), G D Perks (a solicitor and former vice-chairman of AGE), and C W Chapman, technical director and company secretary. Frank succeeded in raising some capital. With three men recruited from Avelings at Rochester, the first diesel engine was built and tested in October 1932, three months after design. Christened the Vixen by Frank in 1933, it was installed in a Hillman Wizard car, one of the first diesel cars in the world. A more powerful engine, named the Wolf was accepted by Commers in October 1933 as an alternative to the standard petrol engine in their trucks.

Frank overcame cash flow problems by bank loans, guaranteed by further sums put up by shareholders, chiefly Alan Richardson and G D Perks. Engines were installed in customers' own vehicles, replacing the existing petrol units and in addition were sold directly to manufacturers such as Commers. Demand grew, because the low cost of diesel fuel, compared to petrol, meant that each engine could 'pay for itself' within a couple of years.

After 1933 Frank started selling engines abroad and made sales visits to the USSR, Europe, North and South America and South Africa. A Wolf engine installed in a racing car driven by Reg Munday in 1935 broke or set up six world records for diesels, and actually exceeded 100 mph on the Brooklands circuit. This demonstrated conclusively that the light, high-speed diesel was a serious proposition.

Sales steadily improved but the Wolf engine was evidently not large enough and a six-cylinder engine which came to be known as the P6 was hurriedly designed by a small team under C W Chapman and put into production in 1936. With a four- and then a three-cylinder version, this became the mainstay of the company's production until the 1950s. Immediately before the outbreak of the Second World War an additional engine, the S6 of some 100 bhp, was designed at the request of the Air Ministry and supplied along with the P6 to the British Government as the power unit for air-sea rescue launches and seaplane tenders. These engines took the bulk of the company's expanded production capacity which now occupied all of the old Barford & Perkins works at Queen Street, Peterborough. With sales rising from £7,006 in 1933 to £206,320 in 1939, topping £1 million in 1942 and reaching £1.3 million in 1945 the company was now well established. Differences between Frank Perkins and Charles Chapman over the handling of a project for a twelve-cylinder Vee engine of 1,000 hp (eventually abandoned when wartime demand ended) were one of the major reasons for Chapman leaving the company.

As the war came to an end, Frank determined to enter world markets for high speed diesels. The first breakthrough came in 1946 when agricultural tractor-makers, like Ford UK and Massey-Harris of Canada, adopted Perkins's engines as the standard diesel power units for their products. Sales reached a figure of 100 diesel engines a week and to handle this a new factory was built on the 33 acres of farm land purchased by the company at Frank's suggestion for £2,780 some ten years earlier.

In 1947 the new Eastfield factory was completed with funds made available by the Finance Corporation for Industry, with flow line production and the latest automatic machines. Above the main office block Frank had inscribed 'Where there is no vision the people perish'. Very soon the company was supplying engines to more than 100 manufacturers of equipment and within two years the company went public. In the next five years its success continued at an almost meteoric rate. Turnover rose from £1.25 million in 1946 to £9.35 million in 1951 and then shot up again to £21.5 million in 1956. During the 1950s overseas plants, sales and service facilities were established in France, India, Spain and Brazil.

Frank Perkins was recognised as a man of integrity. He exuded confidence, even his physical appearance left a firm impression. The atmosphere of paternalism that he inevitably and perhaps unknowingly or deliberately (who can know?) generated in the organisation seems not to have been resented; since it was accompanied by firmness and fairness, it seems to have created a sense of security among employees. Without the impression of integrity, confidence and ability that he was able to create it would have been much more difficult to obtain outside funds for capital expansion {Neufeld (1969) 323}.

Frank's own position was recognised by his election as president of the Society of Motor Manufacturers and Traders in 1956. In the same year also he was appointed High Sheriff of Cambridgeshire and Huntingdonshire.

His other interests included work for the Peterborough Council of Boys Clubs of which he was president in 1955 and Peterborough District National Savings Committee. His benefactions included Peterborough Cathedral, Alwalton Parish Church and other charities. He was created an honorary freeman of the City of Peterborough in 1962.

In 1957 for the first time since 1933 the company made a loss. The following year, along with a marked recovery, came warning signs that some major manufacturing customers were contemplating setting up their own diesel engine plants, demand now having reached sufficient proportions to justify the capital investment involved. In this climate Frank felt that one solution would be to reduce the size of the establishment. In the event the offer of a takeover from one of the manufacturing customers, Massey-Ferguson, was received and accepted in 1958 (when turnover was down to £16 million). Frank Perkins, now approaching seventy, resigned from the active management of the company but retained the office of chairman. He was succeeded as managing director by Monty (later Sir Monty) Prichard whom he had taken on some six years earlier as his own personal assistant.

Frank Perkins held directorships in two other companies, Ambrose Shardlow Ltd of Sheffield, crankshaft suppliers to Perkins, and Lawes Chemical Co, fertiliser manufacturers, of which he eventually became chairman. His shares in that company had been left him by his father who had accepted them in settlement of debt for crushing machinery supplied.

Frank's other interest was farming. To the end of his life he owned and personally managed a small arable farm. He was president of Peterborough Agricultural Society in 1965 and enjoyed shooting and fishing. In later years too he took up sailing a small yacht which he kept on the River Orwell. A countryman at heart he enjoyed dallying in the affairs of big business and the sophistications of city life.

He married twice: firstly in 1915 to Susan Gwynneth Gee, daughter of Hugh Roberts Williams, a Government Inspector; they had a son and three daughters; the son Richard spent his career in his father's firm, rising to become an executive director. After his first wife's death in 1961, Frank remarried in 1965 to Maud V Dixon, a widow and daughter of Robert L Andrews, a retired army captain. Frank Perkins died on 15 October 1967 leaving £137,403 gross.

J C THOMPSON

Sources:

Unpublished

BCe.

MCe.

PrC.

Charles W Chapman, 'The Perkins Story' (1967).

Information from David Phillips.

Published

Edward Barford, *Reminiscences of a Lance-Corporal of Industry* (Hamish Hamilton, 1972).

Laurie W J Hancock, *The Perkins Story* (Peterborough: Perkins Engines Co, 1969).

Edward P Neufeld, *A Global Corporation* (Toronto: University of Toronto Press, 1969).

PERKS, Sir Robert William

(1849-1934)

Solicitor and railway director

Robert William Perks was born at Old Brentford, Middlesex, on 24 April 1849, the elder son of Rev George Thomas Perks (1819-77), a Wesleyan minister who became president of the Wesleyan Conference in 1873, and his wife Mary, daughter of James Alexander Dodds, an Edinburgh architect. He was educated at New Kingswood School, Bath (then exclusively for the sons of Wesleyan ministers), 1858-64, then at a private school in Clapham run by Henry Jefferson (former head of Kingswood) and in 1867 entered the general literature and science department of King's College, London. He graduated with a BA (Hons) (though KCL Archives cannot supply evidence of this) in English Literature and mathematics in 1870 and continued his studies until 1871 with the objective of entering the Indian civil service, but failed to achieve this.

Turning to law, he was articled to a firm of City lawyers, Messrs De Jerseys Micklem, and was admitted a solicitor in 1875. In 1876 he joined Henry Hartley Fowler (1830-1911) in establishing the firm of Fowler, Perks & Co in London. He continued to practise as a solicitor until 1903. Fowler (also the son of a Wesleyan minister) had been admitted a solicitor in 1852 and settled in Wolverhampton in 1856; he became a prominent Liberal statesman and was created Viscount Wolverhampton in 1908. Fowler, Perks & Co specialised in railway and parliamentary practice. Through Fowler, Perks was connected with many of the public works of Staffordshire and took personal charge of numerous engineering Bills in parliament. In view of such experience, he was elected an associate of the Institution of Civil Engineers in March 1878.

Perks had gained powerful patronage when, by chance, while on holiday in North Wales he met George Douglas-Pennant (qv), then MP for Caernarvonshire, and suggested to Douglas-Pennant and his friends a scheme, which proved very successful, for taking Conway Bridge into private ownership. Through this connection Perks was employed by Lord Cranbrook in a dispute with the South Eastern Railway Co in the mid-1870s. His performance so impressed the SER's chairman, Sir Edward Watkin (qv), that when Watkin came to fight a shareholders' election he employed Perks as his chief of staff and among the new directors elected was Perks's future father-in-law William Mewburn, 'Gentleman' {MCe} and the largest shareholder in the SER. Watkin then promised Perks the 'first big thing he had at his disposal' {Perks (1936) 64}. Meantime he introduced Perks to Thomas Andrew Walker (1828-89) and Perks became involved in the legal side of Walker's contracting business. Watkin's 'big thing' came later in connection with the Metropolitan Railway.

In his student days, Perks had developed an interest in railways and spent many Saturday afternoons surveying possible routes for a line to join the two underground rivals, the Metropolitan Railway (which reached Moorgate in December 1865) and the District Railway (which reached Mansion House in July 1871), in order to complete the Inner Circle. However, differences between the two railway companies prevented the prospect of completion until after Sir Edward Watkin became chairman of the Metropolitan Railway in 1872. In 1879 Watkin, keeping his earlier promise, offered Perks the solicitorship of the Metropolitan Railway. The terms under which Perks accepted are revealing of both the man and his business arrangements. At first Perks declined Watkin's offer but then had a private interview with him. According to Perks's much later recollection, it went thus:

> 'Now Perks,' said Sir Edward, 'tell me why you would not take the post I offered you. It is one that a thousand lawyers would jump at.' 'The reason, sir, is this; sometimes you lose your temper and when you do, you say and do some strange things. Now, suppose I left my law business in the City, which is growing rapidly, and went to Paddington as your lawyer, and some day when you did not approve something I had done or advised you to do, you were to dismiss me and I lost my only client. Where should I be then?'
>
> 'Well, Perks, I see the force of that — but tell me what is to be done? For I want you to have the appointment'. I suggested that I would open a legal office at Paddington close to the Railway Company's office. I would always have there two efficient clerks, one of them a solicitor, who would attend solely to the railway business. I would visit the office every day myself, personally, and I would guarantee the work would be well and quickly done. I would also personally attend every Board Meeting. The parliamentary work I would attend to myself. The salary was to be £3,000 a year, plus all my disbursements. But this arrangement was I said not to prevent or

> interfere in any way with me carrying on my usual legal and parliamentary business at Clements Lane, Lombard Street. These were very new and larger offices into which I had lately moved. {Perks (1936) 70-71}

Perks remained solicitor to the Metropolitan Railway from 1879 to 1892 and then a consultant until June 1895. In this role Perks claimed to be the architect of the scheme whereby the surplus lands of the Metropolitan Railway were separated from the company's railway business (under the 1885 Metropolitan Railway Act); the Surplus Lands Co in due course became the nucleus of the present (1983) Metropolitan Estate & Property Corporation Ltd.

With Walker, Perks was concerned in the completion of the Severn Tunnel and in building such works as Barry Docks, Preston Docks, and the Manchester Ship Canal, and also with important railway and docks work in South America, including the harbour works at Buenos Aires and the Transandine Railway. Perks retired from the firm of Walker & Co in 1912 and joined Macarthur, Perks & Co of Ottawa and New York, contractors for docks and railway construction.

Grouping of the underground railways in London evolved from the series of promotions of deep-level tube railways which followed the successful opening of the City & South London Railway in 1890. Perks was associated with the promoters of the Charing Cross, Euston & Hampstead Railway which secured its powers under an Act of 24 August 1893 but failed to raise the necessary capital. The situation changed towards the end of the century with the incursion of American finance, headed by Charles Tyson Yerkes (1837-1905), a deft financier from Chicago whose methods were widely regarded in the USA as devious. Perks negotiated the sale to him and his associates of the powers for the Hampstead Line, which he bought for £100,000 on 1 October 1900. Perks was also the largest individual shareholder in the Metropolitan District Railway and his business friends were large holders. This enabled Yerkes to secure effective control in March 1901 and he immediately announced his intention to modernise the District Line and proceed with its conversion to electric traction. This American control attracted wide interest and *The Globe* (a London evening newspaper) published a humorous verse:

> Said Mr Perks to Mr Yerks
> 'A fortune in the sewer lurks'
> Said Mr Yerks to Mr Perks
> 'I'll boss the job then in those circs'
> So Mr Perks and Mr Yerks
> Cornered the District and its works.

The writer clearly had not then learned that the pronounciation of the American's name was Yerk-ees. Perks (although not previously a director) became chairman of the Metropolitan District Railway Co on 5 September 1901 and held that office until 9 February 1905, but continued as deputy chairman to June 1907. The group also took over the powers for the Brompton & Piccadilly Circus and the Great Northern & Strand Railways in September 1901 and the partly-built Baker Street & Waterloo Railway in March 1902. The Underground Electric Railways Co of London Ltd was incorporated on 9 April 1902 as the holding company of the group and this was effectively the basis for the eventual formation of London Transport in 1933, which Perks lived to see. He also took a prominent part in the financing of the Ealing & South Harrow Railway and in supplying the District Railway moiety of the share capital of the Whitechapel & Bow Railway Co. During the same period he gave both legal and financial guidance to the Lancashire, Derbyshire & East Coast Railway in its difficult situation in 1894. He became a director in that year and held office until the company was taken over by the Great Central Railway as from 1 January 1907. Perks held no office in any railway company after 1907 but, as representing large shareholding interests, he was a frequent speaker at the annual meetings of British railway comapnies and was always heard with attention. He made an important speech at the Underground shareholders' meeting on 1 May 1931, backing Lord Ashfield's (qv) recommendation to accept the terms offered in the London Passenger Transport Bill.

In the political sphere, Perks entered parliament in 1892 as Liberal MP for the Louth Division of Lincolnshire, and held the seat until 1910. When the Liberal League was formed under Lord Rosebery, Herbert Henry Asquith, Sir Edward Grey, Henry Hartley Fowler and Richard Burdon Haldane in February 1902, Perks was appointed treasurer and his skill consistently avoided financial difficulties. He was also the originator and chairman (1906-8) of the parliamentary committee of 200 Nonconformist MPs. He was JP for Oxfordshire and Kent and was created a baronet in 1908, but is believed to have declined a peerage as he disliked pomp and ceremony and maintained a simple life style.

Coincident with his career in commerce, Perks also exercised his business ability in the interests of Methodism. In 1878 he was one of the first laymen to be admitted to the Wesleyan Conference, hitherto confined to ministers, and thereafter continuously agitated for the organic union of the three larger branches of Methodism and latterly gained a reputation as 'Methodism's foremost lay statesman.' In 1900 he launched the Wesleyan Methodist Twentieth Century Million Fund, of which he was treasurer. This campaign to raise a million guineas facilitated the purchase of the site of the Westminster Royal Aquarium (opened on 22 January 1876) which was about $2\frac{1}{2}$ acres. The Aquarium was demolished in 1902 and in its place were built the Wesleyan Central Hall (opened on 3 October 1912), Caxton House, and Portland House. Eventually, his life-long wish for Methodist reunion was accomplished in 1932 with the merger of the Wesleyan Methodist, Primitive Methodist, and United Methodist bodies. Sir Robert was elected unanimously as the first vice-president (1932-33) of the united body.

In 1878 Perks married Edith, the youngest daughter of William Mewburn, prominent and wealthy Methodist layman, of Wykham Park, Banbury. They had one son and four daughters. Sir Robert Perks died at Kensington Palace Gardens on 30 November 1934, aged eighty-five. He left an estate valued at £74,947 gross, family provision and many donations to charity apparently having been made during his lifetime. He was succeeded as second baronet by his son Robert Malcolm Mewburn Perks.

CHARLES E LEE

PERKS Sir Robert William

Writings:

Is it Desirable to Alter the Law which Prohibits Railway Companies from Paying Interest out of Capital? (C F Roworth, 1883).

The Policy and Leadership of the Liberal Party (pp, 1900).

PP, RC London Traffic (1905) Cd 2751, 2752.

The King's Declaration (Hodder & Stoughton, 1910).

Montreal, Ottawa, and Georgian Bay Canal (RSA address, pp, 1914).

The Re-Union of British Methodism (Epworth Press, 1920).

The Aim of the Methodist Church. An Address (Epworth Press, 1933).

Sir Robert Perks, Baronet (Epworth Press, 1936).

Sources:

Unpublished

BCe.

MCe.

PrC.

Published

Theodore C Barker and Michael Robbins, *A History of London Transport* (2 vols, George Allen & Unwin, 1963-74).

Denis Crane, *The Life Story of Sir Robert W Perks* (Robert Culley, 1909).

DAB.

DNB.

George Dow, *Great Central* (3 vols, Locomotive Publishing Co, 1959-65).

Alexander Edmonds, *History of the Metropolitan District Railway to June 1908* (London Transport, 1973).

The Law Society Gazette 32 (Jan 1935).

Charles E Lee, *The Metropolitan District Railway* (The Oakwood Press, 1956).

The Methodist Recorder 6 Dec 1934.

The Railway Gazette 7 Dec 1934.

The Railway News 24 Aug 1901.

Times 1 Dec 1934.

WWMP.

WWW.

Sir Michael Perrin, ca 1966 (courtesy of the Wellcome Foundation Ltd).

PERRIN, Sir Michael Willcox

(1905-)

Pharmaceutical company executive

Michael Willcox Perrin was born in Victoria, British Columbia, Canada, on 13 September 1905, the only son of the Right Rev William Willcox Perrin, then Bishop of British Columbia, and his wife, Isolene Harriet née Bailey. The family returned to England in 1910, following his father's appointment as Bishop of Willesden. Perrin gained his first interest in science at his prep school, Twyford, in Hampshire. From Winchester College he won a scholarship to New College, Oxford, where he took a second class BA in chemistry and then completed a one-year BSc research degree in the physics department. While at Oxford he was already interested in a research career in industry and he met, and favourably impressed, ICI's research manager, Dr Francis A Freeth FRS. After Oxford, he spent a year (1928-29) at Toronto University working for his MA in physics, under the distinguished physicist, Professor J C McLennan FRS, studying the effect of high-speed cathode rays on chemical reactions.

Perrin was tempted to stay longer in Toronto but Freeth offered him a post with Professor A M J F Michels, whose work (in the field of high pressure) at Amsterdam University was being subsidised by ICI. He worked with Michels for four years, gaining valuable research and laboratory administration experience. In January 1932, while Perrin was spending a short holiday in England, he and Dr J C Swallow, Deputy Research Director at Winnington, Cheshire (ICI Alkali Group's research centre), presented a paper to the Alkali Group's board suggesting a research programme on the effect of high pressure on chemical reactions. This coincided with a memorandum, submitted to the Dyestuffs Group's Research Committee by Professor Robert Robinson FRS, suggesting that a number of organic reactions which needed catalysts might take place under high pressure alone. It was decided that the research should be done at Winnington and the programme was duly commenced by Dr R O Gibson and E W Fawcett (an organic chemist seconded from Dyestuffs). As a result of their work, polythene (the polymer of ethylene) was first discovered, on 27 March 1933, while studying the effects of high pressure on the reaction between ethylene and benzaldehyde. At the time no great importance was attached to the discovery and, after a number of explosions, the work was abandoned.

Perrin joined the staff at Winnington in October 1933 but did not immediately join the high pressure group, working initially on the properties and potential use of heavy water. It was not until October 1935, after Gibson and Fawcett had moved to other work, that he was put in charge of the high pressure research under Swallow. On 19 December 1935 he set up an experiment on ethylene, alone, under high pressure and 8 grams of the polymer were produced. He had 'rediscovered' polythene at the first attempt. This time the work was continued and its success, according to Swallow, was largely due to Perrin's single-mindedness. Polythene's potential as an insulator for submarine cable was soon recognised and on 1 September 1939 the first commercial production plant came into operation. Before then, expectations of imminent war work had prompted Dr R E Slade, Research Controller of ICI, to transfer Perrin, in 1938, to the Research Department headquarters in London. Here he took a wider interest in the company's research programme.

In April 1940 the MAUD Committee was set up to report to the Government on the feasibility of an atomic bomb. Its research was assisted by a number of ICI people including Dr Slade and his assistant, Perrin. After the Committee reported, in July 1941, Sir Wallace Akers (Research Director on the ICI parent board) was asked by Sir John Anderson to become Director of Tube Alloys, which was set up in the Department of Scientific and Industrial Research to work on the atomic project. He took up the post in November, taking Perrin with him as Assistant Director because, as he said, no-one knew the men and work so well. Henceforth, Perrin's career was to turn away from research and towards administration and policy making. Perrin held this post throughout the war, during which time he paid several visits to the United States to co-ordinate the two countries' efforts and to Canada to enlist support for the atomic project and to organise the joint project in Montreal. He worked closely with the Intelligence Services and, in November 1943, helped to arrange the escape of the Danish scientist, Niels Bohr, to England.

In 1946 the Directorate of Tube Alloys became the Division of Atomic Energy in the Ministry of Supply. Akers returned to ICI and Lord Portal (qv), wartime Chief of Air Staff, became Controller. He appointed Perrin Deputy Controller (Technical Policy). Perrin's task was to ensure that the technical policy being followed accorded with the latest scientific information available and to formulate any technical (as opposed to scientific) advice required by Government departments. He worked closely with the three other Deputy Controllers: Professor John Cockcroft, Christopher Hinton (qv) (also a former ICI man), and Dr William Penney, responsible, respectively, for research, production and weapon development. In January 1950 it was to Perrin that the spy Klaus Fuchs insisted on confessing the extent of his revelations to the Russians. Perrin supported the moves made in 1950-51 to make the Atomic Energy Division independent of the Ministry of Supply. When this seemed to have failed and Lord Portal had resigned, Perrin returned to ICI, as Research Adviser, in June 1951. However, this post was to be short-lived.

While working for Tube Alloys, Perrin had often attended Sir John Anderson's Consultative Committee and had become acquainted with the eminent scientist, Sir Henry H Dale (then president of the Royal Society). Sir Henry, who was chairman of the Wellcome Trustees, sole shareholders of the pharmaceutical company The Wellcome Foundation Ltd, had been impressed with Perrin's abilities and this led to Perrin being offered the post of chairman of the Foundation. Despite his own qualms about his lack of knowledge of the pharmaceutical industry, and encouraged by the board of ICI, he took up the post on 1 January 1953.

At this time the Wellcome Foundation was still suffering from the

Head office of Cooper, McDougall & Robertson, Berkhampstead (Herts), acquired by the Wellcome Foundation in 1959 (courtesy of the Wellcome Foundation Ltd).

effects of the massive death duties imposed in 1936 on the death of the founder, Sir Henry Wellcome (qv), together with the effects of the war. Perrin saw that to achieve recovery it would be necessary to plough back a large proportion of the company's profits. His good relationship with the Trustees helped him to persuade them that this would, in the long term, result in greater dividends for them to use for the research they funded. During his chairmanship, ca 70 per cent of the profits were ploughed back. His own research background had taught him that much of this investment needed to go into research and development. This policy paid off: important products introduced during this period included 'Covexin' (1961), a seven-in-one vaccine for sheep; 'Zyloric' (1966), an anti-gout remedy; and 'Septrin' (1968), an anti-bacterial.

Perrin's first year of office (1953) coincided with the centenary of Wellcome's birth and the company's effort to re-establish itself is evident from the well-publicised way in which this was celebrated.

Perrin was determined to build up the company's interests overseas, not only by exports but also by establishing overseas subsidiary companies. In 1953 there were only eight overseas 'houses' (in Australia, South Africa, Italy, Canada, USA, Shanghai, Argentina and India) and none had been established since 1912. The period of Perrin's chairmanship saw a great expansion overseas, starting with New Zealand in 1954 and culminating in a number of Far Eastern branches in 1968. There was also a steady build up of bases in Europe. By 1970 the Group had 68 subsidiaries of which 58 were located abroad (20 in Europe). This expansion was greatly helped by Perrin's own tireless world-wide journeys (at least a dozen overseas tours) during which he utilised and extended the contacts made during his early career.

Photograph of buildings opened at Wellcome Research Laboratories, Beckenham, 1956–59. The four buildings on the right hand side of the photo are, left to right: Poliomyelitis vaccine production, virus vaccine production, virus research and anaerobic bacteriology building (courtesy of the Wellcome Foundation Ltd).

Perrin saw the need for the Wellcome Foundation to diversify and he placed great emphasis on expanding the veterinary side of the business, a policy which was accelerated by the acquisition of the Cooper McDougall & Robertson Group (a company that brought with it more overseas business) in 1959. Emphasis was also placed on consumer products and great success was earned by such products as 'Saxin' and 'Marzine'. This policy was again reflected in the acquisition in 1967 of the Calmic Group, in which Wellcome had had a 25 per cent share since 1964.

In his efforts to improve the efficiency of the company, Perrin laid great emphasis on work-study. In 1967 the company was reorganised and three deputy chairmen were appointed, Dr D E Wheeler (formerly managing director) to co-ordinate central group activities such as research and development, production and finance, Dr Fred Wrigley to co-ordinate medical sales and Wellcome companies world-wide and to be chairman of Calmic, and Mr A A Gray to be responsible for all veterinary sales worldwide and to be chairman of Cooper McDougall & Robertson. Regional managers were appointed for the major regions of the world

(Europe; North America; Australasia; South America; Afro-Asia) to co-ordinate all companies in their region whether Cooper, Calmic or Wellcome. In 1969 a world-wide company house-style was introduced to reinforce its unity. A fitting climax to his career with the company was the Queen's Award to Industry received by the Wellcome Foundation in 1970 for its export achievements in the field of human medical products and diagnostic reagents. This was followed, in 1971, by the Queen's Award for Technological Innovation.

Sir Michael Perrin (he was knighted in January 1967 for his work as chairman of the Board of Governors of St Bartholomew's Hospital and as chairman of the Wellcome Foundation Ltd) retired from the Wellcome Foundation on 31 December 1970, having seen the company sales increase from £10.938 million in 1953 to £85.809 million in 1970. The Trust's faith in him was repaid to the extent that in the period 1968-70 they were able to award grants totalling £5,780,268 in the broad field of medical research (directed into buildings, 7 per cent; equipment, 6 per cent; research assistance, 35 per cent; fellowships, 18 per cent; university awards, 4 per cent; history of medicine, 8 per cent; veterinary medicine, 8 per cent; and other items, 4 per cent). This compared with the total of £1,170,000 paid out for the entire period 1937-56. Evidence of the international spirit and 'family feeling' that he had done so much to foster in the group, as well as the affection in which he was held, were the retirement gifts he received from the Foundation's constituent companies.

In addition to his chairmanship of the Wellcome Foundation, Perrin was a director of Inveresk Research International, a contract research organisation, 1961-74 (chairman, 1971-73); and a director of Radiochemical Centre Ltd, now Amersham PLC, 1971-75, headed by Walter Grove (qv).

Sir Michael has held the following offices (among many others): Treasurer (ie chairman) of the board of Governors and president of the Medical College of St Bartholomew's Hospital, 1960-69; member of the Council of the Royal Veterinary College, London University, 1967-76 (chairman, 1967-72); of the Council of the School of Pharmacy, London University, 1963-76; of the Central Advisory Council for Science and Technology, 1969-70; and of the governing body of the British Postgraduate Medical Federation (chairman, 1972-77); and chairman of the council of Roedean School, 1974-79. He was a trustee of the British (Natural History) Museum, 1974-83. In 1948 he was elected (scientific) fellow of the Zoological Society of London. He served on its Council and Finance Committee, 1957-77, and, as a vice-president, 1967-77. He became a fellow of the Chemical Society in 1952 and served on its Council, 1954-66 (as treasurer, 1954-61, and as a vice-president, 1963-66). He became a life fellow of the Royal Society of Chemistry in 1980.

Before his knighthood Michael Perrin was awarded the OBE in 1946 and the CBE in 1952 for his atomic energy work. In 1969 he was awarded an honorary DSc by the University of British Columbia.

He married in 1934, Nancy May, daughter of the Right Rev Charles Edward Curzon, then Bishop of Stepney and later Bishop of Exeter. They have one son and one daughter.

ROSEMARY C E MILLIGAN

PERRIN Sir Michael Willcox

Writings:

(with J C McLennan and H J C Ireton) 'The Action of High Speed Cathode Rays on Acetylene' *Proceedings of the Royal Society* Series A, 125 (Sept 1929).

(with R O Gibson and E W Fawcett) 'The Effect of Pressure on Reactions in Solution. I Sodium Ethoxide and Ethyl Iodide to 3,000 kg/cm². II Pyridine and Ethyl Iodide to 8,500 kg/cm²' Series A *ibid* 150 (May 1935).

(with E G Williams and R O Gibson) 'The Effect of Pressure up to 12,000kg/cm² on Reactions in Solution' *ibid* Series A, 154 (May 1936).

(with E G Williams) 'The Effect of Pressure up to 12,000 kg/cm² on the Reactions between Amines and Alkyl Halides in Acetone Solution' *ibid* Series A, 159 (Mar 1937).

'The Influence of Hydrostatic Pressure on Reaction Velocity' *Transactions of the Faraday Society* 24 (Jan 1938).

'The Polymerisation of Hydrocarbons' *ibid* 35 (Aug 1939).

'Chemical Effects of High Pressure. New Light on the Mechanism of Reactions' *The Times Science Review* winter 1952.

'The Story of Polythene' *Research* 6 (Mar 1953).

Sources:

Unpublished

Wellcome Foundation archives, London.

Conversations with Sir Michael Perrin and staff of the Wellcome Foundation Ltd.

Published

Foundation News (in-house journal of the Wellcome Foundation).

Margaret Gowing, *Britain and Atomic Energy, 1939-1945* (Macmillan, 1964).

—, *Independence and Deterrence. Britain and Atomic Energy, 1945-1952* (2 vols, Macmillan, 1974).

The ICI Magazine (in-house journal of ICI).

Gilbert Macdonald, *In Pursuit of Excellence: One Hundred Years Wellcome, 1880-1980* (The Wellcome Foundation, 1983 edn).

'Profile: Michael Perrin. The Man to Whom Fuchs Confessed' *New Scientist* 24 Jan 1957.

William J Reader, *Imperial Chemical Industries. A History* (2 vols, Oxford University Press, 1970-75) 2.

Martin Sherwood, 'Polythene and Its Origins' *Chemistry and Industry* 21 Mar 1983.

John C Swallow, 'Ethylene Polymers, Past and Future' *Plastics Institute Transactions and Journal* 31 Feb 1963.

E F Thurston, *Winnington's Research Laboratory. The First Fifty Years 1928-1978* (ICI, 1979).

Spencer R Weart, *Scientists in Power* (Cambridge, Massachusetts: Harvard University Press, 1979).

WW 1982.

PERRY, Percival Lee Dewhurst

Lord Perry of Stock Harvard

(1878-1956)

Motor vehicle manufacturer

Percival Lee Dewhurst Perry was born at Bristol, on 18 March 1878, the son of Alfred Thomas Perry, a clerk, and his wife Elizabeth née Wheeler. He won a scholarship to King Edward VI's School in Birmingham and on leaving school worked for a Birmingham solicitor. Lacking money he looked around for a job to support himself and, by answering an advertisement in the *Birmingham Post*, found one in the London office of Harry J Lawson (qv), who was attempting to corner the infant British motor industry by buying up all the valuable patents recently taken out by Continental manufacturers. While with Lawson, Perry worked alongside Charles Jarrott, later to be a leading figure in the motor trade and a co-founder of the Automobile Association, and took part in a number of demonstrations of motorcars. Next Perry was briefly employed in his uncle's printing business in Hull and then with a company concerned with developing dustless road surfaces. By 1900 he was in the Coventry motor industry.

He returned to London with a reputation as a 'motor expert', and when the first Ford Model A cars were imported to Britain in 1903 Perry was invited to give a technical report on them for the backers of a prospective importing company, the American Motor Car Agency & Central Motor Car Emporium, headed by one Aubrey Blakiston. The American Motor Car Agency was unsuccessful — American cars were regarded as 'cheap and nasty' by British customers, then all wealthy individuals — and was reorganised as the Central Motor Car Co Ltd, registered in November 1904 with a capital of £10,000 in £1 ordinary shares, of which Blakiston had 2,400 and Perry 500.

Neither did the Central Motor Car Co prosper. It had to issue debentures to raise new funds and Blakiston withdrew. Perry was appointed managing director early in 1906. Sales remained low, and in an attempt to publicise the Ford car, Perry put three Model B Fords on the road as taxicabs, one of the first fleets of motor cabs to operate in London.

In 1906 Perry decided to seek financial support from the Ford Motor Co in the USA and went to Detroit. Henry Ford invited Perry (and possibly his wife Catherine, daughter of John Meals, a postmaster of Hull whom he had married in 1902) to stay at his home but Ford would not invest overseas at this point. Nevertheless, Perry established a lasting friendship with Ford who apparently introduced him to Gordon McGregor, head of Ford of Canada, who had sales rights throughout the British Empire. McGregor, described by Perry as 'one of the finest men who ever lived' {Fawcett}, ceded his United Kingdom rights to Perry, declaring that 'the rest of the British Empire is enough for me' {ibid}. Early in 1907, Perry formed a new company, Perry Thornton & Schreiber, to replace the Central Motor Car Co, which was put into voluntary liquidation.

The advent of the four-cylinder Model N Ford in 1906 gave Perry a product which was more acceptable to British tastes, and sales of Ford cars started to increase. In October 1908 Ford introduced his mass-produced Model T to the American public and the following month exhibited it in England at the Olympia Motor Show in London. The Model T became a huge success and in 1908 the Ford Motor Co's profits were so large that the company declared dividends of £2.5 million. Now Henry Ford was ready to branch overseas. In 1909 Perry, who had left Thornton and Schreiber and was selling Reo cars (put out by R E Olds), was appointed to take full charge of a new branch of the Ford company. The branch was headquartered at 55-59 Shaftesbury Avenue, London.

Perry started with nine salaried and 13 hourly employees. Model T Fords were imported from Detroit, partly knocked down, uncrated at Vauxhall Wharf, and sufficiently assembled to enable them to be driven to Shaftesbury Avenue or to a Ford dealership. Perry laid the foundations of a nationwide exclusive dealer organisation, and demand for Ford Model Ts was soon large enough — over 400 cars were sold in the first twelve months at Shaftesbury Avenue — to justify the establishment of a British assembly plant. Perry found a suitable plant site of $5\frac{1}{2}$ acres on the Trafford Park industrial estate on the southern outskirts of Manchester. In October 1911, the new factory went into operation. The Shaftesbury Avenue premises were retained as showrooms and offices.

Meanwhile Detroit officials had decided to replace their British branch with a company: this offered tax advantages and the prospect of greater strength through independence for the English firm. In March 1911 the Ford Motor Co (England) Ltd was incorporated, wholly owned by the shareholders of the parent American firm. Its capital of £1,100 was divided into £5 shares of which Henry Ford held 117. Perry, though acquiring no shares, was well rewarded. 'His income in 1912 had risen to $25,000 and for the year ending 30 September 1914 Perry was paid $15,000 in salary and $18,000 bonus. During the two years he had operated the English enterprise as a branch, it had sold 1,023 Model T cars and made profits of $145,333' {Wilkins and Hill (1964) 47-48}.

Henry Ford visited Britain with his family in summer 1912, Perry meeting them at Plymouth with a Rolls Royce. After visiting the Ford plant and then touring the Coventry and Birmingham motor industry districts, Henry Ford decided that the English company should eventually move to a larger freehold site with room for expansion. At this time the English company was still only assembling, rather than manufacturing, cars and with a capacity of 15,000 per annum, compared to Detroit's 250,000. However, under close American supervision the Manchester factory slowly edged into manufacturing. Ford's new mass-production methods, which pioneered the moving production line, were introduced in the Manchester plant in 1913-14. Production was 3,000 vehicles in 1912 and 6,000 in 1913. Only the outbreak of war in 1914 prevented 10,000 being reached that year. On the eve of the war the firm employed 1,500. Under production pressures a number of strikes broke out. Perry refused to bargain with the unions and Ford in 1913 and 1914 sent over Charles E

Sorenson to break union power — which he did by 'assuring strategically placed workers of both job security and high wages' {*ibid*, 49}.

During the First World War, Perry faced a dilemma. While the war effort called upon his own resources and those of Ford in England he sold chassis to the War Office for ambulances, worked in the Food Production Department and the Agricultural Machinery Department of the Ministry of Munitions his boss, Henry Ford became a militant pacifist. Despite any tensions he may have felt Perry remained loyal and active in building up the Ford organisation in England. He was instrumental in bringing the Fordson tractor to Britain, where a manufacturing plant was established in Cork, Ireland. He became Deputy Controller of the Mechanical Warfare Department and Director of Traction of the Ministry of Munitions in 1918: simultaneously he directed the Ford Motor Co (England) Ltd, Henry Ford & Son Ltd (set up in 1917 to make Fordson tractors) and he watched over Ford activities in France, all of which imposed a great strain. For his war work Perry was knighted in 1918.

After the war, the Manchester factory was extended and production rose steeply. In 1919, however, a long-submerged conflict came to the surface. Henry Ford wanted to run the English company as a branch of Detroit and to make his chief executives in Britain no more than managers. Perry, for his part, wanted to direct expansion in Britain. Confronted by Henry Ford's imperious disapproval of his plans, and dogged by ill-health, Perry resigned in May 1919. A wealthy man, he next headed a group which bought the Slough Motor Co Repair Depot, later the Slough Trading Estate, with 600 acres of land, 15,000 cars and 30 buildings, for £7 million. It developed a huge trading estate and disposed of government-surplus vehicles. In August 1922, however, Sir Percival resigned as chairman and managing director of the Slough Estates Ltd and took over Compton Mackenzie's lease on the Channel Island of Herm, where he lived in retirement.

British demand for Ford cars continued to grow. It became imperative to set up a new factory specially designed for large scale production. In 1924, Henry Ford deputised Edward Grace, manager of the Cork plant, to purchase a suitable site. The final choice of Dagenham came as a surprise to many people. Ford already had land at Southampton. The 310-acre Essex site, acquired in 1925, was mostly low-lying marsh. Some experts said it was unworkable, but the geographical advantages of the site proved decisive. Its proximity to London's docks gave easy access to European ports — and it was as a great exporting centre that the idea of such a factory was conceived.

For a decade Henry Ford ran the English company with a series of salaried American managers who tried to replicate Detroit methods in Manchester. The strategy failed. None of Perry's successors possessed his vision and resourcefulness. With a new phase of expansion envisaged, Henry Ford, now advised by Sorensen (a pro-Perry man) reversed his judgement of Perry. In May 1928 on one of his rare trips to Europe Henry Ford contacted Perry and offered him the chairmanship of the new organisation — Ford Motor Co Ltd, which was formed in 1928 — 'the expansion that Perry had wanted to undertake in 1919 was now being offered to him' {*ibid*, 189}. Perry accepted. The Ford empire had grown rapidly throughout the world and, to create order, a decentralisation strategy was adopted. Henry Ford would have three centres for international business. Ford Detroit was to supply parts for assembly, mainly to Latin America and Japan. Ford Canada was to continue to supply most of the British Empire. Ford England would serve Europe from Dagenham, the largest automobile factory in the world outside the USA. This reorganisation of European operations was called 'The 1928 Plan'. Its principal author was Sir Percival Perry, whose aim was to co-ordinate and unify European operations.

Ford of England would be owned 60 per cent by Ford USA and 40 per cent by the British public. Similarly Ford of England would own 60 per cent of the Ford companies on the Continent and the public in each country would hold the remaining 40 per cent. Henry Ford hoped that this national participation in ownership would remove Ford's image as a 'foreign' corporation. Perry had succeeded in persuading Ford to do in Europe what had been done in Canada twenty-five years earlier: to place Ford subsidiary companies under local management and direction in order to fit national business conditions. In 1936 Perry stated 'The Ford organisation in England has now come to be considered entirely British' {ibid 290}.

At Dagenham the first Ford car produced specifically to meet the laws, needs and preferences of the British market was the Model Y. A small car (with a 4-cylinder 8 hp engine), designed and styled by American engineers aided by A R Smith (later Sir Rowland Smith), it sold for £120 when first marketed in February 1932. It was later credited with carrying Ford of England through the depressed years of the 1930s: by 1934 the Model Y had captured 54 per cent of the market of all vehicles of 8 hp or less. Perry's 1928 Plan looked feasible until nationalist interests intensified in Europe. In Germany and France, government restrictions hit hard and it was a case of manufacturing locally or going out of business. Italy came under similar nationalistic pressure from Mussolini, determined to protect Fiat against Ford's dangerous rivalry. In Spain the Civil War halted Ford's assembly activities.

Despite these setbacks, European operations showed encouraging progress with a separate product line of European cars and local stock interest — Perry, of course, continued to take his orders from Henry Ford, but had a great deal of autonomy as European 'Governor General' and the impact of the modest US foreign sales department was limited. Working under Perry was a remarkable triumverate responsible for the day-to-day running of Ford: Patrick Hennessy (qv), A R Smith and Stanford Cooper. Their achievement can be baldly stated: representing a capital investment of £2 million, full production started at Dagenham in 1932, when 25,571 cars and trucks rolled off the assembly line. By 1936 production reached 94,180 vehicles per annum.

Another venture of Perry's during the 1930s was Fordson Estates which acquired Lord Kenyon's Boreham property near Chelmsford, Essex, and ran it as a co-operative, 'Co-Partnership Farms Ltd', which survived almost unchanged until it was taken over by an agricultural group in the early 1970s.

In January 1938, Perry was created Baron Perry of Stock Harvard, in recognition of his contributions to automotive progress and his stature as a business leader. Perry retained the chairmanship of Ford of Britain throughout the Second World War. Nor was he simply the token chairman. Dagenham was put on a war footing. While manufacturing Fordson tractors essential to the war effort Perry had to fend off Henry Ford's diversionary enthusiasm for the new tractors of Henry Ferguson (qv). For nearly two years, 1940–41, the firm produced a new small car, the Anglia. For the rest of the war the firm was preoccupied with vehicles for military use (144,495 made altogether), tractors (136,811 built) and engines (93,810 V-8s and 30,000 Merlin aircraft engines). After VE Day in 1945, Perry resumed co-ordination of the European Ford organisation. Lord Perry retired as chairman of Ford Motor Co Ltd in April 1948 and was succeeded by Lord Airedaile. That year Ford at Dagenham made 102,531 cars. Lord Perry remained a director of Ford until his death on New Providence, Bahama Islands, on 17 June 1956, when he left £77,699 gross. He was childless.

DAVID BURGESS-WISE

Writings:

(with Catherine Perry) *The Island of Enchantment* (Hutchinson & Co, 1926).

Beware Bureaucracy! (Individualist Bookshop, 1941).

How Many Beans Make Five? (Individualist Bookshop, 1942).

Industry in Reconstruction (1945).

Sources:

Unpublished

BCe.

MCe.

PrC.

Information from Professor Mira Wilkins.

L'Estrange Fawcett, 'Wheels of Fortune'.

Published

Mira Wilkins and Frank E Hill, *American Business Abroad. Ford on Six Continents* (Detroit, Michigan: Wayne State University Press, 1964).

WWW.

PETO, Sir Samuel Morton

(1809-1889)

Contractor

Samuel Morton Peto was born at Whitmore House, Woking, Surrey, on 4 August 1809, the eldest son of William Peto (d 1849) and his wife Mary née Alloway. After attending various schools from the age of six Samuel completed his academic education in his early teens at a boarding school at Brixton run by an Independent, Alexander Jardine. Here he received instruction in Latin, French, simple mathematics and algebra, a syllabus then regarded as appropriate for a business career. In 1823 he was apprenticed to his paternal uncle, Henry, who had a large, well-established building business in the City of London as well as a considerable amount of property. Samuel acquired the practical skills of carpentry and bricklaying, while his applied education was completed through attendance at both a technical school run by a Mr Grayson for building apprentices and classes given by George Maddox, an architect at Furnival's Inn, Holborn. Samuel finished his apprenticeship by acting as a superintendent and foreman in his uncle's business and taking responsibility for the erection of a number of substantial buildings.

About the time Samuel completed his apprenticeship in 1830, his uncle died and left the firm to Samuel and another nephew, Thomas Grissell, who had been a partner since 1825. The estate was considerable, with a gross income of £12,000, but against this were mortgages totalling about £7,500, annuities of £3,000, and a law suit over the Custom House that Henry had built. The two cousins overcame the financial and legal problems of their joint inheritance, while their business relations were reinforced in 1831 by Peto's marriage to his partner's sister and his own cousin, Mary de la Garde Grissell. Peto made his first family home at Albany Terrace, York Road, Lambeth where three daughters and two sons were born, but in 1841 one son died, as did his first wife the following year. In 1844 he married Sarah Ainsworth, daughter of Henry Kelsall of Rochdale, by whom he had six sons and four daughters.

Initially Grissell & Peto followed the lines established by their uncle Henry and on a capital of £50,000 netted an income of £11,000 to £12,000 a year mainly from contracts from large breweries and fire offices. However, they soon branched out and became well known through the construction of important public buildings in the metropolis and the provinces. Their initial contract for railway development was an extension of such activity, namely the building in the 1830s of two stations in Birmingham. Similarly their first contract involving the track bed could be considered as a transition stage between the erection of buildings and the laying of the permanent way; it was for the Wharncliffe viaduct, a Great Western Railway contract, which Grissell & Peto obtained in November 1835.

In the 1840s Grissell & Peto won contracts for the South Eastern and the Eastern Counties railways. In the case of the contract for the Yarmouth &

Norwich Railway, which they completed in 1844, they employed 1,500 men and had to agree to take a large part of their payment in the form of securities. Similarly with a £420,000 contract for the Southampton & Dorchester, gained in mid-1844, Grissell & Peto had to take £25,000 in shares in the company. This practice became increasingly common in Peto's subsequent career and made him not only a contractor, but also a railway financier, manager, and promoter. It led to liquidity problems as during the 1847 crisis when Peto had debts of £200,000 rising to £300,000-£350,000 the following year, forcing him to borrow £140,000. During the late 1840s Peto's cash flow difficulties were apparently eased by the connections that he had developed with the Gurney group of Norfolk banks as a result of his East Anglian contracts. By the 1860s this financial link was with Overend, Gurney, the London discount house.

Clearly it was Peto who was responsible for the growing involvement of Grissell & Peto in railway contracting, one component, albeit the major one, of the partnership's increasing commitment to large scale civil engineering. In 1846 Grissell decided to dissolve the partnership, as he was concerned about the increasing capital commitments of the firm and their finance, especially the railway contracts. With the division of the business Peto took £25,000 of plant and the railway contracts for the South Eastern, the Norfolk, the Southampton & Dorchester, and the Ely to Peterborough section of the Eastern Counties. He then formed a new partnership with Edward Betts, his brother-in-law, with whom he had business associations since the early 1840s. It continued until Betts's death in 1872. As before Peto acted largely as the financier while Betts was the superintendent of works.

Very quickly Peto came to appreciate that railways could either generate traffic and demands for other facilities or require traffic to be generated for them to become financially viable. Between the mid-1840s and the late 1850s Peto's wider development plans largely centred on the re-establishment of Lowestoft as a port and its transformation into a holiday resort. He enlarged and improved Lowestoft harbour, gave the port rail connections with Norwich, and on land to the south of the harbour he developed a resort with the building of a Marine Parade and Esplanade and several hotels. In the 1850s he built the East Suffolk railway which gave Lowestoft a direct link to London as opposed to the previous, more circuitous, route via Norwich. The line, opened on 1 June 1859, was leased by Peto, an arrangement which continued until 1861 when it became part of the Great Eastern. Peto also enlarged the Suffolk port's trade through the North of Europe Steam Navigation Co which provided shipping services between Lowestoft and Denmark where Peto & Betts had built the Royal Danish Railway in the mid-1850s and which they worked by lease on its completion. Similar was Peto's relationship with the Chester & Holyhead for which he considered developing Abergele as a holiday resort while in 1856 he gave priority to the construction of a branch to Llandudno in order to generate tourist traffic. Again, in the case of the London, Tilbury & Southend Railway, Peto, with Brassey, built 124 houses at Cliff Town (the future Westcliff) in 1861 in order to encourage leisure traffic on the line that they had built, were leasing, and on which they were losing £24,000 a year. Other centres where Peto was active in the 1840s and 1850s were Lincolnshire, where he completed several contracts for the Great

Northern Railway, and the West Midlands where he performed work for the Birmingham & Oxford Junction and the Oxford, Worcester and Wolverhampton railways.

As a result of his activities at home and abroad Peto in 1857 was chairman of the Chester & Holyhead, the Severn Valley, and the Wells & Fakenham, the latter a Norfolk line; deputy chairman of the Oxford, Worcester & Wolverhampton; and a director of the Chipping Norton and the Norwegian Trunk railways. In addition Peto & Betts were leasing the Royal Danish and, in conjunction with Brassey, the London, Tilbury & Southend. Over and above this there was Peto's role in the development of Lowestoft and the East Suffolk Railway while in 1856 his firm completed the contract for the West End & Crystal Palace Railway.

It has been estimated that Peto had handled contracts worth over £20 million during the 1840s. These had been undertaken with an air of orderliness almost unique in railway contracting. Generally Peto did not use sub-contractors and insisted upon weekly payment for his labour force. He was a critic of the tommy shop and tried to prevent the sale of beer on the works for which he was responsible. Rather, he went to great lengths to ensure that his men who, in the case of the Eastern Counties contracts, numbered 3,000 for two years, were well fed and provisioned by local merchants and shopkeepers. Moreover, he built temporary barrack accommodation for his navvies (renting it at reasonable rates), mobile temporary halls, which provided shelter against the weather, and libraries. This concern for the well-being of his labour force extended to the provision of sick clubs and went beyond their physical and cultural needs to embrace the spiritual. He employed ten or 11 scripture readers in 1846 for the Eastern Counties contract from Ely to Peterborough and built a chapel at Brandon.

With an Independent schooling in his early teens and attendance at St Mary's (Baptist) Chapel, Norwich in the early 1840s, this side of Peto's character was developed further by his second wife Sarah and his own switch from the Congregationalists to the Baptists. Peto now became heavily involved with the establishment and financial support of orphanages and hospitals and the rehabilitation of newly-released convicts. Between 1846 and 1867 he acted as the treasurer for the Baptist Missionary Society and bore the costs of deputations to India, West Africa and Jamaica. Later between 1853 and 1855, and between 1863 and 1867, he was chairman of the Dissenting Deputies. Responding to a need for Baptist churches in central London, Peto was responsible for the building of Bloomsbury Chapel in 1848, the conversion of the Diorama into Regent's Park Chapel, and the building of a further chapel at Notting Hill. Peto headed the Bloomsbury congregation, provided for a subsidised day school in its basement for poor but 'respectable' children, and financed a mission in the slums of St Giles.

His innovations in the employment of navvies were a major factor in Peto's emergence as a national public figure. He was MP for Norwich 1847-54, for Finsbury 1859-64 and for Bristol 1865-67. He championed steady and progressive reform, civil liberty, and free trade. He acted as a financial guarantor, to the extent of £50,000, for the promotion of the Great Exhibition and subsequently became a Commissioner. Later he built the Crimean military railway. For these services Peto received a barontecy in 1855. After his bankruptcy in 1867 he retired from public life.

The origins of Peto's withdrawal from public life may possibly be traced back to the early 1850s and particularly his involvement with the Grand Trunk Railway of Canada. In 1851 Peto had been approached by the premier of Nova Scotia to secure his influence with the British Government for imperial aid to assist the construction of an intercolonial railway between Quebec and Halifax. Through a local agent, Peto offered to build a line connecting the St Lawrence and the Atlantic seaboard. The premiers of Canada, New Brunswick and Nova Scotia rejected the proposal on cost grounds. However in October 1852 Peto obtained the contract for the Quebec & Richmond Railway, an enterprise controlled by London and Liverpool capital. The Grand Trunk was incorporated the following month, but did not assume its final form until 1853 when, as a result of discussion in London, other Canadian lines, (including the Quebec & Richmond) were absorbed, which increased the capital involved from £3 million to £9.5 million and the mileage from 330 to 1,100, so transforming it into the (then) largest world railway project.

The major contracts, including the Victoria bridge, were let to Peto & Betts in conjunction with Brassey and Jackson. As was becoming increasingly common, the responsibility for financing the enterprise was passed over to the contractors who, in turn, approached Barings and Glyns. The company's prospectus was issued in April 1853, but ten days previously the contractors were forced by their bankers to agree to take up half of the company's equity capital, its B shares, about £1.8 million nominal. Further, the contractors were to be paid 50 per cent in cash, 33 per cent in bonds and 16 per cent in more B shares and were required to pay £12 10s per share on the last. Peto let sub-contracts to Canadians for grading work and the construction of wooden bridges and culverts, but the English contractors established an engineering works at Birkenhead, Cheshire, to supply locomotives and ironwork for the Victoria bridge. This manufacturing enterprise had a capital of £270,000 of which a third was contributed by Peto. The Canada Works at Birkenhead were laid out in 1853, employed 600 and equipped the Grand Trunk and other lines, in Britain and overseas, built by its contracting owners.

In 1855 the share price of the Grand Trunk collapsed, the result of a number of factors. On the sections opened revenue fell due to declining immigration and the effects of cholera, while, more broadly, a Canadian lumber boom had run its course. It would appear that these adverse economic conditions in Canada forced sales by local holders of the railway's securities. The English contractors may also have been selling in order to cover their liquidity position. Costs had greatly exceeded estimates, which was common enough, but the company was not in a position to pay for a higher standard of civil engineering. The various issues involved resulted in arbitration of the Victoria Bridge contract for which Peto had sought additional aid. By the award the contractors were forced to reduce their price and to waive their claim of £100,000 for contingencies. Their only gain was that henceforth they were to be paid only in cash and bonds and so the burden of having to pay £12 10s on each B share was lifted.

The Victoria Bridge over the St Lawrence was not opened until October

1860, two years after the railway was completed. The problems of the poorly-built, over-capitalised Grand Trunk continued but led to Peto's involvement with the American Atlantic & Great Western Railroad one of the few lines on whch construction proceeded during the Civil War. It was both a rival to the Grand Trunk and a possible feeder of traffic to it. Peto assisted MacHenry, its contractor, in raising money for the building of the line in the 1860s, with Peto & Betts themselves making advances of £331,000 to the company against its securities as collateral.

Peto's finances were under considerable strain from the late 1850s. He had liabilities of £11 million during the 1857 crisis and personally regarded the late 1850s as a difficult time. In 1861, when he had income of £10,000 a year, he stated that he was doing better than he had been over the previous seven. Nevertheless his financial problems continued and in 1862 he sold Somerleyton, his Suffolk estate, while the partnership, Peto & Betts, realised their investment in the Clay Cross Colliery for £70,000. Although his biographer and Portuguese sources are in some dispute, it seems that financial reasons were in part responsible for Peto being unable to fulfil a contract to build a line between Lisbon and Oporto in the late 1850s which involved a £20,000 deposit and a guarantee of 7 per cent on the contractor's part. The only result of the affair was a rather sordid dispute between Peto and the Portuguese Government over the costs of the necessary preliminary surveys which led to the matter being raised in the Commons and involved the Foreign Office and the British Minister at Lisbon.

Although Peto's Portuguese initiatives came to nothing, his contracting firm in the 1850s was responsible for lines in Australia (with Brassey) and in the 1860s for the Algiers to Blida railway, the Orel to Vitebsk line in western Russia, and the Varna to Ruse railway on the Black Sea littoral. The Algerian line's capital was underwritten by Peto which led to him subscribing 80 per cent because of a poor public response. The Russian concession was generous, involving a 5 per cent guarantee on estimated costs, as the Government was anxious both to facilitate grain exports in order to gain hard currency and to reduce the losses on the already completed state-guaranteed Riga to Vitebsk line. In the case of the Varna railway, which Peto & Betts built with Crampton, the contractors turned to two of the finance companies of the 1860s to float the balance of the railway company's equity capital on the London market. Further, Peto & Betts, with Brassey, obtained £300,000 from another of the finance companies in order to assist them with their continuing Danish contracts.

One of the major roles played by the English finance companies of the 1860s was to act as contractors' banks. The International Financial Society consulted Peto regarding the prospects for a Moldavian railway and the Lisbon to Cintra concession, while Peto was a major shareholder in the Imperial Mercantile Credit. His connections seemed to have been largely with the second rank of these institutions and with Overend, Gurney, which, with its change of management in the mid-1850s shifted increasingly into the provision of investment funds, away from 'pure' discounting. Peto, with Brassey and Overend, Gurney, took an initial interest in the development of the Millwall Dock, East London, in the early 1860s, a continuation of an involvement in the expansion of the metropolis's port facilities since the 1840s. Peto & Betts had built the

Victoria Dock in 1850 and then along with Brassey leased it in 1855; their other activities in this sphere included the Woolwich and the Thames graving docks.

The increasing strain on Peto's financial resources in the early 1860s and his consequent complicated relations with the finance companies are indicated by the methods that he used to finance contracts for the London, Chatham & Dover Railway. Peto & Betts were drawn into the construction of this line by the locomotive engineer Thomas Russell Crampton. They built the Strood to Elephant and Castle section of the railway and then, in the 1860s, again with Crampton, took on contracts for its metropolitan extensions. Since the 1850s the railway had come to rely on its contractors for finance, adopting a procedure whereby the contractors applied for its equity capital, which allowed the company to utilise its borrowing powers, but the debentures were in turn passed over to the contractors who then issued them to the public. One result was that the company over-issued debentures with new bonds being sold before old ones, often deposited with banks as collateral for loans, had been retired. The consequence was that the London, Chatham & Dover exceeded its statutory borrowing powers, although this did not become evident until it collapsed in the 1866 crisis.

Generally Peto used Coleman, a stockbroker and a director of the Imperial Mercantile Credit, for the public flotation of London, Chatham & Dover securities which resulted in the railway paying, over and above Peto's own charges, two further issuing commissions, one to the stockbroker and one to the finance company. By the spring of 1865 the expensive independent entry of the London, Chatham & Dover into London was draining severely the resources of all involved. Peto guaranteed 6 per cent on a public issue of £1.2 million a stock undertaken by the Credit Foncier & Mobilier of England but, although this was 1 per cent above the normal rate on such securities, little of the issue was taken up by the public. Privately he sought loans from the finance and insurance companies but a request for £375,000 was refused by both the International Financial Society and the Royal Exchange Assurance. There was a growing stringency on the London financial markets from the summer of 1865 which led to even more involved arrangements for financing construction. In order to erect its own metropolitan goods depot, the London, Chatham & Dover in February 1866 sold what was considered to be 'surplus' land to Peto who then used it as security for loans totalling £295,000 from both the Imperial Mercantile Credit and the General Credit & Finance. However what in fact the two finance companies passed to Peto were accepted foreign bills of exchange, drawn largely by men of no financial substance which the contractor then discounted with Overend, Gurney. Ultimately the whole arrangement was to be funded by a mortgage on the completed premises from the Rock Insurance Co, of which Peto was a director, but it was interrupted by the 1866 crisis.

Railway finance had increasingly centred upon the contractor since the early 1850s and the perverted structure of finance in the 1860s, in which bills of exchange acted as mortgages, crumbled during the first half of 1866. The whole edifice gave way on 11 May with the failures of Peto & Betts and Overend, Gurney. Initially Peto was regarded in terms of 'That he will emerge from the cloud still a very rich man, with the a character for honour beyond the reach of any question' {*Economist* 16 June 1866}. The statement of the affairs of his partnership showed creditors and liabilities of £483,375 as against assets of £1,562,064 but of which only £7,744 was liquid. The only criticism made of him was that 'he engaged in operations beyond the force even of his great capital, and in consequence he borrowed at rates of interest so high as to be injurious to his credit as well as destructive of his profit.' {*ibid*}

From the autumn of 1866 a wave of criticism of Peto's conduct began to gather as a result of the investigations into Overend, Gurney and the London, Chatham & Dover which was now bankrupt. Peto accepted the blame for the railway company having overissued debentures, although a railway solicitor pointed that what the London, Chatham & Dover had done was the general practice of railway companies, while the *Economist* held the company's directors equally responsible as their agent Peto. In October 1866 further details of Peto's financing of the London, Chatham & Dover emerged, showing how the capital of the company had been watered with a difference on one section of line of £4.6 million between nominal receipts of £15.25 million and capital received and expended of £10.625 million. In one case '£2,207,300 of stock was publicly sold, in respect of which Messrs Peto & Co claim to give the company credit for only £27 10s per cent of its nominal account, less £38,500 further deducted as the expense of placing it' {*ibid* 6 Oct 1866}

Contractor and company now made claims against one another with the railway asking for £186,000 from Peto and Peto £384,000 from the company. Still anxious to preserve Peto's public standing all the *Economist* could comment was: 'Perhaps he did not himself know, at least not in full and exactly, how his name was being used, though he was bound to know. But the result is the same. By virtue of Peto's name, the public have been robbed and they should hereafter be slow to give a similar trust to any other name.' {*ibid* 13 Oct 1866} Peto defended his conduct in the following way:

> with regard to the over-issue of debentures, he told them on the last occasion that he accepted the responsibility personally, and that on good grounds. In the first place, he felt that he was prepared to justify all he had done, and if he could not, he was not going to allow another individual to bear his responsibilities. They all recollected the crisis that occurred in the spring of the year. During that period loans matured with his acceptance on them to the amount of £150,000, and his firm must either collapse itself or meet them; and, besides, he was bound to, and did, provide for a great necessity of the company of £210,000. He must tell them that the debentures which had been placed with a financial company were not lost, as that company held an enormous amount of his Sir M Peto's securities, more than sufficient to redeem them. He felt, therefore, that no loss could accrue, and that therefore he was justified in using the money in the way he had done.' {*ibid* 20 Oct 1866}

Within a week Peto backtracked on his position by now claiming that there had not been an over-issue of debentures but rather the debentures were used as collateral for loans from financial institutions and were either not fully filled out or not adequately registered. The *Economist* described them as imitation debentures, pawned until the general public would subscribe for them. A year later details of the financing of the London, Chatham &

Dover's metropolitan goods depot became public, with further revelations in February 1868.

In March 1868 Peto was examined in the Bankruptcy Court which led to further public exposure of the intricate and involved relations between the contractor and the London, Chatham & Dover.

> What was being done was wrong, and all concerned were quite well aware of the fact. The most marvellous part of the transaction, indeed, is the facility afforded to Sir Morton Peto by the various people whose assistance was necessary, and some of whom may be supposed to have represented the public interest in the matter. There never seems to have been any difficulty. The contract prices were raised 20 per cent above the original proposal, on the mere 'suggestion of Mr Betts'. When Sir Morton Peto applied for a rebate of 50 per cent on the A shares, the application was at once acceded to. All parties were mutually complaisant in tiding over difficulties. One of the most formidable of these was the necessity of a subscription contract, in order to use the compulsory powers of the Act. It was got over by the simple expedient of Peto and Co subscribing the contract themselves, and paying £206,000 to the Union Bank as the first deposit on 82,000 shares. But whence came the money? In the first day's examination Sir Morton Peto said he could not remember whether he borrowed the money upon the shares, but on the same day he got a sum of £100,000, and on the following day a sum of £51,000. In the second examination, a document was shown which cleared up the doubt. The amount was for commission on the deposit of the shares. That is, apparently, Sir Morton Peto pays a deposit on certain shares, but gets back most of the cash he parts with in the name of commission, so that the deposit became a mere form' {*ibid* 14 Mar 1868}

The dispute between the London, Chatham & Dover and Peto & Betts was settled finally by a compromise. In August 1868 Peto's personal balance sheet was published covering the period from 1864 to 3 July 1867 but it was unintelligible, neglected to estimate contingent liabilities and attempted 'to show how the existing conditions of affairs was brought about innocently from a more prosperous period' {*ibid* 22 Aug 1868}.

The tangled nature of Peto's affairs was also investigated by the Bloomsbury Chapel through the treasurer and one deacon, one of whom was a businessman. Peto co-operated fully with this investigation although the chapel's inquirers found difficulty in comprehending the verbatim reports of the Examinations in Bankruptcy. They found that Peto had followed normal business practice when contributing to various 'legal fictions', cleared him of the charge of dishonest conduct, but could not in the last resort 'declare our brother to have been free from blame' {Bowers (1982) 10}. Peto, along with Betts and Crampton, was discharged as a bankrupt in July 1868.

Following his bankruptcy Peto's career as a railway contractor virtually came to an end. Surveys in Russia made before 1866 did not subsequently yield contracts. Peto spent 1868 and 1869 in Budapest working on a regulation scheme for the Danube, with the expectation of obtaining the contract along with Brassey, but again this came to nothing. In 1869 he went to Paris to try for contracts for the Palais de Justice in Algiers and a hospital in the French capital but their adjudication was interrupted by the Franco-Prussian War. The only contract that Peto & Betts did manage to obtain was one for minor alterations on the Metropolitan Railway. Betts died in 1872 and Peto alone became involved in the speculative Cornwall Minerals Railway in the mid-1870s.

With his bankruptcy Peto had been forced to sell his house in Kensington Palace Gardens which had been built for him. In the mid-1870s he moved home nearly every other year but finally in 1877 settled at Eastcote House, Pinner, where some of his time was occupied as JP for Middlesex. In 1884 he moved again to Blackhurst, Tunbridge Wells, but with failing health spent two winters in Cannes. From November 1888 he became increasingly ill and died at Blackhurst on 13 November 1889.

P L COTTRELL

Writings:

Taxation: Its Levy and Expenditure, Past and Future; Being an Enquiry into Our Financial Policy (Chapman & Hall, 1863).

The Resources and Prospects of America Ascertained during a Visit to the States in the Autumn of 1865 (Alexander Strahan, 1866).

Sources:

Unpublished

Brian and Faith Bowers, 'Bloomsbury Chapel and Mercantile Morality. The Case of Sir Morton Peto' (unpublished paper prepared for a seminar on Christianity and Business held in the Business History Unit, LSE, 26 Mar 1982).

Philip L Cottrell, 'Investment Banking in England 1856-1882' (Hull PhD, 1974).

Antonio Lopes Vieira, 'The Role of Britain and France in the Finance of Portuguese Railways 1850-1890' (Leicester PhD, 1983).

Published

Peter E Baughan, *North and Mid Wales. Regional History of the Railways of Great Britain* II (Newton Abbot: David & Charles, 1980).

Bradshaw's Shareholders' Guide (various volumes and years).

Eric D Brant, *Railways of North Africa* (Newton Abbot: David & Charles, 1971).

D R Butcher, 'A Great Victorian' *East Anglian Magazine* 33 (1973-74).

John M Cooper, *London Railways* (B T Batsford, 1962).

Philip L Cottrell, 'Railway Finance and the Crisis of 1866: Contractors' Bills of Exchange and the Finance Companies' *Journal of Transport History* new ser 3 (1975).

Edwin Course, *London Railways* (B T Batsford, 1962).

John G Cox, *Castleman's Corkscrew. The Southampton and Dorchester Railway 1844-1848* (City of Southampton, 1975).

Archibald W Currie, *The Grand Trunk Railway of Canada* (Toronto: University of Toronto Press, 1957).

DNB.

Economist 16 June, 6, 13, 20 Oct 1866, 14 Mar, 22 Aug 1868.

Donald I Gordon, *The Eastern Counties. Regional History of Railways of Great Britain* V (Newton & Abbot: David & Charles, 1977).

Charles H Grinling, *The History of the Great Northern Railway 1845-1922* (George Allen & Unwin, 1966).

Richard S Joby, *The Railway Builders* (Newton & Abbot: David & Charles, 1983).

James W Lowe, *British Steam Locomotive Builders* (Goose & Son, 1975).

Edward T MacDermot, *History of the Great Western Railway* (repr, 2 vols, Ian Allan, 1964) I.

Sir Henry Peto, *Sir Morton Peto, a Memorial Sketch* (Elliot Stock, 1893).

S Richards, 'Samuel Morton Peto (1809-1889): A Biographical Note' *Journal of the Railway and Canal Historical Society* 27 (1982).

Michael Robbins, 'The Balaclava Railway' *Journal of Transport History* I (1953).

D J Smith, *The Severn Valley Railway* (Bracknell: Town & Country Press, 1968).

Douglas C Sparkes, 'Samuel Morton Peto: A Note' *The Baptist Quarterly* 24 (1972).

John N Westwood, *A History of Russian Railways* (George Allen & Unwin, 1964).

Henry P White, *Southern England. Regional History of Railways of Great Britain* (Phoenix House, 1961).

John Wrottesley, *The Great Northern Railway* I, *Origins and Development* (B T Batsford, 1979).

WWMP.

PETTER, Sir Ernest Willoughby

(1873-1954)

and

PETTER, Percival Waddams

(1873-1955)

Engine and aircraft manufacturers

Ernest Willoughby Petter and Percival Waddams Petter were identical twins born at Yeovil, on 26 May 1873; they were third and fourth of the fifteen children of James Bayeley Petter, an ironmonger, and his wife

Charlotte Waddams née Branscombe, daughter of a Bristol rubber merchant and a member of the Exclusive Brethren. After local schooling, and two years at Mount Radford School, Exeter, they were brought back aged sixteen as apprentices in the family business. This had flourished and as well as the ironmonger's shop, the Yeovil foundry and engineering works dealing mainly in agricultural machinery had been acquired and the Nautilus Stove Co had been set up. The father was an innovative engineer and in the ten years from 1881 he had taken out 17 patents, the majority being for grates and kitchen ranges for the Nautilus Co.

Ernest and Percy became very interested in engines and Percy late in life described how, inspired by articles in the 1894 *Boys' Own Paper* and with the help of the foundry foreman, Benny Jacobs who was a skilled engineer draughtsman and mechanic, they made their first oil engine. By the end of 1895 this engine had been installed in a carriage body made by a local coachbuilder and despite the Red Flag Act they were allowed by the local police to drive it on the roads before 8.0 am without the flag. This was one of the first internal combustion vehicles built in England. In 1896 the *Engineer* journal offered 1,000 guineas in prizes for the best self-propelled road vehicle and the Petter brothers as the Yeovil Motor Car & Cycle Co entered a paraffin oil engined car. Despite over 70 entries, only five vehicles, including oil, petrol, steam and electric drive, appeared for the trials at the Crystal Palace in June 1897. Daimlers refused to participate. The judges decided no vehicle was sufficiently satisfactory and did not award the prize, to the disappointment of the Petters. Although they made a few more custom-built oil-engined cars and a couple of electric cars, one of which appeared in the 1897 Lord Mayor's Show in London, they found their resources inadequate to tackle standardised large-scale production of petrol-engined vehicles. Instead they concentrated on small oil engines of 1 hp and 2.5 hp for agricultural and dairy applications where there was no competition from gas engines such as those made by Crossleys (qv). Soon they had a thriving business in which they were assisted by their brothers Guy (1872-1948), who had trained as a mining engineer, Harry and Hugh.

The Petters preferred direct selling, achieved through demonstrations at agricultural shows up and down the country but in two areas they turned to agents. Ernest, who was more concerned with the financial side of the business set up a London agency for Petters engines and Nautilus stoves. For Ireland, they appointed William and James Kennan of Dublin as their selling agents. Percy married Emily Kennan in 1904.

Percy, under his father's eye, was held responsible for the engine business while the father concentrated mainly on the ironmongery and hot water heating side. The engine business flourished but required considerable capital; the shifting of the business bank account to obtain adequate overdraft facilities caused problems with the father who was determined to maintain a patriarchal right of veto over his sons' business activities. A little later a loss of £3,000, largely attributed to the engine side of the business, led the father to instruct Percy to shut it down. Instead, after a painful disagreement Percy and Ernest offered to buy the engine business for £3,850 from their father; with the help of family, Christian Brethren and City acquaintances they formed in 1901 James B Petter & Sons Ltd, raised £4,000 (to which the two brothers were able to contribute £300 — their father had never paid them more than £2 a week) and set up

independently. By working hard and curbing expenses, they made a profit of £2,000 in their first year and the business expanded steadily. The range of engines manufactured was increased and technical improvements were made (from 1898-1918 Ernest, Percy and Guy took out 39 patents, almost all for improvements to internal combustion engines and vehicles — thereafter patents were taken out in the name of Petters Ltd).

In 1903 the company came under heavy competition from the American Fairbanks Morse petrol engines; Percy launched a hard sales campaign, pressuring their agents to place bulk orders for batches of 50 of their own 'Handy Man' 2 hp engine. The campaign was successful, orders increased dramatically not only in England but in many overseas markets. In response to the needs of the Russian trade, two-stroke engines were made; these were found to be more effective and largely displaced four-stroke engines. By 1910 fresh capital was needed and the company was reconstructed under the name of Petters Ltd with an authorised capital of £150,000 of which £76,805 represented the purchase money for the predecessor firm. Trade proved so buoyant that their factory and particularly the foundry working day and night was unable to keep pace with orders. Some 1,500 engines were sold in 1911 and the workforce was around 500. In 1913 a 75-acre site was purchased at West Hendford not only for a new foundry but also for a garden village to be managed by a separate private company similar to the Bournville project of the Cadburys (qv). The site was named Westland and the foundry started work but only a handful of houses were built because of the outbreak of the First World War.

The immediate effect on the business was the cancellation of many home and foreign orders but government contracts, at first for engines, compensated. When the company accepted a munitions contract to make shell cases in 1915, W R Moore, who had been a major subscriber in 1901 and chairman since then, resigned for conscientious reasons; like Ernest and Percy he was an active member of the Christian Brethren. Ernest was elected chairman and the manufacture of munitions proceeded. Petters then offered their resources to the War Office and Admiralty and were advised to build aeroplanes. The Admiralty assumed that the firm had patternmakers who would be very suitable for this class of work which was presumed not to be difficult.

Percy and another brother John, an architect, visited Oswald Short and his brothers near Rochester and were given a contract for 15 seaplanes.

Westland Wapiti made by the Westland Aircraft Co (from Michael J H Taylor Warplanes of the World*).*

Under R A Bruce, who had been the pre-war manager of the British & Colonial Aeroplane Co at Bristol, the Petter aviation business (soon known as the Westland Aircraft Works) built nearly 1,000 aeroplanes and the Petter works made thousands of engines, as well as production of shell cases and gun carriage equipment, employing in all some 3,000 people by 1918.

After the war Percy and Ernest Petter tried to find work for nearly 600 demobilised employees by starting the manufacture of pianos at Westland Aircraft but, encountering a labour demarcation dispute, they returned to the manufacture of engines. Petters, in a deal with Vickers in 1920, formed Vickers-Petters Ltd at Ipswich operating independently of Petters Ltd at Yeovil, and purchased a large local ex-Vickers factory to manufacture a more powerful range of semi-diesel engines up to 2,000 hp. These larger engines were used in ocean-going ships and factory and municipal electricity generators, a significant proportion being exported. In 1926 the Vickers's interest was bought out by Petters to give greater freedom of action, but the venture was not a success. Labour unrest in the engineering industry pushed up costs; the return to gold in 1925 eroded overseas profits; and a national grid, authorised by the Electricity Supply Act of 1926 and completed within seven years, wiped out much of the domestic demand for heavy gasoline engines. The Petters' attempts to sell the Ipswich works were thwarted by the depression and the firm survived only on the strength of its Yeovil business.

At Yeovil Ernest and Percy Petter, with R A Bruce as managing director of their subsidiary the Westland Aircraft Works, continued manufacture of aeroplanes despite the falling peacetime demand, and were sustained by orders for the DH 9A and its subsequent Westland developments, the Widgeon, offered for £750 complete with tools and airworthiness certificate, and the Wapiti, of which at one period there were more in the RAF than any other type (over 500 were supplied to the Air Ministry).

A Cierva CL 20 helicopter (courtesy of Westland Helicopters Ltd).

Equally successful in the early 1930s was the production of Petter oil engines, from 2 to 60 hp, for use as stationary or portable agricultural engines in smaller powers, and marine engines for the larger, or as electricity generating or pumping units for rural use at home and in the colonies. By 1935 standard engines of up to 15 hp were being assembled on moving conveyer belts. In 1935 the Petter aircraft interests were separated out and a new company, Westland Aircraft Ltd was registered with a share capital of £250,000. An offer of 500,000 5s shares at 7s was oversubscribed. Already in 1935 the company was experimenting with unconventional aircraft; it was associated with the Cierva Autogiro Co Ltd from 1933 and had already built its first machine of which it had great hopes. The prospectus reported Westland's intention to manufacture autogiros in quantity and foresaw a large market for machines 'which the private owner can operate with safety and comfort' {Times *Prospectuses* 90 (1935)} (helicopters in which Westland now (1984) specialises differ from autogiros as the rotor is powered).

In 1937 Ernest retired from the chairmanship of Petters and Westland and Percy from his directorship of Petters. Ernest's eldest son, Edward, was already technical director of Westland; he had an important career as aircraft designer, being responsible inter alia for the English Electric Canberra.

Ernest, like his father was very interested in politics and three times attempted to win election to parliament as an Independent Conservative; on the third occasion in 1931 he stood at Westminster against Duff Cooper, the successful official Conservative candidate, and 'conducted the campaign with all the fire-eating vigour used by others of Baldwin's enemies elsewhere' {*Times* 19 July 1954}. He was president of the British Engineers' Association, 1923-25, and received a knighthood for organising the engineering section of the 1925 British Empire Exhibition at Wembley. He was a vice-president of the Institution of Mechanical

Engineers and a member of the executive of the Federation of British Industries.

In 1907 he married Angela Emma, daughter of Henry Petter of Calcutta; they had three sons and one daughter. She died in 1934 and the following year he married Lucy Ellen, daughter of Charles Hopkins of Portsmouth who survived him. Following his retirement he lived in British Columbia until just before his death on 18 July 1954. He left £859 in England.

Percy played a very active role in the civic life of Yeovil. He was elected to the council in 1916 and became alderman and mayor in 1925-27 and was a JP. Although a confirmed Anglican, he was a very active member of the Christian (or Open) Brethren throughout his life and believed in the power of prayer in his business as well as his private life. In 1919 he was one of the 'Pilgrim Preachers', a band of evangelists who preached on a walking tour between Bath and London. The Pilgrim Preachers made a number of other journeys in 1919-21 but Percy had to limit his further participation because of his business obligations. He took a strong public stand on ritualism in the Church of England and wrote a number of pamphlets. At the time of his death he was president of the National Union of Protestants. He married first Emily Kennan of Dublin by whom he had two sons and four daughters; following his first wife's death he married Ruth Penson-Harris who survived him. Percy Petter died on 15 September 1955 and left £23,502.

DAVID J JEREMY *and* FRANCIS GOODALL

Writings:

Ernest Willoughby Petter, *The Disease of Unemployment and the Cure* (Hutchinson & Co, 1925).

Percival Waddams Petter, *The Story of the Pilgrim Preachers and Their Message* (Marshall Bros, 1922).

—, *Assembly Service [On the Assemblies of the "Open Brethren"]* (Marshall, Morgan & Scott, 1930).

—, *The Counsel of Sapiens, the Christian* (Yeovil: Channel Publishers, 1939).

—, *Eternal Life, the Gift of God* (Stirling: Stirling Tract Enterprise, 1942).

—, *Guilty Clergy* (Yeovil: Channel Publishers, 1943).

—, *Essential Amendments in the Canon Law Proposed for the Church of England in the Report of the Archbishop's [sic] Commission on Canon Law* (National Union of Protestants, 1947).

Sources:

Unpublished

BCe.

PrC.

P W Petter, 'The Story of Petters Limited — Told for My Children' (typescript in the possession of Dr Norah Sims).

Correspondence with Dr Norah Sims (née Petter) and Harald J Penrose (formerly of Westland Aircraft Ltd).

Published

Chartered Mechanical Engineer 2 (1955).

Engineer 81 (1896), 82 (1897), 159 (1935), 187 (1949), 198 (1954).

Engineering 178 (1954), 180 (1955).

Patent Office *Registers* 1880-1920.

Petters Monthly News Jan-Dec 1927.

Stock Exchange Official Year Book 1934, 1936.

Times 19 July 1954.

Times *Prospectuses* 90 (1935).

WWW.

PHILIPPS, Sir Ivor

(1861-1940)

Industrialist

Ivor Philipps was born at Warminster, Wiltshire, on 9 September 1861, the second son of Canon Sir James Erasmus Philipps, Twelfth Baronet, Vicar of Warminster and later Prebendary of Salisbury Cathedral, and his wife the Honourable Mary Margaret née Best. (The family's background is outlined in the entries on John Wynford Philipps and Owen Cosby Philipps.)

Ivor Philipps attended Felsted School, Essex, which offered reduced fees to the sons of clergymen. He then entered the Militia and, after two years, received a regular commission. Serving in Burma and the North-West Frontier, he fought in the China Expedition, 1900-1, and was awarded the DSO for his part in the relief of Peking. He retired from the regular army in 1903 to command the Pembroke Yeomanry and to pursue a political career, representing Southampton as a Liberal MP, 1906-22. He had a house in London but resided mainly at Cosheston Hall, Pembroke, and took a prominent part there as an alderman on Pembrokeshire County Council and later as Vice-Lieutenant of the county. He is remembered particularly for his painstaking restoration of Pembroke Castle.

In 1906, at the age of forty-five, he entered business life and by 1914 was director of 16 companies, chairman of nine and vice-chairman of one. In 1933 his 14 chairmanships included Ilford Ltd, British Alkaloids, British Industries & General Investment Trust, Schweppes, four rubber companies and World Marine & General Insurance Co. Many of these companies were controlled or connected with other members of the family, particularly his elder brother, John.

Ivor Philipps apparently held no managerial responsibilities in the companies with which he was connected. He was always interested in 'productivity' and introduced typewriters into the War Office during the First World War. He spent a great deal of his time at his farm in Pembrokeshire, coming up to London periodically to his house in Ebury Street, Victoria, for parliamentary duties; he also had an office in the City, reported to be small and only used as a base from which to make sorties to his various companies to spur them on. While he regularly made tours of inspection of some of his companies' factories, he rarely spent more than one day a week on industrial premises and never visited most of the subsidiaries of the major companies in which he took an interest. An impression is left with those who knew him of a major-general visiting his staff officers and troops — and this approach worked well, especially after 1920. It may be significant that he was assisted by members of the Kemp-Welch family at both the major manufacturing companies with which he was associated — Ilford and Schweppes.

Ivor Philipps's involvement with Ilford Ltd started purely by chance. He happened to meet one of the firm's solicitors in London in 1905. The Ilford board was unsettled at the time and the shareholders restive. Philipps agreed to take on the job of chairman. Ilford Ltd had been making photographic materials successfully since 1879. Then, Kodak Ltd had made bids for the company in 1902 and 1903, leading to a dispute between the directors and the shareholders. A new board had been elected who knew very little of the business and was beset by technical and financial problems. Ilford had not followed Kodak into the manufacture of roll films at the end of the nineteenth century, being content with a successful business in glass plates and sensitised papers. However, by 1912, Philipps evidently decided upon new policies. The company altered course by engaging two German specialists to set up an experimental film factory at Brentwood, Essex, but they were repatriated in 1914 without having achieved their aim.

When the First World War started, Philipps was recalled from the army reserve and appointed brigadier-general in command of the 115th Brigade. In 1915, he was promoted major-general and appointed Parliamentary Secretary (military) to the Ministry of Munitions, resigning his executive position at Ilford. Later that year he raised the 38th Welsh Division, went with it to France and took part in the battle of the Somme in July 1916. He was created a KCB in 1917.

He returned to Ilford as joint managing director in November 1921. By that time, the profits, which had risen from £14,000 in 1907 to £48,000 in 1915, had slipped back to £35,000. He decided that this must be rectified and used his organising abilities, learned from his army experience, to revitalise the company. He did so by taking-over smaller rivals, thereby reducing competition, and achieving economies of scale.

Just before Philipps had joined Ilford in 1905, a committee of shareholders had recommended, in a strongly-worded memorandum, that British manufacturers of photographic materials, cameras and lenses, as well as distributors, should combine to meet outside competition. Very little had been done and, in 1919, there were still nearly 30 independent UK manufacturers of sensitised materials. Sir Ivor first negotiated with the Imperial Dry Plate Co and, shortly afterwards, with Thos Illingworth Ltd. Both companies were soon effectively under his control. The idea of producing roll films was revived and a new company, Selo Ltd, based on the pre-war Brentwood factory, was set up jointly with Imperial and four other companies. This led to the purchase by Ilford in 1927 of a controlling interest in all the companies concerned. In 1930, Wellington & Ward Ltd was purchased. Thus by 1930 Sir Ivor had succeeded in amalgamating into Ilford Ltd all the major British photographic companies which had not already been purchased by Kodak earlier in the century.

The next ten years were a period of consolidation and rationalisation. The research and development organisation, which had always been strong, was strengthened still further by the addition of bright, young scientists to the teams headed by the brilliant chemists, F F Renwick and Olaf Bloch. The smaller factories were closed, leaving the company with five major sites. The administration was overhauled and export business rapidly expanded throughout the world. As a result, profits rose steadily, in spite of the recession, from £95,000 at the start of the decade to £131,000 in 1939.

Similarly Philipps revived Schweppes, the mineral water business. Run as a partnership by John Kemp Welch and William Evill, it had been floated as a public company in 1897 by Ernest Terah Hooley (qv). With an authorised capital of £1.25 million, the new company was over-capitalised and for years the board was unable to meet by a long way either their liability for the cumulative deferred dividend or their responsibility to finance the business. Eventually in 1918 there was a revolt among the shareholders and the board which, except for C D Kemp-Welch, resigned. A new board under the chairmanship of Sir Ivor Philipps was appointed. Sir Ivor came in with a firm hand and immediately reformed the balance sheet, disclosing a huge goodwill (£1,039,000) which from the first year he wrote down as fast as possible. He reduced the loans, built up the reserves, paid off the arrears of dividend on the deferred shares, and expanded the business. Within ten years he built new factories at Glasgow, Brighton, Cardiff, Leeds and Dublin, expanded the factories at Hendon and Vauxhall in London, and added cider to the range of table waters produced. Overseas he formed operating companies in Belgium, France and South Africa, in addition to two Australian factories which were expanded. As a result, Schweppes's profits rose from £55,000 in 1918 to £173,000 in 1928 and the market value of the company from £479,000 to £1,855,000 over the same period.

In 1891, he married Marian Isobel, daughter of J B Mirrlees of Glasgow; they had one daughter. Major-General Sir Ivor Philipps died on 15 August 1940, at the age of seventy-eight, leaving £26,563 gross.

GEORGE A JONES

Sources:

Unpublished

Ilford Ltd, Brentwood, board minutes, 1906-40.

BCe.

Information from W H Dimsdale, nephew of Sir Ivor Philipps, and Mr Douglas Simmons.

Published

Burke's Peerage and Baronetage 1975.

Crockford's Clerical Directory 1905.

Peter N Davies, 'Business Success and the Role of Chance: The Extraordinary Philipps Brothers' *Business History* 23 (1981).

DD 1914, 1921, 1931, 1933.

DNB.

Financial News 10 May 1929.

Robert J Hercock and George A Jones, *Silver by the Ton: The History of Ilford Limited 1879-1979* (McGraw-Hill, 1979).

Douglas A Simmons, *Schweppes. The First 200 Years* (Springwood Books, 1983).

Times 16 Aug 1940.

WWMP.

WWW.

PHILIPPS, John Wynford

1st Viscount St Davids of Lydstep Haven

(1860-1938)

Financier

John Wynford Philipps was born at Warminster on 30 May 1860, the eldest son of the six sons and five daughters of Canon Sir James Erasmus Philipps, Twelfth Baronet. The family were the junior branch of an old Welsh landowning family but much of their property at Picton in Pembrokeshire had passed out of the male line in the early nineteenth century and for some time family members had pursued careers in the Church of England. An impoverished member of the minor gentry, Sir James became Vicar of Warminster and Prebendary of Salisbury Cathedral and was married to Mary Margaret, the eldest daughter of the Honourable the Rev Samuel Best, Rector of Abbotts Ann, Hampshire; her brother became the Fifth Baron Wynford. Sir James's father and two of his uncles had been in the Church, and his sisters had married clergymen. It was perhaps surprising that none of his sons followed him into the Church.

John (known as Jack in the family) was educated at Felsted School in Essex, 1873-78, and read modern history at Keble College, Oxford, 1878-82, gaining a third class degree. He then studied law, qualifying as a barrister in the Middle Temple in 1886. Two years later he married Leonora Gerstenberg, younger daughter and joint heiress of Isidor Gerstenberg, the founder of the Council of Foreign Bondholders, who died tragically in 1876 leaving £140,000 gross. This marriage brought Philipps financial independence in the form of his wife's inheritance which by 1888 was worth nearly £100,000. An earlier biographer asserted that, 'As a young man Philipps's tastes lay in the direction of politics, sport, and society ... His connection with finance seems to have been almost accidental' {*DNB*} and his marriage into wealth was undoubtedly important in establishing him in business.

In 1890 Philipps became involved in business through joining the board of Government Stocks & Other Securities Investment Co, one of the earliest investment trusts. Twelve months later the company was in difficulties because of the Baring crisis and he became chairman in order to initiate a rescue. Although it is not clear why the board should have chosen such a young man as their chairman, he was evidently successful. He was elected a director of the associated Omnium Investment Co later that year and became its chairman in 1892. He rapidly began to consolidate his own position and to build up the basis of a substantial business grouping by forming Premier Investment in 1892 and by joining the board of Consolidated Trust (also associated with the GSOSI Co) in 1893. These trusts were important in the financing of his brother Owen, later Lord Kylsant (qv) in his ventures into shipping, and in 1897 the two brothers jointly formed London Maritime Investment. These business associations were instrumental in the creation of Kylsant's Royal Mail shipping group.

Besides shipping, Philipps entered other business sectors, primarily through the activities of his growing investment group. During the 1890s he became chairman of several railway companies operating in Costa Rica and Argentina. These companies, in which his investment trusts held shares, were given extra finance and were reorganised, Philipps instigating major extensions of the Argentine line towards Chile. In the following years the investment group became involved in the finance of Associated Portland Cement (later Blue Circle Industries), which had originally been promoted by Henry O'Hagan (qv), and British Electric Traction, managed by Emile Garcke (qv). Philipps's group took an active interest in its investments and was rarely a purely passive shareholder. Its association with BET was particularly close and enduring. BET built up a mass of associates and subsidiaries in electricity supply, electrical engineering, tramways and motor buses, and its leading directors were drawn from the Philipps investment group. Philipps became a director of International

John W Philipps. 1st Viscount St Davids (right) with Lloyd George in 1926 (from E Green and M Moss, A Business of National Importance Methuen, 1982).

Financial Society in 1907-8 and of Municipal Trust in 1912. By this date the investment group was based on Dashwood House in the City and was already coming to be known by its address as the '69 Old Broad Street group'. Lord St Davids (he received a peerage in 1908) held the group together as a tightly co-ordinated system of interests through cross-shareholdings and interlocking directorships. Although still associated with the affairs of his brother Owen, the fact that both brothers had significantly expanded the scale of their interests meant that they drew apart.

During the 1920s the 69 Old Broad Street group, or the St Davids group as it was also known, continued to grow. St Davids held a commanding position in the City and few of his contemporaries were as prominent financiers as he. Lord St Davids himself remained as chairman of all the major trusts, though an important role was played by John ('Jack') Austen. The two men had been contemporaries at Felsted School and they had a close relationship — St Davids's third son was given the name Austen as one of his forenames. Philipps's autocratic behaviour, however, led him on occasion to regard Austen with suspicion. St Davids's brothers Ivor and Lawrence had shareholdings and directorships within the group, and the group's interests were represented on the boards of its associated companies by them and by men such as Sir Arthur Stanley and Ferdinand Stanley (brothers of the Seventeenth Earl of Derby). Through its own investments and those of the Phillips family, the group was closely associated with such firms as Ilford, Court Line, and Schweppes. The group was allied closely with other investment interests in the City: with the former Morton Rose trusts (later the basis of the F & C management group); with Schroders and Balfour Boardman on the board of Anglo Scottish Amalgamated Corporation; and with the Robert Fleming and Robert Benson groups on the board of Metropolitan Trust.

The South American railways which St Davids ran experienced difficulties in 1932 which resulted in extensive reconstructions, but a major problem for the trusts occurred during the troubles of the Royal Mail shipping group, which had been built up by Lord Kylsant and Lord Pirrie (qv) with some financial backing from St Davids. At the height of the Royal Mail's difficulties in 1929, St Davids, as trustee of its 4.5 per cent and 5 per cent debentures, expressed concern at the accounts. He demanded an investigation into the Royal Mail's problems, but refused to meet his brother to discuss matters. The public dispute between the brothers continued throughout the year and did little to restore confidence in Royal Mail. The dispute came to a head when St Davids resigned as 5 per cent trustee at the beginning of 1930, an event that was followed by the collapse of the Royal Mail group later in the year. St Davids remained trustee of the 4.5 per cent debentures and pressed for receivership and liquidation as an alternative to the rescue plan forced on Kylsant by the Government, the Bank of England, and the Midland Bank, and backed by a consortium of City institutions. His demands were rejected, as the voting trustees who now controlled the Royal Mail felt that his opposition owed more to personal and political differences between the brothers than to the interests of the debenture holders. Whatever the truth, the St Davids group was henceforth only marginally involved in the rescue and reconstruction of the Royal Mail and its various subsidiaries and associates.

Throughout his adult life, Philipps was politically active. Having failed to get elected in the Devizes division of East Wiltshire in 1886, he became Liberal MP for Mid-Lanarkshire in 1888 (his Labour rival was Keir Hardie). He owed the nomination to his brother Owen, who was active in the Glasgow Liberal Association. His real desire, however, was a seat closer to his London business interests and he was, in any case, forced to resign on health grounds in 1894. Four years later he was returned to parliament for Pembrokeshire, and by 1908 there was a solid phalanx of

Philipps family members on the Liberal benches: Owen was MP for the neighbouring constituency of Pembroke District, and their brother Ivor was MP for Southampton. John Philipps seems to have been forced to resign his seat by his local party, following press speculation that he intended to resign in order to free a seat for Winston Churchill. Whatever the truth in this, his resignation in 1908 was followed by his entry to the House of Lords, with the title of Baron St Davids, amidst renewed press debate over the prime ministerial use of political honours. His peerage was followed by a series of honorary titles and appointments: he became Lord Lieutenant for Pembrokeshire in 1911 (his brother Ivor was made DL), was sworn of the Privy Council in 1914, was promoted to a viscountcy in 1918, and received a GBE in 1922. He was a president of the Welsh National Liberal Council, which remained faithful to Lloyd George, was offered government office, and was a member of Lloyd George's 'Policy for Government' Committee. His brother Owen joined the Unionists in 1921, but St Davids remained a Liberal. The political division between the two brothers was a major factor aggravating their business antagonism. St Davids held a number of administrative posts, although he never held government office. From 1913 he was a member of the Investment Committee set up under the Insurance Act; until 1919 he was a member of the Roads Board (along with Lord Pirrie) which was in that year incorporated into the Ministry of Transport headed by Sir Eric Geddes (qv); in 1920-32 he was chairman of the Unemployment Grants Committee; and for some time he was chairman of the Organisation for the Employment of Retired Officers.

Undoubtedly his most controversial appointment was one which brought together his business and political interests. He was chairman of the Lloyd George Fund, which had developed from the National Liberal Political Fund and was intended to provide Lloyd George with a financial base independent of the Liberal Party. St Davids was active in determining the investments of the fund and was closely associated with the purchase of the *Daily Chronicle*. The Lloyd George Fund formed a company called United Newspapers in 1918 to acquire control of the newspaper from Frank Lloyd (qv), and the St Davids investment group was involved as purchaser of some of the shares. The paper remained under the control of the Fund and the trusts until 1928, when most of the Fund's controlling block was sold to Inveresk Paper. In 1936 the paper was merged with the *Daily News*, controlled by the Cadbury family, to form the *News Chronicle*. The St Davids group and BET remained as substantial shareholders until the present (1984). When St Davids died and the chairmanship of the Fund became vacant there was much controversy as to whether the Fund was truly a 'trust' or simply the personal property of Lloyd George.

St Davids's first wife Leonora died in 1915 and, to his great distress, their two sons were killed shortly after in the course of the war. He remarried in 1916, to Elizabeth, daughter of Pawlyn Rawdon-Hastings; they had a son and a daughter. Elizabeth succeeded in having the baronies of Strange, Hungerford, and De Moleyns brought out of abeyance in her favour in 1921, and these titles were inherited by the Second Lord St Davids on her death in 1975.

Viscount St Davids died on 28 March 1938, aged seventy-seven. The investment group had grown considerably and consisted of 16 trusts with total capital of more than £20 million, making it the second largest trust group in Britain — just behind the Touche group, and just ahead of the Robert Benson, Govett, and Brown Fleming & Murray groups. Despite the great size of the business which he had built, the gross value of the estate was proved at the relatively modest level of £123,736. His title and most of his wealth were inherited by his son, though the latter did not play an active part in running the trusts. He was succeeded in the business first by Jack Austen and, after Austen died in 1942, by 'Harley' (Harold) Drayton (qv).

JOHN P SCOTT

Sources:

Unpublished

BCe.

MCe.

PrC.

Philip L Cottrell, 'Investment Banking in England, 1856-1882' (Hull PhD, 1974).

Published

Burke's Peerage and Baronetage.

Peter N Davies, 'Business Success and the Role of Chance: The Extraordinary Philipps Brothers' *Business History* 23 (1981).

—, *The Trade Makers. Elder Dempster in West Africa 1862-1972* (George Allen & Unwin, 1973).

DNB.

Economist Sept 1936.

Edwin Green and Michael Moss, *A Business of National Importance. The Royal Mail Shipping Group, 1902-1937* (Methuen, 1982).

Henry O O'Hagan, *Leaves From My Life* (2 vols, John Lane, The Bodley Head, 1929).

Frank Owen, *Tempestuous Journey. Lloyd George, His Life and Times* (Hutchinson, 1954).

WWMP.

WWW.

PHILIPPS, Laurence Richard

1st Baron Milford of Llanstephan

(1874-1962)

Financier and shipowner

Laurence Richard Philipps was born on 24 January 1874, the sixth son of Canon Sir James Erasmus Philipps, Vicar of Warminster, Wiltshire, and his wife, the Honourable, Mary Margaret Best, daughter of Rev the Honourable Samuel Best, Rector of Abbotts Ann, Hampshire. His father was an enterprising Anglo-Catholic who established a convent and a College for training missionary priests in Warminster. He instilled in all his children strong Liberal Christian ideals which projected them towards careers in business and public life. His was a remarkable family. His sons were all exceptionally tall and four of them, including Laurence, became business leaders. Three of them were created peers, John Wynford as Lord St Davids and Owen Cosby as Lord Kylsant (qqv) (see the entries on John and Owen for more on the family background) as well as Laurence.

Laurence was educated at Felsted School and the Royal School of Mines. In 1897 in co-operation with his elder brother, Ivor (qv) he established Northern Securities Trust Ltd, which was to be a vehicle for investments by members of the family in a range of companies, particularly Ilford Ltd, Kia-Ora Ltd, and Schweppes Ltd. Laurence was appointed chairman. The following year he acted for his brother Owen Cosby (founder of the King Line of steamers) in the purchase of the London & Thames Haven Petroleum Wharf Ltd. Also in 1898 he started Laurence Philipps & Co and in 1903 became a full member of Lloyds founding a syndicate called L R Philipps & Others while his broking business carried on at 23 Birchin Lane, London, specialising in shipping. In 1903 Laurence also became a director of Motor Union Insurance which, as chairman, he did much to build up. It was eventually sold to the Royal Exchange Co. Later Lawrence joined Ivor on the boards of Ilford, Kia-Ora and Schweppes.

With his insurance broking business flourishing and Northern Securities Trust expanding, Laurence Philipps, followed Owen into shipping. In 1905 Owen introduced him to Philip Haldinstein and together Laurence and Haldinstein founded the Court Line in 1905. This concern was totally separate from Owen's Royal Mail Shipping Group and was managed by Haldinstein & Co of Leadenhall Street. Starting with two steamships of 7,000 tons, the first of which cost £38,000, its fleet had grown to seven ships by the outbreak of the First World War. During the war a sister concern Cressington Steamship Co was founded to own the *Dorrington Court* and the management company's name was changed because of its German association, to Haldin & Co. At the end of the war the fleet had been reduced to five ships. Unlike his brother, Laurence did not invest in new tonnage after the war, but sold off two of his remaining vessels. When prices collapsed in 1923 he began to buy recently-built and new tonnage. Another subsidiary, United British Steam Ship Co, was formed. By 1927 the joint fleet totalled 14 vessels. The Court Line was liquidated in 1929 and its assets transferred to the United British Steam Ship Co. At the same time the name of the management company was changed to Haldin & Philipps Ltd. The name of the United British Steam Ship Co was changed in 1936 to Court Line Ltd. By this time the company had a fleet of 22 vessels, built between 1918 and 1930. (Philip Haldin was knighted in 1939 for services to the shipping industry.) At the end of the Second World War Haldin Philipps managed 20 vessels, half for the Government. After the war Laurence Philipps withdrew from shipping, Court Line Ltd was liquidated in 1947 and the management company continued as Haldin & Co. James Philipps, Laurence's son, succeeded as chairman of Court Line.

Outside shipping, Laurence Philipps in 1906 formed the British East Africa Corporation which pioneered the growing of cotton in Uganda and had much to do with the development of the port of Mombasa. In 1909 he became a member of the Aero Club and sponsored a number of flying competitions. He later became a member of the Air Registration Board under the Air Ministry. In 1914 on the outbreak of war he was a pioneer in war risks insurance which was later taken over by the Government.

Laurence, like his eldest brother, was a keen race-goer. This enthusiasm led him at the request of the Jockey Club and the Racecourse Betting Control Board, to establish studs at Dalham Hall and Derisley, Suffolk in 1928 and to establish Tote Investors Ltd, which gave credit for betting on the totalisator. This highly successful concern was taken over by the Horse Race Totalisator Board after his death. For his services to the sport he was made a member of Tattersall's Committee and the Jockey Club. He was also a member of the Wye Fishing Board. He undertook many public duties, especially in Wales. He founded the Hospital for Paralysed Ex-Servicemen at Rookwood, Llandaff and the National Welsh Plant Breeding Institute at Aberystwyth. He served as a governor of the University College of Wales and received its honorary LLD in 1939. He was vice-president of the Wales and Monmouthshire Conservative Association and of the Suffolk Conservative and Unionist Association.

Philipps was a JP of Hampshire (1910) and Radnorshire (1918) and High Sheriff of Hampshire (1915). He was created a baronet in 1919 and Baron Milford of Llanstephan in 1939. In 1901 he married Ethel Georgina, only daughter of Rev Benjamin Speke, Rector of Dowlish Wake, Somerset. They had five sons and one daughter. The three younger sons who survived into adult life suceeded their father into the businesses with which he was connected. Laurence Philipps died on 7 December 1962 at the age of eighty-eight leaving £281,167 gross.

MICHAEL MOSS

Sources:

Unpublished

PrC.

Information from the Honourable Hanning Philipps.

Published

Burke's Peerage and Baronetage 1980.

P N Davies, 'Business Success and the Role of Chance: the Extraordinary Philipps Brothers' *Business History* 23 (1981).

WWW.

Owen Cosby Philipps, 1st Baron Kylsant in E Green and M Moss, A Business of National Importance Methuen, 1982).

PHILIPPS, Owen Cosby

Lord Kylsant of Carmarthen

(1863-1937)

Shipowner

Owen Cosby Philipps was born at Warminster on 25 March 1863, the third of six sons (and eleven children) of Canon Sir James Erasmus Philipps (1824–1912), Twelfth Baronet and his wife the Honourable Mary Margaret née Best. The eldest son, John Wynford Philipps and the youngest Laurence Richard (qqv) also became prominent in business.

At one time the Philipps family owned much property at Picton in Pembrokeshire but these possessions passed out of the male line early in the nineteenth century. The Twelfth Baronet was, therefore, a member of what might be described as the minor aristocracy and had little in the way of a family fortune. Sir James graduated at Oxford and then entered the Church. At the age of thirty-five in 1859 he was appointed Vicar of Warminster and the income and house which went with this living enabled him to marry. His wife was the eldest daughter of Rev and Honourable Samuel Best, Rector of Abbotts Ann, Hampshire; her brother later became the Fifth Baron Wynford. During his forty-two years at Warminster Sir James, an Anglo-Catholic, made distinctive contributions in a number of fields. He established the St Boniface Missionary College and St Denys Training Home to provide facilities for the training of priests and women helpers to work overseas. He later opened a boarding school and subsequently transformed St Denys into a Community for the training of nuns. The cost of these enterprises was provided by a series of appeals which were assisted by his supplementary appointment as a prebendary of Salisbury Cathedral. In addition he issued a series of books including a *Missionary Manual of Hymns and Prayers and Time Books, Seven Common Faults* and *Your Duty and Mine* which had the dual advantage of raising finance and of conveying his ideals to a wider public. By the 1880s his work in this direction had been sufficiently recognised to justify the regular publication of a magazine and *Warminster Work: At Home and Abroad* provided a further outlet for his ideas.

These activities did not lead to the neglect of his parishioners and he not only rebuilt the local church but had a second one constructed in a growing area of the town. He was also busy on a number of other fronts and his efforts resulted in the opening of a cottage hospital and an orphanage and he supported both the setting-up of soup kitchens and the establishment of National Schools. Sir James served on the town council as a Liberal and took a great interest in such diverse pursuits as the Wiltshire Rifle Volunteers and the Cottagers' Garden Society.

Sir James's enormous energies and wide talents were never directed towards personal gain and his income was never enough to satisfy all the needs and aspirations of his eleven children. The shortage of money helped to ensure that Owen, who was regarded as rather 'slow', was not sent to the highly-regarded Felsted School like his brothers. Instead, all his schooling was undertaken at the newly-established Newton College at Newton Abbot, Devon, and even in that inferior atmosphere he failed to make any significant progress. Consequently he was withdrawn from the school in 1880 and then apprenticed to Dent & Co, ship managers and ship brokers, in Newcastle upon Tyne.

The factors and pressures which enabled a titled clergyman's son from the rural part of Southern England to make the transition to a shipping office in the North East cannot now be explained. What is certain is that Owen rapidly demonstrated a great aptitude for the business and after completing his training in 1886 he joined Allan C Gow & Co in Glasgow. Owen undoubtedly moved to gain experience in a larger shipping centre and it was the combination of his new situation, together with the activities of his eldest brother, that was to form the foundation of his subsequent career. John Philipps's marriage to a wealthy heiress, Leonora Gerstenberg, had by then provided him with a sound financial base and he decided to seek a parliamentary constituency. Owen's position as an active member of the Glasgow Liberal Club was a large factor in securing John's nomination and, after the seat had been won, it was only natural that the two brothers should join together in a locally-based business venture.

The resulting firm, Philipps & Co, was essentially organised by Owen and backed by John. They began in a small way in ship broking and the management of shipping property but in July 1889, they took a major step forward by establishing the King Alfred Steamship Co Ltd, to acquire a vessel that was under construction at Blyth. The firm's name was changed to the King Line Ltd in 1893: simultaneously its articles of association were altered so that it could own more than one ship at a time. During the ensuing five years the King Line expanded quite rapidly and also established a subsidiary, the Scottish Steam Ship Co — and it was during this period of growth Owen relocated himself and his firm to London.

There were sound commercial reasons for this move but the timing was probably influenced by the loss of John Philipps's parliamentary seat in 1894. His subsequent adoption for a Pembrokeshire constituency then made a London venue more attractive and diminished the need for a base in Glasgow for either of the brothers. The capital city proved to be a favourable environment for the enterprises of both John and Owen and, in

shareholdings and the high-gearing that had been employed and successfully concealed.

In the circumstances, Kylsant decided to attempt to maintain the apparent profitability of the Group until such times as trade, and freight rates, improved. Reasonable, though prudent dividends were paid throughout the 1920s being financed from refunds of wartime taxation, from 'secret' reserves and exceptional cash receipts and from provisions for depreciation. The inadequacies of company law at that time permitted this to be accomplished without serious impediment so that from 1921 to 1928 the Group paid dividends to the value of £5 million which had not been found from current earnings but from non-recurring items of revenue and undisclosed transfers of hidden resources.

However these tactics only concealed the difficulties of the Group which remained in a loss-making and illiquid situation. Consequently Kylsant borrowed substantial sums to finance new construction under the provisions of the Trade Facilities Act and it was when he was unable to repay £2.55 million which was due in 1930 that an impartial investigation was undertaken by Sir William McLintock (qv). His report indicated the true state of affairs and the Group was then put under the control of 'Voting Trustees' who were nominated by the Government and Banks. Kylsant was then given leave of absence and was subsequently charged with issuing misleading accounts and a false prospectus. He was eventually convicted in 1931 for issuing a false prospectus in 1927 and served twelve months in prison. On his release from Wormwood Scrubs he continued to be accepted into the best society, for his offence was regarded as only a technical one. Nevertheless it resulted in the loss of his control and in the break-up of the 'Royal Mail Group' with enormous consequences for the British shipping and shipbuilding industries. Furthermore the shareholders in the constitutent companies lost practically all of their investments — the net loss of between £50 million and £70 million at 1931 prices was probably the biggest commercial bankruptcy ever recorded in this country.

In 1902 Owen Philipps married Mai Alice, daughter of Thomas Morris of Coomb, near Carmarthen, the place from which the Philipps family originated. His wife was wealthy in her own right having succeeded to a large part of the fortune accumulated by David Morris II through the family banking business in Carmarthen. Owen and Mai Philipps had two daughters.

Owen was anxious to emulate his brother and become an MP. He stood unsuccessfully for Montgomery Boroughs in 1895 and for Darlington in 1898. In 1906 he was returned in the Liberal interest for Pembroke and Haverfordwest. Subsequently he was a conscientious member of the Royal Commission on Shipping Rings as well as vice-chairman of the newly-formed Port of London Authority. Partly as a reward for these services he was knighted in 1910 (KCMG). In 1916 he was returned as the Unionist MP for Chester holding the seat until 1923, when he was created Baron Kylsant of Carmarthen.

Lord Kylsant died on 5 June 1937 at his home at Coomb near Llanstephan (this very substantial residence is now a 'Cheshire' home). It is clear that his personal fortune was little affected by the collapse of the 'Royal Mail Group'. However this fact is not reflected in his will and only a nominal amount of £53,570 was returned with his wife as the sole beneficiary.

P N DAVIES

Writings:

PP, RC Shipping Rings and Deferred Rebates (1909) Cd 4669 Cd 4670 Cd 4685.

Sources:

Unpublished

Mrs Fisher-Hoch (eldest daughter of Lord Kylsant) holds the personal MSS of her father at Plas Llanstephan.

BCe.

MCe.

PrC.

Published

Collin Brook, *The Royal Mail Case* (William Hodge & Co, 1933).

Peter N Davies and A M Bourn, 'Lord Kylsant and the Royal Mail' *Business History* 14 (1972).

Peter N Davies, 'Business Success and the Role of Chance: The Extraordinary Philipps Brothers' *Business History* 23 (1981).

—, *The Trade Makers, Elder Dempster in West Africa, 1852-1972* (Allen & Unwin, 1973).

DNB.

Edwin Green and Michael Moss, *A Business of National Importance: The Royal Mail Shipping Group, 1902-1937* (Methuen, 1982).

M Murray, *Union Castle Chronicle* (Longmans, Green & Co, 1953).

WWMP.

WWW.

John Spencer Phillips (from the
Institute of Bankers 1879-1929
(Blades, East & Blades, 1929).

PHILLIPS, John Spencer

(1847-1909)

Clearing banker

John Spencer Phillips was born at Ludlow, Shropshire, on 18 August 1847, the eldest son of Rev John Phillips, Rector of Ludlow, and his wife Frances née Anderson. From Shrewsbury School, he went to Trinity College, Cambridge, in 1865, where he read law. Returning to Shropshire, he joined the partners of the Shrewsbury & Welshpool Old Bank (established in 1800). Phillips became a director of Lloyds Banking Co in 1880 when the Old Bank was taken over.

Phillips's rise through Lloyds Banking Co was more steady than dramatic. He had a vigorous personality and was known as a strong and clear-headed negotiator, but the acquisition of the Birmingham Joint Stock Bank in 1889, in a deal concluded with his friend and neighbour, Joseph Beattie, led to criticism from Howard Lloyd who was then managing director. Although Lloyd later admitted that the purchase had been right, he wrote about this particular amalgamation 'perhaps the less said the better' {Lloyd (1917) 53}, so manifestly was the advantage on the other side.

After Phillips became chairman of Lloyds in 1898 his dogmatic and self-confident public style led him to break with tradition in the substance of his address at the Annual General Meeting. There was little of national importance which Phillips did not cover in his address and repeatedly he returned to matters of principle in fiscal affairs. Chief among these were defects in the law of limited liability, accusations of extravagance in municipal borrowing and the weakness of national gold reserves. As president of the Institute of Bankers, 1904-6 (a third successive year was an unusual honour), Phillips developed these topics further in his annual address, arguing persistently that every bank should publish each month a balance sheet or, better still, average weekly figures, and keep larger reserves of capital. The press looked forward to his addresses, both at the Institute and at the bank's annual meeting. Although sometimes not in agreement with his views ('we altogether dissent from two or three points ...' {*Statist* Nov 1906}), his lively style was refreshing ('The whole speech was ... of interest ... part approached the sensational' {*The World* Jan 1908}).

During his chairmanship of Lloyds Bank Ltd, Phillips saw deposits rise from £37 million in 1898 to £69 million in 1908, and he steered the company through 15 amalgamations. He was the last chairman to act also as chief executive. He worked mainly from the bank's Birmingham head office, but also from home, and every fortnight he visited London from Wednesday until Friday, staying at the flat above the bank's branch at 16 St James's Street. Here he had informal and clandestine meetings with business colleagues while negotiating mergers, and the proximity of the branch, to which he directed visitors, seemed not to inhibit him. 'I tell you this', he wrote to a banker at Southampton, 'lest you may be nervous at seeing a Bank there; but all sorts of people are constantly coming to see me there, so you need not be the least afraid of anyone taking the slightest notice of you calling' {Lloyds Bank Archives: file 5393}. When he did call in a bank officer as co-negotiator, it was Alexander Duff, the general manager, 'an old Cambridge friend of mine ... {ibid}.

Although often in Birmingham and London, Phillips never lost sight of his Shropshire origins. He lived at The Mount, Shrewsbury, he was a JP for the borough, he was a director and later deputy chairman of the North Staffordshire Railway Co, and was chairman of the Shrewsbury Gas Light Co and of the local board of the Alliance Assurance Co; however, according to an obituary 'he took no part in the public life of the town' {*Times* 1 June 1909}.

As a young man Phillips had been a good athlete at school and was later a keen huntsman. He liked rowing and walking and was opening bat for the Shropshire Eleven at late as 1896.

In 1872 Phillips married Kathleen Harriet, daughter of Major-General T H Tidy, and had one daughter. Phillips died unexpectedly on 31 May 1909 leaving £154,550 gross.

JOHN BOOKER

Sources:

Unpublished

Lloyds Bank archives, Spencer Phillips Scrapbook, ref Book no 1430; amalgamation papers, files 2514, 5044, 5369, 5393.

SSRC Elites data.

BCe.

PrC.

H Lloyd, 'Notes and Reminiscences of Lloyds Bank, 1862-1892' (typescript, 1917 Lloyds Bank archives, ref Book no 29).

Published

Bankers' Magazine 38 (1909).

Birmingham Gazette and Express 1 June 1909.

Journal of the Institute of Bankers 30 (1909).

Richard S Sayers, *Lloyds Bank in the History of English Banking* (Oxford: Clarendon Press, 1957).

Statist Nov 1906.

Times 1 June 1909.

Venn, *Alumni Cantabrigienses*.

The World Jan 1908.

Frank Pick (courtesy of London Transport).

PICK, Frank

(1878-1941)

Transport manager

Frank Pick was born at Spalding, Lincolnshire, on 23 November 1878, the eldest child of Francis Pick, draper, and his wife, Fanny née Clarke. The family moved in 1883 to York where Frank won a scholarship to St Peter's School. He was articled in 1897 to George Crombie, solicitor of York, and qualified with an LLB London in 1902. He joined the North Eastern Railway in the same year; after working as booking-clerk at Knaresborough, under the company's training scheme, he became personal assistant to the general manager, Sir George Gibb (qv), in 1904 and followed him to the Underground Electric Railways Co of London Ltd in 1906. In 1908 he became responsible for the Underground's traffic publicity and in 1909 was put in charge of all traffic promotion and development. On the inclusion of the London General Omnibus Co in the Underground group in 1912, Pick became commercial manager of the combined undertaking.

From 1917 to 1919 he was in charge of the household fuel and lighting branch of the Coal Mines Department of the Board of Trade. He became joint assistant managing director of the Underground group in 1921, with a wider range of responsibilities, and joined the board in 1928 as managing director, the chairman, Lord Ashfield (Albert Stanley (qv)), retaining the title of managing director also. In 1933 he was appointed vice-chairman of the London Passenger Transport Board, under Ashfield, at a salary of £10,000 a year.

Pick was an administrator with great powers of intelligence, ability to assimilate detail, and understanding of statistics. Moreover, 'the power of decision came easily to him', the phrase of Sir John Elliot (qv) {*DNB*}. He developed a kind of omnicompetence which, while admired and respected, made it difficult for the talents of other men to grow in his shade. As Lord Ashfield wrote, 'work was his hobby and inspiration' {*Times* 10 Nov 1941}. Though he enjoyed walking, foreign travel, and going to the opera, he indulged in none of the usual sociable recreations. He was a shy and austere man. He appeared to be unapproachable, and he was not good at the ordinary skills of man-management; unlike Ashfield, he had no gift of the 'common touch'. Yet he was no desk-bound administrator; from his traffic development days before 1914, he would regularly get out on to the ground to keep himself informed of what he was making decisions about. Every other Friday was set aside for going outdoors to see things with his own eyes. His administrative gifts and command of detail, allied to Ashfield's more intuitive and 'political' approach to affairs, made a formidable business combination.

At York, Rev John Hunter, minister of the Salem Congregational Chapel, had deeply imbued Pick with a consciousness of social duty, and

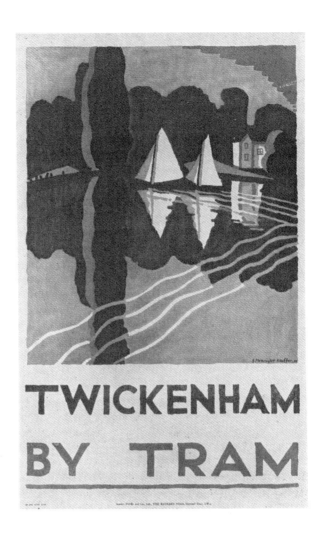

One of E McKnight Kauffer's posters, Twickenham by Tram, 1924 (from T C Barker and M Robbins, A History of London Transport 2).

he always questioned the ultimate purposes of immediate policies and tried to establish that every activity of his management was directed towards an intelligible and proper goal. He wanted his actions in business life to be coherent and consistent with his ideas about human life, and he was constantly thinking of the possibilties of harnessing commercial methods to the achievement of large social objectives.

From early in his career Pick had been concerned about ugliness and poor quality in everyday things, from buildings and printing to crockery and the like. Under his direction the Underground's posters, while always strictly directed to the commercial purpose of promoting travel, became adventurous in technique and compelling as publicity, and his patronage, especially of the American-born Edward McKnight Kauffer (1890-1954), from whom he first commissioned posters in 1915, produced work that set new and demanding standards in what was until then a chaotic and generally tasteless activity. He persuaded the calligrapher Edward Johnston (1872-1944) to design in 1916 a new sans-serif display type which,

ABCDEFGHIJKLMN OPQRSTUVWXYZ abcdefghijklmnopq rstuvwxyz 123456 7890 (&£.,:;'!?-*"")

The Johnston alphabet, designed 1916 (from T C Barker and M Robbins, A History of London Transport *2).*

with the 'roundel' or bar-and-circle device developed from station name-boards, is London Transport's motif — a very early example, if not the earliest in Britain, of a consistent 'house style' and one which, despite changes in fashion, has held its own with only minor modifications. Pick brought in Charles Holden (1875-1960) as architect for a series of stations, beginning with the Bond Street exterior (1924) and the headquarters building at 55 Broadway, Westminster (1929), which are admired as outstanding examples of 1920s and 1930s design. Both the 'house style' and the architecture were based on fitness for purpose and simplicity of forms. Pick's critical eye was quick to note whatever was visually crude or ill-fitted to its purpose in every department of his undertaking, and he had the authority to insist on correction. But he was not so authoritarian that he could not on occasion give way to others' expert judgement against his own; the controversial Epstein sculptures at 55 Broadway showed deference to Holden's advocacy and were not to Pick's taste.

Pick left the London Transport Passenger Board in 1940 and, after reporting to Sir John Reith (qv), then Minister of Transport, on the operation of ports, became Director-General of the Ministry of Information from August to December 1940. In 1941 he inspected and reported on canals and inland waterways.

He was active in the Design and Industries Association from 1915, serving as chairman in 1932-34, and he became the first chairman of the Council for Art and Industry (1934). He was a founder member of the Institute of Transport in 1920 and president, 1931-32. He was a member of the Royal Commission on Police Powers and Procedures (1928). He was made honorary associate of the Royal Institute of British Architects in 1932; but he received no public or academic honour. No portrait from life is known to exist.

Pick married in 1904 Mabel Mary Caroline, daughter of C S Woodburn, solicitor of York; there were no children. Frank Pick died at his home in Hampstead Garden Suburb on 7 November 1941, leaving £36,434 gross.

MICHAEL ROBBINS

Writings:

Pick wrote numerous articles and speeches on transport and on art, architecture, and design. The most important are listed in Theodore C Barker and Michael Robbins, *History of London Transport* vol 2 (George Allen & Unwin, 1974) Appendix 4 pp 501-3. A more detailed catalogue by J H Clancey and B C Johnson is noted below.

Sources:

Unpublished

Greater London RO, Minutes of Underground group and associated companies (formerly in British Transport Historical Records and so cited in Barker & Robbins, *History of London Transport*; now at Greater London RO with same record number).

London Transport, 55 Broadway, London, SW1, Minutes of London Passenger Transport Board, 1933-40.

Victoria & Albert Museum Library, correspondence.

BCe.

MCe.

PrC.

J H Clancey and B C Johnson, 'Catalogue of the Papers of Frank Pick' (London Transport Museum).

Conversations with London Transport officers and staff.

Personal knowledge; private information (the writer's father knew Pick well).

Published

Theodore C Barker and Michael Robbins, *A History of London Transport: Passenger Travel and the Development of the Metropolis* (2 vols, George Allen & Unwin, 1963-74).

Christian Barman, 'Frank Pick' *Architectural Review* 92 (1942).

—, *The Man Who Built London Transport* (Newton Abbot: David & Charles, 1979).

DNB.

A Forty, 'Lorenzo of the Underground' *London Journal* 5 (1979).

Frederick A A Menzler, 'Lord Ashfield and the Public Corporation' *Public Administration* 9 (1951).

Nikolaus B L Pevsner, 'Patient Progress: The Life Work of Frank Pick' *Architectural Review* 92 (1942).

Railway Gazette 14 Nov 1941.

P M Shand, 'Under Ground' *Architectural Review* 66 (1929).

Times 10 Nov 1941, 17 Jan 1942.

WWW.

PICKERSGILL, William

(1847-1936)

Shipbuilder

William Pickersgill was born at Monkwearmouth, Sunderland, on 28 August 1847, the eldest child of William Pickersgill Sr (1823-1880), shipbuilder, and his wife Mary née Bedingfield.

William Pickersgill Sr is reputed to have been of Scottish descent and a member of a farming family. Born at Chester-le-Street, he is said to have founded a shipbuilding firm at North Dock in 1838, but the evidence points rather to the establishment of the firm of Pickersgill & Miller at Southwick in 1852. Their first ship was launched in 1854, when the partnership with Miller was dissolved. During the 1850s there were some 75 shipbuilding firms on the Wear, many of them only in business for a brief period. William Pickersgill Sr, who trained with the firm headed by James Laing (qv), succeeded in establishing his business on a secure basis.

On leaving school William Pickersgill was apprenticed to the timber trade. He then worked as a carpenter and later as foreman in his father's yard. In eighteen consecutive years he was never off work. A skilled craftsman himself, he later insisted that his own son should serve as a plater, riveter, foreman and under-manager as well as serving five years in the drawing office. He believed than any man destined for an executive position should be able to bring the eye of a practical man to the work. He prided himself on knowing all the employees by name, and indeed several generations of Southwick families were employed by the firm. He became a junior partner in 1869 and managing director in 1880 when his father was killed in an accident in the yard. He was joined by his younger brothers, Charles and Frederick. Charles died in 1895 and Frederick left the firm in 1907, when it was turned into a private company. William Pickersgill retained the chairmanship of the company until his death in 1936. His son William John became managing director in 1907, but William Pickersgill took an active part in the work of the yard until 1915.

William Pickersgill Jr took over the firm at a crucial time. In 1880 large numbers of orders were being placed after a strike and poor trade levels the previous year. Moreover by 1879 Pickersgills was the only firm on the Wear still working solely in wood, and the only survivor of the last ten firms to work exclusively in this material. In 1880 they launched the *Coppername* (316 tons), the last wooden ship to be built on the Wear. In the same year, a few months before the death of William Pickersgill Sr, the yard had been extended (the original covered only two acres) to accommodate iron vessels. William Pickersgill succeeded in guiding the firm through the depression of the mid-1880s (when the total tonnage for the years 1885-87 dropped to 5,000 tons) and through the changeover from iron to steel construction in 1887-88.

The closing decades of the nineteenth century saw shipbuilders engaged in developing designs for small steamers with a low net tonnage which could carry large cargoes, and for three- or four-masted iron and steel barques capable of competing with the steam vessels for speed, cargo capacity and low maintenance costs. Pickersgills made a distinguished contribution in both these areas.

Only ten weeks before his father's sudden death, the SS *Carmago*, the yard's first iron ship, was launched. Built for a Newport owner, it was an iron screw steamer intended for general work and classed AI at Lloyds. It was designed to carry a large cargo on a light draught of water, was equipped with McIntyre water-ballast tanks and with engines from George Clark's (qv) Southwick Engine Works. It was the first of many steamers built at the yard during the next thirty years for well-known shipping lines. Repeat orders for 'Castles', 'Cairns', 'Dales', 'Counts' and 'Pools' were indications of their success. William Pickersgill's greatest contribution came in the designing and building of high-class iron and steel sailing ships between 1880 and 1900. During the 1880s several medium-sized iron clippers were built for Wakenham & Sons of Liverpool for the copper ore and nitrate trade. *Samanco*, *Chala* and *Chepica* were built in 1884-85, and their sister ship, the *Inca*, in 1889. The poet John Masefield knew the *Chepica* and praised her as a 'steel grey lovely barque' {Masefield (1946) 295}.

The 1890s saw the yard producing large steel barques with steel rigging for Liverpool owners. They were designed to carry nitrates from Chile and coal from New South Wales. The first of them, the *Dunmarlis* (2,530 tons) and the great *Andorinha* (3,400 tons), the largest sailing vessel ever built on the Wear, gave particularly fine performances against stiff competition.

Clippers designed for speed and cargo capacity were also in demand for the fishing grounds. Pickersgill perfected a model of the Newfoundland clipper. These ships performed so well that his design was adopted by the Fleetwood owners. Sunderland's last contribution to the era of the tall ships, the *Marguerita*, was launched in 1893.

In 1881 Pickersgills, with a gross tonnage of 3,907, were eleventh in the progress table of Wearside shipbuilders. By 1900 they were in fifth place with 20,845 gross tonnage.

In 1870 William Pickersgill married Ellen, the daughter of Joseph Lincoln, a Southwick farmer and butcher, at Bethesda Free Church, an independent evangelical church founded in 1845 by Rev A A Rees. They remained members there throughout the sixty-two years of their marriage. Unlike many of his fellow shipbuilders, William Pickersgill shunned public life; he did not join any professional institutions as both he and his wife preferred the domestic scene. He did, however, serve twice on the Urban District Council because of his lifelong interest in Southwick affairs. But he was well known in Sunderland both as a sportsman and as a shipbuilder. He was one of the original members, and became vice-president, of the Sunderland Cricket and Football Club. Renowned as an all-round sportsman, he played cricket until well into his fifties. In the winter he played football for the Sunderland club. In later life he played golf and finally bowls, being the regular skip for the Sunderland team until two years before his death. A colourful character, he delighted to speak in the local dialect and was said to be upset by mice. William Pickersgill died on 28 May 1936, the doyen of Wearside shipbuilders. He was survived by four sons and left £4,070.

S P RUSSELL

Sources:

Unpublished

Sunderland Public Library, Corder Manuscript on 'Wear Shipbuilders'.

BCe.

MCe.

PrC.

Information from Joe F Clarke.

Published

Joseph F Clarke, 'Shipbuilding on the Wear, 1780-1870' in R W Sturgess (ed), *The Great Age of Industry in the North East* (Durham Local History Society, 1981).

John Masefield, *Collected Poems* (Heinemann, 1946).

River Wear Commissioners, *The Port of Sunderland* (Sunderland: Reed, 1949).

Shipbuilder June 1936.

J W Smith and T S Holden, *Where Ships Are Born 1346-1946: A History of Shipbuilding on the River Wear* (Sunderland: Thomas Reed & Co, 1946).

Sunderland Daily Echo 28 June 1880, 29 May 1936.

PIERCY, William Stuckey

1st Lord Piercy of Burford

(1886-1966)

Financier

William Stuckey Piercy was born in Bermondsey, London, on 7 February 1886. He was brought up by his mother, Mary Ann Piercy and Augustus Edward Piercy, an engineer at Vickers Ltd, as the only son and eldest of four children. Augustus Piercy was killed in a works accident in 1893. William left school at the age of eleven to go to work, living in Hoxton between 1903 and 1909 and being employed in the wood-broking trade from 1906 to 1912. When not at work, he spent much of his time singing in the choir at St John the Baptist Church, Hoxton and attending evening classes, in particular those at the City of London College. He matriculated in 1909 and aided by two small scholarships from the Mitchell Trust and the City Parochial Foundation began a part-time BSc Economics course at the London School of Economics in 1910. In 1912, aged twenty-six, he became a full-time student. He had a brilliant undergraduate career at the LSE, winning a University Scholarship in 1912, the Gladstone Memorial Prize in 1911 and 1913 and graduating with a BSc (Econ) first class honours in 1913. Specialising in economic history, he was one of a distinguished quartet of 'firsts' taught by Dr Lilian Knowles, the others later achieving fame as Dr Vera Anstey, Sir Theodore Gregory and Lady (Mary) Stokes. In addition to his academic studies, Piercy was also active in the Students' Union, becoming secretary and the president in 1913-14. A well-known undergraduate figure, he was one of a distinguished generation of LSE students, which also included Clement Attlee and Hugh Dalton. After graduating, Piercy began on his chosen career as an academic, obtaining a Mitchell research studentship and being appointed as an assistant and lecturer in history and public administration at the London School of Economics. However, the outbreak of the First World War and personal circumstances diverted him from this promising academic career.

Piercy's practical and academic experience was employed in high-level government administration during the war. Between 1915 and 1917 he worked in the Ministry of Munitions, where he was one of the architects of the Munitions Levy, which financed a high proportion of wartime capital expenditure and was later succeeded by the Excess Profits Levy. In 1917, after America's entry into the war, he went to Washington as secretary of a mission to Herbert C Hoover, US Food Administrator (and later President), to negotiate the purchase of food, staying in America after completing this task to help with the establishment of the British Ministry of Food and the Allied Co-ordinating Committee. He returned to England in 1919.

Piercy had married in 1915 and by 1919 he was a father. The necessity of providing for his family persuaded him to leave academia and enter business. In 1919 he joined Harrisons & Crosfield, East India merchants, as marketing director. His duties involved several trips to the Far East, Malaya and the Dutch East Indies. In February 1925, after failing to secure the position of company secretary at Nobel Industries (it went to W H Coates (qv)), he became a working director of Pharaoh Gane, brokers for manufacturers and shippers of timber and plywood. At Pharaoh Gane Piercy was successful in repairing much of the damage caused to the softwood trade by the Russian Revolution, by establishing a consortium of timber brokers to organise a central softwoods financing, marketing and purchasing agency. His years at Pharaoh Gane took him to Scandanavia, the Russian borderlands and Germany, and provided him with an introduction to the world of industrial and trade financing. Following disagreements in the boardroom, Percy left Pharaoh Gane in 1933. He considered going to America to learn about the teaching and practice of business administration at university level, with the intention of introducing a similar system in Great Britain. After a couple of months' rest, however, he decided to enter the City, becoming a member of the Stock Exchange and a partner in Capel Cure & Terry in 1934. As a member of the Stock Exchange between 1934 and 1942 he was to make a personal fortune. As a partner in Capel Cure & Terry from 1934 until 1941, and in Fenns Crosthwaite from 1937 to 1942, Piercy played a pioneering role (with others like G M Booth (qv)) in the development of the unit trust movement, which was then in its infancy. Acting in effect as a unit trust consultant, he was personally responsible for designing more than 20 trusts, including the formation of the Trust of Insurance Shares Ltd. Employing his very precise and analytical mind, Piercy quickly emerged as an innovator in the intricate technique of management and selling, shaping geared trusts and helping to plan the first block offer.

Once again war interrupted and changed his career. During 1940 and the first half of 1941 he worked as a Special Assistant in the Export Credit Guarantee Department. From May 1941 he headed the British Petroleum Mission to Washington as an impartial negotiator from outside the oil business, charged with negotiating and organising the purchase of petrol under the Lend Lease arrangements. Piercy also played an important part in the successful introduction of 'pooled', rather than brand, distribution of petrol during the war. He went on to serve as a principal assistant to the deputy Prime Minister, Clement Attlee, working under the supervision of Evan Durbin, then a lecturer at the LSE. In January 1945, Durbin and Piercy swapped positions because Durbin wished to spend more time teaching and Piercy became the full-time salaried assistant. During this period, Piercy, hitherto a Liberal, joined the Labour Party and quickly became an important member of Nicholas Davenport's XYZ group, a financial policy group of Labour economists which included Piercy's long-standing friend Hugh Dalton, Hugh Gaitskell, Evan Durbin, Douglas Jay, Thomas Balogh and Nicholas Kaldor. As a member of this group Piercy became directly involved in the projected National Investment Board as well as being responsible for drafting the legislation for the nationalisation of the Bank of England. He flirted briefly with the idea of standing as a Labour candidate in the 1945 General Election, but in the summer accepted the offer from Lord Catto (qv), then Governor of the Bank of England and a good friend of Piercy, to become the first chairman of the Industrial & Commercial Finance Corporation.

The Industrial & Commercial Finance Corporation (ICFC), formed to fill the so-called 'Macmillan Gap' in the financing of small- and medium-sized businesses, was in a very delicate position during Piercy's first years as chairman. Created and backed by the banks, before they were forced to do so by the Government, it was regarded by many of the banks as being unnecessary and unwanted. Working with a small and capable team, Piercy employed his mental skills, his practical experience and his immense capacity for efficient hard work to sift through the many applications for funds to identify the small percentage of genuinely feasible ventures, as well as drawing on his natural astuteness to ensure that the ICFC retained markets. Under his leadership, the ICFC prospered after some difficult early years until it became an established financial corporation, having assets of some £70 million and having lent over £120 million by the time Piercy vacated the chair in 1964. The ICFC owed much of its eventual success to Piercy's shrewd leadership. Piercy's personality was extremely complex. Highly intelligent, astute, capable of both abstract thought and hard-headed business dealings, he combined a straightforward, friendly manner with a capacity to be devious when he felt this to be necessary. During his time at the ICFC he also had the energy and enthusiasm to establish (in 1952) the Estates Duties Investment Trust (EDITH) whose function was to acquire minority interests in private and small public companies to enable the shareholders to make provision for estate duty. EDITH received powerful backing from a group of insurance companies as well as from the ICFC and Piercy acted as its chairman until his death. The ICFC also put up £200,000 of the £1 million capital for the Ship Mortgage Co which provided medium-term loans on first mortgages of ships constructed in the United Kingdom, the whole scheme being the brain-child of Piercy and his City friend, Sir Charles Hambro.

Piercy was honoured for his services in both world wars. In 1919 he was made a CBE and in November 1945 he became Baron Piercy of Burford, 'Great House', Burford, Oxfordshire being his place of residence. Despite working long hours at the ICFC, Piercy was also a director of the Bank of England, 1946-56. In 1947 and 1948 he was considered seriously as a successor to his friend Catto as Governor of the Bank of England, his case being strongly pressed by Dalton, who was overruled by Cripps, Dalton's successor as Chancellor.

Outside his business career, Piercy maintained a continuous interest in university life and teaching. While at Harrisons & Crosfield, he and the company secretary E C Cleveland-Stevens (another pre-1914 research student at the LSE), together with their chairman (Sir) H Eric Miller, fostered the development at the LSE of the commerce degree. While in America during the First World War, Piercy had become interested in the field of management studies, following the progress of Mrs Ethel Woods's Management Research Groups in the 1920s, and in the late 1920s helped to establish the business administration department of the LSE. Piercy also devoted considerable time to the administrative side of education, being a member of the Court and Senate of the University of London (1947-66), trustee of the friends of the LSE (1957-66) and a governor of the LSE (1955-66), Birmingham University (1960-63), Gordonstoun School (1947-66) and Regent Street Polytechnic. He was also a member of St Anne's College Investment Committee (1957-65) and he was associated with the Administrative Staff College, Henley (1945-65). His visit to America also increased Piercy's abiding interest in the psychological influences which shape economic behaviour and he became a founder-member of the executive council of the National Institute of Industrial Psychology being its president, 1945-66. Piercy was also a fellow (elected 1922) and president (1954-55) of the Royal Statistical Society. His other professional and public offices included the presidency of the Market Research Society (1954-66), of the Association of Technical Institutions (1955-60) and of the Institute of Works Managers (1957-66); trustee and chairman of the Wellcome Trust (1946-65), the Fabian Society's Dartmouth Street Trust (1946-58) and the Industrial Training Board; a council member of the British Institute of Management (1947-52) and the

BBC General Advisory Council (1947-56); and a committee member of the Government of Ghana's Investment Committee (1957-58), Homes for Working Boys in London (1946-55) and the World Refugee Year Finance Committee (1956-60). His official appointments ranged from chairmanship of the Reorganisation Commission for Hops (1946-7), through his work on the National Youth Employment Council (1947-56), to his chairmanship of the Committee of Inquiry on the Rehabilitation, Training and Resettlement of Disabled Persons (1951-56), as well as giving evidence to a series of government financial committees and enquiries.

Piercy in 1915 married Mary Louisa Pelham (1885-1953), who had been secretary of the LSE Students' Union while Piercy had been president. She was the daughter of the Honourable Thomas Pelham, CB, third son of the Third Earl of Chichester, a barrister and civil servant, and through her mother was related to the Balfours of Burleigh. William and Mary Piercy had one son and three daughters. In 1964, William Piercy married Veronica, daughter of John Handley Warham, a bank manager, who both as secretary at the ICFC and later as his wife did much to ease his life as a reluctantly ageing man with a tendency to overwork.

Lord Piercy died on 7 July 1966 at Stockholm, aged eighty, while attending a meeting of the Kuwait International Advisory Committee, of which he was a member. He left £14,300 gross.

MARTIN CHICK

Writings:

'The Macmillan Gap and the Shortage of Risk Capital' *Journal of the Royal Statistical Society* Series A 118 (1955).

Sources:

Unpublished

BLPES, the Piercy papers; Dalton diaries.

BCe.

MCe.

PrC.

Published

DNB.

Journal of the Royal Statistical Society. Series A 130 part 2 (1967).

John Kinross, *Fifty Years in the City; Financing Small Business* (John Murray, 1983).

LSE Magazine Jan 1967.

William J Reader, *Imperial Chemical Industries. A History* (2 vols, Oxford University Press, 1970-75) 2.

Times 9 July 1966.

Philip M Williams (ed), *The Diary of Hugh Gaitskell, 1945-56* (Jonathan Cape, 1983).

WWW.

Sir Alastair Pilkington (courtesy of Pilkington Brothers PLC).

PILKINGTON, Sir Lionel Alexander Bethune

(1920-)

Businessman and inventor

Lionel Alexander Bethune (known as Alastair) Pilkington was born in Calcutta on 7 January 1920. His father and paternal grandfather were both engineers who did much of their work in the Empire. His father, Lionel G Pilkington, had been born in Australia. His mother Evelyn Bethune, of a family with Indian business connections, came from Blebo, Fife. Both parents were Christian Scientists. Alastair grew up in an extremely happy home and was to follow their beliefs, teaching in the Sunday School later in his life.

The family moved to London when Alastair was three years old and then, when he was twelve, to the Newbury area when his father became managing director of Pulsometer Pumps at Tilehurst, Reading. He went to prep school at St Michael's, Uckfield and to Sherborne. He there showed a facility for mathematics, learned to play the clarinet and developed an interest in music. This was considerably nourished during the year he spent in Zurich (1937-38) before going up to Trinity College, Cambridge, to read mechanical sciences. The war was already looming and, preferring to fight with professionals, he volunteered and was commissioned in the Supplementary Reserve of the Royal Artillery. He was posted to Egypt a week before war was declared and fought in the Desert, Greek and Crete campaigns. The rest of the war was spent in prisoner of war camps in Germany where he improved his musicianship in the camp orchestra. He returned to Cambridge in 1945 to complete his degree course. He also won Blues for tennis, squash and fives and in 1947 was Fives Amateur Champion of England.

His appointment to the Pilkington glass business at St Helens as a family trainee, though not in any way related to the St Helens Pilkingtons, is one of the most remarkable coincidences of modern British business history. Alastair's father had become interested in his family tree and so had Sir Richard Pilkington, a shareholding member of the St Helens glassmaking family. When it became clear that there was no traceable link between their respective ancestors (as the Pilkington board minutes quaintly put it, 'Col L G Pilkington's branch of the family broke away at least 15 generations ago'), the two men got round to discussing the rising generation. Would Pilkingtons be interested in employing an up and coming engineer when he had completed his degree? As it happened, the company was then very concerned about its shortage of well-qualified engineers. Harry Pilkington (qv), the future chairman and his cousin, Douglas Phelps, saw Alastair's father and subsequently had Alastair himself up to St Helens for close scrutiny over a three-day period. More remarkable, the board decided that 'a member of the Pilkington family, however remote, could be accepted only as a potential family director'. So it came about that Alastair having passed the preliminary test, started work at Pilkington Bros Ltd in August 1947 as a family trainee.

He began as technical assistant ('an unusual status for an ex-officer') working on brick gas producers where pokers six feet long were needed to clear the clinker ('quite rugged') and was gradually introduced to all branches of glass manufacture. It did not take him long to learn that there was much about glassmaking that was still little understood, an art rather than a science. His enquiring, analytical brain started to ponder some of these problems and especially the one which was then exercising the minds of the technical directors: how to produce a continuous ribbon of high quality, plate glass without the enormous cost then expended in its grinding and polishing. The twin grinder and polisher developed by Pilkington between the wars though capable of making polished plate glass remarkable for its planimetry, involved a succession of grinding and polishing heads stretching in length for 1,400 feet and consuming electrical energy in large quantities.

As part of his training, Alastair Pilkington was posted in 1949 as production manager at Pilkington's Doncaster works and therefore had the opportunity to conduct a certain amount of experimental work to investigate the interaction of molten glass and molten tin at high temperatures. (It was already known that tin could be used as a satisfactory conveyor of a ribbon of glass at 600° C.) His act of invention, which came to him in a flash at the beginning of 1952, soon after his return to St Helens, was to use one end of a long bath of tin at about 1,000° C to form a glass ribbon, and then to float it down a temperature gradient so that it could be taken off on rollers at the other end at 600° C. The satisfactory execution of this idea, however, was to pose formidable technical problems, for little was known about the interaction of molten glass and molten tin at such high temperatures. The inventor later confessed: 'If we had known all the horrors at the beginning, we would certainly not have gone ahead' {Privately communicated to the writer}. Fortunately he had the resources and know-how of one of the world's leading glassmaking businesses behind him, though not of its scientists who had a better theoretical realisation of the huge difficulties involved.

At the beginning of 1953 Alastair Pilkington became a sub-director of the company (director 1955) and a member of its executive committee. So he was well placed to plead the case for the new process, against the specialist scientific opinion from the company's research department, which increased as it ran into development difficulties. But he was a superb advocate, was supported throughout by Sir Harry Pilkington, the

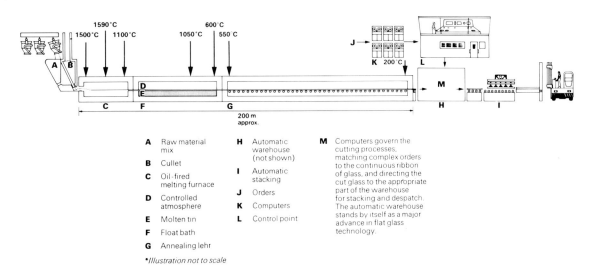

A Raw material mix	**H** Automatic warehouse (not shown)	**M** Computers govern the cutting processes, matching complex orders to the continuous ribbon of glass, and directing the cut glass to the appropriate part of the warehouse for stacking and despatch. The automatic warehouse stands by itself as a major advance in flat glass technology.
B Cullet	**I** Automatic stacking	
C Oil-fired melting furnace	**J** Orders	
D Controlled atmosphere	**K** Computers	
E Molten tin	**L** Control point	
F Float bath		
G Annealing lehr		

Illustration not to scale

Diagram to show the float glass process (courtesy of Pilkington Brothers PLC).

company chairman, and was lucky that the worst development losses were sustained during the 1950s when the glass industry was buoyant and profits were good. Nevertheless it was not until January 1959 that enough saleable Float glass was made to justify a public announcement, not until July 1962 that the process was first licensed to another company (Pittsburgh Plate Glass), nor until that financial year that the company managed to make uninterrupted profits from it. Alastair Pilkington played a vital role in all these licensing negotiations. Licences were soon granted to other international glassmaking giants and, as the process came to be further developed and worked more efficiently, it began to replace the cheaper sheet glass as well as plate. The proceeds from licensing were eventually to reach a peak of £38 million per annum. In 1973 Sir Alastair Pilkington (he was knighted in 1970) became chairman of Pilkington Bros, a position he held for seven years. During his chairmanship the company developed still further its many activities, particularly abroad and especially in Europe where in 1979 it bought from BSN Gervais Danone, the French glass and food group, control of 18 glassmaking and processing plants in Belgium, Holland and Germany, including the main German producer, Flachglas. He also took up influential appointments outside the company as his predecessor had done, becoming a director of the Bank of England (1974), British Petroleum (1976) and Business International (1980). During 1973-76 he was a (not very happy) part-time member of the British Railways board.

He was a keen advocate of closer links between industry and the academic world, and served on the Science Research Council in 1970-73, the Central Advisory Council for Science and Technology and the committees of the London University Business History Unit, in the setting up of which he played a crucial part. He was also interested in encouraging industry and commerce to become involved in helping the communities in which they operated. During his chairmanship, and some

691

time before it became national policy to do so, Pilkington Bros made arrangements for helping those who wished to set up small businesses by providing financial and managerial assistance. In 1982 he became chairman of the Council for Business in the Community.

Many honours and prizes came his way. He received the Royal Society's Mullard Award in 1968, and became a FRS in the following year. He also received the John Scott Award from the board of directors of City Trusts, City of Philadelphia (1969) and the Phoenix Award, USA (1981), presented annually to the 'Man of the Year' in the glass industry. He became a fellow of the University of Manchester Institute of Science and Technology (1969), of Imperial College of Science and Technology (1975) and of the London School of Economics (1979). The universities of Bristol, Liverpool, London, Loughborough and the CNAA conferred honorary degrees upon him. In 1980 he became Pro-Chancellor of Lancaster University and in 1984 chairman of the CNAA. He was also chairman of the British Association for the Advancement of Science in 1983-84.

Retirement in 1980 at the age of sixty from the chairmanship and executive management (but not from the board) of Pilkington Brothers evidently did not mean retirement in any real sense, the more so as he was prevailed upon, in 1979, to become non-executive chairman of the Chloride Group at a particularly difficult time in that company's history. At the same time as moving from St Helens to a splendidly situated house in the Lake District, he also acquired a flat in Eaton Place, London, from where he continued to pursue his interests in the business and academic worlds as well as to cultivate his particular private passion, music. His first wife, Patricia Nicholls née Elliot, whom he had married in 1945, died of cancer in 1977. They had one son and one daughter. He remarried in 1978, an American lady, Kathleen, widow of Eldridge Haynes.

T C BARKER

Writings:

'The Float Glass Process' *Proceedings of the Royal Society* 314 (Dec 1969).

'Float: An Application of Science, Analysis and Judgement' *Glass Technology* 12 (4 Aug 1971).

'The Future of the Glass Industry' *The Indian and Eastern Engineer* Dec 1973.

'Floating Windows' *Proceedings of the Royal Institution of Great Britain* 48 (1975).

'The Future of the Glass Industry' *Engineering in Britain Information Services* TBN 197.

'The Float Glass Process Today' *Times Higher Education Supplement* 22 Jan 1976.

'Float Glass: Evolution and Revolution over 60 Years' *Glass Technology* 17 (Oct 1976).

Sources:

Unpublished

Pilkington Brothers PLC, archives.

Personal knowledge.

Published

Theodore C Barker, 'Business Implications of Technical Developments in the Glass Industry, 1945-65: A Case Study' in Barry Supple (ed), *Essays in British Business History* (Oxford: Clarendon Press, 1977).

—, *The Glassmakers. Pilkington: The Rise of an International Company, 1826-1976* (Weidenfeld & Nicolson, 1977).

WW 1982.

PILKINGTON, William Henry

1st Lord Pilkington of St Helens

(1905-1983)

Glass manufacturer and industrialist

W H Pilkington, Lord Pilkington (courtesy of Pilkington Brothers PLC).

William Henry (Harry) Pilkington was born at St Helens, Lancashire, on 19 April 1905, the eldest son of Richard Austin Pilkington and Hope, daughter of Sir Herbert Hardy (later First Lord) Cozens-Hardy of Letheringsett Hall, Holt, Norfolk, an eminent lawyer and future Master of the Rolls. His father, grandson of one of the original Pilkington brothers who had founded the glassmaking business in St Helens in 1826, suffered from tuberculosis which by 1909 had become so bad that the family went to live for several years in the dry, thin air of Colorado in a last, desperate bid to save his life. He made a complete recovery, the family returned to England and in due course Harry Pilkington was sent to Rugby (1919-23). There he distinguished himself neither at his studies nor at games. A private tutor accompanied him on at least one summer holiday and he took a year off between leaving school and going up to Magdalene College, Cambridge. There he did not shine either (he got a third in both parts of his tripos — history (1925) and economics (1927) — though he was a keen rower for the College). The failure of either Rugby or Cambridge to make the most of his undoubted powers of memory and his considerable mathematical ability, is hard to explain, for after his entry into the business in 1927 few were left for long in any doubt about his talent and promise. His memory proved phenomenal and he developed a keen, analytical brain, able to penetrate quickly to the heart of a problem. His remarkable head for figures enabled him to take in a table of statistics at a

693

glance. He possessed iron self discipline and a great sense of responsibility. Perhaps it was this which caused him to blossom, for he saw the business as a trust which should be handed on in a better state than it had been inherited. He had been brought up to believe that a Pilkington should perform, and be seen to perform, better than others. For him this did not pose any serious problem.

Henry Pilkington entered the company, along with his cousin, Douglas Phelps the son of a Pilkington daughter, at a critical point in its history. It had been the sole British producer of a polished plate glass, the quality product, since the beginning of the century and had also emerged as the main manufacturer of the cheaper, sheet glass from which most windows were made. Most of the competition then came from abroad, especially Belgium, rather than from Chance Bros Ltd of Spon Lane, Smethwick, the only other surviving British manufacturer. During the 1920s Pilkington did well in plate glass but failed to develop its own continuous method of sheet glassmaking or to secure a licence for the Libbey-Owens or Fourcault continuous processes. Both were being operated with increasing commercial success on the Continent and attempts were being made by a rival to operate the latter at a factory at Queenborough on the Isle of Sheppey. In 1927, when Harry Pilkington entered the company, there was a real prospect that Pilkington would very soon have to abandon sheet glass manufacture altogether.

Although Pilkington Bros had been a limited company in law since 1894, its shareholding was still restricted to the family and it continued to be run on partnership lines. The Pilkington directors kept control in their own hands and there was as yet no committee structure which would give other executives an opportunity to participate in policy making. During the 1920s Harry Pilkington's father had become chairman, and his uncle, Cecil, technical director. Harry Pilkington himself underwent a three-year probationary period and became a sub-director in 1930. By then the worst of the company's troubles were over, for the company managed in the nick of time to acquire rights to the Pittsburgh Plate Glass Co's new window glassmaking process, better than the other two. It was not, however, installed in time to prevent a loss being returned for the half year ending March 1931, an almost unheard-of event. Harry Pilkington's father and uncle resigned. Another uncle, his mother's brother, the Third Lord Cozens-Hardy, an electrical engineer by training who had been brought in when his father was ill with TB and had stayed, formed an executive committee and became its chairman. He also set about creating the beginnings of a committee structure and extended Harry Pilkington's probationary period for a further three years. He became a full member of the board in 1934, but then, on the unexpected retirement of the head of the sales department in the following year, found himself the senior executive on the commercial side. He was just thirty.

In the meantime he had married, in 1930, Rosamund Margaret Rowan, daughter of Colonel H D Rowan, an army medical officer, and they had spent their honeymoon on a voyage to Australia to visit Pilkington's selling agencies there and in New Zealand. Their son, John, was born in 1931, and a daughter, Jennifer, in 1933. A second daughter, Catherine, was to follow in 1938.

Authority in the company was soon to pass to the fourth generation.

Lord Cozens-Hardy retired from the chairmanship of the executive committee in 1939 and R M Weeks (qv), his successor — General Weeks, as he became during the war — never returned to the Pilkington executive after the war was over. Douglas Phelps became chairman of the executive in 1947 and Harry Pilkington chairman of the company itself in 1949. There then followed a period of quite remarkable progress as more glass was needed all over the world both for the rapidly growing motor industry (more vehicles and more glass per vehicle) and for building. This involved the new chairman in frequent visits abroad, and not just to Europe or the eastern parts of North America but on longer trips to South Africa, India, Australia and New Zealand where, as in Canada, the company developed factories, usually operated by wholly-owned subsidiaries. (Air travel now made possible such frequent long journeys. Harry Pilkington had, in 1935, been one of the first fare-paying passengers on the newly-opened Qantas route to Australia and he remained an enthusiast for flying. He later kept a record of the prodigious number of miles he covered every year.)

While chairman of the company, Sir Harry Pilkington (as he became in 1953) was also a very active member of its executive committee. He was particularly responsible for financial matters and was among the first businessmen to introduce inflation accounting. He was also concerned with the need to develop the company's committee structure in order to keep pace with its rapid expansion at home and (especially) overseas. (The capital employed in the business grew from £7.5 million just after the Second World War to nearly £60 million in 1960 and to £174 million ten years later; the sales turnover grew from £9 million to £58 million and £123 million in the same periods. These were very impressive figures even when discounted for inflation.) Above all, in the later 1950s and early 1960s, he was giving his unhesitating support to the Float process, the revolutionary new method of making a continuous ribbon of glass by pouring molten glass upon molten tin at over 1,000° C. Without it, Alastair Pilkington (qv), the inventor would never have weathered the academic criticisms he encountered from scientists within the company or the horrible development losses. The company would have been deprived of an asset which was to be licensed to its competitors all over the world, bringing in at its peak £38 million a year in licence income. Float glass also gave the chairman a pre-eminent position in international glassmaking circles.

Sir Harry suffered a personal tragedy in 1953 when his wife died suddenly from a heart attack. His reaction was to throw himself with even more vigour into governmental and other tasks in London. He had first become nationally known as president of the Federation of British Industries (1953-55), although he had already chaired the National Council of Building Material Producers from 1944 to 1952 and had attracted attention in Whitehall in May of the latter year by his report upon the methods and costs of school building. Expected to criticise the Ministry's officials adversely, he came down decisively on their side and, indeed, recommended that their methods be adopted by other departments. He was later to serve on the important Crichel Down Enquiry (1954) before being invited to chair the Royal Commission on Doctors' and Dentists' Remuneration (1957-60), which recommended large pay increases in those professions. Immediately after that he chaired the Committee on

Broadcasting which bears his name. It held 78 full meetings between August 1960 and May 1962 with much homework to be read and visits to various parts of the United Kingdom and to the United States and Canada. Its unanimous, carefully reasoned report, though not widely welcomed, led to the setting up of BBC 2 and decided the future of television for the next decade. Between 1955 and 1972 he was a director of the Bank of England. All these important and time-consuming activities coincided with the particularly critical years of expansion within the company outlined in the previous paragraph. There were times when Sir Harry seemed to be spending his life on the sleeper, or flying, between Lancashire and London (when he was not flying farther afield) and spending very full working days at each end.

He was by nature rather shy, and a strict Congregationalist upbringing, which no doubt had contributed to making him one of the world's leading workaholics, had not helped his shyness. Many people were to remark upon the great change which was to come about after his second marriage, in 1961, to Mrs Mavis Wilding, daughter of Gilbert Caffrey, a company director. This brought him the support he needed, a broader outlook on life and greater happiness. There were fewer duties in London, though he still had his regular weekly commitment at the Bank and he continued for some years as chairman of the National Council on Education for Industry and Commerce (1955-66). His flights to various parts of the world (sometimes with his wife) continued, and jet travel now made them all the easier. His greatest achievement in the 1960s, however, was undoubtedly the highly successful presentation of the Pilkington case, for which he was personally responsible, when flat glass was referred to the Monopolies Commission. Its report in 1966 not only acquitted the company of any charge of acting against the public interest but even included warm commendation of the way in which it conducted its affairs as a large-scale producer and exporter.

During Sir Harry Pilkington's chairmanship, lasting almost a quarter of a century, Pilkington Bros Ltd, still a family concern, achieved unprecedented prosperity and, with the Float process, world leadership in flat glass. In 1970 the company went public. If present profit is the true yardstick of success, the fourth generation of the family was more successful than any of its predecessors, contrary to received opinion among historians. To some extent, as he would have been the first to point out, this success was due to the remarkable international growth of Pilkington's two main markets, building and the motor trade, in both of which, by international agreement among the world's small and select band of glassmakers, Pilkington Bros enjoyed the lion's share throughout the Commonwealth markets. With the luxury of hindsight, however, critics may come to fault Pilkington management in this most prosperous period for specialising too narrowly upon flat glass at the expense of diversifying more vigorously into kindred industries which would serve the company in good stead when demand from the building industry and the motor trade fell away and the spread of the less capitalised and more scientific Float process made it easier for newcomers to become glassmakers, bringing with them keener competitive attitudes.

Sir Harry Pilkington was a tall man with a very deep, softly-spoken voice, shaggy brows, a twinkle in his eye and a beautiful smile. Indeed, a smile was never far from his lips. One member of his Committee on Broadcasting likened him to 'an overgrown schoolboy with a good face, wrinkled around the eyes ... full of energy, wit and brain' {Grenfell (1980) 128}. He was a cultivated person with a great curiosity and wide interests. He prided himself on the speed with which he could complete even the most difficult crossword puzzles. When he went to visit Pilkington subsidiaries abroad, the local staff never knew what questions they would be expected to answer on all subjects under the sun (those in New Zealand had a hard time with all the flora there); but woe betide anyone who presented guesses as if they were well-informed answers. He had a good sense of humour, though he was also quite capable of leaving people in no doubt that serious matters were not to be joked about. He enjoyed a particular accord with his cousin, Arthur Pilkington, the director in charge of sales, whom he invariably consulted on a wide range of matters and whose opinions and advice he particularly valued. The two were in many ways complementary, and their collaboration contributed considerably to the strength of the company at that time.

Harry Pilkington's views on management were summarised by him in the Chuter Ede Lecture in 1963. The days were already past, he believed, when managers selected themselves within a business 'by their obvious ability and character and learning the whole of their profession inside the firm, by example, by industry and by instinctive genius'. In most cases they would have to be pre-selected but often not trained in management as such. He went on:

> I do not know how far management can be taught. I am sure it can be to some extent. I am sure it cannot be completely ... Management is partly a science and partly an art ... At the very least teachers in management can point to a large number of expensive mistakes that should not have been made ... Management needs, especially, individual qualities. By definition, it requires judgement and decisiveness. It involves choosing, often enough, not between the good and the bad but between two courses one of which is good and the other better. To choose the wrong course is expensive but to hesitate is often fatal. We can no longer afford to learn from our mistakes. A mistake whether in works management or, more particularly ... in personal relations, is so costly that there can be no excuse for failing to learn routine methods that will avoid them. Management moreover, even more than most other careers, requires a liberal education, giving an understanding of the larger context in which decisions are taken {Sir Harry Pilkington, Chuter Ede Lecture (1963)}.

Sir Harry Pilkington possessed a superabundance of physical, as well as cerebral, energy. In his heyday he thought nothing of having colleagues play tennis with him before breakfast in London at the start of a hard day's work or in the evening until it grew too dark to see. He liked to drive any car in which he was riding, even if this meant the chauffeur shivering in the back (he was a demon for fresh air). On occasion he would get his secretary to accompany him to the station or airport so that she could read out correspondence to him while he, at the wheel, rattled off quick replies. His devotion to the bicycle became legendary. This was his preferred mode of local travel, even in London, for he believed it was the quickest way of getting around in heavy traffic. City swells were sometimes taken aback, however, when, after some splendid evening-dress function, he would put on his clips and cycle off into the night. Among his hobbies, rose growing was a favourite and on one occasion he won the Royal National Rose Society's trophy in the amateur competition for specimen blooms. He had been known to pick his exhibits at first light from his garden, bring them to London, show them in the office during the day and then ride with them tied to his handlebars to Chelsea where they were to be shown. He was particularly delighted when, on his retirement from the company chairmanship in 1973, Pilkington's Australian company arranged to have a Wheatcroft rose named after him.

Lord Pilkington (he was made a life peer in 1968) was made the company's honorary life president after his retirement and remained on the board as a non-executive director until 1980. He also continued as Chancellor of the Loughborough University of Technology. (He had become its first Chancellor in 1966.) He maintained many of his local interests in and around St Helens which he had never really dropped even when he had been most preoccupied by business and public affairs. He had been a JP since 1937 and was a regular worshipper at the Congregational (United Reformed) Church in the town on Sunday mornings. The local YMCA, hospitals, Marriage Guidance Council and many other organisations (not least the St Helens Rugby Football Club) had his personal support and he was Vice-Lord Lieutenant of Merseyside from 1974 to 1979 and chairman of the North-West Regional Council for Sport and Recreation from 1976 to 1982. He was given the freedom of the County Borough of St Helens in 1968. Much of his time latterly was spent writing in his own hand to pensioners when they reached the age of eighty or subsequent milestones, and sometimes delivering these letters in person.

He lived at Windle Hall, just outside St Helens, where Dr William Pilkington, father of the two founders of the business, had first gone to live in 1826. He died on 22 December 1983, leaving £1,879,873 gross. None of his children followed him into the company.

T C BARKER

Writings:

PP, Crichel Down Report of Public Inquiry (1954) Cmd 9176.

PP, RC Doctors' and Dentists' Remuneration (1957-60) Cmnd 939, 1064.

PP, Commission on Broadcasting (1960-62) Cmnd 1753.

PP, *HC* 1968 (83) Monopolies Commission Report on the Supply of Flat Glass.

'Manpower, Modernisation and Productivity' 4th Annual Willis Jackson Lecture, 11 Dec 1972 *British Association for Commercial and Industrial Education*.

'The Chain of Change' 27th William Menelaus Memorial Lecture, *Proceedings of the South Wales Institute of Engineers* (86).

Sources:

Unpublished

Pilkington Brothers PLC, St Helens, Lancashire, speeches of Lord Pilkington:

'The Challenge of Change and the Development of the Individual' 1963 Chuter Ede Lecture.

'The Role of Management in Shaping Modern Industrial Society' 13th CIOS Management Congress, New York, 16-20 Sept 1963.

'Education: The Responsibility of Industry' Address to the British Academy for the Advancement of Science, Southampton 2 Sept 1964.

Presidential address to the Association of Technical Institutes, 24 Feb 1966.

Speech on Installation as Chancellor of the University of Technology, Loughborough, 14 July 1966.

Speech on Broadcasting, House of Lords, 21 May 1969.

Speech at the 50th Annual Dinner of the Institution of Production Engineers, Dorchester Hotel, London, 23 Sept 1970.

Keynote address to the Hong Kong Management Association Conference, 8 Nov 1972.

Speech to the Society of Investment Analysts, London, 14 Dec 1972.

'East-West Trade' Speech to the International Industrial Conference jointly sponsored by the Conference Board and Stanford Research Institute, 17-21 Sept 1973.

'The Four Freedoms' University of Technology, Loughborough, July 1974.

'Management's Challenges' Alfred Watson Memorial Lecture, 24 Mar 1975.

Funeral oration by Lord Benson, The City Temple United Reformed Church, London, 1 Feb 1984.

BCe.

MCe.

PrC.

Information from Sir Antony Part, John Parry, Maurice A Shillington and members of the Pilkington family.

Personal knowledge of over forty years.

Published

Theodore C Barker, *The Glassmakers. Pilkington: The Rise of an International Company, 1826-1976* (Weidenfeld & Nicolson, 1977).

Cambridge Historical Register Supplement 1921-30 (Cambridge: Cambridge University Press, 1932).

Joyce Grenfell, *In Pleasant Places* (Macmillan, 1979).

WW 1982.

Samuel James Pipkin (courtesy of Hugh Cockerell).

PIPKIN, Samuel James

(1847-1927)

Insurance Company executive

Samuel James Pipkin was born at Leighton Buzzard, Bedfordshire on 14 October 1847, the son of James Pipkin, a maltster, and his wife Louisa née Price. At the age of eighteen he came to London as a temporary invoice clerk at £1 a week with Walker, Parker & Co, shot manufacturers of Lambeth. He soon left for a temporary appointment with Kemp, Ford & Co, public accountants, who were engaged in liquidation work after the Overend Gurney collapse in 1866. The work was heavy; often he did not leave the City until midnight. When the job came to an end the senior partner of his original employers nominated him for a clerkship at the Atlas Assurance Co where the partner was a director. Pipkin was accepted in 1868 after an examination which consisted of casting a column in a cash book and writing from dictation a paragraph from *The Times*. Recalling his early years there he said, 'Oh, it was awful. Nearly all above me young — no sign of business development to create chances of promotion — a dismal vision of rounded shoulders, narrowed chest and atrophied muscles ...' {*Journal of the Federation of Insurance Institutes* 9 (1907) 292}.

In 1873, needing a higher salary in order to get married, he applied for and was appointed directors' auditor at the Commercial Union Assurance Co, a growing office, where he made rapid progress, being appointed secretary in 1881. Three years later he accepted an invitation to return to Atlas as secretary, that is, chief executive.

The Atlas, founded in 1808 to transact fire and life insurance, had acquired a good business in its early years but more recently had lapsed into torpidity, perhaps because of the longevity of its principal officers. Pipkin was the third man to hold the secretaryship. The first secretary had held office for fifty years and the second for twenty-five. It was time for a shake-up and this Pipkin's energy supplied. At home the Atlas opened branch offices in 1885 and the appointment of an agency superintendent (that is, a sales manager) was revived. The company embarked on a policy of advertising on railway stations and appointed many new agents. The Atlas had hitherto transacted little overseas fire insurance. Pipkin began to travel the world in search of suitable agents. He was particularly successful in India and the Far East in building up a profitable business. Pipkin also reorganised the life business, in particular identifying the need to train agents. But the company's fire business accounted for well over 83 per cent of the increase in premium income from £215,096 in 1886 to £2,033,073 in 1918. Between 1886 and 1918 shareholders' assets rose nearly tenfold, from £361,457 to £3,456,000. In the first eight years of Pipkin's tenure the Atlas raised its dividend by 50 per cent and though the San Francisco earthquake and fire of 1906 cost the Atlas £400,000 its dividend was not reduced.

Pipkin, although an excellent organiser, was not an innovator. An early sally into personal accident insurance, unprecedented for a fire insurance company, was soon discontinued and his company was late in developing casualty insurance at the turn of the century. It eventually had to buy its way in by acquiring the Manchester Fire & Life Assurance Co in 1904 and the Essex & Suffolk Equitable Insurance Society in 1911. Pipkin disapproved of loss of profits insurance which had been pioneered at Lloyd's in the 1880s. In 1905 he was still condemning such policies as 'against public morals because they afford incentives to arson' {Pipkin (1916) 880}. He also expressed disapproval of fire policies under which the value of the insured property was agreed in advance. He considered them a form of gambling likely to lead to fraud.

Pipkin was given the title of general manager in 1896. On his retirement in 1918 he was appointed a director and remained on the board until his death. He was also chairman of the Essex & Suffolk Co, 1912-22, the company operating separately from the Atlas.

Although he took no part in activities unconnected with insurance he made signal contributions to the insurance community. He was the first general manager to support the idea of a fund for the benefit of orphans of insurance men. He set on foot the Insurance Clerks' Orphanage in 1902 and served it first as chairman and then as an active president until his death, by which time it had become well established. Similarly he gave positive support to the Federation of Insurance Institutes of Great Britain and Ireland which had never succeeded in interesting the insurance community in London until it prevailed on Pipkin to become president in 1905-6. In 1907, the Insurance Institute of London was established at his insistence and the foundation laid for the Chartered Insurance Institute which received its charter in 1912. Pipkin served as chairman of the London Salvage Corps for more than twenty years.

Pipkin's management style was robust. He was hot-tempered and mercurial but those who worked for him saw beyond the tantrums to the kind heart that governed his actions in the long run. He in turn treated them as human beings and sought to develop their qualities. A colleague described him as irascible but lovable. Among his fellow insurance company managers he was popular.

He became an Associate of the Institute of Actuaries in 1883 by virtue of position rather than actuarial knowledge.

Pipkin served on two government committees, one appointed to assess the losses arising out of the Irish rebellion in 1916 and the other to advise on aircraft and bombardment losses during the First World War.

Samuel Pipkin in 1873 married Emma, the daughter of William Stratford, a straw manufacturer. They had one daughter. Samuel Pipkin died at his home at Folkestone on 13 December 1927, leaving £60,075 gross.

HUGH COCKERELL

Writings:

A Run Round the World (pp, 1890).

'The Average Conditions of a Fire Insurance Policy' *Journal of the Federation of Insurance Institutes* (1898).

'Some Modifications and Developments in Fire Insurance Business' *Journal of the Federation of Insurance Institutes* (1906).

'Fifty Years' Reminiscences in the City' *Post Magazine and Insurance Monitor* 23 Dec 1916.

Sources:

Unpublished

Records of the Insurance Clerks' Orphanage (now the Insurance Orphans' Fund).

BCe.

MCe.

PrC.

Published

R B Caverly and George N Bankes, *Leading Insurance Men of the British Empire* (Index Publishing Co, 1892).

Hugh A L Cockerell, *Sixty Years of the Chartered Insurance Institute 1897-1957* (Chartered Insurance Institute, 1957).

Bernard Drew, *The Fire Office. Being the History of the Essex & Suffolk Equitable Insurance Society Ltd 1802-1952* (Colchester: Essex & Suffolk Equitable Insurance Society, 1952).

Barry Supple, *The Royal Exchange Assurance* (Cambridge: Cambridge University Press, 1970).

Alfred W Yeo, *Atlas Reminiscent. An Account of the Development of the Atlas Assurance Company 1808-1908* (J M Dent & Co, 1908).

PIRRIE, William James

Viscount Pirrie

(1847-1924)

Shipbuilder and shipowner

William James Pirrie was born of Presbyterian Irish parentage in Quebec on 24 May 1847. His father, James Alexander Pirrie, had emigrated to Canada in the early 1840s to manage a family shipping concern. In 1844 he married Eliza née Montgomery also an Ulster-born immigrant by whom

W J Pirrie, Viscount (courtesy of the Ulster Museum, Belfast).

he had two children, Eliza (b 1845) and William James. The family moved to New York, where James Pirrie died of cholera in 1849. After his death the family returned home to Conlig in County Down. The Pirries were of some substance in the city of Belfast. William Pirrie's grandfather, also William (1780-1858), was a retired Scottish sea captain who had made his fortune in the American and later in the Spanish trade (partly by helping to break the Napoleonic blockade). He settled in Belfast as representative of the family's Liverpool-based shipping and insurance firm, becoming a shipowner and prominent in public affairs in the town. He was a member of the Belfast Harbour Commissioners from 1847 until his death and played a leading role in creating the Victoria Channel (which was the foundation of the modern port of Belfast). One of the by-products of the drainage scheme involved reclaiming large amounts of land from the sea which became, thanks to a clause inserted by Pirrie in the parliamentary bill authorising it, the property of the Harbour Commissioners. Named in 1849 as Queen's Island, this later became the site of Harland & Wolff's shipyard. Thus William Pirrie Sr's career neatly dovetailed into that of his more illustrious grandson.

William James Pirrie's background, then, was relatively prosperous and very much rooted in shipbuilding in the port of Belfast. Between 1858 and 1862 he studied at the Royal Belfast Academical Institution where he showed promise in mathematics. When he left school in June 1862 his mother purchased for him an apprenticeship at the shipbuilding firm owned by Edward Harland and Gustav Wolff (qqv). More, she wrote for him a little book of maxims for his guidance which he carried with him for the rest of his life. Typical ones are: 'You have your own way to make. It depends on your own exertions whether you starve or not', 'Simple industry and studious exactness would be the making of Ireland', 'An ounce of pluck is worth a ton of luck' {*Belfast Newsletter* 27 June 1924}. William rapidly passed through the firm's hierarchy of staff functions, as draughtsman, assistant manager, sub-manager and works manager. In 1874, aged only twenty-seven, he was promoted to a partnership at the same time as a young draughtsman, Walter Wilson, who was to be responsible for the design of many of the vessels built by Harland & Wolff. The two promotions complemented each other. Pirrie, though always keenly aware of technical developments, was to excel at salesmanship and later at wheeling and dealing within the international shipping world; Wilson's expertise was primarily in naval architecture.

The early history of the firm has been told elsewhere (see entries under Sir Edward Harland and Gustav Wolff). In 1885 it was incorporated in Dublin as the Queen's Island Shipbuilding & Engineering Co Ltd, and in 1888 it changed its name to Harland & Wolff Ltd. Pirrie, with prime responsibility on the selling side, was frequently away from Belfast, particularly in Liverpool and London. In addition, from 1872 he paid many 'educational visits', as they were termed, to foreign countries, in order to ascertain what improvements could be made in the construction of vessels for the comfort of passengers. In essence this was the beginning of the process, culminating in the *Olympic* and *Titanic*, of building 'floating hotels'. The overseas voyages were also undertaken to discover the need to modify ships' designs to take account of peculiarities of the ports for which they were destined. A visit to South Africa in 1893-94, for example, led to the construction of a purpose-built 400-foot vessel capable of surmounting the bar at Durban.

In some respects Harland & Wolff's products were not difficult to sell. The firm already had a reputation for quality and through its intimate connection with the White Star and Bibby Lines, for whom it built exclusively, had a ready-made market. Later Pirrie was responsible for establishing similar links with other shipping companies, most notably, through his contacts with Owen Phillips, later Lord Kylsant (qv), the Royal Mail Shipping Group. In this respect his activity in the field of shipowning was intimately connected with the prosperity of Harland & Wolff as the relationships he created established markets for the company's products. The firm rarely tendered for contracts, operating instead a system of full cost plus an agreed mark-up for profit; such arrangements required complete confidence between shipowner and shipbuilder. Pirrie frequently provided the bridge between the two.

From the late 1880s Pirrie played an increasingly important role in the firm. In 1887 Harland became an MP and in 1892 Wolff followed him into parliament, making a conscious decision to withdraw from a close connection with the yard. 'Sir Edward Harland builds the ships for our firm' he is quoted as saying, 'Mr Pirrie makes the speeches, and, as for me, I smoke the cigars' {Jefferson (1948) 59}. After Harland's death in 1895, Pirrie became chairman and undisputed head of the firm; two years later the company launched more tonnage than any yard in the United Kingdom, and the largest on record to that date.

Under Pirrie's leadership Harland & Wolff became the greatest shipbuilders in the world. The firm's speciality was the large passenger liner. Beginning in 1899 in close co-operation with T H Ismay (qv), and later his son Bruce, Harland & Wolff began to build ships larger than had ever been known. The company commenced with the 17,040-ton *Oceanic*, at 705 feet the first ship to exceed in length Brunel's *Great Eastern*. Establishing new standards of excellence in accommodation, and marking a great advance in steam propulsion, she has been called 'the crowning success of the nineteenth century in naval architecture and marine engineering' {Anderson (1964) 84}. Her financial success led to even more enormous vessels: the *Celtic* 21,000 tons, the *Baltic* 24,000, the *Adriatic* 25,000, culminating in the *Olympic* and *Titanic*, both 46,400 tons, and the *Britannic* 50,000 tons. During the pre-war period the firm began to expand its activities by establishing branches in mainland Britain. This began in 1907 when, in order to secure a supply of materials necessary for shipbuilding, steel products and turbines for example, Pirrie entered into an agreement with John Brown & Co which established interlocking shareholdings between the Sheffield-based group and Harland & Wolff. (This move, incidentally, involved Pirrie in a heavy personal financial commitment of £250,000, which he later found difficult to honour as he had stretched his resources even further by the acquisition of the Union Castle Line in 1912.) Through its connection with John Brown, which had interests in Glasgow shipbuilding, and to overcome shortages of skilled labour in Belfast, Harland & Wolff began to expand its activities on the Clyde. The move may also have been influenced by the growing political instability in Ulster in the wake of the Home Rule crisis. In 1912 it purchased the London & Glasgow Engineering & Iron Shipbuilding Co of

Govan, a step followed by the acquisition of smaller companies in Greenock, Scotstoun and Dunbarton. The same year, in what was to prove a move of great foresight, the company acquired the right to produce under licence the diesel engine patented by Burmeister & Wain of Copenhagen. This gave Harland & Wolff a lead over many of its competitors in the transition from coal to oil as a source of motive power. Additionally, repair yards were established at Southampton, Liverpool and Woolwich.

During the immediate pre-war period Pirrie's concern was less with the day-to-day running of the firm than with broader aspects of company policy. He had behind him in Belfast an able team of managers and technicians, first Wilson, then his brother-in-law, Alexander Carlisle, and his nephew, Thomas Andrews (who died on the maiden voyage of the *Titanic* which he had designed). Pirrie's primary role in the company was as salesman and financier. As one Scottish industrialist put it: 'Lord Pirrie has a sort of magic by which I think he charms orders for ships out of his customers' {Green and Moss (1982) 28}. The contacts he built up in the international shipping community necessitated lengthy absences from Belfast, and he established homes in Belgravia and Witley Park, in Surrey, a huge mansion on which he lavished £250,000. During the First World War, Harland & Wolff maintained its position as the country's leading builder of mercantile tonnage. In 1918, for example, it built over 200,000 out of a national total for merchant shipbuilding of 1.5 million tons; its nearest rival built only 78,000 tons. In 1917 the company embarked on the construction of a new 2,000-acre site. Employment in the yard, which had been only 3,000 when Pirrie became a partner in Harland & Wolff in 1874, rose to 12,000 in 1914 and 15,000 in 1920. The firm's capitalisation increased from £500,000 at the turn of the century to £8.1 million in 1921. Pirrie's pre-eminence in the industry was recognised by his appointment in March 1918 as Comptroller-General of Merchant Shipbuilding, responsible for co-ordinating the national effort to produce more ships and repair those damaged by enemy action; at the same time he was sworn of the Privy Council with direct access to the Cabinet. Acting on a plan devised by the Glasgow shipbuilder, James Lithgow, ship designs were standardised and productivity notably increased. Pirrie's work was rewarded with a viscountcy in 1921.

Plans for the expansion of Harland & Wolff continued after the war. Whatever private reservations Pirrie may have had, he acted as though he thought the great shipping boom would never end. Facilities at the yard were upgraded and plans to complete the 1917 scheme put into operation. In 1920 after negotiations (which commenced in 1917) to provide supplies of steel for the anticipated growth in demand, Harland & Wolff acquired David Colville & Sons, the 'apparently rudderless' West of Scotland steelmaking company {Payne (1979) 135}. With hindsight these moves appear excessively optimistic. When the boom ended in 1921, Harland & Wolff experienced excess capacity, falling profits, and the need to shed labour. By the time of Pirrie's death the firm was in serious financial difficulties, in part a consequence of the expansionary programme undertaken by him at the end of the war. Nonetheless, looked at more generally, the firm performed creditably in the depressed conditions of the 1920s, thanks, in part, to Pirrie's early conversion of the business to the advantages of the diesel engine. After his death in 1924 he was succeeded as chairman of Harland & Wolff by his friend and business associate Lord Kylsant. The firm for the first time became public with a nominal capital of £12.1 million. Because of the shipbuilding industry's precarious financial position, however, the launch of the new company was not a success.

Increasingly, Pirrie's role as shipbuilder was combined with that of shipowner. In many ways this combination of occupations was natural as it helped secure markets for Harland & Wolff's products. This aspect of his career began as early as 1886 when he was involved in the establishment of the North Western Shipping Co, which went into voluntary liquidation in 1895. In 1891 he became a director of the African Steamship Co, and assumed the chairmanship in 1901. Between 1901 and 1902 he was engaged with Bruce Ismay and the German shipowner Albert Ballin in an attempt to limit competition in the North Atlantic trade routes. Later, after Ballin's withdrawal from the proposed scheme, Pirrie, knowing that J P Morgan & Co were trying to buy Cunard, encouraged, perhaps even pressured, Ismay to come to an arrangement with the American company. In February 1902 an agreement was signed between Morgan, White Star, the Dominion Line, the American Line, the Mississippi & Dominion Steam Ship Co, and the Atlantic Transport Co of Baltimore, establishing the International Mercantile Marine Co. Morgan later alleged that Pirrie's great enthusiasm for the deal stemmed from personal financial embarrassment and that 'if the combine had not gone through he [Pirrie] would have been bankrupt six months ago as he could not have carried the load he had on his shoulders' {Oldham (1961) 148}. However, he was also motivated by the desire to extend Harland & Wolff's markets; under the agreement all orders for new vessels and repairs requiring to be done in British yards were to go to the company. American dominance of this new organisation brought Pirrie's patriotism into question; *Fairplay* magazine alleged he had as much of the sentiment 'as a Muscovy duck' {Green and Moss (1982) 21}. Guarantees were, however, given with respect to use of the company's British-based shipping in the event of war. Cunard stayed outside the scheme, influenced partly by political pressure and partly by the lucrative subsidies it was offered. IMM was not a success. It was overcapitalised, its share issue was unsuccessful, and its financial performance poor.

Pirrie was also interested in the African trade. In 1901 he became chairman of the African Steamship Co and had also built up a 14 per cent shareholding in Elder Dempster Shipping Ltd. His interest in the trade broadened in 1909, when together with Owen Philipps (qv), he took over the business interests of Sir Alfred Jones (qv), establishing Elder Dempster & Co as the owner of the firm's operating companies in March 1910. This was the beginning of an association between Phillips and Pirrie which was only to end with the latter's death. In 1912 they jointly acquired for Royal Mail and Elder Dempster the Union Castle Line with its 44 vessels totalling 319,514 tons. The move was criticised at the time as it involved the creation of a higher proportion of fixed interest stock and loan capital than was usual for public companies; this heavy indebtedness was to prove burdensome in the depressed post-war years. Pirrie's fortunes became increasingly intertwined with those of Philipps, as the connection between Harland & Wolff and the Royal Mail group grew closer. In 1918 they jointly bid for all the United Kingdom companies in IMM for which they offered the huge sum of £27 million. This move was vetoed by Woodrow Wilson himself: a blessing in disguise as the burden of debt the bid entailed could not have been sustained after 1920.

Pirrie's business interests were enormously wide-ranging. With respect to shipping at one time or another he held the following posts: chairman of the African Steamship Co, the Ocean Transport Co and the Glen Line; director of the White Star Line, the IMM, Frederick Leyland & Co, the British & North Atlantic Steam Navigation Co, the Mississippi & Dominion Steamship Co, Wilson & Furness, Leyland Line, Elder Dempster & Co, Lamport & Holt, A & J Inglis & Co, the Atlas Mercantile Co, the Union Castle Mail Steamship Co, and John Brown & Co. Outside shipping he was a director of the London & South Western Railway Co (and of the Southern Railway, 1923–24), the London City & Midland Bank, the London City & Midland Executor & Trustee Co, the Eastern Telegraph Co, the Scottish Widows' Life Assurance Co, the Alliance Debenture Co, the British American Petroleum Co (British Union Oil), the Watertight Door Co, and the Fibre Co of Ireland. A list of shareholdings, derived from his will, shows even broader involvement in industry and trade. This ceaseless accumulation of business offices was almost certainly counter-productive and led to a dissipation of his talents. Not all his investments were profitable. His £50,000 holding in British Union Oil was valued in his estate at £1 'no market value'. The £46,000 nominal value held in the Fibre Co of Ireland was worth 'say' £100.

Pirrie's career outside business was equally varied. He became involved in Unionist politics at the time of the second Home Rule Bill (1892) when he was honorary treasurer of the Ulster Defence Union. In 1893 he was elected a Conservative member of the Belfast Harbour Commissioners and also an alderman on the Corporation, where he did useful work on the Electricity Committee and was also instrumental, together with his wife, in modernising and extending the Royal Victoria Hospital. In 1896 and 1897 he was Lord Mayor and in 1898 became the first freeman of the City (the second was T H Ismay) as well as High Sheriff for County Antrim. In 1899 he was made High Sheriff for County Down. The same year, however, Pirrie fell out with the Conservative establishment that controlled the city's politics. The quarrel began over a nomination for a vacant seat on the corporation, and was aggravated in 1902 when Pirrie was rejected as Conservative nominee for the South Belfast seat in favour of a County Down landowner who had no connections with the city. Pirrie took this very badly. His anger was increased when he was passed over in the list of those Belfast citizens honoured during King Edward VII and Queen Alexandra's visit to the town in 1903. Whether in temper, or whether by conviction (he was an ardent free trader, opposed all forms of subsidies, and disliked government intervention even to the extent of opposing trademarks!) he became a Liberal and helped finance the party candidates in the province in the 1905 election. His reward from the Campbell-Bannerman Government was a barony in 1906 (motto 'Deeds not Words'). Being a Liberal in Belfast inevitably meant political estrangement from his fellow citizens, but by going one stage further and becoming an outspoken Home Ruler, Pirrie created active antagonism. The hostility culminated in the violent scenes which greeted the visit of

PIRRIE William James

Winston Churchill, John Redmond and other prominent Home Rulers to the city in 1912. (Pirrie was chairman of the meeting at which the MPs spoke.) Later Pirrie and his wife were pelted with rotten eggs in the cross-channel port of Larne. After the war, however, Pirrie returned once more to Unionism, became a senator in the Northern Ireland parliament, and was reconciled to his former colleagues.

Though denied, at least until 1918, the significant position in public life he coveted, his list of minor offices (like his directorships) is lengthy. He was a member of the following: the Committee of Lloyd's Register of British Shipping, the Committee of the Institution of Mechanical Engineers, the Board of Trade Conciliation Court Panel, the Advisory Committee on New Lighthouse Work; the Vice-Regal Commission on Irish Railways; the Committee on Irish Finance. Between 1907 and 1913 he was Comptroller General of the Household of of the Lord Lieutenant in Dublin. In 1908 he became Pro-Chancellor of the newly-formed Queen's University of Belfast. He was made a knight of St Patrick the following year and in 1911 was appointed HM Lieutenant for Belfast.

Pirrie in 1879 married Margaret Montgomery, daughter of John Carlisle, MA, of Belfast; they had no children and his peerage became extinct after his death. He died while passing through the Panama Canal on 7 June 1924; his body was returned to Belfast for burial and, old differences forgotten, large crowds lined the city streets as the cortège passed. His widow received messages of sympathy from inter alia the King and Queen and the Prime Ministers of Britain and Northern Ireland.

Pirrie's fortunes were severely reduced by the post-war depression, and in the 1920s he had to raise large loans and overdrafts in order to support his investments. In common with other shipbuilders, Harland & Wolff were making losses, and the shipping companies in which he had an interest were also in difficulties as freight rates fell. At his death Pirrie was far from being the multi-millionaire contemporaries believed him to be; indeed consideration was given to declaring his estate bankrupt in order to avoid death duties. This never took place because of the adverse affect it was felt the declaration would have on the fortunes of Harland & Wolff. Bankruptcy was averted only by Kylsant forming a trust to purchase Pirrie's shares in Harland & Wolff for £500,000. In his will Pirrie left £175,841 gross.

William Pirrie was the greatest Irish businessman of his generation. His ventures into shipowning were not without their failures, the IMM being the most notable example. His optimism in the conditions of 1918-20 was excessive and created during the 1920s problems for the companies with which he was involved. But as a shipbuilder he was unrivalled in his generation as his appointment as Comptroller General of Shipbuilding in 1918 testifies. Together with his team at Queen's Island, he helped set new standards in shipbuilding size and design and in passenger comfort. He foresaw earlier than most of his contemporaries the replacement of coal by oil as a source of motive power. His greatest achievement was that, in an unlikely part of the United Kingdom, he helped create, and, even more significantly, sustained for thirty years, Harland & Wolff's position as the greatest shipbuilders in the world.

D S JOHNSON

Writings:

PP, HC 1896 (233) VIII, SC Belfast Corporation Bill and the Londonderry Improvement Bill.

PP, HC 1902 (385) IX, SC Steamship Subsidies.

PP, Vice-Regal Commission on Irish Railways. Final Report (1910) Cd 5247.

PP, HC 1912-13 (6,799) XXX, Committee on Irish Finance.

Sources

Unpublished

PrC; Will.

Private communication from Michael Moss, Archivist of Glasgow University.

Published

Roy Anderson, *White Star* (Prescot: I T Stephenson & Sons, 1964).

Belfast Newsletter 23, 27 June 1924.

Belfast Telegraph 12 Apr 1945.

R D C Black, 'William James Pirrie' in Conor Cruise O'Brien (ed), *The Shaping of Modern Ireland* (Routledge & Kegan Paul, 1960).

Peter N Davies, *The Trade Makers. Elder Dempster in West Africa 1862-1972* (George Allen & Unwin, 1973).

—, *Sir Alfred Jones. Shipping Entrepreneur Par Excellence* (Europa, 1978).

—, 'Group Enterprise: Strengths and Hazards. Business History and the Teaching of Business Management' in Sheila Marriner (ed), *Business and Businessmen: Studies in Business, Economic and Accounting History* (Liverpool: Liverpool University Press, 1978).

Peter N Davies and A M Bourn, 'Lord Kylsant and the Royal Mail' *Business History* 14 (1972).

DNB.

Charles E Fayle, *The War and the Shipping Industry* (Humphrey Milford, 1927).

Charles R V Gibbs, *Passenger Liners of the Western Ocean. A Record of the North Atlantic Steam and Motor Passenger Vessels from 1838 to the Present Day* (Staples Press, 1952).

Edwin Green and Michael Moss, *A Business of National Importance: The Royal Mail Shipping Group 1902-1937* (Methuen, 1982).

Francis E Hyde, *Cunard and the North Atlantic 1840-1973* (Macmillan, 1975).

Irish News 10 June 1924.

Irish Times 22 Apr 1922.

Herbert Jefferson, *Viscount Pirrie of Belfast* (Belfast: W Mullan & Son, 1948).

Northern Whig 9, 23 June 1924.

C H Oldham, 'The History of Belfast Shipbuilding' *Journal of the Statistical and Social Inquiry Society of Ireland* 12 (1911).

Wilton J Oldham, *The Ismay Line. The White Star Line and the Ismay Family Story* (Liverpool: Journal of Commerce, 1961).

Peter L Payne, *Colvilles and the Scottish Steel Industry* (Oxford: Clarendon Press, 1979).

Sidney Pollard and Paul Robertson, *The British Shipbuilding Industry 1870-1914* (Cambridge, Massachusetts: Harvard University Press, 1979).

Denis Rebbeck, 'Harland and Wolff's Shipyard and Engine Works at Belfast' *Engineering* 16, 26 Sept 1952.

WWW.

PITMAN, Sir Isaac

(1813-1897)

Publisher

Isaac Pitman was born at Trowbridge, Wiltshire, on 4 January 1813, the second son of Samuel and Maria Pitman. His father, a handloom weaver by trade, was overseer at John Edgell's cloth factory in the town. Isaac's parents were Baptists (although his father taught at an Anglican Sunday-school as well as founding a Baptist one); their piety, and his father's interest in education and temperance reform, greatly influenced him. He attended a day-school until he was thirteen, but his real education came from his own reading and studies, which included shorthand. Put to work in Edgell's counting-house, and then in the counting-house of the cloth-factory his father set up in 1829, Isaac continued to study before and after his twelve-hour office day. Having little contact with educated people, he read through Walker's *Dictionary* — twice — noting the phonetic symbols carefully to correct his mispronunciation of many of the words he had learnt from his reading.

Although Isaac's father resisted his son's pleas to be allowed to continue his schooling, he was generous in providing books for study, and in 1831 he sent Isaac to the Borough Road Training College of the British and Foreign School Society. (Five of Isaac's brothers and sisters were to follow him to Borough Road.) After four years' teaching at Barton-on-Humber in North Lincolnshire (where he married Mary Holgate, the widow of a local solicitor, in 1835) he moved to Wotton-under-Edge in Gloucestershire. His career as a British School teacher ended there soon after he made public his conversion to the ideas of Swedenborg, of whom he remained a devoted disciple for the rest of his life.

It was while running a private school at Wotton-under-Edge in 1837, that he invented his own system of shorthand, based on the sound rather than the spelling of words. His promotion of this system took on the character of an evangelistic crusade. He travelled the country, lecturing and teaching, in the school holidays, as well as conducting free postal tuition which was greatly assisted by the introduction of the Penny Post in January 1840. (He was to oppose paid postal teaching of his method until the late 1860s.) Later the work of itinerant lecturing was taken up by a group of devoted followers, until the numbers of Pitman's own publications and the general acceptance of the system by the early 1850s made this superfluous. Pitman's shorthand had its ever-increasing band of fervent disciples and, eventually, its schisms. Twice, in 1855 and 1862, he issued revised versions of the system and refused to reprint earlier editions, despite the fact that many 'phonographers' continued to use the old system.

It is hard to assess the financial success of Pitman's business, because for many years most of the profits from the sale of his 'phonographic' publications went into his efforts to promote the reform of spelling on phonetic principles, and to perfect a system of printing in 'phonetic' characters. For the first ten years after he closed his school in 1843 and devoted all his time to 'phonography' he allowed himself only £80 a year out of the profits, £100 for the next five years, and £150 for the next three. During this period he never took a holiday, and until 1864 worked without the assistance of a clerk or foreman, personally supervising the printing and binding of his publications. At first this was done from two rooms of his house in Nelson Place, Bath, where by 1849-50 he employed 18 people; in 1851 he rented a house, Albion Place, in Bath to hold his presses. In 1858 he rented a room of 1,500 square feet on the top floor of premises at Parsonage Lane, Bath and continued to work in these cramped and unsuitable conditions for fifteen years, still with only 18 employees. By 1873 over 80,000 'phonographic' manuals a year were being produced here, as well as *The Phonographic Journal*, and literature on spelling reform. All this had to be produced on hand presses, and Pitman felt the time had come to find new premises which could take steam-powered presses. In 1874 he bought 6 and 7 Kingston Buildings, which provided him with 5,000 square feet of space, for £600.

From now on, more of the profits seem to have been put back into the business, although no accounts survive by which its growth can be charted. This new approach to the dissemination of Pitman's shorthand literature — more and more an ordinary business, rather than a crusade — is perhaps attributable to the entry of Isaac's sons, Alfred and Ernest, into the firm. They were concerned, for example, at their father's continuing improvements and modifications of his system, because they regarded them as 'bad for business' {*As Fast As Speech* (1977) 14}. The firm was renamed Isaac Pitman & Sons in 1886, the year that the *Phonographic Teacher*, one of Pitman's leading manuals, reached its first million copies. In 1889 new premises were opened near Bath, this time purpose-built for the production of books and periodicals. Isaac handed over his interest in the business to his sons in 1894, the year the *Teacher* reached its second million. In 1896 they set up a limited liability company, Sir Isaac Pitman & Sons Ltd, with a nominal capital of £120,000, of which £100,000 was taken up in equal parts by Alfred and Ernest themselves; they were to be governing directors for life.

All Pitman's brothers and sisters, his father, and his second wife, Isabella Masters of Bath (the mother of his two sons, Alfred and Ernest), whom he married in 1861, learnt his system of 'phonography'. His brother Benn was particularly active in its promotion, first lecturing in England, then publishing Pitman's manuals in America (he continued to publish the ninth edition rather than Isaac's later revised versions of the system). In 1847 another brother, Frederick, took over from Benn the management of the London depot of the publisher Samuel Bagster from which Pitman's manuals were issued. He opened his own business in 1849, and until his death in 1886 published all Isaac's phonographic books and periodicals. After Frederick's death, Isaac Pitman & Sons opened their own London publishing-house at 1 Amen Corner.

Throughout his long life, Pitman was rarely ill; he attributed his excellent health and his ability to work for very long hours to his vegetarian diet and his abstinence from alcohol. He was a strict disciplinarian in the office; and although he would listen to advice he always did things in his own way in the end. He was greatly interested in promoting not only spelling reform and the doctrines of Swedenborg, but a wide range of causes from liberal politics to campaigns against drink, tobacco, vivisection and vaccination.

Working 'with remarkable success in an industrial bye-path of his own' {*Times* 23 Jan 1897}, through his system of shorthand Pitman had a considerable effect on the work of countless offices in every kind of organisation. By the beginning of the twentieth century his system was by far the most widely-used, especially among clerks and secretaries, in English-speaking countries, and had been adapted to several European and Asian languages. Pitman's 'great services to Stenography' {Baker (1908) 296} were rewarded by a knighthood in 1894. Sir Isaac Pitman died on 22 January 1897.

CHRISTINE SHAW

Writings:

A summary bibliography of Pitman's publications is given in Alfred Baker, *The Life of Sir Isaac Pitman* (Sir I Pitman & Sons, 1908).

Sources:

Unpublished

C Reg: (50,690) Pitman Ltd.

Published

David Abercrombie, *Isaac Pitman, a Pioneer in the Scientific Study of Language* (Sir I Pitman & Sons, 1937).

As Fast as Speech: An Outline History of Shorthand from 2400 BC (Pitmans, 1977).

Alfred Baker, *The Life of Sir Isaac Pitman Inventor of Phonography* (Sir I Pitman & Sons, 1908).

DNB.

Thomas Allen Reed, *A Biography of Isaac Pitman* (Griffin & Farran, 1890).

Times 23 Jan 1897.

Wreford J C Pittard (courtesy of the Pittard Group Limited).

PITTARD, Wreford John Charles

(1877-1959)

Leather merchant

Wreford John Charles Pittard was born at Yeovil on 10 October 1877, the younger son of Charles Wreford Pittard, a leather merchant, and his wife Fanny née Mogridge. At the age of nine he was sent to board at John Aldridge's School, now Yeovil School. The family had lived in Yeovil for over two hundred years and the family business which he joined in 1892 had been founded by his great-grandfather. The business had two factories in Yeovil, at Middle Street and Sherborne Road, and was well-established in fell-mongering and leather-dressing. On 5 April 1909, the business became a private limited company under the title of C W Pittard & Co, Wreford Pittard being one of the founder directors.

In 1912 his father died suddenly whilst in London attending the Raw Skin and Hide Auctions. Wreford Pittard, then thirty-six years old, was left in complete charge of the firm, being chairman and managing director, although his elder brother, Harold, a glove manufacturer, was made an executive director. During the First World War, the production of sheepskins (with the wool retained) for making trench coats and mittens was carried on. After the war, Wreford Pittard decided that fell-mongering, the initial dressing of rougher leathers, should cease and the entire output of the factories should be in gloving leathers, as Yeovil was one of the main UK centres of this craft industry. His judgement was sound and by the mid-1920s other producers in the area, and as far away as Marlborough, were undertaking contract dressing for C W Pittard & Co.

In 1922 his eldest son, Douglas Wreford Pittard (b 1904), joined the business. During the period 1920-24, Wreford Pittard decided to enlarge the Sherborne Road premises by building a large warehouse and office block, and also by enlarging the production area and installing modern machinery for fleshing the skins, and hair or wool drying. This enabled

The dye shop at the Highfield works, as it was rebuilt in 1936 (courtesy of the Pittard Group Limited).

Hand-staking at the Highfield factory in the mid 1930s (courtesy of the Pittard Group Limited).

him to sell the Middle Street property, and in addition reduce the transport and administrative costs.

Wreford Pittard's second son, John (b 1908), joined the firm in 1926 and as was the custom he spent several years becoming familiar with the dressing processes, going to another leather producer in the Midlands to gain experience in chrome tanning and dyeing, and returning to Yeovil in 1928. John was put in charge of a small chroming and dyeing plant in the Yeovil Highfield area. This development enabled the company to expand its business considerably by selling finished leather to glove manufacturers throughout the British Isles, who themselves had no leather-producing facilities. The Highfield factory was considerably enlarged, and was producing high-quality dyed and finished leather for making-up, both at home and overseas. At the outbreak of the Second World War, specialised leathers were produced for the fighting services — aircrew gloves, waterproof leather for fighter pilot suits, transport and despatch riders' gloves, and ski gloves. In addition, the company made leather for the face pieces of oxygen masks and for many other uses.

Wreford Pittard chaired the UK Light Leather Producers' Committee, advising the Leather Controller at the Ministry of Supply. At the end of the war, he and his colleagues turned their attention to further rebuilding both the Sherborne Road and Highfield factories so that leather production could be increased considerably. This permitted the development of volume sales to overseas markets, particularly the USA and Canada. In ensuing years approximately 40 per cent of production was exported.

In 1892, when Wreford Pittard joined the business, approximately 25 people were employed handling 2,000 skins a week. By 1959, the number had increased to 250, handling 24,000 skins a week, using the most modern machines and techniques. In 1955 Pittards were able to guarantee that their glove leathers were washable, a major breakthrough in gloving leather technology. The firm was converted into a public company in 1962, three years after Wreford's death. As well as his own company, Wreford Pittard was also a director of Clark Son & Morland, another local firm manufacturing sheepskin goods which had been founded in 1825, about the same time as the Pittard business.

Wreford Pittard, like his father, took an active part in public life serving as councillor on both the Yeovil Borough and Somerset County Councils, being elected an alderman in 1922 and made a freeman of the borough in 1949. He served as a magistrate for twenty years and chairman of the bench, 1950-52. He was chairman of the Yeovil Liberal Association, the Tone Vale Hospital Management Committee and the governors of his old school. He was a generous benefactor to local organisations and often helped his local Baptist church. He retained a lifelong interest in sport and as a young man had played football for another local firm founded by the Petter brothers (qv).

He married in 1902 Ethel Mary, daughter of John Hiskett, a compositor's overseer, at the Baptist Church, Frome. He died on 25 September 1959, leaving £35,835 gross, and was survived by his wife and two sons.

D W PITTARD

Sources:

Unpublished

MCe.

PrC.

Published

Pittards 1826-1976. A Commemorative History (Yeovil: pp C W Pittard & Co, nd).

Stock Exchange Official Year Book 1968.

Western Gazette 2 Oct 1959.

PLATT, Sir Frank

(1890-1955)

Cotton spinner

Frank Platt was born on 9 June 1890, the son of Thomas Platt, a mule spinner, and his wife Rachel. Frank was educated at Derby Street Board School and the Central Higher Grade School in Rochdale, Lancashire. At the age of fourteen he left school to work in the counting house of the Clover Mill where he made rapid progress and 'while still a youth showed signs of great organising powers' {*Textile Weekly* 15 July 1955}. In 1914 he joined Higher Crompton Mills Ltd, at Shaw, as mills manager and by the post-war boom of 1919-20 he had become a director, not only of Higher Crompton Mills but also of other spinning companies in the Oldham and Rochdale districts, which were foremost centres of coarse spinning in Lancashire.

During the post-war boom Platt participated in the rush of mill re-flotations, 'turning over' about a dozen mill companies. In what appears to have been an uncharacteristic move he then retired from the cotton industry to become a gentleman farmer in North Wales where he bred racehorses and Alsatians. However, for one reason or another he soon abandoned the life of the gentrified entrepreneur and by the mid-1920s he was once again a director of several spinning companies in the Oldham district. From this vantage point he must have been closely acquainted with the difficulties of the Lancashire cotton industry in the 1920s, when Lancashire was unable to recover its former hegemony over world markets for cotton goods.

By the late 1920s there was a strong current of opinion, influenced by the contemporary vogue for industrial 'rationalisation', which attributed the industry's continuing depression to its outmoded internal structure and organisation, inherited from the heyday of nineteenth-century competitive capitalism. The industry's highly specialised and competitive structure should, it was argued, be superseded by large-scale corporate enterprise, capable of recovering lost export markets by reaping economies of scale. This theme was taken up by successive Conservative and Labour Governments, both of which looked to the Bank of England to bring their policies into effect by reorganising the industry. It was from this scenario that Platt was to emerge as one of the leading figures in the British cotton industry.

In 1928-29 the Bank of England was instrumental in launching the Lancashire Cotton Corporation (LCC) which, its promoters hoped, would play a major part in rationalising the cotton industry by amalgamating a large number of spinning companies and then integrating forward into the weaving and merchanting of cotton goods. In its first three years the LCC acquired mill companies at a dramatic pace until, by 1932, it had absorbed 96 companies controlling nearly 10 million spindles in 109 mills, representing between a quarter and a third of the country's cotton spindles, excluding those engaged in the production of fine yarns from Egyptian cotton. The merger was highly unpopular in Lancashire where many spinning companies were forced into the LCC by creditor banks acting under the aegis of the Bank of England, which itself appointed more than half of the Corporation's board.

Meanwhile, various other proposals for cotton industry mergers were laid before the Bank of England which set up two subsidiaries — the Securities Management Trust (SMT) and the Bankers' Industrial Development Corporation (BIDC) — as the official channels for its rationalising activities. The most promising scheme was put forward by Platt, who sought £1,250,000 of new capital to merge about 5 million spindles owned by 44 companies, most of them Midland Bank customers, into a new spinning amalgamation, to be known as Allied Spinners. However, after prolonged negotiations the Allied Spinners scheme had to be abandoned because neither the BIDC nor the Midland was prepared to finance the merger, notwithstanding the fact that it was recognised as a sounder project than the LCC.

Indeed, by the middle of 1932 the LCC was in a crisis. It had failed to realise the forecast economies of scale and had all but exhausted its cash resources following heavy losses in its first three years. Furthermore, its internal controls were stretched to breaking point, and beyond in some cases; it was burdened with many shut down mills, most of which were too inefficient to be competitive; it had cut its prices below costs of production in an effort to increase its volume of business; and it had made unsuccessful incursions into weaving and merchanting. To make matters worse, it had also alienated the rest of the spinning section in which the LCC was widely regarded as an unfair competitor, controlled and subsidised by London-based financial interests, and intent on driving other spinning companies out of business by its policy of price-cutting.

In the midst of this crisis the Bank of England intervened, through Barings' merchant bank, to reorganise the LCC's board. One of the Bank's

proposals had to be abandoned. Platt nevertheless continued to support the cause of industrial reorganisation and self-regulation, putting the industrial weight of the LCC behind the Cotton Spinning Industry Act of 1936, under which a Spindles Board was set up to purchase and scrap surplus spinning plant. Although this measure fell well short of Platt's earlier proposals for amalgamations and statutory controls he did, at least, play a major part in bringing a measure of unity to the spinning section of the 1930s, when internecine competition was replaced by minimum price agreements and an organised reduction in capacity. Whilst he was unable to reverse the secular decline of the Lancashire cotton industry there was

> No denying that Frank Platt and the men who followed his ascendant star from 1932 onwards saved the spinning trade — and the cloth market — from sinking further into the abyss { *Textile Mercury* 15 July 1955}.

Shortly after the outbreak of the Second World War Platt was appointed Deputy Cotton Controller and an executive member of the Cotton Board. These appointments were full-time and the LCC board therefore agreed that whilst Platt would remain a director, the Corporation would 'loan' him to the Government for the duration of the war. However, in 1942 Platt resigned his directorship of the LCC, receiving £17,500 compensation for the cancellation of his service agreement, following his appointment as Cotton Controller. In this capacity he led the Ministry of Production's Cotton Textile Mission which was sent to examine methods of production in the American cotton industry in 1943, the same year in which Platt was knighted. The Mission's Report, known as the Platt Report, was published in 1944 and addressed itself, not only to immediate wartime needs but also to the longer term reorganisation of the British cotton industry which, the Report recommended, should re-equip with modern machinery, standardise its output, introduce new working conditions and establish closer vertical co-operation between the spinning, weaving and merchanting sections.

Following the end of the war in Europe Platt resigned as Cotton Controller in June 1945 and returned to the LCC as managing director and vice-chairman at a salary of £10,000 per annum plus director's fees. In January 1954 he was appointed chairman of the LCC, a position which he combined with that of managing director until June 1955 when he resigned from the latter position following a protracted illness. He nevertheless continued as chairman until his death on 8 July 1955. As managing director he continued, of course, to play an active part in the LCC during his last ten years. Meanwhile, however, little progress was made along the lines recommended in the Platt Report of 1944. Indeed, after his return to the LCC in 1945 Platt 'rather surprisingly withdrew from the limelight' {*ibid*} in the affairs of the cotton industry at large, prompting one obituary writer to comment

> Latterly, it could be complained that the Lancashire cotton industry could have used the gifted leadership he brought to his earlier successful efforts to unite the trade. {*ibid*}

Notwithstanding his relative quiescence in the post-war years Platt had been a powerful figure in the cotton industry for nearly a quarter of a century and in the words of Sir John Grey, 'His work for the cotton spinning industry was greater than that of any other individual of this generation' {'Short History' (nd) 31}. Nine years after Platt's death the LCC was acquired by Courtaulds as part of the latter company's strategy of forward integration in the Lancashire textile industry.

Outside his business interests Platt owned racehorses, was a keen farmer and horticulturalist, and between 1919 and 1933 he was a director of Oldham Athletic Football Club. In his later years he played 'an excellent game of tennis' { *Times* 11 July 1955}. In 1915 he married Mary, daughter of Benjamin Lord. They had one daughter. Sir Frank Platt died on 8 July 1955, leaving £36,591 gross.

J H BAMBERG

Writings:

'Cotton Textiles Mission to the United States of America' *Report* (HMSO, 1944).

Sources:

Unpublished

Bank of England Archives, SMT and BIDC papers.

Courtaulds plc, Northern Spinning Division, Manchester, LCC Board Minutes 1929-55, Minutes of Cloth Sales Committee 1929-32.

Midland Bank Archives, Parkes' diary 30/98 (1930-32), Lederer's diary 30/127 (1933).

PRO, Kew, BT56/33/CIA/1768/14, BT56/36/CIA/1768/87, BT64/3/IM/651/33.

BCe.

'Short History and Chronicle of Events Concerning the Lancashire Cotton Corporation Limited and an Appreciation of the Contribution made by Sir Alan Tod CBE, DL, LLD, Director 1929-61' (Courtaulds plc, Coventry, nd).

Henry Clay, 'Report on the Position of the English Cotton Industry' SMT Ltd, 1931.

J H Bamberg, 'The Government, the Banks and the Lancashire Cotton Industry 1918-39' (Cambridge PhD, 1984).

Published

Henry Clay, *Lord Norman* (Macmillan, 1957).

Donald C Coleman, *Courtaulds: An Economic and Social History* (3 vols, Oxford: Clarendon Press, 1969-80) 3.

George W Daniels and J Jewkes, 'The Post-war Depression in the Lancashire Cotton Industry' *Journal of Royal Statistical Society* 91 (1928).

Leslie Hannah, 'Managerial Innovation and the Rise of the Large-Scale Company in Interwar Britain' *Economic History Review* 2nd ser 27 (1974).

—, *The Rise of the Corporate Economy* (Methuen, 1976).

— (ed), *Management Strategy and Business Development* (Macmillan, 1976).

Arthur Knight, *Private Enterprise and Public Intervention. The Courtaulds Experience* (Allen & Unwin, 1974).

A F Lucas, 'The Bankers' Industrial Development Company' *Harvard Business Review* 11 (1933).

A Ormerod, 'The Prospects of the British Cotton Industry' *Yorkshire Bulletin of Economic and Social Research* 15 (1963).

PD 1926-31.

PP, Economic Advisory Council Committee on the Cotton Industry *Report* (1930) Cmd 3615.

PEP, *Report on the British Cotton Industry* (1934).

Robert Robson, *The Cotton Industry in Britain* (Macmillan, 1957).

J Ryan, 'Combination in the Cotton Trade' *Journal of the National Federation of Textile Works Managers Associations* 8 (1928-29).

Richard Sayers, *The Bank of England, 1891-1944* (3 vols, Cambridge: Cambridge University Press, 1976).

Skinners Cotton Trade Directory of the World 1923-32.

Textile Mercury 15 July 1955.

Textile Recorder Aug 1955.

Textile Weekly 15 July 1955.

Times 11, 15 July, 8 Sept 1955.

Leonard A C Tippett, *A Portrait of the Lancashire Textile Industry* (Oxford University Press, 1969).

WWW.

PLATT, James Westlake

(1897-1972)

Oil industry manager and pioneer of management education

James Westlake Platt was born in Northern Ireland on 13 June 1897. His father, W T Platt, was born into a Protestant family of small farmers and shopkeepers in Donegal, but, when James was two, the family emigrated to New Zealand, where the Platt brothers opened a general store at Opotiki. W T Platt later became a Presbyterian cleric, moving to a

J W Platt, a portrait by Anthony Buckley ('A Shell photograph').

ministry at St Helier's Bay, Auckland, after the First World War. James Platt was very much the product of a Presbyterian upbringing; he was immensely hard-working (he worked until 10 or 10.30 every night), absolutely honest, and fanatically loyal. He was educated at Auckland Grammar School, and served with the New Zealand Division in France during the last years of the First World War. He received his commission shortly before the end of the war and, as the holder of one of the four scholarships allotted to the New Zealand Expeditionary Force, went up to Balliol College, Oxford, in 1919 to read history. He graduated in 1922, narrowly missing the predicted first. James Platt had a great love of poetry and he was widely read, but theatre did not interest him, and he was tone deaf. He was an accurate but stilted linguist, and took immense trouble, beyond the great majority of his fellow Britons, to master the language of the people among whom he lived, including Cantonese and Spanish.

Platt's loyalty and honesty were important elements in his successful career. But he had also the clearest of minds; from the beginning he knew exactly where he wanted to go — to the top of whatever he undertook. As a New Zealander of modest family he could expect no patronage; characteristically, he was a great admirer of Alfred Milner and his 'kindergarten', able young men from Oxford, selected for their ability rather than their connections. When he left Oxford he thought of academic life (at Harvard) and of a post in the meritocratic Indian Civil Service. But he wanted an active and enduring career. He joined the Royal Dutch-Shell Group of oil companies, serving first in China (to 1938) and then in Argentina (to 1945). Once Platt had decided on a career, he put everything into it, perhaps at some cost socially to himself and his family. He was gentle, quiet, and unassuming, modest and matter of fact; but he was shy and uneasy with people and not always perceptive in his private relationships. He could be very distant and unapproachable. Compassion for honest weakness stopped short of tolerance; sharp practice or personal betrayal were never forgiven. Integrity in himself and others he prized highly.

It was his clear mind and great loyalty which, during the Second World War, singled him out to Frank Hopwood (later Lord Southborough) as by far the most promising of the current generation of Shell managers in Latin America. Hopwood, himself a man of singular integrity and ability, brought Platt home to the Eagle Oil & Shipping Co, a Shell subsidiary (bought from Weetman Pearson (qv) in 1919), and, in 1949, was influential in inviting him to serve as one of the seven managing directors of the Shell Group. Platt's responsibilities included world marketing (outside Europe), the tanker fleet, and personnel (in all non-technical areas). It was his responsibility for personnel which awakened him to the importance of high-quality education. He was a good judge of men, or at any rate of a man's qualities for business. He chose the right man for the right job, and he was genuinely tough; if a man slipped into error, he did not pass it over, even at a very high level. In business generally he was extremely thoughtful, the reverse of the erratic brilliance of Shell's great eccentric, Henri Deterding.

When he retired as a managing director in 1957, he remained on the board for a further decade, but now threw himself, body and soul, into the cause of education for managers. He was very aware in Shell of the importance of team effort, but he felt the shortage of good, trained men and determined to remedy it.

He was one of the group who met together regularly in the late 1950s and gave a critical impetus to the efforts which produced the remarkable and swift growth of management education at university level during the 1960s and 1970s. Others included Sir Keith Joseph MP, John Bolton, Peter (later Sir Peter) Parker, Sir John Rodgers MP, and Sir Keith Murray (now (1984) Lord Murray of Newhaven) who was at that time chairman of the University Grants Committee. They decided that, to get management education accepted by the universities as an important field of intellectual endeavour, industry would have to enter an informal partnership with the UGC for the purpose.

The Foundation for Management Education was therefore formed as a private body financed by industry, and in 1960 about £250,000 was raised in order, jointly with the UGC, to start some pilot projects at a small number of universities (Bristol, Cambridge and Leeds). Jim Platt threw himself into the work of FME and was its chairman from 1960 until 1968. In 1962 he was appointed by the Minister of Education as chairman of the Advisory Council on Education for Management, retaining this position until 1967.

In the early 1960s other groups became interested in promoting university management education, one of them being the 'Savoy Group' whose leading lights were Sir Anthony Bowlby and Jim Parsons of GKN. These various groups decided to invite Lord Franks to advise them on the development of university management education and he produced a report in 1963 which, amongst other things, recommended the setting up of the London and Manchester business schools. In 1964 the Federation of British Industries (forerunner of the CBI), the British Institute of Management and FME appealed to industry for funds to found these two schools jointly with the UGC, and £5 million was raised to do this and other work at university level.

In 1967 with the encouragement of the then Secretary of State for Education and Science, Anthony Crosland, the CBI, the BIM and FME sponsored a body to represent industry in matters of management education — the Council of Industry for Management Education. Platt played a major part in the discussions which preceded the formation of CIME but he did not, at his own request, become a member of the Council.

Platt was elected to an honorary fellowship of his old college, Balliol, in 1963; he was awarded a CBE in 1965; and he received an honorary DSc from the City University (London) in 1969. In his seventieth year he retired voluntarily and completely from all his occupations. He died in Jersey (Channel Islands) on 17 December 1972, leaving his wife, Veronica Norma Hope (whom he married in 1927), and four sons (businessmen and academics). His estate was worth nearly £750,200 gross.

D C M PLATT

Writings:

Education for Business Management (British Institute of Management, 1967).

Sources:

Unpublished

Interviews and correspondence with members of the family, Lord Southborough, John Loudun, John Marsh, Philip F Nind, Sir William Haley.

Published

Management Today Mar 1973.

Times 20 Dec 1972.

WWW.

John Platt ca 1865 (courtesy of the Local Studies Library Oldham).

PLATT, John

(1817-1872)

Textile machinery maker

John Platt was born at the Pennine village of Dobcross, in Saddleworth, a seed-plot of entrepreneurs, on 15 September 1817, the second son of Henry Platt (1793-1842), of the younger or Saddleworth branch of the Platts of Manchester, and his wife Sarah née Whitehead. After being educated at Dunham Massey, Cheshire, he learned the trade of ironmoulder and was admitted in 1837 to the family business. Henry Platt had abandoned the making of woollen machinery on his removal to Oldham in 1821 in favour of the manufacture of cotton machinery, especially carding engines; he had formed a partnership in 1822 with Elijah Hibbert (1801-46) under the name of Hibbert & Platt. John Platt became the senior partner after the successive deaths of his father in 1842, of his elder brother in 1845 and of Elijah Hibbert. He proved to be a man of great business faculty, of broad and far-reaching perception and of astute judgement, especially of character. He recruited between 1839 and 1854 five men of outstanding technical and managerial ability in Eli Spencer (1823-87), W F Palmer (1815-94), George Little (1823-96), J W Nuttall (1828-99) and John Dodd (1837-1912). He secured the invaluable support of his younger brother,

James Platt (1824-57), whose abilities 'both as a mechanician and a merchant were of the highest order' {*Manchester City News* 1 Apr 1865}. He bought out the Hibbert interest in 1854, renamed the firm Platt Brothers & Co and admitted his managers as partners, so generating an unrivalled esprit de corps and preventing the firm from becoming a recruiting ground for rivals.

In 1845 Platt opened the Hartford New Works, Oldham, where he adopted the use of machine-tools as well as the railway. He had first exported spinning machinery under licence to Europe in 1842. He began the manufacture of self-acting mules from 1843 and took out seven patents (1846-51) for improvements in cotton spinning. He took out his first patent for power-loom weaving in 1851 and added the manufacture of looms in 1857, so becoming able to supply clients with a full line of machinery, unlike any other contemporary British textile engineer. The powerlooms were largely manufactured for foreign firms, especially in Russia. Platt Bros improved the inventions made by others, such as Ryder's spindle-forging machine (1840), the Parr & Curtis self-acting mule (1847), Evan Leigh's finisher lap machine (1850) and the Crighton opener (1861). Under the direction of John Platt the firm was transformed from an assembler of parts made by other manufacturers into a fully integrated engineering firm by the addition (1854-57) of ironfounding and iron-forging, as well as the manufacture of rollers, spindles, flyers and tin-plate. Platt made a pioneer installation of a steel boiler in 1860. After establishing a brickworks in 1859 he began to manufacture brickmaking machinery. He maintained an efficient system of departmental organisation as the firm's range of activity expanded. The firm became the largest employer of labour in the Oldham district after the opening of the new works but increased its capital even faster than its labour, raising the number of its employees at an annual average rate of 8.8 per cent between 1837 and 1870 from 400 to 6,000 but its capital at a rate of 10.5 per cent from £37,263 to £911,844. Platt organised the Central Association of Employers of Operative Engineers in 1851 and defeated the Amalgamated Society of Engineers in the four months' lock-out of 1852. He remained hostile to unions extending their function beyond that of simple benefit societies. He developed the use of self-acting tools to the fullest extent, so economising in the use of skilled labour. He also endowed Oldham with an advanced system of technical education by means of a works library in 1848, a new Science and Art School in 1865 and a works school in 1866. In 1859 he became a member of the Institution of Mechanical Engineers and contributed to its proceedings, reading in 1866 the first paper on cotton spinning machinery. He served as president of the Oldham Lyceum in 1865-68 and helped to endow in 1868 a chair of civil engineering at Owens College, where he was commemorated in the Platt exhibitions first awarded in 1875.

Platt's greatest achievement was to establish the supremacy of his firm in the world market after the abolition in 1843 of restrictions on the export of machinery. That end was attained by the manufacture of machinery of the highest quality, by the use of iron instead of wood in construction, by the establishment of close links with the steam-engine makers of Bolton, by the supply of an after-sales service through the dispatch abroad of machine-erectors, and by the use of enterprising foreign agents. The firm captured the Russian market after 1843 and the Indian market after 1854: it equipped the first spinning mill in Japan in 1867. After a sensational success at the Great Exhibition of 1851 it made its displays at international exhibitions into a main instrument of marketing, winning an unparalleled series of honours. In the late 1840s the firm surpassed Dobson & Barlow of Bolton in size to become the largest textile machinist in Lancashire; in the 1850s it outdistanced the competition of Belgian and Swiss firms to become the largest machine-maker in the world. Such a marked degree of primacy in the world market enabled it to charge higher prices than its competitors could afford. John Platt responded to the challenge of the Cotton Famine by helping to found the Manchester Cotton Co Ltd (1860-64) in order to develop the supply of cotton from India, by adapting the preparatory machinery of the trade to the use of short-stapled Surat and by encouraging Oldham mills to pioneer the use of Indian cotton in place of the American staple. The firm diversified its range of products by adding the manufacture of cotton gins, of woollen powerlooms in 1863, of linen powerlooms in 1864 and self-acting woollen mules in 1864. Between 1864 and 1868 the firm perfected the self-acting mule and made it into the most productive of machines for the spinning of coarse counts, so assisting Oldham to become by 1865 the metropolis of cotton spinning. Between 1868 and 1872 total sales rose by 53 per cent to reach £966,538, of which 54 per cent were made abroad, while dividends averaged 11 per cent per annum.

Platt was as active in the political as in the economic sphere. He became chairman of the Oldham Liberal Party in 1847 and so began twenty-five years of public service. He was the prime mover in securing the incorporation of Oldham as a chartered borough in 1849. He was the first member of his family to serve on the borough council (1849-62) and the first Liberal mayor of the borough, serving as mayor three times (1854-55, 1855-56, 1861-62) and ushering in forty years of Liberal control of the council. He established municipal control of the gas and water supply and fostered the development of railways and technical education to a greater degree than any other person. He was the prime mover in the construction of the rail links of 1856-63 and served in 1862-67 as a director of the LNWR. He also became a director of the Ebbw Vale Co Ltd established by David Chadwick (qv) in 1864. A convinced radical in politics, he served as MP for Oldham from 1865 until his death. He was the second textile machine maker to enter the House of Commons, his younger brother having served as an MP for five months before his untimely death in 1857. It is, however, misleading to identify John Platt's fellow-MP, J T Hibbert (1824-1904), the eldest son of his father's partner, as another representative of the firm, since the Hibbert interests had been bought out in 1854. As an MP Platt encouraged Gladstone to visit Oldham in 1867. The incorporation of the firm in 1868 gave him more leisure for his parliamentary duties; it also enabled him to reward the enterprise of his best managers by making them directors and it gave to the engineering industry its first limited company. Platt had become a member of the Council of the Anti-Corn Law League in 1843 and he remained a lifelong advocate of free trade: he helped Cobden to negotiate the Anglo-French Commercial Treaty of 1860, he criticised the advocates of 'reciprocity' in 1869 and he opposed a demand made in the House of Commons in 1870 for an enquiry into the effect of the Treaty of 1860 upon British commerce and manufactures. He abandoned the Congregational faith of his fathers and became an Anglican, probably in 1842. He remained an Anglican of the radical variety; he presented the site for St Thomas's Church, Werneth, which was built in 1855 and extended in 1860, but he favoured the disestablishment and even the disendowment of the Church of England. In 1857 he acquired a country estate at Llanfairfechan which he transformed from a hamlet into a summer resort. He became a JP and, in 1863, a High Sheriff of Caernarvon as well as a JP and DL of Lancashire.

In Oldham he evoked intense opposition from local Tories as 'the Nabob of Werneth Park' {*Oldham Standard* 11 Mar 1871} but was presented on 4 March 1871 with an address signed by 8,000 working men. If any one man may be credited with founding the industrial power and commercial prosperity of Oldham; then it should be John Platt: he compensated Oldham for its comparative lack of advantages, he supplied its cotton industry with an external economy of unrivalled efficiency and he employed by 1871 an estimated 42 per cent of the borough's population.

Platt in 1842 married Alice (1822-1902), the daughter of Samuel Radcliffe, the leading local cotton manufacturer; they had six daughters and seven sons, of whom four became country squires.

He died suddenly from typhoid in Paris at the age of fifty-four on 18 May 1872. His estate was valued at under £800,000 where as his father in 1842 had left an estate under £10,000. John Platt was honoured by a public funeral and was commemorated in a bronze memorial, inaugurated in 1878 outside the town hall, giving Oldham its second public statue.

D A FARNIE

Writings:

'On Machinery for the Preparing and Spinning of Cotton' *Proceedings of the Institution of Mechanical Engineers* (1866).

PP, HC 1868 (432) XV SC on Scientific Instruction.

PD, 3rd ser 182, col 866 (23 Mar 1866); 197, cols 1364-66 (7 July 1869); 198, cols 1356-57 (5 Aug 1869); 201, cols 140-42 (3 May 1870); 202, cols 1739-41 (5 July 1870); 204, cols 1532-34 (7 Mar 1871); 207, cols 612-13 (26 June 1871).

Sources:

Unpublished

Lancashire RO, Platt-Saco-Lowell archives, especially balance-sheets for 1834-44, 1847-53, 1867-72.

Manchester Central Library, Archives Department, S E Cottam Records, especially balance-sheets for 1853-72.

PrC.

Information from Dr D J Jeremy and J Hunt.

Douglas A Farnie, 'The English Cotton Industry, 1850-1896' (Manchester MA, 1953).

Published

Douglas A Farnie, 'The Metropolis of Cotton Spinning, Machine Making and Mill Building' *The Cotton Mills of Oldham* (Oldham: Oldham Libraries, 1985 2nd ed).

John Foster, *Class Struggle and the Industrial Revolution. Early Industrial Capitalism in Three English Towns* (Weidenfeld & Nicolson, 1974).

London Society Jan 1885 'The Platts of Oldham' reprinted in J Burnley (ed), *Fortunes Made in Business. A Series of Sketches by Various Authors* (3 vols, Sampson Low, 1884) 3.

Manchester City News 1, 8, 15 Apr 1865 'The Workshops of Lancashire' No 5 (Messrs Platt Bros & Co of Oldham).

Oldham Chronicle 21 Jan, 15 Jul 1865, 11 Mar 1871, 25 May, 1 June 1872, 14, 21 Sept 1878.

Oldham Evening Express 20 May 1872.

Oldham Standard 26 Dec 1863, 11 Mar 1871.

W O Williams, 'The Platts of Oldham. A Chapter in the History of a Caernarvonshire Parish' *Transactions of the Caernarvonshire Historical Society* 1957.

WWMP.

S R Platt ca 1885 (courtesy of the Local Studies Library Oldham).

PLATT, Samuel Radcliffe

(1845-1902)

Textile machinery maker

Samuel Radcliffe Platt was born at Greenhill, Oldham, on 1 July 1845, the second son of John Platt (qv) and his wife, Alice née Radcliffe (1822-1902). He was given a non-classical education at Cheltenham College (1856-59) and a technical education at the Friedrich Wilhelm Realschule, Berlin (1859-62).

Between 1862 and 1865 he worked his way through every department of the firm of Platt Bros, proving to be the only one of John Platt's seven sons with a decided mechanical bent in marked contrast to the eldest son, Henry. He became a partner in 1867, a director in 1868 and, on the unexpected death of his father in 1872, chairman at the age of twenty-six. Under his direction the impetus given by his father was maintained through the influence of six senior managers, especially William Richardson (1811-92) and John Dodd (1837-1912). He continued the policy of appointing the best managers as directors and from 1873 he made the best foremen into shareholders. He created a trust fund in 1894 to provide pensions. The number of hands employed rose from 6,000 in 1872 to nearly 15,000 in 1902. The process of vertical integration was completed with the extension into coal mining from 1874. Dividends rose to a relative peak in 1876-77 under the influence of the boom in the formation of joint-stock spinning companies and reached their absolute peak in 1891-92, averaging 18 per cent per annum over the thirty years 1873-1902. When the firm was reincorporated in 1898 its capital of £3,091,800 was more than treble the £912,306 of 1868. The range of products was extended to include the fine spinning mule from 1874, the revolving flat card from 1881, the carpet loom and the ring spinning frame from 1882, the Heilmann comber from 1885, the exhaust opener from 1889, the hopper feeder from 1894 and the Nasmith comber from 1901. Rival machine-makers were so discouraged by the spectacle of their competitive incapacity that they ceased in the 1890s to display their products at international exhibitions: Platt Bros were the sole British exhibitors of cotton machinery at Milan in 1881 and at Chicago in 1893.

The international eminence of the firm was recognised by foreign powers: Austria created Platt a knight of the Order of Francis Joseph in 1873 and France awarded him in 1878 the Cross of the Légion d'Honneur. But he failed to recruit anyone of comparable calibre to his father's managers and he lived to some extent upon the paternal inheritance. The value of sales certainly rose in an era of declining prices from £966,538 in 1872 to £1,255,449 in 1901. Foreign sales became decidedly more important than domestic sales from 1886 and reached their peak proportion of 83 per cent of total sales in 1896, under the influence of German and Japanese demand. Foreign markets took 63 per cent of the firm's sales between 1873 and 1902, Europe taking 66 per cent, Asia 24 per cent and America 10 per cent. The production of powerlooms doubled between 1872 and 1879 but the firm reached its peak production and export of looms in 1879, its peak export of mule spindles in 1889 and its peak export of ring and mule spindles taken together in 1896. The share of direct sales abroad sank from 32 per cent of foreign sales in 1877 to 10 per cent in 1894 as sales through agents increased. From 1894 profits fell off sharply as competition increased in the marketing of the ring frame from Howard & Bullough of Accrington as well as from Tweedale & Smalley of Rochdale. From 1895 the number of ring spindles exported regularly surpassed the number of mule spindles but the total production of mule spindles continued to exceed that of ring spindles until 1915. The firm's exports of £9,710,200 during the decade 1893-1902 nevertheless represented some 16.7 per cent of the total exports of textile machinery.

Platt became a member of the Institution of Mechanical Engineers in 1867 and a member of the Iron and Steel Institute in 1873. He subscribed for £25,000 of shares in the Manchester Ship Canal in 1887, served as a director of the company from 1886 to 1891, precipitating the crisis of 1891-92 by his report of 21 November 1890 on the slow progress of the works. He carried the directors on his yacht *Norseman* on the inaugural voyage of 1 January 1894 and diverted the trade of his firm in timber and machinery through the new port. Platt was elected president of the Oldham Chamber of Commerce on its formation in 1883, holding office until his death and serving as an ex officio director of the Manchester Chamber of Commerce. He was elected president of the Oldham District Engineering Trades Association and served as one of three representatives of Oldham on the executive board of the Engineering Employers' Federation established in 1896 by Colonel Dyer (qv). He emerged victorious from the strikes of 1897 and 1897-98 and was elected in 1900 to the Council of the Institution of Mechanical Engineers. He also served as a director of the British & North Atlantic Steam Navigation Co Ltd, the Chatterley-Whitfield Collieries Ltd and the Manchester Public Hall Co.

Like his father, Platt fostered the development of technical education. He became a director of the Oldham Lyceum in 1868 and its president in 1888-89, after enlarging the School of Science and Art in 1878-81 at the cost of £10,000 in memory of his father. In politics he inherited his father's position as leader of the local Liberals. He was the fourth and last member of his family to serve on the borough council (1882-92), being twice elected mayor, in 1887 and 1888. In 1873 he became a county magistrate, in 1886 a borough magistrate and in 1897 High Sheriff of Lancashire. He served as president of the Oldham Reform Club from 1881 until 1886 when he adopted the Unionist view on Home Rule and so lost any chance of becoming a Liberal MP. He remained a staunch free trader and an Anglican.

Platt did not devote himself exclusively to business but developed his interest in cricket, foreign travel, music and drama. He became chairman of Werneth Cricket Club from its foundation in 1864, bringing to Oldham an All-England eleven in 1866 and the Australian eleven in 1878 on their first overseas tour. From 1865 onwards Platt travelled extensively abroad in his ocean yacht, tending to neglect the works during the travel season in summer. Excelling on the oboe, he organised works orchestras in 1865 and 1873 and works choirs in 1878 and 1884. In 1870 he presented a £3,000 organ with four manuals, suitable for a cathedral organ, to St Thomas's Church, Werneth. In 1892 he became a founder member and trustee of the Royal Manchester College of Music as well as founder and president of the Oldham School of Music. He organised weekly winter concerts in Oldham and served from 1895 as president of the Oldham Orchestral Society. He built up a music library of over a thousand works and was included in 1897 in a dictionary of British musical biography, which omitted any mention of his business career. After his death he was commemorated in the S R Platt Scholarship at the Oldham School of Music.

In 1884 he married Helen May Hodder Roberts, by whom he had one son and two daughters. Platt died at the age of fifty-seven on 5 September 1902, on board his yacht in the Menai Straits, leaving £648,643 gross, more than double the average size of estate left by his six brothers: his widow left £178,726 when she died in 1926. Samuel Platt was the last member of the family to preside over the destinies of the firm and was succeeded as chairman by John Dodd under whom production reached its all-time peak in 1906.

D A FARNIE

PLATT Samuel Radcliffe

Writings:

'Fencing or Guarding Machinery Used in Textile Factories, with Special Reference to Machinery Use by Cotton Spinners and Manufacturers' *Proceedings of the Institution of Mechanical Engineers* (1902).

Sources:

Unpublished

Lancashire RO, Platt-Saco-Lowell Archives, especially minute books of company meetings 1868-1902; minute books of directors' meetings 1897-98; balance sheets 1867-98; and directors' reports to shareholders 1867-1909.

PrC.

Published

J D Brown and S S Stratton, *British Musical Biography* (Birmingham: Stratton, 1897).

Engineer 30 Dec 1887.

Douglas A Farnie, 'Platt Bros & Co of Oldham, Machine Makers to Lancashire and to the World: An Index of Production of Cotton Spinning Spindles, 1880-1914' *Business History* 23 (1981).

—, 'The Emergence of Victorian Oldham as the Centre of the Cotton Spinning Industry' *Saddleworth Historical Society Bulletin* Autumn 1982.

Manchester Faces and Places 13 Sept 1902.

Manchester Guardian 8 Sept 1902.

Oldham Chronicle 28 May 1884, 6, 13 Sept 1902.

Oldham Express 25 Feb 1882.

Oldham Standard 8 Sept 1902.

Proceedings of the Institution of Mechanical Engineers 1902.

Textile Recorder 15 May 1897, 15 Sept 1902.

WWW.

John Player (courtesy of John Player & Sons).

PLAYER, John

(1839-1884)

and

PLAYER, John Dane

(1864-1950)

and

PLAYER, William Goodacre

(1866-1959)

Tobacco manufacturers

John Player was born at Saffron Walden, Essex, on 11 July 1839, the son of John Dane Player and his wife Sophia née Clare. His father was a solicitor who died young, and in the census enumerator's, return for 1851 John Dane Player's widow Sophia was described as a schoolmistress with four children aged between eight and thirteen, including John. Nothing is known of John's early life at Saffron Walden but he appears to have left there about 1859 for Nottingham, apparently because of a connection with a solicitor, Joseph Bright, who was to become an important figure in the town's business and civic life. Young Player first appears as one of the five male assistants living at 42 Long Row, a house and general draper's shop owned by Robert Dickinson, which eventually became Nottingham's leading departmental store as Griffen & Spalding. John Player was then described as a general draper's clerk. By 1862 Player had premises on Beastmarket Hill, overlooking the large market place, where he began business as an agent for lace thread and for Prentice's artificial manures. His immediate neighbour was Mrs Ann Whiteley, a milliner and lacedealer, and widow ten years his senior, whom he married in 1863. About this time Player added tobacco to his other lines, but the exact date is not on record.

At the time that John Player began to sell tobacco it was sold loose from jars, weighed and handed over in small screws of plain paper, rather like a sweet bag, but it was evident from the activities of other manufacturers that customer allegiance to a particular type of tobacco was extremely strong and he also began to pre-pack. Before very long this tobacco sideline took over as the main business of the shop, by now very prosperous, so much so that in 1877 Player purchased as a going concern the tobacco manufactuary of William Wright, which had been established in the Broad March in 1823 and already employed 150 workers. At this period Nottingham boasted of some 19 firms engaged in the processing of tobacco, though there was no bonded warehouse for any kind of goods.

John Dane Player (courtesy of John Player & Sons).

With the purchase of the Broad Marsh Factory and rapidly growing experience of the trade, Player developed his advertising and marketing. A plain packet of tobacco containing a particular blend was obviously a ripe vehicle for a name and for that name to be printed on the packet. Player's first brand name to be registered was Gold Leaf, although in 1877, when he first began to manufacture under his own name, John Player registered his first actual trade mark, the familiar drawing of Nottingham Castle. 'Gold Leaf' was evidently an immediate success, for a Player price list of 1881 shows a dozen other varieties of branded packet tobaccos had already appeared. The Gold Leaf packet of 1885 was a work of art, printed in nine colours and gold with an overall design resembling a dove in gold on the reverse and completely hidden side. Player followed the other cigarette manufacturers of the 1880s in using coloured cards as stiffeners in his cigarette packets. These cards became an additional incentive to brand loyalty. The most famous of all the Player trade marks was the sailor's head. In 1883 John Player was attracted to a painting of a bearded sailor produced by an artist called Wright of Clapham some thirty years or so earlier when uniform had just been adopted by the Royal Navy. The portrait was being used by a small tobacoo company, Parkins of Chester, to advertise their 'Jack's Glory' brand. John Player immediately bought and registered the painting as a trademark. Over the years many variations of the background and frame appeared, including the lifebelt and two of HM ships in the background. Its greatest impact came after 1918.

From the acquisition of the Wright business in 1877, Player's marketing and advertising methods were so successful that he was able to purchase some 30 acres of land in the then undeveloped suburb of Radford. On this site he built the three blocks which became No 1 Factory along a square fronting to Radford Boulevard, then called Victoria Boulevard. As he was not yet ready to occupy his new factory, John Player let out standings to small co-operatives of lacemakers and finishers. In April 1884 production was transferred to the new site but the whole factory was not occupied by Players until towards the end of the century.

John Player died of lung cancer on 12 November 1884 at the early age of forty-five, leaving £43,802. For the next nine years the business was continued by family friends and senior employees. It was an interregnum during which the heirs, John Player's two sons, John Dane (b 29 November 1864) and William Goodacre (b 26 January 1866), were educated at Nottingham High School and evidently groomed to succeed their father. Though John Player died before his sons reached their majority, he left a carefully prepared will in which two executors, Joseph Bright and a local bank manager, were appointed to oversee the business until the boys became twenty-five. When the business was incorporated in 1895 the sons became joint managing directors. Six years later, when the prosperity and independence of the British tobacco industry was threatened by the powerful American Tobacco Co, while retail chains like Salmon & Gluckstein were making inroads on manufacturers' resale price maintenance, 13 leading firms federated to form the Imperial Tobacco Co. J D Player was one of the original directors of the combine and was also appointed advertising manager to the parent company. His younger brother became a director following the first board meeting. Imperial Tobacco 'leaned heavily on the advertising skills of Messrs J D and W G

William Goodacre Player (courtesy of John Player & Sons).

Player' {Alford (1973) 275}, but this did not prevent Players's brands competing with those of other members of the group, or apparently dilute the quality of the Nottingham firm's advertising.

Until after the First World War John Player & Sons Ltd lay well behind the market leaders, W D & H O Wills Ltd. When the Imperial Tobacco Co (of Great Britain & Ireland) Ltd was formed, in 1901, Players were purchased for £601,456, somewhat less than Lambert & Butler Ltd and Stephen Mitchell & Son, and far less than Wills which accounted for £6,992,221 of the £11,957,022 purchase price for the 13 original federating firms. Between 1905 and 1920, however, Player's share of Imperial's total cigarette and tobacco sales by weight rose from 7.8 per cent (4.8 cigarettes and 3.2 tobaccos) to 20.2 (17.3 cigarettes and 2.9 tobaccos). By 1938 Players were rivalling Wills, with 40.9 per cent. This dramatic growth came largely from the demand for up-market (class B brand) cigarettes — especially Player's Medium Cut — created by rising real incomes. Players overtook Wills in 1955 when sales of Players Medium Navy Cut cigarettes reached 27 million lb and their cheaper selling line 'Weights', 10 million lb. However, this was not attained until a generation after the founders' sons had retired.

Father and sons had the reputation of enlightened employers. The popular practice of paying every employee an annual bonus on earnings was started in 1910, and holidays with pay began in 1922. Sports clubs associated with the firm started in the early 1900s and led to a comprehensive welfare and sports organisation with well-equipped grounds. The firm became noted for its high wages and excellent working conditions. John Player & Sons, as the branch became known, continued to expand with the growing demand for cigarettes. Under the regime of the two brothers its workforce reached 2,500 by 1914 and 5,000 by 1928. Both brothers retired from active participation in the tobacco business in 1926 although they continued to serve on the board of the Imperial Tobacco Co.

In 1934 they were both made honorary freemen of the City of Nottingham in recognition of their considerable charitable donations to hospitals and churches in the city. John Dane was also granted a similar honour by his father's native town of Saffron Walden in recognition of his public services and his family's interest in the town's Literary Institution and Library. In 1934 he was also made a DL for Nottinghamshire, and having been a JP since 1905. Having no children of his own, one of his particular interests was Nottingham Children's Hospital, to which he gave £50,000 for rebuilding. His interest was not confined to monetary gifts as he used to visit the children regularly.

Both brothers married in the 1890s: John Dane to Margaret Page and William Goodacre to Mabel Askley (in 1894). John took a house, Fernleigh, in Alexandra Park, Nottingham, whilst William bought Lenton Hurst, a house which now forms part of Nottingham University. He later moved to Whatton Manor, about 10 miles east of Nottingham, and also had another country house, Ednaston Manor in Derbyshire.

J D Player died at the age of eighty-five on 6 April 1950, leaving £2,501,621 and W G Player died at the age of ninety-three on 29 June 1959, leaving £1,606,739. W G Player had four daughters and four sons, two of whom entered the firm. John Dane Player II was killed during the Second

World War but John Ashley Player spent his career with Imperial Tobacco and reached the main board.

S D CHAPMAN *and* G OLDFIELD

Sources:

Unpublished

John Player & Sons, especially 'Guard Books' (advertising material) and accounts.

PrC; Wills.

Census returns 1851-81.

P Alan Dobson, 'John Player & Sons — A Short History and Appreciation' (typescript, 1975).

Published

Bernard W E Alford, *W D & H O Wills and the Development of the UK Tobacco Industry 1786-1965* (Methuen, 1973).

Maurice Corina, *Trust in Tobacco. The Anglo-American Struggle for Power* (Michael Joseph, 1975).

Sheila A Mason, 'Tobacco and Lace: The Growth of John Player and Sons, 1881-1903' *Transactions of the Thoroton Society* 85 (1981).

John Player & Sons, *From Plantation to 'Players'* (John Player & Sons, 1953).

PP, HC 1960-61 (218) XIX, Monopolies Commission Report on the Supply of Cigarettes and Tobacco and of Cigarette and Tobacco Machinery.

PLENDER, William

Lord Plender of Sundridge, Kent

(1861-1946)

Accountant

William Plender was born at Felling on Tyne on 20 August 1861, eldest of nine children of William Plender, grocer and draper, and his wife Elizabeth Agnes Smallpiece née Varday. He was educated at the Royal Grammar School, Newcastle upon Tyne. He left school at sixteen, denied

what he later called the 'supreme advantage' of an Oxbridge education, and spent seven years with the Newcastle firm of John G Benson & Co, chartered accountants. He passed the December 1883 examinations of the Institute of Chartered Accountants in England and Wales (ICAEW) and was admitted as an associate member the following spring. This allowed him to fulfil his second youthful ambition, to work in London, whence he travelled in spring 1884, with only a letter of introduction from G B Monkhouse, a leading practising accountant in Newcastle. He had a number of interviews for his first job in London, but received just two offers. He rejected an appointment of £2 per week and went instead to Deloitte, Dever, Griffiths & Co (established by Deloitte (qv)) at £100 per annum, the current rate of remuneration for newly-qualified accountants, because he considered the latter a more gentlemanly proposal. He travelled widely on the firm's business: to Canada, the USA and many parts of Europe. Although his seniors respected him, progress within the firm was slow. Some years later, he recalled 'how hard it was to climb the ladder that led to a Partnership' {Kettle (1958) 83}. He reached the top of the ladder in 1897, and seven years later he became senior partner. Apprehension among members of staff that a change of name (after thirty-two years) to Deloitte, Plender, Griffiths & Co, would irretrievably damage goodwill proved totally unjustified. The firm prospered and expanded at a rapid rate during his period of leadership, to become an international organisation with offices in many parts of the world. It is likely that the firm's other partners played a substantial part in Deloitte's success in view of Plender's heavy commitment to Government and Institute affairs detailed below. The firm also suffered setbacks, of course. For example, in 1913 a sum of £20,000 was paid to the liquidators of the Law Guarantee Trust and Accident Society 'in settlement of a claim which might have amounted to £52,000.' {ibid, 98} This is an early example of a payment made by a firm of auditors to avoid prosecution for negligence, though the harbinger of many more to come.

On a broader front, Plender's career paralleled a massive growth in the size and influence of the accountancy profession. The Institute was formed in 1880 and when Plender qualified, three years later, there were 453 members; by the 1940s the membership exceeded 14,000. In 1903 Plender became a member of the Council of the ICAEW, and in 1910 he became president for the first time. He was then forty-nine years of age and the first president to have passed through the turnstile of the examinations as opposed to having been a founder member. The *Accountant* described his rise to the position of president as 'almost meteoric'. He remained a member of Council for forty-three years, and served twice more as president, in 1911-12 and 1929-30 when he was widely regarded as the most fitting person to preside during the Jubilee year of the Institute. He was chairman of perhaps the Institute's most important committee, the parliamentary and law committee, from 1913 until 1931.

Government use of Plender's financial and administrative talents came at an early stage. In 1903 he acted for the Metropolitan Water Board which acquired the London water companies, and in 1908 he again acted for the purchasers to help establish the Port of London Authority. He was a member of the committee appointed to inquire into the problems of Irish Finance, 1911, and, in the same year, he officially investigated conditions of

Sir William Plender, later Lord Plender laying the foundation stone of the Institute of Chartered Accountants in 1930 (from E Green and M Moss A Business of National Importance *Methuen, 1982).*

medical work and remuneration under the National Insurance Act. He served on the Royal Commission on Railways (1913) and was Commissioner under the Welsh Church Act (1914-42).

The First World War immensely increased the volume of Plender's commitments, and he found himself at the centre of a political controversy following his appointment as Controller of the large London branches of German, Austrian and Turkish banks. Their affairs were complicated and the liquidation was slow. This resulted in a certain amount of press criticism, and even pro-German proclivities were imputed to Plender. The most swingeing attack was contained in a letter to the *Times* from Lord Northcliffe who then controlled that paper. Northcliffe warned Plender that he would remove Deloittes from their positions as auditor of the *Times* and of Associated Newspapers Ltd, which controlled the *Daily Mail* and other newspapers, if 'the Government policy of keeping alive the German business is to be continued'. {ibid, 101} An inquiry, instigated by the Lords Commissioners of His Majesty's Treasury, proved beyond doubt that Plender was performing his specified duties in an entirely satisfactory manner. Northcliffe nevertheless carried out his threat, provoking a stinging criticism of his high-handed behaviour from the *Economist*. Nevertheless the continued presence of the German banks stirred strong emotions, and even the *Accountant*, while defending Plender for properly carrying out government policy, complained of 'these enemy (financial) strongholds in our midst'. {*Accountant* 23 Feb 1918} Undoubtedly the Government was fully satisfied with Plender's performance as he continued to be showered with commissions which resulted in a list of public activities amazing in its length and variety: member of the Postmaster-General's Committee on the organisation of the telegraph service and of the Foreign Trade Debts Committee (1914); member of the Liquor Trade Finance Committee (England and Wales), of the Clerical and Commercial Employments Committee and a government representative on the Metropolitan Munitions Committee (1915); member of the Advisory Committee and chairman of the Panel on Military Service (Civil Liabilities) Committee, member of the Enemy Debts Committee (1916); member of the Company Law Amendment Committee, of the Surplus Government Property Disposal Board, chairman of the Civil Liabilities (Demobilisation) Committee, a nominated director of United Services Trustee and honorary financial adviser to the Board of Trade (1918); chairman of the Panel Ministry of Labour Grants Committee and a member of the Public Trustee Organisation Inquiry Committee (1919). In the 1920s and 1930s he was chairman of the Advisory Committee of the Enemy Debt Clearing Office (1920); member of the Tribunal on the Ministry of Munitions, of the Lord Chancellor's Committee on Remuneration of Solicitors, chairman of the Advisory Committee Trade Facilities Act and chairman of the National Board for the Coal Industry (1921); member of the commission on Property and Finance of the Church of England (1923); member of the Royal Commission on Cross-River Traffic in London (1926); chairman of the Durham Coal Industry Inquiry (1927); member of the Committee of Inquiry on Export Credits Guarantee (1928); member of the Iron and Steel Committee of the Economic Advisory Council (1929); member of the Committee on National Expenditure and chairman of the Northumberland Minimum Wage Board (1931); member of the Committe of Enquiry on the Post Office (1932); chairman of the German Debts Committee (1935); member of the Coal Mining Royalties Tribunal (1937). Much more was unrecorded by these official positions. For example, it was Plender whom Lord Pirrie (qv) commissioned to draft a scheme for the amalgamation of the Scottish steel works, a project aborted by Pirrie's death in 1924.

Despite his heavy professional commitments, Plender succeeded in making a substantial contribution to the accounting literature in speeches, presidential addresses and papers presented to the Third and Fourth International Congresses of Accountants. 'The Accountant's Certificate in Connection with the Accountant's Responsibility', presented to the Amsterdam Congress (1926), is particularly interesting in view of Plender's involvement with the Royal Mail Shipping Group whose contemporary accounting practices entangled Lord Kylsant (qv) in a legal action which shook the accounting profession to its foundations in the early 1930s. Plender's paper reflected on the nature of the auditor's responsibility, and he concluded that

> the reputation enjoyed by the Professional Accountant does not rest upon his adherence to legal principles, however important; it is mainly by reason of the Accountant's regard for his much wider moral duty and responsibility that he enjoys the confidence of the business community and the public generally. The mere observance of legal requirements may develop into a formality and render easy the evasion of responsibility upon technical grounds. No such limitation of our responsibilities should be permitted to

influence the conduct of our professional business {*Accountant* 10 July 1926}.

On 20 July 1931, Lord Kylsant (the chairman of the Royal Mail Co) and Harold Morland (the auditor) stood in the dock at the Old Bailey charged with publishing balance sheets which were false and fraudulent. The essence of the prosecution, following an important report by Sir William McLintock (qv), was that the balance sheet for 1926 was intentionally misleading, and therefore fraudulent, because it showed a trading profit for the year of approximately £439,000 whereas, in reality, the company had suffered a trading loss of about £300,000. The difference was brought about by an undisclosed transfer, from reserves, of nearly £750,000. The case turned on the wording used to describe the profit for the year. It was as follows: 'Balance for the year, including Dividends on Shares in Allied and other Companies, adjustment of Taxation Reserves, less Depreciation of Fleet, etc ... £439,213'. The case for the defence was that the phrase 'adjustment of Taxation Reserves' was inserted, at the auditor's insistence, to render the description technically correct. The prosecution contended that the wording was grossly misleading, since it implied that the company was thriving, and had earned a substantial profit, subject to some modest adjustment to taxation reserves, whereas it was on the verge of ruin. Plender, as the leading professional figure, was naturally called as an expert witness.

Plender undoubtedly found himself in an uncomfortable position. He was chairman of the Trade Facilities Act (TFA) Advisory Committee, which was responsible for monitoring Treasury-guaranteed loans to the Royal Mail Group. Research has shown that he was slow to grasp the extent of the Group's financial problems, so that firm action was delayed while matters got worse: an outcome which could presumably have been avoided if Morland had acquainted the TFA, of which he was a member, with the real position of the Group. Plender was also 'saddened' by Morland's failure 'to ensure that the shareholders were given a more forthright view of the Group'. {Green and Moss (1982) 107} Certainly, the extract from his 1926 paper suggests that Plender would have considered Morland guilty of failing to discharge his moral responsibilities. Nevertheless, secret reserves were in widespread use during the 1920s and, under cross-examination, Plender confirmed that the wording used to describe the transfer was technically correct. In defence counsel's view, it was this piece of evidence which secured the acquittal, on a technicality, of Kylsant and Morland (Kylsant was found guilty of issuing a false prospectus, for which he went to prison in 1931). Nevertheless, the fact that the Crown believed the prosecution necessary, shocked the accounting profession and brought about a more widespread recognition of a broad moral, rather than a narrow technical, responsibility towards users of accounting reports. Plender was at the forefront encouraging change in a series of speeches delivered during 1932. He saw it as the duty of the accounting profession to put its own house in order and argued against demands for a legislative solution to the problem.

In other areas also, Plender believed that government intervention should be kept to a minimum. He was a strong advocate of the balanced budget and, contrary to the theories expressed by 'Keynesian economists', he urged the Government to reject doing the things which appeared desirable and instead to spend only on things which were absolutely essential. His argument that the problem of unemployment could best be solved by reducing taxation in order to boost private sector business also has a modern ring. At the same time, he was quite willing to advocate novel methods of raising finance to provide funds for the Exchequer during the First World War. His advocacy of a Premium Loan, as a means of appealing to the sporting instincts of the British public, was not however acted upon until the Premium Bond was introduced by Viscount Mackintosh (qv) in 1956.

Plender showed a keen interest in the education and training of young accountants. As president of the Chartered Accountant Students' Society of London, 1909-28, his addresses, although sometimes a little dry, are presented in a clear, direct and concise fashion. In them, Plender emphasised qualities and behavioural characteristics which he endeavoured to display throughout his own business career:

> Much learning you may get, brilliancy may be counted among your possessions; but the simpler qualities of industry, integrity, self-restraint, and tenacity of will form the foundations which, as a rule, are more lasting than the former gifts, great as they are ... Do not aspire to be a smart man, but aim at being a good professional business man ... Avoid extremes, be fair and moderate in your views and judgements, tactful in behaviour, cultivate concentration, and remember that compromise plays no unimportant part in outlook. {*Accountant* 13 May 1922}

Plender was kindly, even-tempered and generous with both his time and in the financial sense. Arthur (later Sir Arthur) Cutforth, a future partner in Deloitte and president of the Institute, recalled his first meeting with Plender with some affection. Cutforth, as a young qualified clerk, was instructed to take a report for Plender to sign. The partner was speaking on the telephone and motioned to Cutforth to pass him the report. In an effort to respond quickly to the signal, Cutforth succeeded only in catching his foot in the telephone flex and destroying the telephone. Plender showed no annoyance, but observed in a tone of voice that was sad to the verge of pathetic: 'You know, Cutforth, if you first take away my telephone when I am talking to a very important client and you then break it, I entirely fail to see how I am going to carry on my business' {Murphy (1953) 14}. Apparently, further apologies were dismissed with a smile and a wave of the hand. His ability to stay calm under pressure proved invaluable during the war. According to the *Times* 'Never flustered or irritated at a time when the nerves of so many good workers were on edge, Plender was one of the figures that made all with whom he came into contact feel that victory was assured to a country that had such inperturbable advisers' {*Times* 21 Jan 1946}.

Plender's public services were rewarded by a knighthood in 1911, the GBE in 1918, a baronetcy in 1923 and a barony in 1931. He was honorary LLD of Birmingham University, honorary member of the Institution of Civil Engineers, High Sheriff of Kent 1928-29, Lieutenant of the City of London, High Sheriff of the County of London and DL 1927-28, president of the Fourth International Congress of Accountants, London, 1933, a Knight of Grace of the Order of St John of Jerusalem, chairman of the

City of London War Savings Association, 1916-41, retiring as vice-president, an honorary member of the Institute of Journalists, honorary treasurer, of the Royal Society of Painter-Etchers and Engravers, vice-president of the Poplar Hospital for Accidents, governor of St Thomas's Hospital, president of the Kent County Cricket Club, chairman of the governing body of the City of London School, 1935-41, and a governor of the King's School, Canterbury, 1936-46. Plender was also an active freemason, being member of a number of masonic lodges and one of the founder members and first master of the Chartered Accountants' Lodge in 1906.

Plender in 1891 married Marion Elizabeth Channon, the daughter of John Channon. His first wife died at Cannes on 31 December 1930 and he married Mable Agnes Stevens (née Laurie), the widow of George Norton Stevens and daughter of Peter George Laurie, in 1932 at St Margaret's, Westminster. In 1940 Plender was persuaded to leave London for the relative safety of Torquay for the duration of the war. It was not a happy time. Both his London and country homes were rendered uninhabitable by bomb damage and much of his collection of seventeenth century furniture and objets d'art was badly damaged. His health was poor and he died in a nursing home in Tunbridge Wells on 19 January 1946 at the age of eighty-four, leaving £325,788 gross. There were no children from either of his two marriages and, on his death, his titles became extinct.

J R EDWARDS

Writings:

President's address to the Tenth Autumnal Meeting of the Institute of Chartered Accountants in England and Wales *Accountant* 8 Oct 1910.

PP, Existing Conditions in Respect of Medical Attendance and Remuneration in Certain Towns (1912-13) Cd 6305.

PP, Irish Finance (1912-13) Cd 6153.

PP, Enemy Banks (London Agencies) (1916) Cd 8430.

PP, Enemy Banks (London Agencies), Second Report (1917-18) Cd 8889.

PP, Company Law (1918) Cd 9138.

'The Presentment of Facts' *Accountant* 15 Apr 1922.

'President's Address to the Chartered Accountant Students' Society of London' *ibid* 13 May 1922.

PP, Cross River Traffic in London (1926) Cmd 2772.

'The Accountant's Certificate in Connection with the Accountant's Responsibility' *The International Accountants Congress, Amsterdam 1926* (Amsterdam: Musses, 1926). Also published in *Accountant* 10 July 1926.

'Constructive Accounting' *Accountant* 31 Dec 1928.

PP, Export Credits Guarantee Scheme 1928-29 (1929-30) Cmd 3450.

'Depreciation and Obsolescence — From the Viewpoint of the Investor in Securities' *International Congress on Accounting* 1929 (Ronald Press, 1930). Also published in *Accountant* 9 Nov 1929.

PP, International Committee of Experts: Supervision of Certain Inter-Governmental Debts (1930-31) Cmd 3947.

PP, National Expenditure (1930-31) Cmd 3920.

'Address to the Leicester Society of Chartered Accountants' *Accountant* 22 Mar 1930.

'President's Address to the Forty-Ninth Annual Meeting of the Institute of Chartered Accountants in England and Wales' *ibid* 10 May 1930.

'Functions of the Accountant' *ibid* 10 May 1930.

'Remarks at the Chartered Accountants of Scotland Dinner' Edinburgh, 1930 *Accountants' Magazine* Dec 1930.

PP, Post Office (1931-32) Cmd 4149.

'Some Observations on Balance Sheets' *Accountant* 23 Feb 1932.

'President's Address to the London Chartered Accountant Students' Society' *ibid* 14 May 1932.

'National Expenditure' (Maiden speech in the House of Lords) *ibid* 2 July 1932.

'Observations on Half a Century of Business Life in the City' *ibid* 6 Jan 1934.

'Remarks at the Bankers' Dinner' *ibid* 12 Oct 1935.

Lady Plender (ed), *Lord Plender, Some Writings and Speeches* (Gee, 1951).

Sources:

Unpublished

PrC.

Published

Accountant 7 July 1906, 23 Feb 1918, 26 Jan 1946.

DNB.

Economist 14 Nov 1916.

J R Edwards, 'The Accounting Profession and Disclosure in Published Reports, 1925-35' *Accounting and Business Research* 1976.

Edwin Green and Michael Moss, *A Business of National Importance, the Royal Mail Shipping Group 1902-37* (Methuen, 1982).

Sir Patrick Hastings, 'The Case of the Royal Mail' in W T Baxter and Sidney Davidson (eds), *Studies in Accounting Theory* (Sweet & Maxwell, 1962).

The History of the Institute of Chartered Accountants in England and Wales and Its Founder Bodies 1870-1965 (Heinemann, 1966).

[Sir Russell Kettle], *Deloitte & Co 1845-1956* (Oxford: pp for Deloitte Plender Griffiths & Co at the University Press, 1958).

Mary E Murphy, 'Lord Plender: A Vignette of an Accountant and His Times, 1861-1948' *Business History Review* 27 (1953).

Peter L Payne, *Colvilles and the Scottish Steel Industry* (Oxford: Clarendon Press, 1979).

Times 21 Jan 1946.

WWW.

PLOWDEN, Edwin Noel August

Lord Plowden of Plowden

(1907-)

Industrialist

Edwin Noel August Plowden was born on 6 January 1907, the fourth son of Roger Herbert Plowden (1853-1921), of Strachur Park, Loch Fyne, Argyllshire, who left £3,533. The Plowdens were a Roman Catholic family, who had lived at Plowden in Shropshire for many centuries, and were involved in banking. Edwin's grandfather had been a banker at Blounts Bank in Paris and later on his own account in Florence and Rome; his father had pursued a similar career before becoming a landowner. Plowden's mother was Helen, the daughter of William Stanley Haseltine, an American sea and landscape painter.

Plowden was educated in Switzerland and at Pembroke College, Cambridge. In 1930 he worked for Standard Telephones as a salesman after training on the shop floor. In 1931 he joined the merchant firm of C Tennant Son & Co Ltd, as a salesman in the chemical department. After a period which involved much travelling and administrative work, he became a director in 1938 at the relatively early age of thirty-one.

At the beginning of the Second World War, Plowden left Tennants to join the Ministry of Economic Warfare. He moved to the Ministry of Aircraft Production in 1940, where he was responsible for the supply of light alloys, and a year later he became Director of Materials Production, a post which gave him responsibility for all hardware supplies for aircraft. He was later appointed Director-General of Materials Production, then Director-General of Materials and Engine Production, and, finally, in 1945, he succeeded Air Chief Marshal Sir Wilfred Freeman as the Ministry's chief executive. Plowden was also a director of the Government-controlled Power Jets (R & D) Ltd, set up to develop Frank Whittle's jet engine. He received the KBE for his wartime activities in 1946.

After the war the Ministry of Aircraft Production was merged with the Ministry of Supply and Plowden returned to the City. He was re-appointed to Tennant's board and also became a member of the boards of British South American Airways Corporation, British Aluminium Co Ltd, and the Commercial Union Assurance Co Ltd. When in 1947 the Labour Government set up the Central Economic Planning Staff and Economic Planning Board Plowden was appointed chairman and Chief Planning Officer, accordingly resigning his seat on the BSAAC board and taking leave of absence from his other companies. Originally the appointment was to be only for a year but Plowden was asked to stay on by each successive Government and remained until October 1953. In autumn 1947 the CEPS became part of the Treasury, as Plowden had urged.

During his years with the Economic Planning Board Plowden was responsible for the co-ordination of economic policy, long-term planning for the use of manpower resources and the preparation of annual economic surveys. He drew up the four-year plan for the Co-ordination of Britain's Economic and Industrial Resources which Stafford Cripps used as the basis for the Washington discussions on Marshall Aid in 1948. Plowden attended many conferences and high-level negotiations abroad: he represented Britain at the Paris Organisation for European Economic Co-operation conference on Marshall Aid in 1948; he went with Stafford Cripps and Ernest Bevin to the USA in 1949 for discussions with the Americans and Canadians on Britain's dollar crisis and subsequent devaluation of sterling; and attended similar discussions in the USA with Attlee in 1950 during the Korean War, with Sir Roger Makins (then head of the Foreign Office Economics Department) in 1951, and with Eden and Butler in 1953. In 1951 Plowden became vice-chairman of the Temporary Council Committee of NATO (the 'Three Wise Men') formed to attempt to reconcile the military requirements with the political and economic capabilities of the 12 member states. Plowden was awarded the KCB in 1951.

By 1953 there had been considerable development in Britain's atomic energy project, primarily for military purposes, under the direction of Lord Portal (qv), and Britain had tested her first atomic bomb late in 1952. Military demands were expanding and there were now good hopes of civil nuclear power. On 19 July 1954 the United Kingdom Atomic Energy Authority (UKAEA) came into existence and took over responsibility from the Ministry of Supply for the Atomic Energy Research Establishment (AERE) at Harwell under Dr (later Sir) John Cockcroft, the Atomic Weapons Research Establishment at Aldermaston under Dr (later Sir) William Penney, and the atomic production group at Risely under Sir Christopher Hinton (qv).

In post-war Britain nuclear power appeared to have enormous economic, political and military significance. Such was Plowden's reputation and experience, both at home and abroad, that as early as 1953 he was asked to become the first chairman of the UKAEA. As chairman-designate he was appointed to the staff of the Lord President of the Council to assist in the establishment of the new organisation so that by the time the new Corporation came into being he had familiarised himself with the problems involved.

During Plowden's chairmanship (1953-59) there were rapid strides in military and civilian atomic energy. Relations between Britain and the USA were a crucial factor. They were very poor when the UKAEA was set up, because the 1946 US Atomic Energy Act (McMahon Act) prevented transatlantic exchanges of atomic energy information. Plowden played a key role in the renewal of co-operation and friendship with the USA and relations improved dramatically. In 1955 a bilateral agreement for civil purposes, and in 1958 and 1959 bilateral agreements for defence purposes were signed; nuclear collaboration now became close.

At home the period 1954-59 saw major developments in the atomic weapons programme — Britain's first thermonuclear weapon was tested in 1957. It also saw the beginning of a huge expansion of the civil nuclear power programme. Calder Hall's No 1 reactor was completed in 1956 and having been authorised primarily to produce military plutonium it became the world's first nuclear power station to feed electricity into a national grid. In February 1955, even before Calder Hall was opened, the Government announced a ten-year programme for building nuclear power stations, which was to provide a capacity of 1,500-2,000 MW of electricity at a cost of about £300 million. Plowden used his great influence within Whitehall to press hard for the nuclear programme. His task was made easier by the impact of the Suez crisis on oil supply, which 'led to the partial collapse of rationality within Westminster, the Atomic Energy Authority and, to a lesser but still noticeable extent, within Whitehall' {Hannah (1982) 178}. The result was that a programme of 5,000-6,000 MW of generating capacity was envisaged by the end of 1965. The drive to expand was fuelled by another feature of Plowden's chairmanship — the establishment of nuclear consortia.   Plowden was awarded a life peerage in 1959 and remained chairman of the UKAEA until the end of that year. By then the enthusiasm for nuclear power had begun to wane. More than half the world's supply of nuclear power was generated in Britain in the early 1960s, but the massive commitment to a nuclear programme was seen to have been mis-timed at a time of cheap and plentiful oil. The accident to Britain's first plutonium-producing reactor at Windscale in October 1957 had caused alarm about the possible dangers of nuclear power and the Campaign for Nuclear Disarmament voiced opposition to nuclear weapons.

In 1963 Lord Plowden became chairman of Tube Invesments, one of the biggest engineering firms in the UK, and one of the largest manufacturers of precision tubing in the world. TI had extensive domestic and overseas interests in electrical products, aluminium, capital goods, iron and steel, and machine tools. Under Plowden further acquisitions were made to the machine tool side when, in 1966, TI purchased Charles Churchill & Co Ltd, which was headed by J B S Gabriel (qv), and also Maschinenfabrik Froriep GmbH of Rheydt, West Germany. In 1952 TI employed about 32,000 with a capital of about £40 million; by 1967 69,000 were employed and capital had increased to about £217 million; and by 1976, the year of Plowden's retirement from the chairmanship, TI employed 53,431, with a capital of £300 million and an annual turnover of about £500 million. Plowden subsequently became president of the TI group.

Lord Plowden was frequently asked to chair important government enquiries. In 1964 the Wilson Government appointed him as head of a committee to examine the future of the British aircraft industry, a position that was to make Plowden's name a household word. The committee's terms of reference were to consider the future place and organisation of the aircraft industry in relation to the country's economy, taking into account the demands of national defence, export prospects, the comparable industries of other countries, and the relationship of the industry with Government activities in aviation. The main burden of the final report — that Government support for the aircraft industry should be reduced and that the British industry must turn to collaboration with other countries in Europe — was bitterly attacked for being negative and defeatist, especially by those within the aircraft industry, such as Sir George Edwards and Lord Nelson (qqv).

Lord Plowden has held, among other posts: a directorship of National Westminster Bank; and the chairmanship of Equity Capital for Industry Ltd, 1976-82, of the CBI Companies Committee, 1976-80, and of the Top Salaries Review Body since 1981; chairmanship of the Police Complaints Board, 1976–81 and independent chairmanship of the Police Negotiating Board, 1980–83. He has been an honorary fellow of Pembroke College, Cambridge, since 1958 and a visiting fellow at Nuffield College, Oxford, 1956-64; president of the London Graduate School of Business Studies since 1976; and has been awarded honorary degrees by Pennsylvania State University, the University of Aston, and Loughborough.

Plowden married on 20 June 1933 Bridget Horatia, the daughter of the late Admiral Sir Herbert William Richmond. They have two sons, William Julius Lowthian (b 1935) and Francis John (b 1945), and two daughters, Anna Bridget (b 1938) and Penelope Christina (b 1941). Lady Plowden is a leading figure in the arts and education world.

GEOFFREY TWEEDALE

Writings:

remarks on atomic power in Corbin Allardice (ed), *Atomic Power: An Appraisal* (Pergamon, 1957).

PP, Report on Treasury Control of Public Expenditure (1961) Cmnd 1432.

PP, Report of the Committee on Representational Service Overseas (1962-63) Cmnd 2276.

PP, Report of the Committee of Inquiry into the Aircraft Industry (1964-65) Cmnd 2853 (chairman).

PP, Report of the Committee of Enquiry into the Structure of the Electricity Supply Industry in England and Wales (1976) Cmd 6388.

Sources:

Unpublished

Research notes on Plowden's atomic energy career compiled by Stephanie Zarach.

SSRC Elites data.

Lord Plowden, 'Tube Investments Ltd' (Edwards Seminar Paper 390, 9 May 1967).

Published

Leonard Bertin, *Atom Harvest* (Secker & Warburg, 1955).

Burke's Baronetage and Peerage 1980.

Charles Gardner, *The British Aircraft Corporation: A History* (Batsford, 1981).

Margaret Gowing, *Independence and Deterrence: Britain and Atomic Energy, 1945-1952* (2 vols, Macmillan, 1974).

Leslie Hannah, *Engineers, Managers and Politicians* (Macmillan, 1982).

UKAEA Annual Reports.

WW 1984.

Sir Felix J C Pole (courtesy of the National Railway Museum).

POLE, Sir Felix John Clewett

(1877-1956)

Railway manager

Felix John Clewett Pole was born at Little Bedwyn near Marlborough, Wiltshire, on 1 February 1877, the second son of Edward Pole, the local schoolmaster and an active Churchman, and his wife Emma, the youngest daughter of Charles Clewett of Wincanton, Somerset. He attended school in the villages of Little Bedwyn and Ramsbury and at the age of fourteen, upon the nomination of Walter Hume Long, MP for North Wiltshire and later a director of the Great Western Railway, joined the GWR as a telegraph lad clerk at Swindon on 12 October 1891 with a salary of £35 a year.

Within two years he was promoted to a post in the telegraph superintendent's office at Paddington, London, the company's headquarters. In May 1896, upon passing the senior clerk's examination, he was transferred to the chief engineer's office. Eight years later he joined the small general manager's office, a more promising department for a man who was not qualified in technical subjects. There, under James Charles Inglis (general manager, 1903-11) (qv), he showed his talent for publicity and industrial relations. He edited and revived the moribund staff magazine using it to promote a 'family' corporate image and later to publicise his views as general manager, especially on labour matters. At the same time he became deeply involved in industrial relations, in particular from 1909 in the work of the conciliation boards, and when Frank Potter became general manager in 1912, Pole was made head of the staff and labour department in the general manager's office at £400 a year. In June 1913 he was appointed chief clerk, a position which he retained throughout the First World War, having been rejected for military service because of poor eyesight. As well as his involvement in labour questions, it was his particular responsibility to see that Potter was provided with information for the Railway Executive Committee. In March 1919 he was made assistant to the general manager, then in the following August, after Potter's death, assistant general manager to Charles Aldington at a salary of £2,000 rising to £2,500 a year. Aldington's ill-health (he was absent for ten of the twenty-two months he held the office) provided Pole with many opportunities to show his paces and when Aldington was forced to retire Pole was appointed his successor at the age of forty-four in June 1921 at £6,000 a year, thus following a company tradition by which chief officers were recruited internally.

Pole's first task as general manager was the merger of the 33 companies which were to form an enlarged Great Western system (4,044 route miles, £319,341,766 paid up capital and 109,376 employees in 1923) under the Railways Act of 1921. The adjustments were relatively straightforward because of the much greater size of the GWR compared with the aggregate of the others and because of the dominance of the departmental, functionally centralised administration that characterised all of the merging concerns, including the GWR. However, Pole was dissatisfied with the existing administrative arrangements, notably the separation of the spending from the revenue departments, over-centralisation in departments and the lack of control by his office of major decisions and expenditure. His mentor Inglis had failed to effect the administrative reforms which he believed were required to control several of the heads of department; his efforts were cut short by his death while in office at the age of sixty. Pole attempted, with modest success, to overcome these inherited problems, through, for example, regular meetings of the Chief Officers' Conference, more careful budgeting and account control and the participation of himself or his representative in the meetings of the various functional sub-committees of the board. He also moved towards the creation of co-terminous areas of responsibility for the district and divisional organisations of the departments, in an effort to encourage a limited degree of decentralised 'general' management.

Consistent with his belief that the company needed men with managerial as well as technical skills, from 1921 Pole implemented a four-year special training scheme which enabled six men chosen from the ranks annually to gain experience across the company. Although he accepted that in normal negotiations trade unions had an essential role to play, he was a firm negotiator and during the General Strike (May 1926), when he was chairman of the railways' General Managers' Conference, he was severely critical of the men's involvement in 'a deep conspiracy against the state' {*Great Western Railway Magazine*}. Their action seemed to threaten the corporate paternalism that Pole advocated and tried to implement through schemes such as those to assist employees in house purchases. Good customer relations and publicity were also given high priority. Pole failed though to convince the ailing coal and iron and steel industries of South Wales through the offer of rebates (1923) and reduced terminal charges (1925) that larger capacity wagons were mutually beneficial: a good example of how the failure to secure co-operation between vertically related but separate industries may mean the sacrifice of a cost-saving development. During his general managership there were substantial fluctuations in profitability and in the stock market's valuation of the company. The high nominal capitalisation and leverage, established under the 1921 Act, meant that with faltering net revenues, ordinary dividends between 1923 and 1926 could only be maintained with appropriations from the general reserve fund to the extent of £2,623,143; and in 1926, a disastrous year for the company, £979,144 was taken from reserves to pay dividends and interest on the preference and guaranteed stocks. However, in Pole's last full year (1928), the rate of return on revenue account (before, that is, allocations for dividends etc) was 20.8 per cent, and the return on capital account expenditure was 3.5 per cent — a creditable outcome in view of the depressed condition of the South Wales coal industry, and an improvement over the position that he had inherited in 1921.

He had difficulty in co-ordinating a group of individualistic heads of department, and relations between Pole and his active, non-executive chairman, Viscount (Victor Spencer) Churchill, may have been strained. Pole, who was earning £8,000 a year at the time, left the GWR with a gratuity of £5,000 and a pension of £1,000 to become the executive chairman of Associated Electrical Industries Ltd in July 1929 at a salary of £10,000. He was retained by the GWR as a consultant but not, to his disappointment, as a director. However, he kept alive the interests developed in his railway career: in 1931 he visited the Sudan, Egypt and Palestine to advise on railway policy; in 1933 he became a director of Airports Ltd, the company formed by Morris Jackaman to develop Gatwick into an airport for scheduled services; in 1934 he reported to the Northern Ireland Government on transport conditions in the province (advocating co-ordination); and was chairman (1936-45) of the Government's Central Housing Advisory Committee on Private Enterprise Housing.

Associated Electrical Industries Ltd was formed by the General Electric Co of America, headed by Gerard Swope (1872-1957), from its subsidiaries British Thomson-Houston Co and three other companies (Ferguson Pailin, Edison Swan and Metropolitan Vickers Co) it acquired in 1926-28, thereby creating the second largest electrical group in Britain in the late 1920s. It is estimated that the market value of AEI's capital in 1930 was £9.8 million, placing the group in twenty-ninth position in the top 50 industrial companies. The group was a full-line producer and innovator of electrical goods. Pole's predecessor, Howard C Levis, and managing director, Sir Philip Manley Nash (who was sacked in October 1931), had favoured centralisation. However, initially Pole pursued a policy, supported by the group's American parent, of retaining autonomous units, with separate trading identities, bank accounts, competing products and local executive committees at Rugby (British Thomson-Houston) and Manchester (Metropolitan Vickers). Nonetheless, he established an executive committee of the holding company's board (which recommended large capital outlays) and inter-company committees for engineering (design), manufacturing, purchasing and accounting. Significantly, it was only later that the optimistically-titled Commercial Co-ordinating and Policy Committee was added.

Through personal contact, Pole tried to create a sense of identity within the group and inter-firm co-operation — but the recession of the early 1930s rekindled old rivalries. However, American control was removed in

1934 and by 1936, through a moderate degree of product concentration, innovations, the group's involvement in national and international rings (which led Pole to travel widely) and the recovery of the home market, AEI's profits were good (10 per cent ordinary dividend). Indeed, Pole came to believe in planned capitalism based on large co-operating firms, and in 1934 he was on the executive committee of Harold Macmillan's Industrial Reorganisation League. AEI further benefited from the rearmament boom and made a large contribution to the war effort of 1939-45, in particular by developing radar.

Pole resigned from the chairmanship of AEI in 1945 due to blindness but remained a director until 1955. He was succeeded by Captain Oliver Lyttelton (later Lord Chandos (qv)). He mastered braille and continued as chairman of the *Reading Standard*. He had been knighted in 1924 in Stanley Baldwin's dissolution list (Baldwin had been a GWR director, 1908-18) and was selected as High Sheriff of Berkshire in 1947 but could not accept because of his disability. Pole had a lifetime interest in fishing and natural history, and like his father, was a conscientious Anglican. He married in 1899 Ethel Maud, the daughter of Horace Flack, a shoemaker in the West End of London; they had a son and two daughters. Sir Felix Pole died in Reading on 15 January 1956, leaving £153,305 gross.

GEOFFREY CHANNON

Writings:

'The Conversion of the Gauge of the Great Western Main-Line' in Archibald Williams (ed), *Engineering Wonders of the World* (3 vols, Thomas Nelson & Sons, 1909-10) I.

Cardiff and the Great Western Railway Great Western Pamphlets no 12 (1924).

(with James Milne) 'The Economics of Passenger Transport' *Modern Railway Administration: A Practical Treatise by Leading Railway Experts* 2 (Gresham, 1925).

'The Administrative Reorganisation of the Railways Following the War' *ibid* 2 (1925).

A Few Observations on Railways (pp, 1927).

PP, Northern Ireland, Transport Conditions in Northern Ireland (1934) NI Cmd 160.

Report on Proposed Railway Improvements in Palestine (1935).

Felix J C Pole: His Book (Reading: privately circulated, 1954; Bracknell: Town & Country Press, 1968).

Pole also contributed numerous articles to the *Great Western Railway Magazine*, *Railway News*, *Railway Times* and *Modern Transport*.

Sources:

Unpublished

General Electric Co Ltd, records of AEI.

POLE Sir Felix John Clewett

PRO, GWR Board Minutes and Traffic Committee Minutes, RAIL 250/53; GWR Chief Officers' Conference Minutes, RAIL 250/143; GWR Reports and Accounts, RAIL 1110/197.

BCe.

MCe.

PrC.

Information from John King.

Published

Derek F Channon, *The Strategy and Structure of British Enterprise* (Macmillan, 1973).

Geoffrey Channon, 'The Reorganisation of British Railways under the 1921 Railways Act: The Case of the Great Western' *Business History Review* 55 (1981).

DNB.

Great Western Railway Magazine especially 25 (1913), 32 (1921) and 41 (1929).

Leslie Hannah, *The Rise of the Corporate Economy* (2nd ed, Methuen, 1984).

Robert Jones and Oliver Marriott, *Anatomy of a Merger. A History of GEC, AEI and English Electric* (Jonathan Cape, 1970).

Harold Macmillan, *Winds of Change 1914-1939* (Macmillan, 1966).

Modern Transport 21 Jan 1956.

Oswald S Nock, *The Great Western Railway in the Twentieth Century* (Ian Allan, 1971).

E R Pole, *Little Bedwyn School Centenary, 1854-1954, and a Supplement to the Memory of Sir Felix J C Pole* (Reading: privately circulated, 1956).

Reading Standard 20 Mar 1956.

Jack Simmons, *The Railway in England and Wales 1830-1914: The System and Its Working* (Leicester: Leicester University Press, 1978).

Times 20 Mar 1956.

G Walker, 'Development and Organisation of Associated Electrical Industries Limited' in Ronald S Edwards and Harry Townsend (eds), *Business Enterprise: Its Growth and Organisation* (Macmillan & Co, 1958).

WWW.

Arthur Pollen (from Anthony Pollen The Great Gunnery Scandal. The Mystery of Jutland *Collins, 1980).*

POLLEN, Arthur Joseph Hungerford

(1866-1937)

Manufacturer and inventor

Arthur Joseph Hungerford Pollen, who was often known as Arthur Hungerford Pollen, came from a Wiltshire family which had received a baronetcy in 1795, and was born on 13 September 1866. His father John Hungerford Pollen (1820-1902), of Pembridge Crescent, Notting Hill, was a former Anglican clergyman, fellow of Merton and Proctor of Oxford University who was converted to Roman Catholicism in 1852 and became a distinguished artist. His mother, the daughter of Rev C J La Primaudaye of St John's College, Oxford, was of Huguenot descent. His father left £10,285 in 1902, and his mother £2,530 in 1919. Pollen's great-uncle Lord Addington was Governor of the Bank of England 1853-55; his cousins included Samuel Pepys Cockerell of the British Bank for Foreign Trade, Lord Rendel of Armstrong Whitworth and Evelyn Hubbard, chairman of Guardian Assurance, 1900-30. Of his seven brothers three became Roman Catholic priests and three were soldiers. Both his parents wrote on artistic subjects, and literary influences were strong in the family. His father was the lifelong confidante of Cardinal Newman, and a friend of Thackeray, Ruskin and Gladstone; his mother was seduced by Wilfred Scawen Blunt; and he was himself secretary of the Crabbet Club 1887-89 and the oldest friend of Hilaire Belloc.

Educated at the Oratory School, Birmingham, and Trinity College, Oxford, he worked as a private tutor, was called to the Bar at Lincolns Inn in 1893, visited Canada and the USA in 1893 (where he hunted bears in the Rockies with Theodore Roosevelt), and India in 1894. Afterwards he contributed musical, artistic, literary and dramatic criticism to London's quality evening newspaper, the *Westminster Gazette*. He also wrote light articles about legal life, and joined the editorial staff of the *Daily Mail* shortly after its inception. His parents, under Scawen Blunt's influence, were strong supporters of Irish Home Rule, and in 1895 Pollen unsuccessfully contested Walthamstow as a Gladstonian Liberal parliamentary candidate.

His career was transformed by his marriage in 1898 to Maud Beatrice, only child and heiress of Sir Joseph Lawrence (qv), who had made a fortune developing the American linotype patents in Britain. Lawrence made Pollen managing director of his linotype company in 1898, believing that Pollen's journalistic expertise would be useful in a company which made newspaper print machinery. The original Linotype Co had been registered in Britain in 1889, and amalgamated in December 1896 with the Machinery Trust Ltd (formed 1893) in the newly-created Linotype & Machinery Ltd. When Pollen joined the company, its capital consisted of £980,000 in ordinary shares, £100,000 in 6 per cent preference shares, £20,000 in founders shares and £500,000 in recently issued debentures;

another £179,205 debentures were created in 1901. Ordinary dividends of 10 per cent were paid in 1898-1900, and 7 per cent in 1901. The capital was increased in 1902 to £500,000 in 5 per cent cumulative preference, £1 million of non-cumulative preferred ordinary and £1 million of deferred ordinary shares. There was a further capital reorganisation in 1903. Pollen thus swiftly gained experience in a fast-expanding and technologically advanced business, whose financial needs were all too complicated. He also joined the board of *Black and White Magazine* Ltd in 1898.

After 1900 Pollen made a study of naval gunnery, and devised a brilliant and sophisticated system of naval fire control which he offered to the Admiralty. The early stages of his research were helped by his Linotype co-director, the scientist Lord Kelvin, but the greater part of inventive imagination and practical application came from Pollen. In its final and most advanced form the Pollen system produced constantly up-to-date ranges and bearings of the enemy, correcting them automatically for the changes produced by the movements of both sides' ships during the projectiles' time of flight. In a disastrous and unnecessary mistake of 1912, Pollen's system was discarded by the Admiralty in favour of the cheaper, derivative and cruder Dreyer system, whilst the Argo Co which marketed his invention was struck off the list of Admiralty contractors in 1913. It is significant of the two inventors' merits that whereas Dreyer got £5,000 for his design in 1916, Pollen was awarded £30,000 in 1925 by the Royal Commission on Awards and Inventions on top of £11,500 paid to him by the Admiralty in 1908. Yet this cash award was poor recompense for the spite and injustice with which he had been treated.

To create time for his gunnery researches, Pollen resigned his executive responsibilities with Linotype in 1904, although remaining a director. For a time he was a director of the Standard Construction Corporation, and later he was concerned with Daimler Motors of Coventry. Around 1911 he bought control of the York optical instrument makers Thomas Cooke & Son, to supply components when his naval rangefinder went into production. Following the Admiralty's rejection of him, he sold Cooke in 1915 to Vickers, who merged it with Troughton & Simms in 1922.

A prolific writer on naval topics for the *Westminster Gazette* and *Sunday Times*, from May 1915 until February 1919 he was a regular and authoritative contributor to an acclaimed wartime publication, *Land and Water*. He was sedulous in upholding official Admiralty war propaganda, although some of his well-informed criticism so annoyed the Admiralty that in 1916 his arrest was urged under the Defence of the Realm Act. His naval work meant so much to him that in substitution for the armorial bearings of his father's family, he obtained a new grant from the College of Arms featuring 'a naval crown' and a scattering of 'anchors erect' {Fox-Davis (1930) 1569}.

For a time Pollen was the European representative of the Guaranty Trust of New York. He visited the USA on business in 1914, and returned on unofficial, but effective, propaganda work from June to December 1917. He again visited the USA in 1921 and 1927. His admiration of the American business system became so pronounced that he repeatedly tried to apply its practices in Britain.

His father-in-law Sir Joseph Lawrence helped to start 'the process of incubation' in 1918 whereby rich industrialists advocating Imperial

Protection and other business reforms formed a pressure group called the British Commonwealth Union {HLRO, Bonar Law 83/6/6, Lawrence to Law, 2 Aug 1918}. Pollen applied in 1919 for a senior post in the Union's permanent directorate, and although he was not appointed, later had charge with (Sir) Patrick Hannon of its propaganda against labour extremism and nationalisation, and in favour of private enterprise and increased production. Pollen's BCU work largely duplicated that of Sydney Walton and the National Propaganda organisation chaired by Lord Inchcape (qv). He was also vice-president of the Federation of British Industries, and Master of the Coachmakers Company in 1926.

Also in 1926 Pollen became chairman of International Linotype Ltd at an annual salary in 1932 of £6,000 plus a company house. International Linotype originated from the merger in 1908 of Linotype & Machinery with the Mergenthaler Linotype Co of New York. Under this deal, which practically created a world linotype monopoly, 98 per cent of L&M's capital was transferred to International Linotype, which was registered in March 1909. During Pollen's chairmanship, the company had £555,668 issued ordinary capital, on which 6 per cent was paid in 1926, 6.5 per cent in 1927, 1928 and 1931, 7 per cent in 1929, 7.5 per cent in 1930, and 5.5 per cent in 1932. Pollen used a management consultant, T Gerald Rose (author of *Higher Control*) to rationalise the business, and applied American business methods when possible.

Daimler Motors, with whom he had pre-war contacts, was owned from 1910 by Birmingham Small Arms, a company whose directors included BCU luminaries such as Lincoln Chandler, Dudley Docker (qv), Hannon, Sir Edward Manville (qv) and Sir Hallewell Rogers (qv). Early in the 1920s Pollen was put in charge of the foreign trade of BSA and Daimler, visiting America on their behalf in 1921. In April of that year he submitted a long but inconclusive report on BSA's sales organisation, and in 1923 he joined the company's board. Under Rogers's effete chairmanship, BSA had undertaken a post-war diversification programme (1919-21) so careless that ordinary dividends were passed throughout 1921-24 and 1926-28. Most of the directors were incompetent, management was loose and undisciplined, products were over-diversified and marketing was defective. Manville replaced Rogers as chairman in 1928 but failed to make satisfactory reforms. BSA's purchase of Lanchester Motors in 1931 — a characteristically precipitate and desperate attempt to widen Daimler's market appeal — aggravated the group's position. A net loss of £204,194 recorded in 1931 was followed by a net trading loss of £797,928 in 1932.

In this crisis BSA turned to its former deputy-chairman, Dudley Docker, himself a major shareholder, who ran the Birmingham Advisory Committee of the Midland Bank which had sanctioned much of BSA's borrowing. Docker arranged for Sir Mark Webster Jenkinson (qv) to report on the group structure and strategy, and had searching discussions with the BSA directors and other financiers. Docker regarded Pollen as the 'strongest' of the BSA board who would 'pull the business round if anyone can' {MBA, Astbury diary 1 July 1932}. In July 1932 Docker persuaded Pollen to relinquish the International Linotype chair for that of BSA.

A critical position confronted Pollen. Compared with 1931, BSA's output of motor cycles was down by 24 per cent in 1932; steel output declined by 40 per cent; and the output of machinery and small-tools by 50 per cent. His reorganisation proposals were furiously resented by Percy Martin (qv), while his 'impulsive and dictatorial methods' (so tough that Manville was reduced to tears by one board meeting) upset his sedentary colleagues {HLRO, Hannon papers 31/1, Patrick Hannon to Arthur Wood, 4 Oct 1932}. Pollen gradually forfeited their loyalty, and at the board meeting of 6 December 1932 (from which he was absent), Martin announced that he would no longer co-operate with Pollen as chairman and obtained a resolution from his co-directors which criticised Pollen sharply. 'Terribly overwrought', and feeling that he had been ruined (as with the Dreyer case) by a 'pack of lies', Pollen resigned the BSA chair, although he remained on the BSA and Daimler boards until his death {ibid, Hannon 31/1, Hannon to Martin, 7 Dec 1932}. His successor as chairman, Sir Alexander Roger (qv), introduced by Docker from the Midland Bank, was opposed and insulted by Martin throughout 1933 until Docker forced Martin to retire from executive responsibilities in December.

Pollen, who received Coronation medals in 1902 and 1911 and a General Service medal in 1914, was also a director of the Car & General Insurance Corporation (whose chairman in 1907-33 was Manville), and of the Motor Union Insurance Co. He did not regain his position at Linotype after 1932, and instead became chairman of Follsain Metals Ltd, and a director of the Follsain Syndicate and of Bensonite Ltd. From 1936 he chaired the board of the *Tablet*, the leading Catholic weekly newspaper, but died on 28 January 1937 at his flat in St James's Court, leaving £12,340 gross. His widow left £35,723 in 1962. Their elder son married into the Baring family and was a sculptor: the younger son was an assurance general manager.

Belloc thought Pollen 'remarkable for the rapidity and exactitude of his judgement' {*Times* 4 Feb 1937}. Hannon found him 'capable and efficient but somewhat aggressive' at the BCU in 1919 {HLRO, Hannon 12/5, Hannon, memorandum of 1919}, but after the rows at BSA in 1932 wrote of 'baffling negotiations with an impossible personality' {ibid 31/1, Hannon to Martin, 10 Dec 1932}. Leo Maxse called Pollen 'not only a remarkable man of altogether exceptional competence on his subject but a brilliant inventor' {*National Review*, 66 (Feb 1916) 838}. To Lord Clark Pollen seemed 'a rich and forceful man' with eccentric religious views: he believed Woodrow Wilson was diabolically possessed, and when Sargent's portrait of the American president was hung at the Royal Academy, Pollen said he offered 'any pure young woman a hundred pounds if she would sit for five minutes looking at the picture, and they all ran screaming from the room' {Clark (1974) 176}. A biography of this remarkable polymath was published by his younger son in 1980.

R P T DAVENPORT-HINES

Writings:

This list is not definitive. Pollen contributed prolifically to newspapers and magazines for over forty years, and it is impossible to trace all the writings to which he appended his name, still less those which were anonymously published. It is known, for example, that he contributed to the *Spectator* of 16 Jan 1925, but it is not now clear which unsigned paragraphs in that magazine were written by him. His contributions to *Land and Water* during 1915-19 are filed in the Pollen papers at Churchill College and are too numerous to list here.

Preface to Henry Charles Somers Augustus Somerset, *The Land of the Muskeg* (1895).

Memorandum on a Proposed System of Finding Ranges at Sea and Ascertaining the Speed and Course of Any Vessel in Sight. (pp, 1904).

The Jupiter Letters (pp, 1907).

Notes on a Proposed Method of Studying Naval Tactics (pp, 1907).

The Gun in Battle (pp, nd 1912-13).

Handbook for Argo A1 Rangefinder Mounting (pp, 1912).

The Necessity of Fire Control (pp, nd 1913).

letter on fire control and the Royal Navy *Times* 1 July 1913.

'The Submarine Myth' *Dublin Review* 156 (Apr 1915).

'The Submarine Campaign' *ibid* 157 (July 1915).

'The Needs of our Navy' *North American Review* March 1916.

'The Spirit of the Nation' *Dublin Review* 159 (July 1916).

'The Two Views' *North American Review* Oct 1917.

'America and the Naval Revolution' *Metropolitan Magazine* Feb 1918.

'A Plea for First Principles' *Colliers Weekly* May 1918.

The Navy in Battle (Chatto & Windus, 1918).

'Jutland' *Harpers Magazine* Aug 1919.

letter on Lord Jellicoe and Jutland *Times* 2 Nov 1920.

letter on Jutland and Pollen's range-finder invention *ibid* 12 Nov 1920.

Five articles on US naval policy in *New York Evening Post*, 21-25 Feb 1921 (reprinted as a pamphlet in April 1921 by the American Association for International Conciliation).

'Disarmament Doubts' *Sperlings Journal* Sept 1921.

'England's Navy and Disarmament' *Atlantic Monthly* Dec 1921.

'Three Lessons of the Naval War' book review in *Foreign Affairs* June 1924.

'Back to First Principles: Admiral Sir Reginald Custance's *Study of War*' book review in *Spectator* 29 Nov 1924.

naval book review *ibid* 8 Oct 1926.

'Jutland and the Unforeseen' *19th Century and After* 102 (1927).

'The Tragedy of Lord Fisher' *Naval Review* Feb 1930.

'Convoy and Battle Turn' *ibid* Nov 1930.

'The Retort Courteous' *ibid* Feb 1931.

book review in *ibid* May 1931.

article in *Sunday Times* 26 Feb 1933.

POLLEN Arthur Joseph Hungerford

letters on 'profiteering in armaments' *Times* 19 Nov, 26 Nov, 28 Nov and 15 Dec 1936.

Sources:

Unpublished

Churchill College, Cambridge, Pollen papers.

Coventry City RO, Daimler papers.

House of Lords RO, Bonar Law and Hannon papers.

Midland Bank Archives, Astbury diary.

PRO, Admiralty papers.

University of Warwick, Modern Records Centre, BSA papers.

MCe.

PrC.

Published

Anthony Bird and Francis Hutton-Stott, *Lanchester Motor Cars* (Cassell, 1965).

Kenneth Mack Clark (Lord Clark), *Another Part of the Wood* (Murray, 1974).

Richard Davenport-Hines, *Dudley Docker* (Cambridge: Cambridge University Press, 1984).

Arthur C Fox-Davies, *Armorial Families* (Hurst & Blackett, 1930) 2.

Countess of Longford, *A Pilgrimage of Passion: The Life of Wilfred Scawen Blunt* (Weidenfeld & Nicolson, 1979).

National Review 66 (Feb 1916).

New York Evening Post 3 Feb, 15 Mar 1921 (interviews with Pollen).

New York Morning World 2 Feb 1921 (interview with Pollen).

J A L Pollen, *The Great Gunnery Scandal* (Collins, 1980).

Stephen W Roskill, *Admiral of the Fleet Earl Beatty. The Last Hero* (Collins, 1980).

Jon T Sumida, 'British Capital Ship Design in the Dreadnought Era' *Journal of Modern History* 51 (1979).

Times 26 May 1910, 21, 24 June 1913, 29 Jan, 4 Feb 1937.

Times Literary Supplement 12, 26 Dec 1918, 29 May 1919.

Westminster Gazette 21 Jan 1916.

Andrew N Wilson, *Hilaire Belloc* (Hamish Hamilton, 1984).

WWW.

Viscount Portal (from Alexander Howard and Ernest Newman, British Enterprise *(Lincolns Praeger, 1952)).*

PORTAL, Charles Frederick Algernon

1st Viscount Portal of Hungerford

(1893-1971)

Industrial executive

Charles Frederick Algernon ('Peter') Portal was born at Eddington House, near Hungerford, Berkshire, on 21 May 1893, the son of Edward Robert Portal (1854-1953) and his second wife, Ellinor Kate, the daughter of Captain Charles West Hill, the governor of Winchester prison. The Portals were of Huguenot origin and could trace their direct ancestry to the fifteenth century. After the family's arrival in England in 1695 the various Portals became involved in paper manufacture, silversmithing, landowning, and public service.

Peter Portal's boyhood, shared with his two half-brothers and four brothers, was comfortable and uneventful. His father, who had qualified as a barrister but led the life of a country gentleman on the proceeds of the Portals' Northampton wine business (when he died on 26 March 1953 he left an estate valued at £134,609 gross) was the dominant influence, though his strictness towards his children was tempered by the warmth and devotion of their mother. Peter attended preparatory school at Banstead, Surrey, and then Winchester, where he developed a life-long passion for falconry and sport. His time at Christ Church, Oxford (1912-14), where he read for a BA degree with the intention of becoming a barrister, and indulged in hawking, beagling, and motor-cycling, was interrupted by the First World War.

Portal enlisted as a dispatch-rider in the motor-cyclist section of the Royal Engineers on 6 August 1914. By November he had been promoted to motor cyclist officer, had been mentioned in dispatches, and had narrowly escaped death when a shell blew him through the door of a house. He joined the RFC as an observer in July 1915, qualifying as a pilot the following year. His outstanding fighting qualities — he won an MC and DSO in 1917, and a bar to the DSO in 1918 — ensured his rapid promotion in 1918 to lieutenant-colonel, RAF, at the age of twenty-five. He amassed over a thousand wartime flying hours and after his night-bombing exploits he returned home in 1918 as a war hero.

In August 1919, Portal received a permanent post-war commission as a squadron-leader at Cranwell. Duty at the Air Ministry in 1923-26 introduced him to the machinery of Government and brought him to the attention of Air Marshal Sir Hugh Trenchard, who quickly formed a high opinion of the rising officer. In a variety of posts Portal advanced steadily in his chosen profession between the wars, joining the ranks of the Air Council in 1939, when he was made a CB.

The outbreak of the Second World War brought Portal into national prominence when in 1940 he became Air Officer Commanding-in-Chief,

Bomber Command. But he was there only seven months before his return to the Ministry as Chief of the Air Staff. He remained as the professional head of the RAF until January 1946. On him more than any other fell the burden of directing the RAF in the Second World War and in presenting to Churchill and the War Cabinet the advice of the Chiefs of Staff on allied strategy and on other matters of military policy.

The war demonstrated Portal's two outstanding characteristics: 'first, his astonishing efficiency in any and every service task which he had to compete with ... [and] ... Secondly, his extraordinary equanimity under the tremendous burden of work and responsibility which he supported virtually throughout the war' {*Times* 24 Apr 1971}. He was promoted to KCB in 1940, to GCB in 1942, and to the highest rank of Marshal of the RAF in 1944. In Churchill's resignation honours list he was created a baron, and in 1946 raised to a viscountcy and also made a member of the OM. In the same year he was one of the seven war leaders who were appointed Knights of the Garter. He also received numerous foreign honours and honorary doctorates.

Only eleven days after Portal had ceased to be Chief of Air Staff Attlee requested his help in developing an atomic programme. He at first declined, looking forward as he was to a business career in the City. However, he eventually accepted, as from March 1946, the post of Controller of Production, Atomic Energy, Ministry of Supply, at a salary of £3,000.

Although there was some hope of future peaceful nuclear power and although the formal decision to make a bomb was taken — at Portal's prompting — as late as January 1947, the production programme was from the outset primarily military. A reactor for plutonium production had been approved at the end of 1945. Portal's familiarity with the technical and military background of the subject and his sympathy with the idea of a national nuclear deterrent made him an obvious candidate.

Portal's position was peculiar. He was responsible to the Prime Minister not to the Minister of Supply, and he had no written terms of reference. Although he was Controller of Production it was expected that he would exercise general co-ordination between the various parts of the emerging project: research under John Cockcroft, production of fissile material under Christopher Hinton (qv) and bomb fabrication under William Penney. In this Portal was not very successful: as one critic writes '... the overall direction and control of the atomic energy project within the Ministry of Supply was weak. Apart from the organisational difficulties, Portal himself was drained by the war, had no experience of a production organisation and had little taste for the atomic energy job ... In general ... he was remote and unbending and made little attempt to interfere' {Gowing (1974) 1, 45}. In particular, Hinton, who came directly under Portal, felt that he had little enthusiasm for the work and did not give him the necessary support.

However, at the level of Cabinet Ministers and the Chiefs of Staff, Portal's prestige was very high and his views carried great weight. He always won his battles for top priority rating for atomic weapons against other military claims. By the time Portal resigned in August 1951 the production of plutonium was assured and the design of the bomb well advanced, leading to the first British test in October 1952.

Portal, quietly refusing an offer from Churchill to take over at the Ministry of Defence, now turned his attention to a career in the City. He had accepted his first directorship at Barclays Bank DCO within three weeks of resigning as the Chief of Air Staff — a result of his friendship with the chairman, Sir William Goodenough (qv). During 1949-60 he was on the board of Commercial Union Assurance. In 1949 he was invited to serve on the board of the Ford Motor Co of Britain which was progressing rapidly under the skilful direction of Sir Patrick Hennessy (qv). In 1960 when Ford Motors of USA made a takeover bid for the equity of Fords of Dagenham, Portal sold his personal holding of 2,000 shares for £14,500, finally retiring from the board in 1964. Portal derived much satisfaction from these directorships and boardroom friendships, though his experiences were less than happy as chairman from 1953 of the British Aluminium Co. In 1958 his lack of business and commercial experience became evident when British Aluminium unsuccessfully fought off a take-over bid by the American giant Reynolds Metal. Portal relinquished the post in 1959 with compensation of £30,000 and within two months became chairman of the British Match Corporation, succeeding his sponsor Lord Kindersley (qv).

The Reynolds Metal takeover had exposed Portal's limitations in the role of figurehead, but he was more successful as an 'independent' chairman at the British Aircraft Corporation, a post he accepted on 1 June 1960, four months after its formation. Since it was envisaged that the early problems of the BAC — a Government-backed merger of Vickers, English Electric and Bristols, designed to create a firm efficient enough to compete in the international market — would be more concerned with higher policy and financial, contractual, and sales aspects than manufacture, Lord Knollys (qv), chairman of Vickers and a fellow director of Portal's at Barclays, suggested making the chairmanship non-executive and inviting Portal to take it on. Portal, though now sixty-seven, heavily influenced by the claims of duty and the national interest, agreed, resigning from Commercial Union, but at first retaining his other directorships including a newly-acquired seat at Portals Ltd (the paper firm run by the other branch of the family).

From 1960 Portal steered the BAC through its formative problems, and then through the successive crises of the cancellation of the TSR2 and the period when it nearly went out of business as the Government attempted to squeeze it into compliance and merger with its rivals at the end of 1965. One of the mainsprings of the BAC's comeback from these reverses was the exceptionally harmonious relationship between Portal and his ebullient managing director, Sir George Edwards (qv). According to Edwards: 'the inspired choice of Lord Portal as BAC's first chairman — and his selfless acceptance of the invitation to take the chair (which he regarded as a duty) — was the biggest single unifying factor around which we all gathered' {Gardner (1981) 9}. In 1965 profit after tax was only £104,000 and in 1966 it was little better at £201,000. But matters improved towards the end of the decade: by 1968 net profit after tax was £4.2 million and thereafter performance was good, with new orders exceeding £200 million for the first time in 1971, heralding an outstanding order book position in the early 1970s. Portal retired at the end of 1968 and was succeeded by Sir Reginald Verdon-Smith.

Portal spent his retirement at his restored eighteenth century house at West Ashling, Chichester. He was heavily involved in Service charities, serving as deputy chairman of the Council of the RAF Benevolent Fund and president of the RAF Escaping Society, and in benevolent work for the Dominion Students Hall Trust and King Edward VII Hospital at Midhurst.

In his prime Portal was tall, slim, and dark-haired, his features dominated by the famous 'Portal' nose. At work he was a punctilious man, invariably courteous, but also withdrawn (uniquely amongst his contemporaries he wrote no record of his life) and made little attempt to talk to others about his outside life and interests, leading one friend to conclude that 'except for his family and close friends [he was] more interested in things than in people'{Richards (1977) 175}.

He married on 22 July 1919 Joan Margaret, youngest daughter of Sir Charles Glynne Earle Welby, Fifth Baronet, in a family of Lincolnshire landowners. Apart from a son who died in infancy, they had two daughters: Rosemary Ann (b 1923) and Mavis Elizabeth Alouette (b 1926), who was handicapped. Portal died from cancer at his home on 22 April 1971, leaving £85,438 gross.

GEOFFREY TWEEDALE

Writings:

letter on Middle East *Times* 6 Nov 1956.

farewell address *Airframe* Dec 1968.

Portal also published a number of articles on military matters and falconry, which are listed in Richards, below.

Sources:

Unpublished

BCe.

MCe.

PrC.

Published

Airframe June 1971.

George Bull and Anthony Vice, *Bid for Power* (Elek Books, 3rd ed, 1961).

Burke's Peerage and Baronetage 1980.

Charles Gardner, *British Aircraft Corporation. A History* (Batsford, 1981).

Margaret Gowing, *Independence and Deterrence. Britain and Atomic Energy, 1945-1952* (2 vols, Macmillan, 1974).

Denis Richards, *Portal of Hungerford* (Heinemann, 1977).

Times 24 Apr 1971.

WWW.

POSNETT, Robert Harold

(1869-1929)

Leather manufacturer

Robert Harold Posnett was born at Wakefield on 1 April 1869, the third son of Rev Robert Posnett, a Wesleyan Methodist minister, and his wife May Annie whose father, William Walker, had moved from Darlington to Bolton in 1823 and started a tanning business. His father was posted to several different churches in Robert's childhood and Robert attended Grove School and Kingswood School, Bath, the school for Wesleyan Methodist ministers' sons. After matriculating in 1885 he commenced his apprenticeship under his cousin, C E Parker, at the Penketh Tanning Co Ltd, near Warrington. Three years later he became managing foreman, at 25s a week, to the Highfield Tanning Co, Runcorn, which had just been taken over by his uncles Thomas and William Walker of Bolton. Under Robert Posnett's management the tannery increased enormously in size and efficiency and his interests expanded rapidly. In 1894 he became one of the first directors of the Liverpool Tanning Co Ltd and over the next twenty years became a director, or associated with Highfield, Tanning Co, Penketh Co, Union Tanneries, Guest Bros, Oak Tanning Co, the Latchford Tanning Co and the Camden Tanning Co. In Liverpool, Warrington and the north-west counties during the period 1891-1911 the number of workers employed in tanning and fellmongering increased sharply from 21 per cent to 33 per cent of the national total which remained almost unchanged. Liverpool and Warrington became the main centres for heavy leather tanning; not only was there increasing demand which was met by imported hides especially from South America but the port charges in Liverpool were lower than those at London. Liverpool also brought in dressed hides from the United States which posed a severe threat to the English industry. In 1900-4 when the competition was most severe, 418,000 cwt of dressed leather (valued at £3.75 million) was imported against 890,000 cwt of undressed leather (valued at £4.3 million).

This period brought the closure of many small businesses while the possibilities of economies of scale through mechanisation were greater in the heavy leather sector; the Highfield and Penketh works were amongst the earliest provided with the most modern equipment available. Experiments were also being undertaken at this time in using mixed tannage extracts in the manufacture of heavy leather leading to a recognition of the importance of leather chemistry. Generally the British tanning industry was slower than the German or American industries to take up mineral rather than vegetable tanning. Chrome tanning required technical understanding and scientific control and there were technical problems in the manufacture of chrome-tanned leather for shoes. It was not until 1918 in response to a request from the War Office that Posnett started production of chrome sole leather at Central Tanneries, Warrington. He was certainly not alone in being slow to adopt chrome tanning methods which had been common for twenty years in the United States and Germany, which provided the main competition to the English tanneries. Rimmer and Church suggest that there was a 'generation gap', an unwillingness to abandon methods which had brought prosperity in the past and an inability to accept the need for close technical control of the process.

During the First World War, Posnett was very active in meeting the demands of the War Office, for example through starting chrome tanning, and was also very active through the United Tanners' Federation (formed in 1908 from the Manchester, Liverpool and District Tanneries Federation to recapture the home market from the Americans). He negotiated with the Government's Raw Materials Department, especially the fixing of fair prices. In view of his many trips to London, he managed to persuade the railway to stop the sleeper express especially for him at Runcorn.

In 1920 Posnett was a leading figure in the establishment of British Tanners Ltd, a buying house designed to reduce competition among the tanners and to secure better prices in their raw material markets; this supplied a number of independent tanneries which, however, had family links. He also joined the board of Lotus Ltd which was headed by Henry Bostock (qv) . In 1929 the Highfield Tanning Co (registered 1888) had an authorised capital of £500,000; the issued capital included £4,850 of employees' shares. In addition to a director from Lotus, Highfield also had a Walker from William Walkers of Bolton, Posnett's maternal grandfather's tanning business (registered as a limited company in 1895) which had an authorised capital of £600,000. Neither Walkers nor Highfield published accounts.

Posnett's development of successful tanneries employing 1,000 men in Runcorn was particularly welcome, as the chemical trade had been diverted elsewhere on the formation of the United Alkali Co and unemployment was rife.

Posnett was elected a member of the Runcorn Council when he was only twenty-seven and served for thirty years, five times as chairman. He became a JP in 1907, a county councillor on 1910 and a county alderman in the year of his death.

Posnett was a liveryman of the Worshipful Company of Leathersellers, and a freeman of the City of London. Throughout his life he was a keen sportsman. He strongly supported the Wesleyan Church at Runcorn and for twenty-five years represented the Liverpool district at the Wesleyan Conference. His younger brother, Charles, became a prominent missionary in India. He was a very generous benefactor to his church, his old school at Bath, of which he was a governor, and the town. He purchased land at Runcorn, cleared the slum dwellings and presented the land to the town for recreation purposes. 'He has been the leader of every movement which has been for the betterment of its inhabitants' {Gittings (1925)}.

In 1894 he married Fanny, the third daughter of Robert Garnett, a cabinet manufacturer of Penketh; they had two sons and two surviving daughters. The son, Charles Christopher (b 1903), succeeded his father in his various tanning interests.

Robert Harold Posnett died on 17 May 1929, leaving £470,469 gross.

FRANCIS GOODALL *and* DAVID J JEREMY

Sources:

Unpublished

BCe.

PrC.

Memorandum on his father by Charles Christopher Posnett.

Memorandum: Matters Personal and Public in the Life of R H Posnett submitted by William Gittings, Chairman of Runcorn UDC, 1925: copy in *DBB* files.

Published

British Sports and Sportsmen 1930.

Arthur B Butman, *Shoe and Leather Trade in the United Kingdom* (Washington: US Department of Commerce and Labour, Special Agent Series 9, 1912).

Roy A Church, 'The British Leather Industry and Foreign Competition, 1870-1914' *Economic History Review* 2nd ser 24 (1971).

DD 1929.

W G Rimmer, 'Leeds Leather Industry in the Nineteenth Century' *Thoresby Society Miscellany* 46 (1960).

Runcorn Guardian 18 May 1929.

F Colyer Sackett, *Posnett of Medak* (Cargate Press, 1951).

Stock Exchange Official Intelligence 1929.

Warrington Examiner 25 May 1929.

PREECE, Sir William Henry

(1834-1913)

Consulting electrical engineer

Sir William Preece (from the Electrician *vol 18, 8 April 1887).*

William Henry Preece was born at Caernarvon, North Wales, on 15 February 1834, the eldest surviving son of Richard Mathias Preece, then on the staff of a local bank but formerly a school teacher in Glamorgan, and a well-known Wesleyan Methodist preacher (in Welsh and English), and his wife Jane, daughter of John Hughes, a Caernarvon shipbuilder. Richard Preece, having twice been mayor of Caernarvon, decided in 1845 to move to London to give more scope for himself and his numerous family. William was sent to the strictly Anglican King's College School and received some training at King's College, London. His father suffered heavy financial losses in 1848 and 1851 with the result that William had to leave college and could not be commissioned into the army as his father had hoped. Instead he entered the engineering profession in 1852 in the office of Edwin Clark (1814-94), engineer with the Electrical & International Telegraph Co. Here in 1853-54 he worked closely with Faraday who was studying electromagnetism at the Royal Institution.

Preece was promoted to superintendent of the Southern district of the E&ITCo in 1856, with headquarters at Southampton; in 1858 he was additionally appointed engineer to the Channel Islands Telegraph Co; and in 1860 he was also appointed to the post of superintendent in the London & South Western Railway Co, with the task of organising a telegraph system for that company. He held all three posts simultaneously for a time. On the nationalisation of telegraphs in 1870, Preece became a Divisional Engineer in the Post Office, becoming Electrician in 1877 and Engineer-in-Chief in 1892; he retired from the Post Office in 1899.

In his official career in the Post Office, Preece was responsible for many technical innovations, and although not an inventor himself, he was quick to see the possibilities of other people's ideas. The British telegraph system was technically one of the best in the world, and Preece adopted several advanced systems (eg quadruplex working in 1879 and the Delany multiplex system in 1886) to preserve its leadership. He took up telephony actively after Bell's demonstration of 1876, although he appeared to subscribe to the general British Government view of the 1880s that telephony had somewhat limited potential in comparison with telegraphy. Nevertheless, he made experiments in long-distance telephony, developed an erroneous theory of it, and in spite of this, engineered a highly-successful cross-Channel telephone link providing speech communication between London and Paris in 1891. When the Post Office obtained the monopoly of trunk telephony in 1895, Preece was responsible for the upgrading and extension of the national long-distance telephone network.

Preece had developed ideas on wireless communication from his observation of interference effects between telegraph and telephone lines, and demonstrated wireless telegraphy from Portsmouth to the Isle of Wight in 1882. Later on he set up a permanent wireless link to the island of Flat Holm in the Bristol Channel. These were conductive or inductive systems. When Marconi approached him in 1896 with his wireless system based on electromagnetic radiation, Preece seems to have seen the potential of this new approach and collaborated in experiments in 1897; unfortunately by 1900 he had lost faith in Marconi.

Preece had a private consulting practice for many years while in the Post Office, and continued consulting long after his retirement. He had been taking an interest in the developments in electricity generation and in electric lighting in the 1870s and had started to take part in the discussions at meetings concerned with these topics at least as early as the end of 1878. As with telecommunications, he was sometimes badly wrong in his opinions; for instance, in 1879 he stated that 'a subdivision of the electric light is an absolute ignis fatuus' { *Telegraphic Journal* (1879) 60}, by which he meant that parallel operation of incandescent lamps was impossible; yet it was precisely on the basis of parallel operation of incandescent lamps that electric lighting systems developed. He published his first paper on electric lighting in 1881, but had given a public lecture on the subject at the Albert Hall in 1880.

He was consultant to the Bristol Corporation in 1884 and submitted his first report to them on 4 December 1884, recommending them not to proceed with setting up an electric lighting system until the science and art were more advanced. He submitted similar reports on 16 October 1885 and on 20 September 1887, but on 31 May 1889 he advised that the time was now ripe for the Corporation to go ahead, the recent improvements in plant having been very significant and the financial situation being more suitable. Preece then became responsible for the preparation of plans and specifications and for supervising the contractors; he employed Gisbert Kapp (qv) as his assistant. He managed to find time to attend meetings of the Corporation and its committees at Bristol every few weeks. The Bristol Central Electric Lighting Station opened in 1893, but Preece remained as consultant at Bristol for many years. Although demand quickly outstripped the capacity of the station, it was technically very satisfactory.

Preece was adviser and supervisor for the Worcester electricity undertaking, 1892-94. This was Britain's largest nineteenth century hydro-electric station used for public supply, with a water-generated capacity of about 400 kW. It was partially successful, and endured for over fifty years, but the hydraulic calculations were defective, and it was often short of water.

As an example of his activity, during the two years 1892-93, Preece was, in addition to his work at Bristol and Worcester, consultant to at least 11 other electric light schemes, having in every case to visit the place concerned, study its problems, and prepare a report making definite technical and financial recommendations — sometimes a good deal more than this. In one or two cases he worked with his son, A H Preece, who was also a consulting engineer.

In slightly different fields, Preece was consultant to the Government on lighting the House of Commons as well as lighting in Malta and Gibraltar, the British Museum and the Dublin Museum; in 1894 he was consultant to the Commission of Sewers regarding gas explosions in the City of London;

and in 1895 was a member, with Lord Kelvin and Major Cardew, of the Board of Trade Committee appointed to report on the proposed new electric lighting regulations.

Preece's extensive private practice did not escape the eye of parliament; questions were asked in the Commons as to how a full-time civil servant could be allowed to do this private work, which was against the rules. The official answer on 20 May 1892 was 'That the case of Mr Preece is exceptional' {*PD* 4th ser 4 col 1442} and no action was to be taken to hinder him.

Preece was distinguished by administrative ability and some scientific and technical insight, but above all by his immense industry, incredible activity, and remarkable breadth of interest. Throughout most of his working life he successfully conducted several professional careers simultaneously, each one of which would be regarded as a full-time job by most people. In addition to various branches of electrical engineering, he took an interest in several other technical fields; eg sanitary engineering, on which subject — concentrating mainly on water supply and sewage disposal — he gave the inaugural address as president to the 1899 Congress of the Sanitary Institute. He published profusely. It is difficult to make an accurate count of his published papers and lectures, for not only were most of them reprinted in several journals, but he frequently gave substantially the same paper to several societies and institutions. However, a reasonably reliable figure is 136 separate papers and printed lectures, although their contents overlap a good deal. Of these, no fewer than 99 belong to his specially-productive period, 1877-94. In addition to the papers and printed lectures, there were innumerable published contributions to discussions and many unpublished lectures. He was a very popular public speaker.

In recognition of his work, Preece was elected president of the Society of Telegraph Engineers (later the Institution of Electrical Engineers) in 1880 and again in 1893, and of the Institution of Civil Engineers in 1898-99. He was elected FRS in 1881 and knighted in 1899.

Preece was connected by his sisters' marriages to the leading telegraph engineers, Latimer Clark and F C Webb. He himself in 1863 married Agnes, daughter of George Pocock, a solicitor, of Southampton; she died in 1874 after bearing seven children. Thereafter Preece's eldest sister, Jane Elizabeth, herself unmarried, looked after him and his family at Gothic Lodge, Wimbledon. Sir William Preece died at Caernarvon on 6 November 1913 leaving £32,320 gross.

D G TUCKER

Writings:

Preece's writings were extremely numerous. A comprehensive bibiliography was compiled in 1974 by Mary Lane and Joyce Bartle and is available in typescript form in the Library of the Department of Electronic and Electrical Engineering at the University of Birmingham and in the Archives Department of the Institution of Electrical Engineers. A select bibliography is appended to Baker, *Preece*, below.

(with Sir James Sivewright) *Telegraphy* (Longmans Green & Co, 1870 and many other editions until 1914).

Sources:

Unpublished

Institution of Electrical Engineers, London, archives.

Post Office RO, London, Preece Collection.

MCe.

PrC.

Published

Edward C Baker, *Sir William Preece, FRS* (pp, 1976).

Engineer 14 Nov 1913.

P D, 4th Ser, 4, Col 1442 (20 May 1892).

Telegraphic Journal 1879.

D G Tucker, 'The First Cross-Channel Telephone Cable: The London-Paris Telephone Links of 1891' *Transactions of the Newcomen Society* 47 (1974-76).

—, 'Sir William Preece (1834-1913)' *ibid* 53 (1981-82).

WWW.

PRICE, Sir William

(1865-1938)

Milk retailer and wholesaler

William Price was born in the parish of Llanwrtyd Wells, near Brecon in 1865, the sixth of at least nine children born to William Price, a farmer and his wife Magdalene. Little else is known of his background or early education. His migration to London in the early 1880s followed a well-worn path trodden by generations of other Welshmen of similarly humble rural origins. The milk trade was their introduction to the harsh realities of city life, but at least it was a familiar employment in an otherwise alien environment. When he first came to London (he and his wife, whom he married in 1885, became members of the Welsh Presbyterian Church in Shirland Road, Paddington, in 1886) William Price found himelf staring at the premises of the famous Aylesbury Dairy Co in St Petersburgh Place, but lacking the courage to go in and ask for a job. He later had the unusual experience of buying the Aylesbury for United Dairies, and using those same offices as his headquarters.

Rather than risk rebuff by the prestigious Aylesbury Dairy Co, Price decided to set up a business on his own. He bought a small retail dairy in

West London and, helped by his wife, he was able to build up wholesale custom also. Eventually he joined John Hopkins as a partner in Great Western & Metropolitan Dairies, which in 1915 was one of the firms to join the new United Dairies combine. William Price was the moving spirit behind the subsequent merger of several large London retail milk companies with United Dairies, which in 1917 gave it a quasi-monopoly over London's milk trade.

William Price had a genius for friendship; he had friends in every walk of life, and his contacts and ability to communicate his ideas were of assistance throughout his career. He was confident, assured and determined, and acquired the nickname of 'the General' in the trade. His formidable organisational abilities were enhanced by the delegation of everyday details to his assistants and by his forthrightness in business dealings.

These various qualities of character and personality were tested to the limit during the First World War when the need to supply London with milk had to be balanced against the demand for milk products by the Forces in France. Price helped to organise collections of milk from small producers all over the country whose supplies had hitherto not been called upon for town consumption. In those years he was never far from the telephone and regularly worked a seventeen-hour day. During the General Strike of 1926 he repeated the exercise and, as chairman of the London Milk (Emergency) Committee and London's milk controller, was second in command to Wilfred Buckley (1873-1933) as Emergency Milk Commissioner at the Board of Trade. Price organised a milk pool in Hyde Park and kept the milk flowing at a time when it might otherwise have been thought that the intricate structure of the city's supply must inevitably break down.

He was knighted in 1922 for services to the nation's milk industry and in 1923 500 people attended a dinner to celebrate the honour. His contribution to the various trade organisations was energetic. He was a president of the Metropolitan Dairymen's Benevolent Institution (Incorporated), a delegate at the foundation of the National Milk Publicity Council in 1920, an initiator of the United Dairies Benefit Society, a president of the National Federation of Dairymen's Associations, and a leader of the distributor's side of the Permanent Joint Milk Committee, formed in 1922. His bitter disappointment was the failure of his National Scheme for the Sale and Purchase of Milk, first recommended by the Permanent Joint Milk Committee in June 1929. This scheme was never put into operation because of the opposition of vested interests in the trade.

He was a JP for London (1916). From 1901 he was an elder of the Presbyterian Church of Wales in Shirland Road, Paddington, and later its treasurer. In 1912 he was instrumental in clearing the debt of £42,000 burdening the denomination's churches in the London Association. He had residences in Cambridge Gardens, North Kensington, and Church End, Finchley, where he retired after ill-health forced him to leave active business after 1929. His work was continued by his sons Ivor and Tudor. Sir William Price died on 16 April 1938, leaving £48,165 gross.

P J ATKINS

Writings:

'The Settlement' *Milk Industry* 6 (1925).

'A Few Words to the Trade' *Milk Industry* 6 (1926).

Sources:

Unpublished

PRO, 1871 census returns.

PrC.

Information from Mr Meurig Owen and Mrs Gwenda Thompson, London.

Published

Brecon and Radnor Express and County Times 28 Apr 1938.

Burke's Peerage, Baronetage and Knightage 1931.

Dairyman, Cowkeeper and Dairyman's Journal 60 (1938).

Dairy World 47 (1938).

Ben Davies, 'Sir William Price' *Our Notebook* (United Dairies Ltd house magazine) 18 (July 1938).

A G Enock, *This Milk Business: A Study from 1895 to 1943* (H K Lewis & Co, 1943).

Kelly's Handbook to the Titled, Landed and Official Classes 1924.

A Jenkins, *Drinka Pinta: The Story of Milk and the Industry That Serves It* (Heinemann, 1970).

Milk Industry 18 (1938).

B Morgan, *Express Journey 1864-1964* (Newman Neame, 1964).

Times 18 Apr 1938.

WWW.

PRIESTMAN, Francis

(1855-1936)

Colliery owner

Francis Priestman was born at Shotley Bridge in County Durham on 25 August 1855, the son of Jonathan Priestman, the founder of Priestman Collieries Ltd, and his wife Lucy Ann née Richardson. He came from a

Quaker family and was educated at Hollymount School, Malvern, and at Rugby.

He became chairman of Priestman Collieries in County Durham when his father died in 1888 leaving an estate valued at £103,236 gross. At the same time Francis became a partner in, and later chairman of, the Ashington Coal Co in Northumberland in which his father had purchased an eighth share in 1869. It was to these two companies that the bulk of his working life was devoted. Under his management both expanded, the former to command an annual output in 1913 of some 1.25 million tons, whilst the latter was to become the leading export firm in the North East with an annual production of 2.25 million tons. Both were privately-owned family firms in which the Priestmans held the majority of shares.

Francis Priestman's public life was not an intensive one, although he did become a JP for the County of Durham, a life governor of the Newcastle Infirmary, and in 1914 DL and High Sheriff of Durham. In addition to his chairmanship of the Priestman Collieries and the Ashington Coal Co, he was chairman of the Priestman Power Co Ltd, and a director of the Newcastle & Gateshead Gas Co, Martin's Bank, the North British & Mercantile Insurance Co Ltd, and the Tyneside Industrial Trust Ltd.

Priestman in 1883 married Cecil Marguerite, daughter of Dr Shiel of Chester-le-Street in County Durham. They had two sons, Francis Noel (who died an infant) and Jonathan Lee, and two daughters, Faith Hadwyn and Zaida Nell. Francis Priestman died on 28 February 1936 and left a personal estate valued at £219,988 gross.

A A HALL

Sources:

Unpublished

Northumberland CRO, Ashington Coal Co papers.

BCe.

MCe.

PrC.

R W Martin (comp), 'Northern Worthies' vol 1 (1932), Newcastle upon Tyne City Library.

Published

Burke's Landed Gentry.

James Jamieson, *Northumberland at the Opening of the Twentieth Century* (Brighton: W T Pike & Co, 1905).

Sir John Priestman (courtesy of J F Clarke).

PRIESTMAN, Sir John

(1855-1941)

Shipbuilder and industrialist

John Priestman was born at Bishop Auckland, County Durham, on 22 March 1855, the son of Robert Priestman, a master baker, and his wife Jane née Smith. His father died when he was young and nothing is known of his education. As a boy he entered the shipyard of J Bulmer on Wearside at the time when the yard was beginning to build ships of iron.

Priestman must have displayed ability for he secured the necessary drawing office experience to enable him to move as chief draughtsman to the nearby shipyard of William Pickersgill (qv). At the age of twenty-five, he designed Pickersgills' first iron ship the *SS Camargo*. Only two years later, in a rising boom of shipbuilding, Priestman opened his own shipyard at Southwick on the River Wear and launched a total of 2,984 tons in 1882. During the next year output increased to 7,553 tons, which was more than the total output during the following five years; in 1887 Priestman's yard was idle. Much determination was displayed by the young man in persisting in such a hazardous industry. He was one of the Wear shipbuilders who restored the wood shipyard practice of day rates rather than piecework during the late 1880s depression. By 1890 he had recovered and that year his yard's output exceeded 10,000 tons, a level that was doubled by the end of the decade, largely due to Priestman's business connections with many Continental shipowners. His yard, of which he remained sole proprietor, had three berths up to 450 feet long and was capable of an annual output of up to 40,000 tons. The yard's output in the First World War was 16 ships, totalling 67,255 tons, with four more under construction at the Armistice.

Priestman's main contribution to shipbuilding lay in the design of tramp steamers. He built the first 'self-trimming trunk vessel', according to the specifications of his 1894 patent, for a Norwegian owner. These vessels incorporated characteristics of the cantilever designs of Raylton Dixon (qv), and reportedly 'found great favour with owners' {*Shipbuilder* 48 (1941) 30}. He also introduced a tower deck design in response to Doxford's (qv) 'turret deck design' of 1892.

The post-1920 depression in shipbuilding did not spare Priestman's yard: only 4,274 tons were built in 1921 and none at all in 1922 and 1926. Output for the whole of the 1920s averaged only 9,608 tons per annum; in 1930-34 the annual average was 9,016 tons and in two of these years the yard was idle. The last ship built was sold by auction in 1933 after standing for years on the stocks. Playing tennis on the empty slipway in the early years with his manager and building on 'spec' may have reflected an underlying optimism in John Priestman, who clearly wanted to design and build ships. However, his very large fortune was being made elsewhere, largely in South African gold mine investments. Surprisingly he did not participate in or belong to any of the technical institutions.

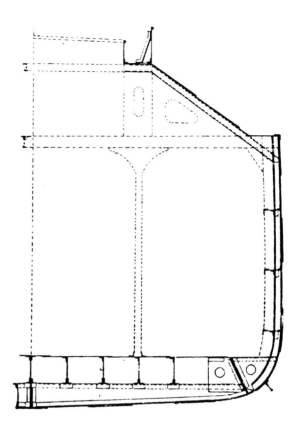

*Priestman's self trimmer SS
'Universe' 1898 from the transactions
of Royal Institute of Naval
Architects.*

His many widespread shipping interests resulted in chairmanships of the
Enfield Steamship Co (of Sunderland), Cliffside Steamship Co (of
Newcastle upon Tyne) and the Brinkburn SS Co. His colliery investments
led to his chairmanship of Bullock's Hall Colliery Co Ltd. He was also a
director of Elswick Coal Co, the Newcastle upon Tyne branch of the
Phoenix Assurance Co and the Sunderland & South Shields Water Co.

A Conservative in politics, Priestman served on the Southwick Urban
District Council for twenty-three years, twenty-one of these as chairman;
he was also a county councillor and a member of the local School Board. A
member of the River Wear Commission, and for many years a JP in
Sunderland (from 1901), he was made a freeman of the town in 1933. He
was a keen organist, serving as president of the Sunderland Organists'
Association, and donated organs to many churches. An active Anglican,
his second wife was the sister of the vicar of St Andrews, Roker, where he
himself was organist and where he endowed a parish hall. It was estimated
that he distributed half a million pounds in his charitable bequests, which
included churches, hospitals (including £50,000 to Durham County and
Sunderland Eye Infirmary and £100,000 used for building Haig homes for
ex-servicemen) and clothing for the poor children (for which he set up a
£100,000 trust in the early 1930s). He donated £20,000 for the Sunderland
Technical College Library which was opened in 1939.

John Priestman was knighted in 1923 and made a baronet in 1934.

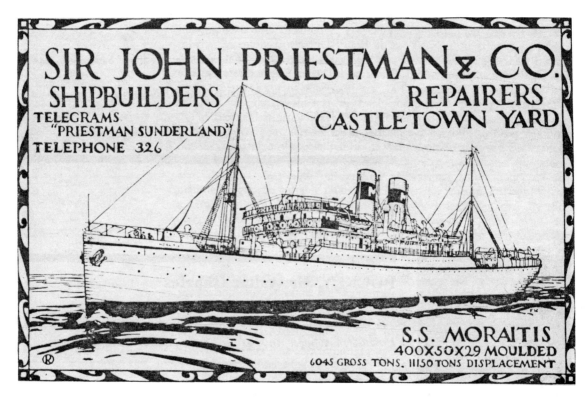

Advertisement for Sir John Priestman & Co shipbuilders from 'Port of Sunderland Handbook' (1929).

Priestman married twice, firstly in 1880 to Naomi, fourth daughter of D T Huntley, and secondly in 1915 to Sarah Marie, daughter of Dr Arthur Pownall of Manchester. Their only child was a daughter, Barbara Marie.

Sir John Priestman died at Tyringham, Harrowgate, County Durham, on 5 August 1941, leaving £1,504,774 gross.

J F CLARKE

Sources:

Unpublished

Sunderland Public Library, Corder MSS.

BCe.

MCe.

PrC.

Published

Engineer 172 (1941).

the sitting MP and the local Liberal association, Pugh put up an alternative official Liberal candidate in opposition to the former MP who stood as an independent Liberal — neither was elected. Pugh was keenly interested in education (he served on the education committee from 1904 onwards). He pressed for the establishment of a new technical college and was a member of the Board of Governors of Birmingham University.

Charles Pugh died at Bognor on 23 August 1921 leaving a widow, Mary Frances (daughter of Edward Smith, a farmer) whom he had married in 1902, five sons and two daughters. His estate was valued at £48,990 gross.

J LOWE

Sources:

Unpublished

BCe.

MCe.

PrC.

Published

Anthony C Bird and Francis H Scott, *Lanchester Motor Cars — A History* (Cassell & Co, 1965).

Coventry Herald 26 Aug 1921.

Coventry Standard 26 Jan, 9 Nov 1900, 8 Nov 1901, 26 Aug 1921.

Cycle Manufacturers' and Dealers' Review 30 Mar 1895, 26 Apr 1902.

Cycling 1 Sept 1921.

A E Harrison, 'Joint-Stock Company Flotation in the Cycle, Motor Vehicle and Related Industries 1882-1914' *Business History* 23 (1981).

Peter W Kingsford, *F W Lanchester: A Life of an Engineer* (Edward Arnold, 1960).

Midland Daily Telegraph 24 Aug 1921.

Bryan Reynolds, *Don't Trudge It, Rudge It* (Yeovil: Haynes Publishing Group, 1977).

The Rudge Record — The Monthly House Journal of Rudge-Whitworth Ltd Aug and Sept 1908.

Stock Exchange Official Year Book 1961, 1962.

Times 25 Aug 1921.

Tit-Bits 11 Jan 1896.

PYBUS, Sir Percy John

(1880-1935)

Electrical and cement manufacturer, insurance chairman and newspaper publisher

Percy John Pybus (usually known as John Pybus) was born at Kingston-upon-Hull, Yorkshire, on 25 January 1880, one of the three sons of John Pybus (1845-1929), stationer and newspaper compositor of Sculcoates, and his wife Alice née Posthill (1850-1926). His father was a leading Wesleyan in Hull, becoming a town councillor for Beverley Ward (1898), a member of Hull Board of Guardians (1896), an alderman (1918) and sitting on numerous municipal and charitable committees, including Hull Electricity Committee. He left £688 in 1929.

As a boy in Hull, young Pybus neglected his homework to study electricity, and his father, on discovering this, built him a shed where he could experiment and then apprenticed him to a firm of Hull engineers. He later entered the Woolwich works of Siemens as a junior, and was subsequently transferred by the company to their works at Stafford, where during the First World War he was engaged on munitions contracts. Under the wartime Trading with the Enemy Acts, Siemens' Stafford factory passed first into the control of the Public Trustee and then in 1917 into that of the financier Birch Crisp (qv). In 1919 it was absorbed into the newly formed English Electric Co (EECo), together with other factories at Rugby, Preston, Bradford, Coventry and Scotstoun. Pybus was appointed managing director of English Electric in March 1921, and succeeded Sir Charles Ellis as chairman in April 1926.

The constituent companies of EECo included the former Willans & Robinson steam turbine and oil engine factory at Rugby; the United Electric Car Co of Preston; the Phoenix Dynamo Manufacturing Co of Bradford (alternators and motors); the Coventry Ordnance Works; and the Dick Kerr lamp factory at Preston (capable of making 5 million lamps per annum). English Electric's board included nominees from the four armament companies which had been interested in Coventry Ordnance before 1918: Lionel Hichens (qv) of Cammell Laird, Sir Charles Ellis and John Sampson of John Brown, Bernard Firth of Firths, and Sir Alexander Gracie of Fairfield Shipbuilding. From the outset EECo specialised in heavy electrical equipment under a twenty-five year agreement with Siemens which allocated light equipment as the latter's speciality. The two businesses collaborated in a joint lamp business until 1927, when EECo made an unwise decision to sell their half-share for £75,000.

EECo failed to justify the hopes of its promoters in 1919. It suffered 'from an insufficient understanding of the need for careful costing in this highly competitive industry and from a top management overweighed with prestige and too far away from the operating centres' {Jones and Marriott (1970) 130}. It had insufficient capital available for investment, and

suffered from the high cost of annually servicing debentures totalling
£2,180,816 in 1925. It was consistently less successful than its main British
rivals, General Electric of Hugo Hirst (qv) and Metropolitan-Vickers,
whose managing director was then Robert Hilton (qv). Although Pybus
was an energetic and conscientious businessman, he was also self-critical,
over-anxious and highly strung. His responsibilities at EECo, and its bad
results in the 1920s, preyed on his nerves. Pybus was sent abroad for a rest
in the summer of 1925, in which year EECo passed its ordinary dividend;
in 1926 even the preference shareholders received a mere 3 per cent; and in
the following five years to 1931, EECo met no more than its interest
charges. Pybus seems to have broken down in 1927, when he was
succeeded as chairman in October by Lionel Hichens, and again in 1929
when he finally left the EECo board. Before his resignation in 1929, he
spent some weeks in Egypt trying to win railway electrification contracts
for EECo which had been jeopardised by a clumsy attempt at bribery by
EECo's joint managing director, Vernon Watlington. There was
'abominable mud-slinging and vituperation' in Egypt between Pybus and
the Duke of Atholl (representing Dudley Docker (qv) on behalf of
Metropolitan-Vickers and the Belgian trust, Sofina), and Pybus's
'despicable' part in 'this disgusting bickering' may have accelerated his
nervous collapse {PRO FO 371/13877, Lord Lloyd to Sir Ronald Lindsay,
21 Apr and 5 May 1929}. As it was, on a turnover of £2.75 million in 1929,
EECo lost £47,000 and with the assistance of Robert Brand of Lazards and
Sir Guy Granet (qqv) of Higginsons, it was reconstructed in 1930. George
Nelson (qv) then became managing director instead of Pybus and
Watlington, and Sir Holberry Mensforth (qv) succeeded Hichens as
chairman.

Pybus collected other business interests in the 1920s. He was a director
of The Times Publishing Co and its associates, and his representation of
the newspaper in the management of the *British Gazette* during the
General Strike of 1926 led one bureaucrat to write: 'He is a little terrier
and not afraid to bite' {Middlemas (1969) 55}. He was also on the boards
of Associated Portland Cement, British Portland Cement and Humber
Portland Cement. Other directorships such as of Société Hellénique
Générale, the Sudan Light & Power Co (from 1925), and of Power &
Traction Finance (and its Polish subsidiary), derived from his work with
EECo before 1929. Power & Traction financed and executed large
engineering schemes involving civil, mechanical and electrical work, and
in 1924-25 promoted the Lanarkshire Hydro-Electric Power Act to develop
the Falls of the Clyde.

In March 1927 Pybus joined the board of Phoenix Assurance, becoming
joint deputy chairman in November 1929 and chairman in June 1931.
Having contested Shipley as a Liberal in the general elections of 1923 and
1924, Pybus had won the Harwich seat for the Liberals in June 1929; in
September 1931, only three months after assuming the Phoenix
chairmanship, when he was in mid-Atlantic on his way to America on
Phoenix business, he received a wireless cable from the Prime Minister,
Ramsay MacDonald, asking him to become Minister of Transport in the
new National Government. He agreed, and immediately returned to
England, resigning all his directorships. As Minister of Transport, Pybus
guided through the House of Commons the controversial London

Passenger Transport Act of 1933 which effectively nationalised the transport interests headed by Lords Ashfield and Aberconway (qqv). His nervous and sensitive disposition suffered agonies from the hurly-burly of front-bench politics, and although he enjoyed and was reasonably competent at departmental administration, his resignation as Minister in February 1933 was no surprise. He had received a CBE in 1917 for his munitions work, and was created a baronet for political services in 1934.

Having left government office, Pybus rejoined the Phoenix board in March 1933, becoming chairman in June 1933, and was elected president of the Advertising Association in November 1934. He also returned to the boards of the *Times* and the cement companies, and was recruited to that of Metal Traders Ltd. Before receiving ministerial office, Pybus sat on the Royal Commission on the Civil Service in 1929-31, and was a member of the Balfour committee on trade and industry from 1924, the Development (Public Utility) Advisory Committee, the Committee on Education for Salesmanship in 1928-31, and the Unemployment Grants Committee during 1920-31. He was also a member of the Committee on the Classification and Definition of Firearms of 1934, and was largely responsible for ensuing legislation prohibiting the sale of firearms to persons aged under seventeen years or the possession of firearms by children under fourteen. Pybus was a delegate of King's College, London, from around 1924.

> He was the architect of his own fortunes, but was preserved from the worst failings and the most resounding triumphs of such men by an unusually keen sense of humour. His life was moulded by ... his experience as an apprentice in a general engineering shop 40 years ago, when hard work with no amenities was the rule ... He had a catholic appreciation of ingenious design and fine craftsmanship, whether in a machine, in furniture or in old silver, or in the latest attachment to a radio gramophone. He was once seen ... in some Continental Grand Babylonian Hotel to take from a waistcoat pocket and relight the snuffed out fag-end of a cigarette — a quite unconscious survival from the days when smoking in the shops was a practice both furtive and expensive {*Times* 26 Oct 1935}.

Quick in manner, excessively conscientious about his responsibilities, a severe asthmatic, Pybus seems to have been haunted by private anxieties and inner insecurities; in the last decade of his life he drove himself at his work despite almost incapacitating neurosis. The nervous strain broke his physical health in 1935, and after some months illness he died in a London nursing home on 23 October 1935, when his baronetcy became extinct. Pybus was unmarried, but for twelve years had a romance with Miss L E Bowyer-Bailey who lived in a flat above a Pimlico shop. Perhaps from some unspoken fear, he resisted her pleas for marriage, although very shortly before his death he apparently relented and agreed to a private engagement. Pybus left £93,951 gross. After bequests totalling £45,00 (including £10,000 each to Miss Bowyer-Bailey and his brother Sydney, and £5,000 to his brother Herbert), he left the residue in trust to assist the education and advancement of artisan youths aged under twenty-five born within twenty-five miles of Hull or Bradford.

R P T DAVENPORT-HINES

Writings:

articles on 'Trade Union Policy' *Times* 7, 8 Aug, 21 Sept 1923, reissued as a pamphlet, *Payment by Results* (1923).

letter on fiscal policy and wage inequalities *Times* 3 Apr 1924.

letter on industrial peace *ibid* 30 Mar 1925.

letters on British cars abroad 31 Dec 1930, 13 Jan 1931.

PP, Reports of Unemployment Grants Committee (1930) Cmd 3744,(1932) Cmd 4029, (1933) Cmd 4354.

PP, RC on the Civil Service (1931) Cmd 3909.

PP, Committee on Education for Salesmanship (1931).

letter on legible handwriting and the university franchise *Times* 21 Feb 1931.

letter on firearms sold to children *ibid* 13 Nov 1933.

letter on shorter working hours *ibid* 28 Nov 1934.

PP, Departmental Committee on Statutory Definition and Classification of Firearms and Ammunition (1934-35) Cmd 4758.

letter on business honesty *Times* 3 Apr 1935.

speech on medical advertising *ibid* 5 July 1935.

Sources:

Unpublished

Cambridge University Library, papers of Phoenix Assurance.

PRO, Kew, papers of Foreign Office.

BCe.

PrC.

Information from Mrs Hermione Hichens, Dec 1982.

Published

Burke's Peerage 1935.

Daily Express 7 Dec 1935.

Richard Davenport-Hines, *Dudley Docker* (Cambridge: Cambridge University Press, 1984).

Eastern Morning News 21 Sept 1929.

Robert Jones and Oliver J D Marriott, *Anatomy of a Merger: A History of GEC, AEI and English Electric* (Cape, 1970).

Robert Keith Middlemas (ed), *Thomas Jones's Whitehall Diary* (Cambridge: Cambridge University Press, 1969) 2.

Times 21 Sept 1929, 24, 25, 26 Oct 1935.

WWMP.

WWW.

Harold J Pye (courtesy of Mr H J Pye).

PYE, Harold John

(1901-)

Scientific instrument and radio manufacturer

Harold John Pye was born in Cambridge on 27 November 1901, the youngest son of William George Pye (qv) and his wife Annie Eliza née Atkins. His father, partnered by his grandfather, William Thomas Pye, had established the scientific instrument firm of W G Pye & Co in Cambridge. Harold early showed he had inherited their craft skills. Preparatory schooling in Cambridge preceded five years at Oundle, then three years at St John's College, Cambridge. In 1923 aged twenty-one, he graduated BA in physics, chemistry and physiology. His tutor E V Appleton who contributed much to radio science was technical adviser to W G Pye & Co.

Harold joined the family firm in 1923, shortly after it started wireless manufacturing, and he records that in five weeks on the road he sold not one of the '500' series receivers, beautifully made though they were. For a replacement, he designed the more sensitive '700' series which soon established the company's success as quality wireless manufacturers. In 1924 he became a partner. Always innovative, he sometimes failed to have his ideas adopted; his introduction of moulded bakelite components was not the precursor of a large plastics moulding plant as he wished. His university background, and mechanical precision, facilitated co-operation with leading medical and scientific figures in the development of specialised research instrumentation, notably in encephalography, cardiography, pH metering and X-ray analysis. The introduction of fire loaded Timken Taper roller-bearings as now used on most machine tools was his idea. For tool making he introduced a method of optical measurement for precision setting of a simple jig boret maintaining accuracy regardless of wear or inaccuracy of the machine, it could be applied to any machine.

In 1928, after much uncertainty, William sold the flourishing radio side to Charles Orr Stanley, who registered it as Pye Radio Ltd in 1929. In partnership with William, Harold retained the high-quality scientific instrument business, moving to Newmarket Road and maintaining the name Granta Works. The succeeding depression years proved frustrating, although limited development continued on sophisticated devices, often involving electronics. A second period of uncertainty ended in 1936 when William retired and sold his share of the company to Harold. Harold registered his firm as W G Pye & Co Ltd with an issued share capital of £3,300; in the following year he acquired Clifton Instruments Ltd.

Even before 1938, W G Pye & Co were warned to be prepared for war; their special skills, with Harold's characteristic clear-sightedness, allowed them to undertake new and exacting tasks alongside established production. They had already developed an aircraft speed and course calculator based on the 1934 design of a Cambridge University Air Squadron member; in addition 15,000 Air Ministry patterns calculators were produced for use on warplanes. At the end of hostilities an automatic pilot, as still used today, was developed for aircraft to home on to a radio beacon within an accuracy of half a degree of arc. Other wartime products included test gear, navigation aids, telescopes, anti aircraft sights, radar components and precision-machined components, some for the neighbouring, but quite independent, Pye Ltd (as it was known from 15 June 1937). As well as controlling the firm, Harold inaugurated supply department committees for co-ordinating work from individual manufacturers and for avoiding duplication of resources. He also applied his ingenuity to solving problems of a secret nature, notably in a test range for aerial torpedo-launching.

After 1945 work resumed on a delayed range of laboratory instruments and in 1947, with a gross turnover of £94,000, W G Pye & Co Ltd was purchased by Pye Ltd in order to terminate restrictive covenants waived during the war. At forty-six, and with earnings of £26,000 in his last year, Harold retired, before his target age of fifty.

Harold married twice: firstly in 1927 Jennie, daughter of Clowes Garner Milson, a clergyman; the couple, who had no family, lived at 6 Grange Road, Cambridge. After Jenny's death in 1948 he moved to Elm Farm at Burnham-on-Crouch, where for twelve years he enjoyed a second career in farming. He remarried in 1955, to Edith Pinney née Flight, a widow and daughter of Hauson Flight, an ironmonger and great-granddaughter of the founder of Worcester porcelain. Edith, who brought him step-children, Janet and John, died in 1969. Harold sold the farm but continued to live in the farmhouse before moving nearer the River Crouch. Here, as a member of the Royal Burnham Club, he still enjoys a day's sailing; his other interests include tennis and golf and watching rugby and snooker.

GORDON BUSSEY

Sources:

Unpublished

BCe.

MCe.

Some personal and business documents presented by Harold J Pye to the author.

Published

Gordon Bussey, *The Story of Pye Wireless* (Pye Ltd, 1979).

Maldon and Burnham Standard 26 July 1979.

W G Pye in Cambridge in the twenties (courtesy of Mr Gordon Bussey).

PYE, William George

(1869-1949)

Scientific instrument and radio manufacturer

William George Pye was born at Battersea, Surrey, on 27 October 1869, the eldest son and third in a family of eight of William Thomas Pye and his wife Elizabeth née Wilson. As a young man his father had some wealth and developed his hobby of scientific model-making including optical instruments; ca 1880 his fortunes suffered a reversal and when his collaborator A G Dew Smith (with Horace Darwin (qv)) formed the Cambridge Scientific Instrument Co in 1881, W T Pye became their associate. William George soon showed he had inherited these skills and, trained by his father, became at twenty-three an instrument-maker at the Cavendish Laboratory of the University. In the same year, 1892, he married Annie Eliza daughter of John Atkins, a joiner.

In 1896, with the help of Annie and his brothers Henry and Frederick, he started part-time in his own business, making scientific instruments for teaching and research: advertisements of these appeared in catalogues, the first catalogue being hand-written by Annie. A garden shed at the family home, 19 Humberstone Road, Chesterton, Cambridge, was the first factory, replaced within a year by premises at 30, St Andrews Street.

William Thomas joined his son in partnership in 1898 and a year later William George left the Cavendish to work full-time in W G Pye & Co. They leased yet larger property in Mill Lane, Cambridge, called the Granta Works, a name (from the Saxon place-name for Cambridge) retained for subsequent factories, all in Cambridge. W G Pye's father retired in 1909 and by 1913 the company, with 40 employees, expanded further into a factory in Cam Road. War in 1914 created an urgent need for precision instruments and W G Pye & Co provided a large range of optical and electrical equipment to military specifications.

Following the First World War, a resurgence of traditional demand faded by 1921, so the company, now employing 100 and seeking other markets, turned to wireless. Initially it catered for teaching and research by a 'unit system' of individual panels, containing some novel features, which easily interconnected to build multi-valve apparatus. These units were already popular with wireless amateurs when public broadcasting started (November 1922). Following this development the company responded with a range of complete wireless receivers, the '500' series. These were crafted with the same precision as all Pye instruments, but very strict observance of the Postmaster General's limitations made them relatively insensitive and thus unattractive. At this critical time, Harold John Pye (qv) joined the company and designed the much more satisfactory '700' series. From August 1924 they sold well and helped to ensure success for the enterprise.

The wireless factory expanded from 13,000 to 57,000 square feet in

addition in 1842 he was also listed as secretary of the Edinburgh Silk Yarn Co.

The growth of Quilter's practice was based on its handling of insolvencies during the commercial crisis of 1847-48. Although the total volume of their work is not known, of the 43 cases chronicled by D M Evans, eight were dealt with by Quilter, Ball, more than any other firm, resulting in the promotion of two clerks, G H Jay and W Crosbie, to the partnership. Some of the firm's fees and expenses for their work were substantial; £2,000 in the largest case they handled where liabilities were in excess of £450,000. By 1849 Quilter could state that he believed that his practice was the most extensive in England. During the crisis of 1857-58 Quilter, Ball again handled more cases than any other firm, 31 of the 147 cases examined by Evans. At both periods, however, the largest insolvencies were dealt with by J E Coleman who had an invaluable connection with the Bank of England and whose partnership with Turquand, Youngs (formed in 1857) provided Quilter Ball with an important rival for many years. Both Coleman and Ball gave evidence to the Select Committee on the Bank Acts in 1858 which included summaries of the cases they had handled in 1857. For Quilter, Ball the total liabilities of their largest cases amounted to £4,496,000; in Coleman's 12 largest cases the total was £6,726,840.

The collapse of the railway mania in 1847 provided Quilter with a new field of opportunity as his firm was commissioned by shareholder committees to investigate the accounting manipulations which had been used to sustain dividends. The most publicised of these investigations was into Hudson's frauds at the Eastern Counties Railway Co, but the firm was also involved at the South Eastern, the Midland, the London, Chatham & Dover and probably at the London Brighton & South Coast Railway companies. In many of these cases the firm revealed that the distinction between capital and revenue expenditures had been deliberately confused, a process facilitated by the absence of any legal requirement specifying their nature until the double account system was embodied in law in 1868. Although the obituaries of both Quilter and W W Deloitte (qv) credited both men with the invention of this system, it had been in use before their personal involvement with the railways, but Quilter may have advised the Government on the final form adopted. Quilter's real achievement was that his pioneering investigations were important in familiarising the shareholders with the advantages of using accountants to assist shareholder auditors, against a barrage of opposition from some of the railway press. Quilter had explained to the Select Committee on the Audits of Railway Accounts in 1849 his opposition to the requirement that the auditors of railway companies should be shareholders, on the grounds that this compromised their independence and his firm never became permanent auditors to any of the major British railways. Indeed the firm's experience when Quilter, Ball made an extraordinary audit of the Eastern Counties Railway in 1854 was not a happy one. He was criticised by a shareholders' committee for failing to detect some examples of misclassified expenditure which he had been so adept at discovering during his investigations. Later in the 1860s, the firm did become auditor to several of the major South American railways, the Buenos Ayres & Rosario and the Buenos Ayres Great Southern, the latter a joint audit with Deloitte as was that of the Central Uruguay. Quilter's own personal interests were heavily involved with railway investment and this was a more likely source of his wealth than income from his practice. On his death Quilter owned railway shares valued at over £276,000. His views on the independence of the auditor seem to have modified over time since he had shareholdings in railways where his partners were the auditors, a position that most contemporary accountants would not have found unethical. He was also a director of the Smyrna & Cassaba Railway from 1867 and of the Colchester & Stour Valley from 1869 until his death, when he was chairman — the position he then also held on the board of the St Lawrence & Ottawa Railway.

During the 1860s Quilter began developing a substantial audit practice as companies were formed to take advantage of the provision of limited liability under the 1855 and 1856 Companies Acts. The many failures of new companies provided an additional source of insolvency work, although the firm was placed only sixth in an analysis made in 1866 of the number and value of liquidations in the hands of the leading London practices. Quilter had been appointed with W Turquand (qv) as the first investigating inspectors of companies under the 1856 Companies Act, although the occasional nature of investigations of any sort, could not provide the regular work that auditing generated. The firm's last large-scale investigation was commissioned in 1859 by the Government into the accounts of the army clothing store at Weedon after the storekeeper absconded, the firm also having to design a new and effective accounting system.

The first large audits that Quilter obtained seem to have been those of the Hudson's Bay Company in 1863 after the company's reconstruction and that of the Birmingham Joint Stock Bank in 1866. Other audits followed gradually: a joint audit of the Alliance Bank with Harmood-Banner (qv) from 1869, the Bank of Australia, the Huddersfield Bank, the London Joint Stock — a joint audit with Deloittes, as was the audit of Eastern Telegraph. Apart from the foreign railway audits the firm obtained, there were several audits of companies in railway-related industries: the Midland Wagon Co, General Credit & Discount and the railway investment trust London Financial. Quilter was also the auditor of several companies to which he was linked by family ties. His stockbroker son, Sir W C Quilter MP, was a director of several of these companies, including United Telephone and many of its provincial licensees and Swan United Electric Light. Another was Eley Brothers the cartridge makers of which Quilter was also a shareholder and director; in addition he was the father-in-law to Charles Eley. At the time of his death Quilter's practice audited over 70 quoted companies and an unknown number of private ones.

In June 1870 Quilter called a meeting at his offices of nine leading practitioners and proposed to form an Institute of Accountants in London and apply for a royal charter. This would enable its carefully selected members, as 'chartered accountants', to distinguish themselves from other accountants who were taking advantage of the substantial opportunities for fraud under the Bankruptcy Act of 1869 and bringing the practice of accountancy into disrepute. Although the Scottish societies of accountants had obtained charters during 1855-65, the Government was quick to

RADFORD Francis

gross estate of £225,618, and his long and complex will contains a hint of character traits which may have assisted him in achieving such a large measure of success. He gave bequests to several past and present members of staff and to workmen, including a labourer to whom he left an annuity of £36, and he made the manager of his Holland Park estate an executor. He also left legacies to five hospitals and decreed that several loans which he had made to relatives should be regarded as free gifts.

Francis Radford was survived by three sons. The eldest, William, was also a speculative builder, and he lived until 1939, when he died at the age of ninety, leaving a gross estate of £160,048.

VICTOR BELCHER

Sources:

Unpublished

Devon CRO, parish registers of Kentisbeare.

Greater London RO, Middlesex Deeds Register.

Kensington Central Library, MSS 15624/707, 16323.

PRO, wills of Charles Radford, 1846, and Francis Radford Sr, 1857; census enumerators' books, 1871.

MCe.

PrC; Will.

Inscriptions on grave at Kensal Green Cemetery.

Alfred Moor Radford, 'Kensington' Lecture of unknown date given to London Society (copy of typescript in Kensington Central Library).

Published

Building News 5 Feb 1858, 14 Jan, 22 July 1859.

Rev Edwin S Chalk, *Kentisbeare and Blackborough* (Parochial Histories of Devonshire, 3 and 4, Devonshire Association, 1934).

Kensington News 12 Jan 1900.

London Post Office Directories 1876-78.

Ian Nairn, *Nairn's London* (Penguin Books, 1966).

Irene Scouloudi and A P Hands, 'The Ownership and Development of Fifteen Acres at Kensington Gravel Pits' *London Topographical Record* 22 (1965).

Francis H W Sheppard (ed), *Survey of London* vol 37: *Northern Kensington* (Athlone Press, 1973).

RAE, Edward

(1847-1923)

Provincial stockbroker

Edward Rae was born in Claughton, the Wirral, on 20 March 1847, the second son of George Rae (qv), chairman of the North & South Wales Bank and the author of the classic work, *The Country Banker*, and his wife Elspet née Kynoch. He was educated locally in Birkenhead. At the early age of eighteen, following an interest in iron shipbuilding and engineering, he spent some time on the Continent preparing a report (it is not clear for whom) on the condition of shipbuilding in French and Italian dockyards. Pursuing this interest he went to Egypt in the following year to superintend the construction of vessels for the provisional traffic on the Suez Canal. It was this experience which led him on his return to advocate the dredging of the Mersey Bar as a means to advance the development of Liverpool as a major port. For a short time he also worked in his father's bank.

Already well travelled, an interest in primitive people coupled with a linguistic facility prompted him to embark on a series of explorations to Iceland, Lapland, Russia and North Africa. From these travels came three books. By all accounts he was a particularly self-reliant traveller, with a bent for the daring, such as secretly visiting the sacred Mosque of Okhbah in the city of Kairouan, near Tunis, where no Westerner had ever set foot. In 1874 he was elected a fellow of the Royal Geographical Society; he was also a fellow of the Society of the Antiquaries of London.

His broking career began in 1870 when he went into partnership with Henry Bingham Parr (son of the founder of Parr's Bank) to form the firm of Parr & Rae on the Liverpool Stock Exchange. In 1890 he was elected vice-chairman of the Stock Exchange and chairman in 1894, holding this office until 1915, an indication of his stature both within and outside the Stock Exchange.

National prominence in financial circles arose from his tireless efforts to secure the passing of the Forged Transfers Act. The need for it arose from the Barton frauds, perpetrated by Samuel Barton between 1874 and 1885 in the stock of the London & North Western Railway Co. As joint trustee under a will Barton sold portions of the stock, forging the signatures of the other trustee and the attesting witnesses. Since he had also signed the dividend warrants and accounted for all the dividends the frauds remained undetected until he absconded in 1886 and new trustees were appointed. They brought a successful action against the company which was ordered to replace the trustees' names on the company's register as the owners of the stock, thus dispossessing those to whom the stock had been transferred. While legally correct, the action of the company caused widespread alarm, especially since railway stocks at the time were regarded as first-class investments.

Several Liverpool firms of stockbrokers were concerned at the threat to themselves and their clients posed by the court's decision and they initiated moves which led to consultations with the Exchanges of Manchester and Glasgow. Representatives of the three Exchanges met in Liverpool in 1890 and decided to form the Council of Associated Stock Exchanges, initially to canvas for a Forged Transfers Act, and in the long term to promote the general interests of the provincial markets. Since a bill had already been introduced into the Commons by Pitt Lewis, which had the same objectives in view, the Council threw its weight behind the bill. Edward Rae mobilised impressive support for the parliamentary campaign, the only lukewarm response coming from the London Stock Exchange. Passed in August 1891, the act empowered companies to compensate shareholders for losses arising from forged transfers. In effect it rendered stock and share certificates absolute evidence of title provided companies adopted its provisions. Adoption was at first slow due to the continued opposition of many company directors and Edward Rae had to campaign vigorously at company general meetings to get the protection of the act extended to a wider circle of shareholders. By 1904 some £1,000 million of securities were covered by its provisions. In the campaign for the legislation and its subsequent adoption Edward Rae was acknowledged as being 'the moving spirit throughout' {Thomas (1972) 195}.

Rae saw the long term aims of the Council as bringing the practices of the provincial exchanges closer together and promoting their interests, particularly in any negotiations with the London market. In 1890 the Council numbered eight exchanges with 550 members; by 1922 there were 28 exchanges with 1,077 members. Between 1890 and 1914, the period when Edward Rae was most active in its work, he was elected to the annual office of president on five separate occasions, 1896, 1897, 1902, 1908 and 1912, plain testimony of his dominant role in its affairs and his eminence in broking circles.

After the adoption of the Forged Transfer Act the Council turned its attention to achieving a greater degree of uniformity in the regulations governing the member exchanges. It was appreciated that complete uniformity was not possible due to variation in local practice, with the added complication of some exchanges being subject to the Scottish legal system, but uniformity of principle seemed desirable. After Glasgow withheld its approval, several of the English exchanges began to waver on the idea of the Code Laws and it was only after considerable exertions by Rae that the Council was persuaded to proceed on an English basis.

Two other subjects dominated the Council's activities in the pre-war years and in both Edward Rae was the leading participant. The first concerned relations with outside brokers. The general feeling at the time was that they took more business from provincial markets than they brought to them and it was therefore decided to attempt to limit their access to market floors. However, in Rae's view success depended on seeking the co-operation of London since any attempt to charge minimum commissions to outside brokers would be fruitless without London's participation; but he also realised that London's interest in outside brokers started and ended within the City. Even within provincial ranks there was not complete agreement since each Exchange viewed the role of the outside broker differently. The matter drifted on without action for some years and was shelved in 1914 until the major conferences with London in the inter-war years.

More significant were the protracted and occasionally thorny negotiations with London over its new rules, introduced between 1908 and 1912, to enforce single capacity dealing (the separation of jobbing and broking activity) and to adopt a minimum scale of commission not only for the public but also for inter-market dealings hitherto conducted on a 'free trade' basis. Several conferences were held between London and representatives from the Council of Associated Stock Exchanges, of which Edward Rae was the main spokesman. A significant effect of London's new rules was the end of shunting business between London dealers and provincial brokers. Increasingly London had viewed this practice as a drain on its turnover and they therefore decided to close off any outside access to the jobbers, at the same time imposing a fixed scale for all dealings done with the provinces, at half the public rate. A delegation from the provinces managed to get this reduced to 37.5 per cent but London then changed its mind and shifted back to 50 per cent, a reversal which greatly disappointed the Council and prompted Edward Rae to advise against sending any further delegations to plead with London. In return for the lower rate the provinces had been prepared to introduce a minimum scale for the public but this was then dropped. Instead they directed their energy to channelling a greater flow of business within the provinces. The rift with London over the commission issue and shunting was a disappointment to Rae but he was determined that having been snubbed by London they should not go south to beg for better terms.

Under his guidance the Council of Associated Stock Exchanges had achieved a useful degree of co-operation and while relations with London were clouded, without the Council to speak for them the treatment of provincial exchanges by London might have been far worse. The credit for the considerable measure of provincial unity was largely Rae's and the provincial exchanges' decision not to subjugate themselves completely to London's wishes stemmed from his view of the viability of provincial floors at the time.

Apart from his love of travel, particularly in the Near East, Rae's other great interest outside business was art. He built up a valuable collection of paintings, and was himself skilled in painting, oak carving, and designing.

He married in 1882 Margaret, daughter of James Leathart (qv), a lead manufacturer of Gateshead-on-Tyne; they had four sons.

Edward Rae died on 26 June 1923 leaving £83,422 gross.

W A THOMAS

Writings:

The Land of the North Wind; or, Travels among the Laplanders and Samoyedes (John Murray, 1875).

Siberia in Europe: Impressions of the Samoyedes and Their Country (1876).

The Country of the Moors, a Journey from Tripoli in Barbary to the City of Kairwan (1877).

RAE Edward

The White Sea Peninsulas: A Journey in Russian Lapland and Karelia (John Murray, 1881).

Sources:

Unpublished

Guildhall Library, London, minutes of the Council of Associated Stock Exchanges.

Liverpool Stock Exchange minutes.

BCe.

MCe.

PrC.

Published

Daily Courier (Liverpool) 28 June 1923.

Liverpool Daily Post and Mercury 28 June 1923.

Benjamin G Orchard, *Liverpool's Legion of Honour* (Birkenhead: the author, 1893).

W Arthur Thomas, *The Provincial Stock Exchanges* (Cass, 1972).

RAE, George

(1817-1902)

Banker

George Rae, a portrait by Frank Holl (1883) (courtesy of the Midland Bank plc).

George Rae was born in Aberdeen, on 21 October 1817, the son of George Rae, messenger at arms. He was educated at the 'Classical and Commercial Academy', Aberdeen. After a brief apprenticeship in a lawyer's office, in 1836 he was recruited as branch accountant at the Peterhead office of the newly-established North of Scotland Bank. The new bank rapidly established a branch network throughout North-East Scotland, and Rae was appointed accountant at new branches at Keith and Elgin. 'Though a young man', the bank's general manager wrote of Rae, 'we have more than once employed him in opening branches, by which he has acquired a complete knowledge of our system of accounts and books' {Keith (1936) 174}.

Although the North of Scotland Bank was to experience a long and successful history (it was eventually merged with the Clydesdale Bank Ltd in 1950), Rae was keenly aware of the astonishing growth of joint-stock banking in England and Wales in the 1830s. In April 1839 he successfully applied for the appointment of inspector of branches at the North & South Wales Bank, Liverpool, at a salary of £130. The 'Wales Bank' was one of the more enterprising new country banks, claiming when it was founded in 1836 that it would 'combine the best features of the Scotch system' {Midland Bank Archives, M139 North & South Wales Bank Shareholders' Minutes, Mar 1836} and would operate both in agricultural and industrial districts. By 1839 it had already opened 13 branches, mostly in North Wales.

Rae's experience of Scottish branch banking earned him rapid promotion and in 1842 he became manager at the Oswestry branch in Shropshire. He also benefited from the unimpressive performance of the bank's senior management between 1840 and 1844, a period when dividend payments were suspended. The directors looked to Rae for a remedy. At the age of only twenty-eight, Rae was appointed general manager at a salary of £400 in 1845.

After less than two years as general manager, Rae was confronted with the greatest single crisis in the history of the Wales Bank, which was caught up in the general financial crisis afflicting the city of London during October 1847. At that time, the London money market suspended its practice of discounting bills drawn on country banks. In Liverpool the immediate result of the suspension was the failure of the Royal Bank of Liverpool and the Liverpool Banking Co. The Wales Bank survived the initial rush to withdraw deposits, but on 22 October a London newspaper reported that it had already stopped payment. Although the report was false, and was strenuously denied both by Rae and by the bank's London agents, the panic was renewed and within two days the Wales Bank was forced to suspend payment of deposits.

Although the Wales Bank had therefore been a victim of external pressures, its difficulties were also a longer-term result of the old management's failure to restrict lending. The auditors, for example, had given good warning against 'extending its business beyond what the limits of its capital justified' {ibid, M5, 19 Aug 1842}. There was also evidence that a number of directors owed large debts to the bank. Rae himself escaped the censure of the shareholders and concentrated upon the reconstruction of the bank. Preference shares worth £100,000 were issued, depositors were asked to accept post-dated bills, and Rae closed a number of Welsh branches in the attempt to reduce expenses. These efforts allowed the bank to reopen in January 1848, but rehabilitation was a slow process. The Cefn Collieries (where Rae had acted as manager since the owners had failed in 1846) were sold in 1850, and the bank eventually realised its securities for heavy debts owed by the Birkenhead Commissioners. Rae became Commissioner for Birkenhead in an attempt to improve the account, and by 1852 most of the bank's doubtful debts had been extinguished.

After the 1847 débâcle Rae sought new income from Liverpool-based industry and commerce in preference to reopening or extending the bank's Welsh branch network. From 1863 this approach was underpinned by new 'town branches' in the Liverpool area (an early example outside London of suburban branch banks). Rae also pioneered a savings scheme for dock workmen in Birkenhead, helping to give the bank a local reputation as 'the tradesman's bank'. When combined with elaborate financial and bookkeeping controls within the bank, these measures stabilised earnings and enabled the bank to survive the financial crises of 1857 and 1866, despite the collapse of no less than three other Liverpool-based joint stock banks. Between 1850 and 1865, when Rae was rewarded with promotion to managing director at a salary of £2,000, the bank's deposits showed a five-fold increase to £1.5 million.

By the 1860s Rae already had a wide range of interests outside the bank. In 1862, for example, he had joined a syndicate of Liverpool merchants and cotton brokers to form the Tryddyn Oil & Coke Co. The new concern was promoted to explore shale and cannel deposits at Tryddyn, Flintshire, for the purpose of refining the minerals as paraffin oil. Numbers of similar oil companies were then being promoted in North Wales in anticipation of the expiry of James Young's paraffin patents. Rae became chairman of the Tryddyn Co in September 1863, yet before production had begun he entered negotiations with the Mineral Oil Co of Saltney. As a result the assets of the Tryddyn and Mineral Oil companies were sold to a new promotion, the Flintshire Oil & Cannel Co Ltd, in November 1866. Rae joined the board of the new company. Although the Tryddyn shareholders appeared to profit from the deal, Rae himself was drawn into a long and unrewarding association with the Flintshire Co. The Tryddyn seams proved unworkable as early as 1867, the board was rent by disputes over property valuations, and by the early 1870s the company's remaining production was made fruitless by the rapid fall in world oil prices. The Flintshire Co was not wound up until 1885 but its career was effectively over by 1875.

The downfall of Rae's interests in the Flintshire oil industry did not appear to damage his reputation as a banker. Neither did the stream of defamatory circulars which were issued to shareholders between 1876 and 1879, denouncing Rae for not registering the bank with limited liability. The circulars were eventually traced to Matthew Harrison, chairman of the Wales Bank during the disastrous early 1840s. Harrison's invective reached a crescendo after the failure of the City of Glasgow Bank (an unlimited company, like the Wales Bank) in 1878. He ridiculed the bank for employing 'a Scotch Bank officer' {ibid, M159/62, M Harrison to North and South Wales Bank, 22 Oct 1878} and warned that the Wales Bank shareholders would suffer the same fate as the luckless owners of the City of Glasgow Bank. Harrison did not finally give up his allegations until Rae had prepared a libel action and the bank's auditors had published a statement to demonstrate the strength of the bank's balance sheet.

The Wales Bank's shareholders, customers and staff remained loyal to Rae throughout Harrison's maverick campaign. The 1870s were perhaps his most creative period at the bank. In addition to opening a series of new branches, Rae negotiated the acquisition of Williams & Son, bankers at Dolgellau and Barmouth in 1873, Cassons & Co of Portmadoc, Pwllheli, Festiniog, Blaenau and Harlech in 1875, and the Bala Banking Co in 1877. These extensions were supplemented by a 'truce' with the National Provincial Bank for the sharing of North Welsh business; the agreement survived from 1873 until 1900.

Rae's appointment as chairman and managing director in 1873 significantly increased his control over the financial management of the Wales Bank. He was especially energetic in improving the quality of statistical information about the distribution of funds. Detailed weekly statements were instituted in 1875, with the result that advances were held in closer check while gilt-edged investments increased. Rae also defined the hierarchy of management more clearly. Routine decision-making was delegated to a daily committee of three directors and the managing director ex officio. The committee's work was reported to the bank's general board once a week.

Under this regime the balance sheets of the Wales Bank remained healthy, and shareholders regularly received dividends of 17.5 per cent between 1870 and 1895. Total deposits advanced from £2,025,000 in 1870 to £6,643,000 in 1890. In the years of stringency following the Glasgow failure, Rae increased holdings of consols and pegged the limit of total advances at 20 per cent of deposits, capital and reserves. Cash in hand was fixed at 33.3 per cent of liabilities until the late 1890s. Strict precautions were also taken against forgery and fraud. Shortly after the detection of a fraud at the Bank of Liverpool, for example, Rae's staff confirmed that the Wales Bank was protected against similar crimes by not allowing any ledger-keeper to balance his own weekly ledger, and by preventing any one officer from balancing the same ledger two weeks running.

In the 1880s and 1890s, under Rae's guidance, the Wales Bank's business continued to move away from its original agricultural base towards industrial and commercial business in Liverpool and its region. Whereas 67 per cent of deposits had come from country branches in 1870, they accounted for only 42 per cent of deposits by 1890. This alteration was matched by an expansion of the bank's facilities in Liverpool and the Wirral, with a consequent increase in working expenses. In June 1895, Rae acknowledged the extent of the change: 'a large proportion of our business is of a mercantile and commercial character, so that our figures would not be a fair criterion in the case of banks having a larger agricultural connection' {ibid, M222, George Rae letter book, June 1895}.

In the 1890s Rae took a less active role in the day-to-day management of the bank. Many of his responsibilities passed to T R Hughes, the Liverpool manager, and Thomas Brocklebank, a senior and influential member of the board. More seriously Rae's health was poor, and he suffered from long bouts of asthma and other nagging illnesses. Failing health forced him to give up his dual responsibilities as chairman and managing director in March 1898. By then the bank had built up a network of 77 branches and was responsible for £7.8 million in deposits, placing it amongst the largest and most influential of the country banks in England and Wales. The North & South Wales Bank was subsequently acquired by the Midland Bank in 1908.

Outstanding as he was as a manager in his long career at the Wales Bank, George Rae emerged as a major influence on the banking community as a whole in the later nineteenth century. This was partly a reflection of his activities as an organiser and lobbyist. He was a promoter of the short-lived Banking Institute in 1851, and in 1874 he was a prime mover in the Association of English Country Bankers, the first serious attempt to represent the interests of provincial joint stock and private banks. He remained a dominant figure in the Association until his retirement. He was also a founder and trustee of the Institute of Bankers in 1879, and four years later he inaugurated an Institute prize for the best essay on bank bookkeeping. This concern for the development of the banking profession was a constant theme; in 1902 he established a prize in practical banking for entrants in the Institute's examinations and endowed a lectureship in banking and currency at the University College of North Wales.

Rae was equally busy as a spokesman for banking interests. He gave evidence to the 1875 Parliamentary Select Committee on Banks of Issue. Crucially, he also intervened to influence the 'reserved liability' legislation which was introduced in 1879 in the aftermath of the City of Glasgow Bank failure. The proposed system of reserved liability provided for the division of a bank's uncalled capital into shares at call at the discretion of the directors and shares which could only be called in the event of bankruptcy. Rae's contribution was to persuade the Irish banks' representatives to drop their opposition and in his clarificaton of the provisions of the bill. He was especially anxious to see more widespread introduction of published balance sheets as a result of the legislation. He had introduced published balance sheets at the Wales Bank as early as 1891. 'You need have no hesitation about giving publicity to your balance sheet', he wrote later; 'a bank is not strong by reasons of its magnitude, but by the proportion which its 'liquid assets' bear to its liabilities ... a strong balance sheet, I feel persuaded, attracts business' {ibid, M222, George Rae letter book, July 1891}.

George Rae's most durable influence on the banking community was as an author. An early edition of the *Banker's Magazine* in 1847 had contained articles on currency legislation over the signature 'R A E', and he also contributed letters to the magazine in the name of 'Thomas Bullion'. In 1850 these letters were published anonymously as *The Internal Management of a Country Bank*. Parts of this pamphlet reappeared thirty-five years later in Rae's classic textbook, *The Country Banker: His Clients, Cares and Work*. This guide to practical banking was designed both for branch officials and for general managers. The clarity and realism of Rae's writing ensured that the first edition was 'pirated' in the USA, while in the United Kingdom *The Country Banker* appeared in seven editions between 1885 and 1930.

Outside banking Rae was an enthusiastic traveller and student of the arts. With his wife and family, he undertook major expeditions to Europe, Russia and the Middle East. A diary of his tours from 1865 onwards was published privately in 1891 as *Holiday Rambles by Land and Sea*. In later years Rae preferred yachting cruises in Scotland, but he was also increasingly involved in patronage of the pre-Raphaelite school of painting. His friends included Ford Madox Brown and Edward Burne-Jones. Above all, Rae was proud of his friendship with Rossetti, and his collection contained a number of the artist's important pictures. *The Beloved*, for example, had been commissioned by Rae as early as 1863. This painting and ten other Rossettis in Rae's collection were acquired by the Tate Gallery in 1916.

Rae's first wife, Elspeth Kynoch of Keith, Banffshire, died in about 1851 leaving two sons George Bertram and Edward, and a daughter Alice. In 1854 he married Julia, daughter of John Williams of Ferryside,

Carmarthen. Their home Redcourt, Claughton, Cheshire, was designed by Edmund Kirby and built between 1876 and 1879. George Rae died there on 4 August 1902. The net value of his estate was £192,000, the gross value being £198,092.

EDWIN GREEN

Writings:

The International Management of a Country Bank (Groombridge & Son, 1850).

PP, HC 1875 (351) IX, SC on Banks of Issue.

The Country Banker: His Clients, Cares and Work (John Murray, 1885, 7th ed 1930).

Holiday Rambles by Land and Sea (2 vols, pp, D Marples, 1891).

contributions to:

Bankers Magazine.

Economist

Murray's Magazine.

Times.

Sources:

Unpublished

Midland Bank Archives, London.

Guy S O Rippon, 'The Flintshire Oil and Cannel Co Ltd 1864-1872' (London MA, 1977).

Published

Wilfred F Crick and John E Wadsworth, *A Hundred Years of Joint Stock Banking* (Hodder & Stoughton, 1936, 4th ed 1964).

Edwin Green, *Debtors to their Profession. A History of the Institute of Bankers 1879-1979* (Methuen, 1979).

Alexander Keith, *The North of Scotland Bank Limited, 1836-1936* (Aberdeen Journals, 1936).

Liverpool Daily Post 5 Aug 1902.

Liverpool Mercury 5 Aug 1902.

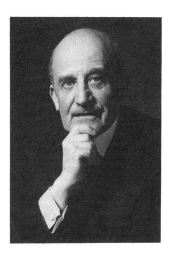

Sir Harry Railing (courtesy of General Electric Co plc).

RAILING, Max John

(1868-1942)

and
RAILING, Sir Harry

(1878-1963)

Electrical equipment manufacturers

Max John and Harry Railing were the sons of Isaac Railing, a Jewish hop merchant of Munich, and Hannah née Bing; Max John was born in 1868, and his younger brother Adolf (he later adopted the more English-sounding name of Harry) on 10 December 1878. No details are recorded of their early lives, though it is known that Harry attended Munich University and graduated as a doctor of engineering in 1901, before acquiring experience in the USA.

In 1892 Max Railing left Germany for England and shortly after his arrival joined the General Electric Co in the accounts department. His quick grasp of figures, his energy, and his sound business sense soon marked him out for promotion. He helped in the foundation of the electrical fittings department and developed the policy of establishing showrooms for their display. After the building of the Witton Works, near Birmingham in 1900, he was entrusted with the task of inducing reluctant electricity supply authorities and other buyers to give the GEC orders for heavy electrical machinery which had never been designed and constructed in Britain. His success during this critical period led to his transfer to London at the age of forty-two as general manager — a post which he retained until he was promoted to joint managing director in 1929.

At about the time Max Railing was appointed general manager, Hugo Hirst (qv) was consolidating his grip on the GEC. By 1906 he had become sole managing director, having emerged as victor in a struggle with the more conservative founder of the company, Gustav Byng. Railing became the director's right-hand man, in Hirst's words 'my alter ego' {Whyte (1930) 143}. They were not only close in business matters. In 1900 Max had married Amanda, daughter of Herman Hirsch, whose sister Leontine had married Hugo (her cousin) in 1892, the year both Leontine and Max had left Germany. At GEC Railing became the counterbalance, with, to a lesser degree, Byng, to Hirst's flamboyance and adventurousness. With his accountant's mind Railing meticulously watched and controlled the finances of every part of the organisation, acting as a restraint on some of Hirst's more ambitious schemes. In 1917, for example, it was Max and his brother Harry who blocked Hirst's plan to absorb British Westinghouse. He was also the most influential adviser when GEC attracted the attentions of General Electric of America in 1929. As Hirst moved increasingly into the role of industrial statesman in the inter-war period it was Max who kept his eye on the day-to-day running of the business.

Railing did not complain: he had none of his boss's ostentation, hated social life (though he played some golf and curling), worked extremely long hours, and had no special interest in becoming a part of English society (unlike Hirst he never lost his strong guttural accent). He held a number of directorships in other companies and was also a vice-president of the British Electrical and Allied Manufacturers Association, and of the Radio Manufacturers Association. He was an active member of the Institution of Electrical Engineers; a member of the Board of Trade Advisory Council, 1935-37; and master of the Worshipful Company of Makers of Playing Cards, 1935-36.

Max Railing was the obvious choice as Hirst's successor; however, he predeceased Hirst on 14 January 1942, leaving £291,186 gross, and was survived by his wife. He had two daughters.

Hirst's successor as chairman, at the age of sixty-three, was Max's younger brother Harry Railing. He had joined GEC in 1905 as chief of the test room at Witton, bringing with him a wide knowledge of American and Continental practice, and was soon appointed adviser to all engineering departments. He later transferred to London as a technical assistant to Hirst, before returning to Witton as manager. In 1911 he was elected to the board, and so became the director responsible for the engineering activities of the whole company. Later, when the Chamberlain & Hookham Meter Works was taken over, he became chairman of that company. In 1941 Hirst appointed him as joint general manager with Leslie Gamage, Hirst's son-in-law. After the death of Max, Harry came next in the informal line of succession decided by Hirst. In 1942 Harry Railing became vice-chairman, and then, on Hirst's death in 1942, chairman of Britain's largest electrical manufacturing enterprise with a capital of £7.8 million and nearly 40,000 employees.

Harry Railing was well-fitted for GEC's immediate task of responding to the war effort. Pioneering work on radar was perhaps the most notable achievement, though nearly all branches of activity were expanded, so that by the end of the war the number employed had risen to about 50,000. But GEC did not grow rich on war output: trading profits of £1.9 million were virtually the same in 1944-45 as they had been in 1939-40. Harry Railing was knighted in 1944 and received the OBE in 1946.

Once the war was over Railing greatly expanded the productive capacity of GEC to meet the booming demand for electrical equipment of all kinds, especially household appliances. Soon a majority interest was taken in Woods of Colchester Ltd, a firm which manufactured ventilating equipment of all kinds. Enormous amounts of money were also expended on re-equipment and extensions. During 1947-55 the company spent £20 million on plant and buildings alone, and in 1952 authorised and issued capital was increased to £23.6 million.

Much of the increased capital was spent on the engineering side, reflecting Harry Railing's chief interest. A completely new generating shop with testing plant was added at Witton and opened in 1950, whilst a new heavy turbine shop was completed at Erith at the same time. In the mid-1950s the GEC under Railing's guidance and that of (later Sir Arnold) Lindley, an engineer from the GEC's South Africa Co, moved into the

Clarence Mill (from The Master Millers. The Story of the House of Rank 1875–1955 *Harley Publishing Co Ltd).*

Direction of the company meanwhile was passing increasingly from Joseph Rank to his sons, son-in-law (Sidney Bruce Askew), and other executives. Yet Rank did not retire and played an active part in the affairs of the business until he died. At his death, Ranks was the largest flour milling business in the country, said to be capable of supplying one-seventh of the population with flour.

Why Joseph Rank of all the thousands of small millers should have reached pre-eminence perhaps owed something to fortune. But chance was aided and abetted by Rank's skills and character. He was a first-class dealer in commodities which enabled him to make a profit despite the over-capacity and competition in the industry. He thoroughly understood marketing and established a market for his flour before building a new mill to serve it. He was quick to see the trend towards large roller mills with deep water access to receive shipments of foreign grain, and although not a trail-blazing innovator, he did ensure that his mills were well-sited and well-equipped both with machinery and storage. He was wise in his choice of lieutenants who could be entrusted with much of the development of the business. Some of these, like John Kemp and W H Raylor, who joined him in the early years in Hull, remained throughout their careers, eventually becoming directors of the company.

Joseph Rank was deeply interested in the welfare of the milling trade as a whole. He was an active member of the National Association of British and Irish Millers, becoming their president for the year 1904-5. In the Association he was an active, though not always successful, supporter of schemes for mutual benevolent funds and for rationalising the forms of trade in the industry. Similar motives of hoping to improve the conditions in the trade as a whole led Joseph Rank into his one excursion into political affairs as a member of Joseph Chamberlain's (qv) Tariff Commission. During the First World War he advised the Government on the management of wheat supplies, becoming a member of the Wheat Control Board.

Outside his business life religion was Rank's main concern. He was an active member of his local Wesleyan Methodist church both in Hull and in London, and took especial delight in working with the Sunday School.

Deeply-held religious convictions led Joseph to devote much of his wealth to charitable purposes. He supported many causes great and small, but those dearest to his heart were his church and his home town of Hull. The Methodist Missionary Society alone received well over £2 million in cash and shares in Joseph Rank Ltd over the years, and other sections of Methodism, particularly the Central Hall and other church building programmes, were handsomely supported. In Hull the Royal Infirmary was one of Rank's especial interests, and he supported many welfare funds until he consolidated his gifts by the endowment of the Joseph Rank Benevolent Fund. In recognition of these services he was granted the freedom of the City of Hull in 1935. The extent of his giving can be gauged from the fact that he left an estate of only £70,954.

Personally, Joseph was frugal and lived modestly: 'the reputation was that he travelled third class on the railways until the end and always took sandwiches to prevent having to pay for his lunch' {Sir Joseph Lockwood, 18 Sept 1984}. He certainly complained about his eldest son's taste for a fine house, and breeding and racing horses.

Joseph Rank married twice. His first wife was Emily, daughter of Robert Voase, a Holderness farmer, whom he married on 15 June 1880. She died in 1916, and in 1918 Joseph married Emily's sister Annie M Witty, who had been widowed some time before; his second wife died in 1940. He had three sons and five daughters (one of whom died young), all by his first wife. The sons were all active in the family business. However, one, Rowland, set up his own business and died comparatively young in 1939. James Voase Rank (qv) succeeded his father as chairman of Joseph Rank Ltd, and Joseph Arthur Rank (qv) eventually became a British film magnate. Joseph Rank died on 13 November 1943, aged eighty-nine.

JONATHAN BROWN

Sources:

Unpublished

MCe.

PrC.

Information from members of Ranks Hovis McDougall Ltd, especially Mr Joseph Rank (grandson of the firm's founder); also from Sir Joseph Lockwood in letter to *DBB* editor, 18 Sept 1984.

Published

Burke's Peerage and Baronetage.

Richard G Burnett, *Through the Mill: The Life of Joseph Rank* (Epworth Press, 1945).

Farmers' Weekly 19 Nov 1943.

Hull Daily Mail 11 July 1935, 15 Nov 1943.

The Miller 4 Jan, 1 Feb 1904 and passim.

Milling 25 Nov 1934 and passim.

Joseph Rank Ltd, *The Master Millers: the Story of the House of Rank* (Harley Publishing Co, 1956).

Times 15 Nov 1943.

Times *Prospectuses* 86 (1933).

WWW.

Joseph Arthur Rank, Lord Rank (courtesy of Joseph Rank).

RANK, Joseph Arthur

Lord Rank of Sutton Scotney

(1888-1972)

Milling and film companies chairman

Joseph Arthur (known as Arthur) Rank was born at Hull on 22 December 1888, the third and youngest son of Joseph Rank (qv), a corn miller, and his wife Emily, daughter of Robert Voase, a farmer at Ellerby in Yorkshire. The Ranks had been flour millers for three generations, and before that farmers since the mid-sixteenth century. Although his father's early years as an independent miller had been an uphill stuggle, by the time of Arthur's birth he had built his first steam-driven roller-mill in Hull and thereby laid the foundation stone of his future commercial success. A fervent Wesleyan Methodist, he instilled into all his children an enduring sense of religious obligation and moral values. Sundays were an unbreakable routine of religious services morning and evening, relieved only by Bible classes in the afternoon. A devoted family man, he also taught his children the pleasures of cricket, tennis and croquet and took them on picnics and to the circus.

Joseph Rank's own formal education had been perfunctory and he saw to it that his children fared better. Arthur was sent to a Methodist boarding school, the Leys, Cambridge (as was his brother Rowland), before joining his father's business in 1905. By that time it was established as a private limited company under the name of Joseph Rank Ltd, with a capital of £700,000, and its head office had moved from Hull to London. As training in the business of flour milling, Arthur spent six months in the London office, six months on the London Corn Exchange and a year as apprentice with another miller, W Looker, at Luton. This was followed by eighteen months working in all the processes of milling at Joseph Rank Ltd's recently-erected Premier Mills in Royal Victoria Docks, London, and a year at Hull in charge of production at Clarence Mills, so rounding off an extensive and thorough grounding in the business.

During the course of the First World War, Arthur Rank was appointed a director of the company. Soon after, he enlisted in the army with an ambulance unit raised by Sir Arthur du Cros (qv) and served in France, reaching the rank of captain in the Royal Field Artillery.

Despite the world trade recession of the 1930s, Joseph Rank Ltd continued to flourish and expand. Arthur Rank's main responsibilities were for the technical aspects of production. His first important contribution to the expansion of the company followed the acquisition in 1932 of Associated London Flour Mills Ltd, itself a merger of seven small and previously independent milling businesses in the London area. With it Joseph Rank Ltd acquired the Blue Cross trade mark for animal feeds (provender and feed traditionally were by-products of flour milling). Under Arthur's direction the newly-acquired trade mark was brought into use at all the mills in the company and sales developed vigorously. Separate feed mills were established in close proximity to the flour mills and a policy of national marketing adopted with considerable commercial success.

In common with his older brothers, Arthur had his father's entrepreneurial spirit in great measure. The eldest son, James, accepted the natural role of managing director and eventual successor to his father as head of the business, which in 1933 was incorporated as a public limited company capitalised at £7,295,000. The two other sons sought and found fields of endeavour in which to express their own desire for personal achievement. Rowland, the middle son, controlled his own independent milling company, Mark Mayhew Ltd, at Battersea, London, and but for his early death in 1939 might have built a commercial enterprise to rival that of his father. Arthur Rank, while remaining a director of Ranks Ltd, as it had by then become, turned his attention to the fast-expanding film industry. His interest sprang originally from his Methodist convictions and his first intention was to sponsor films with a religious and moral content.

To this end he joined in 1934 the board of a new film production company, British National, whose first production was a prize-winning film on a religious theme, *The Turn of the Tide*. It failed to obtain general distribution since the distributors and exhibitors considered it unlikely to be a commercial success. In 1935 Rank, together with Lord Luke (of Bovril) (qv), Lord Portal of Lavenham and Paul Lindenburg of Japhets bank, established a holding company, the General Film Finance Corporation, which acquired a 25 per cent share in the US Universal Pictures, and a controlling interest in General Film Distributors, managed by C M Woolfe (qv). He also bought a West End cinema and, in 1936, became one of the founders of Pinewood Studios.

As his knowledge of the commercial cinema grew, Arthur Rank became impatient of Hollywood's dominance of film-making and determined to reinvigorate the British film industry in order to present a British point of view to the millions of cinema-goers in this country. In 1941 he acquired control of Gaumont British Picture Corporation, developed by Isidore Ostrer (qv) and its subsidiary companies and, early in 1942, control of Odeon Theatres Ltd, founded by Oscar Deutsch (qv). He was now a leading force in film production, distribution and exhibition in Britain, with over 600 cinemas and studios at Pinewood, Shepherds Bush,

Islington, Denham and later at Highbury. He also acquired and subsequently developed important interests in optics and other technical aspects of film shooting and projection.

Throughout the Second World War Rank was greatly encouraged by the Government, which regarded the making and showing of films as a most important contribution to national morale and the war effort. Towards the end of the war, he and his close colleague, John Davis, began to build up a worldwide distribution organisation to market British-made films effectively overseas, again with a view to challenging the domination of Hollywood.

However, the post-war Labour Government abruptly changed its policy towards the British film industry and in 1947 revoked the 75 per cent ad valorem duty on imported films, replacing it with a quota of 45 per cent of British screen time for imported films. This came at a time when Rank had embarked on a most ambitious programme of film production and the resulting financial difficulties (including overdrafts of £13.5 million with the National Provincial Bank) for the Rank companies brought about an enforced period of retrenchment and diversification of interests. Nevertheless, the J Arthur Rank symbol of the man with the gong had become known around the world. The feature films which his initiative encouraged included classics like *Henry V, Hamlet, The Way to the Stars* and *In Which We Serve*. At the same time he backed Sir Michael Balcon (qv) at Ealing Studios and was directly responsible for the production of the news and current affairs series *This Modern Age* to counter what he considered the excessively American viewpoint of the *March of Time* newsreel series. Nor were his earliest intentions in entering the film world forgotten, for he pioneered the Children's Film Foundation to bring a new and more worthwhile type of film to young audiences. On the technical side of the business, Rank factories were making excellent lenses and these were in demand by Hollywood production studios.

Rank left his producers and directors a free hand. According to Sir John Davis, who worked with him, he did so as 'a matter of business philosophy ... as he believed film production being a creative activity, [they] need their freedom' {Sir John Davis to Joseph Rank, 1982}. Rank's biographer, Alan Wood, attributes Rank's liberality to his awareness of his own ignorance of film-making. Rank himself once told a gathering of his directors and other notables of the film industry, 'I know I have no talent for making films; but I *can* help you get what money you want' {Wood (1952) 127}. Sometimes his generosity and ignorance were exploited, and his money went into some very bad films, as well as some very good ones, and there were those in the film industry, including some who worked for Rank, who resented his influence and financial strength, seeing him as a monopolist who threatened to crush the creative talents of the industry. But Rank 'gave the money, and he gave a free hand' and these were his 'essential contributions which made the British film industry renaissance possible' {*ibid*}.

In 1952 the family flour milling business demanded a renewal of Arthur's attention, following the death of his only surviving brother. He made over his and his wife's controlling interests in the Rank film companies in 1953 to a company limited by guarantee, with the objective of ensuring that the control of the Rank Organisation, as it was renamed, would remain in British hands. The right to receive the major part of the income from these interests was vested in trustees to distribute for charitable purposes.

At the time of life when most men retire from active work, Arthur returned to the family business with a new vigour, while remaining non-executive chairman of the Rank Organisation. His eldest brother, James, had become chairman of Ranks Ltd in 1943 on the death of their father, and held this office until his own death in 1952, when Arthur, aged sixty-four, succeeded him and devoted himself wholeheartedly to the business. The next twenty years were a period of unprecedented expansion and diversification for Ranks. Under his guidance the company acquired bakery businesses in all parts of Britain within the space of a few years to protect its outlets for flour against imports from Canada. Over 100 bakery businesses were bought from their previous owners and integrated into British Bakeries Ltd, a new division of the company. The ablest of the former owners were retained in directorial and senior managerial positions. A second major expansion was the acquisition of about 20 agricultural merchanting companies to form another division. Rank's first important contribution to the company a quarter of a century before had been to organise the production and sale of branded animal feeds. In its final integrated form the new agricultural division extended its interests beyond animal feed into cereal and herbage seed production and sales, extensive grain trading and the merchanting of several important products to farmers, including fertilisers.

In 1962 Hovis-McDougall Ltd, the result of an earlier merger between two long-established flour milling companies, was acquired and the company renamed Ranks Hovis McDougall Ltd (with a share capital increased from £30 million to £45 million). This was followed by the acquisition in 1968 of Cerebos Ltd, a company which made a variety of packaged grocery products and had overseas manufacturing facilities. (Following this acquisition Ranks Hovis McDougall's share capital stood at £65,574,771.) The Cerebos interests in Britain became the nucleus of a fourth division of the company, grocery products, and its overseas interests became the building-point for an overseas division.

Rank relinquished control of the company in 1969, when he was in his eightieth year, to his nephew and managing director, Joseph MacArthur Rank. His annual salary at that time as chairman of Ranks Hovis McDougall was £30,000 and as president of the Rank Organisation, £2,750. He had personal holdings of over 200,000 RHM shares and an interest in several beneficial family trusts totalling another million shares. To this must be added his shareholdings in the Rank Organisation of 431,000 shares of various categories.

By the time of his death in 1972 at the age of eighty-four, Rank had seen the transformation of the company from Ranks Ltd, a large flour milling concern, to RHM, an international company with very widely diversified food processing interests. His main role in this development was to provide the broad vision and will to break out of the closed commercial world of flour-milling and to open up unlimited possibilities at home and abroad. A few trusted senior colleagues were in his confidence and through them he expected his far-ranging plans to be executed with despatch and without fail, yet his inclinations towards authoritarianism were tempered by a genuine regard for those employed by the company. In a sense he viewed his 60,000 employees rather as a Nonconformist minister views his flock, to be urged unrelentingly onwards towards an unquestionable goal, chided for any perceived backsliding, but always to be valued as unique human beings. Following the example of his father, throughout his lifetime he was a benefactor on a large scale of charities, mainly those of the Methodist Church, in which he held local and national offices. He shunned publicity for his good works and it is not possible to form an estimate of the sums he gave from his own pocket. He was given a barony in 1957, taking the title Lord Rank of Sutton Scotney. He was also a JP of Surrey and received honorary doctorates from the universities of Boston and Southampton.

In 1917 he married Laura Ellen, eldest daughter of Horace Marshall (later First Baron Marshall of Chipstead). Their marriage lasted for over half a century until her death in 1971 and they were notably devoted to each other; they had two daughters. Lord Rank died on 29 March 1972 leaving £5,993,323 gross.

ROGER MANVILLE *and* JOSEPH RANK

Sources:

Unpublished

BCe.

MCe.

PrC.

Information from Sir John Davis.

Published

Burke's Peerage and Baronetage, 1980.

Richard G Burnett, *Through the Mill. The Life of Joseph Rank* (Epworth Press, 1945).

Stock Exchange Official Year Book 1971.

Times 30 Mar 1972.

Alan Wood, *Mr Rank: A Study of J Arthur Rank and British Films* (Hodder & Stoughton, 1952).

WWW.

John Rankin from George Chandler,
Four Centuries of Banking
*(courtesy of Barclays Bank PLC and
B T Batsford).*

RANKIN, John

(1845-1928)

Shipowner

John Rankin was born at Greenbank, New Brunswick, Canada, on 14 February 1845, the son of James Rankin (1787-1870) of Mearns, Renfrewshire. His grandfather, also called James Rankin (1752-1815) had been a small landowner in Mearns. Out of this small parish and mostly educated by the same schoolmaster came all the partners in the great Scottish Canadian timber merchanting house of Pollok Gilmour & Co, to whom the Rankins were allied. This firm, taking advantage of the Canadian timber preferences, established many branches in eastern Canada in the early nineteenth century. In 1838 they also established a branch in Liverpool, Rankin Gilmour & Co, which sold Southern cotton as well as Canadian timber. Pollok Gilmour & Co were in addition one of Britain's largest shipowners, building their own ships in their Canadian yards and either using them to freight timber or selling them in Liverpool. James Rankin was brought up in Mearns but emigrated to New Brunswick in 1830. He went out in one of the firm's ships but was wrecked on the way, losing his accumulated property, a complete outfit of farming implements and a considerable quantity of valuable livestock. John Rankin's biography of the firm is silent on his father's occupation in Canada, but he himself spent his early days at Greenbank, New Brunswick. However, in 1854 when he was nine years old he was sent to Liverpool and was educated at Dr Ihne's School and Madras College. He then briefly attended St Andrews University in New Brunswick, before joining Rankin Gilmour in Liverpool in 1861.

At this time the Liverpool firm consisted of Robert Rankin (1801-70), John Rankin's uncle, who had spent his early years in Mirimichi before opening the Liverpool branch; George Hoghton (1817-76), who until the Civil War had managed the firm's New Orleans' branch, and from 1861 sold the firm's cotton on the Exchange Flags in Liverpool; and Robert Rankin Jr (1830-1898), John Rankin's elder brother, who had also been brought up in Canada and had joined the Liverpool firm in 1847. John Rankin was therefore almost certainly given his chance in the firm because of family connections, and with the hope that in due course, if successful, he would be able to help to buy out the senior partners. He went through the normal mercantile apprenticeship, at first copying bills, then (in 1865) becoming cashier. For a time he made the annual round of small Irish ports selling the firm's timber. He counted his most valuable early commercial experience as 'dunning at other offices for freight balances or rent accounts, etc' {Rankin (1921) 146}. In 1871 he became a partner and in 1898 on the death of his brother, senior partner. Robert Rankin Sr had died in 1870 and George Hoghton had retired in 1866.

John Rankin joined the firm at a difficult and challenging time. Both the

Liverpool firm and the Pollok Gilmour houses generally faced the problem of changing generations and adapting to new commercial methods. Until 1860 the firms had been dominated by the strong characters of Allan Gilmour Sr (1775-1849), who first developed the Canadian branches, John Pollok (1778-1858) and Arthur Pollok (1780-1870) who managed the Glasgow firm, and Alexander Rankin (1788-1852) and Allan Gilmour Jr (1805-84) who organised timber purchases in Canada and the firms' shipping. However the Polloks retired in 1853 and Allan Gilmour only nominally took over the management of the Glasgow house, leaving the leadership of the firms with Robert Rankin Sr in Liverpool. However, by 1860 the Canadian timber trade, suffering from the repeal of the timber duties, was no longer so profitable and the junior partners in Liverpool, facing the need to finance the imminent retirement of Robert Rankin Sr and Allan Gilmour Jr, lost interest in the Canadian branches. In 1870 Allan Gilmour retired and the Canadian partnerships ceased connection with the Glasgow, London and Liverpool branches, and over the next decade were shut down one by one. The Glasgow branch also closed in 1873, and the London branch in 1889. The Liverpool partners as the active remnant of the firm were simultaneously faced with considerable changes in commercial methods. They made handsome profits out of cotton in the early years of the Civil War, but their offices in the South were never fully reinstated after the war. This was partly because of personalities, and the retirement of Robert Rankin Sr and George Hoghton who had been interested in merchant business, partly because with the establishment of the telegraph and the growth of futures in the early 1870s, the old mercantile profits were no longer available. Their large warehouses which were built above the office were initially left empty and then let to outsiders. Similarly in timber they found their trade dwindling as their former customers in Britain purchased direct from Canada. Of this decline, and the changes it imposed on the company, Rankin commented:

> My good fortune it was to have dropped in about this period, and without undue humility I cannot profess having assisted towards regaining the magnitude of the old firm. The business worked out or was allowed to lapse — R, G & Co have strayed into new fields. The evidences of the departure may be best understood when I say that when I entered the office the business was entirely with British North America. The US Southern ports were then closed by the War, and the New Orleans and Mobile houses were inoperative. Today our business is practically only that of steamship owners, and practically the only warranty in the steamers' insurance runs: "No British North America" (this on account of the dangers of the St Lawrence) which means that we have a world wide range of ports where we may trade to, except the ports of British North America. The irony of it! {*ibid*, 248}.

The firm's move towards iron steamships began before John Rankin became a partner. The first step was the run down of their fleet of wooden sailing ships. In the 1830s they may have had as many as 100 ships, and in the 1840s, 50. However when Robert Rankin Jr gave evidence to the Unseaworthy Ships Commission (Plimsoll Commission) in 1873 they only had 15 ships. Six of these were large iron sailing ships recently built by yards in England but the remainder were old wooden ships built by the firm in Canada. The wooden ships were generally used in the timber and cotton trades, the iron ships in trade to the East and India. The change

opposition from the Admiralty, but he was not to be thwarted. Contrary to their wishes, he constructed new permanent buildings of brick with concrete floors and laid out new arterial and internal roads made almost entirely of concrete, earning the nickname 'King Concrete'. For his swift action in bringing the yard into production, Rebbeck was knighted in 1941. Later in the war the Admiralty and the Ministry of Supply became concerned at Harland & Wolff's heavy costs. Sir Charles Craven, who chaired the Ministry of Supply Committee on efficiency, and Sir James Lithgow, Controller of Merchant Shipbuilding and Repair, would have liked to dismiss Rebbeck. Instead it was agreed that C J G Palmour, an accountant, should be appointed chairman and Rebbeck step down to the post of managing director. The relationship was not happy. When Palmour resigned in 1944, Rebbeck resumed the chairmanship.

By this time he was already shaping plans for post-war trading, intending to concentrate on the construction of large diesel engined tankers. In the first ten years after the war this policy was an outstanding success. Under Rebbeck's leadership the company built up strong links with Scandinavian owners.

In the mid-1950s the company ran into difficulties. Rebbeck was now an old man and not capable of controlling the business. Gradually the deputy chairman, J S Baillie, began to take command, securing funds for the badly-needed improvements of the Musgrave Yard at Belfast. Rebbeck became ill in 1961 and retired the following year at the age of eighty-four.

Sir Frederick Rebbeck's style as chairman was autocratic. Like many of his contemporaries in British business, Sir Frederick stayed too long, believing that the good years that followed the war would never end.

Sir Frederick was a director of Colvilles Ltd, Short Brothers & Harland Ltd, and the Harland & Wolff's subsidiaries Ocean Transport Co Ltd, the Watertight Door Co Ltd and Heaton Tabb & Co Ltd. He was a member of the General Committee of Lloyd's Register of Shipping and of the Shipbuilding Conference executive board. His professional and trade honours included the presidency of the Institution of Marine Engineers and of the Shipbuilding Employers' Federation as well as vice-presidency of the Royal Institution of Naval Architects. He was also a Belfast Harbour Commissioner and a JP. His knighthood was advanced to KBE in 1953 and he received at least two honorary doctorates.

In 1907 Rebbeck married Amelia Letitia Glover, daughter of Robert Glover; they had two sons and three daughters. His wife died in 1955. His son, Dr Denis Rebbeck, succeeded him as managing director and later chairman.

Sir Frederick Rebbeck died on 27 June 1964, leaving £391 in England.

MICHAEL MOSS

Sources:

Unpublished

Harland & Wolff, Belfast archives.

Midland Bank, London archives, 30/58 letter McKee to Hyde, 21 July 1930.

Published

Michael S Moss and J R Hume, *A History of Harland and Wolff 1853-1985* (Blackstaff Press, 1985).

WWW.

RECKITT, Sir James

(1833-1924)

Starch manufacturer

James Reckitt was born at Nottingham on 14 November 1833, the youngest son of Isaac Reckitt (1792-1862), a corn factor, and his wife Ann née Coleby. The business of Reckitt & Sons Ltd was founded in 1840 when Isaac Reckitt moved from Nottingham and rented a small starch factory in Dansom Lane, Hull. Isaac had a ten-year struggle before the business showed any sign of being viable and, indeed, at one time, when almost in despair, he took up stockbroking as a second string to his bow. It was largely due to the hard work of his two elder sons, George and Francis, who went out 'on the road' to sell the starch to grocers, that success was ultimately achieved.

James attended Packer's Academy in Nottingham, a 'Dame' school in Hull and in 1845, at the age of eleven and a half, was sent to Ackworth, the Quaker school near Pontefract, where George and Francis had been educated before him. He left in 1848, aged fifteen, and entered the starch business as a junior clerk. The company was still very small, employing six or so men and perhaps 25 girls. From 1850 onwards James also did his share of travelling, mainly in the Midlands and the North of England, but his real talent lay in administration rather than selling.

By 1858 the company was firmly established. All loans had been paid off and there was a credit of over £2,000 at the bank. Four years later Isaac Reckitt died, leaving the business in equal shares to his sons, George, Francis and James. Frederic Isaac, the eldest son, who was an epileptic, continued as chief chemist. Within two years, George, after a disagreement with his brothers, realised his share in the business and took up a directorship in a London insurance company. However, in 1870 he was back in the business as manager of the London office (his branch of the family continued to be responsible for the London area until 1947). James and Francis, his older brother, were now sole partners and the business grew steadily under their leadership.

After his father's death James lived at Brough, and in 1865 married Kathleen Saunders, daughter of Robert Saunders of Darlington and Lilling Farm, York. Shortly afterwards he built himself a house at Hessle called 'Mentone', next door to his brother Francis's house, 'Crag View'. The two brothers used to have the firm's mail sent out to them each morning and they would open it and discuss it as they drove into Hull.

In 1879 the business was formed into a private joint stock company with an authorised capital of £200,000, with Francis and James as alternating chairmen, and George as a director. James and his family moved to Swanland Manor (since demolished) in 1884. Francis moved from the Hull area in 1888 to live for the rest of his life in Highgate and elsewhere in the South. He continued as joint chairman until his death in 1917, but James was left in sole executive control of the company, strongly supported but never over-shadowed by T R Ferens (qv), who had joined the firm in 1868 as shorthand clerk to James, and rose to be works manager and a director of the company and eventually chairman. There is no doubt that James had a strong, forceful and even dominating character and it may well be that both George and Francis found him difficult to work with as an equal.

The First World War was a difficult time for James. His whole upbringing as a Quaker had been orientated against everything military but he seems to have accepted the inevitable. When visiting the Canister Works in Hull, where the company's tins were made, he made no comment when he saw part of the factory devoted to producing war-like articles. 'His personal attitude towards the war was that he left it alone' {Reckitt (1981) 6}.

James's life was devoted to the company, to politics (he was an ardent Liberal) and to helping causes which he considered worthy of help. He headed a campaign for a public library in Hull and when he failed to persuade the City authorities of the need, built one at his own cost in Holderness Road. He took a great interest in the distribution of land and published a pamphlet which advocated the break-up of the big estates into smaller owner-occupied holdings. He was much concerned with the Hull Royal Infirmary, of which he was chairman from 1900 until his death, and he and his brother Francis together bought a derelict hotel in Withernsea, converted it into a convalescent home and handed it over to the Infirmary. They were both also strong supporters of the Sailors' Children's Society in Hull, and James was its first president (1904). James established a Garden Village in Hull. His many other charitable activities were not confined to the Quakers, to his own country or to established bodies. Many individuals in need received his help. In 1894 he was offered a baronetcy which, after some hesitation, he accepted.

Sir James Reckitt died on 18 March 1924, only fourteen months after the death of his wife Kathleen, leaving an estate valued at £487,152 gross and a charitable foundation.

BASIL N RECKITT

Writings:

Our Land Laws and British Interest (S Harris & Co, 1880).

Sources:

Unpublished

MSS in private hands.

PrC.

Published

Desmond Chapman-Huston, *Sir James Reckitt: A Memoir* (Faber & Gwyer, 1927).

Basil N Reckitt, *History of Reckitt & Sons Ltd* (A Brown & Sons Ltd, 1953).

—, *A History of the Sir James Reckitt Charity, 1921-1979* (Hull: pp, 1981).

REDDISH, Sir Halford Walter Lupton

(1898-1978)

Cement manufacturer

Halford Walter Lupton Reddish was born at Rugby on 15 August 1898, the son of Henry Walter Lupton Reddish, a solicitor, and his wife Millicent Emma née Luckman. His education at Rugby School was cut short at the age of sixteen by the First World War and, after military service, Halford Reddish took articles under a chartered accountant. He moved from employee through partnership and consultancy to become an entrepreneur. The professional disciplines and ethics established during that decade explain much of his subsequent management style. On a personal level he remained, for instance, self-employed for the rest of his career despite his chairmanship of Rugby Cement, and his relations with senior colleagues often had more in common with private practice than modern industry.

Halford Reddish qualified in November 1920, but remained a clerk with Edward Thomas Peirson & Co (a small Coventry firm) for only two years before he and H G W Teverson, a fellow clerk and exact contemporary, established a practice in Rugby as Reddish Teverson. The partnership appeared to flourish, for by 1928 there were additional offices at Coventry, Tunbridge Wells and Oxford Street, London. However, Halford Reddish was increasingly directing his own energies towards consultancy and he began to develop his own entrepreneurial talents. Reddish Teverson was dissolved in 1929 and in 1930 Reddish & Co informed its clients that it was confining itself to consultancy work; the conventional practice was sold to another local firm, H H Sherwood & Co.

Halford Reddish's own entrepreneurial activities had started with the conversion of his own house into the Northfield Nursing Home, which was sold along with his practice in 1930. Following this he moved into the cinema business, which was to give him control of three of Rugby's four cinemas in two years. The Plaza was built in Northfield's grounds in 1933 and the years before and after saw the purchase of the Regent and Regal Cinemas. Out of the regular showing of the Bernstein films developed a close friendship with Sidney Bernstein who was to buy the Plaza Group in 1945; Reddish remained on the Granada board until his death.

Halford Reddish had been invited on to the board of the Rugby Portland Cement Co as a non-executive director in 1929. This appointment might have remained a minor interest but for the unexpected death of Rugby's general managing director. In 1933 Reddish found himself in control of a one-works cement company with an out-of-date capacity of barely 30,000 tons; sales in that first year were little more than 11,000 tons and profits £1,500.

The first three years proved a period of hectic activity, in which were taken the basic decisions which determined the shape of Rugby's UK operations over the subsequent quarter century. The modernisation and re-equipment of the original Rugby plant was complemented by the purchase of a works at nearby Southam from the receiver of Kaye & Co; and in 1936, while the Rugby works investment programme was still in full swing, the Rochester Cement Co was acquired; finally, the neighbouring Gillingham Portland Cement Co was bought in June 1938 and merged with Rochester. The first phase of the Group's capital spending was not completed until 1938, when capacity had risen from 30,000 to 130,000 tons. The pre-war period ably demonstrated the entrepreneurial side of Halford Reddish, with his nose for a strategic acquisition (Southam cost only £27,000) but he was no adventurer buying companies just for excitement and a quick profit. Reddish was a strong believer in the policy of investing in the most modern plants and each of Rugby Cement's three main sites had, in effect, been rebuilt by the onset of the Second World War. He became chairman in 1939.

Without detracting from Halford Reddish's achievements, the pre-war period which laid the foundations of Rugby's growth could scarcely have offered more favourable conditions. In 1932, the year before Reddish became managing director, construction output and building materials production had fallen to their lowest levels since the mid-1920s and the cement industry was characterised by severe price competition, which had intensified with the collapse of the export market at the beginning of the 1930s. Yet from 1932 the construction industry, led by the housing market, enjoyed a substantial rise in output and by 1939 production of cement had almost doubled. Additionally, the Cement Makers' Federation was formed in 1934 with the express (and successful) intention of ending the ruinous price competition amongst manufacturers.

The expansion programme was to continue unabated after the war and, by the time that the next UK acquisition was made in 1962, capacity at the three pre-war sites had reached one million tons, half of which was at Southam. There then followed the purchase of Eastwoods Cement Ltd in

1962 and Chinnor Industries Ltd in 1963, contributing four works in Cambridgeshire, Sussex, Humberside and Oxfordshire; these added 80 per cent to capacity and took Rugby's market share from 7 per cent to 12.5 per cent. By then Rugby Cement was beginning to challenge Tunnel for second place in the industry league table. Progress from then on remained steady, though in the context of the slow-changing cement industry the increase in market share to over 15 per cent by Sir Halford's final year (1976) remains impressive and reflects the continued insistence on the modernisation of older kilns and the introduction of new capacity well ahead of demand. When he retired, Rugby's UK capacity had exceeded 3 million tons, one hundred times greater than when he took command, and Rugby was the industry's undisputed number two producer.

Reddish's management philosophy was no secret; he would expound on it with both enthusiasm and frequency and he took great pride in a 1958 Harvard Business School study of the Rugby management philosophy — the first ever made of a British company. The concept of business as a partnership between management and labour was by no means original, yet to Reddish it was a concept that had to be followed vigorously on his appointment as managing director — though as with others who believed in teamwork, there was never any question as to who was making the rules. At that time, the custom of the industry was to close down the kilns in the winter months, laying off the men. Reddish introduced a policy of continuous working through the year. Indeed, no-one but he had authority to release people during slack periods and during the whole of his time at Rugby, he never authorised a lay-off. At the same time works committees were established at each plant (he never admitted trade unions into the group) and in 1935 a profit-sharing scheme was introduced. The scheme included the allocation of notional ordinary shares in the company, the number of shares being related to salary and length of service, the bonus to be the exact equivalent of the dividend paid on those notional shares. The scheme was taken a stage further in 1954 with the creation of Rugby 'A' shares, a security unlike any other seen in the Stock Exchange, combining paternalism and financial originality in equal measure. Shares were available in set tranches at a nominal price of 1s but the complicated formula by which attributable profits were calculated took the market value on the Stock Exchange to over £6 at one point. However, that market value could only be realised on retirement (or earlier death) and any employee leaving Rugby received back only his 1s a share — participation with a powerful sting in the tail.

Reddish's homilies on the responsibilities of labour, management and, for that matter, Government, were well-known. More than any other company chairman, he was prepared to write publicly what many preferred to say privately. Emotive headlines like 'Grasping Hands', 'Troublemakers' and 'Moral Decay' give the flavour of his lengthy discourses, yet looking back at the substance of his written work, it must be recognised that his warnings, forebodings and pleas have stood the test of time and showed a percipience sadly clouded by his dramatic style — witness his vigorous analysis of the impact of government expenditure on the rate of inflation, first voiced in 1946.

Once the initial post-war settling-in period had passed and the next phase of the domestic expansion was initiated, Reddish turned his attention to overseas manufacture, establishing Trinidad Cement in 1951 with the co-operation of the then colonial government. In the following year, Cockburn Cement was incorporated in Western Australia. He was easiest overseas in an Empire or Commonwealth environment and his other close connections were in Canada and New Zealand — where he unsuccessfully tried to buy into a local producer in 1962. Both the Caribbean and Western Australia were selected as areas of potential growth, though they had the added advantage, from a corporate view, of limited competition — Trinidad was actually a local monopoly. Cockburn proved a highly-successful development, with capacity reaching almost one million tons by 1971, and forged close links with Western Australia. By contrast, he became disenchanted with Trinidad when the country achieved independence and Trinidad Cement was eventually nationalised in 1976. Indeed, unlike Blue Circle, its large competitor, Reddish never felt at ease investing in emerging nations and neglected opportunities successfully pursued by other cement companies.

Sir Halford's (he was knighted in 1958) last decade at Rugby brought highly-publicised and embarrassing problems over succession. Nominal measures to devolve management responsibility had been taken in 1968 and in 1969 Sir Basil Smallpeice (qv) was appointed to the board with a view to becoming non-executive chairman in 1970. Sir Halford was to remain in the conceptually unusual role of executive life president; the anomalies this created led to the speedy resignation of Sir Basil. Sadly, this was to be only the forerunner of a bitter clash between Sir Halford and the rest of the Rugby board in 1976. He announced his intention to retire later that year but was opposed in his wish to appoint as his successor an employee below board level. The resignation statement made in November 1976 was as forthright as any of his annual reports: 'I regret that I am unable to name my successor but it has been made clear to me that a majority of the directors would not elect to the board the men, including the new chairman, whom I wished to follow me' {*Financial Times* 30 Nov 1976}. Sir Halford continued to attend his office at Rugby, and maintained his outside directorships at Granada Group, Meldrum Investment Trust and Warburg Investment Management.

During his life Reddish made substantial charitable donations and though he expressly instructed that these should remain completely private, his £5 million gift for a research institute at the King Edward VII Hospital at Midhurst did become public. In 1977 he was made an honorary fellow of the Royal College of Physicians. He was a member of the Council of the Imperial Society of Knights Bachelor and a freeman of the City of London in the Livery of the Pattenmakers.

Sir Halford Reddish died on 12 October 1978 at the age of eighty. His second wife, Valerie, eldest daughter of Arthur Grosart Lehman Smith, had died in 1971 and there were no children. He left an estate of £2,171,571 gross.

FRED WELLINGS

Writings:

This Is Industrial Partnership (Staples Press, 1955).

(with Henry Teverson) *Principles and Practice of Income Tax, Super Tax and Corporation Profits Tax* (1st edn, St Albans: Metropolitan College, 1924; 13th edn, Gregg Publishing Co, 1939).

Sources:

Unpublished

BCe.

PrC.

Published

Financial Times 30 Nov 1976.

Times 14 Oct 1978.

WWW.

REDWOOD, Sir Thomas Boverton

(1846-1919)

Oil consultant

Thomas Boverton (known as Boverton) Redwood was born at St Giles, Middlesex (now in Bloomsbury, London), on 26 April 1846, the son of Professor Theophilus Redwood (1806-92), of Boverton, Glamorgan and Montague Street, London, and his wife Charlotte Elizabeth, daughter of Thomas Newborn Robert Morson of Queen Square, London and Hornsey, Middlesex. His father had become professor in the school of pharmacy of the Pharmaceutical Society of Great Britain, a position he held for forty years. Boverton Redwood was educated at University College School and was a fellow of the Chemical Society before he was twenty. After a period in his father's laboratory, in 1869 he joined the Petroleum Association which required a secretary with a knowledge of analytical chemistry and thenceforward he determined to specialise in mineral oil. The oil industry was still in its infancy and many of his friends considered he had chosen too narrow a field for his professional career.

His earliest work was in connection with the testing of the flashpoint of mineral oils. In 1872 he first gave evidence to a Select Committee and in 1876-77 he was called to advise on legislation; his experimental work with Sir Frederick Abel resulted in the Abel apparatus being adopted as the standard method of testing. He studied the effect of barometric pressure on the evolution of volatile constituents of oil at various altitudes in the Alps and in a pressure chamber at Berlin and visited India to study the effects of climatic conditions. In 1886 he designed the Redwood viscometer as an adaptation of equipment used in a London candle works; this was adopted as a British Government and petroleum industry standard and even today viscosity is often described in seconds (eg 35 second oil), the time for 50 cc of oil to pass through a Redwood standard aperture; the viscometer is included in the Spy Cartoon of Sir Boverton which is simply entitled 'Petroleum'. Again with Sir Frederick Abel, he investigated the causes of accidents with lamps using mineral oil. In 1892 he studied the risk of explosion from the accumulation of petroleum vapour in oil tankers, which was of topical and urgent concern with the opening of the Suez Canal and advised the Board of Trade about accidents on ships carrying petroleum. He worked closely with successive Chief Inspectors of Explosives, with one of whom, Captain J H Thomson, he wrote a handbook in 1901.

He patented (with Professor Sir James Dewar) a process of refining under pressure to increase kerosene yields from crude petroleum which according to Sir Frederick W Black 'is to a large extent the foundation of the modern "cracking processes"' {Redwood (1922) vii}. Redwood established a consultancy firm which, at a time when British oil companies rarely if ever employed full-time geologists or any other kind of technical expert, was used before 1914 by most British oil companies (but not Shell). His relations with the Burmah Oil Co, for whom he was part-time consultant from 1893 to 1919, were particularly close, and he seems to have played a prominent role on occasion in decision-making in that company. Redwood's advice and geologists were utilised by the British syndicate searching for oil in Persia in the early 1900s on the basis of the concession granted to William Knox D'Arcy (qv). Redwood's most significant achievements came in 1904-5 when he was a vital intermediary between the D'Arcy Syndicate, rapidly running out of funds in its search for oil in Persia, the Admiralty and Burmah Oil. In 1905 Burmah Oil agreed to take over the struggling Persian company, and three years later oil was found. Redwood's technical assessment of the value of the oilfield discovered in Persia in 1908 was included in the prospectus which launched the Anglo-Persian Oil Co in 1909. Redwood's firm was similarly used by Weetman Pearson (qv) after Pearson acquired large oil concessions in Mexico in the mid-1900s. According to a junior contemporary in the same field, Redwood virtually 'monopolised petroleum consulting work in England' {Beeby-Thompson (1961) 75}.

Redwood had firm views on the future of the oil industry. He recognised early on the advantages for the Royal Navy in using oil rather than coal. He was, however, worried that Britain's supply position was vulnerable because the British Empire lacked significant oil reserves, and depended on oil supplied by firms either entirely foreign, such as Standard Oil of the USA, or with foreign associations, such as the Shell Transport & Trading

Co (which became a minority partner in the Anglo-Dutch group in 1907). Consequently Redwood used his influence with Government to support independent British oil companies and to encourage the development of oilfields in the British Empire. Redwood's position as a 'walking encyclopaedia of oil knowledge' {Corley (1983) 39} made him the first choice when the British Government sought advice on petroleum matters. He gave evidence to every important committee on petroleum established between 1870 and 1919, including the Select Committees of the House of Lords in 1872 and 1883, the Royal Commission on Coal in 1903-5 and the Admiralty Committees on Oil in 1903-6 and in 1911-12. As Adviser on Petroleum to the Home Office he performed numerous assignments for government departments.

In 1912 Redwood served on Admiral Lord Fisher's Commission on Fuel and Engines considering oil fuel for the navy. Despite his age, he was active during the First World War and became Director of Technical Investigations at the newly-formed Petroleum Executive in 1917. In the same year he became chairman of the Interdepartmental Committees on Gas Traction and Alcohol Motor Fuel.

Professionally he was consulted on the occurrence, real or supposed, of petroleum in nearly every part of the world and his opinions were deservedly trusted by clients. He published many books and assisted in the establishment of curricula devoted to petroleum at Birmingham University and the Imperial College of Science. Redwood was a technical polymath rather than an entrepreneur, yet his oil consultancy business was the first of its kind in Britain and provided important services to British oil companies. His influence helped shape British oil policy and the structure of the early British oil industry.

In addition to his consultancy work, Redwood was very active in the fields of chemistry, geology and related subjects. As well as being a founder and first president of the Institution of Petroleum Technology he was connected with 20 other scientific societies and was president of the Society of the Chemical Industry. In 1899 he received an honorary DSc from the Normal University of Ohio. He was knighted in 1905 and granted a baronetcy in 1911. He owned one of the first four-cylinder Daimler cars made in England and demonstrated it to the Prince of Wales. He also owned a succession of motor yachts and was a keen member of the Royal Thames Yacht Club. Redwood was reported to have a resemblance to the actor Sir Henry Irving (qv) for whom he was often mistaken, 'something that he was vain enough to encourage' {ibid, 39}. A young American oil consultant contrasted 'Sir Boverton Redwood, immaculately attired, with an orchid in his button hole, speaking in a slightly affected but impressive manner with a provincial accent', with William d'Arcy, 'the tough, shrewd, plainspeaking Australian mining man' {Beeby-Thompson (1961) 80}. Redwood married in 1873 Mary Elizabeth, daughter of Frederick Letchworth. They had two daughters and a son, Bernard, who died in 1911; on Sir Boverton Redwood's death on 4 June 1919 (when he left £165,014 gross) the title passed to his grandson Thomas Boverton Redwood (1906-74).

GEOFFREY JONES *and* FRANCIS GOODALL

Writings:

PP, HL 1872 (135) IX, SC on Petroleum Bill.

PP, HL 1883 (180) IX, SC on Petroleum Bill.

PP, HC 1896 (311) XII, SC on Petroleum.

Treatise on Petroleum (2 vols, Charles Griffin & Co, 1896, 4th ed (intro by Sir Frederick W Black), 3 vols, 1922).

(with Captain J H Thomson) *The Handbook on Petroleum for Inspectors under the Petroleum Acts* (Charles Griffin & Co, 1901).

PP, RC Coal Resources of the United Kingdom 1903-5 (1904) Cd 1991.

PP, Alcohol Motor Fuel (1919) Cmd 218 (chairman).

PP, Gas Traction (1919) Cmd 263 (chairman).

A complete list of Boverton Redwood's works is set out in the *Journal of the Institution of Petroleum Technology* 1918-19.

Sources:

Unpublished

BCe.

MCe.

PrC.

Published

A Beeby-Thompson, *Oil Pioneer* (Sedgwick & Jackson, 1961).

Burke's Peerage and Baronetage.

T A B Corley, *A History of the Burmah Oil Company 1886-1924* (Heinemann, 1983).

Ronald W Ferrier, *The History of the British Petroleum Company* (Cambridge: Cambridge University Press, 1982).

Robert Henriques, *Marcus Samuel, First Viscount Bearsted and Founder of the Shell Transport and Trading Company, 1853-1927* (Barrie & Rockliff, 1960).

Geoffrey Jones, *The State and the Emergence of the British Oil Industry* (Macmillan, 1981).

Journal of the Institution of Petroleum Technology 5 (1918-19).

Petroleum Times 24 May 1954.

Times 5 June 1954.

WWW.

Albert E Reed (courtesy of Reed International PLC).

REED, Albert Edwin

(1846-1920)

Paper manufacturer

Albert Edwin Reed was born at Cullompton, Devon, on 13 January 1846, the third of nine children of Edward Reed, an excise officer, and his wife Eliza née Saunders. His father was periodically transferred in the course of his duties, which included supervision of the excise on papermaking. Albert's education was consequently sporadic but he finally spent two years at the Blue School, Wells. Under his father's influence he was Liberal, Nonconformist and musical; in fact had he not been the son of a dissenter the Dean of the Cathedral would have accepted him for a musical education.

Forced to look elsewhere for his career, Albert got his first job, at the age of fourteen, as a junior clerk earning £30 a year at Lower Wookey paper mill (now St Cuthbert's). He was appointed manager of the mill in 1867 at the age of twenty-one. It was one of the earliest users of esparto pulp and operated two machines, one at that time the biggest in the world. In 1873 Samuel Evans and Robert Owen, who owned the store Evans & Owen in Bath and were friends of the Reed family in the Methodist Wesleyan Chapel, gave Albert financial support to take over Trevarno mill (now Bathgate). Here, he and his bride, Emma Vickery, made their first home. In 1877 Owen appointed him manager of the larger mill at Ely, Cardiff, making newsprint, printings and wrappings.

At this time difficulties in the supply of the raw materials, rag and esparto, were beginning to be recognised. Ground wood had already been used as a constituent of certain papers. The effective utilisation of the unlimited forest potential depended, however, upon the discovery of a successful chemical means of removing the unwanted components of wood to leave relatively pure cellulose or 'chemical woodpulp'. At Ely, Reed undertook pioneering work in this direction. Although he achieved only limited success he gained experience, which later proved valuable.

In 1889 Reed broke with Owen. With severance pay of £639 and shares in profits, he had resources of £7,000 with which he bought the bankrupt Riverside mill, Dartford, Kent. He incorporated the London Paper Mills Co to which he sold the assets profitably, retaining a minority holding and joint managing directorship. By now a method had been worked out in several countries for producing 'sulphite', the form of chemical woodpulp which was to become for many years the major papermaking raw material. The first large-scale sulphite mill was being erected by Ekman at Northfleet and Reed was appointed manager at £600 a year.

In 1894 Reed bought Upper Tovil mill, Maidstone, Kent, and founded a private company. By skilful choice of pulps and installation of supercalenders, adopted from the textile industry, to impart a smooth surface, he produced a superior newsprint which he later sold to Alfred

Tovil Mill (courtesy of Reed International PLC).

Harmsworth's (qv) *Daily Mirror*. This was the only paper suitable for high speed printing of half-tone illustrations, thus enabling photographic reporting of news to be created and the *Daily Mirror* to be saved from collapse.

The incorporation of Albert E Reed & Co Ltd was made in 1903. Authorised capital was £300,000, the consideration paid to Reed being £295,000 made up of cash and all the voting shares. The mills sold to the company were Tovil, Horton Kirby, Wycombe Marsh and Merton — all predominantly making newsprint and other printing papers. At various times Reed was manager, owner or a major shareholder in 19 mills in the UK and became known as the 'Wizard of the South' because of his record in acquiring derelict mills and, by modern equipment, efficient management and astute sales, converting them into profitable enterprises.

Reed's UK business was co-ordinated with overseas woodpulp ventures. Having witnessed first rag and then esparto fail to keep up with the expanding demands of the paper industry, Reed concluded that he must ensure supplies by owning forests and pulp mills. He launched ventures in Norway, USA, Canada and Newfoundland, the latter with capital of £400,000 and scheduled annual output of 40,000 tons of pulp. The project involved a dam at Bishop's Falls on the Exploits River, electric turbines to generate 13,600 hp to drive 18 grinders for producing mechanical pulp direct from wood cut from the 1,300 square miles of timber lands over which cutting rights were held. It also included, jointly with Harmsworth's Anglo-Newfoundland Development Co mill, the construction of a railway to a port built for shipping to UK. In all it was an ambitious enterprise.

The First World War severed the links between Reed's overseas pulp production and UK paper mills with the threat of ruin to both. He disposed of the Newfoundland company to the Harmsworth Anglo-Newfoundland Development Co (owners of the neighbouring mill) for £56,000, plus repayment of a personal Reed loan of £31,000. Record

Bridge Mill (courtesy of Reed International PLC).

demands, however, brought temporary prosperity to the UK paper trade and enabled Reed to sell three of his mills at boom prices and prolong profitable production in the others.

He thus saw his company enter the post-war period with only five mills but with record profits, minimal debt and high liquidity. He and his son, Albert Ralph (qv), agreed on a new strategy of creating one very large modern UK paper mill as the basis of future growth, and initiated the building of Aylesford mill near Maidstone, Kent.

Reed's main colleagues were Charles Stevens, responsible for the technical side of production, Stanley Cousins, responsible for sales, and in later years his twin sons, Albert Ralph and Percy. Albert Reed himself retained absolute control. In the early stages he was assisted by his brothers, William and Ernest, for whom he bought mills. William founded Reed & Smith and in turn his sons, particularly Sir Arthur, became prominent papermakers and citizens in the West Country.

Albert Reed's principal contributions to the industry were probably his active part in the development (though not the origination) of first esparto pulp, and then chemical woodpulp, as papermaking materials and, secondly, his use of large efficient machines and supercalenders which enabled his company to produce newsprint successfully for so long against foreign competitors in spite of the latter's natural advantages.

Reed served on many industrial committees, such as the British Wood Pulp Association (president, 1918-19) and the Paper Makers' Association, and was a Royal Commissioner for paper during the war. He narrowly missed election as a Liberal in the 1906 general election. He was a devoted family man with three daughters and two sons, an accomplished musician and above all, a pious and ardent supporter and benefactor of the Wesleyan Church and various related charities.

Albert Reed died on 21 February 1920, leaving an estate of £399,320 gross, represented predominantly by shares in his company.

PHILIP SYKES

Sources:

Unpublished

Albert E Reed diary 1861-64, in possession of Kathleen Judd, grand-daughter.

BLPES, Tariff Commission papers, evidence of Albert E Reed, TC3 1/88.

PRO, BT 31/4655/30601, 31/15807/53240, 31/18076/93115.

Reed International PLC, Albert E Reed memorandum book; statutory declaration 1903 (description of layout and procedures of Mendip Mill in 1860s); Albert E Reed & Co Ltd, memorandum and articles of association, 1903, prospectus, annual reports.

Wiggins Teape Ltd, description of Ely Paper Mill, Cardiff, by Albert E Reed, for Cardiff Naturalist Society, 23 June 1880.

BCe.

PrC.

Information from Percy Reed (supplied by Mrs Van den Arend, grand-daughter of Albert Reed, 1975).

Published

Methodist Recorder 26 Feb, 4 Mar 1920.

Methodist Times 26 Feb 1920.

Paper Mills Directory.

Paper Record 8 Mar, 8 June 1893.

Reginald Pound and Geoffrey Harmsworth, *Northcliffe* (Cassell, 1959).

Philip Sykes, *Albert E Reed and the Creation of a Paper Business 1860-1960* (Reed International Ltd, 1981).

Times 23 Feb 1920.

Woking Herald 27 Feb 1920.

World's Paper Trade Review 26 July, 12 Aug 1889, 15 July 1898, 27 Feb 1920.

Harpenden and Gerrards Cross. He was also a considerable supporter of the City Temple where a stained glass window stands in his memory. After he met Dr Frank Buchman, founder of Moral Rearmament, in 1933, Austin Reed came to believe that 'the true function of business was to distribute the resources of the world for the benefit of all and the exploitation of none'. {*Times* 6 May 1954} As one move towards this objective, he was responsible in 1949, when the firm's capital was increased to £1.2 million, for the issue of 10,000 Austin Reed employee shares. He was a liberal in his political views, although he took no active part in politics. He was a keen golfer and, in his youth, an active oarsman.

He married Emily, sixth daughter of Alfred Wilson, a butcher of Bridlington, Yorkshire, in 1902. They had two sons (one of whom was killed in North Africa during the war) and four daughters. Austin Reed died on 5 May 1954, leaving an estate valued at £108,663 gross.

G TONGE and DAVID J JEREMY

Sources:

Unpublished

C Reg: Austin Reed (164,291).

BCe.

MCe.

PrC.

Published

DNB.

John H Dunning and E Victor Morgan (eds), *An Economic Study of the City of London* (George Allen & Unwin, 1971).

Times 6 May 1954.

WWW.

REITH, John Charles Walsham

1st Lord Reith of Stonehaven, Kincardineshire

(1889-1971)

Pioneer manager of broadcasting

John Charles Walsham Reith was born at Stonehaven, near Aberdeen, on 20 July 1889, fifth son of Rev George Reith (1842-1919), a minister (and later Moderator) of the Free Church of Scotland and his wife Adah Mary née Weston (d 1935). He was educated at Glasgow Academy, Gresham's School, Holt, and the Royal Technical College of Glasgow, and, while he afterwards gained an MSc from Lafayette College, USA, in 1917, he was to regret later that he had no university education. It was important for his development, however, that his initial training was as an engineer and that he spent his long apprenticeship in a locomotive works. He did not take up a post in London until 1916 and he was to return to Glasgow as the general manager of the Coatbridge works of the large and varied engineering firm, William Beardmore & Co, in 1920. Engineering interested him less than decision-taking and management, and he never confused training, the kind of training he had had, and education. His own education, as he himself conceived it, was a continuing education going through different phases. There was an obvious analogy with broadcasting, which itself rested on a technology and the science that underlay it, but which blossomed in its output as cultural expression. Reith believed, however, that both the advance of technology and the promotion of culture had to be in the right hands. The Manse had left him with a strong, at times almost obsessive, sense of the burden of personal responsibility. Soon after he had joined the new BBC, when he wrote his most cheerful, interesting and challenging book *Broadcast Over Britain* (1924), he stressed how heavily 'the responsibility of pioneering a new broadcasting enterprise 'weighs with us': 'it is realised to the full, it is apt to become an obsession. Whether we are fit or not, is for reasoned judgment only ... Pronouncement may be reserved till the proofs of the efforts are established.' {Reith (1924) 34}

During the First World War, when Reith served in France as a lieutenant in the Royal Engineers, he had learned in a different way of the weight of responsibility, as he described in his book *Wearing Spurs* (1966). He saw how serious it was for everyone when it was missing. Badly wounded in October 1915, he was left with a conspicuous facial scar for the rest of his life. He widened his experience, however, when, declared unfit for further military service, he was sent as a major to the United States to take charge of contracts for munitions, and in 1918 he joined the Admiralty in the Department of the Civil Engineer-in-Chief. In 1919 he was in charge of the liquidation of ordnance and engineering contracts for the Ministry of Munitions.

It was the new post-1918 medium of broadcasting which provided Reith with his great opportunity, although he did not know what broadcasting meant when he joined the newly-founded British Broadcasting Co as first general manager in December 1922 at a salary of £1,750 a year. Fortunately for Reith, broadcasting involved growth, not liquidation. It also involved giving orders, not taking them. There were, indeed, no standing orders providing him with any initial guidance as to how to operate his new venture. The British Broadcasting Co, formed in October 1922 and registered in December, had seven directors, with Lord Gainford, an ex-Postmaster-General, as its chairman, but Reith was already very much in charge when the Company received its licence, a monopoly licence, from the Post Office in January 1923. It had been formed by radio manufacturing interests after difficult and protracted negotiations at the Post Office, with an initial capital of £100,000, but its dividends were restricted by Post Office ruling to 7.5 per cent. It was by will of Reith, however not of the Post Office, that from the start it set out to act as a 'public service'. In practice, during the first four years of its life it never concerned itself primarily with the interest either of radio manufacturers or, since it was financed by listeners' licence fees not by advertising, with the manufacturers of anything else. During the last months of its existence, following two official enquiries, the directors connived at their own extinction and did not seek to interfere with the constitutional rearrangements which by Royal Charter transformed the Company into a Corporation on 1 January 1927.

Reith remained — with a new and more difficult board of Governors and with the new title of Director-General. There had been no break in his own philosophy. Indeed, he had been one of the chief advocates of the change. The philosophy, which distinguished broadcasting from publishing or from the cinema business, was to offer people not what they wanted but balanced fare and high standards. 'Few know what they want and very few what they need.' {*ibid*} To have run it differently would have been prostitution. As the trustees of a public service the Director-General and the Governors were not out to make money, they were determined to provide a national coverage and they were seeking 'unified control'. {*PP*, (1923) Cmd 1951}

Nonetheless, for Reith the absence of the profit motive did not minimise the importance of sound management. He was keenly interested in resources, in structures, in recruitment and in human relationships, and he set out to fashion a broadcasting institution which would be outstanding on the international scene. His task was not an easy one, for as the number of licence-holders grew from over 2 million in 1926 to over 8.5 million at the end of 1938 the size of the BBC's staff rose also from 773 to 4,060. There were extensions of provision also: from 1932 onwards an Empire Service was provided on his own initiative, and from 1936 onwards a small regular television service was made available in the London area in parallel with sound broadcasting. Reith carried out one major review of BBC organisation in 1933-34. 'Creative' and 'administrative' staff and functions were separated from each other 'in order to enable creative staff to concentrate on their creative work' {BBC internal memorandum, 29 Aug 1933}, and a new top post, that of Controller (Output), was created alongside that of Controller (Administration). Each Controller was put in charge of a Division and in each Division there were to be five Branches.

After carrying out this 'reorganisation', as he called it, Reith became less interested in staff recruitment and in the daily routines of the Corporation he had served so faithfully. The staff had been housed in a 'temple of the Muses', a new purpose-built Broadcasting House, since 1932, a landmark date in the history of the BBC which marked the end of the old informal Savoy Hill days which soon became shrouded in nostalgia. Yet there were more staff problems between 1933 and 1938 than during the previous twelve years of broadcasting, with some of Reith's critics inside and outside Broadcasting House accusing him of being too authoritarian. He was, indeed, a firm disciplinarian in a period when there was no countervailing trade union power. There was no Staff Association until 1939 (and no Director of Staff Administration until 1936). It should be added that there was no Listener Research Group until 1936.

Reith delivered a number of lectures on the structure and management of the BBC, never without its critics, before he left it in 1938 a highly centralised, though not monolithic, organisation, which he preferred to call an organism. He drew a strong distinction between his executive responsibilities as Director-General and those of the chairman of the Governors, primarily those of a public trustee, and at the top of the organisation he attached the utmost importance to narrowing 'the span of control'. He believed that the BBC in operation represented 'an ideal combination of co-operative management and definite leadership and direction. There was nothing statutory about it' {*PP* (1935-36) Cmd 5091, 8 May 1935}. He and other writers on the BBC as a public corporation distinguished it formally from commercial broadcasting companies on American lines and national propaganda broadcasting institutions operating on Russian or on German lines. Reith prized the independence and related it directly to what he was to call later 'the brute force of monopoly' {Reith (1949) 99}. He was not surprised when the last official committee of enquiry examining broadcasting policy before the Second World War — the Ullswater Committee of 1936 — paid a tribute to the BBC and to the prudence and idealism which have characterised its operations and enabled it to overcome the many difficulties which surround a novel and expanding public service' {*PP* (1935-36) Cmd 5091, para 7}.

Between 1936 and 1938 Reith was ready for a change of responsibilities, but he did not consider that he was offered the right type of task by politicians, of most of whom he had a low opinion. When he moved at Neville Chamberlain's suggestion to become chairman of Imperial Airways in 1938 he never entirely settled down and he was contemptuous of the change of regime in Broadcasting House. He remained with Imperial Airways and its successor, the BOAC, until 1940. It was Chamberlain, however, who drew him into Government, after the Second World War broke out, as Minister of Information in January 1940. A safe parliamentary seat was found for him at Southampton: he was returned as National MP, unopposed, in February 1940 and his prestige in the country was high. Moreover, he had had much to do behind the scenes with the preparations for the creation of the new Ministry, which never under him or later became a popular institution. He carried out considerable reorganisation in its already unwieldy structure before being transferred by Winston Churchill to the Ministry of Transport, where he stayed for only a short, highly frustrating time (May-October 1940). The two men were incompatible, and although Reith had a great deal to offer when he was moved (in October 1940) to the Ministry of Works and Buildings and had his role extended when post-war planning procedures were added to his responsibilities, he lost his job two weeks after the extension was implemented (in February 1942). Churchill remarked curtly that he found Reith difficult to work with. Reith never forgave him. They had first clashed at the time of the General Strike in 1926 when Reith struggled hard to maintain the young BBC's (relative) independence.

Soon afterwards, in 1942, Reith joined the RNVR as a lieutenant-commander in 1942 and served with the rank of captain as Director of Combined Operations Material Department at the Admiralty from 1943 to 1945. After the war he was chairman of the Commonwealth Telecommunication Conference in 1945 and on its board from 1946 to 1950. He was also returned to one of his most important wartime responsibilities, that of planning, when in 1946 he was appointed chairman of the New Towns Committee: it issued three important reports in quick succession. Not surprisingly he became chairman of the Hemel Hempstead Development Corporation in 1947 and stayed in the post until 1950. In the latter year he became chairman of the Colonial Development Corporation remaining in the post, greatly respected but still seeking wider responsibilities until 1959. He was chairman of the State Building Society, 1960-64; a director and vice-chairman of the British Oxygen Co Ltd, 1956-66, and a director of the Phoenix Assurance Co and Tube Investments.

Reith's gifts were more appreciated by the post-war Labour Party than by the Conservatives, and he forged new links when he headed a Labour Party enquiry into advertising and bitterly opposed the introduction of commercial television. Yet he was never a Socialist and he retained his low opinion of most politicians. He liked to think of himself as being in the Viceroy tradition, a deeply-rooted tradition of public service, which did not prevent him from holding a number of commercial directorships at various times after 1945.

A son of the Manse, Reith never lost the imprint of his origins. He was Lord Rector of the University of Glasgow in 1965-68, and in an appointment that gave him great satisfaction he became Lord High Commissioner of the Church of Scotland in 1967. These were culminating experiences, however, relieving a continuing sense of disappointment that his exceptional talents had never been adequately used after he left the British Broadcasting Corporation in 1938.

Although Reith had what to other men would have been important appointments after that date in administration and business, he did not feel, in his own favourite words, that they 'fully stretched him'. His autobiography *Into the Wind* (1949) was a bleak but impressive book, written when he still had high hopes of a challenging job: his voluminous diaries, published in edited form in 1975, did not add to his posthumous reputation, although they had meant much to him from the day he started keeping them in December 1911 and revealed more than most diaries do both of ambition and doubt.

Those who knew Reith personally realised that neither the book nor the diaries as they were generally interpreted did full justice to the forcefulness and magnetism of Reith's complex personality. They were too intimate and too selective. Six feet six inches in height, he towered physically over most of his contemporaries, and he could tower over many of them mentally and psychologically as well. Yet having 'warmed both hands before the fire of life' {*Times* 17 June 1971}, another of his memorable phrases, he was not always gloomy. Moreover, he could give his confidence and friendship without reserve to those whom he trusted. He could also command loyal and willing support. There was outstanding character behind all the caricatures.

He married in 1921 Muriel Katherine, younger daughter of the publisher John Lynch Odhams; they had one son and one daughter. He was knighted in 1927, created GBE in 1934 and GCVO in 1939, and sworn of the Privy Council in January 1940. He was raised to the peerage as Lord Reith of Stonehaven in October 1940. He was made a CB in 1945 and a KT in 1969. In addition he received numerous honorary doctorates and professional honours. It would be wrong to claim that he despised such honours, for he attached considerable weight to them. It was little consolation, nonetheless, for him to conclude that 'he or she whom public opinion regards as successful may know themselves to have failed.' {Rectorial address at Glasgow University 1966}

Lord Reith died on 16 June 1971, leaving £6,155 gross.

ASA BRIGGS

Writings:

Broadcast Over Britain (Hodder & Stoughton, 1924).

Personality and Career (George Newnes, 1925).

Broadcasting Policy and Development — A Report (Pretoria: Government Printer, 1935).

Report of the New Towns Committee (HMSO, 1946).

Into the Wind (Hodder & Stoughton, 1949).

Wearing Spurs (Hutchinson, 1966).

(Charles Stuart ed), *The Reith Diaries* (Collins, 1975).

Sources:

Unpublished

Numerous BBC memoranda and lectures.

PrC.

Personal knowledge.

Published

Andrew Boyle, *Only the Wind Will Listen* (Hutchinson, 1972).

Asa Briggs, *The History of Broadcasting in the United Kingdom* (4 vols, Oxford University Press, 1961-79).

REITH John Charles Walsham

Burke's Peerage and Baronetage 1980.

PP, Departmental Committee on Broadcasting (1923) Cmd 1951.

PP, Committee on Broadcasting (1935-36) Cmd 5091.

Times 17 June 1971.

WWMP.

WWW.

RENOLD, Sir Charles Garonne

(1883-1967)

Precision chain manufacturer

Sir Charles G Renold (courtesy of Renold PLC).

Charles Garonne Renold was born at Altrincham, Cheshire, on 29 October 1883, the eldest son of Hans Renold, a precision chain manufacturer, and his first wife, Mary Susan, daughter of Charles Herford. Hans Renold had come to England from his native Switzerland in 1873, and had bought for £300 a small textile chainmaking business in Salford in 1879. The business soon outgrew its premises, and was moved to Brook Street, Manchester; it was further expanded in 1895. Life in the Renold household was materially austere, the business always having first claim on Hans Renold's earnings, but Hans was a cheerful man, and he and his wife, both Unitarians, took a keen interest in the welfare of the Renolds workpeople, as well as in their own family.

After education at Abbotsholme School, Charles went to America and graduated Master of Engineering at Cornell University. In 1905 he joined the staff of Hans Renold Ltd (the private company had been formed in 1903) and he became a director in 1906, the year work began on a new factory at Burnage near Didsbury. From the first he was interested above all in the problems of industrial management: he worked throughout his career to raise the level of effectiveness of British industrial managers by the example of his own firm, and by the promotion of management education.

In 1910 (when Renolds' turnover was about £105,000), Charles Renold introduced a personnel department, then called the 'employment department', into the family firm and a beginning was made in holding 'management meetings', foreshadowing the conciliar arrangements now (1984) governing the detailed execution of board policies in the Renold group. In 1912 he re-visited the USA to study the work of F W Taylor, the American pioneer of modern factory production methods, and on his return persuaded his father to allow the introduction of time-and-motion study. He became an early enthusiast of 'scientific management', arguing that the application of some of its principles to the Renolds engineering works (of some 1,000 employees at this time) had beneficial effects for the company and no adverse effects on the workers.

In the First World War the Renold works at Burnage, at that time the company's only factory, was chiefly occupied with munitions making and the workforce grew to 2,380. This brought its own management problems, and Charles Renold began to examine the whole subject of what he came to call 'constitutional management' in the company. In 1916 he became works director, and, in that year, formed a welfare committee to consider working conditions in general. The policy of constitutional management was formally introduced in 1917, and a shop stewards' committee was established.

In 1919, Charles Renold became managing director. Like many other companies, Hans Renold Ltd faced a difficult period of transition from munitions manufacture to the resumption of their peacetime production. In 1919, the business registered its first loss, of £3,000, on the year's trading. As well as the reconversion of the works to chain manufacture, efforts were made to recover and extend former markets. Branch sales offices in Birmingham and Leeds were added to those opened in London and Glasgow in the years before the war. In 1921 a subsidiary selling company, Renold Chains Ltd, was formed to handle exports other than to the USA and Canada. Particular attention was paid to sales in France and Belgium, and, in 1928, a German agency, Renold Industrie Ketten GmbH, was formed. In that year, in which turnover reached some £560,000 and 1,750 workers were employed, Charles Renold succeeded his father as chairman.

His first period of office was short because of the success of his own efforts in negotiating a merger, which he had been trying to bring about for ten years, with the rival Coventry Chain Co. He became the first managing director as well as deputy chairman of the Renold & Coventry Chain Co Ltd, which had a capital of £1.1 million. The chair was taken by Arthur Brampton, the leading figure among the Coventry Chain Co directors.

The organisation of the 13 subsidiaries was simplified, and production rationalised with chainmaking being concentrated at the Manchester and Coventry works. Efforts were made to improve the quality and standardise the design of the cycle fittings manufacture which had come with the Coventry Chain Co, but this was a long process, and costly in investment and in trading losses sustained during reconstruction. In 1937, an offer from a competitor to acquire the fittings business was accepted, and the company concentrated solely on the production of precision chains and wheels. Turnover lost by this sale was recovered within a year, and the net profit for 1938 was £231,124. In the Second World War, chain manufacture continued alongside munitions manufacture and the production of tooling equipment for small arms manufacture at premises leased for the duration of the war at Newton Mill in Cheshire. Some 500 were employed here, 3,300 at the Renold Works near Manchester and 1,200 at Coventry.

Photo-elasticity test equipment for chain (courtesy of Renold PLC).

After his father's death in May 1943 and the retirement of Arthur Brampton the following month, Charles Renold was appointed chairman; he resigned the position of managing director. Post-war reorganisation was easier after the Second World War than after the First, partly because most of the firm's capacity had been devoted to production of the firm's usual products; Renold estimated that 'Measured in terms of establishment strength our total activities increased by about 60 per cent, the activity concerned with our normal types of product having increased by about 30 per cent, the other 30 per cent being devoted to special products' {Tripp (1956) 154}. In 1946 a five-day week was introduced, and a new factory of some 130,000 square feet was acquired at Cardiff. In 1948, sales were more than twice the figure for 1938. By 1955, Renold Chains Ltd (as the Renold & Coventry Chain Co was re-named the preceding year) employed about 5,000 workers in UK: 2,400 at the Renold Works, 1,400 at Coventry, 550 at Cardiff and 660 at the head office, Renold House, at Wythenshawe. About 800 workers were employed in the French factory at Calais and 125 in a new factory in Australia. There were sales subsidiaries in France, Holland, Belgium, Germany and Canada, and agencies in over 70 countries.

During the final period of his chairmanship from 1955 to 1967 the company established its position as a world leader in power transmission engineering expanding its chain-making capacity and merging with two important gear manufacturers to extend its product range. In 1955 work started on the construction of a purpose-built factory to meet the increased demand for conveyor and agricultural machinery chain. In the same year the Anchor Chain Co Ltd, a specialist manufacturer of chain for fork-lift trucks and for the textile industry, was acquired. Four years later, the important chain and cycle component manufacturer Perry & Co (Holdings) Ltd was taken over. At the same time the Group was expanding overseas, establishing a plant in Canada in 1961 and in 1963 acquiring Arnold & Stolzenberg GmbH, one of the largest and old-established chain manufacturers in Germany. Further expansion occurred in France, Spain and Austria.

However, the most significant single development in the reorientation of the Renold Group was the merger with John Holroyd & Co Ltd in 1964, which expanded the company's product range into machine tools, worm gears and other gears and bronze castings. In the final few months, when Sir Charles was honorary president, the development of the Group was enhanced by the merger with Crofts Engineers (Holdings) Ltd, manufacturer of gears, clutches and couplings. Sir Charles was an active principal up to and including the formation of this new grouping, renamed Renold Ltd and the significance of this period of expansion can be judged by the fact that in 1967-68 the Group was able to report sales of £37 million and employed nearly 12,000.

Outside his business activities, Charles Renold had a long association with the Manchester College of Technology (now the University of Manchester Institute of Science and Technology). He was one of the business members of the committee which established the department of industrial administration in 1918 (serving as chairman of that committee for some thirty years), and was appointed a member of the Manchester Education Committee's sub-committee for MCT in 1925. He was chairman of the MCT planning and development committee from its formation in 1946 until July 1965, when he became its deputy chairman. He also served as vice-president and deputy chairman of the College Council. From 1936 he was a member of the Court of Manchester University and from 1938 of the University Council, and chairman of the University Buildings Committee from its establishment in 1946 until 1962. In 1960 he received an honorary LLD from the University of Manchester.

Renold was also an active member of Management Research Groups and became interested in both the department of business administration set up at the London School of Economics in the early 1930s and the Administrative Staff College at Henley (1945). In 1946 he was appointed the first chairman of the new British Institute of Management and, later, its first vice-president. In 1948 he was knighted for his services to the cause of good management and the development of humane and progressive ideals and practices in industry.

Renold was married twice: firstly in 1909 to Margaret Hilda Hunter (d 1958) (they had three sons and one daughter); and secondly in 1960 to Noel Garry (d 1966). His recreations were fishing and gardening. Sir Charles remained chairman of the Renold Group until shortly before his death on 7 September 1967. He left an estate of £109,050 gross.

L J TOLLEY *and* SHIRLEY KEEBLE

Writings:

Workshop Committees (Pitman, 1921).

'Relations in the Workshop' *Manchester Guardian* Industrial Relations Supplement 30 Nov 1927.

'Some Aspects of Budgetary Control' *Transactions of the Manchester Association of Engineers* 1934-35.

'Labour Management' paper delivered to Management of Labour Conference *Institute of Labour Management Review* Apr 1935.

'I and the Economic Crisis' *Journal of the Industrial Co-Partnership Association* Jan-Mar 1947.

'Function of Management' address to London District Society of Chartered Accountants *Accountant* 27 Nov 1948.

'Managers and Men' broadcast on BBC Home Service *British Management Review* 7 no 2 (1948).

'Management in a Buyers' Market' paper to Cotton Board Conference *Textile Weekly* 4 Nov 1949.

'Conception of Management' *Machinist* 15 Apr 1950.

Joint Consultation over Thirty Years (George Allen & Unwin, 1950).

'New Management for Industry' *Financial Times* 1 Dec 1950.

'Training for Management' *ibid* 13 Oct 1952.

'Management as a Career' *ibid* Careers in Industry Supplement 31 Oct 1955.

A full list of Sir Charles Renold's writings on management is held in the *DBB* files.

Sources:

Unpublished

PrC.

Published

Times 8 Sept 1967.

Basil H Tripp, *Renold Chains: A History of the Company and the Rise of the Precision Chain Industry 1879-1955* (George Allen & Unwin, 1956).

WWW.

Paul Julius Reuter at fifty-three, painted by Rudolf Lehmann (from Graham Storey, Reuters Century 1851–1951 *Max Parrish, 1951).*

REUTER, Paul Julius

1st Baron de Reuter

(1816-1899)

News agency proprietor

Israel Beer Josaphat (who changed his name to Paul Julius Reuter in later life) was born in Cassel, in the Electorate of Hesse, on 21 July 1816, the third son of Samuel Levi Josaphat, then provincial Rabbi of Cassel. The family had a tradition of learning, and presumably Israel was given the groundings of a good education before, when his father died in 1829, he was sent to join a cousin, a banker in Göttingen. While there, he met Karl Friedrich Gauss, one of the pioneers of telegraphy.

In the early 1840s Israel settled in Berlin, where in 1844 he was baptised a Christian and took the name Paul Julius Reuter. The following year he married Ida Maria Mangus, daughter of a Berlin banker. With some capital from his father-in-law, Reuter took a share in a bookshop and publishing business in Berlin that became known as Reuter & Stargardt. This was commercially successful, but in 1848 Reuter & Stargardt published some political booklets and pamphlets, apparently on Reuter's initiative, which met the disapproval of the authorities as the revolutionary fervour of that year died away. Reuter and his wife joined the growing circle of political émigrés in Paris.

Here he began working as a translator in the news agency of Charles Havas. The agency collected extracts from the European Press and supplied them to other newspapers, mainly inside France, ran a carrier pigeon service between London, Brussels and Paris, and had its own correspondents in most European capitals. Too energetic and ambitious to remain in another man's employment for long, Reuter left to establish his own news-sheet in Paris in early 1849. Inadequately financed, staffed only by himself and his wife working from their dilapidated lodgings, the enterprise failed within a few months.

Reuter then turned to the provision of commercial news. Others had also seen the opportunities for a commercial news service to feed the increasingly active financial and commercial exchanges of Europe. Havas for one supplied the Paris Bourse with European exchange rates, and in Berlin Bernhard Wolff founded the 'first telegraphic bureau proper in Europe' {Storey (1951) 9} to send commercial news along the Prussian state telegraph line from Berlin to Aachen where it was opened to the public in October 1849. Reuter set up a small telegraphic office at Aachen, supplying financial information to local clients. His insistence that all his clients should be treated the same, that no one should have preferential access to the information he supplied, helped to establish his reputation. When the French Government opened its telegraph line from Paris to Brussels to the public in early 1850 Reuter organised a carrier pigeon service to bridge the hundred-mile gap between Aachen and Brussels. By

ELECTRIC NEWS.

——◆——

The following Telegram was received at Mr. REUTER's Office, October 8th.

BERLIN, October 8th, 4.7. PM.

The official Prussian Correspondence announces that the King recognizing the necessity has charged the Prince of Prussia to act as regent with full powers, according to his own views, until the re-establishment of his (the King's) health.

The necessary publications of this resolution is expected.

The Chambers will probably be convoked on the 20th inst.

Printed at Mr. REUTER's Office,
1, Royal Exchange Buildings, City.

Reuter's first 'Electric News' telegram, 8 October 1858 (from Graham Storey, Reuters Century 1851–1951 *Max Parrish, 1951).*

the end of the year, extensions to existing lines had narrowed the gap to five miles; Reuter switched from pigeons to relays of horses to cover it, moving to Verviers, the new terminus of the Berlin wire. The gap was finally closed in late December 1850 and Reuter, with the disappearance of his commercial opportunity, moved to London.

In October 1851 Reuter rented two rooms in 1 Royal Exchange Buildings in the City, where he set up his 'telegraphic office' with one office-boy, John Griffiths. It was a propitious moment, for the first successful cable was just being laid between Dover and Calais, and came into use in November. One of his first agreements was with the Stock Exchange to provide the latest news from Continental exchanges; soon he was supplying brokers and merchants in London, Paris, Amsterdam, Vienna, Berlin and Athens with commercial information.

While running his service at Aachen, Reuter had been planning to extend his activities into the supply of political news, using the agents he had in most European cities to supply original information, not simply extracts from the local newspapers. He wanted to develop this in London, but had problems in getting his political news service established, largely because Mowbray Morris, manager of the *Times*, satisfied with the *Times*'s own arrangments for news-gathering, refused to subscribe. Before the abolition of the newspaper stamp in 1855, the *Times* accounted for half the total sales (about 100,000) of daily newspapers in the United Kingdom; if it refused Reuter's news, other newspapers would be very unlikely to accept it. The new provincial and London dailies that sprang up after the abolition of the stamp were soon building up their circulation and in October 1858, Reuter persuaded all the London dailies except the *Times* to accept his news telegrams on a fortnight's free trial. If they were satisfied by the trial, he would supply them with a regular service at £30 a month each. His first news telegram was issued to the London press on 8 October; on 13 October, Mowbray Morris's diary recorded 'Saw Reuter about telegrams of foreign news' {*ibid*, 26}. The despatches of his correspondents, especially those from the battlefields of the Franco-Austrian war of 1859 — short, factual, accurate — and his insistence on simultaneous publication of his news to all his subscribers, made his reputation for impartiality. 'Soon the public regarded Reuter's name as a token of reliability, thus strengthening his position in his dealings with the newspapers' {*ibid*, 30}. He was able to raise the terms of his subscriptions to the newspapers, particularly as he extended his news-gathering to America, Australia and the Far East. If one newspaper accepted a news service, the others could not afford to refuse and by the late 1860s were paying £1,000 a year each to him.

The extension of the network of telegraph cables to link the world proceeded apace. In 1865, the first overland telegraph to India, via Russia, Constantinople and the Persian Gulf was completed; in 1866, attempts to lay a cable across the Atlantic were finally successful (a cable laid in 1858 had functioned for only a few weeks). In order to exploit the overland wire to India, Reuter planned his own line, to link with it in North Germany. By early 1865, he had secured a concession from the King of Hanover to lay a cable to the island of Norderney, off the north coast of Germany, which the Hanoverian Government would connect by land wires to Hanover, Hamberg, Bremen and Cassel. These land wires were to be used solely for Norderney cable messages.

In order to finance this venture, Reuter incorporated his agency in February 1865, with a nominal capital of £250,000, of which £80,000 was paid up. Reuter was paid £65,000 for his business; he became managing director and in the running of the company had virtually unfettered control. However, by the time the cable was laid, in September 1866, Prussia had annexed Hanover and the concession had to be re-negotiated. The wire was moved to Berlin; Reuter would not be permitted to set up an office in Hanover, and it was clear that the Prussians would prefer him not to send representatives to reside in Germany. The cable, opened for traffic on the last day of 1866, was within a year giving the Agency a revenue of £2,000 a month from telegram fees of outside customers alone. In 1870, following the British Government's acquisition of the inland telegraph lines under the Electric Telegraph Acts of 1868 and 1869, Reuter, apprehensive of further political difficulties in Germany, persuaded it to acquire the Norderney cable as well. Reuters received £726,000 for it, though it had cost them only £153,000.

The realisation of Reuter's plans to expand into Germany was obstructed by the Prussian King's support for the Berlin-based agency of

Bernhard Wolff. Reuter, Wolff and Havas had agreed in 1856 to exchange stockmarket quotations and market prices, and in 1859 to exchange political news. As Reuter expanded first into Belgium and the Netherlands, setting up a joint office in Brussels with Havas, buying a local agency in Amsterdam from Alexander Delamar (who, with his brother Herman, joined Reuters) and then expanding into Germany, laying the Norderney Cable and opening offices in Hamburg, Frankfurt and Hanover, the Prussian Chancellor, Bismarck and his King, decided to oppose what they viewed as encroachment by British interests on their territory. The King encouraged Prussian bankers to help Wolff incorporate his Continental Telegraph Co in May 1865, and Wolff's political telegrams were treated as official correspondence and given priority over all private telegrams, including Reuters'. When the American cable was brought into operation, although the very high rates charged — £20 for ten words — made co-operation between the major agencies highly desirable, Wolff refused to join with Havas and Reuter in their contract with the New York Associated Press, making a separate contract with a rival US agency, Western Associated Press. Despite this disadvantage, Reuter maintained his German office, and developed his office in the free city of Hamburg as his major base. He made an agreement with an agency in Bremen, another with the agency of Ritzans of Copenhagen, and eventually won over Havas to his side as well. By 1869 Wolff was ready to negotiate again with his two major rivals.

The three agencies agreed that Wolff should 'exploit' Austria, Scandinavia and Russia. Reuter was to close all his German and Austrian offices, except Hamburg. He was to have a monopoly of the British Empire and the Far East, Havas the French Empire, Italy, Spain and Portugal. The agreement was signed in January 1870. Reuters and Havas were still closer to each other then either was to Wolff, particularly after the Franco-Prussian War. For a while they operated a separate 'joint purse' agreement, sharing all profits from all sources. This financed expansion into South America, following the laying of a cable from Europe to Brazil in 1874; a joint office was set up in Rio de Janeiro. But the agreement was brought to an end after Reuter's scheme for a private telegraph service between South America, North America, the West Indies and Europe foundered, largely due to the incompetence of the man selected to run the crucial New York end of the operation, and Havas were displeased at having to bear half the losses. Nevertheless, relations between the two agencies continued to be amicable. Henceforth Reuter concentrated on improving and developing services with the British Empire.

Reuter's international business and reputation was based on quite insubstantial resources. After the sale of the Norderney cable, the capital of the company was reduced to £72,000, of which £65,000 represented Reuter's goodwill. Most of its offices were leased (though its head office from 1871, at 24 Old Jewry, where Reuter himself worked, was bought). No profits came from the news service; it was the commercial department and the private telegram service to and from the Far East that provided the modest annual profit (about £7,000 a year in the 1870s). When profits from the private telegram service were threatened in the mid-1870s by competition from the cable companies and the Post Office, the company's financial position was threatened. They were saved by the development of a more compact code for telegrams, which halved the number of words used; this was developed by John Griffiths, Reuter's first office boy in London and secretary of the company since its formation. The windfall from the sale of the Norderney cable had largely been distributed to the shareholders. Despite the modest financial scale of his business, Reuter kept a large house, 18 Kensington Palace Gardens, in London, where he entertained frequently and lavishly. He was particularly fond of musical parties and gave receptions for famous visiting musicians and singers. He also loved to throw family parties, to which he would invite his staff and where 'with enormous zest, he insisted on playing Christmas games at any season of the year' {*ibid*, 88}. His great vitality found vent, too, in frequent travelling, particularly round Europe, where he would pay sudden informal visits to his agents and staff. He took no part in public life; he firmly believed that 'Our [ie the agency's] character for impartiality, on which we mainly depend for success, would be seriously imperilled by any suspicion of political partisanship' {*ibid*, 59}.

In 1871 he was granted a barony by the Duke of Saxe-Coburg-Gotha, 'in acknowledgement of his extraordinary qualities' {*ibid*, 60}; he became known as Baron Julius de Reuter rather than Baron von Reuter. It was not until 1891 that he and his heirs were granted the privileges of the foreign nobility in England.

The most astonishing demonstration of Reuter's enterprise and courage was not connected with his news agency, but was a concession he negotiated with the Shah of Persia, ratified at Teheran on 25 July 1872. (Reuter was one of a number of British businessmen who had been approached by the Persian Minister in London, Mohsin Khan.) Curzon described it as 'the most complete and extraordinary surrender of the entire industrial resources of a kingdom into foreign hands that has probably ever been dreamed of, much less accomplished, in history' {Curzon (1892) I, 480}. Reuter was given the exclusive right to build a railway from the Caspian Sea to the Persian Gulf, with such branches as he saw fit, as well as to build roads and other public works, and the right to carry out irrigation schemes, develop the forests and mineral resources, and to farm the State Customs for twenty years. He was authorised to raise a £6 million loan in London, on which the Persian Government nominally guaranteed 5 per cent interest. One of Reuter's backers was Hugh Mackay Matheson (qv) of Jardine Matheson & Co. 'He was so sure of success that he would not even launch a special Company'{Storey (1951) 72} though the history of a whole series of previous concessions in Persia to Europeans should have warned him that, as the British minister at Teheran remarked, such projects 'have been entertained principally as a means of profit to the Persian Ministers and the agents employed by them' {Frechtling (1938) 519}.

It soon became clear that the Shah did not intend Reuter to enjoy his concession. Though a survey was made for the railway, and a thousand men employed on constructing the preliminary earthworks, the Persian Government argued that some part of the rails should have been laid by the deadline set for November 1873, and that Reuter clearly had no intention of fulfilling his part of the bargain. Reuter tried in vain to enlist the support of the British Government in making good his claims. Only when the Shah in 1874 granted a new concession to build a railway to a Russian, General Falkenhagen, did the Foreign Office, ever on the alert for the spread of Russian influence in that region, support him. Reuter's claim was a useful diplomatic weapon, as pressure could be put on to the Persian Government to cancel the Russian concession as conflicting with the outstanding concession to a British citizen (Reuter was granted naturalisation in 1857). But still Reuter could get no real help from the Government in making good his claims and he had to settle them as best he could. Negotiations dragged on for over a decade and Reuter did not receive any compensation until in 1888 he sent his second son, George, to Teheran with full powers to conclude a settlement. After another year, it was finally agreed that Reuter would be given the right to found the Imperial Bank of Persia. It was incorporated the same year, with offices in Teheran and London, and after Reuter's death would play an important part in Persian finances.

Reuter retired from the Agency in May 1878, being succeeded as managing director by his eldest son Herbert (1852-1915) who had joined the firm, reluctantly, as assistant manager without a salary, in 1875 when the Persian concession was taking up much of his father's time. After about a year his initial reluctance gave way to deep interest in and commitment to the Agency, and he remained managing director until 1915, when, distraught at the death of his wife, he committed suicide.

Baron Julius de Reuter died on 25 February 1899, at his villa on the Promenade des Anglais at Nice, leaving £262,604 gross. His body was brought back to South London for burial.

CHRISTINE SHAW

Writings:

PP, Correspondence between HM Government and Baron de Reuter on Persian Concession (1873) C 803.

Sources:

Unpublished

PrC.

Published

Oliver Boyd-Barrett, 'Market Control and Wholesale News: The Case of Reuters' in George Boyce, James Curran and Pauline Wingate, *Newspaper History from the Seventeenth Century to the Present Day* (Constable, 1978).

Hon George N Curzon, *Persia and the Persian Question* (2 vols, Longmans, Green & Co, 1892).

Louis E Frechtling, 'The Reuter Concession in Persia' *Asiatic Review* 34 (1938).

James Grant, *The Newspaper Press: Its Origin, Progress and Present Position* (2 vols, Tinsley Brothers, 1871) 2.

PD, 3rd ser 215, cols 517-18 (3 Apr 1873); 217, cols 290-301 (14 July 1873).

Graham Storey, *Reuter's Century 1851-1951* (Max Parrish, 1951).

WWW.

REVELSTOKE, 2nd Lord Revelstoke
see **BARING, John**

REYROLLE, Alphonse Constant

(1864-1919)

Electrical engineering equipment manufacturer

Alphonse Constant Reyrolle was born at Juillac, Corrèze, France in 1864, although the exact date of his birth and details of his education and parentage, other than that his father was a soldier during the Franco-Prussian war, are unknown. At the age of nineteen he came to London as an improver with the firm of Légé & Co, scientific instrument makers in Turk's Head Yard, Farringdon Street. There he learned the craft skills which enabled him to get into business. Three years later he set up his own workshop in Charlotte Street off Fitzroy Square. Amongst other work he undertook subcontract manufacture on behalf of electrical firms. Certainly the scale of production was small — with one employee and an apprentice in the late 1880s — but subsequent expansion took him to larger premises in Union Street and then, in 1897, to Pancras Street off Tottenham Court Road. Some growth came from meeting the requirements of several of the early electrical engineering companies, since Reyrolle established a reputation for high-quality craftsmanship and the ability to produce for design requirements. It seems likely, however, that this was only a part of the business, since Reyrolle's early patents (three in the years 1896-98, when he gave a Paris address) relate to the construction of bicycles. The firm was also known for the production of vitrines steel framework for the exhibition of jewels and curios.

REYROLLE Alphonse Constant

In 1901 Reyrolle went to Tyneside and founded the firm of A Reyrolle & Co Ltd (registered in May 1901 with a nominal capital of £20,000), of which he was managing director, on a site of $5\frac{1}{2}$ acres at Hebburn, with 58 employees. There is no clear evidence as to why he chose Tyneside, although there are suggestions that he was attracted by the expansion of the electricity supply industry in the area and that he needed an area of heavy engineering for the manufacture of the tanks for switchgear in which the firm was to make its reputation. The latter suggestion is untenable since Reyrolle knew nothing of metal-clad switchgear when he came to Tyneside. It does, however, seem possible that Reyrolle was encouraged to go to Tyneside by C H Merz (qv), the electrical pioneer, whose views on large-scale generation of electricity, which had been made practical by the development of the large unit turbo-generator by Sir Charles Parsons (qv), helped to establish Tyneside's reputation. Merz, a Tynesider by birth, had already developed many contacts in the supply of electricity and in electrical engineering in various parts of the United Kingdom by the end of the 1890s and set up a London ofice in 1901. In view of Reyrolle's growing reputation among London electrical engineers, it is likely that Merz met him, recognised his potential and encouraged him to go to Tyneside, where the scope for his services was about to become considerable. The influence of Merz is made more credible by the fact that his brother, Norbert, an accountant, joined Reyrolle in 1901 in the management of the Hebburn company. After Reyrolle's death, Norbert Merz was to replace him as managing director.

The new firm was specifically concerned with the manufacture of equipment for the electricity supply industry and users of electrical equipment. Its emphasis on innovation was evidenced by the laboratory set up at the outset and by Reyrolle's seven patents taken out between 1902 and 1908 which related to electrical switches, resistances and motors. No doubt, under the influence of Charles Merz, who was much involved with the design of electricity generating capacity on Tyneside, Reyrolle's reputation for craftsmanship developed in the North-East and the firm prospered. By 1905 Charles Merz had persuaded Reyrolle to employ H W Clothier (1872-1938), an outstanding electrical equipment designer with whom Merz had worked. The result of this relationship was the expansion of the firm into the field which really made its name, the construction of high voltage, metal-clad, draw-out switchgear. Merz promoted the concept of the large scale, regional supply of electricity for lighting and power purposes as pioneered by Sebastian de Ferranti (qv); Clothier designed the high capacity circuit breakers that such a scheme necessitated; and Reyrolle provided the engineering and production skills and facilities needed to produce the equipment.

With the expansion of the scale of electricity generation involved in Merz's plans, which were put into effect with the opening of the Neptune Bank power station on Tyneside in 1901, the question of safety in operation became a crucial one. The new industry needed to avoid risks and the interruption of electricity supply. There were dangers of accidents to power station attendants, the possibility of the failure of switchgear to clear short circuits, the risk of fire from circuit-breaker explosions and many other problems. Merz complained that protection 'entailed vast concrete structures full of guards, screens and isolating switches' {Hunter

(1949) 9}. Clothier's idea for metal-clad protection was discussed with Reyrolle and his designers and prototype switchboards for both low and high voltage were developed and put into experimental use with the Newcastle Electric Supply Co which ran the Neptune Bank station. To contemporary switchboard engineers the new designs were unrecognisable as compared with traditional structures. The switching elements was entirely contained in earthed metal enclosures which were oil-filled. The result was a high degree of safety, together with significant savings in cleaning and maintenance costs. The first metal-clad switchgear was produced by the firm in 1906 and an initial reluctance to accept the design change by other manufacturers of switchgear enabled Reyrolle to exploit an early monopoly which recovered development costs and initially produced good profits. Probably again through the influence of Merz the design was rapidly accepted in the North-East, from which it spread, becoming known world-wide as Reyrolle 'C' type.

When Reyrolle first came to Hebburn he retained the London works but about 1904 this was sold and a London office and depot for the supply of products from the Hebburn works opened. This enabled Reyrolle to concentrate on Tyneside and under the impetus of metal-clad switchgear the firm expanded rapidly. In 1910 its sales totalled £52,662. By the time of Reyrolle's death there were some 700 employees and shortly afterwards a neighbouring site had to be purchased to accommodate continuing expansion. Switchgear remained the main production, being applied not only to power stations but also to underground installations in coal mines where the importance of safety was paramount and metal-cladding enabled electrification to be developed. Dust, fire and water risks in mines made the early introduction of electrical equipment hazardous but the firm developed flame-proof joints with wide machined flanges for protection of switchgear in places where open sparking would be dangerous. There were, however, many other developments. As a result of early problems with the performance of oil circuit-breakers — where breaking capacity was known only very approximately and there was no standard for the assessment of different types — Reyrolles, in conjunction with C A Parsons & Co Ltd, 'designed a short-circuit generator capable of closely imitating the short-circuit performance of a large power-station' {*ibid*, 12}. This was a major breakthrough which enabled experimental information and records to be obtained, in turn leading to improved designs with higher breaking capacities. Again with the emphasis on safety, the firm moved into the production of protected plugs and sockets with earthing facilities. With the expansion of generating capacity there was considerable scope for the firm's products and the First World War, in particular, provided much scope for expansion with repairs to the electrical equipment of warships. By the time of Reyrolle's death his firm had representatives and agents in many countries.

In all this development Reyrolle was an organiser and developer rather than an inventor (although the number of his personal patents shows that he was not just a craftsman as some have suggested). It is clear that his firm's reputation was built on a thoroughness, quality of production, and ability to meet design specification which stemmed from its head. It is said that Reyrolle, until his death, inspected every new pattern which was made in the works and imbued all the employees with a consciousness of the importance of what they were doing and the need to do it well. Reyrolle was undoubtedly a practical mechanic who paid considerable attention to the detail of the work. The story is told of an apprentice at work with a file, who was stopped with the words, 'My boy, I pay for that file from one end to the other. You're only using the middle of it' {*50 Years on Tyneside* (1951) 4}. The managing director then took of his coat, took the file and set the example of how to produce outstanding work. Just before his death he organised a practical school for his apprentices. It was important to Reyrolle to build a close relationship with his employees and as early as 1902 there was a works annual dinner and annual outings were arranged in an attempt to build up the company esprit de corps. One part of this close contact with employees led Reyrolle to bring a number of French workmen to Tyneside (some of whose descendants still work for the firm today) although this may well have caused difficulties with local employees in building up a company spirit. He was elected a member of the Institution of Electrical Engineers in 1911 (though he apparently did not offer any papers or contribute to discussions) and referred to his life's work as 'a contribution in no small measure to the conversion of electrical apparatus from the old "string and resin" to the "good job" state'. {Clothier (1919) 623}.

Reyrolle appears to have been a very private man about whom almost no evidence seems to have survived. He married in August 1906 and had one son. He lived in substantial villas in Beech Grove Road, Newcastle, firstly 'Netherton Lodge' and then 'Grindon'. He was a freemason, being a member of the Queen's Westminster Lodge No 2021 and also the Hotspur Lodge. Alphonse Reyrolle died on 27 February 1919, leaving £17,358 gross.

D J ROWE

Sources:

Unpublished

Tyne and Wear Archives, Newcastle upon Tyne, Reyrolle & Co papers.

PrC.

Information from Joe F Clarke.

Published

J R Beard, *The North Eastern Centre 1899-1959* (Institution of Electrical Engineers, 1959).

H Clothier, obituary of Reyrolle *Journal of the Institution of Electrical Engineers* 57 (1919).

Electrical Review 84 (7 Mar 1919).

Electrical Times 55 (6 Mar 1919).

Engineer 92 (1901).

50 Years on Tyneside (A Reyrolle & Co Ltd, 1951).

P V Hunter, *A Jubilee Address. The North Eastern Centre 1899-1949* (Institution of Electrical Engineers, 1949).

Newcastle Daily Chronicle 1 Mar 1919.

Stock Exchange Official Intelligence 1920.

Stock Exchange Year Book 1920.

RHONDDA, 1st Viscount Rhondda
see THOMAS, David Alfred

RICHARDS, Edward Windsor

(1831-1921)

Iron and steel manufacturer

E W Richards (from Journal of the Iron and Steel Institute*).*

Edward Windsor Richards was born at Dowlais in Glamorgan in August 1831, the son of an engineer and general manager of the Rhymney Iron Works (who died soon after the birth of Edward). Richards was sent to school in Monmouth and at Christ's Hospital in London, before beginning his industrial experience in 1847 as an apprentice in the Rhymney Iron Co's works. He moved to the Tredegar Iron Works in 1854 to become assistant engineer to his brother Edwin Richards (d January 1916), becoming chief engineer in 1858. Shortly afterwards, he joined the Ebbw Vale Co, where he rose to become works manager and then, in 1871, general manager. At Ebbw Vale works in 1870 he was responsible for building a Bessemer-steel department, and started the first British production of spiegeleisen, or manganese-rich iron, needed for the Bessemer process, but in short supply from Germany because of the Franco-Prussian War of 1870-71.

On 1 January 1876, Windsor Richards became manager of mining and metallurgical works for Bolckow, Vaughan & Co in the Cleveland district of North-East England, succeeding another Welsh migrant, Edward Williams (qv). Richards thus took responsibility for the technical running of one of the largest ironmaking plants in the world, with substantial colliery output in County Durham. Another employee, the company secretary Thomas Richardson, was in charge of the commercial side but before long Richards became commonly referred to as 'general manager'.

At Bolckow, Vaughan a policy of producing bulk steel had been embarked upon, but not implemented. It was Richards who undertook in 1877 the building and commissioning of three new blast furnaces and four eight-ton Bessemer converters, together with a rail-rolling mill, at Eston Junction some three miles east of Middlesbrough. At the time these were the largest steelworks of their kind in Britain. The Cleveland Works used low-phosphorus iron, obtained by smelting hematitic ores mainly imported from Spain. Under John Vaughan in 1851 Bolckow, Vaughan had been the first to exploit the adjacent Cleveland ironstone, and in the 1870s the company's blast furnaces produced large quantities of iron for foundry purposes as well as for laborious refining in puddling furnaces to yield malleable iron for engineering applications. There was thus strong incentive to use the iron made from local ores in the Bessemer converters, but the large proportion of phosphorus in Cleveland iron precluded this, for in established converting practice the phosphorus was not removed from the metal, producing brittle steel.

At the 1878 meeting of the Iron and Steel Institute, held in Paris, Windsor Richards met the young S G Thomas (qv), a man who claimed to have devised a method for removing phosphorus during steelmaking. On return from France, Richards arranged to be shown what Thomas had achieved, travelling to South Wales with Bolckow, Vaughan's consultant chemist, J E Stead (1851-1923). At Blaenavon Works three trial blows were made using Cleveland iron, while at Dowlais, Richards spoke on the subject with the general manager William Menelaus (qv). The two Middlesbrough men were impressed, and Richards obtained his directors' approval for Thomas and his cousin Gilchrist (qv) to be offered facilities to continue their experimental work in Middlesbrough. In return, Bolckow, Vaughan secured the right to make 150,000 tons a year of steel using the technique free from royalty fee, together with a one-fifth share in royalties from elsewhere that might ensue from a successful solution to the phosphorus problem.

Sufficient progress was made during the winter of 1878-79 for public demonstrations of the new procedures to be given on 4 April 1879 and again in May. By this time there was international interest in what was being done, and continental steelmakers paid visits to Middlesbrough, using the technique themselves on their return home. Although Bolckow, Vaughan's results were erratic, in December 1879 the company announced the decision to build at Eston Junction a new converting plant to make steel from Cleveland iron on a large scale. Portions of this plant soon came into use, so that in 1882 the company was able to claim a yearly output of 100,000 tons of this steel and 60,000 tons of Bessemer 'acid' steel made from hematitic iron.

Besides providing all the practical engineering support, Richards was evidently deeply concerned with the experimental work. Writing forty years afterwards, in 1920, J E Stead stated, 'Only those who were working with him in the inner circle knew that at times he was so much discouraged as to feel inclined to discontinue the experiments and give up hope; but he struggled on until success was eventually assured' {*Journal of*

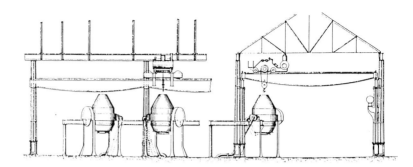

Arrangement of 15-ton converters for basic working at Cleveland Steelworks of Bolckow, Vaughan & Co, near Middlesbrough (from Proceedings of the Cleveland Institution of Engineers *November 1880).*

the Iron and Steel Institute (1920) 58}. Because of Richards's persistence, Bolckow, Vaughan became the first firm in Britain to achieve the commercial production of bulk steel by 'the basic process' or, as it was to be known abroad, 'the Thomas process'.

Bolckow, Vaughan had spent £300,000 on the original Eston steel plant for producing rails; by the early 1880s it had spent another £300,000 on equipment for 'basic-steel' products. As a diversification, cast-steel railway sleepers began to be made. In addition, to meet the changed demand for ships' plates rather than rails, Richards supervised the installation of rolling mills for the new product, as well as the erection of open-hearth steelmaking furnaces. The exploitation of salt was also started, the raw material being obtained from beneath the company's properties as brine. In 1882 Bolckow, Vaughan had 13,000 employees and a weekly wage bill of £19,000. The company claimed to be the largest world producer of steel (with capacity exceeding 200,000 tons), iron (half a million tons) and coal (two million tons).

In 1883, S G Thomas wrote to the president of the Iron and Steel Institute that 'the present position of dephosphorisation has only been rendered possible by the frank, generous, and un-reserved co-operation of Mr Richards ..., of our earliest and consistent supporter Mr Martin,' and others {*Journal of the Iron and Steel Institute* (1883) 490}. The following year, jointly with E P Martin of South Wales, Richards was awarded the Bessemer gold medal of the Iron and Steel Institute for the leading part he had played in bringing the 'basic process' to large-scale commercial success.

In late 1888, at the age of fifty-seven, Windsor Richards resigned from the managership of Bolckow, Vaughan on health grounds, stating that he wanted a less arduous job. The following year he became general manager of the Low Moor Iron Co, with works situated just south of Bradford in Yorkshire. The long-established Low Moor Co was one of five concerns in the Bradford-Leeds area which produced 'Best Yorkshire' wrought iron for engineering purposes, originally using local ores and coal. It is curious that the man who had done so much to promote the new bulk steel in competition with wrought iron should make such a change, but he remained with the Low Moor Co for ten years, retiring in 1898.

He did not, however, sever his connection with Bolckow, Vaughan, being appointed a director of the company in 1888 on his resignation from the managership. During the 1890s he urged on the board the need to adopt new techniques and practices in an endeavour to compete with

America. From 1903 to 1906 he was chairman of Bolckow, Vaughan, only retiring on medical advice at the age of seventy-five.

In 1901 Richards became a director of Guest, Keen & Co, at the time of the reorganisation of the Dowlais interests, and continued after 1902 as a director of Guest, Keen & Nettlefolds Co Ltd until 1918. He was also a director of the Harvey Steel Co Ltd and of the Glengarnock Iron & Steel Co Ltd, whose Ayrshire works were one of the five in Britain which used basic-Bessemer converters between 1885 and 1920. At Glengarnock a relative, Edgar J W Richards, was manager.

Windsor Richards had become a member of the Institution of Mechanical Engineers in 1866, and a member of the Iron and Steel Institute on its formation in 1869. He was president of the Cleveland Institution of Engineers for 1880-81, vice-president of the Iron and Steel Institute from 1884 to 1892, president of the same institute in 1893 and 1894, and president of the Mechanical Engineers in 1896 and 1897. He was a member of the Iron and Steel Institute's committee on steel rails in 1896, and a Royal Commissioner at the Paris Exhibition in 1900. For some time he served as chairman of Eston Urban District Council; in 1902 he was High Sheriff of Monmouthshire. For his metallurgical services in Belgium and Spain he was made a Knight Commander of the Order of Leopold and given the Royal Order of the Grand Cross of Isabella la Catolica.

Besides links with the Continent, by 1901 Richards had made five visits to the steel industry in the USA, some in company with his friend Arthur Keen (qv). Over many years he was a contributor to meetings of the Iron and Steel Institute and, in the years around 1900, argued that Britain occupied an increasingly vulnerable position because of steel competition from the USA and Germany, and that to protect British makers reciprocal import duties were needed.

Richards was one of a number of Welshmen who, following training and experience in the works of the South Wales valleys, migrated to influential positions in other parts. When he retired from active work at Low Moor he returned to Monmouthshire, to live at Plas Llecha, Tredunnock, Caerleon near Newport. His wife had died suddenly in Bradford in August 1893, and his second son, Frederic Windsor, died in 1898 at the age of thirty-one. His eldest son, Arthur Windsor, was employed by Bolckow, Vaughan until 1910, being works manager for some years before this.

Edward Windsor Richards died at his home at Tredunnock on 12 November 1921, aged ninety, leaving £87,811 gross.

J K ALMOND

Writings:

'President's Address' *Proceedings of the Cleveland Institution of Engineers* 1880-81.

'Presidential Address' *Journal of the Iron and Steel Institute* 43 (1893).

'Presidential Address' *ibid* 45 (1894).

'President's Address' *Proceedings of the Institution of Mechanical Engineers* 1896.

'Best Yorkshire Iron and How It Is Made' (report of address given in Glasgow) *Engineer* 16 Oct 1896.

'President's Address' *Proceedings of the Institution of Mechanical Engineers* 1897.

Sources:

Unpublished

British Steel Corporation, Northern Regional Record Centre, Middlesbrough, Bolckow, Vaughan & Co Ltd, Annual Reports 1875-1910-11.

PrC.

Published

Engineer 132 (18 Nov 1921).

Iron and Coal Trades Review 103 (18 Nov 1921).

William T Jeans, *The Creators of the Age of Steel* (Chapman & Hall, 1884).

Journal of the Iron and Steel Institute 1883, 1921.

North-Eastern Daily Gazette 14 Nov 1921.

John A Owen, *The History of the Dowlais Iron Works 1759-1970* (Newport, Gwent: The Starling Press, 1977).

Proceedings of the Institution of Mechanical Engineers Jan-May 1922.

J E Stead, 'Presidential Address' *Journal of the Iron and Steel Institute* 1920.

Times 14 Nov 1921.

WWW.

RICHARDSON, James Nicholson

(1846-1921)

Linen manufacturer

James Nicholson Richardson was born in Belfast on 7 February 1846, the son of John Grubb Richardson, scion of an old-established linen manufacturing family of Ireland; he had inherited the family bleachworks business and in 1846 he took up flax spinning, buying Mount Caulfield estate from Lord Charlemont and constructing the model village of Bessbrook for this purpose. James's mother, Helena née Grubb, originally from Cahir Abbey, County Tipperary, died in childbirth in 1849. His father remarried in 1853, and had one son and seven daughters by this

James Nicholson Richardson (from Charlotte Fell Smith, James Nicholson Richardson of Bessbrook *Longmans, Green & Co, 1925).*

marriage. James lived with his father and stepmother at Brookhill, Lisburn and was tutored at home until 1857 when he was sent to a small private school which closed after James had been there for nine months. He was then sent to Grove House School, Tottenham where he remained as a pupil until late 1862. Early in 1863 he began working for his father in Bessbrook.

John Richardson took a particular interest in the business at Bessbrook, where in 1852-53 linen powerloom weaving was introduced. James began his apprenticeship in the firm in 1863. In this 'he passed through all the different stages of hackling, sorting, preparing and spinning in the same manner as an ordinary apprentice, observing every rule as to hours and routine' {Smith (1925) 199}. He became particularly expert at judging and buying flax. During his apprenticeship 'he began to evince that aptitude for industrial management and for dealing with men of all shades of opinion and creed which afterwards were to make him so excellent a chairman' {*ibid*, 40}.

In the year James Nicholson Richardson entered his apprenticeship, John Grubb bought out the entire business, works and village of Bessbrook, thus separating the operations of the mill from those of J N Richardson, Sons & Owden, and formed the Bessbrook Spinning Co. After this John Richardson increasingly left the running of the mill to his elder son. The formation of the Bessbrook Spinning Co coincided with a sudden upturn in the fortunes of the Irish linen industry caused by the cotton famine in Britain. Bessbrook reaped its share of the benefits. In the first two years of operation annual profits rose from just over £8,000 to over £41,000. In 1867 damask weaving was introduced in the mill and two years later the 'Bessbrook' machine for damask weaving was invented by an employee there, Henry Barcroft. In 1868 the company bought the Craigmore factory to extend its powerloom weaving activities.

Like his father, James Richardson was a benevolent paternalistic employer. Early in the 1870s he visited Belgium and France to compare working hours and conditions in the flax mills there with those in Ireland. From this visit he came to the conclusion (unlike most of the other linen lords who went) that state intervention in business on behalf of the employees was amply justified.

In 1878 the firm was incorporated as a limited liability company. James Richardson had several reasons for doing this. Firstly, the revival of the British cotton industry after the American Civil War had adversely affected the fortunes of the Irish linen industry and by having the firm incorporated he could reduce his own personal financial risk should the firm collapse. Secondly, and perhaps of more significance, Richardson had political aspirations which he could not fulfil if he was totally occupied with the running of the business. Consequently, after incorporation he became chairman of the board, leaving the actual management of the firm to a carefully selected team.

In 1884, despite the generally depressed state of the Irish linen industry the Bessbrook Spinning Co Ltd embarked on a programme of expansion. However, in 1886 the directors cut the programme short because 'they dared not go on extending the works until they knew who their rulers were to be. So capital went from the little country needing it so much to American Rails and Australian Bush Irrigation'. {*ibid*, 57} During the

1870s and 1880s employment in the Bessbrook Spinning Co reached a peak of about 4,500 workers. By 1921 when Richardson died, it had fallen to about half this number. In 1896, at the age of fifty, Richardson decided it was time for a younger man to take over as chairman but the other directors refused to accept his resignation and persuaded him to stay on. His resignation was eventually accepted twenty years later in 1916.

From his early years, James Richardson was imbued with the virtues of work and thrift. By the time he was sixteen he was showing 'strongly Protestant characteristics: a deep ingrained love of liberty and justice ... qualities of leadership, self-reliance and command'. {*ibid*, 30} As chairman of the Bessbrook Spinning Co he was 'clever at forming conclusions of the 'mind of the meeting' as well as holding the balance between conflicting opinions and in reconciling opposing elements'. {*ibid*, 199} However, he tended to be conservative and slow to come to definite commitments.

One of Richardson's greatest advantages in running the business was his family links in the linen industry. The linen produced at Bessbrook was bleached at Glenmore Bleach Works, which were owned by his cousins, and sold through James Nicholson Richardson, Sons & Owden, in which he had retained an interest. Several of his uncles had, with the encouragement of his father, established linen importing concerns in various parts of the world (including Liverpool, Philadelphia and New York). Thus the market for Richardson's linens in these areas had already been established before James Richardson took over at Bessbrook. Indeed by the late nineteenth century Richardson's linen had gained a virtual monopoly of the fine Irish linen market in the United States.

The Richardson family had been members of the Society of Friends for several generations and had lived their lives and conducted their business affairs on Quaker principles. John Richardson had founded Bessbrook village as 'an ideal self-contained industrial colony' {*ibid*, 7} run on temperance principles. It was built without the three Ps — a public house, a police station, or a pawnbroker's shop. James Nicholson Richardson continued to uphold these Quaker traditions. In his business life he showed 'great opposition to anything short of moral rectitude and fair dealing' {*ibid*, 199} and he was always concerned with the accuracy of the firm's accounts. He and his first wife established a Sunday School and he founded a home for orphan children. He laid out cricket and football pitches and a bowling green, provided the village with its own electric lighting scheme and built an institute with billiards, reading and writing rooms.

Having unburdened himself of sole responsibility for the Bessbrook Spinning Co in 1878 James Nicholson Richardson turned his attention to politics. A Liberal, with a strong commitment to Irish land reform, he was also a Unionist. He was elected Liberal MP for County Armagh in April 1880, and for four years he took a very active part in political life. However, in 1883 he began to suffer from nervous depression and so in 1884 he spent a year on a world tour. When he returned he went back into politics but became disillusioned because of Gladstone's neglect of the temperance question and his support for Irish Home Rule. Richardson therefore retired from politics in 1885.

Richardson's wife, Sophia Malcolmson of Portlaw, died in 1886, and his father, to whom he had always been very close, died four years later. Both of these events greatly depressed Richardson, so that he again took to travelling. He toured the Holy Land in 1886-87 and took another trip round the world in 1890. In 1893 he married again, to Sarah Alexander Bell of Lurgan. After a honeymoon in Palestine, James Nicholson Richardson settled down and devoted his energies to life at Bessbrook. He died in a Birmingham hospital, after an unsuccessful operation, on 11 October 1921, aged seventy-five. His estate was valued at just under £75,000 (£32,665 in England). He had no children by either marriage.

EMILY BOYLE

Sources:

Unpublished

Emily Boyle, 'The Economic Development of the Irish Linen Industry 1825-1913' (Queens University, Belfast PhD, 1979).

Published

Belfast Telegraph 12 Oct 1921.

Fibres and Fabrics Journal Apr, May 1942.

J N Richardson, *Bessbrook* (pp, Bessbrook Spinning Co Ltd, and J N Richardson Sons & Owden Ltd, 1945).

Charlotte Smith, *James Nicholson Richardson* of Bessbrook (Longmans, 1925).

WWMP.

WWW.

RICHARDSON, John Wigham

(1837-1908)

Shipbuilder

John Wigham Richardson was born at Torquay, Devon (where his family wintered for health reasons), on 7 January 1837, the second son in the family of ten children of Edward Richardson (1806-63), a Newcastle upon Tyne Quaker, and his wife Jane née Wigham (1808-73). A sickly child, he attended three schools (including Dr Bruce's Academy) before having

J Wigham Richardson (courtesy of Mr J F Clarke).

private tuition with a few other children in the Carlisle home of the biscuit manufacturer J D Carr (qv). This was followed by two years as a boarder at the Friends School, York, where he attended some science lectures and experiments.

In 1852 at the age of fifteen his industrial training began in Liverpool with Senhouse Martindale, a distant relation who was a Lloyds surveyor and a former Tyneside shipyard foreman. Returning to Newcastle, Wigham Richardson began an engineering apprenticeship at the steam-tug building works of Jonathan Robson and finished his 'time' in the summer of 1856. Despite a twelve-hour working day, he used his evenings for a great deal of reading and private coaching was arranged in preparation for attending university. His stay at University College, London, was suddenly ended in 1857 by the failure of the Northumberland & District Bank, in which his family were large shareholders. His father's friend, the engineer Robert Hawthorn (1796-1867), agreed to allow the young Wigham Richardson to work in his machine drawing office of the Forth Banks Work, initially without pay; soon after Hawthorn entrusted the young man with the drawings for a pumping engine ordered by the Altona Waterworks on the Elbe. These three periods of diverse industrial experience proved invaluable in later years, especially in providing an understanding of the attitudes of workingmen and a much closer appreciation of working practices than many nineteenth century employers ever gained.

Richardson went into partnership with the Scot, C J D Christie (1830-1905), with £5,000 capital provided by his father and in March 1860 they began as shipbuilders. Nearly one-third of the capital went on the lease and the necessary capital equipment for the Neptune yard at Wallcar on the north bank of the Tyne. Christie, a naval architect, set the highest design standards but for Richardson he was 'far too much a scientific naval architect to make ... business a commercial success' {Richardson (1911) 143}. After two years all the initial capital was gone and only by great personal efforts by the partners (with Richardson himself delivering vessels to Continental ports) did the yard survive. The depression following the American Civil War would have ended the shipyard but for support from their bankers which the personal standing of Richardson's family no doubt helped to secure. To get the firm out of depression a 850 ton deadweight steamer was built on speculation.

The Neptune Yard was a small one at this time, consisting of four acres with a river frontage of 320 feet and three berths which could build ships up to 335 feet in length. It provided employment for 200 to 250 when fully occupied. Output in 1865 just exceeded 4,000 tons. In the 1870s two further berths were added and in 1872 a marine engine works was opened. Seven years later Richardson recruited John Tweedy (1850-1916), a first-class marine engine designer, who soon produced his own design of triple expansion engine. In 1882 Richardson became the principal shareholder in the Tyne Pontoons & Dry Docks Co which brought business in ship-repairing and so offset falls in the demand for new shipping.

Until 1883 orders were usually secured from overseas customers rather than British owners. They included ferries for carrying trains across the Rhine. In the 1880s business increased: by 1882-83 output was up to 16,000 tons per annum and exceeded 20,000 tons in 1889, the highest for the yard.

The south bay of the machine shop of the Neptune engine works, Wigham Richardson & Co, Newcastle on Tyne (from Shipping World*).*

The yard's largest vessel to date was the Spanish mail steamship *Alfonso XII* launched in 1887 and powered by one of Tweedy's triple expansion engines. Faced with growing demand, Richardson extended his facilities. With the addition of the North Yard in 1898 the berths were extended to 540 feet in length. In 1898 Richardson employed under 2,000 and his yards had a capacity for 30,000 gross tons of shipping and 30,000 ihp of marine engines. The following year a limited liability company was formed and four years later the company, together with the Tyne Pontoons, was merged with Swan, Hunter (of which Richardson became vice-chairman) with a shares allocation of £364,250 out of an initial issue of £994,000 (and an authorised capital of £1.5 million). The new combine, organised by George Burton Hunter (qv), survived until nationalisation in 1977.

Richardson was contemplating the formation of a limited liability company in the late 1880s and in a speech at the launching of the SS *Alfonso XII* linked this with his attitude to labour questions: 'If we ever go into a limited liability company we would like if possible, to do so in the form of letting the workmen be our co-shareholders' {*Shipping World* 1 Jan 1889, 260}. When finally £1 shares were offered, few workmen except foremen took up the offer. Richardson corresponded with his friend the pioneer of co-partnership, Sir George Livesey (qv), and later persuaded his co-directors of the Walker & Wallsend Union Gas Co to adopt co-partnership. He built housing for his workers both for rent and purchase, which paid a regular 5 per cent. Prizes were awarded for the decoration of the dwellings, and Richardson exemplified his goals by constructing at the entrance of his own office a conservatory of shrubs and evergreens.

Under his influence (no doubt affected by his connections with the Merz family), the Walker & Wallsend Gas Co moved towards the supply of electricity with a parliamentary application in 1898, at which Charles H

The north yard of the Neptune works, with a steamer of 5,000 tons gross register ready for launching, Wigham Richardson & Co, Newcastle on Tyne (from Shipping World).

Merz (qv) was the Gas Co's technical expert. When parliamentary permission was given, Merz was appointed consulting engineer and brought with him from Cork (where he had been designing an electric tramway system) William McClellan — thus initiating a famous firm. The Gas Co was persuaded to accept the building of Neptune Bank, the first central, large-scale electricity generating station for lighting and industrial power (opened in 1901) which paved the way for the North East's reputation in the supply of electricity for industry; Richardson's shipyard became an early customer.

Wigham Richardson was an unusually cultured industrialist. A serious bibliophile, his library was described as that of 'a true student and scholar' {Richardson (1911) 253}. He was particularly knowledgable on military and naval history. Friends, including Sir Benjamin Browne (qv) and the family of Richardson's nephew Charles Merz, gathered at his house regularly for Virgil evenings. On one occasion he used his Latin to find his way in Poland. He was a considerable linguist, fluent in French and nearly so in German and with a sound knowledge of several other languages. He travelled widely, having sufficient confidence in his managers at one time to stay in Russia for six months. He also visited both Canada and the USA, the West Indies and North and South Africa. On these trips he always took his sketch pad and watercolour box. Interested in architecture, he designed a number of houses. His private pursuits also included the study of sundials and fox hunting.

His literary and commercial interests came together in the part he played in the founding of the journal *The Shipping World* of which he was the first chairman in 1882. Always keenly interested in economic and social matters, he became the second president of the Newcastle Economic Society in 1896-97. As a member of the Northumberland County Council for a number of years he concerned himself particularly with education matters (being on both Walker and Wallsend Local Boards and chairman of Longbenton school board) and as a Northumberland magistrate he chaired the Licensing Committee and also belonged to the prison visiting committee. A Unionist in politics, he 'did not take a very active part in public life' {*Newcastle Journal* 16 Apr 1908}. Although a member of the Society of Friends he became an Anglican later in life — attending Benwell Parish Church. He was particularly generous in donations to religious organisations, especially to Christ Church at Walker and gave many gifts to local schools.

Richardson was a most active member of the North East Coast Institution of Engineers and Shipbuilders from its foundation in 1884; as fourth president he gave a very wide-ranging address in which he stressed the need for the beauty of trees in towns, a pure water supply and scientific sanitation as well as the economy of fuel. A member also of the North of England Institute of Mining Engineers and the Institution of Naval Architects, to all three technical societies he contributed important papers and regularly drew on his wide experience in contributions to the discussions. In his early years he conducted experiments on the strength of materials and in a 1874 pamphlet took issue with Lloyds Register of Shipping.

When in 1902 the lease expired on his life-long home of Wingrove House, he removed to Hindley Hall near Stocksfield and after that played a less active role in running his company, but he did visit Walker on one day each week. By that time the company employed a workforce in excess of 2,000 with a turnover of about £400,000 per annum, and occupied a site of 27 acres. In 1902 it completed its largest vessel, which also reflected the yard's diversity, the twin-screw *Colonia*, a cable laying ship of about 8,000 tons.

John Wigham Richardson in 1864 married Marian Henrietta, eldest daughter of J P Thol of High Wycombe Marsh, Buckinghamshire. They had five sons and two daughters; two of the sons predeceased their father. Following an operation in London, Richardson died on 15 April 1908, leaving £92,001 gross.

J F CLARKE

Writings:

'The Overloading of Steamers' *Transactions of the Institution of Naval Architects* 14 (1873).

Lloyds Register of Shipping: Its Effect, with Other Societies for the Classification of Vessels, upon the Art of Shipbuilding (1874).

'The Strains and Strengths of Ships' *Transactions of the Institution of Naval Architects* 16 (1875).

'The Load Line of Steamers' *ibid* 19 (1878).

'The Modes of Estimating Strains to which Steamers are Subject' *ibid* 24 (1883).

Practical Directions for the Construction and Fixing of Sundials (1889).

appendix on the construction of sundials in Mrs Alfred Gatty, *The Book of Sundials* (G Bell & Sons, 1889).

(ed), *Handbook to Industries of Newcastle and District* (British Association, 1889).

President's Inaugural Address *Transactions of the North East Coast Institution of Engineers and Shipbuilders* 7 (1890-91).

PP, RC on Poor Laws (1910) Cd 5066.

Memoirs of John Wigham Richardson (1837-1908) (first seven chapters based on Richardson's own papers, particularly 'A Colloquy on Strikes and Trade Unions') (Glasgow: Hugh Hopkins, 1911).

Sources:

Unpublished

Tyne & Wear Archives, papers of E & J Richardson; records of the North East Coast Institution of Engineers and Shipbuilders.

PrC.

Information from Dr D J Rowe.

Published

Engineering 85 (1908).

Roger A S Hennessey, *The Electric Revolution* (Newcastle upon Tyne: Oriel Press, 1972).

Mid-Tyne Link 2 (Newcastle upon Tyne: Swan Hunter & Wigham Richardson, 1906).

Newcastle Journal 16 Apr 1908.

William Richardson, *The History of the Parish of Wallsend* (Newcastle upon Tyne: Northumberland Press, 1923).

Shipbuilder 3 (1908).

Shipping World 1883-89.

Times 16 Apr 1908.

Transactions of the Institution of Naval Architects 14-35 (1874-94).

Transactions of the North East Coast Institution of Engineers and Shipbuilders 1-24 (1884-1908).

Riddell was twice married. In 1888 he married Grace Edith, daughter of Thomas Williams; they were later divorced. When his name was offered to the King in 1920 for elevation to the peerage there were objections because of the nature of the divorce action in which Riddell had been involved and Lloyd George went to great lengths to obtain support for the elevation from other Press Lords. Riddell thus became the first divorced peer to enter the House of Lords. In 1900 he had married his cousin, Anne Molison, daughter of William Allardine of Valparaiso, Chile, and Rock Ferry, Cheshire. She survived him. There were no children of either marriage. Lord Riddell died on 5 December 1934, leaving £1,838,901 gross. There were bequests to the National Playing Fields Association, the London Library, the Newspaper Press Fund and the Royal Free Hospital as well as to friends and employees. After his death his widow, Lady Riddell, gave £1,000 in his memory to the Child Emigration Society's Fund to establish a cottage on a farm school in Vancouver.

DEIAN HOPKIN

Writings:

Law for the Million by a Practical Lawyer (News of the World, 1904).

Some Studies in Remarkable Minds (Birkbeck College Foundation Orations, 1922).

Some Things that Matter (Hodder & Stoughton, 1922).

More Things that Matter (Hodder & Stoughton, 1925).

Dame Louisa Aldrich-Blake (Hodder & Stoughton, 1926).

Looking Round. A Miscellany (George Newnes, 1928).

Medico-Legal Problems (H K Lewis & Co, 1929).

The Story of the Western Mail (Cardiff: Western Mail & South Wales News, 1929).

The Curious Story of Helen Tulk. A Panorama not a Novel (George Newnes, 1932).

Lord Riddell's Intimate Diary of the Peace Conference and After, 1918-23 (Victor Gollancz, 1933).

Lord Riddell's War Diary, 1914-18 (I Nicholson & Watson, 1933).

More Pages from My Diary, 1908-14 (Country Life, 1934).

The Treaty of Versailles and After (G Allen & Unwin, 1935).

Sources:

Unpublished

BCe.

Published

Annual Register 1934.

Lord Beaverbrook, *Men and Power 1917-18* (Hutchinson, 1956).

DNB.

Keith Middlemas (ed), *Thomas Jones, Whitehall Diaries* (3 vols, Oxford University Press, 1969-71).

Kenneth O Morgan (ed), *Lloyd George Family Letters 1885-1936* (Cardiff: University of Wales Press, 1973).

Peter Rowland, *Lloyd George* (Barrie & Jenkins, 1975).

Stock Exchange Year Book passim.

Alan J P Taylor (ed), *My Darling Pussy. The Letters of Lloyd George and Frances Stevenson, 1913-41* (Weidenfeld & Nicolson, 1975).

Times 6 Dec 1934.

Western Mail passim.

Trevor Wilson (ed), *The Political Diaries of C P Scott, 1911-28* (Collins, 1970).

WWW.

Utrick A Ritson (courtesy of R W Rennison).

RITSON, Utrick Alexander

(1843-1932)

Coalowner and utility companies director

Utrick Alexander Ritson was born at Dursley, Gloucester, on 7 March 1843, the second of the seven children of William Ritson (1811-93) and his wife Jane née Alexander. His father was initially a stonemason but later became a civil engineering contractor involved in the construction of docks and railways; the son, too, adopted contracting as a career and, amongst other works, built the Hexham to Allendale railway, a 12-mile long branch of the North Eastern Railway, opened in 1869. With his uncle, he was also involved in the construction of the Thames Embankment.

Later, Ritson became interested in the coal trade, owning collieries at Burnhope, South Pontop and New Pelaw in County Durham and at Preston, North Shields; the first two collieries Ritson inherited from his father but it was the Preston Colliery which proved the most profitable. It was established in 1860 and by 1885 was one of the leading concerns in the North East coal trade, coals being shipped from both the Tyne and Wear.

Ritson was active in politics as well as business. He became one of the first members of the Durham County Council, was elected an alderman at its first meeting in February 1889, served as a DL and in 1899-1900 was

High Sheriff. He was also a member of the Newcastle Town Council for five years from 1878 and was a JP for both Newcastle and Gateshead.

Of his business interests, one, the vice-chairmanship of Northern Counties Conservative Newspapers Co Ltd, was linked with politics. His newspaper interests, principally the *Newcastle Journal*, served the Newcastle & Gateshead Water Co well in times of crisis; of this company Ritson was a director from 1895 until 1912. He was also a director of the Newcastle & Gateshead Gas Co from 1898 until 1910, when he resigned due to his growing deafness. Like other directors of these last-named companies, he was a director of the Redheugh Bridge Co — both utilities had a financial interest in it — which constructed and operated a major crossing of the river between Newcastle and Gateshead. In 1887 he was elected by the region's coalowners as one of their representatives on the Tyne Improvement Commission, founded in 1850 and responsible for the improvement of and navigation upon the river Tyne; he remained a member until his death.

Ritson was an active Wesleyan Methodist, attending the church in Jesmond, Newcastle, where he lived, and he erected a memorial on the spot from which John Wesley, on his first visit to Newcastle, preached in 1742. In addition to his town house, Ritson maintained a home at Calf Hall, Muggleswick, which became, over the years, his principal residence.

Ritson married in 1867 Annie Ridley of Hexham; they had eleven children. Two of his sons followed him into the colliery business, John Ridley (1870-1937), who became chairman of the Newcastle & Gateshead Gas Co and a director of the Water Co, and Cuthbert Ward (1882-1970) who succeeded his brother as a director of the latter concern. Both sons served in the army, the elder during the First World War and the younger as a regular officer until 1922. Utrick Ritson died on 16 November 1932 at Calf Hall, leaving to his large family an estate valued at £106,832 gross.

R W RENNISON

Sources:

Unpublished

Newcastle & Gateshead Water Co, minute books 1895-1912.

Tyne and Wear Archives, minute books of Newcastle & Gateshead Gas Co, 1898-1910.

BCe.

PrC.

Information from Col C W Ritson (1968) and John S Stephenson (1978).

Published

Newcastle Council Reports 1878-82.

Tyne Improvement Commission Reports 1887-1909.

Tyneside Industries (Newcastle upon Tyne, 1885).

RIVERDALE, 1st Lord Riverdale of Sheffield
see **BALFOUR, Arthur**

Sir Alexander Roger (from C Addison, Politics From Within*).*

ROGER, Sir Alexander Forbes Proctor

(1878-1961)

Financier and industrialist

Alexander Forbes Proctor Roger was born at Rhynie, Aberdeenshire, on 30 January 1878, the third and posthumous son of James Paterson Roger, of Rhynie. One of his brothers was manager of St James's Court for Sir Harry Mallaby-Deeley (qv), and on the maternal side he was a cousin of Sir Patrick Ashley Cooper, Governor of the Hudson's Bay Company in 1931-52 and a director of the Bank of England in 1932-55. He was educated at Robert Gordon's College, Aberdeen, with financial help from the Cooper family. At the age of eighteen he went to work in the City of London for the Law Guarantee, Trust & Accident Society, where he was engaged on the accountancy side. Law Guarantee, which in addition to ordinary insurance business, undertook fidelity and other guarantees and mortgages, fell into financial straits until in 1909 it was acquired in a rescue operation by Guardian Assurance. During Law Guarantee's financial crisis, its senior director suffered a breakdown and Roger found himself in a position of responsibility which entailed considerable nervous strain.

Although Roger had no formal accountancy training, he could analyse and dissect balance sheets or company accounts within a few minutes, and on the recommendation of the merchant banker Robert Fleming, he became a junior partner of Sir John Philipps (qv), Viscount St Davids, in the investment trusts known as the St Davids or 69 Old Broad Street group. The group acted in association with British Electric Traction Co, and through a meticulous system of cross-shareholding and interlocking directorships, was active in many companies associated with electrical supply utilities, electrical engineering, tramways and motor buses, in Britain, South America and elsewhere. Among the directors of the Old Broad Street Group, St Davids himself was particularly keen on investing in South America. Roger was far closer to St Davids' associate, J S Austen, who had a great influence on Roger's business outlook, and whom Roger imitated to the extent of his household furnishings. His lifelong belief that one should separate one's business and domestic life entirely derived from Austen. Harley Drayton (qv) was another brilliant tyro financier and industrialist nurtured by Austen within the St Davids group, and to some extent Drayton served as a substitute in Austen's affections after Roger had moved elsewhere.

When war was declared in 1914, Roger and his wife were en route to inspect the Smyrna railway, in which the St Davids group were interested: the Rogers escaped internment by the Turks and Austro-Hungarians and returned to England only with difficulty, discomfort and some discriminate bribery. Shortly after Roger reached London he was appointed unpaid Director of the Motor Ambulance Department of the British Red Cross Society, and organised the department's work on the Western Front until July 1915. In that month he was recruited to the Ministry of Munitions as Director General of Trench Warfare Supplies, with a seat on the Council of the Ministry. Mortars, grenades and other light-weight weapons, such as phosphorus bombs or catapults, were the main concern of the Trench Warfare Supplies Department. Roger inherited an appalling deficiency in these weapons, for which the War Office had previously relied on the Royal Arsenal at Woolwich. With his cousin Patrick Cooper as his deputy, Roger initiated a policy of spreading contracts among civilian businesses of all types, so that within five months of becoming Director General, his department employed over 200 different contractors in grenade production alone. Under Roger's energetic re-organisation, national productive capacity in trench warfare equipment was hugely multiplied, and Woolwich Arsenal was freed to concentrate on shells and other heavier armament. He was knighted in June 1916. On one occasion at this time Roger was badly gassed when the wind changed direction at a gas demonstration which he attended in France. The gravity of the gassing was not at first realised, and his life was probably saved by his cousin, Rudolf Wingfield, a pioneer in the technique of collapsing lungs, who happened to meet him just after his return from France. Thereafter Roger survived with one lung. In October 1917 the retiring Minister of Munitions, Dr Christopher Addison, who had been appointed first Minister of Reconstruction, persuaded Roger to take responsibility for financial policy at the new ministry. In November 1917 Roger was also appointed to the government committee on financial facilities chaired by Sir Richard Vassar-Smith (qv). Addison wrote at this time that although Roger was 'a little too talkative', his work with Percy Martin, Lord Weir (qqv), 'and some others whom nobody knows anything about' had established British air superiority in the war {Bodleian, Addison diary 16 Jan, 11 Apr 1918}. Roger left government service shortly after the Armistice in 1918, and returned to business.

Lord St Davids' elder sons were killed in action in 1915-16, and Austen warned Roger that St Davids' vindictive resentment that Roger had three healthy sons would make his future within the Broad Street group unpleasant and uncertain. At this hint from Austen, Roger therefore loosened his connections with St Davids. He joined the board of the Commercial Bank of London in May 1920, in which month he resigned from Lord St Davids's companies such as Premier Investment Co (registered 1892) and Union Commercial Investment Co (registered 1914).

He however remained until after the Second World War on the board of the Aberdeen Trust, formed in 1911 by Sir Thomas Jaffrey and Sir James Taggart, two Aberdeen worthies. He was also a director of its allied East of Scotland Trust, formed in 1913 with Sir James Campbell as chairman, and joined the board of the related Aberdeen Edinburgh & London Trust when it was formed in 1928 under the chairmanship of Sir Alexander Lewis. These were interlocking general investment trusts, not part of the Broad Street group (although St Davids was their London correspondent for a time); Roger largely owed his introduction to them to his wife's brother-in-law, an Aberdonian lawyer called Alexander Cruikshank. In this period Roger declined an approach to recruit him from Sir James Dunn (qv). Roger was also a director of the Midland Bank from March 1932 until December 1958, serving as deputy chairman from 1948. His eldest son believed that Roger enjoyed his association with the Midland Bank, and his attendance at its board meetings, more than any other aspect of his business life. Roger was the main protagonist behind the appointment of Lord Linlithgow, who as Viceroy helped Roger on an official mission to India in 1941, to the chairmanship of the Midland Bank in 1945. Roger was also close to Linlithgow's successors, Lords Harlech and Monckton, whose selection he supported.

More centrally to Roger's industrial career, he became a director in 1918 of British Insulated & Helsby Cables, a Liverpool-based company which changed its name in 1925 to British Insulated Cables (BIC). Its other directors included Sir John Harmood-Banner (qv). Roger became vice-chairman of BIC in May 1928, and chairman on the death of Dane Sinclair in 1930. The company had widespread interests, and had expanded from a workforce of 2,150 in 1902 (when wages and salaries amounted to £232,000) to 8,200 employees in 1928 (costing £1,023,000 annually). Tax paid by BIC rose from £7,400 to £120,000 a year during 1902-28. Its subsidiaries included the Midland Electric Corporation for Power Distribution and the Electric Supply Co of Victoria, with Roger as chairman, which had owned valuable supply concessions in Australia since 1900. BIC also undertook rail electrification in South Africa, Australia and elsewhere. In the early 1920s he was much involved with the ambitious and complicated railway schemes of a flamboyant Spanish adventurer, Pedro Pedreza. In India BIC electrified Bombay's suburban railways (Roger visited India in 1929), and in 1931 completed the mainline electrification of the Great Indian Peninsula Railway. Other major Far Eastern contracts of the late 1920s included transmission lines in the Federated Malay States for the Perak River Hydro-Electric Power Co. In Britain, following the Electricity Act of 1926, BIC won the contract for the Scottish section of the national overhead grid, which was finished by 1932. In 1929 the Central Electricity Board gave BIC a large order for cables in London. After discovering that the output of Northern Rhodesia's Roan Antelope Copper Mines (which was opened by Chester Beatty (qv) at Luangwa in 1927) was of a purity peculiarly suited to electrical work, BIC formed British Copper Refiners Ltd, with Roger as chairman and a factory at Prescot, to refine Roan Antelope's ore. Roger was also a director of other BIC related businesses, such as the Alton Battery Co from 1928.

An area of BIC's operations in which Roger was specially interested was their telephone subsidiaries. Previously, in 1911, BIC had transferred its telephone business to a separate company, Automatic Telephone Manufacturing, to which it remained connected by interlocking directorships and close business associations. ATM was controlled by Automatic Electric Co of Chicago and when BIC made this deal in 1911 they felt they could not compete with the Americans' world-wide commercial power, patent experience and superior technical expertise. Roger was chairman of ATM during the 1920s, his co-directors including Sir Max Muspratt (qv). In 1926 BIC, ATM and other British companies entered a marketing alliance with various American financial and operating interests in the telephone business: Associated Telephone & Telegraph was incorporated in Delaware, with a large international board including Roger, and holding interests in telephone companies in British Columbia, Portugal, Colombia, Santo Domingo, Britain and Belgium. During the Slump, Roger saw BIC's opportunity to recover control of their telephone business, and in 1935 BIC bought the Americans' entire holding in ATM. BIC, however, maintained its close working relations with the Americans, and Roger visited the USA many times.

Roger was chairman of the Anglo-Portuguese Telephone Co from 1927, and a director of the Constantinople Telephone Co until 1930. Anglo-Portuguese Telephone was formed in 1887 to acquire from Edison-Gower-Bell Telephone Co of Europe Ltd certain established exchanges and Portuguese government concessions. It had acquired a new concession in 1901, and in January 1928 Roger extracted a further concession, expiring in 1968, subject to renewal for a further twenty-five years, providing for freedom from government taxation, and royalties of between 3 and 5 per cent on gross earnings. APT operated systems in Lisbon and Oporto, and by December 1932 had provided 33,400 telephones to serve a population of about 1.5 million. Roger in due course developed a confidential friendship with the Portuguese dictator, Salazar. The Constantinople Telephone Co had received a thirty-year concession in 1911, and was last visited by Roger in 1926; it came under the control of International Telephone & Telegraph (ITT), the American giant, in 1931.

During the General Strike of 1926 Roger was temporarily put in charge of the London docks. Throughout the inter-war years he attributed Britain's high industrial costs and poor competitiveness to it being 'the most highly taxed nation in the world'. He opposed 'profligate and ruinous social and other legislation for which all political parties are guilty' as causing 'excessive taxation, imperial, local and municipal, which is crushing the life out of industry' {*Economist* 21 Mar 1931}.

In December 1932 Roger was approached by a Midland Bank associate, Dudley Docker (qv), to become chairman of Birmingham Small Arms (in which Docker was a major shareholder), a troubled giant of Midland engineering with interests in small arms, motorbicycles, bicycles, motor cars (Daimler and Lanchester), machine-tools, special alloys and cognate products. There had been three previous BSA chairmen since 1928: Sir Hallewell Rogers, Sir Edward Manville and Arthur Pollen (qqv) had all departed amidst rancour and recrimination as the group's results steadily deteriorated. BSA's worst troubles involved personalities, but its widely variegated product line was ill-coordinated, while its marketing strategy had been acknowledged as inadequate for over a decade. Roger took the job as a challenge, but was only able to assert his control at BSA after a year of struggle. In December 1933 he removed his most difficult and jealous colleague, Percy Martin, from executive responsibilities; he introduced new management; and started a co-ordinating sub-committee, with a remit to look at the sales organisation. In the following years, BSA's superficial position improved considerably, and it returned from the brink of ruin; but its managerial vices were merely made latent, rather than extinct, by Roger. BSA provided the only occasions in his business career when he was provoked to real fury, and he had little liking or respect for the individuals involved, except the managing director, Sir Geoffrey Burton. In 1938 he visited Czechoslovakia to finalise purchasing the Bren gun rights for the War Office. After he relinquished the BSA chair in 1940 to head the Tank Board, his successor Bernard Docker (qv) revivified all BSA's fatal history of personal ill-will, bad strategy, ignorant marketing and careless finance.

The Tank Board, with Roger as first chairman from May 1940, was appointed by the War Office and Ministry of Supply as a body akin to a Royal Commission advising on tank production and design. It made its influential first report early in June 1940, and was reconstituted in January 1941 when Sir James Lithgow succeeded Roger as chairman.

Previously, in August 1940, Roger had left Britain as leader of a Ministry of Supply industrial mission including Sir Guy Locock (qv) of the FBI and experts from business and Whitehall. After visiting South Africa, Roger's mission acted as the British delegation to the Viceroy of India's Conference at Delhi on munitions supply, and then proceeded to Australia, New Zealand, Hongkong, Malaya, and Burma before returning to Britain later in 1941. Just as in 1915-16 Roger had spread trench warfare supply contracts over a wide range of civilian manufacturers, so in India he tried to broaden the lines of supply and develop mass production. Although the Indian Civil Service greeted his mission with much ceremony, many officials, especially Sir Hugh Dow, the Director General of Supply, resented outside advice, while others resisted any change. In particular officials doubted that businessmen would accept the price control and regimentation contingent on mass production. There were serious misunderstandings and disagreements, although Roger's mission included Sir William Barton, late of the Indian Civil Service, whose political advice was invaluable. The Viceroy, Linlithgow, also supported Roger, and indeed Dow was transferred to become Governor of Sind later in 1941. Despite these obstacles, Roger's mission increased the Eastern hemisphere's supply of armaments for the British Empire until Japan's entry into the war in December 1941. Roger returned to Britain via Australia and the USA: 'The official world rejoiced when the Roger Mission departed ... Red tape reigns and peace if not progress is restored' {*Statesman* 22 June 1942}. During his mission's visit, Indian newspapers nicknamed him 'Ginger Roger' in allusion to his energy. As a result of his work at the Delhi Conference, Roger was created KCIE in 1941.

When his mission's work was complete, Roger vigorously but unsuccessfully urged upon Lord Beaverbrook (qv) the institution within the Ministry of Supply of 'a high central authority' to co-ordinate supply activities in India, the Dominions and Colonies. 'There is no one at the Ministry of Supply particularly charged with the interests of India', he warned, while the Dominions must be treated with tact and encouraged in every way ... They are extremely touchy and should never be given reason to think that they are not looked upon as most important partners in the common war effort ... They are moreover somewhat jealous of one another and the only country able to supply the essential constant liaison between them is England {Roger papers, memorandum to Beaverbrook, 11 Sept 1941}.

Before his recruitment to the Tank Board, Roger was also chairman of the Transport of Wounded Department in the special war organisation of the British Red Cross Society and Order of St John of Jerusalem in 1939-40. Roger's interest in medical charities was reflected in his chairmanship from 1934 until the nationalisation of the health service in 1947 of the Appeals Council of Great Ormond Street Hospital for Sick Children. J M Barrie gave to the hospital the performing rights of *Peter Pan* which financed rebuilding and extensions, especially when Walt Disney made a cartoon film of the story. Arising from his industrial and munitions work, he received decorations from Tsarist Russia, Poland (1934) and Portugal. He was vice-president of the Federation of British Industries (1939), of the Anglo-Portuguese Society and of the Hispanic and Luso-Brazilian Councils. He was a candidate for the rectorship of Aberdeen University in 1936.

Following the amalgamation in June 1945 of BIC with Callenders, he was elected chairman of the new British Insulated Callender's Cables (BICC) Co. The amalgamation had been agreed in principle in 1943, and had been foreshadowed both by merger discussions held in 1935 and the Cable Research Closer Working Agreement signed by BIC, Callenders and Henleys in 1927. In the immediate post-war years, BICC's performance was handicapped by manpower shortages, and by severe bottlenecks in the supply of raw materials and component parts. Roger was exasperated by the Attlee administration's restrictive controls, and in 1947 urged 'that the Government pause in their doctrinaire policies and instead ... help all industry to maximum production in the ways which industries understand'. He besought Whitehall to cease disrupting the supply of materials: 'Restore the merchants and dealers and middle men to their old and experienced functions ... Revivify the metal markets, the produce markets, the cotton market and shipping'. For Roger it was axiomatic that 'Production cannot be done in Whitehall' {*Economist* 7 June 1947}. Although Roger was a supporter of Conservative Government policy of the early 1950s to dismantle direct controls of economic activity and revert to the market mechanism, he vigorously opposed a Report of the Monopolies and Restrictive Practices Commission which recommended an end to various price-fixing arrangements by cable manufacturers. Despite these difficulties BICC was able to achieve a record trading profit of £9.5 million in 1952 and £8.3 million in 1953; in Roger's last full year as chairman (1953) it secured a net profit of £3.7 million, compared with £3 million in 1952.

Roger slowed down in business after an illness around 1944, and took increasing pleasure in recalling old times with his cronies at the Carlton Club. He disliked, but was unable to prevent, the senior engineers and managers at BICC's provincial factories relocating themselves for reasons of personal prestige at the London head office, and felt that this necessitated a new and confusing layer of management in the provincial factories. He retired as chairman in May 1954, and thereafter served as first honorary president of BICC until his death. By 1956 its sales to outside customers were worth £129 million. He was also chairman of the Telephone & General Trust until 1960, and remained connected with telephone operating subsidiaries in Portugal and the West Indies.

In business Roger was a delegator who was usually a good judge of character. His one weakness was a sentimental bias in favour of fellow Scots, especially Aberdonians (his successor at BICC and the Midland Bank, for example, William (later Lord) McFadzean (qv), came from Stranraer), and some of the Scottish swans whom he favoured or promoted proved to be geese. He preferred finance to industry and his early love of investment work never left him: although he could produce a good paper scheme for reorganising an industrial company, his real talent was reading between the lines of a company's accounts. On one occasion in the late 1920s he was crossing the Atlantic when his friends at Automatic Electric telegraphed from Chicago asking him to contrive to meet the Swedish match king, Ivar Kreuger, who was travelling on the same liner. Roger telegraphed back a refusal, saying that he had read a recent Kreuger balance-sheet and would not touch him. This was at a time when Kreuger's reputation appeared unassailable, and Chicago was annoyed by Roger's response, but the discovery of massive frauds within Swedish Match, following Kreuger's suicide in 1932, vindicated Roger's prescience. Indeed Kreuger's fall was precipitated by the rejection of some of his figures by ITT in his abortive sale of the L M Ericsson Co, and Roger may have planted the original scepticism of Kreuger among Sosthenes Benes and his Chicago telephone people. Roger absorbed from Jack Austen a slightly old-fashioned streak of financial puritanism about such matters as directors' expenses, and disapproved of knighthoods for businessmen except in recognition of voluntary public work. He was motivated by the pleasure of achievement, and liked taking on challenges, but was not interested in the accumulation of power or riches for their own sake: he had the opportunities to become a millionaire, but never took them. Although somewhat shy and blushing in youth, he became a self-confident and extrovert man holding strong views, with 'the reputation of being a great driving force' {*PD, HC* 24 Feb 1942 col 170}. According to a description written when he was sixty-two, 'Sir Alexander, slim and well-groomed, can still dance well and play with vigour on the tennis and squash court. As a Highlander, he has a natural ability for deer stalking ... [He] has a lively prose style. His letters are fluent, witty and vigorous' {*Evening Standard* 26 Oct 1940}.

In 1908 Roger married Helen Stuart (1884-1975), youngest daughter of James Campbell Clark, of Connel Ferry, Argyllshire. They had three sons. Sir Alexander Roger died at his house at Binfield, Berkshire on 4 April 1961, leaving £221,644 gross.

R P T DAVENPORT-HINES

ROGER Sir Alexander Forbes Proctor

Writings:

PP, Report of Ministry of Reconstruction Committee on Financial Facilities (1918) Cd 9227.

letter on bank amalgamations *Times* 25 July 1918.

letter on capital levy *ibid* 15 Nov 1922.

article on electric cables *ibid* (Faraday Number) 21 Sept 1931.

letter on J M Barrie and Peter Pan *ibid* 26 June 1937.

letters on Germany *ibid* 20 Mar, 8 July 1938.

letter on Ministry of Supply *ibid* 22 Oct 1938

letter on economic warfare *ibid* 2 Dec 1939.

letter on aircraft production *ibid* 30 Jan 1942.

Sources:

Unpublished

Bodleian, Oxford, papers of Viscount Addison.

House of Lords RO, papers of Sir Patrick Hannon.

PRO, papers of Foreign Office, Ministry of Munitions and Ministry of Reconstruction.

University of Warwick, Modern Records Centre, papers of Birmingham Small Arms.

Papers of Sir Alexander Roger, held by his son Alan.

PrC.

Information from Alan Roger, and R M Morgan.

Published

Christopher Addison, *Politics from Within 1911-18* (Herbert Jenkins, 1924).

—, *Four and a Half Years* (1934).

Sir William Barton (anonymously), 'India as a Workshop' *Times* 22 June 1942.

Burke's Peerage and Baronetage.

Richard Davenport-Hines, *Dudley Docker* (Cambridge: Cambridge University Press, 1984).

Economist 21 Mar 1931, 7 June 1947.

Evening Standard 26 Oct 1940.

Charles S Goldman, 'What is Wrong with the Telephone?' *Nineteenth Century* 76 (1914).

R M Morgan, *Callender's 1882-1945* (Prescot: BICC, 1982).

PD, HC, 5th ser 378 col 170 (24 Feb 1942).

Barry Ryerson, *The Giants of Small Heath: The History of BSA* (Sparkford, Yeovil, Somerset: Haynes Publishing, 1980).

I de Sola Pool (ed), *The Social Impact of the Telephone* (Cambridge, Massachusetts: MIT Press, 1977).

Statesman (Calcutta) 22 June 1942.

Joseph Sykes, *The Amalgamation Movement in English Banking 1825-1924* (P S King, 1926).

Times 6 Apr 1961.

Geoffrey W Tyson, *India Arms for Victory* (Allahabad, Kitabistan, 1943).

Donovan M Ward, *The Other Battle* (York 1946).

World's Press News 19 Mar 1942 (interview with Roger).

WWW.

ROGERS, Sir Hallewell

(1864-1931)

Small arms, vehicles and machine tool company chairman

Hallewell Rogers was born in Hampstead on 25 February 1864, son of George Rogers, a bank manager of Hampstead, and his wife Maria née Robinson. He was educated at Stanfield's private school in Hampstead, but at the age of seventeen moved to Birmingham where he joined Jesse Collings & Wallis, who were factors. He was apparently employed by them as a salesman. This was a traditional way into the purchase of local businesses, and five years later Rogers bought the firm of Howes & Burley, carriage lamp makers of Bishop Street. Subsequently he acquired two brush businesses, John Lea's and William James's, which he ran in addition to his earlier trade; none of these operations was on a large scale. He also became chairman of Thomas Carlyle Ltd of Aston, and director of Harris & Sheldon Ltd, J B Brooks and of Chamberlain, King & Jones, in which latter firm his brother-in-law Sir James Smith was also interested.

Rogers was a Liberal Unionist supporter of Joseph Chamberlain (qv), and was drawn into politics through his former employer, Collings. He had served on the committee of Collings's Rural Labourers' League before his election as a Birmingham city councillor for St Martin's Ward in 1893. His reputed business acumen was such that he was soon recruited to the Council's gas and water committees without training on lesser committees, as was usual with newcomers; Rogers proved an active chairman of the former during 1901-19. During that time the Gas Committee established its own Industrial Research Laboratory, and Rogers was chairman of the British Commercial Gas Association in 1915-18. He was a magistrate from 1901, alderman from 1902 and served as Lord Mayor during 1902-4, although only second choice for the office. He was knighted by King Edward VII in July 1904 on the inauguration of the city's water supply from the upper reaches of the Elan and Claerwen rivers in Wales. The three years of Rogers' mayoralty coincided with his election to the boards of two prominent Birmingham companies.

He became a director of the well-established Birmingham District & Counties Banking Co, which was then chaired by his brother-in-law Sir James Smith. During 1906-7 Birmingham District & Counties absorbed other local banks at Wakefield, Barnsley and Bradford, and consequently in 1907 altered its name to the United Counties Bank. Rogers remained a director until early 1916 when as part of the wartime banking amalgamations it was bought by Barclays Bank. In October 1919 Rogers resumed his active connection by joining the Barclays main board, where he remained until 1929. He was a Birmingham local director of Barclays during 1916-31.

In January 1904 Rogers joined the board of Birmingham Small Arms, and was chairman from May 1906. 'He was not ... a vigorous or constructive Chairman, and must be judged for his kindly qualities more than his efficiency' {HLRO, H 33/4, Sir Patrick Hannon to Sir Bernard Docker 21 May 1951}; his tenure of the post for over two decades would not have been tolerated in a better-run company, or by more able and united co-directors. BSA had been formed in 1861 by J D Goodman who had started business in 1831 and had in 1855 led promotion of the parliamentary Act establishing the Birmingham Proof House. Neither Goodman, nor his successors as chairman in 1900-6, Herbert Chamberlain and T F Walker, succeeded in drawing colleagues of great imagination or ability to the BSA board. Although the company had been formed with official encouragement from the War Office, from its earliest days it suffered from fluctuating and uncertain government orders. After the Small Heath factory had shut for a year for lack of small-arms work in 1879, BSA produced their first safety bicycle in 1880, diversified into producing bicycle components around 1893, took a pioneering interest in motorcycles after 1895 and made their first motor-cycle frames in 1903.

In the Edwardian period, especially under Rogers' chairmanship, BSA steadily reduced its reliance on the erratic and precarious armaments business, which accounted for an average of only 27.2 per cent of annual turnover by 1910-13. Nevertheless, this civilian diversification, well-judged in itself, was not always well-managed, and there were constant marketing and financial difficulties. As Rogers once declared, 'Our policy in connection with the motor-cycle is the same as with our other manufactures, namely to produce only the best and spare no expense in embodying the improvements and perfecting the machines, rather than attempt to cheapen the cost with a view to reducing the selling price' {Ryerson (1980) 29}. This policy was perhaps the proud reaction of a Lord Mayor of Birmingham to the city's reputation for producing cheap but nasty goods: its commercial consequences were eventually disastrous. Periodically throughout the seventy years from Rogers's election in 1904, BSA (which collapsed in 1973, merged with the motor cycle interests of Manganese Bronze to form Norton Villiers Triumph, and vanished into the ill-starred Meriden Co-operative) suffered serious crises as the result of boardroom rows, poorly-judged purchases of new subsidiaries, bad marketing failures, and worse financial planning. 'The management of BSA' in Rogers's time as well as after 1945 'was very highly skilled, and was very bad' {*ibid*, 137}.

In July 1906 BSA bought the Royal Small Arms Factory at Sparkbrook from the Government, but sustained a loss as the War Office did not maintain its orders to Sparkbrook at the level expected. In February 1907 BSA absorbed Eadie Manufacturing of Redditch, headed by Albert Eadie (qv) and famed for their patent coaster hub; and as a result in 1908 marketed the first complete BSA bicycle for twenty-one years. In an attempt to utilise the Sparkbrook facilities, BSA opened a motorcar department there: this, however, was ill-organised, lacked commercial bearings and suffered a production crisis in 1909. Largely as a result of this, BSA's deputy chairman, Dudley Docker (qv), arranged for the company to buy Daimler Motors of Coventry in 1910. Thereafter Edward Manville (qv) of Daimler became increasingly powerful alongside Rogers in BSA's boardroom.

During the Boer War BSA had produced 2,500 Lee-Metford rifles weekly, but for the five years prior to the outbreak of war, British government orders to BSA averaged only 7,000 rifles (135 rifles weekly). At the height of the munitions effort of 1914-18, BSA's weekly production reached 10,000 Lee Enfield rifles, which they had begun making in 1907. In 1912 BSA bought the sole manufacturing rights of the air-cooled automatic machine-gun invented by the American Colonel I N Lewis from a Belgian syndicate headed by Joseph Waterkeyn. Weekly output by BSA of Lewis guns was raised from 50 in August 1914 to 2,000. BSA supplied all British needs in Lewis machine-guns during the First World War, besides some for the Belgian and Russian Governments. BSA's cycle department was converted to produce aircraft parts such as aero-engines, oil pumps and Interrupter Drive Sets: at the height of hostilities BSA weekly produced 150,000 aircraft parts. Their motorcar factories produced ambulances, tractors and other vehicles for the war effort, as well as engines for the first tanks. In the spring of 1916 the motorcar body, painting and upholstery shops, and some of the chassis erecting shops, were adapted to produce 12-inch shells. Other plant made 18-pounder high explosive shell and fuses. Even these figures do not tell the whole story of BSA's war work. The Lee Enfield rifle used 1,250 gauges, and consisted of 131 distinct parts, so that to reach their weekly output of 10,000 rifles, BSA were producing 1,310,000 rifle components weekly, involving over 15 million machine operations.

BSA's post-war development was troubled. 'We framed our 1919 policy', Rogers explained, 'to make the smallest possible range of products on the largest possible scale' {*Economist* 29 Apr 1922}; but the grandeur of BSA's strategy was more evident than clear or detailed thinking about the future. While their Daimler Car Hire Co formed in 1919 reaped some rewards, their purchase from George Holt Thomas (qv) in 1920 of the Air Transport & Travel group (Airco) instantly proved a mistake, leading to an overall deficit of £469,168 for the financial year 1921-22 and passed ordinary dividends for 1921-24. As a result, however, of their Airco investment BSA controlled Daimler Hire's air passenger services which were absorbed in 1924 into Imperial Airways under Eric Geddes (qv). BSA also determined in 1919 to add machine tools to their other civilian businesses, and bought for about £1.4 million the Sheffield steel firm of William Jessop & Son Ltd, headed by Sir Albert Hobson, an associate of Manville in the Association of British Chambers of Commerce, and former colleague of Rogers on a government committee on engineering. BSA also bought the machinery merchants, Burton Griffiths & Co, and J J Saville, makers of steel tools. The formation in 1926 of BSA Radios Ltd, in conjunction with Standard Telephone & Cables, was another new venture. Yet throughout the BSA group there was ill-definition of responsibilities among management and poor communication attributable to the attitude of the managing director, Percy Martin (qv), who resented any suggestion that the board should supervise medium-term planning. Martin frustrated Rogers's feeble attempts at financial control, just as he obstructed later BSA chairmen such as A J H Pollen and A F P Roger (qqv). After ordinary dividends had again been passed for two successive years, Rogers was replaced as chairman of BSA in 1928 by Manville, who was himself supplanted when the group approached ruin in 1931.

Rogers however survived on the BSA board until the summer of 1931, when he was only dislodged with difficulty. Personally unexceptionable in a colourless way, he lacked dynamism or strength of leadership, and presided over a board of directors drawn from a narrow and rather complacent circle of Birmingham businessmen. To adapt Lloyd George's jibe at Rogers's BSA co-director Neville Chamberlain, Rogers's career proved that to be a good Lord Mayor of Birmingham in a lean year was no qualification for high industrial responsibility.

Rogers was a 'personal friend and commercial confrère' of Dudley Docker {*Midland Advertiser* 28 Oct 1911}, and for example on 10 February 1912 they were the joint speakers at the annual dinner of the Birmingham Association of Mechanical Engineers. Rogers owed at least part of his position at BSA to Docker and was a supporter of the latter's campaign before 1914 for Business Government and a Business Party in parliament. 'In the next House of Commons they ought to elect business men', Rogers declared: he similarly backed Docker's wartime corporatism and his formation of the Federation of British Industries. 'Unless we were going to allow our trade to be crippled as it had been in the past, unless we were going to allow the Germans to take our trade from us after the war, then some combination of this kind was absolutely ... essential' for Britain to survive 'as one of the principal commercial nations' {*Economist* 3 June 1916}. He was appointed to the departmental committee on the engineering trades of 1916-17 which considered post-war international competition and safeguarding. As a member of the Board of Trade's advisory committee on Commercial Intelligence during 1913-17, he joined the foundation board of the imperialist and anti-German export bank, the British Trade Corporation, whose Governor Lord Faringdon (qv) had Docker as his deputy. Arising from his commercial intelligence work, Rogers was also a wartime adviser to the Board of Trade on patents and trade marks. Rogers was active in the right-wing business pressure-group, the British Commonwealth Union, of which Docker was president. Rogers was on its official list of parliamentary candidates at the 1918 general election, and was chairman of its executive committee in 1918-26. He was elected Unionist MP for the Moseley division of Birmingham in

December 1918, but never spoke in the Commons; he resigned in February 1921 to create a parliamentary vacancy for Patrick Hannon, Director of the British Commonwealth Union and soon a director of BSA. Rogers politically was an Imperialist, with vague views on many topics, although as a municipal worthy he favoured decentralisation of power from London. Together with J Norton Griffiths (qv) he was one of 54 members of the Royal Colonial Institute elected to parliament in the general election of 1918. He said in 1921 that 'all industrial wages are a speculative investment by capital' {University of Warwick, MRC, BSA papers 19A/4/6}.

Rogers was interested in various Midlands charities, and for ten years from 1908 was chairman of the Hospital Saturday Committee. He was involved in the management of the Skin Hospital from 1888, sat on the committee of the District Nursing Institute, and was active in the Town Mission and the Girls' Night Shelter in Bath Row. He was active in the City Aid Society (later Citizens' Society); for years he was associated with the Church of the Redeemer, and later Carrs Lane Chapel, but was later described as belonging to the Anglican church of St Martin's. Like many of his contemporaries he apparently moved from Nonconformity and Liberal Unionism to become a Conservative Anglican. He also taught at Clark Street Early Morning School. A member of the Territorial Force Association for Warwickshire, he was honorary colonel during 1913-26 of the 3rd South Midland Royal Field Artillery Brigade, and a DL of Warwickshire from 1925.

He married, at the age of twenty-one, in July 1885, Lydia Watton (1855-1908), daughter of Thomas Smith, a stationer and printer of Edgbaston, and his wife Elizabeth Watton, and sister of Sir James Smith (1847-1932), a bedstead maker who was first Lord Mayor of Birmingham in 1896-97. Their only son Esmond was killed in action in France on 3 July 1916. Rogers married secondly, in 1927, Phyllis Daisy, widow of James Louis Mortimer Reeve of Shepherds Bush (who died when his ship was torpedoed off the Welsh coast in October 1918) and elder daughter of W H Burton of Ravenscroft Park, West London. Docker, and perhaps other business friends, disapproved of his second wife.

Rogers was greatly distressed by his enforced retirement from BSA in April 1931: he was left 'in a very shaky condition and very depressed'. Soon afterwards he was 'asked to resign from the Birmingham board of Barclays' and found 'the ordeal of parting pretty severe' {HLRO, H 31/1, Hannon to Martin 13 May 1931}. He died a few months later, after a seizure at his house at Edgbaston, on 16 November 1931, leaving £22,226.

R P T DAVENPORT-HINES

Writings:

PP, Report by Advisory Committee on Commercial Intelligence (1917) Cd 8815.

PP, Report of Departmental Committee on the Engineering Trades (1918) Cd 9073.

ROGERS Sir Hallewell

Sources:

Unpublished

House of Lords RO, papers of Sir Patrick Hannon.

University of Warwick, Modern Records Centre, papers of Birmingham Small Arms.

BCe.

MCe.

PrC.

Information from Dr Linda J Jones.

Published

Arms and Explosives passim.

Birmingham Gazette 17 Nov 1931.

Birmingham Mail 16 Nov 1931.

Birmingham Post 17 Nov 1931.

Burke's Peerage and Baronetage.

Richard P T Davenport-Hines, *Dudley Docker* (Cambridge: Cambridge University Press, 1984).

George A B Dewar, *The Great Munitions Feat 1914-1918* (1921).

Economist 3 June 1916, 29 Apr 1922.

Edgbastonia passim.

George H Frost, *Munitions of War: A Record of the Work of the BSA and Daimler Companies during the World War 1914-1918* (Birmingham: BSA, 1921).

John D Goodman, 'Small-Arms Manufacture' in Samuel Timmins (ed), *The Resources, Products and Industrial History of Birmingham and the Midland Hardware District* (Birmingham: Robert Hardwick, 1866).

Isaac F Marcossan, *The Business of War* (Lane, 1918).

Midland Advertiser 28 Oct 1911.

Barry Ryerson, *The Giants of Small Heath: The History of BSA* (Sparkford, Yeovil: Haynes Publishing, 1980).

W T Stead, 'Cycles and Science; or, Coventry Awake' *Review of Reviews* 27 (1903).

WWMP.

WWW.

Hon Charles Stewart Rolls (from H F Morris, Two Brave Brothers *Clifton Publishing House).*

ROLLS, The Honourable Charles Stewart

(1877-1910)

Motorcar promoter and manufacturer

Charles Stewart Rolls was born at 35 Hill Street, Berkeley Square, in London's West End on 27 August 1877, the third son among four children of John Allan Rolls (1837-1912), great grandson of the Seventh Earl of Northesk, of the Hendre, Monmouth and of Llangattock Manor, (later Conservative MP for Monmouthshire, 1880-85, and raised to the peerage as Lord Llangattock in 1892), and his wife Georgiana Marcia, fourth daughter of Sir Charles Fitzroy Maclean, Ninth Baronet. He was educated at Eton (where he became intrigued by things electrical), 1890-93, and at Trinity College, Cambridge, 1895-98, where he matriculated in 1895 and in 1898 took the Special Examination in mechanism and applied science for the ordinary BA degree, achieving a second class.

Rolls grew up in the age of the bicycle and greedily imbibed the spirit of individualism, science and speed which it symbolised. At Cambridge he won a half blue for cycling in 1896 and captained the university bicycle team the following year. As an undergraduate he was introduced to the motorcar by Sir David Salomons (qv) in February 1896 and later owned the first car seen in Cambridge — a 3.75 hp Peugeot which he imported from France in October 1896 and in doing so broke the Locomotive 'Red Flag' Act (of 1878) on his $11\frac{3}{4}$ hour journey from Victoria Station, London, to Cambridge. When, late in 1896, the Locomotives on Highways Act raised the maximum speed limit from 4 mph to 12 mph, Rolls emerged as one of the small band of wealthy English enthusiasts whose exploits popularised the motor car among their class. At Christmas 1896 he drove from London to the family home at Monmouth, descending Birdlip Hill without brakes and getting run over by his own car in the yard of the *New Inn*, Gloucester.

Rolls joined the Self-Propelled Traffic Association founded by Sir David Salomons and Harry Lawson (qv) in December 1895 to repeal the legal restrictions on road vehicles; became a member of the Automobile Club of France (formed in 1895); and was a founder member (and on the club committee until 1908) of the Automobile Club of Great Britain and Ireland (later the RAC), organised by Frederick Simms (qv) in August 1897. While speed lured him, Rolls was equally fascinated in discovering the limits of the new motorcar technology. In the Thousand Mile Reliability Trial, London to Edinburgh, of 1900, Rolls in a 12 hp Panhard won the Automobile Club's gold medal for the best amateur performance. In 1905 he was British representative in the race in France for the International Trophy offered by James Gordon Bennett (1841-1918), proprietor of the *New York Herald*. The other 'goggles and dust' trials in which he participated tested many of the incremental modifications, mostly French, that were then refining the technical structure of the early motorcar. For a decade (1896-1906) those races and trials also sifted the possibilities of the three major forms of propulsion for road vehicles — petrol, steam or electricity. Petrol emerged triumphant, proved in Britain by the work of S F Edge, Montague Napier (qqv) and Frederick Lanchester.

His flamboyant image as racing car driver and his aristocratic connections, together with £6,500 from his father, readily enabled Rolls to establish (in January 1902) a successful agency for petrol-driven motor cars, C S Rolls & Co, of Lillie Hall, Fulham, with himself publicising, and his partner, Claude Johnson (qv), organising the business. To improve sales Rolls introduced a scheme for car purchase by instalment. In spring 1904 Rolls heard about a new and unusually reliable car built in Manchester. That May, without enthusiasm, he visited its designer and builder Henry Royce (qv), having unsuccessfully approached another engineer, William Weir (qv), the previous March.

A test run convinced Rolls that the vehicle would realise his ambition for 'a good high-class quality car to replace the Panhard, preferably of three or four cylinders' {Lloyd (1978) 11}. Royce agreed to manufacture for Rolls who became his sole agent — the separation of manufacturing and marketing was an arrangement copied from Edge and Napier. Rolls contemplated giving up his other agencies as soon as Royce's output justified, 'for the 1904 agreement required Royce to design and manufacture four different chassis of 10, 15, 20 and 30 hp'. {ibid} The 10 hp and 20 hp models were exhibited at the Paris Show in December 1904, eliciting high praise from the technical press. Although the Rolls-Royce Co was not formed until the following year, a distributing agency, the Rolls-Royce Distributing Co Ltd, operated under the control of C S Rolls & Co. Rolls continued to sell other makes but increasingly advertised Rolls-Royce models, concentrating on a four-cylinder 20 hp machine, named the 'Grey Ghost' and retailing at £650 in December 1904.

Rolls and Johnson then proceeded to advertise the new car 'both by competing with it in all the important endurance long-distance, reliability and Tourist Trophy competitions, and by placing the car at the disposal of the press wherever occasion offered' {ibid, 13}. By the end of 1905 orders greatly exceeded the works' capacity and Rolls announced that he would thereafter trade only in British cars. Rolls-Royce Ltd was registered with a nominal capital of £60,000 in March 1906. Exactly how much was held by C S Rolls personally is unclear, but again his father gave him financial backing. In December 1906 the firm made a public flotation which, instead of the expected £100,000, raised only £51,000. Supplemented by a loan of £9,000, it was just sufficient to finance the necessary expansion of Royce's manufacturing facilities. Rolls became technical managing director with a salary of £750 per annum plus 4 per cent of profits in excess of £10,000.

Meanwhile Rolls gave the motorcars magnificent publicity. In May 1906 he broke the Monte Carlo-London record in a Rolls-Royce; one of the two Rolls-Royce cars entered for the 1906 (August) Tourist Trophy on the Isle of Man won the race; in October that year Rolls took the car to New York to demonstrate its speed at the Empire City Track; and in London he leased a second showroom, in Conduit Street. The following year Rolls helped to test drive the new 40-50 hp Silver Ghost, the model with which Rolls-Royce challenged the Napier 40-60 hp cars, hitherto the leaders at the top end of the market. Rolls also returned to the USA to race and to explore the potential of the American market — which he rated as good but underestimated American indifference to quality, the very essence of the

*Hon C S Rolls with the Wright Brothers in a Silver Ghost at Sheppey in May 1909. Orveille is seated next to Rolls and Wilbur is behind in a bowler hat (from H F Morris, *Two Brave Brothers* Clifton Publishing House).*

Rolls-Royce product. After the works were moved from Manchester to Derby in 1908 and adverse trading conditions curbed demand, one of the London showrooms was closed.

By this time Rolls's interest in the motorcar was waning. His fascination with speed and novel technological means of pursuing it had drawn him into aviation. In 1901 he had begun making balloon ascents, achieving 170 before he died, and in 1906 won the French Aero Club's medal for the longest balloon journey. In July 1908 the Rolls-Royce board gave him permission to become consulting engineer of a company proposing to build an airship.

Late in 1908 Rolls visited Le Mans in France to meet Wilbur Wright and study his aeroplane. He became one of the first to fly with Wright, imported a Wright aeroplane to England and learned to fly. In February 1909 it was suggested to the Rolls-Royce board (almost certainly by Rolls) that the company should acquire the British rights to manufacture the Wright aeroplane. The proposal was rejected forthwith, probably because of a lack of working capital and the danger of undermining Royce's health by overwork. Rolls, however, had arranged for the company to manufacture the gearing for the War Office aeroplane and dirigible balloon, which brought strong protests from fellow directors. This divergence of view led Rolls to resign from the Rolls-Royce board in April 1910. The following June he made the first return flight across the Channel in his Wright aeroplane. However, the promise of a major contribution to aviation was tragically extinguished a month later.

Characteristically, Rolls's recreations included amateur dramatics and football as well as motoring and ballooning, and on the last two he wrote a number of pieces. He was a fellow of the Royal Geographical Society and of the Royal Metallurgical Society as well as an associate member of the Institution of Mechanical Engineers. Rolls was a keep-fit enthusiast, seldom drank and patronised a vegetarian restaurant. He was treasurer of the National Food Reform Association and supporter of the National Anti-Vivisection Society. He was unmarried and was described by Sir Thomas Sopwith (qv) as a 'natural solitary' {Montagu (1966) 231}. Rolls became the first Englishman to be killed flying an aeroplane when his Wright biplane crashed at a flying tournament at Bournemouth on 12 July 1910. He left £30,936 gross.

DAVID J JEREMY

Writings:

'The Caprices of the Petrol Motors' in Alfred C W Harmsworth (ed), *Motors and Motor Driving* (Badminton Library, 1902).

Roadside Experiences. A Paper Read at the Automobile Club of Great Britain and Ireland (G Shield, 1904).

'Un Vol en Aéroplane Wright' *La Conquête de l'Air* (Brussels, Nov 1908).

'In the Days of My Youth' *Pearson's Weekly* (ca 1908).

Motor Notes (1908).

'My Voyage in the World's Greatest Airship' *London Magazine* May 1908 (and pp).

'Pleasure Motors' *Encyclopaedia Britannica* (11th ed, 1910-11).

(with R H Royce) *Instructions for Care of Rolls-Royce Cars, 40-50 hp* (1908).

Sources:

Unpublished

PrC.

Published

W W Rouse Ball and J A Venn, *Admissions to Trinity College, Cambridge 1546-1900* (5 vols, Macmillan, 1911-16).

Cambridge University Reporter 1 June 1898.

Roy Church, 'Markets and Marketing in the British Motor Industry before 1914 with Some French Comparisons' *Journal of Transport History* 3rd ser 3 (1982).

Complete Peerage.

DNB.

Ian Lloyd, *Rolls-Royce. The Growth of a Firm* (Macmillan, 1978).

Edward J B D S Montagu, *Rolls of Rolls-Royce* (Cassell, 1966).

Henry F Morris, *Two Brave Brothers* (Clifton Publishing House, 1918).

Harold Nockolds, *The Magic of a Name* (G T Foulis & Co, 1950).

William J Reader, *The Weir Group. A Centenary History* (Weidenfeld & Nicolson, 1971).

Kenneth Richardson, *The British Motor Industry, 1896-1939* (Macmillan, 1977).

Samuel B Saul, 'The Motor Industry in Britain to 1914' *Business History* 5 (1962).

Charles H Wilson and William J Reader, *Men and Machines. A History of D Napier & Son, Engineers, Ltd, 1808-1958* (Weidenfeld & Nicolson, 1958).

WWW.

ROOTES, Sir Reginald Claud

(1896-1977)

Motor vehicle manufacturer and distributor

Reginald Claud Rootes was born at Goudhurst, Kent, on 20 October 1896, younger son of William Rootes (1869-1955), a cycle and motor engineer, and his wife Jane née Catt. He was educated at Cranbrook School and in 1915 entered the Civil Service, where he worked in the Admiralty.

In 1919 he was persuaded to leave the Civil Service to join his brother, William (qv), as joint managing director of Rootes Ltd. Throughout the 1920s, as the motor distributing business was expanding, Reginald's main activity was in administering the firm. Although never visibly a world traveller like William, he did attend the British Empire Exhibition held in Buenos Aires during 1931 and founded Rootes Argentina SA. This branch was one of the earliest British vehicle distributing organisations in Latin America.

Following the reorganisation of Humber Ltd in 1932, Reginald became managing director and devoted much of his life to the manufacturing arm of the new Rootes Group. The development of common components, integration of factories and the creation of a more identifiable 'house design' of vehicles were largely achieved by the end of the decade.

Reginald took over full direction of the firm when William left to head the supply council of the Ministry of Supply early in the Second World War. He played a major part in the application of quantity production methods to aero-engine and aircraft building. In addition to its pre-war plants, by 1943 Rootes was operating two shadow factories in Coventry employing over 6,000 workers. The Rootes contribution to the war effort was substantial — 60 per cent of all British armoured cars, 30 per cent of scout cars, 14 per cent of bombers in addition to the 50,000 aero-engines manufactured. Reginald's war work earned him a knighthood in 1946.

The post-war expansion of the company required a great deal of attention to the details of new designs of cars and trucks, re-tooling of factories and the organisation of supply systems to produce and then distribute the finished vehicles. The pre-war geography of the Rootes Group was already complex and this was accentuated afterwards. Car engines and transmissions were made in Coventry, truck engines were produced in Luton. Some body parts came from the subsidiary in Acton, but most were hauled by road from Oxford and Swindon to the main car assembly plant on the outskirts of Coventry. Planning regulations imposed after 1947 restricted the physical expansion of Coventry and Luton. All factory extensions required government approval and, although permission to build a new truck assembly plant at Dunstable near Luton was granted, extra manufacturing capacity had to be sought through the acquisition of existing factories. Demand for new factory space was an element in the purchase of Tilling Stevens Motors Ltd in Maidstone during 1951 and Singer Motors with factories in Coventry and Birmingham in 1955. By the late 1950s, Rootes Group production came from over a dozen plants scattered between Coventry and Folkestone. The detailed co-ordination of these plants in a period of industrial growth and growing labour problems imposed a major burden on Reginald and his staff in Devonshire House.

The Rootes brothers fought hard in 1959-60 to breach the Coventry greenbelt in order to erect a new plant for the mini car then being developed for the corporate strategy of expansion. In 1961 Rootes was persuaded by strong government influence to build its assembly plant at Linwood, Renfrew. At least £25 million was spent on the factory complex which was opened by the Duke of Edinburgh in May 1963. While the new plant was expected to contribute to the industrial regeneration of Clydeside, only 20 per cent of the materials used in the new Hillman Imp were produced in Scotland. Most of the materials had to be transported at least 300 miles from the West Midlands and the bulk of the finished vehicles also had to be shipped southwards. Linwood was an expensive venture at a difficult time in the company's history and its distant location from the other centres of Rootes's activity must have increased the stresses on management. Some commentators suggest that the Linwood plant was the main factor in the financial problems of Rootes which led Lord Rootes just before his death in 1964 to turn to Chrysler for new investment. Chrysler, then in a phase of rapid worldwide expansion, announced in June 1964 that it was taking a £12.3 million interest in Rootes. At this time 30 per cent of the ordinary (voting) shares and 50 per cent of the non-voting shares were acquired. The transfer of control from the family to Chrysler occurred within a few years and in 1970 the Rootes name was replaced by the new corporate symbol of the Chrysler Pentastar. Following the death of his brother in 1964, Sir Reginald continued as a member of the board until he retired from Rootes Motors at the age of seventy.

Like his elder brother, Reginald played a part in the wider activities of the British motor industry. Elected a vice-president of the Society of Motor Manufacturers and Traders in 1943, he became president in 1945-46 and served as deputy-president until 1950. In 1952-53 he was president of the Motor Industry Research Association, the co-operative research organisation which had a proving ground and laboratories at Lindley, near Nuneaton. Reginald Rootes was also a vice-president of the Engineering and Allied Employers' Federation during the 1950s.

As the close business partner of his brother, Sir Reginald Rootes played an important role in the industry and in the family firm for nearly fifty years. In physical characteristics and personality, he complemented William. Slightly taller than his brother, Reginald had a quieter temperament and a discreet personality. Although always the less visible partner in the Rootes Group, his significance in the successful administration of all the complex operations over a long period of time should not be overlooked. He was aptly described as providing the 'steering and braking system to Sir William's power unit' {*Coventry Standard* 29 June 1956}.

Sir Reginald was interested in farming and throughout his life maintained a country residence in Kent, from the 1950s at Hothfield, near

Ashford. He was married twice, firstly in 1922 to Ruth Joyce, daughter of William Harding Bensted, a stone merchant, whom he divorced in 1938; secondly, in 1938 to Nancy Norris Beadle. A son of the first marriage, Timothy David (b 1925), who was educated at Harrow, was also active in the Rootes Group from 1947. Sir Reginald was a wealthy man, with a substantial holding in Rootes Motors. In 1951 he held 10.9 per cent of the voting shares. He died on 20 December 1977, leaving £1.33 million gross.

G T BLOOMFIELD

Sources:

Unpublished

MCe.

PrC.

Published

Burke's Peerage and Baronetage 1980.

Coventry Evening Telegraph 21 Dec 1977.

Coventry Standard 29 June 1956.

P Sargant Florence, *Ownership, Control and Success of Large Companies* (Sweet & Maxwell, 1961).

Times 21 Dec 1977.

WWW.

S Young and N Hood, *Chrysler UK: A Corporation in Transition* (New York: Praeger, 1977).

ROOTES, William Edward

1st Lord Rootes of Ramsbury

(1894-1964)

Motor vehicle manufacturer and distributor

William Edward Rootes was born at Hawkhurst, Kent, on 17 August 1894, elder son of William Rootes, a cycle and motor engineer, and his wife Jane née Catt. He was educated at Cranbrook School and in 1913 began an apprenticeship with Singer Motors Ltd in Coventry. At this time he was also active in motor cycle racing. In 1915 he volunteered as a pupil engineer in the Royal Naval Volunteer Reserve, becoming a lieutenant, and was transferred to the Royal Naval Air Service in 1917.

After the war he persuaded his younger brother, Reginald (qv), to join him as joint managing director of Rootes Ltd, a family business formed at Maidstone and registered in 1917 to take over the motor distributorship begun earlier in the century by their father. Billy Rootes was a salesman par excellence and became the key figure in the rapid growth of the firm. Rootes sold Singer, Austin, Humber, Hillman, Clyno and other makes in a period when the mass car market was beginning to develop on a large scale. A firm in Rochester was one of Rootes's earliest acquisitions and was followed by other garage and distribution businesses in London, Birmingham, Manchester and other parts of England. By 1926 Rootes had acquired a London base in Long Acre, and the firm moved into the newly-built Devonshire House in Piccadilly as its head office and prestige West End showroom. Within ten years of founding, Rootes was the largest distributor in Britain and the biggest export agency in the country. Although increasingly involved in other business affairs, William Rootes always maintained the loyalty of his dealers.

It was clear from the success of Morris, Austin and the American companies that there were benefits for a firm which integrated distribution and production of vehicles. The Rootes brothers therefore decided to acquire Thrupp & Maberly, an old-established London coach builder, in 1925, and from this time they gradually developed a production base. The investment of £1 million in Rootes Ltd by the Prudential Assurance Co provided new capital in 1929, not only for immediate use but also for 'the particular object of fostering the export of British cars' {*Times* 25 Oct 1929}. Since Rootes was already directing the export organisation of Humber Ltd, it was not unexpected that some of the new capital went into this firm. Humber was an old-established cycle and motor company in Coventry and had two subsidiaries, Hillman which was also in Coventry, and Commer in Luton. The company was still small compared with the leading firms in the industry and despite reorganisation was in financial difficulties. When Rootes acquired an interest in Humber Ltd, William became directly involved in the testing and promotion of cars, notably the Hillman Minx introduced in 1931. This design and its successors formed the basis of the successful entry of Rootes into the mass production of a popular low-priced car.

By 1932 Rootes Ltd held 60 per cent of the ordinary shares of Humber Ltd and was able to insist on a new scheme of financing and management. In August 1932 the Rootes brothers took direct control of Humber with William as deputy chairman and Reginald as managing director. From this time William added responsibilities for the manufacturing activities of the group.

Further corporate re-organisation followed in April 1933 when Rootes Securities Ltd was formed as a private holding company. The Rootes Group now had two related arms — Humber Ltd, controlling the manufacturing sector, and Rootes Ltd, which owned subsidiaries in motor vehicle distribution, property and hire purchase financing. Overall management was in the hands of the Rootes brothers and controlled from

Devonshire House. Following this consolidation of business interests, other firms were acquired: Karrier Motor Ltd in 1934, Clement Talbot Ltd and the Sunbeam Motor Car Co Ltd in 1935. These firms were old-established manufacturers with respected names — perhaps the most valuable asset they possessed. British Light Steel Pressings Ltd was acquired in 1937 to provide some car body making capability for the group.

By the late 1930s the Rootes Group had an integrated organisation, output had increased fourfold and the company was clearly one of the 'Big Six' British vehicle manufacturers, with nearly 43,000 motor vehicles produced in 1938, accounting for about 10 per cent of total national vehicle production.

William Rootes had an early interest in the overseas expansion of the British motor industry. In 1927 he represented the industry on a Board of Trade mission to Australia and New Zealand. Between 1931 and 1934 and in 1939-40 he was the motor industry representative on the Advisory Council of the Board of Trade and in 1933 he joined the Overseas Trade Development Council. British motor vehicle exports more than doubled in volume in the decade after 1927 as a result of Empire trade preferences and British manufacture by US subsidiaries, as well as the efforts of promotion groups such as those joined by Rootes. By the late 1930s the Rootes group had a significant export market in Australia, New Zealand and Latin America.

As a member and, later, chairman of the Joint Aircraft Engine Committee (Shadow Industry) 1936-41, William played an active part in the shadow factory scheme. Two shadow factories were built for Rootes in Coventry, the larger at Ryton-on-Dunsmore becoming the post-war car assembly plant for the group. At the outbreak of war Rootes became virtually a full-time member of the several government committees organising the supply of aircraft, motor vehicles and other war material. He was chairman of the supply council of the Ministry of Supply in 1941-42 and received a knighthood in 1942 for his contribution to the war effort.

After the war, Rootes shared in the substantial expansion of the British motor industry. In 1949, Rootes Securities Ltd was reorganised as Rootes Motors Ltd, to bring a new capital participation required for investment in modernised plants, overseas distribution networks and new designs. In 1960 Rootes was the twelfth largest world motor corporation by volume of output, considerably larger than the little-known Toyota Motor Co. At this time the group owned six million square feet of manufacturing space, had some 1,000 dealers in the UK, was involved in hire purchase, car hire, driving schools, made air conditioners, owned nine assembly plants overseas and employed a labour force of some 20,000 people. The direction of the group at this time was still controlled by the Rootes brothers in their adjacent suites of offices in Devonshire House.

In this expansion William's role was that of international salesman and promoter both for the company and for British exports generally. Assembly operations were established in many parts of the world, ranging from Australia (1946) to Venezuela (1963). Isuzu Motors in Japan became a licensee for Hillman cars and built 50,000 units by 1963. Some of the greatest of Rootes's efforts were devoted to establishing a strong position in the North American market. Parts and service depots were opened in New York, Chicago, Los Angeles and Toronto by 1950. At the end of the decade Rootes had over 700 dealers in every state of the Union and was selling 20 per cent of its output through this network. William became chairman of the Dollar Exports Council in 1951 and headed a concerted drive to sell British goods in the USA. He continued as chairman of this organisation (renamed the Western Hemisphere Exports Council in 1960) until his retirement in March 1964. Few major trade events did not have his active presence, and he was travelling up to 70,000 miles a year in order to promote exports.

The post-war growth of Rootes was not achieved without some problems. While the firm grew substantially, its relative standing in the British industry remained steady. Overseas assembly and distribution networks, essential to the survival of the company, were costly to develop, especially in the face of increasing competition from the mid-1950s. Volkswagen, which in 1950 was producing the same volume as Rootes, was a decade later manufacturing more than four times the number of vehicles. Rootes in 1960 was an awkward size, attempting to cover world markets with a full range of vehicles at volumes of output which lost many of the economies of scale in production and distribution. The cycle of low sales volumes leading to low overall returns and reduced investment became an increasing problem in the late 1950s. Profits were marginal at best and were vulnerable to rapid changes in sales (as in the decline in US imports in 1960), difficult labour relations (such as the prolonged strike at the Acton plant in 1961) and catastrophes (like the big fire at Ryton in 1960).

There were several strategies open to the firm if it was to develop a stronger market position. One direction was to follow the example of Peugeot, a company of similar size and to concentrate production on a more limited range of vehicles for a higher-value segment of the market. An alternative was to attempt to expand further into the highly competitive mass market with a new car design. The latter strategy was chosen and a rear-engined mini car, the Hillman Imp, was designed and produced in a newly-built plant in Scotland opened in 1963. Although the plant was supported by a government grant to promote economic re-development in the West of Scotland, the construction of the factory and the development of a new vehicle were costly not only in financial terms but in extra management time and effort. Early returns on this new investment were low as the volume of output failed to reach planned targets.

Rootes Motors Ltd made losses in 1962 and 1963 and it was becoming clear to outside observers that the company would have to seek new sources of capital or merge with another motor firm in order to survive. With the increased concentration in the British industry the range of potential partners was limited. The long-standing connections of Rootes in the United States made it no surprise that attempts might be made to interest an American firm. One of his last major activities in 1964 was to negotiate with the Chrysler Corporation for the infusion of new capital into Rootes Motors Ltd.

Rootes was also involved in the activities of the Society of Motor Manufacturers and Traders, the trade association for the British motor industry. He was vice-president, 1934-36, president, 1939-42 and continued as a member of its council until 1964. He served as a member of the Board of Trade's National Advisory Council for the Motor

Manufacturing Industry, 1947-64 and the Engineering Advisory Council of the Board of Trade, 1947-62.

Although Rootes never lived in Coventry, his business activities there gave him a close interest in the city. By the 1950s he was part of the folklore of Coventry since he was then one of the last entrepreneurs actively directing a large firm there. After the heavy air raids in November 1940, Rootes served as chairman of the Coventry Industrial Reconstruction and Co-ordinating Committee and had a major role in restoring essential services in the devastated city. In 1961 he was invited to become chairman of the promotion committee of the new University of Warwick. He was a galvanising force and raised over £1 million for the Foundation Fund. At the time of his death he was chancellor-designate.

His work for exports was recognised by advancement to GBE in 1955 and his elevation to the peerage as Baron Rootes of Ramsbury in 1955. In 1962 the Royal Society of Arts awarded him the Benjamin Franklin medal for his activities in furthering Anglo-American commerce. He was also a member of the council and executive committee of the British Council.

Rootes had a long-standing interest in farming and was well known as a breeder of pedigree livestock. He acquired an estate at Stype Grange, near Hungerford in the 1930s and moved to the nearby Ramsbury Manor in Wiltshire during the 1950s. He also acquired property at Glenalmond, Perthside, for his other hobby of shooting. He married Nora, daughter of Horace Press, a miller, in 1916, and after their divorce in 1951 he married Ann Peck. The sons of his first marriage, William Geoffrey (b 1917) and Brian Gordon (b 1919), were both active in the business. William Rootes was a wealthy man with substantial holdings in Rootes Motors. In 1951 he held 18.7 per cent of the voting shares and when he died on 12 December 1964 he left £1.84 million gross.

William Rootes was unquestioned head of the Rootes dynasty, which included not only his brother but by late the 1950s his two sons and nephew. It was a distinctive partnership in business — he provided the power unit for the firm while his brother supplied some of the checks and balances. He was a super salesman for the firm and acted as its spokesman on almost every issue, having a very good relationship with the press. Rootes was physically smaller than his brother, friendly and approachable, restless and remarkably energetic. Few individuals could have sustained his role, not only in the firm, but also in the wide range of activities in British industrial affairs and the promotion of British exports.

G T BLOOMFIELD

Sources:

Unpublished

MCe.

PrC.

ROOTES William Edward

Published

Gerald T Bloomfield, 'The Changing Spatial Organisation of Multinational Corporations in the World Automotive Industry' in F E I Hamilton and G R S Linge (eds), *Spatial Analysis, Industry and the Industrial Environment* (Chichester: Wiley, 1981) 2.

Burke's Peerage and Baronetage 1980.

Coventry Evening Telegraph 12 Dec 1964.

Coventry Standard 29 June 1956.

DNB.

P Sargant Florence, *Ownership, Control and Success of Large Companies* (Sweet & Maxwell, 1961).

PEP, *Motor Vehicles* (1950).

Kenneth Richardson, *Twentieth Century Coventry* (Macmillan, 1972).

—, *The British Motor Industry, 1896-1939* (Macmillan, 1977).

Stock Exchange Official Year-Book 1935.

Times 25 Oct 1929, 11 Aug 1932, 14 Dec 1964.

WWW.

S Young and N Hood, *Chrysler UK: A Corporation in Transition* (New York: Praeger, 1977).

ROPNER, Sir Robert

(1838-1924)

Shipowner and shipbuilder

Emil Hugo Oscar Robert (known as Robert) Ropner was born at Magdeburg in Prussia on 16 December 1838, the son of an army officer. His parents died in 1848 during a cholera epidemic and he was brought up by an aunt in Helmstedt where he attended the grammar school. In 1857 at the age of eighteen he emigrated to England. His reasons for doing so have been variously given as avoidance of ministry in the Church, romantic visions of going to sea, and (a favoured reason during the First World War) a dislike of Prussian militarism. There is no evidence to suggest that he had received any prior commercial training, and although his English was often complimented in later life he does not appear to have had any special tuition in the language.

On landing at Hartlepool, he took employment in a bakery, and in 1858 married Mary Ann Craik, the daughter of the owner of another bakery in the town. His first son, John Henry, was born in 1861. Meanwhile, Ropner made his first move towards a commercial career by joining Geipels, a firm of colliery fitters and coal exporters, as a clerk. Much of the coal trade of the North East at this time was done with Germany and the Baltic and one of his first duties for the firm was a trip to Germany.

In 1860 Ropner joined another coal exporter, Thomas Appleby. With Appleby, Ropner's duties were again intimately connected with the trade in coal with Germany and the other countries bordering on the Baltic. Early in 1866 Ropner was admitted into partnership by Appleby. First steps towards vertical integration of the coal exporting business can be detected at the end of 1867. There is surviving correspondence between Ropner and the shipbuilders Messrs Denton, Gray & Co negotiating the price of a 800 deadweight tons steamer to be built for Appleby, Ropner & Co. This was the iron screw steamer *Amy*, launched in July 1868. Her owners were Ropner and Appleby, each with 24/64ths shares, J P Denton and William Gray (qv) with 8/64ths each. The close relationship between shipbuilder and shipowner indicated here was a common feature of the shipping industry of the period. The economies possible by negotiating repeat orders, with the consequent simplicity of specifications, were considerable. Such arrangements also served to smooth the worst fluctuations in the highly cyclical demand for new ships. Shipyards were afforded guaranteed orders, and shipowners could take quick delivery of better built and more efficient tonnage in advance of any rise in freight rates. Moreover, shipbuilders, when orders were scarce, were often prepared to participate in ownership and to offer extended credit terms, as they did in the case of *Amy*. Ropner's first venture into shipowning was extremely short-lived however, as *Amy* was wrecked in the Baltic in September 1868. Moreover, Ropner's second steamship, *Magdala*, 703 tons gross, launched in April 1870, also had a short life, being wrecked in the Baltic in October 1872.

These first tentative moves into shipowning, in collaboration with Appleby and Denton, Gray & Co, held until 1874, when Ropner felt confident enough to break away on his own. Nevertheless, Ropner maintained a close interest in the coal industry as fitter, or agent, for the Haswell, Shotton & Easington Coal Co, and coal was to remain the principal export cargo carried by his steamers for more than one generation.

Much shipping during this period was financed by the 'sixty-fourth' system of ownership and management rather than setting up 'single ship' companies as many other shipowners like Henry Radcliffe (qv) did. Ropner was able to rely upon a network of investors mainly located in the textile towns of the North of England, such as Wakefield, Huddersfield, Ilkley and Leeds. These steadfast supporters of Ropner's shipowning ventures were rewarded with regular, if unspectacular, dividends, and they clearly benefited from Ropner's judgement and dedication in a notoriously speculative industry.

The Ropner fleet of tramp steamers grew remarkably in numbers, in aggregate tonnage and in average size per ship. By 1884, Ropner was the part-owner and manager of 18 steamers of 29,380 tons gross register.

Sir Robert Ropner's steamer Moorby, *built in his shipyard in 1896 and owned by him, seen here on the River Avon (courtesy of York collection, Bristol Museum).*

Unlike many other shipowners of his day, Ropner made very little use of the secondhand market in procuring tonnage, so that his new-built vessels embodied each new technological advance consistent with reliability, thus securing maximum carrying capacity at the minimum cost. Although many shipowners were adopting single-ship, limited liability company organisation from the 1880s, Ropner resisted the trend, thanks to the confidence reposed in him by those who invested in his ships. He did, however, form the Pool Shipping Co Ltd in 1903, a firm whose directorships were disposed strictly within Ropner's own family. The authorised capital was £250,000 in £10 shares, but the articles of association stipulated a subscription of £100,000, so that it was clearly intended to be a tightly-knit family organisation. Subsequently, as new ships were acquired, the capital was raised to £937,500. The formation of the Pool Shipping Co did not mean that Ropner relinquished altogether the older form of ownership in 64ths. Indeed, in 1914 of his vast fleet of steamers, numbering 58 vessels of 193,423 gross tons, 42 of 128,045 were still owned by R Ropner & Co, a partnership to which his sons were admitted between 1886 and 1902, and only 14 vessels of 60,517 tons were owned by the joint-stock company. By this time the distinctive nomenclature of Ropner vessels had been established: Ropner's vessels having names with the suffix 'by' and Pool Shipping Co Ltd ships having the suffix 'pool'.

To judge by surviving balance sheets, Ropner's management of the Pool Shipping Co Ltd was distinguished by the same sagacity and prudence that had characterised his professional life from the outset. He carefully marshalled his resources and by ploughing back profits in the enterprise he was able to add new units to the fleet even when such new vessels cost as much as £43,000 each, as they did in the 1900s. He took pains to depreciate his assets realistically (at 4 per cent per annum), and when times were good, placed money in reserves.

One contemporary view of the success of R Ropner & Co as shipowners cites in particular Ropner's method of reducing the overall cost of marine insurance by extending coverage to the particular average of his vessels. This, according to *Fairplay*, had contributed to the success of their vessels as dividend-earning concerns.

Ropner needed to keep in close touch both with the freight market and the export trade in coal. To meet the latter need, he first opened an office in Cardiff, the centre of the export coal trade, in 1879. As Ropner himself wrote, ' ... there is little doubt that the bulk of the overseas boat trade will in future be done from South Wales and my steamers will more frequently load there' {Ropner family papers}. However, it is not entirely clear that Ropner's initiative in Cardiff met with much success since his office there seems to have been closed for much of the period between 1880 and 1886. In response to the need to be close to the centre of chartering and shipbroking, he did open an office in London in the 1880s so that he could maintain vital contact with the Baltic Exchange, the international centre for shipping chartering.

Ropner's fleet suffered terrible losses in the First World War. Altogether 26 of his vessels, aggregating 83,343 tons, were lost by enemy action, a grievous blow to the companies. Only two new units were added to the fleet during the course of the war, and, exceptionally, one vessel was acquired secondhand. Ropner stood altogether aloof from the highly-speculative shipping boom which followed the end of hostilities, and in this he vouchsafed further evidence of his prudence and farsightedness. New vessels were not acquired until 1924, when five new vessels were ordered, and another secondhand vessel acquired. At the time of his death in 1924, the Ropner fleet comprised 14 steamships of 61,980 gross registered tons, all but one of which were now owned by the Pool Shipping Co Ltd.

In 1888 Ropner had added materially to his activities by purchasing the medium-sized Stockton-on-Tees shipyard of Pearse & Co, which for some time had stood idle. This enterprise was run as a partnership with his sons, Leonard and Robert Jr, in charge. It was his son Robert who was largely responsible for introducing a new type of tramp steamer, known as the 'trunk-deck' ship, which was really a variant of Doxford's (qv) 'turret deck' design. Of the many trunk-deck steamers launched between 1896 and 1908, 23 were absorbed in the fleets of the parent companies, and several more were acquired by other shipowners, such as Henry Radcliffe of Cardiff.

Although trunk-deck ships proved sea-kindly, strong and of enhanced carrying capacity, they suffered the disadvantage of being fundamentally single-deck ships and appropriate only for the homogeneous bulk cargoes that were Ropner's staple trades. The shipyard enjoyed modest success, although it suffered from the same volatile demand that characterised other tramp shipbuilding enterprises. Ropner's shipyard constructed hulls only, and never engaged in marine engine building, but the firm obtained extremely reliable engines, mainly from Messrs Blair of Stockton, or, occasionally, from William Gray's Central Marine Engineering Works. In 1896 Ropner's shipyard ranked eighth on the North-East Coast in terms of tonnage launched. In 1907, 32,127 gross tons were constructed, but in the depressed year of 1908, only 5,005 gross tons of shipping came from the yard. However, in 1912, Ropners produced ten steamships of 43,547 tons, putting it in thirteenth place among all British shipyards in tonnage launched. The best year during the First World War was an output of 33,372 tons in 1917, but by the early 1920s the yard finally closed. Previously, in October 1907, Ropner adopted for his shipyard joint-stock, limited liability company structure, with a capital of £150,000 in £1 shares and himself as permanent director and chairman.

From 1890 onwards Ropner's attention turned away from his business, pursuit of his outside interests becoming possible now that he could leave much of the day-to-day running of the company to his sons (who now numbered five). The practical management of the West Hartlepool offices was entrusted to John Henry and William; Robert Jr and Leonard managed the shipyard; Walter managed the London office (opened in 1887). Ropner's public career moved in two directions. He was particularly active in the institutions of the shipping industry. He was chairman of the Hartlepool Port and Harbour Commission, of the Hartlepool Shipowners' Society, and of the East Coast Well Deck, and West Hartlepool Freight and Demurrage Insurance Associations. He served on the executive council of the United Kingdom Chamber of Shipping and was president of the Chamber in 1901 and 1902.

Secondly, like Christopher Furness (qv) and William Gray, Ropner went into politics. He became mayor of Stockton in 1892. A confirmed Unionist and tariff reformer, he twice stood for parliament before his eventual election as MP for Stockton-on-Tees in 1900. He was knighted in 1902 and created a baronet in 1904. He retired from parliament in 1910.

The picture which emerges from a study of Ropner's private life is that of an immigrant anxious to assimilate into an English way of life. He became naturalised in 1861. Early in his career he became a town councillor for West Hartlepool, and he also served as a JP. He joined the Durham Volunteer Light Infantry Regiment in 1873 and eventually rose to the rank of colonel. By the late 1880s he had moved to Preston Hall, Stockton, and he also owned estates in the country. He was noted for acts of philanthropy including the donation of £10,000 to the governors of the Stockton and Thornaby Hospital for the building of a new surgical wing, on the occasion of his diamond wedding anniversary. In a retrospective view of his life, dating from 1918, he wrote that he hoped he had been a loyal British subject. Sir Robert Ropner died on 26 February 1924, leaving £3,615,828. Before his death he had the satisfaction of seeing two of his three grandsons, Colonel Leonard Ropner and Major Guy Ropner, join the company which today (1984) still plays its full part in the British mercantile marine.

ROBIN CRAIG *and* MICHAEL ROBSON

Sources:

Unpublished

PrC.

Ropner family papers.

Published

'Fairplay's' Annual Summary of British Shipping Finance 1925.

Leonard Gray, *The Ropner Fleet 1874-1974* (Kendal: World Ship Society, 1975).

Syren and Shipping passim.

WWMP.

WWW.

ROSENTHAL, James Hermann
see KEMNAL, James H R

ROTHERHAM, 1st Lord Rotherham
see HOLLAND, William Henry

ROTHERMERE, 1st Viscount Rothermere
see HARMSWORTH, Harold Sidney

Nathan Meyer Rothschild (from Jules Ayer, A Century of Finance 1804–1904 *Neely, 1905).*

ROTHSCHILD, Nathan Meyer

1st Lord Rothschild of Tring, Hertfordshire

(1840-1915)

Merchant banker

Nathan Meyer ('Natty') Rothschild was born in London on 8 November 1840, the eldest son of Baron Lionel Nathan de Rothschild (1808-79) and his wife and cousin Charlotte née Rothschild. For the most part he was privately educated, but also attended King's College School (London) and Trinity College, Cambridge, and spent some time in Germany as a young man. From an early age it was expected that he would enter the family merchant bank, N M Rothschild & Sons, which had been founded in London by his grandfather in 1805. When the founder died suddenly in 1836, the family lost its financial genius, and the principal initiative passed to Baron James, N M's younger brother, in Paris. In London the reins were cautiously taken up by Baron Lionel who dedicated himself entirely to the business throughout his life, but lacked the founder's virtuosity and outstanding business ability.

During the long period (1836-79) in which Baron Lionel ruled 'New Court' (Rothschild's offices in the City of London), his firm became increasingly conservative. It has become customary for historians to write of the London, Paris, Frankfurt, Vienna and Naples branches of the Rothschild family as if they pursued a single policy, but in this period most of the entrepreneurship ascribed to them emanated from Baron James de Rothschild (1792-1868) in Paris, who survived his elder brother N M by more than thirty years, and James's son, Baron Alphonse. All the Rothschild houses lost a great deal of money when Arnstein & Eskelles of Vienna went bankrupt in the crisis of 1848, and the London Rothschilds are said to have lost heavily on Confederate bonds in the American Civil War. Baron Lionel's boldest initiative, to judge from the shelves of his business correspondence still at New Court, was in extending commercial credits for trade in Europe and North America. Even so, he was invariably resistant to the business propositions sent by the firm's energetic American agent, August Belmont, and acceptances fell away during his last years. By and large Lord 'Natty' Rothschild maintained his father's conservative business policies.

Apart from the bullion trade and loans to Brazil, N M Rothschild & Sons showed little interest in opportunities outside Europe until after the death of Baron Lionel in 1879. 'Natty' Rothschild took some new initiatives at the beginning of his long reign at New Court, though largely in the trade in which his family had already showed most interest over the years, that in precious metals and diamonds. The London partner's most conspicuous success was achieved in South Africa. From 1882 a stream of technical experts was diverted from California to Kimberley and the Rand, and the family began to take a small speculative interest in mining shares, which in the early 1880s were at a low level. But Rothschilds' celebrated sponsorship of the De Beers diamond monopoly (1888) was not such a bold venture as it may seem, for the merger initiative in fact began with the Paris Erlangers, and Rothschilds' syndicate was paid £250,000 for advancing £750,000 for the key purchase. The real value of the South African connection was soon recognised as shipping, refining and marketing gold for Wernher, Beit & Co, which by 1900 had overtaken the Standard Bank as the leading Rand dealers. The De Beers's issue of 1889 was arranged by Rothschilds' most able clerk of the period, Hamburg-born Carl Meyer, who became a director of De Beers in 1888 and deputy chairman from 1901 until his death in 1921. However, far from capitalising on his expertise, the Rothschild brothers declined to offer him a partnership in the bank, or even procuration, instead allowing their most dynamic rival, Sir Ernest Cassel (qv), to capture Meyer for his Egyptian and other projects.

Most of Rothschilds' subsequent investments in mining appear to have been conducted through a City syndicate called the Exploration Co Ltd. It was founded in 1886 by Hamilton Smith, an American engineer whom Lord Rothschild first employed to report on the El Callao gold mining in Venezuela, and who earned a reputation in Britain for his early advocacy of deep level mining on the Rand. The company consisted of some 20 members, among whom it was said were some of the best-known names in the City but investments in Mexico, Alaska, Western Australia, Burma, South Africa and German South-West Africa, do not seem to have produced outstanding results anywhere. However, the formation of this syndicate, one of two major ones active in the City at the period, was probably Lord Rothschild's most original economic undertaking. Elsewhere he seems to have relied even more on the enterprise or risk-taking of others.

The Rothschild group bought a 20 per cent interest in the lucrative Rand Mines Ltd, but the initial connection was between Wernher Beit & Co and the Continental Rothschilds, rather than their English cousins. Similarly the Rothschilds' well-known interest in the Russian (Baku) oil industry and the building of the Trans-Caucasian Railway (1883) was the outcome of Baron Alphonse's enterprise and it seems that London had little to do with it. It is, moreover, significant that the British-based oil companies of Marcus Samuel and Frederick Lane (qqv), were supported by the Paris Rothschilds and not by their London cousins. Where it is possible to identify initiatives that began in London rather than Paris, they appear to have been projects already tried and proved by other merchant banks. Thus Rothschild investment in the famous Rio Tinto Mining Co, was only a late sequel to the bold entrepreneurship of Matheson & Co, while Rothschilds' issue for the Burma Ruby Mines (1889) represented a take-over of the development work by Ogilvy Gillanders & Co and the loan to the Transvaal National Bank (1892) began with Schroders' connection.

The fairest assessment of the policy of the second and third generation of London Rothschilds is that, fraternising with European royalty, entertained and flattered by the peerage, and considered financially inviolate by the commercial aristocracy of the age, they had little need to search for new business in America or trouble themselves with risky ventures in the old world. As Baron Alphonse wrote to his London cousins in 1872, 'Notwithstanding the many new banking houses, the governments always turn to us' {Rothschild Archives, T10/389, 11 Apr 1872}. Such was their prestige, they could maintain the upward momentum of their business without taking any client that suggested the possibility of significant risk. It was an ideal business environment in which to operate, and the London Rothschilds did not care to look for trouble outside it.

In the second and third generations the business was progressively simplified to minimise administration and eliminate risks. The number of ledger accounts was reduced from 115 in 1835 (the last full year before N M's sudden death) to 41 at the turn of the century, with the earlier concentration on the German states and the Low Countries turning to Russia, Southern Europe (Austria-Hungary, Italy, Spain and the Balkans), Latin America and the USA. Following a visit to Russia in 1873-74, Baron Edmond wrote to his London cousins that the 'Minister of Finance particularly is very pleased with himself and his connection with our Houses, enabling him to conclude his loans by a mere exchange of telegrams' {ibid, T11/62, 18 Feb 1874}. By 1900 a handful of favoured clients accounted for much of the turnover; three St Petersburg financial agencies (£14.4 million), three Latin American banks (£7.2 million) and M Guggenheim & Sons of New York (£7.1 million). (Meyer Guggenheim was a Swiss Jew who found his way into New York's financial elite through his good luck and shrewdness in the US silver and copper mining.) In 1885 Baron Alphonse Rothschild had complained to his London cousins about the Frankfurt house having made themselves the 'satellite' of Hansemann and his Discontogesellschaft, a house 'not of our standing' {ibid, T13/163, 203, 16 Jan and 10 Dec 1885}, but by 1900 N M Rothschild & Co's largest business in Germany (£2.2 million) was being conducted through this joint-stock bank. The old Jewish private banks (Warburgs, Bleichröders, Behrens, and Mendelsohns) maintained their accounts but were steadily diminishing in overall importance.

A dozen years after N M's death, a well-known City journalist fairly observed that while the banker's sons inherited his business, 'they do not inherit his position in the stock market. They are competitors for government loans, but though with the name remains a certain amount of its former power, they do not appear willing to entertain the extensive and complicated business in which their father delighted' {Francis (1849) 308}. When Lord 'Natty' Rothschild died in 1915, the *Times* recorded that 'He was not a man of genius in the sphere of finance like his father, and in a still higher degree his grandfather ...' {*Times* 1 Apr 1915}. Even so, his younger brothers 'were somewhat eclipsed by the masterful character of Lord Rothschild' {Schroder Wagg Archives, Wagg, 'History of the Firm'}, who pontificated over his following of stockbrokers in much the same way that his father had done. A R Wagg, who became a partner in Helbert Wagg, Rothschilds' principal stockbrokers, in 1903, recorded that 'everybody was in considerable awe of Baron Lionel', while 'the manners of Lord Rothschild were not calculated to put a person at all sensitive at his ease' {ibid}. Private records reinforce the picture of growing autocracy within the firm and aloofness to almost all other firms outside. In 1905 Carl Meyer wrote 'One after the other of the principal employees retires finding it impossible to get on with Alfred [de Rothschild] who is becoming more unbearable than ever to the staff and treats men of 30 years service like office boys' {Meyer letters}. The brothers lunched regularly together at New Court, often calling in the experts who served them, but the names of other merchant bankers seldom figured in the invitation lists.

Family compacts prevented outside partners being brought into the business, so there were scarcely any critics of this autocracy and, not surprisingly, a failure to innovate. In addition to De Beers, Rothschilds involved themselves in company promotion in the late 1880s with the Manchester Ship Canal, but found the business more troublesome than they expected and retired from the scene. The later Ship Canal issues were shared with Barings, who now took the initiative in this area, though not always without losses. Rothschild also issued stock for the armaments industry (Maxim Nordenfeldt, 1888) and maintained an avuncular eye on Vickers's activities, but the latter's letterbooks reveal no sustained or specific correspondence on policy matters or special ventures. From 1890 Rothschilds were less active as an issuing house as the Brazilian revolution of 1889 was 'a cause of serious anxiety to Lord Rothschild' {*Times* 1 Apr 1915}. He 'often said that the trouble was largely due to the excessive growth of the practice of underwriting, which made it fatally easy to bring out almost any loan' {*ibid*}. It was no doubt for this reason and the general caution induced by the Baring crisis that he declined for some years to take the initiative in Chinese and Japanese loans to be raised in London in the fifteen years or so before the First World War. This of course was the opportunity of the Hong Kong & Shanghai Banking Corporation and for specialist stockbrokers like Panmure Gordon (qv), from whom 'Natty' Rothschild belatedly acquired a holding in Japanese stock. More generally, it seems fair to accept the *Times* verdict in 1915 that 'It is probably true that London as a money centre, though enormously powerful, was not so powerful as it would have been if Rothschilds had thought fit to initiate and control some of the big new business of the last 25 years' {*ibid*}.

N M Rothschild & Sons decline to release any information on the capital or profits of the nineteenth century partnership, but it is possible to offer data on the size of the firm's acceptances and loans to compare with those of leading competitors. Down to the death of Lord Rothschild, the firm continued to be the most important loan contractor operating in London. In the 1870s and 1880s, Baring Bros, led by the First Lord Revelstoke, strove to overtake their traditional rivals, but at the Baring Crisis (1890) this competition was effectively removed. Thereafter Lord Rothschild's principal rival was Morgan Grenfell & Co. By the turn of the century, Morgan's American house occupied a position 'immensely more predominant than Rothschilds in Europe' {Bodleian Library, Milner MSS, 214/42, 41, 8 Feb and 22 Mar 1901}, while the Rothschilds were never strong in America. At the close of the Boer War, Morgans forced Rothschilds to share two major British government loans, which was seen as an immense blow to the prestige of New Court. In acceptances, Rothschilds had always been behind Barings and after 1890 lost the initiative to more enterprising Anglo-German houses, notably Kleinworts and Schroders. The problem was not only lack of enterprise, but also Lord Rothschild's arrogance in disdaining syndicates (unless in his firm's name) and underwriting.

'Natty' Rothschild was elected to parliament as Liberal MP for Aylesbury in 1865 and sat for twenty years, until he was elevated to the peerage in 1885. On the introduction of the Home Rule Bill (1886), Lord Rothschild became a Liberal Unionist and 'remained a loyal and, for the most part, silent member of the party' for the rest of his life {*DNB*}. However, from the perspective of his business career, the most interesting aspect of Rothschild's politics was his connection with imperialism, especially in Africa. The Liberal outlook of the English Rothschilds did not restrain them from a close connection with the Conservative leader, Disraeli; indeed when the former Prime Minister died in 1881 Baron Alphonse described him as 'the best and truest friend of our family' {Rothschild Archives, RAL T13/81 19 Apr 1881}. The famous purchase of the Khedive of Egypt's shares in the Suez Canal (1875) was the product of the friendship between Disraeli and Baron Lionel and, for the Rothschilds, opened the way to a sequence of state loans to Egypt in the 1880s and 1890s. In the later 1880s, Lord Rothschild's name was closely linked with that of Cecil Rhodes and the finance of diamond and gold mining in South Africa. Rothschild was broadly sympathetic with Rhodes's imperialist ambitions in southern Africa, but it is a mistake to regard the two men as friends or close collaborators. Rothschild was too orthodox a businessman to be happy with Rhodes's cavalier treatment of his shareholders, while Rhodes thought Rothschild a wet blanket, 'honest but without sufficient brains' {Davis (1983) 214}. The De Beers board of directors saw recurrent rows between the orthodox (Rothschild) and entrepreneurial (Rhodes) factions.

Another aspect of the Rothschilds' financial support of imperialism is revealed in their relations with King Leopold of Belgium. Rothschild loans had missed the credit of the small state from its creation, and when the King sought to establish an overseas empire, Lord Rothschild was prepared to support this as well, first in an aborted initiative in the Philippines (1873), then in the Congo (1888). 'Votre famille m'a toujours gâté', the King very fairly observed to Lord Rothschild's brother Alfred at a reception in Brussels in 1892 {Rothschild Archives, RAL T16/25 5 Dec 1892}. Rothschilds also missed the credit of the young state of Brazil for many years (1824-1914), but a recent historian of the country's economy believes that while Rothschild loans oiled the wheels of the country's overseas trade, Lord Rothschild's opposition to the industrial loans of 1892 may have 'contributed to the lack of confidence which surrounded them' and so put a brake on industrialisation {Graham (1968) 321}. In a word, Rothschild policy was governed by concepts of safe business rather than ideology.

The *Encyclopaedia Judaica* maintains that Lord Rothschild not only succeeded his father as head of N M Rothschild & Sons, but also as 'effective lay head of Anglo-Jewry'. The *DNB* goes further, claiming that following the death of Sir Moses Montefiore in 1885 Lord Rothschild 'may almost be said to have been the generally acknowledged leader of the Jews of the world', though it is conceded that he 'was for long out of sympathy with the Zionist movement'. The importance of this aspect of Rothschild's life in the context of business history lies in the relations of the firm, who continued to be the leading international loan contractors, with Tsarist Russia, which down to 1917 was one of the world's major debtor nations. When Russia embarked on a policy of persecution of her six million Jews in 1881, international Jewry looked to the famous bankers for leadership. The family was not unaware of its unique position of influence; as one of them (Lady Constance Battersea) wrote, 'Their vast financial undertakings in the five European capitals brought them into close touch with the rulers and statesmen of those countries ... they were on a different social plane from their co-religionists, and gradually became habitués of a world still closed to many of their own Jewish friends and connections' {Battersea (1922) 66}. The *DNB* article on Lord Rothschild piously concludes that 'largely through his influence the doors of the City of London were closed to anti-Semitic powers seeking loans'.

However, the fact remains that Tsarist Russia *did* succeed in raising a sequence of large loans in London, so bold assertions about Lord Rothschild's influence evidently need some qualification. There can be no question that the family earnestly desired to prevent or alleviate the plight of poor Russian Jews, but it is proper to recognise the limits of their power as they themselves did. In October 1882, only three years after Rothschild succeeded his father, Natty's cousin Baron Alphonse wrote from Paris:

> Our friend Shuvaloff is in Paris ... with a mission of the Russian Minister of Finances, viz to ask us whether we still lay an interdict upon the Russian Government, to which we can but reply that we wish for nothing better than to conclude a financial operation with the Russian Government but are not able to do so in view of the persecution of our Russian co-religionists ... We should be very glad indeed if our influence was as all-powerful as others would like it to be { Rothschild Archives, T13/117, 4 Oct 1882}.

The main consequence of this policy was that Barings (Rothschilds' main rival) took over their Russian business, so in 1889 Lord Rothschild shifted his position and with Rothschild Frères shouldered two major Russian Government conversion loans. Another conversion loan was successfully negotiated in 1890 and the links with Russia became even closer when the looming Baring crisis led the Tsarist regime to transfer large deposits from Barings to New Court. When the 1891 loan was cancelled, the Rothschilds' last minute withdrawal was popularly attributed to the order by the Governor-General of Moscow to all Jewish artisans to leave the capital (28 March 1891). René Girault has speculated that the persecution was only the pretext for breaking off a connection that had been deteriorating for some months following the Russian Government's belief that the French Rothschilds' grip on key sectors of the economy (the Trans-Siberian Railway contracts, Baku oil pipeline, and grain exports) might be used against their interests. In fact, the letters of Baron Alphonse to Lord Rothschild show much simpler calculations: the new conversion loan was cancelled because a coincidence of events on the Continent (a bad harvest predicted and civil disorder on the Belgian coalfields) led the French Rothschilds to believe that the timing for the proposed issue was wrong. In London, Lord Rothschild was kept informed but was essentially a partner syndicated to Parisian transactions. Antagonism to the Russian Government's anti-semitic policies was evidently tempered by financial considerations.

When Witte, the most able of a sequence of Russian finance ministers, sought British capital for investment in the development of his country, Lord Rothschild did not allow the Jewish problem to stifle his connection. The English Rothschilds participated in the 1894 loan to Russia, and Lord Rothschild expressed an interest in Siberian mineral wealth and asked to send an agent to study the possibilities. Another Jewish merchant banker (Leopold Hirsch) and John Hays Hammond (the American mining engineer) toured Russia in 1893, while Rothschild retained a keen personal interest. Then Witte's financial agent asked Lord Rothschild if the Jewish question could create obstacles to a further Russian issue and was told 'No I would not make public business dependent on my personal feelings ... After all, although I am a Jew I understand that England can only act in the European East as a Christian power' {Anan'ich (1970) 28-32}. His private view was that 'financial necessities never weigh and never will weigh with blind and despotic autocrats' {Rothschild Archives, XI/130A/o, 18 Sept 1906}. Rothschild continued to maintain an interest in Russian investment opportunities, but was inhibited by political uncertainties (Anglo-Russian tension in the Middle East and Far East) rather than by religious scruples. Diplomatic relations between Britain and Russia did not encourage the migration of capital until 1910, when the seventy-year-old Rothschild still showed interest but now feared Russian discrimination against Jewish bankers. Rothschild's diffidence as a business man may have been the final factor in a complex equation.

Baron Lionel provided country houses for all his sons and in 1872, five years after marriage to his Frankfurt cousin Emma, Natty acquired Tring Park. Meanwhile his two brothers and cousins became the owners of other proud edifices at Ascott, Anton Clinton, Mentmore, Halton and Waddesdon, together forming a Rothschild enclave in rural Buckinghamshire. Lord Rothschild also inherited his father's mansion in Piccadilly, London, and built up a rich collection of art treasures and old masters.

The First Lord Rothschild died on 31 March 1915 leaving an estate valued at £2.5 million. His two brothers and partners in the bank, Leopold and Alfred de Rothschild, each left £1.5 million. In the absence of a better guide, the sum of these valuations (£5.5 million) may offer an indication of what the City used to call the partners' 'responsible capital', ie resources available to guarantee their financial activities. Despite the Rothschild brothers' guarded policies, this capital continued to be larger than that of any other London merchant bank through the period of Lord Rothschild's control (1879-1915), and in the final analysis this superiority may count as his most significant achievement, for without such a huge capital the prestige of the house would not have been sustained.

S D CHAPMAN

Writings:

'The Persecution of the Jews in Russia' *Times* 11, 13 Jan 1882.

Sources:

Unpublished

Bodleian Library, Milner papers.

N M Rothschild & Sons, New Court, St Swithin's Lane, London, business records; Lord Rothschild's private correspondence was destroyed.

Rhodes House Library, Oxford, Rhodes Archives.

Schröder Wagg Archives, A R Wagg, 'History of the Firm'.

Letters of Sir Carl Meyer (in private ownership).

J W McCarty, 'British Investment in Overseas Mining 1880-1914' (Cambridge PhD, 1961).

Published

B V Anan'ich, *Rossiya i Mezmdynarodnyi Kapital 1897-1914* (*Russia and International Capital 1897-1914*) (Leningrad, 1970).

David Avery, *Not On Queen Victoria's Birthday: The Story of the Rio Tinto Mines* (Collins, 1974).

Jules Ayer, *A Century of Finance 1804-1904: The London House of Rothschild* (Neely, 1905).

Lady Constance Battersea, *Reminiscences* (Macmillan & Co, 1922).

Stanley D Chapman, *The Rise of Merchant Banking* (Allen & Unwin, 1984).

—, 'Rhodes and the City of London: Another View of Imperialism' *Historical Journal* 28 (1985).

DAB.

Richard Davis, *The English Rothschilds* (Collins, 1983).

Dictionary of South African Biography (ed) W J deKock et al (Cape Town: Nasionale Boekhandel Bpk and Butterworths & Co (SA) (Pty) Ltd, 1968 —).

DNB.

Encyclopaedia Judaica (Jerusalem, 1971).

John Francis *Characters of the Stock Exchange* (1849).

René Girault, *Emprunts Russes et Investissements Français en Russie 1887-1914* (Paris: Librairie Armand Colin, 1973).

Charles S Goldman, *South African Mines and Finance* (3 vols, E Wilson & Co, 1896) 3.

Richard Graham, *Britain and the Onset of Modernisation in Brazil 1850-1914* (Cambridge: Cambridge University Press, 1968).

John H Hammond, *The Autobiography of John Hays Hammond* (2 vols, New York: Farrar & Rinehart, 1935).

Charles E Harvey, *The Rio Tinto Company: An Economic History of a Leading International Mining Concern 1873-1954* (Penzance: Alison Hodge, 1981).

Jewish Encyclopaedia (1905 edn) 10 sv 'Rothschild'.

PP, HC, 1887 (535) LXIII, Correspondence Respecting the Ruby Mines of Upper Burmah.

Victor, Third Lord Rothschild, *You Have It, Madam. The Purchase, in 1875, of Suez Canal Shares by Disraeli and Baron Lionel de Rothschild* (pp, 1980).

Times 1 Apr 1915.

R V Turrell, 'Rhodes, De Beers, and Monopoly' *Journal of Imperial and Commonwealth History* 10 (1982).

WWMP.

WWW.

ROUTLEDGE, Thomas

(1819-1887)

Paper manufacturer

Thomas Routledge was born in London on 22 September 1819, the son of a wine merchant, and was educated by Rev Dr Lord of Tooting. From 1839 to 1856 he was connected with the manufacture of imitation stone and terracotta, copper smelting and metal brokerage and designed a machine for crushing plaintain stalks. In these activities he sought ways of saving labour. During the 1850s the shortage of rags for papermaking became serious, and Routledge, like many others, began to search for substitutes. He experimented with sugar-cane waste, and then in 1856, at his Eynsham paper mill, he began work on esparto grass procurable from Spain and North Africa. He took out his first esparto patent in 1856, with improvements in 1860 and 1861. Up to 1860 he supplied half-stuff (pulp) from his mill at Eynsham, near Oxford.

He met prejudice against esparto, but changes in economic and technical conditions worked in his favour. In 1862 he was fully recompensed for his pioneering work with esparto by receiving honourable mention for his esparto half-stuff, and a medal for paper made exclusively from esparto. In

Pulp manufacture from esparto grass — top floor of a typical esparto digestion 'house', c 1950.

954

that year he moved to Sunderland, and in 1864 the Ford paper mill, South Hylton, Sunderland became a limited liability company with Routledge as managing director and John Evans (qv) as chairman. The mill supplied half-stuff to the Dickinson mills in Hertfordshire.

In 1866 Routledge joined with George Noble in establishing the Esparto Trading Co Ltd to trade in esparto grass; this was wound up in 1876 because the company had failed to forward its returns (in accordance with the Companies Act, 1862) for 1875. Other importers of esparto had been established and had gained the major hold upon the market. In the 1870s Routledge turned his attention to bamboo, which he thought, wrongly, would be the fibre of the future. But his esparto had introduced a fibre that formed the basis of a speciality manufacture in Britain for over a century. More importantly he had bridged the gap between the rag shortages of around 1860 and the arrival of wood pulp imports around 1880. Stimulated by his activities, imports of esparto rose from 50 tons in 1856 to 200,000 tons in 1887.

Routledge took little part in politics, but was a committee member of the Paper Makers' Association and the Paper Makers' Club, and belonged to numerous learned societies. Thomas Routledge died on 17 September 1887, in London aged sixty-seven. His wife predeceased him, and he was survived by a son and a daughter. He left £5,872 gross.

JOHN WALTON

Writings:

Comments on J Forbes Royle, 'Indian Fibres, Being a Sequel to Observations "On Indian Fibres Fit for Textile Fabrics, or for Rope and Paper Making"' *Journal of the Royal Society of Arts* 5 (28 Nov 1856).

Comments on Robert Johnston, 'Esparto: A Series of Practical Remarks on the Nature, Cultivation, Past History, and Future Prospects of the Plant; Including a Demonstration of the Importance to the Paper-Making Trade of Prompt and Vigorous Measures for its Preservation' *ibid* 20 (22 Dec 1871).

Bamboo, Considered as a Paper-Making Material. With Remarks upon its Cultivation and Treatment. Supplemented by a Consideration of the Present Position of the Paper Trade in Relation to the Supply of Raw Material (1875).

'Paper Making Fibre from the Bamboo of British Burma' *Paper Makers' Monthly Journal* 19 (15 June 1881).

Sources:

Unpublished

National Paper Museum, Manchester Museum of Technology, Routledge v Sommerville and Son, Copy of Pursuers Statement of Facts (1866).

Royal Botanic Gardens, Kew, archives, English letters 37 (1857); English letters L-Z 42 (1862-65); English letters red-rye 100 (1856-1900); North Europe letters NAE-YOU 137 (1845-1900). Munro correspondence.

ROUTLEDGE Thomas

PRO, BT 31/1288/3245X/K 1757, Memorandum and Articles of Association of the Esparto Trading Co Ltd and Summary of Capital and Shares, etc (1866-76).

PrC.

Published

Boase.

British and Colonial Printer and Stationer 29 Sept 1887.

Harry Carter, 'Thomas Routledge and the Introduction of Esparto in Papermaking' in J S G Simmons (ed), *VII International Congress of Paper Historians Communications* (Oxford: Taylor Institution, 1967).

J P Cornett (comp), *A Short Account of the Introduction of Esparto as a Paper-Making Material by Mr Thomas Routledge* (Sunderland: Thomas Reed & Co Ltd, 1909).

J Edington Aitken, 'History of Esparto and Esparto Paper' *British Paper* 1 (Mar 1933).

'Esparto — An Historical and Economic Review' *Paper* 9 (2 Oct 1912).

'Esparto and Its History' *British and Colonial Printer and Stationer* 15 Aug, 31 Oct, 14, 21 Nov 1895, 7 May, 11 June 1896.

Joan Evans, *The Endless Web: John Dickinson & Co Ltd, 1804-1954* (Jonathan Cape, 1955).

Carl Hofmann, *Praktisches Handbuch der Papier-Fabrikation. II Band* (Berlin: Verlag der Papier-Zeitung, 1897).

London International Exhibition 1862. Reports by the Juries (Society for the Encouragement of Arts, Manufactures and Commerce, 1863).

G R Noble, 'Concerning Bagasse, Cornstalks etc' *World's Paper Trade Review* 11 June 1909.

'Paper-Making Progress: Hylton Firm's Role' *Sunderland Echo* 20 Oct 1950.

Paper Record 30 Sept 1887.

PP, HC 1861 (467) XI, SC on Paper (Export Duty on Rags).

Proceedings of the Institution of Civil Engineers 92 (1888).

Proceedings of the Institution of Mechanical Engineers Aug 1887.

James Reid, 'Some Contributions to the History of Esparto' *Proceedings of the Technical Section of the British Paper and Board Makers' Association* 29 (1948).

Sunderland Weekly Echo and Times 23 Sept 1887.

B G Watson, 'The Search for Papermaking Fibers: Thomas Routledge and the Use of Esparto Grass as a Papermaking Fiber in Great Britain' *Paper Maker* 26 (1957).

Sir Herbert Rowell (courtesy of Mr J F Clarke).

ROWELL, Sir Herbert Babington

(1860-1921)

Shipbuilder

Herbert Babington Rowell was born at Warburton House, Carr's Hill, Gateshead, on 24 November 1860, the son of Robert Rowell, a shipbroker, and his wife Jane née Laidlaw. He attended the Mill Hill School and completed his education in Switzerland, acquiring competency in speaking and writing both French and Italian. During his five-year apprenticeship at the Walker upon Tyne shipyard of Wigham Richardson (qv) he worked at the various shipbuilding trades. Rowell took the then relatively unusual step of spending six months at Glasgow University attending the 'advanced course' in naval architecture.

Rowell next worked for Sir W G Armstrong Mitchell & Co, first at their Walker shipyard, 1883-85, and then at Elswick, 1885-90; at Elswick he spent two years in the designing department. In charge of design at that time were two future Directors of Naval Construction, William (later Sir William) White (1845-1913) and Philip (later Sir Philip) Watts (1846-1926); White became one of the greatest warship designers. Just before entering Hawthorn-Leslie Ltd in January 1891, Rowell was sent out to the Armstrong-Italian Works at Pozzuoli to arrange the erection and equipping of gun barges. On his return to Newcastle he offered his services as an assistant shipyard manager to Sir Benjamin Browne (qv) of Hawthorn-Leslie Ltd and was appointed at £500 per annum.

Browne clearly hoped he had recruited a man who could take charge of the shipyard and transform the loss of £69,815 on the new ship account over the previous five years into a profit. Three months later Rowell was given complete charge of the construction of a warship, a step which precipitated the resignation of the shipyard manager. Rowell became general manager of the Hebburn shipyard in May 1891 at an annual salary of £800 plus 2 per cent of the profits for two years and thereafter 4 per cent. Losses were eliminated by the end of 1893 and for the rest of Rowell's life the yard never made a loss, although profits were frequently low. A visit to the yard by the Director of Naval Construction, William White, resulted in a contract for the torpedo boat destroyer *Sunfish*. Rowell went on to establish a high reputation for destroyer construction, and the yard built more than 30 destroyers for the Admiralty by 1913.

Many fine ships for the Russian Volunteer Fleet were produced under Rowell, who gave pride of place to the 7,270 ton *Smolensk*, launched within sixty weeks of laying the keel and on her 1901 trial exceeding 20 knots. Rowell wanted the company to compete in foreign markets much more, especially for warships and large vessels. He pioneered the construction of radical new designs of open decked ore carriers such as the SS *Sir Ernest Cassel*. Under Rowell there was substantial capital investment in cranage and pneumatic equipment and, just before the First

The Sir Ernest Cassell *(courtesy of Mr J F Clarke).*

World War, a shipyard modernisation programme in which he was ably assisted by J T Batey (qv).

Once profits were flowing, pressures to revise his contract were perhaps inevitable and Browne, anxious to keep such an able colleague, successfully negotiated a new contract. From 1896 Rowell's annual salary was to be £1,500 plus £300 for every 1 per cent dividend paid, and he became a director in 1899. Under the new arrangement Rowell received £1,750 in 1896 and over the next five years his income averaged £2,450; this was almost doubled over the next two years and reached £9,373 in 1906.

The First World War brought a vast increase in work for the seemingly tireless Rowell, who in addition to running the shipyard was soon managing the whole company. More than 500 men left the shipyard by February 1915 in response to the call to the colours and during the first year of war the workforce fell from 2,314 to 2,044 but this was built up to almost 2,800 in 1918. Two light cruisers, two leader destroyers, and 19 torpedo boat destroyers, together with 12 merchant vessels, were completed during the war. At this time Rowell served on numerous committees including the Admiralty's Shipbuilding Council, the Merchant Ships Advisory Committee and the Privy Council Committee on Scientific and Industrial Research. After the war he served on the Committee on the Engineering Trades and was a member of two labour inquiries.

When Browne resigned in 1916 Rowell became both chairman and managing director of R & W Hawthorn-Leslie & Co Ltd and guided the company successfully through the immediate post-war period. Not long after becoming chairman he attempted to arrange a merger with Armstrong, Whitworth; an earlier attempt in this direction had failed and so indeed did Rowell's negotiations. Before his death he secured orders from the Cunard and the P & O lines for the large ships he had long wanted the Hebburn yard to build. However, he had to start a long (and eventually successful) resistance against the efforts of Lord Inchcape (qv) to cancel the P & O contract.

Sir Herbert Rowell's job application (November 1890) for the post of assistant manager at Hawthorne Leslie Ltd (courtesy of Mr J F Clarke).

Discussing scientific management, Rowell argued that analysis could be taken too far and offered some advice for winning orders:

> The time to make friends with your customer is when he is *not* in the market. Always remember in which joint his gout takes him. Leave his office before he wants you to go. {*Transactions of the North East Coast Institution of Engineers and Shipbuilders* (1916) 94}

He himself played a very active part in winning orders for the shipyard and, always anxious to learn about new techniques, toured both American and Japanese shipyards in 1918.

Having a more sympathetic understanding of labour attitudes, Browne occasionally had to restrain Rowell's hardline policies on industrial relations within the company. Rowell regularly negotiated with the trade unions on behalf of the employers at a regional, and later national, level. Within the employers' associations, he became chairman of the Tyne Shipbuilders' Association (1911-12), and later president of the Shipbuilding Employers' Federation (1912-14); on the foundation of the Federation of British Industries in 1916 (set up by charter in 1923), he became a vice-president. During the early 1900s he discussed collaboration within the industry to share available work (a policy realised among the warship builders long after his death) with Summers Hunter (d 1940) of the North Eastern Marine Co; he also mooted the possibility of amalgamating the Shipbuilding and Engineering Employers' Federations, schemes of which Browne disapproved.

Rowell was keenly interested in promoting professional education. He himself was the first lecturer, part-time, in naval architecture at the Armstrong College (later part of the University of Durham). During his presidency the North East Coast Institution of Engineers and Shipbuilders produced a major report on the education of apprentices. He served on the council of the Institution of Naval Architects; was a member of the Institution of Civil Engineers; and played a prominent, if unsuccessful, part in efforts to establish an industrial research organisation on the North East coast. He was, however, successful in helping to form the British Marine Engineering Design and Construction Committee. He was a member of Lloyds Technical Committee and of the Council of the Industrial Welfare Society founded by Robert Hyde (qv).

A member of the Northumberland Territorial Force Association and a magistrate for the County of Durham, Rowell was awarded the KBE in 1918. As a young man he was very interested in athletics and won prizes in cycling, walking, running, swimming and tennis. His early love of nature and the countryside, especially Northumberland, continued throughout his life. He was a member of the Royal Automobile and Royal Societies Club, had a flat in St James' Court in London, the Manor House in Jesmond, Newcastle upon Tyne, and Redesmouth House in the North Tyne valley.

Herbert Rowell in 1891 married Mary Dobree Robin of Naples; they had two sons and two daughters. His elder son, Sir H B Robin Rowell (1894-1981), later held the posts in Hawthorn-Leslie which his father had occupied. Sir Herbert Rowell died on 23 June 1921, leaving £97,634 gross.

J F CLARKE

Writings:

'The Russian Volunteer Fleet' *Transactions of the Institution of Naval Architects* 47 (1905).

'Oil-Tight Work in Ships of Light Construction' *ibid* 48 (1906).

Presidential address *Transactions of the North East Coast Institution of Engineers and Shipbuilders* 32 (1915).

From an Old Drawer (a volume of poetry) (pp, ca 1920).

Sources:

Unpublished

Tyne and Wear Archives, papers of Hawthorn-Leslie & Co Ltd; papers of the Tyne Shipbuilders' Association; records of the North East Coast Institution of Engineers and Shipbuilders.

BCe.

PrC.

Published

Joseph F Clarke, *Power on Land and Sea: 160 Years of Industrial Enterprise on Tyneside: A History of R & W Hawthorn-Leslie & Co Ltd* (Wallsend: Clark-Hawthorn Ltd, 1979).

Engineer 1921.

Engineering 1921.

Shipbuilder 8 (1913), 25 (1921).

Shipbuilding and Shipping Record 30 Jan 1921.

Transactions of the Institution of Naval Architects 58 (1921).

Transactions of the North East Coast Institution of Engineers and Shipbuilders 1-38 (1884-1922).

ROWNTREE, Benjamin Seebohm

(1871-1954)

Promoter of management research and confectionery company chairman

Benjamin Seebohm Rowntree was born at York on 7 July 1871, the third child of Joseph Rowntree (qv) and Emma Antoinette Seebohm, both of whom were members of the Society of Friends. His education was in the care of governesses until 1882, when he became a day boy at the Quaker School, Bootham. In 1887, he enrolled at Owens College, Manchester, to read chemistry, but left after two years without a degree.

Rowntree's career in the family chocolate and confectionery firm began in 1889, when he was eighteen. He was employed initially on chemical research, but his stronger interest in 'the human factor' in business brought him out of the laboratory and into the personnel function in his company. In 1897, when the firm was converted into a limited liability company, he became a director of the company and assumed responsibility for the Labour Department at the Cocoa Works, the new factory which his father began to lay out from the 1890s onwards. He succeeded his father as chairman in 1923 and remained a board member until his retirement in 1941. By this time, the company 'had established itself as the second largest chocolate and confectionery concern in the United Kingdom ... and the third largest business of its kind in the world' {Briggs (1961) 9}. To Seebohm Rowntree is due some measure of the company's success, but the greater part of his energies were spent outside the firm — on his work to promote better methods of management in British industry.

Rowntree's commitment was very much influenced by his Quaker religious beliefs and Quaker business ethics, together with his findings on the extent of poverty in nineteenth-century York and what he believed to be two of the underlying causes of poverty — the low wages paid to

The Rowntrees on 31 May 1923, from left to right: Stephen, Benjamin Seebohm, Joseph (father), Arnold and Oscar (from Anne Vernon, A Quaker Businessman George Allen & Unwin, 1958).

working men and women, and the insecurity of their employment. He began to see the true function of industry as a form of social service, a means of providing for the worker on the one hand 'earnings sufficient to maintain a reasonable standard of comfort' and 'reasonable economic security during the whole working life and in old age' {Rowntree, *Industrial Unrest* (1922) 12}, and providing for society on the other 'useful commodities, made under good conditions and sold at reasonable prices' {Rowntree, *Human Factor* (1921) 99}. For this to be possible, Rowntree thought, employers would need to adopt much better managerial practices, particularly in the area of industrial relations. The authority of management, he believed, would only be respected if management were composed of men possessing 'not only the necessary technical qualifications but the power of leading men' {*ibid,* 98}. Industry needed able administrative officers, trained in the best management methods and committed to the ideal of industrial progress through co-operation. The worker would co-operate if he had 'a reasonable share with the employer in determining the conditions of work, and an interest in the prosperity of the industry in which he is engaged' {Rowntree, *Industrial Unrest* (1922) 12}. It was essential for management to establish more democratic conditions within the workplace, but without impairing efficiency.

Lyndall Urwick (qv) has written (somewhat generously) that Seebohm Rowntree had 'a greater influence than any other business man who has lived in our time towards guiding this country to a wider, wiser and more enlightened view of the task of business leadership' {*B Seebohm Rowntree* (1954) 29}. This influence, however, was exerted primarily through other workers: his own direct attempts to influence industrialists met with limited response. Rev Robert Hyde (qv) recalled the reaction by some industrialists (and some Civil Servants) towards Rowntree during his period as Director of the newly-established Welfare Department at the recently-created Ministry of Munitions, 1915-18. 'I find it hard to believe now that these bitter personal attacks made by some of the employers met, were directed against him ... BSR was very conscious that in some quarters he was regarded as a rebel, as a crank, as an innovator, and as a menace to certain vested interests ... ' {*ibid*, 18}. Occasionally, in later years, Rowntree deliberately remained in the background of certain causes to give them a better chance of succeeding.

Rowntree's main contribution to modern management came through education and research, through the support of others and through personal example. In 1919, for example, he initiated the Oxford Conferences for Works Managers, at which the aim was 'to educate the foremen in new ideas' {Briggs (1961) 169}. In the mid-1920s he became a member of the Liberal Industrial Inquiry (his aversion to socialism was very strong), and his influence in the report *Britain's Industrial Future* is very apparent. At the same time as this report was being prepared, Rowntree was, with the help of Urwick and C F Merriam, setting up Management Research Groups in this country. These were groups of manufacturing companies interested in improving efficiency in their enterprises through research and exchange of views and experience; the first was set up in 1927. By 1935, eight such groups were successfully established: Group 1, in particular, made a significant impact on the efficiency of its member companies; Groups 2-8 still (1983) survive. The National Institute of Industrial Psychology, which offered firms a consultancy service between 1921 and the 1970s, owed its survival from infancy partly to Seebohm Rowntree's practical advice and support. A number of individuals whom Rowntree picked out for encouragement (for example, Robert Hyde, Oliver Sheldon (qv), Lyndall Urwick and William Wallace) are themselves noted for their contribution to modern industrial management. His own company was, in the words of a contemporary, as efficient as might be expected.

Through these avenues, Seebohm Rowntree helped to raise the level of efficiency in British industrial management. A certain reluctance to seek the limelight and an inclination to avoid confrontation, may have prevented his making an even more significant contribution than he did. He was given an honorary LLD by the University of Manchester in 1942, and was made a CH in 1931.

Rowntree married in 1897 Lydia, daughter of Edwin Potter, an engineer. There were four sons and one daughter of the marriage. Seebohm Rowntree died on 7 October 1954, leaving £90,812 gross.

SHIRLEY KEEBLE

Writings:

Poverty. A Study of Town Life (Macmillan & Co, 1901).

Betting and Gambling: A National Evil (Macmillan & Co, 1905).

Land and Labour: Lessons From Belgium (Macmillan & Co, 1910).

(with Bruno Lasker) *Unemployment. A Social Study* (Macmillan & Co, 1911).

Introduction to *The Destitute of Norwich and How They Live. A Report into the Administration of Outrelief* (Jarrold & Sons, 1912).

(with May Kendall) *How the Labourer Lives. A Study of the Rural Labour Problem* (Thomas Nelson & Sons, 1913).

The Labourer and the Land (Manchester: National Labour Press, 1914).

The Way to Industrial Peace and the Problem of Unemployment (T Fisher Unwin, 1914).

(with A C Pigou) *Lectures on Housing* (Manchester: Victoria University, 1914).

The Human Needs of Labour (T Nelson & Sons, 1919).

The Human Factor in Business (Longmans & Co, 1921, 3rd edn, 1938).

(with Frank D Stuart) *The Responsibility of Women Workers for Dependents* (Oxford: Clarendon Press, 1921).

Industrial Unrest. A Way Out (Longmans & Co, 1922).

Introduction to *Practical Profit Sharing. A Survey of the Existing Schemes* (Manchester: *Manchester Guardian*, 1922).

Poverty (Longmans & Co, 1922).

The Unemployment Problem: Some Practical Steps Towards Its Solution (1923).

Society and Human Relations (Leeds: H Olaf Hodgkin, 1924).

(with David Lloyd George et al) *How to Tackle Unemployment* (Press Printers, 1930).

The Human Needs of Labour (Longmans & Co, 1937).

The Condition of the People (Liberal Publication Department, 1938).

(ed, with Viscount Astor) *Smallholdings Studies: Reports of Surveys Undertaken by Some Agricultural Economists* (Longmans & Co, 1938).

Poverty and Progress. A Second Social Survey of York (Longmans & Co, 1941).

The Price of Full Employment (Liberal Publication Department, 1944).

Portrait of a City's Housing: Being the Results of a Detailed Survey in the City of York 1935-9 (Faber & Faber, 1945).

(with George Russell Lavers) *English Life and Leisure. A Social Study* (Longmans Green & Co, 1951).

—, *Poverty and the Welfare State. A Third Social Survey of York Dealing Only with Economic Questions* (Longmans Green & Co, 1951).

Sources:

Unpublished

BLPES, papers of National Institute of Industrial Psychology.

Business History Unit, London School of Economics and Political Science, papers of Management Research Group No 1.

Published

Asa Briggs, *Social Thought and Social Action: A Study of the Work of Seebohm Rowntree, 1871-1954* (Longmans, 1961).

John Child, 'Quaker Employers and Industrial Relations' *Sociological Review* new ser 12 (1964).

DNB.

B Seebohm Rowntree, *1871-1954: In Memoriam* (Rowntree & Co Ltd, 1954).

WWW.

ROWNTREE, Joseph

(1836-1925)

Chocolate manufacturer and industrial relations pioneer

Joseph Rowntree (from Anne Vernon, A Quaker Businessman *George Allen & Unwin, 1958).*

Joseph Rowntree was born above the family's grocery shop in the centre of York on 24 May 1836, second of the three sons and five children of Joseph Rowntree Sr (1801-59) and his wife Sarah née Stephenson. Joseph Rowntree Sr had opened the shop in 1822. Of Quaker stock, like his wife, he was actively interested in education, especially among the Society of Friends for whom he established two Quaker Schools in York (Bootham and the Mount).

Joseph Sr's three sons and two daughters enjoyed a good measure of freedom and independence as well as security in the busy community of the family shop and household of twelve, several of whom were living-in apprentices. In the 1830s the Quakers were very much a closed community, marrying into Quaker families, and sending their children to Quaker schools. Barred from Oxford and Cambridge, opposed to service in the army or navy, they usually went into trade — where their associations were chiefly with other Quaker families.

Joseph's education started at home, but at the age of eleven he went to Bootham School which, though old fashioned in some ways, set no bounds on intellectual curiosity. While Joseph was at Bootham, his father took him and his elder brother John Stephenson Rowntree (1834-1907) to Ireland where the sights of the Great Famine affected him deeply and lay behind his later studies of poverty. At sixteen, Joseph left Bootham and was apprenticed to his father. He remained at the grocer's shop until 1868, becoming a partner with his older brother, and taking over its management with him after their father's death in 1859.

In 1869 he became a partner of his younger brother Henry Isaac Rowntree (1838-1883), who had acquired a 'Cocoa, chocolate and chicory works' on the banks of the Ouse, from the Tuke family, also Quakers, for whom Henry had worked the previous eight years. The business was not very large, having total sales of £3,000 in 1862. Joseph took his capital out of the grocery business and put it into the new venture and at the age of thirty-three he had to learn a new trade. He looked after the accounts, and began to study production costs, using his knowledge of figures and meticulous attention to detail, to understand how the business was going and how it could be improved. At that time, only 12 people were employed in the factory, and their weekly output of cocoa was around 12 cwt. The number of employees soon rose to 30. The Rowntree brothers both believed that it would be the quality of their products which would guarantee future sales; they were suspicious of advertising their products, partly on grounds of principle, but also because of the many false claims made by other manufacturers for their goods. The business was barely profitable, and in 1873 made a loss, despite increased sales.

A stroke of fortune came in 1879, when a Frenchman, Claude Gaget, produced some samples of gums and pastilles — hitherto a French monopoly — which he made: the Rowntree brothers decided to manufacture them; they were put on the market in 1881, and sold well. Two years later, in the midst of a difficult trading year, the partnership was sundered when Henry Isaac was suddenly taken ill and died of peritonitis in May 1883. Joseph became sole owner and carried on alone, now employing 200 people. He started his two older sons, John Wilhelm and Benjamin Seebohm (qv) in the business in 1885 and 1889 respectively; they spent time in every department of the factory, becoming thoroughly acquainted with all the practical aspects. The business flourished as the result of Joseph's systematic approach and reliance on facts and figures; by 1887 a horse-drawn lorry was needed to take each day's output to the station. The factory was expanded, new manufacturing processes were acquired, and a new brand of Cocoa, 'Elect', was successfully introduced in 1887. In 1892 Joseph took full page space in the daily papers for advertisements which included coupons and a list of retailers willing to exchange coupons for a sample of Elect and an unused penny stamp, all under the slogan, 'A cup of Cocoa and your morning paper for nothing!'

Three years later Joseph bought 33 acres of land to the north of the city on Haxby Road and construction of a new factory commenced. The new factory, built between 1891 and 1898, was equipped with the latest chocolate processing plant. Manufacture continued in the old factory at Tanners Mount until 1910, posing some administrative problems for sixteen years. Trade continued to expand, one measure of growth being the size of the workforce which rose from 200 in 1883 to 894 in 1894 and 4,000 in 1906, suggesting a quadrupling of business every decade. In 1897 the business of H I Rowntree & Co was converted into a limited company, Rowntree & Co Ltd, with an authorised capital of £300,000 in 14,980 £10 ordinary shares (10,000 issued), 15,000 £10 preference shares (12,600 issued) and 200 £1 deferred shares (all issued). Joseph became chairman with his two oldest sons, John Wilhelm and Benjamin Seebohm and two nephews, Francis Henry Rowntree (1868-1918) and Arnold Stephenson Rowntree (1872-1951) as directors. A third nephew, Theodore Hotham Rowntree (1867-1949), became company secretary. The only director outside the family was J B Morrell.

The new factory provided scope for putting into practice Joseph's long-

View of Haxby Road works from a drawing (from Anne Vernon, A Quaker Businessman *George Allen & Unwin, 1958).*

maturing plans for translating his Quaker and liberal principles into practical policies. He was able to change his outlook from one of giving his employees what he thought was good for them to one of basing his policy on the needs of the time. Problems of size and communication concerned him before he moved his factory from the centre of the city to its northern fringe; some of his solutions were failures, others startlingly successful. His first personnel worker was appointed in 1891, a house magazine was started in 1902, and a suggestion scheme the same year. A pension fund was set up in 1904.

Joseph Rowntree carried into his growing business the same scientific and deliberate approach he used in his earlier days. He would carry out a thorough-going job analysis before making an appointment, and he attempted to put the selection of his staff on a more systematic basis long before modern methods of assessment were known. He coupled this with a rare capacity for delegating authority. Once he was assured that his young executives were properly placed, they were 'not fussed by constant commands and prohibitions from above; and Joseph himself was left with the relatively uncluttered desk which is essential for progress'. {Vernon (1958) 126}

Nor was he a believer in welfare for its own sake. He never forgot that all the facilities he provided depended on the firm making a profit. Welfare was good business as he openly admitted. The services which he originated were certainly of benefit to the men and women he employed, but they also benefited the firm. The Psychological Department, established in 1922 and the first of its kind in any firm, certainly helped men and women to take up work which fitted them; but good selection helped the firm as much as the workers.

Joseph Rowntree first became interested in adult education while working in his father's grocery shop, and he continued to teach in the Quaker Adult School until he was over sixty. His interest broadened to cover what could be done to give British workers a higher standard both of health and general education, to meet the growing competition from Germany and the United States. His solution was characteristically direct

— he appointed his son-in-law as the firm's factory physician in 1904, and later provided free dental as well as medical services. The following year he established a domestic school for factory girls, and in 1907 one for boys. The former aimed to provide training for the management of a future married home, the latter primarily to increase physical fitness, but eventually to teach practical and mathematical skills. These day continuation classes were compulsory, and survived until the 1960s when state education at last caught up and made them unnecessary.

Much of the success of the firm in the early years of this century was due to the new ideas and enthusiasm of his fellow directors, all under thirty as the new century began, and all with practical experience. His nephew Arnold persuaded Joseph to accept the need for advertising and mounted some remarkable advertising campaigns. Joseph Rowntree, as he grew older, delegated much of his authority to his two sons, but was determined to maintain his personal touch despite the growth of the firm. He soon had to face the problems of co-ordinating technical experts with his line and other managers to form an effective team. The factory was becoming more specialised, and expert techniques were replacing improvisation. Most of his production managers had come from the shop floor, and this could have led to friction between them and the specialists now needed. His success in welding together a promising team was certainly helped both by his long participation in Quaker business meetings, and by his pioneer efforts at 'management development'. His method was idiosyncratic: he took his executives on regular Saturday afternoon walks, many along Scarborough sea-front, which he started years before when his companions had been his brother or a pupil from his Adult School. He continued this practice until his death.

If in his earlier years, his outlook had been paternalistic, it was never wholly based on giving his work people what he thought best for them, however much his Quaker concern for others led him in that direction. He regarded his business as one held in trust. He gave practical expression to this essentially Quaker belief, by setting aside, in 1904, almost half his property, to found three trusts: the growing prosperity of his business now allowed him to take such steps. He had originally intended to found a single trust which would cover all his main interests; but as some of these lay outside the boundaries set by the laws governing charities, he was obliged to change his plans. He set up a non-charitable trust, the Joseph Rowntree Social Service Trust Ltd, to undertake social and political work outside the scope of a charitable trust; and the Joseph Rowntree Charitable Trust, which financed social research, fostered adult education and supported the work of the Society of Friends. Both of these trusts were designed to come to an end after thirty-five years; Joseph believed that money was best spent during a person's lifetime: in his sixty-ninth year he considered that he was unlikely to be able to do that, so he decided to establish the Trust to use his growing resources in ways he would have wished. The third Trust was the Joseph Rowntree Village Trust, established to administer and develop his interests in proper housing; as property had been acquired, a permanent body was needed to hold and manage it. The assets of the other two Trusts were intended to pass to it after they expired. The Village Trust built New Earswick, a mile to the north of the new factory; it was not a philanthropic venture, still less a

Elect Cocoa motorcar advertisement, 1897 (courtesy of Rowntree Mackintosh PLC).

means of providing houses for his employees: it was an experiment in creating a well-housed and socially-mixed community. It contained no public house, church or chapel, but had a Folk Hall which could be used by any denomination. In 1913 the Village Trust set up its own school in line with Rowntree's deep belief that education mattered for the fulfilment of the individual as well as the good of society.

Joseph Rowntree was essentially an innovator, but the new ideas and practices he introduced were the product of thought and research, guided by a conviction that his workers had the right to know what went on in the business, and to have an interest in its prosperity. In 1907, he first discussed profit-sharing with his fellow directors. He saw it as a means of giving his work people a share in whatever success the firm might achieve. His directors were not in favour, the trade unions were opposed to it

(Beatrice and Sydney Webb felt that profit-sharing would undermine the solidarity of the working class), so the matter was dropped until a more suitable moment.

During the First World War, although by then nearly eighty, he remained company chairman, and was still mentally alert and full of practical ideas and suggestions and was still very much in command, as was clear when in 1918 he decided not to proceed with negotiations with Cadbury and Fry on closer association for the mutual benefit of the three firms. (In 1919 Cadbury and Fry merged their financial interests in a holding company.) In 1930 Rowntree made a direct (unsuccessful) approach to Cadbury, and notes prepared by S B Rowntree included this reference:

> You will recall that you approached us in 1918. At that time the whole Board, except Joseph Rowntree, were favourably inclined to accept your proposals. He made it a personal matter (not at all I need hardly say out of any feeling against you, but because of certain ideas and principles with which he had grown up) and out of affection for him we accepted his view, though it was against our own business judgement {Cadbury archives}.

His last years saw three measures which Benjamin Seebohm Rowntree regarded as the foundation of industrial democracy. The first was a Works Council set up during the war. Joseph instituted the practice of an open meeting for all employees after the annual general meeting; at these he would describe the year's work and answer questions. In 1919 a Central Works Council was established; it revised the Works Rules and in the same year, voted and secured a five-day week. Secondly, an Appeal Committee (half workers, half management) was established, to which those who felt they had been unjustly punished for breach of the rules or for conduct which did not affect job performance, could refer their case. Those who were dismissed for poor work, could appeal 'up the line' to Joseph himself (or his successors), if need be. Thirdly, in 1923 a rule was introduced (after discussion in the Central Works Council) by which a foreman could not be appointed until the workroom's view on his suitability had been sought.

Nor was profit-sharing forgotten; when Joseph raised the matter again, in 1916, he still faced opposition; so he decided to investigate existing or previous schemes elsewhere, some of which had succeeded, some had not. Those that had failed were soon to be found to have been introduced for the wrong reasons: to counter trade unionism, or as incentives to greater production. Those that worked were in firms where trust and confidence existed between management and men, and the share, however small, was recognised as a symbol of the worker's status in the company. The profit-sharing scheme was eventually introduced in 1923.

Joseph Rowntree relinquished the chairmanship of Rowntree & Co Ltd in 1923, when he was eighty-seven and the firm was still growing with a turnover of £3.2 million, profits of £101,000 (or 3 per cent) and a workforce of 7,000.

Active in public affairs from his early twenties, Joseph succeeded his father on the committee which ran the two Quaker schools in York; he served forty-two years on the management committee of the Retreat, the mental hospital in York; he founded, and was for many years chairman of the Liberal Association in York; he was a governor of York's only undenominational school and active in the setting up of the city's public library.

Rowntree's encounter with the Irish famine helped to instigate his investigations into poverty, particularly its connection with drink. In 1897, he and Arthur Sherwell began an investigation, described in their book *The Temperance Problem and Social Reform*, into attempts made to reduce drinking in other countries. Four other books on the same topic followed in the next seven years; their dispassionate approach gave them a wide readership, but their advocacy of government control of the liquor trade (established in Carlisle during the First World War) foundered on the polarised opposition of brewing and temperance interests.

Joseph Rowntree was not a controversialist but on occasion his actions aroused strong criticism. The Rowntree Social Service Trust acquired an interest (with Cadburys) in two London newspapers, the *Morning Leader* and the *Star*. In view of the latter's tipsters, who continued their racing columns, both the Rowntree and Cadbury families, strong supporters of the Anti-Gambling League, were accused of hypocrisy. Their defence was that the *Star*, in particular, had for years been a champion of social reform and armaments reduction. Had they not acquired the paper, it would have passed into opposing hands at a time when few daily newspapers took minority views.

Joseph Rowntree, unlike most successful businessman of his day, cared nothing for status and honours. Nonetheless, in 1911 he was made an honorary freeman of the City of York, an award hitherto rarely bestowed except on royalty, the peerage and Church dignitaries. In his speech at the ceremony he dwelt briefly on poverty and destitution in York, to whose alleviation he was deeply committed.

Rowntree was an avid reader and garnered a wide and deep, though limited, store of knowledge: he rarely read novels, preferring scientific and historical works, biographies and travel books. He was a fluent speaker, a prolific writer (confining much of his output to the circles within which he moved) and an intensely 'curious' man who liked to find out about things and to trace back their causes. Above all he was diligent and fastidious in all he did, said and wrote.

Joseph Rowntree was twice married: in 1856 to Julia Seebohm, daughter of a German Quaker from Bad Pyrmont, by whom he had a daughter (who died in 1869). After his first wife's death in 1863, he married in 1867 Antoinette Seebohm (d 1924), a first cousin of his first wife and daughter of William Seebohm, a wool merchant. They had four sons, John Wilhelm (1868-1905), Benjamin Seebohm (1871-1954), Joseph Stephenson (1875-1951) and Oscar Frederic (1879-1947), and two daughters, Agnes Julia (1870-1960) and Winifred (1884-1915); their sons went into the business, the second one, Seebohm, succeeding his father as the company's chairman. Joseph Rowntree died on 24 February 1925, leaving £220,336 gross.

MARTIN HIGHAM

ROWNTREE Joseph

Writings:

(with Arthur Sherwell) *The Temperance Problem and Social Reform* (Hodder & Stoughton, 1899).

(with Arthur Sherwell) *State Prohibition and Local Option* (Hodder & Stoughton, 1900).

(with Arthur Sherwell) *British 'Gothenburg' Experiments and the Public House Trade* (Hodder & Stoughton, 1901).

(with Arthur Sherwell) *Public Control of the Liquor Traffic* (Grant Richards, 1903).

(with Arthur Sherwell) *The Taxation of the Liquor Trade* (Macmillan & Co Ltd, 1906).

Official Opening of the New Earswick School (pp, 1912).

(with Arthur Sherwell) *State Purchase of the Liquor Trade* (Allen & Unwin Ltd, 1919).

Sources:

Unpublished

Cadbury archives, Bournville.

Rowntree Mackintosh archives, York.

PrC.

L A G Strong, 'The Story of Rowntree' (unpublished MS in Rowntree plc archives).

Published

Asa Briggs, *Seebohm Rowntree* (Longman & Co Ltd, 1961).

DNB.

T Martin Higham, 'Review of Anne Vernon, *A Quaker Business Man*' *Occupational Psychology* 34 (1960).

Anne Vernon, *A Quaker Business Man. The Life of Joseph Rowntree, 1836-1925* (Allen & Unwin Ltd, 1958).

Lewis Waddilove, *One Man's Vision* (Allen & Unwin Ltd, 1954).

WWW.

ROYCE, Sir Frederick Henry

(1863-1933)

Motorcar and aero engine manufacturer and designer

Frederick Henry Royce (known as Henry Royce) was born at Alwalton near Peterborough, on 27 March 1863, youngest of the two boys and three girls born to James Royce (b 1830), a farmer and miller, and owner of the Castor & Alwalton Flour Mills, and his wife Mary (d 1904), third daughter of Benjamin King, formerly of Edwin's Hall, Woodham Ferrers, Essex. When Henry was four his father, intent upon running a metropolitan flour mill, took his two sons to London; financial trouble followed and Henry became a W H Smith newspaper boy first at Clapham and then Bishopsgate and, after a year's schooling, a Post Office telegraph boy in Mayfair. When his father died on 22 July 1872 leaving under £20, a kindly aunt arranged for Henry to be apprenticed in the Great Northern Railway Co's locomotive workshops at Peterborough for a premium of £20 per annum. After three years, financial stringency compelled the aunt to terminate his apprenticeship but the enthusiasm and interest of a railway works craftsman, with whom he boarded, sparked Royce's commitment to an engineering career. He tramped in search of work and found it with a machine tool firm in Leeds, at 11s for a fifty-four-hour week, but soon decided that London held better prospects. In 1882 he became a tester for the Electric Light & Power Co, then installing electric arc and incandescent lighting in London's streets; simultaneously he set out to improve his technical education by attending night classes at the newly-opened Finsbury Technical College. Within a year he was promoted chief electrical engineer for the Lancashire Maxim & Western Electric Co, EL&P Co's subsidiary, formed to bring electric lighting to Liverpool. Royce mainly worked on theatre lighting until months later the company went into liquidation and he was again thrown back on his own resources.

Meantime, his Liverpool work had introduced him to Ernest Albert Claremont (d 1921), a young man with £50 capital (to add to Royce's £25) and some electrical experience. They set themselves up as electricians in Cooke Street, Manchester, as F H Royce & Co, making electric bell sets, lampholders, switches, fuses and registering instruments and, later, dynamos of Royce's design for a drum-wound armature for continuous current 'which had sparkless commutation before the days of carbon brushes' {Lloyd (1978) I, 3}. Their dynamos were widely used in lighting cotton mills, factories and ships and acquired a reputation (in the English tradition) for reliability and longevity, thereby adumbrating the quality of Royce's future work. The partnership gained strength from ties of kinship and an additional £1,500 capital on 16 March 1893 when Royce married Minnie Grace (d 1936) daughter of Alfred Punt, a licensed victualler of London, another of whose daughters married Claremont. Royce purchased a house in Knutsford with a fine garden of which he was very proud and soon after brought his mother from London to live there.

In 1894 the partners converted their business into a limited company, Royce Ltd, bringing a friend with capital onto the board and making a young cashier and accountant, John De Looze, company secretary. De Looze liberated Royce from the minutiae of paperwork so that he could develop new technical ideas. Among these were electrical cranes and motors for lock gates which demonstrated again his special qualities as an engineer: an interest in adapting new technology to pre-existing techniques; a commitment to reliability and durability of product; and inventive skills in designing and building the new components required by his work. Between October 1897 and February 1899 the value of the firm's orders rose from £6,000 to £20,000 and the directors raised company capital to £30,000 in order to finance an increase in productive capacity. Then came setbacks: the Boer War reversed the trend of rising domestic investment and imports of cheaper cranes (many incorporating Royce's modifications) from Germany and the USA drastically reduced Royce's sales. Royce refused to reduce the quality of his cranes in order to make his prices more competitive. For several years financial results deteriorated and in the meantime Royce, the key figure in the firm, had apparently lost interest in cranes and electrical matters. To the vexation of his associates he was tinkering with road vehicles.

At this point French manufacturers dominated the infant car industry. Royce's interest began early in 1903 when he bought his first motorcar, a secondhand 10 hp Decauville. 'He considered his Decauville to be a brilliant achievement completely marred by careless workmanship (the flywheel of this car was held on by a taper-ended set screw). He admired French cars and maintained that they were the first vehicles to be properly designed for the purpose. He showed no interest in American cars, whose engineering he regarded as primitive' {*ibid*, I, 6-7}. Royce set out to rebuild the Decauville in his spare time and ended up redesigning the vehicle. Late in 1903 he informed Claremont and De Looze that he intended to build his own motorcar. The two-cylinder 10 hp model emerged from the Cook Street works on 1 April 1904 after months of overtime in which components were ruthlessly tested by multifarious experiments. Royce made most of it himself, aided by two apprentices, T S Haldenby and Eric Platford, and a toolmaker, Arthur Wormald, recruited from the Westinghouse works. Altogether three experimental machines were made. In the first months they tended to break down frequently but Royce persisted with his improvising, innovating, fitting and testing and, for their day, the vehicles became unusually reliable.

The first car completed became Royce's personal vehicle; the second was taken by Ernest Claremont and used for experiments; the third was purchased by Henry Edmunds, a newcomer to the board of Royce Ltd, who was a member of the Automobile Club committee. Discovering its merits, Edmunds sent a photograph and specification of the machine to his friend the Honourable Charles Stuart Rolls (qv) who was then running a London agency for French motorcars with Claude Johnson (qv). In the first week of May 1904 Rolls (who had previously approached William Weir (qv) in March) and Edmunds went to Manchester. Rolls was so impressed that he agreed with Royce to become his sole agent and in this manner the famous partnership, echoing that between Edge and Napier (qqv), began.

Henry Royce at his Cooke Street factory, 1904 (from R W Harker The Engines Were Rolls-Royce*).*

While Rolls, flamboyant and impetuous, advertised Royce's cars in a series of trials in 1904-6, ably understudied by Johnson who was more directly involved in selling, Royce concentrated on production. At first he brought out a variety of models based on four different chassis of 10, 15, 20 and 30 hp in 1904; 'in 1905 and 1906 he continued to manufacture several distinct types including an extraordinary eight-cylinder, constant-speed V-8 type known as the 'Legallimit'' {*ibid*, I, 13} which was not a success. When Rolls-Royce Co was formed in 1906 Royce became chief engineer and works director with a salary of £1,250 and 4 per cent of the profits in excess of £10,000 — the most highly-paid man in the firm. After the difficulties in raising capital for the formation of the Rolls-Royce Co in

Sir Henry Royce at the Wheel of a 40/50 horsepower Silver Ghost, ca 1925 (from R W Harker The Engines Were Rolls-Royce).

December 1906, Johnson decided that the best way to secure a market share and simultaneously cut costs would be to standardise the production of a very superior motorcar. Royce set to work and designed the 40/50 hp Silver Ghost 'his greatest achievement' {*ibid*, I, 22} which remained in production substantially unchanged until 1925. After being test driven, non-stop for over 14,000 miles in June-August 1907, the first Silver Ghost required the replacement of parts costing £2 2s 7d, equivalent to 4.5d a mile for maintenance costs, which underlined the elitist nature of motoring, for third-class railway travel then cost 1d a mile. Demand for the Silver Ghost was so strong that between 1907 and 1916 2,813 and between 1919 and 1925 3,360 were produced, the price rising from £985 to £1,450 as a result of wartime inflation.

Manufacture of the Silver Ghost was moved from Manchester to Derby in June 1908 and by this time Royce, so long oblivious to the discipline of the balance sheet, was well recognised by the company's board as a poor production engineer. When he fell seriously ill in September, his health having suffered from four years of incessant work and overwork, Claude Johnson persuaded him to work in a drawing office at home with the assistance of a team of draughtsmen. News of Rolls's death in 1910 triggered a breakdown in Royce's health and in 1911 he underwent a major operation. Johnson, who realised that Royce's design talents were now the greatest asset of the firm, persuaded him to live in a villa in the South of

France with a drawing office and with a personal staff of eight. This unusual separation of design and production lasted for the remainder of Royce's career: he divided his time between Knutsford or West Wittering in Sussex (in summer) and the villa at Le Canadel on the French Riviera (in winter) and never again came within a hundred miles of Derby.

With the outbreak of war in 1914 Royce turned to the design of an aero-engine, preferring the more compact liquid (as against air) cooling arrangement. Starting with a 12-cylinder V engine he designed the Eagle (6,100 ordered) in 1914, the Falcon (2,175 ordered) and Hawk in 1915 and later the Condor. Eagle engines powered the Vickers Vimy bomber which took Alcock and Brown on the first west-east crossing of the Atlantic in 1919. At Royce's instigation the company entered for the Schneider Cup competition in 1929 — the first race in 1927 had been won for Britain by a Supermarine seaplane powered by a Napier series VII Lion, the most popular aeroengine of the 1920s. With Hives (qv) in charge of its development, Royce modified the 850 hp Kestrel engine (which he designed in 1925) into the 'R' engine. Installed in the Supermarine S6 seaplane designed by R J Mitchell, it won the trophy. Further design work by Royce and metallurgical research at Derby improved the engine again and enabled Britain to win and keep the Schneider Cup in 1931. Out of the experience gained from transatlantic and Schneider cup competitions, Royce laid down the prototype designs for the Merlin engine, 'an exact scale-up of the Kestrel' {*ibid*, II, 160}, which powered Spitfires and Hurricanes in the Second World War. As the company's chief engineer, Royce remained jealous of his position to the last. When the firm acquired Bentley Motors in 1931 he harshly subordinated W O Bentley, a rival designer and engineer, to the position of sales assistant in the Rolls-Royce London showroom.

Royce had only two directorships throughout his career — of Royce Ltd, Trafford Park, Manchester and Rolls-Royce Ltd of Derby. He was a member of the Institutions of mechanical, electrical and aeronautical engineers. Royce was appointed OBE in 1918 and created a baronet in 1930. His marriage produced no children; his wife survived him. He listed his *WW* recreations as gardening (roses and fruit trees were his specialities) and designing. In the last twenty years of his life he was nursed through his bouts of ill health by Ethel Aubin who was rewarded handsomely in his will. Sir Henry Royce died at his home at West Wittering, Sussex, on 22 April 1933, aged sixty-nine, leaving £112,598 gross.

DAVID J JEREMY

Sources:

Unpublished

MCe.

PrC.

Information from Lt Colonel Eric Barrass.

Published

Walter Owen Bentley, *W O: An Autobiography* (Hutchinson, 1958).

Burke's Peerage and Baronetage 1931.

DD 1914, 1931.

DNB.

Ian Lloyd, *Rolls-Royce*. I *The Growth of a Firm* (Macmillan, 1978).

—, *Rolls-Royce*. II *The Years of Endeavour* (Macmillan, 1978).

Harold Nockolds, *The Magic of a Name* (G T Foulis & Co, 1950).

Max Pemberton, *The Life of Sir Henry Royce* (Selwyn & Blount Ltd, 1934).

William J Reader, *The Weir Group. A Centenary History* (Weidenfeld & Nicolson, 1971).

Samuel B Saul, 'The Motor Industry in Britain to 1914' *Business History* 5 (1962).

WWW.

Sir Walter Runciman (from Walter Runciman, Collier Brigs and Their Sailors *T Fisher Unwin, 1926).*

RUNCIMAN, Walter

1st Lord Runciman of Shoreston

(1847-1937)

Shipowner

Walter Runciman was born at Dunbar, Scotland, on 6 July 1847, the fourth of five sons and two daughters of Walter Runciman, a sea captain, and his wife Jean, daughter of John Finlay, a shipowner of Dunbar. When he was six years old his father, who had joined the coastguard service, moved to the station at Cresswell, a small village on the Northumberland coast. Here Walter was brought up and went to a local school although he quickly showed an interest in finding employment. At the age of nine he left school for work on a local farm but he was soon sacked for inattention to his duties, having been found asleep by the farmer. He returned to school but was shortly to run away with the aim of going to sea, although his father caught up with him and brought him home. It seems clear that the sea was in the family blood and young Walter had heard sea stories, not only from his father but also from his grandfather and uncles. At the age of twelve he successfully ran away from home (not, it would appear, because of unhappiness or ill-treatment) in the early hours of a winter morning, ending up at the local port of Amble where he signed on as a cabin boy on a sailing collier, the 450 ton brig *Harperley*. He discovered that a life at sea was not all that he had expected, and after a few voyages he broke his indentures and ran away from the ship in order to avoid the ill-treatment of the captain.

After signing on with a different captain he found greater satisfaction, sailing to a variety of European and North American ports. His apprenticeship over, he became an able seaman and studied navigation from books with the help of officers on various ships on which he served. He passed the Board of Trade examination and obtained his mate's ticket in 1867, following this with his master's certificate in October 1871. Immediately after this he obtained the command of a sailing barque. For the next thirteen years he remained a sea captain, shifting from sail to the 1,650 ton steamer *Coanwood* in 1876. After a period of ill-health he retired from the sea on medical advice in 1884.

Runciman returned to South Shields where he had been living with his wife, Ann Margaret, elder daughter of John Lawson of Blakemoor Hall, Northumberland, whom he had married on 26 March 1869, and their only son, Walter. The drive and initiative, which had stood him well in his career at sea, led him into a variety of local activities. Following his father, he was a keen Wesleyan Methodist and preached on the local circuit. He was a life-long teetotaller and became much involved in the temperance movement at South Shields, advocated non-sectarian religious education in the local board schools and became deeply involved in local politics, standing for the council on a reform ticket, especially sanitary reform.

With improving health, however, it was inevitable that a man of Runciman's drive was not going to be satisfied merely with dabbling in local politics. In 1885, with some of the money he had saved from his time at sea, he began business as a shipowner with the purchase of the *Dudley*, a 1,200 ton steamer, which, at a time of depression in the industry, had been laid up for three-and-a-half years. As an owner, however, Runciman was able to benefit from the practical experience of twenty-five years at sea and was able to make a profit. With some aid from his bankers and the use of the sixty-fourths system of ownership, he rapidly built up a fleet of a dozen steamers. He then began to purchase new steamers, the first of which, the *Blakemoor* (named after his father-in-law's estate) inaugurated a new company, the South Shields Steam Shipping Co Ltd.

Formed in 1889, the company had a nominal capital of £150,000 in £10 shares and soon proved itself a very successful venture, paying a dividend of 27.5 per cent in its first year. The nominal capital was soon raised to £500,000, although no more than £366,000 was ever issued. In 1892 Runciman was joined in the firm by his son. The head office was moved from South Shields to Newcastle and in 1895 the name of the firm was changed to Moor Line Ltd. By this time the company (which was not a true shipping line running a regular service between specific ports, but a tramp shipping firm) owned 25 steamers and had a constant policy of replacing older vessels with new ones purchased largely from local shipbuilders. The expansion of the firm made it the second largest shipowner in the North East behind Sir James Knott's (qv) Prince Line. A London office, in Leadenhall Street, run by another member of

Runciman's near family, was opened and by 1914 the line owned 40 steamers. Of these, 26 were sunk during the First World War and at its end pressure from a number of shareholders led to the company being wound-up and its reserves and assets distributed.

Although Runciman was opposed to this decision, it was a blessing in disguise. The company avoided having to replace vessels at the high price of the post-war boom and between 1921 and 1924, with prices of new shipping at a low, Runciman resurrected the Moor Line and purchased 23 steamships. Despite advancing age he remained actively involved in the management of the company and in 1935 was responsible for the purchase of a controlling interest in the Anchor Line, of which he also became chairman.

Inevitably a man of Runciman's personality and significance in the shipping industry was invited to join the institutions of the industry. Apart from being the founder of the Moor Line Ltd and North Moor Steamships Ltd, as well as being senior partner in Walter Runciman & Co, he was chairman of the United Kingdom Freight Association, United Kingdom Protection and Indemnity Association, UK War Risks Association, North of England Shipowners' Association, Newcastle Protection and Indemnity Association and Newcastle 100 A1 Insurance Association. He was president of the UK Chamber of Shipping and Commerce, 1910-11, and president of the Shipping Federation from 1932. He was a director of the British Steamship Owners' Association, the London Steamship Owners' Association and the North Eastern Freight Insurance Association. He was also chairman, director and member of a variety of shipping chambers and associations. Outside the immediate area of shipowners, Runciman was chairman of International Stores Ltd, and a director of Tyneside Engineering Works, Cardiff and of Blyth Shipbuilding Co Ltd. He was a member of the North East Coast Institution of Engineers and Shipbuilders and of the Tyne Improvement Commission.

Out of his early interest in the local politics of South Shields, Runciman had developed a support for the Liberal interest but this did not really come to the fore until he was sufficiently well established in business to spare the time and until his son stood as Liberal candidate for Gravesend in 1898. Then Runciman brought his yacht, the *Asthore*, down to the Thames in support of his son's canvass. Although he had not time to consider becoming a MP himself, Runciman became heavily involved in the organisational work of the Liberal Party, was vice-president and president of Newcastle Liberal and Radical Association for many years, and became chairman of the Northern Liberal Federation. In 1906 he was made a baronet as a result of his services to the Liberal Party and in 1914 he became Liberal MP for the Hartlepools in an unopposed election caused by the death of his fellow shipowner, Sir Stephen Furness. He retired from the Commons in 1918, not wishing to contest an election since he was too busy with his shipowning work. His election as an MP when his son was already a Cabinet Minister created a situation which was unique in British political history. Runciman already had a number of links with national politics before his election, having been a member of the Departmental Committee of the Board of Trade on the Employment of Boy Seamen, 1906-7 (he was a lifelong advocate of the apprenticeship of seamen and his ships always carried a full complement of apprentices in order to train a sufficiently large group of future seamen) and he was a member of the Advisory Committee of the Marine Department of the Board of Trade. Runciman was a strong free-trader but in 1931, shortly before it came, he accepted the need for protection.

In addition to his shipowning and political activities, Runciman was an author of some note. Beginning in 1902, he wrote a number of books which were largely based on his own sea-going experiences and included racy tales of the old sailing-ship captains, of storms at sea and the life of a young sailor. They were very successful and sold well.

After moving from South Shields, Runciman lived in Newcastle at Fernwood House but in the 1900s he purchased several North-Eastern estates: firstly Doxford Hall, which subsequently became the home of his son and then Shoreston Hall (near Seahouses, Northumberland, where he overlooked the Farne Islands, grave of many ships) and the Springwell and Brunton estates. When he was raised to the peerage in 1933, he took as his title Lord Runciman of Shoreston. He was a JP for Newcastle upon Tyne as well as for the counties of Northumberland and Durham. His major leisure interest, unusually for a man who had been a professional sailor, was yachting. In the 1890s he purchased a schooner yacht, the *Ashore* and later the *Sunbeam*, a yacht previously belonging to Lord Brassey; in 1929 he had a yacht *Sunbeam II*, designed and built to his own requirements. True to his beliefs all his yachts carried a full number of apprentice sailors and Runciman published an annual edition of his yachts' logs. He was a member of many yacht clubs, including the Royal Clyde, Royal Thames, Royal Victoria and Royal Yorkshire, while he was a commodore of the Royal Northumbrian Yacht Club. He was a member of the National Liberal and City Clubs, London and of the Union and Liberal Clubs, Newcastle upon Tyne.

Runciman became known as a philanthropist in his later years, most especially for his donation of £50,000 towards the cost of the extension scheme for the Royal Victoria Infirmary, Newcastle upon Tyne, in 1929, followed by a further sum of £25,000 in 1931.

Runciman died, at the age of ninety, on 13 August 1937 at Newcastle upon Tyne, leaving £286,431 gross (excluding settled land), and settled land to the value of £18,440.

D J ROWE

Writings:

Windjammers and Sea Tramps (At the Unicorn, 1902).

The Shellback's Progress in the Nineteenth Century (Newcastle upon Tyne: Walter Scott Publishing Co, 1904).

Looking Seaward Again (Felling-on-Tyne: Walter Scott Publishing Co, 1907).

The Tragedy of St Helena (T Fisher Unwin, 1911).

Drake, Nelson and Napoleon (T Fisher Unwin, 1919).

Before the Mast and After: The Autobiography of a Sailor (T Fisher Unwin, 1924).

Collier Brigs and Their Sailors (T Fisher Unwin, 1926, repr Conway Maritime Press, 1971).

Sources:

Unpublished

University of Glasgow, Moor Line Ltd and Walter Runciman & Co Ltd, papers.

PrC.

Published

Border Magazine 20 (1915).

DNB.

James Jamieson, *Northumberland at the Opening of the Twentieth Century: Contemporary Biographies* (Brighton: W T Pike & Co, 1905).

Transactions of the North East Coast Institution of Engineers and Shipbuilders 54 (1937-38).

WWMP.

WWW.

RUSHBROOKE, Frederick William

(1861-1953)

Cycle parts retailer

F W Rushbrooke (courtesy of Halfords Ltd).

Frederick William Rushbrooke was born at Willenhall, Staffordshire, on 9 December 1861, the son of Joshua Rushbrooke, the owner of a local bakery, confectionery and grocery business, and his wife Harriet née Tildersley. He was educated at Queen's College, Taunton and raised as a Wesleyan Methodist. Unlike other members of the Rushbrooke family, Frederick did not work in his father's firm, but instead served an apprenticeship with a local wholesaler, dealing in ironmongery products for the building trade. He completed his apprenticeship in the minimum required time, and then secured a job with a larger ironmongery wholesaler in Wolverhampton. After a few years in this post, Frederick was appointed manager of J Bates & Son's hardware factoring business, also based in Wolverhampton.

In 1892, at the age of thirty-one, Frederick decided to give up this job and establish a hardware business of his own, exploiting the expertise he

The Halford Cycle Company Ltd (courtesy of Halfords Ltd).

had gained in the trade and his contacts with local customers. This enterprise was financed partly by Frederick's modest savings and partly by a loan from his father. The business, Rushbrooke & Co, was operated initially from small premises in Charlotte Street, Birmingham; however, by 1894 it had outgrown these premises and was transferred to a larger property in Moor Street, Birmingham. Shortly after this move, Frederick Rushbrooke assigned the day-to-day management of the firm to another local businessman, F D Tippetts, whose knowledge of the operation and supply of retail outlets complemented Rushbrooke's wholesaling skills. In the early years, Rushbrooke's firm traded in a wide range of ironmongery products, such as cauldrons, mangles, horse harnesses and even bedsteads. Around the turn of the century, the firm began to specialise in cycle parts. Rushbrooke had, from an early age, been a very keen cyclist, and is reported to have cycled on one occasion from Rhyl to Willenhall, a distance of around a hundred miles, on a penny-farthing. Following the advent of the 'safety cycle' in the mid-1880s and the later introduction of the pneumatic tyre, cycling grew rapidly in popularity. Rushbrooke was quick to exploit the expanding market for cycles and their accessories.

In 1902 Rushbrooke opened a branch warehouse in Halford Street, Leicester, to sell cycle parts to local traders. As a result mainly of dishonest management, this offshoot failed. To hasten its closure, it was decided to sell off the remaining stock direct to the public. This unplanned entry into the retail trade proved fortunate because the goods sold quickly and at higher margins. So successful was this operation that the branch in Halford Street was retained, converted to a retail outlet and renamed the Halford Cycle Co. Local wholesalers strongly objected to Rushbrooke's diversification into retailing and urged the manufacturers of cycle parts to withhold supplies from him, but this did not seriously constrain the growth of Rushbrooke's business. New retail outlets were soon established in Liverpool, Nottingham, Derby, Manchester, Bristol, Birmingham and Sheffield.

The main constraint on the development of this incipient retail chain was a lack of finance. Since founding his company, Rushbrooke had suffered liquidity problems. On one occasion his financial position was so precarious that his bank manager denied him further credit and discouraged even his father from lending him money. The switch from wholesaling to retailing improved Rushbrooke's cash flow and generally enhanced the profitability of his business. His financial position was further strengthened in 1906 as a result of a chance conversation on a train with a fellow traveller. This conversation led to a meeting with a group of interested businessmen who provided enough finance to enable Rushbrooke to establish a public company. The new company, renamed the Halford Cycle Co Ltd, was registered in March 1907. The wholesale side of the business was run down, allowing Rushbrooke thereafter to concentrate his efforts and investment on the development of retail outlets. Rushbrooke rapidly expanded the Halford chain, increasing the number of outlets from nine in 1906 to 48 in 1910 and 93 in 1913. Between 1919 and 1939 the number of branches rose from 114 to 236 and employees from 660 to 1,435. He was strongly supported in this work by F D Tippetts, with whom he shared the managing directorship of the firm until Tippetts's death in 1928. Following the death of the chairman shortly afterwards, Rushbrooke was appointed chairman and sole managing director. He held the post of managing director until his retirement, at the age of eighty-six, in 1947, and remained chairman until his death in 1953, by which time he was believed to be the oldest company chairman in Britain. During the period 1907–53 the firm's capitalisation was increased from £15,000 to £100,000 which bore no relation to its turnover (figures for which are unobtainable).

Rushbrooke was married to L J Wilkinson and had a son and four daughters. He was an abstemious man, active throughout his life in the Methodist church and a strong advocate of principles of determination and honesty. Frederick Rushbrooke died on 15 July 1953, leaving £154,876 gross.

ALAN C MCKINNON

Sources:

Unpublished

BCe.

PrC.

Information from the Library, Burmah Oil Trading Ltd.

Published

B Alcwyn Jones, *The Story of Halfords* (Redditch: Halfords Ltd, 1982).

—, *Halfords 1907-82* (Redditch: Halfords Ltd, 1982).

Who's Who in Methodism, 1933 (*Methodist Times* and *Leader*, 1933).

*Sir S Gordon Russell, 1965
(courtesy of Gordon Russell Ltd).*

RUSSELL, Sir Sydney Gordon

(1892-1980)

Furniture designer and manufacturer

Sydney Gordon (known as Gordon) Russell was born at Cricklewood, Middlesex, on 20 April 1892. He was the eldest of the three sons (the younger brothers being Donald George Shefford and Richard Drew) of Sydney Bolton Russell and his wife Elizabeth née Shefford. Sydney Bolton Russell was employed as a clerk at the Knightsbridge branch of the London & County Bank. To supplement an income of £150 per annum, he had taken on private work, keeping the accounts of a number of the bank's clients. One of them, the brewers Samuel Allsopp & Sons, offered him the position of agency manager which he accepted and the family moved to Repton, Derbyshire. The post involved travelling throughout the country, reporting on the efficient running of the firm's licensed premises, one of which was the *Lygon Arms* at Broadway, Worcestershire in the Cotswolds. Seeing development potential there, S B Russell suggested its up-grading to an hotel; when Allsopps failed to take up the suggestion, he bought the *Lygon Arms* himself (with financial backing from one of his clients, R C Drew) in January 1904. The family moved from Repton to Broadway and Gordon Russell transferred from Burton on Trent Grammar School to Chipping Campden Grammar School, where he was a weekly boarder. The antique furniture, block-printed fabrics and hand-made glass with which his father furnished the *Lygon Arms* led to customer enquiries for similar furnishings and in 1907 S B Russell set up an antiques restoration and selling business with himself and his wife as partners. It was a natural step for Gordon Russell on leaving school in 1908 to be put in charge of the antiques repair workshop, then employing three or four joiners only. He remained there until the outbreak of war, when he served in the territorial battalion of the Worcestershire Regiment. He was offered and accepted a commission in 1917, saw active service in France and was awarded the MC.

After demobilisation, both Gordon and Don Russell returned to Broadway and became partners in the family business, now renamed Russell & Sons. The achievements of the Cotswold designer-craftsmen, working in an arts and crafts tradition nearby, provided Gordon Russell with the impetus to try his own hand at designing, despite having had no formal training. During the period 1923-30, the firm first produced joinery pieces, then traditional rush-seated, turned chairs and later, with the availability of skilled cabinet-makers, one-off high quality cabinet-work. The firm was also involved in series production (up to twelve pieces at a time) of simpler designs using a combination of hand and machine techniques, aimed in particular at the contract market. This Gordon Russell was developing through his own efforts as a salesman, often using personal contacts made through the design reform group (Design and Industries Association) (the DIA), which he had joined in 1920, and also as a result of publicity given to his work and writings in leading decorative art and furniture trade journals such as *The Studio* and *The Cabinet Maker*. Such pieces were exhibited at Cheltenham (1922), London (1923), Wembley (1924) and with great success in the British Pavilion of the Paris Exhibition (1925). At the latter, Russell & Sons were awarded one gold and two silver medals for pieces made to Gordon Russell's design. In 1928 he held a one-man show at the Arlington Gallery, Bond Street — a seemingly strange venue for a furniture exhibition, but his designs were radical in a trade where reproduction antiques, often ill-constructed, were the norm. Meanwhile, profits from the successful antiques restoration and retailing business provided the capital for experimentation in 'modern' furniture design.

By 1926, gross profits of Russell & Sons had reached £5,808, double the level of two years previously. That year the Russells formed a small private company to deal with the furniture side of the business, thus separating the transactions of furniture making and retailing from the running of the *Lygon Arms*. R H Bee was appointed company secretary to the newly-formed enterprise, the Russell Workshops Ltd, incorporated on 4 November 1927 with a nominal capital of £25,000. Gordon Russell became managing director, his father and brother Don, directors.

Gordon Russell Ltd, factory in 1935 (courtesy of Gordon Russell Ltd).

For the year ending March 1929, profits before tax were £3,195 compared with £605 for the previous year; sales stood at £46,383. Contract commissions were sufficiently regular for the company to make a substantial investment in wood-working machinery during 1928 and 1929, the largest items of capital investment being a planing and thicknessing machine and a tenoner. A London showroom, at 28 Wigmore Street rented from Debenhams, was opened in October 1929. Previously retailing had been through a single outlet at Broadway. Gordon Russell's policy was to produce well designed modern furniture, and unlike arts and crafts purists he was willing to use modern machine methods as well as traditional cabinet-making techniques. It was presumably to reflect this policy that the company changed its name from Russell Workshops Ltd to Gordon Russell Ltd on 28 September 1929. With the return to the company in 1928 of his youngest brother Dick, who had just completed an architectural training at the Architectural Association, the drawing office was expanded. Soon after, Gordon Russell took on an additional small group of AA-trained designers who injected a new visual style into the company's design catalogue. This was typical of Gordon Russell's lifetime encouragement of young designers and new design ideas. Unfortunately the opening of the London showroom coincided with a downturn in the United States economy, on which the firm depended. A large proportion of the turnover and profits was derived from factored goods, most of which went to the American market. Simultaneously the British market for high priced furniture almost disappeared as the depression intensified. The company was left with newly-acquired machinery laying idle, high stock levels and poor demand.

Only a combination of Gordon Russell's highly-developed network of personal contacts and his brother Dick's design skills saved the company from extinction. In 1930 they began to produce radio cabinets for Murphy Radio (headed by Frank Murphy (qv)), an association which lasted throughout the 1930s and continued after the Second World War. It was their only involvement in mass production, with up to 40,000 units produced of a single design model. Total cabinets delivered to Murphy rose from 7,636 in 1931 to 55,000 in 1934 and reached a peak of 118,500 in 1937. In 1931, these radio cabinets accounted for 30 per cent of the company's turnover and by 1932 for 65 per cent of a total turnover of £72,833. In 1935 it was decided to open a separate factory at Park Royal, London, to accommodate the demand for radio cabinets. Some 600 workers were employed in a manufacturing system totally alien to the tradition of the Broadway factory. The workshop environment of hand-work and mechanised hand tools was exchanged for the systematic flow production of Park Royal's mill, veneer shop, assembly shop, polishing shop, fitting and silking shop, and despatch departments.

By 1935 too, the furniture and furnishings trade had revived sufficiently for a lease to be taken out on larger retail premises at 40 Wigmore Street, but Gordon Russell and his management were never able to agree fully on a well-defined marketing policy. The perennial and largely unresolved problem was the matter of balancing the benefits of quantity production with the limitations of having only two retail outlets (Broadway and London) serving geographically and culturally distinct markets. Gordon Russell's ideals of producing well-designed, well-made furniture for a domestic mass market remained largely unfulfilled. In his efforts to construct a long term marketing plan, he appointed Nikolaus Pevsner, the architectural historian, as buyer for Wigmore Street in 1935. Pevsner, a refugee from Nazi Germany, had lately been researching British industrial design on behalf of the University of Birmingham. It was Pevsner who encouraged the stocking of modern German- and Czech-designed products to the benefit of sales figures. In 1938, Gordon Russell founded the Good Furnishing Group with the intention that his company should mass-produce a range of well-designed, low cost furniture to be sold through leading department stores which would circumvent the problem of having to establish their own chain of retail outlets. The possibility was explored, but extinguished by the war and the bombing of the Wigmore Street showroom in July 1940. Material shortages and government restrictions in wartime meant that Gordon Russell's overriding interest in high quality furniture production could not be pursued, and he resigned as managing director in October 1940. R H Bee, then company secretary, took over the post and reorganised the company for war work. They were soon producing ammunition boxes and sections for Mosquito aircraft under government contract. Gordon Russell remained a director but did not hold the managing directorship again, although he acted as company chairman between 1967 and 1977.

In 1942, his gifts as an administrator and qualities as a diplomat and public ambassador for good design, led to his involvement with the wartime Utility furniture scheme. He sat on the organising committee set up by Hugh Dalton, then President of the Board of Trade. The intention of the scheme was to provide, on a coupon basis, low cost well-designed and well-constructed furniture for bombed-out families and newly-married couples. The acute timber shortage made it necessary to limit the range of designs available and the quantity of timber used. It was intended that a range of standard designs be chosen, which were capable of being made up to strict government specifications by a variety of hand and machine methods. Although it was not possible to use mass production techniques (as highly-mechanised factories had been switched to aircraft production) the scheme gave Gordon Russell the opportunity to put his ideals into practice on a massive scale. Following its success, Gordon Russell suggested that a six-member design panel be set up to consider the production of future standard designs in the eventuality of prolonged hostilities and for blue-print furniture designs using materials which would become available when restrictions were lifted. It was agreed, and Gordon Russell chaired the panel. This post was followed by a seat on the Board of Trade's Furniture Production Committee in 1944 and the Design Committee of the Furniture Trade Working Party in the following year.

Such positions made him a natural choice for membership of the Council of Industrial Design formed in 1944 and for its directorship in 1947, when its first director, S C Leslie, left to head the Information Division at the Treasury. During his term of office (he retired in 1959), he promoted the concept of Design Weeks in industrial towns, acted as foreign ambassador for British design abroad, and attempted to raise the status and publicise the work of the industrial design profession by his initiatives in the 'Britain Can Make It' (1946) and the 'Design at Work' (1948) exhibitions. He was also an original member of the executive committee of the 1951 Festival of Britain and originated the Design Index, which provided the basis of selection of goods on display at the Festival sites. In addition he was responsible for the creation of London's Design Centre which was opened in the Haymarket in 1956.

On his retirement he was co-opted on to a diverse range of councils, committees and boards concerned with design standards. These included the Royal Society of Arts (from whom he received the Albert gold medal in 1962), the Art Workers Guild, the Royal College of Art (by whom he was made the first Honorary Des RCA in 1952), the DIA (president 1959-62), the Arts Council, the Crafts Council (its first chairman), and the British Council. He was made a Royal Designer for Industry (RDI) in 1940, was appointed the first fellow of the Society of Industrial Artists in 1945, was awarded a CBE in 1947 and knighted in 1955. Academic awards included an honorary doctorate from the University of York in 1969 and from the Royal College of Art in 1980.

As a result of his brother Don's ill health, he took over the chairmanship of Gordon Russell Ltd in 1967. By the end of his stewardship in 1977, he had seen the firm develop over seventy years from a workshop employing three people into an organisation of 200 employees with a turnover of £1.3 million and net current assets of almost half a million pounds. He remained the largest shareholder (15,960 shares) in a predominantly family-owned enterprise. During his lifetime he had witnessed the re-orientation of the firm away from a largely middle-class British domestic market to a foreign contract market.

Despite his heavy involvement in public life as a propagandist for good design, he remained an intensely practical man in the creative sense. He spent over fifty years working on his family home, Kingcombe, whose site had been purchased in 1924. As an avid gardener in the Gertrude Jekyll tradition, he was largely responsible for the designing, building and planting of his own garden at Kingcombe. The muddy-gloved, wellington-clad figure was as much an expression of the man as the physically dominant well-groomed public persona.

In 1920 he had employed Elizabeth Jane Vere (Toni) Denning as his assistant. They were married on 8 August 1921 and had three sons and one daughter. He was diagnosed as suffering from motor neurone disease in

1978 and died at his home on 7 October 1980 aged eighty-eight. His wife and three of his children survived him. He left £49,738 gross.

ANNE CHANNON

Writings:

Honesty and the Crafts (pp, Broadway, 1923).

'The Designer and His Problem. 1. Designing a Radio Cabinet' *Design for Today* May 1933.

'Design Policy For New Techniques' *Design* 60 (Dec 1933).

'The Trend of Design in Modern Furniture' *Studio* 117 (1939).

'Taste in Design' *Art and Industry* Aug 1944.

(with Jacques Groag) *The Story of Furniture* (Harmondsworth, Middlesex: Penguin Books, 1947).

The Things We See: Furniture (Harmondsworth, Middlesex: Penguin Books, 1948).

'What is Good Design?' *Design* 1 Jan 1949.

'The Problems of Raising Design Standards in Industry' in the *Eighth Annual Report of the Council of Industrial Design* 1952-53.

'Modern Trends in Industrial Design' *Journal of the Royal Society of Arts* 108 (1960).

Looking At Furniture (Lund Humphries, 1964).

Designer's Trade: An Autobiography (George Allen & Unwin, 1968).

'Skill' Address delivered to the Faculty of Royal Designers for Industry, 1 Nov 1978, repr in *Journal of the Royal Society of Arts* Dec 1978.

Sources:

Unpublished

Gordon Russell Ltd, Broadway, Worcestershire, company minute books, ledgers, letters, memoranda.

C Reg: Gordon Russell Ltd (225,605).

PrC.

Anne Channon, 'R D Russell, Designer For Industry 1930-35' (RCA, London, MA, 1984).

Published

Ken and Kate Baynes, *Gordon Russell* (Design Council, 1980).

Geoffrey Boumphrey, 'The Designers 2: Gordon Russell' *Architectural Review* 78 (1935).

'Furniture by Russell and Sons' *Studio* 93 (1927).

Corin Hughes-Stanton, 'Gordon Russell Today' *Design* 233 (1968).

Gillian Naylor, *A History of Gordon Russell Limited* (Gordon Russell Ltd, 1976).

Nikolaus Pevsner, *An Enquiry Into Industrial Art in England* (Cambridge: Cambridge University Press, 1937).

—, 'Roots and Branches' *Design* 132 (1959).

—, 'Patient Progress Two: Gordon Russell' in *Studies in Art, Architecture and Design, Volume 2: Victorian and After* (Thames & Hudson, 1968).

R D Russell, Marian Pepler (Geffrye Musuem Exhibition Catalogue, ILEA, 1983).

Times 8 Oct 1980.

J Woudhuysen, 'Beginning at the Bench' *Design* 382 (Oct 1980).

WWW.

RUSSELL, Thomas Baron

(1865-1931)

Advertising consultant

Thomas Baron Russell was born in Camberwell, Surrey, on 15 November 1865, son of Thomas Russell, a librarian at a circulating library in Regent Street, London, and his wife Mary née Everett. Under his father's influence he read widely and gained a love of literature which, had it not been for his father's serious illness when Thomas was aged fifteen, would have led to a university career. Instead Thomas went out to work and after trying several jobs he obtained a post with John Morgan Richards, a firm of importing chemists, in January 1882.

He spent twenty-three years with this firm, the success of which depended on the skilful advertising of the American patent medicines it imported. Russell gained immense practical experience of advertising in working for Morgan Richards and on the visits he made to the USA, Canada, India, and Australia. Among those friends he made overseas was John Irving Romer, editor of the influential advertising magazine, *Printer's Ink*, for which Russell wrote regularly. At Morgan Richards, Russell introduced the 'house organ' to the advertising world when, on behalf of Lacto-Peptine, he suggested supporting the product with a special magazine, in this instance called *Medical Reprints* which carried articles culled from American medical journals. The first number of *Medical Reports* reportedly doubled sales of Lacto-Peptine and 4,000 doctors became subscribers at 2s 6d a year.

By the turn of the century Russell was a leading expert on advertising.

When William Berry (qv) started his periodical *Advertising World* in 1901 he took advice from Russell who contributed, anonymously, a series of articles 'Confessions of an Advertising Manager'. In the May 1902 article he attacked the system by which the agent received his commission from the newspaper (thereby aligning his interests with those of the sellers of advertising space) rather than from the advertiser; instead he urged that agents should receive an agreed fee and that all discounts and commissions should be deducted before the advertiser was charged. For the rest of his career he campaigned for this reform. He also contended that trustworthy advertising depended partly on the publication of accurate newspaper circulation figures, and in this respect especially attacked the *Times*.

Soon after writing another series of articles on advertising practice, published in the *Times* in 1904-5, Horace E Hooper, newly-appointed advertising director at the *Times*, offered him the post of advertising manager. Russell stayed at the *Times* for three years, inaugurating the 'Times Book Club' (book loans being available to all who paid a year's subscription to the *Times* in advance) and increasing the amount of display (black and white illustration) advertising. He never persuaded management to produce net circulation figures. In addition he originated the *Times*'s 'gold brick' advertisements — carrying information researched by *Times* staff and therefore 'guaranteed' as reliable, Russell's ideal advertisement. With Hooper he sold the *Encyclopaedia Britannica* (copyright to which Hooper acquired for the *Times* from Adam & Charles Black) by mail order and in instalments, an innovation in England at the time. Russell left the *Times* in 1908, when Hooper did, and with Hooper worked on several more publicity ventures. For eighteen months he organised the promotion of the *Historians' History of the World* and other encyclopaedias.

Then in 1910 he set himself up as an independent advertising consultant — not quite the first since A L Teele, an American, recorded in 1892 how he had set himself up as 'the only professional advertising expert in England with an office distinct and separate from an advertising agency' {quoted in Nevett (1982) 108}. Whereas the agent bought advertising space on behalf of his clients, the advertising consultant confined himself to writing and designing advertising material and providing advice about general aspects of a business. Working for the advertiser or for an advertising agency, the consultant received no commission from the media but was paid instead by a fee for each project or consultation or else received an annual retainer fee. In September 1910, Russell founded and became the first president of the Incorporated Society of Advertisement Consultants which laid down professional standards, qualifications, and code of conduct for its members; these prescribed practices included flat fees rather than commissions.

As a consultant Russell won a high reputation for his thoroughness, skill and integrity. His method was to investigate his customer's business carefully in order to discover the nature of his customer's market, before recommending any particular form of advertising. He was often hired as arbitrator between agencies and their customers. He was the first advertising agent to be employed by a political party (the Liberals, in 1910) and during the First World War he sat on the six-man Committee on Recruiting Propaganda set up by the War Cabinet.

After the war (in 1919) he was invited to give a series of lectures on advertising at the London School of Economics, the first course of its kind in a British university. He argued, inter alia, that advertising had an informative function and that 'it acted as a guarantor of quality in the case of branded goods' {Watson (1973) 28}; that dishonesty in advertising would be suicidal for a manufacturer and that advertising agents and consultants were guardians of the quality of products; and he promulgated the need for professionalism in advertising. Research, using economics and statistics, was, he thought, 'an integral element in advertising' {*ibid*, 29}. To Russell's regret, the universities did little to develop the study of advertising. Despite the blandishments of Fleet Street newspapers in the 1920s, Russell resolutely refused to form his own advertising agency. His objective was to separate the broking and creative aspects of advertising, with agents specialising in broking and consultants in the creative side. To his chagrin, he saw agencies, not consultants, becoming the predominant force in advertising before ill health forced him to retire in 1931.

He received little recognition beyond being the first recipient of a cup awarded annually by the Publicity Club of London for distinguished services to advertising.

Thomas Baron Russell died at home at Farnham, Surrey, on 31 December 1931. His funeral was at Aylesford Church. He was survived by a widow, a daughter and two sons (Gilbert Russell and McDonagh Russell). He left £3,878 gross.

DAVID J JEREMY

Writings:

'Confessions of an Advertising Manager' *Advertising World* 1901-2.

letters to the *Times* 1904-5.

A Hundred Years Hence: The Expectations of an Optimist (1905).

The Curious Side of Advertising (articles in *Evening News* Nov 1910).

(ed), *Advertising and Publicity* (Educational Book Co Ltd, 1911).

The Twentieth Century Shop. A Book for Modern Retailers (1914).

Advertising and Advertisements (1924).

Commercial Advertising (6 lectures given at LSE, 1919; 2nd ed 1925).

The Advertising World Dec 1931.

Russell also contributed to the *Times* Trade and Engineering Supplement.

Sources:

Unpublished

Times, London, archives.

BCe.

MCe.

PrC.

Published

William Ewert Berry, note in *Times* 23 Sept 1931.

Herman Kogan, *The Great E B. The Story of the Encyclopaedia Britannica* (Chicago: University of Chicago Press, 1958).

Terry R Nevett, *Advertising in Britain. A History* (Heinemann, 1982).

Times 1, 8 Jan 1932.

John Watson, 'Thomas Baron Russell and British Advertising in the Early Years of this Century' *Business Archives* new ser 2 (1973).

RUSTON, Joseph

(1835-1897)

Steam engine and agricultural machinery manufacturer

Joseph Ruston (courtesy of the Institute of Agricultural History and Museum of English Rural Life, University of Reading).

Joseph Ruston was born at Chatteris, Cambridgeshire in February 1835, the son of Robert Ruston, a farmer and local Wesleyan preacher. He forsook any ideas of the ministry after a short attendance at Wesley College, Sheffield and became an apprentice with Wostenholm & Son, of Sheffield, cutlers, headed by George Wostenholm (qv).

In 1857, having accumulated a modest sum of capital, Ruston moved to Lincoln where he entered into a ten-year partnership with a firm of agricultural millwrights and general smiths, Burton & Proctor, established in 1840. The new partnership traded as Ruston, Burton & Proctor, with Ruston responsible for the commercial side of the business. Ruston had no experience of agricultural engineering and his initial value to the partnership was the injection of welcome capital. However, he also injected a mixture of dynamism and new ideas that caused Theophilus Burton to retire from the concern within a matter of seven months, prophesying that Ruston would be the ruin of the firm. The company then became Ruston, Proctor & Co, a style that was retained even after James Proctor retired in 1864. Ruston remained in sole financial and managerial control for the following twenty-five years, annual profits averaging £50,000 during 1882-89 at a time when several of his competitors were just about breaking even on trading. A public limited company, styled Ruston, Proctor & Co Ltd, was formed in 1889, with a share capital of £500,000. Ruston received £415,000 as the purchase price for the old concern and became chairman of the new company.

Ruston's transformation of the firm was remarkable by any standards. He seems to have been a shrewd and single-minded entrepreneur, who was content for the most part to leave technical matters to his subordinates. From as early as 1857, Ruston decided that the firm's future lay in the rapidly expanding area of agricultural steam engineering, no doubt influenced by the substantial profits being made both at home and abroad in this line of business by another Lincoln firm, Clayton, Shuttleworth & Co. During the 1860s and 1870s, Ruston travelled widely, building up the firm's overseas business, with the result that by the 1890s the firm had branches in Pest and Milan with agencies scattered throughout Europe, South America and Australia.

He also realised that the production of portable steam engines and thrashing machines provided a more regular trade and involved less complicated manufacturing processes than the more technically prestigious production of self-moving steam engines. Indeed Alfred Fowler, of John Fowler & Co of Leeds, wrote in 1904, in a mixture of commercial envy and technical disparagement, that Rustons 'have had for forty years orders for hundreds of portable engines which go together in the shop like sewing machines' {Institute of Agricultural History and Museum of English Rural Life, business records of John Fowler & Co (Leeds) Ltd}. By March 1897, Rustons had produced 20,500 steam engines (nearly all portable), 19,700 steam boilers and 10,750 thrashing machines, were employing 2,550 men and had works covering 17 acres. Ruston, however, did not neglect the firm's future and by the 1890s the company was moving away from agricultural into industrial engineering, reflected at the same time in experimental work on oil engine design.

A noteworthy example of a late nineteenth century self-made industrialist, Ruston was ambitious and single-minded with a paternalistic attitude towards his employees. He viewed agricultural engineering as both an industry and a science, adopting as his business maxim, 'My customer is my best friend'.

Ruston had a noteworthy local public career. He was Liberal MP for Lincoln, 1884-86, and at various times Mayor of Lincoln, Deputy Lord Lieutenant, High Sheriff, a JP, a town councillor and an alderman. He was a supporter of Congregationalism and his beneficence helped build the Drill Hall in Lincoln in 1890 and a children's ward at the County Hospital in 1892. In return he was made an honorary freeman of the City of Lincoln. He did not lose his interest in the cutlery trade and became chairman of Joseph Rodgers & Sons Ltd of Sheffield.

Ruston married Jane, daughter of William Brown, a bank manager, of Sheffield, in 1859; on Ruston's death on 10 June 1897, she, two sons and five daughters survived him. He left an estate valued at £929,348 gross.

D C PHILLIPS

Sources:

Unpublished

Lincolnshire Archives Office, business records of Ruston, Proctor & Co.

University of Reading, Institute of Agricultural History and Museum of English Rural Life, business records of John Fowler & Co (Leeds) Ltd.

MCe.

PrC.

Published

Engineer 83 (1897).

Implement and Machinery Review 23 (1897-98).

Bernard Newman, *One Hundred Years of Good Company* (Ruston & Hornsby Ltd, 1957).

WWMP.

Sir F W Pascoe Rutter (courtesy of Professor H Cockerell).

RUTTER, Sir Frederick William Pascoe

(1859-1949)

Insurance company chairman

Frederick William Pascoe Rutter was born on 28 June 1859, the son of William Roger Pascoe Rutter. He was educated at Liverpool College, but left school in 1873 when barely fourteen for an apprenticeship at the Liverpool head office of the London & Lancashire Fire Insurance Co, a twelve-year-old company without reserves and with a hazardous portfolio of fire insurance. Fortunately, in the following year a new manager, C G Fothergill, formerly the sub-manager of the Royal Insurance Co, was appointed and pulled the company into shape.

Rutter came to specialise in overseas fire insurance, making his first foreign visit (to Paris) in 1879; he was appointed head of the foreign department in 1885. In 1890 he was appointed assistant secretary and, two years later, sub-manager. In 1899, on Fothergill's retirement, he became general manager and secretary.

Although Rutter had left school early he educated himself by wide reading and his later publications were spattered with quotations from classical authors. As a manager he was exacting and severe, expecting ready obedience. He placed great store by rigorous training. He took a paternal interest in the company's employees, instituting an annual staff dinner as one of his first acts of management and holding garden parties for the staff at his house. He was very good at negotiation and claimed to have special powers of thought-reading which he had cultivated as a young man. Small of stature, he was lively in mind and popular among his peers, though not necessarily among those who worked under him.

Rutter was quick to see and seize the opportunities for expansion that presented themselves at the turn of the century. His financial timing and judgement were good. Between 1901 and 1914 his company's premium income rose from £1.2 million to £2.6 million. Early in his tenure of office as general manager the company moved into the US fire insurance market, in time to take the brunt of the San Francisco earthquake and its resultant fires in 1906. The company had to pay losses of £1.75 million but these were reduced by reinsurance to £925,000. Within a year two further earthquakes affected Valparaiso and Kingston, Jamaica, but the company's policies were well drafted to distinguish between earthquake damage, which was not covered, and fire damage, which was. The losses were held to less than £100,000. Rutter called payment of the San Francisco losses 'a great investment' {Francis (1962) 55}. Certainly the reputation gained by British insurance companies for solidity and payment of claims served them well in the ensuing decades.

Rutter also saw the potentiality of accident insurance, which until 1900 had hardly been transacted by the old-established fire offices. The stimulants to growth were parliamentary pressure for a system of compensation to all employees injured in accidents at work, culminating in the Workmen's Compensation Act of 1906, and the demand for motor insurance as motor vehicle traffic, freed in 1897 from irksome restrictions, increased rapidly. He began a policy of judicious purchases of accident insurance companies: the Manchester Equitable Fire & Accident Office Ltd (1901), the Scottish Employers & Accident Insurance Co Ltd (1904), and the Law Accident Insurance Society Ltd, a pioneer of motor insurance (1907). In 1908 a separate guarantee and accident company was formed by the London & Lancashire in Canada. A local accident company in Ontario was bought in the following year and a move into the US casualty business made on a limited scale in 1915. In the years 1909-27 many other companies were acquired in Australia, Canada and South Africa.

Diversification into marine insurance came in 1907 with the acquisition of the Standard Marine Insurance Co Ltd, a Liverpool company. The example was soon to be copied by other fire offices. Entry into life insurance was more difficult as the London & Lancashire Fire had a twin company, the London & Lancashire Life, from which it had been separated soon after birth. However, in 1919 Rutter was able to acquire the Law Union & Rock Insurance Co Ltd, an amalgamation of nineteenth-century life companies. The chief administration of the London & Lancashire was then moved to the Law Union & Rock office in Chancery Lane. In 1933 the London & Lancashire ranked fourth among British insurance companies in terms of dividends paid out and fire insurance premium income.

Rutter was a loyal supporter of the fire insurance tariff but he was more far-sighted than many of his contemporaries in perceiving the need for industry-wide co-operation in matters other than rating, such as education. He was a prime mover in the foundation of the Insurance Institute of Liverpool in 1907 which was a prelude to the petition for a charter by the Insurance Institute of Great Britain and Ireland. When the petition was opposed on the ground that some local institutes excluded from membership employees of non-tariff insurers it was Rutter who as president of the institute in 1910-11 broke the deadlock, so enabling the charter to be granted in 1912.

In 1919 Rutter, in an address to the Insurance Institute of London, said 'This institute should become an obvious institute, with its own building, or at any rate, adequate premises or accommodation' {Rutter (1920) 73}. It was not until 1932 that the Chartered Insurance Institute found a suitable site for itself and the London institute. Rutter took a leading role in raising the money needed and served as active chairman of the premises committee. His knighthood dates from 1934 when the hall was opened by King George V.

Similarly, it was Rutter who at a meeting of the Fire Offices' Committee on 28 July 1916 suggested the creation of an association of composite offices; this took shape in 1917 as the British Insurance Association, in the formation of which Rutter was a moving spirit.

His annual speeches as chairman, written in distinctive style, were frequently quoted. He travelled widely both for business and pleasure. One journey, undertaken soon after the First World War, led to the publication in 1921 of his book *A World in Travail*. In 1937 he published a light-hearted autobiography, *The Twinkle*. The proceeds of both books went to the insurance charities. He was a generous benefactor both of the charities and the Chartered Insurance Institute. Rutter liked to receive credit for his actions, and once quoted Bacon saying 'He who seeks glory for himself is seeking at the same time the welfare of others' {Rutter (1921) 36}.

Rutter married in 1893 Mary Agnes Robertson, of Peterhead, by whom he had two sons. She died in 1928 and in 1935 he married Lillian Hendrick of Washington, USA.

Rutter died on 24 June 1949 at Coombe Ridge House, Kingston-upon-Thames, where he had lived since his company's move to London in 1919. He left £397,324 gross.

HUGH COCKERELL

Writings:

'The Versatility of an Insurance Career' *Journal of the Insurance and Actuarial Society* 4th ser 6 (1897).

The Evolution of a Great Profession (Liverpool, 1909).

Presidential address in *Journal of the Chartered Insurance Institute* 1911.

'The Chartered Insurance Institute: Its Right to Work' *ibid* 1920.

A World in Travail: Being the Spontaneous Impression of a Rapid Tour of the Globe under Abnormal Conditions (McCorquodale & Co, 1921).

The Twinkle (Hazell, Watson & Viney, 1937).

Sources:

Unpublished

PrC.

Published

W L Catchpole and E Elverston, *BIA Fifty: 1917-1967. Fifty Years of the British Insurance Association* (Stockport: P H Press, 1967).

Hugh A L Cockerell, *Sixty Years of the Chartered Insurance Institute 1897-1957* (pp, the Institute).

Eric V Francis, *London and Lancashire History: The History of the London and Lancashire Insurance Company Limited* (pp, Newman Neame for the company, 1962).

Times 25 June 1949.

WWW.

RYLANDS, John

(1801-1888)

Textile merchant and manufacturer

John Rylands, 1887 (from H Guppy, The John Rylands Library, 1899–1935 *Manchester, 1935).*

John Rylands was born on 7 February 1801 in the village of Parr, near St Helens, the third and youngest son of Joseph Rylands (1767-1847) and Elizabeth Pilkington (1761-1829), whose nephew, Richard Pilkington (1795-1869), became a glass manufacturer. John Rylands was educated at St Helens Grammar School and became in 1817 a linen manufacturer on the handloom, like his father and grandfather. He also mastered the arts of the retail draper and the commercial traveller. In 1819 the firm of Rylands & Sons was established by Joseph Rylands and his three sons: in 1824 it moved from St Helens to Wigan. John Rylands opened a warehouse in Manchester in 1822 and developed an aggressive style of marketing, extending the activity of the firm from linen manufacture into dyeing and bleaching in 1824, into cotton spinning in 1830 and into powerloom weaving as well as coal mining in 1839. He took up residence in Manchester in 1834 and became the senior partner in Rylands & Son from 1843, when he also leased Gorton Mills in Manchester. In 1849 he opened a warehouse in London and in 1853 expanded the interests of the firm from the heavy trade into the prestigious and profitable fancy trade. In 1854 he withdrew from linen manufacture in order to concentrate upon the cotton industry. By then he had become a self-made textile millionaire, the first native of Lancashire to attain to that status, and after the death of James

Morrison (1789-1857) he became the largest textile merchant in the country.

During the crisis of the Cotton Famine Rylands profited by the low price of mills and machinery to expand his operations further. He built the Gidlow Works in 1863-65 at Wigan where he employed women as minders on self-acting mules in an economical departure from Lancashire practice.

In 1865 he acquired three more mills in Manchester. In 1868 he opened a branch in Liverpool. He then acquired a bleaching works near Chorley in 1870 and a clothing factory in Crewe in 1872. On 25 October 1873 the properties held by the firm and valued at £1,024,788 were incorporated under the management of Rylands & Sons Ltd with a nominal capital of £2 million which remained the largest single capital in the trade until the creation of the Coats combine in 1896. The new company remained a private partnership until 1920 but extended the privilege of shareholding to both its draper-clients and to its principal employees, in harmony with the contemporary enthusiasm for 'industrial partnership'. The articles of association gave to the 'Governor' supreme power within the company and made it impossible for the firm to secure a quotation on the London Stock Exchange in 1890. The shares nevertheless proved an excellent bargain for their fortunate holders, since no charge was made for 'goodwill'. The 'Governor' had suffered the loss of his two sons in 1861 and 1872: he therefore provided for the future management of the company by appointing as directors his fellow Congregationalist Reuben Spencer (1830-1901) in 1873 and the Wesleyan William Carnelley (1821-1919) in 1874.

In 1874-76 the firm bought six more mills in Chorley, Swinton, Manchester and Bolton. It opened branches in Paris in 1874 and in Glasgow in 1877. The acquisition of clothing factories in East London in 1874 and 1881 completed the construction of what was the greatest commercial structure originating during the first quarter of the nineteenth century and perhaps the largest in the world. John Rylands had succeeded to the position of leadership held first by Arkwright, then by Peel and for fifty years by the firm of Horrockses of Preston. The organisation of 200,000 spindles and 5,000 looms in 17 mills represented the most extensive factory system under the control of a single firm but embraced less than 1 per cent of the industry's aggregate spindleage and loomage. In manufacture, in finishing, and in distribution Rylands & Sons Ltd, with 15,000 employees, had become 'the recognised and undisputed head and leader of the cotton trade' {*Manchester of Today* (1888) 79}. The firm was unusual not only in its vast size and in the vertical integration of its operations, extending its interests over the whole range of dry goods, but also in the markets it served: it catered mainly for the home market but also engaged in the export trade to Europe, America and the colonies.

Rylands did not dissipate his energies by wasteful activity outside the sphere of his own vast commercial empire. Nor did he favour outside investments. He did however become a director of the Pearson & Knowles Coal & Iron Co Ltd, formed at Warrington in 1874, and of the Liverpool firm of cotton brokers, William Reynolds & Co Ltd, founded in 1810. He also became the leading shareholder in the Manchester Ship Canal Co in 1885 as well as a director.

John Rylands achieved much more as a merchant than as a

manufacturer. He developed normal mercantile abilities to the point of genius. A superb organiser and an exceptional judge of men, he excelled in financial acumen. He rigorously controlled costs and scrupulously avoided waste. Properties were always acquired at depressed prices. Labour costs were reduced by the employment of women wherever possible and by firm resistance to any attempt at dictation by the unions. He blamed trade combinations for the depression of 1877-79, prophesying that 'unless some check were brought to bear upon them the prosperity of the country would be undermined and the trade of England ruined'. {John Rylands Library, Ryland & Sons Ltd archives, General Meetings Minute Book (4 Feb 1878) 46} Transport costs were kept low by the location of works in the railway junction towns of Wigan, Bolton and Manchester. Rylands employed working directors, recruited them from within the firm, so establishing a tradition maintained until 1929, and paid no directors' fees: he himself drew no salary. He compelled each of the 42 departments to stand upon its own feet and never permitted the profits of one department to be swallowed by the losses made by another. He never traded upon credit, avoided the use of bank overdrafts and paid accounts in cash in return for a discount. Above all, he built up a high reputation for the quality of his goods, especially for Dacca calicoes, and maintained it through the use of trade marks: he never wasted money upon advertising. He sought small gains from quick returns, aimed to turn over his stock at least five times in each year and sought 'to make two per cent on our returns five times a year' {ibid, General Meetings Minute Book (9 Dec 1875) 20}. Thus he was able to capture the trade of other home trade houses which went bankrupt in the 1870s and 1880s.

The firm made average annual profits on its capital of 3.6 per cent, 1873-88. It also built up, at an average annual rate of 26 per cent, a reserve fund from £8,774 in 1873 to £265,516 in 1888, a fund which was buttressed by a further reserve of £500,000 in uncalled share capital and by a concealed reserve in the site value of its property in Manchester and in London, where the freehold was bought in 1883. Dividends averaged 10 per cent, 1873-76, but then declined to 5.6 per cent, 1877-88. Dividends exceeded profits in seven of the ten half years between 1877 and 1881 and the reserve fund was raided on three occasions, in 1878, 1879 and 1881, to maintain the level of dividends. On the paid-up share capital of £1.5 million the dividends paid between 1873 and 1888 aggregated £1,273,547. On the Manchester Stock Exchange the £15 shares were quoted at £18 by 1890 and at £40 by 1897.

After 1876 John Rylands did not renew his subscription to the Manchester Royal Exchange. He last attended a meeting of his directors on 1 March 1877 and he spoke little at shareholders' meetings after 1878, although he continued to preside over them until his death in 1888. In 1882 he acquired a country seat near Ryde on the Isle of Wight. Upon his death the shareholders paid tribute to his ability. 'This meeting desires to place on record its high appreciation of the great business capacity, the unwearied diligence, the fine courtesy, the inflexible firmness, the wise sagacity, the high integrity, the pure sincerity and the unostentatious charity which being united to a character of high moral tone served to endear him to all who were brought into any kind of relation with him' {ibid, General Meetings Minute Book (Feb 1889) 115}.

The succession to John Rylands affords further proof of his capacity. No other 'governor' of the company was ever appointed. The chairmanship of the board devolved in rotation during the next twelve years upon three different directors, Reuben Spencer, William Carnelley and James Horrocks (1832-95). Only after the death of Horrocks in 1895 and of Spencer in 1901 did Carnelley become permanent chairman from 1900 to 1915, during which years the firm paid out dividends totalling £2,581,000 on its share capital of £1,500,000. The mercantile and manufacturing interests of the firm had come into conflict in the 1880s as its sales of outside makes of goods increased faster than the sales of its own products. Several changes of policy were made after the death of the 'Governor'. Regular weekly meetings of the directors began on 11 June 1887 and regular monthly summaries of profit and loss were introduced from September 1887. Director's fees were paid from 1888 and sub-committees of the board established from 1890. Four unprofitable mills were sold off in 1888-89. Price-fixing agreements with Horrockses were first concluded in 1888 and expenditure upon advertising was first authorised in 1889. The firm joined the United Cotton Manufacturers' Association in 1890 and the Dyers' & Finishers' Association in 1891. From 1891 it also began to invest capital outside the firm.

The influence of religion permeated the whole life and work of John Rylands. He 'accepted his work and calling as divine' in the opinion of the Baptist minister, Dr S G Green. In his unresting activity he approaches the ideal type of Weberian entrepreneur inspired by other-worldly ideals. As an adult he had embraced the Baptist faith (1830-42) but he then returned to the Congregational tradition of his family. He became a generous supporter of the Liberation Society but he also developed latitudinarian and even ecumenical sympathies. His deep interest in the Bible and in hymns of worship led him to make their texts more widely available. At his own expense he published three editions of a Paragraph Bible (1863, 1878, 1886), arranged for ease of reference as a 'self-interpretng bible': the accompanying Index served as both an epitome and a concordance. He also distributed French and Italian editions of the New Testament (1875, 1878). His extensive charitable activities catered especially for orphans, for widows, for the aged poor and for ministers of religion. For his benefactions to the poor of Rome he was created a Knight of the Order of the Crown of Italy in 1880. He also became a great benefactor to the township of Stretford where he had built Longford Hall in 1857. There he inaugurated the Congregational Church in 1861 and there he became a patron of the Union Church formed by secession in 1865. Most of the honours he was offered he declined but he did become a JP in 1869.

He married three times, firstly in 1825, Dinah Raby (1803-43), secondly in 1848, the widow Martha Carden (1806-75), daughter of Isaac Greenough, a brewer, and finally in 1875, Enriqueta Augustina (1843-1908), daughter of Stephen Cattley Tennant (1800-1848), a merchant. He died on 11 December 1888 at the age of eighty-seven and left a personal estate of £2,574,922 gross which represented the largest fortune left by any cotton manufacturer down to that date and a striking contrast to the estate of £30,000 left by his own father in 1847 and of £5,000 left by his elder brother, Richard (1798-1863). His widow immortalised the memory of one of the most unassuming of Manchester men by creating the John Rylands Library, which was inaugurated in 1899. She invested £1 million in the library and left an estate of £2,574,922.

D A FARNIE

Writings:

'An Address Delivered by John Rylands Esq on the Occasion of his Laying the Foundation Stone of the Congregational Church, Stretford, on March 29th 1861' in Joseph Parker (ed), *Our Own* I (1861).

The Holy Bible: Containing the Old and New Testaments Arranged in Paragraphs (Manchester: Cave, 1863; Chilworth: Unwin, 1878, 1886).

Hymns of the Church Universal (Chilworth: Unwin, 1885).

An Index Designed to Accompany the Holy Bible Arranged in Paragraphs (Chilworth: Unwin, 1886).

Hymns for the Young (Chilworth: Unwin, 1887).

Sources:

Unpublished

Greater Manchester Archives, Manchester Ship Canal Co, Minutes of the Board of Directors, 1885-88.

John Rylands Library, Manchester, Archives of Rylands & Sons Ltd, especially the Governor's Minute Book, 1873-88, Minutes of Directors' Meetings, 1873-92, the General Meetings Minute Book, 1874-1913 and Balance Sheets, 1873-88; Wills of John Rylands and Mrs E A Rylands.

C Reg: Rylands & Sons Ltd (7,748).

MCe.

Information from Dr J C G Binfield, Miss Glenis A Matheson, P T Sinker, Dr J Frank Taylor and P L Tennant.

Published

Terence S Ashton, 'Rylands & Sons Ltd' *Manchester Guardian Commercial* 5 May 1934.

J Clyde G Binfield, *So Down to Prayers. Studies in English Nonconformity, 1780-1920* (Dent, 1977).

Boase.

'British Industries No clxxvii — Messrs Rylands & Sons (Limited), Manchester, London &c' *British Trade Journal* 1 Apr 1887.

The Century's Progress: Lancashire (London Printing & Engraving Co, 1892).

Henry T Crofton, *A History of the Ancient Chapel of Stretford in Manchester Parish* (Manchester: Chetham Society, 1903).

DD.

RYLANDS John

DNB.

Douglas A Farnie, 'John Rylands of Manchester' *Bulletin of the John Rylands Library* 1973.

Samuel G Green, *In Memoriam John Rylands* (Chilworth: Unwin, 1889).

—, 'The Late Mr John Rylands of Manchester' *Sunday at Home* 23 Mar 1889.

Kazuhiko Kondo, 'John Rylands and "The Protestant Ethic and the Spirit of Capitalism"' [in Japanese] *Shiso* [Thought] 714 (Dec 1983).

Manchester City News 1, 8, 15 Apr 1865, 15 Dec 1888, 1 Jan 1916.

Manchester Examiner 12 Dec 1888.

Manchester of Today (Historical Publishing Co, 1888).

S Massey, *A History of Stretford* (Altrincham: Sherratt, 1976).

'Our Album. John Rylands Esq' *Momus* 15 May 1879.

J Parker, 'The Story of the Cotton King: Recollections of John Rylands of Manchester' *The Young Man* Apr 1893.

Godfrey H Pike, *Dr Parker and his Friends* (Unwin, 1904).

Daniel Puseley, *The Commercial Companion* (Hall, 1858).

A W B Simpson, 'Legal Liability for Bursting Reservoirs: The Historical Context of *Rylands v Fletcher*' *The Journal of Legal Studies* 13 No 2 (June 1984).

Reuben Spencer, *The Home Trade of Manchester* (Simpkin, 1890).

Sir W Peter Rylands (courtesy of CBI).

RYLANDS, Sir William Peter

(1868-1948)

Wire manufacturer

William Peter Rylands, usually known as Peter, was born at Warrington on 23 October 1868, third and youngest son of Peter Rylands (1821-87), of Massey Hall, Thelwall, near Warrington, and Caroline Wright (1841-1920), daughter of William Reynolds, of Penketh House, Warrington, and Pinhoe, Devon. The family firm had diversified from linen manufacture to wire drawing around 1805; after 1843 three brothers John (1814-98), Thomas Glazebrook (1818-1900) and Peter expanded their trade to all classes of wire and wire products, forming the private company of Rylands Brothers in 1868. Their slogan 'Warrington for Wire' became known nationally. In 1864 the Rylands opened the Bewsey works at Warrington to supply puddled iron for their wire mills, to which was later added the manufacture of sheets and hoops; these ironworks were amalgamated in 1874 with the Dallam Forge at Warrington and the Pearson & Knowles collieries at Wigan to form the Pearson & Knowles Coal & Iron Co Ltd. John Rylands was chairman of Pearson & Knowles (1884-98) and Peter Rylands Sr was a director. He also joi⌐ the board of the Manchester & Liverpool District Bank, and ⌐ active part in Lancashire affairs, sitting as Liberal Union⌐ for Warrington (1868-74) and Burnley (1876-87). He left £80 ⌐ 1887.

Peter Ryland⌐ ⌐as educated at Charterhouse (1881-87), and in 1887 matricula⌐ ⌐rinity College, Cambridge (BA 1892). In 1891 he visited M⌐⌐' ⌐and to hunt big game. He was called to the Bar at the Inner ⌐⌐ple in 1894, and practised on the Northern Circuit, with a special interest in patent law. His eldest brother Louis Gordon (1862-1942) was secretary of Rylands Bros (1884-87) before becoming a science schoolmaster and private tutor; the other brother Thomas Kirkland (1866-1933) was a land agent.

Following the death in 1898 of his uncle John, Rylands left legal practice to become managing director of the family wire business, which had four distinct branches. Wire up to 9 gauge was used for fencing and telegraph; gauges 10-14 were for barb fencing; gauges 15-19 were for netting; while fine wires went up to gauge 40. 'The English trade' in the first category, as Rylands told the Tariff Commission in 1904, 'is actually dwindling while the trade of the world is enormously increasing', and his company's orders which had averaged 163 tons a week in 1883 had sunk to a weekly average of 76 tons for the five years to 1898. Under the stimulus of orders for telegraph wire for the India Office and War Office (for use in the Boer War) average weekly orders increased to 92 tons for 1898-1903, but thereafter relapsed. This decline contrasted with the experience of the market in other classes of wire over the period 1883-1904: orders for gauges 10-14 remained constant, for gauges 15-19 increased 50 per cent, 20-50 increased 700 per cent and netting wire orders over 1,000 per cent. At the same time the wire nail trade in Britain had been 'killed' by the German nail syndicate, and Rylands averred 'unless I had some [tariff] security I would not spend the money to put down plant even if the price of nails was remunerative'. German competition had appeared in the British wire business after 1880 (and American competition after 1890), and according to Rylands the former had ousted the British from domination of the world wire trade by the end of the nineteenth century. In the next few years British wire exports stagnated at about 50,000 tons which represented only 10 per cent of the exports of their two main rivals. Having lost the Australian market to the Germans as the result of a strike around 1884, the only major overseas market remaining in the early twentieth century was Argentina. The German success was unsurprising, since their price of £6 5s a ton of fencing wire was a pound sterling cheaper then the price that Rylands managed to quote. In the British home market, the Germans and Americans made a 'dead set' at the major wire consumers and made inroads into Rylands' business; but foreign suppliers could not touch the trade in finer wire. He estimated in 1904 that he had 'about 5,000 ... little customers all over England, tinsmiths, men who make bird cages, who use bell wire, and all sorts of small men' giving orders of 3 or 5 cwts at a time, 'an enormous aggregation of small customers' whom the Germans were unable to reach {BLPES, Tariff Commission, TC3 1/27 Rylands evidence of 1 June 1904}.

Rylands found his wire business 'undoubtedly hampered by having to deal with a Trade Union ... of the most ... conservative and arbitrary type' which was 'determined not to give away anything more than it can help', and had particular trouble with restrictive practices and union rules on the number of apprentices. But the main menace to his company came, he felt, from the German bounty system, and he wanted a countervailing tariff to bring about 'fair competition'. He warned that without protection for the British home market, the metal trades would be increasingly retarded by insufficient investment.

> Unless there is some security for business it is impossible to expect people to put their money into it. It is a reproach sometimes to the English manufacturer that he does not keep up to date - that he does not put down new plant and so on, and we hear wonderful stories about Americans scrapping plant and expending millions of pounds in betterments. But if works are run on very close lines, and make only small profits and sometimes losses, such a policy is impossible {ibid}.

He was an admirer, too, of the tendency to form trade associations, as epitomised by the Canadian Hardware Association, and believed in the necessity for manufacturing combinations. Both of these, he judged, would be fostered by protective tariffs. He regarded British industrialists' reluctance to associate as a fault of national character aggravated by the lack of tariff protection: 'as competitive rates are permanently very low' under free trade, 'the advantage to be derived from combination is very small too' {ibid}. As demonstration of Rylands's belief in combination, the wire company was bought in 1906-7 by Pearson & Knowles, which had owned the Rylands's ironworks since 1874. Peter Rylands had joined the Pearson & Knowles board on the death of his uncle John, and kept responsibility for Rylands Brothers as the wire department of Pearson & Knowles throughout the chairmanship of his uncle's successor, Sir John Harmood-Banner (qv). He was concerned in the erection of the Partington Steelworks during 1910-13, and in other operations of the group.

Rylands was president of the Iron and Steel Wire Manufacturers' Association from 1900, and was one of the chief supporters of Sir Charles Macara (qv) in forming the Employers' Parliamentary Association (1912-13) to lobby for the Lancashire business interest. As he told the EPA, he 'deplored the absence of businessmen from the Legislative councils, which made it possible for the government of the country to fall into the hands of men who might be eminently qualified in one sense, but who were without practical business experience. The only method left was for them to combine as one great force whose powers could not be gainsaid by any Government' {*Times* 4 July 1913}. As representative of Rylands Brothers, he was a founding member of the Executive Council of the Federation of British Industries in 1916, and took an active part in forming its policies. He was vice-chairman of its first general committee (July 1916), a member of the organising committee (September 1916), chairman of the labour committee (1917-18) and of the overseas trade and consular committee